TENTH EDITION

A World of Ideas

ESSENTIAL READINGS FOR COLLEGE WRITERS

LEE A. JACOBUS

University of Connecticut

bedford/st.martin's
Macmillan Learning
Boston | New York

For Bedford/St. Martin's

Vice President, Editorial, Macmillan Learning Humanities: Edwin Hill
Senior Publisher for Composition, Business and Technical Writing,
    Developmental Writing: Leasa Burton
Editorial Director, English and Music: Karen S. Henry
Executive Editor: John E. Sullivan III
Developmental Editor: Alicia Young
Production Editor: Pamela Lawson
Media Producer: Rand Thomas
Production Supervisor: Carolyn Quimby
Marketing Manager: Joy Fisher Williams
Project Management: Jouve
Photo Researcher: Susan Barlow
Text Permissions Researcher: Jenn Kennett
Senior Art Director: Anna Palchik
Text Design: Laura Shaw Design, Inc.
Cover Design: William Boardman
Cover Art/Cover Photo: Villa Farnese (Palazzo Farnese), by Barozzi Jacopo known
    as Vignola, 1550–1559, 16th Century / Villa Farnese, Caprarola, Lazio, Italy /
    Mondadori Portfolio / Electa / Andrea Jemolo / Bridgeman Images
Composition: Jouve
Printing and Binding: LSC Communications

Manufactured in the United States of America.

1 0 9 8 7
f e d c b

For information, write: Bedford/St. Martin's, 75 Arlington Street, Boston,
MA 02116   (617-399-4000)

ISBN 978-1-319-04740-5

Acknowledgments

Text acknowledgments and copyrights appear at the back of the book on pages 818–20, which constitute an extension of the copyright page. Art acknowledgments and copyrights appear on the same page as the art selections they cover.

Preface

Among the pleasures of editing *A World of Ideas* are the discussions I have had over the years with students and teachers who have used the book in their writing classes. A student once wrote to tell me that the book meant a great deal to her and that her experience with it impelled her to wonder what originally inspired me to assemble the first edition. I explained that my teaching of first-year writing has always inclined toward ideas that serious writers and thinkers have explored and contemplated throughout the ages; early on, I could not find a composition reader that introduced students to the important thinkers whose writing I believe should be basic to everyone's education. As a result of that need, *A World of Ideas* took shape and has continued to grow and develop through ten editions, attracting a wide audience of teachers and students who value the thought-provoking ideas that affect the way we interpret the world.

In preparing the tenth edition of *A World of Ideas*, I have benefited, as usual, from the suggestions of hundreds of users of earlier editions. The primary concern of both teachers and students is that the book remain centered on the tradition of important ideas and on the writers whose work has had a lasting influence on society. To that end, I have chosen writers whose ideas are central to our most important and lasting concerns. A new edition offers the opportunity to reevaluate old choices and make new ones that expand and deepen what has always been the fundamental purpose of this composition reader: to provide college students in first-year writing courses with a representative sampling of important ideas examined by men and women who have shaped the way we think today.

The selections in this volume are of the highest quality. Each was chosen because it clarifies important ideas and can sustain discussion and stimulate good writing. Unlike most composition readers, *A World of Ideas* presents substantial excerpts from the work of each of its authors. The selections are presented as they originally appeared; very rarely are they edited and marked with ellipses. They average fifteen pages in length, and their arguments are presented completely, as the authors wrote them. Developing a serious idea in writing takes time and a willingness to experiment. Most students are willing to read deeply into the work of important thinkers to grasp their ideas better because the knowledge yielded by the effort is vast and rewarding.

A Text for Readers and Writers

Because students perceive writers such as Plato and Thoreau as serious and important, they take more seriously the writing course that uses texts by these authors: such students learn to read more attentively, think more critically, and write more effectively. But more important, this may be a student's only opportunity to encounter the thinkers whose ideas have shaped civilization. No other composition reader offers a comparable collection of important readings along with the supportive apparatus students need to understand, analyze, and respond to them.

CLASSIC READINGS. *A World of Ideas* draws its forty-nine selections from the writing of some of the world's most important thinkers. Among them are Hannah Arendt, Aristotle, Francis Bacon, Andrew Carnegie, Charles Darwin, Frederick Douglass, Ralph Waldo Emerson, Sigmund Freud, Howard Gardner, Thomas Jefferson, Carl Jung, Martin Luther King Jr., Hsün Tzu, Niccolò Machiavelli, Karl Marx, Margaret Mead, Philip Kitcher, Michio Kaku, Iris Murdoch, Friedrich Nietzsche, Robert B. Reich, Jean-Jacques Rousseau, Jacob Riis, F. A. Hayek, Francis Fukuyama, Lisa Randall, Adam Smith, Mary Wollstonecraft, Eric Kandell, Kwame Appiah, and Virginia Woolf.

A FOCUS ON SIX GREAT IDEAS.   The unique structure of *A World of Ideas* highlights seminal ideas as developed by great thinkers throughout history and facilitates cross-disciplinary comparisons. Each of the six parts of the book focuses on one great idea — Government, Culture, Wealth, Mind, Science, and Ethics. Part introductions ground students in the history of each idea and connect the philosophies of individual writers and offer questions prompting students to consider their own assumptions about each idea before they begin reading the selections.

"Evaluating Ideas: An Introduction to Critical Reading."   This introduction demonstrates a range of methods students can adopt to participate in a meaningful dialogue with each selection. This dialogue — an active, questioning

approach to texts and ideas—is one of the keys to critical reading. In the introduction, a portion of Machiavelli's "The Qualities of the Prince" is annotated to help students follow the key ideas of the piece and to model for students a critical reading process that they can adapt to other essays in the book. The introduction encourages students to mark what they think are the most interesting and important ideas in an essay and highlight or underline all sentences that they might want to quote in an essay of their own.

"Writing about Ideas: An Introduction to Rhetoric."   In the tenth edition, this section, which now immediately follows "Evaluating Ideas: An Introduction to Critical Reading," has been much expanded, with an emphasis on developing thesis statements, using rhetorical methods of development, and thinking critically to construct a strong argument. Many new examples based on current selections in the tenth edition help students find fruitful approaches to the material. This section explains how a reader can make annotations while reading critically and then use those annotations to write effectively in response to the ideas presented in any selection in the book. "Writing about Ideas" draws on the annotations of the Machiavelli selection illustrated in "Evaluating Ideas: An Introduction to Critical Reading." A sample student essay on Machiavelli, using the techniques taught in the context of reading and writing, gives students a model for moving from a critical response to a selection to writing their own material. In addition, this section helps students understand how they can apply some of the basic rhetorical principles discussed throughout the book.

SELECTION HEADNOTES.   Each selection is preceded by a detailed headnote on the author's life and work and by comments about the primary ideas presented in the reading. The rhetorical techniques of the author are described in some detail with a careful emphasis on the kinds of techniques that students themselves can use. The discussion of the author's rhetoric is usually keyed to the rhetorical skills introduced in Writing about Ideas. One emphasis is on examining how an author's rhetorical techniques can achieve specific effects.

PREREADING QUESTIONS.   To emphasize critical thinking, reading, and writing, prereading questions precede every selection. The content of the selections is challenging, and these prereading questions can help students in first-year writing courses overcome minor difficulties in understanding the author's meaning. These brief questions are designed to help students focus on central issues during their first reading of each selection.

EXTENSIVE APPARATUS.   At the end of each selection is a group of discussion questions designed for use inside or outside the classroom. Questions for Critical Reading focus on key issues and ideas and can be used to stimulate general class discussion and critical thinking. Suggestions for Critical Writing help students practice some of the rhetorical strategies employed by the author of a given selection. These suggestions ask for personal responses, as well as complete essays that involve research. A number of these assignments, labeled "Connections," promote critical reading by requiring students to connect particular passages in a selection with a selection by another writer, either in the same part of the book or in another part. The variety of connections is intriguing—Lao-tzu with Machiavelli, Aristotle with Andrew Carnegie, Adam Smith with Thomas Jefferson, F. A. Hayek with John Maynard Keynes, Francis Bacon with Howard Gardner, Kwame Anthony Appiah with Iris Murdoch and Michael Gazzaniga, Judith Butler with Margaret Mead, Gilbert Ryle with Eric Kandel, Hsün Tzu with Aristotle, and many more.

In this edition, I ask a number of questions in each of the six sections of the book before the student reads any of the essays. This helps give them a baseline for their own thoughts about government, culture, wealth, mind, science, and ethics before they begin examining those ideas. Then, I provide a number of follow-up questions at the end of each section to help students see how much they have absorbed from the authors they have studied.

INSTRUCTOR'S RESOURCE MANUAL. I have prepared an extensive manual, *Resources for Teaching A WORLD OF IDEAS*, that contains further background on the selections, examples from my own classroom responses to the selections, and more suggestions for classroom discussion and student writing assignments. Sentence outlines for the selections—which have been carefully prepared by Michael Hennessy, Carol Verberg, Ellen Troutman, Ellen Darion, and Jon Marc Smith—can be photocopied or downloaded from the Instructor Resources tab on the book's catalog page at **macmillanlearning.com** and given to students. The idea for these sentence outlines came from the phrase outlines that Darwin created to precede each chapter of *On the Origin of Species*. These outlines may be used to discuss the more difficult selections and to provide additional guidance for students. At the end of the manual, brief bibliographies are provided for all forty-eight authors. These bibliographies may be photocopied or downloaded and distributed to students who wish to explore the primary selections in greater depth.

New in the Tenth Edition

The tenth edition offers a number of new features to help students engage and interact with the texts as they learn to analyze ideas and develop their own thoughts in writing.

NEW ESSENTIAL READINGS.   The selections in *A World of Ideas* explore the key ideas that have defined the human experience and shaped civilization. Of the forty-nine selections, twenty-two are new to this edition, including works by Aristotle, Milton and Rose Friedman, Hsün Tzu, Ralph Waldo Emerson, F. A. Hayek, Jacob Riis, John Maynard Keynes, Francis Fukuyama, Friedrich Nietzsche, Karen Horney, John Rawls, Gilbert Ryle, Robert Nozick, Erik Kandel, Howard Gardner, Richard Feynman, Edward O. Wilson, Michio Kaku, Philip Kitcher, Lisa Randall, Hsün Tzu, and Carol Gilligan.

REORGANIZED FOUNDATIONAL IDEAS.   The selections in the six sections — Government, Culture, Wealth, Mind, Science, and Ethics — cover considerable historical periods and attitudes toward their subjects. All six sections contain ideas that affect every one of us in a number of important ways.

- **Government**, with an emphasis on democracy, for example, is, as Aristotle and Plato both knew, in many respects one of the most important ideas of modern times (which is why the book starts with it).

- **Culture** includes a number of social issues: gender studies, issues of justice, prejudice, and a range of historical perspectives that affect all of us.

- **Wealth** centers on the history of economics and how people have interpreted the effects of money on society. In a society facing massive inequalities, it helps to understand how important thinkers square the stress that great wealth has put upon democratic governments.

- **Mind** introduces several important issues: the question of the unconscious and its effect on our lives; the mind-body problem, which has an effect on faith; and the question of how a physical body can produce consciousness. I also introduce basic ideas in classical psychology.

- **Science** focuses more on the scientific way of thinking than on specific details. Darwin's ideas about evolution and Newtonian and Einsteinian theories of gravity stand next to a major modern concern: how our understanding of genetics will ultimately change the genes of human beings.

- Finally, **Ethics** appropriately follows the first five sections because the behavior of government, cultural forces, economists, brain and mind studies, and scientific upheavals all must be governed by the best understanding of ethical principles that will avoid injustice and oppression.

It is important to see how these six great themes intersect in everyone's life. The new "Considerations" and "Reflections" questions I have provided at the beginning and end of each of these sections are designed to provide a way of reflecting on the great ideas that are explored in detail, but they also are designed to help students understand how much they have learned from the ideas in each section.

MORE "CONNECTIONS" QUESTIONS. Throughout the book, students are asked to make connections and comparisons between writers addressing the same great idea within the same great idea topic and between writers addressing different ideas, helping to stimulate comparative critical thinking and writing.

NEW "CONSIDERATIONS" AND "REFLECTIONS" QUESTIONS. This edition features new chapter-wide questions at the end of each part introduction and after the last reading in each section. "Considerations" questions at the end of each chapter introduction ask students to examine their own assumptions about the theme before they begin reading. "Reflections" questions after the last reading in each chapter ask students to reflect on what they have learned about the theme and prompt them to find connections to the readings within their own lives.

Acknowledgments

I am grateful to a number of people who made important suggestions for earlier editions, among them Shoshana Milgram Knapp of Virginia Polytechnic and State University and Michael Hennessy of Texas State University–San Marcos. I want to thank Michelle McSweeney for her work on the sentence outlines for this edition's instructor's manual, and I again thank Jon Marc Smith of Texas State University–San Marcos and Chiara Sulprizio of the Loyola Marymount University for assisting with the manuals for previous editions. I also remain grateful to Michael Bybee, formerly of St. John's College in Santa Fe, for suggesting many fascinating pieces by Eastern thinkers, all of which he has taught to his own students. Thanks to him, this edition includes Lao-tzu.

Like its predecessors, the tenth edition is indebted to a great many creative people at Bedford/St. Martin's, whose support is invaluable. I want to thank Charles Christensen, former president, whose concern for the excellence of this book and whose close attention to detail were truly admirable. I continue to appreciate the advice of Joan E. Feinberg, former copresident of Macmillan Higher Education, and Denise Wydra, former president of Bedford/St. Martin's, whose suggestions over the years were always timely and excellent. Edwin Hill, vice president of editorial for the humanities; Karen Henry, editorial director for English; and Steve Scipione, senior executive editor, offered many useful ideas and suggestions as well, especially in the early stages of development, and kept their sharp eyes on the project throughout. My editor for the eighth edition, Maura Shea, is the professional's professional. My editor for the ninth and tenth editions, Alicia Young, has been a steady guiding hand, discussing material with me and helping me make wise choices. She has been an inspiration in dealing with sometimes intractable problems and responding with encouragement and the kind of help only the very best editors can provide.

Assisting her were a number of hardworking individuals, including Jennifer Prince. Pamela Lawson, production editor, also helped with innumerable important details and suggestions. Caroline Define, copy editor, improved the prose and watched out for inconsistencies. Thanks also to several staff members and researchers: Jenn Kennett cleared text permissions, William Boardman found the cover artwork and designed the marvelous cover, and Susan Barlow secured permission for all the new images. In earlier editions, I had help from Diane Kraut, Maura Shea, Sarah Cornog, Rosemary Winfield, Michelle Clark, Professor Mary W. Cornog, Ellen Kuhl, Mark Reimold, Andrea Goldman, Beth Castrodale, Jonathan Burns, Mary Beth McNulty, Beth Chapman, Mika De Roo, and Greg Johnson. I feel I had a personal relationship with each of them. I also want to thank the students — quite a few of them — who wrote me directly about their experiences reading the first nine editions. I have attended carefully to what they told me, and I am warmed by their high regard for the material in this book.

Earlier editions named hundreds of users of this book who sent their comments and encouragement. I would like to take this opportunity to thank them again. In addition, the following professors were generous with criticism, praise, and detailed recommendations for the tenth edition: Caroline Alphin, Radford University; Deborah Barrett, Rice University; Jon Brammer, Three Rivers Community College; David Calonne, Eastern Michigan University; Jason Casem, Long Beach City College; Jane Cleland, Lehman College; Laurie Lopez Coleman, San Antonio College; Jeanie Crain, Missouri Western State University; Brian Curtis, Nashville State Community College; Kathryn Denton, Ohio State University; Ajit Dhillon, University of South Carolina; Heide Estes, Monmouth University; Allison Fraiberg, University of Redlands; John Gist, Western New Mexico University; Bruce Glenn, Arizona State University; Auston Habershaw, MCPHS University; Deana Holifield, Pearl River Community College; Pam Mathis, North Arkansas College; Lois McDonald, Pearl River Community College; John Metoyer, City Colleges of Chicago–Wright & Washington; Margaret Morlier, Reinhardt University; Garry Partridge, San Antonio College; Ayaz Pirani, Hartnell College; Donna Pittman, Nashville State Community College; Phil Poulos, California State University Los Angeles; Lillian Ruiz, Greenfield Community College; Provvidenza Scaduto, MiraCosta College; Suocai Su, Harold Washington College; Lantz Simpson, Santa Monica College; Greg Underwood, Pearl River Community College; and Stephen Wells, Community College of Allegheny County.

I want to mention particularly the past experiences I had visiting Professor Elizabeth Deis and the faculty and students of Hampden-Sydney College in connection with their writing and humanities programs. Professors James Kenkel and Charlie Sweet were gracious in welcoming me to Eastern Kentucky

University for workshops and classes using *A World of Ideas*. These were delightful and fruitful experiences that helped me shape the book. I am grateful to all who took part in these workshops.

—LEE JACOBUS

With Bedford/St. Martin's, You Get More

At Bedford/St. Martin's, providing support to teachers and their students who use our books and digital tools is our top priority. The Bedford/St. Martin's English Community is now our home for professional resources, including Bedford *Bits*, our popular blog with new ideas for the composition classroom. Join us to connect with our authors and your colleagues at **community.macmillan .com** where you can download titles from our professional resource series, review projects in the pipeline, sign up for webinars, or start a discussion. In addition to this dynamic online community and book-specific instructor resources, we offer digital tools, custom solutions, and value packages to support both you and your students. We are committed to delivering the quality and value that you've come to expect from Bedford/St. Martin's, supported as always by the power of Macmillan Learning. To learn more about or to order any of the following products, contact your Bedford/St. Martin's sales representative or visit the Web site at **macmillanlearning.com**.

CHOOSE FROM ALTERNATIVE FORMATS OF *A WORLD OF IDEAS*. Bedford/St. Martin's offers a range of affordable formats, allowing students to choose the one that works best for them. For details of our e-book partners, visit **macmillanlearning.com/ebooks**.

SELECT VALUE PACKAGES.   Add value to your text by packaging one of the following resources with *A World of Ideas*. To learn more about package options for any of the following products, contact your Bedford/St. Martin's sales representative or visit **macmillanlearning.com**.

   Writer's Help 2.0.   This powerful online writing resource helps students find answers whether they are searching for writing advice on their own or as part of an assignment.

- Smart search

  Built on research with more than 1,600 student writers, the smart search in Writer's Help 2.0 provides reliable results even when students use novice terms, such as *flow* and *unstuck*.

- **Trusted content from our best-selling handbooks**

Choose *Writer's Help 2.0, Hacker Handbooks* or *Writer's Help 2.0, Lunsford Handbooks* and ensure that students have clear advice and examples for all of their writing questions.

- **Adaptive exercises that engage students**

Writer's Help 2.0 includes *LearningCurve*, gamelike online quizzing that adapts to what students already know and helps them focus on what they need to learn.

Student access is packaged with *A World of Ideas* at a significant discount. Order ISBN 978-1-319-11231-8 for *Writer's Help 2.0, Hacker Version* or ISBN 978-1-319-11232-5 for *Writer's Help 2.0, Lunsford Version* to ensure your students have easy access to online writing support. Students who rent a book or buy a used book can purchase access and instructors may request free access by at **macmillanlearning.com/writershelp2**.

LaunchPad Solo for Readers and Writers. This resource allows students to work on whatever they need help with the most. At home or in class, students learn at their own pace, with instruction tailored to each student's unique needs. *LaunchPad Solo for Readers and Writers* features:

- **Pre-built units that support a learning arc**

Each easy-to-assign unit is comprised of a pretest check, multimedia instruction and assessment, and a posttest that assesses what students have learned about critical reading, writing process, using sources, grammar, style, mechanics, and help for multilingual writers.

- **A video introduction to many topics**

Introductions offer an overview of the unit's topic, and many include a brief, accessible video to illustrate the concepts at hand.

- **Adaptive quizzing for targeted learning**

Most units include *LearningCurve*, gamelike adaptive quizzing that focuses on the areas in which each student needs the most help.

- **The ability to monitor student progress**

Use our gradebook to see which students are on track and which need additional help with specific topics.

Order ISBN 978-1-319-11230-1 to package *LaunchPad Solo for Readers and Writers* with *A World of Ideas* at a significant discount. Students who rent or buy a used book can purchase access and instructors may request free access at **macmillanlearning.com/readwrite**.

INSTRUCTOR RESOURCES.   You have a lot to do in your course. Bedford/ St. Martin's wants to make it easy for you to find the support you need—and to get it quickly.

Resources for Teaching A World of Ideas is available as a PDF that can be downloaded from the Bedford/St. Martin's online catalog at the URL above. In addition to chapter overviews and teaching tips, the instructor's manual includes sample syllabi, sentence outlines, suggestions for further reading, suggestions for short and long essays, and classroom activities.

MACMILLAN LEARNING CURRICULUM SOLUTIONS.   Curriculum Solutions brings together the quality of Bedford/St. Martin's content with Hayden-McNeil's expertise in publishing original custom print and digital products. Developed especially for writing courses, our ForeWords for English program contains a library of the most popular, requested content in easy to use modules to help you build the best possible text. Whether you are considering creating a custom version of *A World of Ideas* or incorporating our content with your own, we can adapt and combine the resources that work best for your course or program. Some enrollment minimums apply. Contact your sales representative for more information.

To the Student

When the first edition of *A World of Ideas* was published, the notion that students in first-year composition courses should be able to read and write about challenging works by great thinkers was a radical one. In fact, no other composition reader at the time included selections from such important thinkers as Hannah Arendt, Aristotle, Friedrich Nietzsche, Karl Marx, Plato, Charles Darwin, or Mary Wollstonecraft. I had expected a moderate response from a small number of people. Instead, teachers and students alike sent me a swarm of mail commending the book for the challenge it provided and the insights they gained.

One of the first letters I received was from a young woman who had read the book after she graduated from college. She said she had heard of the thinkers included in *A World of Ideas* but in her college career had never read any of their works. Reading them now, she said, was long overdue. Another student wrote me an elaborate letter in which he demonstrated that every one of the selections in the book had been used as the basis of a *Star Trek* episode. He sagely connected every selection to a specific episode and convinced me that whoever was writing *Star Trek* had read some of the world's most important thinkers. Other students have written to tell me that they found themselves using the material in this book in other courses, such as psychology, philosophy, literature, and history, among others. In many cases, these students were the only ones among their peers who had read the key authors in their discipline.

Sometimes, you will have to read the selections in *A World of Ideas* more than once. Works by influential thinkers, such as Jean-Jacques Rousseau, John Rawls, Judith Butler, Adam Smith, Sigmund Freud, Francis Bacon, Iris Murdoch, and Howard Gardner, can be very challenging. But do not let the challenge discourage you. In "Evaluating Ideas: An Introduction to Critical Reading," I suggest methods for annotating and questioning texts that are designed to help you keep track of what you read and to help you master the material. In addition, each selection is accompanied by a headnote on the author's life and work, comments about the primary ideas presented in the selection, and a host of questions to help you overcome minor difficulties in understanding the author's meaning. Some students have written to tell me that their first reading of the book was off-putting, but most of them have written later to tell me how they eventually overcame their initial fear that the selections would be too difficult for them. Ultimately, these students agreed with me that this material is important enough to merit their absolute attention.

The purpose of *A World of Ideas* is to help you learn to write better by giving you something really significant to think and write about. The selections not only are avenues into some of the most serious thought on their subjects but also are stimulating enough to sustain close analysis and to produce many good ideas for writing. For example, when you think about democracy, it helps to know what Aristotle said about it while Athens enjoyed it, just as it is important to understand the ideals Thomas Jefferson was championing when he penned the Declaration of Independence. Mary Wollstonecraft was also a radical political thinker of her time, advocating for greater respect and better opportunities for women in a society that did not value their gifts and talents. Indeed, social justice is integral to thinking about culture; John Rawls, the most important modern philosopher of justice, measures justice always by its effect on the neediest and least powerful segment of any society. Frederick Douglass speaks from the perspective of a former slave when he cries out against the injustice of an institution that existed in the Americas for hundreds of years. And a hundred years after Douglass, the Reverend Martin Luther King Jr. sent his "Letter from Birmingham Jail," still demanding justice for African Americans and freedom seekers everywhere. The questions of ethics that still haunt us are treated by Iris Murdoch in relation to religion and by Kwame Anthony Appiah in relation to situational and virtue ethics, each of which concentrates on the relation of ones' character to one's ethical behavior. All these writers place their views in the larger context of a universal dialogue on the subject of justice. When you write, you add your own voice to the conversation. By commenting on the selections, expressing and arguing a position, and pointing out contradictions or contrasts among texts, you are participating in the world of ideas.

Keep in mind that I prepared *A World of Ideas* for my own students, most of whom work their way through college and do not take the idea of earning an education lightly. For that reason, I felt I owed them the opportunity to encounter the very best minds I could put them in touch with. Anything less seemed to me a missed opportunity. I hope you, like so many other writing students, find this book both educational and inspiring.

Contents

PART TWO

CULTURE

PART THREE

WEALTH   **319**

PART FOUR

MIND   **453**

PART FIVE

SCIENCE

PART SIX

ETHICS   **683**

Some Considerations about the Nature of Ethics   687

Evaluating Ideas

AN INTRODUCTION TO CRITICAL READING

T HE SELECTIONS IN THIS BOOK demand a careful and attentive reading. The authors, whose works have changed the way we view our world,
our institutions, and ourselves, make every effort to communicate their views
with clarity and style. But their views are complex and subtle, and we must
train ourselves to read them sensitively, responsively, and critically. Critical
reading is basic for approaching the essays in this book. Indeed, it is fundamental for approaching any reading material that deserves serious attention.

Reading critically means reading actively: questioning the premises of the
argument, speculating on the ways in which evidence is used, comparing the
statements of one writer with those of another, and holding an inner dialogue
with the author. These skills differ from the passive reception we employ when
we watch television or read lightweight materials. Being an active, participating
reader makes it possible for us to derive the most from good books.

Critical reading involves most of the following processes:

- **Prereading** Developing a sense of what the piece is about and what its
  general purposes seem to be.

- **Annotating** Using a pencil or a pen to mark those passages that seem
  important enough to return to later. Annotations establish a dialogue
  between you and the author.

- **Questioning** Raising issues that you feel need to be taken into consideration. These may be issues that you believe the author has treated either
  well or badly and that you feel are important. Questioning can be part
  of the annotation process.

1

- **Reviewing** Rereading your annotations and underlinings in order to grasp the entire "picture" of what you've just read. Sometimes writing a summary of the piece as you review makes the meaning even clearer.
- **Forming your own ideas** Reviewing what you have read, evaluating the way that the writer presents the issues, and developing your own views on the issues. This is the final step.

The Process of Critical Reading

PREREADING

Before you read a particular selection, you may find it useful to turn to the beginning of the part in which it appears. There you will find an introduction discussing the broader issues and questions central to all the selections in the part. This may help you focus your thoughts and formulate your opinions as you read the essays themselves.

Begin any selection in this book by reading its headnote. Each headnote supplies historical background on the writer, sets the intellectual stage for the ideas discussed in the essay, and comments on the writer's main points. The second part of each headnote introduces the main rhetorical or stylistic methods that the writer uses to communicate his or her thoughts. In the process of reading the headnote, you will develop an overview that helps prepare you for reading the essay.

This kind of preparation is typical of critical reading. It makes the task of reading more delightful, more useful, and much easier. A review of the headnote to Niccolò Machiavelli and part of his essay "The Qualities of the Prince" (p. 84) will illustrate the usefulness of such preparation. This essay appears in Part One—"Government"—so the content can already be expected to be concerned with styles of government. The introduction to Machiavelli provides the following points, each followed here by the number of the paragraph in which it appears:

> Machiavelli was an Italian aristocrat in Renaissance Italy. (para. 1)
> Machiavelli describes the qualities necessary for a prince—that is, any ruler—to maintain power. (para. 2)
> A weak Italy was prey to the much stronger France and Spain at this time. (para. 2)
> Machiavelli recommends securing power by whatever means necessary and maintaining it. (para. 3)
> His concern for moralizing or acting out of high moral principle is not great. (para. 3)

He supports questionable means of becoming and remaining prince.
  (para. 3)
Machiavelli does not fret over the means used to achieve his ends and
  sometimes advocates repression, imprisonment, and torture. (para. 3)
Machiavelli has been said to have a cynical view of human nature.
  (para. 4)
His rhetorical method is to discuss both sides of an issue: cruelty and
  mercy, liberality and stinginess. (para. 8)
He uses aphorisms to persuade the reader that he is saying something
  wise and true. (para. 9)

With these observations in mind, the reader knows that the selection that
follows will be concerned with governance in Renaissance Italy. The question
of ends versus means is central to Machiavelli's discussion, and he does not
idealize people and their general goodness. Yet because of Machiavelli's rhetorical methods, particularly his use of aphorism,[1] the reader can expect that
Machiavelli's argument will be exceptionally persuasive.

Thus, as a critical reader, you will be well advised to keep track of these
basic statements from the headnote. You need not accept all of them, but you
should certainly be alert to the issues that will probably be central to your
experience of the essay. Remember: it is just as reasonable to question the
headnote as it is to question the essay itself.

Before reading the essay in detail, you might develop an overview of its
meaning by scanning it quickly. In the case of "The Qualities of the Prince,"
note the subheadings, such as "On Those Things for Which Men, and Particularly Princes, Are Praised or Blamed." Checking each of the subheadings
before you read the entire piece might provide you with a map or guide to
the essay.

Each passage is preceded by two or three prereading questions. These
are designed to help you keep two or three points in mind as you read. Each
of these questions focuses your attention on an important idea or interpretation in the passage. For your reading of Machiavelli, the questions are as
follows:

1. Why does Machiavelli praise skill in warfare in his opening pages? How
   does that skill aid a prince?

2. Is it better for a prince to be loved or to be feared?

In each case, a key element in Machiavelli's argument is the center of each
question. By watching for the answer to these questions, you will find yourself
focusing on some of the most important aspects of the passage.

---

[1] **aphorism**   A short, pithy statement of truth.

ANNOTATING AND QUESTIONING

As you read a text, your annotations establish a dialogue between you and the author. You can underline or highlight important statements that you feel help clarify the author's position. They may be statements to which you will want to refer later. Think of them as serving one overriding purpose: to make it possible for you to review the piece and understand its key points without having to reread it entirely.

Your dialogue with the author will be most visible in the margins of the essay, which is one reason the margins in this book are so generous. Take issue with key points or note your assent—the more you annotate, the more you free your imagination to develop your own ideas. My own methods involve notating both agreement and disagreement. I annotate thoroughly, so that after a quick second glance I know what the author is saying as well as what I thought of the essay when I read it closely. My annotations help me keep the major points fresh in my mind.

Annotation keeps track both of what the author says and of what our responses are. No one can reduce annotation to a formula—we all do it differently—but it is not a passive act. Reading with a pencil or a pen in hand should become second nature. Without annotations, you often have to reread entire sections of an essay to remember an argument that once was clear and understandable but after time has become part of the fabric of the prose and thus "invisible." Annotation is the conquest of the invisible; it provides a quick view of the main points.

When you annotate,

- Read with a pen or a pencil.
- Underline key sentences—for example, definitions and statements of purpose.
- Underline key words that appear often.
- Note the topic of paragraphs in the margins.
- Ask questions in the margins.
- Make notes in the margins to remind yourself to develop ideas later.
- Mark passages you might want to quote later.
- Keep track of points with which you disagree.

Some sample annotations follow, again from Niccolò Machiavelli's "The Qualities of the Prince." A sixteenth-century text in translation, *The Prince* is challenging to work with. My annotations appear in the form of underlinings and marginal comments and questions. Only the first few paragraphs appear here, but the entire essay is annotated in my copy of the book.

A Prince's Duty Concerning Military Matters

A prince, therefore, must not have any other object nor any other thought, nor must he take anything as his <u>profession but war,</u> its institutions, and its discipline; because that is the only profession which befits one who commands; and it is of such importance that not only does it maintain those who were born princes, but many times it enables men of private station to rise to that position; and, on the other hand, it is evident that <u>when princes have given more thought to personal luxuries than to arms, they have lost their state.</u> And the first way to lose it is to neglect this art; and the way to acquire it is to be well versed in this art.

Francesco Sforza became Duke of Milan from being a private citizen because he was armed; his sons, since they avoided the inconveniences of arms, became private citizens after having been dukes. For, among the other bad effects it causes, being disarmed makes you despised; this is one of those infamies a prince should guard himself against, as will be treated below: for between an armed and an unarmed man there is no comparison whatsoever, and it is not reasonable for an armed man to obey an unarmed man willingly, nor that an unarmed man should be safe among armed servants; since, when the former is suspicious and the latter are contemptuous, it is impossible for them to work well together. And therefore, a prince who does not understand military matters, besides the other misfortunes already noted, cannot be esteemed by his own soldiers, nor can he trust them.

He must, therefore, never raise his thought from this exercise of war, and in peacetime he must train himself more than in time of war; this can be done in two ways: one by <u>action, the other by the mind.</u> And as far as actions are concerned, besides <u>keeping his soldiers well disciplined and trained,</u> he must always be out hunting, and must accustom his body to hardships in this manner; and he must also <u>learn the nature of the terrain, and know how mountains slope, how valleys open, how plains lie,</u> and understand the nature of rivers and swamps; and he should devote much attention to such activities. <u>Such knowledge is useful in two ways:</u> first, one learns to know one's own country and can better understand how to defend it; second, with the knowledge and experience of the terrain, one can easily comprehend the characteristics

---

Margin notes:

The prince's profession should be war.

Examples

Being disarmed makes you despised. Is this true?

Training: action/ mind

Knowledge of terrain

Two benefits

of any other terrain that it is necessary to explore for the first time; for the hills, valleys, plains, rivers, and swamps of Tuscany, for instance, have certain similarities to those of other provinces; so that by knowing the lay of the land in one province one can easily understand it in others. And a prince who lacks this ability lacks the most important quality in a leader; because this skill teaches you to find the enemy, choose a campsite, lead troops, organize them for battle, and besiege towns to your own advantage.

[There follow the examples of Philopoemon, who was always observing terrain for its military usefulness, and a recommendation that princes read histories and learn from them. Three paragraphs are omitted.]

On Those Things for Which Men, and Particularly Princes, Are Praised or Blamed

Now there remains to be examined what should be the <u>methods and procedures of a prince</u> in dealing with his subjects and friends. And because I know that many have written about this, I am afraid that by writing about it again I shall be thought of as presumptuous, since in discussing this material I depart radically from the procedures of others. But since my intention is to write something useful for anyone who understands it, it seemed more suitable to me to search after the effectual truth of the matter rather than its imagined one. And many writers have imagined for themselves republics and principalities that have never been seen nor known to exist in reality; for there is such a gap between how one lives and how one ought to live that anyone who abandons what is done for what ought to be done learns his ruin rather than his preservation: for <u>a man who wishes to make a vocation of being good at all times will come to ruin among so many who are not good.</u> Hence it is necessary for a <u>prince</u> who wishes to maintain his position <u>to learn how not to be good,</u> and to use this knowledge or not to use it according to necessity.

Leaving aside, therefore, the imagined things concerning a prince, and taking into account those that are true, I say that all men, when they are spoken of, and particularly princes, since they are placed on a higher level, are judged by some of

Those who are good at all times come to ruin among those who are not good.

Prince must learn how not to be good.

Note the
prince's
reputation.

these qualities which bring them either <u>blame or praise.</u> And this is why one is considered generous, another miserly (to use a Tuscan word, since "avaricious" in our language is still used to mean one who wishes to acquire by means of theft; we call "miserly" one who excessively avoids using what he has); one is considered a giver, the other rapacious; one cruel, another merciful; one treacherous, another faithful; one effeminate and cowardly, another bold and courageous; one humane, another haughty; one lascivious, another chaste; one trustworthy, another cunning; one harsh, another lenient; one serious, another frivolous; one religious, another unbelieving; and the like. And I know that everyone will admit that it would be a very praiseworthy thing to find in a prince, of the qualities mentioned above, those that are held to be good, but since it is neither possible to have them nor to observe them all completely, because human nature does not permit it, <u>a prince must be prudent enough to know how to escape the bad reputation of those vices that would lose the state for him, and must protect himself from those that will not lose it for him, if this is possible; but if he cannot, he need not concern himself unduly if he ignores these less serious vices. And, moreover, he need not worry about incurring the bad reputation of those vices without which it would be difficult to hold his state;</u> since, carefully taking everything into account, <u>one will discover that something which appears to be a virtue, if pursued, will end in his destruction;</u> while some other thing which seems to be a vice, if pursued, will result in his safety and his well-being.

Prince must avoid
reputation for
the worst vices.

Some vices may be
needed to hold the
state. True?

Some virtues may
end in destruction.

REVIEWING

The process of review, which takes place after a careful reading, is much more useful if you have annotated and underlined the text well. To a large extent, the review process can be devoted to accounting for the primary ideas that have been uncovered by your annotations and underlinings. For example, reviewing the Machiavelli annotations shows that the following ideas are crucial to Machiavelli's thinking:

- The prince's profession should be war, so the most successful princes are probably experienced in the military.

- If they do not pay attention to military matters, princes will lose their power.

- Being disarmed makes the prince despised.
- The prince should be in constant training.
- The prince needs a sound knowledge of terrain.
- Machiavelli says he tells us what is true, not what ought to be true.
- Those who are always good will come to ruin among those who are not good.
- To remain in power, the prince must learn how not to be good.
- The prince should avoid the worst vices in order not to harm his reputation.
- To maintain power, some vices may be necessary.
- Some virtues may end in destruction.

Putting Machiavelli's ideas in this raw form does an injustice to his skill as a writer, but annotation is designed to result in such summary statements. We can see that there are some constant themes, such as the insistence that the prince be a military person. As the headnote tells us, in Machiavelli's day Italy was a group of rival city-states, and France, a larger, united nation, was invading these states one by one. Machiavelli dreamed that one powerful prince, such as his favorite, Cesare Borgia, could fight the French and save Italy. He emphasized the importance of the military because he lived in an age in which war was a constant threat.

Machiavelli anticipates the complaints of pacifists—those who argue against war—by telling us that those who remain unarmed are despised. To demonstrate his point, he gives us examples of those who lost their positions as princes because they avoided being armed. He clearly expects these examples to be persuasive.

A second important theme pervading Machiavelli's essay is his view on moral behavior. For Machiavelli, being in power is much more important than being virtuous. He is quick to admit that vice is not desirable and that the worst vices will harm the prince's reputation. But he also says that the prince need not worry about the "less serious" vices. Moreover, the prince need not worry about incurring a bad reputation by practicing vices that are necessary if he wishes to hold his state. In the same spirit, Machiavelli tells us that there are some virtues that might lead to the destruction of the prince.

FORMING YOUR OWN IDEAS

One of the most important reasons for critically reading the texts in this book is to enable you to develop your own positions on issues that these writers raise. Identifying and clarifying the main ideas is only the first step; the next step in critical reading is evaluating those ideas.

For example, you might ask whether Machiavelli's ideas have any relevance for today. After all, he wrote nearly five hundred years ago and times have changed. You might feel that Machiavelli was relevant strictly during the Italian Renaissance or, alternatively, that his principles are timeless and have something to teach every age. For most people, Machiavelli is a political philosopher whose views are useful anytime and anywhere.

If you agree with the majority, then you may want to examine Machiavelli's ideas to see whether you can accept them. Consider just two of those ideas and their implications:

- Should rulers always be members of the military? Should they always be armed? Should the ruler of a nation first demonstrate competence as a military leader?

- Should rulers ignore virtue and practice vice when it is convenient?

In his commentary on government, which is also included in Part One, Lao-tzu offers different advice from Machiavelli because his assumptions are that the ruler ought to respect the rights of individuals. For Lao-tzu the waging of war is an annoying, essentially wasteful activity. Machiavelli, on the other hand, never questions the usefulness of war: to him, it is basic to government. As a critical reader, you can take issue with such an assumption, and in doing so you will deepen your understanding of Machiavelli.

If we were to follow Machiavelli's advice, then we would choose American presidents on the basis of whether or not they had been good military leaders. Among those we would not have chosen might be Thomas Jefferson, Abraham Lincoln, and Franklin Delano Roosevelt. Those who were high-ranking military men include George Washington, Ulysses S. Grant, and Dwight D. Eisenhower. If you followed Machiavelli's rhetorical technique of using examples to convince your audience, you could choose from either group to prove your case.

Of course, there are examples from other nations. It has been common since the 1930s to see certain leaders dressed in their military uniforms: Benito Mussolini (Italy), Adolf Hitler (Germany), Joseph Stalin (the Soviet Union), Idi Amin (Uganda), Muammar al-Qaddafi (Libya), Saddam Hussein (Iraq). These were all tyrants who tormented their citizens and their neighbors. That gives us something to think about. Should a president dress in full military regalia all the time? Is that a good image for the ruler of a free nation to project?

Do you want a ruler, then, who is usually virtuous but embraces vice when it is necessary? This is a very difficult question to answer. President Richard Nixon tried to hide the Watergate break-in scandal, President Ronald Reagan did not reveal the details of the Iran-Contra scandal, President Bill Clinton lied about his relations with Monica Lewinsky, and George W. Bush misrepresented intelligence to invade Iraq. Yet all these presidents are noted for important achievements while in office. How might Machiavelli have handled these problems differently? How much truthfulness do we expect from our presidents? How much do we deserve?

These are only a few of the questions that are raised by my annotations in the few pages from Machiavelli examined here. Many other issues could be uncovered by these annotations and many more from subsequent pages of the essay. Critical reading can be a powerful means by which to open what you read to discovery and discussion.

Once you begin a line of questioning, the ways in which you think about a passage begin expanding. You find yourself with more ideas of your own that have grown in response to those you have been reading about. Reading critically, in other words, gives you an enormous return on your investment of time. If you have the chance to investigate your responses to the assumptions and underlying premises of passages such as Machiavelli's, you will be able to refine your thinking even further. For example, if you agree with Machiavelli that rulers should be successful military leaders for whom small vices may be useful at times, and you find yourself in a position to argue with someone who feels Machiavelli is mistaken in this view, then you will have a good opportunity to evaluate the soundness of your thinking. You will have a chance to see your own assumptions and arguments tested.

In many ways, this entire book is about such opportunities. The essays that follow offer you powerful ideas from great thinkers. They invite you to participate in their thoughts, exercise your own knowledge and assumptions, and arrive at your own conclusions. Basically, that is the meaning of education.

Writing about Ideas

AN INTRODUCTION TO RHETORIC

WRITING ABOUT IDEAS has several functions. First, it helps make our thinking available to others for examination. The writers whose works are presented in this book benefited from their first readers' examinations and at times revised their work considerably as a result of such criticism. Writing about ideas also helps us refine what we think—even without criticism from others—because writing is a self-instructional experience. We learn by writing in part because writing clarifies our thinking. When we think silently, we construct phrases and then reflect on them; when we speak, we both utter these phrases and sort them out in order to give our audience a tidier version of our thoughts. But spoken thought is difficult to sustain because we cannot review or revise what we said an hour earlier. Writing has the advantage of permitting us to expand our ideas, to work them through completely and possibly to revise in the light of later discoveries. It is by writing that we truly gain control over our ideas.

Generating Topics for Writing

Filled with sophisticated discussions of important ideas, the selections in this volume endlessly stimulate our responses and our writing. Reading the works of great thinkers can also be chastening to the point of making us feel sometimes that they have said it all and there is no room for our own thoughts. However, the suggestions that follow will assist you in writing your response to the ideas of an important thinker.

Thinking Critically: Asking a Question. One of the most reliable ways to start writing is to ask a question and then to answer it. In many ways, that is what the writers in this book have done again and again. Edward O. Wilson uses a question for the title of his selection, "What Is Science?" (p. 631). Then, he uses the entire idea of questioning to help define what science is: the asking of questions and the effort to answer them. He includes a number of questions in his essay, such as, "What is this grand enterprise called science that has lit up heaven and earth and empowered humanity?" and "Does biology also have laws?" He asks the second question because it is well established that physics and chemistry have laws, but biology is different. After having discussed a number of important ideas in the world of science, he asks, as a kind of summing up, "What, then, in broadest terms is the scientific method?" His essay essentially answers his question. Adam Smith asks what the principles of accumulating wealth really are (p. 325) and proceeds to examine the economic system of his time in such detail that his views are still valued. He is associated with the capitalist system as firmly as Marx is with the communist system. Henry David Thoreau, in "Civil Disobedience" (p. 720), considers the role of conscience in government. He asks, "Can there not be a government in which majorities do not virtually decide right and wrong but conscience?— in which majorities decide only those questions to which the rule of expediency is applicable? Must the citizen ever for a moment, or in the least degree, resign his conscience to the legislator? Why has every man a conscience, then?" (para. 4). These are profound questions.

When Charles Darwin begins his meditation on the power of natural selection (p. 606), he starts with the most obvious question: "How will the struggle for existence . . . act in regard to variation? Can the principle of selection, which we have seen is so potent in the hands of man, apply in nature?" His previous discussion concerns the ways in which people can create variation in dogs by selecting for desirable traits, just as they do for variations in horses, livestock, flowers, and all vegetables used for food. If people can create variability, what happens when nature does it? Such questioning is at the center of all critical thinking.

As a writer stimulated by other thinkers, you can use the same technique. For example, turn back to the Machiavelli excerpt annotated in "Evaluating Ideas: An Introduction to Critical Reading" (p. 2). All the annotations can easily be turned into questions. Any of the following questions, based on the annotations and our brief summary of the passage, could be the basis of an essay:

- Should a leader be armed?
- Is it true that an unarmed leader is despised?
- Will those leaders who are always good come to ruin among those who are not good?
- To remain in power, must a leader learn how not to be good?

One technique is to structure an essay around the answer to such a question. Another is to develop a series of questions and to answer each of them in various parts of an essay. Yet another technique is to use the question indirectly—by answering it, but not in an obvious way. In "Why the Rich Are Getting Richer and the Poor, Poorer" (p. 422), for example, Robert B. Reich answers a question we may not have asked. In the process he examines the nature of our current economy to see what it promises for different sectors of the population. His answer to the question concerns the shift in labor from manufacturing to information, revealing that "symbolic analysts" have the best opportunities in the future to amass wealth.

Many kinds of questions can be asked of a passage even as brief as the sample from Machiavelli. For one thing, we can limit ourselves to our annotations and go no further. But we also can reflect on larger issues and ask a series of questions that constitute a fuller inquiry. Out of that inquiry we can generate ideas for our own writing.

Two important ideas are isolated in our annotations. The first is that the prince must devote himself to war. In modern times, this implies that a president or other national leader must put matters of defense first—that a leader's knowledge, training, and concerns must revolve around warfare. Taking that idea in general, we can develop other questions that, stimulated by Machiavelli's selection, can be used to generate essays:

- Which modern leaders would Machiavelli support?
- Would Machiavelli approve of our current president?
- Do military personnel make the best leaders?
- Should our president have a military background?
- Could a modern state survive with no army or military weapons?
- What kind of a nation would we have if we did not stockpile nuclear weapons?

These questions derive from "The prince's profession should be war," the first idea that we isolate in the annotations. The next group of questions comes from the second idea, the issue of whether a leader can afford to be moral:

- Can virtues cause a leader to lose power?
- Is Machiavelli being cynical about morality, or is he being realistic (as he claims he is)? (We might also ask if Machiavelli uses the word *realistic* as a synonym for *cynical*.)
- Do most American leaders behave morally?
- Do most leaders believe that they should behave morally?
- Should our leaders be moral all the time?

- Which vices can we permit our leaders to have?
- Are there any vices we want our leaders to have?
- Which world leaders behave most morally? Are they the ones we most respect?
- Could a modern government govern well or at all if it were to behave morally in the face of immoral adversaries?

One reason for reading Machiavelli is to help us confront broad and serious questions. One reason for writing about these ideas is to help clarify our own positions on such important issues.

Using Suggestions for Writing. Every selection in this book is followed by a number of questions and a number of writing assignments. The questions are designed to help clarify the most important issues raised in the piece. Unlike the questions derived from annotation, their purpose is to stimulate a classroom discussion so that you can benefit from hearing others' thoughts on these issues. Naturally, subjects for essays can arise from such discussion, but the discussion is most important for refining and focusing your ideas. The writing assignments, on the other hand, are explicitly meant to provide a useful starting point for producing an essay of five hundred to one thousand words.

A sample suggestion for writing about Machiavelli follows:

> Machiavelli advises the prince to study history and reflect on the actions of great men. Do you support such advice? Machiavelli mentions a number of great leaders in his essay. Which leaders would you recommend a prince should study? How do you think Machiavelli would agree or disagree with your recommendations?

Like most of the suggestions for writing, this one can be approached in several ways. It can be broken down into three parts. The first question is whether it is useful to study, as Machiavelli does, the performance of past leaders. If you agree, then the second question asks you to name some leaders whose behavior you would recommend studying. If you do not agree, you can point to the performance of some past leaders and explain why their study would be pointless today. Finally, the third question asks how you think Machiavelli would agree or disagree with your choices.

To deal successfully with this suggestion for writing, you could begin by giving your reasons for recommending that a political leader study "the actions of great men." George Santayana once said, "Those who cannot remember the past are condemned to repeat it." That is, we study history in order not to have to live it over again. If you believe that a study of the past is important, the first part of an essay can answer the question of why such study could make a politician more successful.

The second part of the suggestion focuses on examples. In the sample from Machiavelli in "Evaluating Ideas," we omitted the examples, but in the complete essay they are very important for bringing Machiavelli's point home. Few things can convince as completely as examples, so the first thing to do is to choose several leaders to work with. If you have studied a world leader, such as Indira Gandhi, Winston Churchill, Franklin Delano Roosevelt, or Margaret Thatcher, you could use that figure as one of your examples. If you have not done so, then use the research library's sections on history and politics to find books or articles on one or two leaders and read them with an eye to establishing their usefulness for your argument. An Internet search can help you gather information efficiently. The central question you would seek to answer is how a specific world leader could benefit from studying the behavior and conduct of a modern leader.

The third part of the suggestion for writing—how Machiavelli would agree or disagree with you—is highly speculative. It invites you to look through the selection to find quotations or comments that indicate probable agreement or disagreement on Machiavelli's part. You can base your argument only on what Machiavelli says or implies, and this means that you will have to reread his essay to find evidence that will support your view.

In a sense, this part of the suggestion establishes a procedure for working with the writing assignments. Once you clarify the parts of the assignment and have some useful questions to guide you, and once you determine what research, if any, is necessary, the next step is to reread the selection to find the most appropriate information to help you write your own essay. One of the most important activities in learning how to write from these selections is to reread while paying close attention to the annotations that you've made in the margins of the essays. It is one way in which reading about significant ideas differs from reading for entertainment. Important ideas demand reflection and reconsideration. Rereading provides both.

Developing Ideas in Writing

QUESTIONING THE TEXT

In many ways, the authors of the selections that follow respond to important questions. Sometimes, as with Darwin's essay, there is one question that controls the entire piece, but in many of the selections there is a range of questions that seem to arise from other questions. That is the nature of inquiry, and it helps not only to shape the essay but also to focus our attention as we read it. By observing the nature of the texts that you read and the ways in which questions function as touchstones for the author, you can soon see how valuable the act of questioning can be for you as a writer. The selections in this book are often controversial and demand a response. When you question a text, you are responding to it and your response can be used to develop ideas of your own that can be the basis for your own writing.

Useful Questions. The following questions can be applied to virtually any important material that you read.

- What are the most important ideas presented in this selection?
- Is this article an argument or is it simply an observation of fact?
- What is the main point being presented here?
- What seems to be the author's purpose in writing this piece?
- Is the author's purpose explicit?
- What claim or claims does the author make?
- What specifically supports the author's claims?
- Does the author omit arguments and evidence that might contradict the claims?
- Does the author satisfactorily analyze and reject contradictory arguments?
- To what extent is there a bias for or against a position in the author's argument?
- What assumptions does the author make about his subject matter?
- Has the author provided clear support for the argument in terms of evidence, example, or expert testimony?
- Which details in the argument are the most important? Are they convincing?
- How significant is this argument for me personally? For society generally?

Questioning Freud. At the beginning of "The Oedipus Complex" (p. 477) by Sigmund Freud, three questions suggest points that the reader might use to focus attention on the essay:

- What is the Oedipus complex?
- How does it express itself in dreams?
- How do the examples of *Oedipus Rex* and *Hamlet* illustrate the Oedipus complex?

But these questions are not the same ones you might ask yourself after reading the essay. The most important question you would probably ask is

- Is Freud right? Is there such a thing as an Oedipus complex?

Freud himself is answering a question indirectly: What is the cause of neurosis in the people he has psychoanalyzed? In response, he says that most mental illness arises from the role parents play in a person's childhood. Psychoneurotic children experience an unconscious love for their opposite-sex parent and a hatred for their same-sex parent. In the Greek drama, for which the complex is named, Oedipus kills his father and marries his mother. In the Elizabethan drama by Shakespeare, Hamlet has an unnatural concern for his mother and kills the king, his stepfather. Here is how Freud opens his discussion:

> In my experience, which is already extensive, the chief part in the mental lives of all children who later become psychoneurotics is played by their parents. Being in love with the one parent and hating the other are among the essential constituents of the stock of psychical impulses which is formed at that time and which is of such importance in determining the symptoms of the later neurosis. It is not my belief, however, that psychoneurotics differ sharply in this respect from other human beings who remain normal — that they are able, that is, to create something absolutely new and peculiar to themselves. It is far more probable — and this is confirmed by occasional observations on normal children — that they are only distinguished by exhibiting on a magnified scale feelings of love and hatred to their parents which occur less obviously and less intensely in the minds of most children. (para. 1)

Sample Questions. Here are a few questions that naturally arise from reading Freud's opening paragraph:

- Does Freud claim that parents play a major role in the neuroses of their children?
- Do children seem to grow up hating one parent and loving the other?
- Does my experience help support Freud's views, or does it contradict them?
- When they grow up, are psychoneurotics who suffer from the Oedipus complex likely to kill one of their parents?
- Could Freud's "occasional observations" of children confirm the wide-ranging claim that he makes?
- How do normal children seem to differ from neurotic children?

Once you have read the entire passage, you will formulate other questions that should help you develop ideas of your own as to whether or not what Freud says makes good sense to you. *Oedipus Complex* is a term that is used often, and sometimes used irresponsibly, so it is important for you to decide how valid Freud's thinking is. Once you have read Freud's entire discussion — an argument that employs important examples to support its claim that parents play a major role in the neuroses of their children — you will want to consider the examples carefully. Here are some questions that might be useful after reading the essay:

- Does a discussion of fictitious characters help us understand a cause of neurosis?
- Is Hamlet a neurotic who fits Freud's description?
- Did Oedipus's parents cause his problems?
- Is Oedipus a neurotic?
- If Oedipus and Hamlet are clearly neurotic, does that prove Freud's theory?

You could probably add more questions to these two lists, and if you do, you will be helping yourself not only to better understand the selection but also to better approach writing something of your own about the piece.

A Sample Beginning for a Brief Essay on Freud. The following paragraphs are the beginning of an essay in response to Freud's theory of the Oedipus Complex. A few of the questions above are implied in this sample.

MY OEDIPUS COMPLEX

Freud's theory of the Oedipus Complex is a bit unsettling for me. I grew up knowing that I loved my father more than I loved my mother. It was not a really major difference, but it was noticeable to my younger brother, who says he can relate to our mother more than to our father. According to Freud, that seems to be the pattern of the Oedipus complex, but neither I nor my brother have mental problems. Should I be worried? Should my brother be worried? I hope not, but I'm not entirely sure. After reading about Oedipus and Hamlet, I realize that they are extreme cases, what Freud says is on "a magnified scale." There is nothing magnified about my relation with my dad, who drove me to school and met my roommates and took us to dinner and then went home. My mother stayed home with my brother, Tim, and that's what usually happens.

But there have been some things that I see now may be problems that my brother may have that I don't have. For example, Tim no longer goes with Dad to fish or to hunt in spring and fall. Now I can see how disappointed Dad has been to see that Tim does not want to do some of the same things he does. Mom likes to go to plays, which I don't usually have time for, so Tim goes with her, and I think he really enjoys them. Dad and I would rather go to a movie, and when I was in middle school we used to see action adventure films that

Mom didn't like. Dad and I are more interested in the same kinds of things than are Tim and Mom, who like different things. Is this normal, or should I be worried that sometime in the future Tim will suddenly explode and let go on Dad? Or that I will on Mom? Should I be frightened?

—Alice F.

The rest of the essay examines Alice's and Tim's relationships with their parents and compares them with Freud's examples. Alice aimed at establishing what she thought were normal patterns of behavior toward parents by questioning some of her roommates and by discussing how the literary examples Freud chose were convincing on one level but how they needed to be balanced with Alice's own experience.

Questioning Carnegie. Alice's essay was primarily a personal response to a theory that she was trying to understand. The following is an examination of a problem in political and economic terms that affects many of us. The economic debate today is often posed in terms of inequity — the fact that in recent decades the ultra-rich have come to control an exorbitant amount of the wealth of the nation, with perhaps more than 90 percent of the wealth in the hands of less than 5 percent of the people. For Robert Reich (p. 422), whose selection examines the process of the wealthy growing more wealthy, the problem of economic inequality is serious and perhaps political.

In the late nineteenth and early twentieth centuries, Andrew Carnegie (p. 360) was one of the richest men in the world — he controlled massive wealth and wielded extraordinary influence. Like many of modern society's ultra-rich, he made his money by taking advantage of new technologies and remarkable opportunities. Also like many of today's ultra-rich, he felt that he deserved his wealth because he felt himself to be in many ways a superior person.

In the following paragraph, Carnegie praises the current situation in society that allows an individual such as he to amass as much wealth as possible. He regards possession of such wealth as a hallmark of advanced civilization:

Objections to the foundations upon which society is based are not in order, because the condition of the race is better with these than it has been with any others which have been tried. Of the effect of any new substitutes proposed we cannot be sure. The Socialist or Anarchist who seeks to overturn present conditions is to be regarded as attacking the foundation upon which civilization itself rests, for civilization took its start from the day that the capable, industrious workman said to his incompetent and lazy fellow, "If thou dost not sow, thou shalt not reap," and thus ended primitive Communism by separating the drones from the bees. One who studies this subject will soon be brought face to face with the conclusion that upon the sacredness of property civilization itself depends—the right of the laborer to his hundred dollars in the savings-bank, and equally the legal right of the millionaire to his millions. To those who propose to substitute Communism for this intense Individualism the answer, therefore, is: the race has tried that. All progress from that barbarous day to the present time has resulted from its displacement. Not evil, but good, has come to the race from the accumulation of wealth by those who have the ability and energy that produce it. But even if we admit for a moment that it might be better for the race to discard its present foundation, Individualism—that it is a nobler ideal that man should labor, not for himself alone, but in and for a brotherhood of his fellows, and share with them all in common, realizing Swedenborg's idea of Heaven, where, as he says, the angels derive their happiness, not from laboring for self, but for each other—even admit all this, and a sufficient answer is, This is not evolution, but revolution. It necessitates the changing of human nature itself—a work of aeons, even if it were good to change it, which we cannot know. It is not practicable in our day or in our age. Even if desirable theoretically, it belongs to another and long-succeeding sociological stratum. (para. 7)

Sample Questions. Many of the issues Carnegie treats in this passage require close examination and a serious response because they assume important truths about our society. Carnegie's assumptions about the way our civilization should work may have been reasonable when this essay was written in 1889, but we may question whether those assumptions are still relevant today. As a start, here are a few questions this paragraph raises:

- Why does the Socialist attack the foundations of society?
- Why did civilization get its start from "If thou dost not sow, thou shalt not reap"?
- Who are the drones and who are the bees in civilization?
- Why does civilization depend on the sacredness of property?
- What is "primitive communism"?
- What are the rights of laborers and millionaires?
- What does Carnegie mean by "intense Individualism"?
- How does the accumulation of wealth produce good rather than evil?
- Why is the idea of sharing in common revolution rather than evolution?
- What does Carnegie mean by "human nature"?
- Why would Socialism need to change human nature?

A Sample Beginning for a Brief Essay on Carnegie. Carnegie argues earlier in this essay that the dramatic inequity between the rich and the poor is an example of the progress of the human race. For instance, he comments on a visit to the Sioux in which he visited the chief only to find that the chief lived in a simple dwelling that was almost identical with every other dwelling. On that basis, Carnegie felt that the Sioux were primitive people and that Carnegie's society was advanced. As a strong believer in evolution, Carnegie saw the production of wealth as an example of evolution and progress. While not everyone today might agree with Carnegie, there are arguments on both sides of the issue. In the beginning of the following brief essay, some other specific questions led the author to a consideration of Carnegie's views:

- Is Carnegie's argument a defense of capitalism?
- Is the amassing of great wealth a natural result of the progress of society?
- Why should the laborer be content with his hundreds?
- How do the values of individualism compare with the values of community or collectivism?
- Why does Carnegie call property a sacred right?

The following is the beginning of an essay that takes issue with Carnegie's position.

INDIVIDUALISM AND PROGRESS

Andrew Carnegie defends his style of capitalism by telling us that communism is typical of primitive societies and that capitalism is a natural evolution. Over time, individualism operates to separate the "drones from the bees." Most people, who do not have the skills to produce wealth, are the drones, while the bees who do the work transform society, which is one of his main ideas. Those who produce wealth deserve their millions because without them there would be no millions. Carnegie emphasizes that all of society benefits from its millionaires by saying, "Today the world obtains commodities of excellent quality at prices which even the generation preceding this would have deemed incredible" (para. 3). Some of what Carnegie says is true because we can see that average people in developed societies today enjoy comforts that only royalty could enjoy hundreds of years ago.

However, Carnegie does not discuss the ways in which he amassed his wealth. It is true that he gave away most of his money before he died, and it is also true that he endowed colleges and libraries. But an examination of the way in which he made his money shows that he did all he could to make sure his workers had low-paying jobs because he felt that, being drones, they would not know how to spend their money if he raised their wages. In other words, he was sure that he deserved his wealth because he thought himself superior to his laborers, who he thought should be content with what he gave them. In "The Gospel of Wealth," he is not only defending capitalism as he understood it but also defending his view of himself as almost god-like in his ability to make millions and thereby dictate what is good for the rest of the people. Calling his essay a "Gospel" tells us that he speaks from on high to the lowly people who are not millionaires like him.

Today there are more millionaires and billionaires like Carnegie than there were in the 1870s. Most of them have avoided writing essays such as Carnegie did, but most of them still defend the view that "upon the sacredness of property civilization itself depends" (para. 7). Like Carnegie, they spend time defending their rights to their wealth, asking, "Since when has it become a crime to be wealthy in America?" Meanwhile, as Robert Reich says, the poor get poorer while the rich defend individualism and, to an extent, pay little attention to the relief of the growing numbers of those living at the poverty level. The defense of extravagant wealth is not as easy today as it was when Carnegie wrote his essay.

–Margaret B.

This writer was influenced by some of the current discussion of the shrinking of the middle class and also by the essay by Robert Reich called "Why the Rich Are Getting Richer and the Poor, Poorer" (p. 422). She saw that some of what Andrew Carnegie said could be defended, such as that modern industry produced a great many comforts for the average person. But she also criticized Carnegie's sense of entitlement to extreme wealth because he regarded himself as a superior being. She was concerned that Carnegie, despite his contributions to the nation's culture, did little to relieve the day-to-day limitations of low wages that characterized the late nineteenth century in America. Ironically, Carnegie's portrait of the Sioux chief living like the rest of his people stands in stark contrast to Margaret's portrait of Carnegie living like an emperor while the rest of his people lived much like the Sioux chief's people.

Margaret used many questions to help her establish ways to examine the selection critically in order to produce a useful essay.

CREATING A THESIS STATEMENT

One of the most important steps in writing an essay is creating your thesis. Sometimes you will be able to approach your first draft with a thesis in mind, and sometimes you will not discover your thesis until you have reread the selection you are responding to as well as your own first draft.

Your thesis statement is an assertion that will be made good by the specifics of your essay. The specifics may include references to facts, to the opinions of other important writers, or to your analysis of the text itself. What would not be among the specifics would be your own unsupported opinion. Your thesis statement makes a claim that you back up with careful use of evidence and testimony.

Your thesis may come at the beginning of your essay, as is typical, or it may appear in the middle or at the end. Some professional writers spread their thesis throughout the essay as a series of claims, but the best way to start a brief essay is by telling your reader what you are asserting and how you plan to support those assertions.

In the selections in this book you will find several different kinds of thesis statements that demonstrate the range and complexity of theses.

- **A thesis that states a position** In "The Origin of Civil Society" (p. 99), Jean-Jacques Rousseau opens with one of the most famous assertions in history: "Man is born free, and everywhere he is in chains." This dramatic assertion precedes his discussion of how social order developed from its primitive beginnings to the circumstances of the kinds of governments he observes in his own world. Defending this position is his job in this essay.

- **A thesis that establishes a cause** Henry David Thoreau offers a cause for his refusal to obey certain laws: "The government itself, which is only the mode which the people have chosen to execute their will, is equally liable to be abused and perverted before the people can act through it." This is only one of several thesis statements Thoreau makes in the first paragraph of "Civil Disobedience" (p. 720), an essay explaining why he rejects certain laws. Behind this assertion is his earlier statement: "That government is best which governs not at all." The rest of his essay is a discussion of his complaints against the laws he cannot ethically obey while still maintaining his own moral position.

- **A thesis that states an opinion** In "The Gospel of Wealth" (p. 360), Andrew Carnegie asserts, "The problem of our age is the proper administration of wealth, so that the ties of brotherhood may still bind together the rich and poor in harmonious relationship." Carnegie's first sentence expresses his opinion that the "administration of wealth" is the "problem of our age." With so many problems of any age, this statement will need a great deal of support from Carnegie's analysis of the recent events and the circumstances of his time.

- **A thesis that analyzes circumstance** For this example, we turn to a passage by Virginia Woolf: "But for women, I thought, looking at the empty shelves, these difficulties were infinitely more formidable.

In the first place, to have a room of her own, let alone a quiet room or a sound-proof room, was out of the question, unless her parents were exceptionally rich or very noble, even up to the beginning of the nineteenth century." This statement, Woolf's famous "A Room of Her Own" declaration in "Shakespeare's Sister" (p. 220), comes very deep in her essay (para. 12), after her careful discussion of the history of Shakespeare's time and her analysis of the difficulties any woman of genius would have had trying to become a noted author of important books or plays.

- **A thesis that defines a condition** Henry David Thoreau, in "Civil Disobedience" (p. 720), tries to define the kind of government that would please him most: "I heartily accept the motto — 'That government is best which governs least,' and I should like to see it acted up to more rapidly and systematically. Carried out, it finally amounts to this, which also I believe — 'That government is best which governs not at all'; and when men are prepared for it, that will be the kind of government which they will have." The rest of his essay examines the nature of government as he saw it in his own day, a time when slavery laws forced him to act against his conscience. He explains the conditions of his government to which he would submit and those to which he could not.

- **A thesis that establishes a conclusion** In "The Personal and the Collective Unconscious" (p. 487), Carl Jung explores the unconscious mind through dream analysis and waits until the end to state his thesis, which he feels is a reasonable conclusion to his discussion: "I have therefore advanced the hypothesis that at its deeper levels the unconscious possesses collective contents in a relatively active state. That is why I speak of the collective unconscious." The collective unconscious, he says earlier in the piece, contains archetypal patterns that most people in a given culture will experience in their dreams. In the larger body of his work, he asserts that these archetypes are universal and inherited as part of our mental biology.

Your Thesis Statement. Generally, your own thesis statement will be more direct and assertive than those of the writers in this book. One of the best ways for you to start is by creating a thesis statement that establishes your writing aims. A good modern thesis statement tells your reader what to expect from your essay and controls the scope and focus of your writing, making it easier for you and your reader to know what you are trying to say and when you are finished saying it.

Your thesis identifies your subject and what you want to say about it. Put in a slightly different way, your thesis identifies what is to be argued, explained, or focused on in your writing. It may tell your reader what your approach is and give a hint of your conclusions. In a sense, it acts as a signpost for your writing, guiding your reader throughout the rest of your essay.

Suggestions for Formulating a Thesis. Most of the time, creating a strong, clear thesis before writing is not a luxury but a necessity. Good writers realize that as it develops a thesis statement is dynamic, not carved in stone, not static and permanent. Just as every aspect of your writing is subject to review and revision, the thesis is capable of being recast, again and again, especially if you change your position as you argue your case. In that situation, your changed position would dictate that a new thesis statement be written.

You have several choices regarding the form of your thesis statement. For one, you may wish to break it into several sentences or craft it as a self-contained, single sentence. Further, you may choose to state your thesis plainly and openly — especially if your primary purpose is to be clear in what you are writing — or you may choose to imply it. To some extent, the choice of whether or not to use a strong thesis statement depends on your purpose as a writer. A clearly formulated thesis statement is most useful when your purpose is to persuade or to inform. An implied thesis is more commonly used in an expressive piece of writing in which the end purpose of informing or persuading is either secondary or omitted. Whatever your purpose, the concept of the thesis statement should be regarded as dynamic. There is not just one kind of thesis any more than there is just one place to state it.

Sample Theses. A thesis needs defense, elaboration, example, support, and development. For that reason, the thesis is not always a declarative factual statement. Rather, it is a statement that permits you to explore the issues that interest you and identify the key elements that will constitute your essay. A thesis can be stated in a single sentence or in a group of sentences or phrases. The point is that it shows what your concerns are and how you plan to approach discussing them.

The following sample thesis statements are appropriate for brief essays. They all stake some kind of claim and have the potential to be developed into full-length pieces of writing.

- Because of his belief that people benefit from governing their own behavior and should oppose unjust laws, it is clear that Henry David Thoreau would have championed the cause of Mary Wollstonecraft.

- Although John Rawls may be correct in saying that justice depends on fairness and must benefit the least among us, very few systems could work that way because the needs of the least among us are vast and cannot be fully satisfied. Instead, the utilitarian view that we must provide the greatest good for the greatest number has been workable in society and I think is defensible as a system of justice.

- Margaret Mead says that gender-linked temperaments develop because society reinforces them and essentially imposes them on individuals. That may be true to some extent, but my observations, and those of Judith Butler, suggest that there is a significant genetic factor that has to be taken into account.

- Andrew Carnegie would be very pleased with the distribution of wealth in our country today because it is approximately the same as it was in his time. He would have specifically approved of the decisions of Bill Gates and Warren Buffett to give away their wealth posthumously to benefit the public. Here are my suggestions for how their money should be spent.

- The question of whether or not democracy could give way to an oligarchy, as Aristotle implies, is extremely important to consider because some of the same conditions that deprived Athens of its democracy seem to be at work today. I want to examine several of those conditions and explain why they are threats to our democracy.

- The writer who I feel is most in sympathy with Iris Murdoch's views on morality and religion is Martin Luther King Jr. King, even more often than Murdoch, refers to religion and the Bible, which essentially agrees with Murdoch's view on the existence of evil. By examining the details of King's writing, I will show how close he is to Murdoch's position on morality.

Supporting Your Thesis. Each of these statements is flexible enough to appear at the beginning of an essay, within the first paragraph or somewhere deeper in the piece. Each has the advantage of implying what is to follow. In the first case, the writer's job is to analyze Thoreau's views in order to connect them with Mary Wollstonecraft's. The fact that they are both classic authors will help with the argument, but the challenge is to show that Thoreau felt women should enjoy the equality that Wollstonecraft felt was the only just position that society could take. The writer's thesis needs support to make it effective. Here are some points from Thoreau's essay that support the thesis:

- When Wollstonecraft declares that civil laws forbidding women to control property in society are unnatural and therefore have no force, Thoreau plainly agrees, having himself written that unjust laws exist and that we have a choice of whether to obey them.

- Wollstonecraft calls for change and Thoreau agrees with her when he says, "Abolitionists should at once effectually withdraw their support, both in person and property, from the government of Massachusetts, and not wait till they constitute a majority of one before they suffer the right to prevail through them" (para. 20). Wollstonecraft's view is that the time for action is now, not later, and in that, Thoreau agrees.

- Thoreau begins his essay by quoting John L. O'Sullivan, "That government is best which governs least." Wollstonecraft might agree with that idea but amend it to say, "That government is best that governs all equally." Thoreau would certainly applaud that idea.

These examples are happy ones in that they help the writer shape the remainder of the essay. However, every thesis statement represents a claim, and in order to make the claim stick, the writer has to provide warrants that support the claim. In other words, what are the truths that warrant a writer's claim that Henry David Thoreau would have been likely to support Mary Wollstonecraft? The rest of the essay must answer that question.

A successful thesis must be accompanied by

- Evidence that supports the thesis, either from the selection or from outside sources, either factual or drawn from the opinions of experts,
- Statements and testimony from authoritative texts that address the thesis concept,
- Careful and balanced analysis of the text of the author in question,
- Discussion and analysis of counterarguments that might alter the thesis.

No matter how it is supported, you must realize that your thesis statement is dynamic: it can change. The best thesis statements will establish your purpose and restrict the scope of your essay. A good thesis statement will also reveal some of your conclusions and clarify your approach to your subject. And ultimately, the whole purpose of the thesis is to give you—and your reader—a clear sense of direction for your writing.

Methods of Development

Every selection in this book—whether by Francis Bacon or Margaret Mead, Frederick Douglass or Karl Marx—employs specific rhetorical techniques that help the author communicate important ideas. Each introduction identifies the special rhetorical techniques used by the writer, partly to introduce you to the way in which such techniques are used.

Rhetoric is a general term used to discuss effective writing techniques. For example, an interesting rhetorical technique that Machiavelli uses is illustration by example, usually to prove his points. Francis Bacon (p. 591) uses the technique of enumeration by partitioning his essay into four sections. Enumeration is especially useful when the writer wishes to be very clear or to cover a subject point by point, using each point to accumulate more authority in the discussion. Martin Luther King Jr. (p. 252) uses the technique of allusion, reminding the religious leaders who were his audience that St. Paul wrote similar letters to help early Christians better understand the nature of their faith. By alluding to the Bible and St. Paul, King effectively reminds his audience that they all were serving God.

A great many more rhetorical techniques may be found in these readings. Some of the techniques are familiar because many of us already use them, but we study them to understand their value and to use them more effectively. After all, rhetorical techniques make it possible for us to communicate the significance of important ideas. Many of the authors in this book would surely admit that the effect of their ideas actually depends on the way they are expressed, which is a way of saying that they depend on the rhetorical methods used to express them.

Most of the rhetorical methods used in these essays are discussed in the introductions to the individual selections. Several represent exceptionally useful general techniques. These are methods of development and represent approaches to developing ideas that contribute to the fullness and completeness of an essay. You may think of them as techniques that can be applied to any idea in almost any situation. They can expand on the idea, clarify it, express it, and demonstrate its truth or effectiveness. Sometimes a technique may be direct, sometimes indirect. Sometimes it calls attention to itself, sometimes it works behind the scenes. Sometimes it is used alone, sometimes in conjunction with other methods. The most important techniques are explained and then illustrated with examples from the selections in the book.

Development by Definition. Definition is essential for two purposes: to make certain that you have a clear grasp of your concepts and that you communicate a clear understanding to your reader. Definition goes far beyond the use of the dictionary in the manner of "According to Webster's, . . ." Such an approach is facile because complex ideas are not easily reduced to dictionary definitions. A more useful strategy is to offer an explanation followed by an example. Because some of the suggestions for writing that follow the selections require you to use definition as a means of writing about ideas, the following tips should be kept in mind:

- Definition can be used to develop a paragraph, a section, or an entire essay.

- It considers questions of function, purpose, circumstance, origin, and implications for different groups.

- Explanations and examples make all definitions more complete and effective.

It is not uncommon for an entire essay to devote itself to the act of definition. For example, Edward O. Wilson's essay "What Is Science?" (p. 631) addresses itself to defining this abstruse subject in a letter to a young scientist. The use of definition begins with the first paragraph:

> What is this grand enterprise called science that has lit up heaven and earth and empowered humanity? It is organized, testable knowledge of the real world, of everything around us as well as ourselves, as opposed to the endlessly varied beliefs people hold from myth and superstition. It is the combination of physical and mental operations that have become increasingly the habit of educated peoples, a culture of illuminations dedicated to the most effective way ever conceived of acquiring factual knowledge.

In this opening paragraph, Wilson uses a rhetorical question that, in essence, repeats the question posed in the title of the essay. But then, he moves quickly to provide some definitions, beginning with separating fact from myth and superstition. He then talks about science in terms not of what it has produced in our world, but of how it affects our thought process. There is a scientific way of thinking. This point is made again in the very last paragraph of the essay when, with references to "idols of the mind," he alludes to Francis Bacon (p. 591):

> As a scientist, keep your mind open to any possible phenomenon remaining in the great unknown. But never forget that your profession is exploration of the real world, with no preconceptions or idols of the mind accepted, and testable truth the only coin of the realm.

An essay on the annotated selection from Machiavelli might define a number of key ideas. For example, to argue that Machiavelli is cynical in suggesting that his prince would not retain power if he acted morally, we would need to define what it means to be cynical and what moral behavior means in political terms. When we argue any point, it is important to spend time defining key ideas.

Martin Luther King Jr., in "Letter from Birmingham Jail" (p. 252), takes time to establish some key definitions so that he can speak forcefully to his audience:

> Let us consider a more concrete example of just and unjust laws. An unjust law is a code that a numerical or power majority group compels a minority group to obey but does not make binding on itself. This is *difference* made legal. By the same token, a just law is a code that a majority

compels a minority to follow and that it is willing to follow itself. This is
sameness made legal. (para. 17)

This is an adequate definition as far as it goes, but most serious ideas need
more extensive definition than this passage gives us. And King does go further, providing what Machiavelli does in his essay: examples and explanations.
Every full definition will profit from the extension of understanding that an
explanation and example will provide. Consider this paragraph from King:

> Let me give another explanation. A law is unjust if it is inflicted on a
> minority that, as a result of being denied the right to vote, had no part in
> enacting or devising the law. Who can say that the legislature of Alabama
> which set up that state's segregation laws was democratically elected?
> Throughout Alabama all sorts of devious methods are used to prevent
> Negroes from becoming registered voters, and there are some counties
> in which, even though Negroes constitute a majority of the population,
> not a single Negro is registered. Can any law enacted under such circum-
> stances be considered democratically structured? (para. 18)

King makes us aware of the fact that definition is complex and capable of
great subtlety. It is an approach that can be used to develop a paragraph or an
essay.

The following excerpt is by a student writer whose essay is developed
using the method of definition. Using Jean-Jacques Rousseau's distinction
between natural liberty and civil liberty (p. 99), the writer tries to establish
exactly what those different kinds of liberties are.

> Jean-Jacques Rousseau makes an interesting distinction between two kinds
> of liberty. The first is connected with the origin of society, which Rousseau
> takes to be the family, and it is called natural liberty. I take this to mean the
> kind of liberty we feel when we are alone in nature, or when we live in the
> country in a very remote place. Natural liberty is the freedom we feel when we
> alone determine what is permitted in terms of behavior and what is not. On the
> other hand, the second kind of liberty is called civil liberty and that is the kind
> of liberty we experience when we live in a city or a group. In the second case,
> everyone has to give up a bit of individual freedom in order to "fit in" to soci-
> ety. In today's society we can see interesting examples of both kinds of liberty.
>
> –Rashida G.

In this case, the writer goes on to discuss aspects of Libertarian politics and
how they connect with ideas that Rousseau developed. She also uses her personal experience of a train ride during which other passengers behaved in
ways that annoyed her but that they felt entitled to. Ultimately, she discusses
the idea of liberties in conflict with each other.

Development by Comparison. Comparison is a natural operation of the mind. We rarely talk for long about any topic without comparing it with something else. We are fascinated with comparisons between ourselves and others and come to know ourselves better as a result of such comparisons. Machiavelli, for example, compares the armed with the unarmed prince and shows us, by means of examples, the results of being unarmed.

Comparison usually includes the following:

- A definition of two or more elements to be compared (by example, explanation, description, or any combination of these),
- Discussion of shared qualities,
- Discussion of unique qualities,
- A clear reason for making the comparison.

Virginia Woolf's primary rhetorical strategy in "Shakespeare's Sister" (p. 220) is to invent a comparison between William Shakespeare and a fictional sister that he never had. Woolf's point is that if indeed Shakespeare had had a sister who was as brilliant and gifted as he was, she could not have become famous like her brother. The Elizabethan environment would have expected her to remain uneducated and to serve merely as a wife and mother. In the sixteenth century, men like William Shakespeare could go to London and make their fortune. Women, in comparison, were prisoners of social attitudes regarding their sex. As Woolf tells us,

> He was, it is well known, a wild boy who poached rabbits, perhaps shot a deer, and had, rather sooner than he should have done, to marry a woman in the neighborhood, who bore him a child rather quicker than was right. That escapade sent him to seek his fortune in London. He had, it seemed, a taste for the theatre; he began by holding horses at the stage door. Very soon he got work in the theatre, became a successful actor, and lived at the hub of the universe, meeting everybody, knowing everybody, practicing his art on the boards, exercising his wits in the streets, and even getting access to the palace of the queen. Meanwhile his extraordinarily gifted sister, let us suppose, remained at home. She was as adventurous, as imaginative, as agog to see the world as he was. But she was not sent to school. She had no chance of learning grammar and logic, let alone of reading Horace and Virgil. She picked up a book now and then, one of her brother's perhaps, and read a few pages. But then her parents came in and told her to mend the stockings or mind the stew and not moon about with books and papers. (para. 7)

Woolf's comparison makes it clear that the social circumstances of the life of a woman in Shakespeare's time worked so much against her personal desires and ambitions that it would be all but impossible for her to achieve anything of distinction on the London stage — or in any other venue in which men dominated. Even though a woman was monarch of England, it was a man's world.

A natural comparison can be made between Sigmund Freud's "The Oedipus Complex" (p. 477) and Carl Jung's "The Personal and Collective Unconscious" (p. 487). The following writer begins his essay trying to work out the comparison because he sees that these selections tend to reinforce each other even though Freud and Jung were often in disagreement.

> Even though Carl Jung seems to be treating the idea of the unconscious differently from Sigmund Freud, I think that they have more in common than they seem to. For example, when Jung talks about the collective unconscious containing archetypes that are supposed to be universal, Freud seems to be talking about just such an archetype. His discussion of the Oedipus complex seems to me to be the pattern he describes — of the child loving one parent and hating the other — to be a basic archetype of human behavior. I may be wrong, but if it is not an archetype, what is it? Both Sophocles and Shakespeare, almost two thousand years apart, came up with basically the same idea. Jung does not refer to Freud's examples, but he sees archetypes the way Freud does. They both think the archetypes are built in to us as people.
>
> –Brian J.

Development by Example. Examples make abstract ideas concrete. When Machiavelli talks about looking at history to learn political lessons, he cites specific cases and brings them to the attention of his audience, the prince. Thomas Jefferson in the Declaration of Independence (p. 116) devotes most of his text to examples of the unacceptable behavior of the English king toward the colonies. Margaret Mead (p. 236) structures her essay almost entirely on examples. She discusses the Plains Indians and how they raise their children, explaining that the Dakotas were "frantic" about insisting that every male child be "an indubitable male" (para. 4). She also provides examples of the "masculine" woman and the "feminine" man, especially in the *berdache*, who is capable of performing the jobs of both a man and woman in the tribe. Some of the examples support the idea that "the personalities of the two sexes are socially produced" (para. 7). Some do not. Mead's interest is in examining how the rigid social classifications affect the individual, and the examples she offers provide us a chance to understand sexual patterns along with Mead. Every selection in this book offers examples either to convince us of the truth of a proposition or to deepen our understanding of a statement.

Examples need to be chosen carefully because the burden of proof and of explanation and clarity often depends on them. When the sample suggestion given earlier for writing on Machiavelli's essay asks who among modern world leaders Machiavelli would approve, it is asking for carefully chosen examples.

When doing research for an essay, it is important to be sure that your example or examples really suit your purposes.

Examples can be used in several ways. One is to do as Charles Darwin (p. 606) does and present a large number of examples that force readers to a given conclusion. This indirect method is sometimes time-consuming, but the weight of numerous examples can be effective. A second method, such as Machiavelli's, also can be effective. By making a statement that is controversial or questionable and that can be tested by example, you can lead your audience to draw a reasonable conclusion.

When using examples, keep these points in mind:

- Choose a few strong examples that support your point.
- Be concrete and specific — naming names, citing events, and giving details where necessary.
- Develop each example as fully as possible, and point out its relevance to your position.

In some selections, such as Darwin's discussion of natural selection, the argument hinges entirely on examples, and Darwin cites one example after another. Carl Jung (p. 487), however, concentrates on a single example when he begins to explain the nature of the collective unconscious. He establishes that Sigmund Freud's view of the nature of the unconscious mind is centered on the personal and is a result of the repression of material that he calls "incompatible" to the conscious mind of the individual. During childhood bad things happen and we repress them as we grow up. Sometimes these repressions cause psychic damage and sometimes they do not. Usually they surface in dreams that are personal in nature. But Jung is sure that the unconscious is collective and not only personal. As a way of arguing his case, he presents us with an example of a "father complex" that could be virtually universal in nature:

> Casting about in my mind for an example to illustrate what I have just said, I have a particularly vivid memory of a woman patient with a mild hysterical neurosis which, as we expressed it in those days, had its principal cause in a "father complex." By this we wanted to denote the fact that the patient's peculiar relationship to her father stood in her way. She had been on very good terms with her father, who had since died. It was a relationship chiefly of feeling. In such cases it is usually the intellectual function that is developed, and this later becomes the bridge to the world. Accordingly our patient became a student of philosophy. Her energetic pursuit of knowledge was motivated by her need to extricate herself from the emotional entanglement with her father. (para. 5)

Jung develops this example extensively. This paragraph is more than a page and a half long and Jung continues his discussion of the example for another page because he sees it as a key to his argument.

Considering the claim that Robert B. Reich (p. 422) makes about symbolic analysts, the following writer develops his ideas about what work those analysts do and who in his immediate college environment would qualify as symbolic analysts. This paragraph is within an essay that explores the idea of the symbolic analyst and takes the position that Reich is accurate in his analysis.

Symbolic analysts work with ideas, not with their hands. But as Robert B. Reich says, there are higher and lower symbolic analysts and their economic success will be different depending on who they are. Reich talks about some analysts getting incredibly rich, and I think he means analysts like Mark Zuckerberg, who worked with computer symbols and came up with the idea for Facebook. Some of my friends who major in computer science expect that they may be able to develop ideas that will make them rich or at least help them find good jobs as coders. But there are other symbolic analysts like my friends who major in history. They also analyze symbols, but I'm not sure there will be a good market for their talents even though they know a lot and enjoy what they do. I think they might have to get an MBA or a law degree, both of which would make them symbolic analysts who can earn a living.

–Hector D.

Development by Analysis of Cause and Effect. People are interested in causes. We often ask what causes something, as if understanding the cause will somehow help us accept the result. Yet cause and effect can be subtle. With definition, comparison, and example, we can feel that the connections between a specific topic and our main points are reasonable. With cause and effect, however, we need to reason out the cause. Be warned that development by analysis of cause and effect requires you to pay close attention to the terms and situations you write about. Because it is easy to be wrong about causes and effects, their relationship must be examined thoughtfully. After an event has occurred, only a hypothesis about its cause may be possible. In the same sense, if no effect has been observed, only speculation about outcomes with various plans of action may be possible. In both cases, reasoning and imagination must be employed to establish a relationship between cause and effect.

The power of the rhetorical method of development through cause and effect is such that you will find it in every section of this book, in the work of virtually every author. Keep in mind these suggestions for using it to develop your own thinking:

- Clearly establish in your own mind the cause and the effect you wish to discuss.

- Develop a good line of reasoning that demonstrates the relationship between the cause and the effect.
- Be sure that the cause-effect relationship is real and not merely apparent.

In studying nature, scientists often examine effects in an effort to discover causes. Darwin, for instance, sees the comparable structure of the skeletons of many animals of different species and makes every effort to find the cause of such similarity (p. 606). His answer is a theory: evolution. Andrew Carnegie (p. 360), the defender of wealth and modern capitalism, praises the results of the modern industrial model of manufacture. He reminds us that in former times most manufacture was conducted at home and in small shops in an environment that was stable and suffered little change or upheaval.

> But the inevitable result of such a mode of manufacture was crude articles at high prices. To-day the world obtains commodities of excellent quality at prices which even the generation preceding this would have deemed incredible. In the commercial world similar causes would have produced similar results, and the race is benefited thereby. The poor enjoy what the rich could not before afford. What were the luxuries have become the necessaries of life. The laborer has now more comforts than the farmer had a few generations ago. The farmer has more luxuries than the landlord had, and is more richly clad and better housed. The landlord has books and pictures rarer, and appointments more artistic, than the King could then obtain. (para. 4)

Carnegie's examples of laborer, farmer, and landlord stand for the lower, middle, and upper classes in a modern society. He then shows that the modern industrial mode of manufacture has benefited not just one class, but everyone, from the poor to the rich.

Everywhere in this collection authors rely on cause and effect to develop their thoughts. Thomas Jefferson (p. 116) establishes the relationship between abuses by the British and America's need to sever its colonial ties. Karl Marx (p. 335) establishes the capitalist economic system as the cause of the oppression of the workers who produce the wealth enjoyed by the rich. Henry David Thoreau (p. 720) establishes the causes that demand civil disobedience as an effect.

Although Plato presents us with an allegory of captives in a cave staring at shadows on a wall, it is clear that he intends for us to understand that the condition he describes causes the captives to see a false world, not a real world. This allegory has long been inspiring to philosophers who are concerned with the nature of reality. The job of scientists, for example, is to understand reality and to be sure that they are not beguiled by illusory information. The following writer sees one point of Plato's message.

> At first, I did not understand what Plato was trying to say. I was unaware of what an allegory is and how it works, but after a while I began to make sense of the situation he presents to his readers. In his cave, Plato's people see shadows, not reality, and therefore their thinking is limited. My first thought was that Plato's cave is a lot like our movie theater, or even like our living room when the TV is on. Either on the movie screen or the TV screen what we see are shadows. They are realistic, but they are not real. If we take them to be real, we will make some serious mistakes because the people who created these "shadows" want to convince us of their own "truth," whether it is political, economic, psychological, or anything else. These "shadows" want us to believe in their "reality," rather than to encourage us to think critically for ourselves. It took a long time for Plato's captives to make themselves free, and for many of us we accept what our films and our TVs tell us because they are in front of us all the time. To get free, we need to begin a program of critical analysis that points us to the truth. How do we do this? Let me make some suggestions.
>
> –Hal M.

This writer interprets Plato in a way that makes sense to many other people. Hal is interested primarily in the political power of the "shadows" he responds to. He sees how political films, political TV shows, and political advertisements ask him to look at the "shadows" and not veer to any position that offers an alternative. Hal sees that Plato invites him to observe the truth rather than artificial simulations.

Development by Analysis of Circumstances. Everything we discuss exists as certain circumstances. Traditionally, the discussion of circumstances has had two parts. The first examines what is possible or impossible in a given situation. Whenever you try to convince your audience to take a specific course of action, it is helpful to show that given the circumstances, no other action is possible. If you disagree with a course of action that people may intend to follow because none other seems possible, however, you may have to demonstrate that another is indeed possible.

The second part of this method of development analyzes what has been done in the past: if something was done in the past, then it may be possible to do it again in the future. A historical survey of a situation often examines circumstances.

When using the method of analysis of circumstances to develop an idea, keep in mind the following tips:

- Clarify the question of possibility and impossibility.
- Review past circumstances so that future ones can be determined.
- Suggest a course of action based on an analysis of possibility and past circumstances.
- Establish the present circumstances, listing them if necessary. Be detailed, and concentrate on facts.

Martin Luther King Jr. examines the circumstances that led to his imprisonment and the writing of "Letter from Birmingham Jail" (p. 252). He explains that "racial injustice engulfs this community," and he reviews the "hard brutal facts of the case." His course of action is clearly stated and reviewed. He explains why some demonstrations were postponed and why his organization and others have been moderate in demands and actions. But he also examines the possibility of using nonviolent action to help change the inequitable social circumstances that existed in Birmingham. His examination of past action goes back to the Bible and the actions of the Apostle Paul. His examination of contemporary action is based on the facts of the situation, which he carefully enumerates. He concludes his letter by inviting the religious leaders to whom he addresses himself to join him in a righteous movement for social change.

Machiavelli is also interested in the question of possibility, because he is trying to encourage his ideal prince to follow a prescribed pattern of behavior. As he constantly reminds us, if the prince does not do so, it is possible that he will be deposed or killed. Taken as a whole, "The Qualities of the Prince" (p. 84) is a recitation of the circumstances that are necessary for success in politics. Machiavelli establishes this in a single paragraph:

> Therefore, it is not necessary for a prince to have all of the above-mentioned qualities, but it is very necessary for him to appear to have them. Furthermore, I shall be so bold as to assert this: that having them and practicing them at all times is harmful; and appearing to have them is useful; for instance, to seem merciful, faithful, humane, forthright, religious, and to be so; but his mind should be disposed in such a way that should it become necessary not to be so, he will be able and know how to change to the contrary. And it is essential to understand this: that a prince, and especially a new prince, cannot observe all those things by which men are considered good, for in order to maintain the state he is often obliged to act against his promise, against charity, against humanity, and against religion. And therefore, it is necessary that he have a mind ready to turn itself according to the way the winds of Fortune and the changeability of affairs require him; and, as I said above, as long as it is possible, he should not stray from the good, but he should know how to enter into evil when necessity commands. (para. 23)

This is the essential Machiavelli, the Machiavelli who is often thought of as a cynic. He advises his prince to be virtuous but says that it is not always possible to be so. Therefore, the prince must learn how not to be good when "necessity commands." The circumstances, he tells us, always determine whether it is possible to be virtuous. A charitable reading of this passage must conclude that his advice is at best amoral.

Many of the essays in this collection rely on an analysis of circumstances. Frederick Douglass (p. 743) examines the circumstances of slavery and freedom. When Karl Marx reviews the changes in economic history in *The Communist Manifesto* (p. 335), he examines the circumstances under which labor functions:

> The feudal system of industry, under which industrial production was monopolized by closed guilds, now no longer sufficed for the growing wants of the new market. The manufacturing system took its place. The guild-masters were pushed on one side by the manufacturing middle-class: division of labor between the different corporate guilds vanished in the face of division of labor in each single workshop. (para. 14)

Robert B. Reich (p. 422) examines the circumstances of our contemporary economy. He determines, among other things, that the wages of in-person servers—bank tellers, retail salespeople, restaurant employees, and others—will continue to be low despite the great demand for such workers. Not only are these workers easily replaced, but automation has led to the elimination of jobs—including bank teller jobs made redundant by automatic tellers and by banking with personal computers and routine factory jobs replaced by automation. Under current circumstances, these workers will lose out to the "symbolic analysts" who know how to make their specialized knowledge work for them and who cannot be easily replaced.

The question about the lack of outstanding men in politics that Alexis de Tocqueville raises in "Government by Democracy in America" (p. 139) led the writer of the following excerpt to consider whether what Tocqueville said in 1835 is true today.

> People have been complaining about politicians in Washington, saying that they are not getting anything done and that we don't have the leadership that we did in the 1980s or even in the 1990s. Alexis de Tocqueville says, "the most outstanding men in the United States are rarely summoned to public office."
> I think he may be right. For example, anyone who runs for a major public office has to expect that the opponents will run attack ads that will do everything to ruin that person's reputation. What person seeking public office is so moral and upright that some dirt can't be found that could be used to make that person look bad? I think, for example, that there have been some politicians who

could have won office who refuse to run because of the possibility that they will be hurt and their family hurt in the process. What surprises me is that Tocqueville seems aware of the effects of dirty politics in his own time and now we have even more ways of attacking "outstanding men" running for office.

–Linda R.

Development by Analysis of Quotations. Not all the essays in this collection rely on quotations from other writers, but many do. "Letter from Birmingham Jail" (p. 252), for example, relies on quotations from the Bible. In that piece, Martin Luther King Jr. implies his analysis of the quotations because the religious leaders to whom he writes know the quotations well. By invoking the quotations, King gently chides the clergy, who ought to be aware of their relevance. In a variant on using quotations, Robert B. Reich (p. 422) relies on information taken from various government reports. He includes the information in his text and supplies numerous footnotes indicating the sources, which are usually authoritative and convincing.

When you use quotations, remember these pointers:

- Quote accurately, and avoid distorting the original context.
- Unless the quotation is absolutely self-evident, offer your own clarifying comments.
- To help your audience understand why you have chosen a specific quotation, establish its function in your essay.

Carol Gilligan, in "Concepts of Self and Morality" (p. 770), is quick to use quotations from a number of her former students reacting to the question of what morality means to them. In the first few pages of her essay, she presents quotations from six different female students. Gilligan's method is notable in that she quotes extensively, presenting readers with paragraphs of testimony rather than just one or two trenchant sentences. Her method is to offer the reader the opportunity to respond to what her students say and then provide a bit of clarifying commentary. Her first student connects morality with the abstract idea of obligations to others. Two other students emphasize the general question of hurt and damage to others: "My main principle is not hurting other people as long as you aren't going against your own conscience" (para. 4). Other students talk about resisting absolutes but suggest that the "sanctity of human life" is an important measure. As one reads Gilligan's essay, her students' paragraphs reveal greater and greater complexity in terms of what morality means to each woman. Further, Gilligan introduces the less abstract and more personal question of the moral issues surrounding abortion. The subtleties of her students' understanding of moral choices then begin to be reflected in their writing as they face the moral complexities presented to them in real life.

Kwame Anthony Appiah (p. 801) uses quotations in an interesting variety of ways. He frequently refers to other authorities and quotes from their work, but in his selection "The Case against Character," he does something very unusual and quotes an entire short story by the fiction writer Lydia Davis. The story is short enough to be included in his first sentence and it helps illustrate Appiah's focus on the "virtuous person" and the nature of the virtuous character. His analysis of the story leads to the statement, "A virtuous act is one that a virtuous person would do, done for the reasons a virtuous person would do it." In other words, virtuous acts arise from virtuous character. For comparison, Appiah then refers to Aristotle's *Ethics* and quotes extensively from Rosalind Hursthouse's *On Virtue Ethics*, which essentially questions whether virtue arises from character. Moreover, Appiah goes on to refer to Aristotle's term *eudaimonia*, which he defines as flourishing and which other ethicists sometimes define as happiness. Appiah then examines in depth the concepts implied by that crucial word and analyzes the ways Aristotle uses it to connect the ethical issues of virtue with human character in an effort to see if character is the fundamental issue or not.

In the process of his analysis and discussion of the ethical issues connected with virtue, Appiah refers to many sources and quotes them to clarify his argument. He even goes so far as to refer to the popular film *Schindler's List*, which portrays a German businessman who works for the Nazis building war material while shielding more than one thousand Jews from the death camps. Examining the character of Schindler, a man widely regarded as heroic, Appiah says that he "was mercenary, arrogant, hypocritical, and calculating sometimes . . . but not always." The question of virtue needs closer examination.

In your own writing you will find plenty of opportunity to cite passages from an author whose ideas have engaged your attention. In writing an essay in response to Machiavelli, Carl Jung, or any other author in the book, you may find yourself quoting and commenting in some detail on specific lines or passages. This is especially true if you find yourself disagreeing with a point. Your first job, then, is to establish what you disagree with—and usually it helps to quote, which is essentially a way of producing evidence.

Finally, it must be noted that only a few aspects of the rhetorical methods used by the authors in this book have been discussed here. Rhetoric is a complex art that warrants fuller study. But the points raised here are important because they are illustrated in many of the texts you will read, and by watching them at work you can begin to learn to use them yourself. By using them you will be able to achieve in your writing the fullness and purposiveness that mark mature prose.

Establishing an Argument

Most of the selections in this book are constructed as arguments, although they take a variety of forms. Some assume a hostile audience, some a friendly audience. Some assume their subject is controversial, some assume they are primarily uncovering the truth, and some are simply being informative by explaining something complex. Machiavelli's selection from *The Prince* argues for a strongman political leader. In her analysis of Nazism, Hannah Arendt argues that terror is necessary for the state to achieve total domination over the people. Henry David Thoreau argues for civil disobedience as a means of achieving justice. It is one of the most powerful arguments for justice that any American has written. Martin Luther King Jr.'s "Letter from Birmingham Jail" is itself one of the premier arguments in favor of nonviolent action. Its presentation of reasoned argument is outstanding. Andrew Carnegie argues that the wealthy must give their money back to the community in their lifetimes so they can see that their money is well spent.

Karl Marx's *The Communist Manifesto* is still relevant long after the demise of communism. His arguments against globalization are probably the most telling for today's audience. Robert B. Reich addresses globalization and argues that the people who will prosper in our economy are the "symbolic analysts" who can interpret and master texts. One of the most impressive arguments in the book is Virginia Woolf's insistence that if Shakespeare's imaginary "gifted sister" had the same advantages of education and independence that Shakespeare enjoyed she might have become as accomplished and as well known. Woolf knew that the mores of the age in which Shakespeare lived denied both education and independence for women and assigned them to supporting roles in the family. What Woolf argued for was equality, something still wanting in her own society. In reality, Woolf is arguing not so much for Shakespeare's sister as for herself and other women in her own age. Mary Wollstonecraft in her essay on the subjection of women in the eighteenth century is arguing much the same case as Woolf is.

Iris Murdoch conducts an experimental argument asking whether religion is essential for morality to be relevant. Can there be morality without religion? By contrast, Michael Gazzaniga ignores the question of religion entirely when he discusses the nature of morality in his "Toward a Universal Ethics" (p. 784). He addresses the question of how our genes function to produce a sense of altruism in the human race. Gazzaniga sees the role of evolution as developing the kind of ethical behavior that guaranteed the survival of the race throughout hundreds of thousands of years. Studies of the function of the brain during moral reasoning, while not entirely providing an answer, help him in examining the virtue theory of ethical behavior. It is nature rather than religion that spurs Gazzaniga's research. Charles Darwin argues with masses of collected evidence to derive an argument in favor of natural selection and, thus, evolution.

Most of the selections use one or more of the three basic forms of argument. **Classical arguments** rely on facts and evidence as well as on logic and reasoning to convince the reader of a specific position. Andrew Carnegie's argument in favor of unequal distribution of wealth is a case in point. He begins by remarking that the Sioux Indians make no distinction between the habitation or the dress of the rich or the poor. He argues that "civilized man" was once in that condition but that with industry and civilization comes wealth and inequality. Carnegie can tolerate these inequities, but he ultimately points to the fact that wealthy people are able to be philanthropists and improve the lot of everyone. And his argument extends to trying to convince the wealthy that they are merely stewards of wealth, not its owners. Their responsibility is to use it wisely for the benefit of society. In fact, Carnegie did exactly that, giving all his money to public service.

Henry David Thoreau refuses to support a government with which he does not agree, particularly when he sees it acting unjustly. As a result, in his classical argument he declares, "That government is best which governs not at all." But he realizes that such a government can exist only when people are so good and so just that they do not need a government.

The second common form, like classical argument, is designed to convince someone of a specific position on a subject. This form, known as the **Toulmin argument**, has three parts:

- Claim: what you are trying to prove (often contained in the thesis statement),
- Grounds: the data—facts, observations, or conditions—you use to prove your claim, and
- Warrant: an assumption or belief that underlies the claim and is taken for granted.

Thomas Jefferson's claim in the Declaration of Independence is that America deserves to be just that: independent from Britain. The extraordinary volume of grounds, or data, he presents demonstrates that King George III has become a tyrant and "is unfit to be the ruler of a free people." His warrant is the underlying belief that "all men are created equal" and must be free, not victims of a tyranny. Jefferson has a great deal at stake here. He proposes rebellion and independence from a much more powerful nation and therefore must be convincing, especially to the Americans themselves, most of whom emigrated from Great Britain and felt they owed it allegiance. If other Americans were not convinced by his argument, his life was forfeit.

The third form, the **Rogerian argument,** differs in that it tries to find common ground within a subject that most people would agree with. Thus, this kind of argument may not seem to be an argument at all. It usually functions by establishing basic positions that most people would find nonthreatening, and in the process, such arguments appear to be simple discussions. However, the ultimate goal of a Rogerian argument is still for potentially differing sides to come to mutual agreement. That is the case with Judith Butler's essay from *Undoing Gender.* The underlying question in her discussion of the surgical mishaps perpetrated on her case study, David, who had been so badly maimed surgically when young that he was raised as a girl, is whether gender is a socialization or an "essentialism." The argument is not designed to press us toward accepting that gender is established by the society in which we live or that, regardless of society, gender is somehow innate and decreed by biology. The complexity of David's childhood, including the intervention of those who continued to study his development and who directed much of his growth and tried to craft his sense of self, makes the example very difficult to pin down. That is Butler's point. Because she is not contentious, we are able to consider the example of David from many angles. What we come away with is a sense of how very difficult the entire issue of gender assignment is.

Whatever the form, the structure of most argument will follow this pattern:

Beginning of an argument

- Identify the subject and its importance.
- Suggest (or imply) how you plan to argue your case.

Middle of an argument

- Explain the main points of your argument with accompanying evidence.
- Argue each point in turn with the analysis of evidence.
- Rebut arguments against your position.

Conclusion of an argument

- Review the claims basic to your argument.
- Summarize your arguments, what they imply, and what you then conclude.

The following sample essay, "The Qualities of the President," modeled on Machiavelli's "The Qualities of the Prince" (p. 84), is an example of a Rogerian argument. The author reviews examples of the behavior of various kinds of modern leaders and then develops common ground with the reader to foster agreement on the qualities that seem most desirable in a modern president.

The writer is not confrontational and does not demand absolute agreement but instead offers an exploration of the subject while nonetheless driving to a reasonable conclusion.

A Sample Essay

The following sample essay is based on the first several paragraphs of Machiavelli's "The Qualities of the Prince" that were annotated in "Evaluating Ideas: An Introduction to Critical Reading" (pp. 5–7). The essay is based on the annotations and the questions that were developed from them:

- Should a leader be armed?
- Is it true that an unarmed leader is despised?
- Will those leaders who are always good come to ruin among those who are not good?
- To remain in power, must a leader learn how not to be good?

Not all these questions are addressed in the essay, but they serve as a starting point and a focus for writing. The methods of development that are discussed above form the primary rhetorical techniques of the essay, and each method that is used is labeled in the margin. The sample essay does two things simultaneously: it attempts to clarify the meaning of Machiavelli's advice, and then it attempts to apply that advice to a contemporary circumstance. Naturally, the essay could have chosen to discuss only the Renaissance situation that Machiavelli describes, but to do so would have required specialized knowledge of that period. In this sample essay, the questions prompted by the annotations serve as the basis of the discussion.

THE QUALITIES OF THE PRESIDENT

Introduction   Machiavelli's essay "The Qualities of the Prince" has a number of very worrisome points. The ones that worry me most have to do with the question of whether it is reasonable to expect a leader to behave virtuously. I think this is connected to the question of whether the leader should be armed. Machiavelli emphasizes that the prince must be armed or else face the possibility that someone will take over the government. When I think about how that advice applies to modern times, particularly in terms of how our president should behave, I find Machiavelli's position very different from my own.

Circumstance First, I want to discuss the question of being armed. That is where Machiavelli starts, and it is an important concern. In Machiavelli's time, the late fifteenth and early sixteenth centuries, it was common for men to walk in the streets of Florence wearing a rapier for protection. The possibility of robbery or even attack by rival political groups was great in those days. Even if he had a bodyguard, it was still important for a prince to know how to fight and to be able to defend himself. Machiavelli seems to be talking only about self-defense when he recommends that the prince be armed. In our time, sadly, it too is important to think about protecting the president and other leaders.

Examples In recent years there have been many assassination attempts on world leaders, and our president, John F. Kennedy, was killed in Dallas in 1963. His brother Robert was killed when he was campaigning for the presidency in 1968. Also in 1968 Martin Luther King Jr. was killed in Memphis because of his belief in racial equality. In the 1980s Pope John Paul II was shot by a would-be assassin, as was President Ronald Reagan. They both lived, but Indira Gandhi, the leader of India, was shot and killed in 1984. This is a frightening record. Probably even Machiavelli would have been appalled. But would his solution — being armed — have helped? I do not think so.

Cause/Effect For one thing, I cannot believe that if the pope had a gun he would have shot his would-be assassin, Ali Acga. The thought of it is almost silly. Martin Luther King Jr., who constantly preached the value of nonviolence, logically could not have shot at an assailant. How could John F. Kennedy have returned fire at a sniper? Robert Kennedy had bodyguards, and both President Reagan and Indira Gandhi were protected by armed guards. The presence of arms obviously does not produce the desired effect: security. The only thing that can produce that is to reduce the visibility of a leader. The president could speak on television or, when he must appear in public, use a bulletproof screen. The opportunities for would-be assassins can be reduced. But the thought of an American president carrying arms is unacceptable.

Comparison The question of whether a president should be armed is to some extent symbolic. Our president stands for America, and if he were to appear in press conferences or state meetings wearing a gun, he

would give a symbolic message to the world: look out, we're dangerous. Cuba's Fidel Castro often appeared in a military uniform with a
gun during his presidency, and when he spoke at the United Nations
in 1960, he was the first, and I think the only, world leader to wear
a pistol there. I have seen pictures of Benito Mussolini and Adolf
Hitler appearing in public in military uniform, but never in business
suits. The same was true of the Libyan leader Muammar al-Qaddafi
and Iraq's Saddam Hussein. Today when a president or a head of
state is armed there is often reason to worry. The current leaders of
Russia usually wear suits, but Joseph Stalin always wore a military
uniform. His rule in the Soviet Union was marked by the extermination of whole groups of people and the imprisonment of many more.
We do not want an armed president.

Use of
quotations

Comparison

Yet Machiavelli plainly says, "among the other bad effects it
causes, being disarmed makes you despised . . . for between an
armed and an unarmed man there is no comparison whatsoever"
(para. 2). The problem with this statement is that it is more relevant
to the sixteenth century than to the twenty-first. In our time the
threat of assassination is so great that being armed would be no
sure protection, as we have seen in the case of the assassination of
President Sadat of Egypt, winner of the Nobel Peace Prize. On the
other hand, the pope, like Martin Luther King Jr., would never have
appeared with a weapon, and yet it can hardly be said they were
despised. If anything, the world's respect for them is enormous.
America's president also commands the world's respect, as does
the prime minister of Great Britain. Yet neither would ever think of
being armed. If what Machiavelli said was true in the early 1500s, it
is pretty clear that it is not true today.

Definition

All this basically translates into a question of whether a leader
should be virtuous. I suppose the definition of *virtuous* would differ
with different people, but I think of it as holding a moral philosophy that you try to live by. No one is ever completely virtuous, but
I think a president ought to try to be so. That means the president
ought to tell the truth, since that is one of the basic virtues. The
cardinal virtues — which were the same in Machiavelli's time as in
ours — are justice, prudence, fortitude, and temperance. In a president, the virtue of justice is absolutely a must or else what America
stands for is lost. We definitely want our president to be prudent,

to use good judgment, particularly in this nuclear age, when acts of imprudence could get us blown up. Fortitude, the ability to stand up for what is right, is a must for our president. Temperance is also important; we do not want an alcoholic for a president, nor do we want anyone with excessive bad habits.

Conclusion   It seems to me that a president who was armed or who empha-sized arms in the way Machiavelli appears to mean would be threat-ening injustice (the way Stalin did) and implying intemperance, like many armed world leaders. When I consider this issue, I cannot think of any vice that our president ought to possess at any time. Injustice, imprudence, cowardice, and intemperance are, for me, unacceptable. Maybe Machiavelli was thinking of deception and lying as necessary evils, but they are a form of injustice, and no compe-tent president — no president who was truly virtuous — would need them. Prudence and fortitude are the two virtues most essential for diplomacy. The president who has those virtues will govern well and uphold our basic values.

The range of this essay is controlled and expresses a viewpoint that is focused and coherent. This essay of about one thousand words illustrates each method of development discussed in the text and uses each one to fur-ther the argument. The writer disagrees with one of Machiavelli's positions and presents an argument based on personal opinion that is bolstered by example and by analysis of current political conditions as they compare with those of Machiavelli's time. A longer essay could have gone more deeply into issues raised in any single paragraph and could have studied more closely the views of a specific president, such as President Ronald Reagan, who opposed stricter gun control laws even after he was shot.

The range of the selections in this volume is great, constituting a signifi-cant introduction to important ideas in many areas. These readings are espe-cially useful for stimulating our own thoughts and ideas. There is an infinite number of ways to approach a subject, but observing how writers apply rhetor-ical methods in their work is one way to begin our own development as writers. Careful analysis of each selection can guide our exploration of these writers, who encourage our learning and reward our study.

GOVERNMENT

Introduction

He who exercises government by means of his virtue may be compared to the north polar star, which keeps its place and all the stars turn towards it.
　—CONFUCIUS (551–479 B.C.E.)

When a government becomes powerful it is destructive, extravagant, and violent; it is an usurer which takes bread from innocent mouths and deprives honorable men of their substance, for votes with which to perpetuate itself.
　—MARCUS TULLIUS CICERO (106–43 B.C.E.)

All the ills of mankind, all the tragic misfortunes that fill the history books, all the political blunders, all the failures of the great leaders have arisen merely from a lack of skill at dancing.
　—MOLIERE (1622–1673)

Society in every state is a blessing, but Government, even in its best state, is but a necessary evil; in its worst state, an intolerable one.
　—THOMAS PAINE (1737–1809)

A Bill of Rights is what the people are entitled to against every government, and what no just government should refuse, or rest on inference.
　—THOMAS JEFFERSON (1743–1826)

No government can be long secure without formidable opposition.
　—BENJAMIN DISRAELI (1804–1881)

A government is the most dangerous threat to man's rights: it holds a legal monopoly on the use of physical force against legally disarmed victims.
　—AYN RAND (1902–1982)

At the core of any idea of government is the belief that individuals need an organized allocation of authority to protect their well-being. However, throughout history, the form of that allocation of authority has undergone profound shifts, and each successive type of government has inspired debates and defenses. The first civilizations in Mesopotamia and Egypt (4000–3000 B.C.E.) were theocracies ruled by a high priest. Gradually these political systems evolved into monarchies in which a king whose role was separate from that of the religious leaders held power. During the sixth century B.C.E., the Greek city-state of Athens developed the first democratic system wherein male citizens (but not women or slaves) could elect a body of leaders. As these forms of government developed, so too did the concept of government as the center of law and administration. However, governments and ideas of governments (actual or ideal) have not followed a straight path. History has witnessed constant oscillations between various forms and functions of government, from tyrannies to republics. In turn, these governments and their relation to the individual citizen have been the focus of many great thinkers.

The thinkers represented in this section concentrate on both the role and form of government. Lao-tzu reflects on the ruler who would, by careful management, maintain a happy citizenry. Machiavelli places the survival of the prince above all other considerations of government and, unlike Lao-tzu, ignores the concerns and rights of the individual. For Machiavelli, power is the issue, and maintaining it is the sign of good government. Rousseau's emphasis on the social contract focuses on the theory that citizens voluntarily submit to governance in the hope of gaining greater personal freedom.

Whereas governing well concerns most of these thinkers, the forms of government are of greater concern to others. Aristotle examines the displacement of democracy with an oligarchy in ancient Athens, expressing concerns about the masses being governed by just a wealthy few. Thomas Jefferson struggled with the monarchical form of government, as did Jean-Jacques Rousseau before him, and envisioned a republic that would serve the people. Kings were a threatened species in eighteenth-century Europe, and with Jefferson's aid, they became extinct in the United States. Alexis de Tocqueville examined the United States in 1831 after the revolution in his own country of France. What impressed him most was the sense of equality that prevailed in America. Democracy was a novelty to a European, and Tocqueville marveled at it. Only a few years after Tocqueville published his work, Ralph Waldo Emerson commented on the American experiment and echoed Thomas Jefferson in saying that the best government is the least government. Hannah Arendt was convinced that the totalitarian governments of the twentieth century needed concentration camps in order to practice total domination. Benazir Bhutto extolls the virtues of democracy and argues for why it aligns with the teachings of the Koran, the Muslim holy book.

Lao-tzu (sixth century B.C.E.), whose writings provide the basis for Taoism, one of three major Chinese religions, was interested primarily in political systems. His work, the *Tao-te Ching*, has been translated loosely as "The Way of Power." One thing that becomes clear from reading his work—especially the selections presented here—is his concern for the well-being of the people in any government. He does not recommend specific forms of government (monarchic, representative, democratic) or advocate election versus the hereditary transfer of power. But he does make it clear that the success of the existing forms of government (in his era, monarchic) depends on good relations between the leader and the people. He refers to the chief of state as *Master* or *Sage*, implying that one obligation of the governor is to be wise. One expression of that wisdom is the willingness to permit things to take their natural course. His view is that the less the Master needs to do — or perhaps the less government needs to intervene — the happier the people will be.

When he was writing about politics in the fourth century B.C.E., Aristotle's (384–322 B.C.E.) own teacher, Plato, was well known for his views about democracy and oligarchy. They had experienced both forms of government. Plato, in *The Republic* (380 B.C.E.), was wary of democracy because he feared a tyranny of the majority. Aristotle disagreed with Plato in thinking that government by the majority was preferable to government by a minority oligarchy, the rich and powerful. His views are carefully developed in his analysis and definition of the systems of government and the classes of people who would be ruled in a democracy. What Aristotle says is worth paying attention to if only because he lived through Athens's loss of democracy because of long and unnecessary wars that bankrupted the state. Athens was not the only democracy in ancient Greece, but it has become the one on which all other iterations of democracy are based.

Niccolò Machiavelli (1469–1527) was a pragmatic man of the Renaissance in Italy. As a theoretician and as a member of the political court, he understood government from the inside and carefully examined its philosophy. Because his writings stress the importance of gaining and holding power at any cost, Machiavelli's name has become synonymous with political cunning. However, a careful reading of his work as a reflection of the instability of his time shows that his advice to wield power ruthlessly derived largely from his fear that a weak prince would lose the city-state of Florence to France or to another powerful, plundering nation. His commitment to a powerful prince is based on his view that in the long run strength will guarantee the peace and happiness of the citizen for whom independence is otherwise irrelevant. Therefore, Machiavelli generally ignores questions concerning the comfort and rights of the individual.

In contrast, Jean-Jacques Rousseau (1712–1778) is continually concerned with the basic questions of personal freedom and liberty. A fundamental principle in his essay "The Origin of Civil Society" is that the individual's agreement with the state is designed to increase the individual's freedoms, not to diminish them. Rousseau makes this assertion while at the same time admitting that the individual forfeits certain rights to the body politic in order to gain overall freedom. Moreover, Rousseau describes civil society as a body politic that expects its rulers — including the monarch — to behave in a way designed to benefit the people. Such a view in eighteenth-century France was revolutionary. The ruling classes at that time treated the people with great contempt, and the monarch rarely gave any thought to the well-being of the common people. Rousseau's advocacy of a republican form of government in which the monarch served the people was a radical view and would find its ultimate expression decades later in the French Revolution.

Thomas Jefferson's (1743–1826) views were also radical for his time. Armed with the philosophy of Rousseau and others, his Declaration of Independence advocates the eradication of the monarch entirely. Not everyone in the colonies agreed with this view. Indeed, his political opponents, such as Alexander Hamilton and Aaron Burr, were far from certain such a view was correct. In fact, some efforts were made to install George Washington as king (he refused). In the Declaration of Independence, Jefferson reflects Rousseau's philosophy by emphasizing the right of the individual to "life, liberty, and the pursuit of happiness" and the obligation of government to serve the people by protecting those rights.

Ralph Waldo Emerson (1803–1882) spent much of his life as a public figure in nineteenth-century America. He was known as a poet, and he seemed almost to be a model for Plato's idea of the poet-philosopher. His essays were widely read throughout the English-speaking world and elsewhere in translation. "Politics" is a consideration of the role of the state in the life of the individual. Unlike Machiavelli, Emerson's emphasis is on the individual, not on power. Emerson was concerned that laws may sometimes infringe on the rights of honest citizens. His views about government correspond to some current views in our political debates: he favored less rather than more government.

Alexis de Tocqueville (1805–1859) visited the United States in 1831 after a brief career in politics in France. He was born shortly after the French Revolution (1789) and, while himself an aristocrat, was completely aware that in France and elsewhere the old system of government that was dependent on rule by the aristocracy was quickly being replaced. He saw that the common people were moving into a position of power in France, and when he came to the United States, he was surprised that democracy worked in a way that did not oppress the rich or the wellborn. Equality is a word that he uses frequently in his famous book, *Democracy in America* (1835). He has much to say about how the system works, but what is most interesting is how much he understood about how democracy worked in America after his few years wandering the nation. He was in touch with the rich, the poor, the Native Americans, the African slaves, and the various social classes among the nation's workers and the nation's politicians. He saw the Senate and the House of Representatives and was surprised at the difference between the men who populated each part of our legislature.

The issues of freedom, justice, and individual rights were all virtually irrelevant in the totalitarian regimes that served as the focus of Hannah Arendt's (1906–1975) work. Arendt argued that the fascist states, especially Nazi Germany, and the communist states, especially the Soviet Union, represented a form of government in which individual rights were sacrificed for the good of "the state." In "Total Domination," Arendt argues that the power of totalitarian states depends on the use of terror to enforce the state's ideology. The result is a form of government that eclipses the tyrannical extremes Rousseau and Jefferson sought to eradicate and exceeds even Machiavelli's imaginings of absolute power.

Benazir Bhutto (1953–2007), twice prime minister of Pakistan, explains in "Islam and Democracy" why the teachings of the Koran, the holy book of Muslims, are receptive to democracy, diversity, equality, and fairness. She recognizes that most Westerners will not expect Islam to produce democratic governments because of what the West considers religious restrictions, but she insists that the religion does not limit the possibility of the existence of democracies in Muslim nations. However, she also recognizes that, while Pakistan has a constitution that insists on democracy, there are few if any Muslim democracies. She has a number of theories about why this is so, and she outlines them in her essay. Her greatest fears center on the extremists among Muslims, such as those who attacked her when she first returned to Pakistan and who, shortly after, killed her in a suicide bombing. Currently, a number of Muslim nations are in turmoil as a result of trying to establish some form of democratic government.

Some Considerations about the Nature of Government

Before reading the selections that follow in this section, consider what your views of government are. Reflect on the following questions and write out your responses. Discuss your answers with your classmates.

1. What is your perception of the responsibility of the individual to the state?
2. How well do you think your form of government serves the individual?
3. What is the role of government in protecting the rights of individuals?
4. What is the responsibility of government to protect the rights of minorities?
5. Under what conditions does the government have the right to use force?
6. What is the source of power in a democracy?
7. What freedoms can a democratic government legitimately restrict from its citizens?
8. Which rights do you as an individual willingly surrender to the government?
9. How much influence is it possible for you to have in your government?
10. How do you define "good" government?

LAO-TZU

Thoughts from the Tao-te Ching

© Charles Walker/Topfoto/The Image Works

T HE AUTHOR of the *Tao-te Ching* (in English often pronounced "dow deh jing") is unknown, although the earliest texts ascribe the work to Lao-tzu (sixth century B.C.E.), whose name can be translated as "Old Master." However, nothing can be said with certainty about Lao-tzu (lou′ dzu′) as a historical figure. One tradition holds that he was named Li Erh and born in the state of Ch'u in China at a time that would have made him a slightly older contemporary of Confucius (551–479 B.C.E.). Lao-tzu was said to have worked in the court of the Chou dynasty for most of his life. When he decided to leave the court to pursue a life of contemplation, the keeper of the gate urged him to write down his thoughts before he went into a self-imposed exile. Legend has it that he wrote the *Tao-te Ching* and then left the state of Ch'u, never to be seen again.

Lao-tzu's writings offered a basis for Taoism, a religion officially founded by Chang Tao-ling in about 150 C.E. However, the *Tao-te Ching* is a philosophical document as much about good government as it is about moral behavior. The term *Tao* cannot be easily understood or easily translated. In one sense it means "the way," but it also means "the method," as in "the way to enlightenment" or "the way to live." Some of the chapters of the *Tao-te Ching* imply that the Tao is the allness of the universe, the ultimate reality of existence, and perhaps even a synonym for God. The text is marked by numerous complex ambiguities and paradoxes. It constantly urges us to look beyond ourselves, beyond our circumstances, and become one with the Tao — even though it cannot tell us what the Tao is.

The *Tao-te Ching* has often been called a feminine treatise because it emphasizes the creative forces of the universe and frequently employs the imagery and metaphor of the womb — for example, "The Tao is called the Great Mother." The translator, Stephen Mitchell, translates some of the pronouns associated with the Master as "she," with the

From *Tao-te Ching*. Translated by Stephen Mitchell.

explanation that Chinese has no equivalent for the male- and female-gendered pronouns and that "of all the great world religions the teaching of Lao-tzu is by far the most
female."

The teachings of Lao-tzu are the opposite of the materialist quest for power, dominance, authority, and wealth. Lao-tzu takes the view that possessions and wealth are
leaden weights of the soul, that they are meaningless and trivial, and that the truly free
and enlightened person will regard them as evil. Because of his antimaterialist view, his recommendations may seem ironic or unclear, especially when he urges politicians to adopt
a practice of judicious inaction. Lao-tzu's advice to politicians is not to do nothing but to
intercede only when it is a necessity and then only inconspicuously. Above all, Lao-tzu
counsels avoiding useless activity: "the Master / acts without doing anything / and teaches
without saying anything." Such a statement is difficult for modern Westerners to comprehend, although it points to the concept of enlightenment, a state of spiritual peace and
fulfillment that is central to the *Tao-te Ching*.

Lao-tzu's political philosophy minimizes the power of the state — especially the
power of the state to oppress the people. Lao-tzu takes the question of the freedom
of the individual into account by asserting that the wise leader will provide the people
with what they need but not annoy them with promises of what they do not need.
Lao-tzu argues that by keeping people unaware that they are being governed, the
leader allows the people to achieve good things for themselves. As he writes, "If you
want to be a great leader, / you must learn to follow the Tao. / Stop trying to control. /
Let go of fixed plans and concepts, / and the world will govern itself" (Verse 57); or
in contrast, "If a country is governed with repression, / the people are depressed and
crafty" (Verse 58).

To our modern ears this advice may or may not sound sensible. For those who feel
government can solve the problems of the people, it will seem strange and unwise. For
those who believe that the less government the better, the advice will sound sane and
powerful.

THE RHETORIC OF THE *TAO-TE CHING*

Traditionally, Lao-tzu is said to have written the *Tao-te Ching* as a guide for the ruling sage
to follow. In other words, it is a handbook for politicians. It emphasizes the virtues that the
ruler must possess, and in this sense the *Tao-te Ching* invites comparison with Machiavelli's
efforts to instruct his ruler.

The visual form of the text is poetry, although the text is not metrical or image
laden. Instead of thoroughly developing his ideas, Lao-tzu uses a traditional Chinese
form that resembles the aphorism, a compressed statement weighty with meaning.
Virtually every statement requires thought and reflection. Thus, the act of reading
becomes an act of cooperation with the text.

One way of reading the text is to explore the varieties of interpretation it will sustain. The act of analysis requires patience and willingness to examine a statement to see what lies beneath the surface. Take, for example, one of the opening statements:

> The Master leads
> by emptying people's minds
> and filling their cores,
> by weakening their ambition
> and toughening their resolve.
> He helps people lose everything
> they know, everything they desire,
> and creates confusion
> in those who think that they know.

This passage supports a number of readings. One centers on the question of the people's desire. "Emptying people's minds" implies eliminating desires that lead the people to steal or compete for power. "Weakening their ambition" implies helping people direct their powers toward the attainable and useful. Such a text is at odds with Western views that support advertisements for expensive computers, DVD and Blu-ray players, luxury cars, and other items that generate ambition and desire in people.

In part because the text resembles poetry, it needs to be read with attention to innuendo, subtle interpretation, and possible hidden meanings. One of the rhetorical virtues of paradox is that it forces the reader to consider several sides of an issue. The resulting confusion yields a wider range of possibilities than would arise from a self-evident statement. Through these complicated messages, Lao-tzu felt he was contributing to the spiritual enlightenment of the ruling sage, although he had no immediate hope that his message would be put into action. A modern state might have a difficult time following Lao-tzu's philosophy, but many individuals have tried to attain peace and contentment by leading lives according to its principles.

▚ PREREADING QUESTIONS: WHAT TO READ FOR

The following prereading questions may help you anticipate key issues in the discussion of Lao-tzu's "Thoughts from the *Tao-te Ching.*" Keeping them in mind during your first reading of the selection should help focus your attention.

1. What is the Master's attitude toward action?

2. The Tao is "the way" — how are we to understand its meaning? What does it mean to be in harmony with the Tao?

3. According to Lao-tzu, why is moderation important in government?

Thoughts from the *Tao-te Ching*

3

If you overesteem great men,   1
people become powerless.
If you overvalue possessions,
people begin to steal.

The Master leads   2
by emptying people's minds
and filling their cores,
by weakening their ambition
and toughening their resolve.
He helps people lose everything
they know, everything they desire,
and creates confusion
in those who think that they know.

Practice not-doing,   3
and everything will fall into place.

17

When the Master governs, the people   4
are hardly aware that he exists.
Next best is a leader who is loved.
Next, one who is feared.
The worst is one who is despised.

If you don't trust the people,   5
you make them untrustworthy.

The Master doesn't talk, he acts.   6
When his work is done,
the people say, "Amazing:
we did it, all by ourselves!"

18

When the great Tao is forgotten,   7
goodness and piety appear.

When the body's intelligence declines,
cleverness and knowledge step forth.
When there is no peace in the family,
filial piety begins.
When the country falls into chaos,
patriotism is born.

19

Throw away holiness and wisdom,   8
and people will be a hundred times happier.
Throw away morality and justice,
and people will do the right thing.
Throw away industry and profit,
and there won't be any thieves.

If these three aren't enough,   9
just stay at the center of the circle
and let all things take their course.

26

The heavy is the root of the light.   10
The unmoved is the source of all movement.

Thus the Master travels all day   11
without leaving home.
However splendid the views,
she stays serenely in herself.

Why should the lord of the country   12
flit about like a fool?
If you let yourself be blown to and fro,
you lose touch with your root.
If you let restlessness move you,
you lose touch with who you are.

29

Do you want to improve the world?   13
I don't think it can be done.

The world is sacred.   14
It can't be improved.

If you tamper with it, you'll ruin it.
If you treat it like an object, you'll lose it.

There is a time for being ahead,   15
a time for being behind;
a time for being in motion,
a time for being at rest;
a time for being vigorous,
a time for being exhausted;
a time for being safe,
a time for being in danger.

The Master sees things as they are,   16
without trying to control them.
She lets them go their own way,
and resides at the center of the circle.

30

Whoever relies on the Tao in governing men   17
doesn't try to force issues
or defeat enemies by force of arms.
For every force there is a counterforce.
Violence, even well intentioned,
always rebounds upon oneself.

The Master does his job   18
and then stops.
He understands that the universe
is forever out of control,
and that trying to dominate events
goes against the current of the Tao.
Because he believes in himself,
he doesn't try to convince others.
Because he is content with himself,
he doesn't need others' approval.
Because he accepts himself,
the whole world accepts him.

31

Weapons are the tools of violence;   19
all decent men detest them.

Weapons are the tools of fear;   20
a decent man will avoid them
except in the direst necessity
and, if compelled, will use them
only with the utmost restraint.
Peace is his highest value.
If the peace has been shattered,
how can he be content?
His enemies are not demons,
but human beings like himself.
He doesn't wish them personal harm.
Nor does he rejoice in victory.
How could he rejoice in victory
and delight in the slaughter of men?

He enters a battle gravely,   21
with sorrow and with great compassion,
as if he were attending a funeral.

37

The Tao never does anything,   22
yet through it all things are done.

If powerful men and women   23
could center themselves in it,
the whole world would be transformed
by itself, in its natural rhythms.
People would be content
with their simple, everyday lives,
in harmony, and free of desire.

When there is no desire,   24
all things are at peace.

38

The Master doesn't try to be powerful;   25
thus he is truly powerful.
The ordinary man keeps reaching for power;
thus he never has enough.

The Master does nothing,   26
yet he leaves nothing undone.

The ordinary man is always doing things,
yet many more are left to be done.

The kind man does something,   27
yet something remains undone.
The just man does something,
and leaves many things to be done.
The moral man does something,
and when no one responds
he rolls up his sleeves and uses force.

When the Tao is lost, there is goodness.   28
When goodness is lost, there is morality.
When morality is lost, there is ritual.
Ritual is the husk of true faith,
the beginning of chaos.

Therefore the Master concerns himself   29
with the depths and not the surface,
with the fruit and not the flower.
He has no will of his own.
He dwells in reality,
and lets all illusions go.

46

When a country is in harmony with the Tao,   30
the factories make trucks and tractors.
When a country goes counter to the Tao,
warheads are stockpiled outside the cities.

There is no greater illusion than fear,   31
no greater wrong than preparing to defend yourself,
no greater misfortune than having an enemy.

Whoever can see through all fear   32
will always be safe.

53

The great Way is easy,   33
yet people prefer the side paths.
Be aware when things are out of balance.
Stay centered within the Tao.

When rich speculators prosper   34
while farmers lose their land;
when government officials spend money
on weapons instead of cures;
when the upper class is extravagant and irresponsible
while the poor have nowhere to turn—
all this is robbery and chaos.
It is not in keeping with the Tao.

57

If you want to be a great leader,   35
you must learn to follow the Tao.
Stop trying to control.
Let go of fixed plans and concepts,
and the world will govern itself.

The more prohibitions you have,   36
the less virtuous people will be.
The more weapons you have,
the less secure people will be.
The more subsidies you have,
the less self-reliant people will be.

Therefore the Master says: 37
I let go of the law,
and people become honest.
I let go of economics,
and people become prosperous.
I let go of religion,
and people become serene.
I let go of all desire for the common good,
and the good becomes common as grass.

58

If a country is governed with tolerance,   38
the people are comfortable and honest.
If a country is governed with repression,
the people are depressed and crafty.

When the will to power is in charge,   39
the higher the ideals, the lower the results.
Try to make people happy,

and you lay the groundwork for misery.
Try to make people moral,
and you lay the groundwork for vice.

Thus the Master is content   40
to serve as an example
and not to impose her will.
She is pointed, but doesn't pierce.
Straightforward, but supple.
Radiant, but easy on the eyes.

59

For governing a country well   41
there is nothing better than moderation.

The mark of a moderate man   42
is freedom from his own ideas.
Tolerant like the sky,
all-pervading like sunlight,
firm like a mountain,
supple like a tree in the wind,
he has no destination in view
and makes use of anything
life happens to bring his way.

Nothing is impossible for him.   43
Because he has let go,
he can care for the people's welfare
as a mother cares for her child.

60

Governing a large country   44
is like frying a small fish.
You spoil it with too much poking.

Center your country in the Tao   45
and evil will have no power.
Not that it isn't there,
but you'll be able to step out of its way.

Give evil nothing to oppose

and it will disappear by itself.

61

When a country obtains great power,

it becomes like the sea:

all streams run downward into it.

The more powerful it grows,

the greater the need for humility.

Humility means trusting the Tao,

thus never needing to be defensive.

A great nation is like a great man:

When he makes a mistake, he realizes it.

Having realized it, he admits it.

Having admitted it, he corrects it.

He considers those who point out his faults

as his most benevolent teachers.

He thinks of his enemy

as the shadow that he himself casts.

If a nation is centered in the Tao,

if it nourishes its own people

and doesn't meddle in the affairs of others,

it will be a light to all nations in the world.

65

The ancient Masters

didn't try to educate the people,

but kindly taught them to not-know.

When they think that they know the answers,

people are difficult to guide.

When they know that they don't know,

people can find their own way.

If you want to learn how to govern,

avoid being clever or rich.

The simplest pattern is the clearest.

Content with an ordinary life,
you can show all people the way
back to their own true nature.

66

All streams flow to the sea   53
because it is lower than they are.
Humility gives it its power.

If you want to govern the people,   54
you must place yourself below them.
If you want to lead the people,
you must learn how to follow them.

The Master is above the people,   55
and no one feels oppressed.
She goes ahead of the people,
and no one feels manipulated.
The whole world is grateful to her.
Because she competes with no one,
no one can compete with her.

67

Some say that my teaching is nonsense.   56
Others call it lofty but impractical.
But to those who have looked inside themselves,
this nonsense makes perfect sense.
And to those who put it into practice,
this loftiness has roots that go deep.

I have just three things to teach: 57
simplicity, patience, compassion.
These three are your greatest treasures.
Simple in actions and in thoughts,
you return to the source of being.
Patient with both friends and enemies,
you accord with the way things are.
Compassionate toward yourself,
you reconcile all beings in the world.

75

When taxes are too high,   58
people go hungry.
When the government is too intrusive,
people lose their spirit.

Act for the people's benefit.   59
Trust them; leave them alone.

80

If a country is governed wisely,   60
its inhabitants will be content.
They enjoy the labor of their hands
and don't waste time inventing
labor-saving machines.
Since they dearly love their homes,
they aren't interested in travel.
There may be a few wagons and boats,
but these don't go anywhere.
There may be an arsenal of weapons,
but nobody ever uses them.
People enjoy their food,
take pleasure in being with their families,
spend weekends working in their gardens,
delight in the doings of the neighborhood.
And even though the next country is so close
that people can hear its roosters crowing and its dogs barking,
they are content to die of old age
without ever having gone to see it.

✴ QUESTIONS FOR CRITICAL READING

1. According to Lao-tzu, what must the ruler provide the people with if they are to be happy? See especially Verse 66.

2. To what extent does Lao-tzu concern himself with individual happiness?

3. How would you describe Lao-tzu's attitude toward the people?

4. Why does Lao-tzu think the world cannot be improved? See Verse 29.

5. Which statements made in this selection do you feel support a materialist view of experience? Can they be reconciled with Lao-tzu's overall thinking in the selection?

6. What are the limits and benefits of the expression: "Practice not-doing, / and everything will fall into place"? See Verse 3.

7. To what extent is Lao-tzu in favor of military action? What seem to be his views about the military? See Verse 31.

8. The term *Master* is used frequently in the selection. What can you tell about the character of the Master?

✖ SUGGESTIONS FOR CRITICAL WRITING

1. The term *the Tao* is used often in this selection. Write a short essay that defines what Lao-tzu seems to mean by the term. If you were a politician and had the responsibility of governing a state, how would you follow the Tao as it is implied in Lao-tzu's statements? Is the Tao restrictive? Difficult? Open to interpretation? How well do you think it would work?

2. Write a brief essay that examines the following statements from the perspective of a young person today:

> The more prohibitions you have,
> the less virtuous people will be.
> The more weapons you have,
> the less secure people will be.
> The more subsidies you have,
> the less self-reliant people will be. (Verse 57)

To what extent do you agree with these statements, and to what extent do you feel they are statements that have political importance? Do people in the United States seem to agree with these views, or do they disagree? What are the most visible political consequences of our nation's position regarding these ideas?

3. Some people have asserted that the American political system benefits the people most when the following views of Lao-tzu are carefully applied:

> Therefore the Master says:
> I let go of the law,
> and people become honest.
> I let go of economics,
> and people become prosperous.
> I let go of religion,
> and people become serene.
> I let go of all desire for the common good,
> and the good becomes common as grass. (Verse 57)

In a brief essay, decide to what extent American leaders follow these precepts. Whether you feel they do or not, do you think that they should follow these precepts? What are the likely results of their being put into practice?

4. Some of the statements Lao-tzu makes are so packed with meaning that it would take pages to explore them. One example is "When they think that they know the answers, / people are difficult to guide." Take this statement as the basis of a short essay and, in reference to a personal experience, explain the significance of this statement.

5. What does Lao-tzu imply about the obligation of the state to the individual it governs and about the obligation of the individual to the state? Is one much more important than the other? Using the text in this selection, establish what you feel is the optimum balance in the relationship between the two.

6. **CONNECTIONS**   Ralph Waldo Emerson (p. 124) spent years in Europe reading the classics and the writings of the East. To what extent is it possible to deduce that Emerson probably read Lao-tzu? Consider Verse 67: "Some say that my teaching is nonsense. / Others call it lofty but impractical. / But to those who have looked inside themselves, / this nonsense makes perfect sense." How much of Emerson's thinking on politics seems in agreement with Lao-tzu?

7. **CONNECTIONS**   Compare Lao-tzu's view of government with that of Machiavelli (p. 84). Consider what seems to be the ultimate purposes of government, what seems to be the obligations of the leader to the people being led, and what seems to be the main work of the state. What comparisons can you make between Lao-tzu's Master and Machiavelli's prince?

ARISTOTLE

Democracy and Oligarchy

A RISTOTLE (384–322 B.C.E.) is the great inheritor of Plato's influence in philosophical thought. He was a student at the Academy of Plato in Athens from age seventeen to thirty-seven, and by all accounts he was Plato's most brilliant pupil. He did not agree with Plato on all issues, however, and seems to have broken with his master around the time of Plato's death (347 B.C.E.). In certain of his writings, he is careful to disagree with the Platonists while insisting on his friendship with them. In the *Politics*, for example, Aristotle does not give much thought to Plato's theories of the best kind of government described in the *Republic* because they were based on the best person governing the best people. In a sense, those theories omit the possibility of either democracy or oligarchy.

One interesting point concerning Aristotle's career is that, when he became a teacher, his most distinguished student was Alexander the Great, the youthful ruler who spread Greek values and laws throughout the rest of the known world. Much speculation has centered on just what Aristotle might have taught Alexander about politics. The emphasis on the virtue of the warrior class in this segment of the *Politics* suggests that it may have been a great deal. A surviving fragment of a letter from Aristotle to Alexander suggests that he advised Alexander to become the leader of the Greeks and the master of the barbarians.

In his discussion of democracy and oligarchy, Aristotle is careful to present all the qualities that he feels are essential to defining each term. He speaks carefully about distinctions between the rich and the poor in a society, observing that there will always be a small number of wealthy people and a large number of poor people in any community. What Aristotle calls an *oligarchy* is a government run by a small number of people chosen essentially because they are rich. A *democracy* is governed by the will of the majority, and in most societies, the majority is poor. Aristotle realizes that these definitions are basic and

From the *Politics*.

do not cover all the possibilities for either form of government. In the course of his discussion, he reviews many of the possibilities and characteristics of democracy and oligarchy, including that a democracy can work if the rich and the poor are considered equal before the law. Aristotle is careful to point out the importance of the law as being supreme and as helping government by ensuring that the majority avoids excesses and injustice.

Late in this passage, he also considers governments that are variations of democracy and oligarchy, but his view is that these two forms of government are at the root of all variations of government and that it is important to understand them if one is to comprehend the choices society faces in governance. When one reads the *Politics*, it is important to remember that Aristotle experienced a number of different forms of government in Athens. Twenty years before he was born, Athens had been a model democracy for almost a hundred years, but after the Peloponnesian Wars ended in 404 B.C.E., Athens was governed by the Thirty Oligarchs, thirty people chosen by three thousand aristocratic Athenians. That government lasted only a year, and in its place Athens restored a limited form of democracy. Once again, Athens lost its democratic form of government in 322 B.C.E., the same year Aristotle died in exile.

In another of his writings, the *Nichomachean Ethics,* he tells us that the well-ordered state — the pride of the Greek way of life — is of such noble value that other values must take second place to it. Because current thought somewhat agrees with this view, Aristotle sounds peculiarly modern in this passage. Unlike the Christian theorists of the Middle Ages, the theorists of the Islamic insurgence, or the theorists of the Judaic scriptures, Aristotle does not put divinity or godliness first. He is a practical man whose concerns are with the life that human beings know here on earth. When he considers, for instance, the question of whether a man can be happy before he dies (tragedy can always befall the happy man), Aristotle is thoroughly practical and does not point to happiness in heaven as a substitute for happiness on earth.

ARISTOTLE'S RHETORIC

Even though Aristotle is the author of the single most influential treatise on rhetoric, this document does not have as eloquent a style as might be expected, which has suggested to some that the manuscript was taken from the lecture notes of a student. But, of course, Aristotle does use certain important techniques that demonstrate his awareness of rhetorical effect. Most characteristically, he dedicates himself entirely to being categorical. He concentrates on the categories of governments, focusing on two but admitting that there may be many more and naming five others (para. 11). In the process of writing, he carefully describes each major category of government and considers its potential for producing a happy state.

In terms of style, Aristotle is at a disadvantage — or perhaps the modern world is — because he addresses an audience who has thought very deeply on the issues of politics. As such, his style is rigorous and complex. Fortunately, nothing he says here is beyond the grasp of the careful reader, although modern readers often expect to be provided with a good many concrete examples to help them understand abstract principles. Aristotle purposely avoids using examples so as not to limit too sharply the truths he aims to impart. He also frequently uses aphorisms to focus the reader's attention, such as when he says that it shouldn't be assumed "that democracy is simply that form of government in which the greater number are sovereign."

Aristotle's most prominent rhetorical technique is definition. His overall goal in this work is to define both democracy and oligarchy. But once having done so, and having considered alternatives to these forms of government, Aristotle returns to categorization by considering the kinds of people who make up the state. In the process of doing so, he uses an analogy comparing the different parts of the state (by which he means the different kinds of people) with "the different species of animals" (para. 4). For him, the different species represent different categories that need to be discussed. In paragraph 4, he identifies husbandmen, who produce food; mechanics; traders engaged in buying and selling; serfs, or laborers; warriors, or those who dispense justice; the wealthy; and magistrates and officers. The interests of all of these people must be served by the state, and while Aristotle examines the distinctions between democracy and oligarchy, he clearly implies that the rights of free Athenians are his concern, not the rights of Athenian slaves. Democracy, in its beginning, already limited its participants according to their capacity to qualify as citizens.

❖ PREREADING QUESTIONS: WHAT TO READ FOR

The following prereading questions may help you anticipate key issues in the discussion of Aristotle's "Democracy and Oligarchy." Keeping them in mind during your first reading of the selection should help focus your attention.

1. How does Aristotle define *democracy*?
2. What is the best relationship of the wealthy to the poor in government by the majority?
3. Which form of government does Aristotle think will contribute most to general happiness?

Democracy and Oligarchy

The reason why there are many forms of government is that every state contains many elements. In the first place we see that all states are made up of families, and in the multitude of citizens there must be some rich and some poor, and some in a middle condition; the rich are heavy-armed, and the poor not. Of the common people, some are husbandmen, and some traders, and some artisans. There are also among the notables differences of wealth and property—for example, in the number of horses which they keep, for they cannot afford to keep them unless they are rich. And therefore in old times the cities whose strength lay in their cavalry were oligarchies, and they used cavalry in wars against their neighbors; as was the practice of the Eretrians and Chalcidians, and also of the Magnesians on the river Maeander, and of other peoples in Asia. Besides differences of wealth there are differences of rank and merit, and there are some other elements which were mentioned by us when in treating of aristocracy we enumerated the essentials of a state. Of these elements, sometimes all, sometimes the lesser and sometimes the greater number, have a share in the government. It is evident then that there must be many forms of government, differing in kind, since the parts of which they are composed differ from each other in kind. For a constitution is an organization of offices, which all the citizens distribute among themselves, according to the power which different classes possess, for example the rich or the poor, or according to some principle of equality which includes both. There must therefore be as many forms of government as there are modes of arranging the offices, according to the superiorities and the differences of the parts of the state.

There are generally thought to be two principal forms: as men say of the winds that there are but two—north and south, and that the rest of them are only variations of these, so of governments there are said to be only two forms—democracy and oligarchy. For aristocracy is considered to be a kind of oligarchy, as being the rule of a few, and the so-called constitutional government to be really a democracy, just as among the winds we make the west a variation of the north, and the east of the south wind. Similarly of musical modes there are said to be two kinds, the Dorian and the Phrygian;[1] the other arrangements of the scale are comprehended under one or other of these two. About forms of government this is a very favorite notion. But in either case the better and more exact way is to distinguish, as I have done, the one or two which are true forms, and to regard the others as perversions, whether of the most perfectly attempered mode or of the best form of government: we may compare the severer and more overpowering modes to the oligarchical forms, and the more relaxed and gentler ones to the democratic. 2

It must not be assumed, as some are fond of saying, that democracy is simply that form of government in which the greater number are sovereign, for in oligarchies, and indeed in every government, the majority rules; nor again 3

---

[1] **Dorian and Phrygian**   Greek musical modes; two different classes of musical scales with intervals different from modern scales.

is oligarchy that form of government in which a few are sovereign. Suppose the whole population of a city to be 1,300, and that of these 1,000 are rich, and do not allow the remaining 300 who are poor, but free, and in all other respects their equals, a share of the government—no one will say that this is a democracy. In like manner, if the poor were few and the masters of the rich who outnumber them, no one would ever call such a government, in which the rich majority have no share of office, an oligarchy. Therefore we should rather say that democracy is the form of government in which the free are rulers, and oligarchy in which the rich; it is only an accident that the free are the many and the rich are the few. Otherwise a government in which the offices were given according to stature, as is said to be the case in Ethiopia, or according to beauty, would be an oligarchy; for the number of tall or good-looking men is small. And yet oligarchy and democracy are not sufficiently distinguished merely by these two characteristics of wealth and freedom. Both of them contain many other elements, and therefore we must carry our analysis further, and say that the government is not a democracy in which the freemen, being few in number, rule over the many who are not free, as at Apollonia, on the Ionian Gulf, and at Thera (for in each of these states the nobles, who were also the earliest settlers, were held in chief honor, although they were but a few out of many). Neither is it a democracy when the rich have the government because they exceed in number; as was the case formerly at Colophon, where the bulk of the inhabitants were possessed of large property before the Lydian War.[2] But the form of government is a democracy when the free, who are also poor and the majority, govern, and an oligarchy when the rich and the noble govern, they being at the same time few in number.

    I have said that there are many forms of government, and have explained to what causes the variety is due. Why there are more than those already mentioned, and what they are, and whence they arise, I will now proceed to consider, starting from the principle already admitted, which is that every state consists, not of one, but of many parts. If we were going to speak of the different species of animals, we should first of all determine the organs which are indispensable to every animal, as for example some organs of sense and the instruments of receiving and digesting food, such as the mouth and the stomach, besides organs of locomotion. Assuming now that there are only so many kinds of organs, but that there may be differences in them—I mean different kinds of mouths, and stomachs, and perceptive and locomotive organs—the possible combinations of these differences will necessarily furnish many varieties of animals. (For animals cannot be the same which have different kinds of mouths or of ears.) And when all the combinations are exhausted, there will be as many sorts of animals as there are combinations of the necessary organs. The same, then, is

4

---

[2] **Lydian War** Possibly a reference to the Trojan War, which was in Lydia, now Turkey.

true of the forms of government which have been described; states, as I have repeatedly said, are composed, not of one, but of many elements. One element is the food-producing class, who are called husbandmen; a second, the class of mechanics who practice the arts without which a city cannot exist;—of these arts some are absolutely necessary, others contribute to luxury or to the grace of life. The third class is that of traders, and by traders I mean those who are engaged in buying and selling, whether in commerce or in retail trade. A fourth class is that of the serfs or laborers. The warriors make up the fifth class, and they are as necessary as any of the others, if the country is not to be the slave of every invader. For how can a state which has any title to the name be of a slavish nature? The state is independent and self-sufficing, but a slave is the reverse of independent. Hence we see that this subject, though ingeniously, has not been satisfactorily treated in the *Republic*.[3] Socrates says that a state is made up of four sorts of people who are absolutely necessary; these are a weaver, a husbandman, a shoemaker, and a builder; afterwards, finding that they are not enough, he adds a smith, and again a herdsman, to look after the necessary animals; then a merchant, and then a retail trader. All these together form the complement of the first state, as if a state were established merely to supply the necessaries of life, rather than for the sake of the good, or stood equally in need of shoemakers and of husbandmen. But he does not admit into the state a military class until the country has increased in size, and is beginning to encroach on its neighbor's land, whereupon they go to war. Yet even amongst his four original citizens, or whatever be the number of those whom he associates in the state, there must be some one who will dispense justice and determine what is just. And as the soul may be said to be more truly part of an animal than the body, so the higher parts of states, that is to say, the warrior class, the class engaged in the administration of justice, and that engaged in deliberation, which is the special business of political common sense—these are more essential to the state than the parts which minister to the necessaries of life. Whether their several functions are the functions of different citizens, or of the same—for it may often happen that the same persons are both warriors and husbandmen—is immaterial to the argument. The higher as well as the lower elements are to be equally considered parts of the state, and if so, the military element at any rate must be included. There are also the wealthy who minister to the state with their property; these form the seventh class. The eighth class is that of magistrates and of officers; for the state cannot exist without rulers. And therefore some must be able to take office and to serve the state, either always or in turn. There only remains the class of those who deliberate and who judge between disputants; we were just now distinguishing

---

[3] ***Republic*** Plato's political book, written around 380 B.C.E., which preferred a government run by the best people rather than democracy.

them. If presence of all these elements, and their fair and equitable organization, is necessary to states, then there must also be persons who have the ability of statesmen. Different functions appear to be often combined in the same individual; for example, the warrior may also be a husbandman, or an artisan; or, again, the counselor a judge. And all claim to possess political ability, and think that they are quite competent to fill most offices. But the same persons cannot be rich and poor at the same time. For this reason the rich and the poor are regarded in an especial sense as parts of a state. Again, because the rich are generally few in number, while the poor are many, they appear to be antagonistic, and as the one or the other prevails they form the government. Hence arises the common opinion that there are two kinds of government — democracy and oligarchy.

I have already explained that there are many forms of constitution, and 　5 to what causes the variety is due. Let me now show that there are different forms both of democracy and oligarchy, as will indeed be evident from what has preceded. For both in the common people and in the notables various classes are included; of the common people, one class are husbandmen, another artisans; another traders, who are employed in buying and selling; another are the seafaring class, whether engaged in war or in trade, as ferrymen or as fishermen. (In many places any one of these classes forms quite a large population; for example, fishermen at Tarentum and Byzantium, crews of triremes at Athens, merchant seamen at Aegina and Chios, ferrymen at Tenedos.) To the classes already mentioned may be added day laborers, and those who, owing to their needy circumstances, have no leisure, or those who are not of free birth on both sides; and there may be other classes as well. The notables again may be divided according to their wealth, birth, virtue, education, and similar differences.

Of forms of democracy first comes that which is said to be based strictly 　6 on equality. In such a democracy the law says that it is just for the poor to have no more advantage than the rich; and that neither should be masters, but both equal. For if liberty and equality, as is thought by some, are chiefly to be found in democracy, they will be best attained when all persons alike share in the government to the utmost. And since the people are the majority, and the opinion of the majority is decisive, such a government must necessarily be a democracy. Here then is one sort of democracy. There is another, in which the magistrates are elected according to a certain property qualification, but a low one; he who has the required amount of property has a share in the government, but he who loses his property loses his rights. Another kind is that in which all the citizens who are under no disqualification share in the government, but still the law is supreme. In another, everybody, if he be only a citizen, is admitted to the government, but the law is supreme as before. A fifth form of democracy, in other respects, the same, is that in which, not the law, but the multitude, have the supreme power, and supersede the law by their decrees.

This is a state of affairs brought about by the demagogues. For in democracies which are subject to the law the best citizens hold the first place, and there are no demagogues; but where the laws are not supreme, there demagogues spring up. For the people becomes a monarch, and is many in one; and the many have the power in their hands, not as individuals, but collectively. Homer says that "it is not good to have a rule of many," but whether he means this corporate rule, or the rule of many individuals, is uncertain. At all events this sort of democracy, which is now a monarch, and no longer under the control of law, seeks to exercise monarchical sway, and grows into a despot; the flatterer is held in honor; this sort of democracy being relatively to other democracies what tyranny is to other forms of monarchy. The spirit of both is the same, and they alike exercise a despotic rule over the better citizens. The decrees of the demos correspond to the edicts of the tyrant; and the demagogue is to the one what the flatterer is to the other. Both have great power; — the flatterer with the tyrant, the demagogue with democracies of the kind which we are describing. The demagogues make the decrees of the people override the laws, by referring all things to the popular assembly. And therefore they grow great, because the people have all things in their hands, and they hold in their hands the votes of the people, who are too ready to listen to them. Further, those who have any complaint to bring against the magistrates say, "let the people be judges"; the people are too happy to accept the invitation; and so the authority of every office is undermined. Such a democracy is fairly open to the objection that it is not a constitution at all; for where the laws have no authority, there is no constitution. The law ought to be supreme over all, and the magistracies should judge of particulars, and only this should be considered a constitution. So that if democracy be a real form of government, the sort of system in which all things are regulated by decrees is clearly not even a democracy in the true sense of the word, for decrees relate only to particulars.

These then are the different kinds of democracy. 7

Of oligarchies, too, there are different kinds: — one where the property 8 qualification for office is such that the poor, although they form the majority, have no share in the government, yet he who acquires a qualification may obtain a share. Another sort is when there is a qualification for office, but a high one, and the vacancies in the governing body are filled by co-optation. If the election is made out of all the qualified persons, a constitution of this kind inclines to an aristocracy, if out of a privileged class, to an oligarchy. Another sort of oligarchy is when the son succeeds the father. There is a fourth form, likewise hereditary, in which the magistrates are supreme and not the law. Among oligarchies this is what tyranny is among monarchies, and the last-mentioned form of democracy among democracies; and in fact this sort of oligarchy receives the name of a dynasty (or rule of powerful families).

These are the different sorts of oligarchies and democracies. It should   9
however be remembered that in many states the constitution which is established by law, although not democratic, owing to the education and habits of
the people may be administered democratically, and conversely in other states
the established constitution may incline to democracy, but may be administered in an oligarchical spirit. This most often happens after a revolution: for
governments do not change at once; at first the dominant party are content
with encroaching a little upon their opponents. The laws which existed previously continue in force, but the authors of the revolution have the power in
their hands.

From what has been already said we may safely infer that there are so   10
many different kinds of democracies and of oligarchies. For it is evident that
either all the classes whom we mentioned must share in the government, or
some only and not others. When the class of husbandmen and of those who
possess moderate fortunes have the supreme power, the government is administered according to law. For the citizens being compelled to live by their
labor have no leisure; and so they set up the authority of the law, and attend
assemblies only when necessary. They all obtain a share in the government
when they have acquired the qualification which is fixed by the law—the
absolute exclusion of any class would be a step toward oligarchy; hence all
who have acquired the property qualification are admitted to a share in the
constitution. But leisure cannot be provided for them unless there are revenues to support them. This is one sort of democracy, and these are the causes
which give birth to it. Another kind is based on the distinction which naturally
comes next in order; in this, every one to whose birth there is no objection
is eligible, but actually shares in the government only if he can find leisure.
Hence in such a democracy the supreme power is vested in the laws, because
the state has no means of paying the citizens. A third kind is when all freemen have a right to share in the government, but do not actually share, for
the reason which has been already given; so that in this form again the law
must rule. A fourth kind of democracy is that which comes latest in the history of states. In our own day, when cities have far outgrown their original
size, and their revenues have increased, all the citizens have a place in the
government, through the great preponderance of the multitude; and they
all, including the poor who receive pay, and therefore have leisure to exercise their rights, share in the administration. Indeed, when they are paid, the
common people have the most leisure, for they are not hindered by the care
of their property, which often fetters the rich, who are thereby prevented
from taking part in the assembly or in the courts, and so the state is governed by the poor, who are a majority, and not by the laws. So many kinds
of democracies there are, and they grow out of these necessary causes.

Of oligarchies, one form is that in which the majority of the citizens have   11
some property, but not very much; and this is the first form, which allows to
any one who obtains the required amount the right of sharing in the government. The sharers in the government being a numerous body, it follows that
the law must govern, and not individuals. For in proportion as they are further
removed from a monarchical form of government, and in respect of property
have neither so much as to be able to live without attending to business, nor
so little as to need state support, they must admit the rule of law and not claim
to rule themselves. But if the men of property in the state are fewer than in the
former case, and own more property, there arises a second form of oligarchy.
For the stronger they are, the more power they claim, and having this object
in view, they themselves select those of the other classes who are to be admitted to the government; but, not being as yet strong enough to rule without the
law, they make the law represent their wishes. When this power is intensified
by a further diminution of their numbers and increase of their property, there
arises a third and further stage of oligarchy, in which the governing class keep
the offices in their own hands, and the law ordains that the son shall succeed
the father. When, again, the rulers have great wealth and numerous friends,
this sort of family despotism approaches a monarchy; individuals rule and not
the law. This is the fourth sort of oligarchy, and is analogous to the last sort of
democracy.

There are still two forms besides democracy and oligarchy; one of them   12
is universally recognized and included among the four principal forms of government, which are said to be (1) monarchy, (2) oligarchy, (3) democracy, and
(4) the so-called aristocracy or government of the best. But there is also a fifth,
which retains the generic name of polity or constitutional government; this is
not common, and therefore has not been noticed by writers who attempt to
enumerate the different kinds of government; like Plato, in their books about
the state, they recognize four only. The term *aristocracy* is rightly applied to
the form of government which is described in the first part of our treatise; for
that only can be rightly called aristocracy which is a government formed of the
best men absolutely, and not merely of men who are good when tried by any
given standard. In the perfect state the good man is absolutely the same as the
good citizen; whereas in other states the good citizen is only good relatively to
his own form of government. But there are some states differing from oligarchies and also differing from the so-called polity or constitutional government;
these are termed aristocracies, and in them magistrates are certainly chosen,
both according to their wealth and according to their merit. Such a form of
government differs from each of the two just now mentioned, and is termed
an aristocracy. For indeed in states which do not make virtue the aim of the
community, men of merit and reputation for virtue may be found. And so where

a government has regard to wealth, virtue, and numbers, as at Carthage, that is aristocracy; and also where it has regard only to two out of the three, as at Lacedaemon, to virtue and numbers, and the two principles of democracy and virtue temper each other. There are these two forms of aristocracy in addition to the first and perfect state, and there is a third form, viz. [namely] the constitutions which incline more than the so-called polity towards oligarchy.

I have yet to speak of the so-called polity and of tyranny. I put them in this 13 order, not because a polity or constitutional government is to be regarded as a perversion any more than the above-mentioned aristocracies. The truth is, that they all fall short of the most perfect form of government, and so they are reckoned among perversions, and the really perverted forms are perversions of these, as I said in the original discussion. Last of all I will speak of tyranny, which I place last in the series because I am inquiring into the constitutions of states, and this is the very reverse of a constitution.

Having explained why I have adopted this order, I will proceed to consider 14 constitutional government; of which the nature will be clearer now that oligarchy and democracy have been defined. For polity or constitutional government may be described generally as a fusion of oligarchy and democracy; but the term is usually applied to those forms of government which incline toward democracy, and the term aristocracy to those which incline toward oligarchy, because birth and education are commonly the accompaniments of wealth. Moreover, the rich already possess the external advantages the want of which is a temptation to crime, and hence they are called noblemen and gentlemen. And inasmuch as aristocracy seeks to give predominance to the best of the citizens, people say also of oligarchies that they are composed of noblemen and gentlemen. Now it appears to be an impossible thing that the state which is governed not by the best citizens but by the worst should be well-governed, and equally impossible that the state which is ill-governed should be governed by the best. But we must remember that good laws, if they are not obeyed, do not constitute good government. Hence there are two parts of good government; one is the actual obedience of citizens to the laws, the other part is the goodness of the laws which they obey; they may obey bad laws as well as good. And there may be a further subdivision; they may obey either the best laws which are attainable to them, or the best absolutely.

The distribution of offices according to merit is a special characteristic 15 of aristocracy, for the principle of an aristocracy is virtue, as wealth is of an oligarchy, and freedom of a democracy. In all of them there of course exists the right of the majority, and whatever seems good to the majority of those who share in the government has authority. Now in most states the form called polity exists, for the fusion goes no further than the attempt to unite the freedom of the poor and the wealth of the rich, who commonly take the place of the noble. But as there are three grounds on which men claim an equal share in the government, freedom, wealth, and virtue (for the fourth or good birth is the result of the two last, being only ancient wealth and virtue), it is clear that the admixture of the two elements, that is to say, of the rich and poor, is to be called a polity or constitutional government; and the union of the three is to be called aristocracy or the government of the best, and more than any other form of government, except the true and ideal, has a right to this name.

Thus far I have shown the existence of forms of states other than monarchy, democracy, and oligarchy, and what they are, and in what aristocracies differ from one another, and polities from aristocracies—that the two latter are not very unlike is obvious.   16

Next we have to consider how by the side of oligarchy and democracy the so-called polity or constitutional government springs up, and how it should be organized. The nature of it will be at once understood from a comparison of oligarchy and democracy; we must ascertain their different characteristics, and taking a portion from each, put the two together, like the parts of an indenture. Now there are three modes in which fusions of government may be effected. In the first mode we must combine the laws made by both governments, say concerning the administration of justice. In oligarchies they impose a fine on the rich if they do not serve as judges, and to the poor they give no pay; but in democracies they give pay to the poor and do not fine the rich. Now (1) the union of these two modes is a common or middle term between them, and is therefore characteristic of a constitutional government, for it is a combination of both. This is one mode of uniting the two elements. Or (2) a mean may be taken between the enactments of the two: thus democracies require no property qualification, or only a small one, from members of the assembly, oligarchies a high one; here neither of these is the common term, but a mean between them. (3) There is a third mode, in which something is borrowed from the oligarchical and something from the democratical principle. For example, the appointment of magistrates by lot is thought to be democratical, and the election of them oligarchical; democratical again when there is no property qualification, oligarchical when there is. In the aristocratical or constitutional state, one element will be taken from each—from oligarchy the principle of electing to offices, from democracy the disregard of qualification. Such are the various modes of combination.   17

There is a true union of oligarchy and democracy when the same state may be termed either a democracy or an oligarchy; those who use both names evidently feel that the fusion is complete. Such a fusion there is also in the mean; for both extremes appear in it. The Lacedaemonian constitution, for example, is often described as a democracy, because it has many democratical features. In the first place the youth receive a democratical education. For the sons of the poor are brought up with the sons of the rich, who are educated in such a manner as to make it possible for the sons of the poor to be educated like them. A similar equality prevails in the following period of life, and when the   18 citizens are grown up to manhood the same rule is observed; there is no distinction between the rich and poor. In like manner they all have the same food at their public tables, and the rich wear only such clothing as any poor man can afford. Again, the people elect to one of the two greatest offices of state, and in the other they share; for they elect the Senators and share in the Ephoralty. By others the Spartan constitution is said to be an oligarchy, because it has many oligarchical elements. That all offices are filled by election and none by lot, is one of these oligarchical characteristics; that the power of inflicting death or banishment rests with a few persons is another; and there are others. In a well attempered polity there should appear to be both elements and yet neither; also the government should rely on itself, and not on foreign aid, and on itself not through the good will of a majority—they might be equally well-disposed when there is a vicious form of government—but through the general willingness of all classes in the state to maintain the constitution.

Enough of the manner in which a constitutional government, and in which the so-called aristocracies ought to be framed.   19

✂ QUESTIONS FOR CRITICAL READING

1. According to Aristotle, what seem to be the markers of wealth in Athens?
2. What does the presence of heavy armament and of the cavalry imply for rule by oligarchy?
3. Aristotle admits that there are "many forms of government" (para. 1). What, then, is his explanation for primarily considering only two?
4. In paragraph 4, Aristotle says that some classes are more essential to the state than others. What are they, and do you agree?
5. How important is the idea of equality in a democracy? See paragraph 6.
6. In paragraph 9, Aristotle says the law, not individuals, must govern. What are his reasons?
7. Who can vote in Aristotle's democracy?

✂ SUGGESTIONS FOR CRITICAL WRITING

1. The concept of majority rule is central to Aristotle's discussion of democracy. Explain his views on this question and examine what he says about the limitations of majority rule. Does his thinking on majority rule cause you to change your own ideas about it? What are the strengths and weaknesses of majority rule in a modern democracy?
2. In paragraph 4, Aristotle talks about the different elements in the state, referring to nine classes of people: husbandmen, traders, the military, lawyers, and others. Do these different groups still constitute the modern state in the way in which

Aristotle describes them? Why does he consider these different elements when talking about government? Do you feel he is justified in doing so? What are the most important different "elements" in the state as you understand them?

3. **CONNECTIONS**   Aristotle says, "Because the rich are generally few in number, while the poor are many, they appear to be antagonistic, and as the one or the other prevails they form the government" (para. 4). Do you find that Aristotle is correct about the relationship between the rich and the poor in our modern democracies? Aristotle implies that when the rich govern, we have an oligarchy, and when the poor govern, we have a democracy. Does this view correlate with your observations about government? Compare Aristotle's view with that of Andrew Carnegie in "The Gospel of Wealth" (p. 360). Why does he raise the issue of class warfare between the rich and the poor? Would Carnegie welcome a benevolent oligarchy?

4. **CONNECTIONS**   In paragraph 3, Aristotle discusses the question of how we calculate majority in a democracy in which the majority rules. He points to a variety of such majorities. If the majority in a democracy were to profess a single religion, should then the precepts of that religion guide the entire democracy? Consider Benazir Bhutto's (p. 171) description of the characteristics of the religion of Islam. If Islam were to be the religion of the majority, would a nation then still be democratic? What does Bhutto say that indicates that her under-standing of government is similar to that of Aristotle? What would be the effect on minorities, especially those who profess no religion, in a state with a religious majority? If Evangelical Christians were in the majority, how might that impact democratic government?

5. In paragraph 6, Aristotle says, "Of forms of democracy first comes that which is said to be based strictly on equality." What does he seem to mean by equality? What, in terms of government, do you think the term *equality* means today? Is it possible to have a democracy without equality? Why would equality be such an important issue in any form of government? What is your definition of *equality*? Do you think equality is possible in a modern state?

6. In discussing some of the dangers of majority rule in a democracy, Aristotle raises the issue of the possibility of creating a demagogue. What does he mean? What is a demagogue, and how could a democracy produce one? What harm might a dema-gogue cause a democratic state? What examples of modern demagogues speak to the issues Aristotle raises?

7. Aristotle makes a clear distinction between the minority wealthy class and the majority poor class. When only the wealthy have power, the state is an oligarchy. When the poor have power, the state is a democracy. How would Aristotle's theories be altered if he considered a numerous middle class between the rich and the poor? When the middle class is the majority of the population, how does that affect the distinction between democracy and oligarchy? Would a dominant middle class produce a democracy or an oligarchy?

NICCOLÒ MACHIAVELLI

The Qualities of the Prince

N ICCOLÒ MACHIAVELLI (1469–1527) was an aristocrat whose fortunes wavered according to the shifts in power in Florence. Renaissance Italy was a collection of powerful city-states, which were sometimes volatile and unstable. When Florence's famed Medici princes were returned to power in 1512 after eighteen years of banishment, Machiavelli did not fare well. He was suspected of crimes against the state and imprisoned. Even though he was not guilty, he had to learn to support himself as a writer instead of continuing his career in civil service.

His works often contrast two forces: luck (one's fortune) and character (one's virtues). His own character outlasted his bad luck in regard to the Medicis, and he was returned to a position of responsibility. *The Prince* (1513), his most celebrated work, was a general treatise on the qualities the prince (that is, ruler) must have to maintain his power. In a more particular way, it was directed at the Medicis to encourage them to save Italy from the predatory incursions of France and Spain, whose troops were nibbling at the crumbling Italian principalities and who would, in time, control much of Italy.

The chapters presented here contain the core of the philosophy for which Machiavelli became famous. His instructions to the prince are curiously devoid of any high-sounding moralizing or any encouragement to be good as a matter of principle. Instead, Machiavelli recommends a very practical course of action for the prince: secure power by direct and effective means. It may be that Machiavelli fully expects that the prince will use his power for good ends — certainly he does not recommend tyranny. But he also supports using questionable means to achieve the final end of becoming and remaining the prince. Although Machiavelli recognizes that there is often a conflict between the ends and the means used to achieve them, he does not fret over the possible problems that may

---

From *The Prince*. Translated by Peter Bondanella and Mark Musa.

accompany the use of "unpleasant" means, such as punishment of upstarts or the use of repression, imprisonment, and torture.

Through the years, Machiavelli's view of human nature has come under criticism for its cynicism. For instance, he suggests that a morally good person would not remain long in any high office because that person would have to compete with the mass of people, who, he says, are basically bad. Machiavelli constantly tells us that he is describing the world as it really is, not as it should be. Perhaps Machiavelli is correct, but people have long condemned the way he approves of cunning, deceit, and outright lying as a means of staying in power.

The contrast between Machiavelli's writings and Lao-tzu's opinions in the *Tao-te Ching* is instructive. Lao-tzu's advice issues from a detached view of a universal ruler; Machiavelli's advice is very personal, embodying a set of directives for a specific prince. Machiavelli expounds on a litany of actions that must be taken; Lao-tzu, on the other hand, advises that judicious inaction will produce the best results.

MACHIAVELLI'S RHETORIC

Machiavelli's approach is less poetic and more pragmatic than Lao-tzu's. Whereas Lao-tzu's tone is almost biblical, Machiavelli's is that of a how-to book, relevant to a particular time and a particular place. Yet, like Lao-tzu, Machiavelli is brief and to the point. Each segment of the discussion is terse and economical.

Machiavelli announces his primary point clearly, refers to historical precedents to support his point, and then explains why his position is the best one by appealing to both common sense and historical experience. When he suspects the reader will not share his view wholeheartedly, he suggests an alternate argument and then explains why it is wrong. This is a very forceful way of presenting one's views. It gives the appearance of fairness and thoroughness — and, as we learn from reading Machiavelli, he is very much concerned with appearances. His method also gives his work fullness, a quality that makes us forget how brief it really is.

Another of his rhetorical methods is to discuss opposite pairings, including both sides of an issue. From the first he explores a number of oppositions — the art of war and the art of life, liberality and stinginess, cruelty and clemency, the fox and the lion. The method may seem simple, but it is important because it employs two of the basic techniques of rhetoric — comparison and contrast.

The aphorism is another of Machiavelli's rhetorical weapons. An aphorism is a saying — a concise statement of a principle — that has been accepted as true. Familiar examples are "A penny saved is a penny earned" and "There is no fool like an old fool." Machiavelli tells us, "A man who wishes to make a vocation of being good at all times will come to ruin among so many who are not good."

Such definite statements have several important qualities. One is that they are pithy: they seem to say a great deal in a few words. Another is that they appear to contain a great deal of wisdom, in part because they are delivered with such certainty and in part because they have the ring of other aphorisms that we accept as true. Because they sound like aphorisms, they gain a claim to (unsubstantiated) truth, and we tend to accept them much more readily than perhaps we should. This may be why the speeches of contemporary politicians (modern versions of the prince) are often sprinkled with such expressions and illustrates why Machiavelli's rhetorical technique is still reliable, still effective, and still worth studying.

✖ PREREADING QUESTIONS: WHAT TO READ FOR

The following prereading questions may help you anticipate key issues in the discussion of Niccolò Machiavelli's "The Qualities of the Prince." Keeping them in mind during your first reading of the selection should help focus your attention.

1. Why does Machiavelli praise skill in warfare in his opening pages? How does that skill aid a prince?
2. Is it better for a prince to be loved or to be feared?

The Qualities of the Prince

A Prince's Duty Concerning Military Matters

A prince, therefore, must not have any other object nor any other thought, nor must he take anything as his profession but war, its institutions, and its discipline; because that is the only profession which befits one who commands; and it is of such importance that not only does it maintain those who were born princes, but many times it enables men of private station to rise to that position; and, on the other hand, it is evident that when princes have given more thought to personal luxuries than to arms, they have lost their state. And the first way to lose it is to neglect this art; and the way to acquire it is to be well versed in this art.   1

Francesco Sforza[1] became Duke of Milan from being a private citizen because he was armed; his sons, since they avoided the inconveniences of arms, became private citizens after having been dukes. For, among the other bad effects it causes, being disarmed makes you despised; this is one of those infamies a prince should guard himself against, as will be treated below: for between an armed and an unarmed man there is no comparison whatsoever,   2

---

[1] **Francesco Sforza (1401–1466)**   Became duke of Milan in 1450. He was, like most of Machiavelli's examples, a skilled diplomat and soldier. His court was a model of Renaissance scholarship and achievement.

and it is not reasonable for an armed man to obey an unarmed man willingly, nor that an unarmed man should be safe among armed servants; since, when the former is suspicious and the latter are contemptuous, it is impossible for them to work well together. And therefore, a prince who does not understand military matters, besides the other misfortunes already noted, cannot be esteemed by his own soldiers, nor can he trust them.

He must, therefore, never raise his thought from this exercise of war, and in peacetime he must train himself more than in time of war; this can be done in two ways: one by action, the other by the mind. And as far as actions are concerned, besides keeping his soldiers well disciplined and trained, he must always be out hunting, and must accustom his body to hardships in this manner; and he must also learn the nature of the terrain, and know how mountains slope, how valleys open, how plains lie, and understand the nature of rivers and swamps; and he should devote much attention to such activities. Such knowledge is useful in two ways: first, one learns to know one's own country and can better understand how to defend it; second, with the knowledge and experience of the terrain, one can easily comprehend the characteristics of any other terrain that it is necessary to explore for the first time; for the hills, valleys, plains, rivers, and swamps of Tuscany,[2] for instance, have certain similarities to those of other provinces; so that by knowing the lay of the land in one province one can easily understand it in others. And a prince who lacks this ability lacks the most important quality in a leader; because this skill teaches you to find the enemy, choose a campsite, lead troops, organize them for battle, and besiege towns to your own advantage.

Philopoemon, Prince of the Achaeans,[3] among the other praises given to him by writers, is praised because in peacetime he thought of nothing except the means of waging war; and when he was out in the country with his friends, he often stopped and reasoned with them: "If the enemy were on that hilltop and we were here with our army, which of the two of us would have the advantage? How could we attack them without breaking formation? If we wanted to retreat, how could we do this? If they were to retreat, how could we pursue them?" And he proposed to them, as they rode along, all the contingencies that can occur in an army; he heard their opinions, expressed his own, and backed it up with arguments; so that, because of these continuous deliberations, when leading his troops no unforeseen incident could arise for which he did not have the remedy.

But as for the exercise of the mind, the prince must read histories and in them study the deeds of great men; he must see how they conducted themselves in wars; he must examine the reasons for their victories and for their

3

4

5

---

[2] **Tuscany**   Florence is in the region of Italy known as Tuscany.

[3] **Philopoemon (252?–182 B.C.E.), Prince of the Achaeans**   Philopoemon, from the city-state of Megalopolis, was a Greek general noted for skillful diplomacy. He led the Achaeans, a group of Greek states that formed the Achaean League, in several important expeditions, notably against Sparta. His cruelty in putting down a Spartan uprising caused him to be reprimanded by his superiors.

defeats in order to avoid the latter and to imitate the former; and above all else he must do as some distinguished man before him has done, who elected to imitate someone who had been praised and honored before him, and always keep in mind his deeds and actions; just as it is reported that Alexander the Great imitated Achilles; Caesar, Alexander; Scipio, Cyrus.[4] And anyone who reads the life of Cyrus written by Xenophon then realizes how important in the life of Scipio that imitation was to his glory and how much, in purity, goodness, humanity, and generosity, Scipio conformed to those characteristics of Cyrus that Xenophon had written about.

Such methods as these a wise prince must follow, and never in peaceful   6
times must he be idle; but he must turn them diligently to his advantage in order to be able to profit from them in times of adversity, so that, when Fortune changes, she will find him prepared to withstand such times.

On Those Things for Which Men, and Particularly Princes, Are Praised or Blamed

Now there remains to be examined what should be the methods and proce-   7
dures of a prince in dealing with his subjects and friends. And because I know that many have written about this, I am afraid that by writing about it again I shall be thought of as presumptuous, since in discussing this material I depart radically from the procedures of others. But since my intention is to write something useful for anyone who understands it, it seemed more suitable to me to search after the effectual truth of the matter rather than its imagined one. And many writers have imagined for themselves republics and principalities that have never been seen nor known to exist in reality; for there is such a gap between how one lives and how one ought to live that anyone who abandons what is done for what ought to be done learns his ruin rather than his preservation: for a man who wishes to make a vocation of being good at all times will come to ruin among so many who are not good. Hence it is necessary for a prince who wishes to maintain his position to learn how not to be good, and to use this knowledge or not to use it according to necessity.

Leaving aside, therefore, the imagined things concerning a prince, and   8
taking into account those that are true, I say that all men, when they are spoken of, and particularly princes, since they are placed on a higher level, are

---

[4] **Cyrus (585?–529? B.C.E.)** Cyrus II (the Great), Persian emperor. Cyrus and the other figures featured in this sentence — Alexander the Great (356–323 B.C.E.); Achilles, hero of Homer's *Iliad*; Julius Caesar (100?–44 B.C.E.); and Scipio Africanus (236–184/3 B.C.E.), legendary Roman general — are all examples of politicians who were also great military geniuses. Xenophon (431–350? B.C.E.) was one of the earliest Greek historians; he chronicled the lives and military exploits of Cyrus and his son-in-law Darius.

judged by some of these qualities which bring them either blame or praise. And this is why one is considered generous, another miserly (to use a Tuscan word, since "avaricious" in our language is still used to mean one who wishes to acquire by means of theft; we call "miserly" one who excessively avoids using what he has); one is considered a giver, the other rapacious; one cruel, another merciful; one treacherous, another faithful; one effeminate and cowardly, another bold and courageous; one humane, another haughty; one lascivious, another chaste; one trustworthy, another cunning; one harsh, another lenient; one serious, another frivolous; one religious, another unbelieving; and the like. And I know that everyone will admit that it would be a very praiseworthy thing to find in a prince, of the qualities mentioned above, those that are held to be good, but since it is neither possible to have them nor to observe them all completely, because human nature does not permit it, a prince must be prudent enough to know how to escape the bad reputation of those vices that would lose the state for him, and must protect himself from those that will not lose it for him, if this is possible; but if he cannot, he need not concern himself unduly if he ignores these less serious vices. And, moreover, he need not worry about incurring the bad reputation of those vices without which it would be difficult to hold his state; since, carefully taking everything into account, one will discover that something which appears to be a virtue, if pursued, will end in his destruction; while some other thing which seems to be a vice, if pursued, will result in his safety and his well-being.

On Generosity and Miserliness

Beginning, therefore, with the first of the above-mentioned qualities, I say that it would be good to be considered generous; nevertheless, generosity used in such a manner as to give you a reputation for it will harm you; because if it is employed virtuously and as one should employ it, it will not be recognized and you will not avoid the reproach of its opposite. And so, if a prince wants to maintain his reputation for generosity among men, it is necessary for him not to neglect any possible means of lavish display; in so doing such a prince will always use up all his resources and he will be obliged, eventually, if he wishes to maintain his reputation for generosity, to burden the people with excessive taxes and to do everything possible to raise funds. This will begin to make him hateful to his subjects, and, becoming impoverished, he will not be much esteemed by anyone; so that, as a consequence of his generosity, having offended many and rewarded few, he will feel the effects of any slight unrest and will be ruined at the first sign of danger; recognizing this and wishing to alter his policies, he immediately runs the risk of being reproached as a miser.

A prince, therefore, unable to use this virtue of generosity in a manner   10
which will not harm himself if he is known for it, should, if he is wise, not
worry about being called a miser; for with time he will come to be considered
more generous once it is evident that, as a result of his parsimony, his income
is sufficient, he can defend himself from anyone who makes war against him,
and he can undertake enterprises without overburdening his people, so that
he comes to be generous with all those from whom he takes nothing, who
are countless, and miserly with all those to whom he gives nothing, who are
few. In our times we have not seen great deeds accomplished except by those
who were considered miserly; all others were done away with. Pope Julius II,[5]
although he made use of his reputation for generosity in order to gain the
papacy, then decided not to maintain it in order to be able to wage war; the
present King of France[6] has waged many wars without imposing extra taxes
on his subjects, only because his habitual parsimony has provided for the additional expenditures; the present King of Spain,[7] if he had been considered generous, would not have engaged in nor won so many campaigns.

Therefore, in order not to have to rob his subjects, to be able to defend   11
himself, not to become poor and contemptible, and not to be forced to become
rapacious, a prince must consider it of little importance if he incurs the name of
miser, for this is one of those vices that permits him to rule. And if someone were
to say: Caesar with his generosity came to rule the empire, and many others,
because they were generous and known to be so, achieved very high positions; I
reply: you are either already a prince or you are on the way to becoming one; in
the first instance such generosity is damaging; in the second it is very necessary
to be thought generous. And Caesar was one of those who wanted to gain the
principality of Rome; but if, after obtaining this, he had lived and had not mod-
erated his expenditures, he would have destroyed that empire. And if someone
were to reply: there have existed many princes who have accomplished great
deeds with their armies who have been reputed to be generous; I answer you: a
prince either spends his own money and that of his subjects or that of others; in
the first case he must be economical; in the second he must not restrain any part
of his generosity. And for that prince who goes out with his soldiers and lives
by looting, sacking, and ransoms, who controls the property of others, such
generosity is necessary; otherwise he would not be followed by his troops. And
with what does not belong to you or to your subjects you can be a more liberal
giver, as were Cyrus, Caesar, and Alexander; for spending the wealth of others

---

[5] **Pope Julius II (1443–1513)**   Giuliano della Rovere, pope from 1503 to 1513. Like many
of the popes of the day, Julius II was also a diplomat and a general.

[6] **present King of France**   Louis XII (1462–1515). He entered Italy on a successful military
campaign in 1494.

[7] **present King of Spain**   Ferdinand V (1452–1516). A studied politician; he and Queen
Isabella (1451–1504) financed Christopher Columbus's voyage to the New World in 1492.

does not lessen your reputation but adds to it; only the spending of your own is what harms you. And there is nothing that uses itself up faster than generosity, for as you employ it you lose the means of employing it, and you become either poor or despised or, in order to escape poverty, rapacious and hated. And above all other things a prince must guard himself against being despised and hated; and generosity leads you to both one and the other. So it is wiser to live with the reputation of a miser, which produces reproach without hatred, than to be forced to incur the reputation of rapacity, which produces reproach along with hatred, because you want to be considered as generous.

On Cruelty and Mercy and Whether It Is Better to Be Loved than to Be Feared or the Contrary

Proceeding to the other qualities mentioned above, I say that every prince must desire to be considered merciful and not cruel; nevertheless, he must take care not to misuse this mercy. Cesare Borgia[8] was considered cruel; nonetheless, his cruelty had brought order to Romagna,[9] united it, restored it to peace and obedience. If we examine this carefully, we shall see that he was more merciful than the Florentine people, who, in order to avoid being considered cruel, allowed the destruction of Pistoia.[10] Therefore, a prince must not worry about the reproach of cruelty when it is a matter of keeping his subjects united and loyal; for with a very few examples of cruelty he will be more compassionate than those who, out of excessive mercy, permit disorders to continue, from which arise murders and plundering; for these usually harm the community at large, while the executions that come from the prince harm one individual in particular. And the new prince, above all other princes, cannot escape the reputation of being called cruel, since new states are full of dangers. And Virgil, through Dido, states: "My difficult condition and the newness of my rule make me act in such a manner, and to set guards over my land on all sides."[11]   **12**

Nevertheless, a prince must be cautious in believing and in acting, nor should he be afraid of his own shadow; and he should proceed in such a manner, tempered by prudence and humanity, so that too much trust may not render him imprudent nor too much distrust render him intolerable.   **13**

---

[8] **Cesare Borgia (1476–1507)**   He was known for his brutality and lack of scruples, not to mention his exceptionally good luck. He was a firm ruler, son of Pope Alexander VI.

[9] **Romagna**   Region northeast of Tuscany; includes the towns of Bologna, Ferrara, Ravenna, and Rimini. Borgia united it as his base of power in 1501.

[10] **Pistoia**   (also known as Pistoria) A town near Florence, disturbed in 1501 by a civil war that could have been averted by strong repressive measures.

[11] The quotation is from the *Aeneid* (2.563–64), the greatest Latin epic poem, written by Virgil (70–19 B.C.E.). Dido, a woman general, ruled Carthage.

From this arises an argument: whether it is better to be loved than to be   14
feared, or the contrary. I reply that one should like to be both one and the
other; but since it is difficult to join them together, it is much safer to be feared
than to be loved when one of the two must be lacking. For one can generally
say this about men: that they are ungrateful, fickle, simulators and deceivers,
avoiders of danger, greedy for gain; and while you work for their good they are
completely yours, offering you their blood, their property, their lives, and their
sons, as I said earlier, when danger is far away; but when it comes nearer to you
they turn away. And that prince who bases his power entirely on their words,
finding himself stripped of other preparations, comes to ruin; for friendships
that are acquired by a price and not by greatness and nobility of character are
purchased but are not owned, and at the proper moment they cannot be spent.
And men are less hesitant about harming someone who makes himself loved
than one who makes himself feared because love is held together by a chain
of obligation which, since men are a sorry lot, is broken on every occasion in
which their own self-interest is concerned; but fear is held together by a dread
of punishment which will never abandon you.

A prince must nevertheless make himself feared in such a manner that he   15
will avoid hatred, even if he does not acquire love; since to be feared and not to
be hated can very well be combined; and this will always be so when he keeps
his hands off the property and the women of his citizens and his subjects. And if
he must take someone's life, he should do so when there is proper justification
and manifest cause; but, above all, he should avoid the property of others; for
men forget more quickly the death of their father than the loss of their patrimony. Moreover, the reasons for seizing their property are never lacking; and he
who begins to live by stealing always finds a reason for taking what belongs to
others; on the contrary, reasons for taking a life are rarer and disappear sooner.

But when the prince is with his armies and has under his command a mul-   16
titude of troops, then it is absolutely necessary that he not worry about being
considered cruel; for without that reputation he will never keep an army united
or prepared for any combat. Among the praiseworthy deeds of Hannibal[12] is
counted this: that, having a very large army, made up of all kinds of men, which
he commanded in foreign lands, there never arose the slightest dissention, neither among themselves nor against their prince, both during his good and his
bad fortune. This could not have arisen from anything other than his inhuman
cruelty, which, along with his many other abilities, made him always respected
and terrifying in the eyes of his soldiers; and without that, to attain the same
effect, his other abilities would not have sufficed. And the writers of history,

---

[12] **Hannibal (247–183 B.C.E.)**   An amazingly inventive military tactician who led the
Carthaginian armies against Rome for more than fifteen years. He crossed the Alps
from Gaul (France) in order to surprise Rome. He was noted for use of the ambush
and for "inhuman cruelty."

having considered this matter very little, on the one hand admire these deeds of his and on the other condemn the main cause of them.

And that it be true that his other abilities would not have been sufficient can be seen from the example of Scipio, a most extraordinary man not only in his time but in all recorded history, whose armies in Spain rebelled against him; this came about from nothing other than his excessive compassion, which gave to his soldiers more liberty than military discipline allowed. For this he was censured in the senate by Fabius Maximus,[13] who called him the corruptor of the Roman militia. The Locrians,[14] having been ruined by one of Scipio's officers, were not avenged by him, nor was the arrogance of that officer corrected, all because of his tolerant nature; so that someone in the senate who tried to apologize for him said that there were many men who knew how not to err better than they knew how to correct errors. Such a nature would have, in time, damaged Scipio's fame and glory if he had maintained it during the empire; but, living under the control of the senate, this harmful characteristic of his not only concealed itself but brought him fame.

I conclude, therefore, returning to the problem of being feared and loved, that since men love at their own pleasure and fear at the pleasure of the prince, a wise prince should build his foundation upon that which belongs to him, not upon that which belongs to others: he must strive only to avoid hatred, as has been said.

How a Prince Should Keep His Word

How praiseworthy it is for a prince to keep his word and to live by integrity and not by deceit everyone knows; nevertheless, one sees from the experience of our times that the princes who have accomplished great deeds are those who have cared little for keeping their promises and who have known how to manipulate the minds of men by shrewdness; and in the end they have surpassed those who laid their foundations upon honesty.

You must, therefore, know that there are two means of fighting: one according to the laws, the other with force; the first way is proper to man, the second to beasts; but because the first, in many cases, is not sufficient, it becomes necessary to have recourse to the second. Therefore, a prince must know how to use wisely the natures of the beast and the man. This policy was taught to princes allegorically by the ancient writers, who described how Achilles and many other ancient princes were given to Chiron[15] the Centaur to be raised and

---

[13] **Fabius Maximus (?–203 B.C.E.)**   Roman general who fought Hannibal. He was jealous of the younger Roman general Scipio.

[14] **Locrians**   Inhabitants of Locri, an Italian town settled by the Greeks in c. 680 B.C.E.

[15] **Chiron**   A mythical figure, a centaur (half man, half horse). Unlike most centaurs, he was wise and benevolent; he was also a legendary physician.

taught under his discipline. This can only mean that, having a half-beast and half-man as a teacher, a prince must know how to employ the nature of the one and the other; and the one without the other cannot endure.

Since, then, a prince must know how to make good use of the nature of the   21
beast, he should choose from among the beasts the fox and the lion; for the lion cannot defend itself from traps and the fox cannot protect itself from wolves. It is therefore necessary to be a fox in order to recognize the traps and a lion in order to frighten the wolves. Those who play only the part of the lion do not understand matters. A wise ruler, therefore, cannot and should not keep his word when such an observance of faith would be to his disadvantage and when the reasons which made him promise are removed. And if men were all good, this rule would not be good; but since men are a sorry lot and will not keep their promises to you, you likewise need not keep yours to them. A prince never lacks legitimate reasons to break his promises. Of this one could cite an endless number of modern examples to show how many pacts, how many promises have been made null and void because of the infidelity of princes; and he who has known best how to use the fox has come to a better end. But it is necessary to know how to disguise this nature well and to be a great hypocrite and a liar: and men are so simpleminded and so controlled by their present necessities that one who deceives will always find another who will allow himself to be deceived.

I do not wish to remain silent about one of these recent instances. Alexander   22
VI[16] did nothing else, he thought about nothing else, except to deceive men, and he always found the occasion to do this. And there never was a man who had more forcefulness in his oaths, who affirmed a thing with more promises, and who honored his word less; nevertheless, his tricks always succeeded perfectly since he was well acquainted with this aspect of the world.

Therefore, it is not necessary for a prince to have all of the above-mentioned   23
qualities, but it is very necessary for him to appear to have them. Furthermore, I shall be so bold as to assert this: that having them and practicing them at all times is harmful; and appearing to have them is useful; for instance, to seem merciful, faithful, humane, forthright, religious, and to be so; but his mind should be disposed in such a way that should it become necessary not to be so, he will be able and know how to change to the contrary. And it is essential to understand this: that a prince, and especially a new prince, cannot observe all those things by which men are considered good, for in order to maintain the state he is often obliged to act against his promise, against charity, against humanity, and against religion. And therefore, it is necessary that he have a mind ready to turn itself according to the way the winds of Fortune and the changeability of affairs

---

[16] **Alexander VI (1431–1503)**   Roderigo Borgia, pope from 1492 to 1503. He was Cesare Borgia's father and a corrupt but immensely powerful pope.

require him; and, as I said above, as long as it is possible, he should not stray from the good, but he should know how to enter into evil when necessity commands.

A prince, therefore, must be very careful never to let anything slip from his lips which is not full of the five qualities mentioned above: he should appear, upon seeing and hearing him, to be all mercy, all faithfulness, all integrity, all kindness, all religion. And there is nothing more necessary than to seem to possess this last quality. And men in general judge more by their eyes than their hands; for everyone can see but few can feel. Everyone sees what you seem to be, few perceive what you are, and those few do not dare to contradict the opinion of the many who have the majesty of the state to defend them; and in the actions of all men, and especially of princes, where there is no impartial arbiter, one must consider the final result.[17] Let a prince therefore act to seize and to maintain the state; his methods will always be judged honorable and will be praised by all; for ordinary people are always deceived by appearances and by the outcome of a thing; and in the world there is nothing but ordinary people; and there is no room for the few, while the many have a place to lean on. A certain prince[18] of the present day, whom I shall refrain from naming, preaches nothing but peace and faith, and to both one and the other he is entirely opposed; and both, if he had put them into practice, would have cost him many times over either his reputation or his state.

On Avoiding Being Despised and Hated

But since, concerning the qualities mentioned above, I have spoken about the most important, I should like to discuss the others briefly in this general manner: that the prince, as was noted above, should think about avoiding those things which make him hated and despised; and when he has avoided this, he will have carried out his duties and will find no danger whatsoever in other vices. As I have said, what makes him hated above all else is being rapacious and a usurper of the property and the women of his subjects; he must refrain from this; and in most cases, so long as you do not deprive them of either their property or their honor, the majority of men live happily; and you have only to deal with the ambition of a few, who can be restrained without difficulty and by many means. What makes him despised is being considered changeable, frivolous, effeminate, cowardly, irresolute; from these qualities a prince must guard himself as if from a reef, and he must strive to make everyone recognize in his actions greatness, spirit, dignity, and strength; and concerning the private affairs of his subjects, he must insist that his decision be irrevocable; and he

24

25

---

[17] The Italian original, *si guarda al fine*, has often been mistranslated as "the ends justify the means," something Machiavelli never wrote. [Translators' note]

[18] **A certain prince**   Probably King Ferdinand V of Spain (1452–1516).

should maintain himself in such a way that no man could imagine that he can deceive or cheat him.

That prince who projects such an opinion of himself is greatly esteemed; [26] and it is difficult to conspire against a man with such a reputation and difficult to attack him, provided that he is understood to be of great merit and revered by his subjects. For a prince must have two fears: one, internal, concerning his subjects; the other, external, concerning foreign powers. From the latter he can defend himself by his good troops and friends; and he will always have good friends if he has good troops; and internal affairs will always be stable when external affairs are stable, provided that they are not already disturbed by a conspiracy; and even if external conditions change, if he is properly organized and lives as I have said and does not lose control of himself, he will always be able to withstand every attack, just as I said that Nabis the Spartan[19] did. But concerning his subjects, when external affairs do not change, he has to fear that they may conspire secretly: the prince secures himself from this by avoiding being hated or despised and by keeping the people satisfied with him; this is a necessary matter, as was treated above at length. And one of the most powerful remedies a prince has against conspiracies is not to be hated by the masses; for a man who plans a conspiracy always believes that he will satisfy the people by killing the prince; but when he thinks he might anger them, he cannot work up the courage to undertake such a deed; for the problems on the side of the conspirators are countless. And experience demonstrates that conspiracies have been many but few have been concluded successfully; for anyone who conspires cannot be alone, nor can he find companions except from amongst those whom he believes to be dissatisfied; and as soon as you have uncovered your intent to one dissatisfied man, you give him the means to make himself happy, since he can have everything he desires by uncovering the plot; so much is this so that, seeing a sure gain on the one hand and one doubtful and full of danger on the other, if he is to maintain faith with you he has to be either an unusually good friend or a completely determined enemy of the prince. And to treat the matter briefly, I say that on the part of the conspirator there is nothing but fear, jealousy, and the thought of punishment that terrifies him; but on the part of the prince there is the majesty of the principality, the laws, the defenses of friends and the state to protect him; so that, with the good will of the people added to all these things, it is impossible for anyone to be so rash as to plot against him. For, where usually a conspirator has to be afraid before he executes his evil deed, in this case he must be afraid, having the people as an enemy, even after the crime is performed, nor can he hope to find any refuge because of this.

One could cite countless examples on this subject; but I want to satisfy [27] myself with only one which occurred during the time of our fathers. Messer

---

[19] **Nabis the Spartan**   Tyrant of Sparta from 207 to 192 B.C.E., routed by Philopoemon and the Achaean League.

Annibale Bentivoglio, prince of Bologna and grandfather of the present Messer Annibale, was murdered by the Canneschi[20] family, who conspired against him; he left behind no heir except Messer Giovanni,[21] then only a baby. As soon as this murder occurred, the people rose up and killed all the Canneschi. This came about because of the goodwill that the house of the Bentivoglio enjoyed in those days; this goodwill was so great that with Annibale dead, and there being no one of that family left in the city who could rule Bologna, the Bolognese people, having heard that in Florence there was one of the Bentivoglio blood who was believed until that time to be the son of a blacksmith, went to Florence to find him, and they gave him the control of that city; it was ruled by him until Messer Giovanni became of age to rule.

I conclude, therefore, that a prince must be little concerned with conspiracies when the people are well disposed toward him; but when the populace is hostile and regards him with hatred, he must fear everything and everyone. And well-organized states and wise princes have, with great diligence, taken care not to anger the nobles and to satisfy the common people and keep them contented; for this is one of the most important concerns that a prince has.

28

---

[20] **Canneschi**   Prominent family in Bologna.

[21] **Giovanni Bentivoglio (1443–1508)**   Former tyrant of Bologna. In sequence he was a conspirator against, then a conspirator with, Cesare Borgia.

✂ QUESTIONS FOR CRITICAL READING

1. The usual criticism of Machiavelli is that he advises his prince to be unscrupulous. Find examples for and against this claim.

2. Why do you agree or disagree with Machiavelli when he asserts that the great majority of people are not good? Does our government assume that to be true too?

3. Politicians — especially heads of state — are the contemporary counterparts of the prince. To what extent should successful heads of modern states show skill in war? Is modern war similar to wars in Machiavelli's era? If so, in what ways?

4. Clarify the advice Machiavelli gives concerning liberality and stinginess. Is this still good advice?

5. Are modern politicians likely to succeed by following all or most of Machiavelli's recommendations? Why or why not?

✂ SUGGESTIONS FOR CRITICAL WRITING

1. In speaking of the prince's military duties, Machiavelli says that "being disarmed makes you despised." Choose an example or instance to strengthen your argument for or against this position. Is it possible that in modern society being defenseless is an advantage?

2. Find evidence within this excerpt to demonstrate that Machiavelli's attitude toward human nature is accurate. Remember that the usual criticism of Machiavelli is that he is cynical — that he thinks the worst of people rather than the best. Find quotations from the excerpt that support either or both of these views; then use them as the basis for an essay analyzing Machiavelli's views on human nature.

3. By referring to current events and leaders — either local, national, or international — decide whether Machiavelli's advice to the prince is useful to the modern politician. Consider whether the advice is completely useless or completely reliable or whether its value depends on specific conditions. First state the advice, then show how it applies (or does not apply) to specific politicians, and finally critique its general effectiveness.

4. Probably the chief ethical issue raised by *The Prince* is the question of whether the desired ends justify the means used to achieve them. Write an essay in which you take a stand on this question. Begin by defining the issue: What does the concept "the ends justify the means" actually mean? What difficulties may arise when unworthy means are used to achieve worthy ends? Analyze Machiavelli's references to circumstances in which questionable means were (or should have been) used to achieve worthy ends. Use historical or personal examples to give your argument substance.

5. **CONNECTIONS**   One of Machiavelli's most controversial statements is: "A man who wishes to make a vocation of being good at all times will come to ruin among so many who are not good." How would Lao-tzu (p. 55) respond to this statement? How does the American political environment in the current decade support this statement? Under what conditions would such a statement become irrelevant?

6. **CONNECTIONS**   Thomas Jefferson (p. 116) and Hannah Arendt (p. 159) both read Machiavelli's writings carefully and understood his warnings to those in rule. Jefferson participated in a revolution that overthrew a powerful king, a prince even greater than Borgia. What did Jefferson learn from Machiavelli that helped him achieve his goal? Hannah Arendt describes a state that put principles of power first before everything else. Do the circumstances that she describes seem to be a development based on the principles that Machiavelli asks his prince to follow? Would Machiavelli have approved of some of the applications of power that Arendt discusses?

7. **CONNECTIONS**   For some commentators, the prince that Machiavelli describes resembles the kind of ruler Hannah Arendt deplores in her essay "Total Domination" (p. 159). Examine Machiavelli's views in terms of how his principles would result in a form of government similar to that which Arendt describes. Is terror a legitimate weapon for Machiavelli's prince? How would Machiavelli rationalize the prince's use of terror, should it become necessary?

JEAN-JACQUES ROUSSEAU

The Origin of Civil Society

© Archivo Iconografico, S.A./Corbis

J EAN-JACQUES ROUSSEAU (1712–1778) was
the son of Suzanne Bernard and Isaac Rousseau, a
watchmaker in Geneva, Switzerland. Shortly after his birth, Rousseau's mother died,
and a rash duel forced his father from Geneva. Rousseau was then apprenticed at age
thirteen to an engraver, a master who treated him badly. He soon ran away from his
master and found a home with a Catholic noblewoman who at first raised him as her son
and then, when he was twenty, took him as her lover. In the process Rousseau converted
from Calvinist Protestantism to Roman Catholicism. Eventually, he left Switzerland for
Paris, where he won an important essay contest and became celebrated in society.

Over the course of his lifetime, Rousseau produced a wide variety of literary and
musical works, including a novel, *Emile* (1762), an opera, *The Village Soothsayer* (1752),
and an autobiography, *The Confessions* (published posthumously in 1789). *The Social Contract* (1762) was part of a never-completed longer work on political systems. In many
ways Rousseau wrote in reaction to political thinkers such as Hugo Grotius and Thomas
Hobbes, to whom he responds in the following selection. He contended that the Dutch
philosopher and legal expert Grotius unquestioningly accepted the power of the aristocracy. He felt Grotius paid too much attention to what was rather than what ought to
be. On the other hand, Hobbes, the English political philosopher, asserted that people
had a choice of being free or being ruled. In other words, those who were members of
civil society chose to give up their freedom and submit to the monarch's rule. Either
they relinquished their freedom, or they removed themselves from civil society to live a
brutish existence.

Rousseau argued against Grotius by examining the way things ought to be. He argued
against Hobbes by asserting that both the body politic and the monarch were sovereign
and that when people created a civil society they surrendered their freedom to themselves as a group. If one person acted as sovereign or lawgiver, then that lawgiver had the

---

From *The Social Contract, or Principles of Political Right*. Translated by G. H. D. Cole.

responsibility of acting in accord with the will of the people. In a sense, this view parallels some of the views of Lao-tzu in the *Tao-te Ching*.

Popularly referred to as a defender of republicanism, Rousseau looked to the Republic of Geneva, his birthplace, as a model of government. He also idealized the generally democratic government of smaller Swiss cantons, such as Neuchatel, which used a form of town meeting where people gathered face-to-face to settle important issues. Ironically, Geneva put out a warrant for his arrest upon the publication of *The Social Contract* because although it praised Geneva's republicanism, it also condemned societies that depended on rule by a limited aristocracy. Unfortunately for Rousseau, at that time Geneva was governed by a small number of aristocratic families. Rousseau was deprived of his citizenship and could not return to his native home.

Similarly, Rousseau's controversial views were not easily received by those in power in France. After the publication of *Emile* offended the French parliament, Rousseau was forced to abandon his comfortable rustic circumstances — living on country estates provided by patrons from the court — and spend the rest of his life in financial uncertainty. Ironically, in 1789, a decade after his death, Rousseau's philosophy was adopted by supporters of the French Revolution in their bloody revolt against the aristocracy.

ROUSSEAU'S RHETORIC

Rousseau's method is in many ways antagonistic: he establishes the views of other thinkers, counters them, and then offers his own ideas. An early example appears in the opening of paragraph 8: "Grotius denies that all human power is established in favor of the governed, and quotes slavery as an example. His usual method of reasoning is constantly to establish right by fact." Among other things, Rousseau expects his readers to know who Grotius was and what he said. He also expects his readers to agree that Grotius derives "Right by Fact" by understanding that the fact of monarchy justifies it as being right. As Rousseau tells us, that kind of circular reasoning is especially kind to tyrants because it justifies them by their existence.

Rousseau uses analysis and examination of detail as his main rhetorical approaches. Whether he examines the ideas of others or presents ideas of his own, he is careful to examine the bases of the argument and to follow the arguments to their conclusions. He does this very thoroughly in his section "Slavery," in which he demonstrates that slavery is unacceptable no matter which of the current arguments are used to support it, including the widely held view that it was justifiable to enslave captured soldiers on the grounds that they owed their lives to their captors.

Rousseau also makes careful use of aphorism and analogy. His opening statement, "Man is born free; and everywhere he is in chains," is an aphorism that has been often quoted. It is a powerful and perplexing statement. How do people who are born free lose their freedom? Is it taken from them, or do they willingly surrender it? Rousseau spends considerable time examining this point.

The use of analogy is probably most striking in his comparison of government with the family. The force of the analogy reminds us that the members of a family are to be looked after by the family. As he tells us beginning in paragraph 5, the family is the only natural form of society. But instead of stopping there, he goes on to say that children are bound to the father only as long as they need him. Once they are able to be independent, they dissolve the natural bond and "return equally to independence." This analogy differs from the existing popular view that the monarch was like the father in a family and the people like his children; in fact, the analogy works against the legitimacy of the traditional monarchy as it was known in eighteenth-century France.

Rousseau also refers to other writers, using a rhetorical device known as *testimony:* he paraphrases the views of other authorities and moves on to promote his own. But in referring to other writers, Rousseau is unusually clever. For example, in paragraph 10 he begins with the analogy of the shepherd as the ruler in this fashion: "As a shepherd is of a nature superior to that of his flock, the shepherds of men, i.e., their rulers, are of a nature superior to that of the peoples under them. Thus, Philo tells us, the Emperor Caligula reasoned, concluding equally well either that kings were gods, or that men were beasts." Caligula was a madman and an emperor guilty of enormous cruelty; from his point of view it may have seemed true that kings were gods. But Rousseau, in citing this questionable authority, disputes the validity of the analogy.

He argues as well against the view that might makes right in "The Right of the Strongest." The value of the social contract, he explains, is to produce a society that is not governed by the mightiest and most ruthless and that permits those who are not mighty to live peacefully and unmolested. Thus, those who participate in the social contract give up certain freedoms but gain many more — among them the freedom not to be dominated by physical brutality.

Rousseau concentrates on the question of man in nature, or natural society. His view is that natural society is dominated by the strongest individuals but that at some point natural society breaks down. Thus, in order to guarantee the rights of those who are not the strongest, the political order must change. "The problem is to find a form of association which will defend and protect with the whole common force the person and goods of each associate, and in which each, while uniting himself with all, may still obey himself alone, and remain as free as before" (para. 38). By surrendering some freedom to the group as a whole — to "general will" — the individuals in the group can expect to prosper more widely and to live more happily. According to Rousseau, the establishment of a social contract ensures the stability of this form of civil society.

⸬ PREREADING QUESTIONS: WHAT TO READ FOR

The following prereading questions may help you anticipate key issues in the discussion of Jean-Jacques Rousseau's "The Origin of Civil Society." Keeping them in mind as you read should help focus your attention.

1. When Rousseau says, "Man is born free; and everywhere he is in chains," does he seem to be referring literally to slaves in chains or more figuratively to people in general?

2. How convincing is Rousseau when he claims that the oldest form of government is the family?

3. The "Social Contract" is one of Rousseau's chief ideas. What does it seem to mean?

The Origin of Civil Society

Note

I mean to inquire if, in the civil order, there can be any sure and legitimate rule   1
of administration, men being taken as they are and laws as they might be. In this inquiry I shall endeavor always to unite what right sanctions with what is prescribed by interest, in order that justice and utility may in no case be divided. I enter upon my task without proving the importance of the subject. I shall be asked if I am a prince or a legislator, to write on politics. I answer that I am neither, and that is why I do so. If I were a prince or a legislator, I should not waste time in saying what wants doing; I should do it, or hold my peace.

As I was born a citizen of a free State, and a member of the Sovereign, I   2
feel that, however feeble the influence my voice can have on public affairs, the right of voting on them makes it my duty to study them: and I am happy, when I reflect upon governments, to find my inquiries always furnish me with new reasons for loving that of my own country.

Subject of the First Book

Man is born free; and everywhere he is in chains. One thinks himself the master   3
of others, and still remains a greater slave than they. How did this change come about? I do not know. What can make it legitimate? That question I think I can answer.

If I took into account only force, and the effects derived from it, I should   4
say: "As long as a people is compelled to obey, and obeys, it does well; as soon as it can shake off the yoke, and shakes it off, it does still better; for, regaining its liberty by the same right as took it away, either it is justified in resuming it, or there was no justification for those who took it away." But the social order is a sacred right which is the basis of all other rights. Nevertheless, this right does not come from nature, and must therefore be founded on conventions. Before coming to that, I have to prove what I have just asserted.

The First Societies

The most ancient of all societies, and the only one that is natural, is the family: and even so the children remain attached to the father only so long as they need him for their preservation. As soon as this need ceases, the natural bond is dissolved. The children, released from the obedience they owed to the father, and the father, released from the care he owed his children, return equally to independence. If they remain united, they continue so no longer naturally, but voluntarily; and the family itself is then maintained only by convention.

This common liberty results from the nature of man. His first law is to provide for his own preservation, his first cares are those which he owes to himself; and, as soon as he reaches years of discretion, he is the sole judge of the proper means of preserving himself, and consequently becomes his own master.

The family then may be called the first model of political societies: the ruler corresponds to the father, and the people to the children; and all, being born free and equal, alienate their liberty only for their own advantage. The whole difference is that, in the family, the love of the father for his children repays him for the care he takes of them, while, in the State, the pleasure of commanding takes the place of the love which the chief cannot have for the peoples under him.

Grotius[1] denies that all human power is established in favor of the governed, and quotes slavery as an example. His usual method of reasoning is constantly to establish right by fact. It would be possible to employ a more logical method, but none could be more favorable to tyrants.

It is then, according to Grotius, doubtful whether the human race belongs to a hundred men, or that hundred men to the human race: and, throughout his book, he seems to incline to the former alternative, which is also the view of Hobbes.[2] On this showing, the human species is divided into so many herds of cattle, each with its ruler, who keeps guard over them for the purpose of devouring them.

As a shepherd is of a nature superior to that of his flock, the shepherds of men, i.e., their rulers, are of a nature superior to that of the peoples under them. Thus, Philo[3] tells us, the Emperor Caligula[4] reasoned, concluding equally well either that kings were gods, or that men were beasts.

---

[1] **Hugo Grotius (1583–1645)**　A Dutch lawyer who spent some time in exile in Paris. His fame as a child prodigy was considerable; his book on the laws of war (*De jure belli ac Pacis*) was widely known in Europe.

[2] **Thomas Hobbes (1588–1679)**　An Englishman known as a materialist philosopher who did not credit divine influence in politics. He became famous for *Leviathan,* a study of politics that treated the state as if it were a monster (leviathan) with a life of its own.

[3] **Philo (13? B.C.E.–47? C.E.)**　A Jew who absorbed Greek culture and who wrote widely on many subjects. His studies on Mosaic law were considered important.

[4] **Caligula (12–41 C.E.)**　Roman emperor of uncertain sanity. He loved his sister Drusilla so much that he had her deified when she died. A military commander, he was assassinated by an officer.

The reasoning of Caligula agrees with that of Hobbes and Grotius. 11
Aristotle,[5] before any of them, had said that men are by no means equal naturally, but that some are born for slavery, and others for dominion.

Aristotle was right; but he took the effect for the cause. Nothing can be 12
more certain than that every man born in slavery is born for slavery. Slaves lose
everything in their chains, even the desire of escaping from them: they love their
servitude, as the comrades of Ulysses loved their brutish condition.[6] If then
there are slaves by nature, it is because there have been slaves against nature.
Force made the first slaves, and their cowardice perpetuated the condition.

I have said nothing of King Adam, or Emperor Noah, father of the three 13
great monarchs[7] who shared out the universe, like the children of Saturn,[8]
whom some scholars have recognized in them. I trust to getting due thanks for
my moderation; for, being a direct descendant of one of these princes, perhaps
of the eldest branch, how do I know that a verification of titles might not leave
me the legitimate king of the human race?[9] In any case, there can be no doubt
that Adam was sovereign of the world, as Robinson Crusoe was of his island,
as long as he was its only inhabitant; and this empire had the advantage that the
monarch, safe on his throne, had no rebellions, wars, or conspirators to fear.

The Right of the Strongest

The strongest is never strong enough to be always the master, unless he trans- 14
forms strength into right, and obedience into duty. Hence the right of the strongest, which, though to all seeming meant ironically, is really laid down as a
fundamental principle. But are we never to have an explanation of this phrase?
Force is a physical power, and I fail to see what moral effect it can have. To
yield to force is an act of necessity, not of will—at the most, an act of prudence. In what sense can it be a duty?

---

[5] **Aristotle (384–322 B.C.E.)** A student of Plato; his philosophical method became the
dominant intellectual force in Western thought. See page 70.

[6] **brutish condition** This sentence refers to the Circe episode in Homer's *Odyssey*
(10, 12). Circe was a sorceress who, by means of drugs, enchanted men and turned
them into swine. Ulysses (Latin name of Odysseus), king of Ithaca, is the central
figure of the *Odyssey*.

[7] **father of the three great monarchs** Adam in the Bible (Gen. 4:1–25) fathered Cain,
Abel, Enoch, and Seth. Noah's sons, Shem, Ham, and Japheth, repopulated the world
after the Flood (Gen. 6:9–9:19).

[8] **children of Saturn** Saturn is a mythic god associated with the golden age of Rome
and with the Greek god Cronus. It is probably the children of Cronus—Zeus, Poseidon,
Hades, Demeter, and Hera—referred to here.

[9] **legitimate king of the human race** Rousseau is being ironic; like the rest of us, he is
descended from Adam (according to the Bible).

Suppose for a moment that this so-called "right" exists. I maintain that the   15
sole result is a mass of inexplicable nonsense. For, if force creates right, the
effect changes with the cause: every force that is greater than the first succeeds
to its right. As soon as it is possible to disobey with impunity, disobedience is
legitimate; and, the strongest being always in the right, the only thing that matters is to act so as to become the strongest. But what kind of right is that which
perishes when force fails? If we must obey perforce, there is no need to obey
because we ought; and if we are not forced to obey, we are under no obligation
to do so. Clearly, the word "right" adds nothing to force: in this connection, it
means absolutely nothing.

Obey the powers that be. If this means yield to force, it is a good precept,   16
but superfluous: I can answer for its never being violated. All power comes
from God, I admit; but so does all sickness: does that mean that we are forbidden to call in the doctor? A brigand surprises me at the edge of a wood: must
I not merely surrender my purse on compulsion; but, even if I could withhold
it, am I in conscience bound to give it up? For certainly the pistol he holds is
also a power.

Let us then admit that force does not create right, and that we are obliged   17
to obey only legitimate powers. In that case, my original question recurs.

Slavery

Since no man has a natural authority over his fellow, and force creates no right,   18
we must conclude that conventions form the basis of all legitimate authority
among men.

If an individual, says Grotius, can alienate his liberty and make himself the   19
slave of a master, why could not a whole people do the same and make itself
subject to a king? There are in this passage plenty of ambiguous words which
would need explaining; but let us confine ourselves to the word *alienate*. To
alienate is to give or to sell. Now, a man who becomes the slave of another does
not give himself; he sells himself, at the least for his subsistence: but for what
does a people sell itself? A king is so far from furnishing his subjects with their
subsistence that he gets his own only from them; and, according to Rabelais,[10]
kings do not live on nothing. Do subjects then give their persons on condition
that the king takes their goods also? I fail to see what they have left to preserve.

It will be said that the despot assures his subjects civil tranquility. Granted;   20
but what do they gain, if the wars his ambition brings down upon them, his
insatiable avidity, and the vexatious conduct of his ministers press harder on
them than their own dissensions would have done? What do they gain, if the

---

[10] **François Rabelais (c. 1494–1553)**   French writer, author of *Gargantua* and
    Pantagruel, satires on politics and religion.

very tranquility they enjoy is one of their miseries? Tranquility is found also in dungeons; but is that enough to make them desirable places to live in? The Greeks imprisoned in the cave of the Cyclops[11] lived there very tranquilly, while they were awaiting their turn to be devoured.

To say that a man gives himself gratuitously, is to say what is absurd and   21 inconceivable; such an act is null and illegitimate, from the mere fact that he who does it is out of his mind. To say the same of a whole people is to suppose a people of madmen; and madness creates no right.

Even if each man could alienate himself, he could not alienate his children: 22 they are born men and free; their liberty belongs to them, and no one but they has the right to dispose of it. Before they come to years of discretion, the father can, in their name, lay down conditions for their preservation and well-being, but he cannot give them irrevocably and without conditions: such a gift is contrary to the ends of nature, and exceeds the rights of paternity. It would therefore be necessary, in order to legitimize an arbitrary government, that in every generation the people should be in a position to accept or reject it; but, were this so, the government would be no longer arbitrary.

To renounce liberty is to renounce being a man, to surrender the rights of   23 humanity and even its duties. For him who renounces everything no indemnity is possible. Such a renunciation is incompatible with man's nature; to remove all liberty from his will is to remove all morality from his acts. Finally, it is an empty and contradictory convention that sets up, on the one side, absolute authority, and, on the other, unlimited obedience. Is it not clear that we can be under no obligation to a person from whom we have the right to exact everything? Does not this condition alone, in the absence of equivalence or exchange, in itself involve the nullity of the act? For what right can my slave have against me, when all that he has belongs to me, and, his right being mine, this right of mine against myself is a phrase devoid of meaning?

Grotius and the rest find in war another origin for the so-called right of   24 slavery. The victor having, as they hold, the right of killing the vanquished, the latter can buy back his life at the price of his liberty; and this convention is the more legitimate because it is to the advantage of both parties.

But it is clear that this supposed right to kill the conquered is by no   25 means deducible from the state of war. Men, from the mere fact that, while they are living in their primitive independence, they have no mutual relations stable enough to constitute either the state of peace or the state of war, cannot be naturally enemies. War is constituted by a relation between things, and not between persons; and, as the state of war cannot arise out of simple personal relations, but only out of real relations, private war, or war of man

---

[11] **cave of the Cyclops**   The cyclops is a one-eyed giant cannibal whose cave is the scene of one of Odysseus's triumphs in Homer's *Odyssey*.

with man, can exist neither in the state of nature, where there is no constant property, nor in the social state, where everything is under the authority of the laws.

Individual combats, duels and encounters, are acts which cannot constitute a state; while the private wars, authorized by the Establishments of Louis IX, King of France,[12] and suspended by the Peace of God, are abuses of feudalism, in itself an absurd system if ever there was one, and contrary to the principles of natural right and to all good polity.

26

War then is a relation, not between man and man, but between State and State, and individuals are enemies only accidentally, not as men, nor even as citizens, but as soldiers; not as members of their country, but as its defenders. Finally, each State can have for enemies only other States, and not men; for between things disparate in nature there can be no real relation.

27

Furthermore, this principle is in conformity with the established rules of all times and the constant practice of all civilized peoples. Declarations of war are intimations less to powers than to their subjects. The foreigner, whether king, individual, or people, who robs, kills or detains the subjects, without declaring war on the prince, is not an enemy, but a brigand. Even in real war, a just prince, while laying hands, in the enemy's country, on all that belongs to the public, respects the lives and goods of individuals: he respects rights on which his own are founded. The object of the war being the destruction of the hostile State, the other side has a right to kill its defenders, while they are bearing arms; but as soon as they lay them down and surrender, they cease to be enemies or instruments of the enemy, and become once more merely men, whose life no one has any right to take. Sometimes it is possible to kill the State without killing a single one of its members; and war gives no right which is not necessary to the gaining of its object. These principles are not those of Grotius: they are not based on the authority of poets, but derived from the nature of reality and based on reason.

28

The right of conquest has no foundation other than the right of the strongest. If war does not give the conqueror the right to massacre the conquered peoples, the right to enslave them cannot be based upon a right which does not exist. No one has a right to kill an enemy except when he cannot make him a slave, and the right to enslave him cannot therefore be derived from the right to kill him. It is accordingly an unfair exchange to make him buy at the price of his liberty his life, over which the victor holds no right. Is it not clear that there is a vicious circle in founding the right of life and death on the right of slavery, and the right of slavery on the right of life and death?

29

---

[12] **King Louis IX, King of France (1214–1270)**   Also called Saint Louis. He was considered an ideal monarch.

Even if we assume this terrible right to kill everybody, I maintain that a slave   30
made in war, or a conquered people, is under no obligation to a master, except
to obey him as far as he is compelled to do so. By taking an equivalent for his
life, the victor has not done him a favor; instead of killing him without profit, he
has killed him usefully. So far then is he from acquiring over him any authority in
addition to that of force, that the state of war continues to subsist between them:
their mutual relation is the effect of it, and the usage of the right of war does not
imply a treaty of peace. A convention has indeed been made; but this convention, so far from destroying the state of war, presupposes its continuance.

So, from whatever aspect we regard the question, the right of slavery is   31
null and void, not only as being illegitimate, but also because it is absurd and
meaningless. The words *slave* and *right* contradict each other, and are mutually exclusive. It will always be equally foolish for a man to say to a man or to
a people: "I make with you a convention wholly at your expense and wholly to
my advantage; I shall keep it as long as I like, and you will keep it as long as
I like."

That We Must Always Go Back to a First Convention

Even if I granted all that I have been refuting, the friends of despotism would   32
be no better off. There will always be a great difference between subduing a
multitude and ruling a society. Even if scattered individuals were successively
enslaved by one man, however numerous they might be, I still see no more than
a master and his slaves, and certainly not a people and its ruler; I see what may
be termed an aggregation, but not an association; there is as yet neither public
good nor body politic. The man in question, even if he has enslaved half the
world, is still only an individual; his interest, apart from that of others, is still
a purely private interest. If this same man comes to die, his empire, after him,
remains scattered and without unity, as an oak falls and dissolves into a heap
of ashes when the fire has consumed it.

A people, says Grotius, can give itself to a king. Then, according to Grotius,   33
a people is a people before it gives itself. The gift is itself a civil act, and implies
public deliberation. It would be better, before examining the act by which a
people gives itself to a king, to examine that by which it has become a people;
for this act, being necessarily prior to the other, is the true foundation of
society.

Indeed, if there were no prior convention, where, unless the election were   34
unanimous, would be the obligation on the minority to submit to the choice
of the majority? How have a hundred men who wish for a master the right to
vote on behalf of ten who do not? The law of majority voting is itself something established by convention, and presupposes unanimity, on one occasion
at least.

The Social Compact

I suppose men to have reached the point at which the obstacles in the way of   35
their preservation in the state of nature show their power of resistance to be
greater than the resources at the disposal of each individual for his maintenance in that state. That primitive condition can then subsist no longer; and the
human race would perish unless it changed its manner of existence.

But, as men cannot engender new forces, but only unite and direct existing   36
ones, they have no other means of preserving themselves than the formation,
by aggregation, of a sum of forces great enough to overcome the resistance.
These they have to bring into play by means of a single motive power, and
cause to act in concert.

This sum of forces can arise only where several persons come together: 37
but, as the force and liberty of each man are the chief instruments of his
self-preservation, how can he pledge them without harming his own interests,
and neglecting the care he owes to himself? This difficulty, in its bearing on my
present subject, may be stated in the following terms:

"The problem is to find a form of association which will defend and pro-   38
tect with the whole common force the person and goods of each associate, and
in which each, while uniting himself with all, may still obey himself alone, and
remain as free as before." This is the fundamental problem of which the *Social
Contract* provides the solution.

The clauses of this contract are so determined by the nature of the act   39
that the slightest modification would make them vain and ineffective; so that,
although they have perhaps never been formally set forth, they are everywhere
the same and everywhere tacitly admitted and recognized, until, on the violation
of the social compact, each regains his original rights and resumes his natural
liberty, while losing the conventional liberty in favor of which he renounced it.

These clauses, properly understood, may be reduced to one—the total   40
alienation of each associate, together with all his rights, to the whole community; for, in the first place, as each gives himself absolutely, the conditions are
the same for all; and, this being so, no one has any interest in making them
burdensome to others.

Moreover, the alienation being without reserve, the union is as perfect as   41
it can be, and no associate has anything more to demand: for, if the individuals retained certain rights, as there would be no common superior to decide
between them and the public, each, being on one point his own judge, would
ask to be so on all; the state of nature would thus continue, and the association
would necessarily become inoperative or tyrannical.

Finally, each man, in giving himself to all, gives himself to nobody; and   42
as there is no associate over whom he does not acquire the same right as he
yields others over himself, he gains an equivalent for everything he loses, and
an increase of force for the preservation of what he has.

If then we discard from the social compact what is not of its essence, we   43
shall find that it reduces itself to the following terms:

"Each of us puts his person and all his power in common under the supreme   44
direction of the general will, and, in our corporate capacity, we receive each
member as an indivisible part of the whole."

At once, in place of the individual personality of each contracting party, this   45
act of association creates a moral and collective body, composed of as many
members as the assembly contains votes, and receiving from this act its unity, its
common identity, its life and its will. This public person, so formed by the union of
all other persons formerly took the name of *city*, and now takes that of *Republic*
or *body politic*; it is called by its members *State* when passive, *Sovereign* when
active, and *Power* when compared with others like itself. Those who are associated in it take collectively the name of *people*, and severally are called *citizens*, as
sharing in the sovereign power, and *subjects*, as being under the laws of the State.
But these terms are often confused and taken one for another: it is enough to
know how to distinguish them when they are being used with precision.

The Sovereign

This formula shows us that the act of association comprises a mutual undertak-   46
ing between the public and the individuals, and that each individual, in making
a contract, as we may say, with himself, is bound in a double capacity; as a
member of the Sovereign he is bound to the individuals, and as a member of
the State to the Sovereign. But the maxim of civil right, that no one is bound by
undertakings made to himself, does not apply in this case; for there is a great
difference between incurring an obligation to yourself and incurring one to a
whole of which you form a part.

Attention must further be called to the fact that public deliberation, while   47
competent to bind all the subjects to the Sovereign, because of the two different capacities in which each of them may be regarded, cannot, for the opposite
reason, bind the Sovereign to itself; and that it is consequently against the nature
of the body politic for the Sovereign to impose on itself a law which it cannot
infringe. Being able to regard itself in only one capacity, it is in the position of an
individual who makes a contract with himself; and this makes it clear that there
neither is nor can be any kind of fundamental law binding on the body of the
people—not even the social contract itself. This does not mean that the body
politic cannot enter into undertakings with others, provided the contract is not
infringed by them; for in relation to what is external to it, it becomes a simple
being, an individual.

But the body politic or the Sovereign, drawing its being wholly from the   48
sanctity of the contract, can never bind itself, even to an outsider, to do anything derogatory to the original act, for instance, to alienate any part of itself,

or to submit to another Sovereign. Violation of the act by which it exists would be self-annihilation; and that which is itself nothing can create nothing.

As soon as this multitude is so united in one body, it is impossible to offend against one of the members without attacking the body, and still more to offend against the body without the members resenting it. Duty and interest therefore equally oblige the two contracting parties to give each other help; and the same men should seek to combine, in their double capacity, all the advantages dependent upon that capacity. 49

Again, the Sovereign, being formed wholly of the individuals who compose it, neither has nor can have any interest contrary to theirs; and consequently the sovereign power need give no guarantee to its subjects, because it is impossible for the body to wish to hurt all its members. We shall also see later on that it cannot hurt any in particular. The Sovereign, merely by virtue of what it is, is always what it should be. 50

This, however, is not the case with the relation of the subjects to the Sovereign, which, despite the common interest, would have no security that they would fulfil their undertakings, unless it found means to assure itself of their fidelity. 51

In fact, each individual, as a man, may have a particular will contrary or dissimilar to the general will which he has as a citizen. His particular interest may speak to him quite differently from the common interest: his absolute and naturally independent existence may make him look upon what he owes to the common cause as a gratuitous contribution, the loss of which will do less harm to others than the payment of it is burdensome to himself; and, regarding the moral person which constitutes the State as a *persona ficta*, because not a man, he may wish to enjoy the rights of citizenship without being ready to fulfil the duties of a subject. The continuance of such an injustice could not but prove the undoing of the body politic. 52

In order then that the social compact may not be an empty formula, it tacitly includes the undertaking, which alone can give force to the rest, that whoever refuses to obey the general will shall be compelled to do so by the whole body. This means nothing less than that he will be forced to be free; for this is the condition which, by giving each citizen to his country, secures him against all personal dependence. In this lies the key to the working of the political machine; this alone legitimizes civil undertakings, which, without it, would be absurd, tyrannical, and liable to the most frightful abuses. 53

The Civil State

The passage from the state of nature to the civil state produces a very remarkable change in man, by substituting justice for instinct in his conduct, and giving his actions the morality they had formerly lacked. Then only, when the voice of duty takes the place of physical impulses and right of appetite, does man, 54 who so far had considered only himself, find that he is forced to act on different principles, and to consult his reason before listening to his inclinations. Although, in this state, he deprives himself of some advantages which he got from nature, he gains in return others so great, his faculties are so stimulated and developed, his ideas so extended, his feelings so ennobled, and his whole soul so uplifted, that, did not the abuses of this new condition often degrade him below that which he left, he would be bound to bless continually the happy moment which took him from it forever, and, instead of a stupid and unimaginative animal, made him an intelligent being and a man.

Let us draw up the whole account in terms easily commensurable. What   55
man loses by the social contract is his natural liberty and an unlimited right to everything he tries to get and succeeds in getting; what he gains is civil liberty and the proprietorship of all he possesses. If we are to avoid mistake in weighing one against the other, we must clearly distinguish natural liberty, which is bounded only by the strength of the individual, from civil liberty, which is limited by the general will; and possession, which is merely the effect of force or the right of the first occupier, from property, which can be founded only on a positive title.

We might, over and above all this, add, to what man acquires in the civil   56
state, moral liberty, which alone makes him truly master of himself; for the mere impulse of appetite is slavery, while obedience to a law which we prescribe to ourselves is liberty. But I have already said too much on this head, and the philosophical meaning of the word liberty does not now concern us.

Real Property

Each member of the community gives himself to it, at the moment of its foun-   57
dation, just as he is, with all the resources at his command, including the goods he possesses. This act does not make possession, in changing hands, change its nature, and become property in the hands of the Sovereign; but, as the forces of the city are incomparably greater than those of an individual, public possession is also, in fact, stronger and more irrevocable, without being any more legitimate, at any rate from the point of view of foreigners. For the State, in relation to its members, is master of all their goods by the social contract, which, within the State, is the basis of all rights; but, in relation to other powers, it is so only by the right of the first occupier, which it holds from its members.

The right of the first occupier, though more real than the right of the   58
strongest, becomes a real right only when the right of property has already been established. Every man has naturally a right to everything he needs; but the positive act which makes him proprietor of one thing excludes him from everything else. Having his share, he ought to keep to it, and can have no

further right against the community. This is why the right of the first occupier, which in the state of nature is so weak, claims the respect of every man in civil society. In this right we are respecting not so much what belongs to another as what does not belong to ourselves.

In general, to establish the right of the first occupier over a plot of ground, the following conditions are necessary: first, the land must not yet be inhabited; secondly, a man must occupy only the amount he needs for his subsistence; and, in the third place, possession must be taken, not by an empty ceremony, but by labor and cultivation, the only sign of proprietorship that should be respected by others, in default of a legal title.   59

In granting the right of first occupancy to necessity and labor, are we not really stretching it as far as it can go? Is it possible to leave such a right unlimited? Is it to be enough to set foot on a plot of common ground, in order to be able to call yourself at once the master of it? Is it to be enough that a man has the strength to expel others for a moment, in order to establish his right to prevent them from ever returning? How can a man or a people seize an immense territory and keep it from the rest of the world except by a punishable usurpation, since all others are being robbed, by such an act, of the place of habitation and the means of subsistence which nature gave them in common? When Nuñez Balboa,[13] standing on the seashore, took possession of the South Seas and the whole of South America in the name of the crown of Castile, was that enough to dispossess all their actual inhabitants, and to shut out from them all the princes of the world? On such a showing, these ceremonies are idly multiplied, and the Catholic King[14] need only take possession all at once, from his apartment, of the whole universe, merely making a subsequent reservation about what was already in the possession of other princes.   60

We can imagine how the lands of individuals, where they were contiguous and came to be united, became the public territory, and how the right of Sovereignty, extending from the subjects over the lands they held, became at once real and personal. The possessors were thus made more dependent, and the forces at their command used to guarantee their fidelity. The advantage of this does not seem to have been felt by ancient monarchs, who called themselves Kings of the Persians, Scythians, or Macedonians, and seemed to regard themselves more as rulers of men than as masters of a country. Those of the present day more cleverly call themselves Kings of France, Spain, England, etc.: thus holding the land, they are quite confident of holding the inhabitants.   61

---

[13] **Nuñez Balboa (1475–1519)**   Spanish explorer who discovered the Pacific Ocean.

[14] **Catholic King**   A reference to the king of Spain, probably Ferdinand II of Aragon (1452–1516).

The peculiar fact about this alienation is that, in taking over the goods of   62
individuals, the community, so far from despoiling them, only assures them
legitimate possession, and changes usurpation into a true right and enjoyment
into proprietorship. Thus the possessors, being regarded as depositaries of the
public good, and having their rights respected by all the members of the State
and maintained against foreign aggression by all its forces, have, by a cession
which benefits both the public and still more themselves, acquired, so to speak,
all that they gave up. This paradox may easily be explained by the distinction
between the rights which the Sovereign and the proprietor have over the same
estate, as we shall see later on.

It may also happen that men begin to unite one with another before they   63
possess anything, and that, subsequently occupying a tract of country which
is enough for all, they enjoy it in common, or share it out among themselves,
either equally or according to a scale fixed by the Sovereign. However the
acquisition be made, the right which each individual has to his own estate is
always subordinate to the right which the community has over all: without this,
there would be neither stability in the social tie, nor real force in the exercise
of Sovereignty.

I shall end this chapter and this book by remarking on a fact on which the   64
whole social system should rest: i.e., that, instead of destroying natural inequality, the fundamental compact substitutes, for such physical inequality as nature
may have set up between men, an equality that is moral and legitimate, and that
men, who may be unequal in strength or intelligence, become every one equal
by convention and legal right.

▓ QUESTIONS FOR CRITICAL READING

1. Examine Rousseau's analogy of the family as the oldest and only natural form
   of government. Do you agree that the analogy is useful and that its contentions
   are true? Which aspects of this natural form of government do not work to help
   us understand the basis of government?

2. Rousseau seems to accept the family as a patriarchal structure. How would
   his views change if he accepted it as a matriarchal structure? How would they
   change if he regarded each member of the family as absolutely equal in authority
   from birth?

3. What does it mean to reason from what is fact instead of from what is morally
   right?

4. What features of Rousseau's social contract are like those of a legal contract?
   How does a person contract to be part of society?

5. What distinctions can be made among natural, moral, and legal equality?
   Which kind of equality is most important to a social system?

⠃ SUGGESTIONS FOR CRITICAL WRITING

1. When Rousseau wrote, "Man is born free; and everywhere he is in chains," the institution of slavery was widely practiced and justified by many authorities. Today slavery has been generally abolished. How is this statement relevant to people's condition in society now? What are some ways in which people relinquish their independence or freedom?

2. Clarify the difference between your duty to yourself and your duty to society (your social structure — personal, local, national). Establish your duties in relation to each structure. How can these duties conflict with one another? How does the individual resolve the conflicts?

3. Do you agree with Rousseau when he says, "Every man has naturally a right to everything he needs" (para. 50)? What is necessary to all people, and in what sense do they have a right to what is necessary? Who should provide those necessities? Should necessities be provided for everyone or only for people who are unable to provide for themselves? If society will not provide these necessities, does the individual have the right to break the social contract by means of revolution?

4. What seems to be Rousseau's opinion regarding private property or the ownership of property? Beginning with paragraph 61, Rousseau distinguishes between monarchs with sovereignty over people and those with sovereignty over a region, such as France, Italy, or another country. What is Rousseau's view of the property that constitutes a state and who actually owns it? He mentions that the rights of individual owners must give way to the rights of the community in general. What is your response to this view?

5. Rousseau makes an important distinction between natural liberty and civil liberty. People in a state of nature enjoy natural liberty, and when they bind themselves together into a body politic, they enjoy civil liberty. What are the differences? Define each kind of liberty as carefully as you can, and take a stand on whether you feel civil liberty or natural liberty is superior. How is the conflict between the two forms of liberty felt today?

6. **CONNECTIONS**   Compare Rousseau's views about property in his section "Real Property" (paras. 57–64) with Emerson's (p. 124) views on property. In what ways do they agree, and in what ways do they disagree? Does Rousseau's viewpoint compare favorably with your own views and with those of our culture? How much does Emerson, who read Rousseau and knew his works well, seem to have derived from his understanding of Rousseau? Which of Emerson's ideas seem to be similar to Rousseau's "right of first occupancy"?

7. **CONNECTIONS**   Rousseau's thinking emphasizes the role played by the common people in any civil society. How does that emphasis compare with Machiavelli's (p. 84) thinking? Consider the attitudes each writer has toward the essential goodness of people and the essential responsibilities of the monarch or government leader. In what ways is Rousseau closer in thinking to Lao-tzu (p. 55) than to Machiavelli?

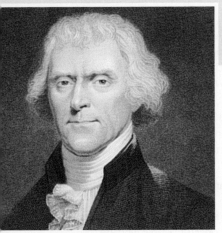

THOMAS JEFFERSON

The Declaration of Independence

THOMAS JEFFERSON (1743–1826) authored one of the most memorable statements in American history: the Declaration of Independence. He composed the work in 1776 under the watchful eyes of Benjamin Franklin, John Adams, and the rest of the Continental Congress, who spent two and a half days going over every word. Although the substance of the document was developed in committee, Jefferson, because of the grace of his writing style, was selected to craft the actual wording.

Jefferson rose to eminence in a time of great political upheaval. By the time he took a seat in the Virginia legislature in 1769, the colony was already on the course toward revolution. His pamphlet "A Summary View of the Rights of British America" (1774) brought him to the attention of those who were agitating for independence and established him as an ardent republican and revolutionary. In 1779 he was elected governor of Virginia. After the Revolutionary War he moved into the national political arena as the first secretary of state (1790–1793). He then served as John Adams's vice president (1797–1801) and was himself elected president in 1800. Perhaps one of his greatest achievements during his two terms (1801–1809) in office was his negotiation of the Louisiana Purchase, in which the United States acquired from France 828,000 square miles of land west of the Mississippi for about $15 million.

One of the fundamental paradoxes of Jefferson's personal and political life has been his attitude toward slavery. Like most wealthy Virginians, Jefferson owned slaves. However, in 1784 he tried to abolish slavery in the western territories that were being added to the United States. His "Report on Government for the Western Territory" failed by one vote. Historians have pointed out that Jefferson probably had an affair with Sally Hemmings, a mixed-race slave, and fathered children with her.

However unclear his personal convictions, many of Jefferson's accomplishments, which extend from politics to agriculture and mechanical invention, still stand. One of the most versatile Americans of any generation, he wrote a book, *Notes on Virginia* (1782); designed and built Monticello, his famous homestead in Virginia; and in large part founded and designed the University of Virginia (1819).

Despite their revolutionary nature, the ideas Jefferson expressed in the Declaration of Independence were not entirely original. Rousseau's republican philosophies greatly influenced the work. When Jefferson states in the second paragraph that "all men are created equal, that they are endowed by their Creator with certain unalienable rights," he reflects Rousseau's emphasis on the political equality of men and on protecting certain fundamental rights (see Rousseau, beginning with para. 40, p. 109). Jefferson also wrote that "Governments are instituted among Men, deriving their just powers from the consent of the governed." This is one of Rousseau's primary points, although it was Jefferson who immortalized it in these words.

JEFFERSON'S RHETORIC

Jefferson's techniques include the use of the periodic sentence, which was especially typical of the age. The first sentence of the Declaration of Independence is periodic — that is, it is long and carefully balanced, and the main point comes at the end. Such sentences are not popular today, although an occasional periodic sentence can still be powerful in contemporary prose. Jefferson's first sentence says (in paraphrase): *When one nation must sever its relations with a parent nation . . . and stand as an independent nation itself . . . the causes ought to be explained.* Moreover, the main body of the Declaration of Independence lists the "causes" that lead to the final and most important element of the sentence. Causal analysis was a method associated with legal thought and reflects Jefferson's training in eighteenth-century legal analysis. One understood things best when one understood their causes.

The periodic sentence demands certain qualities of balance and parallelism that all good writers should heed. The first sentence in paragraph 2 demonstrates both qualities. The balance is achieved by making each part of the sentence roughly the same length. The parallelism is achieved by linking words in deliberate repetition for effect (they are in italicized type in the following analysis). Note how the "truths" mentioned in the first clause are enumerated in the succession of noun clauses beginning with "that"; "Rights" are enumerated in the final clause:

> We hold these truths to be self-evident,
>> *that* all men are created equal,
>> *that* they are endowed by their Creator with certain inalienable
>>> Rights,
>> *that* among these are Life, Liberty, and the pursuit of
>>> Happiness.

Parallelism is one of the greatest stylistic techniques available to a writer sensitive to rhetoric. It is a natural technique: many untrained writers and speakers develop it on their own. The periodicity of the sentences and the balance of their parallelism suggest thoughtfulness, wisdom, and control.

Parallelism creates a natural link to the useful device of enumeration, or listing. Many writers using this technique establish their purpose from the outset — "I wish to address three important issues . . ." — and then number them: "First, I want to say . . . Second . . . ," and so on. Jefferson devotes paragraphs 3 through 29 to enumerating the "causes" he mentions in paragraph 1. Each one constitutes a separate paragraph; thus, each has separate weight and importance. Each begins with "He" or "For" and is therefore in parallel structure. The technique of repetition of the same words at the beginning of successive lines is called *anaphora.* Jefferson's use of anaphora here is one of the best known and most effective in all literature. The "He" referred to is Britain's king George III (1738–1820), who is never mentioned by name. Congress is opposed not to a personality but to the sovereign of a nation that is oppressing the United States and a tyrant who is not dignified by being named. The "For" introduces grievous acts the king has given his assent to; these are offenses against the colonies.

However, Jefferson does not develop the causes in detail. We do not have specific information about what trade was cut off by the British, what taxes were imposed without consent, or how King George waged war or abdicated government in the colonies. Presumably, Jefferson's audience knew the details and was led by the twenty-seven paragraphs to observe how numerous the causes were. And all are serious; any one alone was enough cause for revolution. The effect of Jefferson's enumeration is to illustrate the patience of the colonies up to this point and to tell the world that the colonies have finally lost patience on account of the reasons listed. The Declaration of Independence projects the careful meditations and decisions of exceptionally calm, patient, and reasonable people.

⚎ PREREADING QUESTIONS: WHAT TO READ FOR

The following prereading questions may help you anticipate key issues in the discussion of Thomas Jefferson's Declaration of Independence. Keeping them in mind during your first reading of the selection should help focus your attention.

1. Under what conditions may a people alter or abolish their government?
2. Why does Jefferson consider King George a tyrant?

The Declaration of Independence

In Congress, July 4, 1776

The Unanimous Declaration of the Thirteen United States of America

When in the Course of human events, it becomes necessary for one people to   1
dissolve the political bands which have connected them with another, and to
assume among the Powers of the earth, the separate and equal station to which

the Laws of Nature and of Nature's God entitle them, a decent respect to the opinions of mankind requires that they should declare the causes which impel them to the separation.

We hold these truths to be self-evident, that all men are created equal, that they are endowed by their Creator with certain inalienable Rights, that among these are Life, Liberty, and the pursuit of Happiness. That to secure these rights, Governments are instituted among Men, deriving their just powers from the consent of the governed. That whenever any Form of Government becomes destructive of these ends, it is the Right of the People to alter or to abolish it, and to institute new Government, laying its foundation on such principles and organizing its powers in such form, as to them shall seem most likely to effect their Safety and Happiness. Prudence, indeed, will dictate that Governments long established should not be changed for light and transient causes; and accordingly all experience hath shown, that mankind are more disposed to suffer, while evils are sufferable, than to right themselves by abolishing the forms to which they are accustomed. But when a long train of abuses and usurpations, pursuing invariably the same Object evinces a design to reduce them under absolute Despotism, it is their right, it is their duty, to throw off such Government, and to provide new Guards for their future security. — Such has been the patient sufferance of these Colonies; and such is now the necessity which constrains them to alter their former Systems of Government. The history of the present King of Great Britain is a history of repeated injuries and usurpations, all having in direct object the establishment of an absolute Tyranny over these States. To prove this, let Facts be submitted to a candid world.   2

He has refused his Assent to Laws, the most wholesome and necessary for the public good.   3

He has forbidden his Governors to pass Laws of immediate and pressing importance, unless suspended in their operation till his Assent should be obtained; and when so suspended, he has utterly neglected to attend to them.   4

He has refused to pass other laws for the accommodation of large districts of people, unless those people would relinquish the right of Representation in the Legislature, a right inestimable to them and formidable to tyrants only.   5

He has called together legislative bodies at places unusual, uncomfortable, and distant from the depository of their Public Records, for the sole purpose of fatiguing them into compliance with his measures.   6

He has dissolved Representative Houses repeatedly, for opposing with manly firmness his invasions on the rights of the people.   7

He has refused for a long time, after such dissolutions, to cause others to be elected; whereby the Legislative Powers, incapable of Annihilation, have returned to the People at large for their exercise; the State remaining in the mean time exposed to all the dangers of invasion from without, and convulsions within.   8

He has endeavored to prevent the population of these States;[1] for that purpose obstructing the Laws for Naturalization of Foreigners; refusing to pass others to encourage their migration hither, and raising the conditions of new Appropriations of Lands.

9

He has obstructed the Administration of Justice, by refusing his Assent to Laws for establishing Judiciary Powers.

10

He has made Judges dependent on his Will alone, for the tenure of their offices, and the amount and payment of their salaries.

11

He has erected a multitude of New Offices, and sent hither swarms of Officers to harass our People, and eat out their substance.

12

He has kept among us, in times of peace, Standing Armies without the Consent of our legislature.

13

He has affected to render the Military independent of and superior to the Civil Power.

14

He has combined with others to subject us to a jurisdiction foreign to our constitution, and unacknowledged by our laws; giving his Assent to their acts of pretended Legislation:

15

For quartering large bodies of armed troops among us:

16

For protecting them, by a mock Trial, from Punishment for any Murders which they should commit on the Inhabitants of these States:

17

For cutting off our Trade with all parts of the world:

18

For imposing taxes on us without our Consent:

19

For depriving us in many cases, of the benefits of Trial by Jury:

20

For transporting us beyond Seas to be tried for pretended offenses:

21

For abolishing the free System of English Laws in a neighboring Province, establishing therein an Arbitrary government, and enlarging its Boundaries so as to render it at once an example and fit instrument for introducing the same absolute rule into these Colonies:

22

For taking away our Charters, abolishing our most valuable Laws, and altering fundamentally the Forms of our Governments:

23

For suspending our own Legislatures, and declaring themselves invested with Power to legislate for us in all cases whatsoever.

24

He has abdicated Government here, by declaring us out of his Protection and waging War against us.

25

He has plundered our seas, ravaged our Coasts, burnt our towns, and destroyed the lives of our people.

26

He is at this time transporting large armies of foreign mercenaries to complete the works of death, desolation, and tyranny, already begun with circumstances of Cruelty & perfidy scarcely paralleled in the most barbarous ages, and totally unworthy the Head of a civilized nation.

27

---

[1] **prevent the population of these States**   This meant limiting migration to the colonies, thus controlling their growth.

He has constrained our fellow Citizens taken Captive on the high Seas to   28
bear Arms against their Country, to become the executioners of their friends
and Brethren, or to fall themselves by their Hands.

He has excited domestic insurrections amongst us, and has endeavored to   29
bring on the inhabitants of our frontiers, the merciless Indian Savages, whose
known rule of warfare, is an undistinguished destruction of all ages, sexes, and
conditions.

In every stage of these Oppressions We have Petitioned for Redress in   30
the most humble terms: Our repeated Petitions have been answered only by
repeated injury. A Prince, whose character is thus marked by every act which
may define a Tyrant, is unfit to be the ruler of a free People.

Nor have We been wanting in attention to our British brethren. We have   31
warned them from time to time of attempts by their legislature to extend an
unwarrantable jurisdiction over us. We have reminded them of the circumstances of our emigration and settlement here. We have appealed to their native
justice and magnanimity, and we have conjured them by the ties of our common kindred to disavow these usurpations, which, would inevitably interrupt
our connections and correspondence. They too have been deaf to the voice of
justice and of consanguinity. We must, therefore, acquiesce in the necessity,
which denounces our Separation, and hold them, as we hold the rest of mankind, Enemies in War, in Peace Friends.

We, therefore, the Representatives of the United States of America, in   32
General Congress, Assembled, appealing to the Supreme Judge of the world
for the rectitude of our intentions, do, in the Name, and by Authority of the
good People of these Colonies, solemnly publish and declare, That these
United Colonies are, and of Right ought to be Free and Independent States,
that they are Absolved from all Allegiance to the British Crown, and that
all political connection between them and the State of Great Britain, is and
ought to be totally dissolved; and that as Free and Independent States, they
have full Power to levy War, conclude Peace, contract Alliances, establish
Commerce, and to do all other Acts and Things which Independent States
may of right do. And for the support of this Declaration, with a firm reliance
on the Protection of Divine Providence, we mutually pledge to each other our
Lives, our Fortunes, and our sacred Honor.

■■ QUESTIONS FOR CRITICAL READING

1. What laws of nature does Jefferson refer to in paragraph 1?

2. What do you think Jefferson feels is the function of government (para. 2)?

3. What does Jefferson say about women? Is there any way you can determine
   his views from reading this document? Does he appear to favor a patriarchal
   system?

4. Find at least one use of parallel structure in the Declaration (see p. 117 in the section on Jefferson's rhetoric for a description of parallelism). What key terms are repeated in identical or equivalent constructions, and to what effect?

5. Which causes listed in paragraphs 3 through 29 are the most serious? Are any trivial? Which ones are serious enough to cause a revolution?

6. What do you consider to be the most graceful sentence in the entire Declaration? Where is it placed in the Declaration? What purpose does it serve there?

7. In what ways does the king's desire for stable government interfere with Jefferson's sense of his own independence?

✷ SUGGESTIONS FOR CRITICAL WRITING

1. Jefferson defines the inalienable rights of a citizen as "Life, Liberty, and the pursuit of Happiness." Do you think these are indeed inalienable rights? Answer this question by including some sentences that use parallel structure and repeat key terms in similar constructions. Be certain that you define each of these rights both for yourself and for our time.

2. Write an essay discussing what you feel the function of government should be. Include at least three periodic sentences (underline them). You may first want to establish Jefferson's view of government and then compare or contrast it with your own.

3. Jefferson envisioned a government that allowed its citizens to exercise their rights to life, liberty, and the pursuit of happiness. Has Jefferson's revolutionary vision been achieved in America? Begin with a definition of these three key terms: *life, liberty,* and *the pursuit of happiness.* Then, for each term, use examples — drawn from current events, your own experience, American history — to take a clear and well-argued stand on whether the nation has achieved Jefferson's goal.

4. Slavery was legal in America in 1776, and Jefferson reluctantly owned slaves. He never presented his plan for gradual emancipation of the slaves to Congress because he realized that Congress would never approve it. But Jefferson and Franklin did finance a plan to buy slaves and return them to Africa, where in 1821 returning slaves founded the nation of Liberia. Agree or disagree with the following statement and defend your position: the ownership of slaves by the people who wrote the Declaration of Independence invalidates it. You may wish to read the relevant chapters on Jefferson and slavery in Merrill D. Peterson's *Thomas Jefferson and the New Nation* (1970).

5. What kind of government does Jefferson seem to prefer? In what ways would his government differ from that of the king he is reacting against? Is he talking about an entirely different system or about the same system but with a different

kind of "prince" at the head? How would Jefferson protect the individual against the whim of the state, while also protecting the state against the whim of the individual?

6. **CONNECTIONS**   Write an essay in which you examine the ways in which Jefferson agrees or disagrees with Lao-tzu's (p. 55) conception of human nature and of government. How does Jefferson share Lao-tzu's commitment to judicious inactivity? What evidence is there that the king subscribes to it? Describe the similarities and differences between Jefferson's views and those of Lao-tzu.

7. **CONNECTIONS**   Alexis de Tocqueville (p. 139) and Ralph Waldo Emerson (p. 124) both knew and read the Declaration of Independence. Write a brief essay in which you examine the evidence that demonstrates their knowledge of what Jefferson wrote. What specific issues do they discuss that seem to have come from Jefferson's Declaration? Which of them, Tocqueville or Emerson, writes in a style reminiscent of Jefferson? How does their style help them make the reader pay close attention to their main points? How do these writers use argument to make their case?

8. **CONNECTIONS**   What principles does Jefferson share with Jean-Jacques Rousseau (p. 99)? Compare the fundamental demands of the Declaration of Independence with Rousseau's conceptions of liberty and independence. How would Rousseau have reacted to this declaration?

© Hulton Archive/Getty Images

RALPH
WALDO EMERSON
Politics

R ALPH WALDO EMERSON (1803–1882)
was the son of a Unitarian minister from a fam-
ily that dates back to the Puritans. He was educated at Harvard College and, after a few
years teaching at a girls' school in Boston, went to the Harvard Divinity School to prepare for the ministry. Although he became a popular preacher at the Second Church of
Boston, ill health made it problematic for him to continue. He left that post a few years
after the death of his first wife (at age twenty) and after a later personal crisis of faith.

From 1832 through 1833, he toured Europe and met with some of the most distinguished literary figures of the age: William Wordsworth, Samuel Taylor Coleridge, and
Thomas Carlyle, who became an enduring friend. He also read widely in Eastern religion
and philosophy as well as in Plato and other traditional philosophers.

When he returned from Europe, Emerson rarely preached in church. He married
again and had a family; his first wife's legacy enabled him to devote his time to reading
and writing. His first major essay, *Nature* (1836), was published anonymously but later
appeared in book form (1849) under his name. In this essay, he distilled the thoughts
he had been collecting in his journals since college. He saw himself firmly positioned
in nature and saw that nature reflected the mind of God. In *Nature*, he began to conceive of the idea of the "Over-Soul," the "Universal Mind" that comprehends all things,
and this idea then fed into his concept of the "transcendental man," the intuitive
thinker who could, like Plato, see beyond surface materialism into the "true meaning"
of the world.

Transcendentalism became a movement in New England from the first publication
of *Nature* until the beginning of the Civil War in 1860. It was basically a rejection of the
intense emphasis on pure reason by the eighteenth-century philosophers. Rather, it proposed an intuitive understanding on the part of the individual to perceive directly the
nature of things. Transcendentalism was never codified or made into a coherent philosophy because it was centered on the individual and was seen as an expression of the individual's direct apprehension of the divine spirit in nature.

Before *Nature* was released in book form, Emerson published "Self-Reliance" and other important essays in *Essays: First Series* (1841). Among the other essays in this volume are "History," "Spiritual Laws," "Love," "Friendship," "The Over-Soul," "Intellect," and "Art."

Essays: Second Series (1844) included "The Poet," "Character," "Politics," and others. The subjects of his essays are the concerns of a man in his late thirties, and they sometimes reveal a brashness characteristic of youth empowered by great thoughts. Emerson was widely read throughout much of the English-speaking world. He was one of a remarkable number of "star lecturers" who became famous for speeches delivered in athenaeums throughout the United States as well as in public halls elsewhere.

Emerson was deeply involved in the abolition movement in the United States, and he was also involved in the intellectual life around him. He knew Margaret Fuller and her social living experiment, Brook Farm. Henry David Thoreau was a very close friend and associate; Emerson and Thoreau not only shared transcendental ideas, but also were neighbors. In fact, Thoreau for a time lived with Emerson. Louisa May Alcott, Jones Very, William Hawthorne, and many other American literary notables were also his friends and sometimes his inspiration.

Emerson went his own way and sometimes paid a price for doing so. For example, he delivered one of his most famous lectures to the Divinity School at Harvard in 1838. Now called the "Divinity School Address," this lecture is essentially an attack on all formal religious institutions and a call for the individual to perceive the spirit of divinity intuitively. Religious experience was more important to him than religion itself. As a result of this address, for thirty years, Harvard refused to let him speak there.

EMERSON'S RHETORIC

In his discussion of the state in his essay "Politics," Emerson reminds us that the individual precedes the state both historically and politically. His emphasis on individualism commands his observations throughout the essay, especially when he points to the question of character in any community. His affection for democracy is clear throughout his comments, but he also complains that Americans have a penchant for exploiting their political system. Monarchy, he reminds his readers of 1844, satisfied many older Americans and the inhabitants of many nations elsewhere.

Because Emerson was a gifted speaker, he tends to comment at length in a manner that much resembles someone on a podium. His paragraphs are lengthy, especially by our standards, but they parallel the lengthy expressions of the public speaker of his time. And like many public speakers, his rhetorical approach is explanatory rather than an effort to convince the listener of a specific position. His emphasis on the pronoun "we" connects him to his audience and assures us that he is one with us. His concerns are our concerns.

As many good speakers do, Emerson produces quotable aphorisms. He makes several memorable declarations that punctuate the essay. They do not always demand examination. They are meant to stand on their own. Among them are:

The law is only a memorandum. (para. 1)

One man owns his clothes, and another owns a county. (para. 2)

Property will be protected. (para. 7)

Every actual State is corrupt. Good men must not obey the laws too well. (para. 10)

The wise man is the State. (para. 15)

Emerson also employs metaphor to intensify his views. One of his most famous is "the wise know that foolish legislation is a rope of sand which perishes in the twisting" (para. 1), which he uses to discourage the young from being too eager to pass new laws. He tells us that a "statute is a currency which we stamp with our own portrait" (para. 1), as if a law is to be thought of as a kind of cash that binds us. Emerson borrows another memorable metaphor from his friend, Fisher Ames: "a monarchy is a merchantman, which sails well, but will sometimes strike on a rock and go to the bottom; whilst a republic is a raft, which would never sink, but then your feet are always in water" (para. 12). This last metaphor has a special power in light of the two recent great revolutions that toppled monarchies: the American Revolution of 1776 and the French Revolution of 1789.

As a serious abolitionist in the 1840s, Emerson could hardly imagine that the United States would be on the road to a civil war, a different kind of "rebellion." But his position as an abolitionist colored his views in "Politics" regarding laws, especially those he recommends we not follow too well. For example, Article IV, Section 2, of the U.S. Constitution declared that anyone in "Service or Labor" who ran away must be captured and returned. This was intended as a law forcing citizens to return runaway slaves. It was not strong enough as written and was replaced by the Fugitive Slave Law of 1793, which made it a crime for anyone to harbor a fugitive slave even in a state that did not permit slavery. An even harsher version of that law was enacted in 1850. Henry David Thoreau reacted against such laws in his essay "Civil Disobedience" (p. 720).

A central issue in "Politics" is the question of how the state guarantees the safety of the individual and the protection of property. The Constitution makes special mention of the protection of property and so does Emerson. Yet, he understands the inequities that may result from the state's protection of property. Emerson has been praised in this essay for his emphasis on the individual's personal rights in the state, but he has been criticized for his special pleading for the preservation of property. With reference to the Bible near the end of paragraph 2, Emerson begins what seems to be an argument in favor of property owners and their right to make the laws, a view that many of his countrymen held. But he also observes that the result of giving only property owners the right to vote "allowed the rich to encroach on the poor, and to keep them poor" (para. 6). And although he defends property, he also emphatically claims protection for the individual and individual rights. To that end, he says, "that the highest end of government is the culture of men; and that if men can be educated, the institutions will share their improvement and the moral sentiment will write the law of the land" (para. 6).

⚏ PREREADING QUESTIONS: WHAT TO READ FOR

The following prereading questions may help you anticipate key issues in the discussion of Ralph Waldo Emerson's "Politics." Keeping them in mind during your first reading of the selection should help focus your attention.

1. What is the relationship of the state to the citizen?
2. What are the rights of the citizen?
3. What is the government's role in relation to property?
4. How much government does Emerson recommend?

Politics

Gold and iron are good
To buy iron and gold;
All earth's fleece and food
For their like are sold.
Boded Merlin wise,   5
Proved Napoleon great, —
Nor kind nor coinage buys
Aught above its rate.
Fear, Craft and Avarice
Cannot rear a State.   10
Out of dust to build
What is more than dust, —
Walls Amphion piled
Phoebus stablish must.
When the Muses nine   15
With the Virtues meet,
Find to their design
An Atlantic seat,
By green orchard boughs
Fended from the heat,   20
Where the statesman ploughs
Furrow for the wheat;
When the Church is social worth,
When the state-house is the hearth,
Then the perfect State is come,   25
The republican at home.

In dealing with the State we ought to remember that its institutions are not   1
aboriginal, though they existed before we were born; that they are not superior to the citizen; that every one of them was once the act of a single man;
every law and usage was a man's expedient to meet a particular case; that they
all are imitable, all alterable; we may make as good, we may make better. Society is an illusion to the young citizen. It lies before him in rigid repose, with
certain names, men and institutions rooted like oak-trees to the centre, round
which all arrange themselves the best they can. But the old statesman knows
that society is fluid; there are no such roots and centres, but any particle may
suddenly become the centre of the movement and compel the system to gyrate
round it; as every man of strong will, like Pisistratus or Cromwell,[1] does for a
time, and every man of truth, like Plato or Paul, does forever. But politics rest
on necessary foundations, and cannot be treated with levity. Republics abound
in young civilians who believe that the laws make the city, that grave modifications of the policy and modes of living and employments of the population,
that commerce, education and religion may be voted in or out; and that any
measure, though it were absurd, may be imposed on a people if only you can
get sufficient voices to make it a law. But the wise know that foolish legislation
is a rope of sand which perishes in the twisting; that the State must follow
and not lead the character and progress of the citizen; the strongest usurper is
quickly got rid of; and they only who build on Ideas, build for eternity; and that
the form of government which prevails is the expression of what cultivation
exists in the population which permits it. The law is only a memorandum. We
are superstitious, and esteem the statute somewhat: so much life as it has in the
character of living men is its force. The statute stands there to say, Yesterday
we agreed so and so, but how feel ye this article to-day? Our statute is a currency which we stamp with our own portrait: it soon becomes unrecognizable,
and in process of time will return to the mint. Nature is not democratic, nor
limited-monarchical, but despotic, and will not be fooled or abated by any jot
of her authority by the pertest[2] of her sons; and as fast as the public mind is
opened to more intelligence, the code is seen to be brute and stammering. It
speaks not articulately, and must be made to. Meantime the education of the
general mind never stops. The reveries of the true and simple are prophetic.
What the tender poetic youth dreams, and prays, and paints to-day, but shuns
the ridicule of saying aloud, shall presently be the resolutions of public bodies; then shall be carried as grievance and bill of rights through conflict and
war, and then shall be triumphant law and establishment for a hundred years,
until it gives place in turn to new prayers and pictures. The history of the State

---

[1] **Pisistratus or Cromwell**   Pisistratus (died 527 B.C.E.) was ruler of Athens; Oliver
Cromwell (1599–1658) governed England after the English Revolution.

[2] **pertest**   Impertinence.

sketches in coarse outline the progress of thought, and follows at a distance the delicacy of culture and of aspiration.

The theory of politics which has possessed the mind of men, and which they have expressed the best they could in their laws and in their revolutions, considers persons and property as the two objects for whose protection government exists. Of persons, all have equal rights, in virtue of being identical in nature. This interest of course with its whole power demands a democracy. Whilst the rights of all as persons are equal, in virtue of their access to reason, their rights in property are very unequal. One man owns his clothes, and another owns a county. This accident, depending primarily on the skill and virtue of the parties, of which there is every degree, and secondarily on patrimony, falls unequally, and its rights of course are unequal. Personal rights, universally the same, demand a government framed on the ratio of the census; property demands a government framed on the ratio of owners and of owning. Laban, who has flocks and herds, wishes them looked after by an officer on the frontiers, lest the Midianites shall drive them off; and pays a tax to that end. Jacob has no flocks or herds and no fear of the Midianites, and pays no tax to the officer.[3] It seemed fit that Laban and Jacob should have equal rights to elect the officer who is to defend their persons, but that Laban and not Jacob should elect the officer who is to guard the sheep and cattle. And if question arise whether additional officers or watch-towers should be provided, must not Laban and Isaac, and those who must sell part of their herds to buy protection for the rest, judge better of this, and with more right, than Jacob, who, because he is a youth and a traveller, eats their bread and not his own?

In the earliest society the proprietors made their own wealth, and so long as it comes to the owners in the direct way, no other opinion would arise in any equitable community than that property should make the law for property, and persons the law for persons.

But property passes through donation or inheritance to those who do not create it. Gift, in one case, makes it as really the new owner's, as labor made it the first owner's: in the other case, of patrimony, the law makes an ownership which will be valid in each man's view according to the estimate which he sets on the public tranquillity.

It was not, however, found easy to embody the readily admitted principle that property should make law for property, and persons for persons; since persons and property mixed themselves in every transaction. At last it seemed settled that the rightful distinction was that the proprietors should have more elective franchise than non-proprietors, on the Spartan[4] principle of "calling that which is just, equal; not that which is equal, just."

---

[3] **Laban . . . Jacob**   A reference to Genesis 24:29–31:55.

[4] **Spartan**   A reference to Sparta, a Greek nation-state that was known for its austerity.

That principle no longer looks so self-evident as it appeared in former   6
times, partly because doubts have arisen whether too much weight had not
been allowed in the laws to property, and such a structure given to our usages
as allowed the rich to encroach on the poor, and to keep them poor; but mainly
because there is an instinctive sense, however obscure and yet inarticulate,
that the whole constitution of property, on its present tenures, is injurious, and
its influence on persons deteriorating and degrading; that truly the only interest
for the consideration of the State is persons; that property will always follow
persons; that the highest end of government is the culture of men; and that if
men can be educated, the institutions will share their improvement and the
moral sentiment will write the law of the land.

If it be not easy to settle the equity of this question, the peril is less when   7
we take note of our natural defences. We are kept by better guards than the
vigilance of such magistrates as we commonly elect. Society always consists
in greatest part of young and foolish persons. The old, who have seen through
the hypocrisy of courts and statesmen, die and leave no wisdom to their sons.
They believe their own newspaper, as their fathers did at their age. With such
an ignorant and deceivable majority, States would soon run to ruin, but that
there are limitations beyond which the folly and ambition of governors cannot
go. Things have their laws, as well as men; and things refuse to be trifled with.
Property will be protected. Corn will not grow unless it is planted and manured;
but the farmer will not plant or hoe it unless the chances are a hundred to one
that he will cut and harvest it. Under any forms, persons and property must
and will have their just sway. They exert their power, as steadily as matter its
attraction. Cover up a pound of earth never so cunningly, divide and subdivide
it; melt it to liquid, convert it to gas; it will always weigh a pound; it will always
attract and resist other matter by the full virtue of one pound weight: — and the
attributes of a person, his wit and his moral energy, will exercise, under any
law or extinguishing tyranny, their proper force, — if not overtly, then covertly;
if not for the law, then against it; if not wholesomely, then poisonously; with
right, or by might.

The boundaries of personal influence it is impossible to fix, as persons are   8
organs of moral or supernatural force. Under the dominion of an idea which
possesses the minds of multitudes, as civil freedom, or the religious sentiment,
the powers of persons are no longer subjects of calculation. A nation of men
unanimously bent on freedom or conquest can easily confound the arithmetic of
statists, and achieve extravagant actions out of all proportion to their means; as
the Greeks, the Saracens, the Swiss, the Americans, and the French have done.

In like manner to every particle of property belongs its own attraction. A   9
cent is the representative of a certain quantity of corn or other commodity. Its
value is in the necessities of the animal man. It is so much warmth, so much
bread, so much water, so much land. The law may do what it will with the

owner of property; its just power will still attach to the cent. The law may in a mad freak say that all shall have power except the owners of property; they shall have no vote. Nevertheless, by a higher law, the property will, year after year, write every statute that respects property. The non-proprietor will be the scribe of the proprietor. What the owners wish to do, the whole power of property will do, either through the law or else in defiance of it. Of course I speak of all the property, not merely of the great estates. When the rich are outvoted, as frequently happens, it is the joint treasury of the poor which exceeds their accumulations. Every man owns something, if it is only a cow, or a wheelbarrow, or his arms, and so has that property to dispose of.

The same necessity which secures the rights of person and property   10
against the malignity or folly of the magistrate, determines the form and methods of governing, which are proper to each nation and to its habit of thought, and nowise transferable to other states of society. In this country we are very vain of our political institutions, which are singular in this, that they sprung, within the memory of living men, from the character and condition of the people, which they still express with sufficient fidelity, — and we ostentatiously prefer them to any other in history. They are not better, but only fitter for us. We may be wise in asserting the advantage in modern times of the democratic form, but to other states of society, in which religion consecrated the monarchical, that and not this was expedient. Democracy is better for us, because the religious sentiment of the present time accords better with it. Born democrats, we are nowise qualified to judge of monarchy, which, to our fathers living in the monarchical idea, was also relatively right. But our institutions, though in coincidence with the spirit of the age, have not any exemption from the practical defects which have discredited other forms. Every actual State is corrupt. Good men must not obey the laws too well. What satire on government can equal the severity of censure conveyed in the word politic, which now for ages has signified cunning, intimating that the State is a trick?

The same benign necessity and the same practical abuse appear in the   11
parties, into which each State divides itself, of opponents and defenders of the administration of the government. Parties are also founded on instincts, and have better guides to their own humble aims than the sagacity of their leaders. They have nothing perverse in their origin, but rudely mark some real and lasting relation. We might as wisely reprove the east wind or the frost, as a political party, whose members, for the most part, could give no account of their position, but stand for the defence of those interests in which they find themselves. Our quarrel with them begins when they quit this deep natural ground at the bidding of some leader, and obeying personal considerations, throw themselves into the maintenance and defence of points nowise belonging to their system. A party is perpetually corrupted by personality. Whilst we absolve the association from dishonesty, we cannot extend the same charity

to their leaders. They reap the rewards of the docility and zeal of the masses which they direct. Ordinarily our parties are parties of circumstance, and not of principle; as the planting interest in conflict with the commercial; the party of capitalists and that of operatives: parties which are identical in their moral character, and which can easily change ground with each other in the support of many of their measures. Parties of principle, as, religious sects, or the party of free-trade, of universal suffrage, of abolition of slavery, of abolition of capital punishment, degenerate into personalities, or would inspire enthusiasm. The vice of our leading parties in this country (which may be cited as a fair specimen of these societies of opinion) is that they do not plant themselves on the deep and necessary grounds to which they are respectively entitled, but lash themselves to fury in the carrying of some local and momentary measure, nowise useful to the commonwealth. Of the two great parties which at this hour almost share the nation between them, I should say that one has the best cause, and the other contains the best men. The philosopher, the poet, or the religious man, will of course wish to cast his vote with the democrat, for free-trade, for wide suffrage, for the abolition of legal cruelties in the penal code, and for facilitating in every manner the access of the young and the poor to the sources of wealth and power. But he can rarely accept the persons whom the so-called popular party propose to him as representatives of these liberalities. They have not at heart the ends which give to the name of democracy what hope and virtue are in it. The spirit of our American radicalism is destructive and aimless: it is not loving; it has no ulterior and divine ends, but is destructive only out of hatred and selfishness. On the other side, the conservative party, composed of the most moderate, able and cultivated part of the population, is timid, and merely defensive of property. It vindicates no right, it aspires to no real good, it brands no crime, it proposes no generous policy; it does not build, nor write, nor cherish the arts, nor foster religion, nor establish schools, nor encourage science, nor emancipate the slave, nor befriend the poor, or the Indian, or the immigrant. From neither party, when in power, has the world any benefit to expect in science, art, or humanity, at all commensurate with the resources of the nation.

I do not for these defects despair of our republic. We are not at the mercy of any waves of chance. In the strife of ferocious parties, human nature always finds itself cherished; as the children of the convicts at Botany Bay[5] are found to have as healthy a moral sentiment as other children. Citizens of feudal states are alarmed at our democratic institutions lapsing into anarchy, and the older and more cautious among ourselves are learning from Europeans to look with some terror at our turbulent freedom. It is said that in our license of construing

12

---

[5] **Botany Bay**   A bay in Sydney, Australia. The British originally planned it as a penal colony, but it was untenable.

the Constitution, and in the despotism of public opinion, we have no anchor; and one foreign observer thinks he has found the safeguard in the sanctity of Marriage among us; and another thinks he has found it in our Calvinism. Fisher Ames[6] expressed the popular security more wisely, when he compared a monarchy and a republic, saying that a monarchy is a merchantman, which sails well, but will sometimes strike on a rock and go to the bottom; whilst a republic is a raft, which would never sink, but then your feet are always in water. No forms can have any dangerous importance whilst we are befriended by the laws of things. It makes no difference how many tons' weight of atmosphere presses on our heads, so long as the same pressure resists it within the lungs. Augment the mass a thousand fold, it cannot begin to crush us, as long as reaction is equal to action. The fact of two poles, of two forces, centripetal and centrifugal, is universal, and each force by its own activity develops the other. Wild liberty develops iron conscience. Want of liberty, by strengthening law and decorum, stupefies conscience. "Lynch-law" prevails only where there is greater hardihood and self-subsistency in the leaders. A mob cannot be a permanency; everybody's interest requires that it should not exist, and only justice satisfies all.

We must trust infinitely to the beneficent necessity which shines through all laws. Human nature expresses itself in them as characteristically as in statues, or songs, or railroads; and an abstract of the codes of nations would be a transcript of the common conscience. Governments have their origin in the moral identity of men. Reason for one is seen to be reason for another, and for every other. There is a middle measure which satisfies all parties, be they never so many or so resolute for their own. Every man finds a sanction for his simplest claims and deeds, in decisions of his own mind, which he calls Truth and Holiness. In these decisions all the citizens find a perfect agreement, and only in these; not in what is good to eat, good to wear, good use of time, or what amount of land or of public aid each is entitled to claim. This truth and justice men presently endeavor to make application of to the measuring of land, the apportionment of service, the protection of life and property. Their first endeavors, no doubt, are very awkward. Yet absolute right is the first governor; or, every government is an impure theocracy. The idea after which each community is aiming to make and mend its law, is the will of the wise man. The wise man it cannot find in nature, and it makes awkward but earnest efforts to secure his government by contrivance; as by causing the entire people to give their voices on every measure; or by a double choice to get the representation of the whole; or by a selection of the best citizens; or to secure the advantages of efficiency and internal peace by confiding the government to one, who may

13

---

[6] **Fisher Ames (1758–1808)**   The first Boston representative to the Federal Congress, noted for his eloquence.

himself select his agents. All forms of government symbolize an immortal government, common to all dynasties and independent of numbers, perfect where
two men exist, perfect where there is only one man.

Every man's nature is a sufficient advertisement to him of the character   14
of his fellows. My right and my wrong is their right and their wrong. Whilst I
do what is fit for me, and abstain from what is unfit, my neighbor and I shall
often agree in our means, and work together for a time to one end. But whenever I find my dominion over myself not sufficient for me, and undertake the
direction of him also, I overstep the truth, and come into false relations to
him. I may have so much more skill or strength than he that he cannot express
adequately his sense of wrong, but it is a lie, and hurts like a lie both him and
me. Love and nature cannot maintain the assumption; it must be executed by
a practical lie, namely by force. This undertaking for another is the blunder
which stands in colossal ugliness in the governments of the world. It is the
same thing in numbers, as in a pair, only not quite so intelligible. I can see well
enough a great difference between my setting myself down to a self-control,
and my going to make somebody else act after my views; but when a quarter of
the human race assume to tell me what I must do, I may be too much disturbed
by the circumstances to see so clearly the absurdity of their command. Therefore all public ends look vague and quixotic beside private ones. For any laws
but those which men make for themselves are laughable. If I put myself in the
place of my child, and we stand in one thought and see that things are thus or
thus, that perception is law for him and me. We are both there, both act. But if,
without carrying him into the thought, I look over into his plot, and, guessing
how it is with him, ordain this or that, he will never obey me. This is the history
of governments, — one man does something which is to bind another. A man
who cannot be acquainted with me, taxes me; looking from afar at me ordains
that a part of my labor shall go to this or that whimsical end, — not as I, but as
he happens to fancy. Behold the consequence. Of all debts men are least willing
to pay the taxes. What a satire is this on government! Everywhere they think
they get their money's worth, except for these.

Hence the less government we have the better, — the fewer laws, and the   15
less confided power. The antidote to this abuse of formal government is the
influence of private character, the growth of the Individual; the appearance of
the principal to supersede the proxy; the appearance of the wise man; of whom
the existing government is, it must be owned, but a shabby imitation. That which
all things rend to educe; which freedom, cultivation, intercourse, revolutions,
go to form and deliver, is character; that is the end of Nature, to reach unto this
coronation of her king. To educate the wise man the State exists, and with the
appearance of the wise man the State expires. The appearance of character
makes the State unnecessary. The wise man is the State. He needs no army, fort,
or navy, — he loves men too well; no bribe, or feast, or palace, to draw friends

to him; no vantage ground, no favorable circumstance. He needs no library, for he has not done thinking; no church, for he is a prophet; no statute-book, for he has the lawgiver; no money, for he is value; no road, for he is at home where he is; no experience, for the life of the creator shoots through him, and looks from his eyes. He has no personal friends, for he who has the spell to draw the prayer and the piety of all men unto him needs not husband and educate a few to share with him a select and poetic life. His relation to men is angelic; his memory is myrrh to them; his presence, frankincense and flowers.

We think our civilization near its meridian, but we are yet only at the cock-crowing and the morning star. In our barbarous society the influence of character is in its infancy. As a political power, as the rightful lord who is to tumble all rulers from their chairs, its presence is hardly yet suspected. Malthus and Ricardo[7] quite omit it; the Annual Register is silent; in the Conversations' Lexicon it is not set down; the President's Message, the Queen's Speech, have not mentioned it; and yet it is never nothing. Every thought which genius and piety throw into the world, alters the world. The gladiators in the lists of power feel, through all their frocks of force and simulation, the presence of worth. I think the very strife of trade and ambition is confession of this divinity; and successes in those fields are the poor amends, the fig-leaf with which the shamed soul attempts to hide its nakedness. I find the like unwilling homage in all quarters. It is because we know how much is due from us that we are impatient to show some petty talent as a substitute for worth. We are haunted by a conscience of this right to grandeur of character, and are false to it. But each of us has some talent, can do somewhat useful, or graceful, or formidable, or amusing, or lucrative. That we do, as an apology to others and to ourselves for not reaching the mark of a good and equal life. But it does not satisfy us, whilst we thrust it on the notice of our companions. It may throw dust in their eyes, but does not smooth our own brow, or give us the tranquillity of the strong when we walk abroad. We do penance as we go. Our talent is a sort of expiation, and we are constrained to reflect on our splendid moment with a certain humiliation, as somewhat too fine, and not as one act of many acts, a fair expression of our permanent energy. Most persons of ability meet in society with a kind of tacit appeal. Each seems to say, "I am not all here." Senators and presidents have climbed so high with pain enough, not because they think the place specially agreeable, but as an apology for real worth, and to vindicate their manhood in our eyes. This conspicuous chair is their compensation to themselves for being of a poor, cold, hard nature. They must do what they can.

16

---

[7] **Thomas Malthus (1766–1834)**   Author of *An Essay on the Principle of Population* (1798), which warned of the adverse effects of population growth, especially on the poor; **David Ricardo (1772–1823)** An influential early economist and author of *Principles of Political Economy.*

Like one class of forest animals, they have nothing but a prehensile tail; climb they must, or crawl. If a man found himself so rich-natured that he could enter into strict relations with the best persons and make life serene around him by the dignity and sweetness of his behavior, could he afford to circumvent the favor of the caucus and the press, and covet relations so hollow and pompous as those of a politician? Surely nobody would be a charlatan who could afford to be sincere.

The tendencies of the times favor the idea of self-government, and leave the individual, for all code, to the rewards and penalties of his own constitution; which work with more energy than we believe whilst we depend on artificial restraints. The movement in this direction has been very marked in modern history. Much has been blind and discreditable, but the nature of the revolution is not affected by the vices of the revolters; for this is a purely moral force. It was never adopted by any party in history, neither can be. It separates the individual from all party, and unites him at the same time to the race. It promises a recognition of higher rights than those of personal freedom, or the security of property. A man has a right to be employed, to be trusted, to be loved, to be revered. The power of love, as the basis of a State, has never been tried. We must not imagine that all things are lapsing into confusion if every tender protestant be not compelled to bear his part in certain social conventions; nor doubt that roads can be built, letters carried, and the fruit of labor secured, when the government of force is at an end. Are our methods now so excellent that all competition is hopeless? Could not a nation of friends even devise better ways? On the other hand, let not the most conservative and timid fear anything from a premature surrender of the bayonet and the system of force. For, according to the order of nature, which is quite superior to our will, it stands thus; there will always be a government of force where men are selfish; and when they are pure enough to abjure the code of force they will be wise enough to see how these public ends of the post-office, of the highway, of commerce and the exchange of property, of museums and libraries, of institutions of art and science can be answered.

We live in a very low state of the world, and pay unwilling tribute to governments founded on force. There is not, among the most religious and instructed men of the most religious and civil nations, a reliance on the moral sentiment and a sufficient belief in the unity of things, to persuade them that society can be maintained without artificial restraints, as well as the solar system; or that the private citizen might be reasonable and a good neighbor, without the hint of a jail or a confiscation. What is strange too, there never was in any man sufficient faith in the power of rectitude to inspire him with the broad design of renovating the State on the principle of right and love. All those who have pretended this design have been partial reformers, and have admitted in some manner the supremacy of the bad State. I do not call to mind a single human being who has steadily denied the authority of the laws, on the simple ground of his own moral nature. Such designs, full of genius and full of faith as they are, are not entertained except avowedly as air-pictures. If the individual who exhibits them dare to think them practicable, he disgusts scholars and churchmen; and men of talent and women of superior sentiments cannot hide their contempt. Not the less does nature continue to fill the heart of youth with suggestions of this enthusiasm, and there are now men,—if indeed I can speak in the plural number,—more exactly, I will say, I have just been conversing with one man, to whom no weight of adverse experience will make it for a moment appear impossible that thousands of human beings might exercise towards each other the grandest and simplest sentiments, as well as a knot of friends, or a pair of lovers.

QUESTIONS FOR CRITICAL READING

1. What does Emerson mean by saying "Society is an illusion to the young citizen" (para. 1)?
2. Why does Emerson suggest that the law is in flux?
3. In his opening paragraph, Emerson tells us that nature is not democratic. What is his point?
4. In paragraph 10, Emerson states, "Democracy is better for us." What are his reasons?
5. What are Emerson's views on political parties?
6. What is Emerson's view on the power of personality in politics?
7. How much trust does Emerson give to "[e]very man's nature" (para. 14)?

SUGGESTIONS FOR CRITICAL WRITING

1. Near the end of the essay, Emerson says, "Hence the less government we have the better, — the fewer laws, and the less confided power" (para. 15). Today, politicians say the same thing, but they are referring to laws that they feel stymie trade. Emerson does not suggest less government because of its effect on business. Why does he make this statement? What is his position in the essay in general that causes him to wish for less government?
2. In paragraph 16, Emerson states that "the influence of character is in its infancy." Write a short essay that defines the concept of character as Emerson uses the term. What is the relationship of character to the state? What does Emerson mean by saying that the influence of character is in its infancy? Why is character so important?
3. Throughout the essay, Emerson makes a distinction between the young people in the nation and the older people in the nation. He was barely forty years old

when he wrote this essay. Does he count himself among the young people, or does he think of himself as a wise older man? What differences does he see between younger and older people? What makes the distinction important in an essay on politics and the state? Do you think this distinction holds as much today as it seems to have done in the 1840s?

4. Herman Melville, the author of *Moby-Dick*, satirized Emerson in his novel *The Confidence-Man* because he thought Emerson was too optimistic about the politics of his time. Others also criticized his optimism and sunny outlook on the nation. Examine "Politics" carefully and write an essay that responds to those who feel Emerson is unnecessarily optimistic. What would make any contemporary feel that Emerson was too optimistic about the political realities of democracy as he describes it?

5. In paragraph 17, Emerson talks about "self-government" and "a purely moral force" being brought to bear by the individual. He says, "A man has a right to be employed, to be trusted, to be loved, to be revered." Is Emerson correct in this view? How can a government provide all these rights? Emerson seems to imply that they are possible under self-government. Is he correct? What is self-government, and how does it fit into a democratic state?

6. In the last two paragraphs of the essay, Emerson introduces the power of love and the power of force as alternatives for the "basis of a state." He clearly disapproves of the power of force, but how would the power of love function in a political state? Examine his reasoning in these last paragraphs and write a brief essay that clarifies his views and examines the reasonableness of his suggestions. Is it true that "We live in a very low state of the world, and pay unwilling tribute to governments founded on force" (para. 18)?

7. Do some research to see what important laws were enacted by Congress in the 1830s up to 1840. Among them was the Indian Removal Act of 1830, which was enacted during Andrew Jackson's presidency. What did Emerson think of Andrew Jackson, a president that was explicitly connected to the democratic character of the nation? What child labor laws were passed in that period? What about these laws might have caused Emerson to talk about law as he does in "Politics"?

8. **CONNECTIONS** Among his readings of Eastern philosophical texts, the *Tao-te Ching* may well have been one of the texts that influenced Emerson. We know he read Plato carefully as well as Aristotle. Write an essay that connects Emerson's "Politics" with Lao-tzu (p. 55) and/or Plato (p. 580) and Aristotle (p. 70). What ideas reappear in "Politics" that were also important to these other writers? To what end does Emerson use these ideas?

ALEXIS DE TOCQUEVILLE

Government by Democracy in America

Time Life Pictures/Getty Images

A LEXIS DE TOCQUEVILLE (1805–1859), a French aristocrat, came to see what democracy had produced in America during the early decades of the nineteenth century, when the United States was expanding rapidly westward and developing both agricultural and industrial strength. His family had lived through the French Revolution (1789) and its murderous aftermath. His parents came close to being killed but fled to England for a few years until Napoleon began his wars, which ended in 1814. When they returned to France, they helped Tocqueville begin a career in law that resulted in his appointment to a minor position in Versailles. He spent a good deal of time reading the works of Machiavelli, Montesquieu, Rousseau, and other major political thinkers and began writing in his early twenties. Tocqueville went on to enjoy more important offices in government, including in France's parlement, where he supported the abolishment of slavery. However, the government in France in 1830 became unstable, and Tocqueville's situation proved difficult. He applied for a position that allowed him to visit the United States as an inspector of American prisons.

He chose his best friend, Gustave de Beaumont, to accompany him, and they set out in 1831 to travel across the new nation. Tocqueville did visit some prisons and comment on them, but soon he saw his mission shift to the careful observation of the nature of the government and the people of the United States. Because of the violence of the French Revolution and the unstable governments that followed up to the time of his visit, he was profoundly aware that the world of the aristocracy was crumbling rapidly. Many aristocrats had been guillotined during the French Revolution and many more had been forced out of the country. The rise of a middle class in France in the first decades of the 1800s signaled a change that Tocqueville knew was permanent and imminent. His studies in the

---

From *Democracy in America*.

United States resulted in *Democracy in America* (1835; 1840), still one the most important analyses of the function of democracy as it had been imagined by the framers of the Constitution and the authors of the *Federalist Papers*.

Tocqueville arrived at a propitious time. There were twenty-four states in the Union and the population was thirteen million people. Andrew Jackson (1767–1849) had been elected president in 1829 and was probably the most democratic holder of that office. He had not enjoyed the level of education of the presidents before him nor had he been the heir of great landholdings, like James Madison, or the scion of a brilliant family, like John Quincy Adams. He had been born in the backwoods of Carolina and somehow began the study of law in his teens. He rose in politics, took a commission in the War of 1812, and became famous for his defeat of the British at New Orleans. He was tough, immediate, and sometimes coarse, but the country adored him.

In this environment, Tocqueville traveled freely across the country and recorded his observations. In the absence of an aristocracy, he marveled at the sense of equality that Americans had. He even went so far as to include a chapter in *Democracy in America* on the equality of women. In it he says, "I think that the social change which places father and son, servant and master and, in general, lower and upper classes on the same level, will gradually raise women to make them the equals of men." But he also observed that Americans had a great sense of industry and a love of materialism. "To clear, cultivate, and transform the realm of this vast uninhabited continent of his, the American must have the daily support of some energetic passion which can only be the love of money. This love of money has, therefore, never been stigmatized in America and, provided that it does not exceed the limits set by the public order, it is held in high esteem."

He was impressed by the apparent absence of the hand of government, the freedom that people enjoyed, and the essential practicality of the nation's inhabitants. He was certain that the power of the federal government would diminish over time and felt there could never be a civil war in America — despite the fact that the Civil War began just twenty-one years after his second volume appeared. His opinion that civil war was unlikely was based on his view that the power of the states outweighed the power of the federal government at that time: "If the sovereignty of the Union were to come into conflict with that of the states, one can readily foresee that it would be defeated; I doubt whether the fight would ever be undertaken in any serious fashion." He felt this even though South Carolina threatened war while he was in America in 1832.

Tocqueville returned to France after almost two years in America. There he married and continued his career, taking part in politics during tumultuous times in France. He supported French incursion into Algeria, which he visited. He also visited Ireland in 1835 and deplored the conditions of the Irish tenant farmers in the period before the great famine of the 1840s. He took a leadership role following the French revolution of 1848 and in branches of the government in the 1850s. His last work, a study of recent French history, appeared after he died in 1859.

TOCQUEVILLE'S RHETORIC

Because this is a translation from the French, it is difficult for us to appreciate the direct-ness and skill of Tocqueville's style. However, his principles of organization are clear. He considers only a specific number of issues in this chapter from his book. First, he tackles the question of suffrage, or who can vote. He describes it as universal suffrage because any free male citizen could vote in the United States; there were no restrictions, as in Europe, for men of property, though women, African slaves, and Native Americans could not vote. But Tocqueville also notes that there seem to be fewer distinguished men in office than there were fifty years before, when the Constitution was being written. He implies that when everyone can vote — as opposed to just a limited group of electors — the common people do not choose distinguished men. Tocqueville then develops this point by causal analysis, trying to find what it is that causes fewer men of outstanding quality to assume leadership.

He follows with a discussion of the circumstance of the intervals between elections. The shortness of the intervals between elections, he says, keeps "society in a feverish excitement and public affairs in a continuous state of change" (para. 31). But if there is a long period between elections, the ousted party might try to seize power. Further, with the change that new elections bring, he sees an "instability" of American laws (para. 34). He, like Americans, does not see this as a "great weakness" (para. 34).

Then, considering the "arbitrary power of magistrates," he develops his ideas using a comparison between monarchies, limited monarchies, and democracy, with a reference to the power of New England magistrates, by which he means those "entrusted with the execution of the law." In this section, he compares despotism and democracy by using examples of legislation in New England and continues with a discussion of limited monarchies.

One complaint leads him to devote a section to what he sees as the lack of good record keeping by local governments. Tocqueville points to newspapers as being the only institutions that keep a record of social movements and social issues. As a social scientist, he is himself in the process of recording what he sees at work in America and, in a sense, tries to make up for this lack in contemporary government.

Finally, Tocqueville develops his last idea when he discusses the possibility that Amer-ican democracy may be financially efficient. Again, he relies on comparison to decide whether democracy is inexpensive or overly expensive to maintain. This leads him to con-sider taxation and to reflect on the Aristotelian issue of classes of people. Tocqueville sees three classes: first are the wealthy, whose fortunes are considerable; second are the middle class, who hold only a slight fortune; and third are the general poor, who live on their labor and do not get rich. Tocqueville's analysis of taxation under the government of each of these classes is fascinating. And like both Aristotle and James Madison, Tocqueville is led to consider the question of government by the majority or the minority. Obviously, this question remains central to ideas about democracy.

✖ PREREADING QUESTIONS: WHAT TO READ FOR

The following prereading questions may help you anticipate key issues in the discussion of Alexis de Tocqueville's "Government by Democracy in America." Keeping them in mind during your first reading should help focus your attention.

1. How does universal suffrage affect the choice of who will govern?
2. How might the frequency of elections affect the stability of the laws of the land?
3. To what extent is a democratic form of government economically efficient?

Government by Democracy in America

I realize that I am treading on live cinders. Every single word in this chapter is bound to bruise at some point the different parties which divide my country. Nonetheless I shall speak my thoughts.

In Europe we find it difficult to assess the true character and the permanent instincts of democracy because in Europe two opposed principles are in conflict; it is not precisely known how far this is due to the principles themselves or to the passions aroused by the conflict.

This is not the case in America where the people are in an unimpeded dominance with no dangers to fear nor wrongs to avenge.

Therefore, in America, democracy follows its own inclinations. Its behavior is natural and its movements are free. That is where it must be judged. And who would find such a study more useful and interesting than ourselves since we are daily carried along by an irresistible movement, walking like blind men toward what may prove to be a tyranny perhaps or a republic, but surely toward a democratic social state?

Universal Suffrage

I have previously mentioned that all the states of the Union had adopted universal suffrage. It is found in populations at different stages on the social ladder. I have had the chance to observe its effects in various places and among races of men whom language, religion, or customs turn into virtual strangers to each other, in Louisiana as well as in New England, in Georgia as in Canada. I have noted that universal suffrage was far from producing in America all the benefits or all the ills expected from it in Europe and that its results were in general other than is supposed.

The People's Choice and the Instincts of American Democracy in Its Choices

In the United States the most outstanding men are rarely called upon to direct public affairs—Reasons for this—The envy which, in France, drives the lower classes against the upper classes is not a French instinct but a democratic one—Why, in America, eminent men often keep away from a political career of their own volition.

Many people in Europe believe without saying so, or say so without believing it, that one of the great advantages of universal suffrage is to summon men worthy of public trust to the direction of public affairs. The people could not possibly govern on their own, so it is said, but they do always sincerely support the welfare of the state and their instinct unfailingly tells them which men are fired by a similar desire and thus are the most competent to wield power.   6

For my part, I am bound to say, what I have seen in America does not give me any reason to think that this is the case. When I stepped ashore in the United States, I discovered with amazement to what extent merit was common among the governed but rare among the rulers. It is a permanent feature of the present day that the most outstanding men in the United States are rarely summoned to public office and one is forced to acknowledge that things have been like that as democracy has gone beyond its previous limits. The race of American statesmen has strangely shrunk in size over the last half century.   7

One can point out several reasons for this phenomenon.   8

Whatever one does, it is impossible to raise the intelligence of a nation above a certain level. It will be quite useless to ease the access to human knowledge, improve teaching methods, or reduce the cost of education, for men will never become educated nor develop their intelligence without devoting time to the matter.   9

Therefore the inevitable limitations upon a nation's intellectual progress are governed by how great or small is the ease with which it can live without working. This limitation is further off in certain countries and nearer in others; for it not to exist at all, however, the people would need to be free of the physical cares of life. It would have to cease to be the people. Thus it is as difficult to imagine a society where all men are enlightened as a state where all the citizens are wealthy; those are two related difficulties. I willingly accept that the bulk of the population very sincerely supports the welfare of the country; I might go even further to state that in general the lower social classes seem to be less likely to confuse their personal interests with this support than the   10 upper classes. But what they always lack, more or less, is the skill to judge the means to achieve this sincerely desired end. A long study and many different ideas indeed are needed to reach a precise picture of the character of one single individual! Would the masses succeed where greatest geniuses go astray? The people never find the time or the means to devote to this work. They have always to come to hasty judgments and to latch on to the most obvious of features. As a result, charlatans of all kinds know full well the secret of pleasing the people whereas more often than not their real friends fail to do so.

Moreover, it is not always the ability to choose men of merit which democracy lacks but the desire and inclination to do so.   11

One must not blind oneself to the fact that democratic institutions promote to a very high degree the feeling of envy in the human heart, not so much because they offer each citizen ways of being equal to each other but because these ways continuously prove inadequate for those who use them. Democratic institutions awaken and flatter the passion of equality without ever being able to satisfy it entirely. This complete equality every day slips through the people's fingers at the moment when they think they have a hold on it; it flees, as Pascal[1] says, in an eternal flight. The people become excited by the pursuit of this blessing, all the more priceless because it is near enough to be recognized but too far away to be tasted. The chance of success enthuses them; the uncertainty of success frustrates them. Their excitement is followed by weariness and bitterness. So anything which exceeds their limitations in any way appears to them as an obstacle to their desires and all superiority, however legitimate, is irksome to their eyes.   12

Many people suppose that this secret instinct which persuades the lower classes to remove the upper classes as far as they can from the direction of affairs is found only in France; that is wrong. The instinct I am mentioning is not French, it is democratic; political circumstances may have given it a particularly bitter taste, but they do not bring it into being.   13

In the United States, the people have no especial hatred for the upper classes of society; but they feel little goodwill for them and exclude them from power; they do not fear great talents but have little liking for them. Generally speaking, it is noticeable that anything which thrives without their support has trouble in winning their favor.   14

While the natural instincts of democracy persuade the people to remove distinguished men from power, the latter are guided by no less an instinct to distance themselves from a political career, where it is so difficult for them to retain their complete autonomy or to make any progress without cheapening themselves. This thought is very naively expressed by Chancellor Kent. This celebrated author I speak of, having sung the praises of that part of the Constitution   15

---

[1] **Blaise Pascal (1623–1662)**   French mathematician and philosopher.

which grants the appointment of judges to the executive power, adds: "It is probable, in fact, that the most appropriate men to fill these places would have too much reserve in their manners and too much severity in their principles ever to be able to gather the majority of votes at an election that rested on universal suffrage" (Kent's *Commentaries on American Law,* vol. I, p. 273).

That was what was being printed without contradiction in America in the year 1830.   16

I hold it proved that those who consider universal suffrage as a guarantee of the excellence of the choice made are under a complete delusion. Universal suffrage has other advantages but not that one.   17

Causes Which Are Able Partly to Correct
These Instincts of Democracy

Contrary effects on nations as on men of great dangers—Why America saw so many men at the head of affairs fifty years ago—Influence of intelligence and customs upon the people's choices—Example of New England— States of the Southwest—Influence of certain laws upon the people's choices—Election by two stages—Its effect on the composition of the Senate.

When great dangers threaten the state, the people often make a happy choice of those citizens best suited to save them.   18

It has been noticed that, in the face of imminent danger, a man rarely remains at his normal level; he either rises well above himself or dips well below. The same happens to nations. Extreme dangers, instead of lifting a nation, sometimes end by bringing it low; they arouse its passions without giving them direction and confuse its perceptions without clarification. The Jews were still slitting each other's throats even in the midst of the smoking ruins of the Temple. But more commonly, with nations as with men, extraordinary courage arises from the very imminence of the dangers. Then great characters stand out like those monuments hidden by the darkness of the night and seen suddenly in the glare of a conflagration. Genius no longer disdains to appear on the stage and the people, alarmed by the dangers facing them, momentarily forget their envious passions. At such a time, it is not rare for famous names to emerge from the ballot box. I have said above that statesmen of modern America seem greatly inferior to those who appeared at the head of affairs fifty years ago. Circumstances, as well as laws, were responsible for that. When America was fighting the most just of causes, that of one nation escaping from another's yoke; when it was a question of introducing a new nation into the world, the spirits of all rose to reach the height of the goal to which their efforts aspired. In this general commotion, outstanding men anticipated   19 the nation's call and the people embraced them and adopted them as their leaders. But such events take place at rare intervals and one must judge by the commonplace aspect of things.

If fleeting events sometimes succeed in checking the passions aroused by democracy, the intelligence and customs of the community exercise a no less powerful but more lasting influence upon its inclinations. This is very obvious in the United States.   20

In New England, where education and freedom are the daughters of morality and religion, and where an already ancient and long-settled society has managed to shape its own maxims and customs, the people, while they have avoided all the superiorities which wealth and birth have ever created among men, have become used to respecting intellectual and moral superiorities and to submit to them willingly. Therefore, New England democracy makes better choices than elsewhere.   21

On the other hand, as one goes further south to those states where social ties are less ancient or less secure, where education is not so widespread and where the principles of morality, religion, and freedom are less happily combined, one observes that the aptitudes and virtues of government leaders are increasingly rare.   22

Lastly, when we get right down to the new states of the Southwest where the body of society, formed yesterday, is still no more than a mass of adventurers and speculators, the observer is dismayed to see into what hands public authority has been entrusted and he wonders what force, independent of legislation and of men, will enable the state to grow and society to prosper.   23

Certain laws have a democratic character, yet succeed in correcting partially democracy's dangerous instincts.   24

When you enter the House of Representatives in Washington, you are struck by the coarse appearance of this great assembly. Your eye often seeks in vain a single famous man. Almost all its members are unknown people whose names fail to stimulate any mental picture. For the most part, they are village lawyers, businessmen or even men from the lowest classes. In a country where education is almost universal, it is claimed that the representatives of the people cannot always write correctly.   25

A couple of paces away lies the Senate whose narrow precincts contain a large proportion of America's famous men. There is hardly a single man who does not recall some recent claim to fame. They are eloquent lawyers, distinguished generals, able magistrates, well-known politicians. All the speeches which emanate from this assembly would bring glory to the greatest parliamentary debates of Europe.   26

How does this curious contradiction come about? Why does the nation's elite gather in this house rather than the other? Why does the first assembly attract so many coarse elements whereas the latter has a monopoly of talents   27 and intelligence? Yet both spring from the people, both are the product of universal suffrage and no voice has so far been raised in America to maintain that the Senate might be antagonistic to popular interests. So how does such a wide difference arise? I know of only one explanation: the election for the House of Representatives is direct; the one for the Senate is in two stages. The whole citizen body appoints the legislature of each state and the federal constitution converts one by one these legislatures into electoral colleges, which return members to the Senate. Thus the senators represent, albeit indirectly, the result of universal suffrage, for the legislature which appoints senators is not an aristocratic or privileged body deriving its electoral right from itself; it fundamentally depends upon the totality of citizens; it is generally elected by them every year and they are always able to control its choices by adding new members to its ranks. But it is enough that the will of the people has passed through this elected assembly for it to have become refined in some sense and to have emerged clad in a nobler and more beautiful form. Men thus elected, therefore, represent exactly the ruling majority of the nation but they represent only the highest concepts current in the community, the generous instincts which fire its imagination and not the petty emotions which trouble or the vices which disgrace it.

It is easy to see in the future a moment when American republics will be　28 forced to extend the two tiers in their electoral system for fear of perishing wretchedly on the reefs of democracy.

I have no scruple in confessing that I see in the two-stage electoral system　29 the only means of placing the advantage of political liberty within the reach of all classes of society. Anyone hoping to turn this means into the exclusive weapon of one party, or anyone fearing such an outcome, seems to me to be making an equal mistake.

Influence Which American Democracy Has Exercised on Electoral Laws

Elections at long intervals expose the state to violent crises—Frequency of elections keeps up a feverish agitation—Americans have opted for the latter of these disadvantages—Versatility of the law—Opinions of Hamilton, Madison, and Jefferson on this topic.

When elections occur at long intervals, the state runs the risk of being over-　30 thrown each time. Then the parties make the utmost efforts to seize a prize which comes so rarely within their grasp and, since the outcome is almost beyond remedy for those candidates who lose, their ambition, pushed to the point of desperation, must be a source of fear. If, by contrast, the equal struggle is soon to be repeated, the losers retain their patience.

When elections follow in rapid succession, their frequency keeps society 31 in a feverish excitement and public affairs in a continuous state of change.

Thus, on one side, the state risks the onset of unease or, on the other, 32 revolution; the former system damages the quality of government, the latter threatens its existence.

Americans have preferred to risk the first of these evils to the second. In 33 this choice they have been guided more by instinct than reason, since democracy pushes its inclination for variety to the edge of passion and the consequence is a strange changeability of legislation.

Many Americans consider the instability of their laws as a necessary result 34 of a system whose general effects are useful. Yet there is no one in the United States, I believe, who wishes to deny this instability or who does not regard it as a great weakness.

Hamilton, having demonstrated the usefulness of a power which has been 35 able to prevent or, at least, to impede the promulgation of bad laws, adds: "It may perhaps be said, that the power of preventing bad laws includes that of preventing good ones, and may be used to the one purpose as well as the other. But this objection will have little weight with those who can properly estimate the mischiefs of that inconstancy and mutability in the laws which form the greatest blemish in the character and genius of our governments." *Form the greatest blemish in the character and genius of our government (The Federalist*, No. 73).

"The facility," says Madison, "and excess of law-making seem to be the 36 diseases to which our governments are most liable" *(The Federalist*, No. 62).

Jefferson himself, the greatest democrat to emerge from American democracy, has highlighted the same dangers. 37

"The instability of our laws is really an immense evil," he says. "I think it would 38 be well to provide in our constitution that there shall always be a twelve-month between the engrossing a bill and passing it: that it should then be offered its passage without changing a word: and that if its circumstances should be thought to require a speedier passage, it should take two-thirds of both houses instead of a bare majority."[2]

Civil Servants under the Control of American Democracy

Simplicity of American civil servants—Absence of uniforms—All officials are salaried—Political consequences of this fact—No public career in America—Results of this.

---

[2] **Letter to Madison of 20 December 1787,** M. Conseil's translation. [Tocqueville's note]

American civil servants remain indistinguishable from the mass of the citizens; 39
they have neither palaces nor guards, nor ceremonial uniforms. This simple
government attire does not stem simply from a peculiar twist of the American
character but from the basic principles of their society.

In the eyes of democracy, the government is not a blessing but a necessary 40
evil. Some powers must be granted to civil servants for, without such power,
what use would they be? But the external appearance of power is not vital for
the conduct of affairs and is unnecessarily offensive to the public.

The civil servants themselves are perfectly aware that they have gained the 41
right to hold a superior position in relation to others, which they derive from
their authority only if they place themselves on a level with the whole community through their way of life.

I can imagine no one plainer in his behavior, more approachable, more 42
sensitive to requests than an American civil servant.

I like this unself-conscious approach of democratic government and I per- 43
ceive something admirably manly in this inner strength which characterizes
the office rather than the official, the man rather than the external symbols of
power.

As for the influence that uniforms exert, I believe that the importance they 44
have to carry in a century like ours is much exaggerated. I have not noticed
American officials in the exercise of their authority greeted with any less
respect or regard because they have nothing but their own merit to recommend them.

On the other hand, I very much doubt whether a special garment induces 45
men in public life to respect themselves if they are not naturally disposed to do
so, for I cannot believe that they have more regard for their clothes than their
person.

When I see some of our magistrates harassing or indulging their wit against 46
litigants or shrugging their shoulders at the defense pleas or smiling smugly as
the charges are listed, I should like to try to take their robes from them so as to
find out whether, clothed as ordinary citizens, they might recall the natural dignity of the human race.

Not one American public official wears uniform but they all receive a sal- 47
ary. This flows even more naturally than the preceding example from democratic principles. A democracy may surround its magistrates with pomp and
cover them with gold and silk without directly compromising the principle of
its existence. Such privileges are transitory and belong to the place not the
man. But the creation of unpaid offices is to form a class of wealthy and independent officials; that is the core of an aristocracy. If the people still retain the
right to choose, the exercise of that right has inevitable limitations.

Whenever a democratic republic converts salaried offices to unpaid ones, 48
I think one may conclude that it is veering toward monarchy. And whenever a

monarchy begins to remunerate unpaid offices, it is a sure sign of progression toward a despotism or a republic.

I, therefore, think that to change from salaried to unpaid offices is by itself the instigation of a real revolution.   49

The complete absence of unpaid offices is for me one of the most obvious indications of the absolute sway American democracy holds. Services of whatever kind rendered to the public are rewarded so that everyone has not only the right but also the means of performing such services.   50

If all the citizens of democratic states are able to take up office, all are not tempted to canvas for them. The choice of the electorate is limited not by the qualifications for candidature but by the number and capability of the candidates.   51

In nations where the principle of election is universally applied, properly speaking no public career exists. Men reach office to some degree by accident and have no guarantee of staying there. This is especially true with annual elections. The result is that in times of calm, public office offers little attraction to ambition. In the United States, men of moderate desires commit themselves to the twists and turns of politics. Men of great talent and passion in general avoid power to pursue wealth; it often comes about that only those who feel inadequate in the conduct of their own business undertake to direct the fortunes of the state.   52

These reasons, quite as much as any poor decisions of democracy, have to account for the great number of coarse men holding public office. I do not know whether the people of the United States would choose men of superior qualities who might canvas their votes but it is certain that such men do not bid for office.   53

The Arbitrary Power of Magistrates[3] under the Sway of American Democracy

Why the arbitrary power of magistrates is greater under absolute monarchies and democratic republics than in limited monarchies—Arbitrary power of magistrates in New England.

Under two types of government, magistrates exercise considerable arbitrary power, namely, under the absolute government of a single individual and under that of democracy.   54

This same effect issues from almost analogous causes.   55

In despotisms, no one's fate is secure, whether they be public officials or ordinary individuals. The ruler, holding in his hand the lives, fortunes, and   56

---

[3] Here I mean the word *magistrate* in its widest sense: I apply it to all entrusted with the execution of the law. [Tocqueville's note]

sometimes the honor of those he employs, believes he has nothing to fear from them and allows them great freedom of action because he feels sure they will never use it against him.

In despotisms, the ruler is so enamored of his power that he fears the   57
restrictions of his own regulations; he likes to see his agents acting in an almost random manner so as to be assured that he will never observe in them any inclination which runs against his wishes.

In democracies, since the majority is able to remove power annually   58
from the hands of those entrusted with it, it has no fear of any abuse against itself. Since the majority has the power to indicate its wishes to its rulers from moment to moment, it prefers to leave them to their own efforts rather than bind them to inflexible rules which, by fettering them, would, to some extent, fetter the majority itself.

Looking quite closely, one actually discovers that the arbitrary power of   59
democratic magistrates is even greater than it would be in despotic states, where the ruler can punish at any time all the mistakes he perceives. But he could not possibly flatter himself that he has spotted every mistake he ought to punish. On the other hand, in democracies, the sovereign power is both all-powerful and present everywhere. Thus we see that American officials are much freer in the sphere of action allotted to them by law than any European counterpart. Often they are merely shown the goal to be reached while being left free to choose their own means.

In New England for example, the formation of the jury list is left to the   60
selectmen of each township; the only rule imposed on them is as follows: they should choose juries from citizens who enjoy electoral rights and whose reputation is excellent.[4]

In France, we would consider the life and liberty of men to be in danger, if we   61
entrusted the exercise of such a formidable right to an official, whoever he was.

In New England, these same magistrates are able to have the names of   62
drunkards posted in taverns and to prevent the inhabitants of the town from supplying them with wine.[5]

---

[4] See the law of 27 February 1813 in the *General Collection of the Laws of Massachusetts,* vol. 2, p. 331. It must be added that the jurors are subsequently drawn by lot from the lists. [Tocqueville's note]

[5] Law of 28 February 1787, ibid., vol. 1, p. 302. Here is the text: "The selectmen in each town shall cause to be posted up in the houses and shops of all taverners, innholders, and retailers, within such towns, a list of the names of all persons reputed common drunkards, common tipplers, or common gamesters, misspending their time and estate in such houses. And every keeper of such house or shop, after notice given him, that shall be convicted before one or more Justices of the Peace, of entertaining or suffering any of the persons in such list, to drink or tipple, or game, in his or her house, or any of the dependencies thereof, or of selling them spiritous liquor, shall forfeit and pay the sum of thirty shillings." [Tocqueville's note]

Such a moralistic power would appall people in the most absolute of monar-   63
chies; here, however, people have no difficulty in obeying.

Nowhere has the law left greater scope to arbitrary power than in demo-   64
cratic republics because such power appears not to scare them. It may even be
said that magistrates become freer as voting rights are wider spread and the
duration of the magistracy is shortened.

That is why it is so difficult to convert a democratic republic into a monar-   65
chy. Though they are not elected, magistrates normally retain the rights and the
habits of elected magistrates. That leads to despotism.

Only in limited monarchies does the law define the sphere of action around   66
public officials while at the same time taking care to guide their every step.
This fact is easily explained.

In limited monarchies, power is divided between the people and the prince.   67
Both have a vested interest in the stability of magistrates.

The prince is unwilling to entrust the fate of public officials to the hands of the   68
people for fear that they betray his authority; the people, from their point of view,
are afraid that magistrates, being absolutely dependent upon the prince, might
serve to oppress their liberty; thus they are, in a sense, left dependent upon no one.

The same reason which persuades prince and people to make officials   69
independent induces them to seek guarantees against the abuse of that independence so that they do not turn it against the authority of the former or the
liberty of the latter. Both agree, therefore, upon the necessity of marking out, in
advance, a line of conduct for public officials and find it in both their interests
to impose upon these officials rules they cannot possibly disregard.

Administrative Instability in the United States

*American society often leaves behind fewer records of its proceedings than a
family does—Newspapers are the only historical monuments—How extreme
administrative instability injures the art of government.*

Men reach power for one brief moment before disappearing in a crowd, which   70
changes its appearance daily; the result is that the proceedings of American
society often leave behind fewer records than a private family does. In a sense,
public administration hands down its records via an oral tradition. Nothing is
written or, if it is, it flies off in the slightest gust of wind like Sibylline leaves,[6]
to vanish without recall.

The sole historical monuments in the United States are newspapers. If one   71
number is missing, the chain of events is, as it were, broken; the present and

---

[6] **Sibylline leaves**   A reference to the lost books of the Roman tracks, *The Sibylline Books*.

the past are no longer connected. I am quite certain that in fifty years time it will be more difficult to gather together authentic documents about the details of American social life than about the administration of medieval France. And if a barbarian invasion happened to take the United States by surprise, in order to find out anything about the people who lived there one would have to turn to the history of other nations.

Administrative instability has begun to permeate our thinking; I might almost say that today everyone has ended up with a taste for it. No one has any concern for what happened before his time. No methodical system is in force; no collecting of material takes place; no documents are gathered together when it would be easy to do so. When by chance they are in someone's possession, little care is taken of them. Among my papers I have original documents given to me by public administrators to answer some of my inquiries. American society seems to live from hand to mouth like an army in the field. However, the skill of administration is assuredly a science and all sciences, in order to improve, need to group together the discoveries of the different generations as they follow each other. One man, in the brief span of his life, notes one fact, another conceives an idea; one man invents a method, another finds a formula; the human race collects en route these various fruits of individual experiments and formulates the sciences. It is difficult for American administrators to learn anything from each other. Thus they bring to the conduct of society the enlightenment which they discover widespread in that society and not the knowledge which should be their own. So democracy, pushed to the limits, damages the art of government. In this context, it is better suited to a nation whose administrative education is already complete than to a nation uninitiated in public affairs.

Moreover, this does not apply solely to the science of administration. Democratic government, founded upon such a simple and natural idea, nevertheless always implies the existence of a very civilized and educated society.[7] At first sight, it may be imagined as belonging to the earliest ages of the world; a closer examination allows us to discover that it had to come about last.

Public Expenses under the Rule of American Democracy

In all societies citizens divide into a certain number of classes — The instinct of each of these classes in the organization of state finances — Why public expenses must tend to increase when the people govern — What makes the extravagancies of democracy less of a fear in America — Use of public funds under a democracy.

---

[7] I do not need to say that I am referring here to the democratic government which applies to a nation and not that which applies to a small tribe. [Tocqueville's note]

Is democratic government economical? First we must know with what we are comparing it.   74

The question would be easy to solve if we set out to draw a parallel between a democratic republic and an absolute monarchy. Public expenses would be much higher in the former than in the latter. But such is the case for all free states compared with those which are not so. Despotism certainly brings ruin to men, more by preventing them from producing than by taking away the fruits of their labors; it dries up the source of wealth while it often respects wealth once acquired. On the other hand, freedom spawns a thousand times more goods than it destroys and, in nations where this is understood, the people's resources always grow more quickly than taxes.   75

At present, I am concerned to compare nations which are free and to establish the influence of democracy upon state finances in such nations.   76

Societies, like other organized bodies, are shaped by certain fixed rules which they cannot sidestep and are made up of certain elements found in all places at all times.   77

It will always be simple to divide each nation theoretically into three classes.   78

The first is composed of the wealthy. The second will include those who are, in all respects, comfortably off without being wealthy. In the third are locked those who have only little or no property and who live primarily on the work provided by the first two.   79

The individuals in these various categories may be more or less numerous according to the state of society, but it is impossible for these categories not to exist.   80

Each one of these classes will bring to the handling of state finances certain instincts peculiar to itself.   81

Let us suppose that the first alone makes the laws; it will probably concern itself but little with saving public money because a tax on a substantial fortune removes only part of the surplus without affecting it very much.   82

On the other hand, let us grant that the middle classes alone make the law. You can count on it that they will not raise extravagant taxes because nothing is more disastrous than a heavy tax on a slight fortune.   83

Government by the middle classes has to be, I do not say the most enlightened of free governments, nor especially the most generous, but the most economical.   84

Now, let me suppose that the lowest class is exclusively responsible for making the law; I see clearly opportunities for an increase rather than a decrease in public expenditure for two reasons: 85

As most of the voters then have no taxable property, all the money expended in the interests of society can only profit them without ever harming them; those who do have a little property easily find means of fixing taxes so as to fall upon the wealthy and to profit the poor; this is something the wealthy could not possibly pursue were they to be in charge of the government.   86

Countries where the poor[8] were exclusively responsible for lawmaking   87
could not therefore expect much economy in public expenses, which will
always be extensive, either because taxes cannot touch those who vote for
them or because they are assessed so as not to touch them. In other words,
democratic government is the only one where those who vote for the tax can
evade the obligation to pay it.

It is an empty objection to say that the interest of the people properly   88
understood is to be careful with the fortunes of the wealthy because it would
soon feel an ensuing constriction itself. Is it not also to the advantage of kings
to make their subjects happy and of the nobility to know when it is appropriate
to open their ranks? If a distant advantage could prevail over the passions and
needs of the passing moment, neither tyrannical rules nor exclusive aristocracies would ever have come into being.

Again, someone may stop me and say: Who has ever thought of making the   89
poor solely responsible for lawmaking? Who? Those who introduced universal suffrage. Does the majority or the minority make the law? The majority, of
course; and if I demonstrate that the poor always make up the majority, am I not
right to add that in countries where they have the vote, they alone make the law?

Now, certainly up to this time, in every nation of the world, those with no   90
property or those whose property was too modest to allow them to live comfortably without working always comprised the greatest number. Therefore,
universal suffrage really does entrust the government of society to the poor.

The vexing influence occasionally exercised by the power of the people on   91
state finances was very evident in certain democratic republics of the ancient
world in which the public treasury was drained away to help the poorest citizens or to provide the people with games and public spectacles. It is true that
the representative system was almost unknown in the ancient world. Nowadays, popular passions find it more difficult to thrive in public affairs; however,
you can guarantee that in the long run, the delegate will always in the end
conform to the opinions of his constituents and support their inclinations as
well as their interests.

However, the extravagancies of democracies are less a source of dread   92
as the people become increasingly property-owning because then, on the one
hand, the people need the money of the wealthy less, on the other, they will
experience more difficulty in contriving a tax which will not touch the people themselves. In this respect, universal suffrage should be less dangerous in

---

[8] It should be understood that the word *poor* has here, as in the rest of the chapter, a
relative meaning, not an absolute one. Poor men in America might often appear rich
compared with their European counterparts; nevertheless one would be right to call
them poor in comparison with those of their fellow citizens who are richer than they
are. [Tocqueville's note]

France than in England, where almost all taxable property is concentrated in a few hands. America enjoys a situation more favorable than France because the great majority of citizens own something.

Still more reasons exist for the possible increase of the financial budget in democracies. 93

Under an aristocratic regime, those men who rule the affairs of state are free from all need because of their own position in society; satisfied with their lot, they look to society for power and reputation; placed, as they are, above the dim mass of citizens, they do not always understand clearly how the general well-being must contribute to their own greatness. Not that they view the sufferings of the poor without pity; but they cannot feel their wretchedness as if they shared it themselves. Provided that the people appear to tolerate their lot, they themselves are satisfied and expect nothing more from the government. Aristocracy thinks more about preservation than improvement. 94

On the contrary, when public authority is in the hands of the people, they, as the sovereign power, seek out improvements in every quarter because of their own discontent. 95

The spirit of improvement then infiltrates a thousand different areas; it delves into endless detail and above all advocates those sorts of improvements which cannot be achieved without payment; for its concern is to better the condition of the poor who cannot help themselves. 96

Furthermore, an aimless restlessness permeates democratic societies where a kind of everlasting excitement stimulates all sorts of innovations which almost always involve expense. 97

In monarchies and aristocracies, the men of ambition flatter the sovereign's normal taste for renown and power and thereby often drive him to spend a great deal of money. 98

In democracies where the sovereign power is always in need of funds, its favors can hardly be won except by increasing its prosperity and that can almost never be achieved without money. 99

In addition, when the people start to reflect upon their own position, a host of needs arise which they had not felt at first and which cannot be satisfied except by having recourse to state assets. The result is that public expenditure seems to increase with the growth of civilization and that taxes rise as knowledge spreads. 100

There is one final reason which often makes democratic government more expensive than any other. Sometimes democracy aims to economize in its expenditure but fails to succeed because it has no skill in managing money. As it frequently changes its mind and still more frequently its agents, its enterprises are badly conducted or remain incomplete. Firstly, the state expends more than is warranted by the scope of the intended aim; secondly, its expenditure is unprofitable. 101

✖ QUESTIONS FOR CRITICAL READING

1. Tocqueville was amazed "to what extent merit was common among the governed but rare among the rulers" (para. 7). Is this true today?

2. Tocqueville says, "The people could not possibly govern on their own" (para. 6). What in his essay would convince you that his statement is right or wrong?

3. What does Tocqueville say about the effect of universal suffrage on American democracy?

4. What was the role of newspapers in Tocqueville's time? Is it the same today?

5. How does Tocqueville describe civil servants?

6. Is Tocqueville correct when he says, "Whatever one does, it is impossible to raise the intelligence of a nation above a certain level" (para. 9)? What are his concerns about education in the 1830s?

7. What does Tocqueville think about rule by the majority in a democracy?

✖ SUGGESTIONS FOR CRITICAL WRITING

1. Tocqueville feels all nations must contain three classes: the wealthy, whose fortunes are large; the comfortable, whose fortunes are small; and the poor, who have no fortune and must live by their labors alone. Does this breakdown reflect conditions today? How reasonable is Tocqueville's understanding of how these three groups would vote on taxation? Do you think that if it was true in Tocqueville's time it is true today? Would all three classes vote primarily for their own interests?

2. Tocqueville was disturbed by the fact that when he went into the House of Representatives he met no one who was famous or well known. He felt that universal suffrage was responsible for that. He says that "it is not always the ability to choose men of merit which democracy lacks but the desire and inclination to do so" (para. 11). Do you agree with Tocqueville that universal suffrage works against choosing the most distinguished and accomplished candidate and toward choosing a mediocre candidate? What are his reasons for thinking so?

3. Because elected office is essentially insecure (one may lose an election), Tocqueville says that politics is not a calling that attracts the best men. As he puts it, "In the United States, men of moderate desires commit themselves to the twists and turns of politics. Men of great talent and passion in general avoid power to pursue wealth; it often comes about that only those who feel inadequate in the conduct of their own business undertake to direct the fortunes of the state" (para. 52). Argue either for or against his position using examples from selections in this book or from your own studies and experience.

4. In the section that discusses civil servants (paras. 39–53), Tocqueville makes a number of statements that may be controversial. Examine that section and explain why

he is concerned about the ways in which civil servants are or are not paid and how they present themselves to the general public in the American democracy. How valid do you feel his arguments are?

5. **CONNECTIONS**   The framers of the Constitution as well as Aristotle in "Democracy and Oligarchy" (p. 70) were concerned with the effects of a pure democracy. Tocqueville is similarly concerned, and in paragraph 89 he asks, "Does the majority or the minority make the law?" What is his conclusion regarding this question and how does his analysis affect his thinking about taxation and the economic efficiency of a democracy? With what parts of Tocqueville's analysis would Aristotle take issue, and how would Aristotle correct Tocqueville's thinking? How well might Aristotle and Tocqueville have gotten along had they met?

6. In paragraph 72, while meditating on the failure of the new nation to preserve records of its past, Tocqueville says, "No one has any concern for what happened before his time." Explain what you think Tocqueville means by this statement and see if you can validate or invalidate his view by reference to other selections in Part One. Or consider his statement in light of current national circumstances and your own experience and your experiences with other citizens. Is this statement reasonable and reflective of the way people feel today? How concerned are you that it might be true?

HANNAH
ARENDT

Total Domination

© Oscar White/Corbis

H ANNAH ARENDT (1906–1975) was born and educated in Germany, earning her doctorate from the University of Heidelberg when she was twenty-two years old. She left Germany for Paris after Hitler came to power in 1933 and early in the development of Nazi ideology. In New York City she worked with Jewish relief groups and in 1940 married Heinrich Bluecher, a professor of philosophy. Arendt joined the faculty of the University of Chicago in 1963 and then taught as a visiting professor at a number of universities, eventually settling at the New School for Social Research in New York.

The Origins of Totalitarianism, from which this selection is excerpted, was first published in 1951 and solidified Arendt's reputation as an important political philosopher. She began work on the book in 1945, after Nazism was defeated in Europe, and finished most of it by 1949, during the period of growing tension between the United States and the Soviet Union that began the Cold War. Much of the book analyzes the politics of ideology in fascist and communist countries. Arendt went on to write a number of other influential works, such as The Human Condition (1958) and Crises of the Republic (1972), both of which address the problems she saw connected with a decline in moral values in modern society. One of her most controversial books, Eichmann in Jerusalem (1963), examines Adolf Eichmann, head of the Gestapo's Jewish section, who was tried and executed in Jerusalem. She observed that the nature of Eichmann's evil was essentially banal — that his crime involved going along with orders without taking the time to assess them critically. Her last work, The Life of the Mind, was not completed, although two of its planned three volumes were published posthumously in 1978.

"Total Domination" is part of one of the last chapters in The Origins of Totalitarianism. The first part of the book sets forth a brief history of modern anti-Semitism because the rise of totalitarianism in Germany was based in large part on Hitler's belief that the Aryan race was biologically and morally more evolved than all other races. In this selection

---

From *The Origins of Totalitarianism*

Arendt shows how the totalitarian state derives its power from propagating a set of ideas, or ideology, such as the view that one race is superior to all others. Once that premise is accepted, she demonstrates, then any and all atrocities against people of other races can be permitted and promoted.

In two instances, describing the ideology of German fascism and the ideology of Soviet communism, Arendt demonstrates the ways in which the uncritical acceptance of an ideology provides the core of power for totalitarian states. In the case of Germany, racism led to the theory that if some races are inferior and debased then they must be destroyed for the good of humanity — a theory that was put into brutal practice by the Nazis. Arendt shows how this view derives from a misunderstanding of Darwin's theories of the survival of the fittest (see Darwin's "Natural Selection," p. 606). In the case of the Soviet Union, totalitarianism depended on the "scientific" theory of history put forth by Karl Marx (see Marx's *The Communist Manifesto*, p. 335) that insisted on class struggle and the need of the most "progressive class" to destroy the less progressive classes. Marx was referred to as the "Darwin of history" in part because his views reflected the same scientific logic as Darwin's theories of biology. According to Arendt, both the Nazi and communist totalitarian regimes claimed those laws of biology or history as the justification for their own brutal acts of terror.

ARENDT'S RHETORIC

Arendt is a careful rhetorician. She works in a logical fashion to analyze basic principles to see how they control the outcome of events. In this case, the outcome is the totalitarian institution of the concentration camp in which human dignity is destroyed. For the totalitarian government, the terror and torment of concentration camps demonstrate "that everything is possible" (para. 1), even though it might seem impossible to reduce a person to a thing. Total domination, as she states, is designed to reduce the diversity and complexity of humanity to a single reaction to terror and pain.

Interestingly, Arendt can find no economic virtue in maintaining huge numbers of people in concentration camps. Occasionally in the Soviet Union, inmates' labor was of value, but some 60 percent or more of the inmates died under the harsh labor conditions. In Nazi Germany the work done in the concentration camps was of such poor quality that it usually had to be done again. Further, during World War II, German resources that might have been used to fight the war were diverted to the concentration camps, which functioned as extermination centers even while Germany reeled under potential defeat. In other words, the concentration camps were self-defeating in every important way except that they demonstrated to a populace that total domination was possible.

One important rhetorical principle at work in this essay is the essential definition of total domination by the process of describing the circumstances of the concentration camps as well as the rationale for their construction. The Nazis knew, and Hitler had already trumpeted the news to the world in his book *Mein Kampf* (My Struggle), that if a lie was big enough, large numbers of people would believe it even if it stood against common sense. "The Big Lie" has become a common principle of modern political science. Likewise, if the enormity of the crime is great enough, it is not likely that people will believe it actually occurred. Therefore, it should not have been a surprise that the few people who had escaped the camps before the war were not believed. They told their stories, but even future victims of the camps refused to believe they existed. Western governments thought the accounts of the concentration camps were monstrous exaggerations.

Throughout the book from which this passage comes, Arendt insists that the essence of totalitarianism is terror and that without it the totalitarian state collapses. The concentration camps are the "laboratories" in which absolute terror dominates and that represent total domination. Individual liberty and freedom are erased by the terror of total domination, and in this sense the values that Rousseau and Jefferson argue for are irrelevant. In some states, such as the one Machiavelli imagined (p. 84), terror might be useful for controlling the opposition, but in the totalitarian state it controls everyone. As Arendt states, "a victory of the concentration-camp system would mean the same inexorable doom for human beings as the use of the hydrogen bomb would mean the doom of the human race" (para. 14).

▓ PREREADING QUESTIONS: WHAT TO READ FOR

The following prereading questions may help you anticipate key issues in the discussion of Hannah Arendt's "Total Domination." Keeping them in mind during your first reading of the selection should help focus your attention.

1. What is the role of terror in the totalitarian state?
2. Why is total domination necessary in a totalitarian state?
3. What happens to human beings in concentration camps?

Total Domination

The concentration and extermination camps of totalitarian regimes serve as the laboratories in which the fundamental belief of totalitarianism that everything is possible is being verified. Compared with this, all other experiments are secondary in importance — including those in the field of medicine whose horrors are recorded in detail in the trials against the physicians of the Third Reich — although it is characteristic that these laboratories were used for experiments of every kind.

Total domination, which strives to organize the infinite plurality and differentiation of human beings as if all of humanity were just one individual, is

possible only if each and every person can be reduced to a never-changing identity of reactions, so that each of these bundles of reactions can be exchanged
at random for any other. The problem is to fabricate something that does not
exist, namely, a kind of human species resembling other animal species whose
only "freedom" would consist in "preserving the species." Totalitarian domination attempts to achieve this goal both through ideological indoctrination of
the elite formations[1] and through absolute terror in the camps; and the atrocities for which the elite formations are ruthlessly used become, as it were, the
practical application of the ideological indoctrination—the testing ground in
which the latter must prove itself—while the appalling spectacle of the camps
themselves is supposed to furnish the "theoretical" verification of the ideology.

The camps are meant not only to exterminate people and degrade human   3
beings, but also serve the ghastly experiment of eliminating, under scientifically
controlled conditions, spontaneity itself as an expression of human behavior
and of transforming the human personality into a mere thing, into something
that even animals are not; for Pavlov's dog,[2] which, as we know, was trained to
eat not when it was hungry but when a bell rang, was a perverted animal.

Under normal circumstances this can never be accomplished, because   4
spontaneity can never be entirely eliminated insofar as it is connected not
only with human freedom but with life itself, in the sense of simply keeping
alive. It is only in the concentration camps that such an experiment is at all
possible, and therefore they are not only "*la société la plus totalitaire encore
réalisée*"[3] (David Rousset) but the guiding social ideal of total domination in
general. Just as the stability of the totalitarian regime depends on the isolation of the fictitious world of the movement from the outside world, so the
experiment of total domination in the concentration camps depends on sealing
off the latter against the world of all others, the world of the living in general, even against the outside world of a country under totalitarian rule. This
isolation explains the peculiar unreality and lack of credibility that characterize all reports from the concentration camps and constitute one of the main
difficulties for the true understanding of totalitarian domination, which stands
or falls with the existence of these concentration and extermination camps;
for, unlikely as it may sound, these camps are the true central institution of
totalitarian organizational power.

----

[1] **elite formations**   By this term Arendt seems to mean the SS men and camp guards.

[2] **Pavlov's dog**   Between 1898 and 1930, the Russian psychologist Ivan Petrovich Pavlov
(1849–1936) trained a dog to associate the sound of a ringing bell with food. Eventually the
dog's reflex was to salivate at the sound of the bell even when there was no food.

[3] *la société . . . réalisée*   "The most totalitarian society yet achieved." David Rousset
(1912–1997) survived the concentration camps and wrote *The Other Kingdom* (1947)
about his experience.

There are numerous reports by survivors. The more authentic they are,   5
the less they attempt to communicate things that evade human understanding
and human experience—sufferings, that is, that transform men into "uncom-
plaining animals." None of these reports inspires those passions of outrage
and sympathy through which men have always been mobilized for justice. On
the contrary, anyone speaking or writing about concentration camps is still
regarded as suspect; and if the speaker has resolutely returned to the world of
the living, he himself is often assailed by doubts with regard to his own truthfulness, as though he had mistaken a nightmare for reality.

This doubt of people concerning themselves and the reality of their own   6
experience only reveals what the Nazis have always known: that men determined to commit crimes will find it expedient to organize them on the vastest,
most improbable scale. Not only because this renders all punishments provided by the legal system inadequate and absurd; but because the very immen-
sity of the crimes guarantees that the murderers who proclaim their innocence
with all manner of lies will be more readily believed than the victims who tell
the truth. The Nazis did not even consider it necessary to keep this discovery to themselves. Hitler circulated millions of copies of his book in which he
stated that to be successful, a lie must be enormous—which did not prevent
people from believing him as, similarly, the Nazis' proclamations, repeated *ad
nauseam*,[4] that the Jews would be exterminated like bedbugs (i.e., with poison
gas), prevented anybody from *not* believing them.

There is a great temptation to explain away the intrinsically incredible   7
by means of liberal rationalizations. In each one of us, there lurks such a liberal, wheedling us with the voice of common sense. The road to totalitarian
domination leads through many intermediate stages for which we can find
numerous analogies and precedents. The extraordinarily bloody terror during
the initial stage of totalitarian rule serves indeed the exclusive purpose of
defeating the opponent and rendering all further opposition impossible; but
total terror is launched only after this initial stage has been overcome and
the regime no longer has anything to fear from the opposition. In this context
it has been frequently remarked that in such a case the means have become
the end, but this is after all only an admission, in paradoxical disguise, that
the category "the end justifies the means" no longer applies, that terror has
lost its "purpose," that it is no longer the means to frighten people. Nor does
the explanation suffice that the revolution, as in the case of the French Revolution, was devouring its own children, for the terror continues even after
everybody who might be described as a child of the revolution in one capacity or another—the Russian factions, the power centers of party, the army,
the bureaucracy—has long since been devoured. Many things that nowadays

---

[4] ***ad nauseam***   To the point of sickness.

have become the specialty of totalitarian government are only too well known from the study of history. There have almost always been wars of aggression; the massacre of hostile populations after a victory went unchecked until the Romans mitigated it by introducing the *parcere subjectis*;[5] through centuries the extermination of native peoples went hand in hand with the colonization of the Americas, Australia, and Africa; slavery is one of the oldest institutions of mankind and all empires of antiquity were based on the labor of state-owned slaves who erected their public buildings. Not even concentration camps are an invention of totalitarian movements. They emerge for the first time during the Boer War,[6] at the beginning of the century, and continued to be used in South Africa as well as India for "undesirable elements"; here, too, we first find the term "protective custody" which was later adopted by the Third Reich. These camps correspond in many respects to the concentration camps at the beginning of totalitarian rule; they were used for "suspects" whose offenses could not be proved and who could not be sentenced by ordinary process of law. All this clearly points to totalitarian methods of domination; all these are elements they utilize, develop, and crystallize on the basis of the nihilistic principle that "everything is permitted," which they inherited and already take for granted. But wherever these new forms of domination assume their authentically totalitarian structure they transcend this principle, which is still tied to the utilitarian motives and self-interest of the rulers, and try their hand in a realm that up to now has been completely unknown to us: the realm where "everything is possible." And, characteristically enough, this is precisely the realm that cannot be limited by either utilitarian motives or self-interest, regardless of the latter's content.

What runs counter to common sense is not the nihilistic principle that "everything is permitted," which was already contained in the nineteenth-century utilitarian conception[7] of common sense. What common sense and "normal people" refuse to believe is that everything is possible. We attempt to understand elements in present or recollected experience that simply surpass our powers of understanding. We attempt to classify as criminal a thing which, as we all feel, no such category was ever intended to cover. What meaning has the concept of murder when we are confronted with the mass production of corpses? We attempt to understand the behavior of concentration-camp inmates and SS-men   8

---

[5] *parcere subjectis*   A Roman policy of lenience and mercy toward those they defeated.

[6] **Boer War (1899–1902)**   The British established concentration camps in which some forty thousand people died during their war against the Transvaal and the Orange Free State — which were then controlled by the Boers, who were descended from earlier Dutch settlers — in what is now South Africa.

[7] **utilitarian conception**   Utilitarianism, often known for its doctrine of the greatest good for the greatest number, was a nineteenth-century philosophy rooted in what people felt was essentially common sense.

psychologically, when the very thing that must be realized is that the psyche *can* be destroyed even without the destruction of the physical man; that, indeed, psyche, character, and individuality seem under certain circumstances to express themselves only through the rapidity or slowness with which they disintegrate. The end result in any case is inanimate men, i.e., men who can no longer be psychologically understood, whose return to the psychologically or otherwise intelligibly human world closely resembles the resurrection of Lazarus.[8] All statements of common sense, whether of a psychological or sociological nature, serve only to encourage those who think it "superficial" to "dwell on horrors."

If it is true that the concentration camps are the most consequential institution of totalitarian rule, "dwelling on horrors" would seem to be indispensable for the understanding of totalitarianism. But recollection can no more do this than can the uncommunicative eyewitness report. In both these genres there is an inherent tendency to run away from the experience; instinctively or rationally, both types of writer are so much aware of the terrible abyss that separates the world of the living from that of the living dead, that they cannot supply anything more than a series of remembered occurrences that must seem just as incredible to those who relate them as to their audience. Only the fearful imagination of those who have been aroused by such reports but have not actually been smitten in their own flesh, of those who are consequently free from the bestial, desperate terror which, when confronted by real, present horror, inexorably paralyzes everything that is not mere reaction, can afford to keep thinking about horrors. Such thoughts are useful only for the perception of political contexts and the mobilization of political passions. A change of personality of any sort whatever can no more be induced by thinking about horrors than by the real experience of horror. The reduction of a man to a bundle of reactions separates him as radically as mental disease from everything within him that is personality or character. When, like Lazarus, he rises from the dead, he finds his personality or character unchanged, just as he had left it.

Just as the horror, or the dwelling on it, cannot affect a change of character in him, cannot make men better or worse, thus it cannot become the basis of a political community or party in a narrower sense. The attempts to build up a European elite with a program of intra-European understanding based on the common European experience of the concentration camps have foundered in much the same manner as the attempts following the First World War to draw political conclusions from the international experience of the front generation.[9] In both cases it turned out that the experiences themselves can communicate

9

10

---

[8] **Lazarus**   From the Bible (John 11:18–48). Jesus, urged by Martha, resurrected Lazarus, who had been dead for four days.

[9] **the front generation**   The generation that fought or experienced the fighting in World War I (1914–1918).

no more than nihilistic banalities. Political consequences such as postwar pacifism, for example, derived from the general fear of war, not from the experiences in war. Instead of producing a pacifism devoid of reality, the insight into the structure of modern wars, guided and mobilized by fear, might have led to the realization that the only standard for a necessary war is the fight against conditions under which people no longer wish to live—and our experiences with the tormenting hell of the totalitarian camps have enlightened us only too well about the possibility of such conditions. Thus the fear of concentration camps and the resulting insight into the nature of total domination might serve to invalidate all obsolete political differentiations from right to left and to introduce beside and above them the politically most important yardstick for judging events in our time, namely: whether they serve totalitarian domination or not.

In any event, the fearful imagination has the great advantage to dissolve   11
the sophistic-dialectical[10] interpretations of politics which are all based on the superstition that something good might result from evil. Such dialectical acrobatics had at least a semblance of justification so long as the worst that man could inflict upon man was murder. But, as we know today, murder is only a limited evil. The murderer who kills a man—a man who has to die anyway—still moves within the realm of life and death familiar to us; both have indeed a necessary connection on which the dialectic is founded, even if it is not always conscious of it. The murderer leaves a corpse behind and does not pretend that his victim has never existed; if he wipes out any traces, they are those of his own identity, and not the memory and grief of the persons who loved his victim; he destroys a life, but he does not destroy the fact of existence itself.

The Nazis, with the precision peculiar to them, used to register their oper-   12
ations in the concentration camps under the heading "under cover of the night (*Nacht und Nebel*)." The radicalism of measures to treat people as if they had never existed and to make them disappear in the literal sense of the word is frequently not apparent at first glance, because both the German and the Russian system are not uniform but consist of a series of categories in which people are treated very differently. In the case of Germany, these different categories used to exist in the same camp, but without coming into contact with each other; frequently, the isolation between the categories was even stricter than the isolation from the outside world. Thus, out of racial considerations, Scandinavian nationals during the war were quite differently treated by the Germans than the members of other peoples, although the former were outspoken enemies of the Nazis. The latter in turn were divided into those whose "extermination" was immediately on the agenda, as in the case of the Jews, or could be expected

---

[10] **sophistic-dialectical**   Arendt seems to be referring to Marxist communist views that pit two mighty historical forces—like good and evil—against one another. Her point is that such a dialectic is artificial and dangerous.

in the predictable future, as in the case of the Poles, Russians, and Ukrainians, and into those who were not yet covered by instructions about such an overall "final solution," as in the case of the French and Belgians. In Russia, on the other hand, we must distinguish three more or less independent systems. First, there are the authentic forced-labor groups that live in relative freedom and are sentenced for limited periods. Secondly, there are the concentration camps in which the human material is ruthlessly exploited and the mortality rate is extremely high, but which are essentially organized for labor purposes. And, thirdly, there are the annihilation camps in which the inmates are systematically wiped out through starvation and neglect.

The real horror of the concentration and extermination camps lies in the fact that the inmates, even if they happen to keep alive, are more effectively cut off from the world of the living than if they had died, because terror enforces oblivion. Here, murder is as impersonal as the squashing of a gnat. Someone may die as the result of systematic torture or starvation, or because the camp is overcrowded and superfluous human material must be liquidated. Conversely, it may happen that due to a shortage of new human shipments the danger arises that the camps become depopulated and that the order is now given to reduce the death rate at any price. David Rousset called his report on the period in a German concentration camp "*Les Jours de Notre Mort,*"[11] and it is indeed as if there were a possibility to give permanence to the process of dying itself and to enforce a condition in which both death and life are obstructed equally effectively.   13

It is the appearance of some radical evil, previously unknown to us, that puts an end to the notion of developments and transformations of qualities. Here, there are neither political nor historical nor simply moral standards but, at the most, the realization that something seems to be involved in modern politics that actually should never be involved in politics as we used to understand it, namely all or nothing—all, and that is an undetermined infinity of forms of human living-together, or nothing, for a victory of the concentration-camp system would mean the same inexorable doom for human beings as the use of the hydrogen bomb would mean the doom of the human race.   14

There are no parallels to the life in the concentration camps. Its horror can never be fully embraced by the imagination for the very reason that it stands outside of life and death. It can never be fully reported for the very reason that the survivor returns to the world of the living, which makes it impossible for him to believe fully in his own past experiences. It is as though he had a story to tell of another planet, for the status of the inmates in the world of the living, where nobody is supposed to know if they are alive or dead, is such that it is as though they had never been born. Therefore all parallels create confusion and   15

---

[11] *Les Jours . . . Mort*   Literally, the days of our death.

distract attention from what is essential. Forced labor in prisons and penal colonies, banishment, slavery, all seem for a moment to offer helpful comparisons, but on closer examination lead nowhere.

Forced labor as a punishment is limited as to time and intensity. The convict retains his rights over his body; he is not absolutely tortured and he is not absolutely dominated. Banishment banishes only from one part of the world to another part of the world, also inhabited by human beings; it does not exclude from the human world altogether. Throughout history slavery has been an institution within a social order; slaves were not, like concentration-camp inmates, withdrawn from the sight and hence the protection of their fellow men; as instruments of labor they had a definite price and as property a definite value. The concentration-camp inmate has no price, because he can always be replaced; nobody knows to whom he belongs, because he is never seen. From the point of view of normal society he is absolutely superfluous, although in times of acute labor shortage, as in Russia and in Germany during the war, he is used for work.

The concentration camp as an institution was not established for the sake of any possible labor yield; the only permanent economic function of the camps has been the financing of their own supervisory apparatus; thus from the economic point of view the concentration camps exist mostly for their own sake. Any work that has been performed could have been done much better and more cheaply under different conditions. Especially Russia, whose concentration camps are mostly described as forced-labor camps because Soviet bureaucracy has chosen to dignify them with this name, reveals most clearly that forced labor is not the primary issue; forced labor is the normal condition of all Russian workers, who have no freedom of movement and can be arbitrarily drafted for work to any place at any time. The incredibility of the horrors is closely bound up with their economic uselessness. The Nazis carried this uselessness to the point of open anti-utility when in the midst of the war, despite the shortage of building material and rolling stock, they set up enormous, costly extermination factories and transported millions of people back and forth. In the eyes of a strictly utilitarian world the obvious contradiction between these acts and military expediency gave the whole enterprise an air of mad unreality.

This atmosphere of madness and unreality, created by an apparent lack of purpose, is the real iron curtain which hides all forms of concentration camps from the eyes of the world. Seen from outside, they and the things that happen in them can be described only in images drawn from a life after death, that is, a life removed from earthly purposes. Concentration camps can very aptly be divided into three types corresponding to three basic Western conceptions of a life after death: Hades, Purgatory, and Hell. To Hades correspond those relatively mild forms, once popular even in nontotalitarian countries, for getting undesirable elements of all sorts—refugees, stateless persons, the asocial, and the unemployed—out of the way; as DP camps,[12] which are nothing other than camps for persons who have become superfluous and bothersome, they have survived the war. Purgatory is represented by the Soviet Union's labor camps, where neglect is combined with chaotic forced labor. Hell in the most literal sense was embodied by those types of camp perfected by the Nazis, in which the whole of life was thoroughly and systematically organized with a view to the greatest possible torment.

All three types have one thing in common: the human masses sealed off in   19
them are treated as if they no longer existed, as if what happened to them were no longer of any interest to anybody, as if they were already dead and some evil spirit gone mad were amusing himself by stopping them for a while between life and death before admitting them to eternal peace.

---

[12] **DP camps**   Displaced Persons camps. These camps were common in Europe after World War II.

⊞ QUESTIONS FOR CRITICAL READING

1. Why are concentration camps described as "laboratories" for the totalitarian regime?

2. What is the importance of the concentration camps' goal of removing human spontaneity?

3. In what sense are the concentration camps "the true central institution of total-itarian organizational power" (para. 4)?

4. Arendt implies that the experience of the concentration camp has the effect of "a mental disease." Why would that be so?

5. How is murder different from the mass death that characterizes the concentra-tion camps?

6. Why is the concentration camp "useful" to the totalitarian government?

⊞ SUGGESTIONS FOR CRITICAL WRITING

1. Examine the economic issues Arendt raises that are involved in the establish-ment and operation of concentration camps in a totalitarian state. Decide whether a totalitarian state, whose goal is to achieve total domination, would be able to derive economic advantage from concentration camps. Why would this be an important issue? If there were a considerable economic advantage to maintaining concentration camps, would that fact make them any less terrifying?

2. Arendt reflected the fears of her own time in this essay. For her the most terrifying and immediate totalitarian governments were those of Nazi Germany and the Soviet Union. What evidence do you see in our contemporary world that might suggest totalitarianism is not completely "dead"? Do you perceive any threatening totalitarian governments anywhere in the world today? How do they seem to function and to interact with other nations?

3. Should you establish that a government is functioning as a totalitarian state today, do you feel it is a moral imperative that you do everything possible to overthrow that state? Would it be ethical and moral to go to war against such a state even if it did not immediately threaten you? Would it be ethical and moral for you to turn your back on a totalitarian state and ignore its operation so that it could achieve the kind of total domination Arendt describes?

4. **CONNECTIONS**   How would Machiavelli (p. 84) interpret Arendt's discussion of ends and means in paragraph 8? Would Machiavelli have recommended concentration camps to his prince as a means of maintaining power? If a prince believed that concentration camps would be the means by which a state could achieve stability and power, would he be right in assuming that the stability and power thus achieved were worthwhile ends? Do you think Machiavelli would have accepted a totalitarian prince?

5. Hannah Arendt reminds us that Hitler practiced "The Big Lie," which was predicated on the belief that for a lie to work, it had to be enormous — so big that huge numbers of people would believe it, even if it went against common sense (para. 6). Arendt also notes that spreading vast lies has become a common principle of modern political science. Research current events and write a brief essay that demonstrates the truth of what Arendt says about the big lie. How many instances can you find in recent political statements, either in the United States or abroad? Why do big lies seem to be accepted as true by so many people?

6. Considering Arendt's position regarding the use of violence, would she have applauded the recent revolutions in Syria and Libya, or would she have ridiculed them as being naive and insufficient? A number of governments have been overthrown in recent years and others continue to be threatened in the Middle East because of people's perception that they are oppressive and totalitarian. Choose one of the following recently overthrown leaders and research his career in order to decide how closely it satisfies Arendt's conditions of total domination: Muammar Gaddafi (Libya), Hosni Mubarak (Egypt), or Saddam Hussein (Iraq). You might also consider Bashar al-Assad, the Syrian leader whose fight to maintain rule during the Syrian Civil War has caused hundreds of thousands of refugees to flee abroad beginning in 2015.

BENAZIR
BHUTTO

Islam and Democracy

© Rick Friedman/Corbis

BENAZIR BHUTTO (1953–2007) was the first woman prime minister of Pakistan and thus the first woman leader of an Islamic country. She was educated at Harvard University and Oxford University, where much of her academic attention was focused on political science. Her father, Zulfiqar Ali Bhutto (1928–1979), was prime minister of Pakistan, but after an unfair trial he was hanged on charges of murdering a political dissident. He was denied clemency by the dictator General Zia-ul-Haq (1924–1988), who also imprisoned Benazir Bhutto for more than six years in primitive conditions. She was eventually released in 1984 for medical reasons and permitted to travel out of the country.

In 1986, she returned to Pakistan after her younger brother was poisoned. Upon her return, she was met by some one million people and became active in the Pakistan People's Party, which she had founded in 1982. She was elected prime minister in 1988 and held that office until 1990, when she was accused of corruption and replaced. She was elected again in 1993, however, and held the office until 1996. Both of her terms in office were filled with many struggles. She promoted socialist capitalism, fought against regulation, and dealt with numerous struggles within Pakistan as well as with Pakistan's neighbor India. She was in voluntary exile in Dubai in 1998 when Pakistan acquired nuclear armaments to match those of India. Her enemies then accused her of corruption again and sentenced her to three years' imprisonment. However, she maintained her influence with the Pakistan People's Party while she was abroad, and the party declared her its leader in 2002.

She returned to Pakistan in 2007 and was greeted by crowds, but her entourage was quickly attacked by a suicide bomber who killed 136 people. She survived because

From *Reconciliation: Islam, Democracy, and the West.*

she had been traveling in an armored vehicle and ducked at the last moment. President Pervez Musharraf (b. 1943), who had granted Bhutto amnesty so that she could return to the country, declared a state of emergency and had Bhutto held for a time under house arrest. But in December of 2007, with the Pakistan People's Party far ahead in the upcoming 2008 elections, Bhutto appeared at a major rally for the party and was shot by an assassin who, after shooting her, detonated a bomb that killed almost two dozen bystanders.

For most of her time in public service (and while in detention and exile), Benazir Bhutto represented a powerful voice in favor of democracy in Pakistan. She had a large and enthusiastic following. Her most formidable opponents were fundamentalist extremists, including those who, after several tries, ultimately succeeded in silencing her.

BHUTTO'S RHETORIC

Bhutto wrote much of her book *Reconciliation* only a few months before she was assassinated and during periods of intense political activity and hopefulness for democracy in Pakistan. Yet her writing does not show signs of haste or anxiety. She begins with a review of Islamic religion and its receptiveness to democratic values. She indirectly cites references to Islam's religious book, the Koran, by pointing to the fact that "Muslims believe in the sovereignty of God" (para. 1) but then goes on to point out the responsibilities of humankind on earth to respect the "immutable principles of justice, truth, and equality" (para. 1). In other words, the principles of Islam lead people to create a "just society on earth on which they will be judged in the hereafter" (para. 2).

Knowing, of course, that terrorists had threatened violence for years and indeed had even attacked her, she insists that such actions are irreligious: "They must not sin by taking innocent life, for God alone has the right to give and take life" (para. 2). Thus, terrorists pervert their religion when they kill. Interestingly, Bhutto twice mentions that it is a sin to take innocent life, leaving one to wonder about whether the death of others — those who are far from innocent — can be justified. A fatwa, a religious edict often invoked for the purpose of killing someone, was leveled against her, but she says that such an edict will not protect an assassin on the day of judgment. However, she does not explain the right of a religious leader to issue a fatwa or how it is permitted by Islam.

Bhutto first establishes the principles of her religion and its implementation in secular life and then offers a remarkable piece of testimony to bolster her view that democracy and Islam are compatible: she quotes the preamble of the 1973 Constitution of Pakistan, much of which was written by her father and passed "unanimously" by Pakistan's Parliament. Some of the basic issues are also covered by the U.S. Constitution, but Pakistan's Constitution also includes concerns and issues that do not appear in the U.S. version. Still, the document's design is used to try to convince us that her original premise, her thesis, is sound.

Bhutto makes a clear distinction between the spiritual agenda of Islam and the political agenda of those who are angry at the West; as she says, "[r]eligion is being exploited" (para. 8) by those who become terrorists. She spends some time dealing with the term *secularism*, which she says is a "rhetorical trap" (para. 7) for Muslims. For someone from the West, secularism means a separation from religious issues. But for Muslims that is a nonissue. Their issues are freedom, equal-opportunity education for both sexes, and independence of the judiciary. She uses an interesting rhetorical question, "Who can doubt" (para. 8), when she asserts that Islam has been distorted. Of course, there is much doubt, and a careful analysis of the situation will either remove doubt or reinforce it depending on circumstances.

Bhutto reviews much current history, including the Russian expedition in Afghanistan and the rise of the mujahideen — the warriors who fought and defeated the Russians and who continue to fight Western influences in Afghanistan. Mujahideen literally means "those who wage jihad," or religious war. She fears that extremists may direct themselves toward disabling Pakistan and taking over its nuclear facilities. In speaking of the nuclear capacity of Pakistan, Bhutto says that the Koran promotes education and "encourages knowledge and scientific experimentation" (para. 16).

In the second part of her discussion, she lays out an argument that suggests that the West has somehow made it difficult, if not impossible, for Pakistan and other Muslim countries to fulfill their goal to become democratic. Because the West has colonized countries such as Pakistan and India, it has supported dictators who have made a point of giving the West access to oil and other important resources. While encouraging civil rights in countries where the West has no immediate interests or needs, it tolerates despotism and the deprivation of rights in countries whose resources it needs. This, she says, "has been a major impediment to the growth of democracy in Islamic nations" (para. 21).

She hopes to prove her argument by using the testimony of President George W. Bush (para. 26) supporting "America's belief in human dignity" while at the same time supporting "Pakistan's military dictator, General Musharraf" (para. 27). She follows this with more testimony from an article in the *New York Times Magazine* (para. 28).

Finally, she concludes with evidence from Freedom House's surveys of the level of freedom enjoyed in nations around the world. Freedom House is credentialed by Bhutto's reference to its founders, Eleanor Roosevelt and Wendell Willkie, a Democrat and a Republican who worked together for the common good in an effort to be as politically unbiased as possible. The statistics she reveals are not as encouraging as we might wish, and the difference between Arab and non-Arab Muslims is significant, although she does not explain why such a difference should exist.

Her point, finally, is that the West is somewhat responsible for the lack of democracy in Muslim countries. The religion of Islam is not the root of the problem; however, the exploitation of religion by extremists remains a very significant and ongoing problem. Indeed, Benazir Bhutto paid with her life for the principles she believed in: democracy and equality.

❖ PREREADING QUESTIONS: WHAT TO READ FOR

The following prereading questions may help you anticipate key issues in the discussion of Benazir Bhutto's "Islam and Democracy." Keeping them in mind during your first reading should help focus your attention.

1. Why do some people assume democracy will not work in Islamic countries?
2. Why does Bhutto feel democracy and Islam are compatible?
3. What does Bhutto say about the role of the West in supporting democracy in Islamic countries?

Islam and Democracy

Some people assert that democracy will not work in an Islamic country because Muslims believe in the sovereignty of God and thus cannot accept man's law. God is Master of the Universe, of the known and unknown. Humans share two relationships: one with God and one with one another. They are custodians of God's trust, the earth, which has been placed in their care, as they are created by God. God has sent his principles to humans through thousands of Prophets, including Moses, Abraham, Jesus, and Mohammad (who is the last messenger), to instruct us how we should conduct our lives and the principles by which we should conduct our societies. The immutable principles of justice, truth, and equality must not be transgressed if we are to gain entrance to everlasting life in Paradise.   1

Thus humans must seek and apply knowledge, must use reason, must consult and build a consensus for a just society on earth on which they will be judged in the hereafter. They must not sin by taking innocent life, for God alone has the right to give and take life. Anyone who interferes in God's work by taking a life commits the most heinous crime in Islam.   2

The terrorists who attacked me with two bomb blasts on October 19, 2007, when I returned to Pakistan to a historic reception, committed the most heinous crime of murder by taking the lives of 179 innocent people. So too does anyone who attacks innocent people, whether in the World Trade Center, the tubes in London, or the resorts of Bali, Indonesia.   3

I am told that the terrorists who made the bombs and conspired to kill me took a *fatwa*, or religious edict, to sanctify the terrorist attacks. However, on the Day of Judgment, such an edict will be of no help. God has ordained that each individual will have to account individually for his actions without intercession from any other individual.   4

Under the Constitution of Pakistan, authored by my father and passed   5
unanimously by Pakistan's Parliament in 1973, the democratic right to Muslim
governance is recognized. The Constitution of 1973 states, in its preamble:

> Whereas sovereignty over the entire Universe belongs to Almighty Allah
> alone, and the authority to be exercised by the people of Pakistan within
> the limits prescribed by Him is a sacred trust;
>
> And whereas it is the will of the people of Pakistan to establish an
> order:
>
> Wherein the State shall exercise its powers and authority through
> the chosen representatives of the people;
>
> Wherein the principles of democracy, freedom, equality, tolerance,
> and social justice, as enunciated by Islam, shall be fully observed;
>
> Wherein the Muslims shall be enabled to order their lives in the indi-
> vidual and collective spheres in accordance with the teachings and require-
> ments of Islam as set out in the Holy Quran and Sunnah;[1]
>
> Wherein adequate provision shall be made for the minorities freely
> to profess and practice their religions and develop their cultures;
>
> Wherein the territories now included in or in accession with Pakistan
> and such other territories as may hereafter be included in or accede to
> Pakistan shall form a Federation wherein the units will be autonomous
> with such boundaries and limitations on their powers and authority as
> may be prescribed;
>
> Therein shall be guaranteed fundamental rights, including equality of
> status, of opportunity and before law, social, economic, and political jus-
> tice, and freedom of thought, expression, belief; faith, worship, and asso-
> ciation, subject to law and public morality;
>
> Wherein adequate provision shall be made to safeguard the legiti-
> mate interests of minorities and backward and depressed classes;
>
> Wherein the independence of the judiciary shall be fully secured;
>
> Wherein the integrity of the territories of the Federation, its inde-
> pendence and all its rights, including its sovereign rights on land, sea, and
> air, shall be safeguarded;
>
> So that the people of Pakistan may prosper and attain their right-
> ful and honored place amongst the nations of the World and make
> their full contribution towards international peace and progress and
> happiness of humanity:
>
> Now, therefore, we, the people of Pakistan,
>
> Cognisant of our responsibility before Almighty Allah and men;
>
> Cognisant of the sacrifices made by the people in the cause of Pakistan;
>
> Faithful to the declaration made by the Founder of Pakistan, Quaid-i-
> Azam Mohammad Ali Jinnah,[2] that Pakistan would be a democratic State
> based on Islamic principles of social justice;

---

[1] **Holy Quran and Sunnah**   The Quran, the holy book of Islam, is Allah's word as revealed
to the prophet Muhammad; the Sunnah is a record of the sayings of Muhammad.

[2] **Mohammad Ali Jinnah (1876–1948)**   Indian politician who struggled since the 1920s to
create a separate Muslim state and managed to create Pakistan in 1947.

Dedicated to the preservation of democracy achieved by the unremitting struggle of the people against oppression and tyranny;

Inspired by the resolve to protect our national and political unity and solidarity by creating an egalitarian society through a new order;

Do hereby, through our representatives in the National Assembly, adopt, enact, and give to ourselves, this Constitution.

Thus we can see that there is a perfect constitutional template for democratic governance in the Muslim world. But the current poor relations between much of the West and much of the Islamic world may suggest the need for new terminology if we are to realize the vision. The word *secular*, used to denote separation of state and religion in the Western world, often means "atheism," or rejection of God, when translated into other languages, including into Urdu in Pakistan.

Instead of terms such as *secularism*, the director of the Study of Muslim Civilizations at the Aga Khan University in London, Dr. Abdou Filali-Ansary,[3] believes that we should refer directly to the individual building blocks of democracy—free elections, an independent judiciary, respect for women's and minority rights, the rule of law, and fundamental freedoms—to describe the true meaning of a democratic society. We shouldn't be talking secularism, which to Muslims is a clouded, misleading, and sometimes contentious term. Instead of using terms that fall into the rhetorical trap set by extremists to discredit the elements of modern democratic society, we should rather stress elements such as freedom to travel, freedom to work, opportunity for education for both sexes, the independence of the judiciary, and a robust civil society. These issues, more than the term *secularism*, connote the compatibility of Islam and democratic values.

Who can doubt that Islam—as a religion and as a value structure—has been distorted and manipulated for political reasons by militants and extremists and dictators. The establishment of the Afghan mujahideen by Zia[4] in the 1980s is an example. (After all, the jihad in Afghanistan aimed to rid the country of Soviet occupation, not reject modernity, technology, and pluralism, and to establish "strategic depth" in Pakistan. That was a political agenda of Zia.) Islam is now being used for purely political purposes by a group of people who are angry with the West. Religion is being exploited and manipulated for a political agenda, not a spiritual agenda.

The militants seethe with anger, but their anger is always tied to their political agenda. First, they were angry that the West had abandoned three million Afghan refugees and stopped all assistance to them after the Soviets

---

[3] **Abdou Filali-Ansary**   Professor of Islamic studies active in the Muslim Reformist tradition.

[4] **Muhammad Zia-ul-Haq (1924–1988)**   Dictator of Pakistan from 1979 until his death.

left Afghanistan. Second, they are angry that their offer to the government of Pakistan to send one hundred "battle-hardened mujahideen" to help in the Kashmir uprising of 1989 was rejected. Third, they wanted King Fahd[5] of Saudi Arabia to turn to their "battle-hardened mujahideen" to protect Saudi Arabia after Iraqi president Saddam Hussein[6] invaded Kuwait on August 2, 1990. He refused. Fourth, they went off to fight in Bosnia when the region was engulfed in war (from 1993 to 1996 I lobbied President Bill Clinton, Prime Minister John Major, and other European leaders to intervene to bring the conflict to an end). Fifth, they tried to exploit the Chechen nationalist movement. Sixth, with the fall of my government, they turned their attention to Kashmir and tried to take over the nationalist Kashmiri movement from 1997 onward.

Muslim extremists systematically targeted historical nationalist move- 10 ments to gain credibility and launch themselves into the Muslim heartland with a view to piggybacking off nationalist movements to advance their agenda. However, most Muslims were suspicious and not welcoming of their extreme interpretation of Islam. Thus it was only in Afghanistan, already softened by years of resistance by Afghan mujahideen, that Muslim extremists were able to establish the Taliban dictatorship.

Driven out of Afghanistan after the September 2001 attacks on the United 11 States, they returned to Pakistan, where the journey had begun with General Zia-ul-Haq in 1980.

After the United States invaded Iraq, these same extremists turned their 12 attention to that country. Abu Musab al-Zarqawi[7] went off to fight in Iraq. Presumably others did, too. Again they used religious propaganda to kill, maim, and effectively divide one of the richest Muslim countries, Iraq, into a land of carnage and bloodshed. Sunnis and Shias, who had lived peacefully side by side for centuries, began to kill each other, and Iraq began to fall apart. It is quite easy (and typical) for Muslim extremists to blame the Americans for the sectarian civil war that rages in Iraq today, when actually it is a long-standing tension between Muslim communities that has been exacerbated and militarized to create the chaos under which extremists thrive.

Iraq is not the only goal of the extremists. Pakistan too is in great danger. 13 Pro-Taliban forces have taken over the tribal areas of Pakistan. They occupy the Swat Valley. They have been ceded Waziristan by the Musharraf[8] regime.

---

[5] **King Fahd bin Abdul Aziz Al Saud (1923–2005)**   Ruler of Saudi Arabia from 1982–2005.

[6] **Saddam Hussein (1937–2006)**   Absolute ruler of Iraq from 1979–2003.

[7] **Abu Musab al-Zarqawi (1966–2006)**   An al-Qaeda terrorist.

[8] **Pervez Musharraf (b. 1943)**   A general who took control of the Pakistani government by coup in 1999 and ruled as president until 2008, when he went into self-imposed exile. He has been threatened with arrest if he returns to Pakistan.

They are moving into the settled areas of Pakistan. Their apparent next goal is the cities of my country, including our capital, Islamabad. They thrive on dictatorship; they thrive on terror; they provoke chaos to exploit chaos.

I returned to Pakistan on October 18, 2007, with the goal of moving my   14
country from dictatorship to democracy. I hoped that this transition could take place during the scheduled elections of 2008. I feared that otherwise the extremists would march toward Islamabad. Islamabad is near the town of Kahuta, where Pakistan's nuclear program is being carried out.

It is my fear that unless extremism is eliminated, the people of Pakistan   15
could find themselves in a contrived conflict deliberately triggered by the militants (or other "Islamists") who now threaten to take over Pakistan's nuclear assets. Having a large Muslim nation fall into chaos would be dangerous; having the only nuclear-armed Muslim nation fall into chaos would be catastrophic. My people could end up being bombed, their homes destroyed, and their children orphaned simply because a dictator has focused all his attention and all of the nation's resources on containing democrats instead of containing extremists, and then has used the crisis that he has created to justify those same policies that caused the crisis. It may sound convoluted, but there is certainly method to the madness.

This is such a tragedy, especially because Islam is clearly not only tolerant   16
of other religions and cultures but internally tolerant of dissent. Allah tells us over and over again, through the Quran, that he created people of different views and perspectives to see the world in different ways and that diversity is good. It is natural and part of God's plan. The Quran's message is open to and tolerant of women's full participation in society, it encourages knowledge and scientific experimentation, and it prohibits violence against innocents and suicide, despite terrorists' claims to the contrary.

Not only is Islam compatible with democracy, but the message of the   17
Quran empowers the people with rights (democracy), demanding consultation between rulers and ruled (parliament), and requiring that leaders serve the interests of the people or be replaced by them (accountability).

Islam was sent as a message of liberation. The challenge for modern-day   18
Muslims is to rescue this message from the fanatics, the bigots, and the forces of dictatorship. It is to give Muslims back the freedom God ordained for humankind to live in peace, in justice, in equality, in a system that is answerable to the people on this earth accepting that it is God who will judge us on the Day of Judgment.

It is by accepting that temporal and spiritual accountability are two   19
separate issues that we can provide peace, tranquillity, and opportunity. There are two judgments: the judgment of God's creatures in this world through a democratic system and the judgment by God when we leave this world. The extremists and militants who seek to hijack Islam aim to make their own

judgments. In their failure lies the future of all Muslims and the reconciliation of Islam and the West.

Islam and Democracy: History and Practice

Conventional wisdom would have us believe that democracy has failed to develop in the Muslim world because of Islam itself. According to this theory, somehow Islam and democracy are mutually exclusive because Islam is rooted in an authoritarianism that promotes dictatorship. I reject this thinking as convenient and simplistic, grounded in neither theology nor experience. As a Muslim who has lived under both democracy and dictatorship, I know that the reasons are far more complex.   20

The so-called incompatibility of Islam and democratic governance is used to divert attention from the sad history of Western political intervention in the Muslim world, which has been a major impediment to the growth of democracy in Islamic nations.   21

The actions of the West in the second half of the nineteenth century and most of the twentieth century often deliberately blocked any reasonable chance for democratic development in Muslim-majority countries. It is so discouraging to me that the actions of the West in the pursuit of its various short-term strategic goals have been counterproductive, often backfiring. Western policies have often preserved authoritarianism and contained the growth of nascent democratic movements in the developing world, specifically in the Islamic world. Western nations' efforts to disrupt democratic tides — initially for economic reasons and then for political ones — have fueled and exacerbated tensions between the West and Islam.   22

Despite often grand rhetoric to the contrary, there has been little real Western support for indigenous democratic movements. Indeed, too often there has been outright support for dictatorships. Both during the Cold War and now in the current battle with international terrorism, the shadow between Western rhetoric and Western actions has sowed the seeds of Muslim public disillusionment and cynicism. The double standards have fueled extremism and fanaticism. It accounts, at least in part, for the precipitous drop in respect for the West in the Muslim world. This trend is true even in pro-Western Muslim countries such as Turkey. When I was growing up, I thought of Western nations as inspirations for freedom and development. I still do, but I'm afraid I'm in a shrinking minority of Muslims.   23

There is an abundance of other examples that manifest the inconsistency of Western support for democracy in the Muslim world: specifically, Western actions that undermined democratic institutions, democratic movements, and democratically elected governments in countries that the West considered critical to other policy objectives. The countries range from   24 large to small, from very important to relatively insignificant. What is remarkable is the clear pattern of Western action: perceived pragmatic self-interest trumping the values of democracy, almost without exception. In a nation that is not relatively strategically important, such as Burma, the West will enforce its democratic creed quite enthusiastically, organizing trade embargoes and other forms of political isolation. But in places that are viewed as strategically important for economic or geopolitical factors, the West's commitment to democracy can often be more platitude than policy.

I raise this as not just a strategic inconsistency but a true moral dilemma 25 for the West, especially the United States. On one level the West speaks of democracy almost in the context of the values of religion, using rhetoric about liberty being a "God-given" right. And Western nations often take that standard abroad, preaching democratic values like missionaries preaching religion. The problem arises, of course, in its selective application to bilateral foreign policy relationships. I have always believed, and have publicly argued, that the selective application of morality is inherently immoral.

If dictatorship is bad, then dictators are bad—not just dictators who are 26 impotent and irrelevant but also those who are powerful allies in fighting common enemies. The West makes human rights the centerpiece of its foreign policy selectively. The West also stands four-square with struggling democracies selectively. In his second inaugural address, President George W. Bush said:

> We will encourage reform in other governments by making clear that success in our relations will require the decent treatment of their own people. America's belief in human dignity will guide our policies, yet rights must be more than the grudging concessions of dictators; they are secured by free dissent and the participation of the governed. In the long run, there is no justice without freedom, and there can be no human rights without human liberty.

President Bush's words notwithstanding, Washington supported Pakistan's 27 military dictator, General Musharraf, whom it considered a key ally in the war against terrorism, even as it simultaneously supported democracy in neighboring Afghanistan and in Iraq in the Middle East.

I am not the only one, of course, who has pointed to strategic and moral 28 inconsistencies in the application of Western political values abroad. Recently Noah Feldman wrote in the *New York Times Magazine* that "a republic that supports democratization selectively is another matter. President Bush's recent speech to the United Nations, in which he assailed seven repressive regimes, was worthy of applause—but it also opened the door to the fair criticism that he was silent about the dozens of places where the United States colludes with dictators of varying degrees of nastiness." Feldman specifically cites my homeland of Pakistan as one example but goes on to criticize

American support for Hosni Mubarak[9] of Egypt as Mubarak cracks down on the press and other political parties. Feldman adds that "Saudi Arabia—one [of the United States'] most powerful and durable allies—hasn't moved beyond the largely symbolic local council elections that it held two years ago." The United States, berating Burma and Iran for their undemocratic brutality, has had little to say about U.S. allies. Again, the selective application of morality is criticized as immoral in many nations whose people are also striving for democracy.

There is a clear relationship between dictatorship and religious fanaticism   29
that cannot be ignored. Carl Gershman,[10] the president of the National Endowment for Democracy, has referred to it as a relationship between autocrats and the Islamists. To the extent that international support for tyrannies within Islamic states has resulted in the hostility of the people of these countries to the West—and cynicism about the West's true commitment to democracy and human rights—some might say that the West has unintentionally created its own Frankenstein monster.

I cannot dispute that there have been few sustained democracies in the   30
Islamic world. But the responsibility does not lie in the text of the Muslim Holy Book. It is a responsibility shared by two significant elements that have come together in the context of environmental conditions inhospitable to the establishment, nurturing, and maintenance of democratic institutions in Muslim-majority societies.

The first element—the battle within Islam—is the purportedly theological   31
fight among factions of Islam that also often seeks raw political and economic power at the expense of the people. The second element—the responsibility of the West—includes a long colonial period that drained developing countries of both natural and human resources. During this time the West showed a cold indifference toward supporting democracy among Muslim states and leaders for reasons that were either economic (oil) or political (anticommunism).

We cannot minimize the fault line that has existed within Muslim nations,   32
a fault line of internal factionalism, disrespect for minority rights, and interventionist and often dysfunctional military institutions. These elements have often been accompanied by the presence of authoritarian political leadership. There is obviously a shared responsibility for democracy's weakness in Muslim-majority states, but there can be no disputing the fact that democratic governance in Muslim countries lags far behind that in most other parts of the world.

---

[9] **Hosni Mubarak (b. 1928)**   President of Egypt (1981–2011).

[10] **Carl Gershman (b. 1943)**   President of the National Endowment for Democracy since its founding in 1984.

A useful context for the history of democracy within Muslim countries   33
is provided by a brief review of current categorizations of political rights and
civil liberties around the world. It will then be possible to objectively compare
the Muslim and non-Muslim worlds on standards and criteria of democratic
development. Central to this analysis is something that I have always believed
and strongly endorse: that freedom and liberty are universal values that can
be applied across cultures, societies, religions, ethnic groups, and individual
national experiences. Democracy is not an inherently Western political value;
it is a universal value. Liberty means as much to someone from Indonesia as it
does to someone from Louisiana.

Freedom House (which was founded at the beginning of World War II by   34
First Lady Eleanor Roosevelt and Wendell Willkie,[11] the Republican candidate
whom her husband had just defeated for the presidency) is an international
nongovernmental organization (NGO) dedicated to promoting democracy,
human rights, and freedom around the world. Each year it engages scholars
from around the world to categorize governments on a scale of political rights
ranging from "totally free" to "not free." This useful analytical tool is based
on analyses of electoral processes, political pluralism and participation, and
how the government functions. Countries are scored on a numerical scale that
ranges from one to seven, with the highest number representing the lowest
level of freedom. This number is then used to determine one of three ratings:
free, partly free, or not free. In some cases, additional variables are used to
supplement the data. For example, for traditional monarchies international
scholars are additionally asked if the system provides for genuine, meaningful
consultation with the people, encourages public discussion of policy choices,
and permits petitioning the ruler.

The analysis is especially useful in evaluating political systems in predom-   35
inantly Muslim monarchies, because it integrates the elements of legitimate
secular government with the citizen consultation enshrined in the Quran. The
disparities in Freedom House ratings between the Muslim and non-Muslim
worlds are dramatic and statistically significant, but not particularly surprising.
It is important to remember, of course, that Muslim nations are very different
from Western nations in national experience. Specifically, Islamic law generally
has a role in government, whether in secular Islamic states such as Kazakhstan
or religiously ideological countries such as the Islamic Republic of Iran.

Of the forty-five predominantly Muslim states, only Indonesia, Mali, and   36
Senegal are considered free. Eighteen Muslim nations are considered partly

---

[11] **Eleanor Roosevelt (1884–1962)**   Social activist and wife of President Franklin Delano
Roosevelt; **Wendell Willkie (1892–1944)**   Roosevelt's opponent for the presidency in
1940.

free: Afghanistan, Albania, Bahrain, Bangladesh, Comoros, Djibouti, Gambia, Jordan, Kuwait, Kyrgyzstan, Lebanon, Malaysia, Mauritania, Morocco, Niger, Sierra Leone, Turkey, and Yemen.

Twenty-four predominantly Muslim nations are labeled not free: Azerbaijan, Brunei, Egypt, Palestine, Guinea, Iran, Iraq, Jordan, Kazakhstan, Libya, Maldives, Oman, Pakistan, Qatar, Saudi Arabia, Somalia, Sudan, Syria, Tajikistan, Tunisia, Turkmenistan, United Arab Emirates, Uzbekistan, and Western Sahara.   37

The mean score for political rights (on a scale of 1 to 7, with 1 being the   38
highest level of rights) in the Muslim world is 5.24, compared to 2.82 for the non-Muslim world. The mean score for civil liberties in Muslim countries is 4.78, compared to 2.71 for non-Muslim countries. These are significant differences. I believe that these differences are not the result of theology but rather a product of both Western manipulation and internal Muslim politicization of Islam.

One frequently overlooked detail in the analysis of Freedom House scores   39
is the difference between Arab and non-Arab Muslim-majority countries. In "An 'Arab' More than 'Muslim' Electoral Gap," Alfred Stephan and Graeme Robertson use two different indices of levels of political rights to compare these two types of Muslim-majority countries. The study contrasts the scores of countries in the Freedom House study and also in the Polity IV Indexes relative to GDP from 1972 to 2000, when the competitiveness of an election was questioned. (The Polity IV Project codes and compiles information on the regulation and competitiveness of political participation.)

The authors differentiate between "underachievers" and "over- achievers"   40
in electoral competitiveness, defined by such criteria as whether the government was selected by reasonably fair elections and whether the democratically elected government actually wields political power.

Stephan and Robertson found that a non-Arab Muslim-majority country   41
was astoundingly "almost 20 times more likely to be 'electorally competitive' than an Arab Muslim-majority country." Of the forty-seven Muslim-majority countries that they studied, the Arab Muslim countries formed "the largest single readily identifiable group among all those states that 'underachieve,'" but the world's thirty-one Muslim-majority non-Arab countries form the largest bloc that "greatly overachieves" in electoral competitiveness. In studying the thirty-eight countries in the world that suffer from extreme poverty, they found "no comparative Muslim gap whatsoever when it comes to political rights." Their findings suggest that the success of democracy within certain states has less to do with whether a country has a Muslim majority than was previously thought by Western analysts. The result shatters the hypothesis that religion is a key variable related to democracy and that Islam and democracy are inconsistent. It relegates the Islam-democracy incompatibility theory to the level of mythology.

Democracies do not spring up fully developed overnight, nor is there nec-   42
essarily a bright line between democratic governance and autocracy. More
typical, democracy can be seen on a continuum. Civil society and democratic
institutions such as political parties and NGOs tend to develop slowly over
time, one critical step at a time.

True democracy is defined not only by elections but by the democratic   43
governance that should follow. The most critical elements of democratic governance go beyond just free and fair elections to the protection of political
rights for those in political opposition, the open function of a civil society
and free press, and an independent judiciary. Far too often in the developing
world—including the Islamic developing world—elections are viewed as
zero-sum games. The electoral process is democratic, but that's where democracy ends. What follows is tantamount to one-party authoritarian rule. This is
the opposite of true democratic governance, which is predicated on shared
constitutional power and responsibility. And because democratic governance
rests on a continuum of experience, the length of that experience is directly
related to the sustainability of democratic governance itself. In other words,
the longer democratic governance is maintained, the stronger the democratic
system becomes.

A democracy that is more than two hundred years old is not in serious   44
danger of interruption or of suspension of constitutional norms. It has a
two-century-old firewall of democratic history and practice to protect itself
from extraconstitutional abuse of power. A nation without such a long history of democracy and democratic institutions—political parties; a popularly
elected, legitimate, sovereign parliament; NGOs; free media; and an independent judiciary—is vulnerable to the suspension of the democratic order.
We must think of a new democracy like a seedling that must be nourished,
watered, fed, and given time to develop into a mighty tree. Thus, when democratic experiments are prematurely interrupted or disrupted, the effects can
be, if not permanent, certainly long lasting. Internal or external interruptions
of democracy (both elections and governance) can have effects that ripple and
linger over generations.

We must be realistic and pragmatic about democracy. John F. Kennedy   45
once referred to himself as an "idealist without illusions." To me this is a useful
description as I think in particular of my country moving from the brutality of
dictatorship to the civility of democracy. When confronted with tyranny, one
is tempted to go to the barricades directly, when pragmatism would dictate
exhausting other potential (and peaceful) remedies. As I have grown in maturity and experience, I remain as strongly committed to the cause but more
patient in finding means to achieve goals peacefully.

The colonial experience of many Muslim countries had contributed to   46
their difficulties in sustaining democracy. In the absence of adequate support

and without the time and commitment needed to build a democratic infrastructure, they failed to strengthen their electoral and governing processes. Many of the countries discussed in this chapter were exposed to democratic values, democratic ideals, and the gradual development of political and social institutions while under colonial rule or shortly thereafter. However, their nascent democratic seeds were often smothered by the strategic interests of Western powers (often working with elements within their own societies) before they flowered into viable democratic systems.

✂ QUESTIONS FOR CRITICAL READING

1. How effective is Bhutto's use of examples? Which example is most powerful?

2. How does Bhutto see the relationship between the spiritual and the worldly obligations of Muslims?

3. When Bhutto says it is a sin to take innocent life, do you think she implies that taking a life that is not innocent is somehow acceptable?

4. What seem to be some of the basic religious beliefs that Bhutto credits as Islamic in the early part of her essay? How different are they from the beliefs of other religions?

5. What does the suggestion that the Koran promotes diversity have to do with the possibility of Islam's supporting democracies?

6. Why would people today feel that Islam might not support a democratic government?

7. How convincing is Bhutto in this selection? Besides the Koran, what other sources does she use to bolster her argument?

✂ SUGGESTIONS FOR CRITICAL WRITING

1. In paragraph 15, Bhutto raises the question of extremists getting control of Pakistan's nuclear plants and their nuclear weapons. How serious is this possibility? How worried does she seem about this possibility? How worried are you? What should be done if there is such a threat, and who should respond to the threat?

2. In paragraph 29, Bhutto says that "the West has unintentionally created its own Frankenstein monster." What does she mean by this statement? Examine her position in the paragraphs before and after this comment (which she has often used in speeches). How well has she supported her argument? What methods has she used to support the argument? Do you feel that she is correct, or are you not convinced?

3. **CONNECTIONS**   Compare the preamble of Pakistan's Constitution with the Constitution of the United States. On what issues do the two documents agree?

What seem to be the primary differences between these constitutions? What issues are included in Pakistan's Constitution that are not present in the U.S. Constitution? What is important in the U.S. Constitution that is either omitted from or of lesser importance in the Pakistan Constitution? Does the excerpt from Pakistan's Constitution convince you that its intention is to produce a democratic government?

4. Bhutto says that dictators who are favored by the West help extremists, especially by uniting them in their dislike of the United States. How do dictators help the causes of extremists in Muslim countries? Bhutto talks a good deal about Afghanistan and the Taliban. Research the current situation in Afghanistan and its history since the Russian invasion. Then decide whether or not Afghanistan is a good example for Bhutto to use in her complaint that the West must bear a share of the responsibility for the presence of dictators in Muslim countries.

5. What are the realistic choices for the West in its dealings with nations such as Saudi Arabia, which has a great deal of oil but little in the way of civil rights? Women, for instance, cannot drive cars. There are no elections for a president or prime minister nor for a parliament. Before he was overthrown, Hosni Mubarak ruled Egypt with an iron hand and denied thousands of people their civil rights, but he guaranteed the security of Israel and kept the Suez Canal open for international trade and military shipping. Should the West demand that these nations become democratic and respect human civil rights? If they don't follow through, what should the West do?

6. Read the Koran for evidence to support Bhutto's claim that the Muslim holy book supports diversity, equality of men and women, civil rights, and a democratic approach to government. Argue a case in favor of Bhutto's position or against it. Use testimony from the Koran to bolster your argument.

7. **CONNECTIONS**   In paragraph 7, Benazir Bhutto states that the term "secularism" is a problem for Muslims. Her argument is that the religion of Islam is not an impediment to democracy. Neither Alexis de Tocqueville (p. 139) nor Ralph Waldo Emerson (p. 124) makes distinct references to religion in government. They do, however, comment on the question of freedom, which Bhutto makes a point to emphasize. Write an essay that explains the common ground that Bhutto has with both Tocqueville and Emerson. To what extent is it possible to imagine a separation of church and state in Bhutto's commentary? Why is the separation of church and state important in a democracy?

Reflections on the Nature of Government

Now that you have read the selections in "Government," consider in what ways these writers have helped further inform your views of the role of government in your life.

1. How do these writers help you define what government is?

2. What do these writers say is your own role in government?

3. Where do you think the source of power is in our government?

4. Have these essays made you feel more or less confident in the future of our government?

5. How have your ideas on the "sanctity" of property been affected by these essays?

6. What is the difference between *good* government and *bad* government?

7. Some writers say that the best government is the least government. How do you react to this idea? How little government would you tolerate?

8. How serious is the conflict between individual rights and community rights in today's government?

9. How do you feel about the future of democracy?

10. Which author made the most difference in helping clarify your views of government?

PART TWO

CULTURE

Introduction

Be good, be kind, be humane, and charitable. Love your fellows, console the afflicted, pardon those who have done you wrong.
　—ZOROASTER

Male and female citizens, being equal in the eyes of the law, must be equally admitted to all honors, positions, and public employment according to their capacity and without other distinctions besides those of their virtues and talents.
　—OLYMPE DE GOUGES (1748–1793)

The highest possible stage in moral culture is when we recognize that we ought to control our thoughts.
　—CHARLES DARWIN (1809–1882)

Let us be grateful to people who make us happy. They are the charming gardeners who make our souls.
　—MARCEL PROUST (1871–1922)

I imagine one of the reasons people cling to their hates so stubbornly is because they sense, once hate is gone, they will be forced to deal with pain.
　—JAMES BALDWIN (1924–1987)

It is a sure sign that a culture has reached a dead end when it is no longer intrigued by its myths.
　—GREIL MARCUS (b. 1945)

Class, race, sexuality, gender, and all other categories by which we categorize and dismiss each other need to be excavated from the inside.
　—DOROTHY ALLISON (b. 1949)

In many ways, the question of human culture is embedded in the question of human values. Our modern culture in the Western world is changing in so many ways that it is difficult to understand the implications of change. The values that our grandparents held are often quite different from those that we hold today. Just taking into account the kinds of advertising that appear regularly on commercial television, we can see that our forebears would have been scandalized by ads for Viagra and women's underwear. They would have been mystified by the music and literature that young people enjoy. They would have been puzzled by interracial marriage and the marriage of same-sex partners, both of which are now commonplace and legal throughout all of the country and in Europe. The emergence of transgender people would have been almost incomprehensible.

Gender and racial inequities were accepted by most of the population of the United States until the mid-nineteenth century. Questions of law and justice were beginning to take form around that time, but change seemed a bit slower in those days until the Civil War upended most political values. Yet up through the 1960s, most of the nation remained segregated, and the efforts to change the values associated with segregation resulted in protests in the streets and police brutality to control them.

Mary Wollstonecraft (1759–1797) wrote in a time of extreme political change: when revolution was erupting in the American colonies in 1776 and in France in 1789. Kings and aristocrats were losing their heads, literally. Monarchies were giving way to republics. During this period democracy in its modern forms began to grace the lives of some, whereas tyranny oppressed others. Even though radical changes took place in some areas, a conservative backlash in England and elsewhere threatened to heighten oppression rather than expand freedom. Although Wollstonecraft is known today chiefly for her feminist works, she was also engaged in the radical political thought of the time. For example, her defense of the ideals of the French Revolution in *A Vindication of the Rights of Men* (1790) brought her work to the attention of other radical thinkers such as William Godwin (whom she later married), Thomas Paine, William Blake, and William Wordsworth.

Still, Wollstonecraft's name remains a keystone in the history of feminism. She went on to write one of the most important books of the late eighteenth century, *Vindication of the Rights of Woman* (1792), and is remembered most for her careful analysis of a society that did not value the gifts and talents of women. Her complaint is based on a theory of efficiency and economics: it is a waste to limit the opportunities of women. By making her appeal in this fashion she may have expected to gain the attention of the men who held power in late-eighteenth-century England. Some of them did listen. By the 1830s, at the height of the industrial revolution, women were often employed outside the home. However, they were frequently given the most wretched jobs (such as in mining) and were not accorded the kind of respect and opportunity that Wollstonecraft envisioned. They often became drudges in a process of industrial development that demeaned their humanity.

Twenty-five years after the Civil War in the United States, Jacob A. Riis (1849–1914), a muckraking journalist, studied the conditions of life among the poor in New York. His book *How the Other Half Lives* (1890), which exposed what life was like for people living in extreme poverty in New York City, was shocking for many citizens. The tenement life was marked by unsanitary conditions, rent gouging, and astonishing overcrowding. The world of the slums of New York was almost unknown to those living in comfort, but Riis's work brought it to the attention of Theodore Roosevelt, who was then the police commissioner of New York. Eventually, changes were implemented to alleviate the pain of the poor. In his essay, Riis addresses the attitudes of landlords toward African American tenants, many of whom had migrated from the South in the decades after the end of slavery. In revealing their unethical treatment at the hands of the landlords of the city, Riis also reveals his own admiration for African Americans and points out that they were better tenants than many of the white emigrants who were charged lower rents. At the same time, Riis reveals some of the prejudicial values of his time even while praising "colored citizens."

In 1929, the novelist and essayist Virginia Woolf (1882–1941) considered the question of how gifted women could hope to achieve important works if the current and historical patterns of oppression were to continue. Her book *A Room of One's Own* was addressed originally to a group of women studying at Cambridge in the two colleges reserved for them at the time. Woolf regarded these women appropriately as gifted, but she worried for their future because their opportunities in postwar England were quite limited. In a stroke of brilliance, Woolf demonstrates the pattern that oppresses gifted women by imagining for William Shakespeare an equally gifted sister named Judith and then tracing her probable development in sixteenth-century England. What chance would Judith have had to be a world-famous figure like her brother? Woolf's discussion is so lifelike and so well realized that it stands as a classic in modern feminist literature.

Margaret Mead (1901–1978) brings a very different kind of authority to the gender question because it was one of her primary research topics when she lived among various tribal groups in Papua New Guinea. She is famous for having studied closely the sexual development of women in societies that had not been totally altered by contact with modern Europeans. She discovered that the roles thought appropriate to men and women in our society were not always the same in the Mundugumor (now Biwat) society, which demonstrated a considerable capacity for change. Mead warns against societies that standardize genders and adhere to rigid expectations. She cautions that individuals who do not have the temperaments that their society thinks gender appropriate will suffer great pain and frustration. She points to the berdache, the "men-women" of the Plains Indians who were valued for their all-encompassing skills, which transcended sex roles.

"Letter from Birmingham Jail" was written by Martin Luther King Jr. (1929–1968) while he sat in a cell after a protest against segregation in everyday life in Mississippi in 1963. Although the protest was against the state laws that prohibited the intermingling of blacks and whites in public venues in the South, informal segregation existed in most of the rest of the nation. In the middle of the twentieth century, the changes that Jacob A. Riis had thought were coming were slow to arrive. King addresses his fellow clergy, the people who, despite the Christian values they were expected to uphold, hoped King would modify his demands. Their values had not kept up with his. The clergy prayed for change, but slow change. King knew that meant little change, particularly in the prejudices that held sway against African Americans. An important achievement of Martin Luther King Jr. was to help Americans change their values and create a culture of acceptance and understanding.

While Martin Luther King Jr. was fighting for justice, the modern thinker who has had the most lasting effect on the concept of justice is John Rawls (1921–2002). In his book *A Theory of Justice*, he examines the ideas of Plato and Aristotle and defends the rights of the individual against the demands of the state in insisting on justice as fairness. In this selection from his book, which includes the main idea of his theory of justice, Rawls takes a view that differs from those of many practical thinkers. He feels that any just society will provide certain "Primary Goods," such as freedom, equality, and opportunity, to every citizen. He also feels that the justice of any law ought to be measured by its effect on the least advantaged citizens rather than the greatest number of citizens. His view is radical, and his argument in favor of it is carefully couched. By insisting on a culture of fairness, Rawls touches on some of the most apparently basic human values of any age.

Neil Postman's (1931–2003) essay focuses on the ways language can shape our values and our understanding of the world. Words, he tells us, help us map our environment and, in some ways, both limit and expand our awareness of our world. He explains that language creates our understanding of just about everything. He describes the power of metaphor as controlling meaning in order to convince the reader. He introduces us to the thinking of Alfred Korzybski, the scholar who most helped define the study of semantics, the science of the meaning of words. Postman was fearful that television and other electronic sources of entertainment would rob children of their childhood by introducing them to adult subject matter too early in life. He had thought that television would be a great aid in education, but he changed his mind when he realized that what children need more is early exposure to texts in order to develop more fully their language faculties.

Our cultural values regarding gender identification and gender essentialism are currently in flux. Judith Butler (b. 1956) addresses these values in the selection from her book *Undoing Gender* (2004). She examines a young boy's mutilation in infancy that resulted in his being raised as a girl. The problems that this young child faced were complicated by other children's ridicule as well as by the constant examination by doctors who were supervising the transgender experiment. Butler's essay is essentially an analysis of the narrative of the boy's experiences. She questions the reliability of the boy's narrative and asks us to examine it in depth to reach an understanding of the boy's true experience. The issues of gender dimorphism and society's limiting view of gender are among her primary concerns.

These essays represent a number of ways our culture interprets differences among people. Different ethnic groups are sometimes stereotyped, as in the fashion of Jacob A. Riis, who is himself a completely well-meaning man. Differences in opportunity create distinctions that in earlier times were thought to be inbred rather than the result of environment and chance. For many years, the values that shape our laws have been based on what is good for the greatest number of people, but John Rawls reminds us that the highest human values aim to protect the weakest among us. Martin Luther King Jr. took a Rawlsian position in jail, having been incarcerated for trying to change laws that did not protect the weakest, but protected the strongest among us. Cultural values are in flux in all ages, but in our time, as in the past, changes in values meet resistance, especially from the established people in society. The writers in this section remind us how change happens and why.

Some Considerations about the Nature of Culture

Before reading the selections that follow, consider what your views of culture are. Reflect on the following questions and write out your responses. Discuss your answers with your classmates.

1. To what extent are you in agreement that culture involves the question of human values?

2. How important is fairness to our sense of appropriate values in society?

3. How does society shape its cultural values?

4. Why are there often clashes in values between people in the same community?

5. How does our culture treat differences among peoples?

6. Why do cultural values about, say, sex, gender, or ethnicity change?

7. Which cultural values have changed in an evolutionary way?

8. Which cultural values have changed abruptly?

9. Which values does our culture seem to have adopted that offend your values?

10. Which cultural values do you hold that are not held by older members of your family?

MARY
WOLLSTONECRAFT

Of the Pernicious Effects Which Arise from the Unnatural Distinctions Established in Society

© Hulton Archive/Getty Images

MARY WOLLSTONECRAFT (1759–1797) was born into relatively modest circumstances, with a father whose heavy drinking and spending eventually ruined the family and left her and her sisters to support themselves. She became a governess, a teacher, and eventually a writer. Her views were among the most enlightened of her day, particularly regarding women and women's rights, giving her the reputation of being a very forward-looking feminist for her time, and even for ours. Her thinking, however, is comprehensive and not limited to a single issue.

She was known to the American patriot Thomas Paine (1737–1809), to Dr. Samuel Johnson (1709–1783), and to the English philosopher William Godwin (1756–1836), whom she eventually married. Her views on marriage were remarkable for her time; among other beliefs, she felt it unnecessary to marry a man in order to live happily with him. Her first liaison, with an American, Gilbert Imlay, gave her the opportunity to travel and learn something about commerce and capitalism at first hand. Her second liaison, with Godwin, brought her into the intellectual circles of her day. She married Godwin when she was pregnant, and died in childbirth. Her daughter, Mary, married the poet Percy Bysshe Shelley and wrote the novel *Frankenstein* (1818).

The excitement generated by the French Revolution (1789–1799) caused Wollstonecraft to react against the very conservative view put forward by the philosopher Edmund Burke. Her pamphlet *A Vindication of the Rights of Men* (1790) was well received. She followed it with *Vindication of the Rights of Woman* (1792), which was translated into French.

From *Vindication of the Rights of Woman.*

She saw feminism in political terms. The chapter reprinted here concentrates on questions of property, class, and law. As a person committed to the revolutionary principles of liberty, equality, and fraternity, Wollstonecraft linked the condition of women to the political and social structure of her society. Her aim was to point out the inequities in the treatment of women — which her society simply did not perceive — and to attempt to rectify them.

WOLLSTONECRAFT'S RHETORIC

Mary Wollstonecraft wrote for an audience that did not necessarily appreciate brief, exact expression. Rather, they appreciated a more luxuriant and leisurely style than we use today. As a result, her prose can sometimes seem wordy to a modern audience. However, she handles imagery carefully (especially in the first paragraph) without overburdening her prose. She uses an approach that she calls "episodical observations" (para. 12). These are anecdotes — personal stories — and apparently casual cataloguings of thoughts on a number of related issues. She was aware that her structure was not tight, that it did not develop a specific argument, and that it did not force the reader to accept or reject her position. She also considered this a wise approach because it was obvious to her that her audience was completely prejudiced against her view. To attempt to convince them of her views was to invite total defeat.

Instead, she simply puts forward several observations that stand by themselves as examples of the evils she condemns. Even those who stand against her will see that there is validity to her claims; and they will not be so threatened by her argument as to become defensive before they have learned something new. She appeals always to the higher intellectual capacities of both men and women, directing her complaints, too, against both men and women. This balance of opinion, coupled with a range of thought-provoking examples, makes her views clear and convincing.

Also distinctive in this passage is the use of metaphor. The second sentence of paragraph 1 is particularly heavy with metaphor: "For it is in the most polished society that noisome reptiles and venomous serpents lurk under the rank herbage; and there is voluptuousness pampered by the still sultry air, which relaxes every good disposition before it ripens into virtue." The metaphor presents society as a garden in which the grass is decaying and dangerous serpents are lurking. Good disposition — character — is a plant that might ripen, but — continuing the metaphor — it ripens into virtue. A favorite source of metaphors for Wollstonecraft is drapery (dressmaking). When she uses one of these metaphors she is usually reminding the reader that drapery gives a new shape to things, that it sometimes hides the truth, and that it ought not to put a false appearance on what it covers.

One of her rhetorical techniques is that of literary allusion. By alluding to important literary sources — such as Greek mythology, William Shakespeare, Jean-Jacques Rousseau, and Samuel Johnson — she not only demonstrates her knowledge but also shows that she respects her audience, which she presumes shares the same knowledge. She does not show off by overquoting or by referring to very obscure writers. She balances her allusions perfectly, even transforming folk aphorisms into "homely proverbs" such as "whoever the devil finds idle he will employ."

Wollstonecraft's experiences with her difficult father gave her knowledge of gambling tables and card games, another source of allusions. She draws further on personal experience — shared by some of her audience — when she talks about the degradation felt by a woman of intelligence forced to act as a governess — a glorified servant — in a well-to-do family. Wollstonecraft makes excellent uses of these allusions, never overdoing them, always giving them just the right touch.

‣ PREREADING QUESTIONS: WHAT TO READ FOR

The following prereading questions may help you anticipate key issues in the discussion of Mary Wollstonecraft's "Of the Pernicious Effects Which Arise from the Unnatural Distinctions Established in Society." Keeping them in mind during your first reading of the selection should help focus your attention.

1. What are some of the pernicious effects that Wollstonecraft decries?
2. What kinds of work are women fit for, in Wollstonecraft's view?
3. What happens to people who are born to wealth and have nothing to do?

Of the Pernicious Effects Which Arise from the Unnatural Distinctions Established in Society

From the respect paid to property flow, as from a poisoned fountain, most of the evils and vices which render this world such a dreary scene to the contemplative mind. For it is in the most polished society that noisome reptiles and venomous serpents lurk under the rank herbage; and there is voluptuousness pampered by the still sultry air, which relaxes every good disposition before it ripens into virtue. 1

One class presses on another; for all are aiming to procure respect on account of their property: and property, once gained, will procure the respect due only to talents and virtue. Men neglect the duties incumbent on man, yet are treated like demi-gods; religion is also separated from morality by a ceremonial veil, yet men wonder that the world is almost, literally speaking, a den of sharpers or oppressors. 2

There is a homely proverb, which speaks a shrewd truth, that whoever the devil finds idle he will employ. And what but habitual idleness can hereditary 3 wealth and titles produce? For man is so constituted that he can only attain a proper use of his faculties by exercising them, and will not exercise them unless necessity of some kind first set the wheels in motion. Virtue likewise can only be acquired by the discharge of relative duties; but the importance of these sacred duties will scarcely be felt by the being who is cajoled out of his humanity by the flattery of sycophants.[1] There must be more equality established in society, or morality will never gain ground, and this virtuous equality will not rest firmly even when founded on a rock, if one half of mankind be chained to its bottom by fate, for they will be continually undermining it through ignorance or pride.

It is vain to expect virtue from women till they are in some degree indepen-   4 dent of men; nay, it is vain to expect that strength of natural affection which would make them good wives and mothers. Whilst they are absolutely dependent on their husbands they will be cunning, mean, and selfish, and the men who can be gratified by the fawning fondness of spaniel-like affection have not much delicacy, for love is not to be bought, in any sense of the words; its silken wings are instantly shrivelled up when anything beside a return in kind is sought. Yet whilst wealth enervates men, and women live, as it were, by their personal charms, how can we expect them to discharge those ennobling duties which equally require exertion and self-denial? Hereditary property sophisticates[2] the mind, and the unfortunate victims to it, if I may so express myself, swathed from their birth, seldom exert the locomotive faculty of body or mind; and, thus viewing everything through one medium, and that a false one, they are unable to discern in what true merit and happiness consist. False, indeed, must be the light when the drapery of situation hides the man, and makes him stalk in masquerade, dragging from one scene of dissipation to another the nerveless limbs that hang with stupid listlessness, and rolling round the vacant eye which plainly tells us that there is no mind at home.

I mean, therefore, to infer[3] that the society is not properly organized which   5 does not compel men and women to discharge their respective duties, by making it the only way to acquire that countenance from their fellow-creatures which every human being wishes some way to attain. The respect, consequently, which is paid to wealth and mere personal charms, is a true north-east blast that blights the tender blossoms of affection and virtue. Nature has wisely attached affections to duties to sweeten toil, and to give that vigor to the exertions of reason which only the heart can give. But the affection which is put on merely because it is the appropriated insignia of a certain character, when its duties are not fulfilled, is one of the empty compliments which vice and folly are obliged to pay to virtue and the real nature of things.

---

[1] **sycophants**   Toadies or false flatterers.

[2] **sophisticates**   Ruins or corrupts.

[3] **infer**   Imply.

To illustrate my opinion, I need only observe that when a woman is admired   6
for her beauty, and suffers herself to be so far intoxicated by the admiration
she receives as to neglect to discharge the indispensable duty of a mother, she
sins against herself by neglecting to cultivate an affection that would equally
tend to make her useful and happy. True happiness, I mean all the contentment
and virtuous satisfaction that can be snatched in this imperfect state, must
arise from well regulated affections; and an affection includes a duty. Men are
not aware of the misery they cause and the vicious weakness they cherish by
only inciting women to render themselves pleasing; they do not consider that
they thus make natural and artificial duties clash by sacrificing the comfort and
respectability of a woman's life to voluptuous notions of beauty when in nature
they all harmonize.

Cold would be the heart of a husband, were he not rendered unnatural by   7
early debauchery, who did not feel more delight at seeing his child suckled by
its mother, than the most artful wanton tricks could ever raise; yet this natural
way of cementing the matrimonial tie and twisting esteem with fonder recol-
lections, wealth leads women to spurn. To preserve their beauty and wear the
flowery crown of the day, which gives them a kind of right to reign for a short
time over the sex, they neglect to stamp impressions on their husbands' hearts
that would be remembered with more tenderness when the snow on the head
began to chill the bosom than even their virgin charms. The maternal solicitude
of a reasonable affectionate woman is very interesting, and the chastened dignity with which a mother returns the caresses that she and her child receive
from a father who has been fulfilling the serious duties of his station, is not
only a respectable but a beautiful sight. So singular indeed are my feelings,
and I have endeavored not to catch factitious[4] ones, that after having been
fatigued with the sight of insipid grandeur and the slavish ceremonies that with
cumbrous pomp supplied the place of domestic affections, I have turned to
some other scene to relieve my eye by resting it on the refreshing green everywhere scattered by nature. I have then viewed with pleasure a woman nursing
her children, and discharging the duties of her station with, perhaps, merely a
servant maid to take off her hands the servile part of the household business. I
have seen her prepare herself and children, with only the luxury of cleanliness,
to receive her husband, who returning weary home in the evening found smiling babes and a clean hearth. My heart has loitered in the midst of the group,
and has even throbbed with sympathetic emotion, when the scraping of the
well known foot has raised a pleasing tumult.

Whilst my benevolence has been gratified by contemplating this artless   8
picture, I have thought that a couple of this description, equally necessary
and independent of each other, because each fulfilled the respective duties of

---

[4] **factitious**   False.

their station, possessed all that life could give. Raised sufficiently above abject poverty not to be obliged to weigh the consequence of every farthing they spend, and having sufficient to prevent their attending to a frigid system of economy, which narrows both heart and mind, I declare, so vulgar[5] are my conceptions, that I know not what is wanted to render this the happiest as well as the most respectable situation in the world, but a taste for literature, to throw a little variety and interest into social converse, and some superfluous money to give to the needy and to buy books. For it is not pleasant when the heart is opened by compassion and the head active in arranging plans of usefulness, to have a prim urchin continually twitching back the elbow to prevent the hand from drawing out an almost empty purse, whispering at the same time some prudential maxim about the priority of justice.

Destructive, however, as riches and inherited honors are to the human character, women are more debased and cramped, if possible, by them than men, because men may still, in some degree, unfold their faculties by becoming soldiers and statesmen.   9

As soldiers, I grant, they can now only gather, for the most part, vainglorious laurels, whilst they adjust to a hair the European balance, taking especial care that no bleak northern nook or sound incline the beam.[6] But the days of true heroism are over, when a citizen fought for his country like a Fabricius[7] or a Washington, and then returned to his farm to let his virtuous fervor run in a more placid, but not a less salutary, stream. No, our British heroes are oftener sent from the gaming table than from the plough[8] and their passions have been rather inflamed by hanging with dumb suspense on the turn of a die, than sublimated by panting after the adventurous march of virtue in the historic page.   10

The statesman, it is true, might with more propriety quit the faro bank, or card table, to guide the helm, for he has still but to shuffle and trick.[9] The whole system of British politics, if system it may courteously be called, consisting in multiplying dependents and contriving taxes which grind the poor   11

---

[5] **vulgar**   Common.

[6] **incline the beam**   The metaphor is of the balance—the scale that representations of blind justice hold up. Wollstonecraft's point is that in her time soldiers fought to prevent the slightest changes in a balance of power that grew ever more delicate, not in heroic wars with heroic consequences.

[7] **Fabricius (fl. 282 b.c.e.)**   Gaius Fabricius, a worthy Roman general and statesman known for resistance to corruption.

[8] **from the plough**   Worthy Roman heroes were humble farmers, not gamblers.

[9] **shuffle and trick**   The upper class spent much of its time gambling: faro is a high-stakes card game. Wollstonecraft is ironic when she says the statesman has "still but to shuffle and trick," but she connects the "training" of faro with the practice of politics in a deft, sardonic fashion. She is punning on the multiple meanings of *shuffle*—to mix up a deck of cards and to move oneself or one's papers about slowly and aimlessly—and *trick*—to win one turn of a card game and to do a devious deed.

to pamper the rich; thus a war, or any wild goose chase, is, as the vulgar use the phrase, a lucky turn-up of patronage for the minister, whose chief merit is the art of keeping himself in place. It is not necessary then that he should have bowels for[10] the poor, so he can secure for his family the odd trick. Or should some show of respect, for what is termed with ignorant ostentation an Englishman's birthright, be expedient to bubble the gruff mastiff[11] that he has to lead by the nose, he can make an empty show very safely by giving his single voice and suffering his light squadron to file off to the other side. And when a question of humanity is agitated he may dip a sop in the milk of human kindness to silence Cerberus,[12] and talk of the interest which his heart takes in an attempt to make the earth no longer cry for vengeance as it sucks in its children's blood, though his cold hand may at the very moment rivet their chains by sanctioning the abominable traffic. A minister is no longer a minister than while he can carry a point which he is determined to carry. Yet it is not necessary that a minister should feel like a man, when a bold push might shake his seat.

But, to have done with these episodical observations, let me return to the more specious slavery which chains the very soul of woman, keeping her forever under the bondage of ignorance.   12

The preposterous distinctions of rank, which render civilization a curse by dividing the world between voluptuous tyrants and cunning envious dependents, corrupt, almost equally, every class of people, because respectability is not attached to the discharge of the relative duties of life, but to the station, and when the duties are not fulfilled the affections cannot gain sufficient strength to fortify the virtue of which they are the natural reward. Still there are some loopholes out of which a man may creep, and dare to think and act for himself; but for a woman it is a herculean task, because she has difficulties peculiar to her sex to overcome which require almost superhuman powers.   13

A truly benevolent legislator always endeavors to make it the interest of each individual to be virtuous; and thus private virtue becoming the cement of public happiness, an orderly whole is consolidated by the tendency of all the parts towards a common center. But, the private or public virtue of woman is very problematical; for Rousseau, and a numerous list of male writers, insist that she should all her life be subjected to a severe restraint, that of propriety. Why subject her to propriety—blind propriety, if she be capable of acting from a nobler spring, if she be an heir of immortality? Is sugar always to be produced by vital blood? Is one half of the human species, like the poor African slaves, to be subject to prejudices that brutalize them, when principles would be a surer   14

---

[10] **bowels for**   Feelings for; sense of pity.

[11] **to bubble the gruff mastiff**   To fool even a guard dog.

[12] **Cerberus**   The guard dog of Hades, the Greek hell or underworld.

guard, only to sweeten the cup of man? Is not this indirectly to deny woman reason? For a gift is a mockery, if it be unfit for use.

Women are, in common with men, rendered weak and luxurious by the   15
relaxing pleasures which wealth procures; but added to this they are made slaves to their persons, and must render them alluring that man may lend them his reason to guide their tottering steps aright. Or should they be ambitious, they must govern their tyrants by sinister tricks, for without rights there cannot be any incumbent duties. The laws respecting woman, which I mean to discuss in a future part, make an absurd unit of a man and his wife,[13] and then, by the easy transition of only considering him as responsible, she is reduced to a mere cypher.[14]

The being who discharges the duties of its station is independent; and,   16
speaking of women at large, their first duty is to themselves as rational crea-tures, and the next in point of importance, as citizens, is that which includes so many, of a mother. The rank in life which dispenses with their fulfilling this duty necessarily degrades them by making them mere dolls. Or, should they turn to something more important than merely fitting drapery upon a smooth block, their minds are only occupied by some soft platonic attachment; or, the actual management of an intrigue may keep their thoughts in motion; for when they neglect domestic duties, they have it not in their own power to take the field and march and counter-march like soldiers, or wrangle in the senate to keep their faculties from rusting.

I know that, as a proof of the inferiority of the sex, Rousseau has exultingly   17
exclaimed, How can they leave the nursery for the camp![15] And the camp has by some moralists been termed the school of the most heroic virtues; though, I think, it would puzzle a keen casuist[16] to prove the reasonableness of the greater number of wars that have dubbed heroes. I do not mean to consider this question critically; because, having frequently viewed these freaks of ambition as the first natural mode of civilization, when the ground must be torn up, and the woods cleared by fire and sword, I do not choose to call them pests; but surely the present system of war has little connection with virtue of any denom-ination, being rather the school of *finesse* and effeminacy than of fortitude.

Yet if defensive war, the only justifiable war, in the present advanced state   18
of society, where virtue can show its face and ripen amidst the rigors which purify the air on the mountain's top, were alone to be adopted as just and

---

[13] **absurd unit of a man and his wife**   In English law man and wife were legally one; the man spoke for both.

[14] **cypher**   Zero.

[15] **leave the nursery for the camp!**   Rousseau's Émile complains that women cannot leave a nursery to go to war.

[16] **casuist**   One who argues closely, persistently, and sometimes unfairly.

glorious, the true heroism of antiquity might again animate female bosoms. But fair and softly, gentle reader, male or female, do not alarm thyself, for though I have compared the character of a modern soldier with that of a civilized woman, I am not going to advise them to turn their distaff[17] into a musket, though I sincerely wish to see the bayonet converted into a pruning-hook. I only recreated an imagination, fatigued by contemplating the vices and follies which all proceed from a feculent[18] stream of wealth that has muddied the pure rills of natural affection, by supposing that society will some time or other be so constituted, that man must necessarily fulfill the duties of a citizen or be despised, and that while he was employed in any of the departments of civil life, his wife, also an active citizen, should be equally intent to manage her family, educate her children, and assist her neighbors.

But, to render her really virtuous and useful, she must not, if she discharge her civil duties, want, individually, the protection of civil laws; she must not be dependent on her husband's bounty for her subsistence during his life or support after his death—for how can a being be generous who has nothing of its own? or virtuous, who is not free? 19

The wife, in the present state of things, who is faithful to her husband, and neither suckles nor educates her children, scarcely deserves the name of a wife, and has no right to that of a citizen. But take away natural rights, and duties become null. 20

Women then must be considered as only the wanton solace of men when they become so weak in mind and body that they cannot exert themselves, unless to pursue some frothy pleasure or to invent some frivolous fashion. What can be a more melancholy sight to a thinking mind than to look into the numerous carriages that drive helter-skelter about this metropolis in a morning full of pale-faced creatures who are flying from themselves. I have often wished, with Dr. Johnson,[19] to place some of them in a little shop with half a dozen children looking up to their languid countenances for support. I am much mistaken if some latent vigor would not soon give health and spirit to their eyes, and some lines drawn by the exercise of reason on the blank cheeks, which before were only undulated by dimples, might restore lost dignity to the character, or rather enable it to attain the true dignity of its nature. Virtue is not to be acquired even by speculation, much less by the negative supineness that wealth naturally generates. 21

---

[17] **distaff**   Instrument to wind wool in the act of spinning, notoriously a job only "fit for women."

[18] **feculent**   Filthy, polluted; related to *feces*.

[19] **Dr. Samuel Johnson (1709–1784)**   The greatest lexicographer and one of the most respected authors of England's eighteenth century. He was known to Mary Wollstonecraft and to her sister, Eliza, a teacher. The reference is to an item published in his *Rambler*, essay 85.

Besides, when poverty is more disgraceful than even vice, is not morality   22
cut to the quick? Still to avoid misconstruction, though I consider that women
in the common walks of life are called to fulfill the duties of wives and mothers, by religion and reason, I cannot help lamenting that women of a superior
cast have not a road open by which they can pursue more extensive plans of
usefulness and independence. I may excite laughter by dropping a hint which I
mean to pursue some future time, for I really think that women ought to have
representatives, instead of being arbitrarily governed without having any direct
share allowed them in the deliberations of government.

But, as the whole system of representation is now in this country only a   23
convenient handle for despotism, they need not complain, for they are as well
represented as a numerous class of hard-working mechanics, who pay for the
support of royalty when they can scarcely stop their children's mouths with
bread. How are they represented whose very sweat supports the splendid stud
of an heir apparent, or varnishes the chariot of some female favorite who looks
down on shame? Taxes on the very necessaries of life enable an endless tribe
of idle princes and princesses to pass with stupid pomp before a gaping crowd,
who almost worship the very parade which costs them so dear. This is mere
gothic grandeur, something like the barbarous useless parade of having sentinels on horseback at Whitehall,[20] which I could never view without a mixture
of contempt and indignation.

How strangely must the mind be sophisticated when this sort of state   24
impresses it! But, till these monuments of folly are levelled by virtue, similar
follies will leaven the whole mass. For the same character, in some degree, will
prevail in the aggregate of society; and the refinements of luxury, or the vicious
repinings,[21] of envious poverty, will equally banish virtue from society, considered as the characteristic of that society, or only allow it to appear as one of the
stripes of the harlequin coat worn by the civilized man.

In the superior ranks of life every duty is done by deputies, as if duties   25
could ever be waived, and the vain pleasures which consequent idleness forces
the rich to pursue appear so enticing to the next rank that the numerous scram-
blers for wealth sacrifice everything to tread on their heels. The most sacred
trusts are then considered as sinecures,[22] because they were procured by interest, and only sought to enable a man to keep *good company*. Women, in particular, all want to be ladies. Which is simply to have nothing to do, but listlessly
to go they scarcely care where, for they cannot tell what.

---

[20] **sentinels on horseback at Whitehall**   This is a reference to the expensive demonstration of showmanship that continues to our day: the changing of the guard at Whitehall.

[21] **repinings**   Discontent, fretting.

[22] **sinecures**   Jobs with few duties but good pay.

But what have women to do in society? I may be asked, but to loiter with   26
easy grace; surely you would not condemn them all to suckle fools and chronicle small beer![23] No. Women might certainly study the art of healing, and be
physicians as well as nurses. And midwifery, decency seems to allot to them,
though I am afraid the word midwife in our dictionaries will soon give place to
accoucheur,[24] and one proof of the former delicacy of the sex be effaced from
the language.

They might also study politics, and settle their benevolence on the broadest   27
basis; for the reading of history will scarcely be more useful than the perusal of
romances, if read as mere biography; if the character of the times, the political
improvements, arts, &c., be not observed. In short, if it be not considered as the
history of man; and not of particular men, who filled a niche in the temple of
fame, and dropped into the black rolling stream of time, that silently sweeps all
before it, into the shapeless void called—eternity. For shape, can it be called,
"that shape hath none"?[25]

Business of various kinds they might likewise pursue, if they were edu-   28
cated in a more orderly manner, which might save many from common and
legal prostitution. Women would not then marry for a support, as men accept
of places under government, and neglect the implied duties; nor would an
attempt to earn their own subsistence—a most laudable one!—sink them
almost to the level of those poor abandoned creatures who live by prostitution.
For are not milliners and mantua-makers[26] reckoned the next class? The few
employments open to women, so far from being liberal, are menial; and when a
superior education enables them to take charge of the education of children as
governesses, they are not treated like the tutors of sons, though even clerical
tutors are not always treated in a manner calculated to render them respectable in the eyes of their pupils, to say nothing of the private comfort of the
individual. But as women educated like gentlewomen are never designed for
the humiliating situation which necessity sometimes forces them to fill, these
situations are considered in the light of a degradation; and they know little of
the human heart, who need to be told that nothing so painfully sharpens sensibility as such a fall in life.

Some of these women might be restrained from marrying by a proper spirit   29
or delicacy, and others may not have had it in their power to escape in this
pitiful way from servitude; is not that government then very defective, and very

---

[23] **chronicle small beer!**   *Othello* (II.i.158). This means to keep the household accounts.

[24] *accoucheur*   Male version of the female midwife.

[25] **"that shape hath none"**   The reference is to *Paradise Lost* (II.667) by John Milton
(1608–1674); it is an allusion to death.

[26] **milliners and mantua-makers**   Dressmakers, usually women (whereas tailors
were usually men).

unmindful of the happiness of one half of its members, that does not provide for honest, independent women, by encouraging them to fill respectable stations? But in order to render their private virtue a public benefit, they must have a civil existence in the state, married or single; else we shall continually see some worthy woman, whose sensibility has been rendered painfully acute by undeserved contempt, droop like "the lily broken down by a plowshare."

It is a melancholy truth — yet such is the blessed effect of civilization! — the most respectable women are the most oppressed; and, unless they have understandings far superior to the common run of understandings, taking in both sexes, they must, from being treated like contemptible beings, become contemptible. How many women thus waste life away the prey of discontent, who might have practiced as physicians, regulated a farm, managed a shop, and stood erect, supported by their own industry, instead of hanging their heads surcharged with the dew of sensibility, that consumes the beauty to which it at first gave lustre; nay, I doubt whether pity and love are so near akin as poets feign, for I have seldom seen much compassion excited by the helplessness of females, unless they were fair; then, perhaps pity was the soft handmaid of love, or the harbinger of lust.   30

How much more respectable is the woman who earns her own bread by fulfilling any duty, than the most accomplished beauty! — beauty did I say? — so sensible am I of the beauty of moral loveliness, or the harmonious propriety that attunes the passions of a well regulated mind, that I blush at making the comparison; yet I sigh to think how few women aim at attaining this respectability by withdrawing from the giddy whirl of pleasure, or the indolent calm that stupefies the good sort of women it sucks in.   31

Proud of their weakness, however, they must always be protected, guarded from care, and all the rough toils that dignify the mind. If this be the fiat of fate, if they will make themselves insignificant and contemptible, sweetly to waste "life away," let them not expect to be valued when their beauty fades, for it is the fate of the fairest flowers to be admired and pulled to pieces by the careless hand that plucked them. In how many ways do I wish, from the purest benevolence, to impress this truth on my sex; yet I fear that they will not listen to a truth that dear-bought experience has brought home to many an agitated bosom, nor willingly resign the privileges of rank and sex for the privileges of humanity, to which those have no claim who do not discharge its duties.   32

Those writers are particularly useful, in my opinion, who make man feel for man, independent of the station he fills, or the drapery of factitious sentiments. I then would fain[27] convince reasonable men of the importance of some of my remarks; and prevail on them to weigh dispassionately the whole tenor   33

---

[27] **fain** Happily, gladly.

of my observations. I appeal to their understandings; and, as a fellow-creature, claim, in the name of my sex, some interest in their hearts. I entreat them to assist to emancipate their companion, to make her a *help meet*[28] for them!

Would men but generously snap our chains, and be content with rational   34 fellowship instead of slavish obedience, they would find us more observant daughters, more affectionate sisters, more faithful wives, more reasonable mothers—in a word, better citizens. We should then love them with true affection, because we should learn to respect ourselves; and, the peace of mind of a worthy man would not be interrupted by the idle vanity of his wife, nor the babes sent to nestle in a strange bosom, having never found a home in their mother's.

------

[28] *help meet*   Helper, helpmate.

✂ QUESTIONS FOR CRITICAL READING

1. Who is the audience for Wollstonecraft's writing? Is she writing more for men than for women? Is it clear from what she says that she addresses an explicit audience with specific qualities?

2. Analyze paragraph 1 carefully for the use of imagery, especially metaphor. What are the effects of these images? Are they overdone?

3. Wollstonecraft begins by attacking property, or the respect paid to it. What does she mean? Does she sustain that line of thought throughout the piece?

4. In paragraph 12, Wollstonecraft speaks of the "bondage of ignorance" in which women are held. Clarify precisely what she means by that expression.

5. In paragraph 30, Wollstonecraft says that people who are treated as if they were contemptible will become contemptible. Is this a political or a psychological judgment?

6. What is the substance of Wollstonecraft's complaint concerning the admiration of women for their beauty?

✂ SUGGESTIONS FOR CRITICAL WRITING

1. Throughout the piece Wollstonecraft attacks the unnatural distinctions made between men and women. Establish carefully what those unnatural distinctions are, why they are unnatural, and whether such distinctions persist to the present day. By contrast, establish what some natural distinctions between men and women are and whether Wollstonecraft has taken them into consideration.

2. References are made throughout the piece to prostitution and to the debaucheries of men. Paragraph 7 specifically refers to the "wanton tricks" of prostitutes. What is Wollstonecraft's attitude toward men in regard to sexuality and their

attitudes toward women — both the women of the brothels and the women with whom men live? Find passages in the piece that you can quote and analyze in an effort to examine her views.

3. In paragraph 2, Wollstonecraft complains that "the respect due only to talents and virtue" is instead being given to people on account of their property. Further, she says in paragraph 9 that riches are "destructive . . . to the human character." Determine carefully, by means of reference to and analysis of specific passages, just what Wollstonecraft means by such statements. Then, use your own anecdotes or "episodical observations" to take a stand on whether these are views you yourself can hold for our time. Are riches destructive to character? Is too much respect paid to those who possess property? If possible, use metaphor or allusion — literary or personal.

4. In paragraph 4, Wollstonecraft speaks of "men who can be gratified by the fawning fondness of spaniel-like affection" from their women. Search through the essay for other instances of similar views and analyze them carefully. Establish exactly what the men she describes want their women to be like. Have today's men changed very much in their expectations? Why? Why not? Use personal observations where possible in answering this question.

5. The question of what roles women ought to have in society is addressed in paragraphs 26, 27, and 28. What are those roles? Why are they defined in terms of work? Do you agree that they are, indeed, the roles that women should assume? Would you include more roles? Do women in our time have greater access to those roles? Consider what women actually did in Wollstonecraft's time and what they do today.

6. **CONNECTIONS**   Mary Wollstonecraft wrote more than a century and a half before Karen Horney (p. 500). Examine the assumptions each writer makes about the role and nature of each sex in her historical situation. How much has changed since Wollstonecraft wrote her book? How much does each of these writers agree about the position of power of men and women in their society? How much of what each writer describes about the relationship between men and women do you observe in your own environment?

7. **CONNECTIONS**   Compare Wollstonecraft's views on the ways in which women are victims of prejudice with the views of Martin Luther King Jr. (p. 252). How much do women of Wollstonecraft's time have in common with the conditions of African Americans as described by King? What political issues are central to the efforts of both groups to achieve justice and equal opportunity? Might Wollstonecraft see herself in the same kind of struggle as King, or would she draw sharp distinctions?

JACOB
A. RIIS

The Color Line in New York

© Corbis

J ACOB A. RIIS (1849–1914), as a twenty-one-
year-old Danish immigrant to New York, found him-
self in a desperate situation and unable to get work. He almost gave up hope, subsisting
in shelters brutally run by the police in their station cellars and then eventually living
on the streets. Fortunately, he was befriended by the principal of Cooper Union, who
got him a job writing about a luncheon at Astor House. His article was good enough
to secure him work for the New York News Association. He became editor of *South
Brooklyn News*, but the paper, which was a political news organ, went bankrupt. Riis
bought the company with some promissory notes and his savings of $75 and ran it inde-
pendently for a time. Eventually, the political group decided to buy it back and paid Riis
five times his original investment.

This windfall permitted him to return for a short time to Denmark. The woman he
wanted to marry, Elizabeth Gjortz, had originally refused him when he first left home. But
hearing that her fiancé had died, Riis proposed to her again and she accepted. They soon
returned to the United States and Brooklyn, where Riis found newspaper work. In time, he
became a police reporter on the *New York Tribune*. He was assigned the most dangerous
areas of the city to cover. The Five Points area was notorious. But Riis made a point of walking through the most dangerous areas and the worst slums. He spent a great deal of time
in the locations in which the poor suffered most painfully. As a result of his experience
observing poverty in New York, he published a short piece on tenement life for *Scribner's
Magazine*. It developed into his first, and most famous, book, *How the Other Half Lives:
Studies among the Tenements of New York* (Scribner's, 1890).

Riis was a type of journalist called a "muckraker" because he called society's attention
to unpleasant issues. He became a photographer because photographs provided a more
forceful way to make his point about the miseries of the poor in late-nineteenth-century
New York. He bought a camera when the first flash photography was invented, making
it possible for him to photograph the interiors of many squalid tenements. At that time,
it was not uncommon for ten people to live in a two-room tenement without running

water or an interior bathroom. He brought these conditions to the notice of Theodore Roosevelt, who was then the New York City Police Commissioner. Roosevelt accompanied Riis in his work recording the miseries of the impoverished. Riis is considered one of the first photojournalists.

Riis was concerned with the various ethnic groups he studied and photographed. He had some conventional prejudices regarding the major impoverished groups: the Italians, the Jews, the Bohemians (Czechs and Slovaks), and the African Americans. He often complained of some groups' inability to maintain sanitation and of their unwillingness to make changes that might have improved their lives. But these views did not prevent him from working on their behalf. His journalism is credited with helping to transform the slums of New York and changing the sanitary conditions in which hundreds of thousands lived.

RIIS'S RHETORIC

As a result of his experience as a reporter and as an editor of a newspaper, Riis writes in a no-nonsense fashion. His paragraphs are distinct and long in the fashion of the papers of his day. Because he came to America as a carpenter, he seems to "build" his essay out of distinct parts, but they are not as smoothly held together as they might be. Rarely does one paragraph move in easy transition to the next — each seems a separate entity. He makes some limited use of rhetorical techniques such as metaphor or testimony from other authors. "Rookeries" derives from the multiple nests of birds; "hegira" is a reference to Mohammed; even "ukase" alludes to the power of czarist Russia. But on the whole, the most important rhetorical resource for Riis is the facts.

Riis was not the first to write about the poor in New York. A number of other authors produced books in the 1870s and the 1890s, but most of those books were formal, moralistic, and distant from their subject. What made *How the Other Half Lives* successful was the directness and the simplicity of its language. Riis uses statistics and facts to make his point. He refers to exact streets and, in paragraph 5, compares the exact differences in rents charged to African Americans and whites even while explaining that "negro" tenants were cleaner, less destructive, and better tenants.

Another of his techniques is the use of example. Riis seems to have had a special interest in Christmas (he wrote two books about it) and introduces an old "scrubwoman," Ann, living on Sixteenth Street, who was to be given two dollars from out of town friends for the purpose of buying her a Christmas dinner (para. 6). Riis, who was to deliver this money to her, found that her landlady was all too willing to take the money in Ann's absence. He realized how easy it was for the landlady and her husband to take advantage of their tenant.

Riis is unembarrassed to provide what he feels are the facts about the behavior of all the ethnic groups he describes in his book. He presents a number of generalizations to us as witness of his own personal observation and judgment. Whether or not we accept his observations as fact, they are the cornerstone of his technique.

When it comes to prejudice, he challenges the landlords, who are not exhibiting good business sense according to Riis. Yet, although Riis is unusual for his time in his essential respect and admiration for African Americans, he is also judgmental and possesses some of the same prejudicial attitudes as the general white public at that time and later. He points out that the "negro" has come north to New York in a large migration and is only twenty-five years out of slavery. The progress made in that time by the "negro" is remarkable, but as he tells us, the restriction to menial work limits opportunity. Riis, a trained carpenter, points out that there are very few African American carpenters who can find work in New York. (Riis himself found little work as a carpenter.) His references to recent history and his analysis of circumstances make his work distinctive.

The use of specific detail and attention to location distinguish his book from those by contemporaries. He gives us the street names in lower Manhattan that contain the "rookeries" and slums that he detests. He cites the development of Harlem as offering new and clean housing as "the colored citizen" moves out of the "black-and-tan slums of Thompson and Sullivan Streets," which he describes as "Africa" (para. 3).

Riis approaches the act of writing as a direct and essentially simple task. Each of his paragraphs begins with a controlling or topic sentence that declares the subject of the paragraph. His approach is somewhat naive because most of the paragraphs are detached from the next. The first paragraph introduces the prejudices of the landlord. The second explains that there may be some hope that the "color line" may be weakening and positive change may come. The third paragraph focuses on the migration of African Americans north since the Civil War and describes the qualities he observes in them. Each following paragraph adds information and opinion, but these paragraphs could be seen as standing alone.

Throughout his book, Riis is direct and uncompromising in describing other ethnic groups. Whether fair or unfair, he is often critical of the characteristics of the Chinese and the Italians. However, his praise for the "negro" — "he has his eminently good points" (para. 7) — conjures the stereotyped character of the "negro" as carefree, happy, not planning ahead, addicted to gambling, and dangerous ("When a fight breaks out during the dance a dozen razors are handy in as many boot-legs" [para. 9]). For whatever reason, he treats "the negro" not as an individual, but as a group, expecting his generalizations to be bolstered by the fact of his observations.

✂ PREREADING QUESTIONS: WHAT TO READ FOR

The following prereading questions may help you anticipate key issues in the discussion of Jacob A. Riis's "The Color Line in New York." Keeping them in mind during your first reading should help focus your attention.

1. What does Jacob Riis tell us about tenement life?

2. How distinct and separate are the ethnic groups Riis describes?

3. How does racial prejudice affect the business practices of landlords?

4. What are Riis's own prejudices? How do they affect his reporting?

The Color Line in New York

The color line must be drawn through the tenements to give the picture its proper shading. The landlord does the drawing, does it with an absence of pretence, a frankness of despotism, that is nothing if not brutal. The Czar of all the Russias is not more absolute upon his own soil than the New York landlord in his dealings with colored tenants. Where he permits them to live, they go; where he shuts the door, stay out. By his grace they exist at all in certain localities; his ukase[1] banishes them from others. He accepts the responsibility, when laid at his door, with unruffled complacency. It is business, he will tell you. And it is. He makes the prejudice in which he traffics pay him well, and that, as he thinks it quite superfluous to tell you, is what he is there for.

That his pencil does not make quite as black a mark as it did, that the hand that wields it does not bear down as hard as only a short half dozen years ago, is the hopeful sign of an awakening public conscience under the stress of which the line shows signs of wavering. But for this the landlord deserves no credit. It has come, is coming about despite him. The line may not be wholly effaced while the name of the negro, alone among the world's races, is spelled with a small n. Natural selection will have more or less to do beyond a doubt in every age with dividing the races; only so, it may be, can they work out together their highest destiny. But with the despotism that deliberately assigns to the defenceless Black the lowest level for the purpose of robbing him there that has nothing to do. Of such slavery, different only in degree from the other kind that held him as a chattel, to be sold or bartered at the will of his master, this century, if signs fail not, will see the end in New York.

Ever since the war[2] New York has been receiving the overflow of colored population from the Southern cities. In the last decade this migration has grown to such proportions that it is estimated that our Blacks have quite doubled in number since the Tenth Census. Whether the exchange has been of advantage to the negro may well be questioned. Trades of which he had practical control in his Southern home are not open to him here. I know that it may be answered that there is no industrial proscription of color; that it is a matter of choice. Perhaps so. At all events he does not choose then. How many colored carpenters or masons has anyone seen at work in New York? In the South there are enough of them and, if the testimony of the most intelligent of their people is worth anything, plenty of them have come here. As a matter of fact the colored man takes in New York, without a struggle, the lower level of menial service

---

[1] **ukase**   A command having the force of law.

[2] **the war**   The Civil War, 1861–1865.

for which his past traditions and natural love of ease perhaps as yet fit him best. Even the colored barber is rapidly getting to be a thing of the past. Along shore, at any unskilled labor, he works unmolested; but he does not appear to prefer the job. His sphere thus defined, he naturally takes his stand among the poor, and in the homes of the poor. Until very recent times — the years since a change was wrought can be counted on the fingers of one hand — he was practically restricted in the choice of a home to a narrow section on the West Side, that nevertheless had a social top and bottom to it — the top in the tenements on the line of Seventh Avenue as far north as Thirty-second Street, where he was allowed to occupy the houses of unsavory reputation which the police had cleared and for which decent white tenants could not be found; the bottom in the vile rookeries[3] of Thompson Street and South Fifth Avenue, the old "Africa" that is now fast becoming a modern Italy. To-day there are black colonies in Yorkville and Morrisania. The encroachment of business and the Italian below, and the swelling of the population above, have been the chief agents in working out his second emancipation, a very real one, for with his cutting loose from the old tenements there has come a distinct and gratifying improvement in the tenant, that argues louder than theories or speeches the influence of vile surroundings in debasing the man. The colored citizen whom this year's census man found in his Ninety-ninth Street "flat" is a very different individual from the "nigger" his predecessor counted in the black-and-tan slums of Thompson and Sullivan Streets. There is no more clean and orderly community in New York than the new settlement of colored people that is growing up on the East Side from Yorkville to Harlem.

Cleanliness is the characteristic of the negro in his new surroundings, as it was his virtue in the old. In this respect he is immensely the superior of the lowest of the whites, the Italians and the Polish Jews, below whom he has been classed in the past in the tenant scale. Nevertheless, he has always had to pay higher rents than even these for the poorest and most stinted rooms. The exceptions I have come across, in which the rents, though high, have seemed more nearly on a level with what was asked for the same number and size of rooms in the average tenement, were in the case of tumble-down rookeries in which no one else would live, and were always coupled with the condition that the landlord should "make no repairs." It can readily be seen that his profits were scarcely curtailed by his "humanity." The reason advanced for this systematic robbery is that white people will not live in the same house with colored tenants, or even in a house recently occupied by negroes, and that consequently its selling value is injured. The prejudice undoubtedly exists, but it is not lessened by the house agents, who have set up the maxim "once a colored house, always a colored house."

4

---

[3] **rookeries**   Overcrowded apartments; modeled on the crowded nests of birds.

There is method in the maxim, as shown by an inquiry made last year by   5
the *Real Estate Record.* It proved agents to be practically unanimous in the
endorsement of the negro as a clean, orderly, and "profitable" tenant. Here
is the testimony of one of the largest real estate firms in the city: "We would
rather have negro tenants in our poorest class of tenements than the lower
grades of foreign white people. We find the former cleaner than the latter,
and they do not destroy the property so much. We also get higher prices.
We have a tenement on Nineteenth Street, where we get $10 for two rooms
which we could not get more than $7.50 for from white tenants previously.
We have a four-story tenement on our books on Thirty-third Street, between
Sixth and Seventh Avenues, with four rooms per floor — a parlor, two bed-
rooms, and a kitchen. We get $20 for the first floor, $24 for the second, $23
for the third and $20 for the fourth, in all $87 or $1,044 per annum. The size
of the building is only 21 + 55." Another firm declared that in a specified
instance they had saved fifteen to twenty per cent on the gross rentals since
they changed from white to colored tenants. Still another gave the following case of a front and rear tenement that had formerly been occupied by
tenants of a "low European type," who had been turned out on account of
filthy habits and poor pay. The negroes proved cleaner, better, and steadier
tenants. Instead, however, of having their rents reduced in consequence, the
comparison stood as follows:

Rents under White Tenants		PER MONTH	Rents under Colored Tenants		PER MONTH
Front	1st floor (store, etc.)	$21	Front	1st floor (store, etc.)	$21
	2d floor (store, etc.)	13		2d floor (store, etc.)	14
	3d floor (store, etc.)	13		3d floor (store, etc.)	14
	4th floor (and rear)	21		4th floor (store, etc.)	14
Rear	2d floor (and rear)	12	Rear	2d floor (store, etc.)	12
	3d floor (and rear)	12		3d floor (store, etc.)	13
	4th floor (see front)	—		4th floor (store, etc.)	13
Rear house	1st floor (see front)	8	Rear house	1st floor (store, etc.)	10
	2d floor (see front)	10		2d floor (store, etc.)	12
	3d floor (see front)	9		3d floor (store, etc.)	11
	4th floor (see front)	8		4th floor (store, etc.)	10
	Total	$127		*Total*	$144

An increased rental of $17 per month, or $204 a year, and an advance of nearly thirteen and one-half per cent. On the gross rental "in favor" of the colored tenant. Profitable, surely!

I have quoted these cases at length in order to let in light on the quality   6 of this landlord despotism that has purposely confused the public mind, and for its own selfish ends is propping up a waning prejudice. It will be cause for congratulation if indeed its time has come at last. Within a year, I am told by one of the most intelligent and best informed of our colored citizens, there has been evidence, simultaneous with the colored hegira[4] from the low down-town tenements, of a movement toward less exorbitant rents. I cannot pass from this subject without adding a leaf from my own experience that deserves a place in this record, though, for the credit of humanity, I hope as an extreme case. It was last Christmas that I had occasion to visit the home of an old colored woman in Sixteenth Street, as the almoner[5] of generous friends out of town who wished me to buy her a Christmas dinner. The old woman lived in a wretched shanty, occupying two mean, dilapidated rooms at the top of a sort of hen-ladder that went by the name of stairs. For these she paid ten dollars a month out of her hard-earned wages as a scrubwoman. I did not find her in and, being informed that she was "at the agent's," went around to hunt her up. The agent's wife appeared, to report that Ann was out. Being in a hurry it occurred to me that I might save time by making her employer the purveyor of my friend's bounty, and proposed to entrust the money, two dollars, to her to be expended for Old Ann's benefit. She fell in with the suggestion at once, and confided to me in the fullness of her heart that she liked the plan, inasmuch as "I generally find her a Christmas dinner myself, and this money — she owes Mr.—— (her husband, the agent) a lot of rent." Needless to state that there was a change of programme then and there, and that Ann was saved from the sort of Christmas cheer that woman's charity would have spread before her. When I had the old soul comfortably installed in her own den, with a chicken and "fixin's" and a bright fire in her stove, I asked her how much she owed of her rent. Her answer was that she did not really owe anything, her month not being quite up, but that the amount yet unpaid was — two dollars!

Poverty, abuse, and injustice alike the negro accepts with imperturbable   7 cheerfulness. His philosophy is of the kind that has no room for repining. Whether he lives in an Eighth Ward barrack or in a tenement with a brownstone front and pretensions to the title of "flat," he looks at the sunny side of life and enjoys it. He loves fine clothes and good living a good deal more than he does a bank account. The proverbial rainy day it would be rank ingratitude,

---

[4] **hegira**   Migration; a reference to Mohammed's migration from Mecca.

[5] **almoner**   A person who gives money to the poor.

from his point of view, to look for when the sun shines unclouded in a clear sky. His home surroundings, except when he is utterly depraved, reflect his blithesome temper. The poorest negro housekeeper's room in New York is bright with gaily-colored prints of his beloved "Abe Linkum," General Grant, President Garfield, Mrs. Cleveland, and other national celebrities, and cheery with flowers and singing birds. In the art of putting the best foot foremost, of disguising his poverty by making a little go a long way, our negro has no equal. When a fair share of prosperity is his, he knows how to make life and home very pleasant to those about him. Pianos and parlor furniture abound in the uptown homes of colored tenants and give them a very prosperous air. But even where the wolf howls at the door, he makes a bold and gorgeous front. The amount of "style" displayed on fine Sundays on Sixth and Seventh Avenues by colored holiday-makers would turn a pessimist black with wrath. The negro's great ambition is to rise in the social scale to which his color has made him a stranger and an outsider, and he is quite willing to accept the shadow for the substance where that is the best he can get. The claw-hammer coat and white tie of a waiter in a first-class summer hotel, with the chance of taking his ease in six months of winter, are to him the next best thing to mingling with the white quality[6] he serves, on equal terms. His festive gatherings, pre-eminently his cake-walks, at which a sugared and frosted cake is the proud prize of the couple with the most aristocratic step and carriage, are comic mixtures of elaborate ceremonial and the joyous abandon of the natural man. With all his ludicrous incongruities, his sensuality and his lack of moral accountability, his superstition and other faults that are the effect of temperament and of centuries of slavery, he has his eminently good points. He is loyal to the backbone, proud of being an American and of his new-found citizenship. He is at least as easily moulded for good as for evil. His churches are crowded to the doors on Sunday nights when the colored colony turns out to worship. His people own church property in this city upon which they have paid half a million dollars out of the depth of their poverty, with comparatively little assistance from their white brethren. He is both willing and anxious to learn, and his intellectual status is distinctly improving. If his emotions are not very deeply rooted, they are at least sincere while they last, and until the tempter gets the upper hand again.

Of all the temptations that beset him, the one that troubles him and the police most is his passion for gambling. The game of policy is a kind of unlawful penny lottery specially adapted to his means, but patronized extensively by poor white players as well. It is the meanest of swindles, but reaps for its backers rich fortunes wherever colored people congregate. Between the fortune-teller and the policy shop,[7] closely allied frauds always, the wages of

8

---

[6] **white quality**   *Quality* is a term referring to the upper class, or aristocrats.

[7] **policy shop**   The place in which the betting slips for numbers are bought and paid out from. The three numbers, 4–11–44, represent the bets at that time.

many a hard day's work are wasted by the negro; but the loss causes him few regrets. Penniless, but with undaunted faith in his ultimate "luck," he looks forward to the time when he shall once more be able to take a hand at "beating policy." When periodically the negro's lucky numbers, 4–11–44, come out on the slips of the alleged daily drawings, that are supposed to be held in some far-off Western town, intense excitement reigns in Thompson Street and along the Avenue, where someone is always the winner. An immense impetus is given then to the bogus business that has no existence outside of the cigar stores and candy shops where it hides from the law, save in some cunning Bowery "bro-ker's" back office, where the slips are printed and the "winnings" apportioned daily with due regard to the backer's interests.

It is a question whether "Africa" has been improved by the advent of the   9
Italian, with the tramp from the Mulberry Street Bend in his train. The moral turpitude of Thompson Street has been notorious for years, and the mingling of the three elements does not seem to have wrought any change for the better. The border-land where the white and black races meet in common debauch, the aptly-named black-and-tan saloon,[8] has never been debatable ground from a moral stand-point. It has always been the worst of the desperately bad. Than this commingling of the utterly depraved of both sexes, white and black, on such ground, there can be no greater abomination. Usually it is some foul cellar dive, perhaps run by the political "leader" of the district, who is "in with" the police. In any event it gathers to itself all the law-breakers and all the human wrecks within reach. When a fight breaks out during the dance a dozen razors are handy in as many boot-legs, and there is always a job for the surgeon and the ambulance. The black "tough" is as handy with the razor in a fight as his peaceably inclined brother is with it in pursuit of his honest trade. As the Chinaman hides his knife in his sleeve and the Italian his stiletto in the bosom, so the negro goes to the ball with a razor in his boot-leg, and on occasion does as much execution with it as both of the others together. More than three-fourths of the business the police have with the colored people in New York arises in the black-and-tan district, now no longer fairly representative of their color.

I have touched briefly upon such facts in the negro's life as may serve to   10
throw light on the social condition of his people in New York. If, when the account is made up between the races, it shall be claimed that he falls short of the result to be expected from twenty-five years of freedom, it may be well to turn to the other side of the ledger and see how much of the blame is borne by the prejudice and greed that have kept him from rising under a burden of responsibility to which he could hardly be equal. And in this view he may be seen to have advanced much farther and faster than before suspected, and to promise, after all, with fair treatment, quite as well as the rest of us, his white-skinned fellow-citizens, had any right to expect.

---

[8] **black-and-tan saloon**   The colors refer to skin color, and Riis implies a mixing of races.

✂ QUESTIONS FOR CRITICAL READING

1. What does Riis mean by the term "color line"?

2. What is the economic value of the landlord's prejudice?

3. What is the status of African American tradesmen in Riis's New York?

4. What kind of work did African Americans get in New York?

5. What qualifies the judgment of what kind of tenant the "negro" was?

6. How does Riis portray landlords?

7. Why does Riis pay such attention to cleanliness in tenants?

✂ SUGGESTIONS FOR CRITICAL WRITING

1. In paragraph 3, Riis says that the number of African Americans in New York City has doubled since the Tenth Census. His book was published the year of the Eleventh Census. Research the census records and see how accurate Riis is. What percentage of the population in New York was African American in 1890? In your essay, provide information about the numbers of other ethnic groups singled out by the census. How important is Riis's reference to the census to the points he makes in this selection?

2. If you have experience or personal knowledge of the behavior of landlords in your neighborhood, write an essay that describes the modern attitude of landlords toward minority tenants. If you have no personal experience, search reports in local and national newspapers for articles on rental issues raised by minorities. Is there a good reason to compare modern practice with that described by Riis?

3. Riis complained about the overcrowding of tenants in tenements designed to hold only a single family but that often held two or more. He also complained about lack of outside space, poor quality of inside air, and rooms that had no window. Many of the tenements he visited and photographed had no running water and no indoor bathrooms. He saw the move of residents to Harlem as beneficial, and in theory, he would have been pleased by the development of high-rise projects. If you have experience or knowledge of housing projects with open space and modern conveniences, write an essay that explains why Riis would or would not be satisfied with them.

4. In paragraph 5, Riis gives the actual costs of rent for different apartments in residential tenements. He has one column for "Whites" and one for "Colored Tenants." These costs seem extremely low by modern standards, but the value of the dollar has changed since 1890. Do some research and find out the approximate value in today's money of the 1890 dollar. Then in your essay, write a list of the 1890 costs in today's money. Find out what today's going rental rates in lower Manhattan are for similar apartments. If possible, choose rates on Thompson Street, Sullivan Street, or Mulberry Street. What conclusions do you draw?

5. Riis was a liberal by the standards of his day. Even now, his sympathy for the African American is considerable, just as his dislike for the rapacious landlord is obvious. However, he reveals prejudices common to his time and, for some Americans, even common in our time. Yet he reveals these prejudices while praising African Americans. What are the circumstances of prejudice against people of color in your community? What kinds of praise for minorities indicate prejudice? What aspects of his "praise" seem most unfair to you?

6. Riis wrote his book to call attention to the conditions in which the poor lived in New York in the late nineteenth century. Most prosperous Americans of the day knew that there were many poor people in the city, but they avoided them by avoiding specific neighborhoods. They were not entirely indifferent, but in the nineteenth century, affluent Americans often felt that the conditions endured by the poor were largely of their own doing, that it was their own fault for being poor. To what extent do you get the feeling that Riis might share their view? How much has changed in the attitudes of the general public toward the poor in the United States? What is the general view of the rich toward the poor? Is there anyone today who, similar to Jacob A. Riis, is helping to call attention to the conditions of the poor? Consult some major newspapers and other journalistic media, in print or online, to determine what America's attitude toward the poor, particularly poor African Americans, seems to be.

7. **CONNECTIONS**   Alexis de Tocqueville (p. 139) is another European who came to America and wrote his observations of the circumstances that interested him. Tocqueville made many judgments of the American people as a result of his observations. In what ways can you compare Riis to Tocqueville in terms of the accuracy of their observations? What is similar in their rhetorical approach to their subject? Both writers produced work that has lasted and that seems relevant to our own time. In an essay, explain what makes their work so enduring.

VIRGINIA
WOOLF

Shakespeare's Sister

VIRGINIA WOOLF (1882–1941), one of the most gifted of the modernist writers, was a prolific essayist and novelist in what came to be known as the Bloomsbury group, named after a section of London near the British Museum. Most members of the group were writers, such as E. M. Forster, Lytton Strachey, and the critic Clive Bell, and some were artists, such as Duncan Grant and Virginia Woolf's sister, Vanessa Bell. The eminent economist John Maynard Keynes was part of the group as well, along with a variety of other accomplished intellectuals.

Virginia Woolf published some of the most important works of the early twentieth century, including the novels *Jacob's Room* (1922), *Mrs. Dalloway* (1925), *To the Lighthouse* (1927), *Orlando* (1928), and *The Waves* (1931). Among her many volumes of nonfiction prose is *A Room of One's Own* (1929). In this book Woolf speculates on what life would have been like for an imaginary gifted sister of William Shakespeare.

In discussing the imaginary Judith Shakespeare, Woolf examines the circumstances common to women's lives during the Renaissance. For example, women had little or no say in their future. Unlike their male counterparts, they were not educated in grammar schools and did not learn trades that would enable them to make a living for themselves. Instead, they were expected to marry as soon as possible, even as young as thirteen or fourteen years of age, and begin raising a family of their own. When they did marry, their husbands were men selected by their parents; the wives essentially became the property of those men. Under English law a married couple was regarded as one entity, and that entity was spoken for only by the man. Similarly, the women of the period had few civil rights. As Woolf points out, the history books do not mention women very often, and when they do, it is usually to relate that wife beating was common and generally approved of in all classes of society.

As Woolf comments on the opportunities that women were denied during the Renaissance, she agrees with an unnamed bishop who said that no woman could have

From *A Room of Own's Own.*

written Shakespeare's plays. Woolf explains that no woman could have had enough contact with the theater in those days to be received with anything but disdain and discourtesy. Women could not even act on stage in Shakespeare's time, much less write for it.

It would be all but impossible in a society of this sort to imagine a woman as a successful literary figure, much less as a popular playwright. After all, society excluded women, marginalizing them as insignificant — at least in the eyes of historians. Certainly women were mothers; as such, they bore the male children who went on to become accomplished and famous. However, without a trade or an education, women in Shakespeare's time were all but chattel slaves in a household.

In this setting, Woolf places a brilliant girl named Judith Shakespeare, a fictional character who, in Woolf's imaginative construction, had the same literary fire as her famous brother. How would she have tried to express herself? How would she have followed her talent? Woolf suggests the results would have been depressing, and for good reason. No one would have listened to Judith; in all likelihood her life would have ended badly.

The women of Shakespeare's time mentioned in the history books are generally Elizabeths and Marys, queens and princesses whose power was inherent in their positions. Little is known, Woolf says, about the lives of ordinary middle-class women. In Woolf's time, historians were uninterested in such information. However, many recent books have included detailed research into the lives of people in the Elizabethan period. Studying journals, day-books (including budgets and planning), and family records, modern historians have found much more information than English historian George Trevelyan (to whom Woolf refers in her essay) drew on. In fact, it is now known that women's lives were more varied than even Woolf implies, but women still had precious few opportunities compared to men of the period.

WOOLF'S RHETORIC

This selection is the third chapter from *A Room of One's Own*; thus, it begins with a sentence that implies continuity with an earlier section. The context for the essay's opening is as follows: a male dinner guest has said something insulting to women at a dinner party, and Woolf wishes she could come back with some hard fact to contradict the insult. However, she has no hard fact, so her strategy is to construct a situation that is as plausible and as accurate as her knowledge of history permits. Lacking fact, the novelist Virginia Woolf relies on imagination.

As it turned out, Woolf's portrait of Judith Shakespeare is so vivid that many readers actually believed William Shakespeare had such a sister. Judith Shakespeare did not exist, however. Her fictional character enables Woolf to speculate on how the life of any talented woman would have developed given the circumstances and limitations imposed on all women at the time. In the process, Woolf tries to reconstruct the world of Elizabethan England and place Judith in it.

Woolf goes about this act of imagination with extraordinary deliberateness. Her tone is cool and detached, almost as if she were a historian herself. She rarely reveals contempt for the opinions of men who are dismissive of women, such as the unnamed bishop. Yet, we catch an edgy tone when she discusses his views on women in literature.

On the other hand, when she turns to Mr. Oscar Browning, a professor who believed the best women in Oxford were inferior to the worst men, we see another side of Woolf. She reveals that after making his high-minded pronouncements, Mr. Browning returned to his quarters for an assignation with an illiterate stable boy. This detail is meant to reveal the true intellectual level of Mr. Browning, as well as his attitude toward women.

Woolf makes careful use of simile in such statements as "for fiction, imaginative work that is, is not dropped like a pebble upon the ground, as science may be; fiction is like a spider's web, attached ever so lightly perhaps, but still attached to life at all four corners" (para. 2). Later, she shows a highly efficient use of language: "to write a work of genius is almost always a feat of prodigious difficulty.... Dogs will bark; people will interrupt; money must be made; health will break down" (para. 11). For a woman — who would not even have had a room of her own in an Elizabethan household — the impediments to creating "a work of genius" were insurmountable.

One reason for Woolf's controlled and cool tone is that she wrote with the knowledge that most men were very conservative. In 1929, people would not read what she wrote if she became enraged on paper. They would turn the page and ignore her argument. Thus, her tone seems inviting and cautious, almost as if Woolf is portraying herself as conservative on women's issues and in agreement with men like the historian Trevelyan and the unnamed bishop. However, nothing could be further from the truth. Woolf's anger may seethe and rage beneath the surface, but she keeps the surface smooth enough for those who disagree with her to be lured on to read.

One of the interesting details of Woolf's style is her allusiveness. She alludes to the work of many writers — male writers such as John Keats; Alfred, Lord Tennyson; and Robert Burns; and women writers such as Jane Austen, Emily Brontë, and George Eliot. Woolf's range of reference is that of the highly literary person — which she was; yet the way in which she makes reference to other important writers is designed not to offend the reader. If the reader knows the references, then Woolf will communicate on a special shared level of understanding. If the reader does not know the references, there is nothing in Woolf's manner that makes it difficult for the reader to continue and understand her main points.

Woolf's rhetoric in this piece is singularly polite. She makes her points without rancor and alarm. They are detailed, specific, and in many ways irrefutable. What she feels she has done is nothing less than tell the truth.

❖ PREREADING QUESTIONS: WHAT TO READ FOR

The following prereading questions may help you anticipate key issues in the discussion of Virginia Woolf's "Shakespeare's Sister." Keeping them in mind during your first reading of the selection should help focus your attention.

1. What was the expected role of women in Shakespeare's time?
2. By what means could Shakespeare's imaginary sister have become a dramatist?

Shakespeare's Sister

It was disappointing not to have brought back in the evening some important statement, some authentic fact. Women are poorer than men because—this or that. Perhaps now it would be better to give up seeking for the truth, and receiving on one's head an avalanche of opinion hot as lava, discolored as dish-water. It would be better to draw the curtains; to shut out distractions; to light the lamp; to narrow the enquiry and to ask the historian, who records not opinions but facts, to describe under what conditions women lived, not throughout the ages, but in England, say in the time of Elizabeth.

For it is a perennial puzzle why no woman wrote a word of that extraordinary literature when every other man, it seemed, was capable of song or sonnet. What were the conditions in which women lived, I asked myself; for fiction, imaginative work that is, is not dropped like a pebble upon the ground, as science may be; fiction is like a spider's web, attached ever so lightly perhaps, but still attached to life at all four corners. Often the attachment is scarcely perceptible; Shakespeare's plays, for instance, seem to hang there complete by themselves. But when the web is pulled askew, hooked up at the edge, torn in the middle, one remembers that these webs are not spun in midair by incorporeal creatures, but are the work of suffering human beings, and are attached to grossly material things, like health and money and the houses we live in.

I went, therefore, to the shelf where the histories stand and took down one of the latest, Professor Trevelyan's[1] *History of England*. Once more I looked up Women, found "position of," and turned to the pages indicated. "Wife-beating," I read, "was a recognized right of man, and was practiced without shame by high as well as low. . . . Similarly," the historian goes on, "the daughter who refused to marry the gentleman of her parents' choice was liable to be locked up, beaten, and flung about the room, without any shock being inflicted on public opinion. Marriage was not an affair of personal affection, but of family avarice, particularly in the 'chivalrous' upper classes. . . . Betrothal often took place while one or both of the parties was in the cradle, and marriage when they were scarcely out of the nurses' charge." That was about 1470, soon after Chaucer's time. The next reference to the position of women is some two hundred years later, in the time of the Stuarts. "It was still the exception for women of the upper and middle class to choose their own husbands, and when the husband had been assigned, he was lord and master, so far at least as law and custom could make him. Yet even so," Professor Trevelyan concludes, "neither Shakespeare's women nor those of authentic seventeenth-century

---

[1] **Trevelyan: George Macaulay (1876–1962)**   One of England's great historians. [Woolf's note]

memoirs, like the Verneys and the Hutchinsons, seem wanting in personality and character." Certainly, if we consider it, Cleopatra must have had a way with her; Lady Macbeth, one would suppose, had a will of her own; Rosalind, one might conclude, was an attractive girl. Professor Trevelyan is speaking no more than the truth when he remarks that Shakespeare's women do not seem wanting in personality and character. Not being a historian, one might go even further and say that women have burnt like beacons in all the works of all the poets from the beginning of time—Clytemnestra, Antigone, Cleopatra, Lady Macbeth, Phèdre, Cressida, Rosalind, Desdemona, the Duchess of Malfi, among the dramatists; then among the prose writers: Millamant, Clarissa, Becky Sharp, Anna Karenina, Emma Bovary, Madame de Guermantes—the names flock to mind, nor do they recall women "lacking in personality and character." Indeed, if woman had no existence save in the fiction written by men, one would imagine her a person of the utmost importance; very various; heroic and mean; splendid and sordid; infinitely beautiful and hideous in the extreme; as great as a man, some think even greater.[2] But this is woman in fiction. In fact, as Professor Trevelyan points out, she was locked up, beaten, and flung about the room.

A very queer, composite being thus emerges. Imaginatively she is of the highest importance; practically she is completely insignificant. She pervades poetry from cover to cover; she is all but absent from history. She dominates the lives of kings and conquerors in fiction; in fact she was the slave of any boy whose parents forced a ring upon her finger. Some of the most inspired words, some of the most profound thoughts in literature fall from her lips; in real life she could hardly read, could scarcely spell, and was the property of her husband.   4

It was certainly an odd monster that one made up by reading the historians first and the poets afterwards—a worm winged like an eagle; the spirit of life and beauty in a kitchen chopping up suet. But these monsters, however amusing to the imagination, have no existence in fact. What one must do to bring her to life was to think poetically and prosaically at one and the same moment, thus   5

---

[2] **even greater**   "It remains a strange and almost inexplicable fact that in Athena's city, where women were kept in almost Oriental suppression as odalisques or drudges, the stage should yet have produced figures like Clytemnestra and Cassandra, Atossa and Antigone, Phèdre and Medea, and all the other heroines who dominate play after play of the 'misogynist' Euripides. But the paradox of this world where in real life a respectable woman could hardly show her face alone in the street, and yet on the stage a woman equals or surpasses a man, has never been satisfactorily explained. In modern tragedy the same predominance exists. At all events, a very cursory survey of Shakespeare's work (similarly with Webster, though not with Marlowe or Jonson) suffices to reveal how this dominance, this initiative of women, persists from Rosalind to Lady Macbeth. So too in Racine; six of his tragedies bear their heroines' names; and what male characters of his shall we set against Hermione and Andromaque, Bérénice and Roxane, Phèdre and Athalie? So again with Ibsen; what men shall we match with Solveig and Nora, Hedda and Hilda Wangel and Rebecca West?"—F. L. Lucas, *Tragedy*, pp. 114–15. [Woolf's note]

keeping in touch with fact—that she is Mrs. Martin, aged thirty-six, dressed in blue, wearing a black hat and brown shoes; but not losing sight of fiction either—that she is a vessel in which all sorts of spirits and forces are coursing and flashing perpetually. The moment, however, that one tries this method with the Elizabethan woman, one branch of illumination fails; one is held up by the scarcity of facts. One knows nothing detailed, nothing perfectly true and substantial about her. History scarcely mentions her. And I turned to Professor Trevelyan again to see what history meant to him. I found by looking at his chapter headings that it meant—

"The Manor Court and the Methods of Open-field Agriculture . . . The Cis-   6 tercians and Sheep-farming . . . The Crusades . . . The University . . . The House of Commons . . . The Hundred Years' War . . . The Wars of the Roses . . . The Renaissance Scholars . . . The Dissolution of the Monasteries . . . Agrarian and Religious Strife . . . The Origin of English Sea-power . . . The Armada . . ." and so on. Occasionally an individual woman is mentioned, an Elizabeth, or a Mary; a queen or a great lady. But by no possible means could middle-class women with nothing but brains and character at their command have taken part in any one of the great movements which, brought together, constitute the historian's view of the past. Nor shall we find her in any collection of anecdotes. Aubrey[3] hardly mentions her. She never writes her own life and scarcely keeps a diary; there are only a handful of her letters in existence. She left no plays or poems by which we can judge her. What one wants, I thought—and why does not some brilliant student at Newnham or Girton[4] supply it?—is a mass of information; at what age did she marry; how many children had she as a rule; what was her house like; had she a room to herself; did she do the cooking; would she be likely to have a servant? All these facts lie somewhere, presumably, in parish registers and account books; the life of the average Elizabethan woman must be scattered about somewhere, could one collect it and make a book of it. It would be ambitious beyond my daring, I thought, looking about the shelves for books that were not there, to suggest to the students of those famous colleges that they should rewrite history, though I own that it often seems a little queer as it is, unreal, lopsided; but why should they not add a supplement to history? calling it, of course, by some inconspicuous name so that women might figure there without impropriety? For one often catches a glimpse of them in the lives of the great, whisking away into the background, concealing, I sometimes think, a wink, a laugh, perhaps a tear. And, after all, we have lives enough of Jane Austen; it scarcely seems necessary to consider again the influence of the

---

[3] **John Aubrey (1626–1697)**   English antiquarian noted for his *Brief Lives*, biographical sketches of famous men.

[4] **Newnham or Girton**   Two women's colleges founded at Cambridge in the 1870s. [Woolf's note] Newnham (1871) and Girton (1869) were the first women's colleges at Cambridge University.

tragedies of Joanna Baillie upon the poetry of Edgar Allan Poe; as for myself, I should not mind if the homes and haunts of Mary Russell Mitford were closed to the public for a century at least. But what I find deplorable, I continued, looking about the bookshelves again, is that nothing is known about women before the eighteenth century. I have no model in my mind to turn about this way and that. Here am I asking why women did not write poetry in the Elizabethan age, and I am not sure how they were educated; whether they were taught to write; whether they had sitting-rooms to themselves; how many women had children before they were twenty-one; what, in short, they did from eight in the morning till eight at night. They had no money evidently; according to Professor Trevelyan they were married whether they liked it or not before they were out of the nursery, at fifteen or sixteen very likely. It would have been extremely odd, even upon this showing, had one of them suddenly written the plays of Shakespeare, I concluded, and I thought of that old gentleman, who is dead now, but was a bishop, I think, who declared that it was impossible for any woman, past, present, or to come, to have the genius of Shakespeare. He wrote to the papers about it. He also told a lady who applied to him for information that cats do not as a matter of fact go to heaven, though they have, he added, souls of a sort. How much thinking those old gentlemen used to save one! How the borders of ignorance shrank back at their approach! Cats do not go to heaven. Women cannot write the plays of Shakespeare.

Be that as it may, I could not help thinking, as I looked at the works of Shakespeare on the shelf, that the bishop was right at least in this; it would have been impossible, completely and entirely, for any woman to have written the plays of Shakespeare in the age of Shakespeare. Let me imagine, since facts are so hard to come by, what would have happened had Shakespeare had a wonderfully gifted sister, called Judith, let us say. Shakespeare himself went, very probably — his mother was an heiress — to the grammar school, where he may have learnt Latin — Ovid, Virgil, and Horace — and the elements of grammar and logic. He was, it is well known, a wild boy who poached rabbits, perhaps shot a deer, and had, rather sooner than he should have done, to marry a woman in the neighborhood, who bore him a child rather quicker than was right. That escapade sent him to seek his fortune in London. He had, it seemed, a taste for the theatre; he began by holding horses at the stage door. Very soon he got work in the theatre, became a successful actor, and lived at the hub of the universe, meeting everybody, knowing everybody, practicing his art on the boards, exercising his wits in the streets, and even getting access to the palace of the queen. Meanwhile his extraordinarily gifted sister, let us suppose, remained at home. She was as adventurous, as imaginative, as agog to see the world as he was. But she was not sent to school. She had no chance of learning grammar and logic, let alone of reading Horace and Virgil. She picked up a book now and then, one of her brother's perhaps, and read a few pages. But

7

then her parents came in and told her to mend the stockings or mind the stew and not moon about with books and papers. They would have spoken sharply but kindly, for they were substantial people who knew the conditions of life for a woman and loved their daughter—indeed, more likely than not she was the apple of her father's eye. Perhaps she scribbled some pages up in an apple loft on the sly, but was careful to hide them or set fire to them. Soon, however, before she was out of her teens, she was to be betrothed to the son of a neighboring wool-stapler. She cried out that marriage was hateful to her, and for that she was severely beaten by her father. Then he ceased to scold her. He begged her instead not to hurt him, not to shame him in this matter of her marriage. He would give her a chain of beads or a fine petticoat, he said; and there were tears in his eyes. How could she disobey him? How could she break his heart? The force of her own gift alone drove her to it. She made up a small parcel of her belongings, let herself down by a rope one summer's night and took the road to London. She was not seventeen. The birds that sang in the hedge were not more musical than she was. She had the quickest fancy, a gift like her brother's, for the tune of words. Like him, she had a taste for the theatre. She stood at the stage door; she wanted to act, she said. Men laughed in her face. The manager—a fat, loose-lipped man—guffawed. He bellowed something about poodles dancing and women acting—no woman, he said, could possibly be an actress. He hinted—you can imagine what. She could get no training in her craft. Could she even seek her dinner in a tavern or roam the streets at midnight? Yet her genius was for fiction and lusted to feed abundantly upon the lives of men and women and the study of their ways. At last—for she was very young, oddly like Shakespeare the poet in her face, with the same grey eyes and rounded brows—at last Nick Greene, the actor-manager took pity on her; she found herself with child by that gentleman and so—who shall measure the heat and violence of the poet's heart when caught and tangled in a woman's body?—killed herself one winter's night and lies buried at some cross-roads where the omnibuses now stop outside the Elephant and Castle.[5]

That, more or less, is how the story would run, I think, if a woman in Shakespeare's day had had Shakespeare's genius. But for my part, I agree with the deceased bishop, if such he was—it is unthinkable that any woman in Shakespeare's day should have had Shakespeare's genius. For genius like Shakespeare's is not born among laboring, uneducated, servile people. It was not born in England among the Saxons and the Britons. It is not born today among the working classes. How, then, could it have been born among women whose work began, according to Professor Trevelyan, almost before they were out of the nursery, who were forced to it by their parents and held to it by all the power of law and custom? Yet genius of a sort must have existed among

8

---

[5] **Elephant and Castle**   A bus stop in London. The name came from a local pub.

women as it must have existed among the working classes. Now and again an Emily Brontë or a Robert Burns[6] blazes out and proves its presence. But certainly it never got itself on to paper. When, however, one reads of a witch being ducked, of a woman possessed by devils, of a wise woman selling herbs, or even of a very remarkable man who had a mother, then, I think we are on the track of a lost novelist, a suppressed poet, of some mute and inglorious Jane Austen, some Emily Brontë who dashed her brains out on the moor or mopped and mowed about the highways crazed with the torture that her gift had put her to. Indeed, I would venture to guess that Anon, who wrote so many poems without signing them, was often a woman. It was a woman Edward Fitzgerald,[7] I think, suggested who made the ballads and the folk-songs, crooning them to her children, beguiling her spinning with them, or the length of the winter's night.

   This may be true or it may be false—who can say?—but what is true in it, so it seemed to me, reviewing the story of Shakespeare's sister as I had made it, is that any woman born with a great gift in the sixteenth century would certainly have gone crazed, shot herself, or ended her days in some lonely cottage outside the village, half witch, half wizard, feared and mocked at. For it needs little skill in psychology to be sure that a highly gifted girl who had tried to use her gift for poetry would have been so thwarted and hindered by other people, so tortured and pulled asunder by her own contrary instincts, that she must have lost her health and sanity to a certainty. No girl could have walked to London and stood at a stage door and forced her way into the presence of actor-managers without doing herself a violence and suffering an anguish which may have been irrational—for chastity may be a fetish invented by certain societies for unknown reasons—but were none the less inevitable. Chastity had then, it has even now, a religious importance in a woman's life, and has so wrapped itself round with nerves and instincts that to cut it free and bring it to the light of day demands courage of the rarest. To have lived a free life in London in the sixteenth century would have meant for a woman who was poet and playwright a nervous stress and dilemma which might well have killed her. Had she survived, whatever she had written would have been twisted and deformed, issuing from a strained and morbid imagination. And undoubtedly, I thought, looking at the shelf where there are no plays by women, her work would have gone unsigned. That refuge she would have sought certainly. It was the relic of the sense of chastity that dictated anonymity to women even

9

---

[6] **Emily Brontë (1818–1848)** wrote *Wuthering Heights;* **Robert Burns (1759–1796)** was a Scots poet; **Jane Austen (1775–1817)** wrote *Pride and Prejudice* and many other novels. All three wrote against very great odds.

[7] **Edward Fitzgerald (1809–1883)**   British scholar, poet, and translator who wrote *The Rubaiyat of Omar Khayyam.*

so late as the nineteenth century. Currer Bell, George Eliot, George Sand,[8] all the victims of inner strife as their writings prove, sought ineffectively to veil themselves by using the name of a man. Thus they did homage to the convention, which if not implanted by the other sex was liberally encouraged by them (the chief glory of a woman is not to be talked of, said Pericles, himself a much-talked-of man), that publicity in women is detestable. Anonymity runs in their blood. The desire to be veiled still possesses them. They are not even now as concerned about the health of their fame as men are, and, speaking generally, will pass a tombstone or a signpost without feeling an irresistible desire to cut their names on it, as Alf, Bert, or Chas. must do in obedience to their instinct, which murmurs if it sees a fine woman go by, or even a dog, Ce chien est à moi.[9] And, of course, it may not be a dog, I thought, remembering Parliament Square, the Sieges Allee and other avenues; it may be a piece of land or a man with curly black hair. It is one of the great advantages of being a woman that one can pass even a very fine negress without wishing to make an Englishwoman of her.

That woman, then, who was born with a gift of poetry in the sixteenth century, was an unhappy woman, a woman at strife against herself. All the conditions of her life, all her own instincts, were hostile to the state of mind which is needed to set free whatever is in the brain. But what is the state of mind that is most propitious to the act of creation, I asked. Can one come by any notion of the state that furthers and makes possible that strange activity? Here I opened the volume containing the Tragedies of Shakespeare. What was Shakespeare's state of mind, for instance, when he wrote *Lear* and *Antony and Cleopatra*? It was certainly the state of mind most favorable to poetry that there has ever existed. But Shakespeare himself said nothing about it. We only know casually and by chance that he "never blotted a line." Nothing indeed was ever said by the artist himself about his state of mind until the eighteenth century perhaps. Rousseau perhaps began it. At any rate, by the nineteenth century self-consciousness had developed so far that it was the habit for men of letters to describe their minds in confessions and autobiographies. Their lives also were written, and their letters were printed after their deaths. Thus, though we do not know what Shakespeare went through when he wrote *Lear*, we do know what Carlyle went through when he wrote the *French Revolution;* what Flaubert went through when he wrote *Madame Bovary;* what Keats[10] was

10

---

[8] **Currer Bell (1816–1855), George Eliot (1819–1880),** and **George Sand (1804–1876)**   Masculine pen names for Charlotte Brontë, Mary Ann Evans, and Amandine-Aurore-Lucille Dudevant, three major novelists of the nineteenth century.

[9] **Ce chien est à moi**   That's my dog.

[10] **Thomas Carlyle (1795–1881), Gustave Flaubert (1821–1880),** and **John Keats (1795–1821)**   Important nineteenth-century writers, all men.

going through when he tried to write poetry against the coming of death and the indifference of the world.

And one gathers from this enormous modern literature of confession and self-analysis that to write a work of genius is almost always a feat of prodigious difficulty. Everything is against the likelihood that it will come from the writer's mind whole and entire. Generally material circumstances are against it. Dogs will bark; people will interrupt; money must be made; health will break down. Further, accentuating all these difficulties and making them harder to bear is the world's notorious indifference. It does not ask people to write poems and novels and histories; it does not need them. It does not care whether Flaubert finds the right word or whether Carlyle scrupulously verifies this or that fact. Naturally, it will not pay for what it does not want. And so the writer, Keats, Flaubert, Carlyle, suffers, especially in the creative years of youth, every form of distraction and discouragement. A curse, a cry of agony, rises from those books of analysis and confession. "Mighty poets in their misery dead"—that is the burden of their song. If anything comes through in spite of all this, it is a miracle, and probably no book is born entire and uncrippled as it was conceived. 11

But for women, I thought, looking at the empty shelves, these difficulties were infinitely more formidable. In the first place, to have a room of her own, let alone a quiet room or a sound-proof room, was out of the question, unless her parents were exceptionally rich or very noble, even up to the beginning of the nineteenth century. Since her pin money, which depended on the goodwill of her father, was only enough to keep her clothed, she was debarred from such alleviations as came even to Keats or Tennyson or Carlyle, all poor men, from a walking tour, a little journey to France, from the separate lodging which, even if it were miserable enough, sheltered them from the claims and tyrannies of their families. Such material difficulties were formidable; but much worse were the immaterial. The indifference of the world which Keats and Flaubert and other men of genius have found so hard to bear was in her case not indifference but hostility. The world did not say to her as it said to them, Write if you choose; it makes no difference to me. The world said with a guffaw, Write? What's the good of your writing? Here the psychologists of Newnham and Girton might come to our help, I thought, looking again at the blank spaces on the shelves. For surely it is time that the effect of discouragement upon the mind of the artist should be measured, as I have seen a dairy company measure the effect of ordinary milk and Grade A milk upon the body of the rat. They set two rats in cages side by side, and of the two one was furtive, timid, and small, and the other was glossy, bold, and big. Now what food do we feed women as artists upon? I asked, remembering, I suppose, that dinner of prunes and custard. To answer that question I had only to open the evening paper and to read that Lord Birkenhead is of opinion—but really I am not going to trouble to copy our Lord 12

Birkenhead's opinion upon the writing of women. What Dean Inge says I will leave in peace. The Harley Street specialist may be allowed to rouse the echoes of Harley Street with his vociferations without raising a hair on my head. I will quote, however, Mr. Oscar Browning, because Mr. Oscar Browning was a great figure in Cambridge at one time, and used to examine the students at Girton and Newnham. Mr. Oscar Browning was wont to declare "that the impression left on his mind, after looking over any set of examination papers, was that, irrespective of the marks he might give, the best woman was intellectually the inferior of the worst man." After saying that Mr. Browning went back to his rooms — and it is this sequel that endears him and makes him a human figure of some bulk and majesty — he went back to his rooms and found a stable-boy lying on the sofa — "a mere skeleton, his cheeks were cavernous and sallow, his teeth were black, and he did not appear to have the full use of his limbs. . . . 'That's Arthur' [said Mr. Browning]. 'He's a dear boy really and most high-minded.'" The two pictures always seem to me to complete each other. And happily in this age of biography the two pictures often do complete each other, so that we are able to interpret the opinions of great men not only by what they say, but by what they do.

But though this is possible now, such opinions coming from the lips of important people must have been formidable enough even fifty years ago. Let us suppose that a father from the highest motives did not wish his daughter to leave home and become writer, painter, or scholar. "See what Mr. Oscar Browning says," he would say; and there was not only Mr. Oscar Browning; there was the *Saturday Review;* there was Mr. Greg — the "essentials of a woman's being," said Mr. Greg emphatically, "are that *they are supported by, and they minister to, men*" — there was an enormous body of masculine opinion to the effect that nothing could be expected of women intellectually. Even if her father did not read out loud these opinions, any girl could read them for herself; and the reading, even in the nineteenth century, must have lowered her vitality, and told profoundly upon her work. There would always have been that assertion — you cannot do this, you are incapable of doing that — to protest against, to overcome. Probably for a novelist this germ is no longer of much effect; for there have been women novelists of merit. But for painters it must still have some sting in it; and for musicians, I imagine, is even now active and poisonous in the extreme. The woman composer stands where the actress stood in the time of Shakespeare. Nick Greene, I thought, remembering the story I had made about Shakespeare's sister, said that a woman acting put him in mind of a dog dancing. Johnson repeated the phrase two hundred years later of women preaching. And here, I said, opening a book about music, we have the very words used again in this year of grace, 1928, of women who try to write music. "Of Mlle. Germaine Tailleferre one can only repeat Dr. Johnson's dictum concerning a woman preacher, transposed into terms of music. 'Sir,

13

a woman's composing is like a dog's walking on his hind legs. It is not done well, but you are surprised to find it done at all.'"[11] So accurately does history repeat itself.

Thus, I concluded, shutting Mr. Oscar Browning's life and pushing away the rest, it is fairly evident that even in the nineteenth century a woman was not encouraged to be an artist. On the contrary, she was snubbed, slapped, lectured, and exhorted. Her mind must have been strained and her vitality lowered by the need of opposing this, of disproving that. For here again we come within range of that very interesting and obscure masculine complex which has had so much influence upon the woman's movement; that deep-seated desire, not so much that *she* shall be inferior as that *he* shall be superior, which plants him wherever one looks, not only in front of the arts, but barring the way to politics too, even when the risk to himself seems infinitesimal and the suppliant humble and devoted. Even Lady Bessborough, I remembered, with all her passion for politics, must humbly bow herself and write to Lord Granville Leveson-Gower: ". . . notwithstanding all my violence in politics and talking so much on that subject, I perfectly agree with you that no woman has any business to meddle with that or any other serious business, farther than giving her opinion (if she is ask'd)." And so she goes on to spend her enthusiasm where it meets with no obstacle whatsoever upon that immensely important subject, Lord Granville's maiden speech in the House of Commons. The spectacle is certainly a strange one, I thought. The history of men's opposition to women's emancipation is more interesting perhaps than the story of that emancipation itself. An amusing book might be made of it if some young student at Girton or Newnham would collect examples and deduce a theory — but she would need thick gloves on her hands, and bars to protect her of solid gold.

But what is amusing now, I recollected, shutting Lady Bessborough, had to be taken in desperate earnest once. Opinions that one now pastes in a book labelled cock-a-doodle-dum and keeps for reading to select audiences on summer nights once drew tears, I can assure you. Among your grandmothers and great-grandmothers there were many that wept their eyes out. Florence Nightingale shrieked aloud in her agony.[12] Moreover, it is all very well for you, who have got yourselves to college and enjoy sitting-rooms — or is it only bed-sitting-rooms? — of your own to say that genius should disregard such opinions; that genius should be above caring what is said of it. Unfortunately, it is precisely the men or women of genius who mind most what is said of them.

14

15

---

[11] *A Survey of Contemporary Music*, Cecil Gray, p. 246. [Woolf's note]

[12] *See Cassandra* by Florence Nightingale, printed in *The Cause*, by R. Strachey. [Woolf's note]

Remember Keats. Remember the words he had cut on his tombstone.[13] Think of Tennyson; think—but I need hardly multiply instances of the undeniable, if very unfortunate, fact that it is the nature of the artist to mind excessively what is said about him. Literature is strewn with the wreckage of men who have minded beyond reason the opinions of others.

And this susceptibility of theirs is doubly unfortunate, I thought, returning   16
again to my original enquiry into what state of mind is most propitious for creative work, because the mind of an artist, in order to achieve the prodigious effort of freeing whole and entire the work that is in him, must be incandescent, like Shakespeare's mind, I conjectured, looking at the book which lay open at *Antony and Cleopatra*. There must be no obstacle in it, no foreign matter unconsumed.

For though we say that we know nothing about Shakespeare's state of   17
mind, even as we say that, we are saying something about Shakespeare's state of mind. The reason perhaps why we know so little of Shakespeare—compared with Donne or Ben Jonson or Milton[14]—is that his grudges and spites and antipathies are hidden from us. We are not held up by some "revelation" which reminds us of the writer. All desire to protest, to preach, to proclaim an injury, to pay off a score, to make the world the witness of some hardship or grievance was fired out of him and consumed. Therefore his poetry flows from him free and unimpeded. If ever a human being got his work expressed completely, it was Shakespeare. If ever a mind was incandescent, unimpeded, I thought, turning again to the bookcase, it was Shakespeare's mind.

---

[13] **words . . . tombstone**   "Here lies one whose name is writ on water." [Woolf's note]

[14] **John Donne (1572–1631), Ben Jonson (1572/3–1637), John Milton (1608–1674)**
    Three of the most important seventeenth-century poets.

✖ QUESTIONS FOR CRITICAL READING

1. How did Elizabethan cultural roles limit opportunities for women in the literary arts?

2. Why does Woolf begin by referring to an eminent historian?

3. Why does history treat sixteenth- and seventeenth-century women with so little notice?

4. What is Woolf's point regarding the behavior of Oscar Browning?

5. Why does Woolf worry over the relation of opinions to facts?

6. What is the difference between the way women are represented in history and the way they are depicted in fiction?

7. Why does Woolf have Judith Shakespeare become pregnant?

✖ SUGGESTIONS FOR CRITICAL WRITING

1. Woolf says that a woman "born with a gift of poetry in the sixteenth century, was an unhappy woman, a woman at strife against herself" (para. 10). What does it mean for a woman to be "at strife against herself"? What are the characteristics of such a strife, and what are its implications for the woman? In what ways would she be aware of such inner strife?

2. Look up brief biographies of the women writers who took men's names. Woolf lists three together: Currer Bell, George Eliot, and George Sand. What did they have in common? Why did they feel the need to use a man's name for their pseudonym? What did they do to avoid being stigmatized as women writers? Were they equally successful? Are they now considered feminist writers?

3. Woolf's view is that biology determines one's fate. She is explicitly speaking of the biology of the female in our culture, but how much do you feel she attends to the entire range of gender? Margaret Mead (p. 236) talks about gender deviance and its effect on the individual in a standardized society. Woolf's society was standardized, but she belonged to a subculture of intellectuals, the Bloomsbury group, that practiced many forms of deviant gender behavior. Would she have argued as strongly in support of deviant sexual behavior as she does for equal opportunities for Shakespeare's "sister"? What would her argument be? Present your case, using some of Woolf's rhetorical techniques.

4. Read the book from which this essay comes, *A Room of One's Own*. The last chapter discusses androgyny, the quality of possessing characteristics of both sexes. Woolf argues that perhaps a writer should not be exclusively male or female in outlook, but should combine both. How effective is her argument in that chapter? How much of an impact did the book have on your own views of feminism?

5. Explain why it is so important for a woman to have "a room of one's own." Obviously, the use of the word *room* stands for much more than a simple room with four walls and a door. What is implied in the way Woolf uses this term? Do you think this point is still valid for women in the twenty-first century? Why are so many women in any age denied the right to have "a room of one's own"?

6. Woolf says that "even in the nineteenth century a woman was not encouraged to be an artist. On the contrary, she was snubbed, slapped, lectured, and exhorted. Her mind must have been strained and her vitality lowered by the need of opposing this, of disproving that" (para. 14). Explain the implications of this statement, and decide whether it still describes the situation of many or most women. Use your personal experience where relevant, but consider the situations of any women you find interesting.

7. **CONNECTIONS**   Karen Horney (p. 500) and Woolf both take analytical approaches to their subject matter, despite the fact that Horney is a psychologist and Woolf is a literary figure. What methods of analysis does Woolf use

that are also characteristic of Horney? Does Horney's psychological approach to analyzing the relationship between men and women match Woolf's? How does each author make use of narrative techniques in her analytic approach?

8. **CONNECTIONS**   In what ways are Mary Wollstonecraft (p. 195) and Woolf in agreement about the waste of women's talents in any age? As you comment on this, consider, too, the ways in which these writers differ in their approach to discussing women and the ways in which women sometimes cooperate in accepting their own restrictions. Which of these writers is more obviously a modern feminist in your mind? Which of them is more convincing? Why?

9. **CONNECTIONS**   Based on Woolf's attitudes in this essay, which of the male writers in this collection comes closest to supporting feminist views? Consider especially the work of Karl Marx (p. 335), Martin Luther King Jr. (p. 252), and Henry David Thoreau (p. 720). Which of their views seems most sympathetic to the problems Woolf considers here?

MARGARET
MEAD

Sex and Temperament

MARGARET MEAD (1901–1978) received her Ph.D. in anthropology from Columbia University in 1929. She is renowned for her extensive fieldwork in the South Pacific, especially for her work on Manus, one of the Admiralty Islands, northwest of New Guinea. The fieldwork that she did in 1925 led to her doctoral dissertation and to the book that established her as one of the most visible and readable modern anthropologists, *Coming of Age in Samoa: A Psychological Study of Primitive Youth for Western Civilization* (1928). She learned seven indigenous languages and always used them with the people she studied and lived with so that she could think in their vernacular. Her experiences with the Manus spanned twenty-five years, some of which included a disastrous world war. She first lived with them in 1928, when she began the work that led her to write *Growing Up in New Guinea: A Comparative Study of Primitive Education* (1930).

Mead was married three times, as she tells us in her autobiography, *Blackberry Winter* (1972), which focuses on her early years. All three of her husbands were also anthropologists. With Gregory Bateson, to whom she was married from 1936 to 1950, she had her only child, a daughter. Later, Mead was romantically involved with yet another anthropologist, Rhoda Metraux, with whom she lived from 1955 until her death. She taught as an adjunct professor at Columbia University from 1954 to 1978 and took two years off to found the anthropology department at Fordham University in Lincoln Center, New York. Throughout these years, she was also involved with work in museums, particularly the American Museum of Natural History.

Her primary research interests were the patterns of education of the young and the patterns of socialization of women and women's sexuality, particularly early sexual development. Mead asserted that cultural mores are relative and that there are many ways of working out the details of courtship, sex, marriage, and love. She consistently argued that

---

From *Sex and Temperament in Three Primitive Societies.*

there is no right way, suggesting rather that there are many ways, all of which are right within an individual culture.

Mead emphasizes the psychological model of cultures. To the dismay of some anthropologists, Mead also emphasizes the social, traditional, and historical aspects of a culture while concerning herself less with the biological or genetic. Recent critics have faulted Mead for this emphasis and have charged her with ignoring biological determinism in her research.

Near the end of her life, Mead was the most famous anthropologist in the United States. She wrote columns for popular magazines, published more than twenty books, and lectured widely to various audiences. Mead was popular, but she was also a careful and devoted scientist. Her work in the South Pacific still stands as a major contribution to our knowledge of how different cultures deal with basic social issues.

MEAD'S RHETORIC

Mead has the advantage of writing clearly and with a journalist's skill, focusing on the most interesting details. "Sex and Temperament" explores society's expectations regarding temperament rather than trying to convince the reader that one or another of the points of view is accurate. As she says in her opening paragraph, she is not interested in determining if there are "actual and universal differences between the sexes." Instead, she is concerned with the range of temperaments — "dominance, bravery, aggressiveness, objectivity, malleability" (para. 6) — that human beings can have and all the other temperamental qualities individuals can possess. Then, she goes on to explore whether any specific group of temperaments is explicitly limited to one sex or the other.

She admits that, at the beginning of her study, "[she] too had been accustomed to use in [her] thinking such concepts as 'mixed type,' to think of some men as having 'feminine' temperaments, of some women as having 'masculine' minds" (para. 6). In other words, she originally felt that there was a natural disposition of temperaments that was inbuilt depending on sex. Then, with her work among other cultures, her thinking began to change. Ultimately, she realized that each culture begins shaping individuals at birth to fit the patterns that it has determined as most desirable. As she says, there are several courses of action available to a society. One is to emphasize contrasting temperaments in boys and girls. Another is to de-emphasize differences and concentrate on individual talent and natural temperament in determining occupation and behavior, a condition that Mead seems to imply is in place in her own time. However, she is worried that we may "return to a strict regimentation of women" (para. 9) in the future. Society can also "admit that men and women are capable of being molded to a single pattern as easily as to a diverse one" (para. 11).

Interestingly, Mead offers a view that may not be a counterargument so much as a personal lament. She sees in societies in which men and women dress differently, behave differently, and are given different occupations a beautiful diversity that is lost when those distinctions are lost. She is careful to point out that standard biologically relevant distinctions — the difference in male strength and male height — are rendered vastly less significant in leveling the relationship of men and women today because the law has some of the same force that strength in battle had ages ago. Mead is balanced in her view, pointing to the behavior of societies as being responsible for the shaping of male and female standard temperaments.

Two of her rhetorical techniques are comparison and example. She frequently turns to her experience in the Arapesh or Mundugumor societies. She points to an instance in which the "sacrifice of sex-differences has meant a loss in complexity to the society" (para. 13) of the Mundugumor, and by implication, she seems to say that similar results either have happened or will happen in our own culture. Her discussion of the stereotyping of women and priests as always opposed to war demonstrates that this attitude has no basis in any "natural" endowments of either group. However, in any society in which such rigid temperamental qualities are educated into either sex, there will be a considerable number of rebels. She says that the greater the standardization of temperament, the greater will be the tendency to produce rebels.

She also exhibits considerable concern for individuals in a society that places great emphasis on gender-related temperaments when those individuals do not themselves have the "proper" temperaments. These are people who do not fit the mold, who are not naturally disposed to the roles that society has established for them. When society is inflexible and makes it difficult for such individuals to express themselves, they endure a lifetime of frustration. Her concern extends even to those who are victims of birth, by which she means those born into nobility or into peasantry, with temperaments opposite to those that their society demands. She uses India, with its former caste system, as a specific example.

Mead proposes an experiment in which the temperamental distinctions that our society assumes are natural to men and women were linked to eye color instead of gender. She suggests attributing gentleness, nurturance, and submissiveness to blue-eyed people and arrogance, domination, and purposiveness to brown-eyed people. Thus, these qualities would not be gender linked. Interestingly, in some grade schools similar experiments with eye color were put into place to help young people understand the effect of sanctioned distinctions on people who did not fit the requirements of the group.

Mead's final suggestion is to avoid standardizing society or removing all of society's expectations. Instead, she suggests that society might learn to tolerate and accept the natural diversity within a population of many individuals with differing temperaments, some of whom fit society's expectations and some of whom do not. In any event, she celebrates diversity and sees that societies all have different ways of establishing desired temperaments but that they must make room for people who do not easily fit into sanctioned roles.

⁑ PREREADING QUESTIONS: WHAT TO READ FOR

The following prereading questions may help you anticipate key issues in the discussion of Margaret Mead's "Sex and Temperament." Keeping them in mind during your first reading of the selection should help focus your attention.

1. What does Mead mean by *temperament*?
2. What is a "standardized" society?
3. What alternatives are there to a standardized society?
4. Do all societies regard men and women as different in temperament?

Sex and Temperament

This study is not concerned with whether there are or are not actual and universal differences between the sexes, either quantitative or qualitative. It is not concerned with whether women are more variable than men, which was claimed before the doctrine of evolution exalted variability, or less variable, which was claimed afterwards. It is not a treatise on the rights of women, nor an inquiry into the basis of feminism. It is, very simply, an account of how three primitive societies have grouped their social attitudes towards temperament about the very obvious facts of sex-difference. I studied this problem in simple societies because here we have the drama of civilization writ small, a social microcosm alike in kind, but different in size and magnitude, from the complex social structures of peoples who, like our own, depend upon a written tradition and upon the integration of a great number of conflicting historical traditions. Among the gentle mountain-dwelling Arapesh, the fierce cannibalistic Mundugumor, and the graceful head-hunters of Tchambuli, I studied this question. Each of these tribes had, as has every human society, the point of sex-difference to use as one theme in the plot of social life, and each of these three peoples has developed that theme differently. In comparing the way in which they have dramatized sex-difference, it is possible to gain a greater insight into what elements are social constructs, originally irrelevant to the biological facts of sex-gender.

Our own society makes great use of this plot. It assigns different roles to the two sexes, surrounds them from birth with an expectation of different behavior, plays out the whole drama of courtship, marriage, and parenthood in terms of types of behavior believed to be innate and therefore appropriate for one sex or for the other. We know dimly that these roles have changed even within our history. Studies like Mrs. Putnam's *The Lady*[1] depict woman as an infinitely malleable lay figure upon which mankind has draped ever varying period-costumes, in keeping with which she wilted or waxed imperious, flirted or fled. But all discussions have emphasized not the relative social personalities assigned to the two sexes, but rather the superficial behavior-patterns assigned to women, often not even to all women, but only to women of the upper class. A sophisticated recognition that upper-class women were puppets of a changing tradition blurred rather than clarified the issue. It left untouched the roles assigned to men, who were conceived as proceeding along a special masculine road, shaping women to their fads and whims in womanliness. All discussion of the position of women, of the character and temperament of women, the enslavement or the emancipation of women, obscures the basic issue — the recognition that the cultural plot behind human relations is the way in which the roles of the two sexes are conceived, and that the growing boy is shaped to a local and special emphasis as inexorably as is the growing girl. . . .

. . . We know that human cultures do not all fall into one side or the other   3
of a single scale and that it is possible for one society to ignore completely an issue which two other societies have solved in contrasting ways. Because a people honor the old may mean that they hold children in slight esteem, but a people may also, like the Ba Thonga of South Africa, honor neither old people nor children; or, like the Plains Indians, dignify the little child and the grandfather; or, again, like the Manus and parts of modern America, regard children as the most important group in society. In expecting simple reversals — that if an aspect of social life is not specifically sacred, it must be specifically secular; that if men are strong, women must be weak — we ignore the fact that cultures exercise far greater license than this in selecting the possible aspects of human life which they will minimize, overemphasize, or ignore. And while every culture has in some way institutionalized the roles of men and women, it has not necessarily been in terms of contrast between the prescribed personalities of the two sexes, nor in terms of dominance or submission. With the paucity of material for elaboration, no culture has failed to seize upon the conspicuous facts of age and sex in some way, whether it be the convention of one Philippine tribe that no man can keep a secret, the Manus assumption that only men enjoy playing with babies, the Toda prescription of almost all domestic work as too sacred for women, or the Arapesh insistence that women's heads are stronger than men's. In the division of labor, in dress, in manners, in social and religious functioning — sometimes in only a few of these respects,

---

[1] *The Lady: Studies of Certain Phases of Her History*   Book by Emily James Putnam (1865–1944), the first woman dean of Barnard College, in New York City.

sometimes in all—men and women are socially differentiated, and each sex, as a sex, forced to conform to the role assigned to it. In some societies, these socially defined roles are mainly expressed in dress or occupation, with no insistence upon innate temperamental differences. Women wear long hair and men wear short hair, or men wear curls and women shave their heads; women wear skirts and men wear trousers, or women wear trousers, and men wear skirts. Women weave and men do not, or men weave and women do not. Such simple tie-ups as these between dress and occupation and sex are easily taught to every child and make no assumptions to which a given child cannot easily conform.

It is otherwise in societies that sharply differentiate the behavior of men   4
and of women in terms which assume a genuine difference in temperament. Among the Dakota Indians of the Plains, the importance of an ability to stand any degree of danger or hardship was frantically insisted upon as a masculine characteristic. From the time that a boy was five or six, all the conscious educational effort of the household was bent towards shaping him into an indubitable male. Every tear, every timidity, every clinging to a protective hand or desire to continue to play with younger children or with girls, was obsessively interpreted as proof that he was not going to develop into a real man. In such a society it is not surprising to find the *berdache*,[2] the man who had voluntarily given up the struggle to conform to the masculine role and who wore female attire and followed the occupations of a woman. The institution of the *berdache* in turn served as a warning to every father; the fear that the son might become a *berdache* informed the parental efforts with an extra desperation, and the very pressure which helped to drive a boy to that choice was redoubled. The invert who lacks any discernible physical basis for his inversion has long puzzled students of sex, who when they can find no observable glandular abnormality turn to theories of early conditioning or identification with a parent of opposite sex. In the course of this investigation, we shall have occasion to examine the "masculine" woman and the "feminine" man as they occur in these different tribes, to inquire whether it is always a woman of dominating nature who is conceived as masculine, or a man who is gentle, submissive, or fond of children or embroidery who is conceived as feminine.

. . . [W]e shall be concerned with the patterning of sex-behavior from the   5
standpoint of temperament, with the cultural assumptions that certain temperamental attitudes are "naturally" masculine and others "naturally" feminine. In this matter, primitive people seem to be, on the surface, more sophisticated than we are. Just as they know that the gods, the food habits, and the marriage

---

[2] ***berdache***   American Indian term for a man who dresses as a woman and does a woman's work.

customs of the next tribe differ from those of their own people, and do not insist that one form is true or natural while the other is false or unnatural, so they often know that the temperamental proclivities which they regard as natural for men or for women differ from the natural temperaments of the men and women among their neighbors. Nevertheless, within a narrower range and with less of a claim for the biological or divine validity of their social forms than we often advance, each tribe has certain definite attitudes towards temperament, a theory of what human beings, either men or women or both, are naturally like, a norm in terms of which to judge and condemn those individuals who deviate from it.

Two of these tribes have no idea that men and women are different in   6 temperament. They allow them different economic and religious roles, different skills, different vulnerabilities to evil magic and supernatural influences. The Arapesh believe that painting in color is appropriate only to men, and the Mundugumor consider fishing an essentially feminine task. But any idea that temperamental traits of the order of dominance, bravery, aggressiveness, objectivity, malleability, are inalienably associated with one sex (as opposed to the other) is entirely lacking. This may seem strange to a civilization which in its sociology, its medicine, its slang, its poetry, and its obscenity accepts the socially defined differences between the sexes as having an innate basis in temperament and explains any deviation from the socially determined role as abnormality of native endowment or early maturation. It came as a surprise to me because I too had been accustomed to use in my thinking such concepts as "mixed type," to think of some men as having "feminine" temperaments, of some women as having "masculine" minds. I set as my problem a study of the conditioning of the social personalities of the two sexes, in the hope that such an investigation would throw some light upon sex-differences. I shared the general belief of our society that there was a natural sex-temperament which could at the most only be distorted or diverted from normal expression. I was innocent of any suspicion that the temperaments which we regard as native to one sex might instead be mere variations of human temperament, to which the members of either or both sexes may, with more or less success in the case of different individuals, be educated to approximate.

•   •   •

The knowledge that the personalities of the two sexes are socially produced   7 is congenial to every program that looks forward towards a planned order of society. It is a two-edged sword that can be used to hew a more flexible, more varied society than the human race has ever built, or merely to cut a narrow path down which one sex or both sexes will be forced to march, regimented, looking neither to the right nor to the left. . . .

There are at least three courses open to a society that has realized the   8
extent to which male and female personality are socially produced. Two of
these courses have been tried before, over and over again, at different times
in the long, irregular, repetitious history of the race. The first is to standardize
the personality of men and women as clearly contrasting, complementary, and
antithetical, and to make every institution in the society congruent with this
standardization. If the society declared that woman's sole function was motherhood and the teaching and care of young children, it could so arrange matters that every woman who was not physiologically debarred should become
a mother and be supported in the exercise of this function. It could abolish
the discrepancy between the doctrine that women's place is the home and the
number of homes that were offered to them. It could abolish the discrepancy
between training women for marriage and then forcing them to become the
spinster supports of their parents.

Such a system would be wasteful of the gifts of many women who could   9
exercise other functions far better than their ability to bear children in an
already overpopulated world. It would be wasteful of the gifts of many men
who could exercise their special personality gifts far better in the home than in
the market-place. It would be wasteful, but it would be clear. It could attempt
to guarantee to each individual the role for which society insisted upon training
him or her, and such a system would penalize only those individuals who, in
spite of all the training, did not display the approved personalities. There are
millions of persons who would gladly return to such a standardized method of
treating the relationship between the sexes, and we must bear in mind the possibility that the greater opportunities open in the twentieth century to women
may be quite withdrawn, and that we may return to a strict regimentation
of women.

The waste, if this occurs, will be not only of many women, but also of as   10
many men, because regimentation of one sex carries with it, to greater or less
degree, the regimentation of the other also. Every parental behest that defines
a way of sitting, a response to a rebuke or a threat, a game, or an attempt to
draw or sing or dance or paint, as feminine, is molding the personality of each
little girl's brother as well as molding the personality of the sister. There can
be no society which insists that women follow one special personality-pattern,
defined as feminine, which does not do violence also to the individuality of
many men.

Alternatively, society can take the course that has become especially   11
associated with the plans of most radical groups: admit that men and women
are capable of being molded to a single pattern as easily as to a diverse one,
and cease to make any distinction in the approved personality of both sexes.
Girls can be trained exactly as boys are trained, taught the same code, the
same forms of expression, the same occupations. This course might seem to

be the logic which follows from the conviction that the potentialities which different societies label as either masculine or feminine are really potentialities of some members of each sex, and not sex-linked at all. If this is accepted, is it not reasonable to abandon the kind of artificial standardizations of sex-differences that have been so long characteristic of European society, and admit that they are social fictions for which we have no longer any use? In the world today, contraceptives make it possible for women not to bear children against their will. The most conspicuous actual difference between the sexes, the difference in strength, is progressively less significant. Just as the difference in height between males is no longer a realistic issue, now that lawsuits have been substituted for hand-to-hand encounters, so the difference in strength between men and women is no longer worth elaboration in cultural institutions.

In evaluating such a program as this, however, it is necessary to keep in mind the nature of the gains that society has achieved in its most complex forms. A sacrifice of distinctions in sex-personality may mean a sacrifice in complexity. The Arapesh recognize a minimum of distinction in personality between old and young, between men and women, and they lack categories of rank or status. We have seen that such a society at the best condemns to personal frustration, and at the worst to maladjustment, all of those men and women who do not conform to its simple emphases. The violent person among the Arapesh cannot find, either in the literature, or in the art, or in the ceremonial, or in the history of his people, any expression of the internal drives that are shattering his peace of mind. Nor is the loser only the individual whose own type of personality is nowhere recognized in his society. The imaginative, highly intelligent person who is essentially in tune with the values of his society may also suffer by the lack of range and depth characteristic of too great simplicity. The active mind and intensity of one Arapesh boy whom I knew well was unsatisfied by the laissez-faire solutions, the lack of drama in his culture. Searching for some material upon which to exercise his imagination, his longing for a life in which stronger emotions would be possible, he could find nothing with which to feed his imagination but tales of the passionate outbursts of the maladjusted, outbursts characterized by a violent hostility to others that he himself lacked. 12

Nor is it the individual alone who suffers. Society is equally the loser, and we have seen such an attenuation in the dramatic representations of the Mundugumor. By phrasing the exclusion of women as a protective measure congenial to both sexes, the Arapesh kept their *tamberan*[3] cult, with the necessary audiences of women. But the Mundugumor developed a kind of personality 13

---

[3] *tamberan*   A noise-making device such as a bullhorn used by the Arapesh in rituals that assert male solidarity and masculinity.

for both men and women to which exclusion from any part of life was interpreted as a deadly insult. And as more and more Mundugumor women have demanded and been given the right of initiation, it is not surprising that the Mundugumor ceremonial life has dwindled, the actors have lost their audience, and one vivid artistic element in the life of the Mundugumor community is vanishing. The sacrifice of sex-differences has meant a loss in complexity to the society.

So in our own society. To insist that there are no sex-differences in a society that has always believed in them and depended upon them may be as subtle a form of standardizing personality as to insist that there are many sex-differences. This is particularly so in a changing tradition, when a group in control is attempting to develop a new social personality, as is the case today in many European countries. Take, for instance, the current assumption that women are more opposed to war than men, that any outspoken approval of war is more horrible, more revolting, in women than in men. Behind this assumption women can work for peace without encountering social criticism in communities that would immediately criticize their brothers or husbands if they took a similarly active part in peace propaganda. This belief that women are naturally more interested in peace is undoubtedly artificial, part of the whole mythology that considers women to be gentler than men. But in contrast let us consider the possibility of a powerful minority that wished to turn a whole society whole-heartedly towards war. One way of doing this would be to insist that women's motives, women's interests, were identical with men's, that women should take as bloodthirsty a delight in preparing for war as ever men do. The insistence upon the opposite point of view, that the woman as a mother prevails over the woman as a citizen, at least puts a slight drag upon agitation for war, prevents a blanket enthusiasm for war from being thrust upon the entire younger generation. The same kind of result follows if the clergy are professionally committed to a belief in peace. The relative bellicosity of different individual clerics may be either offended or gratified by the prescribed pacific role, but a certain protest, a certain dissenting note, will be sounded in society. The dangerous standardization of attitudes that disallows every type of deviation is greatly reinforced if neither age nor sex nor religious belief is regarded as automatically predisposing certain individuals to hold minority attitudes. The removal of all legal and economic barriers against women's participating in the world on an equal footing with men may be in itself a standardizing move towards the wholesale stamping-out of the diversity of attitudes that is such a dearly bought product of civilization.

Such a standardized society, in which men, women, children, priests, and soldiers were all trained to an undifferentiated and coherent set of values, must of necessity create the kind of deviant that we found among the Arapesh and the Mundugumor, the individual who, regardless of sex or occupation, rebels because he is temperamentally unable to accept the one-sided emphasis of his culture. The individuals who were specifically unadjusted in terms of their psycho-sexual role would, it is true, vanish, but with them would vanish the knowledge that there is more than one set of possible values.

To the extent that abolishing the differences in the approved personalities   16
of men and women means abolishing any expression of the type of personality once called exclusively feminine, or once called exclusively masculine, such a course involves a social loss. Just as a festive occasion is the gayer and more charming if the two sexes are dressed differently, so it is in less material matters. If the clothing is in itself a symbol, and a woman's shawl corresponds to a recognized softness in her character, the whole plot of personal relations is made more elaborate, and in many ways more rewarding. The poet of such a society will praise virtues, albeit feminine virtues, which might never have any part in a social Utopia that allowed no differences between the personalities of men and women.

To the extent that a society insists upon different kinds of personality so   17
that one age-group or class or sex-group may follow purposes disallowed or neglected in another, each individual participant in that society is the richer. The arbitrary assignment of set clothing, set manners, set social responses, to individuals born in a certain class, of a certain sex, or of a certain color, to those born on a certain day of the week, to those born with a certain complexion, does violence to the individual endowment of individuals, but permits the building of a rich culture. The most extreme development of a society that has attained great complexity at the expense of the individual is historical India, based, as it was, upon the uncompromising association of a thousand attributes of behavior, attitude, and occupation with an accident of birth. To each individual there was given the security, although it might be the security of despair, of a set role, and the reward of being born into a highly complex society.

Furthermore, when we consider the position of the deviant individual in   18
historical cultures, those who are born into a complex society in the wrong sex or class for their personalities to have full sway are in a better position than those who are born into a simple society which does not use in any way their special temperamental gifts. The violent women in a society that permits violence to men only, the strongly emotional member of an aristocracy in a culture that permits downright emotional expression only in the peasantry, the ritualistically inclined individual who is bred a Protestant in a country which has also Catholic institutions — each one of these can find expressed in some other group in the society the emotions that he or she is forbidden to manifest. He is given a certain kind of support by the mere existence of these values, values so congenial to him and so inaccessible because of an accident of birth. For those who are content with a vicarious spectator-role, or with materials upon which to feast the creative imagination, this may be almost

enough. They may be content to experience from the sidewalks during a parade, from the audience of a theatre or from the nave of a church, those emotions the direct expression of which is denied to them. The crude compensations offered by the moving pictures to those whose lives are emotionally starved are offered in subtler forms by the art and literature of a complex society to the individual who is out of place in his sex or his class or his occupational group.

Sex-adjustments, however, are not a matter of spectatorship, but a situation   19 in which the most passive individual must play some part if he or she is to participate fully in life. And while we may recognize the virtues of complexity, the interesting and charming plots that cultures can evolve upon the basis of accidents of birth, we may well ask: Is not the price too high? Could not the beauty that lies in contrast and complexity be obtained in some other way? If the social insistence upon different personalities for the two sexes results in so much confusion, so many unhappy deviants, so much disorientation, can we imagine a society that abandons these distinctions without abandoning the values that are at present dependent upon them?

Let us suppose that, instead of the classification laid down on the "natural"   20 bases of sex and race, a society had classified personality on the basis of eye-color. It had decreed that all blue-eyed people were gentle, submissive, and responsive to the needs of others, and all brown-eyed people were arrogant, dominating, self-centered, and purposive. In this case two complementary social themes would be woven together—the culture, in its art, its religion, its formal personal relations, would have two threads instead of one. There would be blue-eyed men, and blue-eyed women, which would mean that there were gentle, "maternal" women, and gentle, "maternal" men. A blue-eyed man might marry a woman who had been bred to the same personality as himself, or a brown-eyed woman who had been bred to the contrasting personality. One of the strong tendencies that makes for homosexuality, the tendency to love the similar rather than the antithetical persons, would be eliminated. Hostility between the two sexes as groups would be minimized, since the individual interests of members of each sex could be woven together in different ways, and marriages of similarity and friendships of contrast need carry no necessary handicap of possible psycho-sexual maladjustment. The individual would still suffer a mutilation of his temperamental preferences, for it would be the unrelated fact of eye-color that would determine the attitudes which he was educated to show. Every blue-eyed person would be forced into submissiveness and declared maladjusted if he or she showed any traits that it had been decided were only appropriate to the brown-eyed. The greatest social loss, however, in the classification of personality on the basis of sex would not be present in this society which based its classification on eye-color. Human relations, and especially those which involve sex, would not be artificially distorted.

But such a course, the substitution of eye-color for sex as a basis upon   21
which to educate children into groups showing contrasting personalities, while
it would be a definite advance upon a classification by sex, remains a parody of
all the attempts that society has made through history to define an individual's
role in terms of sex, or color, or date of birth, or shape of head.

However, the only solution of the problem does not lie between an accep-   22
tance of standardization of sex-differences with the resulting cost in individual happiness and adjustment, and the abolition of these differences with the
consequent loss in social values. A civilization might take its cues not from
such categories as age or sex, race or hereditary position in a family line, but
instead of specializing personality along such simple lines recognize, train, and
make a place for many and divergent temperamental endowments. It might
build upon the different potentialities that it now attempts to extirpate artificially in some children and create artificially in others.

Historically the lessening of rigidity in the classification of the sexes has   23
come about at different times, either by the creation of a new artificial category, or by the recognition of real individual differences. Sometimes the idea
of social position has transcended sex-categories. In a society that recognizes
gradations in wealth or rank, women of rank or women of wealth have been
permitted an arrogance which was denied to both sexes among the lowly or the
poor. Such a shift as this has been, it is true, a step towards the emancipation
of women, but it has never been a step towards the greater freedom of the individual. A few women have shared the upper-class personality, but to balance
this a great many men as well as women have been condemned to a personality
characterized by subservience and fear. Such shifts as these mean only the substitution of one arbitrary standard for another. A society is equally unrealistic
whether it insists that only men can be brave, or that only individuals of rank
can be brave.

To break down one line of division, that between the sexes, and substi-   24
tute another, that between classes, is no real advance. It merely shifts the
irrelevancy to a different point. And meanwhile, individuals born in the upper
classes are shaped inexorably to one type of personality, to an arrogance that
is again uncongenial to at least some of them, while the arrogant among the
poor fret and fume beneath their training for submissiveness. At one end of
the scale is the mild, unaggressive young son of wealthy parents who is forced
to lead, at the other the aggressive, enterprising child of the slums who is
condemned to a place in the ranks. If our aim is greater expression for each
individual temperament, rather than any partisan interest in one sex or its
fate, we must see these historical developments which have aided in freeing
some women as nevertheless a kind of development that also involved major
social losses.

The second way in which categories of sex-differences have become less rigid is through a recognition of genuine individual gifts as they occurred in either sex. Here a real distinction has been substituted for an artificial one, and the gains are tremendous for society and for the individual. Where writing is accepted as a profession that may be pursued by either sex with perfect suitability, individuals who have the ability to write need not be debarred from it by their sex, nor need they, if they do write, doubt their essential masculinity or femininity. An occupation that has no basis in sex-determined gifts can now recruit its ranks from twice as many potential artists. And it is here that we can find a ground-plan for building a society that would substitute real differences for arbitrary ones. We must recognize that beneath the superficial classifications of sex and race the same potentialities exist, recurring generation after generation, only to perish because society has no place for them. Just as society now permits the practice of an art to members of either sex, so it might also permit the development of many contrasting temperamental gifts in each sex. It might abandon its various attempts to make boys fight and to make girls remain passive, or to make all children fight, and instead shape our educational institutions to develop to the full the boy who shows a capacity for maternal behavior, the girl who shows an opposite capacity that is stimulated by fighting against obstacles. No skill, no special aptitude, no vividness of imagination or precision of thinking would go unrecognized because the child who possessed it was of one sex rather than the other. No child would be relentlessly shaped to one pattern of behavior, but instead there should be many patterns, in a world that had learned to allow to each individual the pattern which was most congenial to his gifts.

Such a civilization would not sacrifice the gains of thousands of years during which society has built up standards of diversity. The social gains would be conserved, and each child would be encouraged on the basis of his actual temperament. Where we now have patterns of behavior for women and patterns of behavior for men, we would then have patterns of behavior that expressed the interests of individuals with many kinds of endowment. There would be ethical codes and social symbolisms, an art and a way of life, congenial to each endowment.

Historically our own culture has relied for the creation of rich and contrasting values upon many artificial distinctions, the most striking of which is sex. It will not be by the mere abolition of these distinctions that society will develop patterns in which individual gifts are given place instead of being forced into an ill-fitting mold. If we are to achieve a richer culture, rich in contrasting values, we must recognize the whole gamut of human potentialities, and so weave a less arbitrary social fabric, one in which each diverse human gift will find a fitting place.

▟ QUESTIONS FOR CRITICAL READING

1. What temperament traits do you have? Are they gender linked?

2. What problems face a society that has established rigid gender-linked expectations?

3. How are gender-linked temperament expectations reinforced by society?

4. How much of a range of difference in gender expectation has Mead found in other cultures?

5. Does our society expect different behavior from men than from women? Are those differences visible in daily behavior?

6. Is it possible for a society to mold similar behavior in men and women?

7. Why does Mead give us all the examples she does from other societies? Do you find them convincing?

8. What problems do people with the "wrong" temperaments face in a society?

9. Do you think gender-linked temperaments are biological and natural? Why or why not?

▟ SUGGESTIONS FOR CRITICAL WRITING

1. Mead contends that gender-linked temperaments exist because a society has promoted and reinforced those distinctions. She suggests that gender-linked distinctions are not specifically biological. In a brief essay, summarize the key points of her argument and then, using your own observations and experiences, argue a case that either defends or attacks her position.

2. Which of the societies Mead refers to seems to have the best solution to dealing with what appear to be gender-linked temperaments? If possible, research that society and clarify the nature of its treatment of men and women. How does it treat men who seem "feminine" and women who seem "masculine" in temperament?

3. As best you can tell from this selection, what would Mead's ideal society be like in regard to the question of individual temperaments? Examine the passages in which she makes statements that you feel express her views and respond to them with your own analysis. Would her society satisfy the needs of our modern culture? Would it benefit a great many people, or would it benefit only the few? Is it a society in which you would be comfortable?

4. Drawing on your own experience, explain what you have observed about the way people you know treat "masculine women" and "feminine men." What has the culture done to those who mistreat such individuals? How do the individuals react? What price do they pay for the fact that their temperaments do not fit in with societal expectations? What price does the entire society pay for insisting on rigid patterns of behavior?

5. In paragraph 12, Mead begins an exploration of societies that erase sex differences between men and women. After describing those societies and the results of their decisions, Mead seems to be rethinking her position. She says, "The sacrifice of sex-differences has meant a loss in complexity to the society" (para. 13). Would our society lose complexity if sex differences were somehow erased? Or would the level of complexity remain the same or even increase?

6. **CONNECTIONS**   Mead talks in her selection about the question of temperament. How would you define temperament? Do you observe other people's temperaments? Can the idea of temperament describe the attitude of a culture? Compare Mead's view of gender issues with that of Judith Butler (p. 298). Which is more scientific? Which author has observed cultural behavior more closely? Which of them has made observations that have more relevance for our own culture? Which has had more of an effect on your thinking on the question of gender differences?

7. **CONNECTIONS**   How does Karen Horney's psychological discussion of the relationships of men and women in society (p. 500) support Mead's view that people's temperaments are developed according to the needs of society? Given Horney's analysis, what predictions might Mead make about the ways in which our current society would probably tend to shape the temperaments of men and women in the future? Do you think that Horney is fearful that, as Mead says, our future culture may "return to a strict regimentation of women" (para. 9)? Could that be the basis for the sense of distrust that Horney references?

MARTIN
LUTHER KING JR.

Letter from Birmingham Jail

MARTIN LUTHER KING JR. (1929–1968) was the most influential civil rights leader in America for a period of more than fifteen years. He was an ordained minister with a doctorate in theology from Boston University. He worked primarily in the South, where he labored steadily to overthrow laws that promoted segregation and to increase the number of black voters registered in southern communities.

From 1958 to 1968, demonstrations and actions opened up opportunities for African Americans who in the South hitherto had been prohibited from sitting in certain sections of buses, using facilities such as water fountains in bus stations, and sitting at luncheon counters with whites. Such laws — unjust and insulting, not to mention unconstitutional — were not challenged by local authorities. Martin Luther King Jr., who became famous for supporting a program to integrate buses in Montgomery, Alabama, was asked by the Southern Christian Leadership Conference (SCLC) to assist in the fight for civil rights in Birmingham, Alabama, where an SCLC meeting was to be held.

King was arrested as the result of a program of sit-ins at luncheon counters and wrote the letter printed here to a group of clergymen who had criticized his position. King had been arrested before and would be arrested again — resembling Henry David Thoreau somewhat in his attitude toward laws that did not conform to moral justice.

King, like Thoreau, was willing to suffer for his views, especially when he found himself faced with punitive laws denying civil rights to all citizens. His is a classic case in which the officers of the government pled that they were dedicated to maintaining a stable civil society, even as they restricted King's individual rights. In 1963, many of the good people to whom King addressed this letter firmly believed that peace and order might be threatened by granting African Americans the true independence and freedom that King insisted were their rights and indeed were guaranteed under the Constitution. This is why King's letter objects to an injustice that was rampant in Frederick Douglass's time but inexcusable in the time of John F. Kennedy.

Eventually the causes King promoted were victorious. His efforts helped change attitudes in the South and spur legislation that has benefited all Americans. His views concerning nonviolence spread throughout the world, and by the early 1960s he had become famous as a man who stood for human rights and human dignity virtually everywhere. He won the Nobel Peace Prize in 1964.

Although King himself was nonviolent, his program left both him and his followers open to the threat of violence. The sit-ins and voter registration programs spurred countless bombings, threats, and murders by members of the white community. King's life was often threatened, his home bombed, his followers harassed. He was assassinated at the Lorraine Motel in Memphis, Tennessee, on April 4, 1968. But before he died he saw — largely through his own efforts, influence, and example — the face of America change.

KING'S RHETORIC

The most obvious rhetorical tradition King assumes in this important work is that of the books of the Bible that were originally letters, such as Paul's Epistle to the Ephesians and his several letters to the Corinthians. Many of Paul's letters were written while he was in prison in Rome, and he established a moral position that could inspire the citizens who received the letters. At the same time, Paul carried out the most important work of the early Christian church — spreading the word of Jesus to those who wished to be Christians but who needed clarification and encouragement.

It is not clear that the clergymen who received King's letter fully appreciated the rhetorical tradition he drew on — but they were men who preached from the Bible and certainly should have understood it. The text itself alludes to the mission of Paul and to his communications to his people. King works with this rhetorical tradition not only because it is effective but also because it resonates with the deepest aspect of his calling — spreading the Gospel of Christ. Brotherhood and justice were his message.

King's tone is one of utmost patience with his critics. He seems bent on winning them over to his point of view, just as he seems confident that — because they are, like him, clergymen — their goodwill should help them see the justice of his views.

His method is that of careful reasoning, focusing on the substance of their criticism, particularly on their complaints that his actions were "unwise and untimely" (para. 1). King takes each of those charges in turn, carefully analyzes it against his position, and then follows with the clearest possible statement of his own views and why he feels they are worth adhering to. "Letter from Birmingham Jail" is a model of close and reasonable analysis of a very complex situation. It succeeds largely because it remains concrete, treating one issue after another carefully, refusing to be caught up in passion or posturing. Above all, King remains grounded in logic, convinced that his arguments will in turn convince his audience.

✂ **PREREADING QUESTIONS: WHAT TO READ FOR**

The following prereading questions may help you anticipate key issues in the discussion of Martin Luther King's "Letter from Birmingham Jail." Keeping them in mind during your first reading of the selection should help focus your attention.

1. What kind of injustice did Martin Luther King find in Birmingham?
2. Why was Martin Luther King disappointed in the white churches?

Letter from Birmingham Jail

April 16, 1963

MY DEAR FELLOW CLERGYMEN:[1]

While confined here in the Birmingham city jail, I came across your recent statement calling my present activities "unwise and untimely." Seldom do I pause to answer criticism of my work and ideas. If I sought to answer all the criticisms that cross my desk, my secretaries would have little time for anything other than such correspondence in the course of the day, and I would have no time for constructive work. But since I feel that you are men of genuine good will and that your criticisms are sincerely set forth, I want to try to answer your statement in what I hope will be patient and reasonable terms.

I think I should indicate why I am here in Birmingham, since you have been influenced by the view which argues against "outsiders coming in." I have the honor of serving as president of the Southern Christian Leadership Conference, an organization operating in every southern state, with headquarters in Atlanta, Georgia. We have some eighty-five affiliated organizations across the South, and one of them is the Alabama Christian Movement for Human Rights. Frequently we share staff, educational, and financial

---

[1] This response to a published statement by eight fellow clergymen from Alabama (Bishop C. C. J. Carpenter, Bishop Joseph A. Durick, Rabbi Hilton L. Grafman, Bishop Paul Hardin, Bishop Holan B. Harmon, the Reverend George M. Murray, the Reverend Edward V. Ramage, and the Reverend Earl Stallings) was composed under somewhat constricting circumstances. Begun on the margins of the newspaper in which the statement appeared while I was in jail, the letter was continued on scraps of writing paper supplied by a friendly Negro trusty, and concluded on a pad my attorneys were eventually permitted to leave me. Although the text remains in substance unaltered, I have indulged in the author's prerogative of polishing it for publication. [King's note]

resources with our affiliates. Several months ago the affiliate here in Birmingham asked us to be on call to engage in a nonviolent direct-action program if such were deemed necessary. We readily consented, and when the hour came we lived up to our promise. So I, along with several members of my staff, am here because I was invited here. I am here because I have organizational ties here.

But more basically, I am in Birmingham because injustice is here. Just as the prophets of the eighth century B.C. left their villages and carried their "thus saith the Lord" far beyond the boundaries of their home towns, and just as the Apostle Paul left his village of Tarsus[2] and carried the gospel of Jesus Christ to the far corners of the Greco-Roman world, so am I compelled to carry the gospel of freedom beyond my own home town. Like Paul, I must constantly respond to the Macedonian call for aid.[3]   3

Moreover, I am cognizant of the interrelatedness of all communities and states. I cannot sit idly by in Atlanta and not be concerned about what happens in Birmingham. Injustice anywhere is a threat to justice everywhere. We are caught in an inescapable network of mutuality, tied in a single garment of destiny. Whatever affects one directly, affects all indirectly. Never again can we afford to live with the narrow, provincial, "outside agitator" idea. Anyone who lives inside the United States can never be considered an outsider anywhere within its bounds.   4

You deplore the demonstrations taking place in Birmingham. But your statement, I am sorry to say, fails to express a similar concern for the conditions that brought about the demonstrations. I am sure that none of you would want to rest content with the superficial kind of social analysis that deals merely with effects and does not grapple with underlying causes. It is unfortunate that demonstrations are taking place in Birmingham, but it is even more unfortunate that the city's white power structure left the Negro community with no alternative.   5

In any nonviolent campaign there are four basic steps: collection of the facts to determine whether injustices exist; negotiation; self-purification; and direct action. We have gone through all these steps in Birmingham. There can be no gainsaying the fact that racial injustice engulfs this community. Birmingham is probably the most thoroughly segregated city in the United States. Its ugly record of brutality is widely known. Negroes have experienced grossly unjust treatment in the courts. There have been more unsolved bombings of Negro   6

---

[2] **village of Tarsus**   Birthplace of St. Paul (?–67 C.E.), in Asia Minor, present-day Turkey, close to Syria.

[3] **the Macedonian call for aid**   The citizens of Philippi, in Macedonia (northern Greece), were among the staunchest Christians. Paul went to their aid frequently; he also had to resolve occasional bitter disputes within the Christian community there (see Phil. 2:2–14).

homes and churches in Birmingham than in any other city in the nation. These are the hard brutal facts of the case. On the basis of these conditions, Negro leaders sought to negotiate with the city fathers. But the latter consistently refused to engage in good-faith negotiation.

Then, last September, came the opportunity to talk with leaders of Birmingham's economic community. In the course of the negotiations, certain promises were made by the merchants—for example, to remove the stores' humiliating racial signs. On the basis of these promises, the Reverend Fred Shuttlesworth and the leaders of the Alabama Christian Movement for Human Rights agreed to a moratorium on all demonstrations. As the weeks and months went by, we realized that we were the victims of a broken promise. A few signs, briefly removed, returned; the others remained.   7

As in so many past experiences, our hopes had been blasted, and the shadow of deep disappointment settled upon us. We had no alternative except to prepare for direct action, whereby we would present our very bodies as a means of laying our case before the conscience of the local and the national community. Mindful of the difficulties involved, we decided to undertake a process of self-purification. We began a series of workshops on nonviolence, and we repeatedly asked ourselves: "Are you able to accept blows without retaliating?" "Are you able to endure the ordeal of jail?" We decided to schedule our direct-action program for the Easter season, realizing that except for Christmas, this is the main shopping period of the year. Knowing that a strong economic-withdrawal program would be the by-product of direct action, we felt that this would be the best time to bring pressure to bear on the merchants for the needed change.   8

Then it occurred to us that Birmingham's mayoral election was coming up in March, and we speedily decided to postpone action until after election day. When we discovered that the Commissioner of Public Safety, Eugene "Bull" Connor, had piled up enough votes to be in the run-off, we decided again to postpone action until the day after the run-off so that the demonstrations could not be used to cloud the issues. Like many others, we waited to see Mr. Connor defeated, and to this end we endured postponement after postponement. Having aided in this community need, we felt that our direct-action program could be delayed no longer.   9

You may well ask, "Why direct action? Why sit-ins, marches, and so forth? Isn't negotiation a better path?" You are quite right in calling for negotiation. Indeed, this is the very purpose of direct action. Nonviolent direct action seeks to create such a crisis and foster such a tension that a community which has constantly refused to negotiate is forced to confront the issue. It seeks so to dramatize the issue that it can no longer be ignored. My citing the creation of tension as part of the work of the nonviolent resister may sound rather shocking. But I must confess that I am not afraid of the word "tension." I have earnestly   10 opposed violent tension, but there is a type of constructive, nonviolent tension which is necessary for growth. Just as Socrates[4] felt that it was necessary to create a tension in the mind so that individuals could rise from the bondage of myths and half truths to the unfettered realm of creative analysis and objective appraisal, so must we see the need for nonviolent gadflies to create the kind of tension in society that will help men rise from the dark depths of prejudice and racism to the majestic heights of understanding and brotherhood.

The purpose of our direct-action program is to create a situation so   11
crisis-packed that it will inevitably open the door to negotiation. I therefore concur with you in your call for negotiation. Too long has our beloved Southland been bogged down in a tragic effort to live in monologue rather than dialogue.

One of the basic points in your statement is that the action that I and my   12
associates have taken in Birmingham is untimely. Some have asked: "Why didn't you give the new city administration time to act?" The only answer that I can give to this query is that the new Birmingham administration must be prodded about as much as the outgoing one, before it will act. We are sadly mistaken if we feel that the election of Albert Boutwell as mayor will bring the millennium[5] to Birmingham. While Mr. Boutwell is a much more gentle person than Mr. Connor, they are both segregationists, dedicated to maintenance of the status quo. I have hoped that Mr. Boutwell will be reasonable enough to see the futility of massive resistance to desegregation. But he will not see this without pressure from devotees of civil rights. My friends, I must say to you that we have not made a single gain in civil rights without determined legal and nonviolent pressure. Lamentably, it is an historical fact that privileged groups seldom give up their privileges voluntarily. Individuals may see the moral light and voluntarily give up their unjust posture; but, as Reinhold Niebuhr[6] has reminded us, groups tend to be more immoral than individuals.

We know through painful experience that freedom is never voluntarily   13
given by the oppressor; it must be demanded by the oppressed. Frankly, I have

---

[4] **Socrates (470?–399 B.C.E.)** The "tension in the mind" King refers to is created by the question-answer technique known as the Socratic method. By posing questions at the beginning of the paragraph, King shows his willingness to share Socrates' rhetorical techniques. Socrates was imprisoned and killed for his civil disobedience (see paras. 21 and 25). He was the greatest of the Greek philosophers.

[5] **the millennium** A reference to Revelation 20, according to which the second coming of Christ will be followed by one thousand years of peace, when the devil will be incapacitated. After this will come a final battle between good and evil, followed by the Last Judgment.

[6] **Reinhold Niebuhr (1892–1971)** Protestant American philosopher who urged church members to put their beliefs into action against social injustice. He urged Protestantism to develop and practice a code of social ethics and wrote in *Moral Man and Immoral Society* (1932) of the point King mentions here.

yet to engage in a direct-action campaign that was "well timed" in the view of those who have not suffered unduly from the disease of segregation. For years now I have heard the word "Wait!" It rings in the ear of every Negro with piercing familiarity. This "Wait" has almost always meant "Never." We must come to see, with one of our distinguished jurists, that "justice too long delayed is justice denied."[7]

We have waited for more than 340 years for our constitutional and   14
God-given rights. The nations of Asia and Africa are moving with jet-like speed toward gaining political independence, but we still creep at horse-and-buggy pace toward gaining a cup of coffee at a lunch counter. Perhaps it is easy for those who have never felt the stinging darts of segregation to say, "Wait." But when you have seen vicious mobs lynch your mothers and fathers at will and drown your sisters and brothers at whim; when you have seen hate-filled policemen curse, kick, and even kill your black brothers and sisters; when you see the vast majority of your twenty million Negro brothers smothering in an airtight cage of poverty in the midst of an affluent society; when you suddenly find your tongue twisted and your speech stammering as you seek to explain to your six-year-old daughter why she can't go to the public amusement park that has just been advertised on television, and see tears welling up in her eyes when she is told that Funtown is closed to colored children, and see ominous clouds of inferiority beginning to form in her little mental sky, and see her beginning to distort her personality by developing an unconscious bitterness toward white people; when you have to concoct an answer for a five-year-old son who is asking, "Daddy, why do white people treat colored people so mean?"; when you take a cross-country drive and find it necessary to sleep night after night in the uncomfortable corners of your automobile because no motel will accept you; when you are humiliated day in and day out by nagging signs reading "white" and "colored"; when your first name becomes "nigger," your middle name becomes "boy" (however old you are) and your last name becomes "John," and your wife and mother are never given the respected title "Mrs."; when you are harried by day and haunted by night by the fact that you are a Negro, living constantly at tiptoe stance, never quite knowing what to expect next, and are plagued with inner fears and outer resentments; when you are forever fighting a degenerating sense of "nobodiness"—then you will understand why we find it difficult to wait. There comes a time when the cup of endurance runs over, and men are no longer willing to be plunged into the abyss of despair. I hope, sirs, you can understand our legitimate and unavoidable impatience.

---

[7] **"justice too long delayed is justice denied"**   Chief Justice Earl Warren's expression in 1954 was adapted from English writer Walter Savage Landor's phrase "Justice delayed is justice denied."

You express a great deal of anxiety over our willingness to break laws. This   15
is certainly a legitimate concern. Since we so diligently urge people to obey the
Supreme Court's decision of 1954 outlawing segregation in the public schools,
at first glance it may seem rather paradoxical for us consciously to break laws.
One may well ask: "How can you advocate breaking some laws and obeying
others?" The answer lies in the fact that there are two types of laws: just and
unjust. I would be the first to advocate obeying just laws. One has not only a
legal but a moral responsibility to obey just laws. Conversely, one has a moral
responsibility to disobey unjust laws. I would agree with St. Augustine[8] that "an
unjust law is no law at all."

Now, what is the difference between the two? How does one determine   16
whether a law is just or unjust? A just law is a manmade code that squares
with the moral law or the law of God. An unjust law is a code that is out of
harmony with the moral law. To put it in the terms of St. Thomas Aquinas:[9]
An unjust law is a human law that is not rooted in eternal law and natural law.
Any law that uplifts human personality is just. Any law that degrades human
personality is unjust. All segregation statutes are unjust because segregation
distorts the soul and damages the personality. It gives the segregator a false
sense of superiority and the segregated a false sense of inferiority. Segregation,
to use the terminology of the Jewish philosopher Martin Buber,[10] substitutes
an "I-it" relationship for an "I-thou" relationship and ends up relegating persons to the status of things. Hence segregation is not only politically, economically, and sociologically unsound, it is morally wrong and sinful. Paul Tillich[11]
has said that sin is separation. Is not segregation an existential expression of
man's tragic separation, his awful estrangement, his terrible sinfulness? Thus
it is that I can urge men to obey the 1954 decision of the Supreme Court, for
it is morally right; and I can urge them to disobey segregation ordinances, for
they are morally wrong.

Let us consider a more concrete example of just and unjust laws. An unjust   17
law is a code that a numerical or power majority group compels a minority
group to obey but does not make binding on itself. This is *difference* made

---

[8] **St. Augustine (354–430)**   Early bishop of the Christian Church who deeply influenced
the spirit of Christianity for many centuries.

[9] **St. Thomas Aquinas (1225–1274)**   The greatest of the medieval Christian philosophers and one of the greatest church authorities.

[10] **Martin Buber (1878–1965)**   Jewish theologian. *I and Thou* (1923) is his most famous
book.

[11] **Paul Tillich (1886–1965)**   An important twentieth-century Protestant theologian who
held that Christianity was reasonable and effective in modern life. Tillich saw sin as an
expression of man's separation from God, from himself, and from his fellow man. King
sees the separation of the races as a further manifestation of man's sinfulness. Tillich,
who was driven out of Germany by the Nazis, stresses the need for activism and the
importance of action in determining moral vitality, just as King does.

legal. By the same token, a just law is a code that a majority compels a minority to follow and that it is willing to follow itself. This is *sameness* made legal.

Let me give another explanation. A law is unjust if it is inflicted on a   18
minority that, as a result of being denied the right to vote, had no part in enacting or devising the law. Who can say that the legislature of Alabama which set up that state's segregation laws was democratically elected? Throughout Alabama all sorts of devious methods are used to prevent Negroes from becoming registered voters, and there are some counties in which, even though Negroes constitute a majority of the population, not a single Negro is registered. Can any law enacted under such circumstances be considered democratically structured?

Sometimes a law is just on its face and unjust in its application. For   19
instance, I have been arrested on a charge of parading without a permit. Now, there is nothing wrong in having an ordinance which requires a permit for a parade. But such an ordinance becomes unjust when it is used to maintain segregation and to deny citizens the First Amendment privilege of peaceful assembly and protest.

I hope you are able to see the distinction I am trying to point out. In no   20
sense do I advocate evading or defying the law, as would the rabid segregationist. That would lead to anarchy. One who breaks an unjust law must do so openly, lovingly, and with a willingness to accept the penalty. I submit that an individual who breaks a law that conscience tells him is unjust, and who willingly accepts the penalty of imprisonment in order to arouse the conscience of the community over its injustice, is in reality expressing the highest respect for law.

Of course, there is nothing new about this kind of civil disobedience. It was   21
evidenced subliminally in the refusal of Shadrach, Meshach, and Abednego to obey the laws of Nebuchadnezzar,[12] on the ground that a higher moral law was at stake. It was practiced superbly by the early Christians, who were willing to face hungry lions and the excruciating pain of chopping blocks rather than submit to certain unjust laws of the Roman Empire. To a degree, academic freedom is a reality today because Socrates practiced civil disobedience. In our own nation, the Boston Tea Party represented a massive act of civil disobedience.

We should never forget that everything Adolf Hitler did in Germany was   22
"legal" and everything the Hungarian freedom fighters[13] did in Hungary was

---

[12] **Nebuchadnezzar (c. 630–562 B.C.E.)**   Chaldean king who twice attacked Jerusalem. He ordered Shadrach, Meshach, and Abednego to worship a golden image. They refused, were cast into a roaring furnace, and were saved by God (see Dan. 1:7–3:30).

[13] **Hungarian freedom fighters**   The Hungarians rose in revolt against Soviet rule in 1956. Soviet forces put down the uprising with great force, which shocked the world. Many freedom fighters died, and many others escaped to the West.

"illegal." It was "illegal" to aid and comfort a Jew in Hitler's Germany. Even so, I am sure that, had I lived in Germany at the time, I would have aided and comforted my Jewish brothers. If today I lived in a Communist country where certain principles dear to the Christian faith are suppressed, I would openly advocate disobeying that country's antireligious laws.

I must make two honest confessions to you, my Christian and Jewish   23
brothers. First, I must confess that over the past few years I have been gravely disappointed with the white moderate. I have almost reached the regrettable conclusion that the Negro's great stumbling block in his stride toward freedom is not the White Citizen's Counciler[14] or the Ku Klux Klanner, but the white moderate, who is more devoted to "order" than to justice; who prefers a negative peace which is the absence of tension to a positive peace which is the presence of justice; who constantly says, "I agree with you in the goal you seek, but I cannot agree with your methods of direct action"; who paternalistically believes he can set the timetable for another man's freedom; who lives by a mythical concept of time and who constantly advises the Negro to wait for a "more convenient season." Shallow understanding from people of good will is more frustrating than absolute misunderstanding from people of ill will. Lukewarm acceptance is much more bewildering than outright rejection.

I had hoped that the white moderate would understand that law and order   24
exist for the purpose of establishing justice and that when they fail in this purpose they become the dangerously structured dams that block the flow of social progress. I had hoped that the white moderate would understand that the present tension in the South is a necessary phase of the transition from an obnoxious negative peace, in which the Negro passively accepted his unjust plight, to a substantive and positive peace, in which all men will respect the dignity and worth of human personality. Actually, we who engage in nonviolent direct action are not the creators of tension. We merely bring to the surface the hidden tension that is already alive. We bring it out in the open, where it can be seen and dealt with. Like a boil that can never be cured so long as it is covered up but must be opened with all its ugliness to the natural medicines of air and light, injustice must be exposed, with all the tension its exposure creates, to the light of human conscience and the air of national opinion, before it can be cured.

In your statement you assert that our actions, even though peaceful, must   25
be condemned because they precipitate violence. But is this a logical assertion? Isn't this like condemning a robbed man because his possession of money

---

[14] **White Citizen's Counciler**   White Citizen's Councils organized in southern states in 1954 to fight school desegregation as ordered by the Supreme Court in May 1954. The councils were not as secret or violent as the Klan; they were also ineffective.

precipitated the evil act of robbery? Isn't this like condemning Socrates because his unswerving commitment to truth and his philosophical inquiries precipitated the act by the misguided populace in which they made him drink hemlock? Isn't this like condemning Jesus because his unique God-consciousness and never-ceasing devotion to God's will precipitated the evil act of crucifixion? We must come to see that, as the federal courts have consistently affirmed, it is wrong to urge an individual to cease his efforts to gain his basic constitutional rights because the quest may precipitate violence. Society must protect the robbed and punish the robber.

I had also hoped that the white moderate would reject the myth concerning time in relation to the struggle for freedom. I have just received a letter from a white brother in Texas. He writes: "All Christians know that the colored people will receive equal rights eventually, but it is possible that you are in too great a religious hurry. It has taken Christianity almost two thousand years to accomplish what it has. The teachings of Christ take time to come to earth." Such an attitude stems from a tragic misconception of time, from the strangely irrational notion that there is something in the very flow of time that will inevitably cure all ills. Actually, time itself is neutral; it can be used either destructively or constructively. More and more I feel that the people of ill will have used time much more effectively than have the people of good will. We will have to repent in this generation not merely for the hateful words and actions of the bad people, but for the appalling silence of the good people. Human progress never rolls in on wheels of inevitability; it comes through the tireless efforts of men willing to be co-workers with God, and without this hard work, time itself becomes an ally of the forces of social stagnation. We must use time creatively, in the knowledge that the time is always ripe to do right. Now is the time to make real the promise of democracy and transform our pending national elegy into a creative psalm of brotherhood. Now is the time to lift our national policy from the quicksand of racial injustice to the solid rock of human dignity.

You speak of our activity in Birmingham as extreme. At first I was rather disappointed that fellow clergymen would see my nonviolent efforts as those of an extremist. I began thinking about the fact that I stand in the middle of two opposing forces in the Negro community. One is a force of complacency, made up in part of Negroes who, as a result of long years of oppression, are so drained of self-respect and a sense of "somebodiness" that they have adjusted to segregation; and in part of a few middle-class Negroes who, because of a degree of academic and economic security and because in some ways they profit by segregation, have become insensitive to the problems of the masses. The other force is one of bitterness and hatred, and it comes perilously close to advocating violence. It is expressed in the various black nationalist groups that are springing up across the nation, the largest and best known being Elijah

Muhammad's Muslim movement.[15] Nourished by the Negro's frustration over the continued existence of racial discrimination, this movement is made up of people who have lost faith in America, who have absolutely repudiated Christianity, and who have concluded that the white man is an incorrigible "devil."

I have tried to stand between these two forces, saying that we need emulate neither the "do-nothingism" of the complacent nor the hatred and despair of the black nationalist. For there is the more excellent way of love and nonviolent protest. I am grateful to God that, through the influence of the Negro church, the way of nonviolence became an integral part of our struggle.

If this philosophy had not emerged, by now many streets of the South would, I am convinced, be flowing with blood. And I am further convinced that if our white brothers dismiss as "rabble-rousers" and "outside agitators" those of us who employ nonviolent direct action, and if they refuse to support our nonviolent efforts, millions of Negroes will, out of frustration and despair, seek solace and security in black nationalist ideologies—a development that would inevitably lead to a frightening racial nightmare.[16]

Oppressed people cannot remain oppressed forever. The yearning for freedom eventually manifests itself, and that is what has happened to the American Negro. Something within has reminded him of his birthright of freedom, and something without has reminded him that it can be gained. Consciously or unconsciously, he has been caught up by the *Zeitgeist*,[17] and with his black brothers of Africa and his brown and yellow brothers of Asia, South America, and the Carribbean, the United States Negro is moving with a sense of great urgency toward the promised land of racial justice. If one recognizes this vital urge that has engulfed the Negro community, one should readily understand why public demonstrations are taking place. The Negro has many pent-up resentments and latent frustrations, and he must release them. So let him march; let him make prayer pilgrimages to the city hall; let him go on freedom rides[18]—and try to understand why he must do so. If his repressed emotions

28

29

30

---

[15] **Elijah Muhammad's Muslim movement**   The Black Muslim movement, which began in the 1920s but flourished in the 1960s under its leader, Elijah Muhammad (1897–1975). Among notable figures who became Black Muslims were the poet Amiri Baraka (1934–2014), the world champion prizefighter Muhammad Ali (1942–2016), and the controversial reformer and religious leader Malcolm X (1925–1965). King saw their rejection of white society (and consequently brotherhood) as a threat.

[16] **a frightening racial nightmare**   The black uprisings of the 1960s in all major American cities, and the conditions that led to them, were indeed a racial nightmare. King's prophecy was quick to come true.

[17] ***Zeitgeist***   German word for the intellectual, moral, and cultural spirit of the times.

[18] **freedom rides**   In 1961, the Congress of Racial Equality (CORE) organized rides of whites and blacks to test segregation in southern buses and bus terminals with interstate passengers. More than 600 federal marshals were needed to protect the riders, most of whom were arrested.

are not released in nonviolent ways, they will seek expression through violence; this is not a threat but a fact of history. So I have not said to my people, "Get rid of your discontent." Rather, I have tried to say that this normal and healthy discontent can be channeled into the creative outlet of nonviolent direct action. And now this approach is being termed extremist.

But though I was initially disappointed at being categorized as an extremist, as I continued to think about the matter I gradually gained a measure of satisfaction from the label. Was not Jesus an extremist for love: "Love your enemies, bless them that curse you, do good to them that hate you, and pray for them which despitefully use you, and persecute you." Was not Amos an extremist for justice: "Let justice roll down like waters and righteousness like an ever-flowing stream." Was not Paul an extremist for the Christian gospel: "I bear in my body the marks of the Lord Jesus." Was not Martin Luther an extremist: "Here I stand; I cannot do otherwise, so help me God." And John Bunyan: "I will stay in jail to the end of my days before I make a butchery of my conscience." And Abraham Lincoln: "This nation cannot survive half slave and half free." And Thomas Jefferson: "We hold these truths to be self-evident, that all men are created equal . . ."[19] So the question is not whether we will be extremists, but what kind of extremists we will be. Will we be extremists for hate or for love? Will we be extremists for the preservation of injustice or for the extension of justice? In that dramatic scene on Calvary's hill three men were crucified. We must never forget that all three were crucified for the same crime — the crime of extremism. Two were extremists for immorality, and thus fell below their environment. The other, Jesus Christ, was an extremist for love, truth, and goodness, and thereby rose above his environment. Perhaps the South, the nation, and the world are in dire need of creative extremists.

I had hoped that the white moderate would see this need. Perhaps I was too optimistic; perhaps I expected too much. I suppose I should have realized that few members of the oppressor race can understand the deep groans and passionate yearnings of the oppressed race, and still fewer have the vision to see that injustice must be rooted out by strong, persistent, and determined action. I am thankful, however, that some of our white brothers in the South have grasped the meaning of this social revolution and committed themselves to it. They are still all too few in quantity, but they are big in quality. Some — such as Ralph McGill, Lillian Smith, Harry Golden, James McBride Dabbs, Ann Braden,

[19] **Amos, Old Testament prophet (eighth century** B.C.E.**); Paul (?–**C.E.** 67); Martin Luther (1483–1546); John Bunyan (1628–1688); Abraham Lincoln (1809–1865); and Thomas Jefferson (1743–1826)**   These figures are all noted for religious, moral, or political innovations that changed the world. Amos was a prophet who favored social justice; Paul argued against Roman law; Luther began the Reformation of the Christian Church; Bunyan was imprisoned for preaching the gospel according to his own understanding; Lincoln freed America's slaves; Jefferson drafted the Declaration of Independence.

and Sarah Patton Boyle—have written about our struggle[20] in eloquent and prophetic terms. Others have marched with us down nameless streets of the South. They have languished in filthy, roach-infested jails, suffering the abuse and brutality of policemen who view them as "dirty nigger-lovers." Unlike so many of their moderate brothers and sisters, they have recognized the urgency of the moment and sensed the need for powerful "action" antidotes to combat the disease of segregation.

Let me take note of my other major disappointment. I have been so greatly disappointed with the white church and its leadership. Of course, there are some notable exceptions. I am not unmindful of the fact that each of you has taken some significant stands on this issue. I commend you, Reverend Stallings, for your Christian stand on this past Sunday, in welcoming Negroes to your worship service on a nonsegregated basis. I commend the Catholic leaders of this state for integrating Spring Hill College several years ago.

33

But despite these notable exceptions, I must honestly reiterate that I have been disappointed with the church. I do not say this as one of those negative critics who can always find something wrong with the church. I say this as a minister of the gospel, who loves the church; who was nurtured in its bosom; who has been sustained by its spiritual blessings and who will remain true to it as long as the cord of life shall lengthen.

34

When I was suddenly catapulted into the leadership of the bus protest in Montgomery, Alabama, a few years ago, I felt we would be supported by the white church. I felt that the white ministers, priests, and rabbis of the South would be among our strongest allies. Instead, some have been outright opponents, refusing to understand the freedom movement and misrepresenting its leaders; all too many others have been more cautious than courageous and have remained silent behind the anesthetizing security of stained-glass windows.

35

In spite of my shattered dreams, I came to Birmingham with the hope that the white religious leadership of this community would see the justice of our cause and, with deep moral concern, would serve as the channel through which our just grievances could reach the power structure. I had hoped that each of you would understand. But again I have been disappointed. . . .

36

There was a time when the church was very powerful—in the time when the early Christians rejoiced at being deemed worthy to suffer for what they believed. In those days the church was not merely a thermometer that recorded the ideas and principles of popular opinion; it was a thermostat that transformed the mores of society. Whenever the early Christians entered a town, the people in power became disturbed and immediately sought to convict the

37

---

[20] **written about our struggle** These are all prominent southern writers who expressed their feelings regarding segregation in the South. Some of them, like Smith and Golden, wrote very popular books with a wide influence. Some, like McGill and Smith, were severely rebuked by white southerners.

Christians for being "disturbers of the peace" and "outside agitators." But the Christians pressed on, in the conviction that they were "a colony of heaven," called to obey God rather than man. Small in number, they were big in commitment. They were too God-intoxicated to be "astronomically intimidated." By their effort and example they brought an end to such ancient evils as infanticide and gladiatorial contests.

Things are different now. So often the contemporary church is a weak, 38 ineffectual voice with an uncertain sound. So often it is an archdefender of the status quo. Far from being disturbed by the presence of the church, the powerful structure of the average community is consoled by the church's silent—and often even vocal—sanction of things as they are.

But the judgment of God is upon the church as never before. If today's 39 church does not recapture the sacrificial spirit of the early church, it will lose its authenticity, forfeit the loyalty of millions, and be dismissed as an irrelevant social club with no meaning for the twentieth century. Every day I meet young people whose disappointment with the church has turned into outright disgust.

Perhaps I have once again been too optimistic. Is organized religion too 40 inextricably bound to the status quo to save our nation and the world? Perhaps I must turn my faith to the inner spiritual church, the church within the church, as the true *ekklesia*[21] and the hope of the world. But again I am thankful to God that some noble souls from the ranks of organized religion have broken loose from the paralyzing chains of conformity and joined us as active partners in the struggle for freedom. They have left their secure congregations and walked the streets of Albany, Georgia, with us. They have gone down the highways of the South on torturous rides for freedom. Yes, they have gone to jail with us. Some have been dismissed from their churches, have lost the support of their bishops and fellow ministers. But they have acted in the faith that right defeated is stronger than evil triumphant. Their witness has been the spiritual salt that has preserved the true meaning of the gospel in these troubled times. They have carved a tunnel of hope through the dark mountain of disappointment.

I hope the church as a whole will meet the challenge of this decisive 41 hour. But even if the church does not come to the aid of justice, I have no despair about the future. I have no fear about the outcome of our struggle in Birmingham, even if our motives are at present misunderstood. We will reach the goal of freedom in Birmingham and all over the nation, because the goal of America is freedom. Abused and scorned though we may be, our destiny is tied up with America's destiny. Before the pilgrims landed at Plymouth, we

---

[21] *ekklesia*   Greek word for "church" meaning not just the institution but the spirit of the church.

were here. Before the pen of Jefferson etched the majestic words of the Declaration of Independence across the pages of history, we were here. For more than two centuries our forebears labored in this country without wages; they made cotton king; they built the homes of their masters while suffering gross injustice and shameful humiliation—and yet out of a bottomless vitality they continued to thrive and develop. If the inexpressible cruelties of slavery could not stop us, the opposition we now face will surely fail. We will win our freedom because the sacred heritage of our nation and the eternal will of God are embodied in our echoing demands.

42   Before closing I feel impelled to mention one other point in your statement that has troubled me profoundly. You warmly commended the Birmingham police force for keeping "order" and "preventing violence." I doubt that you would have so warmly commended the police force if you had seen its dogs sinking their teeth into unarmed, nonviolent Negroes. I doubt that you would so quickly commend the policemen if you were to observe their ugly and inhumane treatment of Negroes here in the city jail; if you were to watch them push and curse old Negro women and young Negro girls; if you were to see them slap and kick old Negro men and young boys; if you were to observe them, as they did on two occasions, refuse to give us food because we wanted to sing our grace together. I cannot join you in your praise of the Birmingham police department.

43   It is true that the police have exercised a degree of discipline in handling the demonstrators. In this sense they have conducted themselves rather "nonviolently" in public. But for what purpose? To preserve the evil system of segregation. Over the past few years I have consistently preached that nonviolence demands that the means we use must be as pure as the ends we seek. I have tried to make clear that it is wrong to use immoral means to attain moral ends. But now I must affirm that it is just as wrong, or perhaps even more so, to use moral means to preserve immoral ends. Perhaps Mr. Connor and his policemen have been rather nonviolent in public, as was Chief Pritchett in Albany, Georgia, but they have used the moral means of nonviolence to maintain the immoral end of racial injustice. As T. S. Eliot[22] has said, "The last temptation is the greatest treason: To do the right deed for the wrong reason."

44   I wish you had commended the Negro sit-inners and demonstrators of Birmingham for their sublime courage, their willingness to suffer, and their amazing discipline in the midst of great provocation. One day the South will

---

[22] **Thomas Stearns Eliot (1888–1965)**   Renowned as one of the twentieth century's major poets, Eliot was born in the United States but in 1927 became a British subject and a member of the Church of England. Many of his poems focused on religious and moral themes. These lines are from Eliot's play *Murder in the Cathedral*, about Saint Thomas à Becket (1118–1170), the archbishop of Canterbury, who was martyred for his opposition to King Henry II.

recognize its real heroes. They will be the James Merediths,[23] with the noble sense of purpose that enables them to face jeering and hostile mobs, and with the agonizing loneliness that characterizes the life of the pioneer. They will be old, oppressed, battered Negro women, symbolized in a seventy-two-year-old woman in Montgomery, Alabama, who rose up with a sense of dignity and with her people decided not to ride segregated buses, and who responded with ungrammatical profundity to one who inquired about her weariness: "My feets is tired, but my soul is at rest." They will be the young high school and college students, the young ministers of the gospel and a host of their elders, courageously and nonviolently sitting in at lunch counters and willingly going to jail for conscience's sake. One day the South will know that when these disinherited children of God sat down at lunch counters, they were in reality standing up for what is best in the American dream and for the most sacred values in our Judaeo-Christian heritage, thereby bringing our nation back to those great wells of democracy which were dug deep by the founding fathers in their formulation of the Constitution and the Declaration of Independence.

Never before have I written so long a letter. I'm afraid it is much too long to take your precious time. I can assure you that it would have been much shorter if I had been writing from a comfortable desk, but what else can one do when he is alone in a narrow jail cell, other than write long letters, think long thoughts, and pray long prayers? 45

If I have said anything in this letter that overstates the truth and indicates an unreasonable impatience, I beg you to forgive me. If I have said anything that understates the truth and indicates my having a patience that allows me to settle for anything less than brotherhood, I beg God to forgive me. 46

I hope this letter finds you strong in the faith. I also hope that circumstances will soon make it possible for me to meet each of you, not as an integrationist or a civil rights leader but as a fellow clergyman and a Christian brother. Let us all hope that the dark clouds of racial prejudice will soon pass away and the deep fog of misunderstanding will be lifted from our fear-drenched communities, and in some not too distant tomorrow the radiant stars of love and brotherhood will shine over our great nation with all their scintillating beauty. 47

Yours in the cause of
Peace and Brotherhood,
MARTIN LUTHER KING, JR.

---

[23] **the James Merediths**   James Meredith (b. 1933) was the first black person to become a student at the University of Mississippi. His attempt to register for classes in 1962 created the first important confrontation between federal and state authorities, when Governor Ross Barnett personally blocked Meredith's entry to the university. Meredith graduated in 1963 and went on to study law at Columbia University.

✖ QUESTIONS FOR CRITICAL READING

1. Define "nonviolent direct action" (para. 2). In what areas of human experience is it best implemented? Is politics its best area of application? What are the four steps in a nonviolent campaign?

2. Do you agree that "law and order exist for the purpose of establishing justice" (para. 24)? Why? Describe how law and order either do or do not establish justice in your community. Compare notes with your peers.

3. King describes an unjust law as "a code that a numerical or power majority group compels a minority group to obey but does not make binding on itself" (para. 17). Devise one or two other definitions of an unjust law. What unjust laws currently on the books do you disagree with?

4. What do you think is the best-written paragraph in the essay? Why?

5. King cites "tension" in paragraph 10 and elsewhere as a beneficial force. Do you agree? What kind of tension does he mean?

6. In what ways was King an extremist (paras. 30–31)?

7. In his letter, to what extent does King consider the needs of women? Would he feel that issues of women's rights are unrelated to issues of racial equality?

8. According to King, how should a government function in relation to the needs of the individual? Does he feel, like Thoreau's "Chinese philosopher," that the empire is built on the individual?

✖ SUGGESTIONS FOR CRITICAL WRITING

1. Write a brief letter protesting an injustice that you feel may not be entirely understood by people you respect. Clarify the nature of the injustice, the reasons that people hold an unjust view, and the reasons your views should be accepted. Consult King's letter, and use his techniques. How are injustice and immorality related?

2. In paragraph 43, King says, "I have consistently preached that nonviolence demands that the means we use must be as pure as the ends we seek." What does he mean by this? Define the ends he seeks and the means he approves. Do you agree with him on this point? If you have read the selection from Machiavelli (p. 84), contrast their respective views. Which view seems more reasonable to you?

3. The first part of the letter defends King's journey to Birmingham as a Christian to help his fellows gain justice. He challenges the view that he is an outsider, using such expressions as "network of mutuality" and "garment of destiny" (para. 4). How effective is his argument? Examine the letter for other expressions that justify King's intervention on behalf of his brothers and sisters. Using his logic, describe other social areas where you might be justified in acting on your own views on behalf of humanity. Do you expect your endeavors would be welcomed? Are there any areas where you think it would be wrong to intervene?

4. In paragraphs 15–22, King discusses two kinds of laws — those that are morally right and those that are morally wrong. Which laws did King regard as morally right? Which laws did he consider morally wrong? Analyze one or two current laws that you feel are morally wrong. Be sure to be fair in describing the laws and establishing their nature. Then explain why you feel they are morally wrong. Would you feel justified in breaking these laws? Would you feel prepared, as King was, to pay the penalties demanded of one who breaks the law?

5. Compare King's letter with sections of Paul's letters to the faithful in the New Testament. Either choose a single letter, such as the Epistle to the Romans, or select passages from Romans, the two letters to the Corinthians, the Galatians, the Ephesians, the Thessalonians, or the Philippians. How did Paul and King agree and disagree about brotherly love, the mission of Christ, the mission of the church, concern for the law, and the duties of the faithful? Inventory the New Testament letters and King's letter carefully for concrete evidence of similar or contrary positions.

6. **CONNECTIONS**   How would King define "the aim of man"? Would he agree with Aristotle (p. 70) that "No one would call a man just who did not take pleasure in doing justice" (para. 21)? Would he agree with Aristotle that to "'live well' and 'do well' are the same as to be 'happy'" (para. 8)? Write a brief essay that defends the view that King, because of the nobility of his actions, is happy while he is in Birmingham Jail. Would King agree with Aristotle that happiness is "the highest of all realizable goods" (para. 8)?

7. **CONNECTIONS**   To what extent do Martin Luther King Jr.'s views about government coincide with those of Lao-tzu (p. 55)? Is there a legitimate comparison to be made between King's policy of nonviolent resistance and Lao-tzu's judicious inactivity? To what extent would King have agreed with Lao-tzu's views? Would Lao-tzu have supported King's position in his letter, or would he have interpreted events differently?

8. **CONNECTIONS**   King cites conscience as a guide to obeying just laws and defying unjust laws. How close is his position to that of Henry David Thoreau? Do you think that King had read Thoreau's "Civil Disobedience" (p. 720) as an important document regarding morality and immorality? Compare and contrast the positions of these two writers.

9. Throughout "Letter from Birmingham Jail," Martin Luther King Jr. stresses the question of justice. In paragraphs 15–22, he raises the question of moral laws and immoral laws. If justice depends on moral laws, can we say that justice is a form of morality or ethical behavior? Are justice and morality the same? Is there a religious issue connected to justice? Is that why King, a minister of the church, constantly refers to justice? How are morality and justice connected? What do they have in common?

JOHN
RAWLS

A Theory of Justice

J OHN RAWLS (1921–2002) was widely considered one of the most distinguished moral philosophers of the second half of the twentieth century. He was educated at Princeton University and served in the 32nd Infantry Division in New Guinea and the Philippines from 1943 to 1946. After returning to Princeton for his doctorate, he taught at Cornell, Oxford, Massachusetts Institute of Technology, and finally Harvard University, where he was Conant University Professor, the highest-level professorship at the university.

Rawls began to work out the ideas that eventually formed his most important book, *A Theory of Justice* (1971), in the 1950s, both in his earliest articles and in his notes for his lectures and teaching. He spent more than ten years refining his thinking on the subject, and in the process began to attract the attention of other thinkers concerned with problems of justice and equality. Much to his surprise, *A Theory of Justice* became a bestseller, and it has affected the discourse in justice and politics so widely that contemporary scholars cannot discuss these issues without paying homage to Rawls's work. In essence, he changed the direction of thought away from the utilitarian — a system of justice that benefits the greatest number with the greatest good — to a system of justice based on fairness, in which any social action must be measured by its effect on the least advantaged people in the society. Rawls argued that if a social action were to harm an individual, that action should be avoided.

In *A Theory of Justice*, Rawls develops two basic ideas: the "original position" and the "veil of ignorance." In what is called a thought experiment similar to Plato's "The Allegory of the Cave" (p. 580), Rawls proposes a version of a social contract much like Rousseau's (p. 99). However, the principles are different. In the "original position" concept, Rawls proposes an original starting point for a society in which the designers of the society make certain assumptions about the "Primary Goods" — freedom, equality, opportunity, wealth, powers, and income — that each person in the society must have. The planners of the society, much like Thomas Jefferson and those who constructed our Constitution,

---

From *A Theory of Justice*.

were to take into consideration all the desirable qualities important to a rational society. Then, to make things more interesting and fair, Rawls devised the concept of the "veil of ignorance" in which the planners and the members of the society made their decisions about the Primary Goods without knowing where they themselves would actually fall in the society in terms of their sex, race, birth, or talent. If they were kept ignorant of those facts, Rawls believed, their decisions would not be biased by personal circumstances. Rawls assumed that every individual was directed by self-interest first, so the "veil of ignorance" would prevent the creation of a social structure that would benefit only those who were deciding how justice would be allocated.

Above all, Rawls believed that justice must be fair and that the rights of the individual should never be sacrificed for the greater good of society. Personal freedom insofar as it did not impinge on the freedom of others was one of his most sacred values. Underlying all these ideas is the insistence that people are equal and should be treated equally.

One of Rawls's most controversial ideas is often referred to as the "difference principle." Rawls felt that any inequality produced by a social structure must be measured by its effect on the least advantaged people in the society. For instance, a tax structure that produced inequality of wealth in a community must be measured by its harmful or beneficial effect on those who are least wealthy, and not on the middle class or those with the most advantages. This position has been attacked in part because it seems to penalize those who have the talent to create wealth for themselves. Rawls responds by suggesting that the society he envisions can accept a certain amount of inequality of distribution of wealth, as long as it does not upset the equilibrium of the society. Exactly how this position is worked out in practice is not clear, but on a theoretical level it seems to suggest that a certain amount of unequal distribution of Primary Goods could result in an internal revolution, thus destroying the equilibrium of the society as a result of a perceived injustice. Justice cannot be fair if only a certain group has most of the wealth, opportunities, power, or income. Such a situation constitutes a loss of equilibrium.

RAWLS'S RHETORIC

Rawls is not considered a stylish writer; his purpose is not to convince us by means of a poetic or graceful style, but to present the basic ingredients of an argument. His approach is methodical in the sense that he begins with principles that are carefully defined, then moves on to show us how these principles would be applied and in what conditions they would be appropriate. In other words, this is a method that demands careful attention from the first sentences onward because everything flows from those early statements.

He begins by alluding to related theories, such as Jean-Jacques Rousseau's social contract, which suggests that people in a society agree to an unspoken contract that binds them to accept the conditions of the society or else leave. But Rawls ignores the bases of the contracts proposed by Rousseau and others, and by contrast alludes to principles that "free and rational persons concerned to further their own interests would accept in an initial position of equality as defining the fundamental terms of their association" (para. 1). Rawls ends his first paragraph with a statement of purpose and definition: "This way of regarding the principles of justice I shall call justice as fairness." This principle is fundamental to his argument.

Rawls develops the concept of the "original position" in the third paragraph: "This original position . . . is understood as a purely hypothetical situation characterized so as to lead to a certain conception of justice." Whereas Rousseau refers to a "state of nature" that may have existed in which people bound themselves to a society, Rawls attempts to formulate an ideal or hypothetical situation that conforms with views that he feels may guarantee fairness.

The fourth paragraph examines the idea that justice should guarantee fairness to everyone in the society. Rawls considers the nature of cooperation that naturally pertains to a social order in which people voluntarily and rationally decide to join. In paragraph 5, he addresses the question of interest, a term he uses to clarify the position of individuals in a just society. When he states that individuals are "rational and mutually disinterested" (para. 5), he means that individuals make decisions based on their own concerns, not those of others. A disinterested decision could only be made by someone who does not benefit from the outcome.

Rawls reminds us that those who are designing the social order from the original position must decide what "conception of justice as fairness" (para. 6) they will choose. To be sure, this is a difficult concept. The framers of the U.S. Constitution faced a similar prospect, and despite their concern with equality and fairness, they ignored the conditions of the least advantaged in their society: slaves. In the sixth paragraph, Rawls mentions the principle of utility, which means the utilitarian view that the best society provides the greatest good to the greatest number of people. In that view, the Constitution achieved a utilitarian end, but that does not satisfy Rawls because it ignores the rights of the least advantaged.

The seventh paragraph establishes the bedrock principles by which Rawls expects justice to be established. The planners of the society must assign "rights and duties" in an equal fashion. Economic inequities can be tolerated only if they benefit the least advantaged members of society. This is a difficult provision to implement — but not to implement it would mean failure to achieve a justice of fairness, which is the demand Rawls makes in his opening pages.

Several of the later paragraphs examine what Rawls calls "the merit of the contract terminology" (para. 10) so that we will have as firm an understanding of the idea of the social contract as we can. This discussion reminds us that when members of a society agree to join a community, those members are expected to abide by an implied contract of behavior.

Rawls does not, in this introductory segment to *A Theory of Justice*, propose concrete judgments as to how justice as fairness would be established. In later sections of his book he undertakes the examination of certain aspects of a social order in which justice as fairness functions. Yet, throughout his book, his principles remain those of the philosopher, essentially abstract and ideal. Nonetheless, his ideas, like those of Plato in his *Republic*, have implications for any society that expects its members to respect those who administer justice, for when justice cannot be achieved in a society, dire consequences ensue.

⠿ PREREADING QUESTIONS: WHAT TO READ FOR

The following prereading questions may help you anticipate key issues in the discussion of John Rawls's "A Theory of Justice." Keeping them in mind during your first reading of the selection should help focus your attention.

1. How does Rawls articulate his idea of "justice as fairness"?
2. What are the "primary goods" that people in a society need?
3. What is Rawls's attitude toward the least advantaged people in society?

A Theory of Justice

My aim is to present a conception of justice which generalizes and carries to a higher level of abstraction the familiar theory of the social contract as found, say, in Locke, Rousseau, and Kant.[1] In order to do this we are not to think of the original contract as one to enter a particular society or to set up a particular form of government. Rather, the guiding idea is that the principles of justice for the basic structure of society are the object of the original agreement. They are the principles that free and rational persons concerned to further their own interests would accept in an initial position of equality as defining the fundamental terms of their association. These principles are to regulate all further agreements; they specify the kinds of social cooperation that can be entered into and the forms of government that can be established. This way of regarding the principles of justice I shall call justice as fairness.

1

---

[1] As the text suggests, I shall regard Locke's *Second Treatise of Government*, Rousseau's *The Social Contract*, and Kant's ethical works beginning with *The Foundations of the Metaphysics of Morals* as definitive of the contract tradition. For all of its greatness, Hobbes's *Leviathan* raises special problems. A general historical survey is provided by J. W. Gough, *The Social Contract*, 2nd ed. (Clarendon Press: Oxford, 1957), and Otto Gierke, *Natural Law and the Theory of Society*, trans. with an introduction by Ernest Barker (Cambridge University Press: Cambridge, 1934). A presentation of the contract view as primarily an ethical theory is to be found in G. R. Grice, *The Grounds of Moral Judgment* (Cambridge University Press: Cambridge, 1967). [Rawls's note]

Thus we are to imagine that those who engage in social cooperation 2 choose together, in one joint act, the principles which are to assign basic rights and duties and to determine the division of social benefits. Men are to decide in advance how they are to regulate their claims against one another and what is to be the foundation charter of their society. Just as each person must decide by rational reflection what constitutes his good, that is, the system of ends which it is rational for him to pursue, so a group of persons must decide once and for all what is to count among them as just and unjust. The choice which rational men would make in this hypothetical situation of equal liberty, assuming for the present that this choice problem has a solution, determines the principles of justice.

In justice as fairness the original position of equality corresponds to the 3 state of nature in the traditional theory of the social contract. This original position is not, of course, thought of as an actual historical state of affairs, much less as a primitive condition of culture. It is understood as a purely hypothetical situation characterized so as to lead to a certain conception of justice.[2] Among the essential features of this situation is that no one knows his place in society, his class position or social status, nor does any one know his fortune in the distribution of natural assets and abilities, his intelligence, strength, and the like. I shall even assume that the parties do not know their conceptions of the good or their special psychological propensities. The principles of justice are chosen behind a veil of ignorance. This ensures that no one is advantaged or disadvantaged in the choice of principles by the outcome of natural chance or the contingency of social circumstances. Since all are similarly situated and no one is able to design principles to favor his particular condition, the principles of justice are the result of a fair agreement or bargain. For given the circumstances of the original position, the symmetry of everyone's relations to each other, this initial situation is fair between individuals as moral persons, that is, as rational beings with their own ends and capable, I shall assume, of a sense of justice. The original position is, one might say, the appropriate initial status quo, and thus the fundamental agreements reached in it are fair. This explains the propriety of the name "justice as fairness": it conveys the idea that the principles of justice are agreed to in an initial situation that is fair. The name does not mean that the concepts of justice and fairness are the same, any

---

[2] Kant is clear that the original agreement is hypothetical. See *The Metaphysics of Morals*, pt. I (*Rechtslehre*), especially §§ 47, 52; and pt. II of the essay "Concerning the Common Saying: This May Be True in Theory but It Does Not Apply in Practice," in *Kant's Political Writings*, ed. Hans Reiss and trans. H. B. Nisbet (Cambridge University Press: Cambridge, 1970), 73–87. See Georges Vlachos, *La Pensée politique de Kant* (Presses Universitaires de France: Paris, 1962), 326–35; and J. G. Murphy, *Kant: The Philosophy of Right* (Macmillan: London, 1970), 109–12, 133–36, for a further discussion. [Rawls's note]

more than the phrase "poetry as metaphor" means that the concepts of poetry and metaphor are the same.

Justice as fairness begins, as I have said, with one of the most general of all choices which persons might make together, namely with the choice of the first principles of a conception of justice which is to regulate all subsequent criticism and reform of institutions. Then, having chosen a conception of justice, we can suppose that they are to choose a constitution and a legislature to enact laws, and so on, all in accordance with the principles of justice initially agreed upon. Our social situation is just if it is such that by this sequence of hypothetical agreements we would have contracted into the general system of rules which defines it. Moreover, assuming that the original position does determine a set of principles (that is, that a particular conception of justice would be chosen), it will then be true that whenever social institutions satisfy these principles those engaged in them can say to one another that they are cooperating on terms to which they would agree if they were free and equal persons whose relations with respect to one another were fair. They could all view their arrangements as meeting the stipulations which they would acknowledge in an initial situation that embodies widely accepted and reasonable constraints on the choice of principles. The general recognition of this fact would provide the basis for a public acceptance of the corresponding principles of justice. No society can, of course, be a scheme of cooperation which men enter voluntarily in a literal sense; each person finds himself placed at birth in some particular position in some particular society, and the nature of this position materially affects his life prospects. Yet a society satisfying the principles of justice as fairness comes as close as a society can to being a voluntary scheme, for it meets the principles which free and equal persons would assent to under circumstances that are fair. In this sense its members are autonomous and the obligations they recognize self-imposed.

One feature of justice as fairness is to think of the parties in the initial situation as rational and mutually disinterested. This does not mean that the parties are egoists, that is, individuals with only certain kinds of interests, say in wealth, prestige, and domination. But they are conceived as not taking an interest in one another's interests. They are to presume that even their spiritual aims may be opposed, in the way that the aims of those of different religions may be opposed. Moreover, the concept of rationality must be interpreted as far as possible in the narrow sense, standard in economic theory, of taking the most effective means to given ends. I shall modify this concept to some extent, but one must try to avoid introducing into it any controversial ethical elements. The initial situation must be characterized by stipulations that are widely accepted.

In working out the conception of justice as fairness one main task clearly is to determine which principles of justice would be chosen in the original position. To do this we must describe this situation in some detail and formulate with care the problem of choice which it presents. . . . It may be observed, however, that once the principles of justice are thought of as arising from an original agreement in a situation of equality, it is an open question whether the principle of utility would be acknowledged. Offhand it hardly seems likely that persons who view themselves as equals, entitled to press their claims upon one another, would agree to a principle which may require lesser life prospects for some simply for the sake of a greater sum of advantages enjoyed by others. Since each desires to protect his interests, his capacity to advance his conception of the good, no one has a reason to acquiesce in an enduring loss for himself in order to bring about a greater net balance of satisfaction. In the absence of strong and lasting benevolent impulses, a rational man would not accept a basic structure merely because it maximized the algebraic sum of advantages irrespective of its permanent effects on his own basic rights and interests. Thus it seems that the principle of utility is incompatible with the conception of social cooperation among equals for mutual advantage. It appears to be inconsistent with the idea of reciprocity implicit in the notion of a well-ordered society. Or, at any rate, so I shall argue.

I shall maintain instead that the persons in the initial situation would choose two rather different principles: the first requires equality in the assignment of basic rights and duties, while the second holds that social and economic inequalities, for example inequalities of wealth and authority, are just only if they result in compensating benefits for everyone, and in particular for the least advantaged members of society. These principles rule out justifying institutions on the grounds that the hardships of some are offset by a greater good in the aggregate. It may be expedient but it is not just that some should have less in order that others may prosper. But there is no injustice in the greater benefits earned by a few provided that the situation of persons not so fortunate is thereby improved. The intuitive idea is that since everyone's well-being depends upon a scheme of cooperation without which no one could have a satisfactory life, the division of advantages should be such as to draw forth the willing cooperation of everyone taking part in it, including those less well situated. Yet this can be expected only if reasonable terms are proposed. The two principles mentioned seem to be a fair agreement on the basis of which those better endowed, or more fortunate in their social position, neither of which we can be said to deserve, could expect the willing cooperation of others when some workable scheme is a necessary condition of the welfare of all.[3] Once we decide to look for a conception of justice that nullifies the accidents of natural endowment and the contingencies of social circumstance as counters in quest for political and economic advantage, we are led to these

---

[3] For the formulation of this intuitive idea I am indebted to Allan Gibbard. [Rawls's note]

principles. They express the result of leaving aside those aspects of the social world that seem arbitrary from a moral point of view.

The problem of the choice of principles, however, is extremely difficult. 8 I do not expect the answer I shall suggest to be convincing to everyone. It is, therefore, worth noting from the outset that justice as fairness, like other contract views, consists of two parts: (1) an interpretation of the initial situation and of the problem of choice posed there, and (2) a set of principles which, it is argued, would be agreed to. One may accept the first part of the theory (or some variant thereof), but not the other, and conversely. The concept of the initial contractual situation may seem reasonable although the particular principles proposed are rejected. To be sure, I want to maintain that the most appropriate conception of this situation does lead to principles of justice contrary to utilitarianism and perfectionism, and therefore that the contract doctrine provides an alternative to these views. Still, one may dispute this contention even though one grants that the contractarian method is a useful way of studying ethical theories and of setting forth their underlying assumptions.

Justice as fairness is an example of what I have called a contract theory. 9 Now there may be an objection to the term "contract" and related expressions, but I think it will serve reasonably well. Many words have misleading connotations which at first are likely to confuse. The terms "utility" and "utilitarianism" are surely no exception. They too have unfortunate suggestions which hostile critics have been willing to exploit; yet they are clear enough for those prepared to study utilitarian doctrine. The same should be true of the term "contract" applied to moral theories. As I have mentioned, to understand it one has to keep in mind that it implies a certain level of abstraction. In particular, the content of the relevant agreement is not to enter a given society or to adopt a given form of government, but to accept certain moral principles. Moreover, the undertakings referred to are purely hypothetical: a contract view holds that certain principles would be accepted in a well-defined initial situation.

The merit of the contract terminology is that it conveys the idea that 10 principles of justice may be conceived as principles that would be chosen by rational persons, and that in this way conceptions of justice may be explained and justified. The theory of justice is a part, perhaps the most significant part, of the theory of rational choice. Furthermore, principles of justice deal with conflicting claims upon the advantages won by social cooperation; they apply to the relations among several persons or groups. The word "contract" suggests this plurality as well as the condition that the appropriate division of advantages must be in accordance with principles acceptable to all parties. The condition of publicity for principles of justice is also connoted by the contract phraseology. Thus, if these principles are the outcome of an agreement, citizens have a knowledge of the principles that others follow. It is characteristic of contract theories to stress the public nature of political principles. Finally there is the long tradition of the contract doctrine. Expressing the tie with this line of thought helps to define ideas and accords with natural piety. There are then several advantages in the use of the term "contract." With due precautions taken, it should not be misleading.

A final remark. Justice as fairness is not a complete contract theory. For it is clear that the contractarian idea can be extended to the choice of more or less an entire ethical system, that is, to a system including principles for all the virtues and not only for justice. Now for the most part I shall consider only principles of justice and others closely related to them; I make no attempt to discuss the virtues in a systematic way. Obviously if justice as fairness succeeds reasonably well, a next step would be to study the more general view suggested by the name "rightness as fairness." But even this wider theory fails to embrace all moral relationships, since it would seem to include only our relations with other persons and to leave out of account how we are to conduct ourselves toward animals and the rest of nature. I do not contend that the contract notion offers a way to approach these questions which are certainly of the first importance; and I shall have to put them aside. We must recognize the limited scope of justice as fairness and of the general type of view that it exemplifies. How far its conclusions must be revised once these other matters are understood cannot be decided in advance.

❖ QUESTIONS FOR CRITICAL READING

1. What is the "original position"? Why do you think Rawls named it so?

2. What personal qualities will people who are planning society in the original position need to have?

3. Rawls says the planners must be disinterested, or totally objective. How does the "veil of ignorance" help them achieve the desired level of objectivity?

4. Why is justice as fairness a desirable goal in society?

5. At the end of paragraph 3, Rawls states that justice and fairness are not the same thing. How does his example of distinguishing between poetry and metaphor explain his position?

6. Rawls states, "In justice as fairness the original position of equality corresponds to the state of nature in the traditional theory of the social contract" (para. 3). What does he mean by this, and what do the terms "state of nature" and "original position" mean to you?

7. One of the qualifications for people planning justice as fairness is that they be "rational and mutually disinterested." Why are these important qualities? How is justice as fairness harmed if the planners are not rational or if they operate only from self-interest?

8. In paragraph 6, Rawls suggests that rational planners would not conceive of a society that gave fewer opportunities to some people for the sake of giving many more to others. Do you agree? Do you think our society operates on this rational principle?

9. What for you is the most important decision a society can make to help guarantee a justice of fairness?

⠶ SUGGESTIONS FOR CRITICAL WRITING

1. Keeping in mind that this selection is theoretical in nature and not a practical description of how justice should be applied in a society, offer a critique of the social order Rawls describes in which some people with the ability to make lots of money may have to share a great deal of it with others who make less. What is Rawls's position on such a situation? What is yours? How can you guarantee justice in a society that permits a small number of people to be extremely wealthy while many are relatively poor?

2. Rawls believes that justice must be fair. Do you feel that the system of justice under which we live is fair? Do you think that our system of justice is based on a workable conception of what fairness should be? Do you think justice should be fair? What prevents it from being so?

3. If you were one of the people given the job of designing a "conception of justice" for a society in which you would choose to live, what would you expect of that society in terms of fairness and justice? Can you possibly construct an ideal society without factoring in your own special circumstances, such as your gender, race, ethnicity, social status, level of privilege, or level of education? Rawls wants to factor those issues out of the process. Can you do that? Can anyone? If not, can any system of justice be fair?

4. The utilitarian position emphasizes a form of justice in which the greatest good for the greatest number of people dictates social decisions. Since the nineteenth century, this view, sometimes called the principle of utility, has been fairly dominant in Western democracies. However, Rawls condemns this view because it does not improve the condition of the least advantaged members of society. In fact, it may even harm such people. What is your position on Rawls's rejection of utility? How carefully must a society that values justice work to prevent enacting laws that might make worse the lives of the least advantaged?

5. One of the most important of the "Primary Goods" Rawls considers is equality. Construct an essay in which you define what you think social equality means, taking into consideration such individual differences as genetic makeup, health, intelligence, and physical attributes. How should differences in gender, sexual orientation, or physical prowess be considered in any society that values equality? Why is equality a desirable goal? How can it be achieved?

6. Many religions have taken considered positions on questions of equality. For example, in some synagogues and mosques, men and women cannot worship together. Some religions hold that women are inferior by nature and therefore must be ruled entirely by their husbands or fathers. A religion may forbid women to work outside the home or discourage educating children of either sex beyond grade school. How should a society that values equality and religious freedom resolve conflicts when such fundamental beliefs intersect and clash?

7. **CONNECTIONS**   Thomas Jefferson was in a position similar to those figures Rawls imagines planning a social order based on justice as fairness. What elements of the Declaration of Independence (p. 116) seem to aim toward goals Rawls would find acceptable? Do you feel Jefferson would have shared Rawls's views about trying to avoid any social decisions that might harm the least advantaged citizen? Would Jefferson have had the most advantaged people in society make sacrifices in order to avoid harming the least advantaged? Would you?

8. **CONNECTIONS**   Rawls suggests that what he describes is not really a total contract theory. Turn to Jean-Jacques Rousseau's "The Origin of Civil Society" (p. 99) and try to see how close these two writers are in their view of how a society forms itself and what kind of implicit contract people make with each other when they decide to create and maintain a social order. How concerned is Rousseau with the concept of justice? How much do Rousseau and Rawls have in common regarding their sense of what society should be like?

NEIL
POSTMAN

The Word Weavers/
The World Makers

NEIL POSTMAN (1931–2003) was a student of the word. In 1958, while a graduate student at Columbia University, he taught at San Francisco State University, which was then at the center of original work in semantics, the science of the study of meaning in words. S. I. Hayakawa (1906–1992) was a leader in the field and a colleague of Postman's at San Francisco State. Both were influenced by the work of Alfred Korzybski (1879–1950), who had founded the Institute for Semantics and had been a highly influential lecturer and writer on meaning in language. Korzybski had taught a course called Language and Human Behavior in the Continuing Education School at New York University (NYU). It was, Postman said, the first course given in semantics at a major university. And in 1959, when Postman accepted a position at NYU, he was delighted to be able to continue the tradition and taught that same course there for more than forty years.

While Postman was teaching at NYU, the Canadian rhetorician and professor of English, Marshall McLuhan (1911–1980) was becoming famous for his work in media and language; his slogan "the medium is the message" was influential on media scholars, especially during the explosion of television broadcasting and the beginning of the computer revolution. McLuhan promoted the idea that the media shape culture. Postman was influenced by McLuhan and other semanticists and developed his own views of the media and the influence of electronic forms of communication.

In 1961, Postman published his first book, *Television and the Teaching of English,* in which he applied the theories of linguistics and semantics to teaching English in primary and secondary schools. He followed this book with a series of related texts called *The New English* for grades 7 to 12, which also focused on English education. Postman was quick to see the power of television and its usefulness in teaching. In these books, he reviews the effects of various media on language and words and describes the power of television to

---

From *The End of Education: Redefining the Value of School.*

deliver meaning and shape language (though he would later come to reverse this stance). *Teaching as a Subversive Activity* (1969), which he wrote with Charles Weingartner, was another highly influential book that questioned many of the assumptions about education across the board, not just those regarding English education. Postman and Weingartner pressed the issue of how language not only carries meaning but also shapes it. Postman's point was that language competence was of enormous importance to K–12 students because it actually shaped the way they perceived and understood their culture.

In the late 1970s, Postman began work on a trilogy of books designed to alert educators to the problems involved with the use of media not only in education but in the public sphere. The first, *Teaching as a Conserving Activity* (1979), announced that his earlier work, which had praised the power of television and electronic media, needed a total revision. He had become aware that children did not need much special training to adapt to television. Instead, they needed much more training to deal with basic texts, such as books and printed material. His second book in the series was *The Disappearance of Childhood* (1982), which discussed the entire idea of childhood, a concept that he felt was essentially recent. In the ancient world, children were not treated in a special way. But, Postman argued, by the middle of the nineteenth century through the beginning of the twentieth century a special place had been created in society specifically to accommodate children. In this book, he points to the power of television to influence children by inundating them with adult content that emphasizes consumerism, materialism, and adult hedonism. The worlds of children and adults were conflated on television, and he thought that as a result TV viewers were stunting their intellectual development. Much of Postman's later work was aimed at revealing the ways in which electronic media hindered the growth of those passively immersed in it.

His third book was *Amusing Ourselves to Death: Public Discourse in the Age of Show Business* (1985). In this volume, Postman deals with the question of the effects on children of constant entertainment as a primary source of knowledge of the world. In addition, he points out that the public in general depends on entertainment to satisfy their intellectual needs. Postman became well known for his positions on the damage he said is done to the intellectual capacity of those who depend on television and other electronic media to describe and represent the world around them. His complaint is in some ways quite simple: television, he said, treats serious subjects with indifference and shallow presentation because it is entirely devoted to light entertainment rather than thoughtful instruction.

POSTMAN'S RHETORIC

One of Postman's constant suggestions to writers is that they stress clarity while writing. He made this suggestion at a time when some academic disciplines were becoming more theoretical and the writing produced was often unclear. Postman follows his own advice in this selection and maintains perfect clarity throughout. His subject is the ways in which the control of language affects our perception of the world. He makes it clear that the world is complex and that we need a means to bring what we observe under control and make the complexities of experience manageable. When he talks about a cup, for instance, he reminds us that no one can really perceive a cup in its entirety and that, even more importantly, no one can perceive the reality of a cup because it is a collection of molecules and atoms in constant motion. And even if we could perceive that, we may not be perceiving reality. We use, he tells us, a process of abstraction to create a concept of a cup, just as we do for other physical objects. Such concepts make it possible for us to maintain some control over our environment.

Because Postman was a lifelong educator, his focus throughout the selection is on the ways in which we learn and develop ideas and concepts of the world. His views on semantics are central to the entire essay. He realizes as he writes that the fashion in English and language studies does not currently favor studies in semantics (which was wildly popular from the 1960s through the 1980s). Semantics, he says, should not be limited to study in graduate school but should in fact be introduced in the lower grades, as he did repeatedly while teaching. As he says, we learn by asking questions and we need to know where the questions come from and how they are phrased — and we hope that the best questions will produce even better questions to help clarify areas of study. In fact, Postman would like schools to pay special attention just to the idea of questions.

The essay has a simple three-part structure, which helps Postman achieve the kind of clarity he respects. The first part of the discussion focuses on three verbal issues: definition, questions, and metaphor. The fact that a word has a definition is interesting, he says, but it is important to know who gave it that definition and what other definitions of the word may be relevant. This is part of the process of understanding the meaning of words. He contends that questions shape the way we understand everything, and he states, "Everything we know has its origins in questions" (para. 3). Finally, he discusses metaphor: a comparison between two different things, the result of which is that one of those things is understood in a new way. He illustrates this concept with "Is the human mind, for example, like a dark cavern (needing illumination)? A muscle (needing exercise)? A vessel (needing filling)?" and continues with more examples. The point is that if we liken the human mind to anything else metaphorically, then we reshape the way we understand the concept of the mind.

The second part of the essay focuses on the work of Alfred Korzybski, the "father" of semantics and an inspiration to Postman. Postman provides a brief biography, then talks about Korzybski's major publications and makes an appeal for better understanding of semantics by clarifying Korzybski's original motivations in studying language. Korzybski's war experience made him wonder why so much progress had been made in science and such little progress in social sciences up to his time. Science was successful, but social sciences failed to prevent World War I — in which Korzybski fought and was wounded. Korzybski and Postman are both convinced that a better education in language would help people have better control over their world and help them avoid the rush to war that characterized much of the twentieth century.

The final part of the essay returns to the three issues that are central to the opening pages: concepts of definition, questions, and metaphor, now developed in light of the ideas suggested by Korzybski's work. This three-part structure makes the most difficult ideas in the selection more intelligible. It is similar to the classic structure of the sonata in music: theme, variation and development, restatement of theme. Postman understands how this three-part structure in an essay can help produce and maintain clarity.

⠿ PREREADING QUESTIONS: WHAT TO READ FOR

The following prereading questions may help you anticipate key issues in the discussion of Neil Postman's "The Word Weavers/ The World Makers." Keeping them in mind during your first reading should help focus your attention.

1. What is a metaphor and how does it shape meaning?
2. How does language shape our understanding of the world?
3. What is the definition of *semantics*?

The Word Weavers/The World Makers

In an effort to clear up confusion (or ignorance) about the meaning of a word, does anyone ask, What is *a* definition of this word? Just about always, the way of putting the question is, What is *the* definition of this word? The difference between *a* and *the* in this context is vast, and I have no choice but to blame the schools for the mischief created by an inadequate understanding of what a definition is. From the earliest grades through graduate school, students are given definitions and, with few exceptions, are not told whose definitions they are, for what purposes they were invented, and what alternative definitions might serve equally as well. The result is that students come to believe that definitions are *not* invented; that they are not even human creations; that, in fact, they are — how shall I say it? — part of the natural world, like clouds, trees, and stars.

In a thousand examinations on scores of subjects, students are asked to give definitions of hundreds of things, words, concepts, procedures. It is to be doubted that there are more than a few classrooms in which there has been any discussion of what a definition is. How is that possible?

Let us take the equally strange case of questions. There will be no disagreement, I think, to my saying that all the answers given to students are the end products of questions. Everything we know has its origin in questions. Questions, we might say, are the principal intellectual instruments available

1

2

3

to human beings. Then how is it possible that no more than one in one hundred students has ever been exposed to an extended and systematic study of the art and science of question-asking? How come Alan Bloom didn't mention this, or E. D. Hirsch Jr.,[1] or so many others who have written books on how to improve our schools? Did they simply fail to notice that *the principal intellectual instrument available to human beings is not examined in school?*

We are beginning to border on absurdity here. And we cross the line when   4 we consider what happens in most schools on the subject of metaphor. Metaphor does, in fact, come up in school, usually introduced by an English teacher wanting to show how it is employed by poets. The result is that most students come to believe metaphor has a decorative function and only a decorative function. It gives color and texture to poetry, as jewelry does to clothing. The poet wants us to see, smell, hear, or feel something concretely, and so resorts to metaphor. I remember a discussion, when I was in college, of Robert Burns's lines: "O, my love is like a red, red rose / That's newly sprung in June. / O my love is like the melodie / That's sweetly play'd in tune."

The first questions on the test were: "Is Burns using metaphors or similes?   5 Define each term. Why did Burns choose to use metaphors instead of similes, or similes instead of metaphors?"

I didn't object to these questions at the time except for the last one, to which   6 I gave a defiant but honest answer: How the hell should I know? I have the same answer today. But today, I have some other things to say on the matter. Yes, poets use metaphors to help us see and feel. But so do biologists, physicists, historians, linguists, and everyone else who is trying to say something about the world. A metaphor is not an ornament. It is an organ of perception. Through metaphors, we see the world as one thing or another. Is light a wave or a particle? Are molecules like billiard balls or force fields? Is history unfolding according to some instructions of nature or a divine plan? Are our genes like information codes? Is a literary work like an architect's blueprint or a mystery to be solved?

Questions like these preoccupy scholars in every field. Do I exaggerate   7 in saying that a student cannot understand what a subject is about without some understanding of the metaphors that are its foundation? I don't think so. In fact, it has always astonished me that those who write about the subject of education do not pay sufficient attention to the role of metaphor in giving form to the subject. In failing to do so, they deprive those studying the subject of the opportunity to confront its basic assumptions. Is the human mind, for example, like a dark cavern (needing illumination)? A muscle (needing exercise)? A vessel (needing filling)? A lump of clay (needing shaping)? A garden (needing cultivation)? Or, as so many say today, is it like a computer that processes data? And

---

[1] **Bloom . . . Hirsch**   Alan Bloom (1930–1992) and E. D. Hirsch Jr. (b. 1928) both wrote books critical of American culture.

what of students? Are they patients to be cared for? Troops to be disciplined? Sons and daughters to be nurtured? Personnel to be trained? Resources to be developed?

There was a time when those who wrote on the subject of education, such   8 as Plato, Comenius, Locke, and Rousseau,[2] made their metaphors explicit and in doing so revealed how their metaphors controlled their thinking. "Plants are improved by cultivation," Rousseau wrote in *Emile,* "and man by education." And his entire philosophy rests upon this comparison of plants and children. Even in such ancient texts as the Mishnah,[3] we find that there are four kinds of students: the sponge, the funnel, the strainer, and the sieve. It will surprise you to know which one is preferred. The sponge, we are told, absorbs all; the funnel receives at one end and spills out at the other; the strainer lets the wine drain through it and retains the dregs; but the sieve—that is the best, for it lets out the flour dust and retains the fine flour. The difference in educational philosophy between Rousseau and the compilers of the Mishnah is precisely reflected in the difference between a wild plant and a sieve.

Definitions, questions, metaphors—these are three of the most potent ele-   9 ments with which human language constructs a worldview. And in urging, as I do, that the study of these elements be given the highest priority in school, I am suggesting that world making through language is a narrative of power, durability, and inspiration. It is the story of how we make the world known to ourselves, and how we make ourselves known to the world. It is different from other narratives because it is about nouns and verbs, about grammar and inferences, about metaphors and definitions, but it is a story of creation, nonetheless. Even further, it is a story that plays a role in all other narratives. For whatever we believe in, or don't believe in, is to a considerable extent a function of how our language addresses the world. Here is a small example:

Let us suppose you have just finished being examined by a doctor. In pro-   10 nouncing his verdict, he says somewhat accusingly, "Well, you've done a very nice case of arthritis here." You would undoubtedly think this is a strange diagnosis, or more likely, a strange doctor. People do not "do" arthritis. They "have" it, or "get" it, and it is a little insulting for the doctor to imply that you have produced or manufactured an illness of this kind, especially since arthritis will release you from certain obligations and, at the same time, elicit sympathy from other people. It is also painful. So the idea that you have done arthritis to yourself suggests a kind of self-serving masochism.

---

[2] **Plato . . . Rousseau**   Plato (429–347 B.C.E.), John Amos Comenius (1592–1670), John Locke (1632–1704), and Jean-Jacques Rousseau (1712–1778) were philosophers of language who wrote widely.

[3] **Mishnah**   An important rabbinic collection of Jewish oral tradition collected in 220 C.E.

Now, let us suppose a judge is about to pass sentence on a man convicted   11
of robbing three banks. The judge advises him to go to a hospital for treatment,
saying with an air of resignation, "You certainly have a bad case of criminality."
On the face of it, this is another strange remark. People do not "have" criminality. They "do" crimes, and we are usually outraged, not saddened, by their
doings. At least that is the way we are accustomed to thinking about the matter.

The point I am trying to make is that such simple verbs as *is* or *does* are, in   12
fact, powerful metaphors that express some of our most fundamental conceptions of the way things are. We believe there are certain things people "have,"
certain things people "do," even certain things people "are." These beliefs do
not necessarily reflect the structure of reality. They simply reflect a habitual
way of talking about reality. In his book *Erewhon*, Samuel Butler[4] depicted a
society that lives according to the metaphors of my strange doctor and strange
judge. There, illness is something people "do" and therefore have moral responsibility for; criminality is something you "have" and therefore is quite beyond
your control. Every legal system and every moral code is based on a set of
assumptions about what people are, have, or do. And, I might add, any significant changes in law or morality are preceded by a reordering of how such
metaphors are employed.

I am not, incidentally, recommending the culture of the people of Erewhon.   13
I am trying to highlight the fact that our language habits are at the core of how
we imagine the world. And to the degree that we are unaware of how our ways
of talking put such ideas in our heads, we are not in full control of our situation.
It needs hardly to be said that one of the purposes of an education is to give us
greater control of our situation.

School does not always help. In schools, for instance, we find that tests   14
are given to determine how smart someone *is* or, more precisely, how much
smartness someone *has*. If, on an IQ test, one child scores a 138 and another a
106, the first is thought to *have* more smartness than the other. But this seems
to me a strange conception—every bit as strange as "doing" arthritis or "having" criminality. I do not know anyone who *has* smartness. The people I know
sometimes *do* smart things (as far as I can judge) and sometimes *do* dumb
things—depending on what circumstances they are in, how much they know
about a situation, and how interested they are. Smartness, so it seems to me,
is a specific performance, done in a particular set of circumstances. It is not
something you *are* or *have* in measurable quantities. In fact, the assumption
that smartness is something you *have* has led to such nonsensical terms as
over- and *underachievers*. As I understand it, an overachiever is someone who

---

[4] **Samuel Butler (1835–1902)**   His utopian novel *Erewhon* (an anagram of *Nowhere*) is
still considered an important cultural statement.

doesn't *have* much smartness but does a lot of smart things. An underachiever is someone who *has* a lot of smartness but does a lot of dumb things.

The ways in which language creates a worldview are not usually part of the schooling of our young. There are several reasons for this. Chief among them is that in the education of teachers, the subject is not usually brought up, and if it is, it is introduced in a cavalier and fragmentary fashion. Another reason is that it is generally believed that the subject is too complex for schoolchildren to understand, with the unfortunate result that language education is mostly confined to the study of rules governing grammar, punctuation, and usage. A third reason is that the study of language as "world-maker" is, inescapably, of an interdisciplinary nature, so that teachers are not clear about which subject ought to undertake it.

As to the first reason, I have no good idea why prospective teachers are denied knowledge of this matter. (Actually, I have *some* ideas, but a few of them are snotty and all are unkind.) But if it were up to me, the study of the subject would be at the center of teachers' professional education and would remain there until they were done—that is, until they retire. This would require that they become well acquainted with the writings of Aristotle and Plato (among the ancients), Locke and Kant (among recent "ancients"), and (among the moderns) I. A. Richards, Benjamin Lee Whorf,[5] and, especially, Alfred Korzybski.

A few paragraphs about Korzybski are in order here, since his work offers the most systematic means of introducing the subject, deepening it, and staying with it. Another reason is that academics at the university level either do not know about Korzybski's work or, if they do, do not understand it (which does not mean, by the way, that fifth graders cannot). If they do understand it, they hate it. The result is that an exceedingly valuable means of exploring the relationship between language and reality goes unused.

Korzybski was born in Poland in 1879. He claimed to be of royal ancestry, referring to himself as Count Alfred Korzybski—another reason why academics have kept him at arm's length. He was trained in mathematics and engineering, and served as an artillery officer in World War I. The carnage and horror he witnessed left him haunted by a question of singular importance. He wondered why scientists could have such astonishing successes in discovering the mysteries of nature while, at the same time, the nonscientific community experienced appalling failure in its efforts to solve psychological, social, and political problems. Scientists signify their triumphs by almost daily announcements of new theories, new discoveries, new pathways to knowledge. The rest of us announce our failures by warring against ourselves and others. Korzybski

15

16

17

18

---

[5] **I. A. Richards (1893–1979)**   A British critic and teacher famous for introducing techniques of close reading of literary texts. One of his books is *How to Read a Page*. **Benjamin Lee Whorf (1897–1941)** An American linguist who advocated the principle of "linguistic relativity."

began to publish his answer to this enigma in 1921 in his book *Manhood of Humanity: The Science and Art of Human Engineering*. This was followed in 1926 by *Time-Binding: The General Theory*, and finally by his magnum opus, *Science and Sanity*, in 1933.

In formulating his answer, Korzybski was at all times concerned that his ideas should have practical applications. He conceived of himself as an educator who would offer to humanity both a theory and a method by which it might find some release from the poignant yet catastrophic ignorance whose consequences were to be witnessed in all the historic forms of human degradation. This, too, was held against him by many academics, who accused him of grandiosity and hubris.[6] Perhaps if Korzybski had thought *smaller*, his name would now appear more frequently in university catalogues.

Korzybski began his quest to discover the roots of human achievement and failure by identifying a critical functional difference between humans and other forms of life. We are, to use his phrase, "time-binders," while plants are "chemistry-binders," and animals are "space-binders." Chemistry-binding is the capacity to transform sunlight into organic chemical energy; space binding, the capacity to move about and control a physical environment. Humans have these capacities, too, but are unique in their ability to transport their experience through time. As time-binders, we can accumulate knowledge from the past and communicate what we know to the future. Science-fiction writers need not strain invention in their search for interesting time-transporting machinery: *we* are the universe's time machines.

Our principal means of accomplishing the binding of time is the symbol. But our capacity to symbolize is dependent upon and integral to another process, which Korzybski called "abstracting." Abstracting is the continuous activity of selecting, omitting, and organizing the details of reality so that we experience the world as patterned and coherent. Korzybski shared with Heraclitus[7] the assumption that the world is undergoing continuous change and that no two events are identical. We give stability to our world only through our capacity to re-create it by ignoring differences and attending to similarities. Although we know that we cannot step into the "same" river twice, abstracting allows us to act as if we can. We abstract at the neurological level, at the physiological level, at the perceptual level, at the verbal level; all of our systems of interaction with the world are engaged in selecting data from the world, organizing data, generalizing data. An abstraction, to put it simply, is a kind of summary of what the world is like, a generalization about its structure.

19

20

21

---

[6] **hubris**   Overweening pride.

[7] **Heraclitus (c. 535–c. 475 B.C.E.)**   Early Greek philosopher who claimed that everything was in change and said, famously, that "no one steps in the same river twice."

Korzybski might explain the process in the following way: let us suppose   22
we are confronted by the phenomenon we call a "cup." We must understand,
first of all, that a cup is not a thing, but an event; modern physics tells us
that a cup is made of billions of electrons in constant movement, undergoing
continuous change. Although none of this activity is perceptible to us, it is
important to acknowledge it, because by so doing, we may grasp the idea
that *the world is not the way we see it*. What we see is a summary—an
abstraction, if you will—of electronic activity. But even what we *can* see is
not what we *do* see. No one has ever seen a cup in its entirety, all at once in
space-time. We see only parts of wholes. But usually we see enough to allow
us to reconstruct the whole and to act as if we know what we are dealing
with. Sometimes, such a reconstruction betrays us, as when we lift a cup to
sip our coffee and find that the coffee has settled in our lap rather than on
our palate. But most of the time, our assumptions about a cup will work, and
we carry those assumptions forward in a useful way by the act of naming.
Thus we are assisted immeasurably in our evaluations of the world by our
language, which provides us with names for the events that confront us and,
by our naming them, tells us what to expect and how to prepare ourselves
for action.

The naming of things, of course, is an abstraction of a very high order   23
and of crucial importance. By naming an event and categorizing it as a "thing,"
we create a vivid and more or less permanent map of what the world is like.
But it is a curious map indeed. The word *cup*, for example, *does not in fact
denote anything that actually exists in the world*. It is a concept, a summary
of millions of particular things that have a similar look and function. The word
tableware is at a still higher level of abstraction, since it includes not only all
the things we normally call cups but also millions of things that look nothing
like cups but have a vaguely similar function.

The critical point about our mapping of the world through language is that   24
the symbols we use, whether *patriotism* and *love* or *cups* and *spoons*, are
always at a considerable remove from the reality of the world itself. Although
these symbols become part of ourselves—Korzybski believed they become
imbedded in our neurological and perceptual systems—we must never take
them completely for granted. As Korzybski once remarked, "Whatever we say
something *is*, it is not."

Thus, we may conclude that humans live in two worlds—the world of   25
events and things, and the world of *words* about events and things. In considering the relationship between these two worlds, we must keep in mind that
language does much more than construct concepts about the events and things
in the world; it tells us what sorts of concepts we ought to construct. For we
do not have a name for everything that occurs in the world. Languages differ
not only in their names for things but in what things they choose to name.

Each language, as Edward Sapir[8] observed, constructs reality differently from all the others.

This, then, is what Korzybski meant by what he called general seman-   26
tics: the study of the relationship between the world of words and the world of "not words," the study of the territory we call reality and how, through abstracting and symbolizing, we map the territory. In focusing on this process, Korzybski believed he had discovered why scientists are more effective than the rest of us in solving problems. Scientists tend to be more conscious of the abstracting process; more aware of the distortions in their verbal maps; more flexible in altering their symbolic maps to fit the world. His main educational objective was to foster the idea that by making our ordinary uses of language more like the scientific uses of language, we may avoid misunderstanding, superstition, prejudice, and just plain nonsense. Some of his followers, S. I. Hayakawa, Irving Lee, and Wendell Johnson,[9] wrote readable texts for use in schools, but their material is not much in fashion these days. I wrote some texts along these lines myself, mostly to find out if these ideas are suitable for younger students, and discovered that they are. (I remember with delight the easy success we had with them in Arlington, Virginia, at the Fort Myer Elementary School.) But, of course, not all of the ideas are useful, and not all of them are good. General semantics, like any other system, has to be applied with a considerable degree of selectivity. Assuming teachers know something about the subject, they will discover what works and what doesn't. It is, in any case, a mistake to assume that profound ideas about language, from general semantics or any other place, cannot be introduced until graduate school.

Of course, there are plenty of "other places" from which profound ideas   27
about language may come. The work of I. A. Richards (generally) and what he says, specifically, on definition and metaphor are good introductions to language as world-maker. On definition (from his *Interpretation in Teaching*):

> I have said something at several places . . . about the peculiar paralysis which the mention of definitions and, still more, the discussion of them induces. It can be prevented, I believe, by stressing the purposive aspect of definitions. We want to do something and a definition is a means of doing it. If we want certain results, then we must use certain meanings (or definitions). But no definition has any authority apart from a purpose, or to bar us from other purposes. And yet they endlessly do so. Who can doubt that we are often deprived of very useful thoughts merely because

---

[8] **Edward Sapir (1884–1939)**   Prominent American linguist also trained as an anthropologist.

[9] **Hayakawa . . . Johnson**   S. I. Hayakawa (1906–1992), Irving Lee (1909–1955), and Wendell Johnson (1906–1965) were all important theoreticians of semantics.

the words which might express them are being temporarily preempted by other meanings? Or that a development is often frustrated merely because we are sticking to a former definition of no service to the new purpose?

What Richards is talking about here is how to free our minds from the 28
tyranny of definitions, and I can think of no better way of doing this than to provide students, as a matter of course, with alternative definitions of the important concepts with which they must deal in a subject. Whether it be molecule,
fact, law, art, wealth, genes, or whatever, it is essential that students understand that definitions are instruments designed to achieve certain purposes,
that the fundamental question to ask of them is not, Is this the real definition?
or Is this the correct definition? but What purpose does the definition serve?
That is, Who made it up and why?

I have had some great fun, and so have students, considering the question 29
of definition in a curious federal law. I refer to what you may not say when
being frisked or otherwise examined before boarding an airplane. You may
not, of course, give false or misleading information about yourself. But beyond
that, you are also expressly forbidden to joke about any of the procedures
being used. This is the only case I know of where a joke is prohibited by law
(although there are many situations in which it is prohibited by custom).

Why joking is illegal when you are being searched is not entirely clear to 30
me, but that is only one of several mysteries surrounding this law. Does the
law distinguish, for example, between good jokes and bad jokes? (Six months
for a good one, two years for a bad one?) I don't know. But even more important, how would one know when something is a joke at all? Is there a legal
definition of a joke? Suppose, while being searched, I mention that my middle
name is Milton (which it is) and that I come from Flushing (which I do). I can
tell you from experience that people of questionable intelligence sometimes
find those names extremely funny, and it is not impossible that a few of them
are airport employees. If that were the case, what would be my legal status?
I have said something that has induced laughter in another. Have I, therefore,
told a joke? Or look at it from the opposite view: suppose that, upon being
searched, I launch into a story about a funny thing that happened to me while
boarding a plane in Chicago, concluding by saying, "And then the pilot said,
'That was no stewardess. That was my wife.'" Being of questionable intelligence myself, I think it is a hilarious story, but the guard does not. If he
does not laugh, have I told a joke? Can a joke be a story that does *not* make
people laugh?

It can, of course, if someone of authority says so. For the point is that in 31
every situation, including this one, someone (or some group) has a decisive
power of definition. In fact, to have power means to be able to define and to
make it stick. As between the guard at the airport and me, he will have the

power, not me, to define what a joke is. If his definition places me in jeopardy, I can, of course, argue my case at a trial, at which either a judge or a jury will then have the decisive authority to define whether or not my words qualified as a joke. But it is also worth noting that even if I confine my joke-telling to dinner parties, I do not escape the authority of definition. For at parties, popular opinion will decide whether or not my jokes are good ones, or even jokes at all. If opinion runs against me, the penalty is that I am not invited to many parties. There is, in short, no escaping the jurisdiction of definitions. Social order requires that there be authoritative definitions, and though you may search from now to doomsday, you will find no system without official definitions and authoritative sources to enforce them. And so we must add to the questions we ask of definition, What is the source of power that enforces the definition? And we may add further the question of what happens when those with the power to enforce definitions go mad. Here is an example that came from the Prague government several years ago. I have not made this up and produce it without further comment:

> Because Christmas Eve falls on a Thursday, the day has been designated a Saturday for work purposes. Factories will close all day, with stores open a half day only. Friday, December 25, has been designated a Sunday, with both factories and stores open all day. Monday, December 28, will be a Wednesday for work purposes. Wednesday, December 30, will be a business Friday. Saturday, January 2, will be a Sunday, and Sunday, January 3, will be a Monday.

As for metaphor, I pass along a small assignment which I. A. Richards   32
used on an occasion when I attended a seminar he conducted. (It is but one of a hundred ways to introduce the subject.) Richards divided the class into three groups. Each group was asked to write a paragraph describing language. However, Richards provided each group with its first sentence. Group A had to begin with "Language is like a tree"; Group B with "Language is like a river"; Group C with "Language is like a building." You can imagine, I'm sure, what happened. The paragraphs were strikingly different, with one group writing of roots and branches and organic growth; another of tributaries, streams, and even floods; another of foundations, rooms, and sturdy structures. In the subsequent discussion, we did not bother with the question, Which is the "correct" description? Our discussion centered on how metaphors control what we say, and to what extent what we say controls what we see.

As I have said, there are hundreds of ways to study the relationship   33
between language and reality, and I could go on at interminable length with ideas on how to get into it. Instead, I will confine myself to three further suggestions. The first is, simply, that the best book I know for arousing interest in the

subject is Helen Keller's *The Story of My Life.*[10] It is certainly the best account we have—from the inside, as it were—of how symbols and the abstracting process work to create a world.

Second, I would propose that in every subject—from history to biology to mathematics—students be taught, explicitly and systematically, the universe of discourse that comprises the subject. Each teacher would deal with the structure of questions, the process of definition, and the role of metaphor as these matters are relevant to his or her particular subject. Here I mean, of course, not merely what are the questions, definitions, and metaphors of a subject but also *how* these are formed and how they have been formed in the past.

Of special importance are the ways in which the forms of questions have changed over time and how these forms vary from subject to subject. The idea is for students to learn that the terminology of a question determines the terminology of its answer; that a question cannot be answered unless there are procedures by which reliable answers can be obtained; and that the value of a question is determined not only by the specificity and richness of the answers it produces but also by the quantity and quality of the new questions it raises.

Once this topic is opened, it follows that some attention must be given to how such terms as *right, wrong, truth,* and *falsehood* are used in a subject, as well as what assumptions they are based upon. This is particularly important, since words of this type cause far more trouble in students' attempts to understand a field of knowledge than do highly technical words. It is peculiar, I think, that of all the examinations I have ever seen, I have never come across one in which students were asked to say what is the basis of "correctness" or "falsehood" in a particular subject. Perhaps this is because teachers believe the issue is too obvious for discussion or testing. If so, they are wrong. I have found that students at all levels rarely have thought about the meaning of such terms in relation to a subject they are studying. They simply do not know in what sense a historical fact is different from a biological fact, or a mathematical "truth" is different from the "truth" of a literary work. Equally astonishing is that students, particularly those in elementary and secondary schools, rarely can express an intelligible sentence on the uses of the word *theory.* Since most subjects studied in school consist largely of theories, it is difficult to imagine exactly what students are in fact studying when they do their history, biology, economics, physics, or whatever. It is obvious, then, that language education must include not only the serious study of what truth and falsehood mean in the context of a subject but also what is meant by a theory, a fact, an inference, an assumption, a judgment, a generalization.

34

35

36

---

[10] *The Story of My Life*   Book written by Helen Keller (1880–1968), who was born deaf and blind but learned language and wrote this inspiring autobiography.

✦ QUESTIONS FOR CRITICAL READING

1. What is a metaphor and how does it affect our understanding?

2. What is Postman's concern about the questions we ask and their effect on the answers we get?

3. Who defines words? What word do you define differently than other people do?

4. Are definitions invented?

5. What does Postman mean by the term *abstraction* (para. 21)?

6. In what ways are we "time-binders"? Why is that metaphor important?

7. What does Postman mean by "world making through language" (para. 9)?

✦ SUGGESTIONS FOR CRITICAL WRITING

1. When Postman says, "Everything we know has its origin in questions," he directs us to consider how we come to an understanding of disciplines such as biology, physics, English, psychology, and sociology. Choose a half-dozen questions that are central to one area of study and explore the ways in which these questions help shape your understanding of that area. What new questions arise when you try to provide answers to those questions?

2. One of Postman's fundamental claims is that "our language habits are at the core of how we imagine the world" (para. 13). Write a brief essay for someone who has not read this selection and explain to that audience what Postman means and then defend or attack Postman's position. How can Postman think that our language habits shape our sense of the world? What evidence does he develop to bolster his position? What observations have you made that help explain Postman's idea?

3. Postman says that "one of the purposes of our education is to give us greater control of our situation" (para. 13). If you feel this is true, examine the details of your own education up to this point and explain how it has given you more control over your situation. Then look to the future and discuss how you think your education will contribute to your gaining more control of your situation. What do you think Postman means by the term *situation*? Is *situation* a metaphor?

4. In paragraph 25, Postman says, "we may conclude that humans live in two worlds — the world of events and things, and the world of *words* about events and things." Explain what Postman means by this statement and then examine your own experience with the world of events and things and the world of words about those events and things. How do the words you use actually "map" the world of your personal experience? You may limit yourself to talking about a single event and the things that are part of that event. For instance, how do you map your first hours of the day when you wake up and have breakfast? How do you map a first romantic encounter? Explain the richness of the word *map* used as a metaphor.

5. Find two different newspapers' accounts of a major national event and examine the use of metaphor in each. Do the same for the questions asked or implied and the definitions stated or implied. Is it possible to see that each newspaper "slants" the story somewhat differently by means of the metaphors used and the language choices made? Which story is the most trustable? Does either newspaper give you a sense of confidence in its general truthfulness? Try to avoid accounts that are "fed" to newspapers through an agency such as the Associated Press or Reuters because the accounts will be essentially the same.

6. Try a variation of I. A. Richards's experiment and write a brief essay that uses each of the following opening sentences:

   (a) Culture is like a tree.   (b) Culture is like a river.

   (c) Culture is like a building.   (d) Culture is like a zoo.

   Are you convinced that any one of your essays is a more accurate and convincing description of culture than the others are?

7. Respond to Postman's complaints about the effects of television on children. Consider your childhood experience or the experiences of young children you know. Did you or the children grow up too fast and miss the pleasures of early childhood? Do you think television programming today emphasizes entertainment over information? Do you think it encourages young people to be consumers, to be materialistic, and to develop adult desires? Do you think television stunts the intellectual growth of people who watch it?

8. **CONNECTIONS**   When Postman tells us that the world is not the way we see it, he seems to invoke the selection known as Plato's Cave — which appears in this book as "The Allegory of the Cave" (p. 580). How much in agreement are Postman and Plato about the question of perception of the world? Examine Plato's metaphors and decide how they help shape the meaning of his selection. In what sense is the cave a metaphor? How convincing is Plato's metaphor? Comment on his definitions and the questions he asks.

9. **CONNECTIONS**   Our understanding of our own culture is linked to the words we use to describe it. Examine the language of Jacob A. Riis in "The Color Line in New York" (p. 209). What words are the most "loaded" with significance for understanding the cultural conditions of late-nineteenth-century New York? Which words clearly aim at helping us create an understanding of the world Riis describes? Margaret Mead (p. 236) also introduces a number of unusual words to help us understand the cultures she studied in the South Pacific. How do these words contribute to creating a cultural significance for us? How do these words create our understanding of the cultures these writers describe?

JUDITH BUTLER

From *Undoing Gender*

J UDITH BUTLER (b. 1956) is Maxine Eliot Professor of Rhetoric and Comparative Literature at the University of California, Berkeley. Currently, she is a visiting professor at Columbia University in New York City. She was originally trained in philosophy, and much of her work has been wide-ranging, considering gender studies and political and psychoanalytic issues, as well as concerns for how language shapes our understanding of not just the world, but ourselves.

Her work is often theoretical and influenced by the modern European theoreticians who have sometimes been described as post-structuralist. As a result, her writing has been criticized for being too indirect, abstract, and obscure. However, her book *Undoing Gender* (2004), from which the following selection is taken, is written in a style marked by clarity and directness, unlike many of her articles and other books. She has done a great deal of work focused on gender identity and on the nature of sexuality and argues that both are largely the result of socialization and the force of language in our society. She admits that this idea seems inherently contrary to common sense, but it is for that very reason that she asks us to listen closely to her reasoning. Given the power of language to shape ideas, and given the fluidity of the concept of gender, her argument is taken very seriously by psychologists and philosophers concerned with how individuals view their own nature.

Gender Trouble: Feminism and the Subversion of Identity (1990) was an immediately influential book, its powerful critique of the feminist movement resounding with both academic and popular audiences alike. In it, Butler argues against a "binary view of gender," or a view that limits the definition of gender to a male body and a female body. Butler's argument is that gender is flexible, a continuum from one pole to another of desire. Feminism in 1990, she felt, limited itself to two absolute categories — women and men — with the subsequent view that the focus of sexual desire was also limited to one of these two categories. However, as a lesbian herself and a researcher into gender issues, she knew that desire takes many forms and that feminists holding to their binary view limited the movement as well as themselves. If feminists rejected the doctrine that biology is destiny on the basis of a male-female model, then it was necessary for them to explore their views of the nature of biology and the demands of society with more vigor.

Current research has shown that rigid categories of sexuality have been impossible to maintain. Transgender operations have proliferated enough that public figures have had national recognition in their efforts to change their perceived gender status. Queer studies has become a valid academic discipline in many major universities, especially now that efforts have been made to remove any stigma from homosexual and lesbian lifestyles. Same-sex marriage has become, if not common, more greatly recognized by state laws. Butler has been in the forefront of trying to change society's awareness of how limitations in attitudes affect the perceptions of all of us.

BUTLER'S RHETORIC

As a professor of rhetoric, Butler is deeply concerned with the ways in which language defines people and things. She points out that in some cases it is only through language that we understand the nature of reality — and at that, we cannot totally trust language to give us the complete truth about things. As a result of her concerns for language, she uses it very carefully and performs complex analyses at crucial points in her argument so as to guarantee us as clear a sense of understanding as possible.

The opening pages of her selection establish the general circumstances that she is interested in treating. She explains that she will focus on the human, on "the conditions of intelligibility by which the human emerges" (para. 1). She points to her subjects as "human love," "norms," and "ways of knowing, modes of truth, that forcibly define intelligibility." Her point is that there may be ways of understanding norms and what it is to be human from a careful consideration of what is said and that what we say stands for the truth about humanity.

Once she has established her focus, she introduces us to a narrative of great interest and some complexity. She tells us the case story of David Reimer, a boy who accidentally had his penis burned and subsequently amputated at the age of eight months. The accident was the result of a doctor's mismanagement of an electrocautery needle that he was unfamiliar with. What should have been a risk-free operation totally changed David. His parents, hoping to find a way for him to have a heterosexual life, took him to Dr. John Money at Johns Hopkins University to consult about what should be done. Money was famous for his sex transformation cases involving infants with anomalous sexual organs (often described as hermaphrodites). Money convinced the parents that David could be raised as a girl with great success. He explained that socialization, along with hormones, would establish gender and that David, renamed Brenda, would grow up as a girl and achieve a sense of female identity and feel normal. Money had a reputation for success in cases similar to this, and Brenda was raised as a girl never knowing about the medical mutilation during his infancy.

But the story was complicated by several things. One was that Brenda, as the subject of Dr. Money's scientific studies, was being studied by others to see how the gender change was working: she was frequently asked to disrobe and was examined by other doctors; she was questioned routinely about her feelings and her progress. Brenda became a medical subject and therefore did not experience what others might have considered a normal upbringing. By age two, Brenda began to show signs of gender-assignment discomfort, rejecting clothes chosen for her and choosing what were thought to be inappropriate toys, such as machine guns. Ultimately, Brenda rejected her female assignment and, at age fourteen, became David once again. He underwent another surgery to return himself to something close to the physical male norm.

Butler comments on all the phases of this narrative and ends her essay with a detailed analysis of the narrative that she presents of David's development. She also analyzes David's own account of his circumstances as it is told in the literature. The story has subtleties that Butler unravels in her quest to answer certain questions about what she calls "gender essentialism" and the relationship of gender and gender assignments to the body itself. The question of what constitutes a norm is also central to her interests in understanding the significance of David's experiences moving from gender to gender. Butler's analysis is detailed and thorough, but she admits that there are many aspects of this case that cannot be easily understood, especially by examining the narratives in which the case is presented. As readers of her narrative and her analysis, we are brought to an understanding of our own limitations in the face of narratives that limit our intelligence of what really happened. That is a major part of Butler's central point. Language comes between us and the reality, but that does not prevent us from trying to understand the reality of David's experiences.

Unfortunately, while Butler was preparing her book for press, David Reimer killed himself. She appends that information in a postscript at the end of the selection, but there is much more to the story that should be known. For example, David's was the first experiment by John Money on a child not born a hermaphrodite or with indeterminate genitals. Moreover, David was never told he was born a boy until he was fourteen years old. Once he was told, he said he knew why he had the feelings he had had when he was young and that now he did not feel like a freak. He had his breasts removed and then insisted on being given the FTM (female-to-male) surgery that restored him to his original gender. John Colapinto, who wrote a best-selling book about David, was not entirely surprised that David killed himself. Colapinto said that David had been taunted relentlessly as a child and that those experiences haunted him. In addition, his mother and brother had been clinically depressed. His twin brother Brian overdosed on antidepressants two years before David took his own life at the age of thirty-eight.

Butler focuses on David as an example of someone who struggled with gender issues while in the care of doctors who held to some fundamental decisions regarding the truth about gender and what it should look like. Butler makes us aware that such decisions are not easily reached nor are they easily defended.

✖ PREREADING QUESTIONS: WHAT TO READ FOR

The following prereading questions may help you anticipate key issues in the discussion of this excerpt from Judith Butler's *Undoing Gender*. Keeping them in mind during your first reading should help focus your attention.

1. What is the relation of gender to personhood?
2. Is there an essential gender core (see para. 9)?
3. What was David Reimer's experience with gender reassignment?

From *Undoing Gender*

I would like to take my point of departure from a question of power, the power of regulation, a power that determines, more or less, what we are, what we can be. I am not speaking of power only in a juridical or positive sense, but I am referring to the workings of a certain regulatory regime, one that informs the law, and also exceeds the law. When we ask, what are the conditions of intelligibility by which the human emerges, by which the human is recognized, by which some subject becomes the subject of human love, we are asking about conditions of intelligibility composed of norms, of practices, that have become presuppositional, without which we cannot think the human at all. So I propose to broach the relationship between variable orders of intelligibility and the genesis and knowability of the human. And it is not just that there are laws that govern our intelligibility, but ways of knowing, modes of truth, that forcibly define intelligibility.

This is what Foucault[1] describes as the politics of truth, a politics that pertains to those relations of power that circumscribe in advance what will and will not count as truth, which order the world in certain regular and regulatable ways, and which we come to accept as the given field of knowledge. We can understand the salience of this point when we begin to ask: What counts as a person? What counts as a coherent gender? What qualifies as a citizen? Whose world is legitimated as real? Subjectively, we ask: Who can I become in such a world where the meanings and limits of the subject are set out in advance for me? By what norms am I constrained as I begin to ask what I may become? And what happens when I begin to become that for which there is no place within

---

[1] **Michel Foucault (1926–1984)**   Important French historian of ideas.

the given regime of truth? This is what Foucault describes as "the desubjugation of the subject in the play of . . . the politics of truth."

Another way of putting this is the following: "What, given the contemporary order of being, can I be?" This question does not quite broach the question of what it is not to be, or what it is to occupy the place of not-being within the field of being. What it is to live, breathe, attempt to love neither as fully negated nor as fully acknowledged as being. This relationship, between intelligibility and the human, is an urgent one; it carries a certain theoretical urgency, precisely at those points where the human is encountered at the limits of intelligibility itself. I would like to suggest that this interrogation has something important to do with justice. Justice is not only or exclusively a matter of how persons are treated or how societies are constituted. It also concerns consequential decisions about what a person is, and what social norms must be honored and expressed for "personhood" to become allocated, how we do or do not recognize animate others as persons depending on whether or not we recognize a certain norm manifested in and by the body of that other. The very criterion by which we judge a person to be a gendered being, a criterion that posits coherent gender as a presupposition of humanness, is not only one which, justly or unjustly, governs the recognizability of the human, but one that informs the ways we do or do not recognize ourselves at the level of feeling, desire, and the body, at the moments before the mirror, in the moments before the window, in the times that one turns to psychologists, to psychiatrists, to medical and legal professionals to negotiate what may well feel like the unrecognizability of one's gender and, hence, the unrecognizability of one's personhood. 3

I want to consider a legal and psychiatric case of a person who was determined without difficulty to be a boy at the time of birth, then determined again within a few months to be a girl, who decided in his teenage years to become a man. This is the story of David Reimer, whose situation is referred to as "the Joan/John case," one that was brought to public attention by the BBC and in various popular, psychological, and medical journals. I base my analysis on several documents: an article written by Dr. Milton Diamond, an endocrinologist, and the popular book *As Nature Made Him*, written by John Colapinto, a journalist for *Rolling Stone*, as well as several publications by John Money, and critical commentaries offered by Anne Fausto-Sterling and Suzanne Kessler in their important recent books.[2] David Reimer has now talked openly to the media and has chosen to live outside the pseudonym reserved for him by Milton Diamond and his colleagues. David became 4

---

[2] **John Money (1921–2006)**   Controversial psychologist and sex researcher; **Anne Fausto-Sterling (b. 1944)**, author of "The Five Sexes: Why Male and Female Are Not Enough" (2000); **Suzanne Kessler (b. 1946)**, author of *Lessons from the Intersexed* (2000). All three are important experts in gender studies.

"Brenda" at a certain point in his childhood which I discuss below, and so instead of referring to him as Joan and John, neither of which is his name, I will use the name he uses.

David was born with XY chromosomes and at the age of eight months, his   5 penis was accidentally burned and severed in the course of a surgical operation to rectify phimosis, a condition in which the foreskin thwarts urination. This is a relatively risk-free procedure, but the doctor who performed it on David was using a new machine, apparently one that he hadn't used before, one that his colleagues declared was unnecessary for the job. He had trouble making the machine work, so he increased the power to the machine to the point that it effectively burned away a major portion of the penis. The parents were, of course, appalled and shocked, and they were, according to their own description, unclear how to proceed. Then one evening, about a year after this event, they were watching television, and there they encountered John Money, talking about transsexual and intersexual surgery, offering the view that if a child underwent surgery and started socialization as a gender different from the one originally assigned at birth, the child could develop normally, adapt perfectly well to the new gender, and live a happy life. The parents wrote to Money and he invited them to Baltimore, and so David was subsequently seen at Johns Hopkins University, at which point the strong recommendation was made by Dr. John Money that David be raised as a girl. The parents agreed, and the doctors removed the testicles, made some preliminary preparation for surgery to create a vagina, but decided to wait until Brenda, the newly named child, was older to complete the task. So Brenda grew up as a girl, and was monitored often, given over on a periodic basis to John Money's Gender Identity Institute for the purposes of fostering adaptation to being a girl. Then between the ages of eight and nine, Brenda found herself developing the desire to buy a toy machine gun. Between the ages of nine and eleven, she started to make the realization that she was not a girl. This realization seems to coincide with the desire to buy certain kinds of toys: more guns, apparently, and some trucks. Although there was no penis, Brenda liked to stand to urinate. And she was caught in this position once, at school, and the other girls threatened to "kill" her if she continued.

At this point, the psychiatric teams that were intermittently monitoring   6 Brenda's adaptation offered her estrogen, and she refused this. Money tried to talk to her about getting a real vagina, and she refused; in fact, she went screaming from the room. Money had her view sexually graphic pictures of vaginas. Money even went so far as to show Brenda pictures of women giving birth, holding out the promise that Brenda might be able to give birth if she acquired a vagina. And in a scene that could have been the model for the recent film *But I'm a Cheerleader!* she and her brother were required to perform mock coital exercises with one another, on command. They both later reported being very frightened and disoriented by this demand and did not tell their parents at the time. Brenda is said to have preferred male activities and not to have liked developing breasts. And all of these attributions to Brenda are made by another set of doctors, this time a team of psychiatrists at Brenda's local hospital. The local psychiatrists and medical professionals intervened in the case, believing that a mistake had been made in sex reassignment here, and eventually the case was reviewed by Milton Diamond, a sex researcher who believes in the hormonal basis of gender identity and who has been battling Money for several years. This new set of psychiatrists and doctors offered her the choice of changing paths, which she accepted. She started living as a boy, named David, at the age of fourteen. At this point, David started requesting, and receiving, male hormone shots, and also had his breasts removed. A phallus, so it was called by Diamond, was constructed for him between the age of fifteen and sixteen. David, it is reported, does not ejaculate, although he feels some sexual pleasure there; he urinates from its base. It is a phallus that only approximates some of its expected functions and, as we shall see, enters David only ambivalently into the norm.

During the time that David was Brenda, Money continued to publish papers extolling the success of this sex reassignment case. The case was enormously consequential because Brenda had a brother for an identical twin, and so Money could track the development of both siblings and assume an identical genetic makeup for both of them. He insisted that both were developing normally and happily into their different genders. But his own recorded interviews, mainly unpublished, and subsequent research, have called his honesty into question. Brenda was hardly happy, refused to adapt to many so-called girl behaviors, and was appalled and angered by Money's invasive and constant interrogations. And yet, the published records from Johns Hopkins claim that Brenda's adaptation to girlhood was "successful," and immediately certain ideological conclusions followed. John Money's Gender Identity Clinic, which monitored Brenda often, concluded that Brenda's successful development as a girl "offers convincing evidence that the gender identity gate is open at birth for a normal child no less than for one born with unfinished sex organs or one who was prenatally over or underexposed to androgen, and that it stays open at least for something over a year at birth." Indeed, the case was used by the public media to make the case that what is feminine and what is masculine can be altered, that these cultural terms have no fixed meaning or internal destiny, and that they are more malleable than previously thought. Even Kate Millett[3] cited the case in making the argument that biology is not destiny. And Suzanne Kessler also cowrote with Money essays in favor of the social constructionist thesis. Later Kessler would disavow the alliance and write one of the most important books on the ethical

7

---

[3] **Kate Millett (b. 1934)**   Important feminist and author of *Sexual Politics* (1990).

and medical dimensions of sex assignment, *Lessons from the Intersexed*, which includes a trenchant critique of Money himself.

Money's approach to Brenda was to recruit male to female transsexuals to talk to Brenda about the advantages of being a girl. Brenda was subjected to myriad interviews, asked again and again whether she felt like a girl, what her desires were, what her image of the future was, whether it included marriage to a man. Brenda was also asked to strip and show her genitals to medical practitioners who were either interested in the case or monitoring the case for its adaptational success.

When this case was discussed in the press, and when psychiatrists and medical practitioners have referred to it, they have done so in order to criticize the role that John Money's institute played in the case and, in particular, how quickly that institute sought to use Brenda as an example of its own theoretical beliefs, beliefs about the gender neutrality of early childhood, about the malleability of gender, of the primary role of socialization in the production of gender identity. In fact, this is not exactly everything that Money believes, but I will not probe that question here. Those who have become critical of this case believe that it shows us something very different. When we consider, they argue, that David found himself deeply moved to become a boy, and found it unbearable to continue to live as a girl, we have to consider as well that there was some deep-seated sense of gender that David experienced, one that is linked to his original set of genitals, one that seems to be there, as an internal truth and necessity, which no amount of socialization could reverse. This is the view of Colapinto and of Milton Diamond as well. So now the case of Brenda/David is being used to make a revision and reversal in developmental gender theory, providing evidence this time for the reversal of Money's thesis, supporting the notion of an essential gender core, one that is tied in some irreversible way to anatomy and to a deterministic sense of biology. Indeed, Colapinto clearly links Money's cruelty to Brenda to the "cruelty" of social construction as a theory, remarking that Money's refusal to identify a biological or anatomical basis for gender difference in the early 1970s "was not lost on the then-burgeoning women's movement, which had been arguing against a biological basis for sex differences for decades." He claims that Money's published essays "had already been used as one of the main foundations of modern feminism." He quotes *Time* magazine as engaging in a similarly misguided appropriation of Money's views when they argued that this case "provides strong support for a major contention of women's liberationists: that conventional patterns of masculine and feminine behavior can be altered. . . ." Indeed, Colapinto proceeds to talk about the failure of surgically reassigned individuals to live as "normal" and "typical" women or men, arguing that normality is never achieved and, hence, assuming throughout the inarguable value of normalcy itself.

When Natalie Angier[4] reported on the refutation of Money's theory in the   10
New York Times (14 March 1997), she claimed that the story of David had
"the force of allegory." But which force was that? And is this an allegory with
closure? In that article, Angier reports that Diamond used the case to make an
argument about intersexual surgery and, by implication, the relative success of
transsexual surgery. Diamond argued, for instance, that intersexed infants, that
is, those born with mixed genital attributes, generally have a Y chromosome,
and the possession of the Y is an adequate basis for concluding that the child
ought to be raised as a boy. As it is, the vast majority of intersexed infants are
subjected to surgery that seeks to assign them to a female sex, since, as Cheryl
Chase, points out, it is simply considered easier to produce a provisional vag-
inal tract than it is to construct a phallus. Diamond argues that these children
should be assigned to the male sex, since the presence of the Y is sufficient
grounds for the presumption of social masculinity.

In fact, Chase, the founder and director of the Intersexed Society of North   11
America, voiced skepticism about Diamond's recommendations. Her view,
defended by Anne Fausto-Sterling as well, is that although a child should be
given a sex assignment for the purposes of establishing a stable social identity,
it does not follow that society should engage in coercive surgery to remake the
body in the social image of that gender. Such efforts at "correction" not only
violate the child but lend support to the idea that gender has to be borne out in
singular and normative ways at the level of anatomy. Gender is a different sort
of identity, and its relation to anatomy is complex. According to Chase, a child
upon maturing may choose to change genders or, indeed, elect for hormonal or
surgical intervention, but such decisions are justified because they are based
on knowing choice. Indeed, research has shown that such surgical operations
have been performed without parents knowing, that such surgical operations
have been performed without the children themselves ever having been truth-
fully told, and without waiting until the child is old enough to offer his or her
consent. Most astonishing, in a way, is the mutilated state that these bodies are
left in, mutilations performed and then paradoxically rationalized in the name
of "looking normal," the rationale used by medical practitioners to justify these
surgeries. They often say to parents that the child will not look normal, that
the child will be ashamed in the locker room, the locker room, that site of pre-
pubescent anxiety about impending gender developments, and that it would
be better for the child to look normal, even when such surgery may deprive
the person permanently of sexual function and pleasure. So, as some experts,
such as Money, claim that the absence of the full phallus makes the social case
for rearing the child as a girl, others such as Diamond argue that the presence

---

[4] **Natalie Angier (b. 1958)**   A science correspondent for the *New York Times* and author
    of *Natural Obsessions* (1988), a study of cancer research.

of the Y is the most compelling evidence, that it is what is being indexed in persistent feelings of masculinity, and that it cannot be constructed away.

Thus, in the one case, how anatomy looks, how it appears to others, and   12
to myself, as I see others looking at me—this is the basis of a social identity as woman or man. In the other case, how the genetic presence of the "Y" works in tacit ways to structure feeling and self-understanding as a sexed person is the basis. Money thus argues for the ease with which a female body can be surgically constructed, as if femininity was always little more or less than a surgical construction, an elimination, a cutting away. Diamond argues for the invisible and necessary persistence of maleness, one that does not need to "appear" in order to operate as the key feature of gender identity itself. When Angier asks Chase whether she agrees with Diamond's recommendations on intersexual surgery, Chase replies: "They can't conceive of leaving someone alone." Indeed, is the surgery performed in order to create a "normal-looking" body after all? The mutilations and scars that remain hardly offer compelling evidence that this is what the surgeries actually accomplish. Or are these bodies, precisely because they are "inconceivable," subjected to medical machinery that marks them for life?

Another paradox emerges here—one that I hope to write about further   13
on another occasion—namely, the place of sharp machines, of the technology of the knife, in debates on intersexuality and transsexuality alike. If the David/Brenda case is an allegory, or has the force of allegory, it seems to be the site where debates on intersexuality (David is not an intersexual) and transsexuality (David is not a transsexual) converge. This body becomes a point of reference for a narrative that is not about this body, but which seizes upon the body, as it were, in order to inaugurate a narrative that interrogates the limits of the conceivably human. What is inconceivable is conceived again and again, through narrative means, but something remains outside the narrative, a resistant moment that signals a persisting inconceivability.

Despite Diamond's recommendations, the intersex movement has been   14
galvanized by the Brenda/David case, able now to bring to public attention the brutality, coerciveness, and lasting harm of the unwanted surgeries performed on intersexed infants. The point is to try to imagine a world in which individuals with mixed genital attributes might be accepted and loved without having to transform them into a more socially coherent or normative version of gender. In this sense, the intersex movement has sought to question why society maintains the ideal of gender dimorphism[5] when a significant percentage of children are chromosomally various, and a continuum exists between male and female that suggests the arbitrariness and falsity of the gender dimorphism as a prerequisite of human development. There are humans, in other words,

---

[5] **gender dimorphism**   Theory that the only genders are male and female, based on the male and female bodies.

who live and breathe in the interstices of this binary relation, showing that it is not exhaustive; it is not necessary. Although the transsexual movement, which is internally various, has called for rights to surgical means by which sex might be transformed, it is also clear—and Chase underscores this—that there is also a serious and increasingly popular critique of idealized gender dimorphism within the transsexuality movement itself. One can see it in the work of Riki Wilchins,[6] whose gender theory makes room for transsexuality as a transformative exercise, but one can see it perhaps most dramatically in Kate Bornstein, who argues that to go from F to M, or from M to F, is not necessarily to stay within the binary frame of gender, but to engage transformation itself as the meaning of gender. In some ways, it is Kate Bornstein who is now carrying the legacy of Simone de Beauvoir:[7] if one is not born a woman, but rather becomes one, then becoming is the vehicle for gender itself. But why, we might ask, has David become the occasion for a reflection on transsexuality?

Although David comes to claim that he would prefer to be a man, it is not clear whether David himself believes in the primary causal force of the Y chromosome. Diamond finds support for his theory in David, but it is not clear that David agrees with Diamond. David clearly knows about the world of hormones, asked for them and takes them. David has learned about phallic construction from transsexual contexts, wants a phallus, has it made, and so allegorizes a certain transsexual transformation without precisely exemplifying it. He is, in his view, a man born a man, castrated by the medical establishment, feminized by the psychiatric world, and then enabled to return to who he is. But in order to return to who he is, he requires—and wants, and gets—a subjection to hormones and surgery. He allegorizes transsexuality in order to achieve a sense of naturalness. And this transformation is applauded by the endocrinologists on the case since they understand his appearance now to be in accord with an inner truth. Whereas the Money Institute enlists transsexuals to instruct Brenda in the ways of women, and *in the name of normalization*, the endocrinologists prescribe the sex change protocol of transsexuality to David for him to reassume his genetic destiny, *in the name of nature*.   15

And though the Money Institute enlists transsexuals to allegorize Brenda's full transformation into a woman, the endocrinologists propose to appropriate transsexual surgery in order to build the phallus that will make David a more legible man. Importantly, it seems, the norms [that] govern intelligible gender for Money are those that can be forcibly imposed and behaviorally appropriated, so the malleability of gender construction, which is part of his thesis, turns   16

---

[6] **Riki Wilchins (b. 1952)**   An activist who focuses on gender norms but who is best known for bringing transgender people into public acceptance.

[7] **Kate Bornstein (b. 1948)**   A transsexual and author of *Gender Outlaw* (1994). **Simone de Beauvoir (1908–1986)** was a celebrated French writer and philosopher and author of *The Second Sex* (1953).

out to require a forceful application. And the "nature" that the endocrinologists defend also needs a certain assistance through surgical and hormonal means, at which point a certain nonnatural intervention in anatomy and biology is precisely what is mandated by nature. So in each case, the primary premise is in some ways refuted by the means by which it is implemented. *Malleability is, as it were, violently imposed. And naturalness is artificially induced.* There are ways of arguing social construction that have nothing to do with Money's project, but that is not my aim here. And there are no doubt ways of seeking recourse to genetic determinants that do not lead to the same kind of interventionist conclusions that are arrived at by Diamond and Sigmundsen. But that is also not precisely my point. For the record, though, the prescriptions arrived at by these purveyors of natural and normative gender in no way follow necessarily from the premises from which they begin, and that the premises with which they begin have no necessity of itself. (One might well disjoin the theory of gender construction, for instance, from the hypothesis of gender normativity and have a very different account of social construction than that offered by Money; one might allow from genetic factors without assuming that they are the only aspect of "nature" that one might consult to understand the sexed characteristics of a human: Why is the "Y" considered the exclusive and primary determinant of maleness, exercising preemptive rights over any and all other factors?)

But my point in recounting this story to you and its appropriation for the   17
purposes of gender theory is to suggest that the story as we have it does not actually supply evidence for either thesis, and to suggest that there may be another way of reading this story, one that neither confirms nor denies the theory of social construction, one that neither affirms nor denies gender essentialism. Indeed, what I hope to underscore here is the disciplinary framework within which Brenda/David develops a discourse of self-reporting and self-understanding, since it constitutes the grid of intelligibility by which his own humanness is both questioned and asserted. It seems crucial to remember, as one considers what might count as the evidence of the truth of gender, that Brenda/David was intensely monitored by psychological teams through childhood and adolescence, that teams of doctors observed her behavior, that teams of doctors asked her and her brother to disrobe in front of them so that genital development could be gauged, that there was the doctor who asked her to engage in mock coital exercises with her brother, to view the pictures, to know and want the so-called normalcy of unambiguous genitalia. There was an apparatus of knowledge applied to the person and body of Brenda/David that is rarely, if ever, taken into account as part of what David is responding to when he reports on his feelings of true gender.

The act of self-reporting and the act of self-observation take place in   18
relation to a certain audience, with a certain audience as the imagined recipient,

before a certain audience for whom a verbal and visual picture of selfhood is being produced. These are speech acts that are very often delivered to those who have been scrutinizing, brutally, the truth of Brenda's gender for years. And even though Diamond and Sigmundsen and even Colapinto are in the position of defending David against Money's various intrusions, they are still asking David how he feels and who he is, trying to ascertain the truth of his sex through the discourse he provides. Because Brenda was subjected to such scrutiny and, most importantly, constantly and repeatedly subjected to a norm, a normalizing ideal that was conveyed through a plurality of gazes, a norm applied to the body, a question is constantly posed: Is this person feminine enough? Has this person made it to femininity? Is femininity being properly embodied here? Is the embodiment working? What evidence can be marshalled in order to know? And surely we must have knowledge here. We must be able to say that we know, and to communicate that in the professional journals, and justify our decision, our act. In other words, these exercises interrogate whether the gender norm that establishes coherent personhood has been successfully accomplished. The inquiries and inspections can be understood, along these lines, as the violent attempt to implement the norm, and the institutionalization of that power of implementation.

The pediatricians and psychiatrists who have revisited the case in recent   19
years cite David's own self-description to support their point. David's narrative about his own sense of being male that supports the theory that David is really male, and that he was, even when he was Brenda, always male.

David tells his interviewers the following about himself: 20

> There were little things from early on. I began to see how different I felt and was, from what I was supposed to be. But I didn't know what it meant. I thought I was a freak or something . . . I looked at myself and said I don't like this type of clothing, I don't like the types of toys I was always being given. I like hanging around with the guys and climbing trees and stuff like that and girls don't like any of that stuff. I looked in the mirror and [saw] my shoulders [were] so wide, I mean there [was] nothing feminine about me. I [was] skinny, but other than that, nothing. But that [was] how I figured it out. [I figured I was a guy] but didn't want to admit it. I figured I didn't want to wind up opening a can of worms.

So now you read how David describes himself. And so, if part of my task   21
here is to do justice, not only to my topic, but to the person I am sketching for you, the person around whom so much has been said, the person whose self-description and whose decisions have become the basis for so much gender theorizing, I must be careful in presenting these words. For these words can give you only something of the person I am trying to understand, some part of that person's verbal instance. Since I cannot truly understand this person, since

I do not know this person, and have no access to this person, I am left to be a reader of a selected number of words, words that I did not fully select, ones that were selected for me, recorded from interviews and then chosen by those who decided to write their articles on this person for journals such as the *Archives of Pediatric Adolescent Medicine*. So we might say that I am given fragments of the person, linguistic fragments of something called a person; what might it mean to do justice to someone under these circumstances? Can we?

On the one hand, we have a self-description, and that is to be honored. 22 These are the words by which this individual gives himself to be understood. On the other hand, we have a description of a self that takes place in a language that is already going on, that is already saturated with norms, that predisposes us as we seek to speak of ourselves. Moreover, we have words that are delivered in the context of an interview, an interview which is part of the long and intrusive observational process that has accompanied Brenda's formation from the start. To do justice to David is, certainly, to take him at his word, and to call him by his chosen name, but how are we to understand his word and his name? Is this the word that he creates? Is this the word that he receives? Are these the words that circulate prior to his emergence as an "I" who might only gain a certain authorization to begin a self-description within the norms of this language? So that when one speaks, one speaks a language that is already speaking, even if one speaks it in a way that is not precisely how it has been spoken before. So what and who is speaking here, when David reports: "There were little things from early on. I began to see how different I felt and was, from what I was supposed to be."

This claim tells us minimally that David understands that there is a norm, 23 a norm of how he was supposed to be, and that he has fallen short of the norm. The implicit claim here is that the norm is femininity, and he has failed to live up to that norm. And there is the norm, and it is externally imposed, communicated through a set of expectations that others have; and then there is the world of feeling and being, and these realms are, for him, distinct. What he feels is not in any way produced by the norm, and the norm is other, elsewhere, not part of who he is, who he has become, what he feels.

But given what we know about how David has been addressed, I might, 24 in an effort to do justice to David, ask, what did Brenda see as Brenda looks at himself, feels as he feels himself, and please excuse my mixing of pronouns here, but matters are becoming changeable. When Brenda looks in the mirror and sees something nameless, freakish, something between the norms, is she not at that moment in question as a human, is she not the spectre of the freak against which and through which the norm installs itself? What is the problem with Brenda such that people are always asking to see her naked, asking her questions about what she is, how she feels, whether this is or is not the same as what is normatively true? Is that self-seeing distinct from the way s/he is seen?

He seems clear that the norms are external to him, but what if the norms have become the means by which he sees, the frame for his own seeing, his way of seeing himself? What if the action of the norm is to be found not merely in the ideal that it posits, but in the sense of aberration and of freakishness that it conveys? Consider where precisely the norm operates when David claims, "I looked at myself and said I don't like this type of clothing." To whom is David speaking? And in what world, under what conditions, does not liking that type of clothing provide evidence for being the wrong gender? For whom would that be true? And under what conditions?

Brenda reports, "I didn't like the toys I was being given," and Brenda is   25 speaking here as someone who understands that such a dislike can function as evidence. And it seems reasonable to assume that the reason Brenda understands this "dislike" as evidence of gender dystopia, to use the technical term, is that Brenda has been addressed time and again by those who make use of every utterance that Brenda makes about her experience as evidence for or against a true gender. That Brenda happens not to like certain toys, certain dolls, certain games, may be significant in relation to the question of how and with what Brenda likes to play. But in what world, precisely, do such dislikes count as clear or unequivocal evidence for or against being a given gender? Do parents regularly rush off to gender identity clinics when their boys play with yarn, or their girls play with trucks? Or must there already be a rather enormous anxiety at play, an anxiety about the truth of gender which seizes on this or that toy, this or that proclivity of dress, the size of the shoulder, the leanness of the body, to conclude that something like a clear gender identity can or cannot be built from these scattered desires, these variable and invariable features of the body, of bone structure, of proclivity, of attire?

So what does my analysis imply? Does it tell us whether the gender here   26 is true or false? No. And does this have implications for whether David should have been surgically transformed into Brenda, or Brenda surgically transformed into David? No, it does not. I do not know how to judge that question here, and I am not sure it can be mine to judge. Does justice demand that I decide? Or does justice demand that I wait to decide, that I practice a certain deferral in the face of a situation in which too many have rushed to judgment? Might it not be useful, important, even just, to consider a few matters before we decide, before we ascertain whether it is, in fact, ours to decide?

Consider in this spirit, then, that it is for the most part the gender essential-   27 ist position that must be voiced for transsexual surgery to take place, and that someone who comes in with a sense of the gender as changeable will have a more difficult time convincing psychiatrists and doctors to perform the surgery. In San Francisco, FTM[8] candidates actually practice the narrative of gender

---

[8] **FTM**   Female-to-male surgical transformation.

essentialism that they are required to perform before they go in to see the doctors, and there are now coaches to help them, dramaturgs[9] of transsexuality who will help you make the case for no fee. Indeed, we might say that Brenda/David together went through two transsexual surgeries: the first based on a hypothetical argument about what gender should be, given the ablated[10] nature of the penis; the second based on what the gender should be, based on the behavioral and verbal indications of the person in question. In both cases, certain inferences are made, ones that suggest that a body must be a certain way for a gender to work, another which says that a body must feel a certain way for a gender to work. David clearly came to disrespect and abhor the views of the first set of doctors and developed, we might say, a lay critique of the phallus to support his resistance:

> Doctor said "it's gonna be tough, you're gonna be picked on, you're gonna be very alone, you're not gonna find anybody (unless you have vaginal surgery and live as a female)." And I thought to myself, you know I wasn't very old at the time, but it dawned on me that these people gotta be pretty shallow if that's the only thing they think I've got going for me; that the only reason why people get married and have children and have a productive life is because of what they have between their legs. . . . If that's all they think of me, that they justify my worth by what I have between my legs, then I gotta be a complete loser.

Here David makes a distinction between the "I" that he is, the person that he is, and the value that is conferred upon his personhood by virtue of what is or is not between his legs. He was wagering that he will be loved for something other than this or, at least, that his penis will not be the reason he is loved. He was holding out, implicitly, for something called "depth" over and against the "shallowness" of the doctors. And so although David asked for and received his new status as male, has asked for and received his new phallus, he is also something other than what he now has, and though he has undergone this transformation, he refuses to be reduced to the body part that he has acquired. "If that's all they think of me," he begins his sentence, offering a knowing and critical rejoinder to the work of the norm. There is something of me that exceeds this part, though I want this part, though it is part of me. He does not want his "worth justified" by what he has between his legs, and what this means is that he has another sense of how the worth of the person might be justified. So we might say that he is living his desire, acquiring the anatomy that he wants in order to live his desire, but that his desire is complex, and his worth

28

---

[9] **dramaturgs**   Those who supplement the dramatic production of a play through research.

[10] **ablated**   Amputated; making a portion of the body nonfunctional.

is complex. And this is why, no doubt, in response to many of the questions that Money posed: Do you want to have a penis? Do you want to marry a girl? David often refused to answer the question, refused to stay in the room where Money was, refused to visit Baltimore at all after a while.

David does not trade in one gender norm for another, not exactly. It would be as wrong to say that he has simply internalized a gendered norm (from a critical position) as it would be to say that he has failed to live up to a gendered norm (from a normalizing, medical position), since he has already established that what will justify his worth will be the invocation of an "I" which is not reducible to the compatibility of his anatomy with the norm. He thinks something more of himself than what others think, he does not fully justify his worth through recourse to what he has between his legs, and he does not think of himself as a complete loser. Something exceeds the norm, and he recognizes its unrecognizability. It is, in a sense, his distance from the knowably human that operates as a condition of critical speech, the source of his worth, as the justification for his worth. He says that if what those doctors believe were true, he would be a complete loser, and he implies that he is not a complete loser, that something in him is winning. 29

But he is also saying something more—he is cautioning us against the absolutism of distinction itself, for his phallus does not constitute the entirety of his worth. There is an incommensurability between who he is and what he has, an incommensurability between the phallus he has and what it is expected to be (and in this way no different from anyone with a phallus), which means that he has not become one with the norm, and yet he is still someone, speaking, insisting, even referring to himself. And it is from this gap, this incommensurability, between the norm that is supposed to inaugurate his humanness and the spoken insistence on himself that he performs that he derives his worth, that he speaks his worth. And we cannot precisely give content to this person at the very moment that he speaks his worth, which means that it is precisely the ways in which he is not fully recognizable, fully disposable, fully categorizable, that his humanness emerges. And this is important because we might ask that he enter into intelligibility in order to speak and to be known, but what he does instead, through his speech, is to offer a critical perspective on the norms that confer intelligibility itself. He shows, we might say, that there is an understanding to be had that exceeds the norms of intelligibility itself. And he achieves this "outside," we might speculate, by refusing the interrogations that besiege him, reversing their terms, and learning the ways in which he might escape. If he renders himself unintelligible to those who seek to know and capture his identity, this means that something about him is intelligible outside of the framework of accepted intelligibility. We might be tempted to say that there is some core of a person, and so some presumption of humanism, that emerges here, that is supervenient to the particular discourses on sexed and gendered intelligibility 30 that constrain him. But that would mean only that he is denounced by one discourse only to be carried by another discourse, the discourse of humanism. Or we might say that there is some core of the subject who speaks, who speaks beyond what is sayable, and that it is this ineffability that marks David's speech, the ineffability of the other who is not disclosed through speech, but leaves a portentious shard of itself in its saying, a self that is beyond discourse itself.

But what I would prefer is that we might consider carefully that when David invokes the "I" in this quite hopeful and unexpected way, he is speaking about a certain conviction he has about his own lovability; he says that "they" must think he is a real loser if the only reason anyone is going to love him is because of what he has between his legs. The "they" is telling him that he will not be loved, or that he will not be loved unless he takes what they have for him, and that they have what he needs in order to get love, that he will be loveless without what they have. But he refuses to accept that what they are offering in their discourse is love. He refuses their offering of love, understanding it as a bribe, as a seduction to subjection. He will be and he is, he tells us, loved for some other reason, a reason they do not understand, and it is not a reason we are given. It is clearly a reason that is beyond the regime of reason established by the norms of sexology itself. We know only that he holds out for another reason, and that in this sense, we no longer know what kind of reason this is, what reason can be; he establishes the limits of what they know, disrupting the politics of truth, making use of his desubjugation within that order of being to establish the possibility of love beyond the grasp of that norm. He positions himself, knowingly, in relation to the norm, but he does not comply with its requirements. He risks a certain "desubjugation"—is he a subject? How will we know? And in this sense, David's discourse puts into play the operation of critique itself, critique which, defined by Foucault, is precisely the desubjugation of the subject within the politics of truth. This does not mean that David becomes unintelligible and, therefore, without value to politics; rather, he emerges at the limits of intelligibility, offering a perspective on the variable ways in which norms circumscribe the human. It is precisely because we understand, without quite grasping, that he has another reason, that he *is*, as it were, another reason, that we see the limits to the discourse of intelligibility that would decide his fate. David does not precisely occupy a new world, since he is still, even within the syntax which brings about his "I," still positioned somewhere between the norm and its failure. And he is, finally, neither one; he is the human in its anonymity, as that which we do not yet know how to name or that which sets a limits on all naming. And in that sense, he is the anonymous—and critical—condition of the human as it speaks itself at the limits of what we think we know.

Postscript: As this book was going to press in June of 2004, I was saddened to learn that David Reimer took his life at the age of 38. The *New York*

Times obituary (5/12/04) mentions that his brother died two years earlier and that he was now separated from his wife. It is difficult to know what, in the end, made his life unlivable or why this life was one he felt was time to end. It seems clear, however, that there was always a question posed for him, and by him, whether life in his gender would be survivable. It is unclear whether it was his gender that was the problem, or the "treatment" that brought about an enduring suffering for him. The norms governing what it is to be a worthy, recognizable, and sustainable human life clearly did not support his life in any continuous or solid way. Life for him was always a wager and a risk, a courageous and fragile accomplishment.

✂ QUESTIONS FOR CRITICAL READING

1. What is most shocking about David Reimer's childhood experiences?

2. What are some of the problems inherent in establishing gender norms?

3. Butler talks about gender essentialism. What does she mean by that term?

4. What seems to be the basis of Dr. John Money's assurance that gender identity is largely socialized?

5. What does David Reimer's experience seem to say about the nature/nurture debate?

6. To what extent do you think a child's choice of toys defines his or her gender?

7. Why did children treat Brenda so badly when she was a child? What motivates children to taunt someone like Brenda when she behaved differently from what they thought was normal?

✂ SUGGESTIONS FOR CRITICAL WRITING

1. In paragraph 14, Butler talks about gender dimorphism. Explain what she means by the term and use the narrative about David Reimer to clarify what you think about the limits of gender identification based on the dimorphism of a male body and a female body. If you feel there are no limits, then explain how David Reimer's story clarifies your position.

2. Judging by the way people behave in your environment, what do you feel the markers of gender difference are? How are they expressed in social situations? How do you think Butler might describe gender differences in our society? How are they expressed in terms of clothing, attitudes, interests, language, and appearance? What are your views on gender-appropriate clothing, attitudes, interests, language, and appearance? Do most of your friends agree or disagree with you?

3. In his narrative, David denies that his value as a human being is limited to "what he has between his legs" (para. 29). Examine his narrative and decide whether you agree with Butler's analysis of this statement and her declaration that in

deciding for a sex change he "does not trade in one gender norm for another." How much does "what he has between his legs" define him as a human being? Butler agrees with David on this issue. Do you? How do you think your peers generally feel about how genitalia define them in the estimation of others? How do you respond to their views on this issue?

4. In paragraph 30, Butler talks about David's sense of worth. She says, "We might be tempted to say that there is some core of a person . . . that emerges here." Reflecting on David's own narrative about himself, defend or attack the view that there is a basic core to a person that may or may not be altered or affected by gender or gender choice. Does David's story shed light on the concept that people have a basic core? What seems to be Butler's view on this issue?

5. Is the feminist movement aided by the story of Dr. Money's treatment of David Reimer? Is Butler correct in feeling that feminists limit themselves by assuming that there are only two genders and that they are based entirely on anatomy? Feminists reject the idea that anatomy is destiny, so would they not agree with Butler on this issue? If gender is not based on anatomy, what might it be based on? Does Butler give you any hints?

6. **CONNECTIONS**   How do the questions of trust and distrust help clarify the principles that Butler develops in her argument? What in Karen Horney's essay (p. 500) helps Butler make her case? How might Horney, as a psychologist, react to the story of David Reimer and his experiences in sex change? To what extent would Butler be likely to be suspicious of the categories that Horney establishes?

7. **CONNECTIONS**   How could Butler use the findings about the behavior of the tribes Margaret Mead studied in "Sex and Temperament" (p. 236)? Mead reviews the ways in which our society "assigns different roles to the two sexes" and then goes on to examine the tribal groups that she lived with. Why would the study of a tribal society shed light on the question of gender difference or sameness in our society? How would Mead analyze Butler's narrative of gender behavior? What would she find to agree with and what would she question? How does reading Mead help you better understand the concerns of Butler? How does reading Mead affect your understanding of what David Reimer experienced at the hands of the medical community?

8. Butler's description of the difficulties David Reimer experienced reveals a great deal about cultural attitudes toward gender and how they affect an individual. In a brief essay, describe what you feel are the cultural attitudes toward gender in your town, city, or state. How do they appear similar to or different from the cultural attitudes you have experienced at your college or university? How do they appear similar to or different from the cultural attitudes toward gender that you experienced in high school? How have you changed since high school in your attitude toward gender issues?

Reflections on the Nature of Culture

Now that you have read the selections in "Culture," consider in what ways these writers have helped further inform your views of your own culture.

1. To what extent do you feel you belong to a specific cultural group within the larger culture?

2. How does the way you formulate questions about cultural behavior color the answers you get?

3. How aware are you of your own specific cultural assumptions?

4. To what extent do these essays help you qualify your assumptions about gender and sexuality?

5. What are the most important gender issues facing our culture today?

6. What forces seem to make major cultural changes in a modern nation?

7. Do you think cultural change happens revolutionarily or evolutionarily?

8. How do shifts in cultural values regarding women affect individuals in our society?

9. How convinced are you that in any society justice must act fairly for all citizens?

10. What are the most important clashes in values currently shaping our culture?

WEALTH

Introduction

In a country well governed, poverty is something to be ashamed of. In a country badly governed, wealth is something to be ashamed of.
—CONFUCIUS (551?–479? B.C.E.)

Wealth is the slave of a wise man. The master of a fool.
—SENECA (4 B.C.E.–65 C.E.)

Great eagerness in the pursuit of wealth, pleasure, or honor, cannot exist without sin.
—DESIDERIUS ERASMUS (1466–1536)

Wealth is the ability to fully experience life.
—HENRY DAVID THOREAU (1817–1862)

If you want to know what a man is really like, take notice of how he acts when he loses money.
—SIMONE WEIL (1909–1943)

The only question with wealth is what you do with it.
—JOHN D. ROCKEFELLER (1839–1937)

Nothing is more admirable than the fortitude with which millionaires tolerate the disadvantages of their wealth.
—REX STOUT (1886–1975)

Bottom line is, I didn't return to Apple to make a fortune. I've been very lucky in my life and already have one. When I was 25, my net worth was $100 million or so. I decided then that I wasn't going to let it ruin my life. There's no way you could ever spend it all, and I don't view wealth as something that validates my intelligence.
—STEVE JOBS (1955–2011)

Ancient writers talk about wealth in terms of a surplus of necessary or desirable goods and products. After the invention of coins—which historians attribute to the Lydians, whose civilization flourished in the eastern Mediterranean region from 800 to 200 B.C.E.—wealth also became associated with money. However, the relationship of wealth to money has long been debated. According to Aristotle, people misunderstand wealth when they think of it as "only a quantity of coin." For him, money was useful primarily as a means of representing and purchasing goods but was not sustaining in and of itself.

Writers like Aristotle have argued that wealth benefits the state by ensuring stability, growth, security, and cultural innovations and that it benefits the individual by providing leisure time, mobility, and luxury. Most societies, however, have struggled with the problems caused by unequal distribution of wealth, either among individuals or between citizens and the state. The Spartan leader Lycurgus is said to have tackled the problem in the ninth century B.C.E. by convincing the inhabitants of the Greek city-state of Sparta that they needed to redistribute their wealth. Land and household goods were redistributed among the citizens, and Lycurgus was hailed as a hero. However, Lycurgus's model has not been the norm in subsequent civilizations, and questions about the nature of wealth and its role and distribution in society have persisted.

The selections in this section present ideas on wealth and poverty from a variety of perspectives. Adam Smith begins by tracing the natural evolution of wealth from farming to trade. Karl Marx expounds on what he feels are the corrosive effects of excessive wealth on the individual and on the problems caused by unequal distribution of wealth between laborers and business owners. Andrew Carnegie, himself an extremely wealthy business owner, and Robert B. Reich further investigate the problems that an unequal distribution of wealth poses for society as a whole.

Adam Smith (1723–1790) was known originally as a moral philosopher with a professorship at Glasgow, but he wrote at a time of extraordinary expansion in Great Britain. As industrial power grew in the late eighteenth century, England became more wealthy and began to dominate trade in important areas of commerce. In his own mind, Smith's interest in wealth may have been connected with his studies in morality, or it may have grown from his considerable curiosity about a broad range of subjects. Regardless, he produced one of the century's most important and extensive books on economics, *The Wealth of Nations*. It is still consulted by economists today.

Smith's "Of the Natural Progress of Opulence" is an attempt to understand the "natural" steps to wealth. Smith posits an interesting relationship between the country, where food and plants, such as cotton and flax, supply the necessities of life, and the city, which produces no food but takes the surplus from the country and turns it into manufactured goods. Smith's ideas concerning this process center on surplus. The farmers produce more than they can consume, and therefore they can market their goods to the city. The city takes some of the goods from the farmers and turns them into manufactured products, which can be sold back to the people in the country. When there is a surplus of manufactured goods, they can be sold abroad. That process can produce wealth — on a grand scale.

Karl Marx's (1818–1883) *Communist Manifesto* clarifies the relationship between a people's condition and the economic system in which they live. Marx saw that capitalism provided opportunities for the wealthy and powerful to take advantage of labor. He argued that because labor cannot efficiently sell its product, management can keep labor in perpetual economic bondage.

Marx knew poverty firsthand, but one of his close associates, Friedrich Engels, who collaborated on portions of the *Manifesto*, was the son of a factory owner and so was able to observe closely how the rich can oppress the poor. For both of them, the economic system of capitalism produced a class struggle between the rich (bourgeoisie) and the laboring classes (proletariat).

In an effort to avoid anything like a class struggle between the rich and the poor, Andrew Carnegie (1835–1919) wrote *The Gospel of Wealth*, defending not only the economic system that permitted a few people to amass great wealth but also praising it for being the highest expression of civilization. Carnegie dismisses communism as a failed system and cites Darwinian theories as supporting the laws of competition and accumulation that permitted men like him to possess vast fortunes. His proposal is that such men should give their wealth back to the community for its benefit in the form of institutions that would contribute to "the improvement of the race." Moreover, the rich should give their money away while they are living so that they can clearly guide their gifts in the directions they feel are most important. Carnegie, for example, concentrated on building public libraries throughout the United States and Canada, while founding a university and supporting others rather generously.

John Maynard Keynes (1883–1946) is probably the best known twentieth-century economist. An instructor at Cambridge University for many years, his most important early work involved an accurate and farsighted analysis of the economics of recovery after World War I. During the period of the Great Depression (1929–1939), when his essay "The End of Laissez-Faire" was published, his most important sphere of influence was not Great Britain but the United States, which adopted his theories, including recommendations to boost public spending, to loosen credit restrictions, and to promote a freer economic environment that could profit from expansion and growth. Keynes's theories are based on production and consumption and remain essential today as the basis of modern capitalism. Keynes held that by permitting ambitious business people to pursue their goals of wealth, the entire community would benefit. His views, despite revisionist trends in recent years, are still central to our economic policies in the West. They are also, as you will see from his essay, essentially optimistic in attitude.

Milton and Rose Friedman (1912–2006 and 1910–2009, respectively) focus on the efforts of the state that aim to produce what they call equality of outcome. They are fierce believers in equality of opportunity, but they assert that any effort to guarantee an equality of outcome will restrict the freedom of high achievers in a society. For them, equality of outcome means guaranteeing the economic well-being of people who may not have earned it, while restricting the economic well-being of those who have. Indirectly, the Friedmans offer an argument whose outcome would help preserve the wealth of those with unusual talents for business. They see their position as close to Thomas Jefferson, who championed independence, and completely opposed to Karl Marx.

Friedrich A. Hayek (1899–1992) also opposed the views of Karl Marx and supported the views of the Friedmans. Hayek and Milton Friedman were colleagues at the University of Chicago in the 1950s and represent a strong conservative view of economics. For Hayek, the threat was socialism, even early steps toward a socialist economy. Hayek, an Austrian, lived in Europe in the early years of the rise of fascism, which began, he asserts, with socialism and ended with totalitarianism. The problem is, Hayek asserts, that socialism involves central planning of the economy and whoever does the planning is certain to become dictatorial. He argues that social planning robs citizens of their independence and freedom to either succeed or fail. Moreover, planned economies rob the people of choice, both of products and of careers.

Robert B. Reich (b. 1946), a lecturer at Harvard University until he was appointed secretary of labor in the first Clinton administration, has taught courses in economics and published widely. His 1991 book, *The Work of Nations*, echoes the title of Adam Smith's eighteenth-century masterpiece of capitalist theory, *The Wealth of Nations*. Although Reich's views on labor are distinct from Smith's, his essay focuses on labor with the same intensity Smith brings to money. His views consider how worldwide economic developments will affect labor in the next decades. According to Reich, labor falls into three groups—routine workers, in-person servers, and symbolic analysts—each of which will fare differently in the coming years.

Francis Fukuyama (b. 1952) is not focused on wealth or poverty, but on the middle class and its relationship to a healthy democracy. He enumerates a range of conditions for why the general European proletarian revolution predicted by Karl Marx never happened. He then goes on to demonstrate some of the difficulties in attempting a definition of the middle class. His analysis of the circumstances of modern societies in Asia, Europe, and the Americas is helpful in our understanding of how the middle-class population is likely to behave and how it is likely to prefer a democratic form of government over any other. His view is that the future is bright for democracy because it is bright for a growing global middle class.

Most of these theorists agree that a healthy economy can relieve the misery and suffering of a population. Most agree that wealth and plenty are preferable to impoverishment and want. But some are also concerned with the effects of materialism and greed on the spiritual life of a nation.

Some Considerations about the Nature of Wealth

Before reading the selections that follow in this section, consider what your views of wealth are. Reflect on the following questions and write out your responses. Discuss your answers with your classmates.

1. Should there be limits on how much a chief executive officer (CEO) should earn in relation to the average worker?

2. Is economic inequality a serious problem in our time?

3. How does economic inequality affect the nature of our democracy?

4. Should there be a different tax structure for the ultra-rich?

5. Who benefits most from the social programs of modern governments?

6. Should government support education, health programs, and welfare for the poor?

7. To what extent is the middle class in danger?

8. Is there a difference between the working class and the middle class?

9. To what extent do programs, such as Social Security and welfare, rob the citizen of independence?

10. Are wealth and poverty inevitable? Is it possible to end poverty in the United States?

ADAM
SMITH

Of the Natural Progress of Opulence

A DAM SMITH (1723–1790) was born in Kirkcaldy on the eastern coast of Scotland. He attended Glasgow University and received a degree from Oxford, after which he gave a successful series of lectures on rhetoric in his hometown. This resulted in his appointment as professor of logic at Glasgow in 1751. One year later, he moved to a professorship in moral philosophy that had been vacated by Thomas Craggie, one of his former teachers. He held this position for twelve years. Smith's early reputation was built entirely on his work in moral philosophy, which included theology, ethics, justice, and political economy.

In many ways, Adam Smith's views are striking in their modernity; in fact, his work continues to inform our understanding of current economic trends. His classic and best-known book, *An Inquiry into the Nature and Causes of the Wealth of Nations* (1776), examines the economic system of the modern nation that has reached, as England had, the commercial level of progress. According to Smith, a nation has to pass through a number of levels of culture — from hunter-gatherer to modern commercial — on its way to becoming modern. In this sense, he was something of an evolutionist in economics.

Wealth of Nations is quite different in both tone and concept from Smith's earlier success, *Theory of Moral Sentiments* (1759). The earlier work postulates a social order based, in part, on altruism — an order in which individuals aid one another — whereas *Wealth of Nations* asserts that the best economic results are obtained when individuals work for their own interests and their own gain. This kind of effort, Smith assures us, results in the general improvement of a society because the industry of the individual benefits everyone in the nation by producing more wealth; the greater the wealth of the nation, the better the lot of every individual in the nation.

There is no question that Smith was an ardent capitalist who felt an almost messianic need to spread the doctrine of capitalism. He maintained throughout his life that *Wealth*

From *An Inquiry into the Nature and Causes of the Wealth of Nations*.

of Nations was one with his writings on moral and social issues and that when his work was complete it would encompass the basic elements of any society.

In "Of the Natural Progress of Opulence," Smith outlines a microcosm of the progress of capitalism as he understood it. His purpose is to establish the steps by which a nation creates its wealth and the steps by which a region becomes wealthy. For the most part, he is interested in the development of capitalism in Great Britain, including his native Scotland. His perspective includes the natural developments that he observed in his own time in the late eighteenth century as well as developments that he could imagine from earlier times. Because he wrote and published his book just before the American Revolution and the subsequent industrial revolution, his primary concerns are farming and agriculture. In earlier sections of *Wealth of Nations*, Smith focused on metal — silver and gold — as a measure of wealth, then later on corn (by which he usually meant wheat or barley) as a measure of wealth. In this selection, he is more emphatic about land as a convenient instrument of wealth.

His primary point is related to what he sees as a natural progression. People in the country have land on which they plant crops, which they sell, in part, to people in the town. The people in the town, lacking land but possessing skills such as weaving, building, and the like, create a market for the goods from the country. They take the product of the land and, with the surplus beyond their daily needs for food and sustenance, manufacture useful goods. In turn, they sell the desirable goods to people in the country, and both manage to accumulate wealth in the process. In this view the manufactures of the town are important but by no means as essential as the food that sustains the nation. Indeed, Smith regards surplus production as the key to the move toward wealth, which accumulates into opulence.

It is interesting that Smith does not emphasize the trade of goods among nations. He does emphasize the fact that the interchange between the country and the town in England also has a counterpart in international trade. However, Smith seems a bit uneasy in contemplating the usefulness of international trade as a means to accumulate wealth. Land, he reminds the reader, is secure, controllable, and not likely to yield to the whimsy of foul winds, leaky ships, or dishonest foreign merchants. One realizes that regardless of what he might say in praise of other possibilities, Smith himself would likely prefer a life in the country on a spread of his own land, collecting rent from tenants who produce food and flax and other goods that help him accumulate wealth.

SMITH'S RHETORIC

Adam Smith is widely regarded as one of the most influential economic thinkers of the eighteenth century. His *Wealth of Nations* is a gigantic book with many complex arguments regarding the nature of money and the role of capital in trade. This selection is a relatively straightforward statement regarding what he feels is the usual progress that all nations experience in the creation and accumulation of wealth. However, the normal eighteenth-century paragraph is much longer than those of today. By the same token, the normal eighteenth-century sentence is more complex in structure than we are used to today. For that reason, many readers will pause for reflection as they read Smith's work.

Still, his sentences are ultimately clear and direct. His opening sentence, for example, is a mighty declaration: "The great commerce of every civilized society, is that carried on between the inhabitants of the town and those of the country." In this sentence Smith makes a clear pronouncement, a statement about *every* society. Such a sweeping generalization is likely to invite attack and skepticism, but he feels totally secure in his assertion and proceeds to argue his position point by point.

On a more modest note, when Smith says, "Upon equal, or nearly equal profits, most men will choose to employ their capitals rather in the improvement and cultivation of land, than either in manufactures or in foreign trade" (para. 3), he expects the reader to see the simple wisdom of trusting the land and distrusting instruments of trade. However, many readers — even in his own time — would see this sentence as revealing a personal preference rather than a general rule. Even in the eighteenth century, many merchants were growing rich by ignoring land and trusting trade on the high seas.

Smith's view on this issue reflects an aspect of his conservatism, a stance that remains recognizably conservative even by today's standards. Nevertheless, his principles have guided traders as well as farmers for more than two hundred years. In his time, the workers in agriculture outnumbered workers in manufactures by a factor of eighty or ninety. But today, workers in agriculture have decreased progressively since the industrial revolution. Now, as a result of more efficient farming methods, only two or three people out of a hundred work on farms producing food and other goods. It would be interesting to know how Smith might react to this dramatic shift in occupations.

In helping the reader to work through his argument, Smith includes inset "summaries" of the content of each paragraph. For paragraph 2, he includes two insets. The first — "*The cultivation of the country must be prior to the increase of the town*" — alerts the reader to look for his explanation of why this claim is true. The second inset — "*though the town may sometimes be distant from the country from which it derives its subsistence*" — helps readers focus on the implications of distances from agriculture and manufacture for the local population. Those who grow corn nearest the city will make more money than those who live at a distance and must pay for its transportation to market. It is interesting to note that later ages developed relatively inexpensive means of transport — such as canals and railroads — to even out the cost of carriage in relation to fixed prices.

Smith depends on the clear, step-by-step argument to hold the attention of his reader. He establishes and examines each major point, clarifies his own position, then moves on to the next related point. For example, he talks about nations with uncultivated land, or large areas of land, and how the procedure he outlines works. Then he introduces the situation of a nation that has no uncultivated land available or land available only at very high cost. Under such circumstances, people will turn to manufacture but not rely on selling their products locally. In those conditions, they will risk foreign sales.

It is also worth noting that when Smith talks about the American colonies, he reminds the reader that there is plenty of land for people to work. As a result, little or no manufacture is produced for sale abroad. He sees this as an indication that the Americans are fiercely independent, demanding land of their own so as to guarantee that they will have adequate sustenance in the future. Throughout the selection Smith establishes a clear sense of the progress of nations toward the accumulation of wealth, and he provides the reader with a blueprint for financial success.

∷ PREREADING QUESTIONS: WHAT TO READ FOR

The following prereading questions may help you anticipate key issues in the discussion of Adam Smith's "Of the Natural Progress of Opulence." Keeping them in mind during your first reading of the selection should help focus your attention.

1. What is the nature of the commerce between the country and the town?
2. What does Smith think is the natural order of things in the development of commerce?

Of the Natural Progress of Opulence

The great commerce is that between town and country, which is obviously advantageous to both.

The great commerce of every civilized society, is that carried on between the inhabitants of the town and those of the country. It consists in the exchange of rude for manufactured produce, either immediately, or by the intervention of money, or of some sort of paper which represents money. The country supplies the town with the means of subsistence, and the materials of manufacture. The town repays this supply by sending back a part of the manufactured produce to the inhabitants of the country. The town, in which there neither is nor can be any reproduction of substances, may very properly be said to gain its whole wealth and subsistence from the country. We must not, however, upon this account, imagine that the gain of the town is the loss of the country. The gains of both are mutual and reciprocal, and the division of labor is in this, as in all other cases, advantageous to all the different persons employed in the various occupations into which it is subdivided. The inhabitants of the country purchase of the town a greater quantity of manufactured goods, with the produce of a much smaller quantity of their own labor, than they must have employed had they attempted to prepare them themselves. The town affords a market for

1

the surplus produce of the country, or what is over and above the maintenance of the cultivators, and it is there that the inhabitants of the country exchange it for something else which is in demand among them. The greater the number and revenue of the inhabitants of the town, the more extensive is the market which it affords to those of the country; and the more extensive that market, it is always the more advantageous to a great number. The corn which grows within a mile of the town, sells there for the same price with that which comes from twenty miles distance. But the price of the latter must, generally, not only pay the expence of raising and bringing it to market, but afford too the ordinary profits of agriculture to the farmer. The proprietors and cultivators of the country, therefore, which lies in the neighborhood of the town, over and above the ordinary profits of agriculture, gain, in the price of what they sell, the whole value of the carriage of the like produce that is brought from more distant parts, and they save, besides, the whole value of this carriage in the price of what they buy. Compare the cultivation of the lands in the neighborhood of any considerable town, with that of those which lie at some distance from it, and you will easily satisfy yourself how much the country is benefited by the commerce of the town. Among all the absurd speculations that have been propagated concerning the balance of trade, it has never been pretended that either the country loses by its commerce with the town, or the town by that with the country which maintains it.

The cultivation of the country must be prior to the increase of the town,

As subsistence is, in the nature of things, prior to conveniency and luxury, so the industry which procures the former, must necessarily be prior to that which ministers to the latter. The cultivation and improvement of the country, therefore, which affords subsistence, must, necessarily, be prior to the increase of the town, which furnishes only the means of conveniency and luxury. It is the surplus produce of the country only, or what is over and above the maintenance of the cultivators, that constitutes the subsistence of the town, which can therefore increase only with the increase of this surplus produce. The town, indeed, may not always derive its whole subsistence from the country in its neighborhood, or even from the territory to which it belongs, but from very distant countries; and this, though it forms no exception from the general rule, has occasioned considerable variations in the progress of opulence in different ages and nations.

though the town may sometimes be distant from the country from which it derives its subsistence.

2

This order of things is favored by the natural preference of man for agriculture.

That order of things which necessity imposes in general, 3 though not in every particular country, is, in every particular country, promoted by the natural inclinations of man. If human institutions had never thwarted those natural inclinations, the towns could no-where have increased beyond what the improvement and cultivation of the territory in which they were situated could support; till such time, at least, as the whole of that territory was completely cultivated and improved. Upon equal, or nearly equal profits, most men will choose to employ their capitals rather in the improvement and cultivation of land, than either in manufactures or in foreign trade. The man who employs his capital in land, has it more under his view and command, and his fortune is much less liable to accidents, than that of the trader, who is obliged frequently to commit it, not only to the winds and the waves, but to the more uncertain elements of human folly and injustice, by giving great credits in distant countries to men, with whose character and situation he can seldom be thoroughly acquainted. The capital of the landlord, on the contrary, which is fixed in the improvement of his land, seems to be as well secured as the nature of human affairs can admit of. The beauty of the country besides, the pleasures of a country life, the tranquillity of mind which it promises, and wherever the injustice of human laws does not disturb it, the independency which it really affords, have charms that more or less attract every body; and as to cultivate the ground was the original destination of man, so in every stage of his existence he seems to retain a predilection for this primitive employment.

Cultivators require the assistance of artificers, who settle together and form a village, and their employment augments with the improvement of the country.

Without the assistance of some artificers, indeed, the 4 cultivation of land cannot be carried on, but with great inconveniency and continual interruption. Smiths, carpenters, wheel-wrights, and plough-wrights, masons, and bricklayers, tanners, shoemakers, and tailors, are people, whose service the farmer has frequent occasion for. Such artificers too stand, occasionally, in need of the assistance of one another; and as their residence is not, like that of the farmer, necessarily tied down to a precise spot, they naturally settle in the neighborhood of one another, and thus form a small town or village. The butcher, the brewer, and the baker, soon join them, together with many other artificers and retailers, necessary or useful for supplying their occasional wants, and who contribute still further to augment the town. The inhabitants of the town and those of the country are mutually the servants of one another. The town is a continual fair or market, to which the inhabitants of the country resort in order to exchange their rude for manufactured produce. It is this commerce which supplies the inhabitants of the town both with the materials of their work, and the means of their subsistence. The quantity of the finished work which they sell to the inhabitants of the country, necessarily regulates the quantity of the materials and provisions which they buy. Neither their employment nor subsistence, therefore, can augment, but in proportion to the augmentation of the demand from the country for finished work; and this demand can augment only in proportion to the extension of improvement and cultivation. Had human institutions, therefore, never disturbed the natural course of things, the progressive wealth and increase of the towns would, in every political society, be consequential, and in proportion to the improvement and cultivation of the territory or country.

In the American colonies an artificer who has acquired sufficient stock becomes a planter instead of manufacturing for distant sale,

In our North American colonies, where uncultivated land is still to be had upon easy terms, no manufactures for distant sale have ever yet been established in any of their towns. When an artificer has acquired a little more stock than is necessary for carrying on his own business in supplying the neighboring country, he does not, in North America, attempt to establish with it a manufacture for more distant sale, but employs it in the purchase and improvement of uncultivated land. From artificer he becomes planter, and neither the large wages nor the easy subsistence which that country affords to artificers, can bribe him rather to work for other people than for himself. He feels that an artificer is the servant of his customers, from whom he derives his subsistence; but that a planter who cultivates his own land, and derives his necessary subsistence from the labor of his own family, is really a master, and independent of all the world.

as in countries where no uncultivated land can be procured.

In countries, on the contrary, where there is either no uncultivated land, or none that can be had upon easy terms, every artificer who has acquired more stock than he can employ in the occasional jobs of the neighborhood, endeavors to prepare work for more distant sale. The smith erects some sort of iron, the weaver some sort of linen or woollen manufactory. Those different manufactures come, in process of time, to be gradually subdivided, and thereby improved and refined in a great variety of ways, which may easily be conceived, and which it is therefore unnecessary to explain any further.

Manufactures are naturally preferred to foreign commerce.

In seeking for employment to a capital, manufactures are, upon equal or nearly equal profits, naturally preferred to foreign commerce, for the same reason that agriculture is naturally preferred to manufactures. As the capital of the landlord or farmer is more secure than that of the manufacturer, so the capital of the manufacturer, being at all times more within his view and command, is more secure than that of the foreign merchant. In every period, indeed, of every society, the surplus part both of the rude and manufactured produce, or that for which there is no demand at home, must be sent abroad in order to be exchanged for something for which there is some demand at home. But whether the capital, which carries this surplus produce abroad, be a foreign or a domestic one, is of very little importance. If the society has not acquired sufficient capital both to cultivate all its lands, and to manufacture in the completest manner the whole of its rude produce, there is even a considerable advantage that that rude produce should be exported by a foreign capital, in order that the whole stock of the society may be employed in more useful purposes. The wealth of ancient Egypt, that of China and Indostan, sufficiently demonstrate that a nation may attain a very high degree of opulence, though the greater part of its exportation trade be carried on by foreigners. The progress of our North American and West Indian colonies would have been much less rapid, had no capital but what belonged to themselves been employed in exporting their surplus produce.

So the natural course of things is first agriculture, then manufactures, and finally foreign commerce.

According to the natural course of things, therefore, the greater part of the capital of every growing society is, first, directed to agriculture, afterwards to manufactures, and last of all to foreign commerce. This order of things is so very natural, that in every society that had any territory, it has always, I believe, been in some degree observed. Some of their lands must have been cultivated before any considerable towns could be established, and some sort of coarse industry of the manufacturing kind must have been carried on in those towns, before they could well think of employing themselves in foreign commerce.

But this order has been in many respects inverted.

But though this natural order of things must have taken place in some degree in every such society, it has, in all the modern states of Europe, been, in many respects, entirely inverted. The foreign commerce of some of their cities has introduced all their finer manufactures, or such as were fit for distant sale; and manufactures and foreign commerce together, have given birth to the principal improvements of agriculture. The manners and customs which the nature of their original government introduced, and which remained after that government was greatly altered, necessarily forced them into this unnatural and retrograde order.

9

✂ QUESTIONS FOR CRITICAL READING

1. How does manufacture eventually help agriculture?
2. Why is it more important to cultivate land than foreign trade?
3. What is special about the civilizations of Egypt, China, and Indostan?
4. Why did the American and West Indian colonies grow so rapidly?
5. In unpopulated countries, what is the natural way people treat the land?
6. How do the town manufactures profit from the country's surplus goods?
7. What is an artificer?

✂ SUGGESTIONS FOR CRITICAL WRITING

1. Explain how you know that Smith favors country living over town life. What seems to be his opinion of each way of living?

2. Explain what Smith means by "subsistence is, in the nature of things, prior to conveniency and luxury, so the industry which procures the former, must necessarily be prior to that which ministers to the latter" (para. 2). Smith makes this claim several times. Is he correct even today?

3. Examine Smith's discussion and write an essay that takes issue with his conclusions. Base your argument on the changes that have occurred in world economy since Smith's time. How have things changed economically to render his arguments less valid or less applicable?

4. In paragraph 3, Smith talks about the "natural inclinations of man." What are they? What relevance do they have to Smith's argument? Have man's "natural inclinations" changed substantially since Smith wrote *Wealth of Nations*?

5. Smith says, "The town affords a market for the surplus produce of the country" (para. 1). What does he mean by this statement? Is it still true today? What are the implications of this statement for the theories that Smith attempts to

establish? Why is a surplus essential for his theory on the natural progress of opulence to be persuasive?

6. **CONNECTIONS**   Examine Thomas Jefferson's Declaration of Independence (p. 116) for issues that relate well to the questions that Smith raises. What are the economic and capitalist underpinnings of Jefferson's statements? In what ways does Jefferson agree or disagree with Smith's concepts of the development of opulence?

7. **CONNECTIONS**   Smith is the most important theorist of capitalism prior to the twentieth century. How do his ideas contrast with Karl Marx's views (p. 335) about capitalism and how capitalists work? What would Marx take issue with in Smith's argument? What can you tell about the nature of capitalism in the worlds of Adam Smith in 1776 and of Karl Marx in 1850?

8. **CONNECTIONS**   How does Adam Smith's concept of a natural progress of opulence agree with Milton and Rose Friedman's ideas about the equality of opportunity in the marketplace (p. 400)? Do both agree that some people in a society will naturally become wealthy while others will naturally become poor? To what extent do the authors agree that a distinction between the wealthy and the poor is a natural outcome of any society? How comfortable do you think Smith would be in accepting the Friedmans' arguments? Which arguments might he reject?

9. **CONNECTIONS**   How does Robert B. Reich's analysis of the "new economy" (p. 422) alter the basic wisdom of Smith's views on the natural progress of an economy's development from agriculture to manufactures to foreign trade? What novelties in the "new economy" alter your view of Smith's theory?

KARL
MARX

The Communist Manifesto

© AP Photo

KARL MARX (1818–1883) was born in Germany to Jewish parents who converted to Lutheranism. A scholarly man, Marx studied literature and philosophy, ultimately earning a doctorate in philosophy at the University of Jena. After being denied a university position, however, he turned to journalism to earn a living.

Soon after beginning his journalistic career, Marx came into conflict with Prussian authorities because of his radical social views, and after a period of exile in Paris he moved to Brussels. After several more moves, Marx found his way to London, where he finally settled in absolute poverty; his friend Friedrich Engels (1820–1895) contributed money to prevent Marx and his family from starving. During this time in London, Marx wrote the books for which he is famous while also writing for and editing newspapers. His contributions to the *New York Daily Tribune* number over three hundred items between the years 1851 and 1862.

Marx is best known for his theories of socialism, as expressed in *The Communist Manifesto* (1848) — which, like much of his important work, was written with Engels's help — and in the three-volume *Das Kapital* (*Capital*), the first volume of which was published in 1867. In his own lifetime, he was not well known, nor were his ideas widely debated. Yet he was part of an ongoing movement composed mainly of intellectuals. Vladimir Lenin (1870–1924) was a disciple whose triumph in the Russian Revolution of 1917 catapulted Marx to the forefront of world thought. Since 1917, Marx's thinking has been scrupulously analyzed, debated, and argued. Capitalist thinkers have found him unconvincing, whereas Communist thinkers have found him a prophet and keen analyst of social structures.

In England, Marx's studies centered on the concept of an ongoing class struggle between those who owned property — the bourgeoisie — and those who owned nothing but whose work produced wealth — the proletariat. Marx was concerned with the forces of history, and his view of history was that it is progressive and, to an extent, inevitable.

Translated by Samuel Moore. Part III of *The Communist Manifesto*, "Socialist and Communist Literature," is omitted here.

This view is prominent in *The Communist Manifesto*, particularly in Marx's review of the overthrow of feudal forms of government by the bourgeoisie. He thought it inevitable that the bourgeoisie and the proletariat would engage in a class struggle, from which the proletariat would emerge victorious. In essence, Marx took a materialist position. He denied the providence of God in the affairs of humans and defended the view that economic institutions evolve naturally and that, in their evolution, they control the social order. Thus, communism was an inevitable part of the process, and in the *Manifesto* he worked to clarify the reasons for its inevitability.

One of Marx's primary contentions was that capital is "not a personal, it is a social power" (para. 78). Thus, according to Marx, the "past dominates the present" (para. 83) because the accumulation of past capital determines how people will live in the present society. Capitalist economists, however, see capital as a personal power, but a power that, as John Kenneth Galbraith might say, should be used in a socially responsible way.

MARX'S RHETORIC

The selection included here omits one section, the least important for the modern reader. The first section has a relatively simple rhetorical structure that depends on comparison. The title, "Bourgeois and Proletarians," tells us that the section will clarify the nature of each class and then go on to make some comparisons and contrasts. These concepts were by no means as widely discussed or thought about in 1848 as they are today, so Marx is careful to define his terms. At the same time, he establishes his theories regarding history by making further comparisons with class struggles in earlier ages.

Marx's style is simple and direct. He moves steadily from point to point, establishing his views on the nature of classes, on the nature of bourgeois society, and on the questions of industrialism and its effects on modern society. He considers wealth, worth, nationality, production, agriculture, and machinery. Each point is addressed in turn, usually in its own paragraph.

The organization of the next section, "Proletarians and Communists" (paras. 60–133), is not, despite its title, comparative in nature. Rather, with the proletariat defined as the class of the future, Marx tries to show that the Communist cause is the proletarian cause. In the process, Marx uses a clever rhetorical strategy. He assumes that he is addressed by an antagonist — presumably a bourgeois or a proletarian who is in sympathy with the bourgeoisie. He then proceeds to answer each popular complaint against communism. He shows that it is not a party separate from other workers' parties (para. 61). He clarifies the question of abolishing existing property relations (paras. 68–93). He emphasizes the antagonism between capital and wage labor (para. 76); he discusses the disappearance of culture (para. 94); he clarifies the questions of the family (paras. 98–100) and of the exploitation of children (para. 101). He brings up the new system of public education (paras. 102–4). He raises the touchy issue of the "community of women" (paras. 105–10), as well as the charge that Communists want to abolish nations (paras. 111–15). He brushes aside religion (para. 116). When he is done with the complaints, he gives us a rhetorical signal: "But let us have done with the bourgeois objections to Communism" (para. 126).

The rest of the second section contains a brief summary, and then Marx presents his ten-point program (para. 131). The structure is simple, direct, and effective. In the process of answering the charges against communism, Marx is able to clarify exactly what it is and what it promises. In contrast to his earlier arguments, the ten points of his Communist program seem clear, easy, and (again by contrast) almost acceptable. Although the style is not dashing (despite a few memorable lines), the rhetorical structure is extraordinarily effective for the purposes at hand.

In the last section (paras. 135–45), in which Marx compares the Communists with other reform groups such as those agitating for redistribution of land and other agrarian reforms, he indicates that the Communists are everywhere fighting alongside existing groups for the rights of people who are oppressed by their societies. As Marx says, "In short, the Communists everywhere support every revolutionary movement against the existing social and political order of things" (para. 141). Nothing could be a more plain and direct declaration of sympathies.

▓ PREREADING QUESTIONS: WHAT TO READ FOR

The following prereading questions may help you anticipate key issues in the discussion of Karl Marx's *The Communist Manifesto*. Keeping them in mind during your first reading of the selection should help focus your attention.

1. What is the economic condition of the bourgeoisie? What is the economic condition of the proletariat?
2. How does the expanding world market for goods affect national identity?
3. What benefits does Marx expect communism to provide the proletariat?

The Communist Manifesto

A specter is haunting Europe—the specter of Communism. All the Powers of old Europe have entered into a holy alliance to exorcise this specter; Pope and Czar, Metternich[1] and Guizot,[2] French Radicals[3] and German police-spies.   1

Where is the party in opposition that has not been decried as communistic by its opponents in power? Where is the opposition that has not hurled back   2

---

[1] **Prince Klemens von Metternich (1773–1859)**   Foreign minister of Austria (1809–1848), who had a hand in establishing the peace after the final defeat in 1815 of Napoleon (1769–1821); Metternich was highly influential in the crucial Congress of Vienna (1814–1815).

[2] **François Pierre Guizot (1787–1874)**   Conservative French statesman, author, and philosopher. Like Metternich, he was opposed to communism.

[3] **French Radicals**   Actually middle-class liberals who wanted a return to a republic in 1848 after the eighteen-year reign of Louis-Philippe (1773–1850), the "citizen king."

the branding reproach of Communism against the more advanced opposition parties, as well as against its reactionary adversaries?

Two things result from this fact.   3

I. Communism is already acknowledged by all European Powers to be   4
itself a Power.

II. It is high time that Communists should openly, in the face of the whole   5
world, publish their views, their aims, their tendencies, and meet this nursery tale of the specter of Communism with a Manifesto of the party itself.

To this end, Communists of various nationalities have assembled in   6
London and sketched the following Manifesto, to be published in the English, French, German, Italian, Flemish, and Danish languages.

Bourgeois and Proletarians[4]

The history of all hitherto existing society is the history of class struggles.   7

Freeman and slave, patrician and plebeian, lord and serf, guild-master and   8
journeyman, in a word, oppressor and oppressed, stood in constant opposition to one another, carried on uninterrupted, now hidden, now open fight, a fight that each time ended, either in a revolutionary re-constitution of society at large, or in the common ruin of the contending classes.

In the earlier epochs of history we find almost everywhere a complicated   9
arrangement of society into various orders, a manifold gradation of social rank. In ancient Rome we have patricians, knights, plebeians, slaves; in the Middle Ages, feudal lords, vassals, guild-masters, journeymen, apprentices, serfs; in almost all of these classes, again, subordinate gradations.

The modern bourgeois society that has sprouted from the ruins of feudal   10
society, has not done away with class antagonisms. It has but established new classes, new conditions of oppression, new forms of struggle in place of the old ones.

Our epoch, the epoch of the bourgeoisie, possesses, however, this dis-   11
tinctive feature; it has simplified the class antagonisms. Society as a whole is more and more splitting up into two great hostile camps, into two great classes directly facing each other: Bourgeoisie and Proletariat.

From the serfs of the Middle Ages sprang the chartered burghers of the   12
earliest towns. From these burgesses the first elements of the bourgeoisie were developed.

---

[4] By bourgeois is meant the class of modern Capitalists, owners of the means of social production and employers of wage labor. By proletarians, the class of modern wage laborers who, having no means of production of their own, are reduced to selling their labor-power in order to live. [Engels's note]

The discovery of America, the rounding of the Cape,[5] opened up fresh   13
ground for the rising bourgeoisie. The East Indian and Chinese markets, the
colonization of America, trade with the colonies, the increase in the means
of exchange and in commodities generally, gave to commerce, to navigation,
to industry, an impulse never before known, and thereby, to the revolutionary
element in the tottering feudal society, a rapid development.

The feudal system of industry, under which industrial production was   14
monopolized by closed guilds, now no longer sufficed for the growing wants of
the new market. The manufacturing system took its place. The guild-masters
were pushed on one side by the manufacturing middle-class: division of labor
between the different corporate guilds vanished in the face of division of labor
in each single workshop.

Meantime the markets kept ever growing, the demand ever rising. Even   15
manufacture no longer sufficed. Thereupon, steam and machinery revolutionized industrial production. The place of manufacture was taken by the giant,
Modern Industry, the place of the industrial middle-class, by industrial millionaires, the leaders of whole industrial armies, the modern bourgeois.

Modern industry has established the world-market, for which the discov-   16
ery of America paved the way. This market has given an immense development
to commerce, to navigation, to communication by land. This development has,
in its turn, reacted on the extension of industry; and in proportion as industry,
commerce, navigation, railways extended, in the same proportion the bourgeoisie developed, increased its capital, and pushed into the background every
class handed down from the Middle Ages.

We see, therefore, how the modern bourgeoisie is itself the product of a   17
long course of development, of a series of revolutions in the modes of production and of exchange.

Each step in the development of the bourgeoisie was accompanied by a cor-   18
responding political advance of that class. An oppressed class under the sway
of the feudal nobility, an armed and self-governing association in the medieval
commune,[6] here independent urban republic (as in Italy and Germany), there
taxable "third estate"[7] of the monarchy (as in France), afterwards, in the period
of manufacture proper, serving either the semi-feudal or the absolute monarchy
as a counterpoise against nobility, and, in fact, corner stone of the great monarchies in general, the bourgeoisie has at last, since the establishment of Modern

---

[5] **the Cape**   The Cape of Good Hope, at the southern tip of Africa. This was a main sea
route for trade with India and the Orient. Europe profited immensely from the opening
up of these new markets in the sixteenth century.

[6] **the medieval commune**   Refers to the growth in the eleventh century of towns whose
economy was highly regulated by mutual interest and agreement.

[7] **"third estate"**   The clergy was the first estate, the aristocracy the second estate, and the
bourgeoisie the third estate.

Industry and of the world-market, conquered for itself, in the modern representative State, exclusive political sway. The executive of the modern State is but a committee for managing the common affairs of the whole bourgeoisie.

The bourgeoisie, historically, has played a most revolutionary part.   19

The bourgeoisie, wherever it has got the upper hand, has put an end to all   20
feudal, patriarchal, idyllic relations. It has pitilessly torn asunder the motley feudal ties that bound man to his "natural superiors," and has left no other nexus between man and man than naked self-interest, than callous "cash payment." It has drowned the most heavenly ecstasies of religious fervor,[8] of chivalrous enthusiasm, of Philistine sentimentalism, in the icy water of egotistical calculation. It has resolved personal worth into exchange value, and in place of the numberless indefeasible chartered freedoms, has set up that single, unconscionable freedom — Free Trade. In one word, for exploitation, veiled by religious and political illusions, it has substituted naked, shameless, direct, brutal exploitation.

The bourgeoisie has stripped of its halo every occupation hitherto honored   21
and looked up to with reverent awe. It has converted the physician, the lawyer, the priest, the poet, the man of science, into its paid wage laborers.

The bourgeoisie has torn away from the family its sentimental veil, and has   22
reduced the family relation to a mere money relation.

The bourgeoisie has disclosed how it came to pass that the brutal display   23
of vigor in the Middle Ages, which reactionists so much admire, found its fitting complement in the most slothful indolence. It has been the first to show what man's activity can bring about. It has accomplished wonders far surpassing Egyptian pyramids, Roman aqueducts, and Gothic cathedrals; it has conducted expeditions that put in the shade all former Exoduses of nations and crusades.

The bourgeoisie cannot exist without constantly revolutionizing the instru-   24
ments of production, and thereby the relations of production, and with them the whole relations of society. Conservation of the old modes of production in unaltered form was, on the contrary, the first condition of existence for all earlier industrial classes. Constant revolutionizing of production, uninterrupted disturbance of all social conditions, everlasting uncertainty and agitation distinguish the bourgeois epoch from all earlier ones. All fixed, fast frozen relations, with their train of ancient and venerable prejudices and opinions, are swept away, all new formed ones become antiquated before they can ossify.

---

[8] **religious fervor**   This and other terms in this sentence contain a compressed historical observation. "Religious fervor" refers to the Middle Ages; "chivalrous enthusiasm" refers to the rise of the secular state and to the military power of knights; "Philistine sentimentalism" refers to the development of popular arts and literature in the sixteenth, seventeenth, and eighteenth centuries. "Philistine" refers to those who were generally uncultured, that is, the general public. "Sentimentalism" is a code word for the encouragement of emotional response rather than rational thought.

All that is solid melts into the air, all that is holy is profaned, and man is at last compelled to face with sober senses, his real conditions of life, and his relations with his kind.

The need of a constantly expanding market for its products chases the bourgeoisie over the whole surface of the globe. It must nestle everywhere, settle everywhere, establish connections everywhere.   25

The bourgeoisie has through its exploitation of the world-market given a cosmopolitan character to production and consumption in every country. To the great chagrin of reactionists, it has drawn from under the feet of industry the national ground on which it stood. All old-established national industries have been destroyed or are daily being destroyed. They are dislodged by new industries, whose introduction becomes a life and death question for all civilized nations, by industries that no longer work up indigenous raw material, but raw material drawn from the remotest zones; industries whose products are consumed, not only at home, but in every quarter of the globe. In place of the old wants, satisfied by the productions of the country, we find new wants, requiring for their satisfaction the products of distant lands and climes. In place of the old local and national seclusion and self-sufficiency, we have intercourse in every direction, universal interdependence of nations. And as in material, so also in intellectual production. The intellectual creations of individual nations become common property. National onesidedness and narrowmindedness become more and more impossible, and from the numerous national and local literatures there arises a world-literature.   26

The bourgeoisie, by the rapid improvement of all instruments of production, by the immensely facilitated means of communication, draws all, even the most barbarian nations into civilization. The cheap prices of its commodities are the heavy artillery with which it batters down all Chinese walls, with which it forces the barbarians' intensely obstinate hatred of foreigners to capitulate. It compels all nations, on pain of extinction, to adopt the bourgeois mode of production; it compels them to introduce what it calls civilization into their midst, i.e., to become bourgeois themselves. In a word, it creates a world after its own image.   27

The bourgeoisie has subjected the country to the rule of the towns. It has created enormous cities, has greatly increased the urban population as compared with the rural and has thus rescued a considerable part of the population from the idiocy of rural life. Just as it has made the country dependent on the towns, so it has made barbarian and semi-barbarian countries dependent on civilized ones, nations of peasants on nations of bourgeois, the East on the West.   28

The bourgeoisie keeps more and more doing away with the scattered state of the population, of the means of production, and of property. It has agglomerated population, centralized means of production, and has concentrated   29 property in a few hands. The necessary consequence of this was political centralization. Independent, or but loosely connected provinces, with separate interests, laws, governments, and systems of taxation, became lumped together in one nation, with one government, one code of laws, one national class interest, one frontier, and one customs tariff.

The bourgeoisie, during its rule of scarce one hundred years, has created   30
more massive and more colossal productive forces than have all preceding generations together. Subjection of Nature's forces to man, machinery, application of chemistry to industry and agriculture, steam-navigation, railways, electric telegraphs, clearing of whole continents for cultivation, canalization of rivers, whole populations conjured out of the ground — what earlier century had even a presentiment that such productive forces slumbered in the lap of social labor?

We see then: the means of production and of exchange on whose founda-   31
tion the bourgeoisie built itself up, were generated in feudal society. At a certain stage in the development of these means of production and of exchange, the conditions under which feudal society produced and exchanged, the feudal organization of agriculture and manufacturing industry, in one word, the feudal relations of property became no longer compatible with the already developed productive forces; they became so many fetters. They had to burst asunder; they were burst asunder.

Into their place stepped free competition, accompanied by a social and   32
political constitution adapted to it, and by the economical and political sway of the bourgeois class.

A similar movement is going on before our own eyes. Modern bourgeois   33
society with its relations of production, of exchange and of property, a society that has conjured up such gigantic means of production and of exchange, is like the sorcerer, who is no longer able to control the powers of the nether world whom he has called up by his spells. For many a decade past, the history of industry and commerce is but the history of the revolt of modern productive forces against modern conditions of production, against the property relations that are the conditions for the existence of the bourgeoisie and of its rule. It is enough to mention the commercial crises that by their periodical return put on its trial, each time more threateningly, the existence of the entire bourgeois society. In these crises a great part not only of the existing products, but also of the previously created productive forces, are periodically destroyed. In these crises there breaks out an epidemic that, in all earlier epochs, would have seemed an absurdity — the epidemic of overproduction. Society suddenly finds itself put back into a state of momentary barbarism; it appears as if a famine, a universal war of devastation, had cut off the supply of every means of subsistence; industry and commerce seem to be destroyed; and why? Because there is too much civilization, too much means of subsistence, too much industry, too much commerce. The productive forces at the disposal of society no longer

tend to further the development of the conditions of the bourgeois property; on the contrary, they have become too powerful for these conditions by which they are fettered, and as soon as they overcome these fetters they bring disorder into the whole of bourgeois society, endanger the existence of bourgeois property. The conditions of bourgeois society are too narrow to comprise the wealth created by them. And how does the bourgeoisie get over these crises? On the one hand by enforced destruction of a mass of productive forces; on the other, by the conquest of new markets, and by the more thorough exploitation of the old ones. That is to say, by paving the way for more extensive and more destructive crises, and by diminishing the means whereby crises are prevented.

The weapons with which the bourgeoisie felled feudalism to the ground are now turned against the bourgeoisie itself. 34

But not only has the bourgeoisie forged the weapons that bring death to itself; it has also called into existence the men who are to wield those weapons—the modern working class—the proletarians. 35

In proportion as the bourgeoisie, i.e., capital, is developed, in the same proportion is the proletariat, the modern working class, developed, a class of laborers who live only so long as they find work, and who find work only so long as their labor increases capital. These laborers, who must sell themselves piecemeal, are a commodity, like every other article of commerce, and are consequently exposed to all the vicissitudes of competition, to all the fluctuations of the market. 36

Owing to the extensive use of machinery and to division of labor, the work of the proletarians has lost all individual character, and, consequently, all charm for the workman. He becomes an appendage of the machine, and it is only the most simple, most monotonous, and most easily acquired knack that is required of him. Hence, the cost of production of a workman is restricted almost entirely to the means of subsistence that he requires for his maintenance, and for the propagation of his race. But the price of a commodity, and also of labor, is equal to its cost of production. In proportion, therefore, as the repulsiveness of the work increases the wage decreases. Nay more, in proportion as the use of machinery and division of labor increases, in the same proportion the burden of toil increases, whether by prolongation of the working hours, by increase of the work enacted in a given time, or by increased speed of the machinery, etc. 37

Modern industry has converted the little workshop of the patriarchal master into the great factory of the industrial capitalist. Masses of laborers, crowded into factories, are organized like soldiers. As privates of the industrial army they are placed under the command of a perfect hierarchy of officers and sergeants. Not only are they the slaves of the bourgeois class and of the bourgeois state, they are daily and hourly enslaved by the machine, by the overlooker, and, above all, by the individual bourgeois manufacturer himself. 38

The more openly this despotism proclaims gain to be its end and aim, the more petty, the more hateful and the more embittering it is.

The less the skill and exertion or strength implied in manual labor, in other words, the more modern industry becomes developed, the more is the labor of men superseded by that of women. Differences of age and sex have no longer any distinctive social validity for the working class. All are instruments of labor, more or less expensive to use, according to their age and sex. 39

No sooner is the exploitation of the laborer by the manufacturer, so far at an end, that he receives his wages in cash, than he is set upon by the other portions of the bourgeoisie, the landlord, the shopkeeper, the pawnbroker, etc. 40

The lower strata of the middle class — the small trades-people, shopkeepers and retired tradesmen generally, the handicraftsmen, and peasants — all these sink gradually into the proletariat, partly because their diminutive capital does not suffice for the scale on which Modern Industry is carried on, and is swamped in the competition with the large capitalists, partly because their specialized skill is rendered worthless by new methods of production. Thus the proletariat is recruited from all classes of the population. 41

The proletariat goes through various stages of development. With its birth begins its struggle with the bourgeoisie. At first the contest is carried on by individual laborers, then by the workpeople of a factory, then by the operatives of one trade, in one locality, against the individual bourgeois who directly exploits them. They direct their attacks not against the bourgeois conditions of production, but against the instruments of production themselves; they destroy imported wares that compete with their labor, they smash to pieces machinery, they set factories ablaze, they seek to restore by force the vanished status of the workman of the Middle Ages. 42

At this stage the laborers still form an incoherent mass scattered over the whole country, and broken up by their mutual competition. If anywhere they unite to form more compact bodies, this is not yet the consequence of their own active union, but of the union of the bourgeoisie, which class, in order to attain its own political ends, is compelled to set the whole proletariat in motion, and is moreover yet, for a time, able to do so. At this stage, therefore, the proletarians do not fight their enemies, but the enemies of their enemies, the remnants of absolute monarchy, the landowners, the non-industrial bourgeois, the petty bourgeoisie. Thus the whole historical movement is concentrated in the hands of the bourgeoisie, every victory so obtained is a victory for the bourgeoisie. 43

But with the development of industry the proletariat not only increases in number; it becomes concentrated in greater masses, its strength grows and it feels that strength more. The various interests and conditions of life within the ranks of the proletariat are more and more equalized, in proportion as machinery obliterates all distinctions of labor, and nearly everywhere reduces wages to the same low level. The growing competition among the bourgeois, and the 44 resulting commercial crisis, make the wages of the workers even more fluctu-ating. The unceasing improvement of machinery, ever more rapidly developing, makes their livelihood more and more precarious; the collisions between indi-vidual workmen and individual bourgeois take more and more the character of collisions between two classes. Thereupon the workers begin to form combi-nations (Trades' Unions)[9] against the bourgeois; they club together in order to keep up the rate of wages; they found permanent associations in order to make provision beforehand for these occasional revolts. Here and there the contest breaks out into riots.

Now and then the workers are victorious, but only for a time. The real fruit   45 of their battle lies not in the immediate result but in the ever-expanding union of workers. This union is helped on by the improved means of communication that are created by modern industry, and that places the workers of different localities in contact with one another. It was just this contact that was needed to centralize the numerous local struggles, all of the same character, into one national struggle between classes. But every class struggle is a political strug-gle. And that union, to attain which the burghers of the Middle Ages with their miserable highways, required centuries, the modern proletarians, thanks to railways, achieve in a few years.

This organization of the proletarians into a class, and consequently into   46 a political party, is continually being upset again by the competition between the workers themselves. But it ever rises up again, stronger, firmer, mightier. It compels legislative recognition of particular interests of the workers by taking advantage of the divisions among the bourgeoisie itself. Thus the ten hours' bill in England[10] was carried.

Altogether collisions between the classes of the old society further, in many   47 ways, the course of development of the proletariat. The bourgeoisie finds itself involved in a constant battle. At first with the aristocracy; later on, with those portions of the bourgeoisie itself whose interests have become antagonistic to the progress of industry; at all times, with the bourgeoisie of foreign coun-tries. In all these battles it sees itself compelled to appeal to the proletariat, to ask for its help, and thus, to drag it into the political arena. The bourgeoisie itself, therefore, supplies the proletariat with its own elements of political and general education; in other words, it furnishes the proletariat with weapons for fighting the bourgeoisie.

---

[9] **combinations (Trades' Unions)**   The labor movement was only beginning in 1848. It consisted of trades' unions that started as social clubs but soon began agitating for labor reform. They represented an important step in the growth of socialism in Europe.

[10] **the ten hours' bill in England**   This bill (1847) was an important labor reform. It limited the working day for women and children in factories to only ten hours, at a time when it was common for some people to work sixteen hours a day. The bill's passage was a result of political division, not of benevolence on the managers' part.

Further, as we have already seen, entire sections of the ruling classes are, 48
by the advance of industry, precipitated into the proletariat, or are at least
threatened in their conditions of existence. These also supply the proletariat
with fresh elements of enlightenment and progress.

Finally, in times when the class struggle nears the decisive hour, the pro- 49
cess of dissolution going on within the ruling class—in fact, within the whole
range of an old society—assumes such a violent, glaring character that a small
section of the ruling class cuts itself adrift and joins the revolutionary class, the
class that holds the future in its hands. Just as, therefore, at an earlier period,
a section of the nobility went over to the bourgeoisie, so now a portion of the
bourgeoisie goes over to the proletariat, and in particular, a portion of the bourgeois ideologists, who have raised themselves to the level of comprehending
theoretically the historical movements as a whole.

Of all the classes that stand face to face with the bourgeoisie today the 50
proletariat alone is a really revolutionary class. The other classes decay and
finally disappear in the face of Modern Industry; the proletariat is its special
and essential product.

The lower middle class, the small manufacturer, the shopkeeper, the arti- 51
san, the peasant, all these fight against the bourgeoisie, to save from extinction
their existence as fractions of the middle class. They are therefore not revolutionary, but conservative. Nay, more; they are reactionary, for they try to roll
back the wheel of history. If by chance they are revolutionary, they are so only
in view of their impending transfer into the proletariat; they thus defend not
their present, but their future interests; they desert their own standpoint to
place themselves at that of the proletariat.

The "dangerous class," the social scum, that passively rotting mass thrown 52
off by the lowest layers of old society, may, here and there, be swept into the
movement by a proletarian revolution; its conditions of life, however, prepare
it far more for the part of a bribed tool of reactionary intrigue.

In the conditions of the proletariat, those of the old society at large are 53
already virtually swamped. The proletarian is without property; his relation to
his wife and children has no longer anything in common with the bourgeois
family relations; modern industrial labor, modern subjection to capital, the
same in England as in France, in America as in Germany, has stripped him of
every trace of national character. Law, morality, religion, are to him so many
bourgeois prejudices, behind which lurk in ambush just as many bourgeois
interests.

All the preceding classes that got the upper hand sought to fortify their 54
already acquired status by subjecting society at large to their conditions of
appropriation. The proletarians cannot become masters of the productive
forces of society, except by abolishing their own previous mode of appropriation, and thereby also every other previous mode of appropriation. They have

nothing of their own to secure and to fortify; their mission is to destroy all previous securities for and insurances of individual property.

All previous historical movements were movements of minorities, or in 55 the interest of minorities. The proletarian movement is the self-conscious, independent movement of the immense majority. The proletariat, the lowest stratum of our present society, cannot stir, cannot raise itself up without the whole superincumbent strata of official society being sprung into the air.

Though not in substance, yet in form, the struggle of the proletariat with 56 the bourgeoisie is at first a national struggle. The proletariat of each country must, of course, first of all settle matters with its own bourgeoisie.

In depicting the most general phases of the development of the proletariat, 57 we traced the more or less veiled civil war, raging within existing society, up to the point where that war breaks out into open revolution, and where the violent overthrow of the bourgeoisie, lays the foundations for the sway of the proletariat.

Hitherto every form of society has been based, as we have already seen, on 58 the antagonism of oppressing and oppressed classes. But in order to oppress a class, certain conditions must be assured to it under which it can, at least, continue its slavish existence. The serf, in the period of serfdom, raised himself to membership in the commune, just as the petty bourgeois, under the yoke of feudal absolutism, managed to develop into a bourgeois. The modern laborer, on the contrary, instead of rising with the progress of industry, sinks deeper and deeper below the conditions of existence of his own class. He becomes a pauper, and pauperism develops more rapidly than population and wealth. And here it becomes evident that the bourgeoisie is unfit any longer to be the ruling class in society, and to impose its conditions of existence upon society as an over-riding law. It is unfit to rule, because it is incompetent to assure an existence to its slave within his slavery, because it cannot help letting him sink into such a state that it has to feed him, instead of being fed by him. Society can no longer live under this bourgeoisie; in other words, its existence is no longer compatible with society.

The essential condition for the existence, and for the sway of the bourgeois 59 class, is the formation and augmentation of capital; the condition for capital is wage labor. Wage labor rests exclusively on competition between the laborers. The advance of industry, whose involuntary promoter is the bourgeoisie, replaces the isolation of the laborers, due to competition, by their involuntary combination, due to association. The development of Modern Industry, therefore, cuts from under its feet the very foundation on which the bourgeoisie produces and appropriates products. What the bourgeoisie therefore produces, above all, are its own grave diggers. Its fall and the victory of the proletariat are equally inevitable.

Proletarians and Communists

In what relation do the Communists stand to the proletarians as a whole? 60

The Communists do not form a separate party opposed to other working 61
class parties.

They have no interests separate and apart from those of the proletariat as 62
a whole.

They do not set up any sectarian principles of their own, by which to shape 63
and mold the proletarian movement.

The Communists are distinguished from the other working class parties by 64
this only: 1. In the national struggles of the proletarians of the different countries,
they point out and bring to the front the common interests of the entire proletariat, independently of all nationality. 2. In the various stages of development which
the struggle of the working class against the bourgeoisie has to pass through,
they always and everywhere represent the interests of the movement as a whole.

The Communists, therefore, are on the one hand practically the most 65
advanced and resolute section of the working class parties of every country,
that section which pushes forward all others; on the other hand, theoretically,
they have over the great mass of the proletariat the advantage of clearly understanding the line of march, the conditions, and the ultimate general results of
the proletarian movement.

The immediate aim of the Communists is the same as that of all the other 66
proletarian parties: formation of the proletariat into a class, overthrow of the
bourgeois of supremacy, conquest of political power by the proletariat.

The theoretical conclusions of the Communists are in no way based 67
on ideas or principles that have been invented or discovered by this or that
would-be universal reformer.

They merely express, in general terms, actual relations springing from an 68
existing class struggle, from a historical movement going on under our very
eyes. The abolition of existing property relations is not at all a distinctive feature of Communism.

All property relations in the past have continually been subject to histori- 69
cal change consequent upon the change in historical conditions.

The French Revolution, for example, abolished feudal property in favor of 70
bourgeois property.

The distinguishing feature of Communism is not the abolition of property 71
generally, but the abolition of bourgeois property. But modern bourgeois private property is the final and most complete expression of the system of producing and appropriating products, that is based on class antagonism, on the
exploitation of the many by the few.

In this sense, the theory of the Communists may be summed up in the sin- 72
gle sentence: abolition of private property.

We Communists have been reproached with the desire of abolishing the   73
right of personally acquiring property as the fruit of a man's own labor, which
property is alleged to be the groundwork of all personal freedom, activity, and
independence.

Hard won, self-acquired, self-earned property! Do you mean the property   74
of the petty artisan and of the small peasant, a form of property that preceded
the bourgeois form? There is no need to abolish that; the development of industry has to a great extent already destroyed it, and is still destroying it daily.

Or do you mean modern bourgeois private property?   75

But does wage labor create any property for the laborer? Not a bit. It cre-   76
ates capital, i.e., that kind of property which exploits wage labor, and which
cannot increase except upon condition of getting a new supply of wage labor
for fresh exploitation. Property, in its present form, is based on the antagonism
of capital and wage labor. Let us examine both sides of this antagonism.

To be a capitalist is to have not only a purely personal, but a social status   77
in production. Capital is a collective product, and only by the united action of
many members, nay, in the last resort, only by the united action of all members
of society, can it be set in motion.

Capital is therefore not a personal, it is a social power.   78

When, therefore, capital is converted into common property, into the prop-   79
erty of all members of society, personal property is not thereby transformed
into social property. It is only the social character of the property that is
changed. It loses its class character.

Let us now take wage labor.   80

The average price of wage labor is the minimum wage, i.e., that quantum   81
of the means of subsistence which is absolutely requisite to keep the laborer
in bare existence as a laborer. What, therefore, the wage laborer appropriates
by means of his labor, merely suffices to prolong and reproduce a bare existence. We by no means intend to abolish this personal appropriation of the
products of labor, an appropriation that is made for the maintenance and reproduction of human life, and that leaves no surplus wherewith to command the
labor of others. All that we want to do away with is the miserable character of
this appropriation, under which the laborer lives merely to increase capital
and is allowed to live only insofar as the interests of the ruling class require it.

In bourgeois society, living labor is but a means to increase accumulated   82
labor. In Communist society accumulated labor is but a means to widen, to
enrich, to promote the existence of the laborer.

In bourgeois society, therefore, the past dominates the present; in Communist   83
society the present dominates the past. In bourgeois society, capital is independent
and has individuality, while the living person is dependent and has no individuality.

And the abolition of this state of things is called by the bourgeois aboli-   84
tion of individuality and freedom! And rightly so. The abolition of bourgeois

individuality, bourgeois independence, and bourgeois freedom is undoubtedly aimed at.

By freedom is meant, under the present bourgeois conditions of production, free trade, free selling and buying. 85

But if selling and buying disappears, free selling and buying disappears also. This talk about free selling and buying, and all the other "brave words" of our bourgeoisie about freedom in general have a meaning, if any, only in contrast with restricted selling and buying, with the fettered traders of the Middle Ages, but have no meaning when opposed to the Communistic abolition of buying and selling, of the bourgeois conditions of production, and of the bourgeoisie itself. 86

You are horrified at our intending to do away with private property. But in your existing society private property is already done away with for nine-tenths of the population; its existence for the few is solely due to its nonexistence in the hands of those nine-tenths. You reproach us, therefore, with intending to do away with a form of property, the necessary condition for whose existence is the nonexistence of any property for the immense majority of society. 87

In one word, you reproach us with intending to do away with your property. Precisely so: that is just what we intend. 88

From the moment when labor can no longer be converted into capital, money, or rent, into a social power capable of being monopolized, i.e., from the moment when individual property can no longer be transformed into bourgeois property, into capital, from that moment, you say, individuality vanishes. 89

You must, therefore, confess that by "individual" you mean no other person than the bourgeois, than the middle-class owner of property. This person must, indeed, be swept out of the way and made impossible. 90

Communism deprives no man of the power to appropriate the products of society: all that it does is to deprive him of the power to subjugate the labor of others by means of such appropriation. 91

It has been objected that upon the abolition of private property all work will cease and universal laziness will overtake us. 92

According to this, bourgeois society ought long ago to have gone to the dogs through sheer idleness; for those of its members who work acquire nothing, and those who acquire anything do not work. The whole of this objection is but another expression of the tautology:[11] that there can no longer be any wage labor when there is no longer any capital. 93

All objections urged against the Communistic mode of producing and appropriating material products have, in the same way, been urged against the Communistic modes of producing and appropriating intellectual products. 94

---

[11] **tautology**   A statement whose two parts say essentially the same thing. The second half of the previous sentence is a tautology.

Just as, to the bourgeois, the disappearance of class property is the disappearance of production itself, so the disappearance of class culture is to him identical with the disappearance of all culture.

That culture, the loss of which he laments, is, for the enormous majority, a   95
mere training to act as a machine.

But don't wrangle with us so long as you apply, to our intended abolition   96
of bourgeois property, the standard of your bourgeois notions of freedom, culture, law, etc. Your very ideas are but the outgrowth of the conditions of your bourgeois production and bourgeois property, just as your jurisprudence is but the will of your class made into a law for all, a will whose essential character and direction are determined by the economical conditions of existence of your class.

The selfish misconception that induces you to transform into eternal laws   97
of nature and of reason the social forms springing from your present mode of production and form of property — historical relations that rise and disappear in the progress of production — this misconception you share with every ruling class that has preceded you. What you see clearly in the case of ancient property, what you admit in the case of feudal property, you are of course forbidden to admit in the case of your own bourgeois form of property.

Abolition of the family! Even the most radical flare up at this infamous   98
proposal of the Communists.

On what foundation is the present family, the bourgeois family, based? On   99
capital, on private gain. In its completely developed form this family exists only among the bourgeoisie. But this state of things finds its complement in the practical absence of the family among the proletarians, and in public prostitution.

The bourgeois family will vanish as a matter of course when its comple-   100
ment vanishes, and both will vanish with the vanishing of capital.

Do you charge us with wanting to stop the exploitation of children by their   101
parents? To this crime we plead guilty.

But, you will say, we destroy the most hallowed of relations when we   102
replace home education by social.

And your education! Is not that also social, and determined by the social   103
conditions under which you educate; by the intervention, direct or indirect, of society by means of schools, etc.? The Communists have not invented the intervention of society in education; they do but seek to alter the character of that intervention, and to rescue education from the influence of the ruling class.

The bourgeois clap-trap about the family and education, about the hallowed   104
correlation of parent and child, become all the more disgusting, the more, by the action of Modern Industry, all family ties among the proletarians are torn asunder and their children transformed into simple articles of commerce and instruments of labor.

But you Communists would introduce community of women, screams the   105
whole bourgeoisie chorus.

The bourgeois sees in his wife a mere instrument of production. He hears   106
that the instruments of production are to be exploited in common, and, naturally, can come to no other conclusion, than that the lot of being common to all
will likewise fall to the women.

He has not even a suspicion that the real point aimed at is to do away with   107
the status of women as mere instruments of production.

For the rest, nothing is more ridiculous than the virtuous indignation of   108
our bourgeois at the community of women which, they pretend, is to be openly
and officially established by the Communists. The Communists have no need to
introduce community of women, it has existed almost from time immemorial.

Our bourgeois, not content with having the wives and daughters of their   109
proletarians at their disposal, not to speak of common prostitutes, take the
greatest pleasure in seducing each others' wives.

Bourgeois marriage is in reality a system of wives in common, and thus, at   110
the most, what the Communists might possibly be reproached with, is that they
desire to introduce, in substitution for a hypocritically concealed, an openly
legalized community of women. For the rest, it is self-evident that the abolition
of the present system of production must bring with it the abolition of the community of women springing from that system, i.e., of prostitution both public
and private.

The Communists are further reproached with desiring to abolish countries   111
and nationalities.

The working men have no country. We cannot take from them what they   112
don't possess. Since the proletariat must first of all acquire political supremacy,
must rise to be the leading class of the nation, must constitute itself the nation,
it is, so far, itself national, though not in the bourgeois sense of the word.

National differences and antagonisms between peoples are daily more and   113
more vanishing, owing to the development of the bourgeoisie, to freedom of
commerce, to the world-market, to uniformity in the mode of production and
in the conditions of life corresponding thereto.

The supremacy of the proletariat will cause them to vanish still faster.   114
United action, of the leading civilized countries at least, is one of the first conditions for the emancipation of the proletariat.

In proportion as the exploitation of one individual by another is put an   115
end to, the exploitation of one nation by another will also be put an end to. In
proportion as the antagonism between classes within the nation vanishes, the
hostility of one nation to another will come to an end.

The charges against Communism made from a religious, a philosophical,   116
and generally, from an ideological standpoint, are not deserving of serious
examination.

Does it require deep intuition to comprehend that man's ideas, views, and conceptions, in one word, man's consciousness, changes with every change in the conditions of his material existence, in his social relations, and in his social life? 117

What else does the history of ideas prove than that intellectual production changes in character in proportion as material production is changed? The ruling ideas of each age have ever been the ideas of its ruling class. 118

When people speak of ideas that revolutionize society they do but express the fact that within the old society the elements of a new one have been created, and that the dissolution of the old ideas keeps even pace with the dissolution of the old conditions of existence. 119

When the ancient world was in its last throes the ancient religions were overcome by Christianity. When Christian ideas succumbed in the eighteenth century to rationalist ideas, feudal society fought its death battle with the then revolutionary bourgeoisie. The ideas of religious liberty and freedom of conscience merely gave expression to the sway of free competition within the domain of knowledge. 120

"Undoubtedly," it will be said, "religious, moral, philosophical, and judicial ideas have been modified in the course of historical development. But religion, morality, philosophy, political science, and law, constantly survived this change. 121

"There are, besides, eternal truths such as Freedom, Justice, etc., that are common to all states of society. But Communism abolishes eternal truths, it abolishes all religion and all morality, instead of constituting them on a new basis; it therefore acts in contradiction to all past historical experience." 122

What does this accusation reduce itself to? The history of all past society has consisted in the development of class antagonisms, antagonisms that assumed different forms at different epochs. 123

But whatever form they may have taken, one fact is common to all past ages, viz., the exploitation of one part of society by the other. No wonder, then, that the social consciousness of past ages, despite all the multiplicity and variety it displays, moves within certain common forms, or general ideas, which cannot completely vanish except with the total disappearance of class antagonisms. 124

The Communist revolution is the most radical rupture with traditional property relations; no wonder that its development involves the most radical rupture with traditional ideas. 125

But let us have done with the bourgeois objections to Communism. 126

We have seen above that the first step in the revolution by the working class is to raise the proletariat to the position of ruling class, to win the battle of democracy. 127

The proletariat will use its political supremacy to wrest, by degrees, all   128
capital from the bourgeoisie, to centralize all instruments of production in the
hands of the State, i.e., of the proletariat organized as a ruling class; and to
increase the total productive forces as rapidly as possible.

Of course, in the beginning, this cannot be effected except by means of   129
despotic inroads on the rights of property, and on the conditions of bourgeois
production; by means of measures, therefore, which appear economically
insufficient and untenable, but which in the course of the movement outstrip
themselves, necessitate further inroads upon the old social order, and are
unavoidable as a means of entirely revolutionizing the mode of production.

These measures will of course be different in different countries.   130

Nevertheless in the most advanced countries the following will be pretty   131
generally applicable:

1. Abolition of property in land and application of all rents of land to public
   purposes.

2. A heavy progressive or graduated income tax.

3. Abolition of all right of inheritance.

4. Confiscation of the property of all emigrants and rebels.

5. Centralization of credit in the hands of the State, by means of a national
   bank with State capital and an exclusive monopoly.

6. Centralization of the means of communication and transport in the hands
   of the State.

7. Extension of factories and instruments of production owned by the State;
   the bringing into cultivation of waste lands, and the improvement of the
   soil generally in accordance with a common plan.

8. Equal liability of all to labor. Establishment of industrial armies,
   especially for agriculture.

9. Combination of agriculture with manufacturing industries; gradual
   abolition of the distinction between town and country by a more equable
   distribution of the population over the country.

10. Free education for all children in public schools. Abolition of children's
    factory labor in its present form. Combination of education with
    industrial production, etc., etc.

When, in the course of development, class distinctions have disappeared,   132
and all production has been concentrated in the hands of a vast association
of the whole nation, the public power will lose its political character. Political
power, properly so called, is merely the organized power of one class for
oppressing another. If the proletariat during its contest with the bourgeoisie

is compelled, by the force of circumstances, to organize itself as a class, if, by means of a revolution, it makes itself the ruling class, and, as such, sweeps away by force the old conditions of production, then it will, along with these conditions, have swept away the conditions for the existence of class antagonism, and of classes generally, and will thereby have abolished its own supremacy as a class.

In place of the old bourgeois society, with its classes and class antagonisms, we shall have an association in which the free development of each is the condition for the free development of all. . . .   133

Position of the Communists in Relation to the Various Existing Opposition Parties

[The preceding section] has made clear the relations of the Communists to   134
the existing working class parties, such as the Chartists in England and the Agrarian Reforms[12] in America.

The Communists fight for the attainment of the immediate aims, for   135
the enforcement of the momentary interests of the working class; but in the movement of the present they also represent and take care of the future of that movement. In France the Communists ally themselves with the Social-Democrats[13] against the conservative and radical bourgeoisie, reserving, however, the right to take up a critical position in regard to phrases and illusions traditionally handed down from the great Revolution.

In Switzerland they support the Radicals,[14] without losing sight of the   136
fact that this party consists of antagonistic elements, partly of Democratic Socialists, in the French sense, partly of radical bourgeois.

In Poland they support the party that insists on an agrarian revolution, as   137
the prime condition for national emancipation, that party which fomented the insurrection of Cracow in 1846.[15]

---

[12] **Agrarian Reforms**   Agrarian reform was a very important issue in America after the Revolution. The Chartists were a radical English group established in 1838; they demanded political and social reforms. They were among the more violent revolutionaries of the day. Agrarian reform, or redistribution of the land, was slow to come, and the issue often sparked violence between social classes.

[13] **Social-Democrats**   In France in the 1840s, a group that proposed the ideal of labor reform through the establishment of workshops supplied with government capital.

[14] **Radicals**   By 1848, European Radicals, taking their name from the violent revolutionaries of the French Revolution (1789–1799), were a nonviolent group content to wait for change.

[15] **the insurrection of Cracow in 1846**   Cracow was an independent city in 1846. The insurrection was designed to join Cracow with Poland and to further large-scale social reforms.

In Germany they fight with the bourgeoisie whenever it acts in a revolu-   138
tionary way, against the absolute monarchy, the feudal squirearchy, and the
petty bourgeoisie.

But they never cease for a single instant to instill into the working class the   139
clearest possible recognition of the hostile antagonism between bourgeoisie
and proletariat, in order that the German workers may straightway use, as so
many weapons against the bourgeoisie, the social and political conditions that
the bourgeoisie must necessarily introduce along with its supremacy, and in
order that, after the fall of the reactionary classes in Germany, the fight against
the bourgeoisie itself may immediately begin.

The Communists turn their attention chiefly to Germany, because that   140
country is on the eve of a bourgeois revolution,[16] that is bound to be carried
out under more advanced conditions of European civilization, and with a
more developed proletariat, than that of England was in the seventeenth and
of France in the eighteenth century, and because the bourgeois revolution
in Germany will be but the prelude to an immediately following proletarian
revolution.

In short, the Communists everywhere support every revolutionary move-   141
ment against the existing social and political order of things.

In all these movements they bring to the front, as the leading question in   142
each, the property question, no matter what its degree of development at the
time.

Finally, they labor everywhere for the union and agreement of the demo-   143
cratic parties of all countries.

The Communists disdain to conceal their views and aims. They openly   144
declare that their ends can be attained only by the forcible overthrow of all
existing social conditions. Let the ruling classes tremble at a Communistic revolution. The proletarians have nothing to lose but their chains. They have a
world to win.

Working men of all countries, unite!   145

---

[16] **on the eve of a bourgeois revolution**   Ferdinand Lassalle (1825–1864) developed the
German labor movement and was in basic agreement with Marx, who was nevertheless
convinced that Lassalle's approach was wrong. The environment in Germany seemed
appropriate for revolution, in part because of its fragmented political structure and in
part because no major revolution had yet occurred there.

✛ QUESTIONS FOR CRITICAL READING

1. Begin by establishing your understanding of the terms *bourgeois* and *proletarian*. Does Marx make a clear distinction between the terms? Are such terms
   applicable to American society today? Which of these groups, if any, do you feel
   that you belong to?

2. Marx makes the concept of social class fundamental to his theories. Can "social class" be easily defined? Are social classes evident in our society? Are they engaged in a struggle of the sort Marx assumes to be inevitable?

3. What are Marx's views about the value of work in the society he describes? What is his attitude toward wealth?

4. Marx says that every class struggle is a political struggle. Do you agree?

5. Examine the first part. Which class gets more paragraphs — the bourgeoisie or the proletariat? Why?

6. Is the modern proletariat a revolutionary class?

7. Is Marx's analysis of history clear? Try to summarize his views on the progress of history.

8. Is capital a social force, or is it a personal force? Do you think of your savings (either now or in the future) as belonging to you alone or as in some way belonging to your society?

9. What, in Marx's view, is the responsibility of wealthy citizens?

✖ SUGGESTIONS FOR CRITICAL WRITING

1. Defend or attack Marx's statement: "The executive of the modern State is but a committee for managing the common affairs of the whole bourgeoisie" (para. 18). Is this generally true? Take three "affairs of the whole bourgeoisie" and test each one in turn.

2. Examine Marx's statements regarding women. Refer especially to paragraphs 39, 98, 105, and 110. Does he imply that his views are in conflict with those of his general society? After you have a list of his statements, see if you can establish exactly what he is recommending. Do you approve of his recommendations?

3. Marx's program of ten points is listed in paragraph 131. Using the technique that Marx himself uses — taking each point in its turn, clarifying the problems with the point, and finally deciding for or against the point — evaluate his program. Which points do you feel are most beneficial to society? Which are detrimental to society? What is your overall view of the general worth of the program? Do you think it would be possible to put such a program into effect?

4. All Marx's views are predicated on the present nature of property ownership and the changes that communism will institute. He claims, for example, that a rupture with property relations "involves the most radical rupture with traditional ideas" (para. 125). And he discusses in depth his proposal for the rupture of property relations (paras. 68–93). Clarify traditional property relations — what can be owned and by whom — and then contrast with these the proposals Marx makes. Establish your own views as you go along. Include your reasons

for taking issue or expressing agreement with Marx. What kinds of property relations do you see around you? What kinds are most desirable for a healthy society?

5. What is the responsibility of the state toward the individual in the kind of economic circumstances that Marx describes? How can the independence of individuals who have amassed great wealth and wish to operate freely be balanced against the independence of those who are poor and have no wealth to manipulate? What kinds of abuse are possible in such circumstances, and what remedies can a state achieve through altering the economic system? What specific remedies does Marx suggest? Are they workable?

6. Do you feel that Marx's suggestions are desirable? Or that they are likely to produce the effects he desires? Critics sometimes complain about Marx's misunderstanding of human nature. Do you feel he has an adequate understanding of human nature? What do you see as impediments to the full success of his program?

7. How accurate is Marx's view of the bourgeoisie? He identifies the bourgeoisie with capital and capitalists. He also complains that the bourgeoisie has established a world market for goods and by doing so has destroyed national and regional identities. Examine his analysis in paragraphs 22–36 in terms of what you see happening in the economic world today and decide whether or not his ideas about how the bourgeoisie functions still apply and ring true. Did Marx foresee the problems of globalization that incited protests and riots such as those aimed at the World Bank, the World Trade Organization, and the International Monetary Fund during the last years of the twentieth century into the early part of the twenty-first century?

8. **CONNECTIONS**   Examine Marx's ten points (para. 131) and determine how the Friedmans argue against each of the points (p. 400). Which of Marx's points do the Friedmans attack most forcefully, and why? What is your position regarding the arguments between Marx and the Friedmans? Which of these authors is most concerned with equality? Which is most concerned about the welfare of the individual? Which of these authors is the more significant champion of personal freedom? How can you tell that the Friedmans have definitely read Marx carefully and disagree with him?

9. **CONNECTIONS**   Marx's philosophy differs from that of Robert B. Reich. How would Marx respond to Reich's analysis (p. 422) of the future of labor in the next few decades? Would Marx see signs of a coming class struggle in the distinctions Reich draws between the routine workers, the in-person servers, and the symbolic analysts? Does Reich's essay take any of Marx's theories into account?

10. **CONNECTIONS**   For Marx, there is no more antagonistic figure of capitalism than Andrew Carnegie. Carnegie himself condemns communism as a failed system, while Marx condemns capitalism as a system designed to keep the rich

rich and the poor poor. Imagine that Marx read Carnegie's *The Gospel of Wealth* (p. 360) and decided to counter it with an argument written as a letter to the editor of a major newspaper. What would be the basis of his attack, and how might he structure his letter? Consider Marx's own techniques in defending communism against the bourgeoisie (paras. 60 onward) as you go about constructing the argument against Carnegie.

11. **CONNECTIONS** The principles of communism are totally unacceptable to economists such as F. A. Hayek (p. 386). But it is also true that there may be points of agreement in other selections presented in this section. What concerns does each selection in this section take into consideration in establishing economic ideas that are designed to improve the lives of people? Which selection seems to be the most concerned about the ultimate happiness of the citizens of the state?

ANDREW CARNEGIE

The Gospel of Wealth

ANDREW CARNEGIE (1835–1919) was a truly self-made man. Born in Scotland, he immigrated with his family to Allegheny, Pennsylvania, when he was thirteen. He went right to work in a cotton mill where he labored twelve hours a day, six days a week, for $1.20. Three years later, he became a messenger boy for $2.20 a week for the local telegraph company in Pittsburgh. His connection with the telegraph company and his self-taught mastery of telegraphy proved fortuitous. This was a cutting-edge technology at the time and it intersected another cutting-edge industry next to which the telegraph wires were strung, the railroads. In 1853, Thomas A. Scott, the president of the Pennsylvania Railroad, employed him as his assistant for $35 per month. His rise through the company was rapid after that.

Through the help of Scott, Carnegie invested money successfully and then reinvested his profits in sleeping cars for the railroad. That led to his buying out part of the company that made the cars. Because his investments were so successful, he was able to move into the iron and iron products industry, manufacturing components for bridges and railroad tracks. By the time the Civil War began, Carnegie had amassed a considerable amount of capital: the key to his later success. During the war, Scott appointed Carnegie superintendent of military transport and the Union telegraph lines, which had to be kept up to speed for communication between Washington and the field commanders.

Late in the war, Carnegie invested $40,000 in property in Pennsylvania that yielded petroleum, and profits from that venture led him to move into the steel business in response to the need for cannon, shells, armor, and other military products. Because he had put some of his investment money into iron companies before the war, he was positioned to make considerable profits. After the end of the war, Carnegie saw an opportunity to expand his business by replacing older wooden railroad bridges with steel and iron

---

Originally published as "Wealth" in the *North American Review*, June 1889.

bridges, further building his fortune. It was then, in the 1870s, that he began to conceive of what was to become in 1892 the Carnegie Steel Company, one of the largest companies in the nation. Before that, however, he had purchased huge fields of iron ore around Lake Superior, so he was positioned as a supplier as well as a manufacturer of steel and iron.

Carnegie was a published author and expressed interest in improving his education and in meeting important literary and philosophical people such as Matthew Arnold (1822–1888), whom he admired, and Herbert Spencer (1820–1903), who became a very important influence on his thinking. Spencer was a utilitarian philosopher who was known as a social Darwinist. Spencer coined the phrase "the survival of the fittest" and applied it to the social sphere. Carnegie found Spencer's views totally congenial since he felt that there were superior people (he said "men") who were indeed the fittest in any economy and who deserved to profit from a laissez-faire economy and to rise in society. He was one of those men.

Carnegie was a serious reader and a lover of music. Late in life, he built and named Carnegie Hall in New York, which he designed specifically for concerts. Moreover, part of his success was due to his personal charm and grace, qualities that permitted him to travel in the highest social circles of his day. He also expressed a strong concern in helping working people educate themselves and enjoy the pleasures of art and music. Even in his thirties, he began to conceive his ultimate plan of giving away his fortune and had already begun giving some of his money away to public programs.

His operations in the steel industry, however, were not as obviously benevolent as his programs to benefit the public. He ruthlessly cut wages for skilled and unskilled workers because he thought that the greater his profits the more money he would have to give away and that he could do more good with that money than his workers could. His purpose was to serve the greatest good for the greatest number. In 1892, his workers held a strike at Homestead Steel that lasted 143 days. Carnegie was in Scotland most of this time, and his next in command, Henry Clay Frick, ordered Pinkerton guards to drive out the workers, who were then replaced with immigrants. There was violence and ten men were killed. After that incident, Carnegie's reputation was never the same.

He sold his holdings in 1901 to the banker J. P. Morgan for $480 million, which in today's money would be about $10.6 billion. Morgan told Carnegie that he was probably the richest man in the world, which may have been true. The only other man at that time who could claim that title was John D. Rockefeller. Carnegie retired at sixty-six and began giving his money away in earnest, a sum ultimately amounting to $350 million. He founded Carnegie Mellon University in Pittsburgh, gave considerable sums to Scottish universities and to his hometown in Scotland, and established pension funds for his workers at Homestead and at universities. In small towns and cities throughout the United States and Canada, he is remembered for having built free public libraries, very few of which existed before he began his program. He built 2,509 libraries in all before he ended his project in 1917. Carnegie was not a religious man, preferring to think of himself as more influenced by science and learning, but he did commission a large number of pipe organs to be installed in churches, ostensibly because he approved of the music they would play.

Interestingly, Carnegie challenged the great holders of fortunes in his day to give their money away while they were still living, as he was planning to do. However, other than John D. Rockefeller, few of them followed his lead. Many established philanthropies after their deaths, but they did not have the pleasure of seeing their wealth perform public service.

CARNEGIE'S RHETORIC

One of the first rhetorical notes is the use of the word *Gospel* in the title. Originally the essay was titled "Wealth," but when it was quickly reprinted to be distributed more widely *Gospel* was added. The effect is to impart an almost divine authority to the text because it echoes the gospels of the New Testament and seems then to connect to the teachings of Jesus. Originally, *gospel* meant "good news," and Carnegie certainly thought his concepts here were the best news he could provide.

The organization of the essay is clear enough. Carnegie begins by posing a problem: "The problem of our age is the proper administration of wealth." This profound declaration focuses our attention, but in 1889 we might have felt that it was not the only, nor the most important, problem of the age. Being hyperbolic in that fashion simply forces us to put aside other considerations and attend to the problem of the "contrast between the palace of the millionaire and the cottage of the laborer" (para. 1). We might expect Carnegie to be critical of this unequal distinction, but instead he says that this is the natural result of civilization. By contrast, the home of the leader of the Sioux is much the same as the most ordinary Indian, and thus Carnegie tacitly implies that the Sioux are not civilized. Hidden in his discussion is the assumption that there is a form of Darwinian evolution at work that has produced a "progress of the race," a theme he touches on constantly, and that the modern industrial leader, such as Carnegie himself, is an example of the "fittest" in society.

Carnegie's Darwinism derives from the teaching of Herbert Spencer and was enthusiastically adopted by other leaders who amassed astonishing fortunes in the years during and after the Civil War. It surfaces in specific rhetorical flourishes that center on the idea of laws of nature that are inevitable and, for Carnegie, desirable. In paragraph 6, Carnegie introduces the "law of competition" and sees it as one of the most beneficial laws because it concentrates wealth into the hands of the few. The few then create capital and capital is what makes civilization the beautiful thing it is in his eyes. In paragraph 7, Carnegie talks about "the Law of Accumulation of Wealth, and the Law of Competition" and admits that, although the laws may be imperfect in some ways, "they are, nevertheless, like the highest type of man, the best and most valuable of all that humanity has yet accomplished." In the next paragraph, he refers to these as "the laws upon which civilization is founded," leaving the reader no other option than to accept his view.

Another crucial issue that Carnegie treats and develops throughout the essay is his concept of individualism. He contrasts the individualism of capitalism with the collectivism of communism, a movement that had been discussed throughout the second half of the nineteenth century. Individualism produced the wealth of the nation, according to Carnegie. It was responsible for the achievements of men like him. He treats it as a sacred principle in itself, although he does not declare it a law, as he does the laws of accumulation and distribution.

After praising the system that has produced so much wealth, he then condemns those who would make a religion of wealth. His main point is that fortunes such as his are only in trust, to be disbursed for the public good. Of course, he is the person to decide what the public should have: parks, works of art, public institutions, and other benefits "in the forms best calculated to do them lasting good" (para. 22). The community gets the benefit, but the philanthropist administers "it for the community far better than it could or would have done for itself" (para. 23).

Carnegie praises wealth but condemns charity. He cites an example of a wealthy man who gave a handout to a stranger on the street and claims that what that man did was "probably one of the most selfish and very worst actions of his life" (para. 20). "Indiscriminate charity" is to be condemned because "[o]f every thousand dollars spent in so-called charity to-day, it is probable that $950 is unwisely spent." Charity only goes to those who can help themselves, and as he says, those who can help themselves rarely need assistance. Charity, he fears, only encourages "the slothful, the drunken, the unworthy."

Among the remarkable experiences Carnegie had in his philanthropic years was his singular effort to help support the Tuskegee Institute, a traditionally African American college in Alabama associated with its founder, Booker T. Washington (1856–1915). Carnegie and Washington worked together on a number of projects, among them the founding of the National Negro Business League. Carnegie was a major contributor to the early development of Tuskegee and an enthusiastic friend of Washington, whose views regarding self-improvement much resembled his own.

Carnegie died in Lenox, Massachusetts, in 1919, and the bulk of his remaining wealth went to the Carnegie Corporation and continued his program of public funding.

⁙ PREREADING QUESTIONS: WHAT TO READ FOR

The following prereading questions may help you anticipate key issues in the discussion of Andrew Carnegie's *The Gospel of Wealth*. Keeping them in mind during your first reading of the selection should help focus your attention.

1. What does Carnegie see as the problem of "our age"?

2. Why does Carnegie accept the great gap between the wealth of the millionaire and the relative poverty of the laborer?

3. What laws does Carnegie feel are at work in society to help produce great wealth?

4. What is the highest obligation of the person who has amassed a great fortune?

The Gospel of Wealth

The problem of our age is the proper administration of wealth, so that the ties of brotherhood may still bind together the rich and poor in harmonious relationship. The conditions of human life have not only been changed, but revolutionized, within the past few hundred years. In former days there was little difference between the dwelling, dress, food, and environment of the chief and those of his retainers. The Indians are to-day where civilized man then was. When visiting the Sioux, I was led to the wigwam of the chief. It was just like the others in external appearance, and, even within, the difference was trifling between it and those of the poorest of his braves. The contrast between the palace of the millionaire and the cottage of the laborer with us to-day measures the change which has come with civilization.

This change, however, is not to be deplored, but welcomed as highly beneficial. It is well, nay, essential for the progress of the race, that the houses of some should be homes for all that is highest and best in literature and the arts, and for all the refinements of civilization, rather than that none should be so. Much better this great irregularity than universal squalor. Without wealth there can be no Maecenas.[1] The "good old times" were not good old times. Neither master nor servant was as well situated then as to-day. A relapse to old conditions would be disastrous to both—not the least so to him who serves—and would sweep away civilization with it. But whether the change be for good or ill, it is upon us, beyond our power to alter, and therefore to be accepted and made the best of. It is a waste of time to criticize the inevitable.

It is easy to see how the change has come. One illustration will serve for almost every phase of the cause. In the manufacture of products we have the whole story. It applies to all combinations of human industry, as stimulated and enlarged by the inventions of this scientific age. Formerly articles were manufactured at the domestic hearth or in small shops which formed part of the household. The master and his apprentices worked side by side, the latter living with the master, and therefore subject to the same conditions. When these apprentices rose to be masters, there was little or no change in their mode of life, and they, in turn, educated in the same routine succeeding apprentices. There was, substantially, social equality, and even political equality, for those engaged in industrial pursuits had then little or no political voice in the State.

But the inevitable result of such a mode of manufacture was crude articles at high prices. To-day the world obtains commodities of excellent quality at

---

[1] **Gaius Maecenas (c. 74–8 B.C.E.)**   Wealthy patron to great Roman authors.

prices which even the generation preceding this would have deemed incredible. In the commercial world similar causes have produced similar results, and the race is benefited thereby. The poor enjoy what the rich could not before afford. What were the luxuries have become the necessaries of life. The laborer has now more comforts than the farmer had a few generations ago. The farmer has more luxuries than the landlord had, and is more richly clad and better housed. The landlord has books and pictures rarer, and appointments more artistic, than the King could then obtain.

The price we pay for this salutary change is, no doubt, great. We assemble   5 thousands of operatives in the factory, in the mine, and in the counting-house, of whom the employer can know little or nothing, and to whom the employer is little better than a myth. All intercourse between them is at an end. Rigid Castes are formed, and, as usual, mutual ignorance breeds mutual distrust. Each Caste is without sympathy for the other, and ready to credit anything disparaging in regard to it. Under the law of competition, the employer of thousands is forced into the strictest economies, among which the rates paid to labor figure prominently, and often there is friction between the employer and the employed, between capital and labor, between rich and poor. Human society loses homogeneity.

The price which society pays for the law of competition, like the price it   6 pays for cheap comforts and luxuries, is also great; but the advantages of this law are also greater still, for it is to this law that we owe our wonderful material development, which brings improved conditions in its train. But, whether the law be benign or not, we must say of it, as we say of the change in the conditions of men to which we have referred: it is here; we cannot evade it; no substitutes for it have been found; and while the law may be sometimes hard for the individual, it is best for the race, because it insures the survival of the fittest in every department. We accept and welcome, therefore, as conditions to which we must accommodate ourselves, great inequality of environment, the concentration of business, industrial and commercial, in the hands of a few, and the law of competition between these, as being not only beneficial, but essential for the future progress of the race. Having accepted these, it follows that there must be great scope for the exercise of special ability in the merchant and in the manufacturer who has to conduct affairs upon a great scale. That this talent for organization and management is rare among men is proved by the fact that it invariably secures for its possessor enormous rewards, no matter where or under what laws or conditions. The experienced in affairs always rate the MAN whose services can be obtained as a partner as not only the first consideration, but such as to render the question of his capital scarcely worth considering, for such men soon create capital; while, without the special talent required, capital soon takes wings. Such men become interested in firms or corporations using millions; and estimating only simple interest to be made upon the capital invested, it is inevitable that their income must exceed their expenditures, and that they must accumulate wealth. Nor is there any middle ground which such men can occupy, because the great manufacturing or commercial concern which does not earn at least interest upon its capital soon becomes bankrupt. It must either go forward or fall behind: to stand still is impossible. It is a condition essential for its successful operation that it should be thus far profitable, and even that, in addition to interest on capital, it should make profit. It is a law that men possessed of this peculiar talent for affairs, under the free play of economic forces, must of necessity soon be in receipt of more revenue than can be judiciously expended upon themselves; and this law is as beneficial for the race as the others.

Objections to the foundations upon which society is based are not in order, because the condition of the race is better with these than it has been with any others which have been tried. Of the effect of any new substitutes proposed we cannot be sure. The Socialist or Anarchist who seeks to overturn present conditions is to be regarded as attacking the foundation upon which civilization itself rests, for civilization took its start from the day that the capable, industrious workman said to his incompetent and lazy fellow, "If thou dost not sow, thou shalt not reap," and thus ended primitive Communism by separating the drones from the bees. One who studies this subject will soon be brought face to face with the conclusion that upon the sacredness of property civilization itself depends—the right of the laborer to his hundred dollars in the savings-bank, and equally the legal right of the millionaire to his millions. To those who propose to substitute Communism for this intense Individualism the answer, therefore, is: the race has tried that. All progress from that barbarous day to the present time has resulted from its displacement. Not evil, but good, has come to the race from the accumulation of wealth by those who have the ability and energy that produce it. But even if we admit for a moment that it might be better for the race to discard its present foundation, Individualism—that it is a nobler ideal that man should labor, not for himself alone, but in and for a brotherhood of his fellows, and share with them all in common, realizing Swedenborg's[2] idea of Heaven, where, as he says, the angels derive their happiness, not from laboring for self, but for each other—even admit all this, and a sufficient answer is, This is not evolution, but revolution. It necessitates the changing of human nature itself—a work of aeons, even if it were good to change it, which we cannot know. It is not practicable in our day or in our age. Even if desirable theoretically, it belongs to another and long-succeeding sociological stratum. Our duty is with what is practicable

7

---

[2] **Emanuel Swedenborg (1688–1771)**   A spiritual awakening late in life made him believe he could speak with angels and visit heaven and hell. His book *Heaven and Hell* (1758) was widely read in the nineteenth century and is still influential.

now; with the next step possible in our day and generation. It is criminal to waste our energies in endeavoring to uproot, when all we can profitably or possibly accomplish is to bend the universal tree of humanity a little in the direction most favorable to the production of good fruit under existing circumstances. We might as well urge the destruction of the highest existing type of man because he failed to reach our ideal as to favor the destruction of Individualism, Private Property, the Law of Accumulation of Wealth, and the Law of Competition; for these are the highest results of human experience, the soil in which society so far has produced the best fruit. Unequally or unjustly, perhaps, as these laws sometimes operate, and imperfect as they appear to the Idealist, they are, nevertheless, like the highest type of man, the best and most valuable of all that humanity has yet accomplished.

We start, then, with a condition of affairs under which the best interests of the race are promoted, but which inevitably gives wealth to the few. Thus far, accepting conditions as they exist, the situation can be surveyed and pronounced good. The question then arises—and, if the foregoing be correct, it is the only question with which we have to deal—What is the proper mode of administering wealth after the laws upon which civilization is founded have thrown it into the hands of the few? And it is of this great question that I believe I offer the true solution. It will be understood that *fortunes* are here spoken of, not moderate sums saved by many years of effort, the returns from which are required for the comfortable maintenance and education of families. This is not *wealth*, but only *competence*, which it should be the aim of all to acquire. 8

There are but three modes in which surplus wealth can be disposed of. It can be left to the families of the decedents; or it can be bequeathed for public purposes; or, finally, it can be administered during their lives by its possessors. Under the first and second modes most of the wealth of the world that has reached the few has hitherto been applied. Let us in turn consider each of these modes. The first is the most injudicious. In monarchical countries, the estates and the greatest portion of the wealth are left to the first son, that the vanity of the parent may be gratified by the thought that his name and title are to descend to succeeding generations unimpaired. The condition of this class in Europe to-day teaches the futility of such hopes or ambitions. The successors have become impoverished through their follies or from the fall in the value of land. Even in Great Britain the strict law of entail[3] has been found inadequate to maintain the status of an hereditary class. Its soil is rapidly passing into the hands of the stranger. Under republican institutions the division of property among the children is much fairer, but the question which forces 9

---

[3] **Law of entail**   A law designed to restrict inheritance to only the heirs of the family who owns the property.

itself upon thoughtful men in all lands is: Why should men leave great fortunes to their children? If this is done from affection, is it not misguided affection? Observation teaches that, generally speaking, it is not well for the children that they should be so burdened. Neither is it well for the state. Beyond providing for the wife and daughters moderate sources of income, and very moderate allowances indeed, if any, for the sons, men may well hesitate, for it is no longer questionable that great sums bequeathed oftener work more for the injury than for the good of the recipients. Wise men will soon conclude that, for the best interests of the members of their families and of the state, such bequests are an improper use of their means.

It is not suggested that men who have failed to educate their sons to earn   10
a livelihood shall cast them adrift in poverty. If any man has seen fit to rear his sons with a view to their living idle lives, or, what is highly commendable, has instilled in them the sentiment that they are in a position to labor for public ends without reference to pecuniary considerations, then, of course, the duty of the parent is to see that such are provided for *in moderation*. There are instances of millionaires' sons unspoiled by wealth, who, being rich, still perform great services in the community. Such are the very salt of the earth, as valuable as, unfortunately, they are rare; still it is not the exception, but the rule, that men must regard, and, looking at the usual result of enormous sums conferred upon legatees, the thoughtful man must shortly say, "I would as soon leave to my son a curse as the almighty dollar," and admit to himself that it is not the welfare of the children, but family pride, which inspires these enormous legacies.

As to the second mode, that of leaving wealth at death for public uses, it   11
may be said that this is only a means for the disposal of wealth, provided a man is content to wait until he is dead before it becomes of much good in the world. Knowledge of the results of legacies bequeathed is not calculated to inspire the brightest hopes of much posthumous good being accomplished. The cases are not few in which the real object sought by the testator is not attained, nor are they few in which his real wishes are thwarted. In many cases the bequests are so used as to become only monuments of his folly. It is well to remember that it requires the exercise of not less ability than that which acquired the wealth to use it so as to be really beneficial to the community. Besides this, it may fairly be said that no man is to be extolled for doing what he cannot help doing, nor is he to be thanked by the community to which he only leaves wealth at death. Men who leave vast sums in this way may fairly be thought men who would not have left it at all had they been able to take it with them. The memories of such cannot be held in grateful remembrance, for there is no grace in their gifts. It is not to be wondered at that such bequests seem so generally to lack the blessing.

The growing disposition to tax more and more heavily large estates left at   12
death is a cheering indication of the growth of a salutary change in public opinion. The State of Pennsylvania now takes—subject to some exceptions— one-tenth of

the property left by its citizens. The budget presented in the British Parliament the other day proposes to increase the death-duties; and, most significant of all, the new tax is to be a graduated one. Of all forms of taxation, this seems the wisest. Men who continue hoarding great sums all their lives, the proper use of which for public ends would work good to the community, should be made to feel that the community, in the form of the state, cannot thus be deprived of its proper share. By taxing estates heavily at death the state marks its condemnation of the selfish millionaire's unworthy life.

It is desirable that nations should go much further in this direction. Indeed, it is difficult to set bounds to the share of a rich man's estate which should go at his death to the public through the agency of the state, and by all means such taxes should be graduated, beginning at nothing upon moderate sums to dependents, and increasing rapidly as the amounts swell, until of the millionaire's hoard, as of Shylock's,[4] at least

> —The other half
> Comes to the privy coffer of the state.

This policy would work powerfully to induce the rich man to attend to the administration of wealth during his life, which is the end that society should always have in view, as being that by far most fruitful for the people. Nor need it be feared that this policy would sap the root of enterprise and render men less anxious to accumulate, for to the class whose ambition it is to leave great fortunes and be talked about after their death, it will attract even more attention, and, indeed, be a somewhat nobler ambition to have enormous sums paid over to the state from their fortunes.

There remains, then, only one mode of using great fortunes; but in this we have the true antidote for the temporary unequal distribution of wealth, the reconciliation of the rich and the poor—a reign of harmony—another ideal, differing, indeed, from that of the Communist in requiring only the further evolution of existing conditions, not the total overthrow of our civilization. It is founded upon the present most intense individualism, and the race is prepared to put it in practice by degrees whenever it pleases. Under its sway we shall have an ideal state, in which the surplus wealth of the few will become, in the best sense, the property of the many, because administered for the common good, and this wealth, passing through the hands of the few, can be made a much more potent force for the elevation of our race than if it had been distributed in small sums to the people themselves. Even the poorest can be made to see this, and to agree that great sums gathered by some of their fellow-citizens and spent for public purposes, from which the masses reap the principal benefit, are more valuable

---

[4] **Shylock**   The moneylender and title character in Shakespeare's *The Merchant of Venice.*

to them than if scattered among them through the course of many years in trifling amounts.

If we consider what results flow from the Cooper Institute,[5] for instance, to   15
the best portion of the race in New York not possessed of means, and compare these with those which would have arisen for the good of the masses from an equal sum distributed by Mr. Cooper in his lifetime in the form of wages, which is the highest form of distribution, being for work done and not for charity, we can form some estimate of the possibilities for the improvement of the race which lie embedded in the present law of the accumulation of wealth. Much of this sum, if distributed in small quantities among the people, would have been wasted in the indulgence of appetite, some of it in excess, and it may be doubted whether even the part put to the best use, that of adding to the comforts of the home, would have yielded results for the race, as a race, at all comparable to those which are flowing and are to flow from the Cooper Institute from generation to generation. Let the advocate of violent or radical change ponder well this thought.

We might even go so far as to take another instance, that of Mr. Tilden's   16
bequest of five millions of dollars for a free library in the city of New York, but in referring to this one cannot help saying involuntarily, How much better if Mr. Tilden[6] had devoted the last years of his own life to the proper administration of this immense sum; in which case neither legal contest nor any other cause of delay could have interfered with his aims. But let us assume that Mr. Tilden's millions finally become the means of giving to New York a noble public library, where the treasures of the world contained in books will be open to all forever, without money and without price. Considering the good of that part of the race which congregates in and around Manhattan Island, would its permanent benefit have been better promoted had these millions been allowed to circulate in small sums through the hands of the masses? Even the most strenuous advocate of Communism must entertain a doubt upon this subject. Most of those who think will probably entertain no doubt whatever.

Poor and restricted are our opportunities in this life; narrow our horizon;   17
our best work most imperfect; but rich men should be thankful for one inestimable boon. They have it in their power during their lives to busy themselves in organizing benefactions from which the masses of their fellows will derive lasting advantage, and thus dignify their own lives. The highest life is probably to be reached, not by such imitation of the life of Christ as Count Tolstoi[7] gives us,

---

[5] **Cooper Institute**   Now Cooper Union, founded in 1858 by Peter Cooper as a free school for the sciences and the arts.

[6] **Samuel Tilden (1814–1886)**   He bequeathed $4 million to found the New York Public Library after he died. His will was contested and only $3 million was given to found the library.

[7] **Leo Tolstoy (1828–1910)**   Author of *War and Peace* and *Anna Karenina*. Tolstoy lived a spare and simple life in his old age.

but, while animated by Christ's spirit, by recognizing the changed conditions of this age, and adopting modes of expressing this spirit suitable to the changed conditions under which we live; still laboring for the good of our fellows, which was the essence of his life and teaching, but laboring in a different manner.

This, then, is held to be the duty of the man of Wealth: first, to set an example of modest, unostentatious living, shunning display or extravagance; to provide moderately for the legitimate wants of those dependent upon him; and after doing so to consider all surplus revenues which come to him simply as trust funds, which he is called upon to administer, and strictly bound as a matter of duty to administer in the manner which, in his judgment, is best calculated to produce the most beneficial results for the community—the man of wealth thus becoming the mere agent and trustee for his poorer brethren, bringing to their service his superior wisdom, experience, and ability to administer, doing for them better than they would or could do for themselves.

We are met here with the difficulty of determining what are moderate sums to leave to members of the family; what is modest, unostentatious living; what is the test of extravagance. There must be different standards for different conditions. The answer is that it is as impossible to name exact amounts or actions as it is to define good manners, good taste, or the rules of propriety; but, nevertheless, these are verities, well known although undefinable. Public sentiment is quick to know and to feel what offends these. So in the case of wealth. The rule in regard to good taste in the dress of men or women applies here. Whatever makes one conspicuous offends the canon. If any family be chiefly known for display, for extravagance in home, table, equipage, for enormous sums ostentatiously spent in any form upon itself—if these be its chief distinctions, we have no difficulty in estimating its nature or culture. So likewise in regard to the use or abuse of its surplus wealth, or to generous, free-handed cooperation in good public uses, or to unabated efforts to accumulate and hoard to the last, whether they administer or bequeath. The verdict rests with the best and most enlightened public sentiment. The community will surely judge, and its judgments will not often be wrong.

The best uses to which surplus wealth can be put have already been indicated. Those who would administer wisely must, indeed, be wise, for one of the serious obstacles to the improvement of our race is indiscriminate charity. It were better for mankind that the millions of the rich were thrown into the sea than so spent as to encourage the slothful, the drunken, the unworthy. Of every thousand dollars spent in so-called charity to-day, it is probable that $950 is unwisely spent; so spent, indeed, as to produce the very evils which it proposes to mitigate or cure. A well-known writer of philosophic books admitted the other day that he had given a quarter of a dollar to a man who approached him as he was coming to visit the house of his friend. He knew nothing of the habits of this beggar; knew not the use that would be made of this money, although he had every reason to suspect that it would be spent improperly. This man professed to be a disciple of Herbert Spencer;[8] yet the quarter-dollar given that night will probably work more injury than all the money which its thoughtless donor will ever be able to give in true charity will do good. He only gratified his own feelings, saved himself from annoyance—and this was probably one of the most selfish and very worst actions of his life, for in all respects he is most worthy.

In bestowing charity, the main consideration should be to help those who will help themselves; to provide part of the means by which those who desire to improve may do so; to give those who desire to rise the aids by which they may rise; to assist, but rarely or never to do all. Neither the individual nor the race is improved by alms-giving. Those worthy of assistance, except in rare cases, seldom require assistance. The really valuable men of the race never do, except in cases of accident or sudden change. Every one has, of course, cases of individuals brought to his own knowledge where temporary assistance can do genuine good, and these he will not overlook. But the amount which can be wisely given by the individual for individuals is necessarily limited by his lack of knowledge of the circumstances connected with each. He is the only true reformer who is as careful and as anxious not to aid the unworthy as he is to aid the worthy, and, perhaps, even more so, for in alms-giving more injury is probably done by rewarding vice than by relieving virtue. 21

The rich man is thus almost restricted to following the examples of Peter Cooper, Enoch Pratt of Baltimore, Mr. Pratt of Brooklyn, Senator Stanford,[9] and others, who know that the best means of benefiting the community is to place within its reach the ladders upon which the aspiring can rise—parks, and means of recreation, by which men are helped in body and mind; works of art, certain to give pleasure and improve the public taste; and public institutions of various kinds, which will improve the general condition of the people—in this manner returning their surplus wealth to the mass of their fellows in the forms best calculated to do them lasting good. 22

Thus is the problem of Rich and Poor to be solved. The laws of accumulation will be left free; the laws of distribution free. Individualism will continue, but the millionaire will be but a trustee for the poor; intrusted for a season with a great part of the increased wealth of the community, but administering it for the community far better than it could or would have done for itself. The best minds will thus have reached a stage in the development of the race in which it is clearly seen that there is no mode of disposing of surplus wealth creditable to thoughtful and earnest men into whose hands it flows save by using it year by year for the general good. This day already dawns. But a little while, and although, without 23

---

[8] **Herbert Spencer (1820–1903)**   British philosopher who applied Darwinian theories of evolution to the social sciences.

[9] **Peter Cooper (1791–1883), Enoch Pratt (1808–1896), Charles Pratt (1830–1891), Leland Stanford (1824–1893)**   All were prominent millionaires and eventual philanthropists, three of whom founded universities.

incurring the pity of their fellows, men may die sharers in great business enterprises from which their capital cannot be or has not been withdrawn, and is left chiefly at death for public uses, yet the man who dies leaving behind him millions of available wealth, which was his to administer during life, will pass away "unwept, unhonored, and unsung," no matter to what uses he leaves the dross which he cannot take with him. Of such as these the public verdict will then be: "The man who dies thus rich dies disgraced."

Such, in my opinion, is the true Gospel concerning Wealth, obedience to   24
which is destined some day to solve the problem of the Rich and the Poor, and to bring "Peace on earth, among men Good-Will."

❚❚ QUESTIONS FOR CRITICAL READING

1. What do you see as the problem of wealth in this age?

2. What were the conditions of production in the age prior to Carnegie's (para. 3)?

3. What was wrong with the products of the age prior to Carnegie's?

4. What is the law of competition? Is it still at work today? Is it a law?

5. Is conformity an important issue for Carnegie? Is he for or against it?

6. How great are the inequalities of wealth in this country today?

7. Why does Carnegie take a hard line on charity? What is your view on charity today?

8. In paragraph 7, Carnegie refers to the "highest existing type of man." Whom do you think he is referring to? Whom would you mean if you used that term?

❚❚ SUGGESTIONS FOR CRITICAL WRITING

1. Is it true that today the "poor enjoy what the rich could not before afford" (para. 4)? What do the poor enjoy today that the rich could not have enjoyed in 1889? To what extent are the things and conditions the poor enjoy now the result of the laws of competition and accumulation that Carnegie says operate in our civilization and make such enjoyment possible? If you feel that Carnegie is right in his contention about the production of benefits for the poor, do you then feel yourself inclined to agree with Carnegie in general?

2. What would Carnegie say about the great inequalities of wealth in this country today? In his time, about 1 percent of the population controlled half the wealth. Today, it is about 3 percent. One person in the United States whose wealth could compare with Carnegie's is Bill Gates, and his fortune is about half of Carnegie's in today's dollars. Would Carnegie feel things are getting better or that conditions are so different that there is no comparison with his age? What would his advice be to those with great wealth today?

3. One of Carnegie's important ideas is that societies evolve in the manner that life on earth evolves. He uses the term "survival of the fittest" (para. 6) and lauds the system in economics that permits competition to weed out the weak and reward the strong. Social Darwinism, which is the theory Carnegie talks about, was very popular in the late 1800s. Learn what you can about the idea and determine whether or not Carnegie is following the main line of social Darwinism or if he is changing the idea to suit himself. After you have done some research, answer this question: Is Carnegie right in what he proposes for the progress of civilization?

4. In paragraphs 6 and 7, Carnegie explains what kind of person will rise to great wealth, enumerating that person's qualities and establishing that such persons are rare enough to be worthy of great reward. He also argues against any criticism of his point of view by talking about how communism would be detrimental to society. He says, "Not evil, but good, has come to the race from the accumulation of wealth by those who have the ability and energy that produce it" (para. 7). Examine his arguments in these paragraphs and decide whether or not he is correct and explain why.

5. Carnegie gave away most of his wealth to support projects he felt would benefit the community. He built over 2,500 libraries, endowed many parks, and gave money to universities and other foundations that he thought would "improve the race." Assuming that you had unlimited wealth to give away, what would your priorities be? Do you approve of Carnegie's priorities, or do you feel they are not appropriate for today's communities? What would you want your wealth to achieve in our world?

6. **CONNECTIONS**   By using the word *Gospel* in his title, Carnegie implies that he follows an ethical and moral pattern in his life and in his attitude toward society. With which of the authors in Part Three, "Ethics and Morality," would Carnegie most sympathize? Which authors(s) would question his recommendations regarding the use of wealth? Imagine one of these writers writing to Carnegie about *The Gospel of Wealth*. What would that author praise and what would he or she condemn? Would that author be likely to regard Carnegie as a hero or as a misguided do-gooder? Is Carnegie really interested in questions of morality and ethical behavior?

7. **CONNECTIONS**   Andrew Carnegie's essay exemplifies the laissez-faire economic policies of his era. The Friedmans might have held Carnegie up as proof that their theories work, and work well (p. 400). Assuming that you choose to defend the arguments of the Friedmans for a free and open economic system, write an essay that establishes Carnegie's career and achievements as the best model for their economic views. What benefits to the individual and what benefits to the general society would the Friedmans say Carnegie has produced? What would Carnegie most appreciate about the Friedmans' arguments for equality and liberty? How convinced are you that the Friedmans

and Carnegie have the right ideas about how society should manage economic opportunity?

8. **CONNECTIONS** F. A. Hayek (p. 386) was not a wealthy man, but his theories can be considered as giving some support for the principles that Andrew Carnegie raises in *The Gospel of Wealth*. Which of their ideas seem to be most in agreement about how a nation's economy should work? What are their views on money and wealth? What are their views on poverty and the question of equal distribution of a nation's wealth? Both of these writers construct an argument in favor of similar positions. How effective are their arguments? How does your thinking change after having studied their positions?

JOHN
MAYNARD
KEYNES

The End of
Laissez-Faire

J OHN MAYNARD KEYNES (1883–1946) became one of the most influential economists in modern times after his extraordinary analyses of economic decisions following World War I. He advised the British government from this time until after World War II. His advice to the United States government was responsible for policies that helped to restore economic prosperity in postwar Europe.

His first famous book, *The Economic Consequences of the Peace* (1919), was written after he left his official position with the government in Britain during negotiations leading to the Treaty of Versailles. That document clarified the political and economic terms of the surrender of Germany and its allies at the end of World War I. Keynes was outraged by the plans demanding reparations from Germany for damages caused by the war, and he was especially appalled at the behavior of President Woodrow Wilson, whom he regarded as both ignorant and hypocritical. The publication of *The Economic Consequences of the Peace* immediately established him not only as the most original economic mind of his generation but also as a kind of prophet. He pointed out that the economic strictures imposed on Germany would produce economic collapse and social disorder. Like many others, he was fearful that Germany might become Communist — as Karl Marx predicted it would — as had Russia during a period of war and social upheaval.

His views were prophetic, but his analysis of the situation in Germany was not completely accurate. He felt that the Treaty of Versailles had been motivated by political and military considerations and that it had ignored the impact of economic issues. This he feared would lead to collapse, and to an extent it did. But the fact is that Britain and France had modified their demands for reparations, and the economic conditions of most Germans before the Great Depression of 1929 were not as bad as he had predicted they would be.

From *Essays in Persuasion.*

"The End of Laissez-Faire" was written before the Great Depression and in anticipation of important changes in the nature of modern democratic capitalism. With Great Britain and other European nations bearing immense debts after World War I, certain radical "socialist" moves, such as the nationalization of the mines, were being proposed in Britain as the socialist Labour party gained power.

Laissez-faire is a policy on the part of government to leave business alone to do what it will, including committing various abuses of the kind that Marx complained of. If a government will not regulate business, then government must let it go; Keynes realized that the period of unregulated business was over. Socialism implies complete control of an economic system and of business; although this occurred to a large degree in Britain after World War II, at the time Keynes wrote the country was not yet ready for such socialization. But the essay, as he said later, was prophetic.

One of his chief points was that the corporation served as an intermediate structure between the state and the individual, and thus corporate groups might best represent the interests of both. Certainly, as Keynes explained, the problems of the economy are beyond the power of the individual to control. Corporations are, he noted, "a mode of government," and a more manageable mode than the state itself. However, he also pointed out that management of corporations is rarely responsible to the owners of its capital, the shareholders, in a direct way. Indeed, corporations sometimes downplay the individual interest so that they appear to be socializing themselves.

Keynes, like Marx and Reich, saw an evolutionary pattern to economics. He expressed this in part by looking backward to the corporate structures of guilds and abbeys in the medieval period and forward to what he called a "natural line of evolution," with socialism winning out "against unlimited private profit." Keynes interpreted the kind of changes that were occurring as the end of laissez-faire but also as a continuation of some qualities of laissez-faire — those qualities that stimulated the growth of wealth, such as individual initiative.

KEYNES'S RHETORIC

Keynes's technique is based on a principle of separating issues into two parts. He begins the essay with a quick analysis of whether or not the policies of laissez-faire — doing economically as you will with regard only to personal profit — are a God-given right. Then he moves to the question of what the state ought to be doing in regard to managing an economic system. He refers to Jeremy Bentham's terms: *Agenda* and *Non-Agenda*. These translate into what government should do versus what it should not do. Then he moves to the proposition that people should begin to rely on "forms of Government within a Democracy" that can actually accomplish what is on the agenda. These forms center on the corporation. At that point (para. 3), the discussion focuses on two examples: first, the nature of the corporation; and second, the distinctions between the social and the individual aspects of the agenda (para. 9).

Within each of these two relatively brief discussions, Keynes offers analyses of the economic situations he knows best. He examines socialism in some detail, then examines the state in relation to the individual. He sees that the powerful individual can serve society badly and that some kind of regulation may be essential. To Keynes, such regulation falls short of socialism. He is intent on assuring the reader that whatever government does, it should be something that the individual is not doing. In this way, government will have a chance of being effective without displacing individual initiative.

Keynes's primary rhetorical stance is analytic. He examines an element, weighs it, compares it with other elements, then makes a pronouncement on its value and potential effectiveness. His was one of the most comprehensive and farseeing minds of our time.

⬛ PREREADING QUESTIONS: WHAT TO READ FOR

The following prereading questions may help you anticipate key issues in the discussion of John Maynard Keynes's "The End of Laissez-Faire." Keeping them in mind during your first reading of the selection should help focus your attention.

1. What does the end of laissez-faire mean for business?
2. What is the agenda of government?
3. How does Keynes regard the force of socialism in his time?

The End of Laissez-Faire

Let us clear from the ground the metaphysical or general principles upon which, from time to time, *laissez-faire*[1] has been founded. It is *not* true that individuals possess a prescriptive "natural liberty" in their economic activities. There is *no* "compact" conferring perpetual rights on those who Have or on those who Acquire. The world is *not* so governed from above that private and social interest always coincide. It is *not* so managed here below that in practice they coincide. It is *not* a correct deduction from the Principles of Economics that enlightened self-interest always operates in the public interest. Nor is it true that self-interest generally *is* enlightened; more often individuals acting separately to promote their own ends are too ignorant or too weak to attain even these. Experience does *not* show that individuals, when they make up a social unit, are always less clear-sighted than when they act separately.

1

---

[1] *laissez-faire*   An economic environment in which government leaves businesses unregulated and unrestrained.

We cannot, therefore, settle on abstract grounds, but must handle on its merits in detail, what Burke[2] termed "one of the finest problems in legislation, namely, to determine what the State ought to take upon itself to direct by the public wisdom, and what it ought to leave, with as little interference as possible, to individual exertion." We have to discriminate between what Bentham,[3] in his forgotten but useful nomenclature, used to term *Agenda* and *Non-Agenda*, and to do this without Bentham's prior presumption that interference is at the same time, "generally needless" and "generally pernicious."[4] Perhaps the chief task of Economists at this hour is to distinguish afresh the *Agenda* of Government from the *Non-Agenda*; and the companion task of Politics is to devise forms of Government within a Democracy which shall be capable of accomplishing the *Agenda*. I will illustrate what I have in mind by two examples.

(1) I believe that in many cases the ideal size for the unit of control and organization lies somewhere between the individual and the modern State. I suggest, therefore, that progress lies in the growth and the recognition of semiautonomous bodies within the State—bodies whose criterion of action within their own field is solely the public good as they understand it, and from whose deliberations motives of private advantage are excluded, though some place it may still be necessary to leave, until the ambit of men's altruism grows wider, to the separate advantage of particular groups, classes, or faculties—bodies which in the ordinary course of affairs are mainly autonomous within their prescribed limitations, but are subject in the last resort to the sovereignty of the democracy expressed through Parliament.

I propose a return, it may be said, towards mediaeval conceptions of separate autonomies. But, in England at any rate, corporations are a mode of government which has never ceased to be important and is sympathetic to our institutions. It is easy to give examples, from what already exists, of separate autonomies which have attained or are approaching the mode I designate—the Universities, the Bank of England, the Port of London Authority, even perhaps the Railway Companies.

But more interesting than these is the trend of Joint Stock Institutions, when they have reached a certain age and size, to approximate to the status of public corporations rather than that of individualistic private enterprise. One of the most interesting and unnoticed developments of recent decades has been

2

3

4

5

---

[2] **Edmund Burke (1729–1797)**   Anglo-Irish statesman who wrote *Reflections on the French Revolution* (1790). His views were influential in causing Britain not to support the Revolution.

[3] **Jeremy Bentham (1748–1832)**   English philosopher, whose *Introduction to the Principles and Morals of Legislation* (1789) with its notion of "the greatest happiness for the greatest number" was a major influence on English law in the mid-nineteenth century.

[4] Bentham's *Manual of Political Economy*, published posthumously, in Bowring's edition (1843). [Keynes's note]

the tendency of big enterprise to socialize itself. A point arrives in the growth of a big institution—particularly a big railway or big public utility enterprise, but also a big bank or a big insurance company—at which the owners of the capital, i.e., the shareholders, are almost entirely dissociated from the management, with the result that the direct personal interest of the latter in the making of great profit becomes quite secondary. When this stage is reached, the general stability and reputation of the institution are more considered by the management than the maximum of profit for the shareholders. The shareholders must be satisfied by conventionally adequate dividends; but once this is secured, the direct interest of the management often consists in avoiding criticism from the public and from the customers of the concern. This is particularly the case if their great size or semimonopolistic position renders them conspicuous in the public eye and vulnerable to public attack. The extreme instance, perhaps, of this tendency in the case of an institution, theoretically the unrestricted property of private persons, is the Bank of England. It is almost true to say that there is no class of persons in the Kingdom of whom the Governor of the Bank of England thinks less when he decides on his policy than of his shareholders. Their rights, in excess of their conventional dividend, have already sunk to the neighborhood of zero. But the same thing is partly true of many other big institutions. They are, as time goes on, socializing themselves.

Not that this is unmixed gain. The same causes promote conservatism and a waning of enterprise. In fact, we already have in these cases many of the faults as well as the advantages of State Socialism. Nevertheless we see here, I think, a natural line of evolution. The battle of Socialism against unlimited private profit is being won in detail hour by hour. In these particular fields—it remains acute elsewhere—this is no longer the pressing problem. There is, for instance, no so-called important political question so really unimportant, so irrelevant to the reorganization of the economic life of Great Britain, as the Nationalization of the Railways.   6

It is true that many big undertakings, particularly Public Utility enterprises and other business requiring a large fixed capital, still need to be semi-socialized. But we must keep our minds flexible regarding the forms of this semisocialism. We must take full advantage of the natural tendencies of the day, and we must probably prefer semiautonomous corporations to organs of the Central Government for which Ministers of State are directly responsible.   7

I criticize doctrinaire State Socialism, not because it seeks to engage men's altruistic impulses in the service of Society, or because it departs from *laissez-faire*, or because it takes away from man's natural liberty to make a million, or because it has courage for bold experiments. All these things I applaud. I criticize it because it misses the significance of what is actually happening; because it is, in fact, little better than a dusty survival of a plan to meet the problems of fifty years ago, based on a misunderstanding of what some one   8 said a hundred years ago. Nineteenth-century State Socialism sprang from Bentham, free competition, etc., and is in some respects a clearer, in some respects a more muddled, version of just the same philosophy as underlies nineteenth-century individualism. Both equally laid all their stress on freedom, the one negatively to avoid limitations on existing freedom, the other positively to destroy natural or acquired monopolies. They are different reactions to the same intellectual atmosphere.

(2) I come next to a criterion of *Agenda* which is particularly relevant to what it is urgent and desirable to do in the near future. We must aim at separating those services which are *technically social* from those which are *technically individual*. The most important *Agenda* of the State relate not to those activities which private individuals are already fulfilling, but to those functions which fall outside the sphere of the individual, to those decisions which are made by *no one* if the State does not make them. The important thing for Government is not to do things which individuals are doing already, and to do them a little better or a little worse; but to do those things which at present are not done at all.

It is not within the scope of my purpose on this occasion to develop practical policies. I limit myself, therefore, to naming some instances of what I mean from among those problems about which I happen to have thought most.

Many of the greatest economic evils of our time are fruits of risk, uncertainty, and ignorance. It is because particular individuals, fortunate in situation or in abilities, are able to take advantage of uncertainty and ignorance, and also because for the same reason big business is often a lottery, that great inequalities of wealth come about; and these same factors are also the cause of the Unemployment of Labor, or the disappointment of reasonable business expectations, and of the impairment of efficiency and production. Yet the cure lies outside the operations of individuals; it may even be to the interest of individuals to aggravate the disease. I believe that the cure for these things is partly to be sought in the deliberate control of the currency and of credit by a central institution, and partly in the collection and dissemination on a great scale of data relating to the business situation, including the full publicity, by law if necessary, of all business facts which it is useful to know. These measures would involve Society in exercizing directive intelligence through some appropriate organ of action over many of the inner intricacies of private business, yet it would leave private initiative and enterprise unhindered. Even if these measures prove insufficient, nevertheless they will furnish us with better knowledge than we have now for taking the next step.

My second example relates to Savings and Investment. I believe that some co-ordinated act of intelligent judgment is required as to the scale on which it is desirable that the community as a whole should save, the scale on which these savings should go abroad in the form of foreign investments, and whether the present organization of the investment market distributes savings along the most nationally productive channels. I do not think that these matters should be left entirely to the chances of private judgment and private profits, as they are at present.

My third example concerns Population. The time has already come when each country needs a considered national policy about what size of Population, whether larger or smaller than at present or the same, is most expedient. And having settled this policy, we must take steps to carry it into operation. The time may arrive a little later when the community as a whole must pay attention to the innate quality as well as to the mere numbers of its future members.   13

These reflections have been directed towards possible improvements in the technique of modern Capitalism by the agency of collective action. There is nothing in them which is seriously incompatible with what seems to me to be the essential characteristic of Capitalism, namely the dependence upon an intense appeal to the money-making and money-loving instincts of individuals as the main motive force of the economic machine. Nor must I, so near to my end, stray towards other fields. Nevertheless, I may do well to remind you, in conclusion, that the fiercest contests and the most deeply felt divisions of opinion are likely to be waged in the coming years not round technical questions, where the arguments on either side are mainly economic, but round those which, for want of better words, may be called psychological or, perhaps, moral.   14

In Europe, or at least in some parts of Europe — but not, I think, in the United States of America — there is a latent reaction, somewhat widespread, against basing Society to the extent that we do upon fostering, encouraging, and protecting the money-motives of individuals. A preference for arranging our affairs in such a way as to appeal to the money-motive as little as possible, rather than as much as possible, need not be entirely *a priori*, but may be based on the comparison of experiences. Different persons, according to their choice of profession, find the money-motive playing a large or a small part in their daily lives, and historians can tell us about other phases of social organization in which this motive has played a much smaller part than it does now. Most religions and most philosophies deprecate, to say the least of it, a way of life mainly influenced by considerations of personal money profit. On the other hand, most men today reject ascetic notions and do not doubt the real advantages of wealth. Moreover it seems obvious to them that one cannot do without the money-motive, and that, apart from certain admitted abuses, it does its job well. In the result the average man averts his attention from the problem, and has no clear idea what he really thinks and feels about the whole confounded matter.   15

Confusion of thought and feeling leads to confusion of speech. Many people, who are really objecting to Capitalism as a way of life, argue as though they were objecting to it on the ground of its inefficiency in attaining its own   16 objects. Contrariwise, devotees of Capitalism are often unduly conservative, and reject reforms in its technique, which might really strengthen and preserve it, for fear that they may prove to be first steps away from Capitalism itself. Nevertheless a time may be coming when we shall get clearer than at present as to when we are talking about Capitalism as an efficient or inefficient technique, and when we are talking about it as desirable or objectionable in itself. For my part, I think that Capitalism, wisely managed, can probably be made more efficient for attaining economic ends than any alternative system yet in sight, but that in itself it is in many ways extremely objectionable. Our problem is to work out a social organization which shall be as efficient as possible without offending our notions of a satisfactory way of life.

The next step forward must come, not from political agitation or prema-   17
ture experiments, but from thought. We need by an effort of the mind to elucidate our own feelings. At present our sympathy and our judgment are liable to be on different sides, which is a painful and paralysing state of mind. In the field of action reformers will not be successful until they can steadily pursue a clear and definite object with their intellects and their feelings in tune. There is no party in the world at present which appears to me to be pursuing right aims by right methods. Material Poverty provides the incentive to change precisely in situations where there is very little margin for experiments. Material Prosperity removes the incentive just when it might be safe to take a chance. Europe lacks the means, America the will, to make a move. We need a new set of convictions which spring naturally from a candid examination of our own inner feelings in relation to the outside facts.

⚒ QUESTIONS FOR CRITICAL READING

1. Does the economic future seem to have been especially uncertain in 1926, when Keynes wrote this essay?

2. How would you explain the meaning of "laissez-faire" to someone unfamiliar with the term?

3. Why does Keynes feel it is beyond his scope to "develop practical policies"? What is one practical policy he might have developed?

4. Is a corporation a form of government? Should it be?

5. According to Keynes, what economic rights does an individual have in terms of making a great deal of money?

6. On which points do you find yourself in disagreement with Keynes? On which points do you agree with him?

7. What does Keynes mean by the terms *Agenda* and *Non-Agenda*?

8. Under what conditions does Keynes believe it is necessary for a nation to control the quantity and quality of its population (para. 13)?

⚡ SUGGESTIONS FOR CRITICAL WRITING

1. Keynes distinguishes between the role of government and the role of the individual in the economy. When he says that he does not want government to perform those functions that individuals are already performing, he implies that individuals are leaving undone much that would improve the economy. What would you recommend that your government do today that individuals are currently not doing? And how would the government's actions benefit the economy?

2. In paragraph 8, Keynes refers to man's "natural liberty to make a million." Do you believe that such a liberty exists and if so, that it is natural? What are the results of such a liberty, and how could any government guarantee it?

3. Which services are technically social and technically individual in economics? That is, what can you do as an individual that government either cannot or will not do? In what senses can these two services conflict, and how can such conflict create an unhealthy economic situation? Have you had any experience of such a conflict?

4. How do you feel about the nature of the corporation as a government of sorts? Do you think it is as good a development as Keynes seems to feel it is? Is this development in any way a substitute for government? In reading the business section of your newspaper, do you see evidence of corporate activity that can be in any way interpreted as governmental? Is the result desirable? Is it the result Keynes seems to have hoped for?

5. In paragraph 12, Keynes reminds us that the extent to which individuals save money affects the general health of the economy. He says he believes that "a co-ordinated act of intelligent judgment" is required to establish a national policy of savings. The United States has long been behind nations such as Japan in terms of the individual's goal to save. Do you feel that the government should intervene in the lives of individuals and determine how much they should save? How could any government achieve that end?

6. **CONNECTIONS**   Karl Marx (p. 335) was especially opposed to the style of capitalism Keynes called laissez-faire, in which capitalists were free to exploit labor and economic conditions for their personal benefit. Do Keynes's views parallel those of Marx in *The Communist Manifesto*? Cite the main issues of agreement and disagreement and argue a case for or against Keynes as a potential follower of Karl Marx.

7. **CONNECTIONS**   F. A. Hayek (p. 386) rejects socialism out of hand as an instrument of oppression. How does John Maynard Keynes treat the idea of socialism? What seem to be the differences in Keynes's and Hayek's views of what socialism is and how it affects a capitalist society? Keynes mentions "semisocialism" in paragraph 7 and then discusses socialism more fully beginning with paragraph 8. How do these writers affect your attitudes toward socialism?

8. In "The End of Laissez-Faire," published in 1926, Keynes writes, "Most religions and most philosophies deprecate, to say the least of it, a way of life mainly influenced by considerations of personal money profit" (para. 15). Clarify what Keynes says about the "money-motive" in society. He talks about "protecting the money-motives of individuals" (para. 15). What is our current view on protecting the money motives of business people today? What is the current view of religious groups about money motives? Do religions deplore such motives as much now as they did in 1926? What is your view on protecting the money motives of other people?

© Hulton-Deutsch Collection/Corbis

F. A.
HAYEK

Economic Control and Totalitarianism

F. A. HAYEK (1899–1992) was born in Vienna, Austria, and served in the artillery in World War I. His experience in the army and then in postwar Vienna, which suffered in an economic collapse, shaped much of his later life. He entered the University of Vienna at age nineteen and took a doctorate in law in 1921 and a doctorate in politics in 1923. At the time, the University of Vienna was one of the best places to study economics. Hayek carried the theories of "The Austrian School" to the London School of Economics, where he gave a series of lectures on the theory of money. As a result of these successful appearances, he became visiting professor and, a year later, was awarded a professorial chair.

His lectures were published as *Prices and Production* (1931) and represented a criticism of some of the theories in John Maynard Keynes's 1930 publication, *A Treatise on Money*. Hayek's critical review of Keynes's book resulted in a public dispute between him and Keynes, whose economic ideas were the most important in England and America in the years before the war. Keynes's theories on money and public spending during economic downturns are still favored by many economists to this day. Hayek's contemporary influence is seen in the rejection of socialist policies by capitalist countries. Early in his career, Hayek favored a version of laissez-faire economics, by which he meant very low government regulation and a rejection of planned economies.

Even though they disputed vigorously, Hayek and Keynes became friends and worked together during the Great Depression to develop economic models that would benefit the recovery in England and elsewhere. Hayek's desire to help the people who suffer most from severe depression carried over from his years in postwar Vienna. His training in law and politics bore fruit in his work in economics. Hayek's most popular book, *The Road to Serfdom*, was published by the University of Chicago Press in 1944. His critique of the developments in Germany in the 1930s, when National Socialism (Nazism) developed into a totalitarian government, led him to condemn planned economies and socialist programs.

From *The Road to Serfdom*.

During World War II, Hayek offered his services to the British government to use his fluency in German to produce propaganda. He was refused and spent the war years teaching in London. Because he was an alien — even though he had become a British subject in 1938 — he could not serve in any military or intelligence capacity.

The University of Chicago Press also published Hayek's *The Pure Theory of Capital* in 1941 and *Individualism and Economic Order* in 1948. In 1950, Hayek left London to join the School of Social Thought at the University of Chicago, where he stayed until 1961, after which he retired to Freiburg, Germany. While at Chicago, he published a great deal on many subjects in philosophy, economics, and sociology. In 1974, he shared the Nobel Prize for Economics with Gunnar Myrdal.

Today, Hayek is regarded as a champion of the conservative view of economics. Another economic conservative, Milton Friedman (whose work you will also read in this section), taught at the University of Chicago with Hayek, but he disapproved of Hayek's theories of money and production and, as a result, would not let him become a member of the economics department. Yet they were friends and in agreement on many other important points of economic theory. For Hayek, the most important point was his condemnation of the government's control of the means of production.

HAYEK'S RHETORIC

Even though he is dealing with a sophisticated subject matter, Hayek writes clearly and simply, with carefully planned paragraphs. Because he wrote this essay in 1944 and in a language not his own, his style is somewhat old-fashioned, and his paragraphs are generally long. Throughout this chapter from *The Road to Serfdom*, he constructs an argument point by point, addressing what he feels are the consequences of a planned economy. The argument is quiet, carefully paced, and uses primarily one rhetorical strategy: development by analysis of circumstances. He addresses the question of a planned economy and then carefully considers the circumstances in which people would live in a society in which the question of choice is limited to the needs of the planners. In many cases, this means that the needs of the society will be those of the general public rather than of the individual.

Hayek implies that in a planned economy the individual would have to give up a number of freedoms for the benefit of being taken care of by the planners, who would estimate the individual's needs and accommodate them. He begins by considering that people might think that economic planning would "free us from less important cares" (para. 2), but then reminds us that economic issues cover an enormous range of personal concerns. He goes on to review them, and ultimately says, "economic planning would involve direction of almost the whole of our life" (para. 8).

The question of freedom of choice is a serious issue that Hayek explains is possible in a competitive society because there are usually many products or services available if one does not satisfy the individual. But in a monopoly, there is little choice, and a planned economy would eventually constitute a monopoly. Interestingly, when discussing the freedom of choice, he includes the freedom to make decisions that might lead to failure. His point is that he prefers that whatever economic decisions there are to be made, he wants to make them himself. It is the individual that takes precedent for him, rather than the community.

Among Hayek's rhetorical skills is his ability to create statements that have the appearance and power of a maxim or proverb. The following are some examples:

- "The ultimate ends of the activities of reasonable beings are never economic" (para. 3).
- "It would be much truer to say that money is one of the greatest instruments of freedom ever invented by man" (para. 3).
- "It is often said that political freedom is meaningless without economic freedom" (para. 25).

In the process of his analysis, he establishes that central planning will decide what products are to be made available. The decisions will be made on what is an essentially utilitarian pattern, choosing what seems best for the largest number of people. The principle of utilitarianism is to provide the greatest good for the greatest number. But in a planned economy, the decisions about what the greatest good will be is in the hands of the planners. The products that will be available to purchase will reflect the decisions of the planners.

In addition, not only will the products be based on the decisions of the central planners, but so will the kinds of work that will be available. People's careers will need to be shaped by the needs of the planners. Therefore some career choices that do not satisfy the needs of the planners will simply not be available. Choice of work, which Hayek is quick to say is extremely important to the individual, will be curtailed and curtailed sharply.

The objective from the point of view of the reader is to examine Hayek's position because he is carefully constructing an argument against central planning and in favor of a competitive capitalism. He argues against socialism, which he describes as a planned economy. His argument builds on several important issues: the question of choice; the nature and consequence of planning; the force of the monopoly; the choice of work; and the distribution of wealth. When he has explored all those issues, he comes back to the idea expressed in the opening sentence: "Most planners who have seriously considered the practical aspects of their task have little doubt that a directed economy must be run on more or less dictatorial lines" (para. 1). When this book was written in the early 1940s, dictatorships existed throughout Europe and provided more than enough evidence for Hayek to believe his argument was sound and a warning to all free nations.

❖ PREREADING QUESTIONS: WHAT TO READ FOR

The following prereading questions may help you anticipate key issues in the discussion of F. A. Hayek's "Economic Control and Totalitarianism." Keeping them in mind during your first reading of the selection should help focus your attention.

1. What constitutes "socialism" for Hayek?
2. Why would central economic planning limit the freedom of the individual?
3. Why would socialism eventually lead to totalitarianism?

Economic Control and Totalitarianism

The control of the production of wealth is the control of human life itself.
—Hilaire Belloc

M ost planners who have seriously considered the practical aspects of their task have little doubt that a directed economy must be run on more or less dictatorial lines. That the complex system of interrelated activities, if it is to be consciously directed at all, must be directed by a single staff of experts, and that ultimate responsibility and power must rest in the hands of a commander-in-chief whose actions must not be fettered by democratic procedure, is too obvious a consequence of underlying ideas of central planning not to command fairly general assent. The consolation our planners offer us is that this authoritarian direction will apply "only" to economic matters. One of the most prominent economic planners, Stuart Chase,[1] assures us, for instance, that in a planned society "political democracy can remain if it confines itself to all but economic matters." Such assurances are usually accompanied by the suggestion that, by giving up freedom in what are, or ought to be, the less important aspects of our lives, we shall obtain greater freedom in the pursuit of higher values. On this ground people who abhor the idea of a political dictatorship often clamor for a dictator in the economic field.

The arguments used appeal to our best instincts and often attract the finest minds. If planning really did free us from the less important cares and so made it easier to render our existence one of plain living and high thinking, who would wish to belittle such an ideal? If our economic activities really concerned only the inferior or even more sordid sides of life, of course we ought to endeavor by all means to find a way to relieve ourselves from the excessive care for material ends and, leaving them to be cared for by some piece of utilitarian machinery, set our minds free for the higher things of life.

Unfortunately, the assurance people derive from this belief that the power which is exercised over economic life is a power over matters of secondary importance only, and which makes them take lightly the threat to the freedom of our economic pursuits, is altogether unwarranted. It is largely a consequence of the erroneous belief that there are purely economic ends separate from the other ends of life. Yet, apart from the pathological case of the miser, there is no

---

[1] **Stuart Chase (1888–1985)**   An American economist and moderate socialist.

such thing. The ultimate ends of the activities of reasonable beings are never economic. Strictly speaking, there is no "economic motive" but only economic factors conditioning our striving for other ends. What in ordinary language is misleadingly called the "economic motive" means merely the desire for general opportunity, the desire for power to achieve unspecified ends.[2] If we strive for money, it is because it offers us the widest choice in enjoying the fruits of our efforts. Because in modern society it is through the limitation of our money incomes that we are made to feel the restrictions which our relative poverty still imposes upon us, many have come to hate money as the symbol of these restrictions. But this is to mistake for the cause the medium through which a force makes itself felt. It would be much truer to say that money is one of the greatest instruments of freedom ever invented by man. It is money which in existing society opens an astounding range of choice to the poor man—a range greater than that which not many generations ago was open to the wealthy. We shall better understand the significance of this service of money if we consider what it would really mean if, as so many socialists characteristically propose, the "pecuniary motive" were largely displaced by "noneconomic incentives." If all rewards, instead of being offered in money, were offered in the form of public distinctions or privileges, positions of power over other men, or better housing or better food, opportunities for travel or education, this would merely mean that the recipient would no longer be allowed to choose and that whoever fixed the reward determined not only its size but also the particular form in which it should be enjoyed.

Once we realize that there is no separate economic motive and that an economic gain or economic loss is merely a gain or a loss where it is still in our power to decide which of our needs or desires shall be affected, it is also easier to see the important kernel of truth in the general belief that economic matters affect only the less important ends of life and to understand the contempt in which "merely" economic considerations are often held. In a sense this is quite justified in a market economy—but only in such a free economy. So long as we can freely dispose over our income and all our possessions, economic loss will always deprive us only of what we regard as the least important of the desires we were able to satisfy. A "merely" economic loss is thus one whose effect we can still make fall on our less important needs, while when we say that the value of something we have lost is much greater than its economic value, or that it cannot even be estimated in economic terms, this means that we must bear the loss where it falls. And similarly with an economic gain. Economic changes, in other words, usually affect only the fringe, the "margin," of our needs. There are many things which are more important than anything which economic gains or losses are likely to affect, which for us stand high above the

4

---

[2] Cf. Lionel Robbins, *The Economic Causes of War* (London: J. Cape, 1939), Appendix.

amenities and even above many of the necessities of life which are affected by the economic ups and downs. Compared with them, the "filthy lucre," the question whether we are economically somewhat worse or better off, seems of little importance. This makes many people believe that anything which, like economic planning, affects only our economic interests cannot seriously interfere with the more basic values of life.

This, however, is an erroneous conclusion. Economic values are less important to us than many things precisely because in economic matters we are free to decide what to us is more, and what less, important. Or, as we might say, because in the present society it is *we* who have to solve the economic problems of our lives. To be controlled in our economic pursuits means to be always controlled unless we declare our specific purpose. Or, since when we declare our specific purpose we shall also have to get it approved, we should really be controlled in everything.

The question raised by economic planning is, therefore, not merely whether we shall be able to satisfy what we regard as our more or less important needs in the way we prefer. It is whether it shall be we who decide what is more, and what is less, important for us, or whether this is to be decided by the planner. Economic planning would not affect merely those of our marginal needs that we have in mind when we speak contemptuously about the merely economic. It would, in effect, mean that we as individuals should no longer be allowed to decide what we regard as marginal.

The authority directing all economic activity would control not merely the part of our lives which is concerned with inferior things; it would control the allocation of the limited means for all our ends. And whoever controls all economic activity controls the means for all our ends and must therefore decide which are to be satisfied and which not. This is really the crux of the matter. Economic control is not merely control of a sector of human life which can be separated from the rest; it is the control of the means for all our ends. And whoever has sole control of the means must also determine which ends are to be served, which values are to be rated higher and which lower—in short, what men should believe and strive for. Central planning means that the economic problem is to be solved by the community instead of by the individual; but this involves that it must also be the community, or rather its representatives, who must decide the relative importance of the different needs.

The so-called economic freedom which the planners promise us means precisely that we are to be relieved of the necessity of solving our own economic problems and that the bitter choices which this often involves are to be made for us. Since under modern conditions we are for almost everything dependent on means which our fellow-men provide, economic planning would involve direction of almost the whole of our life. There is hardly an aspect of it, from our primary needs to our relations with our family and friends, from the nature of our work to the use of our leisure, over which the planner would not exercise his "conscious control."[3]

The power of the planner over our private lives would be no less complete   9 if he chose not to exercise it by direct control of our consumption. Although a planned society would probably to some extent employ rationing and similar devices, the power of the planner over our private lives does not depend on this and would be hardly less effective if the consumer were nominally free to spend his income as he pleased. The source of this power over all consumption which in a planned society the authority would possess would be its control over production.

Our freedom of choice in a competitive society rests on the fact that, if one   10 person refuses to satisfy our wishes, we can turn to another. But if we face a monopolist we are at his mercy. And an authority directing the whole economic system would be the most powerful monopolist conceivable. While we need probably not be afraid that such an authority would exploit this power in the manner in which a private monopolist would do so, while its purpose would presumably not be the extortion of maximum financial gain, it would have complete power to decide what we are to be given and on what terms. It would not only decide what commodities and services were to be available and in what quantities; it would be able to direct their distribution between districts and groups and could, if it wished, discriminate between persons to any degree it liked. If we remember why planning is advocated by most people, can there be much doubt that this power would be used for the ends of which the authority approves and to prevent the pursuits of ends which it disapproves?

The power conferred by the control of production and prices is almost   11 unlimited. In a competitive society the prices we have to pay for a thing, the rate at which we can get one thing for another, depend on the quantities of other things of which by taking one, we deprive the other members of society. This price is not determined by the conscious will of anybody. And if one way of

---

[3] The extent of the control over all life that economic control confers is nowhere better illustrated than in the field of foreign exchanges. Nothing would at first seem to affect private life less than a state control of the dealings in foreign exchange, and most people will regard its introduction with complete indifference. Yet the experience of most Continental countries has taught thoughtful people to regard this step as the decisive advance on the path to totalitarianism and the suppression of individual liberty. It is, in fact, the complete delivery of the individual to the tyranny of the state, the final suppression of all means of escape—not merely for the rich but for everybody. Once the individual is no longer free to travel, no longer free to buy foreign books or journals, once all the means of foreign contact can be restricted to those of whom official opinion approves or for whom it is regarded as necessary, the effective control of opinion is much greater than that ever exercised by any of the absolutist governments of the seventeenth and eighteenth centuries. [Hayek's note]

achieving our ends proves too expensive for us, we are free to try other ways. The obstacles in our path are not due to someone's disapproving of our ends but to the fact that the same means are also wanted elsewhere. In a directed economy, where the authority watches over the ends pursued, it is certain that it would use its powers to assist some ends and to prevent the realization of others. Not our own view, but somebody else's, of what we ought to like or dislike would determine what we should get. And since the authority would have the power to thwart any efforts to elude its guidance, it would control what we consume almost as effectively as if it directly told us how to spend our income.

Not only in our capacity as consumers, however, and not even mainly in   12
that capacity, would the will of the authority shape and "guide" our daily lives. It would do so even more in our position as producers. These two aspects of our lives cannot be separated; and as for most of us the time we spend at our work is a large part of our whole lives, and as our job usually also determines the place where and the people among whom we live, some freedom in choosing our work is, probably, even more important for our happiness than freedom to spend our income during the hours of leisure.

No doubt it is true that even in the best of worlds this freedom will be   13
very limited. Few people ever have an abundance of choice of occupation. But what matters is that we have some choice, that we are not absolutely tied to a particular job which has been chosen for us, or which we may have chosen in the past, and that if one position becomes quite intolerable, or if we set our heart on another, there is almost always a way for the able, some sacrifice at the price of which he may achieve his goal. Nothing makes conditions more unbearable than the knowledge that no effort of ours can change them; and even if we should never have the strength of mind to make the necessary sacrifice, the knowledge that we could escape if we only strove hard enough makes many otherwise intolerable positions bearable.

This is not to say that in this respect all is for the best in our present world,   14
or has been so in the most liberal past, and that there is not much that could be done to improve the opportunities of choice open to the people. Here as elsewhere the state can do a great deal to help the spreading of knowledge and information and to assist mobility. But the point is that the kind of state action which really would increase opportunity is almost precisely the opposite of the "planning" which is now generally advocated and practiced. Most planners, it is true, promise that in the new planned world free choice of occupation will be scrupulously preserved or even increased. But there they promise more than they can possibly fulfill. If they want to plan, they must control the entry into the different trades and occupations, or the terms of remuneration, or both. In almost all known instances of planning, the establishment of such controls

and restrictions was among the first measures taken. If such control were universally practiced and exercised by a single planning authority, one needs little imagination to see what would become of the "free choice of occupation" promised. The "freedom of choice" would be purely fictitious, a mere promise to practice no discrimination where in the nature of the case discrimination must be practiced, and where all one could hope would be that the selection would be made on what the authority believed to be objective grounds.

There would be little difference if the planning authority confined itself   15
to fixing the terms of employment and tried to regulate numbers by adjusting these terms. By prescribing the remuneration, it would no less effectively bar groups of people from entering many trades than by specifically excluding them. A rather plain girl who badly wants to become a saleswoman, a weakly boy who has set his heart on a job where his weakness handicaps him, as well as in general the apparently less able or less suitable are not necessarily excluded in a competitive society; if they value the position sufficiently they will frequently be able to get a start by a financial sacrifice and will later make good through qualities which at first are not so obvious. But when the authority fixes the remunerations for a whole category and the selection among the candidates is made by an objective test, the strength of their desire for the job will count for very little. The person whose qualifications are not of the standard type, or whose temperament is not of the ordinary kind, will no longer be able to come to special arrangements with an employer whose dispositions will fit in with his special needs: the person who prefers irregular hours or even a happy-go-lucky existence with a small and perhaps uncertain income to a regular routine will no longer have the choice. Conditions will be without exception what in some measure they inevitably are in a large organization—or rather worse, because there will be no possibility of escape. We shall no longer be free to be rational or efficient only when and where we think it worth while; we shall all have to conform to the standards which the planning authority must fix in order to simplify its task. To make this immense task manageable, it will have to reduce the diversity of human capacities and inclinations to a few categories of readily interchangeable units and deliberately to disregard minor personal differences.

Although the professed aim of planning would be that man should cease   16
to be a mere means, in fact—since it would be impossible to take account in the plan of individual likes and dislikes—the individual would more than ever become a mere means, to be used by the authority in the service of such abstractions as the "social welfare" or the "good of the community."

That in a competitive society most things can be had at a price—though it   17
is often a cruelly high price we have to pay—is a fact the importance of which

can hardly be overrated. The alternative is not, however, complete freedom of choice, but orders and prohibitions which must be obeyed and, in the last resort, the favor of the mighty.

It is significant of the confusion prevailing on all these subjects that it should have become a cause for reproach that in a competitive society almost everything can be had at a price. If the people who protest against having the higher values of life brought into the "cash nexus" really mean that we should not be allowed to sacrifice our lesser needs in order to preserve the higher values, and that the choice should be made for us, this demand must be regarded as rather peculiar and scarcely testifies to great respect for the dignity of the individual. That life and health, beauty and virtue, honor and peace of mind, can often be preserved only at considerable material cost, and that somebody must make the choice, is as undeniable as that we all are sometimes not prepared to make the material sacrifices necessary to protect those higher values against all injury. 18

To take only one example: We could, of course, reduce casualties by automobile accidents to zero if we were willing to bear the cost—if in no other way—by abolishing automobiles. And the same is true of thousands of other instances in which we are constantly risking life and health and all the fine values of the spirit, of ourselves and of our fellow-men, to further what we at the same time contemptuously describe as our material comfort. Nor can it be otherwise, since all our ends compete for the same means; and we could not strive for anything but these absolute values if they were on no account to be endangered. 19

That people should wish to be relieved of the bitter choice which hard facts often impose upon them is not surprising. But few want to be relieved through having the choice made for them by others. People just wish that the choice should not be necessary at all. And they are only too ready to believe that the choice is not really necessary, that it is imposed upon them merely by the particular economic system under which we live. What they resent is, in truth, that there is an economic problem. 20

In their wishful belief that there is really no longer an economic problem people have been confirmed by irresponsible talk about "potential plenty"—which, if it were a fact, would indeed mean that there is no economic problem which makes the choice inevitable. But although this snare has served socialist propaganda under various names as long as socialism has existed, it is still as palpably untrue as it was when it was first used over a hundred years ago. In all this time not one of the many people who have used it has produced a workable plan of how production could be increased so as to abolish even in western Europe what we regard as poverty—not to speak of the world as a whole. The reader may take it that whoever talks about potential plenty is 21 either dishonest or does not know what he is talking about.[4] Yet it is this false hope as much as anything which drives us along the road to planning.

While the popular movement still profits by this false belief, the claim that a planned economy would produce a substantially larger output than the competitive system is being progressively abandoned by most students of the problem. Even a good many economists with socialist views who have seriously studied the problems of central planning are now content to hope that a planned society will equal the efficiency of a competitive system; they advocate planning no longer because of its superior productivity but because it will enable us to secure a more just and equitable distribution of wealth. This is, indeed, the only argument for planning which can be seriously pressed. It is indisputable that if we want to secure a distribution of wealth which conforms to some predetermined standard, if we want consciously to decide who is to have what, we must plan the whole economic system. But the question remains whether the price we should have to pay for the realization of somebody's ideal of justice is not bound to be more discontent and more oppression than was ever caused by the much-abused free play of economic forces.

We should be seriously deceiving ourselves if for these apprehensions we sought comfort in the consideration that the adoption of central planning would merely mean a return, after a brief spell of a free economy, to the ties and regulations which have governed economic activity through most ages, and that therefore the infringements of personal liberty need not be greater than they were before the age of laissez faire. This is a dangerous illusion. Even during the periods of European history when the regimentation of economic life went furthest, it amounted to little more than the creation of a general and semipermanent framework of rules within which the individual preserved a wide free sphere. The apparatus of control then available would not have been adequate to impose more than very general directions. And even where the control was

22

23

---

[4] To justify these strong words, the following conclusions may be quoted at which Colin Clark, one of the best known among the younger economic statisticians and a man of undoubted progressive views and a strictly scientific outlook, has arrived in his *The Conditions of Economic Progress* (London: Macmillan, 1940), pp. 3–4: The "oft-repeated phrases about poverty in the midst of plenty, and the problems of production having already been solved if only we understood the problem of distribution, turn out to be the most untruthful of all modern clichés. . . . The underutilisation of productive capacity is a question of considerable importance only in the U.S.A., though in certain years also it has been of some importance in Great Britain, Germany and France, but for most of the world it is entirely subsidiary to the more important fact that, with productive resources fully employed, they can produce so little. The age of plenty will still be a long while in coming. . . . If preventable unemployment were eliminated throughout the trade cycle, this would mean a distinct improvement in the standard of living of the population of the U.S.A., but from the standpoint of the world as a whole it would only make a small contribution towards the much greater problem of raising the real income of the bulk of the world population to anything like a civilised standard." [Hayek's note]

most complete it extended only to those activities of a person through which he took part in the social division of labor. In the much wider sphere in which he then still lived on his own products, he was free to act as he chose.

The situation is now entirely different. During the liberal era the progressive division of labor has created a situation where almost every one of our activities is part of a social process. This is a development which we cannot reverse, since it is only because of it that we can maintain the vastly increased population at anything like present standards. But, in consequence, the substitution of central planning for competition would require central direction of a much greater part of our lives than was ever attempted before. It could not stop at what we regard as our economic activities, because we are now for almost every part of our lives dependent on somebody else's economic activities.[5] The passion for the "collective satisfaction of our needs," with which our socialists have so well prepared the way for totalitarianism, and which wants us to take our pleasures as well as our necessities at the appointed time and in the prescribed form, is, of course, partly intended as a means of political education. But it is also the result of the exigencies of planning, which consists essentially in depriving us of choice, in order to give us whatever fits best into the plan and that at a time determined by the plan.

It is often said that political freedom is meaningless without economic freedom. This is true enough, but in a sense almost opposite from that in which the phrase is used by our planners. The economic freedom which is the prerequisite of any other freedom cannot be the freedom from economic care which the socialists promise us and which can be obtained only by relieving the individual at the same time of the necessity and of the power of choice; it must be the freedom of our economic activity which, with the right of choice, inevitably also carries the risk and the responsibility of that right.

---

[5] It is no accident that in the totalitarian countries, be it Russia or Germany or Italy, the question of how to organize the people's leisure has become a problem of planning. The Germans have even invented for this problem the horrible and self-contradictory name of *Freizeitgestaltung* (literally: the shaping of the use made of the people's free time), as if it were still "free time" when it has to be spent in the way ordained by authority. [Hayek's note]

✂ QUESTIONS FOR CRITICAL READING

1. Would economic planning really "free us from the less important cares" (para. 2) of life?

2. How does the promise of economic planning affect our choices?

3. Why might people think that matters of economic life are of secondary importance only?

4. Why does Hayek approve of our striving for money?

5. What evidence does Hayek use to bolster his argument?

6. How would a planned economy constitute a monopoly?

7. What does Hayek have to say about poverty in an unplanned economy?

❖ SUGGESTIONS FOR CRITICAL WRITING

1. Hayek says in his first paragraph that a "directed economy must be run on more or less dictatorial lines." Is this true? Consider that Hayek wrote in 1944 while the great planned economies were run by dictators. Do you consider that a modern planned economy must be dictatorial? If possible, research the economies of some modern nations and examine their nature to determine whether they have the limitations that Hayek expects.

2. The principal point of Hayek's chapter — and the main point of his entire book — is that any planned economy that produces socialist institutions will inevitably run the risk of becoming totalitarian. Decide whether he is right or not. Does every planned economy run the risks that he describes in terms of limiting choice of products to buy, careers to choose, or places to go? What is it in the nature of planning that causes such problems? Why are such economies dictatorial?

3. Why is an unplanned economy superior to a planned economy? Whom does the unplanned economy most benefit? Who is least benefited? In which kind of economy do you feel you would most prosper? Do you feel that your economy is now basically planned or basically unplanned? What would Hayek say about the economy that currently exists in our country? Treat these questions in a carefully reasoned argument.

4. Hayek says that "money is one of the greatest instruments of freedom ever invented by man" (para. 3). Write an essay directed as an open letter to America's poor explaining why Hayek says this and why you agree or disagree with him. How hard do you think it will be for you to defend his statement? Who, in your judgment, would most find strong agreement with Hayek? What social problems are implied in accepting Hayek's declaration?

5. Hayek implies that even a laissez-faire economy would be preferable to a planned economy. What is a laissez-faire economy? Research the term in relation to the economies of Western nations. What are the strengths of a laissez-faire economy? What are its weaknesses? To what extent do you now live in a laissez-faire economy?

6. **CONNECTIONS** In paragraph 22, Hayek begins to talk about the question of distribution of wealth. In an unplanned economy, there can be no discussion of the distribution of wealth. Some people, as Adam Smith (p. 325) and Andrew Carnegie (p. 360) tell us, will become wealthier than others. Some will become

enormously wealthy, while others may become extremely poor. How would Smith and Carnegie react to the points that Hayek makes about unequal distribution of wealth? If you are in favor of an unplanned economy, what do you feel should be done about the extremes of inequality we face in our current economy? How do these three writers justify extreme inequality, and what do they propose to do about it, if anything? Is planning the only way to deal with extreme inequality of wealth?

7. **CONNECTIONS**   In *The Communist Manifesto*, Karl Marx (p. 335) holds views opposite those of F. A. Hayek. Compare their positions on the question of control of production and the role of the individual in society. Are there any points on which they seem to be in agreement? Is Marx proposing a planning committee or a planning person who might become what Hayek calls an economic dictator? How does Marx see his system working? How would Hayek counter Marx's enthusiasm for socialism? Does Hayek take into consideration the class struggle that dominates Marx's thinking? Do you regard the class struggle as significant in contemporary economics?

© Alex Wong/Getty Images

MILTON AND ROSE
FRIEDMAN
Created Equal

MILTON FRIEDMAN (1912–2006) taught from 1946 to 1976 at the University of Chicago, where he also served as a senior research fellow at the Hoover Institution and Paul Snowden Russell Distinguished Service Professor Emeritus of Economics. Friedman won the Nobel Prize for Economics in 1976 and was widely regarded as the leading expert in monetarist economics. (A monetarist is an economist who studies the relation of the supply of money to the growth of the economy.) Friedman's theories regarding money supply have been influential on most U.S. government policy since the 1960s.

ROSE DIRECTOR FRIEDMAN (1910–2009) studied at Reed College and then at the University of Chicago, where she received a Bachelor of Philosophy degree and went on to study for the Ph.D. in economics. She did all the work for the degree except for the thesis. She married Milton Friedman in 1937 and worked with the Federal Deposit Insurance Corporation and the National Bureau of Economic Research. She collaborated with her husband on three books, and together they created the Milton and Rose D. Friedman Foundation, whose focus is on helping parents have a say in the schools their children attend.

Milton Friedman was a prominent laissez-faire economist. The term *laissez-faire* translates loosely as "let them do as they will," and its use in economics implies a policy in which the government avoids interfering with business. Friedman saw the government's primary role as limited to regulating the supply of money in order to balance prices, output, and employment. He championed free-market economy, in which tariffs and trade barriers are removed, and advised a number of conservative politicians, from Barry Goldwater to Richard Nixon to Ronald Reagan. His policies were largely those that Margaret Thatcher put into action in her government in England in the 1980s.

Friedman's most important books are *Taxing to Prevent Inflation* (1943); *Essays in Positive Economics* (1953); *A Theory of the Consumption Function* (1957); the book many

From *Free to Choose: A Personal Statement.*

say is his most influential, *A Monetary History of the United States 1867–1960* (1963), with Anna Schwartz; *The Optimum Quantity of Money* (1969); and *Free to Choose: A Personal Statement* (1980). Rose D. Friedman coauthored the last book as well as *Capitalism and Freedom* (1962) and *Tyranny of the Status Quo* (1984). Milton and Rose Friedman also published a memoir, *Two Lucky People* (1998), recounting their struggles and achievements. The Friedmans' work centers on monetary policy but also encompasses larger issues, such as the relationship of government to business and the relationship of the individual to capital and capitalism. Much of Milton Friedman's early work was written in the shadow of fascism and world communism, and his views strongly support more rather than less freedom: he believed that freedom helps produce wealth and avoid poverty.

The essay that follows, "Created Equal," was published originally in *Free to Choose: A Personal Statement* (1980). The concept of equality interested the French statesman and author Alexis de Tocqueville, whose own essay on democracy appears in this volume in the section on Government (p. 139). Tocqueville wrote in the nineteenth century and responded to the development of the United States as a new nation in which nobility and aristocratic classes had no place and in which people regarded each other as being on an essentially equal footing. For Tocqueville, that situation was a novelty. Thomas Jefferson, too, emphasized issues of equality in the eighteenth century, and it is there that the Friedmans center their opening remarks.

The Friedmans explore exactly what the founding fathers meant by equality when they declared that "all men are created equal." The problems associated with the existence of slavery and its essential contradiction of equality persisted for 150 years until the Civil War and emancipation in 1862. The emphasis on equality before God reminds us that the concept of equality is qualified by a number of distinctions, both politically and economically. The Friedmans review some of those distinctions and attempt to clarify points that are central to their own understanding of equality.

For example, they state that when Jefferson declared that all men are created equal, he also knew that all men were very different from one another and that because they were not the same, they remained distinct in sometimes problematic ways. Jefferson himself was a man of enormous talent. He was an architect, a successful farmer, a scientist and inventor, and a founder of a great university. He also grew wealthy enough to own a large number of slaves. The Friedmans point out that he was successful to such a degree that he might be thought superior in achievement to most contemporary Americans. In other words, he was a member of the wealthy elite.

Rather than seeing this as a problem, the Friedmans insist that this is the nature of the world: "Life is not fair" (para. 35). Some people have more talent, luck, and success than others. Yet all are equal before God and equal before the law. According to the Friedmans, the freedom to succeed — to acquire more wealth than some others, to achieve more good works than some others, to flourish more than some others — is central to the American experiment.

Government policies that restrict the freedom to succeed, whether they be excessive taxation, restrictive laws, or specific prohibitions, are forms of oppression. The Friedmans' greatest fear concerns the distinction of *equality of outcome*. The term simply means that rather than promoting equality of opportunity, the government wishes at times to guarantee that a number of people will achieve the same outcome. This desire necessitates some form of restriction that permits all people to share the wealth relatively equally — something like a handicap in horse racing. For the Friedmans, such constraints are the worst form of economic tyranny and a denial of personal freedom.

THE FRIEDMANS' RHETORIC

The primary strategy of the first parts of the passage centers on definition of terms. The Friedmans present an argument in favor of freedom and free markets, but they realize that their argument will succeed or fail in terms of the clarity of their premises and the intelligibility of their definitions. The terms equality and freedom mean different things to different people, and if the Friedmans do not clarify their terms right away, they could end up arguing at cross purposes with their readers. The Friedmans also help their argument by structuring it carefully, using six subheads to clarify its organization: "Equality before God"; "Equality of Opportunity"; "Equality of Outcome"; "Who Favors Equality of Outcome?"; "Consequences of Egalitarian Policies"; and "Capitalism and Equality."

The authors' first efforts are to establish the importance of liberty for the individual and then to show how various government policies can actually impinge on individual liberty in the name of doing something many feel is desirable: guaranteeing a good outcome for all people equally. Their views generally support the free market, which implies that individuals should be free to build a business as they see fit. They should not be hindered by heavy taxation designed to redistribute wealth from people who earn a great deal to those who earn very little. The Friedmans' argument relies on careful comparisons with Communist countries and undeveloped countries to demonstrate the calamities that can result from such programs.

One of the interesting strategies of the argument is the use of historical comparisons, both with modern nations and with classical civilizations. Milton Friedman introduces examples and comparisons from Asia (Japan has embraced and benefited from his economic theories) as well as from Europe and the United States. However, he also understands the civilizations of early Greece and Rome and comments on the effects that modern "mechanical improvement" might have had on individuals in those cultures. He points out that even in Communist Russia — which still existed when he wrote this essay — the concept of equality was contradicted by the fact that the party members and the politburo represented an upper class with wealth and privileges, whereas the ordinary workers made do with shabby goods and limited choice in the marketplace.

Ultimately, this argument favors freedom of choice, freedom of opportunity, and the free capitalist market. Anything else, the Friedmans imply, suggests a restriction of freedom and ultimate unhappiness. Moreover, and most important, such restrictions contradict the principles of freedom on which the concept of equality is based.

⠏ PREREADING QUESTIONS: WHAT TO READ FOR

The following prereading questions may help you anticipate key issues in the discussion of Milton and Rose Friedman's "Created Equal." Keeping them in mind during your first reading of the selection should help focus your attention.

1. In the Friedmans' view, what is the relationship between equality and liberty?

2. Why do the Friedmans disapprove of the concept of "equality of outcome"?

Created Equal

"Equality," "liberty" — what precisely do these words from the Declaration of Independence mean? Can the ideals they express be realized in practice? Are equality and liberty consistent one with the other, or are they in conflict? 1

Since well before the Declaration of Independence, these questions have played a central role in the history of the United Stales. The attempt to answer them has shaped the intellectual climate of opinion, led to bloody war, and produced major changes in economic and political institutions. This attempt continues to dominate our political debate. It will shape our future as it has our past. 2

In the early decades of the Republic, equality meant equality before God; liberty meant the liberty to shape one's own life. The obvious conflict between the Declaration of Independence and the institution of slavery occupied the center of the stage. That conflict was finally resolved by the Civil War. The debate then moved to a different level. Equality came more and more to be interpreted as "equality of opportunity" in the sense that no one should be prevented by arbitrary obstacles from using his capacities to pursue his own objectives. That is still its dominant meaning to most citizens of the United States. 3

Neither equality before God nor equality of opportunity presented any conflict with liberty to shape one's own life. Quite the opposite. Equality and liberty were two faces of the same basic value — that every individual should be regarded as an end in himself. 4

A very different meaning of equality has emerged in the United States in recent decades — equality of outcome. Everyone should have the same level of living or of income, should finish the race at the same time. Equality of outcome is in clear conflict with liberty. The attempt to promote it has been a major source of bigger and bigger government, and of government-imposed restrictions on our liberty. 5

Equality before God

When Thomas Jefferson, at the age of thirty-three, wrote "all men are created   6
equal," he and his contemporaries did not take these words literally. They did
not regard "men"—or as we would say today, "persons"—as equal in physical characteristics, emotional reactions, mechanical and intellectual abilities. Thomas Jefferson himself was a most remarkable person. At the age of
twenty-six he designed his beautiful house at Monticello (Italian for "little
mountain"), supervised its construction, and, indeed, is said to have done some
of the work himself. In the course of his life, he was an inventor, a scholar, an
author, a statesman, governor of the State of Virginia, president of the United
States, minister to France, founder of the University of Virginia—hardly an
average man.

The clue to what Thomas Jefferson and his contemporaries meant by equal   7
is in the next phrase of the Declaration—"endowed by their Creator with certain unalienable rights; that among these are Life, Liberty, and the pursuit of
Happiness." Men were equal before God. Each person is precious in and of
himself. He has unalienable rights, rights that no one else is entitled to invade.
He is entitled to serve his own purposes and not to be treated simply as an
instrument to promote someone else's purposes. "Liberty" is part of the definition of equality, not in conflict with it.

Equality before God—personal equality[1]—is important precisely because   8
people are not identical. Their different values, their different tastes, their different capacities will lead them to want to lead very different lives. Personal
equality requires respect for their right to do so, not the imposition on them
of someone else's values or judgment. Jefferson had no doubt that some men
were superior to others, that there was an elite. But that did not give them the
right to rule others.

If an elite did not have the right to impose its will on others, neither did any   9
other group, even a majority. Every person was to be his own ruler—provided
that he did not interfere with the similar right of others. Government was established to protect that right—from fellow citizens and from external threat—not
to give a majority unbridled rule. Jefferson had three achievements he wanted
to be remembered for inscribed on his tombstone: the Virginia statute for
religious freedom (a precursor of the U.S. Bill of Rights designed to protect
minorities against domination by majorities), authorship of the Declaration
of Independence, and the founding of the University of Virginia. The goal of
the framers of the Constitution of the United States, drafted by Jefferson's

---

[1] See J. R. Pole, *The Pursuit of Equality in American History* (Berkeley and Los Angeles:
University of California Press, 1978), pp. 51–58. [Friedmans' note]

contemporaries, was a national government strong enough to defend the country and promote the general welfare but at the same time sufficiently limited in power to protect the individual citizen, and the separate state governments, from domination by the national government. Democratic, in the sense of widespread participation in government, yes; in the political sense of majority rule, clearly no.

Similarly, Alexis de Tocqueville, the famous French political philosopher   10
and sociologist, in his classic *Democracy in America*, written after a lengthy visit in the 1830s, saw equality, not majority rule, as the outstanding characteristic of America. "In America," he wrote,

> the aristocratic element has always been feeble from its birth; and if at the present day it is not actually destroyed, it is at any rate so completely disabled, that we can scarcely assign to it any degree of influence on the course of affairs. The democratic principle, on the contrary, has gained so much strength by time, by events, and by legislation, as to have become not only predominant but all-powerful. There is no family or corporate authority. . . .
>
> America, then, exhibits in her social state a most extraordinary phenomenon. Men are there seen on a greater equality in point of fortune and intellect, or, in other words, more equal in their strength, than in any other country of the world, or in any age of which history has preserved the remembrance.[2]

Tocqueville admired much of what he observed, but he was by no means   11
an uncritical admirer, fearing that democracy carried too far might undermine civic virtue. As he put it, "There is . . . a manly and lawful passion for equality which incites men to wish all to be powerful and honored. This passion tends to elevate the humble to the rank of the great; but there exists also in the human heart a depraved taste for equality, which impels the weak to attempt to lower the powerful to their own level, and reduces men to prefer equality in slavery to inequality with freedom."[3]

It is striking testimony to the changing meaning of words that in recent   12
decades the Democratic party of the United States has been the chief instrument for strengthening that government power which Jefferson and many of his contemporaries viewed as the greatest threat to democracy. And it has striven to increase government power in the name of a concept of "equality"

---

[2] Alexis de Tocqueville, *Democracy in America*, 2 vols., 2d ed., trans. Henry Reeve, ed. Francis Bowen (Boston: John Allyn, Publisher, 1863), vol. I, pp. 66–67. (First French edition published in 1835.) [Friedmans' note]

[3] Ibid., pp. 67–68. [Friedmans' note]

that is almost the opposite of the concept of equality Jefferson identified with liberty and Tocqueville with democracy.

Of course the practice of the founding fathers did not always correspond   13
to their preaching. The most obvious conflict was slavery. Thomas Jefferson himself owned slaves until the day he died—July 4, 1826. He agonized repeatedly about slavery, suggested in his notes and correspondence plans for eliminating slavery, but never publicly proposed any such plans or campaigned against the institution.

Yet the Declaration he drafted had either to be blatantly violated by the   14
nation he did so much to create and form, or slavery had to be abolished. Little wonder that the early decades of the Republic saw a rising tide of controversy about the institution of slavery. That controversy ended in a civil war that, in the words of Abraham Lincoln's Gettysburg Address, tested whether a "nation, conceived in liberty and dedicated to the proposition that all men are created equal . . . can long endure." The nation endured, but only at a tremendous cost in lives, property, and social cohesion.

Equality of Opportunity

Once the Civil War abolished slavery and the concept of personal equality—   15
equality before God and the law—came closer to realization, emphasis shifted, in intellectual discussion and in government and private policy, to a different concept—equality of opportunity.

Literal equality of opportunity—in the sense of "identity"—is impossible.   16
One child is born blind, another with sight. One child has parents deeply concerned about his welfare who provide a background of culture and understanding; another has dissolute, improvident parents. One child is born in the United States, another in India, or China, or Russia. They clearly do not have identical opportunities open to them at birth, and there is no way that their opportunities can be made identical.

Like personal equality, equality of opportunity is not to be interpreted lit-   17
erally. Its real meaning is perhaps best expressed by the French expression dating from the French Revolution: *Une carrière ouverte aux talents*—a career open to the talents. No arbitrary obstacles should prevent people from achieving those positions for which their talents fit them and which their values lead them to seek. Not birth, nationality, color, religion, sex, nor any other irrelevant characteristic should determine the opportunities that are open to a person—only his abilities.

On this interpretation, equality of opportunity simply spells out in more   18
detail the meaning of personal equality, of equality before the law. And like personal equality, it has meaning and importance precisely because people are

different in their genetic and cultural characteristics, and hence both want to and can pursue different careers.

Equality of opportunity, like personal equality, is not inconsistent with lib-   19
erty; on the contrary, it is an essential component of liberty. If some people are denied access to particular positions in life for which they are qualified simply because of their ethnic background, color, or religion, that is an interference with their right to "Life, Liberty, and the pursuit of Happiness." It denies equality of opportunity and, by the same token, sacrifices the freedom of some for the advantage of others.

Like every ideal, equality of opportunity is incapable of being fully realized.   20
The most serious departure was undoubtedly with respect to the blacks, particularly in the South but in the North as well. Yet there was also tremendous progress for blacks and for other groups. The very concept of a "melting pot" reflected the goal of equality of opportunity. So also did the expansion of "free" education at elementary, secondary, and higher levels—though . . . this development has not been an unmixed blessing.

The priority given to equality of opportunity in the hierarchy of values   21
generally accepted by the public after the Civil War is manifested particularly in economic policy. The catchwords were free enterprise, competition, laissez-faire. Everyone was to be free to go into any business, follow any occupation, buy any property, subject only to the agreement of the other parties to the transaction. Each was to have the opportunity to reap the benefits if he succeeded, to suffer the costs if he failed. There were to be no arbitrary obstacles. Performance, not birth, religion, or nationality, was the touchstone.

One corollary was the development of what many who regarded them-   22
selves as the cultural elite sneered at as vulgar materialism—an emphasis on the almighty dollar, on wealth as both the symbol and the seal of success. As Tocqueville pointed out, this emphasis reflected the unwillingness of the community to accept the traditional criteria in feudal and aristocratic societies, namely birth and parentage. Performance was the obvious alternative, and the accumulation of wealth was the most readily available measure of performance.

Another corollary, of course, was an enormous release of human energy   23
that made America an increasingly productive and dynamic society in which social mobility was an everyday reality. Still another, perhaps surprisingly, was an explosion in charitable activity. This explosion was made possible by the rapid growth in wealth. It took the form it did—of nonprofit hospitals, privately endowed colleges and universities, a plethora of charitable organizations directed to helping the poor—because of the dominant values of the society, including, especially, promotion of equality of opportunity.

Of course, in the economic sphere as elsewhere, practice did not always   24
conform to the ideal. Government *was* kept to a minor role; no major obstacles

to enterprise were erected, and by the end of the nineteenth century, positive government measures, especially the Sherman Anti-Trust Law, were adopted to eliminate private barriers to competition. But extralegal arrangements continued to interfere with the freedom of individuals to enter various businesses or professions, and social practices unquestionably gave special advantages to persons born in the "right" families, of the "right" color, and practicing the "right" religion. However, the rapid rise in the economic and social position of various less privileged groups demonstrates that these obstacles were by no means insurmountable.

In respect of government measures, one major deviation from free markets 25 was in foreign trade, where Alexander Hamilton's *Report on Manufactures* had enshrined tariff protection for domestic industries as part of the American way. Tariff protection was inconsistent with thoroughgoing equality of opportunity . . . and, indeed, with the free immigration of persons, which was the rule until World War I, except only for Orientals. Yet it could be rationalized both by the needs of national defense and on the very different ground that equality stops at the water's edge—an illogical rationalization that is adopted also by most of today's proponents of a very different concept of equality.

Equality of Outcome

That different concept, equality of outcome, has been gaining ground in 26 this century. It first affected government policy in Great Britain and on the European continent. Over the past half-century it has increasingly affected government policy in the United States as well. In some intellectual circles the desirability of equality of outcome has become an article of religious faith: everyone should finish the race at the same time. As the Dodo said in *Alice in Wonderland*, *"Everybody* has won, and *all* must have prizes."

For this concept, as for the other two, "equal" is not to be interpreted liter- 27 ally as "identical." No one really maintains that everyone, regardless of age or sex or other physical qualities, should have identical rations of each separate item of food, clothing, and so on. The goal is rather "fairness," a much vaguer notion—indeed, one that it is difficult, if not impossible, to define precisely. "Fair shares for all" is the modern slogan that has replaced Karl Marx's "To each according to his needs, from each according to his ability."

This concept of equality differs radically from the other two. Government 28 measures that promote personal equality or equality of opportunity enhance liberty; government measures to achieve "fair shares for all" reduce liberty. If what people get is to be determined by "fairness," who is to decide what is "fair"? As a chorus of voices asked the Dodo, "But who is to give the prizes?" "Fairness" is not an objectively determined concept once it departs from identity. "Fairness," like "needs," is in the eye of the beholder. If all are to have "fair shares," someone or some group of people must decide what shares are fair—and they must be able to impose their decisions on others, taking from those who have more than their "fair" share and giving to those who have less. Are those who make and impose such decisions equal to those for whom they decide? Are we not in George Orwell's *Animal Farm,* where "all animals are equal, but some animals are more equal than others"?

In addition, if what people get is determined by "fairness" and not by what they produce, where are the "prizes" to come from? What incentive is there to work and produce? How is it to be decided who is to be the doctor, who the lawyer, who the garbage collector, who the street sweeper? What assures that people will accept the roles assigned to them and perform those roles in accordance with their abilities? Clearly, only force or the threat of force will do.

The key point is not merely that practice will depart from the ideal. Of course it will, as it does with respect to the other two concepts of equality as well. The point is rather that there is a fundamental conflict between the *ideal* of "fair shares" or of its precursor, "to each according to his needs," and the *ideal* of personal liberty. This conflict has plagued every attempt to make equality of outcome the overriding principle of social organization. The end result has invariably been a state of terror: Russia, China, and, more recently, Cambodia offer clear and convincing evidence. And even terror has not equalized outcomes. In every case, wide inequality persists by any criterion; inequality between the rulers and the ruled, not only in power, but also in material standards of life.[4]

The far less extreme measures taken in Western countries in the name of equality of outcome have shared the same fate to a lesser extent. They, too, have restricted individual liberty. They, too, have failed to achieve their objective. It has proved impossible to define "fair shares" in a way that is generally acceptable, or to satisfy the members of the community that they are being treated "fairly." On the contrary, dissatisfaction has mounted with every additional attempt to implement equality of outcome.

Much of the moral fervor behind the drive for equality of outcome comes from the widespread belief that it is not fair that some children should have a great advantage over others simply because they happen to have wealthy parents. Of course it is not fair. However, unfairness can take many forms. It can take the form of the inheritance of property—bonds and stocks, houses, factories; it can also take the form of the inheritance of talent—musical ability, strength, mathematical genius. The inheritance of property can be interfered

29

30

31

32

---

[4] See Smith, *The Russians,* and Kaiser, *Russia: The People and the Power.* Nick Eberstadt, "Has China Failed?" *The New York Review of Books,* April 5, 1979, p. 37, notes, "In China, . . . income distribution seems *very roughly* to have been the same since 1953." [Friedmans' note]

with more readily than the inheritance of talent. But from an ethical point of view, is there any difference between the two? Yet many people resent the inheritance of property but not the inheritance of talent.

33   Look at the same issue from the point of view of the parent. If you want to assure your child a higher income in life, you can do so in various ways. You can buy him (or her) an education that will equip him to pursue an occupation yielding a high income; or you can set him up in a business that will yield a higher income than he could earn as a salaried employee; or you can leave him property, the income from which will enable him to live better. Is there any ethical difference among these three ways of using your property? Or again, if the state leaves you any money to spend over and above taxes, should the state permit you to spend it on riotous living but not to leave it to your children?

34   The ethical issues involved are subtle and complex. They are not to be resolved by such simplistic formulas as "fair shares for all." Indeed, if we took that seriously, youngsters with less musical skill should be given the greatest amount of musical training in order to compensate for their inherited disadvantage, and those with greater musical aptitude should be prevented from having access to good musical training; and similarly with all other categories of inherited personal qualities. That might be "fair" to the youngsters lacking in talent, but would it be "fair" to the talented, let alone to those who had to work to pay for training the youngsters lacking talent, or to the persons deprived of the benefits that might have come from the cultivation of the talents of the gifted?

35   Life is not fair. It is tempting to believe that government can rectify what nature has spawned. But it is also important to recognize how much we benefit from the very unfairness we deplore.

36   There's nothing fair about Marlene Dietrich's having been born with beautiful legs that we all want to look at; or about Muhammad Ali's having been born with the skill that made him a great fighter. But on the other side, millions of people who have enjoyed looking at Marlene Dietrich's legs or watching one of Muhammad Ali's fights have benefited from nature's unfairness in producing a Marlene Dietrich and a Muhammad Ali. What kind of a world would it be if everyone were a duplicate of everyone else?

37   It is certainly not fair that Muhammad Ali should be able to earn millions of dollars in one night. But wouldn't it have been even more unfair to the people who enjoyed watching him if, in the pursuit of some abstract ideal of equality, Muhammad Ali had not been permitted to earn more for one night's fight—or for each day spent in preparing for a fight—than the lowest man on the totem pole could get for a day's unskilled work on the docks? It might have been possible to do that, but the result would have been to deny people the opportunity to watch Muhammad Ali. We doubt very much that he would have been willing to undergo the arduous regimen of training that preceded his fights, or to subject himself to the kind of fights he has had, if he were limited to the pay of an unskilled dockworker.

Still another facet of this complex issue of fairness can be illustrated by 38 considering a game of chance, for example, an evening at baccarat. The people who choose to play may start the evening with equal piles of chips, but as the play progresses, those piles will become unequal. By the end of the evening, some will be big winners, others big losers. In the name of the ideal of equality, should the winners be required to repay the losers? That would take all the fun out of the game. Not even the losers would like that. They might like it for the one evening, but would they come back again to play if they knew that whatever happened, they'd end up exactly where they started?

This example has a great deal more to do with the real world than one 39 might at first suppose. Every day each of us makes decisions that involve taking a chance. Occasionally it's a big chance — as when we decide what occupation to pursue, whom to marry, whether to buy a house or make a major investment. More often it's a small chance, as when we decide what movie to go to, whether to cross the street against the traffic, whether to buy one security rather than another. Each time the question is, who is to decide what chances we take? That in turn depends on who bears the consequences of the decision. If we bear the consequences, we can make the decision. But if someone else bears the consequences, should we or will we be permitted to make the decision? If you play baccarat as an agent for someone else with his money, will he, or should he, permit you unlimited scope for decision making? Is he not almost certain to set some limit to your discretion? Will he not lay down some rules for you to observe? To take a very different example, if the government (i.e., your fellow taxpayers) assumes the costs of flood damage to your house, can you be permitted to decide freely whether to build your house on a floodplain? It is no accident that increasing government intervention into personal decisions has gone hand in hand with the drive for "fair shares for all."

The system under which people make their own choices — and bear most 40 of the consequences of their decisions — is the system that has prevailed for most of our history. It is the system that gave the Henry Fords, the Thomas Alva Edisons, the George Eastmans, the John D. Rockefellers, the James Cash Penneys the incentive to transform our society over the past two centuries. It is the system that gave other people an incentive to furnish venture capital to finance the risky enterprises that these ambitious inventors and captains of industry undertook. Of course, there were many losers along the way — probably more losers than winners. We don't remember their names. But for the most part they went in with their eyes open. They knew they were taking chances. And win or lose, society as a whole benefited from their willingness to take a chance.

The fortunes that this system produced came overwhelmingly from devel- 41 oping new products or services, or new ways of producing products or services, or of distributing them widely. The resulting addition to the wealth of the community as a whole, to the well-being of the masses of the people, amounted to many times the wealth accumulated by the innovators. Henry Ford acquired a great fortune. The country acquired a cheap and reliable means of transportation and the techniques of mass production. Moreover, in many cases the private fortunes were largely devoted in the end to the benefit of society. The Rockefeller, Ford, and Carnegie foundations are only the most prominent of the numerous private benefactions which are so outstanding a consequence of the operation of a system that corresponded to "equality of opportunity" and "liberty" as these terms were understood until recently.

One limited sample may give the flavor of the outpouring of philanthropic activity in the nineteenth and early twentieth century. In a book devoted to "cultural philanthropy in Chicago from the 1880s to 1917," Helen Horowitz writes: 42

> At the turn of the century, Chicago was a city of contradictory impulses: it was both a commercial center dealing in the basic commodities of an industrial society and a community caught in the winds of cultural uplift. As one commentator put it, the city was "a strange combination of pork and Plato."
>
> A major manifestation of Chicago's drive toward culture was the establishment of the city's great cultural institutions in the 1880s and early 1890s (the Art Institute, the Newberry Library, the Chicago Symphony Orchestra, the University of Chicago, the Field Museum, the Crerar Library). . . .
>
> These institutions were a new phenomenon in the city. Whatever the initial impetus behind their founding, they were largely organized, sustained, and controlled by a group of businessmen. . . . Yet while privately supported and managed, the institutions were designed for the whole city. Their trustees had turned to cultural philanthropy not so much to satisfy personal aesthetic or scholarly yearnings as to accomplish social goals. Disturbed by social forces they could not control and filled with idealistic notions of culture, these businessmen saw in the museum, the library, the symphony orchestra, and the university a way to purify their city and to generate a civic renaissance.[5]

Philanthropy was by no means restricted to cultural institutions. There   43 was, as Horowitz writes in another connection, "a kind of explosion of activity on many different levels." And Chicago was not an isolated case. Rather, as Horowitz puts it, "Chicago seemed to epitomize America."[6] The same period saw the establishment of Hull House in Chicago under Jane Addams, the first

---

[5] Helen Lefkowitz Horowitz, *Culture and the City* (Lexington: University Press of Kentucky, 1976), pp. ix–x. [Friedmans' note]

[6] Ibid., pp. 212 and 31. [Friedmans' note]

of many settlement houses established throughout the nation to spread culture and education among the poor and to assist them in their daily problems. Many hospitals, orphanages, and other charitable agencies were set up in the same period.

There is no inconsistency between a free-market system and the pursuit   44
of broad social and cultural goals, or between a free-market system and compassion for the less fortunate, whether that compassion takes the form, as it did in the nineteenth century, of private charitable activity, or, as it has done increasingly in the twentieth, of assistance through government—provided that in both cases it is an expression of a desire to help others. There is all the difference in the world, however, between two kinds of assistance through government that seem superficially similar; first, 90 percent of us agreeing to impose taxes on ourselves in order to help the bottom 10 percent, and second, 80 percent voting to impose taxes on the top 10 percent to help the bottom 10 percent—William Graham Sumner's famous example of B and C deciding what D shall do for A.[7] The first may be wise or unwise, an effective or an ineffective way to help the disadvantaged—but it is consistent with belief in both equality of opportunity and liberty. The second seeks equality of outcome and is entirely antithetical to liberty.

Who Favors Equality of Outcome?

There is little support for the goal of equality of outcome despite the extent   45
to which it has become almost an article of religious faith among intellectuals and despite its prominence in the speeches of politicians and the preambles of legislation. The talk is belied alike by the behavior of government, of the intellectuals who most ardently espouse egalitarian sentiments, and of the public at large.

For government, one obvious example is the policy toward lotteries and   46
gambling. New York State—and particularly New York City—is widely and correctly regarded as a stronghold of egalitarian sentiment. Yet the New York State government conducts lotteries and provides facilities for off-track betting on races. It advertises extensively to induce its citizens to buy lottery tickets and bet on the races—at terms that yield a very large profit to the government. At the same time it tries to suppress the "numbers" game, which, as it happens, offers better odds than the government lottery (especially when account is taken of the greater ease of avoiding tax on winnings). Great Britain, a stronghold, if not the birthplace, of egalitarian sentiment, permits private gambling

---

7 "The Forgotten Man," in Albert G. Keller and Maurice R. Davis, eds., *Essays of William G. Sumner* (New Haven: Yale University Press, 1934), vol. I, pp. 466–96. [Friedmans' note]

clubs and betting on races and other sporting events. Indeed, wagering is a national pastime and a major source of government income.

For intellectuals, the clearest evidence is their failure to practice what so 47 many of them preach. Equality of outcome can be promoted on a do-it-yourself basis. First, decide exactly what you mean by equality. Do you want to achieve equality within the United States? In a selected group of countries as a whole? In the world as a whole? Is equality to be judged in terms of income per person? Per family? Per year? Per decade? Per lifetime? Income in the form of money alone? Or including such nonmonetary items as the rental value of an owned home; food grown for one's own use; services rendered by members of the family not employed for money, notably the housewife? How are physical and mental handicaps or advantages to be allowed for?

However you decide these issues, you can, if you are an egalitarian, esti- 48 mate what money income would correspond to your concept of equality. If your actual income is higher than that, you can keep that amount and distribute the rest to people who are below that level. If your criterion were to encompass the world—as most egalitarian rhetoric suggests it should—something less than, say, \$200 a year (in 1979 dollars) per person would be an amount that would correspond to the conception of equality that seems implicit in most egalitarian rhetoric. That is about the average income per person worldwide.

What Irving Kristol has called the "new class"—government bureaucrats, 49 academics whose research is supported by government funds or who are employed in government financed "think-tanks," staffs of the many so-called "general interest" or "public policy" groups, journalists and others in the communications industry—are among the most ardent preachers of the doctrine of equality. Yet they remind us very much of the old, if unfair, saw about the Quakers: "They came to the New World to do good, and ended up doing well." The members of the new class are in general among the highest paid persons in the community. And for many among them, preaching equality and promoting or administering the resulting legislation has proved an effective means of achieving such high incomes. All of us find it easy to identify our own welfare with the welfare of the community.

Of course, an egalitarian may protest that he is but a drop in the ocean, that 50 he would be willing to redistribute the excess of his income over his concept of an equal income if everyone else were compelled to do the same. On one level this contention that compulsion would change matters is wrong—even if everyone else did the same, his specific contribution to the income of others would still be a drop in the ocean. His individual contribution would be just as large if he were the only contributor as if he were one of many. Indeed, it would be more valuable because he could target his contribution to go to the very worst off among those he regards as appropriate recipients. On another level compulsion would change matters drastically: the kind of society that would emerge if such acts of redistribution were voluntary is altogether different — and, by our standards, infinitely preferable — to the kind that would emerge if redistribution were compulsory.

Persons who believe that a society of enforced equality is preferable can also practice what they preach. They can join one of the many communes in this country and elsewhere, or establish new ones. And, of course, it is entirely consistent with a belief in personal equality or equality of opportunity and liberty that any group of individuals who wish to live in that way should be free to do so. Our thesis that support for equality of outcome is word-deep receives strong support from the small number of persons who have wished to join such communes and from the fragility of the communes that have been established. 51

Egalitarians in the United States may object that the fewness of communes and their fragility reflect the opprobrium that a predominantly "capitalist" society visits on such communes and the resulting discrimination to which they are subjected. That may be true for the United States but as Robert Nozick[8] has pointed out, there is one country where that is not true, where, on the contrary, egalitarian communes are highly regarded and prized. That country is Israel. The kibbutz played a major role in early Jewish settlement in Palestine and continues to play an important role in the state of Israel. A disproportionate fraction of the leaders of the Israeli state were drawn from the kibbutzim. Far from being a source of disapproval, membership in a kibbutz confers social status and commands approbation. Everyone is free to join or leave a kibbutz, and kibbutzim have been viable social organizations. Yet at no time, and certainly not today, have more than about 5 percent of the Jewish population of Israel chosen to be members of a kibbutz. That percentage can be regarded as an upper estimate of the fraction of people who would voluntarily choose a system enforcing equality of outcome in preference to a system characterized by inequality, diversity, and opportunity. 52

Public attitudes about graduated income taxes are more mixed. Recent referenda on the introduction of graduated state income taxes in some states that do not have them, and on an increase in the extent of graduation in other states, have generally been defeated. On the other hand, the federal income tax is highly graduated, at least on paper, though it also contains a large number of provisions ("loopholes") that greatly reduce the extent of graduation in practice. On this showing, there is at least public tolerance of a moderate amount of redistributive taxation. 53

However, we venture to suggest that the popularity of Reno, Las Vegas, and now Atlantic City is no less faithful an indication of the preferences of the public than the federal income tax, the editorials in the *New York Times* and the *Washington Post*, and the pages of the *New York Review of Books*. 54

---

[8] Robert Nozick, "Who Would Choose Socialism?" *Reason*, May 1978, pp. 22–23. [Friedmans' note]

Consequences of Egalitarian Policies

In shaping our own policy, we can learn from the experience of Western coun-   55
tries with which we share a common intellectual and cultural background,
and from which we derive many of our values. Perhaps the most instructive
example is Great Britain, which led the way in the nineteenth century toward
implementing equality of opportunity and in the twentieth toward implementing equality of outcome.

Since the end of World War II, British domestic policy has been dominated   56
by the search for greater equality of outcome. Measure after measure has been
adopted designed to take from the rich and give to the poor. Taxes were raised
on income until they reached a top rate of 98 percent on property income
and 83 percent on "earned" income, and were supplemented by ever heavier
taxes on inheritances. State-provided medical, housing, and other welfare services were greatly expanded, along with payments to the unemployed and the
aged. Unfortunately, the results have been very different from those that were
intended by the people who were quite properly offended by the class structure
that dominated Britain for centuries. There has been a vast redistribution of
wealth, but the end result is not an equitable distribution.

Instead, new classes of privileged have been created to replace or sup-   57
plement the old: the bureaucrats, secure in their jobs, protected against inflation both when they work and when they retire; the trade unions that profess
to represent the most downtrodden workers but in fact consist of the highest paid laborers in the land—the aristocrats of the labor movement; and the
new millionaires—people who have been cleverest at finding ways around the
laws, the rules, the regulations that have poured from Parliament and the bureaucracy, who have found ways to avoid paying taxes on their income and to
get their wealth overseas beyond the grasp of the tax collectors. A vast reshuffling of income and wealth, yes; greater equity, hardly.

The drive for equality in Britain failed, not because the wrong measures   58
were adopted—though some no doubt were; not because they were badly
administered—though some no doubt were; not because the wrong people
administered them—though no doubt some did. The drive for equality failed
for a much more fundamental reason. It went against one of the most basic
instincts of all human beings. In the words of Adam Smith, "The uniform, constant, and uninterrupted effort of every man to better his condition"[9]—and,
one may add, the condition of his children and his children's children. Smith, of
course, meant by "condition" not merely material well-being, though certainly
that was one component. He had a much broader concept in mind, one that
included all the values by which men judge their success—in particular the

---

[9] *Wealth of Nations*, vol. I, p. 325 (Book II, Chap. III). [Friedmans' note]

kind of social values that gave rise to the outpouring of philanthropic activities in the nineteenth century.

When the law interferes with people's pursuit of their own values, they will try to find a way around. They will evade the law, they will break the law, or they will leave the country. Few of us believe in a moral code that justifies forcing people to give up much of what they produce to finance payments to persons they do not know for purposes they may not approve of. When the law contradicts what most people regard as moral and proper, they will break the law—whether the law is enacted in the name of a noble ideal such as equality or in the naked interest of one group at the expense of another. Only fear of punishment, not a sense of justice and morality, will lead people to obey the law.   59

When people start to break one set of laws, the lack of respect for the law inevitably spreads to all laws, even those that everyone regards as moral and proper—laws against violence, theft, and vandalism. Hard as it may be to believe, the growth of crude criminality in Britain in recent decades may well be one consequence of the drive for equality.   60

In addition, that drive for equality has driven out of Britain some of its ablest, best-trained, most vigorous citizens, much to the benefit of the United States and other countries that have given them a greater opportunity to use their talents for their own benefit. Finally, who can doubt the effect that the drive for equality has had on efficiency and productivity? Surely, that is one of the main reasons why economic growth in Britain has fallen so far behind its continental neighbors, the United States, Japan, and other nations over the past few decades.   61

We in the United States have not gone as far as Britain in promoting the goal of equality of outcome. Yet many of the same consequences are already evident—from a failure of egalitarian measures to achieve their objectives, to a reshuffling of wealth that by no standards can be regarded as equitable, to a rise in criminality, to a depressing effect on productivity and efficiency.   62

Capitalism and Equality

Everywhere in the world there are gross inequities of income and wealth. They offend most of us. Few can fail to be moved by the contrast between the luxury enjoyed by some and the grinding poverty suffered by others.   63

In the past century a myth has grown up that free-market capitalism— equality of opportunity as we have interpreted that term—increases such inequalities, that it is a system under which the rich exploit the poor.   64

Nothing could be further from the truth. Wherever the free market has been permitted to operate, wherever anything approaching equality of oppor- tunity has existed, the ordinary man has been able to attain levels of living never dreamed of before. Nowhere is the gap between rich and poor wider,   65 nowhere are the rich richer and the poor poorer, than in those societies that do not permit the free market to operate. That is true of feudal societies like medieval Europe, India before independence, and much of modern South America, where inherited status determines position. It is equally true of centrally planned societies, like Russia or China or India since independence, where access to government determines position. It is true even where central planning was introduced, as in all three of these countries, in the name of equality.

Russia is a country of two nations: a small privileged upper class of bureaucrats, Communist party officials, technicians; and a great mass of people living little better than their great-grandparents did. The upper class has access to special shops, schools, and luxuries of all kind; the masses are condemned to enjoy little more than the basic necessities. We remember asking a tourist guide in Moscow the cost of a large automobile that we saw and being told, "Oh, those aren't for sale; they're only for the Politburo." Several recent books by American journalists document in great detail the contrast between the privileged life of the upper classes and the poverty of the masses.[10] Even on a simpler level, it is noteworthy that the average wage of a foreman is a larger multiple of the average wage of an ordinary worker in a Russian factory than in a factory in the United States—and no doubt he deserves it. After all, an American foreman only has to worry about being fired; a Russian foreman also has to worry about being shot. 66

China, too, is a nation with wide differences in income—between the politically powerful and the rest; between city and countryside; between some workers in the cities and other workers. A perceptive student of China writes that "the inequality between rich and poor regions in China was more acute in 1957 than in any of the larger nations of the world except perhaps Brazil." He quotes another scholar as saying, "These examples suggest that the Chinese industrial wage structure is not significantly more egalitarian than that of other countries." And he concludes his examination of equality in China, "How evenly distributed would China's income be today? Certainly, it would not be as even as Taiwan's or South Korea's. . . . On the other hand, income distribution in China is obviously more even than in Brazil or South America. . . . We must conclude that China is far from being a society of complete equality. In fact, income differences in China may be quite a bit greater than in a number of countries commonly associated with 'fascist' elites and exploited masses."[11] 67

Industrial progress, mechanical improvement, all of the great wonders of the modern era have meant relatively little to the wealthy. The rich in Ancient Greece would have benefited hardly at all from modern plumbing: running 68

---

[10] See Smith, *The Russians*, and Kaiser, *Russia: The People and the Power*. [Friedmans' note]

[11] Nick Eberstadt, "China: How Much Success," *New York Review of Books*. May 3, 1979, pp. 40–41. [Friedmans' note]

servants replaced running water. Television and radio—the patricians of Rome could enjoy the leading musicians and actors in their home, could have the leading artists as domestic retainers. Ready-to-wear clothing, supermarkets— all these and many other modern developments would have added little to their life. They would have welcomed the improvements in transportation and in medicine, but for the rest, the great achievements of Western capitalism have redounded primarily to the benefit of the ordinary person. These achievements have made available to the masses conveniences and amenities that were previously the exclusive prerogative of the rich and powerful.

In 1848 John Stuart Mill wrote: 69

> Hitherto it is questionable if all the mechanical inventions yet made have lightened the day's toil of any human being. They have enabled a greater population to live the same life of drudgery and imprisonment, and an increased number of manufacturers and others to make fortunes. They have increased the comforts of the middle classes. But they have not yet begun to effect those great changes in human destiny, which it is in their nature and in their futurity to accomplish.[12]

No one could say that today. You can travel from one end of the industrialized world to the other and almost the only people you will find engaging in backbreaking toil are people who are doing it for sport. To find people whose day's toil has not been lightened by mechanical invention, you must go to the noncapitalist world: to Russia, China, India or Bangladesh, parts of Yugoslavia; or to the more backward capitalist countries—in Africa, the Mideast, South America; and until recently, Spain or Italy. 70

Conclusion

A society that puts equality—in the sense of equality of outcome—ahead of freedom will end up with neither equality nor freedom. The use of force to achieve equality will destroy freedom, and the force, introduced for good purposes, will end up in the hands of people who use it to promote their own interests. 71

On the other hand, a society that puts freedom first will, as a happy by-product, end up with both greater freedom and greater equality. Though a by-product of freedom, greater equality is not an accident. A free society releases the energies and abilities of people to pursue their own objectives. 72

---

[12] John Stuart Mill, *The Principles of Political Economy* (1848), 9th ed. (London: Longmans, Green & Co., 1886), vol. II, p. 332 (Book IV, Chap. VI). [Friedmans' note]

It prevents some people from arbitrarily suppressing others. It does not prevent some people from achieving positions of privilege, but so long as freedom is maintained, it prevents those positions of privilege from becoming institutionalized; they are subject to continued attack by other able, ambitious people. Freedom means diversity but also mobility. It preserves the opportunity for today's disadvantaged to become tomorrow's privileged and, in the process, enables almost everyone, from top to bottom, to enjoy a fuller and richer life.

✖ QUESTIONS FOR CRITICAL READING

1. What is the difference between equality of opportunity and equality of outcome?

2. What effect does a policy that guarantees equality of outcome have on freedom?

3. Explain the Friedmans' attitude toward the concept of "Equality before God" (paras. 6–14).

4. What is the meaning of *laissez-faire*?

5. What role should government play in regulating the nation's economic system?

6. What is "personal equality"?

7. What advantages does a free market give the "right people"?

✖ SUGGESTIONS FOR CRITICAL WRITING

1. The Friedmans make a strong case for equality of opportunity. However, some critics might say that they actually make a case for permitting the highly advantaged to exploit the less advantaged. This would give those with exceptional economic talent and skills a free rein to make millions while those who are ordinary would spend a life in relative poverty. The Friedmans explain that life is not fair, so such distinctions will naturally occur. How can you defend their views? How can you attack their views?

2. The Friedmans discuss the inheritance of property and the inheritance of talent in paragraphs 32 to 34. If government stands aside on the question of inheritance of talent — which could contribute considerably to the economic success of an individual — why should it not stand aside on the question of inheritance of property? Compare the two and take your own stand on what role government should have in relation to the inheritance of qualities or property that might give an individual a considerable advantage in life.

3. Examine the question of fairness in this essay. The complex idea of "fair share," which is discussed in detail in paragraphs 34 to 41, is dealt with in a manner that is intended to convince you that the Friedmans' position is accurate and desirable. Analyze their position and decide whether or not they are right.

4. In paragraphs 17 to 25, the Friedmans closely examine whether or not we can expect equality of opportunity "to be interpreted literally." Establish their position on this question and then argue the question for yourself. How do you interpret this idea, and what do you personally believe in? Attempt to convince someone who does not agree with you.

5. The Friedmans argue that "[equality of opportunity, like personal equality, is not inconsistent with liberty; on the contrary, it is an essential component of liberty" (para. 19). Why would they feel it necessary to make this statement? Is there any sense in which equality of opportunity might actually be inconsistent with liberty? Examine the entire essay in an effort to make an argument that contradicts the Friedmans' assumption. If possible, draw on your own research.

6. **CONNECTIONS**   The Friedmans have something to say about the effect of machines and mechanical inventions on working people in underdeveloped countries. Karl Marx (p. 335) also comments on the use of machines and its effect on worker morale. How, ultimately, do machines affect the working class in terms of either limiting or expanding personal opportunity?

7. **CONNECTIONS**   This essay assumes that Jefferson's ideas in the Declaration of Independence (p. 116) generally agree with the positions espoused by the Friedmans. Reread Jefferson and evaluate this assumption for yourself: Does Jefferson seem to be in absolute agreement with the Friedmans, or have the Friedmans reinterpreted Jefferson for their own purposes? Use quotations from Jefferson's Declaration to support your answer.

© Reuters/Corbis

ROBERT B.
REICH

Why the Rich Are Getting Richer and the Poor, Poorer

ROBERT B. REICH (b. 1946), professor of public policy at the Goldman School of Public Policy at the University of California at Berkeley, who served as secretary of labor in the first Clinton administration, holds a graduate degree from Yale Law School, and, unlike his former colleagues in the John F. Kennedy School of Government at Harvard, he does not hold a Ph.D. in economics. Nonetheless, he has written numerous books on economics and has been a prominent lecturer for almost two decades. Reich's books include *The Future of Success: Working and Living in the New Economy* (2000); *Reason: Why Liberals Will Win the Battle for America* (2004); and *Supercapitalism: The Transformation of Business, Democracy, and Everyday Life* (2007). All of these have been best sellers, something unusual for the work of an academic concerned with economics. *Locked in the Cabinet* (1997) is a memoir of his four years as secretary of labor. *The Work of Nations* (1991), from which this essay comes, is the distillation of many years' analysis of modern economic trends.

As a college student, Reich was an activist but not a radical. In 1968, he was a Rhodes scholar, studying at Oxford University with Bill Clinton and a number of others who became influential American policy makers. Reich is a specialist in policy studies — that is, the relationship of governmental policy to the economic health of the nation. Unlike those who champion free trade and unlimited expansion, Reich questions the existence of free trade by pointing to the effect of government taxation on business enterprise. Taxation — like many governmental policies regarding immigration, tariffs, and money supply — directly shapes the behavior of most companies. Reich feels that government must establish and execute an industrial policy that will benefit the nation.

Even though organized labor groups, such as industrial unions, have rejected much of his theorizing about labor, Reich has developed a reputation as a conciliator who can

---

From *The Work of Nations*.

see opposite sides of a question and resolve them. He is known for his denunciation of mergers, lawsuits, takeovers, and other deals that he believes simply churn money around rather than produce wealth. He feels that such maneuvers enrich a few predatory people but do not benefit labor in general — and, indeed, that the debt created by such deals harms labor in the long run.

In *The Next American Frontier* (1983), Reich insists that government, unions, and businesses must cooperate to create a workable program designed to improve the economy. Trusting to chance and free trade, he argues, will not work in the current economy. He also has said that the old assembly-line methods must give way to what he calls "flexible production," involving smaller, customized runs of products for specific markets.

Reich's *The Work of Nations* (1991), whose title draws on Adam Smith's classic *The Wealth of Nations* (1776), examines the borderless nature of contemporary corporations. Multinational corporations are a reality, and as he points out in the following essay, their flexibility makes it possible for them to thrive by moving manufacturing plants from nation to nation. The reasons for moving are sometimes connected to lower wages but more often are connected to the infrastructure of a given nation. Reliable roads, plentiful electricity, well-educated workers, low crime rates, and political stability are all elements that make a location attractive to a multinational corporation.

REICH'S RHETORIC

The structure of "Why the Rich Are Getting Richer and the Poor, Poorer" is built on a metaphor: that of boats rising or falling with the tide. As Reich notes, "All Americans used to be in roughly the same economic boat" (para. 2), and when the economic tide rose, most people rose along with it. However, today "national borders no longer define our economic fates"; Reich therefore views Americans today as being in different boats, depending on their role in the economy, and his essay follows the fates of three distinct kinds of workers.

Examining the routine worker, he observes, "The boat containing routine producers is sinking rapidly" (para. 3). As he demonstrates, the need for routine production has declined in part because of improvements in production facilities. Much labor-intensive work has been replaced by machines. Modern factories often scramble to locate in places where production costs are lowest. People in other nations work at a fraction of the hourly rate of American workers, and because factories are relatively cheap to establish, they can be easily moved.

Reich continues the boat metaphor with "in-person servers." The boat that carries these workers, he says, "is sinking as well, but somewhat more slowly and unevenly" (para. 20). Workers in restaurants, retail outlets, car washes, and other personal service industries often work part-time and have few health or other benefits. Their jobs are imperiled by machines as well, although not as much as manufacturing jobs are. Although the outlook for such workers is buoyed by a declining population, which will reduce competition for their jobs, increased immigration may cancel this benefit.

Finally, Reich argues that the "vessel containing America's symbolic analysts is rising" (para. 28). This third group contains the population that identifies and solves problems and brokers ideas. "Almost everyone around the world is buying the skills and insights of Americans who manipulate oral and visual symbols" (para. 33). Engineers, consultants, marketing experts, publicists, and those in entertainment fields all manage to cross national boundaries and prosper at a rate that is perhaps startling. As a result of an expanding world market, symbolic analysts do not depend only on the purchasing power of routine and in-service workers. Instead, they rely on the same global web that dominates the pattern of corporate structure.

Reich's essay follows the fate of these three groups in turn to establish the pattern of change and expectation that will shape America's economic future. His metaphor is deftly handled, and he includes details, examples, facts, and careful references to support his position.

⚑ PREREADING QUESTIONS: WHAT TO READ FOR

The following prereading questions may help you anticipate key issues in the discussion of Robert B. Reich's "Why the Rich Are Getting Richer and the Poor, Poorer." Keeping them in mind during your first reading of the selection should help focus your attention.

1. Why and how does an individual's position in the world economy depend on the function he/she performs in it?

2. Who are the "routine producers"? What will be their fate in the future?

3. Who are the "symbolic analysts" in our economy? How does one become a symbolic analyst?

Why the Rich Are Getting Richer and the Poor, Poorer

The division of labor is limited by the extent of the market.
—ADAM SMITH
*An Inquiry into the Nature
and Causes of the Wealth of Nations* (1776)

Regardless of how your job is officially classified (manufacturing, service, managerial, technical, secretarial, and so on), or the industry in which you work (automotive, steel, computer, advertising, finance, food processing), your real competitive position in the world economy is coming to depend on the function you perform in it. Herein lies the basic reason why incomes are diverging. The fortunes of routine producers are declining. In-person servers are also becoming poorer, although their fates are less clear-cut. But symbolic analysts—who solve, identify, and broker new problems—are, by and large, succeeding in the world economy.

All Americans used to be in roughly the same economic boat. Most rose or fell together as the corporations in which they were employed, the industries comprising such corporations, and the national economy as a whole became more productive—or languished. But national borders no longer define our economic fates. We are now in different boats, one sinking rapidly, one sinking more slowly, and the third rising steadily.

The boat containing routine producers is sinking rapidly. Recall that by midcentury routine production workers in the United States were paid relatively well. The giant pyramidlike organizations at the core of each major industry coordinated their prices and investments—avoiding the harsh winds of competition and thus maintaining healthy earnings. Some of these earnings, in turn, were reinvested in new plant and equipment (yielding ever-larger-scale economies); another portion went to top managers and investors. But a large and increasing portion went to middle managers and production workers. Work stoppages posed such a threat to high-volume production that organized labor was able to exact an ever-larger premium for its cooperation. And the pattern of wages established within the core corporations influenced the pattern throughout the national economy. Thus the growth of a relatively affluent middle class, able to purchase all the wondrous things produced in high volume by the core corporations.

But, as has been observed, the core is rapidly breaking down into global webs which earn their largest profits from clever problem-solving, -identifying, and brokering. As the costs of transporting standard things and of communicating information about them continue to drop, profit margins on high-volume, standardized production are thinning, because there are few barriers to entry. Modern factories and state-of-the-art machinery can be installed almost anywhere on the globe. Routine producers in the United States, then, are in direct competition with millions of routine producers in other nations. Twelve thousand people are added to the world's population every hour, most of whom, eventually, will happily work for a small fraction of the wages of routine producers in America.[1]

The consequence is clearest in older, heavy industries, where high-volume, standardized production continues its ineluctable move to where labor is cheapest and most accessible around the world. Thus, for example, the Maquiladora

---

[1] The reader should note, of course, that lower wages in other areas of the world are of no particular attraction to global capital unless workers there are sufficiently productive to make the labor cost of producing *each unit* lower there than in higher-wage regions. Productivity in many low-wage areas of the world has improved due to the ease with which state-of-the-art factories and equipment can be installed there. [Reich's note]

factories cluttered along the Mexican side of the U.S. border in the sprawl-
ing shanty towns of Tijuana, Mexicali, Nogales, Agua Prieta, and Ciudad
Juárez—factories owned mostly by Americans, but increasingly by Japanese—
in which more than a half million routine producers assemble parts into
finished goods to be shipped into the United States.

    The same story is unfolding worldwide. Until the late 1970s, AT&T had   6
depended on routine producers in Shreveport, Louisiana, to assemble standard
telephones. It then discovered that routine producers in Singapore would perform the same tasks at a far lower cost. Facing intense competition from other
global webs, AT&T's strategic brokers felt compelled to switch. So in the early
1980s they stopped hiring routine producers in Shreveport and began hiring
cheaper routine producers in Singapore. But under this kind of pressure for
ever-lower high-volume production costs, today's Singaporean can easily end
up as yesterday's Louisianan. By the late 1980s, AT&T's strategic brokers found
that routine producers in Thailand were eager to assemble telephones for a
small fraction of the wages of routine producers in Singapore. Thus, in 1989,
AT&T stopped hiring Singaporeans to make telephones and began hiring even
cheaper routine producers in Thailand.

    The search for ever-lower wages has not been confined to heavy industry.   7
Routine data processing is equally footloose. Keypunch operators located anywhere around the world can enter data into computers, linked by satellite or
transoceanic fiber-optic cable, and take it out again. As the rates charged by
satellite networks continue to drop, and as more satellites and fiber-optic cables
become available (reducing communication costs still further), routine data
processors in the United States find themselves in ever more direct competition
with their counterparts abroad, who are often eager to work for far less.

    By 1990, keypunch operators in the United States were earning, at   8
most, $6.50 per hour. But keypunch operators throughout the rest of the
world were willing to work for a fraction of this. Thus, many potential
American data-processing jobs were disappearing, and the wages and benefits of the remaining ones were in decline. Typical was Saztec International, a
$20-million-a-year data-processing firm headquartered in Kansas City, whose
American strategic brokers contracted with routine data processors in Manila
and with American-owned firms that needed such data-processing services.
Compared with the average Philippine income of $1,700 per year, data-entry
operators working for Saztec earn the princely sum of $2,650. The remainder of
Saztec's employees were American problem-solvers and -identifiers, searching
for ways to improve the worldwide system and find new uses to which it could
be put.[2]

---

2 John Maxwell Hamilton, "A Bit Player Buys into the Computer Age," *New York Times
  Business World*, December 3, 1989, p. 14. [Reich's note]

By 1990, American Airlines was employing over 1,000 data processors   9
in Barbados and the Dominican Republic to enter names and flight numbers
from used airline tickets (flown daily to Barbados from airports around the
United States) into a giant computer bank located in Dallas. Chicago publisher
R. R. Donnelley was sending entire manuscripts to Barbados for entry into computers in preparation for printing. The New York Life Insurance Company was
dispatching insurance claims to Castleisland, Ireland, where routine producers,
guided by simple directions, entered the claims and determined the amounts
due, then instantly transmitted the computations back to the United States.
(When the firm advertised in Ireland for twenty-five data-processing jobs, it
received six hundred applications.) And McGraw-Hill was processing subscription renewal and marketing information for its magazines in nearby Galway.
Indeed, literally millions of routine workers around the world were receiving
information, converting it into computer-readable form, and then sending it
back — at the speed of electronic impulses — whence it came.

The simple coding of computer software has also entered into world com-   10
merce. India, with a large English-speaking population of technicians happy
to do routine programming cheaply, is proving to be particularly attractive to
global webs in need of this service. By 1990, Texas Instruments maintained a
software development facility in Bangalore, linking fifty Indian programmers
by satellite to TI's Dallas headquarters. Spurred by this and similar ventures,
the Indian government was building a teleport in Poona, intended to make it
easier and less expensive for many other firms to send their routine software
design specifications for coding.[3]

This shift of routine production jobs from advanced to developing nations is   11
a great boon to many workers in such nations who otherwise would be jobless or
working for much lower wages. These workers, in turn, now have more money
with which to purchase symbolic-analytic services from advanced nations (often
embedded within all sorts of complex products). The trend is also beneficial
to everyone around the world who can now obtain high-volume, standardized
products (including information and software) more cheaply than before.

But these benefits do not come without certain costs. In particular the bur-   12
den is borne by those who no longer have good-paying routine production jobs
within advanced economies like the United States. Many of these people used
to belong to unions or at least benefited from prevailing wage rates established
in collective bargaining agreements. But as the old corporate bureaucracies
have flattened into global webs, bargaining leverage has been lost. Indeed, the
tacit national bargain is no more.

---

[3] Udayan Gupta, "U.S.-Indian Satellite Link Stands to Cut Software Costs," *Wall Street
Journal*, March 6, 1989, p. B2. [Reich's note]

Despite the growth in the number of new jobs in the United States, union   13
membership has withered. In 1960, 35 percent of all nonagricultural workers in
America belonged to a union. But by 1980 that portion had fallen to just under
a quarter, and by 1989 to about 17 percent. Excluding government employees,
union membership was down to 13.4 percent.[4] This was a smaller proportion
even than in the early 1930s, before the National Labor Relations Act created
a legally protected right to labor representation. The drop in membership has
been accompanied by a growing number of collective bargaining agreements
to freeze wages at current levels, reduce wage levels of entering workers, or
reduce wages overall. This is an important reason why the long economic
recovery that began in 1982 produced a smaller rise in unit labor costs than
any of the eight recoveries since World War II—the low rate of unemployment
during its course notwithstanding.

Routine production jobs have vanished fastest in traditional unionized   14
industries (autos, steel, and rubber, for example), where average wages have
kept up with inflation. This is because the jobs of older workers in such industries are protected by seniority; the youngest workers are the first to be laid off.
Faced with a choice of cutting wages or cutting the number of jobs, a majority
of union members (secure in the knowledge that there are many who are junior
to them who will be laid off first) often have voted for the latter.

Thus the decline in union membership has been most striking among   15
young men entering the workforce without a college education. In the early
1950s, more than 40 percent of this group joined unions; by the late 1980s, less
than 20 percent (if public employees are excluded, less than 10 percent).[5] In
steelmaking, for example, although many older workers remained employed,
almost half of all routine steelmaking jobs in America vanished between 1974
and 1988 (from 480,000 to 260,000). Similarly with automobiles: during the
1980s, the United Auto Workers lost 500,000 members—one-third of their total
at the start of the decade. General Motors alone cut 150,000 American production jobs during the 1980s (even as it added employment abroad). Another
consequence of the same phenomenon: the gap between the average wages of
unionized and nonunionized workers widened dramatically—from 14.6 percent in 1973 to 20.4 percent by end of the 1980s.[6] The lesson is clear. If you drop
out of high school or have no more than a high school diploma, do not expect
a good routine production job to be awaiting you.

---

[4] *Statistical Abstract of the United States* (Washington, D.C.: U.S. Government Printing
Office, 1989), p. 416, table 684. [Reich's note]

[5] Calculations from Current Population Surveys by L. Katz and A. Revenga, "Changes in the
Structure of Wages: U.S. and Japan," National Bureau of Economic Research, September
1989. [Reich's note]

[6] U.S. Department of Commerce, Bureau of Labor Statistics, "Wages of Unionized and
Non-Unionized Workers," various issues. [Reich's note]

Also vanishing are lower- and middle-level management jobs involving rou-   16
tine production. Between 1981 and 1986, more than 780,000 foremen, super-
visors, and section chiefs lost their jobs through plant closings and layoffs.[7]
Large numbers of assistant division heads, assistant directors, assistant managers, and vice presidents also found themselves jobless. GM shed more than
40,000 white-collar employees and planned to eliminate another 25,000 by the
mid-1990s.[8] As America's core pyramids metamorphosed into global webs,
many middle-level routine producers were as obsolete as routine workers on
the line.

As has been noted, foreign-owned webs are hiring some Americans to do   17
routine production in the United States. Philips, Sony, and Toyota factories
are popping up all over—to the self-congratulatory applause of the nation's
governors and mayors, who have lured them with promises of tax abatements
and new sewers, among other amenities. But as these ebullient politicians
will soon discover, the foreign-owned factories are highly automated and
will become far more so in years to come. Routine production jobs account
for a small fraction of the cost of producing most items in the United States
and other advanced nations, and this fraction will continue to decline sharply
as computer-integrated robots take over. In 1977 it took routine producers
thirty-five hours to assemble an automobile in the United States; it is estimated
that by the mid-1990s, Japanese-owned factories in America will be producing
finished automobiles using only eight hours of a routine producer's time.[9]

The productivity and resulting wages of American workers who run such   18
robotic machinery may be relatively high, but there may not be many such
jobs to go around. A case in point: in the late 1980s, Nippon Steel joined with
America's ailing Inland Steel to build a new $400 million cold-rolling mill fifty
miles west of Gary, Indiana. The mill was celebrated for its state-of-the-art technology, which cut the time to produce a coil of steel from twelve days to about
one hour. In fact, the entire plant could be run by a small team of technicians,
which became clear when Inland subsequently closed two of its old cold-rolling
mills, laying off hundreds of routine workers. Governors and mayors take note:
your much-ballyhooed foreign factories may end up employing distressingly
few of your constituents.

Overall, the decline in routine jobs has hurt men more than women. This is   19
because the routine production jobs held by men in high-volume metal-bending
manufacturing industries had paid higher wages than the routine production

---

[7] U.S. Department of Labor, Bureau of Labor Statistics, "Reemployment Increases Among
Displaced Workers," *BLS News*, USDL 86–414, October 14, 1986, table 6. [Reich's note]

[8] *Wall Street Journal*, February 16, 1990, p. A5. [Reich's note]

[9] Figures from the International Motor Vehicles Program, Massachusetts Institute of
Technology, 1989. [Reich's note]

jobs held by women in textiles and data processing. As both sets of jobs have been lost, American women in routine production have gained more equal footing with American men—equally poor footing, that is. This is a major reason why the gender gap between male and female wages began to close during the 1980s.

    The second of the three boats, carrying in-person servers, is sinking as well, but somewhat more slowly and unevenly. Most in-person servers are paid at or just slightly above the minimum wage and many work only part-time, with the result that their take-home pay is modest, to say the least. Nor do they typically receive all the benefits (health care, life insurance, disability, and so forth) garnered by routine producers in large manufacturing corporations or by symbolic analysts affiliated with the more affluent threads of global webs.[10] In-person servers are sheltered from the direct effects of global competition and, like everyone else, benefit from access to lower-cost products from around the world. But they are not immune to its indirect effects.   20

    For one thing, in-person servers increasingly compete with former routine production workers, who, no longer able to find well-paying routine production jobs, have few alternatives but to seek in-person service jobs. The Bureau of Labor Statistics estimates that of the 2.8 million manufacturing workers who lost their jobs during the early 1980s, fully one-third were rehired in service jobs paying at least 20 percent less.[11] In-person servers must also compete with high school graduates and dropouts who years before had moved easily into routine production jobs but no longer can. And if demographic predictions about the American workforce in the first decades of the twenty-first century are correct (and they are likely to be, since most of the people who will comprise the workforce are already identifiable), most new entrants into the job market will be black or Hispanic men, or women—groups that in years past have possessed relatively weak technical skills. This will result in an even larger number of people crowding into in-person services. Finally, in-person servers will be competing with growing numbers of immigrants, both legal and illegal, for whom in-person services will comprise the most accessible jobs. (It is estimated that between the mid-1980s and the end of the century, about a quarter of all workers entering the American labor force will be immigrants.[12])   21

    Perhaps the fiercest competition that in-person servers face comes from labor-saving machinery (much of it invented, designed, fabricated, or assembled   22

---

[10] The growing portion of the American labor force engaged in in-person services, relative to routine production, thus helps explain why the number of Americans lacking health insurance increased by at least 6 million during the 1980s. [Reich's note]

[11] U.S. Department of Labor, Bureau of Labor Statistics, "Reemployment Increases Among Disabled Workers," October 14, 1986. [Reich's note]

[12] Federal Immigration and Naturalization Service, *Statistical Yearbook* (Washington, D.C.: U.S. Government Printing Office, 1986, 1987). [Reich's note]

in other nations, of course). Automated tellers, computerized cashiers, automatic car washes, robotized vending machines, self-service gasoline pumps, and all similar gadgets substitute for the human beings that customers once encountered. Even telephone operators are fast disappearing, as electronic sensors and voice simulators become capable of carrying on conversations that are reasonably intelligent and always polite. Retail sales workers—among the largest groups of in-person servers—are similarly imperiled. Through personal computers linked to television screens, tomorrow's consumers will be able to buy furniture, appliances, and all sorts of electronic toys from their living rooms—examining the merchandise from all angles, selecting whatever color, size, special features, and price seem most appealing, and then transmitting the order instantly to warehouses from which the selections will be shipped directly to their homes. So, too, with financial transactions, airline and hotel reservations, rental car agreements, and similar contracts, which will be executed between consumers in their homes and computer banks somewhere else on the globe.[13]

Advanced economies like the United States will continue to generate sizable numbers of new in-person service jobs, of course, the automation of older ones notwithstanding. For every bank teller who loses her job to an automated teller, three new jobs open for aerobics instructors. Human beings, it seems, have an almost insatiable desire for personal attention. But the intense competition nevertheless ensures that the wages of in-person servers will remain relatively low. In-person servers—working on their own, or else dispersed widely amid many small establishments, filling all sorts of personal-care niches—cannot readily organize themselves into labor unions or create powerful lobbies to limit the impact of such competition.   23

In two respects, demographics will work in favor of in-person servers, buoying their collective boat slightly. First, as has been noted, the rate of growth of the American workforce is slowing. In particular, the number of young workers is shrinking. Between 1985 and 1995, the number of eighteen- to twenty-four-year-olds will have declined by 17.5 percent. Thus, employers will have more incentive to hire and train in-person servers whom they might previously have avoided. But this demographic relief from the competitive pressures will be only temporary. The cumulative procreative energies of the postwar baby-boomers (born between 1946 and 1964) will result in a new surge of workers by 2010 or thereabouts.[14] And immigration—both legal and illegal — shows every sign of increasing in years to come.   24

---

[13] See Claudia H. Deutsch, "The Powerful Push for Self-Service," *New York Times*, April 9, 1989, section 3, p. 1. [Reich's note]

[14] U.S. Bureau of the Census, Current Population Reports, Series P-23, no. 138, tables 2-1, 4-6. See W. Johnson, A. Packer, et al., *Workforce 2000: Work and Workers for the 21st Century* (Indianapolis: Hudson Institute, 1987). [Reich's note]

Next, by the second decade of the twenty-first century, the number 25
of Americans aged sixty-five and over will be rising precipitously, as the
baby-boomers reach retirement age and live longer. Their life expectancies will
lengthen not just because fewer of them will have smoked their way to their
graves and more will have eaten better than their parents, but also because
they will receive all sorts of expensive drugs and therapies designed to keep
them alive — barely. By 2035, twice as many Americans will be elderly as in
1988, and the number of octogenarians is expected to triple. As these decaying baby-boomers ingest all the chemicals and receive all the treatments, they
will need a great deal of personal attention. Millions of deteriorating bodies
will require nurses, nursing-home operators, hospital administrators, orderlies,
home-care providers, hospice aides, and technicians to operate and maintain
all the expensive machinery that will monitor and temporarily stave off final
disintegration. There might even be a booming market for euthanasia specialists. In-person servers catering to the old and ailing will be in strong demand.[15]

One small problem: the decaying baby-boomers will not have enough 26
money to pay for these services. They will have used up their personal savings
years before. Their Social Security payments will, of course, have been used by
the government to pay for the previous generation's retirement and to finance
much of the budget deficits of the 1980s. Moreover, with relatively fewer young
Americans in the population, the supply of housing will likely exceed the
demand, with the result that the boomers' major investments — their homes —
will be worth less (in inflation-adjusted dollars) when they retire than they
planned for. In consequence, the huge cost of caring for the graying boomers
will fall on many of the same people who will be paid to care for them. It will
be like a great sump pump: in-person servers of the twenty-first century will
have an abundance of health-care jobs, but a large portion of their earnings
will be devoted to Social Security payments and income taxes, which will in
turn be used to pay their salaries. The net result: no real improvement in their
standard of living.

The standard of living of in-person servers also depends, indirectly, on 27
the standard of living of the Americans they serve who are engaged in world
commerce. To the extent that these Americans are richly rewarded by the
rest of the world for what they contribute, they will have more money to
lavish upon in-person services. Here we find the only form of "trickle-down"
economics that has a basis in reality. A waitress in a town whose major factory has just been closed is unlikely to earn a high wage or enjoy much job
security; in a swank resort populated by film producers and banking moguls,
she is apt to do reasonably well. So, too, with nations. In-person servers in

---

[15] The Census Bureau estimates that by the year 2000, at least 12 million Americans will
    work in health services — well over 6 percent of the total workforce. [Reich's note]

Bangladesh may spend their days performing roughly the same tasks as in-person servers in the United States, but have a far lower standard of living for their efforts. The difference comes in the value that their customers add to the world economy.

Unlike the boats of routine producers and in-person servers, however, the vessel containing America's symbolic analysts is rising. Worldwide demand for their insights is growing as the ease and speed of communicating them steadily increases. Not every symbolic analyst is rising as quickly or as dramatically as every other, of course; symbolic analysts at the low end are barely holding their own in the world economy. But symbolic analysts at the top are in such great demand worldwide that they have difficulty keeping track of all their earnings. Never before in history has opulence on such a scale been gained by people who have earned it, and done so legally. 28

Among symbolic analysts in the middle range are American scientists and researchers who are busily selling their discoveries to global enterprise webs. They are not limited to American customers. If the strategic brokers in General Motors' headquarters refuse to pay a high price for a new means of making high-strength ceramic engines dreamed up by a team of engineers affiliated with Carnegie Mellon University in Pittsburgh, the strategic brokers of Honda or Mercedes-Benz are likely to be more than willing. 29

So, too, with the insights of America's ubiquitous management consultants, which are being sold for large sums to eager entrepreneurs in Europe and Latin America. Also, the insights of America's energy consultants, sold for even larger sums to Arab sheikhs. American design engineers are providing insights to Olivetti, Mazda, Siemens, and other global webs; American marketers, techniques for learning what worldwide consumers will buy; American advertisers, ploys for ensuring that they actually do. American architects are issuing designs and blueprints for opera houses, art galleries, museums, luxury hotels, and residential complexes in the world's major cities; American commercial property developers, marketing these properties to worldwide investors and purchasers. 30

Americans who specialize in the gentle art of public relations are in demand by corporations, governments, and politicians in virtually every nation. So, too, are American political consultants, some of whom, at this writing, are advising the Hungarian Socialist Party, the remnant of Hungary's ruling Communists, on how to salvage a few parliamentary seats in the nation's first free election in more than forty years. Also at this writing, a team of American agricultural consultants is advising the managers of a Soviet farm collective employing 1,700 Russians eighty miles outside Moscow. As noted, American investment bankers and lawyers specializing in financial circumnavigations are selling their insights to Asians and Europeans who are eager to discover how to make large amounts of money by moving large amounts of money. 31

Developing nations, meanwhile, are hiring American civil engineers to advise   32
on building roads and dams. The present thaw in the Cold War will no doubt
expand these opportunities. American engineers from Bechtel (a global firm notable for having employed both Caspar Weinberger and George Shultz for much
larger sums than either earned in the Reagan administration) have begun helping the Soviets design and install a new generation of nuclear reactors. Nations
also are hiring American bankers and lawyers to help them renegotiate the terms
of their loans with global banks, and Washington lobbyists to help them with
Congress, the Treasury, the World Bank, the IMF, and other politically sensitive
institutions. In fits of obvious desperation, several nations emerging from communism have even hired American economists to teach them about capitalism.

Almost everyone around the world is buying the skills and insights of   33
Americans who manipulate oral and visual symbols—musicians, sound engineers,
film producers, makeup artists, directors, cinematographers, actors and actresses,
boxers, scriptwriters, songwriters, and set designers. Among the wealthiest of
symbolic analysts are Steven Spielberg, Bill Cosby, Charles Schulz, Eddie Murphy,
Sylvester Stallone, Madonna, and other star directors and performers—who are
almost as well known on the streets of Dresden and Tokyo as in the Back Bay
of Boston. Less well rewarded but no less renowned are the unctuous anchors
on Turner Broadcasting's Cable News, who appear daily, via satellite, in places
ranging from Vietnam to Nigeria. Vanna White is the world's most-watched game-
show hostess. Behind each of these familiar faces is a collection of American
problem-solvers, -identifiers, and brokers who train, coach, advise, promote,
amplify, direct, groom, represent, and otherwise add value to their talents.[16]

There are also the insights of senior American executives who occupy   34
the world headquarters of global "American" corporations and the national or
regional headquarters of global "foreign" corporations. Their insights are duly
exported to the rest of the world through the webs of global enterprise. IBM
does not export many machines from the United States, for example. Big Blue
makes machines all over the globe and services them on the spot. Its prime
American exports are symbolic and analytic. From IBM's world headquarters
in Armonk, New York, emanate strategic brokerage and related management
services bound for the rest of the world. In return, IBM's top executives are
generously rewarded.

The most important reason for this expanding world market and increas-   35
ing global demand for the symbolic and analytic insights of Americans has been
the dramatic improvement in worldwide communication and transportation

---

[16] In 1989, the entertainment business summoned to the United States $5.5 billion in foreign
earnings—making it among the nation's largest export industries, just behind aerospace.
U.S. Department of Commerce, International Trade Commission, "Composition of U.S.
Exports," various issues. [Reich's note]

technologies. Designs, instructions, advice, and visual and audio symbols can be communicated more and more rapidly around the globe, with ever-greater precision and at ever-lower cost. Madonna's voice can be transported to billions of listeners, with perfect clarity, on digital compact discs. A new invention emanating from engineers in Battelle's laboratory in Columbus, Ohio, can be sent almost anywhere via modem, in a form that will allow others to examine it in three dimensions through enhanced computer graphics. When face-to-face meetings are still required — and videoconferencing will not suffice — it is relatively easy for designers, consultants, advisers, artists, and executives to board supersonic jets and, in a matter of hours, meet directly with their worldwide clients, customers, audiences, and employees.

With rising demand comes rising compensation. Whether in the form of licensing fees, fees for service, salaries, or shares in final profits, the economic result is much the same. There are also nonpecuniary rewards. One of the best-kept secrets among symbolic analysts is that so many of them enjoy their work. In fact, much of it does not count as work at all, in the traditional sense. The work of routine producers and in-person servers is typically monotonous; it causes muscles to tire or weaken and involves little independence or discretion. The "work" of symbolic analysts, by contrast, often involves puzzles, experiments, games, a significant amount of chatter, and substantial discretion over what to do next. Few routine producers or in-person servers would "work" if they did not need to earn the money. Many symbolic analysts would "work" even if money were no object.

At midcentury, when America was a national market dominated by core pyramid-shaped corporations, there were constraints on the earnings of people at the highest rungs. First and most obviously, the market for their services was largely limited to the borders of the nation. In addition, whatever conceptual value they might contribute was small relative to the value gleaned from large scale — and it was dependent on large scale for whatever income it was to summon. Most of the problems to be identified and solved had to do with enhancing the efficiency of production and improving the flow of materials, parts, assembly, and distribution. Inventors searched for the rare breakthrough revealing an entirely new product to be made in high volume; management consultants, executives, and engineers thereafter tried to speed and synchronize its manufacture, to better achieve scale efficiencies; advertisers and marketers sought then to whet the public's appetite for the standard item that emerged. Since white-collar earnings increased with larger scale, there was considerable incentive to expand the firm; indeed, many of America's core corporations grew far larger than scale economies would appear to have justified.

By the 1990s, in contrast, the earnings of symbolic analysts were limited neither by the size of the national market nor by the volume of production of the firms with which they were affiliated. The marketplace was worldwide, and conceptual value was high relative to value added from scale efficiencies.

There had been another constraint on high earnings, which also gave way   39
by the 1990s. At midcentury, the compensation awarded to top executives and advisers of the largest of America's core corporations could not be grossly out of proportion to that of low-level production workers. It would be unseemly for executives who engaged in highly visible rounds of bargaining with labor unions, and who routinely responded to government requests to moder-ate prices, to take home wages and benefits wildly in excess of what other Americans earned. Unless white-collar executives restrained themselves, moreover, blue-collar production workers could not be expected to restrain their own demands for higher wages. Unless both groups exercised restraint, the government could not be expected to forbear from imposing direct con-trols and regulations.

At the same time, the wages of production workers could not be allowed   40
to sink too low, lest there be insufficient purchasing power in the economy. After all, who would buy all the goods flowing out of American factories if not American workers? This, too, was part of the tacit bargain struck between American managers and their workers.

Recall the oft-repeated corporate platitude of the era about the chief   41
executive's responsibility to carefully weigh and balance the interests of the corporation's disparate stakeholders. Under the stewardship of the corporate statesman, no set of stakeholders—least of all white-collar executives—was to gain a disproportionately large share of the benefits of corporate activity; nor was any stakeholder—especially the average worker—to be left with a share that was disproportionately small. Banal though it was, this idea helped to maintain the legitimacy of the core American corporation in the eyes of most Americans, and to ensure continued economic growth.

But by the 1990s, these informal norms were evaporating, just as (and   42
largely because) the core American corporation was vanishing. The links between top executives and the American production worker were fading: an ever-increasing number of subordinates and contractees were foreign, and a steadily growing number of American routine producers were working for foreign-owned firms. An entire cohort of middle-level managers, who had once been deemed "white collar," had disappeared; and, increasingly, American executives were exporting their insights to global enterprise webs.

As the American corporation itself became a global web almost indistin-   43
guishable from any other, its stakeholders were turning into a large and dif-fuse group, spread over the world. Such global stakeholders were less visible, and far less noisy, than national stakeholders. And as the American corpora-tion sold its goods and services all over the world, the purchasing power of American workers became far less relevant to its economic survival.

Thus have the inhibitions been removed. The salaries and benefits of 44
America's top executives, and many of their advisers and consultants, have
soared to what years before would have been unimaginable heights, even as
those of other Americans have declined.

▝ QUESTIONS FOR CRITICAL READING

1. What are symbolic analysts? Give some examples from your own experience.

2. What is the apparent relationship between higher education and an educated worker's prospects for wealth?

3. To what extent do you agree or disagree with Reich's description and analysis of routine workers and in-service workers?

4. If Reich's analysis is correct, which gender or social groups are likely to be most harmed by modern economic circumstances in America? Which are most likely to become wealthy? Why?

5. Are symbolic analysts inherently more valuable to our society than routine or in-service workers? Why do symbolic analysts command so much more wealth?

6. Which of the three groups Reich mentions do you see as having the greatest potential for growth in the next thirty years?

▝ SUGGESTIONS FOR CRITICAL WRITING

1. Judging from the views that Reich holds about decreasing job opportunities for all three groups of workers, how will increased immigration affect the American economy? Is immigration a hopeful sign? Is it a danger to the economy? How do most people seem to perceive the effect of increased immigration?

2. To what extent do you think Reich is correct about the growing wealth of symbolic analysts? He says, "Never before in history has opulence on such a scale been gained by people who have earned it, and done so legally" (para. 28). Do you see yourself as a symbolic analyst? How do you see your future in relation to the three economic groups Reich describes?

3. Reich says, "Few routine producers or in-person servers would 'work' if they did not need to earn the money. Many symbolic analysts would 'work' even if money were no object" (para. 36). Is this true? Examine your own experience — along with the experience of others you know — and defend or attack this view. How accurate do you consider Reich to be in his analysis of the way various workers view their work?

4. Describe the changes that have taken place in the American economy since 1960, according to this essay. How have they affected the way Americans work and the work that Americans can expect to find? How have your personal opportunities been broadened or narrowed by the changes? Do you feel the changes have been good for the country or not? Why?

5. Reich's view of the great success of Japanese corporations and of their presence as manufacturing giants in the United States and elsewhere is largely positive. He has pointed out elsewhere that Honda and other manufacturers in the United States provide jobs and municipal income that would otherwise go to other nations. What is your view of the presence of large Japanese corporations in the United States? What is your view of other nations' manufacturing facilities in the United States?

6. Why are the rich getting richer and the poor, poorer? Examine the kinds of differences between the rich and the poor that Reich describes. Is the process of increasing riches for the rich and increasing poverty for the poor inevitable, or will it begin to change in the near future?

7. **CONNECTIONS**   Karl Marx (p. 335) warns against globalism in the economy in part because it harms local industry and damages local styles and customs. How would Reich counter those fears? Is it clear that Reich approves of the new economy he describes, or does he accept globalism as a form of economic evolution? Would he be likely to agree with Andrew Carnegie (p. 360) that the laws of competition and accumulation operate in the new economy at least as forcefully as they did in Carnegie's time? Does he in any way seem approving of Marx's theories?

8. **CONNECTIONS**   Robert Reich makes a distinction between symbolic analysts and routine workers. According to the Friedmans (p. 400), which of these are more likely to achieve great wealth? Why? If both have freedom of opportunity, why should there be a difference? Reich approves of the increase of opulence (para. 28); should he not agree with the Friedmans' views about the equality of opportunity and its natural outcome of an inequity of wealth in any nation? What arguments might Reich make against the Friedmans? What arguments might he most fervently support?

9. **CONNECTIONS**   Reich examines what seems to be a new form for the economy now that free trade is essentially a reality and major foreign nations — like Japan, China, and India — are creating enormous wealth while Western industrial nations are losing industries and jobs to those countries. How would Reich respond to Adam Smith's (p. 325) concepts of how a nation produces wealth? What are the differences Reich sees in the current economy as compared with that of Smith's time? Would he feel that any of Smith's principles regarding land, agriculture, and manufactures applies to our new economy? Establish Reich's position regarding Smith's basic theories.

FRANCIS
FUKUYAMA

The Middle Class and Democracy's Future

© Colin McPherson/Corbis

F RANCIS FUKUYAMA (b. 1952) is the Olivier Nomellini Senior Fellow at Stanford University's Freeman Spogli Institute for International Studies. Prior to that, he taught at the Paul H. Nitze School of Advanced International Studies of the Johns Hopkins University and at the George Mason University of Public Policy. Fukuyama was known as a neoconservative political philosopher, until the Iraq War changed his mind. Today, he is more centrist in his thinking. Among his personal interests are not only photography, especially travel photography, but also building antique furniture. His undergraduate degree was in classics at Cornell University where he also studied political philosophy with Alan Bloom. He was awarded his doctorate in government from Harvard University. An early article that became a book proclaiming the end of history catapulted him to fame.

Because he was widely misunderstood, he wrote a number of explanations that clarified his views. When he said that we had reached the end of history, what he meant was not that history was no longer being written. He meant that the evolution of social governmental systems had reached its peak in liberal democratic governments. As he wrote in an article in *The Guardian* (October 11, 2001): "And if we looked beyond liberal democracy and markets, there was nothing else towards which we could expect to evolve; hence the end of history. While there were retrograde areas that resisted that process, it was hard to find a viable alternative civilization that people actually wanted to live in after the discrediting of socialism, monarchy, fascism and other types of authoritarianism."

Among Fukuyama's important books are *The End of History and the Last Man* (1992), *Trust: The Social Virtues and the Creation of Prosperity* (1995), *The Great Disruption: Human Nature and the Reconstitution of Social Order* (1999), *State-Building: Governance and World Order in the Twenty-First Century* (2004), and *America at the Crossroads: Democracy, Power, and the Neoconservative Legacy* (2006). While most of these books concern various issues

From *Political Order and Political Decay: From the Industrial Revolution to the Globalization of Democracy*.

of governance and their effects on large populations, under their surface is a deeper issue: how human nature is adapted to varieties of governments and how human nature actually shapes governments. The democratic state with its market economy seems, to Fukuyama, to have evolved because of what we call human nature. It is basic to our needs.

Political Order and Political Decay (2014), the book in which the following selection appears, is the second volume of a major study of politics begun with *The Origins of Political Order* (2011). Fukuyama's scope includes not just the development of the West and Western political systems, but also the developments in Asia, Africa, and Latin America. He considers issues of geography and of natural resources, as in "Silver, Gold, and Sugar," the title of one of his chapters.

He examines the strong Asian governments and the question of law throughout the world. And in the third part of his *Political Order and Political Decay*, he analyzes the origin and spread of democracy, with a particular look at the periods of disorder and revolution in the nineteenth century. It was in the period after the uprisings in Europe in 1848 that democracy began to be embraced in one form or another as a desirable experiment. Visitors to the United States, such as Alexis de Tocqueville, studied the phenomenon of functional democracy in America and reported their findings, often with surprise and enthusiasm.

In his concern for the middle class and the success of democracy, Fukuyama examines the theories of earlier political thinkers such as Marx, whose focus on workers overlooked the rise of the middle class, something that Marx would not have imagined. In today's politics, there is great anxiety about the middle class in the United States because it seems to be threatened by the inequality in income that has marked the economy since the 1980s, when China welcomed foreign manufacturers and rapidly became the number two economic force in the world.

Fukuyama discusses the rise and fall of government systems. In *Political Order and Political Decay*, he states, "No political institution lasts forever." As a result, the last section of his book concerns itself with the ways in which institutions alter and decay.

FUKUYAMA'S RHETORIC

Beginning with references to Karl Marx, whose views on the middle class were colored by the historical circumstances of nineteenth-century Europe, Fukuyama reviews Marx's position and the historical situation. He uses the rhetorical technique of enumeration in the first few pages. He sets out six "unexpected developments" (para. 3) that need to be taken into consideration in understanding why the prophesies of Marx did not come true. By starting his paragraphs with "Second," "Third," "Fourth," and "Fifth," Fukuyama guides us to the issues that he needs to explain. He analyzes the circumstances in Europe that changed in unpredictable ways and allowed the rise of an unexpected middle class throughout parts of the world.

Fukuyama continues his analysis of the changes in class structure for several pages, emphasizing "identity politics," by which he means that people in the middle class concern themselves more with issues such as gay rights, abortion, gun rights, and special concerns much more than with any class issues. These issues cross all imaginable class lines and therefore make narrow views of class almost unrecognizable in the sense that Marx understands the term.

The blurring of the working class and the middle class is a key issue in the discussion. Fukuyama essentially says that one important modern change is the fact that the working class merged into the middle class in the later nineteenth century. Part of the reason for that was the rise of technology and the movement of large sectors of agricultural workers into factories and technically advanced work.

In the section titled "Who Is Middle Class?," Fukuyama introduces the rhetorical technique of development by definition. We all know that defining the middle class is difficult today if only because most people feel they belong in the middle class. Using a range of income to decide who constitutes the middle class is insufficient in many ways, partly because different nations have different ranges of income, so that a small income might imply a middle-class status in one country but not in another. Fukuyama reviews the general suggestions introduced by sociologists, who treat income as less important than education and what kind of work is available to the majority of workers.

Once Fukuyama establishes the parameters of the modern middle class, he then begins to examine its relationship to the stability and appeal of democracy. His view, unsurprisingly, is that a society with a large middle class is more likely to prefer a "liberal democracy" than anything else. With reference to Aristotle's fear of oligarchic government, he says that "societies with extremes of wealth and poverty are susceptible to oligarchic domination or to populist revolution" (para. 12). As a result of his survey of historical developments in various parts of Europe, Asia, and North and South America, Fukuyama puts us in a position to be able to recognize the existence of a middle class while also helping us understand how it helps stabilize the modern democracies of the world.

▪▪ PREREADING QUESTIONS: WHAT TO READ FOR

The following prereading questions may help you anticipate key issues in the discussion of Francis Fukuyama's "The Middle Class and Democracy's Future." Keeping them in mind during your first reading of the selection should help focus your attention.

1. How have historical changes helped the development of a broad middle class?

2. Why would a prosperous middle class support a democratic form of government?

The Middle Class and Democracy's Future

According to Karl Marx, modern capitalism was headed for an ultimate   1
crisis of what he called "overproduction." Capitalist use of technology
would extract surpluses from the labor of the proletariat, leading to greater
concentrations of wealth and the progressive immiseration of workers. The
bourgeoisie who ran this system could not, despite their wealth, consume
everything that it produced, while the proletariat whose labor made it possible
were too poor to buy its products. Ever-increasing levels of inequality would
lead to a shortfall in demand, and the system would come crashing down upon
itself. The only way out of this crisis, according to Marx, was a revolution that
would give political power to the proletariat and redistribute the fruits of the
capitalist system.

Marx's scenario seemed quite plausible through the middle decades of   2
the nineteenth century in all industrializing countries. Working conditions in
new factory towns were appalling, and huge new agglomerations of impoverished workers appeared out of nowhere. Rules concerning working hours,
safety, child labor, and the like were either nonexistent or poorly enforced.
European conditions were, in other words, very similar to those found in the
early twenty-first century in parts of China, Vietnam, Bangladesh, and other
developing countries.

But a number of unexpected developments occurred on the way to the   3
proletarian revolution. First was the fact that labor incomes began to rise.
Early gains were the result of extensive economic growth as new workers were
mobilized out of the agrarian population, but that process reached natural limits and the price of labor relative to capital began to increase. This dynamic
is happening today in China, as the cost of labor has risen rapidly in the first
decades of the twenty-first century.

Second, many countries, beginning with the United States, began to put   4
into place universal public education systems as well as increasing investments
in higher education. This was not simply a matter of public generosity: new
industries required engineers, accountants, lawyers, clerical staff, and hourly
workers with basic literacy and numeracy skills. Higher labor costs could easily be justified if they were matched by enhanced productivity, which was in
turn the result of better technology and increasing human capital.

Third, the spread of the franchise[1] described in the previous chapter led   5
to expansion of the political power of the working classes. This happened

---

[1] **Franchise**   The right to vote.

through the struggles to legalize and expand trade unions, and in the rise of political parties associated with them like the British Labour Party and the German Social Democratic Party. The nature of conservative parties began to change as well: instead of representing wealthy landowners, they shifted their base of support to the new middle-class elites. The working classes' newfound political power was then used to implement social legislation regulating working conditions, which led to agitation for broader welfare state policies like pensions and publicly provided health care.

Fourth, by the middle decades of the twentieth century, the working class simply stopped growing, both in absolute numbers and as a share of the workforce. Indeed, the relative size of Marx's proletariat shrank as workers saw substantial increases in their standards of living that allowed them to move into the middle class. They now owned property and had better educations, and were therefore more likely to vote for political parties that could protect their privileges rather than ones pushing to overturn the status quo.

Fifth, a new class of poor and underprivileged people emerged below the industrial working class, often consisting of recent immigrants, racial and ethnic minorities, and other marginalized people. These groups worked in lower-paying service jobs or remained unemployed and dependent on government benefits. Workers in manufacturing industries who were represented by trade unions became a kind of aristocracy within the labor force. The vast majority of workers had no such representation; in countries where benefits like pensions were tied to regular jobs, they entered the informal sector. Such individuals had few legally defined rights and often did not possess legal title to the land or houses they occupied. Throughout Latin America and many other parts of the developing world, the informal sector constitutes perhaps 60 to 70 percent of the entire labor force. Unlike the industrial working class, this group of "new poor" has been notoriously hard to organize for political action. Rather than living in large barracks in factory towns, they live scattered across the country and are often self-employed entrepreneurs.

Finally, the political Left throughout the world lost its focus on economic and class issues, and became fragmented as the result of the spread of identity politics. I have noted already how working-class solidarity was undermined by nationalism at the time of World War I. But the rise of new forms of identity in the developed world by the middle of the twentieth century around black empowerment, feminism, environmentalism, immigrant and indigenous rights, and gay rights created a whole new set of causes that cut across class lines. The leadership of many of these movements came out of the economic elites, and their cultural preferences often stood at cross-purposes to those of the working-class electorate that had once been the bulwark of progressive politics.

The displacement of class politics by identity politics has been very confusing to older Marxists, who for many years clung to the old industrial working class as their preferred category of the underprivileged. They tried to explain this shift in terms of what Ernest Gellner[2] labeled the "Wrong Address Theory": "Just as extreme Shi'ite Muslims hold that Archangel Gabriel made a mistake, delivering the Message to Mohamed when it was intended for Ali, so Marxists basically like to think that the spirit of history or human consciousness made a terrible boob. The awakening message was intended for *classes*, but by some terrible postal error was delivered to *nations*." Gellner went on to argue that in the contemporary Middle East, the same letter was now being delivered to religions rather than nations. But the underlying sociological dynamic was the same.

The first four of these six developments unanticipated by Karl Marx all   10
center around a single phenomenon, which was the conversion of the working class into a broad middle class. At the conclusion of the tumultuous first half of the twentieth century, the developed democracies of Europe and North America finally found themselves in a happy position. Their politics was no longer sharply polarized between a rich oligarchy and a large working class or peasant majority, who engaged in a zero-sum struggle over the distribution of resources. The old oligarchies in many developed countries had either evolved into more entrepreneurial capitalist elites or had been physically eliminated through revolution and war. The working classes through unionization and political struggle won greater privileges for themselves and became middle class in political outlook. Fascism discredited the extreme Right, and the emerging cold war and threat from Stalinist Russia discredited the Communist Left. This left politics to be played out among center-Right and center-Left parties that largely agreed on a liberal democratic framework. The median voter—a favorite concept of political scientists—was no longer a poor person demanding systemic changes to the social order but a middle-class individual with a stake in the existing system.

Other regions were not so lucky. Latin America had a legacy of high lev-   11
els of inequality, and in many countries the old landowning oligarchies had not been eliminated through the political struggles that consumed Europe. The benefits of economic growth were shared by the organized working classes but not by the mass of workers in the informal sector, and as a result a highly polarized politics emerged reminiscent of nineteenth-century continental Europe. The persistence of radical, anti-systemic groups—the Communist parties led by Cuba, the Tupamaros in Uruguay, the Sandinistas in Nicaragua, the FMLN in El Salvador, and most recently the Bolivarian movement of Hugo Chávez in Venezuela—was a symptom of this fundamental class conflict.

---

[2] **Ernest Gellner (1925–1995)**   A British philosopher and anthropologist and the author of *Words and Things* (1959), in which he criticized ordinary language philosophy.

From the days of Aristotle, thinkers have believed that stable democracy would have to rest on a broad middle class; societies with extremes of wealth and poverty are susceptible to oligarchic domination or to populist revolution. Karl Marx believed that the middle classes would always remain a small and privileged minority in modern societies. Yet by the second half of the twentieth century, the middle class constituted the vast majority of the population of most advanced societies, thereby undercutting the appeal of Marxism. 12

The emergence of middle-class societies also increased the legitimacy of liberal democracy as a political system. [Previously,] I noted the critique of liberal democracy made by writers as varied as Mosca, Pareto, and Marx[3] that its advent was in the end a fraud, masking the continued rule by elites. But the value of formal democracy and an expanded franchise became evident in the twentieth century. Democratic majorities in Europe and North America used the ballot box to choose policies beneficial to themselves, regulating big business and putting into place redistributive welfare state provisions. 13

Who Is Middle Class?

Before proceeding to analyze further the political consequences of the rise of the middle classes, it is necessary to step back and define what the middle class is. There is a difference in the way that economists and sociologists think about it. The former tend to define middle class in income terms. A typical way is simply to choose some band like the middle three quintiles of the income distribution, or to count those individuals who fall within 0.5 to 1.5 times the median income. This makes the definition of middle class dependent on a society's average wealth and thus incomparable cross-nationally; being middle class in Brazil means a much lower consumption level than in the United States. To avoid this problem, some economists choose an absolute level of consumption, ranging from a low of US$5 a day, or $1,800 in parity purchasing power per year, up to a range of $6,000–$31,000 annual income in 2010 U.S. dollars. This fixes one problem but creates another, since an individual's perception of class status is often relative rather than absolute. As Adam Smith noted in *The Wealth of Nations*, a pauper in eighteenth-century England might have lived like a king in Africa. 14

Sociologists, in a tradition beginning with Karl Marx, tend not to look at measures of income but instead at how one's income is earned—occupational status, level of education, and assets. For the purpose of understanding the 15

---

[3] **Mosca . . . Marx**   Gaetano Mosca (1858–1941) was an Italian political scientist, author of *The Ruling Class* (1939); Vilfredo Pareto (1848–1923), Italian economist, author of *Sociological Writings* (1966); Karl Marx (1818–1883), philosopher and economist, author of *Capital* (1867).

political implications of a growing middle class, the sociological approach is vastly preferable. Simple measures of income or consumption, whether relative or absolute, may tell you something about the consumption habits of the person in question but relatively little concerning his or her political inclinations. Huntington's[4] theory of the destabilizing impact of the gap between expectations and reality is much more closely tied to social and occupational status than to any absolute level of income. A poor person of low social status and education who briefly rises out of poverty and then sinks back is likely to be more preoccupied with day-to-day survival than with political activism. A middle-class person, by contrast—someone, say, with a university education who cannot find an appropriate job and "sinks" to a social level he or she regards as beneath his or her dignity—is far more challenging politically.

Thus, from a political standpoint, the important marker of middle-class status would be occupation, level of education, and ownership of assets (a house or an apartment, or consumer durables) that could be threatened by the government. Marx's original definition of "bourgeoisie" referred to ownership of the means of production. One of the characteristics of the modern world is that this form of property has become vastly democratized through stock ownership and pension plans. Even if one does not possess large amounts of capital, working in a managerial capacity or profession often grants one a very different kind of social status and outlook from a wage earner or low-skilled worker.   16

A strong middle class with some assets and education is more likely to believe in the need for both property rights and democratic accountability. One wants to protect the value of one's property from rapacious and/or incompetent governments, and is more likely to have time to participate in politics (or to demand the right to participate) because higher income provides a better margin for family survival. A number of cross-national studies have shown that middle-class people have different political values from the poor: they value democracy more, want more individual freedom, are more tolerant of alternative lifestyles, etc. Political scientist Ronald Inglehart,[5] who has overseen the massive World Values Survey that seeks to measure value change around the world, has argued that economic modernization and middle-class status produce what he calls "post-material" values in which democracy, equality, and identity issues become much more prominent than older issues of economic distribution. William Easterly[6] has linked what he labels a "middle class   17

---

[4] **Samuel P. Huntington (1927–2008)**   A conservative American political scientist, author of *Political Order in Changing Societies* (2006).

[5] **Ronald Inglehart (b. 1934)**   A political scientist at the University of Michigan and the author of *Modernization and Postmodernization* (1997).

[6] **William Easterly (b. 1957)**   A New York University professor of economics and the author of *The Tyranny of Experts: Economists, Dictators, and the Forgotten Rights of the Poor* (2014).

consensus" to higher economic growth, education, health, stability, and other positive outcomes. Economically, the middle class is theorized to have "bourgeois" values of self-discipline, hard work, and a longer-term perspective that encourages savings and investment.

From the earlier discussion of Europe in the nineteenth century, how-   18
ever, it should be clear that the middle classes are not inevitably supporters of democracy. This tends to be particularly true when the middle classes still constitute a minority of the population. Under these circumstances, opening up a country to universal political participation may lead to large and potentially unsustainable demands for redistribution. In this case, the middle classes may choose to align themselves with authoritarian rulers who promise stability and property rights protection.

Such is arguably the case in contemporary Thailand and China. The Thai   19
political system went from an authoritarian military regime to a reasonably open democracy between 1992 and 1997, preparing the way for the rise of the populist politician Thaksin Shinawatra.[7] Thaksin, one of the country's richest businessmen, organized a mass political party based on government programs to provide debt relief and health care to rural Thais. The middle classes, who had strongly supported the democratic opening in the early 1990s, turned against Thaksin and supported a military coup that forced him from power in 2006. He was charged with corruption and abuse of power, and has had to exercise power from exile since then. The country subsequently became sharply polarized between Thaksin's Red Shirt supporters and middle-class Yellow Shirt adherents, and saw an elected government pushed out of power by the military in 2014.

A similar dynamic may exist in China. The size of the Chinese middle   20
class in 2014 depends obviously on definition but is estimated to be perhaps 300–400 million people out of a population of 1.3 billion. These new middle classes are often the source of resistance to the authoritarian government; they are the ones who are on Sina Weibo (the Chinese Twitter equivalent) and who are likely to publicize or criticize government wrong-doing. Survey data from sources like AsiaBarometer suggest that there is widespread support for democracy in China, but when asked about the specific content of democracy, many respondents associate it either with greater personal freedom or with a government responsive to their needs. Many believe that the current Chinese government is already providing them with these things and do not oppose the system as a whole. Middle-class Chinese are less likely to express support for a short-term transition to multiparty democracy under universal suffrage, although it is very difficult to get accurate polling data on this subject.

---

[7] **Thaksin Shinawatra (b. 1949)**   Prime minister of Thailand from 2001–2006.

The Thai and Chinese cases, as well as the nineteenth-century European   21
ones, suggest that the size of the middle class relative to the rest of the society
is one important variable in determining how it will behave politically. When the
middle class constitutes only 20–30 percent of the population, it may side with
antidemocratic forces because it fears the intentions of the large mass of poor
people below it and the populist policies they may pursue. But when the middle
class becomes the largest group in the society, the danger is reduced. Indeed,
the middle class may at that point be able to vote itself various welfare-state
benefits and profit from democracy. This may help to explain why democracy
becomes more stable at higher levels of per capita income, since the size of
the middle class relative to the poor usually increases with greater wealth.
Middle-class societies, as opposed to societies with a middle class, are the bedrock of democracy.

Such societies appeared in Europe by the early decades after World War II,   22
and they have been gradually spreading to other parts of the world ever since.
The Third Wave of democratization was not "caused" by the rise of the middle
class, since many democratic transitions occurred in countries — like those in
sub-Saharan Africa — that did not have appreciable middle classes at the time.
Contagion, imitation, and the failures of incumbent authoritarian regimes were
all significant factors triggering democratic transitions. But the ability to con-
solidate a stable liberal democracy is greater in countries that have large and
broad middle classes, in contrast to ones in which a relatively small middle
class is sandwiched between a rich elite and a mass of poor people. Spain, the
country that kicked off the Third Wave, had been transformed from a backward
agrarian society at the time of the civil war in the 1930s to a much more modern
one by the early 1970s. Surrounded by examples of successful democracies in
the European Union, it was much easier to contemplate a democratic transition then than it had been a generation earlier.

This suggests that the prospects for democracy globally remain good,   23
despite the setbacks that occurred during the early twenty-first century. A
Goldman Sachs report projects that spending on the part of the world's middle
three income quintiles will rise from the current 31 percent of total income
to 57 percent in 2050. A report by the European Union Institute for Security
Studies projects that the numbers of middle class people will grow from
1.8 billion in 2009 to 3.2 billion in 2020, and 4.9 billion in 2030 (out of a projected global population of 8.3 billion). The bulk of this growth is slated to
occur in Asia, particularly China and India, but all regions of the world will
participate in this trend.

Economic growth by itself is not sufficient to create democratic stability   24
if it is not broadly shared. One of the greatest threats to China's social stability today is its rapid increase in income inequality since the mid-1990s, which
by 2012 had reached Latin American levels. Latin America itself had reached

middle-income status well before East Asia but continued to be plagued by high levels of inequality and the populist policies that flowed from it. One of the most promising developments for the region, however, has been the notable fall in income inequality in the decade of the 2000s, as documented by economists Luis Felipe López-Calva and Nora Lustig.[8] There have been significant gains to the Latin American middle class. In 2002, 44 percent of the region's population was classified as poor; this had fallen to 32 percent by 2010 according to the UN Economic Commission for Latin America. The cause of the decline in inequality is not entirely understood, but a certain portion of it is attributable to social policies like conditional cash transfer programs that have deliberately distributed benefits to the poor.

---

[8] **Luis Felipe López-Calva and Nora Lustig**   Luis Lopez-Calva is affiliated with the World Bank. Nora Lustig (b. 1951) is professor of economics at Tulane University. Their book is *Declining Inequality in Latin America.*

✖ QUESTIONS FOR CRITICAL READING

1. How does the cost of labor affect the growth of a middle class?

2. What is the connection between education and the formation of a middle class?

3. Why is a middle class likely to prefer a democratic form of government?

4. What is identity politics? Why does it cross class lines?

5. What would constitute work in the "informal sectors" mentioned in Latin America?

6. How does the existence of an oligarchy affect the middle class? How does it affect democracy?

7. Why is it difficult to define the middle class?

✖ SUGGESTIONS FOR CRITICAL WRITING

1. When he discusses developments in Latin America (para. 11), Fukuyama mentions that much of the economy of Latin American nations involves the "mass of workers in the informal sector" rather than those in the "organized working classes." Why would the informal sector, which consists of "entrepreneurs" who are self-employed and work for low pay, constitute a problem for supporting a democratic form of government? Why are the inequities in Latin America breeding radical groups in places like Uruguay, Nicaragua, and Venezuela?

2. Fukuyama mentions "the spread of the franchise" in paragraph 5 as being a force in helping develop a middle class. The franchise is the right to vote. How is making the right to vote widespread likely to produce a middle class? And how is it likely to preserve a liberal democratic form of government? What are some of the best ways to spread the right to vote?

3. In paragraphs 6 and 7, Fukuyama tells us that in the middle of the twentieth century the "working class simply stopped growing." They moved into the middle class. According to what you have witnessed in your own working experience, do you think that the middle class is still growing? Is there still a working class that you perceive as different from the middle class? Fukuyama also mentions "a new class of poor and underprivileged people" (para. 7). Are we seeing the growth of this "new class"? What evidence helps establish the existence of these classes of people?

4. Starting in paragraph 14, Fukuyama begins to explore the question of how we define the middle class in any society. How do you define it in your society? Take into account the issues that Fukuyama raises, including income, education, and occupation. Is an analysis of these issues sufficient to provide a useful definition, or is there something more that must be taken into consideration? Which of Fukuyama's three "markers" of the middle class is most important?

5. Contemporary politicians seem concerned about apparent threats to the growth, or even the existence, of a healthy middle class. Some politicians threaten that a diminished middle class will cause harm to our democratic ideals and our democratic government. How serious do you think this threat is? Research some of the political discussion of the health of the middle class and decide for yourself how serious the issue is. Much of this discussion involves the question of growing inequities in income in the first decades of the twenty-first century. Why would inequality be an issue in a discussion of the middle class and democracy?

6. In paragraph 5, Fukuyama says that the growing middle class "led to agitation for broader welfare state policies like pensions and publicly provided health care." How does the middle class in our nation agitate for greater social policies that benefit them? Is the middle class in favor of Social Security? Is it in favor of Medicare and health care? According to Fukuyama's analysis, what will happen to social policies if the middle class shrinks noticeably? Why would there be any change to such policies if the middle class were to become sharply reduced?

7. **CONNECTIONS**   Fukuyama is concerned about inequities in income among people in the United States in the twenty-first century. Robert Reich, in "Why the Rich Are Getting Richer and the Poor, Poorer" (p. 422), was also concerned about this issue in 1991. Are Reich's reasons for being alarmed similar to those of Fukuyama? Does Fukuyama raise issues of importance that Robert Reich did not anticipate? In how much agreement are they? In what ways do they disagree? What are your views on inequities in modern society, and what are we to do about them? Does Fukuyama or Reich offer any suggestions that you feel are workable?

Reflections on the Nature of Wealth

Now that you have read the selections in "Wealth," consider in what ways these writers have helped further inform your views on wealth.

1. When it comes to wealth, how does the question of equality of opportunity relate to equality of outcome?

2. How do you define the middle class now that you have read these authors?

3. Does great wealth in the hands of the few make it impossible for there to be a healthy middle class?

4. Should government take a role in redistributing the wealth of the few to the least wealthy of the many?

5. Do you agree with Andrew Carnegie that the government should have a graduated income tax? Is such a tax fair?

6. What is the obligation of a society to those who cannot become wealthy?

7. To what extent do you feel that democracy is under threat by financial inequality?

8. How much do you see yourself defined by identity politics rather than by class distinctions?

9. What, for you, would constitute a fair distribution of wealth in a healthy democracy?

10. What are the strengths and weaknesses of modern socialism?

Reflections on the Nature of Wealth

MIND

Introduction

We are shaped by our thoughts; we become what we think. When the mind is pure, joy follows like a shadow that never leaves.
　　—SIDDHĀRTHA GAUTAMA, THE BUDDHA (563–483 B.C.E.)

That in the soul which is called the mind is, before it thinks, not actually any real thing.
　　—ARISTOTLE (384–322 B.C.E.)

The mind is not a vessel to be filled, but a fire to be ignited.
　　—PLUTARCH (46–120)

Distinctions drawn by the mind are not necessarily equivalent to distinctions in reality.
　　—ST. THOMAS AQUINAS (1225–1274)

Consciousness is the perception of what passes in a man's own mind. Can another man perceive that I am conscious of any thing, when I perceive it not myself? No man's knowledge here can go beyond his experience.
　　—JOHN LOCKE (1632–1704)

To the dull mind all nature is leaden. To the illumined mind the whole world burns and sparkles with light.
　　—RALPH WALDO EMERSON (1803–1882)

The difference in mind between man and the higher animals, great as it is, is one of degree and not of kind.
　　—CHARLES DARWIN (1809–1882)

The computer takes up where psychoanalysis left off. It takes the ideas of a decentered self and makes it more concrete by modeling mind as a multiprocessing machine.
　　—SHERRY TURKLE (b. 1948)

I deas about the nature of the human mind have abounded throughout history. Philosophers and scientists have sought to discern the mind's components and functions and have distinguished humans from other animals according to the qualities associated with the mind, such as reason and self-awareness. The ancient Greeks formulated the concept of the psyche (from which we derive the term *psychology*) as the center of consciousness and reason as well as emotions. During the Renaissance, René Descartes (1596–1650) concluded *Cogito ergo sum* ("I think, therefore I am") and proposed that the mind was the source of human identity and that reason was the key to comprehending the material world. Influenced by Descartes, John Locke (1632–1704) developed a theory of the mind as a tabula rasa, or blank slate, that was shaped entirely by external experiences. The selections in this section further explore these questions about the nature of the mind and its relationship to consciousness, knowledge, intellect, and the other means by which we work to understand ourselves and our world.

In "Apollonianism and Dionysianism," Friedrich Nietzsche (1844–1900) explores issues that were difficult for the Greeks to resolve. Greek philosophers usually recommended that on the path to enlightenment a person should avoid extremes and practice moderation. But Apollonianism (the rational life associated with Apollo, god of music and poetry) and Dionysianism (the life of passion, personified by Dionysus, god of wine) are profound extremes that the Greeks regarded as forms of divine madness. Nietzsche asserted, then, that there is more than one appropriate psychological path to pursue and that both may be in the minds of all people.

These extremes may be threatening to conventional thought, but Nietzsche argued that they are not immoral. He complicated the issue of morality by demanding consideration for the godliness of the individual and the virtues of inspiration. A divine madness is what he praised, something close to the ecstasy of the ancients, a path that he found more interesting than the paths that were laid out in conventional patterns of psychology. This is not a contrast between the unconscious and the conscious because both states of mind are involved in Apollonianism and Dionysianism at the same time. Nietzsche is talking about psychological circumstances that we might think of as people being possessed.

Explaining the nature of the human mind is the province of Sigmund Freud (1856–1939). One of the best-known results of Freud's study of dreams is his conclusion that all people suffer from an Oedipus complex when they are extremely young. Freud explains that Oedipus, thinking he was escaping his fate, killed his father and married his mother, both of whom were strangers to him. Freud takes this familiar Greek myth and explores its significance in the lives of very young children, showing that it is common for them to wish to do away with their parent of the same sex and have their opposite sex parent all to themselves. As people grow older, both the memory and the desire to follow through on this feeling are repressed and forgotten. They become part of our unconscious and, in some cases, may resurface in the form of guilt. As adults, we know that such feelings are completely unacceptable, and the guilt that results can create psychological illness.

Carl Jung (1875–1961) began his studies with Freud's views of the content of the unconscious, but one of his analyses led him in a novel direction. He concluded that some of the content of the unconscious mind could not have begun in the conscious mind because it was not the product of the individual's conscious experience. Jung reasoned that certain images present in the unconscious were common to all members of a culture. He called these images *archetypal* because they seemed fundamental and universal, such as the archetype of the father and archetype of the mother. He then hypothesized that part of the mind's content is derived from cultural history. Unlike Freud, Jung saw the unconscious as containing images that represent deep instinctual longings belonging to an entire culture, not just to the individual.

Karen Horney (1885–1952), a contemporary of both Freud and Jung, responded in her work to some of Freud's theories concerning the sexual development of women, one of which was that girls naturally developed penis envy when they realized that they lacked this anatomical feature. After reflecting on the behavior of primitive tribespeople, Horney theorized that the boot was actually on the other foot. She asserted that men are envious of the power of women to create a human life out of their bodies and that, as a result, throughout history, men have ascribed extraordinary powers to female deities.

However, Horney did not necessarily disagree entirely with Freud. As her daughter, Marianne Horney Eckardt, put it: "Her early writing did focus on such topics as penis envy among other issues. Her observations concluded that penis envy and other feminine symptomatology did exist, but were determined by cultural factors rather than libidinal conflicts." In Dr. Eckardt's words, then, Horney's interest in feminine psychology as such centered more on the cultural than on the purely psychiatric.

Gilbert Ryle (1900–1976), a modern philosopher, approaches the concept of mind from a somewhat different position. He references René Descartes, the seventeenth-century philosopher who said, "I think, therefore I am." Descartes studied the concept of the mind in relation to the brain and concluded, as did some religious thinkers, that the mind was essentially the same as the soul. Therefore, he saw the mind as a spiritual entity, whereas the brain was a part of nature. Descartes maintained that the brain acted mechanically and that it followed the laws of nature in that it grew, aged, and then died. But the mind, he was sure, did none of those things. Ryle is famous for having introduced the term "the ghost in the machine," because he felt Descartes was wrong, despite the fact that people still believed Descartes when Ryle was writing. Ryle, instead, saw the mind and the brain to be products of nature and subject to nature's laws.

Robert Nozick (1938–2002) broaches the question of mind by examining the nature of emotions. In the process of examining emotions and what he feels is their sometime cognitive value, he establishes a three-part approach. Nozick considers that for an emotion to be complete there must first be a belief in something that matters. Second, the evaluation of the belief controls the intensity of the emotion, and the third part is the feeling, or what we experience as emotion. According to Nozick, whether or not emotions are appropriate depends on the value of the belief and the nature of the stimulation. He examines a nonrational aspect of the mind that goes beyond the concerns of neurologists.

Eric Kandel (b. 1929) approaches the problem of mind from the point of view of the neuroscientist and the psychiatrist. For example, he examines the question of how the unconscious operates on the conscious mind. He is interested in two qualities of consciousness: unity, in which the mind unifies all that is perceived; and subjectivity, the "hard problem," which concerns the nature of our unique conscious experiences. Kandel's approach is largely physiological, with his attention directed toward the specific regions of the brain that, when stimulated, produce the kinds of experiences we have. Underlying most of what he discusses is his deep concern for memory and how it is formed in the brain.

Howard Gardner's (b. 1943) interest is intelligence, which he approaches from a pluralist point of view. His idea of seven distinct intelligences, as opposed to the conventional views as represented by standardized IQ tests, is at once traditional and revolutionary. In drawing on the model of ancient Greek education, he urges us to examine the virtues of all seven forms of intelligence and not rely on the logical-mathematical model that dominates contemporary education. Gardner notes that certain forms of intelligence are culturally linked, but he leaves open the question of whether they are gender linked.

The essays in this section approach the concept of mind from different positions and are concerned with different questions of consciousness, thought, limitation, and intelligence. They raise some of the most basic questions concerning the mind: How do we define it? What is its physical status? What is its relationship to the brain? What can it know? What should we most value in its function? In answering these questions, each essay provides us with ideas that provoke more thought and still more questions.

Some Considerations
about the Nature of Mind

Before reading the selections that follow, consider what your views of mind are. Ask yourself the following questions and respond to each in a reading journal. Discuss your answers with your classmates.

1. How aware are you of possessing an unconscious mind?

2. How do you define consciousness?

3. In what sense is the mind distinct from the brain?

4. Are the processes of mind physical or metaphysical?

5. Are there different forms of intelligence?

6. Will computers become thinking machines?

7. To what extent is the brain like a computer?

8. Are there acceptable forms of madness?

9. How do emotions relate to the mind?

10. What unconscious forces seem to direct portions of our life?

FRIEDRICH
NIETZSCHE

Apollonianism and Dionysianism

© Bettmann/Getty Images

F RIEDRICH NIETZSCHE (1844–1900), one of the most influential modern thinkers, was concerned that the rise of science in the modern world and the changes in attitudes toward religion and the nature of God would leave people with a loss of purpose. Like many historians and philosophers of the day, he feared that modern civilization itself was somehow hanging in the balance, and that unless people struggled to reclaim the spiritual energy that brought progress and prosperity, the foundations of society would collapse.

His solution for the malaise that he felt was settling on modern society involved a search for meaning through a form of introspection and self-understanding that might well have been intelligible to Buddha, Plato, or St. Matthew. For Nietzsche, self-mastery was the key to transcending the confusion of modern thought. Realizing that self-domination was not an easy state to achieve, he called the man who succeeded in mastering himself "superman" — a man who could create his own values instead of blindly following conventional or societal standards.

Nietzsche's own personal life was difficult. His minister-father died when he was four years old, leaving Nietzsche to be raised in a household of women. Some critics have felt that the antifemale tone in certain of his writings is a result of his upbringing, but it also may be related to the syphilis that he may have contracted from a prostitute when he was a young man.

He was a brilliant student, particularly of the classics, and he became a professor at the University of Basel at a young age. His first book, *The Birth of Tragedy from the Spirit of Music* (1872), is the result of his effort to clarify certain aspects of the music of Richard Wagner, the contemporary composer who created a mythology depicting Scandinavian gods for his Ring Cycle of operas. Nietzsche eventually broke with Wagner on philosophical matters, but his regard for Wagner's music remained strong. The insight on which

From *The Birth of Tragedy and the Genealogy of Morals*. Translated by Francis Golffing, 1956.

The Birth of Tragedy rests, presented in the selection reprinted here, is an attempt to clarify the two basic religious forces in humankind: Apollonian intellectuality and Dionysian passion. The first reflects the god Apollo, whose symbols were the bow and the lyre, implying his fierceness as a god of conscience combined with his love of the arts and music. The second reflects the god Dionysus, a deity associated with vegetation, plentifulness, passion, and especially wine. Both were sons of Zeus, and each represented extremes in behavior, whether religious or secular.

Both forces were present in ancient Greek society, which Nietzsche takes as a standard of high civilization, particularly in its Doric phase — a phase of clear, calm, beautiful works of religious expression, such as the Parthenon in Athens. Although Apollonian qualities appear to oppose Dionysian qualities, Nietzsche notes that the Greeks discovered the need for both forces to be present in their culture. Greek tragedy, he says, was the ground on which these forces were able to meet in ancient Greece. In Nietzsche's time — as he points out in a section not included here — they meet in the music of Richard Wagner.

The kinds of personal behavior countenanced by these two gods are quite different, but each god represents an aspect of the larger divinity. The rational qualities of Apollonianism approximate the ideals of Plato and Aristotle, whereas the ecstatic qualities of Dionysianism come closer to the views of some saints. The distinction between these two states of mind is considerable, but both are associated with artistic expression and religious practice throughout the world.

Nietzsche relies on art to help him clarify the distinction between each of these Greek gods. Apollo dominates intellectually. He demands clarity, order, reason, and calm. He is also the god of the individual. Dionysus, on the other hand, is the god of ecstasy and passion. Obscurity, disorder, irrational behavior, even hysteria are encouraged by Dionysus. He is the god of throngs and mobs. After reading this excerpt, we can realize that most of us have both capacities within us and that one of life's challenges is learning how to balance them.

NIETZSCHE'S RHETORIC

The most obvious rhetorical device Nietzsche uses is comparison and contrast. The Apollonian contrasts with the Dionysian, the Greek with the barbarian, the dream with the illusion, the god with the human, the individual with the group, the one with the many, even life with death. In this sense, the subject at hand has governed the basic shape of the work.

Nietzsche's task was to explain the polarities, their form of expression, and their effect. Because these terms were quite new to most contemporary readers, he took time to clarify the nature of the *Apollonian* and the *Dionysian*. In a sense, the first paragraphs are spent in the task of definition. Once each polarity is defined, Nietzsche goes on to explain its sphere of influence, its nature, and its implications. Insofar as those qualities are present in the rhetoric, this essay is itself Apollonian.

There is a surprise in Nietzsche's use of rhetoric here, however. Through rhetorical techniques, he also illustrates some aspects of the Dionysian nature. There are passages in the selection, such as the discussion of Dionysus in paragraph 5, that can best be described as ecstatic, poetic, and if not irrational, certainly obscure and difficult to grasp. The Dionysian aspects of the passage are based on feeling. We all know that some poems cannot be broken down into other words — or even explained to others. What we extract from such poems is not an understanding but a complex feeling or impression. The same is true of the passages we confront in this essay. They challenge us because we know that the general character of any essay must be Apollonian. When we are greeted by Dionysian verbal excursions, we are thrown off. Yet that is part of Nietzsche's point: verbal artifacts (such as Greek tragedy) can combine both forces.

Nietzsche's most important point may be that the original religious forces implied by both gods are expressed in the modern world in terms of art. It has become something of a commonplace for contemporary people to assert that the emotion that went into religion in the time of the Greeks or in the great age of the cathedrals in Europe is now expressed in art. The power of Wagnerian music and Wagnerian opera, whose shape borrows some aspects from Greek tragedy, would have been as much a religious experience as an aesthetic experience for many people. Apollo was the god around whom the muses gathered, and therefore he was a caretaker of music, poetry, and dance. Dionysus was the god to whom the citizens of Athens sacrificed when they put on their great tragic competitions. The City Dionysia was the most important of the celebrations involving Greek drama, and its god was Dionysus.

If it can be said that religious faith can be embodied in dramatic art, then it might be said that for the ancients it was present in the work of the Greek tragedians, for the Elizabethans it was present in Shakespeare, and for Nietzsche's contemporaries it was in Wagner's Ring Cycle. The ultimate effect of using the rhetorical device of comparison and contrast is to emphasize the need for these two forces to be unified in the highest cultures. Diversity is everywhere in nature, as Nietzsche implies throughout, but that diversity has one deep longing: to be one with the One. As he explains (para. 14), the eternal goal of the original Oneness is its redemption through illusion. Illusion is art, not just dream. Great artists of all ages understood that dream and illusion are the means of art and make accessible the inner nature of humanity.

❊ PREREADING QUESTIONS: WHAT TO READ FOR

The following prereading questions may help you anticipate key issues in the discussion on Friedrich Nietzsche's "Apollonianism and Dionysianism." Keeping them in mind during your first reading of the selection should help focus your reactions.

1. How does Apollonianism differ from Dionysianism?

2. How is Apollonian or Dionysian behavior related to conscious and unconscious behavior?

Apollonianism and Dionysianism

Much will have been gained for esthetics once we have succeeded in apprehending directly—rather than merely *ascertaining*—that art owes its continuous evolution to the Apollonian-Dionysiac duality, even as the propagation of the species depends on the duality of the sexes, their constant conflicts and periodic acts of reconciliation. I have borrowed my adjectives from the Greeks, who developed their mystical doctrines of art through plausible *embodiments*, not through purely conceptual means. It is by those two art-sponsoring deities, Apollo and Dionysos,[1] that we are made to recognize the tremendous split, as regards both origins and objectives, between the plastic, Apollonian arts and the non-visual art of music inspired by Dionysos. The two creative tendencies developed alongside one another, usually in fierce opposition, each by its taunts forcing the other to more energetic production, both perpetuating in a discordant concord that agon[2] which the term *art* but feebly denominates: until at last, by the thaumaturgy[3] of an Hellenic art of will, the pair accepted the yoke of marriage and, in this condition, begot Attic tragedy,[4] which exhibits the salient features of both parents.

To reach a closer understanding of both these tendencies, let us begin by viewing them as the separate art realms of *dream* and *intoxication*, two physiological phenomena standing toward one another in much the same relationship as the Apollonian and Dionysiac. It was in a dream, according to Lucretius,[5] that the marvelous gods and goddesses first presented themselves to the minds of men. That great healing sculptor, Phidias,[6] beheld in a dream the entrancing bodies of more-than-human beings, and likewise, if anyone had asked the Greek poets about the mystery of poetic creation, they too would

---

[1] **Apollo and Dionysos (Dionysus)**   Apollo is the god of music, healing, and archery, and, as Phoebus Apollo, is also regarded as the god of light. Dionysus is the god of wine and drunkenness.

[2] **agon**   A contest or opposition of forces.

[3] **thaumaturgy**   A magical change. Nietzsche means that a powerful transformation was needed for Apollo and Dionysus to be able to join together.

[4] **Attic tragedy**   Greek tragedy performed in Athens, in the Greek region of Attica, sixth century to fourth century B.C.

[5] **Lucretius (100?–55 B.C.)**   A Roman philosopher whose book on natural science was standard for more than a millennium.

[6] **Phidias (fl. 430 B.C.)**   Greek sculptor who carved the figures of the gods and goddesses on the Parthenon.

have referred him to dreams and instructed him much as Hans Sachs[7] instructs us in *Die Meistersinger:*

> My friend, it is the poet's work
> Dreams to interpret and to mark.
> Believe me that man's true conceit
> In a dream becomes complete:
> All poetry we ever read
> Is but true dreams interpreted.

The fair illusion of the dream sphere, in the production of which every man   3
proves himself an accomplished artist, is a precondition not only of all plastic art, but even, as we shall see presently, of a wide range of poetry. Here we enjoy an immediate apprehension of form, all shapes speak to us directly, nothing seems indifferent or redundant. Despite the high intensity with which these dream realities exist for us, we still have a residual sensation that they are illusions; at least such has been my experience — and the frequency, not to say normality, of the experience is borne out in many passages of the poets. Men of philosophical disposition are known for their constant premonition that our everyday reality, too, is an illusion, hiding another, totally different kind of reality. It was Schopenhauer[8] who considered the ability to view at certain times all men and things as mere phantoms or dream images to be the true mark of philosophic talent. The person who is responsive to the stimuli of art behaves toward the reality of dream much the way the philosopher behaves toward the reality of existence: he observes exactly and enjoys his observations, for it is by these images that he interprets life, by these processes that he rehearses it. Nor is it by pleasant images only that such plausible connections are made: the whole divine comedy of life, including its somber aspects, its sudden balkings, impish accidents, anxious expectations, moves past him, not quite like a shadow play — for it is he himself, after all, who lives and suffers through these scenes — yet never without giving a fleeting sense of illusion; and I imagine that many persons have reassured themselves amidst the perils of dream by calling out, "It is a dream! I want it to go on." I have even heard of people spinning out the causality of one and the same dream over three or more successive nights. All these facts clearly bear witness that our innermost being, the common substratum of humanity, experiences dreams with deep delight and a sense of real

---

[7] **Hans Sachs**   The legendary singer-hero of Richard Wagner's opera *Die Meistersinger von Nürnberg;* the lines quoted are from that opera.

[8] **Arthur Schopenhauer (1788–1860)**   German philosopher who influenced Nietzsche. His books, *The World as Will and Idea* (1819) and *On the Will in Nature* (1836; tr. 1889), emphasized the power of free will as a chief force in the world.

necessity. This deep and happy sense of the necessity of dream experiences was expressed by the Greeks in the image of Apollo. Apollo is at once the god of all plastic powers[9] and the soothsaying god. He who is etymologically the "lucent" one, the god of light, reigns also over the fair illusions of our inner world of fantasy. The perfection of these conditions in contrast to our imperfectly understood waking reality, as well as our profound awareness of nature's healing powers during the interval of sleep and dream, furnishes a symbolic analogue to the soothsaying faculty and quite generally to the arts, which make life possible and worth living. But the image of Apollo must incorporate that thin line which the dream image may not cross, under penalty of becoming pathological, of imposing itself on us as crass reality: a discreet limitation, a freedom from all extravagant urges, the sapient tranquility of the plastic god. His eye must be sunlike, in keeping with his origin. Even at those moments when he is angry and ill-tempered there lies upon him the consecration of fair illusion. In an eccentric way one might say of Apollo what Schopenhauer says, in the first part of *The World as Will and Idea*, of man caught in the veil of Maya:[10] "Even as on an immense, raging sea, assailed by huge wave crests, a man sits in a little rowboat trusting his frail craft, so, amidst the furious torments of this world, the individual sits tranquilly, supported by the *principium individuationis*[11] and relying on it." One might say that the unshakable confidence in that principle has received its most magnificent expression in Apollo, and that Apollo himself may be regarded as the marvelous divine image of the *principium individuationis*, whose looks and gestures radiate the full delight, wisdom, and beauty of "illusion."

In the same context Schopenhauer has described for us the tremendous   4 awe which seizes man when he suddenly begins to doubt the cognitive modes of experience, in other words, when in a given instance the law of causation seems to suspend itself. If we add to this awe the glorious transport which arises in man, even from the very depths of nature, at the shattering of the *principium individuationis*, then we are in a position to apprehend the essence of Dionysiac rapture, whose closest analogy is furnished by physical intoxication. Dionysiac stirrings arise either through the influence of those narcotic potions of which all primitive races speak in their hymns, or through the powerful approach of spring, which penetrates with joy the whole frame of nature. So stirred, the individual forgets himself completely. It is the same Dionysiac power which in medieval Germany drove ever increasing crowds of people singing and dancing from place to place; we recognize in these St. John's

---

[9] **plastic powers**   Apollo is associated with the arts, which are plastic in that they reshape reality and foster imagination.

[10] **Maya**   A Hindu term for the delusion of the senses by the material world. The veil of Maya is the illusion hiding the reality that lies beneath material surfaces.

[11] *principium individuationis*   The principle of the individual, as apart from the crowd.

and St. Vitus' dancers the bacchic choruses[12] of the Greeks, who had their precursors in Asia Minor and as far back as Babylon and the orgiastic Sacaea.[13] There are people who, either from lack of experience or out of sheer stupidity, turn away from such phenomena, and, strong in the sense of their own sanity, label them either mockingly or pityingly "endemic diseases." These benighted souls have no idea how cadaverous and ghostly their "sanity" appears as the intense throng of Dionysiac revelers sweeps past them.

Not only does the bond between man and man come to be forged once   5
more by the magic of the Dionysiac rite, but nature itself, long alienated or subjugated, rises again to celebrate the reconciliation with her prodigal son, man. The earth offers its gifts voluntarily, and the savage beasts of mountain and desert approach in peace. The chariot of Dionysos is bedecked with flowers and garlands; panthers and tigers stride beneath his yoke. If one were to convert Beethoven's "Paean to Joy"[14] into a painting and refuse to curb the imagination when that multitude prostrates itself reverently in the dust, one might form some apprehension of Dionysiac ritual. Now the slave emerges as a freeman; all the rigid, hostile walls which either necessity or despotism has erected between men are shattered. Now that the gospel or universal harmony is sounded, each individual becomes not only reconciled to his fellow but actually at one with him—as though the veil of Maya had been torn apart and there remained only shreds floating before the vision of mystical Oneness. Man now expresses himself through song and dance as the member of a higher community; he has forgotten how to walk, how to speak, and is on the brink of taking wing as he dances. Each of his gestures betokens enchantment; through him sounds a supernatural power, the same power which makes the animals speak and the earth render up milk and honey. He feels himself to be godlike and strides with the same elation and ecstasy as the gods he has seen in his dreams. No longer the *artist,* he has himself become a *work of art:* the productive power of the whole universe is now manifest in his transport, to the glorious satisfaction of the primordial One. The finest clay, the most precious marble—man—is here kneaded and hewn, and the chisel blows of the Dionysiac world artist are accompanied by the cry of the Eleusinian mystagogues:[15] "Do you fall on your knees, multitudes, do you divine your creator?"

---

[12] **bacchic choruses**   Bacchus was the god of wine and ecstasy (a variant of Dionysus); thus, this term means ecstatic choruses. The St. John's and St. Vitus's dancers were ecstatic Christian dancers of the Middle Ages. Their dance was a mania that spread to a number of major religious centers.

[13] **Sacaea**   A Babylonian summer festival for the god Ishtar. The point is that such religious orgies are ancient.

[14] **"Paean to Joy"**   This is Friedrich von Schiller's (1759–1805) poem, *Ode to Joy,* which Ludwig van Beethoven (1770–1827) set to music in the last movement of his Symphony no. 9 (*Choral*).

[15] **Eleusinian mystagogues**   Those who participate in the ancient Greek Eleusinian secret ceremonies celebrating life after death.

So far we have examined the Apollonian and Dionysiac states as the product of formative forces arising directly from nature without the mediation of the human artist. At this stage artistic urges are satisfied directly, on the one hand through the imagery of dreams, whose perfection is quite independent of the intellectual rank, the artistic development of the individual; on the other hand, through an ecstatic reality which once again takes no account of the individual and may even destroy him, or else redeem him through a mystical experience of the collective. In relation to these immediate creative conditions of nature every artist must appear as "imitator," either as the Apollonian dream artist or the Dionysiac ecstatic artist, or, finally (as in Greek tragedy, for example) as dream and ecstatic artist in one. We might picture to ourselves how the last of these, in a state of Dionysiac intoxication and mystical self-abrogation,[16] wandering apart from the reveling throng, sinks upon the ground, and how there is then revealed to him his own condition—complete oneness with the essence of the universe—in a dream similitude.

Having set down these general premises and distinctions, we now turn to the Greeks in order to realize to what degree the formative forces of nature were developed in them. Such an inquiry will enable us to assess properly the relation of the Greek artist to his prototypes or, to use Aristotle's expression, his "imitation of nature."[17] Of the dreams the Greeks dreamed it is not possible to speak with any certainty, despite the extant dream literature and the large number of dream anecdotes. But considering the incredible accuracy of their eyes, their keen and unabashed delight in colors, one can hardly be wrong in assuming that their dreams too showed a strict consequence of lines and contours, hues and groupings, a progression of scenes similar to their best bas-reliefs.[18] The perfection of these dream scenes might almost tempt us to consider the dreaming Greek as a Homer and Homer as a dreaming Greek; which would be as though the modern man were to compare himself in his dreaming to Shakespeare.

Yet there is another point about which we do not have to conjecture at all: I mean the profound gap separating the Dionysiac Greeks from the Dionysiac barbarians. Throughout the range of ancient civilization (leaving the newer civilizations out of account for the moment) we find evidence of Dionysiac celebrations which stand to the Greek type in much the same relation as the bearded

---

[16] **self-abrogation**   The reveler "loses" his self, his sense of being an individual apart from the throng.

[17] **"imitation of nature"**   A key term in Aristotle's theory of *mimesis*, the doctrine that art imitates nature and that the artist must observe nature carefully. Nietzsche emphasizes dreams as a part of nature and something to be closely observed by the artist.

[18] **bas-reliefs**   Sculptures projecting only slightly from a flat surface; they usually tell a story in a series of scenes.

satyr,[19] whose name and attributes are derived from the he-goat, stands to the god Dionysos. The central concern of such celebrations was, almost universally, a complete sexual promiscuity overriding every form of established tribal law; all the savage urges of the mind were unleashed on those occasions until they reached that paroxysm of lust and cruelty which has always struck me as the "witches' cauldron" *par excellence.* It would appear that the Greeks were for a while quite immune from these feverish excesses which must have reached them by every known land or sea route. What kept Greece safe was the proud, imposing image of Apollo, who in holding up the head of the Gorgon[20] to those brutal and grotesque Dionysiac forces subdued them. Doric art has immortalized Apollo's majestic rejection of all license. But resistance became difficult, even impossible, as soon as similar urges began to break forth from the deep substratum of Hellenism itself. Soon the function of the Delphic god[21] developed into something quite different and much more limited: all he could hope to accomplish now was to wrest the destructive weapon, by a timely gesture of pacification, from his opponent's hand. That act of pacification represents the most important event in the history of Greek ritual, every department of life now shows symptoms of a revolutionary change. The two great antagonists have been reconciled. Each feels obliged henceforth to keep to his bounds, each will honor the other by the bestowal of periodic gifts, while the cleavage remains fundamentally the same. And yet, if we examine what happened to the Dionysiac powers under the pressure of that treaty we notice a great difference: in the place of the Babylonian Sacaea, with their throwback of men to the condition of apes and tigers, we now see entirely new rites celebrated: rites of universal redemption, of glorious transfiguration. Only now has it become possible to speak of nature's celebrating an *esthetic* triumph; only now has the abrogation of the *principium individuationis* become an esthetic event. That terrible witches' brew concocted of lust and cruelty has lost all power under the new conditions. Yet the peculiar blending of emotions in the heart of the Dionysiac reveler — his ambiguity if you will — seems still to hark back (as the medicinal drug harks back to the deadly poison) to the days when the infliction of pain was experienced as joy while a sense of supreme triumph elicited cries of anguish from the heart. For now in every exuberant joy there is heard an

---

[19] **satyr**   Greek god, half man, half goat; a symbol of lechery.

[20] **Gorgon**   Powerful monster in Greek mythology with serpents for hair. There were three Gorgons, all sisters, but only Medusa was not immortal. With the help of the goddess Athena, Perseus beheaded Medusa, whose very glance was supposed to turn men to stone. Later Perseus vanquished his enemies by exposing the head to them and turning them to stone.

[21] **Delphic god**   Apollo. The oracle at the temple to Apollo at Delphi, in Greece, was for more than one thousand years a source of prophecies of the future. It was among the most sacred places in Greece.

undertone of terror, or else a wistful lament over an irrecoverable loss. It is as though in these Greek festivals a sentimental trait of nature were coming to the fore, as though nature were bemoaning the fact of her fragmentation, her decomposition into separate individuals. The chants and gestures of these revelers, so ambiguous in their motivation, represented an absolute *novum*[22] in the world of the Homeric Greeks; their Dionysiac music, in especial, spread abroad terror and a deep shudder. It is true: music had long been familiar to the Greeks as an Apollonian art, as a regular beat like that of waves lapping the shore, a plastic rhythm[23] expressly developed for the portrayal of Apollonian conditions. Apollo's music was a Doric architecture of sound — of barely hinted sounds such as are proper to the cithara.[24] Those very elements which characterize Dionysiac music and, after it, music quite generally: the heart-shaking power of tone, the uniform stream of melody, the incomparable resources of harmony — all those elements had been carefully kept at a distance as being inconsonant with the Apollonian norm. In the Dionysiac dithyramb[25] man is incited to strain his symbolic faculties to the utmost; something quite unheard of is now clamoring to be heard: the desire to tear asunder the veil of Maya, to sink back into the original oneness of nature; the desire to express the very essence of nature symbolically. Thus an entirely new set of symbols springs into being. First, all the symbols pertaining to physical features: mouth, face, the spoken word, the dance movement which coordinates the limbs and bends them to its rhythm. Then suddenly all the rest of the symbolic forces — music and rhythm as such, dynamics, harmony — assert themselves with great energy. In order to comprehend this total emancipation of all the symbolic powers one must have reached the same measure of inner freedom those powers themselves were making manifest; which is to say that the votary of Dionysos[26] could not be understood except by his own kind. It is not difficult to imagine the awed surprise with which the Apollonian Greek must have looked on him. And that surprise would be further increased as the latter realized, with a shudder, that all this was not so alien to him after all, that his Apollonian consciousness was but a thin veil hiding from him the whole Dionysiac realm.

In order to comprehend this we must take down the elaborate edifice of Apollonian culture stone by stone until we discover its foundations. At first the eye is struck by the marvelous shapes of the Olympian gods who stand upon its pediments, and whose exploits, in shining bas-relief, adorn its friezes. The fact

9

---

[22] **an absolute *novum***   A genuine novelty.

[23] **plastic rhythm**   Plastic in this sense means capable of being shaped, responsive to slight changes — not rigid.

[24] **cithara**   An ancient stringed instrument, similar to the lyre, used to accompany songs and recitations.

[25] **Dionysiac dithyramb**   A passionate hymn to Dionysus, usually delivered by a chorus.

[26] **votary of Dionysos**   A follower of Dionysus; one devoted to Dionysian ecstasy.

that among them we find Apollo as one god among many, making no claim to a privileged position, should not mislead us. The same drive that found its most complete representation in Apollo generated the whole Olympian world, and in this sense we may consider Apollo the father of that world. But what was the radical need out of which that illustrious society of Olympian beings sprang?

Whoever approaches the Olympians with a different religion in his heart,   10
seeking moral elevation, sanctity, spirituality, loving-kindness, will presently be forced to turn away from them in ill-humored disappointment. Nothing in these deities reminds us of asceticism, high intellect, or duty: we are confronted by luxuriant, triumphant *existence*, which defies the good and the bad indifferently. And the beholder may find himself dismayed in the presence of such overflowing life and ask himself what potion these heady people must have drunk in order to behold, in whatever direction they looked, Helen[27] laughing back at them, the beguiling image of their own existence. But we shall call out to this beholder, who has already turned his back: Don't go! Listen first to what the Greeks themselves have to say of this life, which spreads itself before you with such puzzling serenity. An old legend has it that King Midas[28] hunted a long time in the woods for the wise Silenus, companion of Dionysos, without being able to catch him. When he had finally caught him the king asked him what he considered man's greatest good. The daemon remained sullen and uncommunicative until finally, forced by the king, he broke into a shrill laugh and spoke: "Ephemeral wretch, begotten by accident and toil, why do you force me to tell you what it would be your greatest boon not to hear? What would be best for you is quite beyond your reach: not to have been born, not to *be*, to be *nothing*. But the second best is to die soon."

What is the relation of the Olympian gods to this popular wisdom? It is that   11
of the entranced vision of the martyr to his torment.

Now the Olympian magic mountain opens itself before us, showing us its   12
very roots. The Greeks were keenly aware of the terrors and horrors of existence; in order to be able to live at all they had to place before them the shining fantasy of the Olympians. Their tremendous distrust of the titanic forces of nature: *Moira*,[29] mercilessly enthroned beyond the knowable world; the vulture which fed upon the great philanthropist Prometheus;[30] the terrible lot drawn by

---

[27] **Helen**   The runaway wife of Menelaus, immortalized in Homer's *Iliad* as the cause of the ten-year Trojan War. She was not "good" or ascetic, but her intensity of living secured her a permanent place in history and myth.

[28] **King Midas**   Midas was a foolish king who kidnapped Silenus, a satyr (half man, half goat) who was a companion of Dionysus. Silenus, a daemon or spirit, granted Midas his wish to have everything he touched turn to gold. Because his food turned to gold, he almost died. Dionysus eventually saved him by bathing him in a sacred river.

[29] *Moira*   Fate personified; the figure who gives each person his or her fate.

[30] **Prometheus**   The god who gave men fire—thus, his generosity is philanthropy, the love of man. He was punished by the gods.

wise Oedipus; the curse on the house of Atreus which brought Orestes to the murder of his mother: that whole Panic philosophy,[31] in short, with its mythic examples, by which the gloomy Etruscans perished, the Greeks conquered— or at least hid from view—again and again by means of this artificial Olympus. In order to live at all the Greeks had to construct these deities. The Apollonian need for beauty had to develop the Olympian hierarchy of joy by slow degrees from the original titanic hierarchy of terror, as roses are seen to break from a thorny thicket. How else could life have been borne by a race so hypersensitive, so emotionally intense, so equipped for suffering? The same drive which called art into being as a completion and consummation of existence, and as a guarantee of further existence, gave rise also to that Olympian realm which acted as a transfiguring mirror to the Hellenic will. The gods justified human life by living it themselves—the only satisfactory theodicy[32] ever invented. To exist in the clear sunlight of such deities was now felt to be the highest good, and the only real grief suffered by Homeric man was inspired by the thought of leaving that sunlight, especially when the departure seemed imminent. Now it became possible to stand the wisdom of Silenus on its head and proclaim that it was the worst evil for man to die soon, and second worst for him to die at all. Such laments as arise now arise over short-lived Achilles,[33] over the generations ephemeral as leaves, the decline of the heroic age. It is not unbecoming to even the greatest hero to yearn for an afterlife, though it be as a day laborer. So impetuously, during the Apollonian phase, does man's will desire to remain on earth, so identified does he become with existence, that even his lament turns to a song of praise.

It should have become apparent by now that the harmony with nature which we late-comers regard with such nostalgia, and for which Schiller has coined the cant term *naïve*,[34] is by no means a simple and inevitable condition to be found at the gateway to every culture, a kind of paradise. Such a belief could have been endorsed only by a period for which Rousseau's Émile was an artist and Homer just such an artist nurtured in the bosom of nature.

13

---

[31] **Panic philosophy**   Belief in fate. Oedipus's fate was to murder his father and marry his mother. He tried to escape it but could not. Orestes murdered his mother, Clytemnestra, because she had murdered his father, Agamemnon. All of these were members of the cursed house of Atreus and provide examples of how fate works.

[32] **theodicy**   Examination of the question of whether the gods are just. Because the gods shared human life, they ennobled it; they suffered evil as well.

[33] **short-lived Achilles**   Achilles' fate was to lead the Greeks to victory at Troy but to die by an arrow shot by Paris, who had taken Helen to Troy. Apollo guided the arrow so that it hit Achilles in the heel, his one vulnerable spot. Achilles, like many heroes, lived a brief but intense life.

[34] *naïve*   Friedrich Schiller's (1759–1805) *On the Naïve and the Sentimental in Poetry* (1795–1796) contrasted the classic (naïve) with the romantic (sentimental) in art. It is not the same as Nietzsche's distinction, but it is similar. Nietzsche uses *naïve* to refer to a kind of classical purity and temper.

Whenever we encounter "naïveté" in art, we are face to face with the ripest fruit of Apollonian culture—which must always triumph first over titans, kill monsters, and overcome the somber contemplation of actuality, the intense susceptibility to suffering, by means of illusions strenuously and zestfully entertained. But how rare are the instances of true naïveté, of that complete identification with the beauty of appearance! It is this achievement which makes Homer so magnificent—Homer, who, as a single individual, stood to Apollonian popular culture in the same relation as the individual dream artist to the oneiric[35] capacity of a race and of nature generally. The naïveté of Homer must be viewed as a complete victory of Apollonian illusion. Nature often uses illusions of this sort in order to accomplish its secret purposes. The true goal is covered over by a phantasm. We stretch out our hands to the latter, while nature, aided by our deception, attains the former. In the case of the Greeks it was the will wishing to behold itself in the work of art, in the transcendence of genius; but in order so to behold itself its creatures had first to view themselves as glorious, to transpose themselves to a higher sphere, without having that sphere of pure contemplation either challenge them or upbraid them with insufficiency. It was in that sphere of beauty that the Greeks saw the Olympians as their mirror images; it was by means of that esthetic mirror that the Greek will opposed suffering and the somber wisdom of suffering which always accompanies artistic talent. As a monument to its victory stands Homer, the naïve artist.

We can learn something about that naïve artist through the analogy of dream. We can imagine the dreamer as he calls out to himself, still caught in the illusion of his dream and without disturbing it, "This is a dream, and I want to go on dreaming," and we can infer, on the one hand, that he takes deep delight in the contemplation of his dream, and, on the other, that he must have forgotten the day, with its horrible importunity, so to enjoy his dream. Apollo, the interpreter of dreams, will furnish the clue to what is happening here. Although of the two halves of life—the waking and the dreaming—the former is generally considered not only the more important but the only one which is truly lived, I would, at the risk of sounding paradoxical, propose the opposite view. The more I have come to realize in nature those omnipotent formative tendencies and, with them, an intense longing for illusion, the more I feel inclined to the hypothesis that the original Oneness, the ground of Being, ever-suffering and contradictory, time and again has need of rapt vision and delightful illusion to redeem itself. Since we ourselves are the very stuff of such illusions, we must view ourselves as the truly non-existent, that is to say, as a perpetual unfolding in time, space, and causality—what we label "empiric reality."[36] But if, for the moment, we abstract from our own reality, viewing our

14

---

[35] **oneiric**   Pertaining to dreams.

[36] **"empiric reality"**   The reality we can test by experience.

empiric existence, as well as the existence of the world at large, as the *idea* of the original Oneness, produced anew each instant, then our dreams will appear to us as illusions of illusions, hence as a still higher form of satisfaction of the original desire for illusion. It is for this reason that the very core of nature takes such a deep delight in the naïve artist and the naïve work of art, which likewise is merely the illusion of an illusion. Raphael,[37] himself one of those immortal "naïve" artists, in a symbolic canvas has illustrated that reduction of illusion to further illusion which is the original act of the naïve artist and at the same time of all Apollonian culture. In the lower half of his "Transfiguration," through the figures of the possessed boy, the despairing bearers, the helpless, terrified disciples, we see a reflection of original pain, the sole ground of being: "illusion" here is a reflection of eternal contradiction, begetter of all things. From this illusion there rises, like the fragrance of ambrosia, a new illusory world, invisible to those enmeshed in the first: a radiant vision of pure delight, a rapt seeing through wide-open eyes. Here we have, in a great symbol of art, both the fair world of Apollo and its substratum, the terrible wisdom of Silenus, and we can comprehend intuitively how they mutually require one another. But Apollo appears to us once again as the apotheosis[38] of the *principium individuationis*, in whom the eternal goal of the original Oneness, namely its redemption through illusion, accomplishes itself. With august gesture the god shows us how there is need for a whole world of torment in order for the individual to produce the redemptive vision and to sit quietly in his rocking rowboat in mid-sea, absorbed in contemplation.

If this apotheosis of individuation is to be read in nominative terms, we   15
may infer that there is one norm only: the individual—or, more precisely, the observance of the limits of the individual: *sophrosyne*.[39] As a moral deity Apollo demands self-control from his people and, in order to observe such self-control, a knowledge of self. And so we find that the esthetic necessity of beauty is accompanied by the imperatives, "Know thyself," and "Nothing too much." Conversely, excess and *hubris*[40] come to be regarded as the hostile spirits of the non-Apollonian sphere, hence as properties of the pre-Apollonian era— the age of Titans[41]—and the extra-Apollonian world, that is to say the world

---

[37] **Raphael (1483–1520)**   A Renaissance artist. Raphael was influenced by classical forms, but his work became progressively more humanistic, in some cases tending to Schiller's "sentimental." *Transfiguration* (1517–1520), his last painting, points to the new age of Baroque painting: an intense, emotional, ecstatic style.

[38] **apotheosis**   Godlike embodiment. Nietzsche is saying that Apollo is the god in whom the concept of the individual is best expressed.

[39] *sophrosyne*   Greek word for wisdom, moderation.

[40] *hubris*   Greek word for pride, especially dangerous, defiant pride.

[41] **age of Titans**   A reference to the gods who reigned before Zeus; an unenlightened, violent age.

of the barbarians. It was because of his Titanic love of man that Prometheus had to be devoured by vultures; it was because of his extravagant wisdom which succeeded in solving the riddle of the Sphinx[42] that Oedipus had to be cast into a whirlpool of crime: in this fashion does the Delphic god interpret the Greek past.

The effects of the Dionysiac spirit struck the Apollonian Greeks as titanic and barbaric; yet they could not disguise from themselves the fact that they were essentially akin to those deposed Titans and heroes. They felt more than that: their whole existence, with its temperate beauty, rested upon a base of suffering and *knowledge* which had been hidden from them until the reinstatement of Dionysos uncovered it once more. And lo and behold! Apollo found it impossible to live without Dionysos. The elements of titanism and barbarism turned out to be quite as fundamental as the Apollonian element. And now let us imagine how the ecstatic sounds of the Dionysiac rites penetrated ever more enticingly into that artificially restrained and discreet world of illusion, how this clamor expressed the whole outrageous gamut of nature — delight, grief, knowledge — even to the most piercing cry; and then let us imagine how the Apollonian artist with his thin, monotonous harp music must have sounded beside the demoniac chant of the multitude! The muses presiding over the illusory arts paled before an art which enthusiastically told the truth, and the wisdom of Silenus cried "Woe!" against the serene Olympians. The individual, with his limits and moderations, forgot himself in the Dionysiac vortex and became oblivious to the laws of Apollo. Indiscreet extravagance revealed itself as truth, and contradiction, a delight born of pain, spoke out of the bosom of nature. Wherever the Dionysiac voice was heard, the Apollonian norm seemed suspended or destroyed. Yet it is equally true that, in those places where the first assault was withstood, the prestige and majesty of the Delphic god appeared more rigid and threatening than before. The only way I am able to view Doric art and the Doric[43] state is as a perpetual military encampment of the Apollonian forces. An art so defiantly austere, so ringed about with fortifications — an education so military and exacting — a polity so ruthlessly cruel — could endure only in a continual state of resistance against the titanic and barbaric menace of Dionysos.

[42] **riddle of the Sphinx**   The sphinx, part woman and part beast, waited outside Thebes for years, killing all who tried to pass by but could not solve its riddle. Oedipus (see note 31) answered the riddle: "What walks on four legs in the morning, two legs in the day, and three legs in the evening?" The answer: man, who crawls in infancy, walks upright in his prime, and uses a cane in old age. The solution freed Thebes from its bondage to the Sphinx, but it brought Oedipus closer to his awful fate.

[43] **Doric**   The Doric styles were unadorned, clear, and intellectual rather than sensual. They represent purity and uprightness.

Up to this point I have developed at some length a theme which was sounded   17
at the beginning of this essay: how the Dionysiac and Apollonian elements, in a
continuous chain of creations, each enhancing the other, dominated the Hellenic
mind: how from the Iron Age,[44] with its battles of Titans and its austere popular philosophy, there developed under the aegis of Apollo the Homeric world of
beauty; how this "naïve" splendor was then absorbed once more by the Dionysiac
torrent, and how, face to face with this new power, the Apollonian code rigidified
into the majesty of Doric art and contemplation. If the earlier phase of Greek history may justly be broken down into four major artistic epochs dramatizing the
battle between the two hostile principles, then we must inquire further (lest Doric
art appear to us as the acme and final goal of all these striving tendencies) what
was the true end toward which that evolution moved. And our eyes will come to
rest on the sublime and much lauded achievement of the dramatic dithyramb and
Attic tragedy, as the common goal of both urges; whose mysterious marriage, after
long discord, ennobled itself with such a child, at once Antigone and Cassandra.[45]

---

[44] **Iron Age**   An earlier age, ruled by sterner, less humane gods, the Titans.

[45] **Antigone and Cassandra**   Children in Greek tragedies; Antigone, daughter of Oedipus,
defied the authorities in *Antigone* by Sophocles (496?–406 B.C.) and suffered death;
Cassandra, daughter of Priam, king of Troy, appears in Homer's *Iliad* and several tragedies by Aeschylus (525–456 B.C.) and Euripides (484?–406 B.C.). She had the gift of prophecy but was doomed never to be believed. She foresaw the destruction of Troy, and after
its fall she was taken prisoner by Agamemnon and was killed with him. She and Antigone
were both heroic in their suffering.

⊞ QUESTIONS FOR CRITICAL READING

1. Define *Apollonianism* and *Dionysianism*. What kind of behavior does each word
   stand for?

2. What are the important distinctions between the self and the mob? Between
   dream and illusion?

3. In paragraph 6, Nietzsche speaks of the "mystical experience of the collective."
   What does he mean by this phrase? Is there such an experience?

4. Which paragraphs in the selection are most obscure and difficult to
   understand? How do they seem to show Dionysian qualities?

5. What contemporary art unifies the Apollonian and the Dionysian? Would
   Nietzsche have thought a modern film could do so?

6. Do the distinctions Nietzsche makes give you useful insights into modern
   psychology? If so, how?

7. What moral issues might the Apollonian person and the Dionysian person
   interpret differently?

8. For which of these polarities of behavior is self-control more likely a virtue?

SUGGESTIONS FOR CRITICAL WRITING

1. Examine paragraph 6 carefully. How valid are Nietzsche's insights concerning the self and the "reveling throng"? Drawing on personal experience, contrast the behavior of yourself or a friend — first as an individual and then as a member of a large gathering of people. Are you (or your friend) "possessed" when you are a member of such an assemblage? Be as specific as possible in writing about this contrast.
2. Establish a principle of moral behavior by which you feel the Apollonian can live. Then establish one for the Dionysian. Compare the two personalities to determine their differences and their similarities. How would the mental states represented by these polarities make their moral behavior different? On what would they agree? Is either of these polarities in danger of appearing immoral to people in general?
3. Music is the inspiration for this essay. Choose a piece of music that is important to you. Consider it as an artifact, and describe the qualities it has that you feel are Apollonian and Dionysian, respectively. Is the range of the music — in terms of exciting or sustaining emotional response — narrow or great? Describe your emotional and intellectual reactions to the music, and ask others about their responses to the same music. Is music an appropriate source for finding the conjunction of these two forces?
4. Examine aspects of our culture that reveal whether it is basically Apollonian or basically Dionysian. Be sure to consider matters of religion, literature, music, faith, and art and any aspects of personal life in your immediate environment. In considering these features of our culture, use Nietzsche's technique of comparison and contrast. For instance, you may find the Apollonian and Dionysian sides of, say, the modern film as interesting contrasts, just as you may wish to contrast rock music and Muzak, or any other related pairs.
5. Which of these two polarities of behavior most resembles your own behavior? Are you Apollonian or Dionysian? Define your behavior with reference to Nietzsche. Ask others who have read this selection to comment on your character in terms of the Apollonian-Dionysian distinction. Do you think that you achieve the kind of control that enables you to realize yourself fully in terms of these polarities, or do you feel that control is not an issue? Is inspiration an issue?
6. **CONNECTIONS** Howard Gardner (p. 556), like all the modern authors in this section, is familiar with Nietzsche's work. Write an essay that connects the idea of multiple intelligences with Nietzsche's descriptions of Apollonianism and Dionysianism. Would these two psychological states constitute forms of intelligence as Gardner understands the term? What evidence can you provide in your essay that establishes Nietzsche's two states of mind as forms of intelligence? Have you experienced both states of mind?

7. **CONNECTIONS**   Write a short essay discussing Carl Jung's (p. 487) concept of the unconscious, personal and collective, as it relates to Nietzsche's theory of Apollonianism and Dionysianism in human experience. Argue a case that explains Nietzsche's ideas as forms of the conscious and the unconscious, both personal and collective. To what extent is it possible that Jung was modeling his thought on that of Nietzsche? How does Jung help you understand Nietzsche better?

SIGMUND
FREUD

The Oedipus Complex

S IGMUND FREUD (1856–1939) is, in the minds of
many, the founder of modern psychiatry. He developed the psychoanalytic method: the examination of the mind using dream analysis, the analysis of the unconscious through free association, and the correlation of findings with attitudes toward sexuality and sexual development. His theories changed the way people treated neurosis and most other mental disorders. Today we use terms he either invented or championed, such as *psychoanalysis*, *penis envy*, *Oedipus complex*, and *wish fulfillment*.

Freud was born in Freiberg, Moravia (now Pribor in the Czech Republic), and moved to Vienna, Austria, when he was four. He pursued a medical career and soon began exploring neurology, which stimulated him to begin his psychoanalytic methods. *The Interpretation of Dreams* (1899) is one of his first important books. It was followed in rapid succession by a number of groundbreaking studies: *The Psychopathology of Everyday Life* (1904), *Three Essays on the Theory of Sexuality* (1905), *Totem and Taboo* (1913), *Beyond the Pleasure Principle* (1920), and *Civilization and Its Discontents* (1930). Freud's personal life in Vienna was essentially uneventful until he was put under house arrest by the Nazis in 1938 because he was Jewish. He was released and then moved to London, where he died the following year.

As a movement, psychoanalysis shocked most of the world by postulating a superego, which establishes high standards of personal behavior; an ego, which corresponds to the apparent personality; an id, which includes the deepest primitive forces of life; and an unconscious, into which thoughts and memories we cannot face are repressed or sublimated. The origin of much mental illness, the theory presumes, lies in the inability of the mind to find a way to sublimate — to express in harmless and creative ways — the painful thoughts that have been repressed. Dreams and unconscious actions sometimes act as releases or harmless expressions of these thoughts and memories.

From *The Interpretation of Dreams.* Translated by James Strachey.

As Freud states in *The Interpretation of Dreams*, the unconscious works in complex ways to help us cope with feelings and desires that our superego deems unacceptable. Dreams are mental events, not necessarily connected to physical events. The repression of important emotions, a constant process, often results in dreams that express repressed feelings in a harmless and sometimes symbolic way. In a sense, dreams help us maintain our mental health.

Further, dreams are a primary subject matter of psychoanalysis because they reveal a great deal about the unconscious mind, especially the material that we repress from our consciousness. His discussion of the Oedipus complex, which follows, is a classic case in point. Most people found Freud's theory of the Oedipus complex very compelling once they began to understand the details of its expression. Freud assumed that when we are infants we love our opposite-sex parent and hate our same-sex parent. These feelings of love and hate change as we grow, but they can still linger and cause neurotic behavior. Because these feelings are repressed into the unconscious, we are not aware of them as adults.

FREUD'S RHETORIC

This selection comes from a section of *The Interpretation of Dreams* in which Freud discusses what he calls "typical dreams." It is here that he speaks directly about his theory of the Oedipus complex and links it specifically with two major pieces of Western literature. *Oedipus Rex* by Sophocles (496–406 B.C.E.) and *Hamlet* by William Shakespeare (1564–1616) are tragedies in which some of the unconscious desires of the hero to marry his mother are either carried out, as in *Oedipus Rex*, or strongly hinted at, as in *Hamlet*.

Freud realizes that many readers will not be convinced that such a compulsion exists. He explains, however, that because most young people outgrow the compulsion and thereafter repress it, most adults are unaware of their own oedipal feelings.

The rhetorical strategy of introducing two classic dramatic works that are centuries apart and demonstrating what they have in common is effective in helping the reader understand that the psychological condition Freud refers to is not unknown to Western culture. His analysis of his patients' dreams has helped dredge up the original content and the connection with the oedipal urge, thus freeing them of a sense of guilt and a need for self-punishment. Paragraphs 2–6 detail the story of King Oedipus and the strange way in which he eventually married his mother and thus brought a plague upon his land. Freud's point is that this ancient text reveals an aspect of the inner nature of the human mind that has not changed for many thousands of years.

As he tells us, his patients have dreams of intercourse with parents and then feel such torrents of guilt and shame that they sometimes become neurotic. The fact that Oedipus severely punishes himself at the end of the play corresponds with the sense of guilt that Freud's patients experience. Hamlet is even more severely punished and suffers even more psychological anguish throughout the play, even though he never commits incest with his mother. The power of thought is enough. Hamlet is described as "a pathologically irresolute character which might be classed as neurasthenic" (para. 7). In other words, he could have benefited from Freud's psychoanalysis.

Freud uses these two great plays as examples of his theories because he sees them as imaginative constructs that work out the repressed feelings people have always had. They are similar to dreams in that they are written by poets; and poets who rely on inspiration have traditionally drawn on the unconscious. Because these two tragedies are so important to Western literature, they have a special value that no minor literature could have. Consequently, they have been enormously convincing to those interested in the way the mind works. What Freud has done with these works is to hold them up as a mirror. In that mirror one can see quite clearly the evidence for the Oedipus complex that would be totally invisible in any self-examination. It is one of Freud's great rhetorical achievements.

In paragraph 8, Freud makes some other observations about the dreams some of his patients have had in which they imagined themselves killing their parents. This is such a horrible idea for most people that Freud is surprised that our internal censor permits such dreams to occur. His theory is that the thought is so monstrous that the dream censor "is not armed to meet" it (para. 8). His analysis suggests that worry about a parent may disguise the unconscious wish that the parent should die. Freud mentions "our explanation of dreams in general" (para. 8), by which he means that dreams are wish fulfillments. If that is true, those who dream about killing a parent are likely to be deeply upset and may make themselves neurotic by their own sense of guilt.

Though most people go through an infantile oedipal stage, they usually grow out of it early in life. Freud suggests, however, that those who do not grow out of it may need psychoanalytic help.

✴ PREREADING QUESTIONS: WHAT TO READ FOR

The following prereading questions may help you anticipate key issues in the discussion of Sigmund Freud's "The Oedipus Complex." Keeping them in mind during your first reading of the selection should help focus your attention.

1. What, exactly, is the Oedipus complex?
2. How does the Oedipus complex express itself in dreams?
3. How do *Oedipus Rex* and *Hamlet* illustrate the Oedipus complex?

The Oedipus Complex

In my experience, which is already extensive, the chief part in the mental lives of all children who later become psychoneurotics is played by their parents. Being in love with the one parent and hating the other are among the essential constituents of the stock of psychical impulses which is formed at that time   1 and which is of such importance in determining the symptoms of the later neurosis. It is not my belief, however, that psychoneurotics differ sharply in this respect from other human beings who remain normal—that they are able, that is, to create something absolutely new and peculiar to themselves. It is far more probable—and this is confirmed by occasional observations on normal children—that they are only distinguished by exhibiting on a magnified scale feelings of love and hatred to their parents which occur less obviously and less intensely in the minds of most children.

This discovery is confirmed by a legend that has come down to us from classical antiquity: a legend whose profound and universal power to move can only be understood if the hypothesis I have put forward in regard to the psychology of children has an equally universal validity. What I have in mind is the legend of King Oedipus and Sophocles' drama which bears his name. 2

Oedipus, son of Laïus, King of Thebes, and of Jocasta, was exposed as an infant because an oracle had warned Laïus that the still unborn child would be his father's murderer. The child was rescued, and grew up as a prince in an alien court, until, in doubts as to his origin, he too questioned the oracle and was warned to avoid his home since he was destined to murder his father and take his mother in marriage. On the road leading away from what he believed was his home, he met King Laïus and slew him in a sudden quarrel. He came next to Thebes and solved the riddle set him by the Sphinx who barred his way. Out of gratitude the Thebans made him their king and gave him Jocasta's hand in marriage. He reigned long in peace and honor, and she who, unknown to him, was his mother bore him two sons and two daughters. Then at last a plague broke out and the Thebans made enquiry once more of the oracle. It is at this point that Sophocles' tragedy opens. The messengers bring back the reply that the plague will cease when the murderer of Laïus has been driven from the land. 3

> But he, where is he? Where shall now be read
> The fading record of this ancient guilt?

The action of the play consists in nothing other than the process of revealing, with cunning delays and ever-mounting excitement—a process that can be likened to the work of a psychoanalysis—that Oedipus himself is the murderer of Laïus, but further that he is the son of the murdered man and of Jocasta. Appalled at the abomination which he has unwittingly perpetrated, Oedipus blinds himself and forsakes his home. The oracle has been fulfilled.

Oedipus Rex is what is known as a tragedy of destiny. Its tragic effect is said to lie in the contrast between the supreme will of the gods and the vain attempts of mankind to escape the evil that threatens them. The lesson which, it is said, the deeply moved spectator should learn from the tragedy is 4 submission to the divine will and realization of his own impotence. Modern dramatists have accordingly tried to achieve a similar tragic effect by weaving the same contrast into a plot invented by themselves. But the spectators have looked on unmoved while a curse or an oracle was fulfilled in spite of all the efforts of some innocent man: later tragedies of destiny have failed in their effect.

If *Oedipus Rex* moves a modern audience no less than it did the contemporary Greek one, the explanation can only be that its effect does not lie in the contrast between destiny and human will, but is to be looked for in the particular nature of the material on which that contrast is exemplified. There must be something which makes a voice within us ready to recognize the compelling force of destiny in the *Oedipus*, while we can dismiss as merely arbitrary such dispositions as are laid down in *Die Ahnfrau*[1] or other modern tragedies of destiny. And a factor of this kind is in fact involved in the story of King Oedipus. His destiny moves us only because it might have been ours—because the oracle laid the same curse upon us before our birth as upon him. It is the fate of all of us, perhaps, to direct our first sexual impulse towards our mother and our first hatred and our first murderous wish against our father. Our dreams convince us that that is so. King Oedipus, who slew his father Laïus and married his mother Jocasta, merely shows us the fulfillment of our own childhood wishes. But, more fortunate than he, we have meanwhile succeeded, insofar as we have not become psychoneurotics, in detaching our sexual impulses from our mothers and in forgetting our jealousy of our fathers. Here is one in whom these primeval wishes of our childhood have been fulfilled, and we shrink back from him with the whole force of the repression by which those wishes have since that time been held down within us. While the poet, as he unravels the past, brings to light the guilt of Oedipus, he is at the same time compelling us to recognize our own inner minds, in which those same impulses, though suppressed, are still to be found. The contrast with which the closing Chorus leaves us confronted—

> . . . Fix on Oedipus your eyes,
> Who resolved the dark enigma, noblest champion and most wise.
> Like a star his envied fortune mounted beaming far and wide:
> Now he sinks in seas of anguish, whelmed beneath a raging tide . . .

—strikes as a warning at ourselves and our pride, at us who since our childhood have grown so wise and so mighty in our own eyes. Like Oedipus, we live in ignorance of these wishes, repugnant to morality, which have been forced upon us by

---

[1] *Die Ahnfrau*   Franz Grillparzer (1791–1872) wrote *Die Ahnfrau* (The Ancestress).

Nature, and after their revelation we may all of us well seek to close our eyes to the scenes of our childhood.[2]

There is an unmistakable indication in the text of Sophocles' tragedy itself   6
that the legend of Oedipus sprang from some primeval dream material which had as its content the distressing disturbance of a child's relation to his parents owing to the first stirrings of sexuality. At a point when Oedipus, though he is not yet enlightened, has begun to feel troubled by his recollection of the oracle, Jocasta consoles him by referring to a dream which many people dream, though, as she thinks, it has no meaning:

> Many a man ere now in dreams hath lain
> With her who bare him. He hath least annoy
> Who with such omens troubleth not his mind.

Today, just as then, many men dream of having sexual relations with their mothers, and speak of the fact with indignation and astonishment. It is clearly the key to the tragedy and the complement to the dream of the dreamer's father being dead. The story of Oedipus is the reaction of the imagination to these two typical dreams. And just as these dreams, when dreamt by adults, are accompanied by feelings of repulsion, so too the legend must include horror and self-punishment. Its further modification originates once again in a misconceived secondary revision of the material, which has sought to exploit it for theological purposes. The attempt to harmonize divine omnipotence with human responsibility must naturally fail in connection with this subject matter just as with any other.

Another of the great creations of tragic poetry, Shakespeare's Hamlet,   7
has its roots in the same soil as Oedipus Rex. But the changed treatment of the same material reveals the whole difference in the mental life of these two widely separated epochs of civilization: the secular advance of repression in the emotional life of mankind. In the Oedipus the child's wishful fantasy that underlies it is brought into the open and realized as it would be in a dream. In Hamlet it remains repressed; and—just as in the case of a neurosis—we only learn of its existence from its inhibiting consequences. Strangely enough, the

---

[2] [*Footnote added* 1914:] None of the findings of psychoanalytic research has provoked such embittered denials, such fierce opposition—or such amusing contortions—on the part of critics as this indication of the childhood impulses towards incest which persist in the unconscious. An attempt has even been made recently to make out, in the face of all experience, that the incest should only be taken as "symbolic." —Ferenczi (1912) has proposed an ingenious "over-interpretation" of the Oedipus myth, based on a passage in one of Schopenhauer's letters. —[*Added* 1919:] Later studies have shown that the "Oedipus complex," which was touched upon for the first time in the above paragraphs in the *Interpretation of Dreams*, throws a light of undreamt-of importance on the history of the human race and the evolution of religion and morality. (See my *Totem and Taboo*, 1912–13.) [Freud's notes]

overwhelming effect produced by the more modern tragedy has turned out to be compatible with the fact that people have remained completely in the dark as to the hero's character. The play is built up on Hamlet's hesitations over fulfilling the task of revenge that is assigned to him; but its text offers no reasons or motives for these hesitations and an immense variety of attempts at interpreting them have failed to produce a result. According to the view which was originated by Goethe[3] and is still the prevailing one today, Hamlet represents the type of man whose power of direct action is paralyzed by an excessive development of his intellect. (He is "sicklied o'er with the pale cast of thought.") According to another view, the dramatist has tried to portray a pathologically irresolute character which might be classed as neurasthenic. The plot of the drama shows us, however, that Hamlet is far from being represented as a person incapable of taking any action. We see him doing so on two occasions: first in a sudden outburst of temper, when he runs his sword through the eavesdropper behind the arras, and secondly in a premeditated and even crafty fashion, when, with all the callousness of a Renaissance prince, he sends the two courtiers to the death that had been planned for himself. What is it, then, that inhibits him in fulfilling the task set him by his father's ghost? The answer, once again, is that it is the peculiar nature of the task. Hamlet is able to do anything—except take vengeance on the man who did away with his father and took that father's place with his mother, the man who shows him the repressed wishes of his own childhood realized. Thus the loathing which should drive him on to revenge is replaced in him by self-reproaches, by scruples of conscience, which remind him that he himself is literally no better than the sinner whom he is to punish. Here I have translated into conscious terms what was bound to remain unconscious in Hamlet's mind; and if anyone is inclined to call him a hysteric, I can only accept the fact as one that is implied by my interpretation. The distaste for sexuality expressed by Hamlet in his conversation with Ophelia fits in very well with this: the same distaste which was destined to take possession of the poet's mind more and more during the years that followed, and which reached its extreme expression in Timon of Athens. For it can of course only be the poet's own mind which confronts us in Hamlet. I observe in a book on Shakespeare by Georg Brandes (1896) a statement that Hamlet was written immediately after the death of Shakespeare's father (in 1601), that is, under the immediate impact of his bereavement and, as we may well assume, while his childhood feelings about his father had been freshly revived. It is known, too, that Shakespeare's own son who died at an early age bore the name of "Hamnet," which is identical with "Hamlet." Just as Hamlet deals with the relation of a son to his parents, so Macbeth (written at approximately the same period) is concerned with the subject of childlessness. But just as all neurotic symptoms, and, for that matter,

---

[3] **Johann Wolfgang von Goethe (1749–1832)**   One of Germany's greatest writers.

dreams, are capable of being "over-interpreted" and indeed need to be, if they are to be fully understood, so all genuinely creative writings are the product of more than a single motive and more than a single impulse in the poet's mind, and are open to more than a single interpretation. In what I have written I have only attempted to interpret the deepest layer of impulses in the mind of the creative writer.[4]

I cannot leave the subject of typical dreams of the death of loved relatives, without adding a few more words to throw light on their significance for the theory of dreams in general. In these dreams we find the highly unusual condition realized of a dream-thought formed by a repressed wish entirely eluding censorship and passing into the dream without modification. There must be special factors at work to make this event possible, and I believe that the occurrence of these dreams is facilitated by two such factors. Firstly, there is no wish that seems more remote from us than this one: "we couldn't even *dream*"—so we believe—of wishing such a thing. For this reason the dream-censorship is not armed to meet such a monstrosity, just as Solon's[5] penal code contained no punishment for parricide. Secondly, in this case the repressed and unsuspected wish is particularly often met halfway by a residue from the previous day in the form of a *worry* about the safety of the person concerned. This worry can only make its way into the dream by availing itself of the corresponding wish; while the wish can disguise itself behind the worry that has become active during the day. We may feel inclined to think that things are simpler than this and that one merely carries on during the night and in dreams with what one has been turning over in one's mind during the day; but if so we shall be leaving dreams of the death of people of whom the dreamer is fond completely in the air and without any connection with our explanation of dreams in general, and we shall thus be clinging quite unnecessarily to a riddle which is perfectly capable of solution.

It is also instructive to consider the relation of these dreams to anxiety-dreams. In the dreams we have been discussing, a repressed wish has found a means of evading censorship—and the distortion which censorship involves. The invariable concomitant is that painful feelings are experienced in the dream. In just the same way anxiety-dreams only occur if the censorship has been wholly or partly overpowered; and, on the other hand, the overpowering

8

9

---

4 [*Footnote added* 1919:] The above indications of a psychoanalytic explanation of *Hamlet* have since been amplified by Ernest Jones and defended against the alternative views put forward in the literature of the subject. [*Added* 1930:] Incidentally, I have in the meantime ceased to believe that the author of Shakespeare's works was the man from Stratford. [*Added* 1919:] Further attempts at an analysis of *Macbeth* will be found in a paper of mine [Freud, 1916*d*] and in one by Jekels (1917). [Freud's notes]

5 **Solon (638–558 B.C.E.)** Greek known as the law giver. His ideas on law continue to influence us today.

of the censorship is facilitated if anxiety has already been produced as an immediate sensation arising from somatic[6] sources. We can thus plainly see the purpose for which the censorship exercises its office and brings about the distortion of dreams: it does so *in order to prevent the generation of anxiety or other forms of distressing affect.*

---

[6] **somatic**   Having to do with the physical body.

✣ QUESTIONS FOR CRITICAL READING

1. What role do parents play in the lives of those who become neurotics?
2. Do psychoneurotics differ substantially from normal people?
3. What does Freud expect his example of *Oedipus Rex* to call up in the mind of the reader?
4. What is a tragedy of destiny?
5. In what ways are all of us like Oedipus?
6. How is literature related to dreams, according to Freud?
7. Why do dreams sometimes need to be overinterpreted?
8. How does censorship operate in dreams?

✣ SUGGESTIONS FOR CRITICAL WRITING

1. Most adults have absolutely no awareness of having had an oedipal period in their infancy. However, you may have observed oedipal behavior in young children. If so, describe how the children behaved and if possible describe how they have grown up and whether they have left the oedipal stage behind. Do your observations help bolster Freud's views, or do they help weaken them?

2. Describe in as much detail as possible any anxiety dreams you may have had. Often anxiety dreams are repetitive and recurrent. What are the circumstances in which you find yourself in your dream? What worries you most in the dream? What threatens you most? How does the dream resolve itself? Does the dream provoke guilt or shame? How would you interpret the dream in the light of what you have read here?

3. If you find yourself unable to remember your dreams, interview some friends and "collect" dreams from them. Ask them for dreams that make them feel uneasy — anxiety dreams. Have them write down their dreams and then ask them to talk about events in their waking life that preceded the dreams. See if there are contributing events or anticipations in the mind of the dreamers that would lead them to have anxiety dreams. See, too, if there are any patterns to dreams of different people. Are there any "typical dreams" shared by your friends?

4. What are your typical dreams? Try to write them out as if they were plays. Identify characters, setting, and time, and then write the dialogue and stage directions that would give a good approximation of the content of the dreams. Do not censor your dreams or try to "overanalyze" them (despite Freud's recommendation). Do your best to make the dreams clear in their expression. Does this approach make your dreams any more meaningful to you? Explain.

5. Does your reading of *Hamlet* help bear out Freud's theory that suggests Hamlet is suffering from an Oedipus complex? What is his relationship to his mother? How does she regard him? Is his killing of King Claudius an act of parricide? Is Hamlet's punishment warranted? Argue for or against Freud's view of the play.

6. In paragraph 6, Freud states, "There is an unmistakable indication in the text of Sophocles' tragedy itself that the legend of Oedipus sprang from some primeval dream material." Examine his evidence for this claim and decide yourself whether this seems a reasonable conclusion.

7. Most horror films involve monstrous actions and severe punishment. Is it possible that one of the functions of horror films is to reveal some of the inner nature of our minds somewhat the way *Oedipus Rex* and *Hamlet* do? Choose a favorite film and analyze it in terms of its revealing hidden desires that might trouble us if we felt them consciously and acted on them in life.

8. **CONNECTIONS**   Plato's concerns in "The Allegory of the Cave" (p. 580) point to a level of reality that humans cannot reach because of the limitations of sensory apprehension. Is it also true that the dream world represents a level of reality that is impossible to reach because of the limitations of the conscious waking mind? Which part of the mind — the conscious or the unconscious — does Freud seem to regard as primary in his discussion of the Oedipus complex? Is there the sense that he regards one or the other as possessing a greater "reality"? How do his views fit with those of Plato?

9. **CONNECTIONS**   Both Freud and Eric Kandel (p. 539) are psychiatrists. Kandel talks about the role of the unconscious in affecting the conscious mind, and Freud also addresses how the unconscious finds its way into consciousness. Kandel says that Freud thought some of the issues of psychiatry would be solved by research into physiology. Write an essay that compares their thinking on the role of the unconscious. What would Freud have learned from Kandel, and what could Kandel learn from Freud? What have you learned from reading both and comparing their ideas?

CARL
JUNG

The Personal and the Collective Unconscious

© Hulton Archive/Getty Images

CARL GUSTAV JUNG (1875–1961), Freud's most famous disciple, was a Swiss physician who collaborated with Freud from 1907 to 1912, when the two argued about the nature of the unconscious. Jung's *Psychology of the Unconscious* (1912) posits an unconscious that is composed of more than the ego, superego, and id. According to Jung, an additional aspect of the unconscious is a collection of archetypal images that can be inherited by members of the same group. Experience clarifies these images, but the images in turn direct experience.

In one of his essays on the collective unconscious, Jung asserts that the great myths express the archetypes of actions and heroes stored in the unconscious by elucidating them for the individual and society. These archetypes represent themselves in mythic literature in images, such as the great father or the great mother, or in patterns of action, such as disobedience and self-sacrifice. They transcend social barriers and exemplify themselves similarly in most people in any given cultural group. For Jung, the individual must adapt to the archetypes that reveal themselves in the myths in order to be psychically healthy.

Like Freud, Jung postulates a specific model of the way the mind works: he claims the existence not only of a conscious mind — which all of us can attest to from experience and common sense — but also of an unconscious component to the mind. He argues that we are unaware of the content of our unconscious mind except, perhaps, in dreams (which occur when we are unconscious), which Freud and others insist speak to us in symbols rather than in direct language. Jung also acknowledges the symbolic nature of the unconscious but disagrees with the source of the content of the unconscious mind.

In "The Personal and the Collective Unconscious" (1916), Jung describes the pattern of psychological transference that most psychoanalysts experience with their patients. In the case presented here, the patient's problems were associated with her father, and the

---

From *The Basic Writings of C. G. Jung*. Translated by Cary F. Baynes.

transference was the normal one of conceiving of the doctor — in this case, Jung — in terms of the father. When this transference occurs, the patient often is cured of the problems that brought her to the psychoanalyst, but in this case the transference was incomplete. Jung offers a detailed analysis of the dreams that revealed the problems with the transference and describes the intellectual state of the woman whose dreams form the basis of the discussion. She is intelligent, conscious of the mechanism of transference, and careful about her own inner life. Yet the dream that Jung analyzes had a content that he could not relate to her personal life.

In an attempt to explain his inability to analyze the woman's dream strictly in terms of her personal life, Jung reexamines Freud's definition of the unconscious. As Jung explains Freud's view, the unconscious is a repository for material that is produced by the conscious mind and later repressed so as not to interfere with the function of the conscious mind. Thus, painful memories and unpleasant fears are often repressed and rarely become problems because they are sublimated — transformed into harmless activity, often dreams — and released. According to Freud, the material in the unconscious mind develops solely from personal experience.

Jung, however, argues that personal experiences form only part of the individual's unconscious, what he calls the "personal unconscious" (para. 17). For the patient in this essay, the images in the dream that he and the patient at first classified as a transference dream (in which the doctor became the father/lover figure) had qualities that could not be explained fully by transference. Instead, the dream seemed to represent a primordial figure, a god. From this, Jung develops the view that such a figure is cultural in nature and not personal. Nothing in the patient's life pointed to her concern for a god of the kind that developed in her dream. Jung proposes that the images that constituted the content of her dream were not a result of personal experience or education but, instead, were inherited. Jung defines this portion of the unconscious as the "collective unconscious" (para. 19).

Jung's theories proved unacceptable to Freud. After their collaboration ended, Jung studied the world's myths and mythic systems, including alchemy and occult literature. In them he saw many of the archetypal symbols that he felt were revealed in dreams — including symbolic quests, sudden transformations, dramatic or threatening landscapes, and images of God. His conclusions were that this literature, most or all of which was suppressed or rejected by modern religions such as Christianity, was a repository for the symbols of the collective unconscious — at least of Western civilization and perhaps of other civilizations.

JUNG'S RHETORIC

Like Freud, Jung tells a story. His selection is a narrative beginning with a recapitulation of Freud's view of the unconscious. Jung tells us that according to the conventional view, the contents of the unconscious have passed "the threshold of consciousness" (para. 2): in other words, they were once in the conscious mind of the individual. However, Jung also asserts that "the unconscious also contains components that have *not yet* reached the threshold of consciousness" (para. 3). At least two questions arise from this assertion: What is that content, and where did it come from?

Jung then provides the "example" (para. 5) of the woman whose therapy he was conducting. He tells us, as one would tell a story, about the woman's treatment and how such treatment works in a general sense. He explains the phenomenon of transference, claiming that "a successful transference can . . . cause the whole neurosis to disappear" (para. 5). Near the end of this patient's treatment he analyzed her dreams and found something he did not expect. He relates the narrative of the dream (para. 10), which includes the image of a superhuman father figure in a field of wheat swaying in the wind. From this he concludes that the image of the dream is not the doctor/father/lover figure that is common to transference — and that the patient was thoroughly aware of — but something of an entirely different order. He connects it to an archetype of God and proceeds to an analysis that explains the dream in terms of a collective unconscious whose content is shared by groups of people rather than created by the individual alone.

Jung's rhetorical strategy here is an argument proceeding from both example and analysis. The example is given in detail, along with enough background to make it useful to the reader. Then the example is narrated carefully, and its content is examined through a process of analysis familiar to those in psychiatry.

Some of the material in this selection is relatively challenging because Jung uses technical language and occasionally obscure references. However, the simplicity of the technique of narrative, telling a story of what happened, makes the selection intelligible, even though it deals with highly complex and controversial ideas.

❖ PREREADING QUESTIONS: WHAT TO READ FOR

The following prereading questions may help you anticipate key issues in the discussion of Carl Jung's "The Personal and the Collective Unconscious." Keeping them in mind during your first reading of the selection should help focus your attention.

1. What are some of the contents of the unconscious?
2. What is the difference between the personal and the collective unconscious?

The Personal and the Collective Unconscious

In Freud's view, as most people know, the contents of the unconscious are limited to infantile tendencies which are repressed because of their incompatible character. Repression is a process that begins in early childhood under the moral influence of the environment and lasts throughout life. Through analysis the repressions are removed and the repressed wishes made conscious.

1

According to this theory, the unconscious contains only those parts of the   2
personality which could just as well be conscious and are in fact suppressed only
through upbringing. Although from one point of view the infantile tendencies of
the unconscious are the most conspicuous, it would nonetheless be incorrect
to define or evaluate the unconscious entirely in these terms. The unconscious
has still another side to it: it includes not only repressed contents, but also all
psychic material that lies below the threshold of consciousness. It is impossible
to explain the subliminal nature of all this material on the principle of repression;
otherwise, through the removal of repressions, a man would acquire a phenome-
nal memory which would thenceforth forget nothing.

We therefore emphatically say that in addition to the repressed material   3
the unconscious contains all those psychic components that have fallen below
the threshold, including subliminal sense perceptions. Moreover we know, from
abundant experience as well as for theoretical reasons, that the unconscious
also contains components that have *not yet* reached the threshold of consciousness. These are the seeds of future conscious contents. Equally we have
reason to suppose that the unconscious is never at rest in the sense of being
inactive, but is continually engaged in grouping and regrouping its contents.
Only in pathological cases can this activity be regarded as completely autonomous; normally it is coordinated with the conscious mind in a compensatory
relationship.

It is to be assumed that all these contents are personal insofar as they   4
are acquired during the individual's life. Since this life is limited, the number
of acquired contents in the unconscious must also be limited. This being so, it
might be thought possible to empty the unconscious either by analysis or by
making a complete inventory of unconscious contents, on the ground that the
unconscious cannot produce anything more than is already known and accepted
in the conscious mind. We should also have to infer, as already indicated, that
if one could stop the descent of conscious contents into the unconscious by
doing away with repression, unconscious productivity would be paralyzed. This
is possible only to a very limited extent, as we know from experience. We urge
our patients to hold fast to repressed contents that have been re-associated with
consciousness, and to assimilate them into their plan of life. But this procedure,
as we may daily convince ourselves, makes no impression on the unconscious,
since it calmly continues to produce dreams and fantasies which, according to
Freud's original theory, must arise from personal repressions. If in such cases
we pursue our observations systematically and without prejudice, we shall find
material which, although similar in form to the previous personal contents, yet
seems to contain allusions that go far beyond the personal sphere.

Casting about in my mind for an example to illustrate what I have just said,   5
I have a particularly vivid memory of a woman patient with a mild hysterical
neurosis which, as we expressed it in those days, had its principal cause in a

"father complex." By this we wanted to denote the fact that the patient's peculiar relationship to her father stood in her way. She had been on very good terms with her father, who had since died. It was a relationship chiefly of feeling. In such cases it is usually the intellectual function that is developed, and this later becomes the bridge to the world. Accordingly our patient became a student of philosophy. Her energetic pursuit of knowledge was motivated by her need to extricate herself from the emotional entanglement with her father. This operation may succeed if her feelings can find an outlet on the new intellectual level, perhaps in the formation of an emotional tie with a suitable man, equivalent to the former tie. In this particular case, however, the transition refused to take place, because the patient's feelings remained suspended, oscillating between her father and a man who was not altogether suitable. The progress of her life was thus held up, and that inner disunity so characteristic of a neurosis promptly made its appearance. The so-called normal person would probably be able to break the emotional bond in one or the other direction by a powerful act of will, or else—and this is perhaps the more usual thing—he would come through the difficulty unconsciously, on the smooth path of instinct, without ever being aware of the sort of conflict that lay behind his headaches or other physical discomforts. But any weakness of instinct (which may have many causes) is enough to hinder a smooth unconscious transition. Then all progress is delayed by conflict, and the resulting stasis of life is equivalent to a neurosis. In consequence of the standstill, psychic energy flows off in every conceivable direction, apparently quite uselessly. For instance, there are excessive innervations of the sympathetic system, which lead to nervous disorders of the stomach and intestines; or the vagus (and consequently the heart) is stimulated; or fantasies and memories, uninteresting enough in themselves, become overvalued and prey on the conscious mind (mountains out of molehills). In this state a new motive is needed to put an end to the morbid suspension. Nature herself paves the way for this, unconsciously and indirectly, through the phenomenon of the transference (Freud). In the course of treatment the patient transfers the father imago[1] to the doctor, thus making him, in a sense, the father, and in the sense that he is *not* the father, also making him a substitute for the man she cannot reach. The doctor therefore becomes both a father and a kind of lover—in other words, the object of conflict. In him the opposites are united, and for this reason he stands for a quasi-ideal solution of the conflict. Without in the least wishing it, he draws upon himself an overvaluation that is almost incredible to the outsider, for to the patient he seems like a savior or a god. This way of speaking is not altogether so laughable as it sounds. It is indeed a bit much to be a father and lover at once. Nobody could possibly stand up to it in the long run, precisely because it is too much of a good thing. One would have to be a demigod at least to sustain

---

[1] **imago**   Idealized image of a person.

such a role without a break, for all the time one would have to be the giver. To the patient in the state of transference, this provisional solution naturally seems ideal, but only at first; in the end she comes to a standstill that is just as bad as the neurotic conflict was. Fundamentally, nothing has yet happened that might lead to a real solution. The conflict has merely been transferred. Nevertheless a successful transference can—at least temporarily—cause the whole neurosis to disappear, and for this reason it has been very rightly recognized by Freud as a healing factor of first-rate importance, but, at the same time, as a provisional state only, for although it holds out the possibility of a cure, it is far from being the cure itself.

This somewhat lengthy discussion seemed to me essential if my example   6
was to be understood, for my patient had arrived at the state of transference and had already reached the upper limit where the standstill begins to make itself disagreeable. The question now arose: What next? I had of course become the complete savior, and the thought of having to give me up was not only exceedingly distasteful to the patient, but positively terrifying. In such a situation "sound common sense" generally comes out with a whole repertory of admonitions: "you simply must," "you really ought," "you just cannot," etc. So far as sound common sense is, happily, not too rare and not entirely without effect (pessimists, I know, exist), a rational motive can, in the exuberant feeling of health you get from transference, release so much enthusiasm that a painful sacrifice can be risked with a mighty effort of will. If successful—and these things sometimes are—the sacrifice bears blessed fruit, and the erstwhile patient leaps at one bound into the state of being practically cured. The doctor is generally so delighted that he fails to tackle the theoretical difficulties connected with this little miracle.

If the leap does not succeed—and it did not succeed with my patient—   7
one is then faced with the problem of severing the transference. Here "psychoanalytic" theory shrouds itself in a thick darkness. Apparently we are to fall back on some nebulous trust in fate: somehow or other the matter will settle itself. "The transference stops automatically when the patient runs out of money," as a slightly cynical colleague once remarked to me. Or the ineluctable demands of life make it impossible for the patient to linger on in the transference—demands which compel the involuntary sacrifice, sometimes with a more or less complete relapse as a result. (One may look in vain for accounts of such cases in the books that sing the praises of psychoanalysis!)

To be sure, there are hopeless cases where nothing helps; but there are   8
also cases that do not get stuck and do not inevitably leave the transference situation with bitter hearts and sore heads. I told myself, at this juncture with my patient, that there must be a clear and respectable way out of the impasse. My patient had long since run out of money—if indeed she ever possessed any—but I was curious to know what means nature would devise for a satisfactory way out of the transference deadlock. Since I never imagined that

I was blessed with that "sound common sense" which always knows exactly what to do in every tangled situation, and since my patient knew as little as I, I suggested to her that we could at least keep an eye open for any movements coming from a sphere of the psyche uncontaminated by our superior wisdom and our conscious plannings. That meant first and foremost her dreams.

Dreams contain images and thought associations which we do not create   9 with conscious intent. They arise spontaneously without our assistance and are representatives of a psychic activity withdrawn from our arbitrary will. Therefore the dream is, properly speaking, a highly objective, natural product of the psyche, from which we might expect indications, or at least hints, about certain basic trends in the psychic process. Now, since the psychic process, like any other life process, is not just a causal sequence, but is also a process with a teleological orientation,[2] we might expect dreams to give us certain indicia about the objective causality as well as about the objective tendencies, because they are nothing less than self-portraits of the psychic life process.

On the basis of these reflections, then, we subjected the dreams to a careful   10 examination. It would lead too far to quote word for word all the dreams that now followed. Let it suffice to sketch their main character: the majority referred to the person of the doctor, that is to say, the actors were unmistakably the dreamer herself and her doctor. The latter, however, seldom appeared in this natural shape, but was generally distorted in a remarkable way. Sometimes his figure was of supernatural size, sometimes he seemed to be extremely aged, then again he resembled her father, but was at the same time curiously woven into nature, as in the following dream: *Her father (who in reality was of small stature) was standing with her on a hill that was covered with wheat fields. She was quite tiny beside him, and he seemed to her like a giant. He lifted her up from the ground and held her in his arms like a little child. The wind swept over the wheat fields, and as the wheat swayed in the wind, he rocked her in his arms.*

From this dream and from others like it I could discern various things.   11 Above all I got the impression that her unconscious was holding unshakably to the idea of my being the father-lover, so that the fatal tie we were trying to undo appeared to be doubly strengthened. Moreover one could hardly avoid seeing that the unconscious placed a special emphasis on the supernatural, almost "divine" nature of the father-lover, thus accentuating still further the overvaluation occasioned by the transference. I therefore asked myself whether the patient had still not understood the wholly fantastic character of her transference, or whether perhaps the unconscious could never be reached by understanding at all, but must blindly and idiotically pursue some nonsensical chimera. Freud's idea that the unconscious can "do nothing but wish,"

---

[2] **teleological orientation**   Possessing a sense of design; directed toward an end or a purpose.

Schopenhauer's[3] blind and aimless Will, the gnostic demi-urge who in his vanity deems himself perfect and then in the blindness of his limitation creates something lamentably imperfect — all these pessimistic suspicions of an essentially negative background to the world and the soul came threateningly near. And indeed there would be nothing to set against this except a well-meaning "you ought," reinforced by a stroke of the ax that would cut down the whole phantasmagoria for good and all.

But as I turned the dreams over and over in my mind, there dawned on me another possibility. I said to myself: it cannot be denied that the dreams continue to speak in the same old metaphors with which our conversations have made both doctor and patient sickeningly familiar. But the patient has an undoubted understanding of her transference fantasy. She knows that I appear to her as a semidivine father-lover, and she can, at least intellectually, distinguish this from my factual reality. Therefore the dreams are obviously reiterating the conscious standpoint minus the conscious criticism, which they completely ignore. They reiterate the conscious contents, not *in toto*, but insist on the fantastic standpoint as opposed to "sound common sense."   12

I naturally asked myself what was the source of this obstinacy and what was its purpose? That it must have some purposive meaning I was convinced, for there is no truly living thing that does not have a final meaning, that can in other words be explained as a mere leftover from antecedent facts. But the energy of the transference is so strong that it gives one the impression of a vital instinct. That being so, what is the purpose of such fantasies? A careful examination and analysis of the dreams, especially of the one just quoted, revealed a very marked tendency — in contrast to conscious criticism, which always seeks to reduce things to human proportions — to endow the person of the doctor with superhuman attributes. He had to be gigantic, primordial, huger than the father, like the wind that sweeps over the earth — was he then to be made into a god? Or, I said to myself, was it rather the case that the unconscious was trying to *create* a god out of the person of the doctor, as it were to free a vision of God from the veils of the personal, so that the transference to the person of the doctor was no more than a misunderstanding on the part of the conscious mind, a stupid trick played by "sound common sense"? Was the urge of the unconscious perhaps only apparently reaching out towards the person, but in a deeper sense towards a god? Could the longing for a god be a *passion* welling up from our darkest, instinctual nature, a passion unswayed by any outside influences, deeper and stronger perhaps than the love for a human person? Or was it perhaps the highest and truest meaning of that inappropriate love we call transference, a little bit of real *Gottesminne*,[4] that has been lost to consciousness ever since the fifteenth century?   13

---

[3] **Arthur Schopenhauer (1788–1860)**   German pessimistic philosopher.

[4] ***Gottesminne***   Love of God.

No one will doubt the reality of a passionate longing for a human person; but that a fragment of religious psychology, a historical anachronism, indeed something of a medieval curiosity—we are reminded of Mechtild of Magdeburg[5]—should come to light as an immediate living reality in the middle of the consulting room, and be expressed in the prosaic figure of the doctor, seems almost too fantastic to be taken seriously.

14

A genuinely scientific attitude must be unprejudiced. The sole criterion for the validity of a hypothesis is whether or not it possesses a heuristic—i.e., explanatory—value. The question now is, can we regard the possibilities set forth above as a valid hypothesis? There is no a priori[6] reason why it should not be just as possible that the unconscious tendencies have a goal beyond the human person, as that the unconscious can "do nothing but wish." Experience alone can decide which is the more suitable hypothesis.

15

This new hypothesis was not entirely plausible to my very critical patient. The earlier view that I was the father-lover, and as such presented an ideal solution of the conflict, was incomparably more attractive to her way of feeling. Nevertheless her intellect was sufficiently clear to appreciate the theoretical possibility of the new hypothesis. Meanwhile the dreams continued to disintegrate the person of the doctor and swell them to ever vaster proportions. Concurrently with this there now occurred something which at first I alone perceived, and with the utmost astonishment, namely a kind of subterranean undermining of the transference. Her relations with a certain friend deepened perceptibly, notwithstanding the fact that consciously she still clung to the transference. So that when the time came for leaving me, it was no catastrophe, but a perfectly reasonable parting. I had the privilege of being the only witness during the process of severance. I saw how the transpersonal control point developed—I cannot call it anything else—a *guiding function* and step by step gathered to itself all the former personal overvaluations; how, with this afflux of energy, it gained influence over the resisting conscious mind without the patient's consciously noticing what was happening. From this I realized that the dreams were not just fantasies, but self-representations of unconscious developments which allowed the psyche of the patient gradually to grow out of the pointless personal tie.

16

This change took place, as I showed, through the unconscious development of a transpersonal control point; a virtual goal, as it were, that expressed itself symbolically in a form which can only be described as a vision of God. The dreams swelled the human person of the doctor to superhuman proportions, making him a gigantic primordial father who is at the same time the wind, and in whose protecting arms the dreamer rests like an infant. If we try to make the

17

---

[5] **Mechtild of Magdeburg (1207–1282)** Thirteenth-century German mystic, writer, and saint.

[6] **a priori** Based on theory rather than on experiment or evidence.

patient's conscious, and traditionally Christian, idea of God responsible for the divine image in the dreams, we would still have to lay stress on the distortion. In religious matters the patient had a critical and agnostic attitude, and her idea of a possible deity had long since passed into the realm of the inconceivable, i.e., had dwindled into a complete abstraction. In contrast to this, the god-image of the dreams corresponded to the archaic conception of a nature demon, something like Wotan.[7] *Theos to pneûma*, "God is spirit," is here translated back into its original form where *pneûma* means "wind": God is the wind, stronger and mightier than man, an invisible breath-spirit. As in the Hebrew *ruach*, so in Arabic *ruh* means breath and spirit. Out of the purely personal form the dreams developed an archaic god-image that is infinitely far from the conscious idea of God. It might be objected that this is simply an infantile image, a childhood memory. I would have no quarrel with this assumption if we were dealing with an old man sitting on a golden throne in heaven. But there is no trace of any sentimentality of that kind; instead, we have a primitive conception that can correspond only to an archaic mentality. These primitive conceptions, of which I have given a large number of examples in my *Symbols of Transformation*, tempt one to make, in regard to unconscious material, a distinction very different from that between "preconscious" and "unconscious" or "subconscious" and "unconscious." The justification for these distinctions need not be discussed here. They have a definite value and are worth refining further as points of view. The fundamental distinction which experience has forced upon me merely claims the value of a further point of view. From what has been said it is clear that we have to distinguish in the unconscious a layer which we may call the *personal unconscious*. The materials contained in this layer are of a personal nature insofar as they have the character partly of acquisitions derived from the individual's life and partly of psychological factors which could just as well be conscious. It is readily understandable that incompatible psychological elements are liable to repression and therefore become unconscious; but on the other hand we also have the possibility of making and keeping the repressed contents conscious, once they have been recognized. We recognize them as personal contents because we can discover their effects, or their partial manifestation, or their specific origin in our personal past. They are the integral components of the personality, they belong to its inventory, and their loss to consciousness produces an inferiority in one or the other respect—an inferiority, moreover, that has the psychological character not so much of an organic mutilation or an inborn defect as of a want which gives rise to a feeling of moral resentment. The sense of moral inferiority always indicates that the missing element is something which, one feels, should not be missing, or which could be made conscious if only one took enough trouble. The feeling of moral inferiority does not come from a collision with the generally accepted

---

[7] **Wotan**   Supreme God; character in Richard Wagner's *Ring* cycle of operas.

and, in a sense, arbitrary moral law, but from the conflict with one's own self which, for reasons of psychic equilibrium, demands that the deficit be redressed. Whenever a sense of moral inferiority appears, it shows that there is not only the demand to assimilate an unconscious component, but also the possibility of assimilating it. In the last resort it is a man's moral qualities which force him, either through direct recognition of the necessity to do so, or indirectly through a painful neurosis, to assimilate his unconscious self and to keep himself fully conscious. Whoever progresses along this road of realizing the unconscious self must inevitably bring into consciousness the contents of the personal uncon- scious, thus widening the scope of his personality. I should add at once that this "widening" primarily concerns the moral consciousness, one's self-knowledge, for the unconscious contents that are released and brought into consciousness by analysis are usually unpleasant—which is precisely why these wishes, mem- ories, tendencies, plans, etc. were repressed. These are the contents that are brought to light in much the same way by a thorough confession, though to a much more limited extent. The rest comes out as a rule in dream analysis. It is often very interesting to watch how the dreams fetch up the essential points, bit by bit and with the nicest choice. The total material that is added to conscious- ness causes a considerable widening of the horizon, a deepened self-knowledge which, more than anything else, is calculated to humanize a man and make him modest. But even self-knowledge, assumed by all wise men to be the best and most efficacious, has different effects on different characters. We make very remarkable discoveries in this respect in practical analysis, . . .

As my example of the archaic idea of God shows, the unconscious   18 seems to contain other things besides personal acquisitions and belongings. My patient was quite unconscious of the derivation of "spirit" from "wind," or of the parallelism between the two. This content was not the product of her thinking, nor had she ever been taught it. The critical passage in the New Testament was inaccessible to her—*to pneûma pneî hopou thelei*[8]—since she knew no Greek. If we must take it as a wholly personal acquisition, it might be a case of so-called cryptomnesia,[9] the unconscious recollection of a thought which the dreamer had once read somewhere. I have nothing against such a possibility in this particular case; but I have seen a sufficient number of other cases—many of them are to be found in the book mentioned above—where cryptomnesia can be excluded with certainty. Even if it were a case of crypto- mnesia, which seems to me very improbable, we should still have to explain what the predisposition was that caused just this image to be retained and

---

[8] ***to pneûma pneî hopou thelei***   The wind blows where it wishes (John 3:8).

[9] Cf. Théodore Flournoy, *Des Indes à la planète Mars: Étude sur un cas de somnambulisme avec glossalalie* (Paris and Geneva, 1900; trans. by D. B. Vermilye as *From India to the Planet Mars*, New York, 1900), and Jung, "Psychology and Pathology of So-called Occult Phenomena," *Coll. Works*, Vol. 1, pp. 81ff. [Jung's note]

later, as Semon puts it, "ecphorated" (*ekphoreîn*, Latin *efferre*, "to produce"). In any case, cryptomnesia or no cryptomnesia, we are dealing with a genuine and thoroughly primitive god image that grew up in the unconscious of a civilized person and produced a living effect—an effect which might well give the psychologist of religion food for reflection. There is nothing about this image that could be called personal: it is a wholly collective image, the ethnic origin of which has long been known to us. Here is a historical image of worldwide distribution that has come into existence again through a natural psychic function. This is not so very surprising, since my patient was born into the world with a human brain which presumably still functions today much as it did of old. We are dealing with a reactivated archetype, as I have elsewhere called these primordial images. These ancient images are restored to life by the primitive, analogical mode of thinking peculiar to dreams. It is not a question of inherited ideas, but of inherited thought patterns.

In view of these facts we must assume that the unconscious contains not 19
only personal, but also impersonal, collective components in the form of inherited categories or archetypes. I have therefore advanced the hypothesis that at its deeper levels the unconscious possesses collective contents in a relatively active state. That is why I speak of the collective unconscious.

QUESTIONS FOR CRITICAL READING

1. What is Jung's view of the relationship of the unconscious mind to the conscious mind? How does it compare to Freud's?
2. What is repression? Why does repression work as it does?
3. How does transference work in psychoanalytic treatment? Is it a good thing or not?
4. What is unusual about Jung's patient's dream? What about it can he not fit into a normal pattern of transference?
5. What is the distinction between the personal unconscious and the collective unconscious?
6. Do you agree that "Dreams contain images and thought associations which we do not create with conscious intent" (para. 9)? Why or why not?

SUGGESTIONS FOR CRITICAL WRITING

1. Jung talks about common sense and its limitations. For some people, common sense denies the existence of an unconscious mind. Relying on Jung, your own personal experiences, and any other sources you choose, defend the existence of an unconscious mind. At the same time, do your best to explain the content of the unconscious and why it is important to the individual.

2. With reference to your own dreams, argue for or against the belief that dreams are products of the conscious mind. Have you had dreams whose content did not pass the "threshold" of your conscious mind?

3. Although the adult Jung was not religious, as the son of a Swiss pastor he was well acquainted with religion. In paragraph 13, Jung asserts that his patient's dream reveals a fundamental human longing for God. As he puts it, "Could the longing for a god be a *passion* welling up from our darkest, instinctual nature?" Examine the possibility that such a psychological phenomenon has affected your attitude toward religion and religious belief.

4. Jung suggests that mythic literature maintains some of the images that make up the collective unconscious of a group of people. Select a myth (consult Ovid's *Metamorphosis*, Grimm's fairy tales, or the Greek myths, or choose a pattern of mythic behavior repeated in popular films) and analyze the instinctual longing it represents for us. What does the myth reveal about our culture?

5. **CONNECTIONS**   Jung was a follower of Freud until he eventually broke from him. The break was not altogether friendly, and the feelings between the two — on professional matters — were often strained. Compare Jung's approach to the subject of the unconscious with Freud's (p. 477). In what respects do they differ? In what ways are their methods either compatible or incompatible with each other? Do you find Jung's methods more or less useful than Freud's? Explain why.

6. **CONNECTIONS**   In "Natural Selection" (p. 606), Charles Darwin suggests that as humans developed over a long period of time they may have continued many traditions that began early in history. How would Darwin's ideas help reinforce the concept of an unconscious that might transcend the ages and thus become part of our collective "memory" gathered through eons of evolution? Would Jung have found Darwin's ideas congenial, or would he have discounted them? Does he show any evidence of having been influenced by Darwin? Explain.

KAREN
HORNEY

The Distrust
between the Sexes

K AREN HORNEY (1885–1952) was a distinguished psychiatrist who developed her career
somewhat independently of the influence of Sigmund Freud. In her native Germany, she
taught in the Berlin Psychoanalytic Institute from the end of World War I until 1932, a year
before Hitler came to power. She was influenced by Freud's work — as was every other
psychoanalyst — but she found that although brilliant, it did not satisfactorily explain
important issues in female sexuality.

In Germany, Horney's early research was centered on questions about female psychology. This selection, first published in German in 1931, is part of these early studies.
Horney's conclusion was that penis envy, like many other psychological issues in women,
was determined by cultural factors and that these issues were not purely psychological or
libidinal in origin. She thought Freud oversimplified female sexuality and that the truth,
demonstrated through her own analysis, was vastly different. She began a significant theoretical shift that saw neurosis as a product of both psychological and cultural conflicts
rather than of psychological stress alone.

In 1932, Horney emigrated to America, where she began writing a distinguished
series of publications on neurosis. Her career in Chicago was remarkable. Not only did
she found the American Institute for Psychoanalysis (1941) and the *American Journal of
Psychoanalysis*, but she also wrote such important books as *The Neurotic Personality of Our
Time* (1937), *New Ways in Psychoanalysis* (1939), and *Self-Analysis* (1942). Her work was
rooted in cultural studies, and one of her principal arguments was that neuroses, including sexual problems, are caused by cultural influences and pressures that the individual
simply cannot deal with. Sigmund Freud thought the reverse, placing the causal force of
neuroses in sexuality.

From *Feminine Psychology*. Translated by Harold Kelman.

Her studies constantly brought her back to the question of interpersonal relations, and she saw neurotic patterns developed in childhood as the main cause of many failed relationships. The selection focuses particularly on the relationship that individuals establish with their mother or their father. Her insistence that childhood patterns affect adult behavior is consonant with Freudianism; however, her interpretations of those patterns are somewhat different. Like Carl Jung, she looks toward anthropological studies of tribal behavior for help in interpreting the behavior of modern people.

Horney claims that the distrust between the sexes cannot be explained away as existing only in individuals but is a widespread phenomenon that arises out of psychological forces present in men and women. She discusses a number of cultural practices in primitive peoples in an effort to suggest that even without modern cultural trappings, the two sexes suffer anxieties in their relationships. She also looks at the individual in a family setting, showing that normal expectations of child-parent relations can sometimes be frustrated, with seriously harmful results.

In addition, she examines the nature of culture, reminding us that early societies were often matriarchal — that is, centered not on men and their activities but on women. Her views about matriarchy, that the mystery of a woman is connected to her biologically creative nature, are quite suggestive in psychological terms. The envy as she sees it is on the part of men, who compensate for their inability to create life by spending their energies creating "state, religion, art, and science" (para. 14).

Horney speaks directly about sexual matters and about what she sees as male anxieties. She holds that there are distinct areas of conflict between men and women and that they are psychological in origin.

HORNEY'S RHETORIC

This is an expository essay, establishing the truth of hypothesis by pointing to a range of evidence from a variety of sources. Horney's view is that the distrust between the sexes is the result of cultural forces of which the individual is only dimly aware. In this sense she aligns herself with the Freudians, who constantly point to influences on the individual that are subconscious in nature and, therefore, not part of the individual's self-awareness.

To some degree her essay is itself an analysis of the relationship between men and women, with a look back at the history of culture. Her technique — a review of older societies — establishes that the current nature of the relationship between men and women is colored by the fact that most modern societies are dominated by patriarchal institutions. In ancient times, however, societies may well have been matriarchal.

This selection was originally delivered as a lecture to the German Women's Medical Association in November 1930, and most of the audience members were women. Consequently, the nature of the imagery, the frankness of the discourse, and the cultural focus concern issues that would have a distinct impact on women. On reading this essay, it becomes clear that Horney is speaking with a particular directness that she might have modified for a mixed audience.

Her method of writing is analytical, as she says several times. She is searching for causes within the culture as well as within the individual. Her range of causal analysis includes the comparative study of cultures (ethnology) as well as personal psychology. Her capacity to call on earlier writers and cultures reveals her enormous scope of knowledge and also helps convince the reader of the seriousness of her inquiry.

▟ PREREADING QUESTIONS: WHAT TO READ FOR

The following prereading questions may help you anticipate key issues in the discussion of Karen Horney's "The Distrust between the Sexes." Keeping them in mind during your first reading of the selection should help focus your attention.

1. How can a woman's attitude toward men be influenced by childhood conflicts?
2. How do patriarchal traditions affect men's attitudes toward women?

The Distrust between the Sexes

As I begin to talk to you today about some problems in the relationship between the sexes, I must ask you not to be disappointed. I will not concern myself primarily with the aspect of the problem that is most important to the physician. Only at the end will I briefly deal with the question of therapy. I am far more concerned with pointing out to you several psychological reasons for the distrust between the sexes.

The relationship between men and women is quite similar to that between children and parents, in that we prefer to focus on the positive aspects of these relationships. We prefer to assume that love is the fundamentally given factor and that hostility is an accidental and avoidable occurrence. Although we are familiar with slogans such as "the battle of the sexes" and "hostility between the sexes," we must admit that they do not mean a great deal. They make us overfocus on sexual relations between men and women, which can very easily lead us to a too one-sided view. Actually, from our recollection of numerous case histories, we may conclude that love relationships are quite easily destroyed by overt or covert hostility. On the other hand we are only too ready to blame such difficulties on individual misfortune, on incompatibility of the partners, and on social or economic causes.

The individual factors, which we find causing poor relations between men and women, may be the pertinent ones. However, because of the great frequency, or better, the regular occurrence of disturbances in love relations, we have to ask ourselves whether the disturbances in the individual cases might not arise from a common background; whether there are common denominators for this easily and frequently arising suspiciousness between the sexes?   3

It is almost impossible to attempt within the framework of a brief lecture to give you a complete survey of so large a field. I therefore will not even mention such factors as the origin and effects of such social institutions as marriage. I merely intend to select at random some of the factors that are psychologically understandable and pertain to the causes and effects of the hostility and tension between the sexes.   4

I would like to start with something very commonplace—namely, that a good deal of this atmosphere of suspiciousness is understandable and even justifiable. It apparently has nothing to do with the individual partner, but rather with the intensity of the affect[1] and with the difficulty of taming them.   5

We know or may dimly sense, that these affects can lead to ecstasy, to being beside oneself, to surrendering oneself, which means a leap into the unlimited and the boundless. This is perhaps why real passion is so rare. For like a good businessman, we are loath to put all our eggs in one basket. We are inclined to be reserved and ever ready to retreat. Be that as it may, because of our instinct for self preservation, we all have a natural fear of losing ourselves in another person. That is why what happens to love, happens to education and psychoanalysis; everybody thinks he knows all about them, but few do. One is inclined to overlook how little one gives of one-self, but one feels all the more this same deficiency in the partner, the feeling of "You never really loved me." A wife who harbors suicidal thoughts because her husband does not give her all his love, time, and interest, will not notice how much of her own hostility, hidden vindictiveness, and aggression are expressed through her attitude. She will feel only despair because of her abundant "love," while at the same time she will feel most intensely and see most clearly the lack of love in her partner. Even Strindberg[2] [who was a misogynist] defensively managed to say on occasion that he was no woman hater, but that women hated and tortured him.   6

Here we are not dealing with pathological phenomena at all. In pathological cases we merely see a distortion and exaggeration of a general and normal occurrence. Anybody, to a certain extent, will be inclined to overlook his own hostile impulses, but under pressure of his own guilty conscience, may project them onto the partner. This process must, of necessity, cause some overt or   7

---

[1] **affects**   Feelings, emotions, or passions

[2] **August Strindberg (1849–1912)**   Swedish playwright and novelist whose dark portraits of women were influenced by his misogyny (hatred of women).

covert distrust of the partner's love, fidelity, sincerity, or kindness. This is the reason why I prefer to speak of distrust between the sexes and not of hatred; for in keeping with our own experience we are more familiar with the feeling of distrust.

A further, almost unavoidable, source of disappointment and distrust in our normal love life derives from the fact that the very intensity of our feelings of love stirs up all of our secret expectations and longings for happiness, which slumber deep inside us. All our unconscious wishes, contradictory in their nature and expanding boundlessly on all sides, are waiting here for their fulfillment. The partner is supposed to be strong, and at the same time helpless, to dominate us and be dominated by us, to be ascetic and to be sensuous. He should rape us and be tender, have time for us exclusively and also be intensely involved in creative work. As long as we assume that he could actually fulfill all these expectations, we invest him with the glitter of sexual overestimation. We take the magnitude of such overvaluation for the measure of our love, while in reality it merely expresses the magnitude of our expectations. The very nature of our claims makes their fulfillment impossible. Herein lies the origin of the disappointments with which we may cope in a more or less effective way. Under favorable circumstances we do not even have to become aware of the great number of our disappointments, just as we have not been aware of the extent of our secret expectations. Yet there remain traces of distrust in us, as in a child who discovers that his father cannot get him the stars from the sky after all.

Thus far, our reflections certainly have been neither new nor specifically analytical and have often been better formulated in the past. The analytical approach begins with the question: What special factors in human development lead to the discrepancy between expectations and fulfillment and what causes them to be of special significance in particular cases? Let us start with a general consideration. There is a basic difference between human and animal development—namely, the long period of the infant's helplessness and dependency. The paradise of childhood is most often an illusion with which adults like to deceive themselves. For the child, however, this paradise is inhabited by too many dangerous monsters. Unpleasant experiences with the opposite sex seem to be unavoidable. We need only recall the capacity that children possess, even in their very early years, for passionate and instinctive sexual desires similar to those of adults and yet different from them. Children are different in the aims of their drives, but above all, in the pristine integrity of their demands. They find it hard to express their desires directly, and where they do, they are not taken seriously. Their seriousness sometimes is looked upon as being cute, or it may be overlooked or rejected. In short, children will undergo painful and humiliating experiences of being rebuffed, being betrayed, and being told lies. They also may have to take second place to a parent or a sibling, and they are threatened and intimidated when they seek, in playing with their own bodies, those pleasures that are denied them by adults. The child is relatively powerless in the face of all this. He is not able to ventilate his fury at all, or only to a minor degree, nor can he come to grips with the experience by means of intellectual comprehension. Thus, anger and aggression are pent up within him in the form of extravagant fantasies, which hardly reach the daylight of awareness, fantasies that are criminal when viewed from the standpoint of the adult, fantasies that range from taking by force and stealing, to those about killing, burning, cutting to pieces, and choking. Since the child is vaguely aware of these destructive forces within him, he feels, according to the talion law,[3] equally threatened by the adults. Here is the origin of those infantile anxieties of which no child remains entirely free. This already enables us to understand better the fear of love of which I have spoke before. Just here, in this most irrational of all areas, the old childhood fears of a threatening father or mother are reawakened, putting us instinctively on the defensive. In other words, the fear of love will always be mixed with the fear of what we might do to the other person, or what the other person might do to us. A lover in the Aru Islands,[4] for example, will never make a gift of a lock of hair to his beloved, because should an argument arise, the beloved might burn it, thus causing the partner to get sick.

I would like to sketch briefly how childhood conflicts may affect the relationship to the opposite sex in later life. Let us take as an example a typical situation: The little girl who was badly hurt through some great disappointment by her father, will transform her innate instinctual wish to receive from the man, into a vindictive one of taking from him by force. Thus the foundation is laid for a direct line of development to a later attitude, according to which she will not only deny her maternal instincts, but will have only one drive, i.e., to harm the male, to exploit him, and to suck him dry. She has become a vampire. Let us assume that there is a similar transformation from the wish to receive to the wish to take away. Let us further assume that the latter wish was repressed due to anxiety from a guilty conscience; then we have here the fundamental constellation for the formation of a certain type of woman who is unable to relate to the male because she fears that every male will suspect her of wanting something from him. This really means that she is afraid that he might guess her repressed desires. Or by completely projecting onto him her repressed wishes, she will imagine that every male merely intends to exploit her, that he wants from her only sexual satisfaction, after which he will

10

---

[3] **talion law**   Law that demands that the criminal be given the same punishment as was suffered by the victim — an eye for an eye.

[4] **Aru Islands**   Islands in Indonesia whose inhabitants were especially interesting for modern anthropologists.

discard her. Or let us assume that a reaction formation of excessive modesty will mask the repressed drive for power. We then have the type of woman who shies away from demanding or accepting anything from her husband. Such a woman, however, due to the return of the repressed, will react with depression to the nonfulfillment of her unexpressed, and often unformulated, wishes. She thus unwittingly jumps from the frying pan into the fire, as does her partner, because a depression will hit him much harder than direct aggression. Quite often the repression of aggression against the male drains all her vital energy. The woman then feels helpless to meet life. She will shift the entire responsibility for her helplessness onto the man, robbing him of the very breath of life. Here you have the type of woman who, under the guise of being helpless and childlike, dominates her man.

These are examples that demonstrate how the fundamental attitude of women toward men can be disturbed by childhood conflicts. In an attempt to simplify matters, I have stressed only one point, which, however, seems crucial to me — the disturbance in the development of motherhood. 11

I shall now proceed to trace certain traits of male psychology. I do not wish to follow individual lines of development, though it might be very instructive to observe analytically how, for instance, even men who consciously have a very positive relationship with women and hold them in high esteem as human beings, harbor deep within themselves a secret distrust of them; and how this distrust relates back to feelings toward their mothers, which they experienced in their formative years. I shall focus rather on certain typical attitudes of men toward women and how they have appeared during various eras of history and in different cultures, not only as regards sexual relationships with women, but also, and often more so, in nonsexual situations, such as in their general evaluation of women. 12

I shall select some random examples, starting with Adam and Eve. Jewish culture, as recorded in the Old Testament, is outspokenly patriarchal. This fact reflects itself in their religion, which has no maternal goddesses; in their morals and customs, which allow the husband the right to dissolve the marital bond simply by dismissing his wife. Only by being aware of this background can we recognize the male bias in two incidents of Adam's and Eve's history. First of all, woman's capacity to give birth is partly denied and partly devalued: Eve was made of Adam's rib and a curse was put on her to bear children in sorrow. In the second place, by interpreting her tempting Adam to eat of the tree of knowledge as a sexual temptation, woman appears as the sexual temptress, who plunges man into misery. I believe that these two elements, one born out of resentment, the other out of anxiety, have damaged the relationship between the sexes from the earliest times to the present. Let us follow this up briefly. Man's fear of woman is deeply rooted in sex, as is shown by the simple fact that it is only the sexually attractive woman of whom he is afraid and who, although 13 he strongly desires her, has to be kept in bondage. Old women, on the other hand, are held in high esteem, even by cultures in which the young woman is dreaded and therefore suppressed. In some primitive cultures the old woman may have the decisive voice in the affairs of the tribe; among Asian nations also she enjoys great power and prestige. On the other hand, in primitive tribes woman is surrounded by taboos during the entire period of her sexual maturity. Women of the Arunta tribe are able to magically influence the male genitals. If they sing to a blade of grass and then point it at a man or throw it at him, he becomes ill or loses his genitals altogether. Women lure him to his doom. In a certain East African tribe, husband and wife do not sleep together, because her breath might weaken him. If a woman of a South African tribe climbs over the leg of a sleeping man, he will be unable to run; hence the general rule of sexual abstinence two to five days prior to hunting, warfare, or fishing. Even greater is the fear of menstruation, pregnancy, and childbirth. Menstruating women are surrounded by extensive taboos—a man who touches a menstruating woman will die. There is one basic thought at the bottom of all this: woman is a mysterious being who communicates with spirits and thus has magic powers that she can use to hurt the male. He must therefore protect himself against her powers by keeping her subjugated. Thus the Miri in Bengal do not permit their women to eat the flesh of the tiger, lest they become too strong. The Watawela of East Africa keep the art of making fire a secret from their women, lest women become their rulers. The Indians of California have ceremonies to keep their women in submission; a man is disguised as a devil to intimidate the women. The Arabs of Mecca exclude women from religious festivities to prevent familiarity between women and their overlords. We find similar customs during the Middle Ages—the Cult of the Virgin[5] side by side with the burning of witches; the adoration of "pure" motherliness, completely divested of sexuality, next to the cruel destruction of the sexually seductive woman. Here again is the implication of underlying anxiety, for the witch is in communication with the devil. Nowadays, with our more humane forms of aggression, we burn women only figuratively, sometimes with undisguised hatred, sometimes with apparent friendliness. In any case "The Jew must burn."[6] In friendly and secret

---

[5] **Cult of the Virgin**   During the medieval period (c. 700–300), the Roman Catholic Church promoted a strong emotional attachment to the Virgin Mary, which resulted in the production of innumerable paintings and sculptures. Horney points out the irony of venerating the mother of God while tormenting human women by burning them at the stake.

[6] **"The Jew must burn"**   This is a quote from *Nathan the Wise* by the eighteenth-century German author Gotthold Ephrairn Lessing, a humanist and a spokesman for enlightenment and rationality. The expression became a colloquialism; it meant no matter how worthy and well-intentioned his acts, by virtue of being a Jew, a man was guilty. [Translator's note]

autos-da-fé,[7] many nice things are said about women, but it is just unfortunate that in her God-given natural state, she is not the equal of the male. Mobius[8] pointed out that the female brain weighs less than the male one, but the point need not be made in so crude a way. On the contrary, it can be stressed that woman is not at all inferior, only different, but that unfortunately she has fewer or none of those human or cultural qualities that man holds in such high esteem. She is said to be deeply rooted in the personal and emotional spheres, which is wonderful; but unfortunately, this makes her incapable of exercising justice and objectivity, therefore disqualifying her for positions in law and government and in the spiritual community. She is said to be at home only in the realm of eros. Spiritual matters are alien to her innermost being, and she is at odds with cultural trends. She therefore is, as Asians frankly state, a second-rate being. Woman may be industrious and useful but is, alas, incapable of productive and independent work. She is, indeed, prevented from real accomplishment by the deplorable, bloody tragedies of menstruation and childbirth. And so every man silently thanks his God, just as the pious Jew does in his prayers, that he was not created a woman.

Man's attitude toward motherhood is a large and complicated chapter. One is generally inclined to see no problem in this area. Even the misogynist is obviously willing to respect woman as a mother and to venerate her motherliness under certain conditions, as mentioned above regarding the Cult of the Virgin. In order to obtain a clearer picture, we have to distinguish between two attitudes: men's attitudes toward motherliness, as represented in its purest form in the Cult of the Virgin, and their attitude toward motherhood as such, as we encounter it in the symbolism of the ancient mother goddesses. Males will always be in favor of motherliness, as expressed in certain spiritual qualities of women, i.e., the nurturing, selfless, self-sacrificing mother; for she is the ideal embodiment of the woman who could fulfill all his expectations and longings. In the ancient mother goddesses, man did not venerate motherliness in the spiritual sense, but rather motherhood in its most elemental meaning. Mother goddesses are earthy goddesses, fertile like the soil. They bring forth new life and they nurture it. It was this life-creating power of woman, an elemental force, that filled man with admiration. And this is exactly the point where problems arise. For it is contrary to human nature to sustain appreciation without resentment toward capabilities that one does not possess. Thus, a man's minute share in creating new life became, for him, an immense incitement to create

14

---

[7] **autos-da-fé**   Literally, acts of faith. It was a term used to refer to the hearing at which the Holy Inquisition gave its judgment on a case of heresy, and its most common use is to refer to the burning of heretics at the stake.

[8] **Paul Julius Möbius (1853–1907)**   German neurologist and student of the pathological traits of geniuses such as Rousseau, Goethe, Schopenhauer, and Nietzsche.

something new on his part. He has created values of which he might well be proud. State, religion, art, and science are essentially his creations, and our entire culture bears the masculine imprint.

However, as happens elsewhere, so it does here; even the greatest satis-   15
factions or achievements, if born out of sublimation, cannot fully make up for something for which we are not endowed by nature. Thus there has remained an obvious residue of general resentment of men against women. This resentment expresses itself, also in our times, in men's distrustful defensive maneuvers against the threat of women's invasion of their domains; hence their tendency to devalue pregnancy and childbirth and to overemphasize male generality. This attitude does not express itself in scientific theories alone, but is also of far-reaching consequence for the entire relationship between the sexes, and for sexual morality in general. Motherhood, especially illegitimate motherhood, is very insufficiently protected by laws — with the one exception of a recent attempt at improvement in Russia. Conversely, there is ample opportunity for the fulfillment of the male's sexual needs. Emphasis on irresponsible sexual indulgence, and devaluation of women to an object of purely physical needs, are further consequences of this masculine attitude.

From Bachofen's[9] investigations we know that this state of the cultural   16
supremacy of the male has not existed since the beginning of time, but that women once occupied a central position. This was the era of the so-called matriarchy, when law and custom were centered around the mother. Matricide was then, as Sophocles[10] showed in the *Eumenides*, the unforgivable crime, while patricide, by comparison, was a minor offense. Only in recorded histor-ical times have men begun, with minor variations, to play the leading role in the political, economical, and judicial fields, as well as in the area of sexual morality. At present we seem to be going through a period of struggle in which women once more dare to fight for their equality. This is a phase, the duration of which we are not yet able to survey.

I do not want to be misunderstood as having implied that all disaster results   17
from male supremacy and that relations between the sexes would improve if women were given the ascendancy. However, we must ask ourselves why there should have to be any power struggle at all between the sexes. At any given time, the more powerful side will create an ideology suitable to help maintain its position and to make this position acceptable to the weaker one. In this ideology the differentness of the weaker one will be interpreted as inferiority, and it will be proven that these differences are unchangeable, basic, or God's

---

[9] **J. J. Bachofen (1815–1887)**   One of the earliest German ethnologists who proposed, in 1861, that a pattern of matriarchy — in which the female was the dominant figure in society — had existed in the earliest societies.

[10] **Sophocles (496?–406 B.C.E.)**   Great Greek tragedian. However, Horney is probably refer-ring to Aeschylus (525–456 B.C.E.), who wrote the *Eumenides*, the play she mentions.

will. It is the function of such an ideology to deny or conceal the existence of a struggle. Here is one of the answers to the question raised initially as to why we have so little awareness of the fact that there is a struggle between the sexes. It is in the interest of men to obscure this fact; and the emphasis they place on their ideologies has caused women, also, to adopt these theories. Our attempt at resolving these rationalizations and at examining these ideologies as to their fundamental driving forces, is merely a step on the road taken by Freud.[11]

I believe that my exposition shows more clearly the origin of resentment than the origin of dread, and I therefore want to discuss briefly the latter problem. We have seen that the male's dread of the female is directed against her as a sexual being. How is this to be understood? The clearest aspect of this dread is revealed by the Arunta tribe. They believe that the woman has the power to magically influence the male genital. This is what we mean by castration anxiety in analysis. It is an anxiety of psychogenic origin that goes back to feelings of guilt and old childhood fears. Its anatomical-psychological nucleus lies in the fact that during intercourse the male has to entrust his genitals to the female body, that he presents her with his semen and interprets this as a surrender of vital strength to the woman, similar to his experiencing the subsiding of erection after intercourse as evidence of having been weakened by the woman. Although the following idea has not been thoroughly worked through yet, it is highly probable, according to analytical and ethnological data, that the relationship to the mother is more strongly and directly associated with the fear of death than the relationship to the father. We have learned to understand the longing for death as the longing for reunion with the mother. In African fairy tales it is a woman who brings death into the world. The great mother goddesses also brought death and destruction. It is as though we were possessed by the idea that the one who gives life is also capable of taking it away. There is a third aspect of the male's dread of the female that is more difficult to understand and to prove, but that can be demonstrated by observing certain recurrent phenomena in the animal world. We can see that the male is quite frequently equipped with certain specific stimulants for attracting the female, or with specific devices for seizing her during sexual union. Such arrangements would be incomprehensible if the female animal possessed equally urgent or abundant sexual needs as does the male. As a matter of fact, we see that the female rejects the male unconditionally, after fertilization has occurred. Although examples taken from the animal world may be applied to human beings only with the greatest of caution, it is permissible, in this context, to raise the following question: Is it possible that the male is sexually dependent on the female to a higher degree than the woman is on him, because in women part of the sexual energy is linked to generative processes? Could it

18

---

[11] **Sigmund Freud (1856–1939)**   See page 477.

be that men, therefore, have a vital interest in keeping women dependent on them? So much for the factors that seem to be at the root of the great power struggle between men and women, insofar as they are of a psychogenic nature and related to the male.

That many-faceted thing called love succeeds in building bridges from the loneliness on this shore to the loneliness on the other one. These bridges can be of great beauty, but they are rarely built for eternity and frequently they cannot tolerate too heavy a burden without collapsing. Here is the other answer to the question posed initially of why we see love between the sexes more distinctly than we see hate — because the union of the sexes offers us the greatest possibilities for happiness. We therefore are naturally inclined to overlook how powerful are the destructive forces that continually work to destroy our chances for happiness.

19

We might ask in conclusion, how can analytical insights contribute to diminish the distrust between the sexes? There is no uniform answer to this problem. The fear of the power of the affects and the difficulty in controlling them in a love relationship, the resulting conflict between surrender and self-preservation, between the I and the Thou[12] is an entirely comprehensible, unmitigatable, and as it were, normal phenomenon. The same thing applies in essence to our readiness for distrust, which stems from unresolved childhood conflicts. These childhood conflicts, however, can vary greatly in intensity, and will leave behind traces of variable depth. Analysis not only can help in individual cases to improve the relationship with the opposite sex, but it can also attempt to improve the psychological conditions of childhood and forestall excessive conflicts. This, of course, is our hope for the future. In the momentous struggle for power, analysis can fulfill an important function by uncovering the real motives of this struggle. This uncovering will not eliminate the motives, but it may help to create a better chance for fighting the struggle on its own ground instead of relegating it to peripheral issues.

20

---

[12] **the I and the Thou**   A reference to Martin Buber's book *I and Thou*. Buber (1878–1965), a Jewish theologian and philosopher, is associated with modern existentialism.

⚙ QUESTIONS FOR CRITICAL READING

1. Do you agree that there is hostility between the sexes? What evidence can you cite?

2. What are some of the most important childhood experiences that can affect adult behavior toward the opposite sex?

3. This selection was originally a lecture delivered in Germany in 1930. To what extent are its concerns no longer relevant? To what extent are they still relevant?

4. Do you think this essay could promote better relations between men and women?

5. What kinds of expectations do women seem to have of men, and vice versa? Do these expectations tend to contribute to hostility in specific ways? Consider Horney's description of expectations in paragraph 8.

6. How do the examples of behavior in primitive cultures contribute to an understanding of the relationship between the sexes in our culture?

7. Is Horney pessimistic or optimistic about relationships between the sexes?

■ SUGGESTIONS FOR CRITICAL WRITING

1. In paragraph 9, Horney says that "unpleasant experiences with the opposite sex seem to be unavoidable." In your experience, is this true? What unpleasant experiences have you had with the opposite sex? What unpleasant experiences have you observed?

2. Horney mentions that the intensity of our feelings can stir up secret longings for, and expectations of, the opposite sex (para. 8). What kinds of secret expectations do you feel each sex might have about the other in a relationship? Why would such expectations remain secret? Does such secrecy contribute to problems? Does it contribute to hostility?

3. Deep in the essay, in paragraph 14, Horney mentions envy as contributing to the hostility between the sexes. She says, "For it is contrary to human nature to sustain appreciation without resentment toward capabilities that one does not possess." Do you agree with her? Do you think envy may have something to do with the hostility between the sexes? Examine your own experience to see whether you recall instances of envy on your part toward a member of the opposite sex (or vice versa).

4. At one point, Horney says, "Man's fear of woman is deeply rooted in sex" (para. 13). Do you think this is true? Is woman's fear of man similarly rooted? Examine this question by comparing two men's magazines and two women's magazines to determine what they reveal about the psychology of men and women. Compare their use of social media and their visual material, particularly photographs of members of the opposite sex. Also compare the fiction, and look for signs of a specifically male or female form of fantasy. Compare the advertising to identify the interests of men and women — and try to relate these to psychological concerns.

5. Horney is very direct in her discussion of male dominance in society, not only saying that it exists but asking, "Could it be that men, therefore, have a vital interest in keeping women dependent on them?" (para. 18). Conduct an interview with one man and one woman. Find out whether they have the same or different feelings about this question. Ask them if they see an effort on the

part of men to keep women dependent, and then ask them what form any such dependency takes. Do they agree? Where do you stand on this issue?

6. At one point, Horney discusses how different men are from women. Write an essay in which you show the extent to which women are different from men. If possible, sample others' opinions and see if they note important differences. To what extent would differences between men and women contribute to hostility?

7. What are the most important psychic phenomena in Horney's discussion? Her concerns are primarily cultural, but she also describes a psychological situation that has its root in mental experience. What are the most important mental experiences, and how do they manifest themselves in the mental life of individuals?

8. **CONNECTIONS**   Jung discusses the personal and collective unconscious (p. 487). Horney's argument is that there are personal and cultural aspects to the development of the minds of men and women. How close is Horney to Jung's position regarding what is personal and what is cultural in gender distinction? Does Jung's or Freud's work with dreams clarify the distinctions?

9. **CONNECTIONS**   Horney's arguments about the differences between the sexes at times seem to be almost Nietzschean. Argue a case that Nietzsche's (p. 459) distinctions between Apollonianism and Dionysianism are veiled distinctions between the sexes. To what extent is it possible that Nietzsche is creating a vision of the mind that is gender neutral? Could Nietzsche be influenced by the idea of a transgender figure embodying one or the other of his distinctions? How sympathetic would Horney be to Nietzsche's distinctions?

© Hulton-Deutsch Collection/Corbis

GILBERT RYLE

The Ghost in the Machine

ILBERT RYLE (1900–1976) was one of
Great Britain's most accomplished and best-
known philosophers. He came from a well-educated family, and his father had amassed
a highly valued library. Ryle was born in Brighton and was a gifted student at Brighton
College. At age nineteen, he went to Queens College, Oxford, where he took on important responsibilities as an undergraduate. His studies were in the classics, but he also found
himself drawn to politics, philosophy, and economics. In 1925, he began teaching philosophy at Christ College, Oxford.

In 1940, he was commissioned in the Welsh Guards and remained in army intelligence
throughout World War II. He returned to teaching when the war was over and resumed
a notable career. His publications were connected to what is known as the ordinary language school of philosophy. He was part of a group of ordinary language philosophers who
stressed very careful language analyses as opposed to the more systemic approaches of
groups such as Marxists and existentialists. Ryle, like his colleagues, felt that language was
more complex than it appeared and that misunderstandings of critical terms led to false
conclusions. He was extremely careful in examining how a given term linked with other
similar terms to produce a view that might be correct if properly understood, but that
might be misleading if any of the terms were vague or ambiguous.

Ryle's most famous book, *The Concept of Mind* (1949; republished in 2009), attacked
René Descartes's seventeenth-century view of the mind, called *Cartesian dualism*. This
view held that the body and the mind were two different things. Ryle felt that Descartes
was essentially adapting the religious concept of the soul and transforming it in philosophy and describing the mind as immaterial. For Descartes, the principal characteristic of
the mind was consciousness, and it was separate from the brain. This view of the mind and
the brain, the concept of dualism, has been widely accepted since Descartes established it
philosophically in the mid-seventeenth century. However, in his book, Ryle basically denies

---

From *The Concept of Mind.*

514

that the mind is something separate from the brain, existing in a different immaterial state. In the process of analyzing Descartes's position, he describes Descartes as proposing that the mind is a "ghost in the machine" of the brain.

Part of that argument appears in the selection presented here. Ryle's argument has been very effective in the second half of the twentieth century, in part as a result of the rise of the calculating machines that have become modern computers. The concept of the mind as a machine was not exactly what Ryle had thought he was promoting, but it gave some impetus to the ideas that compose the research into artificial intelligence. If the mind is a product of the brain, the question arises of whether machines can produce the same kind of intelligence as our brain. This would have been a radical idea in Descartes's day, but, interestingly, in eighteenth-century Europe, the Age of Reason was fascinated with machines of all kinds and began the research that yielded the first proto-computers.

RYLE'S RHETORIC

Because this selection is from the first chapter of Ryle's *The Concept of Mind*, what we have is only the preparation for an argument that encompasses the entire book. Nonetheless, Ryle attempts to convince us that his argument has merit by using a number of rhetorical methods designed to clarify the situation. He begins by pointing to René Descartes and what Ryle calls "the official doctrine." This doctrine tells us that "every human being has both a body and a mind" and that after the body dies the "mind may continue to exist and function" (para. 2). This doctrine is usually called a theory of mind-body dualism: the body is one kind of thing and the mind is a different kind of thing. This is the doctrine that Ryle argues against.

His first strategy is to enumerate three sections that treat the question from different perspectives:

1. The Official Doctrine
2. The Absurdity of the Official Doctrine
3. The Origin of the Category-Mistake

In the first section, Ryle uses a pattern of opposites to illustrate the difficulties we have in approaching this issue. He cites the body as being public because it can be observed and the mind as private because it cannot be observed. The body is external; the mind internal. The body responds to physiology; the mind to psychology. The body is physical; the mind mental. Ryle uses metaphor in paragraph 8 when he compares the opposites as two sides of a coin. He points to his use of metaphor in paragraph 6 when he says, "This antithesis of outer and inner is of course meant to be construed as a metaphor, since minds, not being in space, could not be described as being spatially inside anything else, or as having things going on spatially inside themselves." The inner-outer oppositions are marshaled to demonstrate how Descartes and other thinkers of the seventeenth century conceived the relationship of the mind and body.

In the second section, Ryle begins to work on Descartes's idea, and it is here that he speaks of it "with deliberate abusiveness, as 'the dogma of the Ghost in the Machine'" (para. 15). He establishes Descartes's idea as a form of the category mistake, which he defines as representing "the facts of mental life as if they belonged to one logical type or category" when they belong to another (para. 15).

Ryle then uses a number of examples, or "illustrations," in paragraphs 17 and 18 to help us understand the meaning of the category mistake. He uses the example of the university, the name we give for a collection of institutions and colleges such as Oxford. Other examples include the army, the average taxpayer, and team spirit, all things that have no existence in space. As he says in paragraph 23, "the human body, like any other parcel of matter, is a field of causes and effects, so the mind must be another field of causes and effects, though not (Heaven be praised) mechanical causes and effects."

In the third section, Ryle explains that the scientists of the seventeenth century developed a theory of objects existing in space and operating by laws of mechanics. However, this theory reduced the operation of the mind to a mechanical process because, like the body, it exists in space. However, because this theory appeared to reduce the mind to being a form of "clockwork," it was unacceptable: "The mental could not be just a variety of the mechanical" (para. 24). To solve this problem, Descartes and others conceived the idea of not-mechanical, the opposite of the scientific understanding of mechanical matter. The result, Ryle tells us, is that "minds are not merely ghosts harnessed to machines, they are themselves just spectral machines" (para. 28).

Ryle leaves us with something of the question that puzzled Descartes. If the body operates by mechanical laws, by what laws does the mind operate? Essentially, by relying on the concept of the immaterial soul, Descartes uses a religious concept to solve a scientific problem.

⬛ PREREADING QUESTIONS: WHAT TO READ FOR

The following prereading questions may help you anticipate key issues in the discussion of Gilbert Ryle's "The Ghost in the Machine." Keeping them in mind during your first reading of the selection should help focus your attention.

1. What is Cartesian dualism?
2. What is a category mistake?
3. What is "the ghost in the machine"?

The Ghost in the Machine

(I) *The Official Doctrine.*
There is a doctrine about the nature and place of minds which is so preva-   1
lent among theorists and even among laymen that it deserves to be described
as the official theory. Most philosophers, psychologists and religious teachers subscribe, with minor reservations, to its main articles and, although they
admit certain theoretical difficulties in it, they tend to assume that these can
be overcome without serious modifications being made to the architecture of
the theory. It will be argued here that the central principles of the doctrine are
unsound and conflict with the whole body of what we know about minds when
we are not speculating about them.

The official doctrine, which hails chiefly from Descartes,[1] is something like   2
this. With the doubtful exceptions of idiots and infants in arms every human
being has both a body and a mind. Some would prefer to say that every human
being is both a body and a mind. His body and his mind are ordinarily harnessed together, but after the death of the body his mind may continue to exist
and function.

Human bodies are in space and are subject to the mechanical laws which   3
govern all other bodies in space. Bodily processes and states can be inspected
by external observers. So a man's bodily life is as much a public affair as are
the lives of animals and reptiles and even as the careers of trees, crystals and
planets.

But minds are not in space, nor are their operations subject to mechanical   4
laws. The workings of one mind are not witnessable by other observers; its
career is private. Only I can take direct cognisance of the states and processes
of my own mind. A person therefore lives through two collateral histories, one
consisting of what happens in and to his body, the other consisting of what
happens in and to his mind. The first is public, the second private. The events in
the first history are events in the physical world, those in the second are events
in the mental world.

It has been disputed whether a person does or can directly monitor all or   5
only some of the episodes of his own private history; but, according to the official doctrine, of at least some of these episodes he has direct and unchallenge-
able cognisance. In consciousness, self-consciousness and introspection he is

---

[1] **René Descartes (1596–1650)**   A French philosopher noted for having said, "I think,
therefore I am." He was noted for his rationalist approach to philosophy, especially in his
meditations on the nature of the mind and thought.

directly and authentically apprised of the present states and operations of his mind. He may have great or small uncertainties about concurrent and adjacent episodes in the physical world, but he can have none about at least part of what is momentarily occupying his mind.

It is customary to express this bifurcation of his two lives and of his two worlds by saying that the things and events which belong to the physical world, including his own body, are external, while the workings of his own mind are internal. This antithesis of outer and inner is of course meant to be construed as a metaphor, since minds, not being in space, could not be described as being spatially inside anything else, or as having things going on spatially inside themselves. But relapses from this good intention are common and theorists are found speculating how stimuli, the physical sources of which are yards or miles outside a person's skin, can generate mental responses inside his skull, or how decisions framed inside his cranium can set going movements of his extremities. 6

Even when 'inner' and 'outer' are construed as metaphors, the problem how a person's mind and body influence one another is notoriously charged with theoretical difficulties. What the mind wills, the legs, arms and the tongue execute; what affects the ear and the eye has something to do with what the mind perceives; grimaces and smiles betray the mind's moods and bodily castigations lead, it is hoped, to moral improvement. But the actual transactions between the episodes of the private history and those of the public history remain mysterious, since by definition they can belong to neither series. They could not be reported among the happenings described in a person's autobiography of his inner life, but nor could they be reported among those described in some one else's biography of that person's overt career. They can be inspected neither by introspection nor by laboratory experiment. They are theoretical shuttlecocks which are forever being bandied from the physiologist back to the psychologist and from the psychologist back to the physiologist 7

Underlying this partly metaphorical representation of the bifurcation of a person's two lives there is a seemingly more profound and philosophical assumption. It is assumed that there are two different kinds of existence or status. What exists or happens may have the status of physical existence, or it may have the status of mental existence. Somewhat as the faces of coins are either heads or tails, or somewhat as living creatures are either male or female, so, it is supposed, some existing is physical existing, other existing is mental existing. It is a necessary feature of what has physical existence that it is in space and time; it is a necessary feature of what has mental existence that it is in time but not in space. What has physical existence is composed of matter, or else is a function of matter; what has mental existence consists of consciousness, or else is a function of consciousness. 8

There is thus a polar opposition between mind and matter, an opposition which is often brought out as follows. Material objects are situated in a 9 common field, known as 'space', and what happens to one body in one part of space is mechanically connected with what happens to other bodies in other parts of space. But mental happenings occur in insulated fields, known as 'minds', and there is, apart maybe from telepathy, no direct causal connection between what happens in one mind and what happens in another. Only through the medium of the public physical world can the mind of one person make a difference to the mind of another. The mind is its own place and in his inner life each of us lives the life of a ghostly Robinson Crusoe.[2] People can see, hear and jolt one another's bodies, but they are irremediably blind and deaf to the workings of one another's minds and inoperative upon them.

What sort of knowledge can be secured of the workings of a mind? On the one side, according to the official theory, a person has direct knowledge of the best imaginable kind of the workings of his own mind. Mental states and processes are (or are normally) conscious states and processes, and the consciousness which irradiates them can engender no illusions and leaves the door open for no doubts. A person's present thinkings, feelings and willings, his perceivings, rememberings and imaginings are intrinsically 'phosphorescent'; their existence and their nature are inevitably betrayed to their owner. The inner life is a stream of consciousness of such a sort that it would be absurd to suggest that the mind whose life is that stream might be unaware of what is passing down it. ⟨10⟩

True, the evidence adduced recently by Freud seems to show that there exist channels tributary to this stream, which run hidden from their owner. People are actuated by impulses the existence of which they vigorously disavow; some of their thoughts differ from the thoughts which they acknowledge; and some of the actions which they think they will to perform they do not really will. They are thoroughly gulled by some of their own hypocrisies and they successfully ignore facts about their mental lives which on the official theory ought to be patent to them. Holders of the official theory tend, however, to maintain that anyhow in normal circumstances a person must be directly and authentically seized of the present state and workings of his own mind. ⟨11⟩

Besides being currently supplied with these alleged immediate data of consciousness, a person is also generally supposed to be able to exercise from time to time a special kind of perception, namely inner perception, or introspection. He can take a (non-optical) 'look' at what is passing in his mind. Not only can he view and scrutinize a flower through his sense of sight and listen to and discriminate the notes of a bell through his sense of hearing; he can also reflectively or introspectively watch, without any bodily organ of sense, the current episodes of his inner life. This self-observation is also commonly supposed to be immune from illusion, confusion or doubt. A mind's reports of its ⟨12⟩

---

[2] **Robinson Crusoe**   A fictional character in Daniel Defoe's novel *Robinson Crusoe* (1719).

own affairs have a certainty superior to the best that is possessed by its reports of matters in the physical world. Sense-perceptions can, but consciousness and introspection cannot, be mistaken or confused.

On the other side, one person has no direct access of any sort to the events 13 of the inner life of another. He cannot do better than make problematic inferences from the observed behaviour of the other person's body to the states of mind which, by analogy from his own conduct, he supposes to be signalised by that behaviour. Direct access to the workings of a mind is the privilege of that mind itself; in default of such privileged access, the workings of one mind are inevitably occult to everyone else. For the supposed arguments from bodily movements similar to their own to mental workings similar to their own would lack any possibility of observational corroboration. Not unnaturally, therefore, an adherent of the official theory finds it difficult to resist this consequence of his premises, that he has no good reason to believe that there do exist minds other than his own. Even if he prefers to believe that to other human bodies there are harnessed minds not unlike his own, he cannot claim to be able to discover their individual characteristics, or the particular things that they undergo and do. Absolute solitude is on this showing the ineluctable destiny of the soul. Only our bodies can meet.

As a necessary corollary of this general scheme there is implicitly pre- 14 scribed a special way of construing our ordinary concepts of mental powers and operations. The verbs, nouns and adjectives, with which in ordinary life we describe the wits, characters and higher-grade performances of the people with whom we have do, are required to be construed as signifying special episodes in their secret histories, or else as signifying tendencies for such episodes to occur. When someone is described as knowing, believing or guessing something, as hoping, dreading, intending or shirking something, as designing this or being amused at that, these verbs are supposed to denote the occurrence of specific modifications in his (to us) occult stream of consciousness. Only his own privileged access to this stream in direct awareness and introspection could provide authentic testimony that these mental-conduct verbs were correctly or incorrectly applied. The onlooker, be he teacher, critic, biographer or friend, can never assure himself that his comments have any vestige of truth. Yet it was just because we do in fact all know how to make such comments, make them with general correctness and correct them when they turn out to be confused or mistaken, that philosophers found it necessary to construct their theories of the nature and place of minds. Finding mental–conduct concepts being regularly and effectively used, they properly sought to fix their logical geography. But the logical geography officially recommended would entail that there could be no regular or effective use of these mental–conduct concepts in our descriptions of, and prescriptions for, other people's minds.

(2) *The Absurdity of the Official Doctrine.*

Such in outline is the official theory. I shall often speak of it, with deliberate   15
abusiveness, as 'the dogma of the Ghost in the Machine'. I hope to prove that
it is entirely false, and false not in detail but in principle. It is not merely an
assemblage of particular mistakes. It is one big mistake and a mistake of a
special kind. It is, namely, a category-mistake. It represents the facts of mental
life as if they belonged to one logical type or category (or range of types or
categories), when they actually belong to another. The dogma is therefore a
philosopher's myth. In attempting to explode the myth I shall probably be taken
to be denying well-known facts about the mental life of human beings, and my
plea that I aim at doing nothing more than rectify the logic of mental-conduct
concepts will probably be disallowed as mere subterfuge.

I must first indicate what is meant by the phrase 'Category-mistake'. This I   16
do in a series of illustrations.

A foreigner visiting Oxford or Cambridge for the first time is shown a num-   17
ber of colleges, libraries, playing fields, museums, scientific departments and
administrative offices. He then asks 'But where is the University? I have seen
where the members of the Colleges live, where the Registrar works, where
the scientists experiment and the rest. But I have not yet seen the University
in which reside and work the members of your University.' It has then to be
explained to him that the University is not another collateral institution, some
ulterior counterpart to the colleges, laboratories and offices which he has seen.
The University is just the way in which all that he has already seen is organized.
When they are seen and when their co-ordination is understood, the University
has been seen. His mistake lay in his innocent assumption that it was correct to
speak of Christ Church, the Bodleian Library, the Ashmolean Museum *and* the
University, to speak, that is, as if 'the University' stood for an extra member of
the class of which these other units are members. He was mistakenly allocat-
ing the University to the same category as that to which the other institutions
belong.

The same mistake would be made by a child witnessing the march-past   18
of a division, who, having had pointed out to him such and such battalions,
batteries, squadrons, etc., asked when the division was going to appear. He
would be supposing that a division was a counterpart to the units already seen,
partly similar to them and partly unlike them. He would be shown his mistake
by being told that in watching the battalions, batteries and squadrons marching
past he had been watching the division marching past. The march-past was not
a parade of battalions, batteries, squadrons *and* a division; it was a parade of
the battalions, batteries and squadrons *of* a division.

One more illustration. A foreigner watching his first game of cricket learns   19
what are the functions of the bowlers, the batsmen, the fielders, the umpires
and the scorers. He then says 'But there is no one left on the field to contribute

the famous element of team-spirit. I see who does the bowling, the batting and the wicket-keeping; but I do not see whose role it is to exercise *esprit de corps*.'[3] Once more, it would have to be explained that he was looking for the wrong type of thing. Team-spirit is not another cricketing-operation supplementary to all of the other special tasks. It is, roughly, the keenness with which each of the special tasks is performed, and performing a task keenly is not performing two tasks. Certainly exhibiting team-spirit is not the same thing as bowling or catching, but nor is it a third thing such that we can say that the bowler first bowls *and* then exhibits team-spirit or that a fielder is at a given moment *either* catching *or* displaying *esprit de corps*.

These illustrations of category-mistakes have a common feature which must be noticed. The mistakes were made by people who did not know how to wield the concepts *University, division* and *team-spirit*. Their puzzles arose from inability to use certain items in the English vocabulary. [20]

The theoretically interesting category-mistakes are those made by people who are perfectly competent to apply concepts, at least in the situations with which they are familiar, but are still liable in their abstract thinking to allocate those concepts to logical types to which they do not belong. An instance of a mistake of this sort would be the following story. A student of politics has learned the main differences between the British, the French and the American Constitutions, and has learned also the differences and connections between the Cabinet, Parliament, the various Ministries, the Judicature and the Church of England. But he still becomes embarrassed when asked questions about the connections between the Church of England, the Home Office and the British Constitution. For while the Church and the Home Office are institutions, the British Constitution is not another institution in the same sense of that noun. So inter-institutional relations which can be asserted or denied to hold between the Church and the Home Office cannot be asserted or denied to hold between either of them and the British Constitution. 'The British Constitution' is not a term of the same logical type as 'the Home Office' and 'the Church of England'. In a partially similar way, John Doe may be a relative, a friend, an enemy or a stranger to Richard Roe; but he cannot be any of these things to the Average Taxpayer. He knows how to talk sense in certain sorts of discussions about the Average Taxpayer, but he is baffled to say why he could not come across him in the street as he can come across Richard Roe. [21]

It is pertinent to our main subject to notice that, so long as the student of politics continues to think of the British Constitution as a counterpart to the other institutions, he will tend to describe it as a mysteriously occult institution; and so long as John Doe continues to think of the Average Taxpayer as [22]

---

[3] ***esprit de corps***   Group spirit, or team spirit.

a fellow-citizen, he will tend to think of him as an elusive insubstantial man, a ghost who is everywhere yet nowhere.

My destructive purpose is to show that a family of radical category-mistakes is the source of the double-life theory. The representation of a person as a ghost mysteriously ensconced in a machine derives from this argument. Because, as is true, a person's thinking, feeling and purposive doing cannot be described solely in the idioms of physics, chemistry and physiology, therefore they must be described in counterpart idioms. As the human body is a complex organised unit, so the human mind must be another complex organised unit, though one made of a different sort of stuff and with a different sort of structure. Or, again, as the human body, like any other parcel of matter, is a field of causes and effects, so the mind must be another field of causes and effects, though not (Heaven be praised) mechanical causes and effects.

(3) *The Origin of the Category-mistake.*
One of the chief intellectual origins of what I have yet to prove to be the Cartesian category-mistake seems to be this. When Galileo[4] showed that his methods of scientific discovery were competent to provide a mechanical theory which should cover every occupant of space, Descartes found in himself two conflicting motives. As a man of scientific genius he could not but endorse the claims of mechanics, yet as a religious and moral man he could not accept, as Hobbes[5] accepted, the discouraging rider to those claims, namely that human nature differs only in degree of complexity from clockwork. The mental could not be just a variety of the mechanical.

He and subsequent philosophers naturally but erroneously availed themselves of the following escape-route. Since mental-conduct words are not to be construed as signifying the occurrence of mechanical processes, they must be construed as signifying the occurrence of non-mechanical processes; since mechanical laws explain movements in space as the effects of other movements in space, other laws must explain some of the non-spatial workings of minds as the effects of other non-spatial workings of minds. The difference between the human behaviours which we describe as intelligent and those which we describe as unintelligent must be a difference in their causation; so, while some movements of human tongues and limbs are the effects of mechanical causes, others must be the effects of non-mechanical causes, i.e. some issue from movements of particles of matter, others from workings of the mind.

23

24

25

---

[4] **Galileo Galilei (1564–1642)**   Italian astronomer and scientist who proved the earth moved around the sun, not the reverse. His studies in Pisa revealed some of the laws of physics that influenced the scientists of the seventeenth century and later.

[5] **Thomas Hobbes (1588–1769)**   An English political philosopher and author of *Leviathan* (1651). Hobbes believed man to be an object in nature and subject to its laws.

The differences between the physical and the mental were thus repre- 26
sented as differences inside the common framework of the categories of 'thing',
'stuff', 'attribute', 'state', 'process', 'change', 'cause' and 'effect'. Minds are
things, but different sorts of things from bodies; mental processes are causes
and effects, but different sorts of causes and effects from bodily movements.
And so on. Somewhat as the foreigner expected the University to be an extra
edifice, rather like a college but also considerably different, so the repudiators
of mechanism represented minds as extra centres of causal processes, rather
like machines but also considerably different from them. Their theory was a
para-mechanical hypothesis.

That this assumption was at the heart of the doctrine is shown by the fact 27
that there was from the beginning felt to be a major theoretical difficulty in
explaining how minds can influence and be influenced by bodies. How can a
mental process, such as willing, cause spatial movements like the movements
of the tongue? How can a physical change in the optic nerve have among its
effects a mind's perception of a flash of light? This notorious crux by itself
shows the logical mould into which Descartes pressed his theory of the mind.
It was the self-same mould into which he and Galileo set their mechanics. Still
unwittingly adhering to the grammar of mechanics, he tried to avert disaster
by describing minds in what was merely an obverse vocabulary. The workings
of minds had to be described by the mere negatives of the specific descriptions
given to bodies; they are not in space, they are not motions, they are not modifications of matter, they are not accessible to public observation. Minds are not
bits of clockwork, they are just bits of not-clockwork.

As thus represented, minds are not merely ghosts harnessed to machines, 28
they are themselves just spectral machines. Though the human body is an
engine, it it not quite an ordinary engine, since some of its workings are governed by another engine inside it — this interior governor-engine being one of a
very special sort. It is invisible, inaudible and it has no size or weight. It cannot
be taken to bits and the laws it obeys are not those known to ordinary engineers. Nothing is known of how it governs the bodily engine.

A second major crux points the same moral. Since, according to the doc- 29
trine, minds belong to the same category as bodies and since bodies are rigidly
governed by mechanical laws, it seemed to many theorists to follow that minds
must be similarly governed by rigid non-mechanical laws. The physical world
is a deterministic system, so the mental world must be a deterministic system. Bodies cannot help the modifications that they undergo, so minds cannot
help pursuing the careers fixed for them. *Responsibility, choice, merit* and
demerit are therefore inapplicable concepts — unless the compromise solution
is adopted of saying that the laws governing mental processes, unlike those
governing physical processes, have the congenial attribute of being only rather
rigid. The problem of the Freedom of the Will was the problem how to reconcile

the hypothesis that minds are to be described in terms drawn from the categories of mechanics with the knowledge that higher-grade human conduct is not of a piece with the behaviour of machines.

It is an historical curiosity that it was not noticed that the entire argument was broken-backed. Theorists correctly assumed that any sane man could already recognise the differences between, say, rational and non-rational utterances or between purposive and automatic behaviour. Else there would have been nothing requiring to be salved from mechanism. Yet the explanation given presupposed that one person could in principle never recognise the difference between the rational and the irrational utterances issuing from other human bodies, since he could never get access to the postulated immaterial causes of some of their utterances. Save for the doubtful exception of himself, he could never tell the difference between a man and a Robot. It would have to be conceded, for example, that, for all that we can tell, the inner lives of persons who are classed as idiots or lunatics are as rational as those of anyone else. Perhaps only their overt behaviour is disappointing; that is to say, perhaps 'idiots' are not really idiotic, or 'lunatics' lunatic. Perhaps, too, some of those who are classed as sane are really idiots. According to the theory, external observers could never know how the overt behaviour of others is correlated with their mental powers and processes and so they could never know or even plausibly conjecture whether their applications of mental-conduct concepts to these other people were correct or incorrect. It would then be hazardous or impossible for a man to claim sanity or logical consistency even for himself, since he would be debarred from comparing his own performances with those of others. In short, our characterisations of persons and their performances as intelligent, prudent and virtuous or as stupid, hypocritical and cowardly could never have been made, so the problem of providing a special causal hypothesis to serve as the basis of such diagnoses would never have arisen. The question, 'How do persons differ from machines?' arose just because everyone already knew how to apply mental-conduct concepts before the new causal hypothesis was introduced. This causal hypothesis could not therefore be the source of the criteria used in those applications. Nor, of course, has the causal hypothesis in any degree improved our handling of those criteria. We still distinguish good from bad arithmetic, politic from impolitic conduct and fertile from infertile imaginations in the ways in which Descartes himself distinguished them before and after he speculated how the applicability of these criteria was compatible with the principle of mechanical causation.

He had mistaken the logic of his problem. Instead of asking by what criteria intelligent behaviour is actually distinguished from non-intelligent behaviour, he asked 'Given that the principle of mechanical causation does not tell us the difference, what other causal principle will tell it us?' He realised that the problem was not one of mechanics and assumed that it must therefore be one

30

31

of some counterpart to mechanics. Not unnaturally psychology is often cast for just this role.

When two terms belong to the same category, it is proper to construct conjunctive propositions embodying them. Thus a purchaser may say that he bought a left-hand glove and a right-hand glove, but not that he bought a left-hand glove, a right-hand glove and a pair of gloves. 'She came home in a flood of tears and a sedan-chair' is a well-known joke based on the absurdity of conjoining terms of different types. It would have been equally ridiculous to construct the disjunction 'She came home either in a flood of tears or else in a sedan-chair'. Now the dogma of the Ghost in the Machine does just this. It maintains that there exist both bodies and minds; that there occur physical processes and mental processes; that there are mechanical causes of corporeal movements and mental causes of corporeal movements. I shall argue that these and other analogous conjunctions are absurd; but, it must be noticed, the argument will not show that either of the illegitimately conjoined propositions is absurd in itself. I am not, for example, denying that there occur mental processes. Doing long division is a mental process and so is making a joke. But I am saying that the phrase 'there occur mental processes' does not mean the same sort of thing as 'there occur physical processes', and, therefore, that it makes no sense to conjoin or disjoin the two.

✖ QUESTIONS FOR CRITICAL READING

1. What does Ryle mean by saying "the human body is an engine" (para. 28)?
2. How useful is the metaphor of the coin?
3. In what sense is asking to see the university a category mistake?
4. What are mental processes?
5. What did René Descartes believe about the mind?
6. What does Ryle mean when he describes the mind as private?
7. Why does Ryle raise the question of whether "idiots are really idiotic or 'lunatics' lunatic" (para. 30)?

✖ SUGGESTIONS FOR CRITICAL WRITING

1. In paragraph 30, Ryle says, "Save for the doubtful exception of himself, he could never tell the difference between a man and Robot." Given the rapid advances made in robotic engineering in the past several decades, is it likely that there will soon be a robot whose thought processes will be difficult or impossible to distinguish from those of a person? Research the literature on the progress being made in robotic studies. Argue a case in favor or against the possibility of a machine being able to think much as we do.

2. If it is possible to create a machine that is able to think creatively and in much the manner of the average human being, what does that say about Ryle's argument against there being a "ghost in the machine"? How would your understanding about the nature of the mind change if a mechanical mind could function as well or close to as well as yours? Would you side with Descartes or with Ryle?

3. Research the term "category mistake" or "category error" in philosophy and logic. How does Ryle use the term to apply to the concept of the mind? Is it true that Cartesian dualism relies on a category mistake to make its case for the distinction between mind and body? Do you know of any other kinds of category mistakes similar to the ones Ryle lists? How are they used to convince people of something that may not be true?

4. Analyze the arguments being presented in paragraphs 28 and 29. Ryle talks about the seventeenth-century view that "minds must be similarly governed by rigid non-mechanical laws" (para. 29). But he then goes on to talk about "*Responsibility, choice, merit*, and *demerit*" (para. 29). How does introducing these terms affect the argument? What exactly is Ryle saying in these paragraphs, and to what extent do you agree with him? What are your major points of disagreement?

5. If a machine can play chess at the level of the world's grandmasters, what do we then understand about mental processes and how they function? Does the chess-playing machine behave as a mind would behave? Or does the human mind playing chess behave like the machine? If the chess-playing machine makes choices in the act of playing, is there then a "ghost in the chess-playing machine"? In what ways does the chess-playing machine advance the theory that our mind, like our body, is subject to the mechanical laws of nature?

6. If the mind and body are not the same kinds of things, that is, if mind and matter are totally different, how must we view the widely held idea that the mind may continue to exist after the death of the brain? Would the concept of the "ghost in the machine" be essential for us to expect that the mind exists independent of the brain? What evidence do we have that points to the existence of the mind after the death of the brain?

7. **CONNECTIONS**   Because consciousness is an attribute of the mind, what might Ryle have learned from reading Eric Kandel's "The Problem of Consciousness" (p. 539)? Kandel is working with problems as difficult as those that interest Ryle. What does Kandel say that would support Ryle's argument that mind-body dualism is wrong? How does your understanding of Ryle change after having read Kandel? Write an essay that compares Ryle's and Kandel's attitudes and beliefs about how the mind works and the ways in which we conceive of the idea of the mind in general. How does the idea of consciousness feed into Ryle's argument against Descartes?

ROBERT
NOZICK
Emotions

Martha Holmes/The LIFE Images Collection/
Getty Images

R OBERT NOZICK (1938–2002) was the Joseph
Pellegrino Professor of Philosophy at Harvard
University for his entire career and also served as
president of the American Philosophical Society. He was born in Brooklyn, the son of a
Jewish small businessman who had come from Russia. He attended public schools as a
child and then went on to complete his undergraduate studies at Columbia University,
and he received his PhD at Princeton University in 1963. He then spent a year as a Ful-
bright Scholar at Oxford University.

From the start, Nozick's work attracted considerable attention. His first book,
Anarchy, State, and Utopia (1974), remains his most important contribution to the analysis of political systems. Nozick was an analytic philosopher, like Gilbert Ryle (p. 514), and
used ordinary language to analyze complex ideas. At the time he wrote, it was uncommon
for analytic philosophers to take up problems of social systems. Yet he was not alone. John
Rawls (p. 271) had written on the role of justice in society and set himself in opposition
to Nozick. The two have since been seen as the most important philosophers of their age
writing on social politics.

Nozick's views on politics represent his most lasting and most effective work. When he
was young, his position was left-leaning and largely socialist in nature. But as he studied, he
was influenced by a number of conservative libertarians such as F. A. Hayek (p. 386), whom
he joined in rejecting socialism and extensive government power. Nozick felt that the role
of government should be limited to its "regalian" functions — police, military, and general
administration — and that all the other social functions, such as education, health, and welfare, should be taken over by private institutions and religious organizations. His views are
still influential on politicians who defend a libertarian principle and reject Rawls's view that
any law must be measured by its potential harm on the least advantaged of its citizens.

Nozick's later work left social politics behind. He wrote elegantly about epistemol-
ogy, the question of how one knows anything, and in 1989, he wrote *The Examined Life:
Philosophical Meditations*, a work aimed at the general reader. Its purpose was to meditate

---

From *The Examined Life: Philosophical Meditations.*

on the meaning of life. He covered a wide range of subjects in his book, including dying, creating, the nature of god, sexuality, value and meaning, the Holocaust, and wisdom. The following selection is from this book and concerns itself with emotions. This essay is related to a larger project on the nature of rationality. Considering Nozick's interest in knowledge, the question of how emotions inform us and affect us is of some importance.

Although the rest of Nozick's work was not quite as influential as his first book on social-political issues, it is clear that he was able to encompass a great deal of important philosophical work during a relatively short career.

NOZICK'S RHETORIC

Because Nozick was an analytic philosopher, he examines words carefully and invites us to examine them with him. He also, like Aristotle, thought categorically and thus begins his discussion by pointing to three categories that pertain to emotions: belief, evaluation, and feeling. These categories are not self-evidently connected to the concept of emotion as it is commonly understood, so Nozick must spend time discussing each concept and connecting it to the idea of emotions. Therefore, enumeration becomes a useful means of beginning his essay.

The rhetorical technique of example is the path he takes into the question of how emotions function. He takes the emotion of pride as a starting point, applying the three categories of belief, evaluation, and feeling. But he complicates the matter by asking some very difficult questions. For example, if someone feels pride in having read three books this week, but then admits to reading only one book, is it reasonable that the person should still feel pride? How does one evaluate the difference between reading three books and one book, and further, how does one evaluate the kinds of books that have produced this sense of pride? In the process of this argument, Nozick is raising the question of how we evaluate an emotion like pride.

Enumeration is useful again in paragraph 3 when Nozick says, "An emotion can be defective or inappropriate in three ways: the belief can be false; the evaluation can be false or wrong; or the feeling can be disproportionate to the evaluation." This raises more complex issues that need examination and analysis. In this paragraph, he introduces another example: the person who is ecstatic over having found a one dollar bill. Nozick questions the appropriateness of an ecstatic emotion in response to finding a mere dollar bill. He would be happier if it was a five- or six-figure find — it would be a more appropriate response.

Ultimately, this example leads us to paragraph 11, when Nozick begins an analysis of what he calls "external value." Some values are subjective, especially when it comes to emotions, but then some are also external. Nozick says, "It is an objective matter whether something is valuable" (para. 11), and that statement leads to further analysis of the concept of value and the way in which we respond to it. Nozick claims, "Emotions are to value as beliefs are to facts" (para. 12). This kind of flat statement appears in the middle of an examination of the way in which emotions respond to the idea of value. It is a statement that warrants examination.

The example of Mr. Spock, the *Star Trek* character who serves as first officer on the Starship *Enterprise*, is useful because he has no emotional life. He is a mix of human and Vulcan and can feel pleasure but not emotions. Nozick raises the following question in paragraphs 7 and 8 when he introduces the "Spock problem": What is the value of human emotion to the individual? Nozick states that "a life without emotions would be the poorer" (para. 9), and then goes on to explain why.

⬛ PREREADING QUESTIONS: WHAT TO READ FOR

The following prereading questions may help you anticipate key issues in the discussion of Robert Nozick's "Emotions." Keeping them in mind during your first reading of the selection should help focus your attention.

1. What is the relation of belief to emotions?

2. How should we value our emotions?

3. How can emotions be appropriate or inappropriate?

Emotions

A large part of how we feel about life is shaped by the emotions we have   1
had and expect to have, and that feeling too (probably) is an emotion or a combination of them. What emotions should we desire—indeed, why should we desire *any*—and how should we think about the emotions we do have? The recent philosophical literature describes the structure of emotions in a way that is somewhat illuminating—I am not completely happy with it, but I have nothing better at present to offer. Emotions, these philosophers say, have a common structure of three components: a belief, an evaluation, and a feeling.[1] To get clear about this structure it will be helpful to consider an example of a particular emotion: pride. Suppose you say you feel proud that you read three books last week, and I say that you're misremembering; I counted and you read only one book last week. You grant the correction and reply that nevertheless

---

[1] For a survey and selection of this literature, see C. Calhoun and R. Solomon, eds., *What Is an Emotion?* (New York: Oxford University Press, 1984); and Amelie Rorty, ed., *Explaining Emotions* (Berkeley: University of California Press, 1980). Two relevant books have appeared since my several sections on emotion were written: Ronald de Sousa, *The Rationality of Emotion* (Cambridge, Mass.: M.I.T. Press, 1987); Patricia Greenspan, *Emotions and Reason: An Inquiry into Emotional Justification* (New York: Routledge, 1988). [Nozick's note]

you feel proud that you read three. This is bewildering. Since you no longer believe you read three books last week, whatever you are feeling, it isn't pride, or at least, it isn't being proud *of that*. To be proud of something, you have to think or believe it is the case (well, not exactly, as a general point about emotions, for you might think of a possibility in fantasy and have an emotion about it, without believing it to be the case).

Suppose you did read the books, and when you announce your pride I say 2 it's nothing to be proud of; it's a bad thing to read three books, perhaps because it's bad to do anything in threes, or because books are bad, or it was bad to read the ones you did, or because you should have spent the time doing something else. I negatively evaluate your reading the three books. Suppose you accept this evaluation, agree that it was bad, and say that nevertheless you are proud that you did it. I am bewildered and ask whether there's some good aspect of your act that you are focusing upon, such as the courage to defy convention or whatever. You reply that everything about it is bad, but nonetheless you're proud of having done it. Here, too, whatever you are feeling, it isn't pride. To be proud that something is so is to believe it is so and also to positively evaluate it as somehow valuable or good or admirable. Along with your belief that you read the three books and your favorable evaluation of having done so, there perhaps goes a feeling, a sensation, an inner experience. What makes it an emotion *of pride* rather than of something else is the feeling's connection with this particular belief and evaluation. The simplest connection is when the belief and evaluation give rise to the feeling, when the person has the feeling because of his beliefs and evaluations. More complex is a situation where the feeling arises for some other reason and the person attributes it to that belief and evaluation; if while you're simply thinking positively of having read the three books I electrochemically stimulate you, producing a sensation in your chest, you may identify that as pride. But in whichever direction the connection goes, the emotion is partially constituted not just by the feeling but also by its attendant belief and evaluation: a different belief or evaluation, a different emotion. (This does not mean we first are conscious of beliefs and evaluations and *then* have an emotion; sometimes we may discover our implicit beliefs and evaluations by pondering the emotions we are aware of feeling.) Emotion, therefore, is much more "cognitive" than one might think, and thus it can be judged in certain respects.

An emotion can be defective or inappropriate in three ways: the belief can 3 be false; the evaluation can be false or wrong; or the feeling can be disproportionate to the evaluation. Suppose, walking along the street, I find a dollar bill and feel ecstatic. You ask whether I think it indicates this is my lucky day or that my fortunes have changed or that I am beloved by the gods, but no, it is none of these things. I simply am ecstatic. But finding a dollar isn't *that* wonderful a thing; the strength and intensity of the feeling should bear some proportionate relationship to the evaluation of how good a thing finding a dollar is—to the measure of the evaluation.

Let us say that an emotion *fits* when it has the above threefold structure of belief, evaluation, and feeling, and moreover when the belief is true, the evaluation is correct, and the feeling is proportionate to the evaluation. When the feeling is disproportionately strong, given the evaluation, this often indicates that the fact believed and evaluated is functioning symbolically; unconsciously the person views it as something else to which his degree of feeling *is* proportionate. (Alternately, the disproportionate feeling may be camouflage for the opposite unconscious emotion based upon an opposite unconscious evaluation.) When we have a positive emotion, one whose component evaluation is positive, we want the components to fit; we want the belief to be true, the evaluation to be correct, and the feeling to be proportionate. (On occasion we might want the belief and evaluation not simply to be true but also to be known to be so.)   4

In speaking of our evaluations as correct—that is, as something like objectively true and right—I am aware that I have touched upon controversial matters, but these can be sidestepped for now. Perhaps evaluations are not the sorts of things that can be objectively correct. In that case, we can utilize whatever standards and norms are appropriate for assessing them. Evaluations can be informed, unbiased, supported by reasons, justified, or whatever. Provided that not all evaluations are just matters of arbitrary subjective preference, none better grounded than any other, then we can plug in the strongest standards that are appropriate and say that an emotion is fitting only when its component evaluation satisfies those standards. We want the evaluations our emotions are based upon to be the best kind there can be, however that notion of bestness gets specified eventually.[2]   5

Intense emotions are the ones with evaluations that are *very* positive (or very negative) and also with proportionately great attendant feelings. Despite the special and central place it has been given by the philosophical tradition, happiness is only one of these intense emotions, roughly on a par with the rest.   6

An important part of life is having many intense positive emotions that are fitting (including some it would take Rilke[3] to describe). Why? This is not just because the facts evaluated then would hold true; they could hold without   7

---

[2] We want this, all other things being equal; if these best evaluations can be acquired only at a high cost in time or energy, we might be content to let some emotions rest on somewhat inferior evaluations. The same point also applies to beliefs. We want our beliefs to be based upon the best and most complete evidence or data, but when this comes dear we may be content to let certain beliefs rest upon rougher material, accepting their diminution in accuracy. [Nozick's note]

[3] **Rainer Maria Rilke (1875–1926)**   was a German poet and novelist who suffered from depression but wrote intense lyrical poetry and prose that influenced Nietzsche and other nineteenth-century philosophers.

being evaluated. Nor is it just because when something is valuable, there is a further value when it is responded to as valuable. For this could occur unemotionally, through correct evaluative judgments that are not accompanied by any attendant feelings. The character Spock in the television program *Star Trek* held correct beliefs, made correct evaluations, and acted on these, yet his life lacked emotion and inner feeling. Inner experiences are not the *only* things that matter, but they *do* matter. We would not plug into an experience machine, but we would not plug into an anesthetizing machine either.

Why are emotions important, above and beyond correct evaluations? (Call this the Spock Problem.) We might want to reply, simply, that having emotions is an essential part of being human. Yet even if having an emotional texture is essential to being human, the question of why we should prize emotions still would arise. Why should we especially prize being human, if *that* is what it is, unless it embodies something that objectively merits being prized? We don't have to prize every trait we have; why then should the fact that the trait is part of our essence make a significant difference? We need to investigate further the special value of having emotions.   8

Is it that an emotionless life lacks the feelings that go along with correct evaluations and so is less pleasurable? But an emotionless life might contain other equally pleasurable feelings, provided these feelings are not attendant upon beliefs and evaluations, and so are not themselves components of emotions. Consider the pleasurable sensations and feelings of basking in the sun or floating in the water. These may be no less pleasurable than are the feelings that are components of intense positive emotions, and they are available to Spock, as are certain intellectual pleasures. So an emotionless (Spock) life need not be less pleasurable. Emotions might amplify pleasures and help to recall them more easily during pleasureless times, etc., so that it might be more difficult for a life without emotions to be very pleasurable, but I do not think the story is this simple. Rather, a life without emotions would be the poorer. Why?[4]   9

Emotions typically involve not only a psychological feeling but also physiological changes in respiration, pupil size, skin color, etc. Hence, they provide an especially close integration of the mind and the body. They integrate the psychological and the physical—belief, evaluation, and feeling. If a unity between mind and body is itself desirable and valuable, as I think it is, emotions provide a unique route.   10

---

[4] Emotions inform us of the evaluations we are making, including unconscious ones. Since the feelings involved are present to consciousness, we can use them to monitor, reexamine, and perhaps alter our underlying evaluations. This is a useful function, yet we would not renounce emotions if doing so would afford us an even more effective knowledge of our unconscious evaluations; in any case, that function would equally well be served if we could be aware of our evaluations without any attendant feeling. So this too is not the reason why emotions matter especially. [Nozick's note]

Emotions also can link us closely to external value. When we positively 11
evaluate a situation or fact, an emotional response links us more closely to the
value we perceive than an unemotional evaluative judgment would. By value
I do not mean our own subjective experience or liking of something; I mean
the quality something has in virtue of which it is valuable. (In particular, the
quality something has which makes it valuable in itself, apart from its further
consequences and effects — a kind of value philosophers call "intrinsic value.")
Value judgments are not all subjective, I am supposing; they can be right or
wrong, correct or incorrect, true or false, well-founded or not. It is an objective matter whether something is valuable — that is, has the characteristics that
make something valuable or exhibits the property that value consists in. I think
that something is valuable insofar as it has a high degree of "organic unity,"
unifying and integrating disparate material. More will be said about this later,
but whether or not this particular suggestion about the nature of value turns
out to be correct — some of the things it may seem to leave out fall into a wider
category than value — for present purposes we need only assume that value
is not just a matter of opinion, that it is "out there" and has its own nature.
Our current suggestion is that emotions are a response to value (whatever the
correct theory of objective intrinsic value might turn out to be).

When we respond emotionally to value, rather than merely judging or 12
evaluating it mentally, we respond more fully because our feelings and our
physiology are involved. Emotions are a fitting and appropriate response to
value. Emotions are to value as beliefs are to facts. (I will modify this statement somewhat later: Emotions are the fitting response to a wider category
which includes value as a part but also includes other things such as meaning,
intensity, and depth.) Given the nature of value, given its character — and given
ours — we can be most responsive to value, its content and its contours, through
emotion. While this strikes me as so, it is less clear why it is so. Perhaps we
can use this to learn more about the nature of value. What must value be like
if emotions are the appropriate response to it; what is the difference between
value and facts if emotions stand to value as beliefs do to facts?

Beliefs are our appropriate response to nonevaluative facts. When our 13
belief about a fact is true, and that belief is further linked to the fact in an
appropriate way, then it is a case of knowledge. (Philosophers disagree about
the precise nature of this knowledge-connection.) Our appropriate response to
facts is to believe them and know that they hold. And just as we can hold false
beliefs without impugning the objectivity of the facts out there, so too we can
have unfitting emotions, responses to purported values that are incorrect.

I said earlier that emotions are fuller responses to value than are bare 14
evaluative judgments, since emotions involve our bodily responses also. But
we may wonder whether more complete responses always are more desirable.
Would it be better yet if our heart also pumped out in Morse code a statement of

the positive evaluation? What emotion must provide is not merely an increased quantity of response to value but a response that is peculiarly appropriate.

Emotions provide a kind of picture of value, I think. They are our inter- 15 nal psychophysiological response to the external value, a response that is specially close by being not only due to that value but an analog representation of it.[5] Emotions provide a psychophysical replica of value (or of a wider, more inclusive category I discuss later). One way this might happen is the following: Something's being valuable involves its having a certain mode of structural organization to a certain degree—for example, a degree of organic unity; the responding emotion would be a psychophysical entity with a similar or parallel mode of organization. The emotion would be or contain something like a map of the value, or of the thing's being valuable. This model need not be an *exact* analog, however; it may be only the best analog we can produce or the best one it is worthwhile producing, given the extent of our other tasks, emotional resources, etc. (Perhaps this leaves it an exact analog, only now by a more complicated mapping.)

More needs to be said, however, about the way, in which emotion provides 16 an analog of value. For suppose some extraterrestrials could dance expressively and represent external value though analog movement yet not have any elaborate feelings or emotions themselves. If this were possible, then we should have to claim that the medium of psychological feelings is an *especially* apt and appropriate locus for people's analog representation of value, or concede that other analog representations would do as well as emotions. However, perhaps the assumption that no emotions are involved here is too quick. If writers sometimes can write expressively without there being any emotions they have that they are expressing, or rather if the writing itself is the place where they have emotions, not in any inner psychological happenings but right there on the page, then perhaps the Martians can have them too in their dance motions. Emotions then might involve not necessarily inner feelings but rather analog representations (produced in a *certain* way) through *any* sufficiently rich personal medium; feelings would be only one way to constitute emotions.[6]

---

[5] Roughly put, an analog model or representation of a process somehow replicates that process rather than merely describing it. The model depicts a continuous process or dimension in the world by corresponding continuous changes in itself. The analog nature of emotions is more complicated than this brief statement can indicate; I have relegated some details to an appendix to this section. [Nozick's note]

[6] Gerard Manley Hopkins, we might note, held a particular version of the onomatopoetic theory of the origin of language: A word imitates in its substance and (what he called its) inscape the substance and inscape of what it names, so that some words provide a kinesthetic imitation of their referents. (See J. Hillis Miller, *The Disappearance of God* [Cambridge, Mass.: Harvard University Press, 1975], p. 285.) Words such as Hopkins describes would constitute analog models of what they represented. [Nozick's note]

An intense emotion that is fitting is a close response to particular value,   17
and is valuable in itself. It provides an analog model of the value that depends
on the value's existence and perhaps tracks it closely. This combination of
emotion in relation to value gives us a further integrated structure, added to the
integrated structure of the value itself. If such additional integrated structures
count as valuable — as I think they do — that gives us a *second* value. So it is a
valuable thing that there exist fitting positive emotions.

But is it valuable for us? Fitting responses to value, which are valuable   18
things, would be taking place within our psychophysiological structure, but
are they valuable *for us*? We can (following some recent literature on Aristotle)
distinguish between the way you can be that is best, the one whose existence is
most valuable, and the way that is best and most valuable *for you*, the way that
leaves you best off. Suppose your body could be used as a theater by microorganisms to do an intricate and beautifully interwoven pattern of movement
and interaction. That might be the most valuable thing that could happen there;
from the point of view of the universe it might be best that it occur. Since that
process, however, constitutes a fatal disease for you, it would not be best *for
you* that it occur. (Yet might this other fact help reconcile you to its occurrence?) Our question then is: Is it good *for us* to be beings with an emotional
life or is it merely valuable from the point of the universe that it take place
somewhere while we merely happen to be the theater where these valuable
events occur?

This question overemphasizes our passivity, though. Many of our capaci-   19
ties are drawn upon when we respond emotionally to value, capacities of being
able to recognize and appreciate value, to make evaluative judgments, and also
to feel in tandem. Not just anything can be a "theater" for such fine happenings;
only beings with a feel for value can do it. But still, when we do it, is it good
for us or is it merely a good thing happening? It certainly is good for us if, as
Aristotle thought and John Rawls recently has emphasized, it is good for us to
exercise our intricate capacities on valuable objects. Emotions then would be
an important part of a valuable life. Moreover, these emotions recreate within
us the value they respond to; at least, they create an analog model of it, which is
also valuable. We therefore possess these intricate structures within ourselves.
(Not only do these positive emotions feel pleasurable; they constitute a force
we can utilize and in an important way, I think, they provide us with substance.)
Moreover, we make them; we have the ability to produce — often we can't help
producing — these emotional models of value which have value themselves by
having some of the very same qualities they represent and picture. Our emotional capacity, then, constitutes one portion of our value-creating power; and
being originators of value is part of our own special value. Emotions give us
a certain *depth* and substance, too, a fact that becomes clearer when we also
consider emotions that are not positive.

This leads us to an additional even shorter answer to the Spock problem. 20 Emotions make many things—the situation of having emotions, our lives as they include emotions, and also ourselves as beings with emotion—more valuable, more intense, and more vivid than otherwise. Emotions do not simply feel good; intense and fitting emotions make us more.

⠒ QUESTIONS FOR CRITICAL READING

1. When is an emotion appropriate? When is it inappropriate?

2. What are some of the grounds for feeling pride?

3. How can an emotion be evaluated?

4. Can the evaluation of an emotion be objective?

5. When does an emotion become physiological?

6. What is the Spock problem?

7. How can emotions link us to external value?

⠒ SUGGESTIONS FOR CRITICAL WRITING

1. In paragraph 16, Nozick discusses the idea of emotion as an analog of value. What does he mean by this? He discusses a dance performance that represents expression of emotion but in which the dancers do not feel the emotion. Why is this a problem? Is art an expression of emotion? If so, must the artist feel the emotion while creating the art? Address this question in an essay that discusses a particular form of art.

2. Nozick discusses belief throughout the essay, but says, in paragraph 13, "Beliefs are our appropriate response to nonevaluative facts." What do you think he means by this? In a brief essay, discuss the way in which beliefs affect our emotions. What kinds of beliefs seem to be involved in what kinds of emotions? How does belief function in our emotions? In your essay, use examples drawn from experience.

3. In an essay, decide whether it is possible to say that there are good emotions and bad emotions. Is it possible to rephrase that statement to say there are desirable emotions and undesirable emotions? Explain which emotions are desirable and which are not. How are decisions made about the value of an emotion? Choose an emotion or range of emotions that you have experienced as material for your essay on evaluating emotions.

4. Spend a few days observing yourself and others in an attempt to understand what emotions you experience and what they mean to you. Which of your emotions are the most frequent? Which emotions did you most value? Which emotions gave you the most discomfort? Would you say you have a rich emotional life, or is your emotional life less intense than those, say, of your closest

friends? How would you evaluate your emotions in comparison with those you observe in others?

5. In paragraph 10, Nozick says, "When we respond emotionally to value, rather than merely judging or evaluating it mentally, we respond more fully because our feelings and our physiology are involved." Explain what Nozick seems to mean by referencing your own emotional experiences. If possible, query your peers and ask them to provide examples from their own experiences to help understand Nozick's statement. What are the most significant emotions involving a physiological response?

6. Throughout his essay, Nozick refers to the idea of value and evaluation. He talks about facts and value, as well as subjective value and external value. In a careful essay, explain your own ideas about value and evaluation. What constitutes value in your culture? What do you most value, and how do you regard that value — as subjective or as objective? What are the most important external values in your life? Do they connect with your emotional life?

7. **CONNECTIONS** Friedrich Nietzsche's (p. 459) discussion of Dionysianism is an examination of a particular range of emotion or emotions. What light does Nozick's discussion of emotion shed on the description by Nietzsche of the Dionysian state of mind? What emotions seem to be implied in Nietzsche's description of either the Apollonian or the Dionysian force in human psychology? What values are involved in the Nietzschean dichotomy? How would the three categories of belief, value, and feeling apply to Nietzsche's discussion? Argue your case with reference to the issues Nozick discusses.

ERIC KANDEL

The Problem of Consciousness

E RIC KANDEL (b. 1929) was born in Vienna, Austria, but when the Nazis annexed Austria in 1939, his parents realized that they were at risk because Jews were being persecuted and killed. They abandoned their small toy and luggage store and sailed to the United States. With relatives in Brooklyn, Kandel, at age 9, began grade school at a yeshivah and then attended public high school at Erasmus Hall in Brooklyn, where he was a track star. At the suggestion of a teacher, he applied to Harvard University and was accepted; he graduated with a major in modern European history. However, his interest in the studies of the mind began while he was an undergraduate as a result of his friendship with a young woman whose parents were Freudian analysts.

In 1952, Kandel entered New York University's School of Medicine and began a career that led him into the field of psychiatry. Eventually, he began research in neurobiology that centered on the question of how memory works. In 1957, he joined the Laboratory of Neurophysiology at the National Institutes of Health. Some of the ongoing research postulated that the hippocampus, a structure deep in the brain, is a center of memory storage, but the complexity of the hippocampus made it difficult to study directly. After his residency in psychiatry, Kandel went to Paris to study research with Ladislav Tauc (1926–1999), who was working with a simple sea animal called *Aplysia*. Eventually, Kandel also centered his work on the sea slug *Aplysia*, which is one of the simplest animals capable of learning. This animal was particularly easy to work with because the ganglia and axons that help form memory are large enough to manipulate and study.

On his return from Paris, Kandel became a professor in the departments of physiology and psychiatry at the New York University Medical School. He set up a laboratory to continue his studies of *Aplysia* and, in 1974, moved his lab to Columbia University as the founding director of the Center for Neurobiology and Behavior. As his work progressed, he was winner of many prestigious awards, such as the Lasker Award (1983), National Medal

From *In Search of Memory: The Emergence of a New Science of Mind.*

of Science (1988), Wolf Prize in Medicine (1999), and the Nobel Prize in Physiology or Medicine (2000), which he shared with two other researchers.

In Search of Memory: The Emergence of a New Science of Mind (2006) is an award-winning book by Kandel aimed at a large audience. Kandel begins with his own memories of his life in Austria and his immigration to the United States. He remembers his early education and the help he had in deciding to go to Harvard. His book also goes on to present the current research and understanding of the cellular nature of the brain and its operations in memory. It represents a major introduction to the state of the art in memory research. Kandel begins one cell at a time and continues until he presents his thoughts on the problem of consciousness in the selection that follows.

KANDEL'S RHETORIC

The purpose of Kandel's essay is to inform the reader about the ongoing research into the nature of consciousness. Although he admits that the interest in consciousness has been evident since Hippocrates in the fifth century B.C.E., most of his attention is paid to what has been going on since he began his studies. He begins, in paragraph 2, to define consciousness as "a state of perceptual awareness, or selective attention writ large." Much of the rest of the essay expands on this definition.

Although Kandel does not use an enumerative structure, he does begin with an effort to understand the nature of the problem and explain why it is so difficult to solve. Because the problem of consciousness has not been solved — and may not be solved anytime soon — Kandel brings to our attention a wide range of work done by the most important current scientists working on the problem. He begins with the most well-known of modern genetic researchers, James Crick, who discovered the nature of the gene. After he identified the important aspects of the structure of the gene, Crick devoted himself to trying to solve some of the most difficult aspects of the problem of consciousness.

In the process of his review of what is known, Kandel summarizes the position of René Descartes and his view that the mind is immaterial, like the soul, and therefore cannot be studied. Gilbert Ryle (p. 514) also reviews Descartes's ideas, stating they are false. Kandel then reviews modern philosophers and finds a variety of opinions. Eventually, he considers a recent consensus that ascribes "two characteristics to the conscious state: unity and subjectivity" (para. 10). He describes unity as the easy problem, whereas subjectivity is the hard problem of consciousness. But even the easy problem has some great difficulty, as in the case of a bisected brain that, then, has "two conscious minds" that perceive a uniform experience.

Kandel then goes on to discuss issues such as perception, as when he is in his rose garden in Riverdale both seeing and smelling flowers. He asks how the mind creates the unity of experience that he perceives in that setting. "How is it that I respond to the red image of a rose with a feeling that is distinctive to me?" (para. 15). That question is one of subjectivity and, for him, represents the "hard problem of consciousness" (para. 20).

From that point, Kandel moves into the biology of the brain and observes the activity of brain cells during periods of people's awareness and consciousness of feeling. His interest in emotions parallels some of Robert Nozick's (p. 528) interest, but from the point of view of the physiologist. Most of Kandel's essay on consciousness is part of the study of the physiology of the brain while the mind is conscious. However, he also includes observations of the brain and the mind's activity while unconscious. In this way, he links his early training as a psychiatrist with his later training as a neurologist. He also connects the subject of his research with the work of Freud (p. 477), who postulated that in the future his psychological research would probably be clarified by studies of the physiology of the brain.

Thus, Kandel leaves us with the sense that our understanding of consciousness will come not only from philosophical studies or religious studies, but also from neurological studies that are in progress now and that continue to confront still massive challenges to our understanding.

▪ PREREADING QUESTIONS: WHAT TO READ FOR

The following prereading questions may help you anticipate key issues in the discussion of Eric Kandel's "The Problem of Consciousness." Keeping them in mind during your first reading of the selection should help focus your attention.

1. What is the unity problem of consciousness?
2. What is the hard problem of consciousness?
3. How does Eric Kandel define consciousness?

The Problem of Consciousness

Psychoanalysis introduced us to the unconscious in its several forms. Like many scientists now working on the brain, I have long been intrigued by the biggest question about the brain: the nature of consciousness and how various unconscious psychological processes relate to conscious thought. When I first talked with Harry Grundfest[1] about Freud's structural theory of mind — the ego, the id, and the superego — the central focus of my thinking was: How do conscious and unconscious processes differ in their representation in the brain? But only recently has the new science of mind developed the tools for exploring this question experimentally.

To develop productive insights into consciousness, the new science of mind first had to settle on a working definition of consciousness as a state of

---

[1] **Harry Grundfest (1904–1983)**   Professor of neurology at Columbia University and Eric Kandel's teacher.

perceptual awareness, or selective attention writ large. At its core, consciousness in people is an awareness of self, an awareness of being aware. Consciousness thus refers to our ability not simply to experience pleasure and pain but to attend to and reflect upon those experiences, and to do so in the context of our immediate lives and our life history. Conscious attention allows us to shut out extraneous experiences and focus on the critical event that confronts us, be it pleasure or pain, the blue of the sky, the cool northern light of a Vermeer painting, or the beauty and calm we experience at the seashore.

Understanding consciousness is by far the most challenging task confronting science. The truth of this assertion can best be seen in the career of Francis Crick,[2] perhaps the most creative and influential biologist of the second half of the twentieth century. When Crick first entered biology, after World War II, two great questions were thought to be beyond the capacities of science to answer: What distinguishes the living from the nonliving world? And what is the biological nature of consciousness? Crick turned first to the easier problem, distinguishing animate from inanimate matter, and explored the nature of the gene. By 1953, after just two years of collaboration, he and Jim Watson[3] had helped solve that mystery. As Watson later described in *The Double Helix*, "at lunch Francis winged into the Eagle [Pub] to tell everyone within hearing distance that we had found the secret of life." In the next two decades, Crick helped crack the genetic code: how DNA makes RNA and RNA[4] makes protein.

In 1976, at age sixty, Crick turned to the remaining scientific mystery: the biological nature of consciousness. This he studied for the rest of his life in partnership with Christof Koch,[5] a young computational neuroscientist. Crick brought his characteristic intelligence and optimism to bear on the question; moreover, he made consciousness a focus of the scientific community, which had previously ignored it. But, despite almost thirty years of continuous effort, Crick was able to budge the problem only a modest distance. Indeed, some scientists and philosophers of mind continue to find consciousness so inscrutable that they fear it can never be explained in physical terms. How can a biological system, a biological machine, they ask, feel anything? Even more doubtful, how can it think about itself?

3

4

---

[2] **Francis Crick (1916–2004)**   Nobel Prize–winning geneticist who helped to crack the genetic code.

[3] **Jim Watson (b. 1928)**   Co-discoverer with Crick of the double helix structure of the gene.

[4] **DNA and RNA**   Deoxyribonucleic acid, which contains instructions for the gene; ribonucleic acid, which helps carry out the DNA instructions.

[5] **Christof Koch (b. 1956)**   Chief Scientific Officer of the Allen Institute for Brain Science in Seattle, known for his work in consciousness.

These questions are not new. They were first posed in Western thought during the fifth century B.C. by Hippocrates[6] and by the philosopher Plato, the founder of the Academy in Athens. Hippocrates was the first physician to cast superstition aside, basing his thinking on clinical observations and arguing that all mental processes emanate from the brain. Plato, who rejected observations and experiments, believed that the only reason we can think about ourselves and our mortal body is that we have a soul that is immaterial and immortal. The idea of an immortal soul was subsequently incorporated into Christian thought and elaborated upon by St. Thomas Aquinas[7] in the thirteenth century. Aquinas and later religious thinkers held that the soul—the generator of consciousness—is not only distinct from the body, it is also of divine origin.

In the seventeenth century, René Descartes[8] developed the idea that human beings have a dual nature: they have a body, which is made up of material substance, and a mind, which derives from the spiritual nature of the soul. The soul receives signals from the body and can influence its actions but is itself made up of an immaterial substance that is unique to human beings. Descartes' thinking gave rise to the view that actions like eating and walking, as well as sensory perception, appetites, passions, and even simple forms of learning, are all mediated by the brain and can be studied scientifically. Mind, however, is sacred and as such is not a proper subject of science.

It is remarkable to reflect that these seventeenth-century ideas were still current in the 1980s. Karl Popper,[9] the Vienna-born philosopher of science, and John Eccles,[10] the Nobel laureate neurobiologist, espoused dualism all of their lives. They agreed with Aquinas that the soul is immortal and independent of the brain. Gilbert Ryle,[11] the British philosopher of science, referred to the notion of the soul as "the ghost in the machine."

Today, most philosophers of mind agree that what we call consciousness derives from the physical brain, but some disagree with Crick as to whether it can ever be approached scientifically. A few, such as Colin McGinn,[12] believe that consciousness simply cannot be studied, because the architecture of the

---

[6] **Hippocrates (460–375 B.C.E.)**   Regarded as the greatest ancient physician.

[7] **St. Thomas Aquinas (1225–1274)**   A Dominican friar and follower of Aristotle and Plato. *Summa Theologica* is his major work.

[8] **René Descartes (1596–1650)**   French philosopher who in his meditations proposed the idea of mind-body dualism.

[9] **Karl Popper (1902–1994)**   Austrian-British philosopher of science.

[10] **John Eccles (1903–1997)**   Australian neurophysiologist and winner of the Nobel Prize for work on the brain's synapses.

[11] **Gilbert Ryle (1900–1976)**   British analytic philosopher. See p. 514.

[12] **Colin McGinn (b. 1950)**   British philosopher who has contended that the human mind cannot solve the problem of consciousness.

brain poses limitations on human cognitive capacities. In McGinn's view, the human mind may simply be incapable of solving certain problems. At the other extreme, philosophers such as Daniel Dennett[13] deny that there is any problem at all. Dennett argues, much as neurologist John Hughlings Jackson[14] did a century earlier, that consciousness is not a distinct operation of the brain; rather, it is the combined result of the computational workings of higher-order areas of the brain concerned with later stages of information processing.

Finally, philosophers such as John Searle and Thomas Nagel[15] take a middle   9
position, holding that consciousness is a discrete set of biological processes. The processes are accessible to analysis, but we have made little headway in understanding them because they are very complex and represent more than the sum of their parts. Consciousness is therefore much more complicated than any property of the brain that we understand.

Searle and Nagel ascribe two characteristics to the conscious state: unity   10
and subjectivity. The unitary nature of consciousness refers to the fact that our experiences come to us as a unified whole. All of the various sensory modalities are melded into a single, coherent, conscious experience. Thus when I approach a rosebush in the botanical garden at Wave Hill near my house in Riverdale, I sniff the exquisite fragrance of the blossoms at the same time that I see their beautiful red color—and I perceive this rosebush against the background of the Hudson River and the cliffs of the Palisade mountain ridge behind it. My perception is not only whole during the moment I experience it, it is also whole two weeks later, when I engage in mental time travel to recapture the moment. Despite the fact that there are different organs for smell and vision, and that each uses its own individual pathways, they converge in the brain in such a way that my perceptions are unified.

The unitary nature of consciousness poses a difficult problem, but perhaps   11
not an insurmountable one. This unitary nature can break down. In a surgical patient whose brain is severed between the two hemispheres, there are two conscious minds, each with its own unified percept.

Subjectivity, the second characteristic of conscious awareness, poses the   12
more formidable scientific challenge. Each of us experiences a world of private and unique sensations that is much more real to us than the experiences of others. We experience our own ideas, moods, and sensations directly, whereas we can only appreciate another person's experience indirectly, by observing or

---

[13] **Daniel Dennett (b. 1942)**   Professor of philosophy at Tufts University and a noted atheist.

[14] **John Hughlings Jackson (1835–1911)**   British neurologist who has done influential work in epilepsy and aphasia.

[15] **John Searle and Thomas Nagel**   John Searle (b. 1932) is a philosopher at University of California, Berkeley, and Thomas Nagel (b. 1937) is a philosopher teaching at New York University. Both have written about the mind.

hearing about it. We therefore can ask, Is your response to the blue you see and the jasmine you smell—the meaning it has for you—identical to my response to the blue I see and the jasmine I smell and the meaning these have for me?

The issue here is not one of perception per se. It is not whether we each see a very similar shade of the same blue. That is relatively easy to establish by recording from single nerve cells in the visual system of different individuals. The brain does reconstruct our perception of an object, but the object perceived—the color blue or middle C on the piano—appears to correspond to the physical properties of the wavelength of the reflected light or the frequency of the emitted sound. Instead, the issue is the significance of that blue and that note for each of us. What we do not understand is how electrical activity in neurons gives rise to the meaning we ascribe to that color or that wavelength of sound. The fact that conscious experience is unique to each person raises the question of whether it is possible to determine objectively any characteristics of consciousness that are common to everyone. If the senses ultimately produce experiences that are completely and personally subjective, we cannot, the argument goes, arrive at a general definition of consciousness based on personal experience.

Nagel and Searle illustrate the difficulty of explaining the subjective nature of consciousness in physical terms as follows: Assume we succeed in recording the electrical activity of neurons in a region known to be important for consciousness while the person being studied carries out some task that requires conscious attention. For example, suppose we identified the cells that fire when I look at and become aware of a red image of the blossoms on a rosebush at Wave Hill. We have now taken a first step in studying consciousness—namely, we have found what Crick and Koch have called the neural correlate of consciousness for this one percept. For most of us, this would be a great advance because it pinpoints a material concomitant of conscious perception. From there we could go on to carry out experiments to determine whether these correlates also meld into a coherent whole, that is, the background of the Hudson River and the Palisades. But for Nagel and Searle, this is the easy problem of consciousness. The hard problem of consciousness is the second mystery, that of subjective experience.

How is it that I respond to the red image of a rose with a feeling that is distinctive to me? To use another example, what grounds do we have for believing that when a mother looks at her child, the firing of cells in the region of the cortex concerned with face recognition accounts for the emotions she feels and for her ability to summon the memory of those emotions and that image of her child?

As yet, we do not know how the firing of specific neurons leads to the subjective component of conscious perception, even in the simplest case. In fact, according to Searle and Nagel, we lack an adequate theory of how an objective phenomenon, such as electrical signals in the brain, can cause a subjective experience, such as pain. And because science as we currently practice it is a reductionist, analytical view of complicated events, while consciousness is irreducibly subjective, such a theory lies beyond our reach for now.

According to Nagel, science cannot take on consciousness without a significant change in methodology, a change that would enable scientists to identify and analyze the elements of subjective experience. Those elements are likely to be basic components of brain function, much as atoms and molecules are basic components of matter, but to exist in a form we cannot yet imagine. The reductions performed routinely in science are not problematic, Nagel holds. Biological science can readily explain how the properties of a particular type of matter arise from the objective properties of the molecules of which it is made. What science lacks are rules for explaining how subjective properties (consciousness) arise from the properties of objects (interconnected nerve cells).   17

Nagel argues that our complete lack of insight into the elements of subjective experience should not prevent us from discovering the neural correlates of consciousness and the rules that relate conscious phenomena to cellular processes in the brain. In fact, it is only by accumulating such information that we will be in a position to think about the reduction of something subjective to something physical and objective. But to arrive at a theory that supports this reduction, we will first have to discover the elements of subjective consciousness. This discovery, says Nagel, will be enormous in its magnitude and its implications, requiring a revolution in biology and most likely a complete transformation of scientific thought.   18

The aim of most neural scientists working on consciousness is much more modest than this grand perspective would imply. They are not deliberately working toward or anticipating a revolution in scientific thought. Although they must struggle with the difficulties of defining conscious phenomena experimentally, they do not see those difficulties as precluding all experimental study under existing paradigms. Neural scientists believe, and Searle for one agrees with them, that they have been able to make considerable progress in understanding the neurobiology of perception and memory without having to account for individual experience. For example, cognitive neural scientists have made advances in understanding the neural basis of the perception of the color blue without addressing the question of how each of us responds to the same blue.   19

What we do not understand is the hard problem of consciousness—the mystery of how neural activity gives rise to subjective experience. Crick and Koch have argued that once we solve the easy problem of consciousness, the unity of consciousness, we will be able to manipulate those neural systems experimentally to solve the hard problem.   20

The unity of consciousness is a variant of the binding problem first identi-   21
fied in the study of visual perception. An intimate part of my experiencing the
subjective pleasure of the moment at Wave Hill is how the look and the smell
of roses in the gardens are bound together and unified with my view of the
Hudson, the Palisades, and all the other component images of my perception.
Each of these components of my subjective experience is mediated by different brain regions within my visual and olfactory and emotional systems. The
unity of my conscious experience implies that the binding process must somehow connect and integrate all of these separate areas in the brain.

As a first step toward solving the easy problem of consciousness, we need   22
to ask whether the unity of consciousness — a unity thought to be achieved by
neural systems that mediate selective attention — is localized in one or just a
few sites, which would enable us to manipulate them biologically. The answer
to this question is by no means clear. Gerald Edelman,[16] a leading theoretician
on the brain and consciousness, has argued effectively that the neural machinery for the unity of consciousness is likely to be widely distributed throughout
the cortex and thalamus. As a result, Edelman asserts, it is unlikely that we
will be able to find consciousness through a simple set of neural correlates.
Crick and Koch, on the other hand, believe that the unity of consciousness will
have direct neural correlates because they most likely involve a specific set
of neurons with specific molecular or neuroanatomical signatures. The neural
correlates, they argue, probably require only a small set of neurons acting as a
searchlight: the spotlight of attention. The initial task, they argue, is to locate
within the brain that small set of neurons whose activity correlates best with
the unity of conscious experience and then to determine the neural circuits to
which they belong.

How are we to find this small population of nerve cells that could medi-   23
ate the unity of consciousness? What criteria must they meet? In Crick and
Koch's last paper (which Crick was still correcting on his way to the hospital
a few hours before he died, on July 28, 2004), they focused on the claustrum, a
sheet of brain tissue that is located below the cerebral cortex, as the site that
mediates unity of experience. Little is known about the claustrum except that
it connects to and exchanges information with almost all of the sensory and
motor regions of the cortex as well as the amygdala, which plays an important
role in emotion. Crick and Koch compare the claustrum to the conductor of an
orchestra. Indeed, the neuroanatomical connections of the claustrum meet the
requirements of a conductor; it can bind together and coordinate the various
brain regions necessary for the unity of conscious awareness.

The idea that obsessed Crick at the end of his life — that the claustrum is   24
the spotlight of attention, the site that binds the various components of any

---

[16] **Gerald Edelman (1929–2014)**   Neuroscientist who won the Nobel Prize in Physiology
or Medicine. He was professor at the Scripps Research Institute in California.

percept together—is the last in a series of important ideas he advanced. Crick's enormous contributions to biology (the double helical structure of DNA, the nature of the genetic code, the discovery of messenger RNA, the mechanisms of translating messenger RNA into the amino acid sequence of a protein, and the legitimizing of the biology of consciousness) put him in a class with Copernicus, Newton, Darwin, and Einstein. Yet his intense, lifelong focus on science, on the life of mind, is something he shares with many in the scientific community, and that obsession is symbolic of science at its best. The cognitive psychologist Vilayanur Ramachandran,[17] a friend and colleague of Crick's, described Crick's focus on the claustrum during his last weeks:

> Three weeks prior to his death I visited him in his home in La Jolla. He was eighty-eight, had terminal cancer, was in pain, and was on chemotherapy; yet he had obviously been working away nonstop on his latest project. His very large desk—occupying half the room— was covered by articles, correspondence, envelopes, recent issues of *Nature*, a laptop (despite his dislike of computers), and recent books on neuroanatomy. During the whole two hours that I was there, there was no mention of his illness—only a flight of ideas on the neural basis of consciousness. He was especially interested in a tiny structure called the claustrum which, he felt, had been largely ignored by mainstream pundits. As I was leaving he said: "Rama, I think the secret of consciousness lies in the claustrum—don't you? Why else would this tiny structure be connected to so many areas in the brain?"—And gave me a sly, conspiratorial wink. It was the last time I saw him.

Since so little is known about the claustrum, Crick continued, he wanted   25
to start an institute to focus on its function. In particular, he wanted to determine whether the claustrum is switched on when unconscious, subliminal perception of a given stimulus by a person's sensory organs turns into a conscious percept.

One example of such switching that intrigued Crick and Koch is binoc-   26
ular rivalry. Here, two different images—say, vertical stripes and horizontal stripes—are presented to a person simultaneously in such a way that each eye sees only one set of stripes. The person may combine the two images and report seeing a plaid, but more commonly the person will see first one image, then the next, with horizontal and vertical stripes alternating back and forth spontaneously.

---

[17] **Vilayanur Ramachandran (b. 1951)**   Neuroscientist professor at the University of California, San Diego. He is the director of the Center for Brain and Cognition and author of *Phantoms in the Brain* (1999).

Using MRI, Eric Lumer[18] and his colleagues at University College, London have identified the frontal and parietal areas of the cortex as the regions of the brain that become active when a person's conscious attention switches from one image to another. These two regions have a special role in focusing conscious attention on objects in space. In turn, the prefrontal and posterior parietal regions of the cortex seem to relay the decision regarding which image is to be enhanced to the visual system, which then brings the image into consciousness. Indeed, people with damage to the prefrontal cortex have difficulty switching from one image to the other in situations of binocular rivalry. Crick and Koch might argue that the frontal and parietal areas of the cortex are recruited by the claustrum, which switches attention from one eye to the other and unifies the image presented to conscious awareness by each eye.

27

As these arguments make clear, consciousness remains an enormous problem. But through the efforts of Edelman on the one hand, and Crick and Koch on the other, we now have two specific and testable theories worthy of exploration.

28

As someone interested in psychoanalysis, I wanted to take the Crick-Koch paradigm of comparing unconscious and conscious perception of the same stimulus to the next step: determining how visual perception becomes endowed with emotion. Unlike simple visual perception, emotionally charged visual perception is likely to differ between individuals. Therefore, a further question is, How and where are unconscious emotional perceptions processed?

29

Amit Etkin,[19] a bold and creative M.D.-Ph.D. student, and I undertook a study in collaboration with Joy Hirsch,[20] a brain imager at Columbia, in which we induced conscious and unconscious perceptions of emotional stimuli. Our approach paralleled in the emotional sphere that of Crick and Koch in the cognitive sphere. We explored how normal people respond consciously and unconsciously to pictures of people with a clearly neutral expression or an expression of fear on their faces. The pictures were provided by Peter Ekman[21] at the University of California, San Francisco.

30

Ekman, who has cataloged more than 100,000 human expressions, was able to show, as did Charles Darwin before him, that irrespective of sex or culture, conscious perceptions of seven facial expressions—happiness, fear, disgust, contempt, anger, surprise, and sadness—have virtually the same meaning to everyone (figure 1). We therefore argued that fearful faces should elicit a similar response from the healthy young medical and graduate student volunteers

31

---

[18] **Eric Lumer**   British neuroscientist.

[19] **Amit Etkin (b. 1976)**   Stanford University psychiatrist.

[20] **Joy Hirsch**   Professor at Columbia University, studying neurological disorders.

[21] **Peter Ekman**   American photographer.

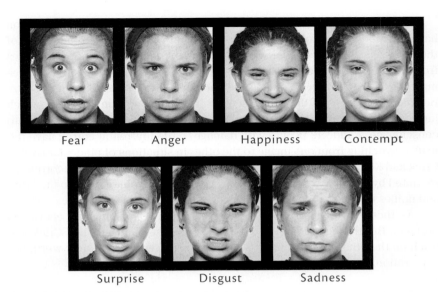

Fig. 1 Ekman's seven universal facial expressions. (© Paul Ekman 2003.)

in our study, regardless of whether they perceived the stimulus consciously or unconsciously. We produced a conscious perception of fear by presenting the fearful faces for a long period, so people had time to reflect on them. We produced unconscious perception of fear by presenting the same faces so rapidly that the volunteers were unable to report which type of expression they had seen. Indeed, they were not even sure they had seen a face!

Since even normal people differ in their sensitivity to a threat, we gave all of the volunteers a questionnaire designed to measure background anxiety. In contrast to the momentary anxiety most people feel in a new situation, background anxiety reflects an enduring baseline trait.   32

Not surprisingly, when we showed the volunteers pictures of faces with fearful expressions, we found prominent activity in the amygdala,[22] the structure deep in the brain that mediates fear. What was surprising was that conscious and unconscious stimuli affected different regions of the amygdala, and they did so to differing degrees in different people, depending on their baseline anxiety.   33

Unconscious perception of fearful faces activated the basolateral nucleus. In people, as in mice, this area of the amygdala receives most of the incoming sensory information and is the primary means by which the amygdala   34

---

[22] **amygdala**   Small almond-shaped nuclei, one in each hemisphere of the brain, associated with emotional responses and the processing of memory.

communicates with the cortex. Activation of the basolateral nucleus by unconscious perception of fearful faces occurred in direct proportion to a person's
background anxiety: the higher the measure of background anxiety, the
greater the person's response. People with low background anxiety had no
response at all. Conscious perception of fearful faces, in contrast, activated
the dorsal region of the amygdala, which contains the central nucleus, and it
did so regardless of a person's background anxiety. The central nucleus of the
amygdala sends information to regions of the brain that are part of the auto-
nomic nervous system—concerned with arousal and defensive responses. In
sum, unconsciously perceived threats disproportionately affect people with
high background anxiety, whereas consciously perceived threats activate the
fight-or-flight response in all volunteers.

We also found that unconscious and conscious perception of fearful faces   35
activates different neural networks outside the amygdala. Here again, the networks activated by unconsciously perceived threats were recruited only by the
anxious volunteers. Surprisingly, even unconscious perception recruits participation of regions within the cerebral cortex.

Thus viewing frightening stimuli activates two different brain systems, one   36
that involves conscious, presumably top-down attention and one that involves
unconscious, bottom-up attention, or vigilance, much as a signal of salience
does in explicit and implicit memory in *Aplysia* and in the mouse.

These are fascinating results. First, they show that in the realm of emotion,   37
as in the realm of perception, a stimulus can be perceived both unconsciously
and consciously. They also support Crick and Koch's idea that in perception,
distinct areas of the brain are correlated with conscious and unconscious
awareness of a stimulus. Second, these studies confirm biologically the importance of the psychoanalytic idea of unconscious emotion. They suggest that the
effects of anxiety are exerted most dramatically in the brain when the stimulus
is left to the imagination rather than when it is perceived consciously. Once the
image of a frightened face is confronted consciously, even anxious people can
accurately appraise whether it truly poses a threat.

A century after Freud suggested that psychopathology arises from conflict   38
occurring on an unconscious level and that it can be regulated if the source
of the conflict is confronted consciously, our imaging studies suggest ways in
which such conflicting processes may be mediated in the brain. Moreover, the
discovery of a correlation between volunteers' background anxiety and their
unconscious neural processes validates biologically the Freudian idea that
unconscious mental processes are part of the brain's system of information
processing. While Freud's ideas have existed for more than one hundred years,
no previous brain-imaging study had tried to account for how differences
in people's behavior and interpretations of the world arise from differences
in how they unconsciously process emotion. The finding that unconscious

perception of fear lights up the basolateral nucleus of the amygdala in direct proportion to a person's baseline anxiety provides a biological marker for diagnosing an anxiety state and for evaluating the efficacy of various drugs and forms of psychotherapy.

In discerning a correlation between the activity of a neural circuit and the unconscious and conscious perception of a threat, we are beginning to delineate the neural correlate of an emotion—fear. That description might well lead us to a scientific explanation of consciously perceived fear. It might give us an approximation of how neural events give rise to a mental event that enters our awareness. Thus, a half century after I left psychoanalysis for the biology of mind, the new biology of mind is getting ready to tackle some of the issues central to psychoanalysis and consciousness.   39

One such issue is the nature of free will. Given Freud's discovery of psychic determinism—the fact that much of our cognitive and affective life is unconscious—what is left for personal choice, for freedom of action?   40

A critical set of experiments on this question was carried out in 1983 by Benjamin Libet[23] at the University of California, San Francisco. Libet used as his starting point a discovery made by the German neuroscientist Hans Kornhuber.[24] In his study, Kornhuber asked volunteers to move their right index finger. He then measured this voluntary movement with a strain gauge while at the same time recording the electrical activity of the brain by means of an electrode on the skull. After hundreds of trials, Kornhuber found that, invariably, each movement was preceded by a little blip in the electrical record from the brain, a spark of free will! He called this potential in the brain the "readiness potential" and found that it occurred 1 second before the voluntary movement.   41

Libet followed up on Kornhuber's finding with an experiment in which he asked volunteers to lift a finger whenever they felt the urge to do so. He placed an electrode on a volunteer's skull and confirmed a readiness potential about 1 second before the person lifted his or her finger. He then compared the time it took for the person to will the movement with the time of the readiness potential. Amazingly, Libet found that the readiness potential appeared not after, but 200 milliseconds before a person felt the urge to move his or her finger! Thus by merely observing the electrical activity of the brain, Libet could predict what a person would do before the person was actually aware of having decided to do it.   42

This finding has caused philosophers of mind to ask: If the choice is determined in the brain before we decide to act, where is free will? Is our sense of willing our movements only an illusion, a rationalization after the fact for what   43

---

[23] **Benjamin Libet (1916–2007)**   A professor of neurology at the University of California, San Francisco; winner of the first Virtual Nobel Prize in psychology.

[24] **Hans Kornhuber (1928–2009)**   Professor at the University of Freiburg, Germany.

has happened? Or is the choice made freely, but not consciously? If so, choice in action, as in perception, may reflect the importance of unconscious inference. Libet proposes that the process of initiating a voluntary action occurs in an unconscious part of the brain, but that just before the action is initiated, consciousness is recruited to approve or veto the action. In the 200 milliseconds before a finger is lifted, consciousness determines whether it moves or not.

Whatever the reasons for the delay between decision and awareness,   44 Libet's findings also raise the moral question: How can one be held responsible for decisions that are made without conscious awareness? The psychologists Richard Gregory and Vilayanur Ramachandran have drawn strict limits on that argument. They point out that "our conscious mind may not have free will, but it does have free won't." Michael Gazzaniga,[25] one of the pioneers in the development of cognitive neuroscience and a member of the American Council of Bioethics, has added, "Brains are automatic, but people are free." One cannot infer the sum total of neural activity simply by looking at a few neural circuits in the brain.

---

[25] **Michael Gazzaniga (b. 1939)**   Heads the Sage Center for the Study of the Mind at the University of California at Santa Barbara. He has done extensive work on the split brain. See p. 784.

▟ QUESTIONS FOR CRITICAL READING

1. How do modern scientists explore the question of consciousness experimentally?

2. What is the relation of the conscious mind to the unconscious mind?

3. How does the conscious mind go beyond just the experience of pleasure and pain?

4. Is consciousness biological?

5. What did René Descartes believe about the mind?

6. Why have we made little headway in understanding consciousness?

7. To what extent may it be possible to identify consciousness with molecular activity?

▟ SUGGESTIONS FOR CRITICAL WRITING

1. Kandel mentions several parts of the brain: the hippocampus, the frontal and parietal lobes, and the amygdala. Research these parts of the brain, and write a brief essay that explains their functions to someone who may not have read this essay. Try to bring your reader up to date on the most contemporary knowledge about these neurological features and how they function.

2. James Crick thought that "the secret of consciousness" (para. 24) was in the claustrum, a little studied portion of the brain. Research the claustrum online and in your library. What functions does it perform in the brain? Crick discusses his understanding of neurobiology in his last book *The Astonishing Hypothesis* (1994). What has been learned about the claustrum since Crick became interested in it?

3. When discussing Descartes, Kandel reviews a position that sees the mind as separate from the brain. Gilbert Ryle (p. 514), on the other hand, sees the mind as a function of the brain. Given what you have understood from your reading on this matter, where do you stand? In a brief essay, relying on the evidence of your reading and/or your research, decide what the status of consciousness is. Is it a product of physiology, or is it a product of something else? What is the primary evidence that convinces you? Make an argument to convince others of your views.

4. In paragraph 37, Kandel talks about conscious and unconscious awareness of a stimulus. He says, "the effects of anxiety are exerted most dramatically in the brain when the stimulus is left to the imagination rather than when it is perceived consciously." What are the chief forms of imagination in your own experience? Would film or literature constitute stimuli of imagination? How responsive are you to your imagination? When do you sense that imagination has produced anxiety? What is the relationship between imagination and consciousness?

5. In paragraphs 41 and 42, Kandel refers to experiments by Libet and Kornhuber that track the path of a person's movement of his or her finger from the person's decision to move the finger to the activity of the brain that moves the finger and, finally, to the actual movement of the finger. Kandel says this experiment calls into question whether or not we have free will. Review what Kandel writes on this subject and then check the literature to see what the current thinking is. Search "Benjamin Libet's experiment." Where do you stand on the question of free will? Is the unconscious mind sometimes dominant over the conscious mind? What does that mean for us?

6. When discussing the possibility that we may not have free will, Ramachandran and his researchers say that although we may not have free will, we have "free won't" (para. 44). What does that really mean? Explore this issue and write a brief essay that explains how "free won't" helps to qualify the question of whether or not people have free will and are responsible for their actions. If, in fact, the unconscious directs our action, should we be held responsible for things we do that we are not consciously aware of doing? What are the legal implications?

7. **CONNECTIONS**   With reference to Robert Nozick's (p. 528) ideas about emotions, how does the information presented in Kandel's essay, in paragraphs 29 to 37, about the conscious and unconscious perception of emotions help

us understand Nozick's ideas? How would Nozick react to the experiments by Amit Etkin and Joy Hirsch as well as to the photographs by Peter Ekman? How do you respond to the expressions on the faces illustrating emotions? Do you agree that each face is properly labeled with the emotion ascribed to it? If possible, take some photographs of yourself consciously expressing a range of emotions. Label each as you take the photo (so you don't forget) and see if others can identify the emotion you are expressing. Do you support Kandel's conclusions about the perception of emotions on people's faces?

© Time-Life Pictures/Getty Images

HOWARD
GARDNER

A Rounded Version: The Theory of Multiple Intelligences

H OWARD GARDNER (b. 1943), Hobbs Professor of Cognition and Education at the Harvard Graduate School of Education, is senior director of Harvard's Project Zero, a program dedicated to improving education in schools by emphasizing creativity in thinking and problem solving. By emphasizing the arts and the newer electronic technologies associated with learning, the program cultivates a "culture of thinking" in the classroom as opposed to a culture of rote learning. Gardner has received a MacArthur Foundation award (1981), which supported his research for five years, and has won a number of important awards in the field of education, including the Grawemeyer Award in Education (1990), given for the first time to an American. Among his many books are *Leading Minds: An Anatomy of Leadership* (1995) and *Extraordinary Minds: Portraits of Exceptional Individuals and an Examination of Our Extraordinariness* (1997).

Perhaps the most important and best-known product of Project Zero is the theory of multiple intelligences, which Gardner first published in *Frames of Mind* (1983). (His more recent book, *Intelligence Reframed: Multiple Intelligence for the 21st Century* [1999], offers a revisitation and more detailed elaboration on multiple intelligence theory and its application.) In *Frames of Mind*, he noted that the general attitude toward intelligence centers on the IQ (intelligence quotient) test that Alfred Binet (1857–1911) devised. Binet believed that intelligence is measurable and that IQ tests result in numerical scores that are reliable indicators of a more or less permanent basic intelligence. Gardner offered several objections to that view. One was that IQ predictors might point to achievement in schools and colleges but not necessarily to achievement in life. For example, students with middling scores performed at extraordinary levels in business, politics, and other walks of

From *Multiple Intelligences: The Theory in Practice.*

life, whereas high-achieving students often settled for middling careers. The reports on high-performing executives indicated a considerable intelligence at work, but it was not necessarily the kind of intelligence that could be measured by the Binet tests.

Gardner also was intrigued by findings that local regions of the brain controlled specific functions of the mind. For example, studies had established that certain regions of the brain were specialized for language functions, whereas others were specialized for physical movement, music, mathematics, and other skills. When those portions of the brain suffered damage, as with stroke or accident, the functions for which they were specialized were adversely affected. These observations, which were plentiful in the work of neurologists during and after World War II, led Gardner to propose the existence of a variety of intelligences rather than only one.

As he explains in the following essay from his book *Multiple Intelligences: The Theory in Practice* (1993), his studies led him to propose seven distinct intelligences. The first is linguistic, which naturally includes language. This intelligence applies not only to learning languages but also to using language well — as, for example, in the case of poets and writers. The second is logical-mathematical, which refers to the applications of mathematics and of logical reasoning. Our society uses these verbal-mathematical forms of intelligence as the practical measure of intelligence: the SATs, for instance, depend almost entirely on measuring these forms.

Gardner adds five more forms of intelligence. Spatial intelligence concerns the ways in which we perceive and imagine spatial relations. Some people, such as architects and sculptors, are clearly more gifted than others at imagining space. Musical intelligence is seen as distinct from other forms of intelligence if only because some people, such as child prodigies, are apparently born with superior musical abilities. Bodily-kinesthetic intelligence shows up in dancers and athletes, like Mikhail Baryshnikov and Jackie Joyner-Kersee, who perform extraordinarily with their bodies. But bodily-kinesthetic intelligence also applies to detailed physical work, such as the manipulations necessary for the work of surgeons, dentists, and craftspeople, such as weavers, potters, metalworkers, and jewelers.

Finally, Gardner also defines two kinds of personal intelligence that are difficult to isolate and study but that he feels must be regarded as forms of intelligence. Interpersonal intelligence concerns the way we get along with other people. People with high interpersonal intelligence might be salespeople, teachers, politicians, or evangelists. They respond to others and are sensitive to their needs and their concerns. They understand cooperation, compromise, and respect for other people's views. The second kind of personal intelligence — intrapersonal — refers to how one understands oneself. The self-knowledge to recognize one's strengths and weaknesses and to avoid an inflated sense of self-importance constitutes a high degree of intrapersonal intelligence.

Gardner sees all these intelligences working together in the individual. As he says, when one of them dominates, the individual can appear freakish, as in the person with autism who easily multiplies huge numbers in his head but cannot relate to other human beings. Because the individual must nurture all these intelligences to develop into a complete person, Gardner is working to revise educational practices to reflect all varieties of intelligence.

Greeks in the time of Plato and Aristotle seem to have understood much of what Gardner says. They included music and dance, for example, in the curriculum of their schools. They developed linguistic and interpersonal skills in the teaching of rhetoric and made logic and mathematics central to their teaching. One of Socrates' most famous statements, in fact — "Know thyself" — admonishes us to develop intrapersonal intelligence.

GARDNER'S RHETORIC

Rather than open the essay by describing the multiple intelligences, Gardner starts with a dramatic scene and a hypothetical story. He describes two eleven-year-old children who take an IQ test and then are regarded in special ways by their teachers: one is expected to do well in school, the other is expected to do less well. The expectations are met. But years later the student with the lower IQ is vastly more successful in business than the student who scored higher. Why is this so? The rest of the essay answers that implied rhetorical question.

One of the most important devices Gardner relies on is enumeration. He has seven different kinds of intelligence to discuss and takes each one in turn. The reader is not aware of a special range of importance to the seven forms of intelligence: the first, musical intelligence, is not necessarily the most important or the first to be recognized in an individual. Bodily-kinesthetic is not necessarily less important because it comes after musical intelligence. By placing logical-mathematical intelligence in the middle of the sequence, Gardner suggests that this form of intelligence, which our society traditionally treats as first in importance, should take its place beside a range of intelligences that are all more or less equal in value.

Just as important as the use of enumeration is Gardner's use of parallelism in the structure of each of the intelligences he enumerates. For each he offers a subhead that identifies the specific intelligence and then a "sketch with a thumbnail biography" that helps establish the nature of the intelligence. Then Gardner discusses the details of each intelligence and suggests ways in which it may relate to other forms of intelligence. This method has the advantage of extreme clarity. Likewise, paralleling examples and quotations in describing each intelligence makes the point over and over and ultimately produces a convincing argument without the appearance of argument.

Gardner makes another important rhetorical decision regarding the size and nature of the paragraphs. Modern readers, conditioned by newspapers and magazines, expect paragraphs to be short and direct. Gardner's paragraphs reflect a decision to communicate with a general reading audience rather than an audience of specialists or specially educated readers. For that reason, a single subject may sometimes be discussed in two or more adjacent paragraphs, with the paragraph break acting as a "breather" (see paras. 19–20 and 22–23).

All these rhetorical devices aid the reader in absorbing complex material. Gardner's primary efforts in this essay are to facilitate communication. He keeps his language simple, his sentences direct, and his paragraphs brief. For the modern reader, this is a recipe for understanding.

⚡ PREREADING QUESTIONS: WHAT TO READ FOR

The following prereading questions may help you anticipate key issues in the discussion of Howard Gardner's "A Rounded Version: The Theory of Multiple Intelligences." Keeping them in mind during your first reading of the selection should help focus your attention.

1. What constitutes an intelligence, according to Gardner?
2. What is the most compelling evidence for the theory of multiple intelligences?

A Rounded Version: The Theory of Multiple Intelligences

Coauthored by Joseph Walters

Two eleven-year-old children are taking a test of "intelligence." They sit at their desks laboring over the meanings of different words, the interpretation of graphs, and the solutions to arithmetic problems. They record their answers by filling in small circles on a single piece of paper. Later these completed answer sheets are scored objectively: the number of right answers is converted into a standardized score that compares the individual child with a population of children of similar age.

The teachers of these children review the different scores. They notice that one of the children has performed at a superior level; on all sections of the test, she answered more questions correctly than did her peers. In fact, her score is similar to that of children three to four years older. The other child's performance is average—his scores reflect those of other children his age.

A subtle change in expectations surrounds the review of these test scores. Teachers begin to expect the first child to do quite well during her formal schooling, whereas the second should have only moderate success. Indeed these predictions come true. In other words, the test taken by the eleven-year-olds serves as a reliable predictor of their later performance in school.

How does this happen? One explanation involves our free use of the word "intelligence": the child with the greater "intelligence" has the ability to solve problems, to find the answers to specific questions, and to learn new material quickly and efficiently. These skills in turn play a central role in school success. In this view, "intelligence" is a singular faculty that is brought to bear in any problem-solving situation. Since schooling deals largely with solving problems of various sorts, predicting this capacity in young children predicts their future success in school.

"Intelligence," from this point of view, is a general ability that is found in   5
varying degrees in all individuals. It is the key to success in solving problems. This ability can be measured reliably with standardized pencil-and-paper tests that, in turn, predict future success in school.

What happens after school is completed? Consider the two individuals in   6
the example. Looking further down the road, we find that the "average" student has become a highly successful mechanical engineer who has risen to a position of prominence in both the professional community of engineers as well as in civic groups in his community. His success is no fluke—he is considered by all to be a talented individual. The "superior" student, on the other hand, has had little success in her chosen career as a writer; after repeated rejections by publishers, she has taken up a middle management position in a bank. While certainly not a "failure," she is considered by her peers to be quite "ordinary" in her adult accomplishments. So what happened?

This fabricated example is based on the facts of intelligence testing.   7
IQ tests predict school performance with considerable accuracy, but they are only an indifferent predictor of performance in a profession after formal school-ing.[1] Furthermore, even as IQ tests measure only logical or logical-linguistic capacities, in this society we are nearly "brain-washed" to restrict the notion of intelligence to the capacities used in solving logical and linguistic problems.

To introduce an alternative point of view, undertake the following "thought   8
experiment." Suspend the usual judgment of what constitutes intelligence and let your thoughts run freely over the capabilities of humans—perhaps those that would be picked out by the proverbial Martian visitor. In this exercise, you are drawn to the brilliant chess player, the world-class violinist, and the champion athlete; such outstanding performers deserve special consideration. Under this experiment, a quite different view of *intelligence* emerges. Are the chess player, violinist, and athlete "intelligent" in these pursuits? If they are, then why do our tests of "intelligence" fail to identify them? If they are not "intelligent," what allows them to achieve such astounding feats? In general, why does the contemporary construct "intelligence" fail to explain large areas of human endeavor?

In this chapter we approach these problems through the theory of multi-   9
ple intelligences (MI). As the name indicates, we believe that human cognitive competence is better described in terms of a set of abilities, talents, or men-tal skills, which we call "intelligences." All normal individuals possess each of these skills to some extent; individuals differ in the degree of skill and in the nature of their combination. We believe this theory of intelligence may be

---

[1] Jencks, C. (1972). *Inequality.* New York: Basic Books. [Gardner's note]

more humane and more veridical[2] than alternative views of intelligence and that it more adequately reflects the data of human "intelligent" behavior. Such a theory has important educational implications, including ones for curriculum development.

What Constitutes an Intelligence?

The question of the optimal definition of intelligence looms large in our inquiry. Indeed, it is at the level of this definition that the theory of multiple intelligences diverges from traditional points of view. In a traditional view, intelligence is defined operationally as the ability to answer items on tests of intelligence. The inference from the test scores to some underlying ability is supported by statistical techniques that compare responses of subjects at different ages; the apparent correlation of these test scores across ages and across different tests corroborates the notion that the general faculty of intelligence, *g*, does not change much with age or with training or experience. It is an inborn attribute or faculty of the individual.

10

Multiple intelligences theory, on the other hand, pluralizes the traditional concept. An intelligence entails the ability to solve problems or fashion products that are of consequence in a particular cultural setting or community. The problem-solving skill allows one to approach a situation in which a goal is to be obtained and to locate the appropriate route to that goal. The creation of a *cultural* product is crucial to such functions as capturing and transmitting knowledge or expressing one's views or feelings. The problems to be solved range from creating an end for a story to anticipating a mating move in chess to repairing a quilt. Products range from scientific theories to musical compositions to successful political campaigns.

11

MI theory is framed in light of the biological origins of each problem-solving skill. Only those skills that are universal to the human species are treated. Even so, the biological proclivity to participate in a particular form of problem solving must also be coupled with the cultural nurturing of that domain. For example, language, a universal skill, may manifest itself particularly as writing in one culture, as oratory in another culture, and as the secret language of anagrams in a third.

12

Given the desire of selecting intelligences that are rooted in biology, and that are valued in one or more cultural settings, how does one actually identify an "intelligence"? In coming up with our list, we consulted evidence from several different sources: knowledge about normal development and development in gifted individuals; information about the breakdown of cognitive skills under

13

---

[2] **veridical**　Telling the truth.

conditions of brain damage; studies of exceptional populations, including prodigies, idiots savants, and autistic children; data about the evolution of cognition over the millennia; cross-cultural accounts of cognition; psychometric studies, including examinations of correlations among tests; and psychological training studies, particularly measures of transfer and generalization across tasks. Only those candidate intelligences that satisfied all or a majority of the criteria were selected as bona fide intelligences. A more complete discussion of each of these criteria for an "intelligence" and the seven intelligences that have been proposed so far is found in *Frames of Mind*.[3] This book also considers how the theory might be disproven and compares it to competing theories of intelligence.

In addition to satisfying the aforementioned criteria, each intelligence   14
must have an identifiable core operation or set of operations. As a neutrally based computational system, each intelligence is activated or "triggered" by certain kinds of internally or externally presented information. For example, one core of musical intelligence is the sensitivity to pitch relations, whereas one core of linguistic intelligence is the sensitivity to phonological features.

An intelligence must also be susceptible to encoding in a symbol system — a   15
culturally contrived system of meaning, which captures and conveys important forms of information. Language, picturing, and mathematics are but three nearly worldwide symbol systems that are necessary for human survival and productivity. The relationship of a candidate intelligence to a human symbol system is no accident. In fact, the existence of a core computational capacity anticipates the existence of a symbol system that exploits that capacity. While it may be possible for an intelligence to proceed without an accompanying symbol system, a primary characteristic of human intelligence may well be its gravitation toward such an embodiment.

The Seven Intelligences

Having sketched the characteristics and criteria of an intelligence, we turn now   16
to a brief consideration of each of the seven intelligences. We begin each sketch with a thumbnail biography of a person who demonstrates an unusual facility with that intelligence. These biographies illustrate some of the abilities that are central to the fluent operation of a given intelligence. Although each biography illustrates a particular intelligence, we do not wish to imply that in adulthood intelligences operate in isolation. Indeed, except for abnormal individuals,

---

[3] Gardner, H. (1983). *Frames of Mind: The Theory of Multiple Intelligences.* New York: Basic Books. [Gardner's note]

intelligences always work in concert, and any sophisticated adult role will involve a melding of several of them. Following each biography we survey the various sources of data that support each candidate as an "intelligence."

Musical Intelligence

When he was three years old, Yehudi Menuhin was smuggled into the San Francisco Orchestra concerts by his parents. The sound of Louis Persinger's violin so entranced the youngster that he insisted on a violin for his birthday and Louis Persinger as his teacher. He got both. By the time he was ten years old, Menuhin was an international performer.[4]

Violinist Yehudi Menuhin's musical intelligence manifested itself even before he had touched a violin or received any musical training. His powerful reaction to that particular sound and his rapid progress on the instrument suggest that he was biologically prepared in some way for that endeavor. In this way evidence from child prodigies supports our claim that there is a biological link to a particular intelligence. Other special populations, such as autistic children who can play a musical instrument beautifully but who cannot speak, underscore the independence of musical intelligence.   17

A brief consideration of the evidence suggests that musical skill passes the other tests for an intelligence. For example, certain parts of the brain play important roles in perception and production of music. These areas are characteristically located in the right hemisphere, although musical skill is not as clearly "localized," or located in a specifiable area, as language. Although the particular susceptibility of musical ability to brain damage depends on the degree of training and other individual differences, there is clear evidence for "amusia" or loss of musical ability.   18

Music apparently played an important unifying role in Stone Age (Paleolithic) societies. Birdsong provides a link to other species. Evidence from various cultures supports the notion that music is a universal faculty. Studies of infant development suggest that there is a "raw" computational ability in early childhood. Finally, musical notation provides an accessible and lucid symbol system.   19

In short, evidence to support the interpretation of musical ability as an "intelligence" comes from many different sources. Even though musical skill is not typically considered an intellectual skill like mathematics, it qualifies under our criteria. By definition it deserves consideration; and in view of the data, its inclusion is empirically justified.   20

---

[4] Menuhin, Y. (1977). *Unfinished Journey*. New York: Knopf. [Gardner's note]

Bodily-Kinesthetic Intelligence

Fifteen-year-old Babe Ruth played third base. During one game his team's pitcher was doing very poorly and Babe loudly criticized him from third base. Brother Mathias, the coach, called out, "Ruth, if you know so much about it, YOU pitch!" Babe was surprised and embarrassed because he had never pitched before, but Brother Mathias insisted. Ruth said later that at the very moment he took the pitcher's mound, he KNEW he was supposed to be a pitcher and that it was "natural" for him to strike people out. Indeed, he went on to become a great major league pitcher (and, of course, attained legendary status as a hitter).[5]

Like Menuhin, Babe Ruth was a child prodigy who recognized his "instrument" immediately upon his first exposure to it. This recognition occurred in advance of formal training.   21

Control of bodily movement is, of course, localized in the motor cortex, with each hemisphere dominant or controlling bodily movements on the contra-lateral side. In right-handers, the dominance for such movement is ordinarily found in the left hemisphere. The ability to perform movements when directed to do so can be impaired even in individuals who can perform the same movements reflexively or on a nonvoluntary basis. The existence of specific *apraxia*[6] constitutes one line of evidence for a bodily-kinesthetic intelligence.   22

The evolution of specialized body movements is of obvious advantage to the species, and in humans this adaptation is extended through the use of tools. Body movement undergoes a clearly defined developmental schedule in children. And there is little question of its universality across cultures. Thus it appears that bodily-kinesthetic "knowledge" satisfies many of the criteria for an intelligence.   23

The consideration of bodily-kinesthetic knowledge as "problem solving" may be less intuitive. Certainly carrying out a mime sequence or hitting a tennis ball is not solving a mathematical equation. And yet, the ability to use one's body to express an emotion (as in a dance), to play a game (as in a sport), or to create a new product (as in devising an invention) is evidence of the cognitive features of body usage. The specific computations required to solve a particular bodily-kinesthetic *problem*, hitting a tennis ball, are summarized by Tim Gallwey: 24

> At the moment the ball leaves the server's racket, the brain calculates approximately where it will land and where the racket will intercept it.

---

[5] Connor, A. (1982). *Voices from Cooperstown.* New York: Collier. (Based on a quotation taken from *The Babe Ruth Story*, Babe Ruth & Bob Considine. New York: Dutton, 1948.) [Gardner's note]

[6] *apraxia*   A neurological disorder characterized by an inability to execute purposeful movements despite having the desire or physical ability to do so.

This calculation includes the initial velocity of the ball, combined with an input for the progressive decrease in velocity and the effect of wind and after the bounce of the ball. Simultaneously, muscle orders are given: not just once, but constantly with refined and updated information. The muscles must cooperate. A movement of the feet occurs, the racket is taken back, the face of the racket kept at a constant angle. Contact is made at a precise point that depends on whether the order was given to hit down the line or cross-court, an order not given until after a split-second analysis of the movement and balance of the opponent.

To return an average serve, you have about one second to do this. To hit the ball at all is remarkable and yet not uncommon. The truth is that everyone who inhabits a human body possesses a remarkable creation.[7]

Logical-Mathematical Intelligence. In 1983 Barbara McClintock won   25 the Nobel Prize in medicine or physiology for her work in microbiology. Her intellectual powers of deduction and observation illustrate one form of logical-mathematical intelligence that is often labeled "scientific thinking." One incident is particularly illuminating. While a researcher at Cornell in the 1920s McClintock was faced one day with a problem: while *theory* predicted 50-percent pollen sterility in corn, her research assistant (in the "field") was finding plants that were only 25- to 30-percent sterile. Disturbed by this discrepancy, McClintock left the cornfield and returned to her office, where she sat for half an hour, thinking:

> Suddenly I jumped up and ran back to the (corn) field. At the top of the field (the others were still at the bottom) I shouted "Eureka, I have it! I know what the 30% sterility is!" . . . They asked me to prove it. I sat down with a paper bag and a pencil and I started from scratch, which I had not done at all in my laboratory. It had all been done so fast; the answer came and I ran. Now I worked it out step by step—it was an intricate series of steps—and I came out with [the same result]. [They] looked at the material and it was exactly as I'd said it was; it worked out exactly as I had diagrammed it. Now, why did I know, without having done it on paper? Why was I so sure?[8]

This anecdote illustrates two essential facts of the logical-mathematical   26 intelligence. First, in the gifted individual, the process of problem solving is often remarkably rapid—the successful scientist copes with many variables at once and creates numerous hypotheses that are each evaluated and then accepted or rejected in turn.

---

[7] Gallwey, T. (1976). *Inner Tennis*. New York: Random House. [Gardner's note]

[8] Keller, E. (1983). *A Feeling for the Organism* (p. 104). Salt Lake City: W. H. Freeman. [Gardner's note]

The anecdote also underscores the *nonverbal* nature of the intelligence. 27
A solution to a problem can be constructed *before* it is articulated. In fact,
the solution process may be totally invisible, even to the problem solver. This
need not imply, however, that discoveries of this sort—the familiar "Aha!"
phenomenon—are mysterious, intuitive, or unpredictable. The fact that it happens more frequently to some people (perhaps Nobel Prize winners) suggests the
opposite. We interpret this as the work of the logical-mathematical intelligence.

Along with the companion skill of language, logical-mathematical reason- 28
ing provides the principal basis for IQ tests. This form of intelligence has been
heavily investigated by traditional psychologists, and it is the archetype of
"raw intelligence" or the problem-solving faculty that purportedly cuts across
domains. It is perhaps ironic, then, that the actual mechanism by which one
arrives at a solution to a logical-mathematical problem is not as yet properly
understood.

This intelligence is supported by our empirical criteria as well. Certain 29
areas of the brain are more prominent in mathematical calculation than others.
There are idiots savants who perform great feats of calculation even though
they remain tragically deficient in most other areas. Child prodigies in mathematics abound. The development of this intelligence in children has been carefully documented by Jean Piaget and other psychologists.

Linguistic Intelligence

At the age of ten, T. S. Eliot created a magazine called "Fireside" to
which he was the sole contributor. In a three-day period during his
winter vacation, he created eight complete issues. Each one included
poems, adventure stories, a gossip column, and humor. Some of this
material survives and it displays the talent of the poet.[9]

As with the logical intelligence, calling linguistic skill an "intelligence" is 30
consistent with the stance of traditional psychology. Linguistic intelligence
also passes our empirical tests. For instance, a specific area of the brain, called
"Broca's Area," is responsible for the production of grammatical sentences. A
person with damage to this area can understand words and sentences quite
well but has difficulty putting words together in anything other than the simplest of sentences. At the same time, other thought processes may be entirely
unaffected.

The gift of language is universal, and its development in children is strik- 31
ingly constant across cultures. Even in deaf populations where a manual sign

---

[9] Soldo, J. (1982). Jovial juvenilia: T. S. Eliot's first magazine. *Biography*, 5, 25–37. [Gardner's
note]

language is not explicitly taught, children will often "invent" their own manual language and use it surreptitiously! We thus see how an intelligence may operate independently of a specific input modality or output channel.

Spatial Intelligence

Navigation around the Caroline Islands in the South Seas is accomplished without instruments. The position of the stars, as viewed from various islands, the weather patterns, and water color are the only sign posts. Each journey is broken into a series of segments; and the navigator learns the position of the stars within each of these segments. During the actual trip the navigator must envision mentally a reference island as it passes under a particular star and from that he computes the number of segments completed, the proportion of the trip remaining, and any corrections in heading that are required. The navigator cannot *see* the islands as he sails along; instead he maps their locations in his mental "picture" of the journey.[10]

32 Spatial problem solving is required for navigation and in the use of the notational system of maps. Other kinds of spatial problem solving are brought to bear in visualizing an object seen from a different angle and in playing chess. The visual arts also employ this intelligence in the use of space.

33 Evidence from brain research is clear and persuasive. Just as the left hemisphere has, over the course of evolution, been selected as the site of linguistic processing in right-handed persons, the right hemisphere proves to be the site most crucial for spatial processing. Damage to the right posterior regions causes impairment of the ability to find one's way around a site, to recognize faces or scenes, or to notice fine details.

34 Patients with damage specific to regions of the right hemisphere will attempt to compensate for their spacial deficits with linguistic strategies. They will try to reason aloud, to challenge the task, or even make up answers. But such nonspatial strategies are rarely successful.

35 Blind populations provide an illustration of the distinction between the spatial intelligence and visual perception. A blind person can recognize shapes by an indirect method: running a hand along the object translates into length of time of movement, which in turn is translated into the size of the object. For the blind person, the perceptual system of the tactile modality parallels the visual modality in the seeing person. The analogy between the spatial reasoning of the blind and the linguistic reasoning of the deaf is notable.

---

[10] Gardner, H. (1983). *Frames of Mind: The Theory of Multiple Intelligences.* New York: Basic Books. [Gardner's note]

There are few child prodigies among visual artists, but there are idiots   36
savants such as Nadia.[11] Despite a condition of severe autism, this preschool
child made drawings of the most remarkable representational accuracy and
finesse.

Interpersonal Intelligence.   With little formal training in special edu-   37
cation and nearly blind herself, Anne Sullivan began the intimidating task of
instructing a blind and deaf seven-year-old Helen Keller. Sullivan's efforts at
communication were complicated by the child's emotional struggle with the
world around her. At their first meal together, this scene occurred:

> Annie did not allow Helen to put her hand into Annie's plate and take
> what she wanted, as she had been accustomed to do with her family. It
> became a test of wills—hand thrust into plate, hand firmly put aside.
> The family, much upset, left the dining room. Annie locked the door
> and proceeded to eat her breakfast while Helen lay on the floor kicking
> and screaming, pushing and pulling at Annie's chair. [After half an hour]
> Helen went around the table looking for her family. She discovered no
> one else was there and that bewildered her. Finally, she sat down and
> began to eat her breakfast, but with her hands. Annie gave her a spoon.
> Down on the floor it clattered, and the contest of wills began anew.[12]

Anne Sullivan sensitively responded to the child's behavior. She wrote   38
home: "The greatest problem I shall have to solve is how to discipline and control her without breaking her spirit. I shall go rather slowly at first and try to
win her love."

In fact, the first "miracle" occurred two weeks later, well before the famous   39
incident at the pumphouse. Annie had taken Helen to a small cottage near the
family's house, where they could live alone. After seven days together, Helen's
personality suddenly underwent a profound change—the therapy had worked:

> My heart is singing with joy this morning. A miracle has happened!
> The wild little creature of two weeks ago has been transformed into a
> gentle child.[13]

It was just two weeks after this that the first breakthrough in Helen's grasp   40
of language occurred; and from that point on, she progressed with incredible

---

[11] Selfe, L. (1977). *Nadia: A Case of Extraordinary Drawing in an Autistic Child.*
New York: Academic Press. [Gardner's note]

[12] Lash, J. (1980). *Helen and Teacher: The Story of Helen Keller and Anne Sullivan Macy*
(p. 52). New York: Delacorte. [Gardner's note]

[13] Lash (p. 54). [Gardner's note]

speed. The key to the miracle of language was Anne Sullivan's insight into the *person* of Helen Keller.

Interpersonal intelligence builds on a core capacity to notice distinctions   41
among others; in particular, contrasts in their moods, temperaments, motivations, and intentions. In more advanced forms, this intelligence permits a skilled adult to read the intentions and desires of others, even when these have been hidden. This skill appears in a highly sophisticated form in religious or political leaders, teachers, therapists, and parents. The Helen Keller–Anne Sullivan story suggests that this interpersonal intelligence does not depend on language.

All indices in brain research suggest that the frontal lobes play a prominent   42
role in interpersonal knowledge. Damage in this area can cause profound personality changes while leaving other forms of problem solving unharmed—a person is often "not the same person" after such an injury.

Alzheimer's disease, a form of presenile dementia, appears to attack pos-   43
terior brain zones with a special ferocity, leaving spatial, logical, and linguistic computations severely impaired. Yet, Alzheimer's patients will often remain well groomed, socially proper, and continually apologetic for their errors. In contrast, Pick's disease, another variety of presenile dementia that is more frontally oriented, entails a rapid loss of social graces.

Biological evidence for interpersonal intelligence encompasses two addi-   44
tional factors often cited as unique to humans. One factor is the prolonged childhood of primates, including the close attachment to the mother. In those cases where the mother is removed from early development, normal interpersonal development is in serious jeopardy. The second factor is the relative importance in humans of social interaction. Skills such as hunting, tracking, and killing in prehistoric societies required participation and cooperation of large numbers of people. The need for group cohesion, leadership, organization, and solidarity follows naturally from this.

Intrapersonal Intelligence.   In an essay called "A Sketch of the Past,"   45
written almost as a diary entry, Virginia Woolf discusses the "cotton wool of existence"—the various mundane events of life. She contrasts this "cotton wool" with three specific and poignant memories from her childhood: a fight with her brother, seeing a particular flower in the garden, and hearing of the suicide of a past visitor:

> These are three instances of exceptional moments. I often tell them over, or rather they come to the surface unexpectedly. But now for the first time I have written them down, and I realize something that I have never realized before. Two of these moments ended in a state of despair. The other ended, on the contrary, in a state of satisfaction.

The sense of horror (in hearing of the suicide) held me powerless. But in the case of the flower, I found a reason; and was thus able to deal with the sensation. I was not powerless.

Though I still have the peculiarity that I receive these sudden shocks, they are now always welcome; after the first surprise, I always feel instantly that they are particularly valuable. And so I go on to suppose that the shock-receiving capacity is what makes me a writer. I hazard the explanation that a shock is at once in my case followed by the desire to explain it. I feel that I have had a blow; but it is not, as I thought as a child, simply a blow from an enemy hidden behind the cotton wool of daily life; it is or will become a revelation of some order; it is a token of some real thing behind appearances; and I make it real by putting it into words.[14]

This quotation vividly illustrates the intrapersonal intelligence — knowledge   46
of the internal aspects of a person: access to one's own feeling life, one's range of emotions, the capacity to effect discriminations among these emotions and eventually to label them and to draw upon them as a means of understanding and guiding one's own behavior. A person with good intrapersonal intelligence has a viable and effective model of himself or herself. Since this intelligence is the most private, it requires evidence from language, music, or some other more expressive form of intelligence if the observer is to detect it at work. In the above quotation, for example, linguistic intelligence is drawn upon to convey intrapersonal knowledge; it embodies the interaction of intelligences, a common phenomenon to which we will return later.

We see the familiar criteria at work in the intrapersonal intelligence. As   47
with the interpersonal intelligence, the frontal lobes play a central role in personality change. Injury to the lower area of the frontal lobes is likely to produce irritability or euphoria; while injury to the higher regions is more likely to produce indifference, listlessness, slowness, and apathy — a kind of depressive personality. In such "frontal-lobe" individuals, the other cognitive functions often remain preserved. In contrast, among aphasics who have recovered sufficiently to describe their experiences, we find consistent testimony: while there may have been a diminution of general alertness and considerable depression about the condition, the individual in no way felt himself to be a different person. He recognized his own needs, wants, and desires and tried as best he could to achieve them.

The autistic child is a prototypical example of an individual with impaired   48
intrapersonal intelligence; indeed, the child may not even be able to refer to

---

[14] Woolf, V. (1976). *Moments of Being* (pp. 69–70). Sussex: The University Press. [Gardner's note]

himself. At the same time, such children often exhibit remarkable abilities in the musical, computational, spatial, or mechanical realms.

Evolutionary evidence for an intrapersonal faculty is more difficult to come by, but we might speculate that the capacity to transcend the satisfaction of instinctual drives is relevant. This becomes increasingly important in a species not perennially involved in the struggle for survival.   49

In sum, then, both interpersonal and intrapersonal faculties pass the tests of an intelligence. They both feature problem-solving endeavors with significance for the individual and the species. Interpersonal intelligence allows one to understand and work with others; intrapersonal intelligence allows one to understand and work with oneself. In the individual's sense of self, one encounters a melding of inter- and intrapersonal components. Indeed, the sense of self emerges as one of the most marvelous of human inventions—a symbol that represents all kinds of information about a person and that is at the same time an invention that all individuals construct for themselves.   50

Summary: The Unique Contributions of the Theory

As human beings, we all have a repertoire of skills for solving different kinds of problems. Our investigation has begun, therefore, with a consideration of these problems, the contexts they are found in, and the culturally significant products that are the outcome. We have not approached "intelligence" as a reified[15] human faculty that is brought to bear in literally any problem setting; rather, we have begun with the problems that humans *solve* and worked back to the "intelligences" that must be responsible.   51

Evidence from brain research, human development, evolution, and cross-cultural comparisons was brought to bear in our search for the relevant human intelligences: a candidate was included only if reasonable evidence to support its membership was found across these diverse fields. Again, this tack differs from the traditional one: since no candidate faculty is *necessarily* an intelligence, we could choose on a motivated basis. In the traditional approach to "intelligence," there is no opportunity for this type of empirical decision.   52

We have also determined that these multiple human faculties, the intelligences, are to a significant extent *independent*. For example, research with brain-damaged adults repeatedly demonstrates that particular faculties can be lost while others are spared. This independence of intelligences implies that a particularly high level of ability in one intelligence, say mathematics, does not require a similarly high level in another intelligence, like language or music.   53

---

[15] **reified**   Regarding an abstraction (e.g., intelligence) as if it were a concrete thing.

This independence of intelligences contrasts sharply with traditional measures of IQ that find high correlations among test scores. We speculate that the usual correlations among subtests of IQ tests come about because all of these tasks in fact measure the ability to respond rapidly to items of a logical-mathematical or linguistic sort; we believe that these correlations would be substantially reduced if one were to survey in a contextually appropriate way the full range of human problem-solving skills.

Until now, we have supported the fiction that adult roles depend largely   54
on the flowering of a single intelligence. In fact, however, nearly every cultural role of any degree of sophistication requires a combination of intelligences. Thus, even an apparently straightforward role, like playing the violin, transcends a reliance on simple musical intelligence. To become a successful violinist requires bodily-kinesthetic dexterity and the interpersonal skills of relating to an audience and, in a different way, choosing a manager; quite possibly it involves an intrapersonal intelligence as well. Dance requires skills in bodily-kinesthetic, musical, interpersonal, and spatial intelligences in varying degrees. Politics requires an interpersonal skill, a linguistic facility, and perhaps some logical aptitude. Inasmuch as nearly every cultural role requires several intelligences, it becomes important to consider individuals as a collection of aptitudes rather than as having a singular problem-solving faculty that can be measured directly through pencil-and-paper tests. Even given a relatively small number of such intelligences, the diversity of human ability is created through the differences in these profiles. In fact, it may well be that the "total is greater than the sum of the parts." An individual may not be particularly gifted in any intelligence; and yet, because of a particular combination or blend of skills, he or she may be able to fill some niche uniquely well. Thus it is of paramount importance to assess the particular combination of skills that may earmark an individual for a certain vocational or avocational niche.

▓ QUESTIONS FOR CRITICAL READING

1. In the heading preceding paragraph 10, Gardner asks, "What Constitutes an Intelligence?" After reading this essay, how would you answer that question? How effectively does Gardner answer it?

2. What is the relation of culture to intelligence? See paragraph 11.

3. Why does society value logical-mathematical intelligence so highly? Do you feel it is reasonable to do so? Why?

4. What relationship do you see between intelligence and problem solving? What relationship do you see between education and problem solving?

5. Do you think that education can enhance these seven forms of intelligence? What evidence can you cite that intelligence is not fixed but can be altered by experience?

6. Why is it important "to assess the particular combination of skills that may earmark an individual" (para. 54)?

⠿ SUGGESTIONS FOR CRITICAL WRITING

1. Gardner says that his theory of MI (multiple intelligences) was shaped by his observations of "the biological origins of each problem-solving skill" (para. 12). Why is this important to his theory? How has he connected each of the intelligences to a biological origin? What biological issues are not fully accounted for in the theory of multiple intelligences?

2. In which of these seven forms of intelligence do you excel? Describe your achievements in these forms by giving specific examples that help your reader relate your abilities to the intelligences you have cited. Now that you have identified your primary intelligences, what implications do they suggest for your later life?

3. Gardner is keenly interested in reforming education in light of his theory of multiple intelligences. How could education be altered to best accommodate the seven forms of intelligence? What would be done differently in schools? Who would benefit from the differences you propose? How would society in general benefit from those differences?

4. Describe a problem-solving situation that requires two or more of the intelligences that Gardner describes. If possible, draw your example from your own experience or the experience of someone you know. Describe how the several intelligences work together to help solve the problem.

5. In some discussions of the forms of intelligence, commentators add an eighth — the naturalist's ability to recognize fine distinctions and patterns in the natural world. What might be the biological origin for that intelligence? In what cultural context might that intelligence be crucial? Do you feel that there is such an intelligence as represented by the naturalist or that it is included in other forms of intelligence?

6. **CONNECTIONS**   Compare Howard Gardner's range of intelligences with Robert Nozick's (p. 528) concepts of emotions. Argue a case defending the idea that emotions can be forms of intelligence. However, if that is so, how do the ideas of Robert Nozick fit in with the ideas of Howard Gardner? Are they both talking about ways of knowing? Where do you stand on the question of how significant an emotional understanding of events is compared with an intellectual understanding of events?

7. **CONNECTIONS**   Many thinkers consider intelligence to be largely conscious in nature. Taking into consideration the concepts of the Jungian unconscious (p. 487) and the views of Eric Kandel (p. 539) on the problems of consciousness, decide which forms Gardner discusses fit the category of the conscious apprehension or the category of the unconscious apprehension. Would Kandel and Jung agree with Gardner's views of intelligence, or would they modify them to suit their own ideas?

Reflections on the Nature of Mind

Now that you have read the selections in "Mind," consider in what ways these writers have helped further inform your views on the workings of the mind.

1. In what ways do your dreams give you insight into your conscious mind?

2. To what extent does great literature, drama, and film inform us about the mind?

3. How aware have you become of your possessing an unconscious mind?

4. Does our understanding of mind and psychology involve gender differences? Why?

5. What are the most important aspects of the relationship between the mind and the brain?

6. How likely do you think it is that a machine will soon be able to replicate the function of the mind? Why?

7. To what extent are your emotions a critical part of your mental functions? Are emotions limited to your mind, or are they somehow distinct?

8. What have you learned about the nature of your own personal consciousness? Have you become more or less aware of your own consciousness?

9. Is it possible for you scientifically to study your own consciousness, or is it only possible to study the consciousness of others?

10. Does a theory of multiple intelligences reveal truths about your own intelligence? How so?

SCIENCE

Introduction

If there be light, then there is darkness; if cold, heat; if height, depth; if solid, fluid; if hard, soft; if rough, smooth; if calm, tempest; if prosperity, adversity; if life, death.
—PYTHAGORAS (C. 580–C. 500 B.C.E.)

Nature and nature's laws lay hid in the night.
God said, Let Newton be! And all was light!
—ALEXANDER POPE (1688–1744)

Science is the great antidote to the poison of enthusiasm and superstition.
—ADAM SMITH (1723–1790)

Every great advance in science has issued from a new audacity of imagination.
—JOHN DEWEY (1859–1952)

To raise new questions, new possibilities, to regard old problems from a new angle, requires creative imagination and marks real advance in science.
—ALBERT EINSTEIN (1879–1955)

Science is a way of thinking much more than it is a body of knowledge.
—CARL SAGAN (1934–1996)

Science is not only a disciple of reason but, also, one of romance and passion.
—STEPHEN HAWKING (b. 1942)

Modern science emerged as a force to change the world in the seventeenth century. Great writers such as the English poet John Donne (1572–1631) showed signs of worry and concern when they began to realize, as Donne said, that science "brings all into doubt." Since the seventeenth century, there have been extraordinary discoveries that have indeed brought much of what was once ordinary belief into doubt. There have been advances that have clarified the nature of the universe, informing us about the moon, the sun, the planets, the stars, galaxies, and previously undreamed-of phenomena. We have learned much about the nature of the earth and its history, the relationship between animals and their development, the mysteries of quantum physics and relativity, the interiority of our genes, and the makeup of the brain itself. And there is undoubtedly much more to discover. Science has called into doubt long-held beliefs, and it has offered answers to questions that, only a comparatively short time ago, could never have been asked.

Plato (428–347 B.C.E.) differed from Aristotle in that he paid less attention to our sensory experiences than he did to ideas. Yet his discussion in the "Allegory of the Cave" was formative to the development of early Greek science because it addressed the manner in which our thoughts can be distorted by our approach to understanding. Plato pictures us as being like people who live in a cave watching shadows on the wall before us. We think those shadows are real because we can see no other features of the real world. In fact, however, the shadows are the appearances of things, the sensory qualities, which are all that we can ever hope to comprehend. Plato tells us that there is something behind sensory qualities, some reality that, because we are limited by our senses, we cannot see or even imagine. Plato insists that the real can exist only in a pure spiritual realm. And because, in the Platonic scheme, we originally came from that realm, we have a dim memory of the real and interpret our sensory experience in accordance with our memory. Thus, there is a resemblance between the spiritual ideal and our sensory experience, but the resemblance is merely as close as the shadows in the cave are to the people who cast them.

At the time Francis Bacon (1561–1626) wrote, before the advent of sophisticated scientific instruments, most scientists relied on their five senses and their theoretical preconceptions to investigate the workings of the world around them. In "The Four Idols," Bacon raises questions about these modes of scientific inquiry by asking: What casts of mind are essential to gaining knowledge? What prevents us from understanding nature clearly? By thus critiquing traditional presumptions and methods of investigation, Bacon challenges his readers to examine nature with new mental tools. He aims to free us from the intellectual limitations that make it difficult, and sometimes impossible, to know the truth.

In "Natural Selection," Charles Darwin (1809–1882) proposes a theory that is still controversial in some parts of the world. While on a voyage around South America in the HMS *Beagle*, Darwin observed remarkable similarities in the structures of various animals. He approached these discoveries with the advantages of a good education, a deep knowledge of the Bible and theology (he was trained as a minister), and a systematic and inquiring mind. Ultimately, he developed his theories of evolution to explain the significance of resemblances he detected among his scientific samples of insects and flowers and other forms of life. Explaining the nature of nature forms the underpinnings of Darwin's work.

Richard P. Feynman (1918–1988) was a colorful character as well as a major figure in American science in the latter part of the twentieth century. He was a physicist working with NASA and solved the problem of why the space shuttle *Challenger* exploded on liftoff in 1986, killing all of the astronauts on board. He also played the frigideira (a small frying pan) in a Brazilian marching band when he was teaching in Rio de Janeiro. Somehow the rhythm instrument fit into his concept of the mathematics of physics. In "The Value of Science," Feynman approaches the most important ways in which science is valuable to individual scientists and to the communities they serve. He cites three major values, including the ability to doubt, which he feels is probably the most important value for making sure that the future is open to all possibilities.

Edward O. Wilson's (b. 1929) letter to a young scientist—"What Is Science?"—introduces a number of important ideas central to the profession of science. Because the essay is a letter, the tone is relaxed and conversational, but the questions Wilson poses are serious. He discusses the nature of the scientific hypothesis and the procedures that the scientist takes to build a theory, test it carefully, and begin to establish the facts revealed by the inquiry. Because he is the world's expert on ants, Wilson begins with an example of his own research and explains to us how he discovered the way in which an ant could tell that another ant was dead. Like Richard Feynman, Wilson conveys that science can be exciting and intellectually rewarding. However, Wilson goes on to compare scientific reality with the creation myths that have, since ancient times, explained the phenomena that are now the province of science.

In "The Theory of the Universe?," Michio Kaku (b. 1947) introduces some of the most extraordinary ideas developed by mathematical physicists in their effort to find a unified theory that will connect quantum mechanics with Einstein's general relativity. Kaku reviews the four fundamental forces that account for all physical reality: gravity, electromagnetism, the strong nuclear force, and the weak nuclear force. He then goes on to explain why quantum theory describes all the particle physical phenomena and why general relativity describes all the cosmic physical phenomena. Then, he explains that each theory is essentially distinct, perhaps even opposed to one another. What is needed is a great unified theory, which Einstein worked on for thirty years without success. Kaku suggests that superstring theory may be the answer that physicists have been looking for.

Eugenics, the practice of genetic selection, is the subject of Philip Kitcher's (b. 1947) "Inescapable Eugenics." In the not so distant past, many people felt that society should make an effort to eliminate defective humans before they were born. For example, in the 1930s in the United States, there was an effort to sterilize women who appeared to be feebleminded and whose progenitors had appeared to be feebleminded. A number of women were sterilized against their wishes before this practice was discontinued. In Nazi Germany in the 1930s and 1940s, a variety of people with "undesirable" traits were killed, while programs were set up to find mates whose offspring would be "superior." Kitcher reviews these practices and projects to the future, asking what kinds of eugenics will be practiced by individuals who have access to genetic testing and who will know in advance what genetic traits their children will have.

Lisa Randall (b. 1962), a theoretical physicist at Harvard, discusses the difference between Newtonian theories of gravitation and those of Albert Einstein in "Newtonian Gravity and Special Relativity." She explains that Newton's ideas assumed that space and time were absolute entities, whereas Einstein established that they were relative to each other. Einstein proposed the idea of spacetime and emphasized the fact that the speed of light was a constant. Randall explores Newton's ideas at some length and then uses the illustration of a moving sailing ship relative to a fixed position as a way of explaining what is important about Einstein's theory of relativity. She is a challenging author writing about a challenging subject, but she calls our attention to the complexities of modern physics.

All of these selections offer a range of ways of thinking in the world of science.

Some Considerations about the Nature of Science

Before reading the selections that follow, consider what your views of science are. Ask yourself the following questions and respond to each in a reading journal. Discuss your answers with your classmates.

1. What indebtedness do you feel to modern science?
2. What is the scientific method?
3. What do politicians think about science?
4. Should geneticists permit parents to choose their child's genes?
5. What are the characteristic mindsets of scientists?
6. When does a theory like evolution become a fact?
7. Are religion and science compatible with each other?
8. In what ways does science threaten you?
9. What are the most important gifts of modern science to our nation?
10. What attracts young people to science?

PLATO

The Allegory of the Cave

PLATO (428–347 B.C.E.) was born into an aristocratic, probably Athenian, family and educated
according to the best precepts available. He eventually
became a student of Socrates and later involved himself closely with Socrates' work and
teaching. Plato was not only Socrates' finest student but also the one who immortalized
Socrates in his works. Most of Plato's works are philosophical essays in which Socrates
speaks as a character in a dialogue with one or more students or listeners.

Both Socrates and Plato lived in turbulent times. In 404 B.C.E. Athens was defeated
by Sparta, and its government was taken over by tyrants. Political life in Athens became
dangerous. Plato felt, however, that he could effect positive change in Athenian politics — until
Socrates was tried unjustly for corrupting the youth of Athens and sentenced to death in
399 B.C.E. After that, Plato withdrew from public life and devoted himself to writing and to
the academy he founded in an olive grove in Athens. The academy endured for almost a
thousand years, which tells us how greatly Plato's thought was valued.

Although it is not easy to condense Plato's views, he may be said to have held the
world of sense perception to be inferior to the world of ideal entities that exist only in
a pure spiritual realm. These ideals, or forms, Plato argued, are perceived directly by
everyone before birth and then dimly remembered here on earth. But the memory, dim
as it is, enables people to understand what the senses perceive, despite the fact that the
senses are unreliable and their perceptions imperfect.

This view of reality has long been important to philosophers because it gives a philosophical basis to antimaterialistic thought. It values the spirit first and frees people from
the tyranny of sensory perception and sensory reward. In the case of love, Plato held that
Eros leads individuals to revere the body and its pleasures; but the thrust of his teaching
is that the body is a metaphor for spiritual delights. Plato maintains that the body is only a
starting point, which eventually can lead to both spiritual fulfillment and the appreciation
of true beauty.

From *The Republic*. Translated and glossed by Benjamin Jowett.

On the one hand, "The Allegory of the Cave" is a discussion of politics: *The Republic*, from which it is taken, is a treatise on justice and the ideal government. On the other hand, it has long stood as an example of the notion that if we rely on our perceptions to know the truth about the world, then we will know very little about it. In order to live ethically, it is essential to know what is true and, therefore, what is important beyond the world of sensory perception.

Plato's allegory has been persuasive for centuries and remains at the center of thought that attempts to counter the pleasures of the sensual life. Most religions aim for spiritual enlightenment and praise the qualities of the soul, which lies beyond perception. Thus, it comes as no surprise that Christianity and other religions have developed systems of thought that bear a close resemblance to Plato's. Later refinements of his thought, usually called Neo-Platonism, have been influential even into modern times.

PLATO'S RHETORIC

Two important rhetorical techniques are at work in the following selection. The first and more obvious — at least on one level — is the device of the allegory, a story in which the characters and situations actually represent people and situations in another context. It is a difficult technique to sustain, although Aesop's fables were certainly successful in using animals to represent people and their foibles. The advantage of the technique is that a complex and sometimes unpopular argument can be fought and won before the audience realizes that an argument is under way. The disadvantage of the technique is that the terms of the allegory may only approximate the situation it represents; thus, the argument may fail to be convincing.

The second rhetorical technique Plato uses is the dialogue. In fact, this device is a hallmark of Plato's work; indeed, most of his writings are called dialogues. The *Symposium*, *Apology*, *Phaedo*, *Crito*, *Meno*, and most of his famous works are written in dialogue form. Usually in these works Socrates is speaking to a student or a friend about highly abstract issues, asking questions that require simple answers. Slowly, the questioning proceeds to elucidate the answers to complex issues.

This question-and-answer technique basically constitutes the Socratic method. Socrates analyzes the answer to each question, examines its implications, and then asserts the truth. The method works partly because Plato believes that people do not learn things but remember them. That is, people originate from heaven, where they knew the truth; they already possess knowledge and must recover it by means of the dialogue. Socrates' method is ideally suited to that purpose.

Beyond these techniques, however, we must look at Plato's style. It is true that he is working with difficult ideas, but his style is so clear, simple, and direct that few people would have trouble understanding what he is saying. Considering the influence this work has had on world thought, and the reputation Plato had earned by the time he wrote *The Republic*, its style is remarkably plain and accessible. Plato's respect for rhetoric and its proper uses is part of the reason he can express himself with such impressive clarity.

▚ PREREADING QUESTIONS: WHAT TO READ FOR

The following prereading questions may help you anticipate key issues in the discussion of Plato's "The Allegory of the Cave." Keeping them in mind during your first reading of the selection should help focus your attention.

1. In what ways are we like the people in the cave looking at shadows?

2. Why is the world of sensory perception somewhat illusory?

3. For Plato, what is the difference between the upper world and the lower world?

The Allegory of the Cave

SOCRATES, GLAUCON. *The den, the prisoners: the light at a distance;*

And now, I said, let me show in a figure how far our nature is enlightened or unenlightened: — Behold! human beings living in an underground den, which has a mouth open towards the light and reaching all along the den; here they have been from their childhood, and have their legs and necks chained so that they cannot move, and can only see before them, being prevented by the chains from turning round their heads. Above and behind them a fire is blazing at a distance, and between the fire and the prisoners there is a raised way; and you will see, if you look, a low wall built along the way, like the screen which marionette players have in front of them, over which they show the puppets.   1

I see.   2

the low wall, and the moving figures of which the shadows are seen on the opposite wall of the den.

And do you see, I said, men passing along the wall carrying all sorts of vessels, and statues and figures of animals made of wood and stone and various materials, which appear over the wall? Some of them are talking, others silent.   3

You have shown me a strange image, and they are strange prisoners.   4

Like ourselves, I replied; and they see only their own shadows, or the shadows of one another, which the fire throws on the opposite wall of the cave?   5

True, he said; how could they see anything but the shadows if they were never allowed to move their heads?   6

And of the objects which are being carried in like manner they would only see the shadows?   7

Yes, he said.   8

And if they were able to converse with one another,   9
would they not suppose that they were naming what was
actually before them?

Very true.   10

And suppose further that the prison had an echo which   11
came from the other side, would they not be sure to fancy
when one of the passers-by spoke that the voice which they
heard came from the passing shadow?

No question, he replied.   12

To them, I said, the truth would be literally nothing but   13
the shadows of the images.

That is certain.   14

And now look again, and see what will naturally follow   15
if the prisoners are released and disabused of their error.
At first, when any of them is liberated and compelled suddenly to stand up and turn his neck round and walk and look
towards the light, he will suffer sharp pains; the glare will distress him, and he will be unable to see the realities of which in
his former state he had seen the shadows; and then conceive
someone saying to him, that what he saw before was an illusion, but that now, when he is approaching nearer to being
and his eye is turned towards more real existence, he has a
clearer vision—what will be his reply? And you may further
imagine that his instructor is pointing to the objects as they
pass and requiring him to name them,—will he not be perplexed? Will he not fancy that the shadows which he formerly
saw are truer than the objects which are now shown to him?

Far truer.   16

And if he is compelled to look straight at the light, will   17
he not have a pain in his eyes which will make him turn away
to take refuge in the objects of vision which he can see, and
which he will conceive to be in reality clearer than the things
which are now being shown to him?

True, he said.   18

And suppose once more, that he is reluctantly dragged   19
up a steep and rugged ascent, and held fast until he is forced
into the presence of the sun himself, is he not likely to be
pained and irritated? When he approaches the light his eyes
will be dazzled, and he will not be able to see anything at all
of what are now called realities.

Not all in a moment, he said.   20

---

*The prisoners
would mistake
the shadows
for realities.*

*And when
released, they
would still
persist in
maintaining
the superior
truth of the
shadows.*

*When dragged
upwards, they
would be dazzled
by excess of light.*

He will require to grow accustomed to the sight of the upper 21
world. And first he will see the shadows best, next the reflections of men and other objects in the water, and then the objects
themselves; then he will gaze upon the light of the moon and
the stars and the spangled heaven; and he will see the sky
and the stars by night better than the sun or the light of the
sun by day?

Certainly. 22

At length they will see the sun and understand his nature.

Last of all he will be able to see the sun, and not mere 23
reflections of him in the water, but he will see him in his own
proper place, and not in another; and he will contemplate him
as he is.

Certainly. 24

He will then proceed to argue that this is he who gives 25
the season and the years, and is the guardian of all that is in
the visible world, and in a certain way the cause of all things
which he and his fellows have been accustomed to behold?

Clearly, he said, he would first see the sun and then rea- 26
son about him.

And when he remembered his old habitation, and the 27
wisdom of the den and his fellow prisoners, do you not suppose that he would felicitate himself on the change, and pity
them?

They would then pity their old companions of the den.

Certainly, he would. 28

And if they were in the habit of conferring honors among 29
themselves on those who were quickest to observe the passing shadows and to remark which of them went before, and
which followed after, and which were together; and who were
therefore best able to draw conclusions as to the future, do
you think that he would care for such honors and glories, or
envy the possessors of them? Would he not say with Homer,

Better to be the poor servant of a poor master,

and to endure anything, rather than think as they do and live
after their manner?

Yes, he said, I think that he would rather suffer anything 30
than entertain these false notions and live in this miserable
manner.

Imagine once more, I said, such a one coming suddenly 31
out of the sun to be replaced in his old situation; would he not
be certain to have his eyes full of darkness?

To be sure, he said. 32

And if there were a contest, and he had to compete in measuring the shadows with the prisoners who had never moved out of the den, while his sight was still weak, and before his eyes had become steady (and the time which would be needed to acquire this new habit of sight might be very considerable), would he not be ridiculous? Men would say of him that up he went and down he came without his eyes; and that it was better not even to think of ascending; and if any one tried to loose another and lead him up to the light, let them only catch the offender, and they would put him to death. 33

No question, he said. 34

This entire allegory, I said, you may now append, dear Glaucon, to the previous argument; the prison house is the world of sight, the light of the fire is the sun, and you will not misapprehend me if you interpret the journey upwards to be the ascent of the soul into the intellectual world according to my poor belief, which, at your desire, I have expressed — whether rightly or wrongly God knows. But, whether true or false, my opinion is that in the world of knowledge the idea of good appears last of all, and is seen only with an effort; and, when seen, is also inferred to be the universal author of all things beautiful and right, parent of light and of the lord of light in this visible world, and the immediate source of reason and truth in the intellectual; and that this is the power upon which he who would act rationally either in public or private life must have his eye fixed. 35

I agree, he said, as far as I am able to understand you. 36

Moreover, I said, you must not wonder that those who attain to this beatific vision are unwilling to descend to human affairs; for their souls are ever hastening into the upper world where they desire to dwell; which desire of theirs is very natural, if our allegory may be trusted. 37

Yes, very natural. 38

And is there anything surprising in one who passes from divine contemplations to the evil state of man, misbehaving himself in a ridiculous manner; if, while his eyes are blinking and before he has become accustomed to the surrounding darkness, he is compelled to fight in courts of law, or in other places, about the images or the shadows of images of justice, and is endeavoring to meet the conceptions of those who have never yet seen absolute justice? 39

But when they returned to the den, they would see much worse than those who had never left it.

The prison is the world of sight, the light of the fire is the sun.

Nothing extraordinary in the philosopher being unable to see in the dark.

Anything but surprising, he replied.   40

Anyone who has common sense will remember that the   41
bewilderments of the eyes are of two kinds, and arise from two
causes, either from coming out of the light or from going into
the light, which is true of the mind's eye, quite as much as of the
bodily eye; and he who remembers this when he sees anyone
whose vision is perplexed and weak, will not be too ready to
laugh; he will first ask whether that soul of man has come out of
the brighter life, and is unable to see because unaccustomed to
the dark, or having turned from darkness to the day is dazzled by
excess of light. And he will count the one happy in his condition
and state of being, and he will pity the other; or, if he have a mind
to laugh at the soul which comes from below into the light, there
will be more reason in this than in the laugh which greets him
who returns from above out of the light into the den.

The eyes may be blinded in two ways, by excess or by defect of light.

That, he said, is a very just distinction.   42

But then, if I am right, certain professors of education   43
must be wrong when they say that they can put a knowledge
into the soul which was not there before, like sight into blind
eyes.

The conversion of the soul is the turning round the eye from darkness to light.

They undoubtedly say this, he replied.   44

Whereas, our argument shows that the power and capac-   45
ity of learning exists in the soul already; and that just as the
eye was unable to turn from darkness to light without the
whole body, so too the instrument of knowledge can only by
the movement of the whole soul be turned from the world of
becoming into that of being, and learn by degrees to endure
the sight of being, and of the brightest and best of being, or in
other words, of the good.

Very true.   46

And must there not be some art which will effect conver-   47
sion in the easiest and quickest manner; not implanting the
faculty of sight, for that exists already, but has been turned
in the wrong direction, and is looking away from the truth?

Yes, he said, such an art may be presumed.   48

And whereas the other so-called virtues of the soul seem   49
to be akin to bodily qualities, for even when they are not originally innate they can be implanted later by habit and exercise,
the virtue of wisdom more than anything else contains a divine
element which always remains, and by this conversion is rendered useful and profitable; or, on the other hand, hurtful and
useless. Did you never observe the narrow intelligence flashing
from the keen eye of a clever rogue—how eager he is, how

The virtue of wisdom has a divine power which may be turned either towards good or towards evil.

clearly his paltry soul sees the way to his end; he is the reverse of blind, but his keen eyesight is forced into the service of evil, and he is mischievous in proportion to his cleverness?

Very true, he said. 50

But what if there had been a circumcision of such natures 51 in the days of their youth; and they had been severed from those sensual pleasures, such as eating and drinking, which, like leaden weights, were attached to them at their birth, and which drag them down and turn the vision of their souls upon the things that are below—if, I say, they had been released from these impediments and turned in the opposite direction, the very same faculty in them would have seen the truth as keenly as they see what their eyes are turned to now.

Very likely. 52

Neither the uneducated nor the over-educated will be good servants of the State.

Yes, I said; and there is another thing which is likely, or 53 rather a necessary inference from what has preceded, that neither the uneducated and uninformed of the truth, nor yet those who never make an end of their education, will be able ministers of State; not the former, because they have no single aim of duty which is the rule of all their actions, private as well as public; nor the latter, because they will not act at all except upon compulsion, fancying that they are already dwelling apart in the islands of the blessed.

Very true, he replied. 54

Then, I said, the business of us who are the founders 55 of the State will be to compel the best minds to attain that knowledge which we have already shown to be the greatest of all—they must continue to ascend until they arrive at the good; but when they have ascended and seen enough we must not allow them to do as they do now.

What do you mean? 56

Men should ascend to the upper world, but they should also return to the lower.

I mean that they remain in the upper world: but this must 57 not be allowed; they must be made to descend again among the prisoners in the den, and partake of their labors and honors, whether they are worth having or not.

But is not this unjust? he said; ought we to give them a 58 worse life, when they might have a better?

You have again forgotten, my friend, I said, the intention 59 of the legislator, who did not aim at making any one class in the State happy above the rest; the happiness was to be in the whole State, and he held the citizens together by persuasion and necessity, making them benefactors of the State, and therefore benefactors of one another; to this end he created them, not to please themselves, but to be his instruments in binding up the State.

True, he said, I had forgotten. 60

Observe, Glaucon, that there will be no injustice in com- 61 pelling our philosophers to have a care and providence of others; we shall explain to them that in other States, men of their class are not obliged to share in the toils of politics: and this is reasonable, for they grow up at their own sweet will, and the government would rather not have them. Being self-taught, they cannot be expected to show any gratitude for a culture which they have never received. But we have brought you into the world to be rulers of the hive, kings of yourselves and of the other citizens, and have educated you far better and more perfectly than they have been educated, and you are better able to share in the double duty. Where- fore each of you, when his turn comes, must go down to the general underground abode, and get the habit of seeing in the dark. When you have acquired the habit, you will see ten thousand times better than the inhabitants of the den,

and you will know what the several images are, and what they represent, because you have seen the beautiful and just and good in their truth. And thus our State, which is also yours, will be a reality, and not a dream only, and will be administered in a spirit unlike that of other States, in which men fight with one another about shadows only and are dis- tracted in the struggle for power, which in their eyes is a great good. Whereas the truth is that the State in which the rulers are most reluctant to govern is always the best and most quietly governed, and the State in which they are most eager, the worst.

Quite true, he replied. 62

And will our pupils, when they hear this, refuse to take 63 their turn at the toils of State, when they are allowed to spend the greater part of their time with one another in the heavenly light?

Impossible, he answered; for they are just men, and the 64 commands which we impose upon them are just; there can be no doubt that every one of them will take office as a stern necessity, and not after the fashion of our present rulers of State.

Yes, my friend, I said; and there lies the point. You must 65 contrive for your future rulers another and a better life than that of a ruler, and then you may have a well-ordered State;

The statesman must be provided with a better life than that of a ruler; and then he will not covet office.

for only in the State which offers this, will they rule who are truly rich, not in silver and gold, but in virtue and wisdom, which are the true blessings of life. Whereas if they go to the administration of public affairs, poor and hungering after their own private advantage, thinking that hence they are to snatch the chief good, order there can never be; for they will be fighting about office, and the civil and domestic broils which thus arise will be the ruin of the rulers themselves and of the whole State.

Most true, he replied.   66

And the only life which looks down upon the life of political ambition is that of true philosophy. Do you know of any other?   67

Indeed, I do not, he said.   68

⁞⁞ QUESTIONS FOR CRITICAL READING

1. What is the relationship between Socrates and Glaucon? Are they equal in intellectual authority? Are they concerned with the same issues?

2. How does the allegory of the prisoners in the cave watching shadows on a wall relate to us today? What shadows do we see, and how do they distort our sense of what is real?

3. Are we prisoners in the same sense that Plato's characters are?

4. If Plato is right that the material world is an illusion, how would too great a reliance on materialism affect ethical decisions?

5. What ethical issues, if any, are raised by Plato's allegory?

6. In paragraph 49, Plato states that the virtue of wisdom "contains a divine element." What is "a divine element"? What does this statement seem to mean? Do you agree with Plato?

7. What distinctions does Plato make between the public and the private? Would you make the same distinctions (see paras. 53–55)?

⁞⁞ SUGGESTIONS FOR CRITICAL WRITING

1. Analyze the allegory of the cave for its strengths and weaknesses. Consider what the allegory implies for people living in a world of the senses and for what might lie behind that world. To what extent are people like (or unlike) the figures in the cave? To what extent is the world we know like the cave?

2. Socrates is concerned at the end of the dialogue about the rulers of the state, explaining that they must be more than simply rulers. They must be philosophers, by which he means they must possess wisdom. Explain how possessing a full understanding of important scientific concepts is equivalent to a ruler's

possessing wisdom. Why should a politician in a modern democracy be aware of the most important developments in science? What has science got to do with politics? What kind of "cave" sometimes imprisons politicians and makes it difficult for them to know the truth about science?

3. As far as Plato is concerned, his tale of captives in a cave relates to their being unable to know the truth about the ideal world. But the allegory may also apply to our own inability, because of an ignorance of science, to know the truth about our world. Plato is talking about our perceptions, our ability to distinguish the true from the false. What does his allegory tell us about how we can understand the true nature of the world around us today? How does science help us see the truth about our existence? What is the equivalent in modern terms of the cave in which Plato's prisoners live?

4. Today, there is a great deal of information about the decisions that ruling politicians make regarding energy exploration, advanced weaponry, human genetics, and agricultural development. These decisions require a great deal of scientific understanding. Pick one of these topics and research the current literature on it and find out what kind of positions our current politicians are taking. What laws have been written (or ignored) that have required sound scientific understanding? Which politicians have held which positions? Are the politicians you read about well versed in the science that is necessary for their making a sound and lasting judgment?

5. Socrates states unequivocally that Athens should compel the best and the most intelligent young men to be rulers of the state. Review his reasons for saying so, consider what his concept of the state is, and then take a stand on the issue. Is it right to compel the best and most intelligent young people to become rulers? If so, would it be equally proper to compel those well suited for the professions of law, medicine, teaching, or religion to follow those respective callings? Would an ideal society result if all people were forced to practice the calling for which they had the best aptitude?

6. **CONNECTIONS**   Plato has a great deal to say about goodness as it relates to government. Compare his views with those of Lao-tzu (p. 55) and Niccolò Machiavelli (p. 84). Which of these thinkers would Plato have agreed with most? In comparing these three writers and their political views, consider the nature of goodness they required in a ruler. Do you think that we hold similar attitudes today in our expectations for the goodness of our government?

7. **CONNECTIONS**   Plato is concerned with the question of how we know what we know. Francis Bacon in "The Four Idols" (p. 591) is concerned with the same question, although he poses it in different terms. Examine the fundamental issues each author raises. How well do these thinkers agree on basic issues? To what extent, for example, does Bacon warn us to beware the evidence of our senses? To what extent is Bacon as concerned about getting to the truth as Plato is?

FRANCIS
BACON

The Four Idols

© ARPL/HIP/The Image Works

FRANCIS BACON, Lord Verulam (1561–1626), lived during one of the most exciting times in history. Among his contemporaries were the essayist Michel Eyquem de Montaigne; the playwrights Christopher Marlowe and William Shakespeare; the adventurer Sir Francis Drake; and Queen Elizabeth I, in whose reign Bacon held several high offices. He became lord high chancellor of England in 1618 but fell from power in 1621 through a complicated series of events, among which was his complicity in a bribery scheme. His so-called crimes were minor, but he paid dearly for them. His book *Essayes* (1597) was exceptionally popular during his lifetime, and when he found himself without a proper job, he devoted himself to what he declared to be his own true work: writing about philosophy and science.

His purpose in *Novum Organum* (The New Organon), published in 1620, was to replace the old organon, or instrument of thought, Aristotle's treatises on logic and thought. Despite Aristotle's pervasive influence on sixteenth- and seventeenth-century thought — his texts were used in virtually all schools and colleges — Bacon assumed that Aristotelian deductive logic produced error. In *Novum Organum* he tried to set the stage for a new attitude toward logic and scientific inquiry. He proposed a system of reasoning usually referred to as induction. This quasi-scientific method involves collecting and listing observations from nature. Once a mass of observations is gathered and organized, Bacon believed, the truth about what is observed will become apparent.

Bacon is often mistakenly credited with having invented the scientific method of inquiring into nature, but although he was right about the need for collecting and observing, he was wrong about the outcome of such endeavors. After all, one could watch an infinite number of apples (and oranges, too) fall to the ground without ever having the slightest sense of why they do so. What Bacon failed to realize — and he died before he could become scientific enough to realize it — is the creative function of the scientist as expressed in the

From *Novum Organum*. Translated by Francis Headlam and R. L. Ellis.

hypothesis. The hypothesis — an educated guess about why something happens — must be tested by the kinds of observations Bacon recommended.

Nonetheless, "The Four Idols" is a brilliant work. It does establish the requirements for the kind of observation that produces true scientific knowledge. Bacon despaired of any thoroughly objective inquiry in his own day, in part because no one paid attention to the ways in which the idols, limiting preconceptions, strangled thought, observation, and imagination. He realized that the would-be natural philosopher was foiled even before he began. Bacon was a farsighted man. He was correct about the failures of science in his time; and he was correct, moreover, in his assessment that advancement would depend on sensory perception and on aids to perception, such as microscopes and telescopes. The real brilliance of "The Four Idols" lies in Bacon's focus not on what is observed but on the instrument of observation — the human mind. Only when the instrument is freed of error can we rely on its observations to reveal the truth.

BACON'S RHETORIC

Bacon was trained during the great age of rhetoric, and his prose (even though in this case it is translated from Latin) shows the clarity, balance, and organization that characterize the prose writing of seventeenth-century England. The most basic device Bacon uses is enumeration: stating clearly that there are four idols and implying that he will treat each one in turn.

Enumeration is one of the most common and most reliable rhetorical devices. The listener hears a speaker say "I have only three things I want to say today" and is alerted to listen for all three, while feeling secretly grateful that there are only three. When encountering complex material, the reader is always happy to have such "road signs" as "The second aspect of this question is . . ."

"The Four Idols," after a three-paragraph introduction, proceeds with a single paragraph devoted to each idol, so that we have an early definition of each and a sense of what to look for. Paragraphs 8–16 cover only the issues related to the Idols of the Tribe: the problems all people have simply because they are people. Paragraphs 17–22 consider the Idols of the Cave: those particular fixations individuals have because of their special backgrounds or limitations. Paragraphs 23–26 address the questions related to Idols of the Marketplace, particularly those that deal with the way people misuse words and abuse definitions. The remainder of the selection treats the Idols of the Theater, which relate entirely to philosophic systems and preconceptions — all of which tend to narrow the scope of research and understanding.

Enumeration is used within each of these groups of paragraphs as well. Bacon often begins a paragraph with such statements as "There is one principal . . . distinction between different minds" (para. 19). Or he says, "The idols imposed by words on the understanding are of two kinds" (para. 24). The effect is to ensure clarity where confusion could easily reign.

As an added means of achieving clarity, Bacon sets aside a single paragraph — the last — to summarize the main points that he has made, in the order in which they were made.

Within any section of this selection, Bacon depends on observation, example, and reason to make his points. When he speaks of a given idol, he defines it, gives several examples to make it clearer, discusses its effects on thought, and then dismisses it as dangerous. He then goes on to the next idol. Where appropriate, in some cases he names those who are victims of a specific idol. In each case he tries to be thorough, explanatory, and convincing.

Not only is this work a landmark in thought, it is also, because of its absolute clarity, a beacon. We can still benefit from its light.

▪▪ PREREADING QUESTIONS: WHAT TO READ FOR

The following prereading questions may help you anticipate key issues in the discussion of Francis Bacon's "The Four Idols." Keeping them in mind during your first reading of the selection should help focus your attention.

1. What are the four idols?
2. Why do the four idols make it difficult for us to see the truth?
3. What are some chief characteristics of human understanding?

The Four Idols

The idols[1] and false notions which are now in possession of the human understanding, and have taken deep root therein, not only so beset men's minds that truth can hardly find entrance, but even after entrance obtained, they will again in the very instauration[2] of the sciences meet and trouble us, unless men being forewarned of the danger fortify themselves as far as may be against their assaults.

There are four classes of idols which beset men's minds. To these for distinction's sake I have assigned names — calling the first class *Idols of the Tribe;* the second, *Idols of the Cave;* the third, *Idols of the Marketplace;* the fourth, *Idols of the Theater.*

---

[1] **idols** By this term Bacon means phantoms or illusions. The Greek philosopher Democritus spoke of *eidola*, tiny representations of things that impressed themselves on the mind (see note 21).

[2] **instauration** Institution.

The formation of ideas and axioms by true induction[3] is no doubt the   3
proper remedy to be applied for the keeping off and clearing away of idols.
To point them out, however, is of great use; for the doctrine of idols is to the
interpretation of nature what the doctrine of the refutation of sophisms[4] is to
common logic.

The *Idols of the Tribe* have their foundation in human nature itself, and in the   4
tribe or race of men. For it is a false assertion that the sense of man is the measure of things. On the contrary, all perceptions as well of the sense as of the mind
are according to the measure of the individual and not according to the measure of the universe. And the human understanding is like a false mirror, which,
receiving rays irregularly, distorts and discolors the nature of things by mingling
its own nature with it.

The *Idols of the Cave* are the idols of the individual man. For everyone   5
(besides the errors common to human nature in general) has a cave or den of
his own, which refracts[5] and discolors the light of nature; owing either to his
own proper and peculiar nature; or to his education and conversation with others; or to the reading of books, and the authority of those whom he esteems and
admires; or to the differences of impressions, accordingly as they take place in
a mind preoccupied and predisposed or in a mind indifferent and settled; or the
like. So that the spirit of man (according as it is meted out to different individuals) is in fact a thing variable and full of perturbation,[6] and governed as it were by
chance. Whence it was well observed by Heraclitus[7] that men look for sciences
in their own lesser worlds, and not in the greater or common world.

There are also idols formed by the intercourse and association of men with   6
each other, which I call *Idols of the Marketplace,* on account of the commerce
and consort of men there. For it is by discourse that men associate; and words
are imposed according to the apprehension of the vulgar.[8] And therefore the ill
and unfit choice of words wonderfully obstructs the understanding. Nor do the

---

[3] **induction**   Bacon championed induction as the method by which new knowledge is
developed. As he saw it, induction involved a patient gathering and categorizing facts in
the hope that a large number of them would point to the truth. As a process of gathering evidence from which inferences are drawn, induction is contrasted with Aristotle's
method, *deduction*, according to which a theory is established and the truth deduced.
Deduction places the stress on the authority of the expert; induction places the stress on
the facts themselves.

[4] **sophisms**   Apparently intelligent statements that are wrong; false wisdom.

[5] **refracts**   Deflects, bends back, alters.

[6] **perturbation**   Uncertainty, disturbance. In astronomy, the motion caused by the gravity
of nearby planets.

[7] **Heraclitus (535?–475? B.C.E.)**   Greek philosopher who believed that there was no
reality except in change; all else was illusion. He also believed that fire was the basis of
all the world and that everything we see is a transformation of it.

[8] **vulgar**   Common people.

definitions or explanations wherewith in some things learned men are wont[9] to guard and defend themselves, by any means set the matter right. But words plainly force and overrule the understanding, and throw all into confusion and lead men away into numberless empty controversies and idle fancies.

Lastly, there are idols which have immigrated into men's minds from the various dogmas of philosophies, and also from wrong laws of demonstration.[10] These I call *Idols of the Theater;* because in my judgment all the received systems[11] are but so many stage-plays, representing worlds of their own creation after an unreal and scenic fashion. Nor is it only of the systems now in vogue, or only of the ancient sects and philosophies, that I speak; for many more plays of the same kind may yet be composed and in like artificial manner set forth; seeing that errors the most widely different have nevertheless causes for the most part alike. Neither again do I mean this only of entire systems, but also of many principles and axioms in science, which by tradition, credulity, and negligence, have come to be received.   7

But of these several kinds of idols I must speak more largely and exactly, that the understanding may be duly cautioned.   8

The human understanding is of its own nature prone to suppose the existence of more order and regularity in the world than it finds. And though there be many things in nature which are singular and unmatched, yet it devises for them parallels and conjugates and relatives[12] which do not exist. Hence the fiction that all celestial bodies move in perfect circles; spirals and dragons being (except in name) utterly rejected. Hence too the element of fire with its orb is brought in, to make up the square with the other three which the sense perceives. Hence also the ratio of density[13] of the so-called elements is arbitrarily fixed at ten to one. And so on of other dreams. And these fancies affect not dogmas only, but simple notions also.   9

The human understanding when it has once adopted an opinion (either as being the received opinion or as being agreeable to itself) draws all things else to support and agree with it. And though there be a greater number and weight of instances to be found on the other side, yet these it either neglects and despises, or else by some distinction sets aside and rejects; in order that by this   10

---

[9] **wont**   Accustomed.

[10] **laws of demonstration**   Bacon may be referring to Aristotle's logical system of syllogism and deduction.

[11] **received systems**   Official or authorized views of scientific truth.

[12] **parallels and conjugates and relatives**   A reference to the habit of assuming that phenomena are regular and ordered, consisting of squares, triangles, circles, and other regular shapes.

[13] **ratio of density**   The false assumption that the relationship of mass or weight to volume was ten to one. This is another example of Bacon's complaint, establishing a convenient regular "relative," or relationship.

great and pernicious predetermination the authority of its former conclusions may remain inviolate. And therefore it was a good answer that was made by one who when they showed him hanging in a temple a picture of those who had paid their vows as having escaped shipwreck, and would have him say whether he did not now acknowledge the power of the gods—"Ay," asked he again, "but where are they painted that were drowned after their vows?" And such is the way of all superstition, whether in astrology, dreams, omens, divine judgments, or the like; wherein men having a delight in such vanities, mark the events where they are fulfilled, but where they fail, though this happen much oftener, neglect and pass them by. But with far more subtlety does this mischief insinuate itself into philosophy and the sciences; in which the first conclusion colors and brings into conformity with itself all that come after, though far sounder and better. Besides, independently of that delight and vanity which I have described, it is the peculiar and perpetual error of the human intellect to be more moved and excited by affirmatives than by negatives; whereas it ought properly to hold itself indifferently disposed towards both alike. Indeed, in the establishment of any true axiom, the negative instance is the more forcible of the two.

    The human understanding is moved by those things most which strike and enter the mind simultaneously and suddenly, and so fill the imagination; and then it feigns and supposes all other things to be somehow, though it cannot see how, similar to those few things by which it is surrounded. But for that going to and fro to remote and heterogeneous instances, by which axioms are tried as in the fire,[14] the intellect is altogether slow and unfit, unless it be forced thereto by severe laws and overruling authority.   11

    The human understanding is unquiet; it cannot stop or rest, and still presses onward, but in vain. Therefore it is that we cannot conceive of any end or limit to the world, but always as of necessity it occurs to us that there is something beyond. Neither again can it be conceived how eternity has flowed down to the present day; for that distinction which is commonly received of infinity in time past and in time to come can by no means hold; for it would thence follow that one infinity is greater than another, and that infinity is wasting away and tending to become finite. The like subtlety arises touching the infinite divisibility of lines,[15] from the same inability of thought to stop. But this inability interferes   12

---

[14] **tried as in the fire**   Trial by fire is a figure of speech representing thorough, rigorous testing even to the point of risking what is tested. An axiom is a statement of apparent truth that has not yet been put to the test of examination and investigation.

[15] **infinite divisibility of lines**   This gave rise to the paradox of Zeno, the Greek philosopher of the fifth century B.C.E. who showed that it was impossible to get from one point to another because one had to pass the midpoint of the line determined by the two original points, and then the midpoint of the remaining distance, and then of that remaining distance, down to an infinite number of points. By using accepted truths to "prove" an absurdity about motion, Zeno actually hoped to prove that motion itself did not exist. This is the "subtlety," or confusion, Bacon says is produced by the "inability of thought to stop."

more mischievously in the discovery of causes:[16] for although the most general principles in nature ought to be held merely positive, as they are discovered, and cannot with truth be referred to a cause; nevertheless, the human understanding being unable to rest still seeks something prior in the order of nature. And then it is that in struggling towards that which is further off, it falls back upon that which is more nigh at hand; namely, on final causes: which have relation clearly to the nature of man rather than to the nature of the universe, and from this source have strangely defiled philosophy. But he is no less an unskilled and shallow philosopher who seeks causes of that which is most general, than he who in things subordinate and subaltern[17] omits to do so.

The human understanding is no dry light, but receives an infusion from the 13 will and affections;[18] whence proceed sciences which may be called "sciences as one would." For what a man had rather were true he more readily believes. Therefore he rejects difficult things from impatience of research; sober things, because they narrow hope; the deeper things of nature, from superstition; the light of experience, from arrogance and pride, lest his mind should seem to be occupied with things mean and transitory; things not commonly believed, out of deference to the opinion of the vulgar. Numberless in short are the ways, and sometimes imperceptible, in which the affections color and infect the understanding.

But by far the greatest hindrance and aberration of the human understand- 14 ing proceeds from the dullness, incompetency, and deceptions of the senses; in that things which strike the sense outweigh things which do not immediately strike it, though they be more important. Hence it is that speculation commonly ceases where sight ceases; insomuch that of things invisible there is little or no observation. Hence all the working of the spirits[19] enclosed in tangible bodies lies hid and unobserved of men. So also all the more subtle changes of form in the parts of coarser substances (which they commonly call alteration, though it is in truth local motion through exceedingly small spaces) is in like manner unobserved. And yet unless these two things just mentioned be searched out and brought to light, nothing great can be achieved in nature, as far as the production of works is concerned. So again the essential nature of our common air, and of all bodies less dense than air (which are very many) is almost unknown. For the sense by itself is a thing infirm and erring; neither can instruments for

---

[16] **discovery of causes**   Knowledge of the world was based on four causes: efficient (who made it?), material (what is it made of?), formal (what is its shape?), and final (what is its purpose?). The scholastics concentrated their thinking on the first and last, whereas the "middle causes," related to matter and shape, were the proper subject matter of science because they alone yielded to observation. (See para. 34.)

[17] **subaltern**   Lower in status.

[18] **will and affections**   Human free will and emotional needs and responses.

[19] **spirits**   The soul or animating force.

enlarging or sharpening the senses do much; but all the truer kind of interpretation of nature is effected by instances and experiments fit and apposite;[20] wherein the sense decides touching the experiment only, and the experiment touching the point in nature and the thing itself.

The human understanding is of its own nature prone to abstractions and   15
gives a substance and reality to things which are fleeting. But to resolve nature into abstractions is less to our purpose than to dissect her into parts; as did the school of Democritus,[21] which went further into nature than the rest. Matter rather than forms should be the object of our attention, its configurations and changes of configuration, and simple action, and law of action or motion; for forms are figments of the human mind, unless you will call those laws of action forms.

Such then are the idols which I call *Idols of the Tribe;* and which take their   16
rise either from the homogeneity of the substance of the human spirit,[22] or from its preoccupation, or from its narrowness, or from its restless motion, or from an infusion of the affections, or from the incompetency of the senses, or from the mode of impression.

The *Idols of the Cave* take their rise in the peculiar constitution, mental or   17
bodily, of each individual; and also in education, habit, and accident. Of this kind there is a great number and variety; but I will instance those the pointing out of which contains the most important caution, and which have most effect in disturbing the clearness of the understanding.

Men become attached to certain particular sciences and speculations, either   18
because they fancy themselves the authors and inventors thereof, or because they have bestowed the greatest pains upon them and become most habituated to them. But men of this kind, if they betake themselves to philosophy and contemplations of a general character, distort and color them in obedience to their former fancies; a thing especially to be noticed in Aristotle,[23] who made his natural philosophy[24] a mere bondservant to his logic, thereby rendering it contentious and well nigh useless. The race of chemists[25] again out of a few

---

[20] **apposite**   Appropriate; well related.

[21] **Democritus (460?–370? B.C.E.)**   Greek philosopher who thought the world was composed of atoms. Bacon felt such "dissection" to be useless because it was impractical. Yet Democritus's concept of the *eidola*, the mind's impressions of things, may have contributed to Bacon's idea of "the idol."

[22] **human spirit**   Human nature.

[23] **Aristotle (384–322 B.C.E.)**   Greek philosopher whose *Organon* (system of logic) dominated the thought of Bacon's time. Bacon sought to overthrow Aristotle's hold on science and thought.

[24] **natural philosophy**   The scientific study of nature in general—biology, zoology, geology, and so on.

[25] **chemists**   Alchemists had developed a "fantastic philosophy" from their experimental attempts to transmute lead into gold.

experiments of the furnace have built up a fantastic philosophy, framed with reference to a few things; and Gilbert[26] also, after he had employed himself most laboriously in the study and observation of the loadstone, proceeded at once to construct an entire system in accordance with his favorite subject.

19   There is one principal and, as it were, radical distinction between different minds, in respect of philosophy and the sciences, which is this: that some minds are stronger and apter to mark the differences of things, others to mark their resemblances. The steady and acute mind can fix its contemplations and dwell and fasten on the subtlest distinctions: the lofty and discursive mind recognizes and puts together the finest and most general resemblances. Both kinds however easily err in excess, by catching the one at gradations, the other at shadows.

20   There are found some minds given to an extreme admiration of antiquity, others to an extreme love and appetite for novelty; but few so duly tempered that they can hold the mean, neither carping at what has been well laid down by the ancients, nor despising what is well introduced by the moderns. This however turns to the great injury of the sciences and philosophy; since these affectations of antiquity and novelty are the humors[27] of partisans rather than judgments; and truth is to be sought for not in the felicity of any age, which is an unstable thing, but in the light of nature and experience, which is eternal. These factions therefore must be abjured,[28] and care must be taken that the intellect be not hurried by them into assent.

21   Contemplations of nature and of bodies in their simple form break up and distract the understanding, while contemplations of nature and bodies in their composition and configuration overpower and dissolve the understanding: a distinction well seen in the school of Leucippus[29] and Democritus as compared with the other philosophies. For that school is so busied with the particles that it hardly attends to the structure; while the others are so lost in admiration of the structure that they do not penetrate to the simplicity of nature. These kinds of contemplation should therefore be alternated and taken by turns; that so the understanding may be rendered at once penetrating and comprehensive, and the inconveniences above mentioned, with the idols which proceed from them, may be avoided.

22   Let such then be our provision and contemplative prudence for keeping off and dislodging the *Idols of the Cave*, which grow for the most part either out

---

[26] **William Gilbert (1544–1603)**   English scientist who studied magnetism and codified many laws related to magnetic fields. He was particularly ridiculed by Bacon for being too narrow in his researches.

[27] **humors**   Used in a medical sense to mean a distortion caused by imbalance.

[28] **abjured**   Renounced, sworn off, repudiated.

[29] **Leucippus (fifth century B.C.E.)**   Greek philosopher; teacher of Democritus and inventor of the atomistic theory. His works survive only in fragments.

of the predominance of a favorite subject, or out of an excessive tendency to compare or to distinguish, or out of partiality for particular ages, or out of the largeness or minuteness of the objects contemplated. And generally let every student of nature take this as a rule — that whatever his mind seizes and dwells upon with peculiar satisfaction is to be held in suspicion, and that so much the more care is to be taken in dealing with such questions to keep the understanding even and clear.

But the *Idols of the Marketplace* are the most troublesome of all: idols   23
which have crept into the understanding through the alliances of words and names. For men believe that their reason governs words; but it is also true that words react on the understanding; and this it is that has rendered philosophy and the sciences sophistical and inactive. Now words, being commonly framed and applied according to the capacity of the vulgar, follow those lines of division which are most obvious to the vulgar understanding. And whenever an understanding of greater acuteness or a more diligent observation would alter those lines to suit the true divisions of nature, words stand in the way and resist the change. Whence it comes to pass that the high and formal discussions of learned men end oftentimes in disputes about words and names; with which (according to the use and wisdom of the mathematicians) it would be more prudent to begin, and so by means of definitions reduce them to order. Yet even definitions cannot cure this evil in dealing with natural and material things; since the definitions themselves consist of words, and those words beget others: so that it is necessary to recur to individual instances, and those in due series and order; as I shall say presently when I come to the method and scheme for the formation of notions and axioms.[30]

The idols imposed by words on the understanding are of two kinds.   24
They are either names of things which do not exist (for as there are things left unnamed through lack of observation, so likewise are there names which result from fantastic suppositions and to which nothing in reality responds), or they are names of things which exist, but yet confused and ill-defined, and hastily and irregularly derived from realities. Of the former kind are Fortune, the Prime Mover, Planetary Orbits, Element of Fire, and like fictions which owe their origin to false and idle theories.[31] And this class of idols is more easily expelled, because to get rid of them it is only necessary that all theories should be steadily rejected and dismissed as obsolete.

But the other class, which springs out of a faulty and unskillful abstraction,   25
is intricate and deeply rooted. Let us take for example such a word as *humid*,

---

[30] **notions and axioms**   Conceptions and definitive statements of truth.

[31] **idle theories**   These are things that cannot be observed and thus do not exist. Fortune is fate; the Prime Mover is God or some "first" force; the notion that planets orbited the sun was considered as "fantastic" as these others or as the idea that everything was made up of fire and its many permutations.

and see how far the several things which the word is used to signify agree with each other; and we shall find the word *humid* to be nothing else than a mark loosely and confusedly applied to denote a variety of actions which will not bear to be reduced to any constant meaning. For it both signifies that which easily spreads itself round any other body; and that which in itself is indeterminate and cannot solidize; and that which readily yields in every direction; and that which easily divides and scatters itself; and that which easily unites and collects itself; and that which readily flows and is put in motion; and that which readily clings to another body and wets it; and that which is easily reduced to a liquid, or being solid easily melts. Accordingly when you come to apply the word—if you take it in one sense, flame is humid; if in another, air is not humid; if in another, fine dust is humid; if in another, glass is humid. So that it is easy to see that the notion is taken by abstraction only from water and common and ordinary liquids, without any due verification.

There are however in words certain degrees of distortion and error. One of the least faulty kinds is that of names of substances, especially of lowest species and well-deduced (for the notion of *chalk* and of *mud* is good, of *earth* bad);[32] a more faulty kind is that of actions, as *to generate, to corrupt, to alter*; the most faulty is of qualities (except such as are the immediate objects of the sense), as *heavy, light, rare, dense*, and the like. Yet in all these cases some notions are of necessity a little better than others, in proportion to the greater variety of subjects that fall within the range of the human sense.   26

But the *Idols of the Theater* are not innate, nor do they steal into the understanding secretly, but are plainly impressed and received into the mind from the play-books of philosophical systems and the perverted rules of demonstration.[33] To attempt refutations in this case would be merely inconsistent with what I have already said: for since we agree neither upon principles nor upon demonstrations, there is no place for argument. And this is so far well, inasmuch as it leaves the honor of the ancients untouched. For they are no wise disparaged—the question between them and me being only as to the way. For as the saying is, the lame man who keeps the right road outstrips the runner who takes a wrong one. Nay, it is obvious that when a man runs the wrong way, the more active and swift he is the further he will go astray.   27

But the course I propose for the discovery of sciences is such as leaves but little to the acuteness and strength of wits, but places all wits[34] and understandings nearly on a level. For as in the drawing of a straight line or perfect   28

---

[32] ***earth* bad**   Chalk and mud were useful in manufacture; hence they were terms of approval. *Earth* is used here in the sense we use *dirt*, as in "digging in the dirt."

[33] **perverted rules of demonstration**   Another complaint against Aristotle's logic as misapplied in Bacon's day.

[34] **wits**   Intelligence, powers of reasoning.

circle, much depends on the steadiness and practice of the hand, if it be done by aim of hand only, but if with the aid of rule or compass, little or nothing; so is it exactly with my plan. But though particular confutations[35] would be of no avail, yet touching the sects and general divisions of such systems I must say something; something also touching the external signs which show that they are unsound; and finally something touching the causes of such great infelicity and of such lasting and general agreement in error; that so the access to truth may be made less difficult, and the human understanding may the more willingly submit to its purgation and dismiss its idols.

Idols of the Theater, or of systems, are many, and there can be and perhaps will be yet many more. For were it not that now for many ages men's minds have been busied with religion and theology; and were it not that civil governments, especially monarchies, have been averse to such novelties, even in matters speculative; so that men labor therein to the peril and harming of their fortunes — not only unrewarded, but exposed also to contempt and envy; doubtless there would have arisen many other philosophical sects like to those which in great variety flourished once among the Greeks. For as on the phenomena of the heavens many hypotheses may be constructed, so likewise (and more also) many various dogmas may be set up and established on the phenomena of philosophy. And in the plays of this philosophical theater you may observe the same thing which is found in the theater of the poets, that stories invented for the stage are more compact and elegant, and more as one would wish them to be, than true stories out of history.   29

In general, however, there is taken for the material of philosophy either a great deal out of a few things, or a very little out of many things; so that on both sides philosophy is based on too narrow a foundation of experiment and natural history, and decides on the authority of too few cases. For the rational school of philosophers[36] snatches from experience a variety of common instances, neither duly ascertained nor diligently examined and weighed, and leaves all the rest to meditation and agitation of wit.   30

There is also another class of philosophers,[37] who having bestowed much diligent and careful labor on a few experiments, have thence made bold to educe and construct systems; wresting all other facts in a strange fashion to conformity therewith.   31

---

[35] **confutations**   Specific counterarguments. Bacon means that he cannot offer particular arguments against each scientific sect; thus he offers a general warning.

[36] **rational school of philosophers**   Platonists who felt that human reason alone could discover the truth and that experiment was unnecessary. Their observation of experience produced only a "variety of common instances" from which they reasoned.

[37] **another class of philosophers**   William Gilbert (1544–1603) experimented tirelessly with magnetism, from which he derived numerous odd theories. Though Gilbert was a true scientist, Bacon thought of him as limited and on the wrong track.

And there is yet a third class,[38] consisting of those who out of faith and veneration mix their philosophy with theology and traditions; among whom the vanity of some has gone so far aside as to seek the origin of sciences among spirits and genii.[39] So that this parent stock of errors — this false philosophy — is of three kinds: the sophistical, the empirical, and the superstitious. . . .

But the corruption of philosophy by superstition and an admixture of theology is far more widely spread, and does the greatest harm, whether to entire systems or to their parts. For the human understanding is obnoxious to the influence of the imagination no less than to the influence of common notions. For the contentious and sophistical kind of philosophy ensnares the understanding; but this kind, being fanciful and tumid[40] and half poetical, misleads it more by flattery. For there is in man an ambition of the understanding, no less than of the will, especially in high and lofty spirits.

Of this kind we have among the Greeks a striking example in Pythagoras, though he united with it a coarser and more cumbrous superstition; another in Plato and his school,[41] more dangerous and subtle. It shows itself likewise in parts of other philosophies, in the introduction of abstract forms and final causes and first causes, with the omission in most cases of causes intermediate, and the like. Upon this point the greatest caution should be used. For nothing is so mischievous as the apotheosis of error; and it is a very plague of the understanding for vanity to become the object of veneration. Yet in this vanity some of the moderns have with extreme levity indulged so far as to attempt to found a system of natural philosophy on the first chapter of Genesis, on the book of Job, and other parts of the sacred writings; seeking for the dead among the living: which also makes the inhibition and repression of it the more important, because from this unwholesome mixture of things human and divine there arises not only a fantastic philosophy but also an heretical religion. Very meet it is therefore that we be sober-minded, and give to faith that only which is faith's. . . .

So much concerning the several classes of Idols, and their equipage: all of which must be renounced and put away with a fixed and solemn determination, and the understanding thoroughly freed and cleansed; the entrance into

32

33

34

35

---

[38] **a third class** Pythagoras (c. 580–500 B.C.E.) was a Greek philosopher who experimented rigorously with mathematics and a tuned string. He is said to have developed the musical scale. His theory of reincarnation, or the transmigration of souls, was somehow based on his travels in India and his work with scales. The superstitious belief in the movement of souls is what Bacon complains of.

[39] **genii** Oriental demons or spirits; a slap at Pythagoras, who traveled in the Orient.

[40] **tumid** Overblown, swollen.

[41] **Plato and his school** Plato's religious bent was further developed by Plotinus (205–270 C.E.) in his *Enneads*. Although Plotinus was not a Christian, his Neo-Platonism was welcomed as a philosophy compatible with Christianity.

the kingdom of man, founded on the sciences, being not much other than the entrance into the kingdom of heaven, whereunto none may enter except as a little child.

✖ QUESTIONS FOR CRITICAL READING

1. Which of Bacon's idols is the most difficult to understand? Do your best to define it.

2. Which of these idols do we still need to worry about? Why? What dangers does it present?

3. What does Bacon mean by implying that our senses are weak (para. 14)? In what ways do you agree or disagree with that opinion?

4. Occasionally Bacon says something that seems a bit like an aphorism (see the introduction to Machiavelli, p. 84). Find at least one such expression in this selection. On examination, does the expression have as much meaning as it seems to have?

5. What kind of readers did Bacon expect for this piece? What clues does his way of communicating provide regarding the nature of his anticipated readers?

✖ SUGGESTIONS FOR CRITICAL WRITING

1. Which of Bacon's idols most seriously affects the way you as a person observe nature? Using enumeration, arrange the idols in order of their effect on your own judgment. If you prefer, you may write about the idol you believe is most effective in slowing investigation into nature.

2. Is it true, as Bacon says in paragraph 10, that people are in general "more moved and excited by affirmatives than by negatives"? Do we really stress the positive and de-emphasize the negative in the conduct of our general affairs? Find at least three instances in which people seem to gravitate toward the positive or the negative in everyday situations. Try to establish whether Bacon has, in fact, described what is a habit of mind.

3. In paragraph 13, Bacon states that the "will and affections" enter into matters of thought. By this he means that our understanding of what we observe is conditioned by what we want and what we feel. Thus, when he says, "For what a man had rather were true he more readily believes," he tells us that people tend to believe what they want to believe. Test this statement by means of observation. Find out, for example, how many older people are convinced that the world is deteriorating, how many younger people feel that there is a plot on the part of older people to hold them back, how many women feel that men consciously oppress women, and how many men feel that feminists are not as feminine as they should be. What other beliefs can you discover that seem to have their origin in what people want to believe rather than in what is true?

4. Bacon's views on religion have always been difficult to define. He grew up in a very religious time, but his writings rarely discuss religion positively. In this work, he talks about giving "to faith that only which is faith's" (para. 34). He seems to feel that scientific investigation is something quite separate from religion. Examine the selection carefully to determine what you think Bacon's view on this question is. Then take a stand on the issue of the relationship between religion and science. Should science be totally independent of religious concerns? Should religious issues control scientific experimentation? What does Bacon mean when he complains about the vanity of founding "a system of natural philosophy on the first chapter of Genesis, on the book of Job, and other parts of the sacred writings" (para. 34)? "Natural philosophy" means biology, chemistry, physics, and science in general. Are Bacon's complaints justified? Would his complaints be relevant today?

5. **CONNECTIONS**   How has the reception of Charles Darwin's work been affected by a general inability of the public to see beyond Bacon's four idols? Read both Darwin's essay (p. 605) and that of Gilbert Ryle (p. 514). Which of these two writers is more concerned with the lingering effects of the four idols? Do you feel that the effects have seriously affected people's beliefs regarding Darwinian theory?

6. **CONNECTIONS**   Both Richard P. Feynman (p. 621) and Edward O. Wilson (p. 631) discuss the nature of science and the value of science in the modern world. Which of the four idols do these two modern writers see as most problematic to establishing a full understanding of how science must be understood today? In what way are these modern authors in debt to the work of Francis Bacon? How might they talk about the problems of coming to an understanding of the truth about science today? Write an essay based on the structure of Bacon's essay but reflecting the concerns of both Feynman and Wilson.

© Mansell/Time Life Pictures/Getty Images

CHARLES
DARWIN
Natural Selection

CHARLES DARWIN (1809–1882) was trained as a minister in the Church of England, but he was also the grandson of one of England's greatest horticulturists, Erasmus Darwin. Partly as a way of putting off ordination in the church and partly because of his natural curiosity, Darwin found himself performing the functions of a naturalist on HMS *Beagle*, which was engaged in scientific explorations around South America during the years 1831 to 1836. Darwin's book *Journal of Researches into the Geology and Natural History of the Various Countries Visited by H. M. S. Beagle, 1832–36* (1839) details the experiences he had and offers some views of his self-education as a naturalist.

His journeys on the *Beagle* led him to note variations in species of animals he found in various separate locales, particularly between remote islands and the mainland. Varieties — his term for any visible (or invisible) differences in markings, coloration, size, or shape of appendages, organs, or bodies — were of some peculiar use, he believed, for animals in the environment in which he found them. He was not certain about the use of these varieties, and he did not know whether the changes that created the varieties resulted from the environment or from some chance operation of nature. Ultimately, he concluded that varieties in nature were caused by three forces: (1) natural selection, in which varieties occur spontaneously by chance but are then "selected for" because they are aids to survival; (2) direct action of the environment, in which nonadaptive varieties do not survive because of climate, food conditions, or the like; and (3) the effects of use or disuse of a variation (for example, the short beak of a bird mentioned in para. 9). Darwin later regarded sexual selection, which figures prominently in this work, as less significant.

The idea of evolution — the gradual change of species through some kind of modification of varieties — had been in the air for many years when Darwin began his work. The English scientists W. C. Wells in 1813 and Patrick Matthew in 1831 had both proposed

From *On the Origin of Species by Means of Natural Selection*. This text is from the first edition, published in 1859. In the five subsequent editions, Darwin hedged more and more on his theory, often introducing material in defense against objections. The first edition is vigorous and direct; this edition jolted the worlds of science and religion out of their complacence. In later editions, this chapter was titled "Natural Selection; or, Survival of the Fittest."

theories of natural selection, although Darwin was unaware of their work. Alfred Russel Wallace (1823–1913), a younger English scientist, revealed in 1858 that he was about to propose the same theory of evolution as was Darwin. They jointly published brief versions of their theories in 1858, and the next year Darwin rushed the final version of his book *On the Origin of Species by Means of Natural Selection* to press.

Darwin did not mention human beings as part of the evolutionary process in *On the Origin of Species*; because he was particularly concerned about the probable adverse reactions of theologians, he merely promised later discussion of that subject. It came in *The Descent of Man and Selection in Relation to Sex* (1871), the companion to *On the Origin of Species*.

When Darwin returned to England after completing his research on the *Beagle*, he supplemented his knowledge with information gathered from breeders of pigeons, livestock, dogs, and horses. This research, it must be noted, involved relatively few samples and was conducted according to comparatively unscientific practices. Yet although limited, it corresponded with his observations of nature. Humans could and did cause changes in species; Darwin's task was to show that nature — through the process of natural selection — could do the same thing.

The Descent of Man stirred up a great deal of controversy between the church and Darwin's supporters. Not since the Roman Catholic Church denied the fact that the earth went around the sun, which Galileo proved scientifically by 1632 (and was placed under house arrest for his pains), had there been a more serious confrontation between science and religion. Darwin was ridiculed by ministers and doubted by older scientists; but his views were stoutly defended by younger scientists, many of whom had arrived at similar conclusions. In the end, Darwin's views were accepted by the Church of England, and when he died in 1882 he was lionized and buried at Westminster Abbey in London. Only recently has controversy concerning his work arisen again.

DARWIN'S RHETORIC

Despite the complexity of the material it deals with, Darwin's writing is fluent, smooth, and stylistically sophisticated and keeps the reader engaged. Darwin's rhetorical method depends entirely on the yoking of thesis and demonstration. He uses definition frequently, but most often he uses testimony, gathering information and instances, both real and imaginary, from many different sources.

Interestingly enough, Darwin claimed that he used Francis Bacon's method of induction in his research, gathering evidence of many instances of a given phenomenon, from which the truth — or a natural law — emerges. In fact, Darwin did not quite follow this path. Like most modern scientists, he established a hypothesis after a period of observation, and then he looked for evidence that confirmed or refuted the hypothesis. He was careful to include examples that argued against his view, but like most scientists, he emphasized the importance of the supportive samples.

Induction plays a part in the rhetoric of this selection in that it is dominated by examples from bird breeding, birds in nature, domestic farm animals and their breeding, and botany, including the breeding of plants and the interdependence of certain insects and certain plants. Erasmus Darwin was famous for his work with plants, and it is natural that such observations would play an important part in his grandson's thinking.

The process of natural selection is carefully discussed, particularly in paragraph 8 and thereafter. Darwin emphasizes its positive nature and its differences from selection by human breeders. The use of comparison, which appears frequently in the selection, is most conspicuous in these paragraphs. He postulates a nature in which the fittest survive because they are best adapted for survival, but he does not dwell on the fate of those who are unfit individuals. It was left to later writers, often misapplying his theories, to do that.

✂ PREREADING QUESTIONS: WHAT TO READ FOR

The following prereading questions may help you anticipate key issues in the discussion of Charles Darwin's "Natural Selection." Keeping them in mind during your first reading of the selection should help focus your attention.

1. What is the basic principle of natural selection?
2. How does "human" selection differ from nature's selection?

Natural Selection

How will the struggle for existence . . . act in regard to variation? Can the principle of selection, which we have seen is so potent in the hands of man, apply in nature? I think we shall see that it can act most effectually. Let it be borne in mind in what an endless number of strange peculiarities our domestic productions, and, in a lesser degree, those under nature, vary; and how strong the hereditary tendency is. Under domestication, it may be truly said that the whole organization becomes in some degree plastic.[1] Let it be borne in mind how infinitely complex and close-fitting are the mutual relations of all organic beings to each other and to their physical conditions of life. Can it, then, be thought improbable, seeing that variations useful to man have undoubtedly occurred, that other variations useful in some way to each being in the great and complex battle of life, should sometimes occur in the course

1

---

[1] **plastic**   Capable of being shaped and changed.

of thousands of generations? If such do occur, can we doubt (remembering that many more individuals are born than can possibly survive) that individuals having any advantage, however slight, over others, would have the best chance of surviving and of procreating their kind? On the other hand, we may feel sure that any variation in the least degree injurious would be rigidly destroyed. This preservation of favorable variations and the rejection of injurious variations, I call Natural Selection. Variations neither useful nor injurious would not be affected by natural selection, and would be left a fluctuating element, as perhaps we see in the species called polymorphic.[2]

We shall best understand the probable course of natural selection by taking the case of a country undergoing some physical change, for instance, of climate. The proportional numbers of its inhabitants would almost immediately undergo a change, and some species might become extinct. We may conclude, from what we have seen of the intimate and complex manner in which the inhabitants of each country are bound together, that any change in the numerical proportions of some of the inhabitants, independently of the change of climate itself, would most seriously affect many of the others. If the country were open on its borders, new forms would certainly immigrate, and this also would seriously disturb the relations of some of the former inhabitants. Let it be remembered how powerful the influence of a single introduced tree or mammal has been shown to be. But in the case of an island, or of a country partly surrounded by barriers, into which new and better adapted forms could not freely enter, we should then have places in the economy of nature which would assuredly be better filled up, if some of the original inhabitants were in some manner modified; for, had the area been open to immigration, these same places would have been seized on by intruders. In such case, every slight modification, which in the course of ages chanced to arise, and which in any way favored the individuals of any of the species, by better adapting them to their altered conditions, would tend to be preserved; and natural selection would thus have free scope for the work of improvement.

We have reason to believe . . . that a change in the conditions of life, by specially acting on the reproductive system, causes or increases variability; and in the foregoing case the conditions of life are supposed to have undergone a change, and this would manifestly be favorable to natural selection, by giving a better chance of profitable variations occurring; and unless profitable variations do occur, natural selection can do nothing. Not that, as I believe, any extreme amount of variability is necessary; as man can certainly produce great results by adding up in any given direction mere individual differences, so could Nature, but far more easily, from having incomparably longer time at

2

3

---

[2] **species called polymorphic**   Species that have more than one form over the course of their lives, such as butterflies.

her disposal. Nor do I believe that any great physical change, as of climate, or any unusual degree of isolation to check immigration, is actually necessary to produce new and unoccupied places for natural selection to fill up by modifying and improving some of the varying inhabitants. For as all the inhabitants of each country are struggling together with nicely balanced forces, extremely slight modifications in the structure or habits of one inhabitant would often give it an advantage over others; and still further modifications of the same kind would often still further increase the advantage. No country can be named in which all the native inhabitants are now so perfectly adapted to each other and to the physical conditions under which they live, that none of them could anyhow be improved; for in all countries, the natives have been so far conquered by naturalized productions, that they have allowed foreigners to take firm possession of the land. And as foreigners have thus everywhere beaten some of the natives, we may safely conclude that the natives might have been modified with advantage, so as to have better resisted such intruders.

As man can produce and certainly has produced a great result by his 4 methodical and unconscious means of selection, what may not nature effect? Man can act only on external and visible characters; nature cares nothing for appearances, except in so far as they may be useful to any being. She can act on every internal organ, on every shade of constitutional difference, on the whole machinery of life. Man selects only for his own good; Nature only for that of the being which she tends. Every selected character is fully exercised by her; and the being is placed under well-suited conditions of life. Man keeps the natives of many climates in the same country; he seldom exercises each selected character in some peculiar and fitting manner; he feeds a long and a short beaked pigeon on the same food; he does not exercise a long-backed or long-legged quadruped in any peculiar manner; he exposes sheep with long and short wool to the same climate. He does not allow the most vigorous males to struggle for the females. He does not rigidly destroy all inferior animals, but protects during each varying season, as far as lies in his power, all his productions. He often begins his selection by some half-monstrous form; or at least by some modification prominent enough to catch the eye, or to be plainly useful to him. Under nature, the slightest difference of structure or constitution may well turn the nicely balanced scale in the struggle for life, and so be preserved. How fleeting are the wishes and efforts of man! how short his time! and consequently how poor will his products be, compared with those accumulated by nature during whole geological periods. Can we wonder, then, that nature's productions should be far "truer" in character than man's productions; that they should be infinitely better adapted to the most complex conditions of life, and should plainly bear the stamp of far higher workmanship?

It may be said that natural selection is daily and hourly scrutinizing, through- 5 out the world, every variation, even the slightest; rejecting that which is bad, preserving and adding up all that is good; silently and insensibly working, whenever and wherever opportunity offers, at the improvement of each organic being in relation to its organic and inorganic conditions of life. We see nothing of these slow changes in progress, until the hand of time has marked the long lapse of ages, and then so imperfect is our view into long past geological ages, that we only see that the forms of life are now different from what they formerly were.

Although natural selection can act only through and for the good of each being, yet characters and structures, which we are apt to consider as of very trifling importance, may thus be acted on. When we see leaf-eating insects green, and bark-feeders mottled-grey; the alpine ptarmigan white in winter, the red-grouse the color of heather, and the black-grouse that of peaty earth, we must believe that these tints are of service to these birds and insects in preserving them from danger. Grouse, if not destroyed at some period of their lives, would increase in countless numbers; they are known to suffer largely from birds of prey; and hawks are guided by eyesight to their prey—so much so that on parts of the Continent[3] persons are warned not to keep white pigeons, as being the most liable to destruction. Hence I can see no reason to doubt that natural selection might be most effective in giving the proper color to each kind of grouse, and in keeping that color, when once acquired, true and constant. Nor ought we to think that the occasional destruction of an animal of any particular color would produce little effect; we should remember how essential it is in a flock of white sheep to destroy every lamb with the faintest trace of black. In plants, the down on the fruit and the color of the flesh are considered by botanists as characters of the most trifling importance; yet we hear from an excellent horticulturist, Downing,[4] that in the United States, smooth-skinned fruits suffer far more from a beetle, a curculio,[5] than those with down; that purple plums suffer far more from a certain disease than yellow plums; whereas another disease attacks yellow-fleshed peaches far more than those with other colored flesh. If, with all the aids of art, these slight differences make a great difference in cultivating the several varieties, assuredly, in a state of nature, where the trees would have to struggle with other trees and with a host of enemies, such differences would effectually settle which variety, whether a smooth or downy, a yellow or purple fleshed fruit, should succeed.

In looking at many small points of difference between species, which, as far as our ignorance permits us to judge, seem to be quite unimportant, we must not forget that climate, food, etc., probably produce some slight and direct effect. It is,

6

7

---

[3] **Continent**   European continent; the contiguous landmass of Europe, which excludes the British Isles.

[4] **Andrew Jackson Downing (1815–1852)**   American horticulturist and specialist in fruit and fruit trees.

[5] **curculio**   A weevil.

however, far more necessary to bear in mind that there are many unknown laws of correlation[6] of growth, which, when one part of the organization is modified through variation and the modifications are accumulated by natural selection for the good of the being, will cause other modifications, often of the most unexpected nature.

As we see that those variations which under domestication appear at   8 any particular period of life, tend to reappear in the offspring at the same period — for instance, in the seeds of the many varieties of our culinary and agricultural plants; in the caterpillar and cocoon stages of the varieties of the silkworm; in the eggs of poultry, and in the color of the down of their chickens; in the horns of our sheep and cattle when nearly adult — so in a state of nature, natural selection will be enabled to act on and modify organic beings at any age, by the accumulation of profitable variations at that age, and by their inheritance at a corresponding age. If it profit a plant to have its seeds more and more widely disseminated by the wind, I can see no greater difficulty in this being effected through natural selection than in the cotton-planter increasing and improving by selection the down in the pods on his cotton-trees. Natural selection may modify and adapt the larva of an insect to a score of contingencies, wholly different from those which concern the mature insect. These modifications will no doubt effect, through the laws of correlation, the structure of the adult; and probably in the case of those insects which live only for a few hours, and which never feed, a large part of their structure is merely the correlated result of successive changes in the structure of their larvae. So, conversely, modifications in the adult will probably often affect the structure of the larva; but in all cases natural selection will ensure that modifications consequent on other modifications at a different period of life, shall not be in the least degree injurious: for if they became so, they would cause the extinction of the species.

Natural selection will modify the structure of the young in relation to the   9 parent, and of the parent in relation to the young. In social animals it will adapt the structure of each individual for the benefit of the community, if each in consequence profits by the selected change. What natural selection cannot do is to modify the structure of one species, without giving it any advantage, for the good of another species; and though statements to this effect may be found in works of natural history, I cannot find one case which will bear investigation. A structure used only once in an animal's whole life, if of high importance to it, might be modified to any extent by natural selection; for instance, the great jaws

---

[6] **laws of correlation**   In certain plants and animals, one condition relates to another, as in the case of blue-eyed white cats, which are often deaf; the reasons are not clear but have to do with genes and their locations.

possessed by certain insects, and used exclusively for opening the cocoon—or the hard tip to the beak of nestling birds, used for breaking the egg. It has been asserted that of the best short-beaked tumbler-pigeons, more perish in the egg than are able to get out of it; so that fanciers[7] assist in the act of hatching. Now, if nature had to make the beak of a full-grown pigeon very short for the bird's own advantage, the process of modification would be very slow, and there would be simultaneously the most rigorous selection of the young birds within the egg, which had the most powerful and hardest beaks, for all with weak beaks would inevitably perish; or, more delicate and more easily broken shells might be selected, the thickness of the shell being known to vary like every other structure.

Sexual Selection

Inasmuch as peculiarities often appear under domestication in one sex and become hereditarily attached to that sex, the same fact probably occurs under nature, and if so, natural selection will be able to modify one sex in its functional relations to the other sex, or in relation to wholly different habits of life in the two sexes, as is sometimes the case with insects. And this leads me to say a few words on what I call Sexual Selection. This depends, not on a struggle for existence, but on a struggle between the males for possession of the females; the result is not death to the unsuccessful competitor, but few or no offspring. Sexual selection is, therefore, less rigorous than natural selection. Generally, the most vigorous males, those which are best fitted for their places in nature, will leave most progeny. But in many cases, victory will depend not on general vigor, but on having special weapons, confined to the male sex. A hornless stag or spurless cock would have a poor chance of leaving offspring. Sexual selection by always allowing the victor to breed might surely give indomitable courage, length to the spur, and strength to the wing to strike in the spurred leg, as well as the brutal cock fighter,[8] who knows well that he can improve his breed by careful selection of the best cocks. How low in the scale of nature this law of battle descends, I know not; male alligators have been described as fighting, bellowing, and whirling round, like Indians in a war-dance, for the possession of the females; male salmons have been seen fighting all day long; male stag-beetles often bear wounds from the huge mandibles[9] of

10

---

[7] **fanciers**   Amateurs who raise and race pigeons.

[8] **brutal cock fighter**   Cockfights were a popular spectator sport in England, especially for gamblers, but many people considered them a horrible brutality.

[9] **mandibles**   Jaws.

other males. The war is, perhaps, severest between the males of polygamous animals,[10] and these seem oftenest provided with special weapons. The males of carnivorous animals are already well armed; though to them and to others, special means of defense may be given through means of sexual selection, as the mane to the lion, the shoulder-pad to the boar, and the hooked jaw to the male salmon; for the shield may be as important for victory as the sword or spear.

Among birds, the contest is often of a more peaceful character. All those who have attended to the subject believe that there is the severest rivalry between the males of many species to attract, by singing, the females. The rock-thrush of Guiana,[11] birds of paradise, and some others, congregate; and successive males display their gorgeous plumage and perform strange antics before the females, which standing by as spectators, at last choose the most attractive partner. Those who have closely attended to birds in confinement well know that they often take individual preferences and dislikes: thus Sir R. Heron[12] has described how one pied peacock was eminently attractive to all his hen birds. It may appear childish to attribute any effect to such apparently weak means: I cannot here enter on the details necessary to support this view; but if man can in a short time give elegant carriage and beauty to his bantams,[13] according to his standard of beauty, I can see no good reason to doubt that female birds, by selecting, during thousands of generations, the most melodious or beautiful males, according to their standard of beauty, might produce a marked effect. I strongly suspect that some well-known laws with respect to the plumage of male and female birds, in comparison with the plumage of the young, can be explained on the view of plumage having been chiefly modified by sexual selection, acting when the birds have come to the breeding age or during the breeding season; the modifications thus produced being inherited at corresponding ages or seasons, either by the males alone, or by the males and females; but I have not space here to enter on this subject.

Thus it is, as I believe, that when the males and females of any animal have the same general habits of life, but differ in structure, color, or ornament, such differences have been mainly caused by sexual selection; that is, individual males have had, in successive generations, some slight advantage over other males, in their weapons, means of defense, or charms; and have transmitted these advantages to their male offspring. Yet, I would not wish to attribute all such sexual differences to this agency: for we see peculiarities arising and

11

12

---

[10] **polygamous animals**   Animals that typically have more than one mate.

[11] **Guiana**   Formerly British Guiana, now Guyana, on the northeast coast of South America.

[12] **Sir Robert Heron (1765–1854)**   English politician who maintained a menagerie of animals.

[13] **bantams**   Cocks bred for fighting.

becoming attached to the male sex in our domestic animals (as the wattle in male carriers, horn-like protuberances in the cocks of certain fowls, etc.), which we cannot believe to be either useful to the males in battle, or attractive to the females. We see analogous cases under nature, for instance, the tuft of hair on the breast of the turkey-cock, which can hardly be either useful or ornamental to this bird; indeed, had the tuft appeared under domestication, it would have been called a monstrosity.

Illustrations of the Action of Natural Selection

In order to make it clear how, as I believe, natural selection acts, I must beg permission to give one or two imaginary illustrations. Let us take the case of a wolf, which preys on various animals, securing some by craft, some by strength, and some by fleetness; and let us suppose that the fleetest prey, a deer for instance, had from any change in the country increased in numbers, or that other prey had decreased in numbers, during that season of the year when the wolf is hardest pressed for food. I can under such circumstances see no reason to doubt that the swiftest and slimmest wolves would have the best chance of surviving, and so be preserved or selected, provided always that they retained strength to master their prey at this or at some other period of the year, when they might be compelled to prey on other animals. I can see no more reason to doubt this, than that man can improve the fleetness of his greyhounds by careful and methodical selection, or by that unconscious selection which results from each man trying to keep the best dogs without any thought of modifying the breed. 13

Even without any change in the proportional numbers of the animals on which our wolf preyed, a cub might be born with an innate tendency to pursue certain kinds of prey. Nor can this be thought very improbable; for we often observe great differences in the natural tendencies of our domestic animals; one cat, for instance, taking to catch rats, another mice; one cat, according to Mr. St. John,[14] bringing home winged game, another hares or rabbits, and another hunting on marshy ground and almost nightly catching woodcocks or snipes. The tendency to catch rats rather than mice is known to be inherited. Now, if any slight innate change of habit or of structure benefited an individual wolf, it would have the best chance of surviving and of leaving offspring. Some of its young would probably inherit the same habits or structure, and by the repetition of this process, a new variety might be formed which would either supplant or coexist with the parent-form of wolf. 14

----

[14] **Charles George William St. John (1809–1856)**   English naturalist whose book *Wild Sports and Natural History of the Highlands* was published in 1846.

Or, again, the wolves inhabiting a mountainous district, and those frequenting the lowlands, would naturally be forced to hunt different prey; and from the continued preservation of the individuals best fitted for the two sites, two varieties might slowly be formed. These varieties would cross and blend where they met; but to this subject of intercrossing we shall soon have to return. I may add, that, according to Mr. Pierce,[15] there are two varieties of the wolf inhabiting the Catskill Mountains in the United States, one with a light greyhound-like form, which pursues deer, and the other more bulky, with shorter legs, which more frequently attacks the shepherd's flocks.

Let us now take a more complex case. Certain plants excrete a sweet juice,   15
apparently for the sake of eliminating something injurious from their sap; this is effected by glands at the base of the stipules[16] in some Leguminosae, and at the back of the leaf of the common laurel. This juice, though small in quantity, is greedily sought by insects. Let us now suppose a little sweet juice or nectar to be excreted by the inner bases of the petals of a flower. In this case insects in seeking the nectar would get dusted with pollen, and would certainly often transport the pollen from one flower to the stigma of another flower. The flowers of two distinct individuals of the same species would thus get crossed; and the act of crossing, we have good reason to believe (as will hereafter be more fully alluded to), would produce very vigorous seedlings, which consequently would have the best chance of flourishing and surviving. Some of these seedlings would probably inherit the nectar-excreting power. Those individual flowers which had the largest glands or nectaries, and which excreted most nectar, would be oftenest visited by insects, and would be oftenest crossed; and so in the long-run would gain the upper hand. Those flowers, also, which had their stamens and pistils[17] placed, in relation to the size and habits of the particular insects which visited them, so as to favor in any degree the transportal of their pollen from flower to flower, would likewise be favored or selected. We might have taken the case of insects visiting flowers for the sake of collecting pollen instead of nectar; and as pollen is formed for the sole object of fertilization, its destruction appears a simple loss to the plant; yet if a little pollen were carried, at first occasionally and then habitually, by the pollen-devouring insects from flower to flower, and a cross thus effected, although nine-tenths of the pollen were destroyed, it might still be a great gain to the plant; and those individuals which produced more and more pollen, and had larger and larger anthers,[18] would be selected.

---

[15] **Mr. Pierce**   Unidentified.

[16] **stipules**   Spines at the base of a leaf.

[17] **stamens and pistils**   Sexual organs of plants. The male and female organs appear together in the same flower.

[18] **anthers**   That part of the stamen that contains pollen.

When our plant, by this process of the continued preservation or natural selection of more and more attractive flowers, had been rendered highly attractive to insects, they would, unintentionally on their part, regularly carry pollen from flower to flower; and that they can most effectually do this, I could easily show by many striking instances. I will give only one—not as a very striking case, but as likewise illustrating one step in the separation of the sexes of plants, presently to be alluded to. Some holly-trees bear only male flowers, which have four stamens producing rather a small quantity of pollen, and a rudimentary pistil; other holly-trees bear only female flowers; these have a full-sized pistil, and four stamens with shrivelled anthers, in which not a grain of pollen can be detected. Having found a female tree exactly sixty yards from a male tree, I put the stigmas[19] of twenty flowers, taken from different branches, under the microscope, and on all, without exception, there were pollen-grains, and on some a profusion of pollen. As the wind had set for several days from the female to the male tree, the pollen could not thus have been carried. The weather had been cold and boisterous, and therefore not favorable to bees; nevertheless every female flower which I examined had been effectually fertilized by the bees, accidentally dusted with pollen, having flown from tree to tree in search of nectar. But to return to our imaginary case: as soon as the plant had been rendered so highly attractive to insects that pollen was regularly carried from flower to flower, another process might commence. No naturalist doubts the advantage of what has been called the "physiological division of labor"; hence we may believe that it would be advantageous to a plant to produce stamens alone in one flower or on one whole plant, and pistils alone in another flower or on another plant. In plants under culture and placed under new conditions of life, sometimes the male organs and sometimes the female organs become more or less impotent; now if we suppose this to occur in ever so slight a degree under nature, then as pollen is already carried regularly from flower to flower, and as a more complete separation of the sexes of our plant would be advantageous on the principle of the division of labor, individuals with this tendency more and more increased, would be continually favored or selected, until at last a complete separation of the sexes would be effected. 16

Let us now turn to the nectar-feeding insects in our imaginary case: we may suppose the plant of which we have been slowly increasing the nectar by continued selection, to be a common plant; and that certain insects depended in main part on its nectar for food. I could give many facts, showing how anxious bees are to save time; for instance, their habit of cutting holes and sucking the nectar at the bases of certain flowers, which they can, with a very little more trouble, enter by the mouth. Bearing such facts in mind, I can see no reason to doubt that an accidental deviation in the size 17

---

[19] **stigmas**   Where the plant's pollen develops.

and form of the body, or in the curvature and length of the proboscis,[20] etc., far too slight to be appreciated by us, might profit a bee or other insect, so that an individual so characterized would be able to obtain its food more quickly, and so have a better chance of living and leaving descendants. Its descendants would probably inherit a tendency to a similar slight deviation of structure. The tubes of the corollas[21] of the common red and incarnate clovers (Trifolium pratense and incarnatum) do not on a hasty glance appear to differ in length; yet the hive-bee can easily suck the nectar out of the incarnate clover, but not out of the common red clover, which is visited by humble-bees[22] alone; so that whole fields of the red clover offer in vain an abundant supply of precious nectar to the hive-bee. Thus it might be a great advantage to the hive-bee to have a slightly longer or differently constructed proboscis. On the other hand, I have found by experiment that the fertility of clover greatly depends on bees visiting and moving parts of the corolla, so as to push the pollen on to the stigmatic surface. Hence, again, if humble-bees were to become rare in any country, it might be a great advantage to the red clover to have a shorter or more deeply divided tube to its corolla, so that the hive-bee could visit its flowers. Thus I can understand how a flower and a bee might slowly become, either simultaneously or one after the other, modified and adapted in the most perfect manner to each other, by the continued preservation of individuals presenting mutual and slightly favorable deviations of structure.

I am well aware that this doctrine of natural selection, exemplified in the above imaginary instances, is open to the same objections which were at first urged against Sir Charles Lyell's noble views[23] on "the modern changes of the earth, as illustrative of geology"; but we now very seldom hear the action, for instance, of the coast-waves, called a trifling and insignificant cause, when applied to the excavation of gigantic valleys or to the formation of the longest lines of inland cliffs. Natural selection can act only by the preservation and accumulation of infinitesimally small inherited modifications, each profitable to the preserved being; and as modern geology has almost banished such views as the excavation of a great valley by a single

18

---

[20] **proboscis**   Snout.

[21] **corollas**   Inner set of floral petals.

[22] **humble-bees**   Bumblebees.

[23] **Sir Charles Lyell's noble views**   Lyell (1797–1875) was an English geologist whose landmark work, *Principles of Geology* (1830–1833), Darwin read while on the *Beagle*. The book inspired Darwin, and the two scientists became friends. Lyell was shown portions of *On the Origin of Species* while Darwin was writing it.

diluvial[24] wave, so will natural selection, if it be a true principle, banish the belief of the continued creation of new organic beings, or of any great and sudden modification in their structure.

[24] **diluvial** Pertaining to a flood. Darwin means that geological changes, such as those that caused the Grand Canyon, were no longer thought of as occurring instantly by flood (or other catastrophes) but were considered to have developed over a long period of time, as he imagines happened in the evolution of the species.

QUESTIONS FOR CRITICAL READING

1. Darwin's metaphor "battle of life" (para. 1) introduces issues that might be thought extraneous to a scientific inquiry. What is the danger of using such a metaphor? What is the advantage of doing so?
2. Many religious groups reject Darwin's concept of natural selection, but they heartily accept human selection in the form of controlled breeding. Why would there be such a difference between the two?
3. Do you feel that the theory of natural selection is a positive force? Could it be directed by divine power?
4. In this work, there is no reference to human beings in terms of the process of selection. How might the principles at work on animals also work on people? Do you think that Darwin assumes this?
5. When this chapter was published in a later edition, Darwin added to its title "Survival of the Fittest." What issues or emotions does that new title raise that "Natural Selection" does not?

SUGGESTIONS FOR CRITICAL WRITING

1. In paragraph 13, Darwin uses imaginary examples. Compare the value of his genuine examples and these imaginary ones. How effective is the use of imaginary examples in an argument? What requirements should an imaginary example meet to be forceful in an argument? Do you find Darwin's imaginary examples to be strong or weak?
2. From paragraph 14 on, Darwin discusses the process of modification of a species through its beginning in the modification of an individual. Explain, insofar as you understand the concept, how a species could be modified by a variation occurring in just one individual. In your explanation, use Darwin's rhetorical technique of the imaginary example.
3. Write an essay that takes as its thesis statement the following sentence from paragraph 18: "Natural selection can act only by the preservation and accumulation of infinitesimally small inherited modifications, each profitable to the

preserved being." Be sure to examine the work carefully for other statements by Darwin that add strength, clarity, and meaning to this one. You may also employ the Darwinian device of presenting imaginary instances in your essay.

4. A controversy exists concerning the Darwinian theory of evolution. Explore your local or college library and the Internet for up-to-date information on the creationist-evolutionist conflict in schools. Look up either or both terms to see what articles you can find. Define the controversy and take a stand on it. Use your knowledge of natural selection gained from this piece. Remember, too, that Darwin was trained as a minister of the church and was concerned about religious opinion.

5. When Darwin wrote this piece, he believed that sexual selection was of great importance in evolutionary changes in species. Assuming that this belief is true, establish the similarities between sexual selection in plants and animals and sexual selection, as you have observed it, in people. Paragraphs 10–12 discuss this issue. Darwin does not discuss selection in human beings, but it is clear that physical and stylistic distinctions between the sexes have some bearing on selection. Assuming that to be true, what qualities in people (physical and mental) are likely to survive? Why?

6. **CONNECTIONS**   Which of Francis Bacon's four idols (p. 591) would have made it most difficult for Darwin's contemporaries to accept the theory of evolution, despite the mass of evidence he presented? Do the idols interfere with people's ability to evaluate evidence?

7. **CONNECTIONS**   To what extent are Darwin's theories a threat to public morality? Consider Iris Murdoch's "Morality and Religion" (p. 757), and examine Darwin for his awareness of the concepts of morality that Murdoch discusses. Would Murdoch find it difficult to accept Darwin's views of evolution? What moral conflicts would Murdoch be likely to find in his theories? If she were to accept Darwin's theories, how would she connect the ideals of religion with the process of natural selection in nature? Write an essay that connects Murdoch's concerns for morality with Darwin's interpretations of the actions of nature.

8. **CONNECTIONS**   In his essay, Darwin discusses natural selection, the way in which genes may alter the biology of individuals in a natural setting. Compare what he has to say about biological change with what Philip Kitcher (p. 656) has to say about artificial selection in which people decide how to change genes to satisfy their own needs or desires. Both processes treat the same issue: how change happens to biological individuals. What might Darwin have said to Kitcher, given Darwin's own comments on the artificial selection of breeders of animals in his own time? What's the difference between the natural selection of a child's genetic gifts and the selection by parents (or politicians) of a child's genetic gifts? Who alarms you more, Darwin or Kitcher?

RICHARD P.
FEYNMAN

The Value of Science

R ICHARD PHILLIPS FEYNMAN (1918–1988), one of the most impressive and colorful physicists of

© Corbis

his age, was generally acknowledged as a genius among geniuses. His research and mathematical formulas thoroughly revised the modern theories of quantum electrodynamics. In fact, he was granted the Nobel Prize in Physics in 1965 for his work in this field.

Born and raised in Far Rockaway, New York, Feynman received his bachelor's degree at the Massachusetts Institute of Technology in 1939 and his doctorate in theoretical physics at Princeton University in 1942. His work on quantum mechanics at both universities was far-reaching and influential on other researchers. During World War II, Feynman worked on the Manhattan Project, which developed the atomic bomb, and was present at the detonation of the first bomb on July 16, 1945, at Alamogordo, New Mexico. His reaction was mixed; he was thrilled to see that his theories actually worked, but at the same time, he was fearful about the bomb's ultimate use.

After the war, Feynman worked at Cornell University as associate professor and then moved to the California Institute of Technology in 1950. He remained at Caltech for the rest of his career. Because he was a charismatic man with a great sense of adventure and humor, stories of Feynman's brilliance and wit entertained many scientists for years. He wrote two books of interesting personal experiences, *"Surely You're Joking, Mr. Feynman": Adventures of a Curious Character* (1985) and *"What Do You Care What Other People Think?": Further Adventures of a Curious Character* (1988), which both became best-sellers. Another best-seller, *The Pleasure of Finding Things Out* (1999), is a collection of his talks and essays that were originally published in magazines. Some of these pieces, especially his essay on miniaturization, "There's Plenty of Room at the Bottom," have proved prophetic.

One of Feynman's most impressive moments came during the investigation of the space shuttle *Challenger*'s explosion in 1986. The *Challenger* was launched in Florida on an unusually cold morning. It exploded moments after liftoff, killing all the astronauts on board. During hearings about the *Challenger* tragedy, Feynman took a piece of the rubber

From *What Do You Care What Other People Think?*

from the O-ring that sealed one of the stages of the booster rocket and dipped it into his ice water. With a flourish, he removed it and showed that sudden temperature change caused the O-ring to crack and fail. By this means, he uncovered the cause of the disaster.

"The Value of Science" is an unusual essay for Feynman. Most of his popular writing centers on his adventures and his experiences with very colorful scientists and friends. He speaks here to an audience with a general interest in science. Feynman is careful to make no absolute claims in the essay. Part of his point is that a good scientist is by nature first curious and second skeptical. Skeptics doubt not only what they are told but also what they see. Doubt is at the center of all scientific inquiry, according to Feynman.

FEYNMAN'S RHETORIC

This selection, "The Value of Science," was originally published in a book called *What Do You Care What Other People Think?*, which was published in the year of Feynman's death. It is a relaxed piece, clearly written as if he were chatting with someone interested in science. As a result, the paragraphs are often short and the language direct. Furthermore, he approaches the piece with a simple idea in mind: How does one answer the question, "What is the value of science?" With this question in mind, he begins with one of the most obvious issues with which the general public is concerned — the responsibility of the scientist to deal with social issues. His approach is to explain that scientists are experts in science, but "a scientist looking at nonscientific problems is just as dumb as the next guy" (para. 3). So, by the third paragraph of the essay, we can see that Feynman's strategy is to raise questions and give only partial answers. This approach is acceptable to him because the entire essay tells us not to be too sure about anything. He wants us to understand the value of doubt and to avoid any authoritarian certainty that might hobble us in the future.

Feynman uses examples to make his points as he moves from one idea to the next. The Buddhist temple provides him with an example of how an idea can clarify a difficult moral concept. Science is a key, not a solution, to problems. His example of how the atoms in our brains change and replace each other at regular intervals cautions us that life is a form of mystery. As an example of how imagination informs him, he places himself on an imaginary seashore reflecting on the creation of the earth and all living things, presenting his thoughts as if in poetic reveries (paras. 13–18). These examples help him convey the sense of awe that science helps us comprehend.

Feynman also uses the convenient rhetorical strategy of subtitles to segment the essay. After the first eighteen paragraphs devoted to a personal experience in a Buddhist temple in Hawaii and a beginning effort to establish the value of science, Feynman relies on subtitles to guide the reader:

- The Grand Adventure
- The Remarkable Idea
- Education, for Good and Evil
- Our Responsibility as Scientists

In such a short essay, this approach helps in clarifying the ideas he wishes to impart. For example, the last section concerning the responsibility of scientists actually picks up from the first few paragraphs that discuss the popular view that scientists have a responsibility to solve social problems. Ending an essay with a consideration of the opening concerns of the essay is a time-honored approach. Each of the other subtitles treats a specific issue, and all are part of the question of what the value of science is for a society.

Feynman also uses another important rhetorical strategy when he enumerates the values he wishes to emphasize. The first value is identified in paragraph 4 when he says, "The way in which science is of value is . . . that scientific knowledge enables us to do all kinds of things." He develops this idea by introducing a "moral choice" that tells us science can be used for good or evil. His example, another rhetorical strategy, of the metaphoric key to heaven that "opens the gates of hell" (para. 6) implies that science, like a key, is an instrument. We use the instrument for our own purposes.

The second value of science is "called intellectual enjoyment" (para. 9), a concept he goes on to examine. The third value of science is the experience with "ignorance and doubt and uncertainty" (para. 26), which he equates with freedom because doubt helps us avoid making the mistake of thinking we know something with absolute certainty when such certainty is what science aims at but can never achieve. Thus, we avoid being locked in by potentially false ideas.

▟ PREREADING QUESTIONS: WHAT TO READ FOR

The following prereading questions may help you anticipate key issues in the discussion of Richard Feynman's "The Value of Science." Keeping them in mind during your first reading of the selection should help focus your attention.

1. What is the responsibility of scientists to solve social problems?
2. What is the relationship of scientific knowledge to certainty?
3. How is science of value to society?

The Value of Science

From time to time, people suggest to me that scientists ought to give more consideration to social problems—especially that they should be more responsible in considering the impact of science upon society. This same suggestion must be made to many other scientists, and it seems to be generally believed that if the scientists would only look at these very difficult social problems and not spend so much time fooling with the less vital scientific ones, great success would come of it.

It seems to me that we do think about these problems from time to time,   2
but we don't put full-time effort into them—the reason being that we know we
don't have any magic formula for solving problems, that social problems are
very much harder than scientific ones, and that we usually don't get anywhere
when we do think about them.

I believe that a scientist looking at nonscientific problems is just as dumb   3
as the next guy—and when he talks about a nonscientific matter, he will sound
as naive as anyone untrained in the matter. Since the question of the value of
science is not a scientific subject, this discussion is dedicated to proving my
point—by example.

The first way in which science is of value is familiar to everyone. It is   4
that scientific knowledge enables us to do all kinds of things and to make all
kinds of things. Of course if we make good things, it is not only to the credit of
science; it is also to the credit of the moral choice which led us to good work.
Scientific knowledge is an enabling power to do either good or bad—but it
does not carry instructions on how to use it. Such power has evident value—
even though the power may be negated by what one does.

I learned a way of expressing this common human problem on a trip to   5
Honolulu. In a Buddhist temple there, the man in charge explained a little bit
about the Buddhist religion for tourists, and then ended his talk by telling them
he had something to say to them that they would *never* forget—and I have
never forgotten it. It was a proverb of the Buddhist religion:

"To every man is given the key to the gates of heaven; the same key opens   6
the gates of hell."

What, then, is the value of the key to heaven? It is true that if we lack clear   7
instructions that determine which is the gate to heaven and which the gate to
hell, the key may be a dangerous object to use, but it obviously has value. How
can we enter heaven without it?

The instructions, also, would be of no value without the key. So it is evi-   8
dent that, in spite of the fact that science could produce enormous horror in
the world, it is of value because it *can* produce *something*.

Another value of science is the fun called intellectual enjoyment which   9
some people get from reading and learning and thinking about it, and which
others get from working in it. This is a very real and important point and one
which is not considered enough by those who tell us it is our social responsibility to reflect on the impact of science on society.

Is this mere personal enjoyment of value to society as a whole? No! But   10
it is also a responsibility to consider the value of society itself. Is it, in the last
analysis, to arrange things so that people can enjoy things? If so, the enjoyment
of science is as important as anything else.

But I would like *not* to underestimate the value of the worldview which   11
is the result of scientific effort. We have been led to imagine all sorts of things
infinitely more marvelous than the imaginings of poets and dreamers of the

past. It shows that the imagination of nature is far, far greater than the imagination of man. For instance, how much more remarkable it is for us all to be stuck—half of us upside down—by a mysterious attraction, to a spinning ball that has been swinging in space for billions of years, than to be carried on the back of an elephant supported on a tortoise swimming in a bottomless sea.

I have thought about these things so many times alone that I hope you will excuse me if I remind you of some thoughts that I am sure you have all had— or this type of thought—which no one could ever have had in the past, because people then didn't have the information we have about the world today.   12

For instance, I stand at the seashore, alone, and start to think. There are the rushing waves . . . mountains of molecules, each stupidly minding its own business . . . trillions apart . . . yet forming white surf in unison.   13

Ages on ages . . . before any eyes could see . . . year after year . . . thunderously pounding the shore as now. For whom, for what? . . . on a dead planet, with no life to entertain.   14

Never at rest . . . tortured by energy . . . wasted prodigiously by the sun . . . poured into space. A mite makes the sea roar.   15

Deep in the sea, all molecules repeat the patterns of one another till complex new ones are formed. They make others like themselves . . . and a new dance starts.   16

Growing in size and complexity . . . living things, masses of atoms, DNA, protein . . . dancing a pattern ever more intricate.   17

Out of the cradle onto the dry land . . . here it is standing . . . atoms with consciousness . . . matter with curiosity.   18

Stands at the sea . . . wonders at wondering . . . I . . . a universe of atoms . . . an atom in the universe.   19

The Grand Adventure

The same thrill, the same awe and mystery, come again and again when we look at any problem deeply enough. With more knowledge comes deeper, more wonderful mystery, luring one on to penetrate deeper still. Never concerned that the answer may prove disappointing, but with pleasure and confidence we turn over each new stone to find unimagined strangeness leading on to more wonderful questions and mysteries—certainly a grand adventure!   20

It is true that few unscientific people have this particular type of religious experience. Our poets do not write about it; our artists do not try to portray this remarkable thing. I don't know why. Is nobody inspired by our present picture of the universe? The value of science remains unsung by singers, so you are reduced to hearing—not a song or a poem, but an evening lecture about it. This is not yet a scientific age.   21

Perhaps one of the reasons is that you have to know how to read the   22
music. For instance, the scientific article says, perhaps, something like this:
"The radioactive phosphorus content of the cerebrum of the rat decreases to
one-half in a period of two weeks." Now, what does that mean?

It means that phosphorus that is in the brain of a rat (and also in mine, and   23
yours) is not the same phosphorus as it was two weeks ago, but that all of the
atoms that are in the brain are being replaced, and the ones that were there
before have gone away.

So what is this mind, what are these atoms with consciousness? Last   24
week's potatoes! That is what now can *remember* what was going on in my
mind a year ago—a mind which has long ago been replaced.

That is what it means when one discovers how long it takes for the atoms   25
of the brain to be replaced by other atoms, to note that the thing which I call my
individuality is only a pattern or dance. The atoms come into my brain, dance
a dance, then go out; always new atoms but always doing the same dance,
remembering what the dance was yesterday.

The Remarkable Idea

When we read about this in the newspaper, it says, "The scientist says that this   26
discovery may have importance in the cure of cancer." The paper is only interested in the use of the idea, not the idea itself. Hardly anyone can understand
the importance of an idea, it is so remarkable. Except that, possibly, some children catch on. And when a child catches on to an idea like that, we have a
scientist. These ideas do filter down (in spite of all the conversation about TV
replacing thinking), and lots of kids get the spirit—and when they have the
spirit when they are in our universities, so we must attempt to explain these
ideas to children.

I would now like to turn to a third value that science has. It is a little more   27
indirect, but not much. The scientist has a lot of experience with ignorance and
doubt and uncertainty, and this experience is of very great importance, I think.
When a scientist doesn't know the answer to a problem, he is ignorant. When
he has a hunch as to what the result is, he is uncertain. And when he is pretty
darn sure of what the result is going to be, he is in some doubt. We have found
it of paramount importance that in order to progress we must recognize the
ignorance and leave room for doubt. Scientific knowledge is a body of statements of varying degrees of certainty—some most unsure, some nearly sure,
none *absolutely* certain.

Now, we scientists are used to this, and we take it for granted that it is   28
perfectly consistent to be unsure—that it is possible to live and *not* know. But
I don't know whether everyone realizes that this is true. Our freedom to doubt

was born of a struggle against authority in the early days of science. It was a very deep and strong struggle. Permit us to question—to doubt, that's all—not to be sure. And I think it is important that we do not forget the importance of this struggle and thus perhaps lose what we have gained. Here lies a responsibility to society.

We are all sad when we think of the wondrous potentialities human beings   29 seem to have, as contrasted with their small accomplishments. Again and again people have thought that we could do much better. They of the past saw in the nightmare of their times a dream for the future. We, of their future, see that their dreams, in certain ways surpassed, have in many ways remained dreams. The hopes for the future today are, in good share, those of yesterday.

Education, for Good and Evil

Once some thought that the possibilities people had were not developed   30 because most of those people were ignorant. With education universal, could all men be Voltaires?[1] Bad can be taught at least as efficiently as good. Education is a strong force, but for either good or evil.

Communications between nations must promote understanding: So went   31 another dream. But the machines of communication can be channeled or choked. What is communicated can be truth or lie. Communication is a strong force also, but for either good or bad.

The applied sciences should free men of material problems at least. Medi-   32 cine controls diseases. And the record here seems all to the good. Yet there are men patiently working to create great plagues and poisons. They are to be used in warfare tomorrow.

Nearly everybody dislikes war. Our dream today is peace. In peace, man   33 can develop best the enormous possibilities he seems to have. But maybe future men will find that peace, too, can be good and bad. Perhaps peaceful men will drink out of boredom. Then perhaps drink will become the great problem which seems to keep man from getting all he thinks he should out of his abilities.

Clearly, peace is a great force, as is sobriety, as are material power, com-   34 munication, education, honesty, and the ideals of many dreamers.

We have more of these forces to control than did the ancients. And maybe   35 we are doing a little better than most of them could do. But what we ought to be able to do seems gigantic compared with our confused accomplishments.

Why is this? Why can't we conquer ourselves?   36

---

[1] **Voltaire**   *Nom de plume* of François-Marie Arouet (1694–1778), author of *Candide*. He was one of France's greatest philosophers and writers of the French Enlightenment.

Because we find that even great forces and abilities do not seem to carry 37
with them clear instructions on how to use them. As an example, the great
accumulation of understanding as to how the physical world behaves only
convinces one that this behavior seems to have a kind of meaninglessness. The
sciences do not directly teach good and bad.

Through all ages men have tried to fathom the meaning of life. They have 38
realized that if some direction or meaning could be given to our actions, great
human forces would be unleashed. So, very many answers must have been
given to the question of the meaning of it all. But they have been of all different
sorts, and the proponents of one answer have looked with horror at the actions
of the believers in another. Horror, because from a disagreeing point of view all
the great potentialities of the race were being channeled into a false and confin-
ing blind alley. In fact, it is from the history of the enormous monstrosities created by false belief that philosophers have realized the apparently infinite and
wondrous capacities of human beings. The dream is to find the open channel.

What, then, is the meaning of it all? What can we say to dispel the mystery 39
of existence?

If we take everything into account, not only what the ancients knew, but all 40
of what we know today that they didn't know, then I think that we must frankly
admit that *we do not know*.

But, in admitting this, we have probably found the open channel. 41

This is not a new idea; this is the idea of the age of reason. This is the 42
philosophy that guided the men who made the democracy that we live under.
The idea that no one really knew how to run a government led to the idea that
we should arrange a system by which new ideas could be developed, tried out,
tossed out, more new ideas brought in; a trial and error system. This method
was a result of the fact that science was already showing itself to be a successful venture at the end of the 18th century. Even then it was clear to socially
minded people that the openness of the possibilities was an opportunity, and
that doubt and discussion were essential to progress into the unknown. If we
want to solve a problem that we have never solved before, we must leave the
door to the unknown ajar.

Our Responsibility as Scientists

We are at the very beginning of time for the human race. It is not unreasonable 43
that we grapple with problems. There are tens of thousands of years in the future.
Our responsibility is to do what we can, learn what we can, improve the solutions
and pass them on. It is our responsibility to leave the men of the future a free
hand. In the impetuous youth of humanity, we can make grave errors that can
stunt our growth for a long time. This we will do if we say we have the answers
now, so young and ignorant; if we suppress all discussion, all criticism, saying,

"This is it, boys, man is saved!" and thus doom man for a long time to the chains of authority, confined to the limits of our present imagination. It has been done so many times before.

It is our responsibility as scientists, knowing the great progress and great value of a satisfactory philosophy of ignorance, the great progress that is the fruit of freedom of thought, to proclaim the value of this freedom, to teach how doubt is not to be feared but welcomed and discussed, and to demand this freedom as our duty to all coming generations.

44

⁑ QUESTIONS FOR CRITICAL READING

1. How do modern scientists treat the question of certainty?
2. Why would people expect scientists to address social problems?
3. Why is it important to know that the atoms of the brain replace themselves?
4. What is the difference between the use of an idea and the idea itself (para. 25)?
5. What is the point of Feynman's experience in the Buddhist temple?
6. What does Feynman mean by "Education, for Good and Evil"?
7. What is the responsibility of scientists?

⁑ SUGGESTIONS FOR CRITICAL WRITING

1. What seems to be the popular view of the obligations of scientists to help solve social problems? Are the issues primarily associated with the problems that are created by scientific discoveries, such as television, computers, smartphones, wireless surveillance, advanced weaponry, and interplanetary exploration? If not, then what does society mean when it asks scientists to be socially responsible?

2. Do some research, particularly in recent newspaper and magazine articles, on the question of how contemporary society regards the achievements of science. Is there a wave of antiscientific attitudes on the part of the general public today? Are contemporary American politicians generally pro-science or antiscience What would move them to one position or the other? What is your position regarding the value of science in your world? Are you pro-science or antiscience?

3. Feynman's writing in paragraphs 13–18 is unusual in that it includes many fragments instead of sentences, and it seems to be very indirect in conveying something that he feels is important. Write a brief essay explaining what Feynman is doing in these paragraphs and what the implications for our scientific understanding of the world are in light of what he is saying. How do you connect these paragraphs with his previous reference in paragraph 11 to "the back of an elephant supported on a tortoise swimming in a bottomless sea"?

4. In paragraph 4, Feynman says, "Scientific knowledge is an enabling power to do either good or bad — but it does not carry instructions on how to use it." This introduces a moral level to the discussion. That idea is also continued in the subtitle, "Education, for Good and Evil." Write an essay in which you establish what you feel are the moral obligations of science. In a sense, Feynman may be saying that there are no moral obligations of science. Do you agree with him in general, or do you disagree?

5. Which of the three values of science that Feynman focuses on is, for you, the most important? Is it that science results in accomplishments that give us a chance to do all kinds of things that the ancients, for example, could not do? Is it "the fun called intellectual enjoyment which some people get from reading and learning and thinking about it" (para. 9)? Or is it the fact that "The scientist has a lot of experience with ignorance and doubt and uncertainty" (para. 26)? Which of these values do you think is most important to Feynman? Are there other values that you think are just as important?

6. **CONNECTIONS** One product of science that is unsettling to many people is Charles Darwin's discussion of evolution in his "Natural Selection" (p. 606). Feynman is primarily a physicist, but his essay seems to move toward natural science and questions of morality. How does reading Feynman make it easier (or more difficult) for you to read and understand Darwin? What moral issues does Darwin raise? Are they similar to Feynman's? How does Feynman's reference to the Buddhist saying that the same key opens the gates of heaven and hell apply to Darwin's essay and the response of society to his ideas?

EDWARD O. WILSON

What Is Science?

© Corbis

One of the most influential and controversial modern scientists, Edward O. Wilson (b. 1929), was born
in Birmingham, Alabama. He went to the University of
Alabama and is today Professor Emeritus at Harvard and a lecturer at Duke University.
When he was young, Wilson was interested in the study of birds, but a fishing accident left
him blind in one eye and he lost some of the hearing in one ear. As a result, he abandoned
ornithology and took an interest in insects and entomology. That interest turned out to
influence the direction of his professional life.

Wilson is known as the major expert on the life of ants. An author of more than thirty
books on nature, Wilson published *The Insect Societies* (1971), his most important early
work on the social order of insects, especially ants. From this work, he began to develop his
theories about what he called sociobiology. He theorized that the complex social structures of ants, termites, bees, and wasps give us insight into the social structures of human
beings. He traces his theories back to evolutionary patterns that he feels are essential to
the survival of all social species. Some scientists have argued with him about this position,
pointing to differences among the species he has studied and the behavior of humans in
a social organization.

Wilson won the Pulitzer Prize for his book *On Human Nature* (1978) and continued
to work out the issues implied in his ideas about sociobiology by applying them to human
behavior, including patterns of aggression and affection. His theory that altruism is an evolutionary development to help preserve the species is another of his controversial ideas.

Later in his career, Wilson began to develop new ways of thinking and knowing. In
his book *Consilience* (1998), Wilson explains how the principles that apply to physics and
chemistry also apply to biology and the social sciences. He sees evolution as central to our
understanding of the world. The modern ideas of evolution became a central issue in his
studies in part because he sees evolution as being progressive. He suggests that evolution
moves from the simple to the complex, from the less organized to the more organized.

From *Letters to a Young Scientist.*

Essentially, his position is that evolution moves forward and improves life. Our job is to be sure to preserve the earth's species and our own species as well. *Creation: An Appeal to Save Life on Earth* (2006) is his most recent statement on this subject.

Wilson's views on religion and science have at times been complicated and, possibly, even contradictory. In 2015, Wilson said that religious faiths impede science and the best social interests of humankind. But he also said that belief in God and religious rituals are a product of evolution and natural selection. He himself is not an atheist, and he holds that science and religion need to work together to help preserve the human race.

WILSON'S RHETORIC

This selection comes from a book called *Letters to a Young Scientist* (2013) and is thus similar in genre to Martin Luther King Jr.'s "Letter from Birmingham Jail." Like most letters, it is written to a particular person, and like most published letters, it is also written with an awareness that others may profit from reading it. The audience of Wilson's letter is a beginning student interested in science. In his letter, Wilson manages to incorporate most of his important ideas about science into the discussion, including his ideas about evolution, the connections of all kinds of knowledge, and the relation of religion and science.

Because this is a letter, the character of the writing is relaxed, sometimes almost intimate. The language is direct and simple, with few technical terms; the technical terms that do appear are usually explained. However, even though it is a letter, the selection has the quality of an essay in that it aims to answer the question posed by its title: "What Is Science?" In addition, because this selection is a letter, Wilson refers to himself frequently, as one would in conversation. He uses the word "I" frequently, as in statements such as, "I have been so bold in recent years to suggest that, yes, biology is ruled by two laws" (para. 13). The effect is to create a sense of intimacy, a feeling that a concerned friend is discussing some important issues that inform but do not threaten the reader.

Wilson uses several examples to make his points. In paragraph 3, he explains how he tried to find out how an ant knows that another ant is dead. This example is extraordinary in that it demonstrates his scientific method of research in such detail that we are caught up in the narrative. His details, references to specific chemicals, help us understand why it is difficult to know how one ant knows another is dead. We see the problem in a concrete way and then observe the method he used to solve it. In this one example, Wilson makes science fascinating.

Because the business of science is asking questions, Wilson often relies on the rhetorical question. Here are a few:

- "What is this grand enterprise called *science* that has lit up heaven and earth and empowered humanity?" (para. 1)

- "So if the hypotheses are true, which of these substances might trigger the undertaker response — all of them, a few of them, or none?" (para. 4)

- "What, then, in broadest terms is the scientific method?" (para. 7)
- "Does biology also have laws?" (para. 12)
- "Why do I and others think in this controversial manner?" (para. 16)

There are others, and each one gives Wilson an opportunity to explore a range of possible questions. We might think of this as a metaphor for scientific research: ask a question and explore the options until the shape of a useful answer begins to appear.

Wilson also relies on the use of definition, as when he defines key terms, such as hypothesis, theory, and law. And, as he writes, he tries to supply useful answers for the questions he continues to pose.

▓ PREREADING QUESTIONS: WHAT TO READ FOR

The following prereading questions may help you anticipate key issues in the discussion of Edward O. Wilson's "What Is Science?" Keeping them in mind during your first reading of the selection should help focus your attention.

1. What is a scientific hypothesis?
2. When does a theory become a fact?
3. What should be science's attitude toward religion?

What Is Science?

What is this grand enterprise called *science* that has lit up heaven and earth and empowered humanity? It is organized, testable knowledge of the real world, of everything around us as well as ourselves, as opposed to the endlessly varied beliefs people hold from myth and superstition. It is the combination of physical and mental operations that have become increasingly the habit of educated peoples, a culture of illuminations dedicated to the most effective way ever conceived of acquiring factual knowledge.

You will have heard the words "fact," "hypothesis," and "theory" used constantly in the conduct of scientific research. When separated from experience and spoken of as abstract ideas they are easily misunderstood and misapplied. Only in case histories of research, by others and soon by you, will their full meaning become clear.

I'll give you an example of my own to show you what I mean. I started with a simple observation: ants remove their dead from the nests. Those of some species just dump the corpses at random outside, while those of other species place them on piles of refuse that might be called "cemeteries." The problem I saw in this behavior was simple but interesting: How does an ant know when another ant is dead? It was obvious to me that the recognition was not by sight. Ants recognize a corpse even in the complete darkness of the underground nest chambers. Furthermore, when the body is fresh and in a lighted area, and even when it is lying on its back with its legs in the air, others ignore it. Only after a day or two of decomposition does a body become a corpse to another ant. I guessed (made a hypothesis) that the undertaker ants were using the odor of decomposition to recognize death. I further thought it likely (second hypothesis) that their response was triggered by only a few of the substances exuded from the body of the corpse. The inspiration for the second hypothesis was an established principle of evolution: animals with small brains, which are the vast majority of animals on Earth, tend to use the simplest set of available cues to guide them through life. A dead body offers dozens or hundreds of chemical cues from which to choose. Human beings can sort out these components. But ants, with brains one-millionth the size of our own, cannot.

So if the hypotheses are true, which of these substances might trigger the undertaker response — all of them, a few of them, or none? From chemical suppliers I obtained pure synthetic samples of various decomposition substances, including skatole, the essence of feces; trimethylamine, the dominant odor of rotting fish; and various fatty acids and their esters[1] of a kind found in dead insects. For a while my laboratory smelled like a combination of charnel house and sewer. I put minute amounts on dummy ant corpses made of paper and inserted them into ant colonies. After a lot of smelly trial and error I found that oleic acid and one of its oleates[2] trigger the response. The other substances were either ignored or caused alarm.   4

To repeat the experiment another way (and admittedly for my and others' amusement), I dabbed tiny amounts of oleic acid on the bodies of living worker ants. Would they become the living dead? Sure enough, they did become zombies, at least broadly defined. They were picked up by nestmates, their legs kicking, carried to the cemetery, and dumped. After they had cleaned themselves awhile, they were permitted to rejoin the colony.   5

I then came up with another idea: insects of all kinds that scavenge for a living, such as blowflies and scarab beetles, find their way to dead animals or dung by homing in on the scent. And they do so by using a very small number of the decomposition chemicals present. A generalization of this kind, widely applied, with at least a few facts here and there and some logical reasoning   6

---

[1] **esters**   Organic compounds that react with water to produce alcohol.

[2] **oleates**   An ester of oleic acid, which is a fatty substance found in animals and plants, one of the most common fats in nature.

behind it, is a theory. Many more experiments, applied to other species, would be required to turn it into what can be confidently called a fact.

What, then, in broadest terms is the scientific method? The method starts   7
with the discovery of a phenomenon, such as a mysterious ant behavior, or a previously unknown class of organic compounds, or a newly discovered genus of plants, or a mysterious water current in the ocean's abyss. The scientist asks: What is the full nature of this phenomenon? What are its causes, its origin, its consequence? Each of these queries poses a problem within the ambit of science. How do scientists proceed to find solutions? Always there are clues, and opinions are quickly formed from them concerning the solutions. These opinions, or just logical guesses as they often are, are the hypotheses. It is wise at the outset to figure out as many different solutions as seem possible, then test the whole, either one at a time or in bunches, eliminating all but one. This is called the method of multiple competing hypotheses. If something like this analysis is not followed—and, frankly, it often is not—individual scientists tend to fixate on one alternative or another, especially if they authored it. After all, scientists are human.

Only rarely does an initial investigation result in a clear delineation of all   8
possible competing hypotheses. This is especially the case in biology, in which multiple factors are the rule. Some factors remain undiscovered, and those that have been discovered commonly overlap and interact with one another and with forces in the environment in ways difficult to detect and measure. The classic example in medicine is cancer. The classic example in ecology is the stabilization of ecosystems.

So scientists shuffle along as best they can, intuiting, guessing, tinkering,   9
gaining more information along the way. They persist until solid explanations can be put together and a consensus emerges, sometimes quickly but at other times only after a long period.

When a phenomenon displays invariable properties under clearly defined   10
conditions, then and only then can a scientific explanation be declared to be a scientific fact. The recognition that hydrogen is one of the elements, incapable of being divided into other substances, is a fact. That an excess of mercury in the diet causes one disease or another can, after enough clinical studies are conducted, be declared a fact. It may be widely believed that mercury causes an entire class of similar maladies, due to the one or two known chemical reactions in cells of the body. This idea may or may not be confirmed by further studies on diseases believed affected in this manner by mercury. Meanwhile, however, when research is still incomplete, the idea is a theory. If the theory is proved wrong, it was not necessarily also altogether a bad theory. At least it will have stimulated new research, which adds to knowledge. That is why many theories, even if they fail, are said to be "heuristic"—they are good for the promotion of discovery. Incidentally, the source of the word

eureka — "I have found it!" — descends from the legend of the Greek scientist Archimedes,[3] who, while sitting in a public bath, imagined how to measure the density of an object regardless of its shape. Put it in water, measure its volume by the rise in the water level, and its weight by how fast it sinks in the water. The density is the amount of weight divided by the amount of volume. Archimedes is said to have then left the bath, running through the streets, hopefully in his robe, while shouting, *Heurika!* Specifically, he'd found how to determine whether a crown was pure gold. The pure substance has a higher density than gold mixed with silver, the lesser of the two noble metals. But of far greater importance, Archimedes had discovered how to measure the density of all solids regardless of their shape or composition.

11   Now consider a much grander example of the scientific method. It has been commonly said, all the way back to the publication of Charles Darwin's *On the Origin of Species* in 1859, that the evolution of living forms is just a theory, not a fact. What could have been said already from evidence in Darwin's time, however, was that evolution is a fact, that it has occurred in at least some kinds of organisms some of the time. Today the evidence for evolution has been so convincingly documented in so many kinds of plants, fungi, animals, and microorganisms, and in such a great array of their hereditary traits, coming from every discipline of biology, all interlocking in their explanations and with no exception yet discovered, that evolution can be called confidently a fact. In Darwin's time, the idea that the human species descended from early primate ancestors was a hypothesis. With massive fossil and genetic evidence behind it, that can now also be called a fact. What remains a theory still is that evolution occurs universally by natural selection, the differential survival and successful reproduction of some combinations of hereditary traits over others in breeding populations. This proposition has been tested so many times and in so many ways, it also is now close to deserved recognition as an established fact. Its implication has been and remains of enormous importance throughout biology.

12   When a well-defined and precisely consistent process is observed, such as ions flowing in a magnetic field, a body moving in airless space, and the volume of a gas changing with temperature, the behavior can be precisely measured and mathematically defined as a law. Laws are more confidently sought in physics and chemistry, where they can be most easily extended and deepened by mathematical reasoning. Does biology also have laws?

13   I have been so bold in recent years as to suggest that, yes, biology is ruled by two laws. The first is that all entities and processes of life are obedient to the laws of physics and chemistry. Although biologists themselves seldom speak of the connection, at least in such a manner, those working at the level of the

---

[3] **Archimedes (c. 287–c. 212 B.C.E.)**   Greek mathematician, engineer, and scientist of ancient Syracuse.

molecule and the cell assume it to be true. No scientist of my acquaintance believes it worthwhile to search for what used to be called the élan vital,[4] a physical force or energy unique to living organisms.

The second law of biology, more tentative than the first, is that all evolu-   14 tion, beyond minor random perturbations due to high mutation rates and random fluctuations in the number of competing genes, is due to natural selection.

A source of the ground strength of science are the connections made not   15 only variously *within* physics, chemistry, and biology, but also *among* these primary disciplines. A very large question remains in science and philosophy. It is as follows: Can this consilience — connections made between widely separated bodies of knowledge — be extended to the social sciences and humanities, including even the creative arts? I think it can, and further I believe that the attempt to make such linkages will be a key part of intellectual life in the remainder of the twenty-first century.

Why do I and others think in this controversial manner? Because science   16 is the wellspring of modern civilization. It is not just "another way of knowing," to be equated with religion or transcendental meditation. It takes nothing away from the genius of the humanities, including the creative arts. Instead it offers ways to add to their content. The scientific method has been consistently better than religious beliefs in explaining the origin and meaning of humanity. The creation stories of organized religions, like science, propose to explain the origin of the world, the content of the celestial sphere, and even the nature of time and space. These mythic accounts, based mostly on the dreams and epiphanies[5] of ancient prophets, vary from one religion's belief to another. Colorful they are, and comforting to the minds of believers, but each contradicts all the others. And when tested in the real world they have so far proved wrong, always wrong.

The failure of the creation stories is further evidence that the mysteries   17 of the universe and the human mind cannot be solved by unaided intuition. The scientific method alone has liberated humanity from the narrow sensory world bequeathed it by our prehuman ancestors. Once upon a time humans believed that light allowed them to see everything. Now we know that the visual spectrum, which activates the visual cortex of the brain, is only a sliver of the electromagnetic spectrum, where the frequencies range across many orders of magnitude, from those of extreme high-frequency gamma rays at one end to those at the extreme low-frequency radiation at the other. The analysis of the electromagnetic spectrum has led to an understanding of the true nature of light. Knowledge of its totality has made possible countless advances in science and technology.

---

[4] **élan vital**   The life spirit.

[5] **epiphanies**   Moments of intense insight.

Once people thought that Earth was the center of the universe and lay flat and unmoving while the sun rotated around it. Now we know that the sun is a star, one of two hundred million in the Milky Way galaxy alone. Most hold planets in their gravitational thrall, and many of these almost certainly resemble Earth. Do the Earthlike planets also harbor life? Probably, in my opinion, and, thanks to the scientific method, furnished with improved optics and spectroscopic analyses, we will know in a short time.   18

Once it was believed that the human race arose full-blown in its present form as a supernatural event. Now we understand, in sharp contrast, that our species descended over six million years from African apes that were also the ancestors of modern chimpanzees.   19

As Freud once remarked, Copernicus demonstrated that Earth is not at the center of the universe, Darwin that we are not the center of life, and he, Freud, that we are not even in control of our own minds. Of course, the great psychoanalyst must share credit with Darwin, among others, but the point is correct that the conscious mind is only part of the thinking process.   20

Overall, through science we have begun to answer in a more consistent and convincing way two of the great and simple questions of religion and philosophy: Where do we come from? and, What are we? Of course, organized religion claims to have answered these questions long ago, using supernatural creation stories. You might then well ask, can a religious believer who accepts one such story still do good science? Of course he can. But he will be forced to split his worldview into two domains, one secular and the other supernatural, and stay within the secular domain as he works. It would not be difficult for him to find endeavors in scientific research that have no immediate relation to theology. This suggestion is not meant to be cynical, nor does it imply a closing of the scientific mind.   21

If proof were found of a supernatural entity or force that affects the real world, the claim all organized religions make, it would change everything. Science is not inherently against such a possibility. Researchers in fact have every reason to make such a discovery, if any such is feasible. The scientist who achieved it would be hailed as the Newton, Darwin, and Einstein, all put together, of a new era in history. In fact, countless reports have been made throughout the history of science that claim evidence of the supernatural. All, however, have been based on attempts to prove a negative proposition. It usually goes something like this: "We haven't been able to find an explanation for such-and-such a phenomenon; therefore it must have been created by God." Present-day versions still circulating include the argument that because science cannot yet provide a convincing account of the origin of the universe and of the setting of the universal physical constants, there must be a divine Creator. A second argument heard is that because some molecular structures and reactions in the cell seem too complex (to the author of the argument, at least) to have been assembled by natural selection, they must have been   22 designed by a higher intelligence. And one more: because the human mind, and especially free will as a key part of it, appear beyond the capability of the material cause and effect, they must have been inserted by God.

The difficulty with reliance on negative hypotheses to support faith-based science is that if they are wrong, they are also very vulnerable to decisive disproof. Just one testable proof of a real, physical cause destroys the argument for a supernatural cause. And precisely this in fact has been a large part of the history of science, as it has unfolded, phenomenon by phenomenon. The world rotates around the sun, the sun is one star out of two hundred million or more in one galaxy out of hundreds of billions of galaxies, humanity descended from African apes, genes change by random mutations, the mind is a physical process in a physical organ. Yielding to naturalistic, real-world understanding, the divine hand has withdrawn bit by bit from almost all of space and time. The remaining opportunities to find evidence of the supernatural are closing fast.

As a scientist, keep your mind open to any possible phenomenon remaining in the great unknown. But never forget that your profession is exploration of the real world, with no preconceptions or idols of the mind accepted, and testable truth the only coin of the realm.

⚝ QUESTIONS FOR CRITICAL READING

1. What does Wilson mean by "consilience" (para. 15)?
2. What is a hypothesis? Why is it important to science?
3. What is the relationship of theory to fact?
4. What does Wilson mean by supernatural explanations for phenomena (para. 22)?
5. In what sciences are laws most confidently asserted?
6. Does biology have laws?
7. What is a negative hypothesis?

⚝ SUGGESTIONS FOR CRITICAL WRITING

1. Wilson talks about creation myths (paras. 16 and 17), but does not mention any of them specifically. Do some research, and write an essay that describes two creation myths in enough detail to demonstrate why they might be convincing to some people. Then examine them in light of what Wilson says about creation myths. Do they tend to contradict each other or other myths? Do they rely on supernatural explanations in order to be plausible? What is your position on their scientific value? What is your position on their general value?

2. If you are a young scientist and therefore the person to whom this letter is addressed, how does Wilson make you feel that your career as a scientist is appropriate, worthwhile, and honorable? How successful is he in making

you glad that you have chosen science as your career? If you are not a young scientist, how successful has Wilson been in making you glad that you have not chosen science as a career?

3. Wilson describes the negative hypothesis in paragraphs 22 and 23. Write an essay that explains why negative hypotheses do not work. In the course of the essay, give as many examples of negative hypotheses as possible. How often do you hear people arguing a position by using negative hypotheses? How effective are they in argument? In what kinds of discussions or arguments are negative hypotheses most often introduced?

4. Examine what Wilson says in paragraph 15, when he discusses consilience. Research the term, and see what critics and others say about it. Write an essay in which you either defend or attack Wilson's view that connections can be "made between widely separated bodies of knowledge" (para. 15). What would it mean if Wilson is right? What would it mean to your education and the ways in which politicians and others must approach vastly different areas of thought? Is there any law or theory that can be applied in both science and social science? If possible, use an example to answer this question.

5. In paragraphs 17 to 20, Wilson surveys what he feels are the accomplishments of science in the modern world. In a brief essay, explain why he introduces these achievements and what they mean to his argument. What other achievements of science do you think he should have included? What has science done for you? How has it improved the way you live as opposed to the way you might have lived in 1500? If you like, you might want to argue this case in reverse.

6. In paragraph 22, Wilson says, "If proof were found of a supernatural entity or force that affects the real world, the claim all organized religions make, it would change everything." To what extent is that statement true? How would it change things? What kind of "entity or force" would be needed to satisfy his claim? What form might it take? What supernatural event would be most convincing that there is a non-natural world apart from our own? How would we know that such an event was truly supernatural?

7. **CONNECTIONS**   Andrew Carnegie, in his "Gospel of Wealth" (p. 360), relies on the principles of Darwinian evolution in his discussion of the social circumstances of his age. In a brief essay, explain how he combines the ideas of science and religion in defending his position as a very wealthy man. Would Wilson consider Carnegie's views an example of consilience? Do you? How scientific is Carnegie in his analysis of modern society, and how convincing is he in using the idea of evolution in his argument?

MICHIO
KAKU

The Theory of the Universe?

Ted Thai/Getty Images

MICHIO KAKU (b. 1947) was born and raised in San Jose, California, received his undergraduate degree from Harvard, and returned to California for his Ph.D. in physics from the University of California, Berkeley, in 1972. Since 1973, he has been professor of theoretical physics at the City College and the Graduate Center of the City University of New York, publishing widely on superstring theory, supergravity, and string field theory. He hosts a weekly national radio show on science called *Science Fantastic* that is carried by ninety radio stations in the United States. Kaku is deeply concerned about the practical ramifications of theoretical physics and has written several books on the dangers of nuclear war. He is active in groups that advocate disarmament.

"The Theory of the Universe?" is in a collection called *Mysteries of Life and the Universe* (1992). In this work, Kaku attempts to explain the complexities of modern physics, with a special look at efforts to resolve the conflicts between two important theories: quantum theory and the theory of relativity. Quantum theory explains the physics of atoms and small particles. The theory of relativity explains cosmic phenomena such as gravity and the universe. However, neither theory works in the other's sphere of influence. Hence, a new theory is needed to resolve the problems; this new theory, called superstring theory, postulates that instead of hard particles existing at the center of atoms "tiny strings of energy" vibrate at an infinite number of frequencies. These strings of energy are at the heart of atoms and consist of everything we know of as matter in the universe.

Because physics involves specialized, advanced mathematics, much of what Kaku says is simplified for a general audience. As a result, we can understand the theories, but only in general terms. Therefore, without the mathematics, we must accept certain ideas at face value, making an effort to imagine, along with Kaku, how modern theories of physics work. Fortunately, he is able to spell out the very complex theories in a fashion that makes them as intelligible as possible for readers who are not experts in mathematics.

From *Mysteries of Life and the Universe.*

Some of the ideas in this essay are also developed in Kaku's best-selling book *Hyperspace* (1994), which discusses the so-called crazy theories of contemporary physicists. Kaku tells us that modern research by contemporary physicists has produced a view of the natural world that virtually defies common sense, just as facts such as the earth's roundness (rather than flatness) and its movement around the sun (rather than the reverse) initially contradicted the common sense of our predecessors. Unfortunately, common sense does not help us understand modern physics or the world of the atom. Because we cannot directly perceive the atom or the molecule, we require sophisticated equipment to make their nature evident. Interestingly, Francis Bacon insisted in *Novum Organum* that until better tools were developed, people would not be able to perceive the truth about the complexities of nature.

In an early chapter of *Hyperspace*, Kaku tells a story about being a young boy and watching fish in a small pond. He realized that for the carp, it was inconceivable that anything existed outside the water in which they swam. Their perceptions were limited entirely to the watery environment of their home. The same is true for people. Our environment may seem larger and more capacious than a pond, but we, like the carp, are limited in our perceptions. Plato realized this when he postulated his allegory of the cave and theorized that human beings' profoundly limited sensory apparatus prevents us from imagining experiences beyond what we know from our senses.

Kaku explains that the problems involved in uniting the quantum theory with the theory of relativity may be solved by postulating a ten-dimensional universe. Because we live in a four-dimensional universe (three dimensions of space and one of time), we are like the carp in their pond and cannot imagine a world of ten dimensions. But Kaku explains that mathematical formulas can deal with extra dimensions easily. However, he ends his essay by saying that we need a new kind of mathematics to fully describe the way in which the two great theories of physics join together.

KAKU'S RHETORIC

Kaku's books are meant for a general reading public and use short paragraphs and intriguing subheads, such as:

- The Four Fundamental Forces
- Two Great Theories
- Superstrings
- Ten-Dimensional Hyperspace
- What Happened Before the Big Bang?

Kaku enumerates the four forces in the universe and gives us examples of what they are and how they affect the modern world. He also implies their possible destructive powers. These rhetorical techniques help readers grasp some of the ideas that the research of Michio Kaku and other modern physicists has developed.

Because the essay offers a general overview of an interesting and elusive subject, Kaku provides a number of analogies and examples designed to give us a chance to understand the complexities of the theories and their implications. His example of a shotput on a bed with a marble rolling toward it is commonly used to explain Einstein's theory of how spacetime can be warped in such a way as to create a gravitational field. His example of the violin string's capacity to have an infinite number of vibrations helps explain part of string theory. Even his example of meeting "some friends for lunch in Manhattan" (para. 41) shows how the three dimensions of space express themselves in our experience. Finally, he ends the essay with an extensive "Parable of the Gemstone," in which he imagines a world in which people live in Flatland in two dimensions and cannot solve the problem of reconstructing an exploded gemstone.

The most important aspect of this essay's rhetoric involves the explanation of complex theories in terms that readers can grasp easily. Although we will not leave this essay with a full understanding of the complexities of a unified theory, we will at least become acquainted with the problems that physicists face in trying to both describe and understand how the universe works.

▞ PREREADING QUESTIONS: WHAT TO READ FOR

The following prereading questions may help you anticipate key issues in the discussion of Michio Kaku's "The Theory of the Universe?" Keeping them in mind during your first reading of the selection should help focus your attention.

1. What are the four fundamental forces?
2. What do quantum theory and general relativity explain?
3. Why are higher dimensions needed to unify the two theories?

The Theory of the Universe?

When I was a child of eight, I heard a story that will stay with me for the rest of my life. I remember my schoolteachers telling us about a great scientist who had just died. They talked about him with great reverence, calling him one of the greatest scientists in all history. They said that very few people could understand his ideas, but that his discoveries had changed the entire world and everything around us.

But what most intrigued me about this man was that he had died before he could complete his greatest discovery. They said he had spent years on this theory, but he died with unfinished papers still sitting on his desk.

I was fascinated by the story. To a child, this was a great mystery. What was   3
his unfinished work? What problem could possibly be so difficult and so important that such a great scientist would dedicate years of his life to its pursuit?

Curious, I decided to learn all I could about Albert Einstein[1] and his unfin-   4
ished theory. Some of the happiest moments of my childhood were spent quietly reading every book I could find about this great man and his ideas. When
I exhausted the books in our local library, I began to scour libraries and book-
stores across the city and state, eagerly searching for more clues. I soon learned
that this story was far more exciting than any murder mystery and more important than anything I could ever imagine. I decided that I would try to get to the
root of this mystery, even if I had to become a theoretical physicist to do it.

Gradually, I began to appreciate the magnitude of his unfinished quest. I   5
learned that Einstein had three great theories. The first two, the special and the
general theories of relativity, led to the development of the atomic bomb and to our
present-day conceptions of black holes and the Big Bang. These two theories by
themselves earned him his reputation as the greatest scientist since Isaac Newton.[2]

However, Einstein was not satisfied. The third, which he called the *uni-*   6
fied field theory, was to have been his crowning achievement. It was to be the
theory of the universe, the Holy Grail[3] of physics that would finally unify all
physical laws into one simple framework. It was to have been the ultimate goal
of all physics, the theory to end all theories.

Sadly, it consumed Einstein for the last thirty years of his life; he spent   7
many lonely years in a frustrating pursuit of the greatest theory of all time. But
he wasn't alone; I learned that some of the greatest minds of the twentieth century, such as Werner Heisenberg and Wolfgang Pauli,[4] also struggled with this
problem and ultimately gave up.

Given the fruitless search that has stumped these and other Nobel Prize   8
winners for half a century, most physicists agree that the Theory of Everything
must be a radical departure from everything that has been tried before. For
example, when Niels Bohr,[5] founder of modern atomic theory, once listened to

---

[1] **Albert Einstein (1879–1955)**   German-born physicist whose theory of relativity helped
in developing nuclear power.

[2] **Isaac Newton (1642–1726)**   English mathematician and scientist who invented calculus and described the mathematical nature of gravity. His laws of mechanics are still
accurate.

[3] **Holy Grail**   The dish or cup from which Christ is supposed to have drunk at the last
supper. Finding it was one of the hopes of the early crusaders. Metaphorically, it is that
which everyone hopes to discover.

[4] **Werner Heisenberg (1901–1976) and Wolfgang Pauli (1900–1958)**   German and
Austrian physicists who were pioneers of quantum physics.

[5] **Niels Bohr (1885–1962)**   Danish Nobel Prize winner (1922) in physics. He was involved
in developing quantum theory.

Pauli's explanation of his own version of the unified field theory, Bohr finally stood up and said, "We are all agreed that your theory is absolutely crazy. But what divides us is whether your theory is crazy enough."

Today, however, after decades of false starts and frustrating dead ends, many of the world's leading physicists think that they have finally found the theory "crazy enough" to be the unified field theory. Scores of physicists in the world's major research laboratories now believe we have at last found the Theory of Everything.

The theory that has generated so much excitement is called the *superstring theory*. Nearly every science publication in the world has featured major stories on the superstring theory, interviewing some of its pioneers, such as John Schwarz, Michael Green, and Yoichiro Nambu.[6] (*Discover* magazine even featured it twice on its cover.) My book *Beyond Einstein: The Cosmic Search for the Theory of the Universe* was the first attempt to explain this fabulous theory to the lay audience.

Naturally, any theory that claims to have solved the most intimate secrets of the universe will be the center of intense controversy. Even Nobel Prize winners have engaged in heated discussions about the validity of the superstring theory. In fact, over this theory we are witnessing the liveliest debate in theoretical physics in decades.

To understand the power of the superstring theory and why it is heralded as the theory of the universe (and to understand the delicious controversy that it has stirred up), it is necessary to understand that there are four forces that control everything in the known universe, and that the superstring theory gives us the first (and only) description that can unite all four forces in a single framework.

The Four Fundamental Forces

Over two thousand years ago, the ancient Greeks thought that all matter in the universe could be reduced to four elements: air, water, earth, and fire. Today, after centuries of research, we know that these substances are actually composites; they in turn are made of smaller atoms and subatomic particles held together by just four and only four fundamental forces.

Gravity is the force that keeps our feet anchored to the spinning earth and binds the solar system and the galaxies together. If the force of gravity could somehow be turned off, we would be immediately flung into outer space at approximately a thousand miles per hour. Furthermore, if gravity did not hold the Sun together, it would explode in a catastrophic burst of energy. Without

---

[6] **John Schwarz (b. 1941), Michael Boris Green (b. 1946), and Yoichiro Nambu (1921–2015)** Physicists who are pioneers in string theory.

gravity, the Earth and the planets would spin out into freezing deep space and the galaxies would fly apart.

Electromagnetism is the force that lights up our cities and energizes our   15
household appliances. The electronic revolution, which has given us the light bulb, TV, the telephone, the computer, radio, radar, the microwave, and the dishwasher, is a byproduct of the electromagnetic force. Without this force, our civilization would be wrenched several hundred years into the past, into a primitive world lit by candlelight and camp fires.

The strong nuclear force is the force that powers the Sun. Without the   16
nuclear force, the stars would flicker out and the heavens would go dark. Without the Sun, all life on Earth would perish as the oceans turned to solid ice. The nuclear force not only makes life on Earth possible, it is also the devastating force unleashed by a hydrogen bomb, which can be compared to a piece of the Sun brought down to Earth.

The weak nuclear force is the force responsible for radioactive decay. The   17
weak force is harnessed in modern hospitals in the form of radioactive tracers used in nuclear medicine. For example, dramatic color pictures of the living brain as it thinks and experiences emotions are made possible by the decay of radioactive sugar in the brain.

It is no exaggeration to say that the mastery of each of these four funda-   18
mental forces has changed every aspect of human civilization. For example, when Newton tried to solve his theory of gravitation, he was forced to develop a new mathematics and formulate his celebrated laws of motion. These laws of mechanics in turn helped to usher in the Industrial Revolution.

Furthermore, the mastery of the electromagnetic force by mathematical   19
physicist James Maxwell[7] in the 1860s has revolutionized our way of life. Whenever there is a power blackout, we are forced to live much like our forebears in the last century. Today, over half of the world's industrial wealth is connected, in some way or other, to the electromagnetic force, without which modern civilization is unthinkable.

Similarly, when the nuclear force was unleashed with the atomic bomb,   20
human history for the first time faced a new and frightening set of possibilities, including the total annihilation of all life on Earth. With the nuclear force, we could finally understand the enormous engine that lies within the Sun and the stars, but we could also glimpse for the first time the end of humanity itself.

Thus, whenever scientists unravel the secrets of one of the four fundamen-   21
tal forces, they irrevocably alter the course of modern civilization. Some of the greatest breakthroughs in the history of the sciences can be traced back to the gradual understanding of these forces.

----

[7] **James Clerk Maxwell (1831–1879)**   Scottish mathematician and physicist who saw that magnetism, electricity, and light were manifestations of the same phenomenon.

Given their importance the next question is, Can these four fundamental
forces be united into one super force? Are they but diverse manifestations of
a deeper reality?   22

Two Great Theories

At present there are two physical frameworks that have partially explained the   23
mysterious features of these four fundamental forces. Remarkably, these two
formalisms, the *quantum theory* and *general relativity,* allow us to explain
the *sum total of all physical knowledge* at the fundamental level. Without
exception.

All the laws of physics and chemistry, which can fill entire libraries with   24
technical journals and books, can in principle be derived from these two fundamental theories—making these the most successful physical theories of all
time, withstanding the test of thousands of experiments and challenges.

Ironically, these two fundamental frameworks are diametrically opposed   25
to each other. The quantum theory, for example, is the theory of the microcosm, with unparalleled success at describing the subatomic world. The theory
of relativity, by contrast, is a theory of the macrocosmic world, the world of
galaxies, superclusters, black holes, and Creation itself.

The quantum theory explains three of the four forces (the weak and strong   26
nuclear forces, and the electromagnetic force) by postulating the exchange
of tiny packets of energy, called *quanta.* When a flashlight is turned on, for
example, it emits trillions upon trillions of photons, or quanta, of light. Lasers,
radar waves, and microwaves all can be described by postulating that they are
caused by the movement of these tiny quanta of energy. Likewise, the weak
force is governed by the exchange of subatomic particles called *W-bosons.* The
strong nuclear force, in turn, binds protons together by the exchange of *gluons.*

However, the quantum theory stands in sharp contrast to Einstein's gen-   27
eral theory of relativity, which postulates an entirely different physical picture
to explain the force of gravity.

Imagine, for the moment, dropping a heavy shotput on a large bedspread.   28
The shotput will, of course, sink deeply into the bedspread. Now imagine
shooting a small marble across the bed. Since the bed is warped, the marble
will execute a curved path. However, for a person viewing the marble from a
great distance, it will appear that the shotput is exerting an invisible "force" on
the marble, forcing it to move in a curved path. In other words, we can now
replace the clumsy concept of a "force" with the more elegant concept of a
bending of space itself. We now have an entirely new definition of this "force."
It is nothing but the byproduct of the warping of space.

In the same way that a marble moves on a curved bedspread, the Earth   29
moves around the Sun in a curved path, because space-time itself is curved.
In this new picture, gravity is not a "force" but a byproduct of the warping of
space-time. In some sense, gravity does not exist; what moves the planets and
stars is the distortion of space and time.

However, the problem that has stubbornly resisted solution for fifty years   30
is that these two frameworks do not resemble each other in any way. The quantum theory reduces "forces" to the exchange of discrete packets of energy,
or quanta, while Einstein's theory of gravity, by contrast, explains the cosmic
forces holding the galaxies together by postulating the smooth deformation
of the fabric of space-time. This is the root of the problem, that the quantum
theory and general relativity have two different physical pictures (packets
of energy versus smooth spacetime continua) and different mathematics to
describe them. This sad state of affairs can be compared to Mother Nature
having two hands, neither of which communicates with the other.

All attempts by the greatest minds of the twentieth century at merging   31
the quantum theory with the theory of gravity have failed. Unquestionably, the
greatest problem facing physicists today is the unification of these two physical
frameworks into one theory.

Superstrings

Today, however, many physicists think that we have finally solved this long-   32
standing problem. A new theory, which is certainly "crazy enough" to be correct, has astounded the world's physics community. But it has also raised a
storm of controversy, with Nobel Prize winners adamantly taking opposite
sides of the issue.

This is the superstring theory, which postulates that all matter and energy   33
can be reduced to tiny strings of energy vibrating in a ten-dimensional universe.

Edward Witten,[8] of the Institute for Advanced Study at Princeton, who   34
some claim is the successor to Einstein, has said that superstring theory will
dominate the world of physics for the next fifty years, in the same way that the
quantum theory has dominated physics for the last half century.

As Einstein once said, all great physical theories can be represented   35
by simple pictures. Similarly, superstring theory can be explained visually.
Imagine a violin string, for example. The note A is no more fundamental than
the note B. What is fundamental is the violin string itself. By studying vibrations or harmonies on a violin string, one can calculate the infinite number of
possible frequencies that can exist.

---

[8] **Edward Witten (b. 1951)**   American physicist working at the Princeton Institute of
Advanced Studies. He studies the mathematics of string theory and quantum physics.

Similarly, the superstring can also vibrate in different frequencies. Each 36
frequency, in turn, corresponds to a subatomic particle, or a quantum. This
explains why there appears to be an infinite number of particles. According
to this theory, our bodies, which are made of subatomic particles, can be
described by the resonances of trillions upon trillions of tiny strings.

In summary, the "notes" of the superstring are the subatomic particles, the 37
"harmonies" of the superstring are the laws of physics, and the universe can be
compared to a "symphony" of vibrating superstrings.

As the string vibrates, however, it causes the surrounding space-time con- 38
tinuum to warp around it. Miraculously enough, a detailed calculation shows
that the superstring forces the space-time continuum to be distorted exactly
as Einstein originally predicted. Thus, we now have a harmonious description
that merges the theory of quanta with the theory of space-time continua.

Ten-Dimensional Hyperspace

The superstring theory represents perhaps the most radical departure from 39
ordinary physics in decades. But its most controversial prediction is that the
universe originally began in ten dimensions. To its supporters, the prediction
of a ten-dimensional universe has been a conceptual tour de force introducing
a startling, breathtaking mathematics into the world of physics. To its critics,
however, the introduction of ten-dimensional hyperspace borders on science
fiction.

To understand these higher dimensions, we must remember that it takes 40
three numbers to locate every point in the universe, from the tip of your nose
to the ends of the universe.

For example, if you want to meet some friends for lunch in Manhattan, you 41
say that you will meet them at the building at the corner of Forty-second and
Fifth Avenue, on the thirty-seventh floor. It takes two numbers to locate your
position on a map, and one number to specify the distance above the map.

However, the existence of the fourth spatial dimension has been a lively 42
area of debate since the time of the Greeks. Ptolemy,[9] in fact, even gave a
"proof" that more than three dimensions cannot exist. Ptolemy reasoned that
only three straight lines that are mutually perpendicular can be drawn (for
example, the three perpendicular lines making up a corner of a room). Since a
fourth straight line cannot be drawn perpendicular to each of the other three
axes—ergo!—the fourth dimension cannot exist.

What Ptolemy actually proved was that it is impossible for us to *visualize* 43
the fourth dimension. Although computers routinely manipulate equations

---

[9] **Ptolemy (c. 100–c. 170)**   Greco–Egyptian mathematician.

in n-dimensional space, humans are incapable of visualizing more than three dimensions.

The reason for this unfortunate accident has to do with biology rather than   44 physics. Human evolution put a premium on being able to visualize objects moving in three dimensions, such as lunging saber-tooth tigers and charging mammoths.

Since tigers do not attack us in the fourth dimension, there was no evolu-   45 tionary correction pressure to develop a brain with the ability to visualize four dimensions.

From a mathematical point of view, however, adding higher dimensions   46 has a distinct advantage: It allows us to describe more forces. There is more "room" in higher dimensions to insert the electromagnetic force into the grav- itational force. (In this picture, light becomes a vibration in the fourth dimen- sion.) In other words, adding more dimensions to a theory always allows us to unify more laws of physics.

A simple analogy may help. The ancients were once puzzled by the weather.   47 Why does it get colder as we go north? Why do the winds blow to the west? What is the origin of the seasons? To the ancients, these were mysteries that could not be solved.

The key to these puzzles, of course, is to leap into the third dimension, to   48 go *up* into outer space, to see that the Earth is actually a sphere rotating around a tilted axis. In one stroke, these mysteries of the weather — the seasons, the winds, the temperature patterns, etc. — become transparent.

Likewise, the superstring is able to accommodate a large number of forces   49 because it has more "room" in its equations to do so.

What Happened Before the Big Bang?

One of the nagging problems of Einstein's old theory of gravity was that it did   50 not explain the origin of the Big Bang.

The ten-dimensional superstring theory, however, gives us a compelling   51 explanation according to which the universe originally started as a perfect ten- dimensional universe with nothing in it.

However, this ten-dimensional universe was not stable. The original   52 ten-dimensional space-time finally "cracked" into two pieces, four- and six- dimensional universes. The six-dimensional universe collapsed into a tiny ball, while the remaining four-dimensional universe inflated at an enormous rate.

The four-dimensional universe (ours) expanded rapidly, eventually creat-   53 ing the Big Bang, while the six-dimensional universe wrapped itself into a ball and collapsed down to infinitesimal size.

The Big Bang is now viewed as a rather minor aftershock of a more cat-   54 aclysmic collapse: the breaking of a ten-dimensional universe into four- and six-dimensional universes.

In principle, it also explains why we cannot measure the six-dimensional   55
universe: it has shrunk down to a size smaller than an atom.

Re-creating Creation

Although the superstring theory has been called the most sensational discovery   56
in theoretical physics in the past decades, its critics have focused on its weakest
point, that it is almost impossible to test. The energy at which the four fundamental forces merge into a single unified force is the fabulous *Planck energy*,[10]
which is a billion billion times greater than the energy found in a proton.

Even if all the nations of the Earth were to band together and single-   57
mindedly build the biggest atom smasher in all history, it would still not be
enough to test this theory.

Because of this, some physicists have scoffed at the idea that superstring theory can be considered a legitimate theory. Nobel laureate Sheldon   58
Glashow,[11] for example, has compared the superstring theory to the former
President Reagan's Star Wars program because it is untestable and drains the
best scientific talent.

The reason the theory cannot be tested is rather simple. The Theory of   59
Everything is necessarily a theory of Creation. It must explain everything, from
the origin of the Big Bang down to that of the lilies of the field. To test this theory on Earth, therefore, means to re-create Creation on Earth, which is impossible with present-day technology.

The SSC: Biggest Experiment of All Time

These questions about unifying the fundamental forces may not be academic if   60
the largest scientific machine ever, the SSC,[12] is built to test some of our ideas
about the instant of Creation. (Although the SSC was originally approved by
the Reagan administration, because of its enormous cost, the project is still
touch-and-go, depending every year on Congressional funding.)

The SSC is projected to accelerate protons to a staggering energy of tens   61
of trillions of electron volts. When these subatomic particles slam into each

---

[10] ***Planck energy***   Unit of energy established by German mathematical physicist Max
Planck (1858–1947).

[11] **Sheldon Glashow (b. 1932)**   Physicist who taught at Harvard University, now
Professor Emeritus.

[12] **SSC**   Superconducting Super Collider, a huge magnetic ring that was to have been built
near Dallas, Texas, but that was discontinued for lack of funding. It was designed to find
more of the basic particles of matter. CERN in Geneva was built instead and has already
been of great use to particle physicists.

other at these fantastic energies, they will generate temperatures that have not been reached since the instant of Creation (although not hot enough to test fully the superstring theory). That is why the supercollider is sometimes called a "window on Creation."

The SSC is projected to cost over eight billion dollars (a large amount of money compared to the government's science budget, but insignificant relative to that of the Pentagon). By every measure, it will be a colossal machine. It will consist of a ring of powerful magnets stretched out in a tube over fifty miles in diameter. In fact, one could easily fit the Washington Beltway, which surrounds Washington, D.C., inside the SSC.

62

At present, the SSC is scheduled to be finished near the turn of the century in Texas, near the city of Dallas. When completed, it will employ thousands of physicists and engineers and cost millions of dollars to operate.

63

At the very least, physicists hope that the SSC will find some exotic sub-atomic particles, such as the Higgs boson and the top quark, in order to complete our present-day understanding of the quantum theory. However, there is also the small chance that physicists might discover "supersymmetric" particles, which are predicted by the superstring theory. In other words, although the superstring theory cannot be tested directly by the SSC, one hopes to find particles (vibrations) predicted by superstring theory among the debris created by smashing protons together.

64

The Parable of the Gemstone

To understand the intense controversy surrounding superstring theory, think of the following parable.

65

Imagine that at the beginning of time there was a beautiful, glittering gemstone. Its perfect symmetries were a sight to behold. However, it possessed a tiny flaw and became unstable, eventually exploding into thousands of pieces. Imagine that the fragments of the gemstone rained down on a flat, two-dimensional world called Flatland, where there lived a mythical race of beings called Flatlanders.

66

These Flatlanders were intrigued by the beauty of the fragments, which could be found scattered all over Flatland. The scientists of Flatland postulated that these fragments must have come from a crystal of unimaginable beauty that shattered in a titanic Big Bang. They then decided to embark upon a noble quest to reassemble all the pieces of the gemstone.

67

After two thousand years of labor by the finest minds of Flatland, they were finally able to fit many, but certainly not all, of the fragments together in two chunks. The first chunk was called the *quantum*, and the second chunk was called *relativity*.

68

Although the Flatlanders were rightfully proud of their progress, they were   69
dismayed to find that these two chunks did not fit together. For half a century,
the Flatlanders maneuvered the chunks in all possible ways and still could not
make them fit.

Finally, some of the younger, more rebellious scientists suggested a hereti-   70
cal solution: perhaps these two chunks could fit together if they were moved
in a *third dimension*.

This immediately set off the greatest scientific controversy in years. The   71
older scientists scoffed at this idea, because they didn't believe in an unseen
third dimension. "What you can't measure doesn't exist," they declared.

Furthermore, even if the third dimension existed, one could calculate that   72
the energy necessary to move the pieces *up* off Flatland would exceed all the
energy available in Flatland. Thus it was an untestable theory.

However, the younger scientists were undaunted. Using pure mathematics,   73
they could show that these two chunks would likely fit together if they were
rotated and moved in the third dimension. The younger scientists claimed that
the problem was therefore theoretical rather than experimental. If one could
completely solve the equations of the third dimension, one could, in principle,
fit the two chunks perfectly together and resolve the problem once and for all.

We Are Not Smart Enough

That is also the conclusion of today's superstring enthusiasts: the fundamental   74
problem is theoretical, not practical. The true problem is in solving the theory
completely and then comparing it with present-day experimental data, not in
building gigantic atom smashers.

Edward Witten, impressed by the vast new areas of mathematics opened   75
up by the superstring theory, has said that the superstring theory represents
"twenty-first-century physics that fell accidentally into the twentieth century."

The superstring theory may very well be twenty-first-century physics, but   76
twenty-first-century mathematics has not yet been discovered.

This situation is not entirely new to the history of physics. When Newton   77
first discovered the universal law of gravitation at the age of twenty-three,
he was unable to solve his equation because the mathematics of the seventeenth century was too primitive. He then labored over the next twenty years
to develop a new mathematical formalism (calculus) that was powerful enough
to solve his universal law of gravitation.

Similarly, the fundamental problem facing the superstring theory is theo-   78
retical. If we could only sharpen our analytical skills and develop more powerful mathematical tools, perhaps we could solve the superstring theory and end
the controversy.

Ironically, the superstring equations stand before us in perfectly well defined form, yet we are too primitive to understand why they work so well, and we are too dim-witted to solve them. The search for the theory of the universe is perhaps finally entering its last phase, awaiting the birth of a new mathematics powerful enough to solve it.

Imagine a child gazing at a TV set. The images and stories conveyed through the screen are easily understood by the child, yet the electronic wizardry inside the TV set is beyond the child's ken. Likewise, we physicists gaze in wonder at the mathematical sophistication and elegance of the superstring equation and are awed by its power, yet we do not understand why it works.

Perhaps some readers will be inspired by this story to read every book in their libraries about the superstring theory. Perhaps some young reader will be the one to complete this quest for the theory of the universe, begun so many years ago by Einstein.

❖ QUESTIONS FOR CRITICAL READING

1. Which theory describes the subatomic world?
2. Which theory explains the cosmos?
3. Why is it so difficult to develop a unified theory?
4. Why does a modern unified theory of physics have to sound crazy?
5. What is the weak nuclear force?
6. How does the electromagnetic force affect our culture?
7. What is the string theory? Why is it interesting to scientists?

❖ SUGGESTIONS FOR CRITICAL WRITING

1. Michio Kaku discusses the "state of the art" of modern science, but in 1992, he imagined that the SSC, or Superconducting Super Collider, would be finished in Texas. However, funds were withdrawn and the collider was built in Geneva. Research the history of the Texas collider and how the CERN was built in Geneva. Write an essay explaining the importance of the Geneva collider and what success it has had.

2. Write an essay that explains quantum theory to a person who has no scientific background. Explain what it tells us about physics and why it is important. Kaku is very simple in his explanation, but include in your essay something of the background and the early explanations for physical events that eventually led to the quantum theory.

3. Albert Einstein is referenced in the essay as trying to establish a unified theory that would combine the conflicting theories of quantum mechanics and general relativity. In a brief essay, introduce Albert Einstein and his theories to

an audience of people interested in science or to an audience of people who are interested in the arts. If possible, use the kind of examples that Kaku uses to explain difficult ideas.

4. Kaku mentions Isaac Newton as a scientist of great importance, second only to Einstein. Write an essay explaining why Newton is so important. What were his achievements in physics and mathematics? How did he develop his theory of gravity? What are his theories of mechanics, and why are they important? Is Newton as important at Kaku says he is?

5. In a brief essay, examine Kaku's explanations of the problems of modern physics. What confuses you? What problems do you note that are not fully explained? What do you need to know in order to better understand the theories that Kaku is trying to explain? He admits that theories of physics today have to be really crazy if they are to be taken seriously. What does he mean by this? How much more do you know about physics now that you have read Kaku compared with before you read this essay? How important to you is a knowledge of physics?

6. The superstring theory has been very attractive to physicists for more than twenty years. Do some research and write an essay that brings us up to date on what is now known about the string theory. Is it still the most attractive theory designed to produce a unified theory? How difficult is it to understand? Does your research convince you that it is a workable theory and that it may lead to the unified theory that Kaku wants?

7. **CONNECTIONS** Write an essay that connects Plato's "Allegory of the Cave" (p. 580) and Francis Bacon's "The Four Idols" (p. 591) with the issues that Michio Kaku is dealing with in his essay. In what ways does referencing Plato and Bacon help you understand the complexities of Kaku's essay? What do Plato and Bacon say about how we know what we know, and how we are sometimes prevented from knowing the truth about the world around us.

Philip Kitcher

PHILIP
KITCHER
Inescapable Eugenics

PHILIP KITCHER (b. 1947), the John Dewey
Professor of Philosophy at Columbia University,
was born in England, studied at Cambridge University, and earned his Ph.D. at Princeton
University. He taught at the University of California, San Diego, and the University of
Minnesota before coming to New York. His range of interests in philosophy is extraordinary. In his early years, he devoted himself to problems in science. In the 1980s, he published a number of influential books: *Abusing Science: The Case Against Creationism* (1982);
The Nature of Mathematical Knowledge (1983); *Vaulting Ambition: Sociobiology and the
Quest for Human Nature* (1985); and *The Advancement of Science* (1993).

In the early part of the twenty-first century, Kitcher's interests broadened into several
related fields. His concerns for social and political issues resulted in the publication of
Science, Truth, and Democracy (2001). But Kitcher continued with explorations of biology
in his book *In Mendel's Mirror: Philosophical Reflections on Biology* (2003), which is a collection of some of his articles, including "Darwin's Achievement" (1985) and "Born Again
Creationism" (2002). "Inescapable Eugenics," the selection in this book, is a chapter from
The Lives to Come: The Genetic Revolution and Human Possibilities (1996).

Kitcher's interests include music, art, and literature. In 2004, he published a book
on Richard Wagner's Ring Cycle of operas, and in 2007, he published a book on James
Joyce's novel *Finnegans Wake*. As John Dewey Professor of Philosophy, Kitcher, in his latest
work, has dedicated himself to examining pragmatism, the American philosophy developed by William James, Charles Sanders Pierce, and John Dewey. *Preludes to Pragmatism:
Toward a Reconstruction of Philosophy* was published in 2012. Kitcher also continues to
produce insights into problems of ethics and in the modern examination of religion. He
has responded to the modern atheist philosophers Richard Dawkins, Daniel Dennett, and
Christopher Hitchens by complaining that their views of religion are much too limited. He
accuses them of concentrating their focus on dogma, false beliefs, and religion's rejection

From *The Lives to Come: The Genetic Revolution and Human Possibilities*.

of evolution. Instead, he points to the comfort and caring community that religions provide for the well-being of a society. A further critique of the atheist philosophers is that they have attacked conventional religion but have not proposed an alternative. Kitcher offers an alternative in his recent book, *Life After Faith: The Case for Secular Humanism* (2014). Humanism, he states, is about values, as is religion. It is about human values and the promotion of ethical behavior to the benefit of all.

In talking about genetics and the future, his concerns are with the well-being of our society. Using genetic science to design our children may be more problematic than it at first seems. For some people, genetic engineering means eliminating dangerous genes that may cause cancer or malformation. However, for others, it may be a means to produce a "designer baby" who may lack many of the qualities we most cherish in our society.

Kitcher's concerns in this selection center on the question of eugenics, the science of hereditary improvement by the use of genetic research. Eugenics was practiced in the late nineteenth century and the first seventy years of the twentieth century, and not always to good effect. The Nazi government wished to purify the "Aryan" race and used draconian means to achieve that end. Kitcher revisits the idea of eugenics in light of modern molecular genetic engineering.

KITCHER'S RHETORIC

Kitcher aims at a clear presentation of the achievements and the problems implied in what he describes as "laissez-faire eugenics," the practice of letting people do what they want when it comes to making decisions about genetic malformations or other genetic issues. In a sense, people in the developed world have been practicing eugenics for some time, but Kitcher is hoping to inform us about the risks and the issues involved in making choices that might involve either the abortion or the birth of a child who will live a short life in constant suffering. These are not just social choices, but moral choices, and none of the choices is easy.

One of the obvious rhetorical strategies Kitcher uses is to provide a brief historical review, particularly of Charles Darwin's cousin, Francis Galton, who had an interest in improving heredity and thereby improving the entire human race. He also reviews the science of eugenics, suggesting that until recently it was not adequate to achieve what Galton hoped for. He then uses an example of a range of eugenic decisions made in the United States to try to eradicate "feeblemindedness" in a family. Three generations of the Buck family were sterilized to prevent what was thought to be a genetic disorder, but later analysis proved that the Bucks were needlessly harmed. This is a situation that Kitcher feels is too common: an "expert" makes decisions for people and coerces them into accepting a damaging procedure.

Kitcher enumerates the ways in which eugenics works (para. 6):

"First, eugenic engineers must select a group of people whose reproductive activities are to make the difference to future generations."

"Next, they have to determine whether these people will make their own reproductive decisions or whether they will be compelled to follow some centrally imposed policy."

"Third, they need to pick out certain characteristics whose frequency is to be increased or diminished."

"Finally, they must draw on some body of scientific information that is to be used in achieving their ends."

After reviewing the ways in which eugenics has been misapplied in the past, Kitcher discusses some of the medical and scientific issues that confront modern parents. Some decisions have a profound effect on parents and those who provide support for children with serious disabling diseases. Other decisions affect the individual who may be diagnosed with a genetic disorder that threatens that person's ability to live a full life. In either event, the decisions to be made are moral as well as scientific.

▓ PREREADING QUESTIONS: WHAT TO READ FOR

The following prereading questions may help you anticipate key issues in the discussion of Philip Kitcher's "Inescapable Eugenics." Keeping them in mind during your first reading of the selection should help focus your attention.

1. What is eugenics?
2. What is laissez-faire eugenics?
3. Who should make decisions about the practice of eugenics?

Inescapable Eugenics

Eugenics was officially born in the writings of Charles Darwin's cousin, Francis Galton,[1] who campaigned for applying knowledge of heredity to shape the characteristics of future generations. In retrospect, we can recognize the new theoretical science as a mixture of a study of heredity and some doctrines about the value of human lives. Galton's approach to studying inheritance, by looking for statistical features of the transmission of phenotypes,[2] was original and was discarded by the growing number of his eugenic descendants who embraced Mendelian genetics.[3] With characteristic Victorian

[1] **Francis Galton (1822–1911)** He coined the term eugenics, and, in his *Hereditary Genius* (1869), he proposed selective mating to produce more intelligent children.

[2] **phenotypes** Observable characteristics of an organism, such as body type, hair color, etc.

[3] **Mendelian genetics** Gregor Mendel (1822–1884), an Austrian scientist, codified the laws of inheritance of genetic traits through several generations.

confidence, however, Galton did not offer a critical discussion of the values underlying his judgments about proper and defective births. Assuming that his readers would agree about the characteristics that should be promoted, he set about the business of promoting them.

Separated from Galton by over a century, we can see how eugenic judgments have mixed science with the values of dominant groups and also how the prejudices have been so powerful as to distort scientific conclusions: Men with a mania for eradicating "feeblemindedness" convinced themselves that there must be genes to be found and duly "found" them. A fundamental objection to eugenics challenges the presupposition that there is *any* system of values that can properly be brought to bear on decisions about genetic worth. Galton's Olympian confidence that he could decide which lives would best be avoided easily provokes the reaction that we should abandon the pretense of being able to judge for others. People with severe disabilities who have attended workshops for human geneticists sometimes pose the question forcefully in words, sometimes even more vividly in their presence and determination: Who are you to decide if I should live?

Yet even as we admire those who have overcome extraordinary adversity to make rewarding lives for themselves, we should remember the dreadful clarity of some examples of genetic disease. Those who watch the inevitable decay of children born with Hurler syndrome or Canavan's disease,[4] those who see the anguish of parents as they care for children whose genes prevent development beyond the abilities of an infant have no difficulty in deciding that similar sufferings should be avoided. In the spring of 1994, at a public discussion of the impact of the Human Genome Project in Washington, D.C., a man in late middle age protested the tendency to see only the problems of the Project, relating how his daughter had given birth to two children with neurofibromatosis.[5] His tone, not his words, conveyed the grief of his family as well as his conviction that abstract fears of eugenic consequences should not block attempts to spare others similar agonies.

As a theoretical discipline, eugenics responds to our convictions that it is irresponsible not to do what can be done to prevent deep human suffering, yet it must face the challenge of showing that its claims about the values of lives are not the arrogant judgments of an elite group. Of course, if eugenics were *simply* a theoretical discipline, pursued by Galton's successors in their studies, there would be little fuss. Precisely because some are concerned about a

2

3

4

---

[4] **Hurler syndrome or Canavan's disease**   Genetic disorders; Hurler syndrome, sometimes called gargoylism, is a genetic disorder that limits mental and physical development by age two to four years; Canavan's is a disease that degenerates an infant's nervous system and leads to early death.

[5] **neurofibromatosis**   A genetic disorder that produces a profusion of tumors.

revival of eugenic *practices*, while others fear that the label "eugenics" will be misapplied to humane and responsible attempts to eliminate pain and grief, questions about the eugenic implications of contemporary molecular biology have more than academic interest. Unless we look past the swastika and achieve a clearer picture of eugenics in action, these important questions will prove irresolvable.

Exactly when are people practicing eugenics? The Nazi doctors, the Americans worried about "racial degeneracy," would-be social reformers like Sidney Webb and George Bernard Shaw,[6] and peasant families in Northern India do not agree on very much, but all of them hope to modify the frequency with which various characteristics are present in future populations. Eugenic practice begins with an intention to affect the kinds of people who will be born.

Translating that intention into social action requires four types of important decision. First, eugenic engineers must select a group of people whose reproductive activities are to make the difference to future generations. Next, they have to determine whether these people will make their own reproductive decisions or whether they will be compelled to follow some centrally imposed policy. Third, they need to pick out certain characteristics whose frequency is to be increased or diminished. Finally, they must draw on some body of scientific information that is to be used in achieving their ends. Practical eugenics is not a single thing. Human history already shows a variety of social actions involving four quite separate components, each of which demands separate evaluation.

Introducing contemporary molecular biology into prenatal testing will lead us to engage in *some* form of eugenics, but that consequence, by itself, does not settle very much. For it is overwhelmingly obvious that some varieties are far worse than others. Greater evils seem to be introduced if we move in particular directions with respect to the four components: More discrimination in the first, more coercion in the second, focusing on traits bound up with social prejudices in the third, using inaccurate scientific information in the fourth. Unsurprisingly, Nazi eugenics was just as bad as we can imagine with respect to each component. The Nazis discriminated among particular populations for their reproductive efforts, selecting the "purest Aryans" for positive programs, using "special treatment" on groups of "undesirables." Starting with compulsory sterilization, they proceeded to the ultimate form of coercion in the gas chambers. The repeated comparison between Jews and vermin and the absurd—but monstrous—warnings about the threats to Nordic "racial health" display the extent to which prejudice pervaded their division of human characteristics. Minor, by comparison, is the fact that much of their genetics was mistaken.

5

6

7

---

[6] **Sidney Webb (1859–1947) and George Bernard Shaw (1856–1940)**   British socialists and reformers with an interest in eugenics.

Scientific inaccuracies infect other past eugenic practices in ways that   8
appear more crucial. Henry Goddard's[7] efforts to keep America pure led him
to administer intelligence tests to newly arriving immigrants; even the staunchest contemporary advocate of IQ would have difficulty defending Goddard's
assumption that his tests measured "innate hereditary tendencies." Those cast
up at the foot of the Statue of Liberty found that their inability to produce facts
about the recent history of baseball indicated their lack of native wit. Likewise,
decisions to sterilize the inmates of state institutions often rested on abysmally
poor evidence. Carrie Buck[8] and her sister Doris were victims of the zeal to
dam up the feebleminded flood, and it was Carrie's case that provoked one of
the most chilling lines in the history of Supreme Court decisions. In 1927, finding in favor of the lower court decision in *Buck* v. *Bell*, Justice Oliver Wendell
Holmes[9] pronounced that "three generations of imbeciles are enough."

The three generations of imbeciles were three members of the Buck fam-   9
ily. Carrie Buck's mother had been diagnosed as "feebleminded," Carrie herself had been placed in the Virginia Colony for Epileptics and Feebleminded;
on the basis of a Stanford-Binet intelligence test, she was assigned a mental
age of nine. The third generation consisted of her illegitimate daughter, Vivian,
seven months old at the time that the original decision for sterilization was
made. Because a Red Cross worker thought that she had "a look" about her
and a member of the Eugenics Record Office claimed, on the basis of a test for
infants, that she had below-average intelligence, Vivian too was classified as
feebleminded. Three generations of feeble-mindedness demonstrated that the
defect was hereditary.

At least the classifications of Carrie Buck and Vivian were quite erroneous.   10
Vivian died while still a young child, but she had completed second grade and
had impressed her teachers. In 1980, when she was in her seventies, Carrie
Buck was rediscovered and was visited by doctors and scholars concerned
with the history of sterilization laws. They found an ordinary woman who read
the newspaper daily and who tackled crossword puzzles. The central figure in
the tragic story was no "imbecile," not even according to the technical criterion
which eugenic enthusiasts employed to grade the feeble-minded (imbeciles
were adults with a mental age between six and nine).

Failure to distinguish the components of eugenic practice blurs our vision   11
of the injustices that have been done. What is the real moral of the case of

---

[7] **Henry H. Goddard (1856–1957)**   Author of *The Kallikak Family: A Study in the Heredity of Feeble-Mindedness* (1912) and an influential eugenicist. He introduced the term "moron."

[8] **Carrie Buck (1906–1983)**   A woman who was sterilized as part of the Racial Integrity Act of 1924 under Virginia law.

[9] **Oliver Wendell Holmes Jr. (1841–1935)**   Associate Justice of the Supreme Court from 1902–1932.

Carrie Buck? Not simply that the judgment was mistaken, that Carrie and her sister Doris, both of whom were sterilized, did not carry genes for "feeble-mindedness." Besides the scientific error, the practice of compulsory sterilization also destroyed something fundamental to people's lives. Even if Carrie, Doris, and Vivian had borne genes that set limits to their mental development, should they have been forced to give up all hopes of bearing children? Like the Nazis, albeit on a far smaller scale, American eugenicists carried out a coercive practice: They compelled some individuals to follow a social policy that was divorced from any aspirations that those who were treated may have had. Doris lived outside the asylum, married, and tried to have children. Only much later did she understand what had been done to her.

The brutal compulsion of the Nazi eugenics program prompted an important change in postwar efforts to apply genetic knowledge. Everyone is now to be her (or his) own eugenicist, taking advantage of the available genetic tests to make the reproductive decisions she (he) thinks correct. If genetic counseling, practiced either on the limited scale of recent decades or in the much more wide-ranging fashion that we can anticipate in the decades to come, is a form of eugenics, then it is surely *laissez-faire* eugenics.[10] In principle, if not in actuality, prenatal testing is equally available to all members of the societies that invest resources in genetic counseling. Ideally, citizens are not coerced but make up their own minds, evaluating objective scientific information in light of their own values and goals. Moreover, the extensive successes of molecular genetics inspire confidence that our information about the facts of heredity is far more accurate than that applied by the early eugenicists. As for the traits that people attempt to promote or avoid, that is surely their own business, and within the limits of available knowledge, individuals may do as they see fit. Laissez-faire eugenics, the "eugenics" already in place and likely to become ever more prominent in years to come, is a very different form of eugenics from the endeavors of Davenport,[11] Goddard, and Hitler's medical minions.

Identifying the gulf between laissez-faire eugenics and the horrors that underlie the stereotype makes room for discussing the important questions surrounding applications of molecular genetics but does not resolve them. Banning prenatal tests by tagging them with the ugly name "eugenics" should not substitute for careful thought about their proper scope and limits. Everything depends on the *kind* of eugenics we practice.

We know that some genetic conditions cause their bearers to lead painful or truncated lives in all the environments that we know how to arrange

12

13

14

---

[10] *laissez-faire* **eugenics**   Practicing eugenics freely at will, with no regulations.

[11] **Charles Davenport (1866–1944)**   The leader of the American Eugenics Movement. He was interested in limiting the passing on of undesirable hereditary traits.

for them. We know also how to identify, before a fetus is sentient, whether or not the fetus carries one of those conditions. Naively, we might try to avoid the smear of eugenics by insisting that nobody should use this information for selective abortions—we shall not interfere with the genetic composition of future populations. But once we have the option of intervening, this allegedly "noneugenic" decision shares important features with eugenic practices. Tacitly, it makes a value judgment to the effect that *unplanned* populations are preferable to *planned* populations. More overtly, it imposes a bar on decisions that individuals might have wished to make, depriving them of the chance to avoid great future suffering by terminating pregnancies in which fetuses are found to carry genes for Sanfilippo syndrome,[12] neurofibromatosis, or any of a host of similarly devastating disorders. When we know how to shape future generations, the character of our descendants will reflect our decisions and the values that those decisions embody. For even if we compel one another to do nothing, that is to judge it preferable not to intervene in the procreation of human life, even to subordinate individual freedom to the goal of "letting what will be, be."

Molecular knowledge pitches us into some form of eugenic practice, and   15
laissez-faire eugenics looks initially like an acceptable species. Yet its character deserves a closer look.

The most attractive feature of laissez-faire eugenics is its attempt to honor   16
individual reproductive freedom. Does it succeed? Are the resources of prenatal testing in affluent societies equally open to all members of the population? Do they help people to make reproductive decisions that are genuinely their own? And is that really a proper goal? Since individual reproductive decisions have aggregate consequences for the composition of the population, should there not be restrictions to avoid potentially disastrous effects? Finally, because individual decisions may be morally misguided—as with those who would select on the basis of sex—will laissez-faire eugenics foster evil on a grand scale?

These serious questions emerge once we have appreciated the dimensions   17
along which eugenic practices may be evaluated, for they correspond to three of the four components: discrimination, coercion, and division of traits. (Concern with the status of our molecular knowledge is less urgent when we concentrate on physiological characteristics, but will reappear later when we consider beliefs about the genetic basis of behavior.) Discrimination and coercion are prominent features of the history of eugenic excesses; only the gullible should believe that simple declarations that genetic testing will be open to all and free from social directives are enough to ensure that history will not repeat itself

---

[12] **Sanfilippo syndrome**   A genetic disease producing aggressive behavior and severe dementia.

in these respects. Most obviously in the United States, but possibly in countries that already assure their citizens access to medical care, the costs of such medical technologies as prenatal tests and *in vitro* fertilization may prove an effective barrier to their broad availability: The poor may lack options that the affluent exercise. Predicting the likely consequences of these kinds of inequalities is not hard. If prenatal testing for genetic diseases is often used by members of more privileged strata of society and far more rarely by the underprivileged, then the genetic conditions the affluent are concerned to avoid will be far more common among the poor—they will become "lower-class" diseases, other people's problems. Interest in finding methods of treatment or for providing supportive environments for those born with the diseases may well wane.

The fault lines that run through our societies may threaten future prenatal   18
decisions in other ways as well. Laissez-faire eugenics promises to enhance reproductive freedom. Prenatal testing is to provide unprecedented choices for prospective parents—and, indeed, it will sometimes spare mothers and fathers the anguish of watching young children degenerate and die. Yet the proclamation of reproductive freedom does not necessarily translate into increased autonomy in the clinic. Although the storm trooper's gun is the least subtle of a variety of ways in which social values may shape individual decisions, simply avoiding official decrees of "racial health" and announcing that prospective parents' decisions are to be their own does not ensure that people will act in ways that correspond to their most fundamental ideals.

There have already been women and couples for whom the bad genetic   19
news has been doubly agonizing. Discovering that a fetus has an extra copy of chromosome 21—that it has Down syndrome[13]—they know that the future person would have a more limited life. However, they also know that, with love, nurture, and support, people with Down syndrome can sometimes defy the gloomy predictions that used to lead some doctors to treat the extra chromosome as a marker for abortion. They are prepared to provide the love and nurture, but they cannot count on the support. For some, it is a matter of economics, of not being able to pay for special programs; for others, the problem stems from the attitudes prevalent in the segment of society they occupy, a tendency to view "mongol" children as defective and to write them off at birth. So, moved by concern for the future happiness of the child who would be born, they decide—reluctantly and against their own deep commitments—to terminate the pregnancy.

Individual choices are not made in a social vacuum, and unless changes   20
in social attitudes keep pace with the proliferation of genetic tests, we can

---

[13] **Down syndrome**   A genetic disorder that produces a range of intellectual limitations. The average life span of someone with this syndrome is fifty to sixty years.

anticipate that many future prospective parents, acting to avoid misery for potential children, will have to bow to social attitudes they reject and resent. They will have to choose abortion even though they believe that a more caring or less prejudiced society might have enabled the child who would have been born to lead a happy and fulfilling life. Laissez-faire eugenics is in danger of retaining the most disturbing aspect of its historical predecessors—the tendency to try to transform the population in a particular direction, not to avoid suffering but to reflect a set of social values. In the actual world unequal wealth is likely to result in unequal access, and social attitudes will probably prove at least partially coercive. How are these problems to be solved?

Not by jettisoning the use of prenatal testing entirely. Parents who have   21
seen their own children grieve over a child with neurofibromatosis or Hurler syndrome, who have watched marriages torn apart, bright lives quenched, rightly remind opponents of prenatal testing of the tragedies that the tests may prevent. Only the callous would refuse to allow some to benefit from the new resources of molecular genetics simply because those resources are not available to all. But even though unequal distribution might be tolerated temporarily, societies that introduce prenatal testing have a moral obligation to work toward making it available to all their citizens.

Similarly, if laissez-faire eugenics is to accord with the advertisement   22
that it promotes individual reproductive freedom, our societies will have to combine attempts to bring into the world children whose lives are not sadly restricted with public commitment to assist those who are born to realize the highest possible degree of development. Disability activists already fear that the spread of prenatal tests will erode the tenuous systems of support that have made it possible for many people to go far beyond the limits once foreseen for them. If those systems decay, prospective parents will experience an ever more relentless pressure to eliminate those whom their society views as "defective." To make their decisions maximally free, they need to know not only how the genetic condition of the fetus would affect the life of the person who would be born, given the range of manageable environments, but also that their society is committed to helping them bring about an environment in which that life will flourish insofar as it can. Only if they are assured that all people have a serious chance of receiving respect and the support they need can prospective parents decide on the basis of their own values.

Social change might make it possible for laissez-faire eugenics to live up   23
to its billing, fastidiously promoting the reproductive freedom of all. But is that really desirable? Prenatal decisions do not affect only the parents; they have consequences, very directly, for the cluster of cells within the uterus and, more remotely, for other members of society who may have to contribute to support for the child who is born.

Those who believe that the cluster of cells already counts as a person view   24
prenatal testing as a means of inspiring evil: Laissez-faire eugenics would hand
out licenses to murder. Others do not oppose the taking of fetal lives in principle but doubt that prospective parents will make socially responsible decisions. One by one, the effects of terminating or continuing a pregnancy may be
small; in the aggregate, they can make profound differences to the lives of our
descendants.

If people proceed myopically, guided by their own dim lights, the conse-   25
quences may prove disastrous. Seventy years ago unregulated breeding was
widely assumed to lead to genetic catastrophe. Eugenicists everywhere suggested that *Homo sapiens* would be buried under a "load of mutations" and,
more chauvinistically, Anglo-Saxons lamented "the passing of the great race."
Today the concerns are expressed less stridently, more apologetically, and in
terms of the *economic* impact on societies. Perhaps the commitment to fostering the full development of those born with genetic disabilities—a commitment which seems morally unassailable—would combine with shortsighted
individual decisions to produce impossible obligations. Prospective parents,
confident that their society will support a child with a genetic disorder, solemnly take on the responsibilities of providing love and care. As the product
of their thoughtful, moral decisions, large social resources—resources that
might have been used to promote the welfare of many other children—are
consumed in compensating for the genetic misfortunes of their offspring.

In the presence of practical constraints, attractive ideals conflict. Repro-   26
ductive freedom is important to us; providing support for all members of society, including people with expensive genetically imposed needs, is equally
important. But our resources are finite. In a callous society, as we have seen,
individual reproductive freedom is severely constrained. In a caring society
individual reproductive freedom may lead to social disaster.

Not all chapters in the history of eugenics are unremittingly bleak, and   27
the reflections of some earlier thinkers indicate a potential solution to our
dilemma. British social reformers—George Bernard Shaw, Sidney and Beatrice
Webb, and others who followed them—hardly correspond to the stereotypes
of eugenic repression: They believed that eugenics, practiced freely, would be
part of a systematic scheme of social reform. The society they envisaged would
provide support for the full development of all its members and would use
eugenic methods to ensure a population in which this commitment could be
met. But they did not intend to dictate reproductive policy. How, then, were the
reformers to guarantee that *right* choices would be made, that parents would
procreate to achieve, collectively, a population of progeny who could be fully
supported by the available resources? Their answer emphasized eugenic education. People would make the right decisions because they would understand
the consequences of their decisions, both for their offspring and for society.

Today's enthusiasts for the use of molecular genetics in prenatal test-   28
ing rarely call themselves "eugenicists," but their vision of future reproductive practice depicts a particular version of laissez-faire eugenics—*utopian
eugenics*—which is remarkably similar to the ideas of Shaw and his friends.
Utopian eugenics would use reliable genetic information in prenatal tests
that would be available equally to all citizens. Although there would be widespread public discussion of values and of the social consequences of individual
decisions, there would be no societally imposed restrictions on reproductive
choices—citizens would be educated but not coerced. Finally, there would be
universally shared respect for difference coupled with a public commitment to
realizing the potential of all those who are born.

Who's afraid of utopian eugenics? Some critics surely fear that utopian   29
eugenics deserves its name, that the conditions it requires cannot be sustained
in any society. They might well concede that, in some attenuated sense, benign
applications of molecular genetics are possible while maintaining that the
results in practice will be far more disturbing. Has any society succeeded in
giving its citizens reasonable access to medical resources, or in providing the
basic support that all its children need to realize their potential? Can education
be expected to succeed in promoting responsible reproductive decisions? Is it
possible that an educational program would enhance reproductive freedom,
rather than collapsing into a system of ideology that would reinforce widely
held prejudices? If we are indeed committed to some form of eugenics, then
utopian eugenics seems the most attractive option. But these questions will
need to be answered if we are to forestall the worry that it will inevitably decay
into something darker.

The chapters that follow address even more fundamental concerns about   30
utopian eugenics. If prenatal tests are to be employed as a prelude to ending
nascent human lives, then abortion must, at least sometimes, be morally defensible. Moreover, our descendants will have to arrive at a clearer conception of
the ways in which genotypes influence human phenotypic[14] traits: Repeating
the determinist errors of earlier versions of eugenics would be truly tragic.
We should also reflect on how the enterprise of choosing people changes our
conceptions of human life and human freedom and of their value. If I am right
in my diagnosis, human molecular genetics is already committed to that enterprise, and before we are carried onward by its momentum, there are important
steps to take.

Most basic is the task of clarifying utopian eugenics, uncovering the con-   31
siderations that should guide our reproductive choices. To envisage a practice

---

[14] **genotypes . . . phenotypic**   A genotype is part of the DNA that determines a phenotype,
a characteristic of an organism.

in which reproductive decisions are both free and educated returns us to the problem with which this chapter began. The trouble is to identify the content of the education, to say what kinds of fetal characteristics would properly lead responsible people to terminate a pregnancy. In thinking about the proper form of eugenics, we have focused thus far on three important components: accurate information, open access, and freedom of choice. The issue of trait discrimination has figured only as an afterthought to the insistence on reproductive freedom: Laissez-faire eugenics allows people to make up their own minds about which traits to promote, which to avoid. Yet matters have proved to be not quite so simple. Utopian eugenics proposes that there should be some encouragement to draw the distinction in a particular way. Which way? The Northern Indians, we believe, do not have it right, whereas the doctors who helped reduce the frequency of Tay-Sachs[15] recognize part of the truth. But exactly where between these polar cases is the line to be drawn?

There is an obvious answer. Abortion is appropriate when the fetus suffers   32
from a genetic disease. Preventing disease has nothing to do with imposing social values, for whether or not something is a disease is a matter of objective fact.

Ultimately, this answer will prove inadequate, but understanding its dif-   33
ficulties will point us toward something better. Once we have left the garden of genetic innocence, some form of eugenics is inescapable, and our first task must be to discover where among the available options we can find the safest home.

---

[15] **Tay-Sachs**   A genetic disorder involving degeneration of nerve cells that usually results in death by age four.

✂ QUESTIONS FOR CRITICAL READING

1. Why is Francis Galton important to eugenics (para. 15)?

2. How do ordinary people practice eugenics?

3. What are the undesirable effects of eugenics?

4. How can molecular genetic testing affect parents' eugenic decisions (para. 25)?

5. What are some of the results of state-controlled eugenics?

6. What is the significance of the story of Carrie Buck?

7. What constitutes a eugenic decision?

✂ SUGGESTIONS FOR CRITICAL WRITING

1. After reviewing what Kitcher says about eugenics, especially laissez-faire eugenics, what kinds of people are most likely to decide in advance what genetic traits their children should inherit? What problems can you foresee if the resources of genetic engineering are not made available to everyone?

2. In northern India, prenatal scanning often results in the abortion of female fetuses. The decision to abort is sometimes made because the family does not value females as much as males. Sometimes it is made because the family knows that the fate of females in the society is brutal and cruel. Write an essay that establishes the moral issues involved in such decisions. If possible, research the abortion practices in India's Punjab region.

3. If you had the means by which you could make decisions regarding the genetic engineering of your children, what would you hope to achieve? If you were to make any decision to alter the normal genetic inheritance of your child, would your decision be considered moral or immoral? What would be the basis of your decision in terms of morality?

4. Children born with Down syndrome often face difficulties in society, but Kitcher points out that many such children also live peaceful and happy lives. If you discovered that you were about to give birth to a child with Down syndrome, would you feel it appropriate to abort the fetus? Are there any acceptable reasons for aborting the fetus? What do you feel your obligation would be to such a fetus, assuming that you did not abort it? What are the moral issues at stake here?

5. In paragraph 20, Kitcher says, "Laissez-faire eugenics is in danger of retaining the most disturbing aspect of its historical predecessors — the tendency to try to transform the population in a particular direction." If Kitcher is correct, and if contemporary eugenics does transform the population in a particular direction, what do you think that direction will be? In a brief essay, explain what you think people will do if they can affect the genetic outcome of their children.

6. Today, some abortions are performed essentially as matters of convenience for those who did not plan their pregnancy. The moral issues in those cases are currently debated. However, some abortions are performed, as Kitcher tells us, to avoid the pain and suffering of malformed and diseased offspring. What is the moral situation of someone who has an abortion because of the certain knowledge that the child will live a mean, painful, and short life? Would you opt for an abortion if you knew you were to have such a child?

7. **CONNECTIONS** Charles Darwin's essay, "Natural Selection" (p. 606) describes the process by which he feels species are changed and presumably improved. Eugenics, as Philip Kitcher explains to us, is not a process of natural selection. It is a process of human selection. Humans have long selected dogs and horses in a manner that produces desired effects. Human selection in animals has generally been approved. With reference to Darwin and Kitcher, write an essay arguing that human selection is more or less desirable than natural selection in producing strong and able human offspring.

© Rick Friedman/Corbis

LISA
RANDALL

Newtonian Gravity and Special Relativity

L ISA RANDALL (b. 1962) was born in Queens, New York, and went from Stuyvesant High School to Harvard University, where she earned her Ph.D. in physics. She taught at Massachusetts Institute of Technology, then at Princeton University, where she was the first woman to earn tenure in the Physics Department. She is currently a professor at Harvard and was also the first woman to earn tenure at Harvard in the field of theoretical physics.

Randall is also said to be the most frequently cited physicist in the world, which means that other physicists routinely reference her in their work. She is best known to the public for her book *Warped Passages: Unraveling the Mysteries of the Universe's Hidden Dimensions* (2005), from which the following selection is drawn. Her work on particle physics has been influential on all major physicists, and her interest in superstring theory has led to discoveries and theories about multiple universes and other baffling concepts. Like Michio Kaku and most modern physicists, she postulates a universe with more dimensions than the four that we live with and can conceive.

Her book *Warped Passages* makes an effort to explain to the rest of us some of the most subtle and unlikely concepts that are currently adopted in science, such as the concept of branes, which are like the surface of a soap bubble. Imagining the universe existing on a brane makes certain insoluble problems of physics easier to understand. In her book, she says, "A Brane is a distinct region of spacetime that extends through only a (possibly multidimensional) slice of space." She uses the metaphor of a brane as a slice of bread in a loaf of other slices. This is only one of the strange ideas that she has explained as part of the exploration of the superstring theory, which suggests that particles in physics are not solid objects, but strings of energy vibrating at different frequencies. Because there is an infinite possible range of frequencies, the theory explains why there seem to be so many particles discovered in the atom.

From *Warped Passages: Unraveling the Mysteries of the Universe's Hidden Dimensions.*

Some of her contemporary research has led her into an interesting area in which her study of dark matter has made her connect that phenomenon to the extinction of the dinosaurs. Dark matter seems to be a substance with gravity that does not emit light or absorb it. It is said to make up 85 percent of our universe, and yet it remains quite mysterious. Its presence can be felt and measured by cosmologists because it is thought to be one of the forces that holds the universe together. In her recent book, *Dark Matter and the Dinosaurs* (2015), she explores what is known about dark matter and hypothesizes that a chunk of dark matter may have been involved in "nudging" an asteroid ten kilometers across into colliding with Earth 66 million years ago, ending the almost 200 million year dominance of the dinosaurs on earth. She admits that she cannot be certain of her theory, but she lays out the evidence that has helped her propose her idea as a strong possibility. Like so much about modern physics, her ideas challenge common sense.

RANDALL'S RHETORIC

Even though Lisa Randall discusses two fundamental issues in physics, the Newtonian and the Einsteinian views of gravity, the complexities that she reveals make this selection challenging. However, her use of short paragraphs and nontechnical language helps her convey her thoughts. Her purpose in this passage is explanatory, so she speaks directly and as simply as possible in an effort to communicate to a general audience. She relies on the basic rhetorical device of separating two principles and examining them one after another. The first is the Newtonian concept, which has been the reigning concept since 1687, when Newton published his theories of gravity.

His discovery was mathematical, and Randall omits the mathematics as a concession for those of us unfamiliar with the equations that Newton relied on for his theories. He discovered that all planets and objects with mass have a gravitational pull, and the pull seems to operate from the center of the object. He also discovered that although we are affected by the gravity of our earth, which keeps us where we are, we are also affected by the gravitational pull of the moon. So it is that we, our earth, and our moon are affected by the gravitational pull of the sun, which keeps the planets spinning steadily in orbit. Some of this was known to scientists in the seventeenth century, but what they did not know was the formulas that permitted people to prophesy the movements and behavior of the planets.

Randall's approach to all this is essentially abstract and, to an extent, a historical summary of Newton's work. As in most explanations, we must follow the progress of the discussion and hope to understand the principles, if not the exact details.

Randall begins her discussion of Einstein's theory of special relativity by mentioning that Einstein began his work by examining and reconsidering Newton's theories of gravity. She points out that his job in the patent office in Bern, Switzerland, made him specially aware of issues of time. In addition, she gives some examples of time as it relates to European and American trains. Einstein, she tells us, refined his ideas of space and time because he saw them less as different than as totally interdependent. To help us understand the relationship of space and time, she uses an example of sailing boats moving at different speeds and at different distances from one another. Einstein posited that time would contract in one case, depending on the speed of the boat. In the ordinary world, such differences would be indistinguishable, but at the speed of light and in the larger world of the cosmos, these differences would be apparent.

Obviously, Randall's job is difficult, and our understanding will be approximate, but the directness and simplicity of her discourse help us gain an appreciation for how scientific research in physics produces unexpected results.

▓ PREREADING QUESTIONS: WHAT TO READ FOR

The following prereading questions may help you anticipate key issues in the discussion of Lisa Randall's "Newtonian Gravity and Special Relativity." Keeping them in mind during your first reading of the selection should help focus your attention.

1. What were Newton's major insights about gravity?
2. What kind of force is gravity?
3. What was different about Einstein's approach to space and time?

Newtonian Gravity and Special Relativity

This chapter will explore Einstein's theory of gravity, a spectacularly accurate theory that applies to a wide range of systems. We'll begin by briefly reviewing Newton's gravitational theory, which works fine for the energies and speeds we encounter in daily life. We'll then move on to the extreme limits in which it fails: namely, very high speed (close to the speed of light) and very large mass or energy. In these limits, Newtonian gravity is superseded by Einstein's theory of relativity. With Einstein's general relativity, space (and spacetime) evolved from a static stage to a dynamical entity that can move and curve and have a rich life of its own. We'll consider this theory, the clues that led to its development, and some of the experimental tests that convince physicists that it's right.

Newtonian Gravity

Gravity is the force that keeps your feet on the ground and is the source of the acceleration that returns a tossed ball to Earth. In the late sixteenth century, Galileo showed that this acceleration is the same for all objects on the surface of the Earth, no matter what their mass.

However, this acceleration does depend on how far the object is from the   3
Earth's center. More generally, the strength of gravity depends on the distance
between the two masses — gravity's pull is weaker when objects are farther
apart. And when what creates the gravitational attraction is not the Earth, but
some other object, gravity's strength will depend on the mass of that object.

Isaac Newton[1] developed the gravitational force law that summarizes how   4
gravity depends on mass and distance. Newton's law says that the force of
gravity between two masses is proportional to the mass of each of them. They
could be anything: the Earth and a ball, the Sun and Jupiter, a basketball and a
soccer ball, or any two objects you please. The more massive the objects, the
greater the gravitational attraction.

Newton's gravitational force law also says how the gravitational force   5
depends on the distance between the two objects. As discussed in Chapter 2,
the law says that the force between two objects is proportional to the inverse
square of their separation. This inverse square law was where the famous apple
entered in.[2] Newton could deduce the acceleration due to the Earth's gravitational pull on an apple located near the Earth's surface and compare it with the
acceleration induced on the Moon, which is located sixty times further away
than the Earth's surface is from its center. The acceleration of the Moon due
to the earth's gravity is 3,600 times smaller (3,600 is the square of 60) than the
acceleration of the apple. This is in accordance with the gravitational force
decreasing as the square of the distance from the Earth's center.

However, even when we know the dependence of the gravitational attrac-   6
tion on mass and distance, we still need another piece of information before
we can determine the overall strength of gravitational attraction. The missing
piece is a number, called *Newton's gravitational constant,* that factors into the
calculation of any classical gravitational force. Gravity is very weak, and this is
reflected in the tiny size of Newton's constant, to which all gravitational effects
are proportional.

The Earth's gravitational pull or the gravitational attraction between the   7
Sun and the planets might seem pretty big. But that's only because the Earth,
the Sun, and the planets are so massive. Newton's constant is very small, and
the gravitational attraction between elementary particles is an extremely
weak force. This feebleness of gravity is itself a big puzzle that we will return
to later on.

Although his theory was correct, Newton delayed its publication for   8
twenty years, until 1687, while he tried to justify a critical assumption of his

---

[1] **Isaac Newton (1642–1726)**   English scientist; inventor of calculus; the greatest scientist
of his age.

[2] The story might be apocryphal, but the reasoning is not. [Randall's note]

theory: that the Earth's gravitational pull was exerted as if its mass were all concentrated at the center. While Newton was hard at work developing calculus to solve this problem, Edmund Halley, Christopher Wren, Robert Hooke,[3] and Newton himself made tremendous progress in determining the gravitational force law by analyzing the motion of the planets, whose orbits Johannes Kepler[4] had measured and found to be elliptical.

These men all made major contributions to the problem of planetary   9
motion, but it is Newton who gets credited with the inverse square law. That is because Newton ultimately showed that elliptical orbits would arise as a result of a central force (that of the Sun) only if the inverse square law was true, and he showed with calculus that the mass of a spherical body did in fact act as if it were concentrated at the center. Newton did, however, acknowledge the significance of others' contributions in his words, "If I have seen further, it is because I have stood upon the shoulders of giants."[5] (However, rumor has it that he said this only because of his intense dislike for Hooke, who was very short.)

In high school physics, we learned Newton's laws and calculated the behav-   10
ior of interesting (if somewhat contrived) systems. I remember my outrage when our teacher, Mr Baumel, informed us that the gravitational theory we had just learned was wrong. Why teach us a theory that we know to be incorrect? In my high school view of the world, the whole merit of science was that it could be true and reliable, and could make accurate and factual predictions.

But Mr Baumel was simplifying, perhaps for dramatic effect. Newton's the-   11
ory was not wrong: it was merely an approximation, one that works incredibly well in most circumstances. For a large range of parameters (speed, distance, mass, and so on), it predicts gravitational forces quite accurately. The more precise underlying theory is relativity, and you only make measurably different predictions with relativity when you are dealing with extremely high speeds or large amounts of mass or energy. Newton's law predicts the motion of a ball admirably well, since neither of the above criteria apply. To use relativity to predict the motion of a ball would be pure silliness.

In fact, Einstein himself initially thought of special relativity merely as an   12
improvement on Newtonian physics—not as a radical paradigm shift. This, of course, grossly underplays the ultimate significance of his work.

---

[3] **Edmund Halley (1656–1742)**   English astronomer and mathematician who calculated the orbit of Halley's Comet; **Christopher Wren (1632–1723)** English astronomer and mathematician as well as an architect; **Robert Hooke (1635–1703)** English scientist who published about gravity before Newton and who disagreed with him.

[4] **Johannes Kepler (1571–1630)**   German astronomer who calculated the movement of the planets.

[5] Letter from Isaac Newton to Robert Hooke, 5 February 1675. [Randall's note]

Special Relativity

A very reasonable thing to expect from physical laws is that they should be the same for everyone. No one could blame us for questioning their validity and utility if people in different countries or sitting on moving trains or flying on an airplane experienced different physical laws. Physical laws should be fundamental and hold true for any observer. Any differences in calculations should be due to differences in environment, not the physical laws. It would be very strange indeed to have universal physical laws that required a particular vantage point. The particular quantities you might measure could depend on your reference frame, but the laws that govern these quantities should not. Einstein's formulation of special relativity ensures that this is the case.

13

In fact, it's somewhat ironic that Einstein's work on gravity is referred to as "the theory of relativity." The essential point that drove both special and general relativity was that physical laws should apply for everyone, independent of their reference frame. In fact, Einstein would have preferred the term *Invariantentheorie*.[6] In a letter Einstein wrote in 1921 in reply to a correspondent who had suggested he reconsider the name, he admitted that the term "relativity" was unfortunate.[7] But by that time, the term was too well entrenched for him to attempt to change it.

14

Einstein's first insight about reference frames and relativity came from thinking about electromagnetism. The well-known theory of electromagnetism from the nineteenth century was based on Maxwell's laws,[8] which describe the behavior of electromagnetism and electromagnetic waves. The laws gave correct results, but everyone initially falsely interpreted the predictions in terms of the motion of an *aether*, a hypothesized invisible substance whose vibrations were supposed to be electromagnetic waves. Einstein realized that if there were an aether, there would also be a preferred observational vantage point, or frame of reference: the one in which the aether is at rest. He reasoned that the same physical laws should apply to people who are moving at constant velocity[9] with respect to each other and with respect to someone at rest — that is, in frames of reference that physicists refer to as inertial frames.[10] By requiring that *all* physical laws, including those of electromagnetism, should hold for

15

---

[6] Gerald Holton, *Einstein, History, and Other Passions* (Cambridge, MA: Harvard University Press, 2000). [Randall's note]

[7] Letter to E. Zschimmer, 30 September 1921. [Randall's note]

[8] **Maxwell's laws**   Equations for electrodynamic events developed by James Clerk Maxwell (1831–1879).

[9] Velocity gives both speed and direction. [Randall's note]

[10] **inertial frame**   A reference frame that moves at fixed velocity with respect to a fixed reference frame, such as the one at rest.

observers in all inertial reference frames, Einstein was led to abandon the idea of the aether and, ultimately, to formulate special relativity.

Einstein's theory of special relativity, with its radical revision of the concepts of space and time, was a major leap. Peter Galison,[11] a physicist and historian of science, suggests that it was not only the aether theory that put Einstein on the right track, but Einstein's job at the time. Galison reasoned that Einstein, who grew up in Germany and worked at the patent office in Bern, Switzerland, must have had time and time coordination on his mind. Anyone who has traveled in Europe knows that precision is valued highly in countries such as Switzerland and Germany, which has the happy consequence that passengers can count on the trains to run on time. Einstein worked in the patent office between 1902 and 1905, during an era when train travel was becoming increasingly important, and coordinating time was at the forefront of new technology. In the early 1900s, Einstein was very likely thinking about real-world problems, such as how to coordinate the time at one train station with that at another.   16

Of course, Einstein did not need to develop relativity to solve the problem of coordinating real trains. (For those of us accustomed to the frequently delayed American trains, coordinated time might sound exotic in any case.[12]) But coordinating time raised some interesting questions. Time coordination of relativistically moving trains is not a straightforward problem. If I were to coordinate my watch with someone on a moving train, I would need to account for the time delay of a signal traveling between us because light has a finite speed. Coordinating my watch with that of the person sitting next to me would not be the same as coordinating watches with someone far away.[13]   17

Einstein's critical insight, the one that led him to special relativity, was that ideas about time had to be reformulated. According to Einstein, space and time could no longer be considered independently. Although they are not the same thing—time and space are clearly different—the quantities you measure depend on the speed at which you are traveling. Special relativity was the result of this insight.   18

---

[11] **Peter Galison (b. 1955)**   The Joseph Pellegrino University Professor in history of science and physics at Harvard University.

[12] Don't get me wrong—I like trains. But I wish they were better supported in the U.S. [Randall's note]

[13] Although American trains don't always coordinate time very well, Amtrak does appear to acknowledge special relativity when they say, "time and the space to use it" in their advertising slogan for the Acela, the high-speed train that travels the Northeast corridor. However, "time" and "space" are not precisely interchangeable. Although the slogan "space and the time to use it" does describe my more heavily delayed train rides, the phrase wouldn't be a very compelling advertisement for a high-speed train. [Randall's note]

Bizarre as they are, one can derive all of Einstein's novel consequences of special relativity from two postulates. To state them, we need to understand the meaning of *inertial frames*—a particular category of reference frames. Let's first choose any frame of reference that moves at constant velocity (speed and direction); the one that's at rest is often a good one. The inertial frames would then be those that are moving at fixed velocity with respect to that first one—someone running or driving by at constant speed, for example.

19

Einstein's postulates then state that:

20

The laws of physics are the same in all inertial frames.
The speed of light, c, is the same in any inertial frame.

The two postulates tell us that Newton's laws are incomplete. Once we accept Einstein's postulates, we have no choice but to replace Newton's laws with new physical laws that are consistent with these rules. The laws of special relativity that follow lead to all the surprising consequences you might have heard of, such as time dilation, the observer dependence of simultaneity, and Lorentz contraction[14] of a moving object. The new laws should look very much like the old classical physics laws when applied to objects moving at speeds that are small compared with the speed of light. But when applied to something moving very fast, at or near the speed of light, the difference between the Newtonian and special relativity formulations should become apparent.

For example, in Newtonian mechanics speeds are simply added together. A car driving towards yours on the freeway approaches you at a speed that's the sum of its speed and yours. Similarly, if someone throws a ball at you from the platform while you are on a moving train, the ball's speed appears to be the sum of the speed of the ball itself plus the speed of the moving train. (A former student of mine, Witek Skiba, can attest to this fact. Witek was nearly knocked out when he was hit by a ball that someone threw at the approaching train he was riding.)

21

According to Newtonian physics, the speed of a beam of light directed at a moving train should be the sum of the speed of light and the speed of the moving train. But this can't be true if the speed of light is constant, as Einstein's second postulate asserts. If the speed of light is always the same, then the speed of the beam aimed at the moving train will be identical to the speed of a light beam that approaches you when you're standing still on the ground. Even though it runs counter to the intuition gained from your experience of the slow speeds you encounter in daily life, light speed is constant, and in special relativity speeds don't simply add up as they do in Newtonian physics. Instead, you add speeds according to a relativistic formula that follows from Einstein's postulates.

22

---

[14] **Lorentz contraction** The contraction of an object moving at speed away from a fixed reference frame.

Many of special relativity's implications don't jibe with our familiar notions   23
of time and space. Special relativity treats time and space differently than they
had been treated before in Newtonian mechanics, and this is what gives rise to
many of its counterintuitive results. Time and space measurements depend on
speed and get mixed up in systems that move relative to each other. Nonetheless, surprising as they are, once you accept the two postulates then a different
notion of space and time is an inevitable consequence.

Here's one argument why. Imagine two identical ships with identical masts.   24
One ship is docked by the shore, while the other is moving away. Also imagine
that the captains of the two ships synchronized their watches when the first
ship sailed off.

Now suppose that the two captains do a rather odd thing: each decides   25
to measure time on her ship by placing a mirror at the top of the mast and a
second mirror at the bottom, shining a light from the bottom mirror to the top
one, and measuring the number of times light hits the mirror and returns. As
a practical matter, of course, this would be absurd, since light would cycle up
and down far too frequently to count. But bear with me, and imagine that the
captains can count extraordinarily fast; I'll be using this somewhat contrived
example to argue that time stretches out on the moving ship.

If each captain knows how long it takes for light to cycle once, she can   26
calculate the passage of time by multiplying the light-cycle time by the number
of times light cycles up and down between the mirrors. Now suppose, though,
that instead of using her own stationary mirror clock, the captain on the docked
ship measures time by the number of times the light on the moving ship hits the
mast's mirror and returns.

Now from the perspective of the captain on the moving ship, the light sim-   27
ply goes straight up and down. However, from the perspective of the captain
on the docked ship, the light has to travel farther (in order to cover the distance
traveled by the moving ship—see figure). But—and this is the counterintuitive part—the speed of light is constant. It is the same for the light sent to the
top of the mast on the docked ship as it is for the light sent to the top of the
mast on the moving ship. Since speed measures distance traveled over time,
and the speed of light for the moving ship is the same as the speed of light for
the stationary one, the moving mirror clock has to "tick" at a slower rate to
compensate for the longer distance the moving light has to travel. This very
counterintuitive conclusion—that moving and stationary clocks must tick at
different rates—follows from the fact that the speed of light in a moving reference frame is the same as the speed of light in stationary one. And although
this is a funny way to measure time, the same conclusion—that moving clocks
run slower—would hold true independently of how time is measured. If the
captains had watches on, they would observe the same thing (again, with the
caveat that for normal speeds, the effect would be tiny).

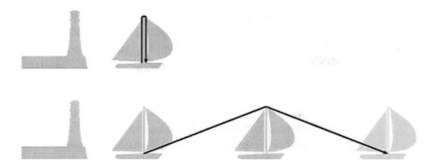

The path of a light beam that bounces off the top of a mast of a stationary ship and of a moving one. The stationary observer (in a boat by the shore or in a lighthouse) would see a longer path in the second case.

While the above example is artificial, the phenomenon described produces genuinely measurable effects. For example, special relativity gives rise to the different time experienced by fast-moving objects—the phenomenon known as time dilation.   28

Physicists measure time dilation when they study elementary particles produced at colliders or in the atmosphere, which travel at relativistic speeds—speeds approaching that of light. For example, the elementary particle called a muon has the same charge as an electron, but is heavier and can decay (that is, it can turn into other, lighter particles). The muon's lifetime, the time before it decays, is only 2 microseconds. If a moving muon had the same lifetime as a stationary one, it would be able to travel only about 600 meters before it disappeared. But muons manage to make it all the way through our atmosphere, and in colliders, to the edges of large detectors, because their near-light-speed velocity makes them appear to us much longer lived. In the atmosphere, muons travel at least ten times further than they would in a universe based on Newtonian principles. The very fact that we see these muons at all shows us that time dilation (and special relativity) gives rise to true physical effects.   29

Special relativity is important both because it was a dramatic deviation from classical physics and because it was essential to the development of general relativity and quantum field theory, both of which play a significant role in more recent developments. Because I won't use specific special relativity predictions when I discuss particle physics and extra-dimensional models later on, I'll resist the urge to go into all the fascinating consequences of special relativity, such as why simultaneity depends on whether an observer is moving and how the sizes of moving objects are different from when they are at rest.   30

✷ QUESTIONS FOR CRITICAL READING

1. Why is Einstein's work on gravity ironic (para. 13)?

2. How does mass affect gravity?

3. Where did Newton think the earth's source of gravity was?

4. Why did Mr. Baumel think Newton's theories of gravity were wrong?

5. What are inertial frames of reference (paras. 16 and 19)?

6. How did Einstein treat space and time?

7. What is the point of the illustration of the stationary and moving ships?

✷ SUGGESTIONS FOR CRITICAL WRITING

1. Begin by writing an essay on Newton's theory of gravity. Explain its key points to a reader who is unaware of who Isaac Newton was. Be sure to explain how Newton treated mass and how he calculated distance in an effort to determine the gravitational pull of an object. How does what you learn in this process help you understand the principles that Lisa Randall talks about in her discussion of Newton?

2. Randall talks about "time dilation" as being a discovery of Einstein and part of his theory of relativity. What is time dilation? How does it relate to Einstein's theories? In a brief essay, explain the concept and its importance to an audience interested in science.

3. In paragraph 22, Randall discusses a problem that arises with Newtonian physics and the question of adding speeds to moving objects. What is the issue that she is describing? Explain why Einstein's concept of the speed of light as a constant creates a problem for Newton's ideas about the speed of a moving object.

4. What is the most problematic of the ideas that Randall discusses? Which of the issues in Newtonian and Einsteinian theories are most relevant to people in general today? Why might a knowledgeable person want to know the differences between the seventeenth-century views of physics and the twentieth-century views of physics? Why would you want to know more about the questions of basic physics that Randall discusses? Argue a case that explains why a modern educated person should know something about the difference between Newtonian physics and Einsteinian physics.

5. In the past, the world has been shaken by scientific discoveries. For example, when Galileo demonstrated that the earth was not the center of the universe, the ultimate result was to undermine one of the most central certainties of his time. Once that certainty was called into question, all kinds of social certainties also gave way — ultimately to revolution. Einstein has called the distinction of

space and time into question, and we now talk about spacetime. What effect does such a distinction have on society today? How can this concept help us imagine other worlds and other universes? How can it inform our awareness of the complexity of the universe?

6. Randall talks about Maxwell's theory of aether (para. 15) as conducting electromagnetic waves. This theory held for many years before Einstein essentially ended it. Research Maxwell's theories and explain why they are important to the development of electricity. But also examine them carefully to see how reasonable they seemed at the time and why the concept of ether was essential for Maxwell to make his theories work. Given that such a theory can hold sway for a long time, what do you conclude about the nature of such theories?

7. **CONNECTIONS**   Compare the way in which Michio Kaku (p. 641) explains the difficult concepts of physics with the way in which Lisa Randall explains them. Both of these physicists are important and both work in the same areas, but they are different in their approaches. Which of them is dealing with the most important ideas? Which of them is clearest in conveying the nature of the ideas to you? What does a careful reading of their selections tell you about how one should go about explaining science to people who do not know much science?

Reflections on the Nature of Science

Now that you have read the selections in "Science," consider in what ways these writers have helped further inform your views on science and its place in our world.

1. In what ways are you aware of your own inquiries as scientific?

2. What should be the best relationship between politicians and scientists?

3. Do you feel that society will soon welcome the chance to select the genes of their children rather than letting nature select their genes?

4. What new scientific discoveries do you imagine will most disturb us in the future?

5. Some physicists have said that if an explanation of a physical fact seems reasonable and understandable, then it is false. Which of the scientific explanations in this text seem most unreasonable? What do you make of them?

6. One definition of modern people living in Plato's cave might be people living without taking advantage of modern science. How could you shape a life without modern science? Would you want to?

7. Which of science's most recent gifts frightens you most? Is it science that frightens you, or is it the people who know how to use it that frighten you?

8. Which of the authors you have read in this part of the book helped you best understand what science is?

9. After reading the authors in this part of the book, how has your attitude toward science changed? Would you consider a career in science?

10. Modern physicists conceive of a world in which there are more than four dimensions. Why is it difficult for us to imagine such a world? Are you convinced that the universe really has more than the dimensions we can perceive?

ETHICS

Introduction

A system of morality which is based on relative emotional values is a mere illusion, a thoroughly vulgar conception which has nothing sound in it and nothing true.
— SOCRATES (469–399 B.C.E.)

God considered not action, but the spirit of the action. It is the intention, not the deed, wherein the merit or praise of the doer consists.
— PETER ABELARD (1079–1142)

If men were born free, they would, so long as they remained free, form no conception of good and evil.
— BARUCH SPINOZA (1632–1677)

All morality depends upon our sentiments; and when any action or quality of the mind pleases us after a certain manner we say it is virtuous; and when the neglect or nonperformance of it displeases us after a like manner, we say that we lie under an obligation to perform it.
— DAVID HUME (1711–1776)

There are no whole truths; all truths are half-truths. It is trying to treat them as whole truths that plays the devil.
— ALFRED NORTH WHITEHEAD (1861–1947)

To set up as a standard of public morality a notion which can neither be defined nor conceived is to open the door to every kind of tyranny.
— SIMONE WEIL (1909–1943)

The establishment of ethical principles that translate into moral behavior constitutes a major step forward for civilization. To be sure, ancient civilizations maintained rules and laws governing behavior, and in some cases those rules were written down and adhered to by the majority of citizens. But the move that major religions made was to go beyond simple rules or laws—to penetrate deeper layers of emotion to make people want to behave well toward each other. The writers and writings in this section have all examined the nature of morality and have come to some interesting conclusions, focusing on various aspects of the ethical nature of humankind.

In the fourth century B.C.E., Aristotle (384–322 B.C.E.) wrote a treatise on ethics aimed at instructing his son Nichomachus. The *Nichomachean Ethics* is the single most famous ancient document that attempts to clarify the nature of ethical behavior and its effect on the individual. In the selection from the *Ethics* included here, Aristotle focuses on defining the good in life, not in the abstract, but in terms of the individual's obligation to participate in statecraft — what we might call politics. Aristotle also felt that in a democracy it is everyone's duty to understand the principles by which people can live happily and well. Once he has defined the good, he proceeds to examine the nature of human happiness, and eventually, he connects it to "virtuous conduct" (para. 23). In the process, he examines virtuous conduct in an effort to enlighten his son on the kind of behavior that is likely to reward him with the most happiness and the best life.

Aristotle emphasizes the soul over the body, in the sense that he emphasizes the spiritual over the material world. Reason, his guide, must be followed if we are to live well, but he realizes it is often disregarded. Therefore, he discusses at some length the irrational aspects of our minds that affect behavior. In the final analysis, Aristotle argues for a reasonable approach to guiding the individual's behavior with respect for others.

In the third century B.C.E., Hsün Tzu (310–c. 220 B.C.E.) was an important Chinese philosopher associated with courts in several Chinese cities. He taught that people are born with natural traits that lead to immoral behavior. Man's nature is evil, and therefore, people must be instructed to follow an ethical and moral path through life. He recommends that individual should read the teachings of the sages and follow the rituals of the culture. Those rituals are not defined, but they imply a proper behavior as established by tradition. Basic human nature leads people to be self-indulgent, self-centered, and committed to sensory pleasure. Therefore, it is clear to Hsün Tzu that an ethical path in life must be regulated by accepting the wisdom and instruction of the elders. As a result, Hsün Tzu is committed to education and recommends a teacher for shaping the individual's basic nature. In other words, he insists on a moral education for everyone as a means to make people behave ethically toward one another so as to live in a peaceful and harmonious community.

Henry David Thoreau (1817–1862) was among the New Englanders who stood firm against slavery and demanded its abolition. Thoreau felt his ethical position threatened by the government's demanding a tax that would go toward supporting laws that he regarded as immoral. But the Fugitive Slave Law of 1850, which was passed a year after Thoreau's "Civil Disobedience" was first published, had grown even fiercer in demanding that every citizen turn in runaway slaves or face punishment. Thoreau influenced many later thinkers and activists who also struggled against injustice and a social failure of ethics, such as Mohandas Gandhi and Martin Luther King Jr.

One victim of what we now think of as immoral behavior was Frederick Douglass (1818–1895), who escaped from slavery by using a deception that his owners considered unethical. Douglass's life was filled with moral conundrums that even now give us pause. But he was a remarkable man who fled slavery and became one of the most famous Americans of his age. When he amassed enough money, he actually bought his freedom from the family who had owned him. While that seems like an ethical act, some people felt that it was not at all ethical—that since he was not a piece of property he should not have paid his "owners" for a right all should unequivocally enjoy: freedom.

Iris Murdoch (1919–1999), one of the twentieth century's most distinguished writers, spent part of her life as an Oxford don teaching philosophy. Her major interests were ethics and morals; in "Morality and Religion" she addresses the question, Can there be morality without religion? Murdoch explores the issues of virtue and duty, both of which she sees as aspects of what we think of as moral behavior, and connects them with the ideals of institutional religion. She then goes on to examine guilt, usually thought of as a religious concept, and the question of sin. That leads her to consider how religion conceives of the struggle of good and evil, aiming as it does to conquer evil through moral behavior. But a paradox arises: If evil can be totally conquered, can there still be a system of morals or a behavior that needs to be called ethical? Murdoch's method is to keep us questioning basic issues until we begin to grasp their significance.

Taking a slightly different approach, Carol Gilligan (b. 1936) in "Concepts of Self and Morality" addresses the question of whether or not men and women see ethical questions differently. She suggests that because of women's upbringing and the fact that they are strongly influenced by three men in their lives—their fathers, their husbands, and their clergymen—they tend to defer to male judgment and perhaps retreat from making some ethical choices when possible. However, Gilligan also introduces the question of abortion and suggests that when contemplating an abortion, women must make their own choices and decide what exactly is involved in making a moral and ethical decision. Gilligan relies on comments made by her own students and by women in an abortion study who had to face their own choices and see how those choices squared with their own moral position.

When Michael Gazzaniga (b. 1939) begins his examination of the nature of ethical behavior in "Toward a Universal Ethics," he brings to bear his extensive experience in brain physiology. He has not only dissected brains but has also written extensively about their various features, especially the nature of the separate left and right hemispheres and their special adaptations. Gazzaniga consults a number of evolutionary neuroscientists who study the brain to see which predilections are inherent. We take the inborn talents of geniuses as examples of brains being "hardwired" to start with, but Gazzaniga ponders the possibility that there may be a moral center in the brain and that, if he is right, there could be a universal ethics that applies to all people regardless of culture or upbringing. In his view, before neuroscience developed a significant knowledge of the functions of the brain, all we knew about ethical and moral philosophy came from people telling "stories." These stories are religious and ethical in import, but they have no scientific basis. Gazzaniga brings science to bear on ethics.

Kwame Anthony Appiah (b. 1954) examines the nature of ethics itself. His excursion into virtue theory tries to work out the relationship between the agent of a good act and the act itself. Is an act virtuous because it is performed by a virtuous character, or is it virtuous in and of itself? The question of character is at the root of his "The Case against Character," but in the process of presenting his argument, Appiah examines evidence from many thinkers on the relationship between a person's character and the virtue of that person's actions. As he examines this relationship, he demonstrates how complex the issue is and how important it is not to take the question of virtue for granted.

Each of these selections offers insights into the ethical underpinnings of modern culture. They clarify the nature of the good and the moral. If our ultimate goal is happiness, then the path to that goal must go through the precincts of ethical and moral behavior.

Some Considerations about the Nature of Ethics

Before reading the selections that follow, consider what your views of ethics are. Ask yourself the following questions and respond to each in a reading journal. Discuss your answers with your classmates.

1. To what extent does happiness depend on ethical behavior?
2. Are human beings naturally good, or are they naturally bad?
3. When is it ethically reasonable to disobey a law of the land?
4. Are ethical principles universal, or do they depend on the customs of various cultures?
5. Does morality depend on religious belief?
6. Is there a difference between ethical behavior and moral behavior?
7. Is ethical behavior built into us through evolution?
8. Do our laws aim at promoting ethical principles?
9. What is the relationship between games we play and our ethical behavior?
10. How does empathy help shape ethical and moral behavior?

Museo Nazionale Romano Rome/Collection Dagli Orti/
The Art Archive at Art Resource, NY

ARISTOTLE
The Aim of Man

A RISTOTLE (384–322 B.C.E.) is the great inheritor of Plato's influence in philosophical thought.
He was a student at the Academy of Plato in Athens from age seventeen to thirty-seven, and by all
accounts he was Plato's most brilliant pupil. He did
not agree with Plato on all issues, however, and seems to have broken with his master
around the time of Plato's death (347 B.C.E.). In certain of his writings he is careful to disagree with the Platonists while insisting on his friendship with them. In the *Nichomachean
Ethics*, for example, the most difficult section (omitted here) demonstrates that Plato is
not correct in assuming that the good exists in some ideal form in a higher spiritual realm.

One interesting point concerning Aristotle's career is that when he became a teacher,
his most distinguished student was Alexander the Great, the youthful ruler who spread
Greek values and laws throughout the rest of the known world. Much speculation has
centered on just what Aristotle might have taught Alexander about politics. The emphasis
on statecraft and political goals in the *Nichomachean Ethics* suggests that it may have been
a great deal. A surviving fragment of a letter from Aristotle to Alexander suggests that he
advised Alexander to become the leader of the Greeks and the master of the barbarians.

The *Nichomachean Ethics* is a difficult document. Aristotle may have written it with
an eye to tutoring his son, Nichomachus, but it is also meant to be read by those who
have thought deeply about human ethical behavior. "The Aim of Man" treats most of the
basic issues raised in the entire document. It is difficult primarily because it is so thoroughly abstract. Abstract reason was thought to be the highest form of reason because
it is independent of sensory experience and because only human beings can indulge in
it. Aristotle, whose studies included works on plants, physics, animals, law, rhetoric, and
logic, to name only some subjects, reminds us often of what we have in common with the
animal and vegetable worlds. But because he values abstract thought so much, his reasoning demands unusual attention from contemporary readers.

Moreover, because he wrote so much on scientific subjects — and, unlike Plato,
emphasized the role of sensory perception in scientific matters — he is careful to warn

From the *Nichomachean Ethics*. Translated by Martin Ostwald.

that reasoning about humankind cannot entail the precision taken for granted in science. That warning is repeated several times in this selection. The study of humankind requires awareness of people's differences of background, education, habit, temperament, and other, similar factors. Such differences will impede the kinds of precision of definition and analysis taken for granted in other sciences.

Aristotle reveals an interesting Greek prejudice when he admits that the highest good for humankind is likely to be found in statecraft. He tells us that the well-ordered state — the pride of the Greek way of life — is of such noble value that other values must take second place to it. Because current thought somewhat agrees with this view, Aristotle sounds peculiarly modern in this passage. Unlike the Christian theorists of the Middle Ages, the theorists of the Islamic insurgence, or the theorists of the Judaic Scriptures, Aristotle does not put divinity or godliness first. He is a practical man whose concerns are with the life that human beings know here on earth. When he considers the question, for instance, of whether a man can be thought of as happy before he has died (tragedy can always befall the happy man), he is thoroughly practical and does not point to happiness in heaven as any substitute for happiness on earth.

ARISTOTLE'S RHETORIC

Even though Aristotle is the author of the single most influential treatise on rhetoric, this document does not have as eloquent a style as might be expected, which has suggested to some that the manuscript was taken from the lecture notes of a student. But, of course, he does use certain minor techniques that demonstrate his awareness of rhetorical effect. He makes careful use of aphorisms — for example, "One swallow does not make a spring" and "Perfect justice is noblest, health is best, / But to gain one's heart's desire is pleasantest" (para. 21).

In terms of style, Aristotle is at a disadvantage — or perhaps the modern world is — because he addresses an audience of those who have thought very deeply on the issues of human behavior, so that his style is elevated and complex. Fortunately, nothing he says here is beyond the grasp of the careful reader, although modern readers expect to be provided with a good many concrete examples to help them understand abstract principles. Aristotle purposely avoids using examples so as not to limit too sharply the truths he has to impart.

Aristotle's most prominent rhetorical technique is definition. His overall goal in this work is to define the aim of man. Thus, the first section of this work is entitled "Definition of the Good." In "Primacy of Statecraft" he begins to qualify various types of good. Later, he considers the relationship between good and happiness (paras. 8–9) and the various views concerning happiness and its definition (paras. 10–11). By then the reader is prepared for a "Functional Definition of Man's Highest Good" (paras. 12–18). He confirms his conclusions in the section entitled "Confirmation by Popular Beliefs" (paras. 19–22). After isolating happiness as the ultimate good, he devotes paragraphs 23–32 to its causes, its effects, and the events that will affect it, such as luck and human decision. The final section (paras. 33–39) constitutes an examination of the soul (the most human element) and its relationship to virtue; he begins that section by repeating, for the third time, his definition of happiness: "happiness is a certain activity of the soul in accordance with perfect virtue."

It could be said that, rhetorically speaking, the body of the work is an exploration and definition of the highest good.

▪▪ PREREADING QUESTIONS: WHAT TO READ FOR

The following prereading questions may help you anticipate key issues in the discussion of Aristotle's "The Aim of Man." Keeping them in mind during your first reading of the selection should help focus your attention.

1. How does Aristotle define the good?
2. What is the relationship of the good to human happiness?
3. What are the two kinds of human happiness Aristotle discusses?

The Aim of Man

Definition of the Good

Every art and every "scientific investigation," as well as every action and "purposive choice," appears to aim at some good; hence the good has rightly been declared to be that at which all things aim. A difference is observable, to be sure, among the several ends: some of them are activities, while others are products over and above the activities that produce them. Wherever there are certain ends over and above the actions themselves, it is the nature of such products to be better than the activities. 1

As actions and arts and sciences are of many kinds, there must be a corresponding diversity of ends: health, for example, is the aim of medicine, ships of shipbuilding, victory of military strategy, and wealth of domestic economics. Where several such arts fall under some one faculty — as bridle-making and the other arts concerned with horses' equipment fall under horsemanship, while this in turn along with all other military matters falls under the head of strategy, and similarly in the case of other arts — the aim of the master art is always more choiceworthy than the aims of its subordinate arts, inasmuch as these are pursued for its sake. And this holds equally good whether the end in view is just the activity itself or something distinct from the activity, as in the case of the sciences above mentioned. 2

Primacy of Statecraft

If in all our conduct, then, there is some end that we wish on its own account,   3
choosing everything else as a means to it; if, that is to say, we do not choose
everything as a means to something else (for at that rate we should go on *ad
infinitum*[1] and our desire would be left empty and vain); then clearly this one
end must be the good—even, indeed, the highest good. Will not a knowledge
of it, then, have an important influence on our lives? Will it not better enable
us to hit the right mark, like archers who have a definite target to aim at? If so,
we must try to comprehend, in outline at least, what that highest end is, and to
which of the sciences or arts it belongs.

Evidently the art or science in question must be the most absolute and   4
most authoritative of all. Statecraft answers best to this description; for it pre-
scribes which of the sciences are to have a place in the state, and which of
them are to be studied by the different classes of citizens, and up to what point;
and we find that even the most highly esteemed of the arts are subordinated
to it, e.g., military strategy, domestic economics, and oratory. So then, since
statecraft employs all the other sciences, prescribing also what the citizens
are to do and what they are to refrain from doing, its aim must embrace the
aims of all the others; whence it follows that the aim of statecraft is man's
proper good. Even supposing the chief good to be eventually the same for the
individual as for the state, that of the state is evidently of greater and more
fundamental importance both to attain and to preserve. The securing of even
one individual's good is cause for rejoicing, but to secure the good of a nation
or of a city-state[2] is nobler and more divine. This, then, is the aim of our present
inquiry, which is in a sense the study of statecraft.

Two Observations on the Study of Ethics

Our discussion will be adequate if we are content with as much precision as is   5
appropriate to the subject matter; for the same degree of exactitude ought no
more to be expected in all kinds of reasoning than in all kinds of handicraft.
Excellence and justice, the things with which statecraft deals, involve so much
disagreement and uncertainty that they come to be looked on as mere conventions, having no natural foundation. The good involves a similar uncertainty,
inasmuch as good things often prove detrimental: there are examples of people
destroyed by wealth, of others destroyed by courage. In such matters, then,

---

[1] ***ad infinitum***   Endlessly; to infinity.

[2] **city-state**   Athens was an independent nation, a city-state (*polis*). Greece consisted of a
great many independent states, which often leagued together in confederations.

and starting from such premises as we do, we must be content with a rough approximation to the truth; for when we are dealing with and starting out from what holds good only "as a general rule," the conclusions that we reach will have the same character. Let each of the views put forward be accepted in this spirit, for it is the mark of an educated mind to seek only so much exactness in each type of inquiry as may be allowed by the nature of the subject matter. It is equally wrong to accept probable reasoning from a mathematician and to demand strict demonstrations from an orator.

A man judges well and is called a good judge of the things about which he   6
knows. If he has been educated in a particular subject he is a good judge of that subject; if his education has been well-rounded he is a good judge in general. Hence no very young man is qualified to attend lectures on statecraft; for he is inexperienced in the affairs of life, and these form the data and subject matter of statecraft. Moreover, so long as he tends to be swayed by his feelings he will listen vainly and without profit, for the purport of these [lectures] is not purely theoretical but practical. Nor does it make any difference whether his immaturity is a matter of years or of character: the defect is not a matter of time, but consists in the fact that his life and all his pursuits are under the control of his passions. Men of this sort, as is evident from the case of those we call incontinent,[3] do not turn their knowledge to any account in practice; but those whose desires and actions are controlled by reason will derive much profit from a knowledge of these matters.

So much, then, for our prefatory remarks about the student, the manner of   7
inquiry, and the aim.

The Good as Happiness

To resume, then: since all knowledge and all purpose aims at some good, what   8
is it that we declare to be the aim of statecraft; or, in other words, what is the highest of all realizable goods? As to its name there is pretty general agreement: the majority of men, as well as the cultured few, speak of it as happiness; and they would maintain that to live well and to do well are the same thing as to be happy. They differ, however, as to what happiness is, and the mass of mankind give a different account of it from philosophers. The former take it to be something palpable and obvious, like pleasure or wealth or fame; they differ, too, among themselves, nor is the same man always of one mind about it: when ill he identifies it with health, when poor with wealth; then growing aware of his ignorance about the whole matter he feels admiration for anyone who proclaims some grand ideal above his comprehension. And to add to the confusion, there have been some philosophers who held that besides the

---

[3] **incontinent**   Uncontrolled, in this case by reason.

various particular good things there is an absolute good which is the cause of all particular goods. As it would hardly be worthwhile to examine all the opinions that have been entertained, we shall confine our attention to those that are most popular or that appear to have some rational foundation.

One point not to be overlooked is the difference between arguments that start from first principles[4] and arguments that lead up to first principles. Plato very wisely used to raise this question, and to ask whether the right way is from or toward first principles — as in the racecourse there is a difference between running from the judges to the boundary line and running back again. Granted that we must start with what is known, this may be interpreted in a double sense: as what is familiar to us or as what is intelligible in itself. Our own method, at any rate, must be to start with what is familiar to us. That is why a sound moral training is required before a man can listen intelligently to discussions about excellence and justice, and generally speaking, about statecraft. For in this field we must take as our "first principles" plain facts; if these are sufficiently evident we shall not insist upon the whys and wherefores. Such principles are in the possession of, or at any rate readily accessible to, the man with a sound moral training. As for the man who neither possesses nor can acquire them, let him hear the words of Hesiod:[5]

> Best is he who makes his own discoveries;
> Good is he who listens to the wise;
> But he who, knowing not, rejects another's wisdom
>   Is a plain fool.

Conflicting Views of Happiness

Let us now resume our discussion from the point at which we digressed. What is happiness, or the chief good? If it is permissible to judge from men's actual lives, we may say that the mass of them, being vulgarians, identify it with pleasure, which is the reason why they aim at nothing higher than a life of enjoyment. For there are three outstanding types of life: the one just mentioned, the political, and, thirdly, the contemplative. "The mass of men" reveal their utter slavishness by preferring a life fit only for cattle; yet their views have a certain plausibility from the fact that many of those in high places share the tastes of

[4] **first principles**   Concepts such as goodness, truth, and justice. Arguments that lead to first principles usually begin with familiar, less abstract evidence.

[5] *Works and Days*, ll. 293–297. [Translator's note] **Hesiod (eighth century B.C.E.)** Well-known Greek author. His *Works and Days* is notable for its portraits of everyday shepherd life and for its moralizing fables. His *Theogony* is a description of the creation, widely taken as accurate in his day.

Sardanapalus.[6] Men of superior refinement and active disposition, on the other hand, identify happiness with honor, this being more or less the aim of a statesman's life. It is evidently too superficial, however, to be the good that we are seeking; for it appears to depend rather on him who bestows than on him who receives it, while we may suspect the chief good to be something peculiarly a man's own, which he is not easily deprived of. Besides, men seem to pursue honor primarily in order to assure themselves of their own merit; at any rate, apart from personal acquaintances, it is by those of sound judgment that they seek to be appreciated, and on the score of virtue. Clearly, then, they imply that virtue is superior to honor: and so, perhaps, we should regard this rather than honor as the end and aim of the statesman's life. Yet even about virtue there is a certain incompleteness; for it is supposed that a man may possess it while asleep or during lifelong inactivity, or even while suffering the greatest disasters and misfortunes; and surely no one would call such a man happy, unless for the sake of a paradox. But we need not further pursue this subject, which has been sufficiently treated of in current discussions. Thirdly, there is the contemplative life, which we shall examine at a later point.

As for the life of money-making, it is something unnatural. Wealth is clearly   11
not the good that we are seeking, for it is merely useful as a means to something else. Even the objects above mentioned come closer to possessing intrinsic goodness than wealth does, for they at least are cherished on their own account. But not even they, it seems, can be the chief good, although much labor has been lost in attempting to prove them so. With this observation we may close the present subject.

Functional Definition of Man's Highest Good

Returning now to the good that we are seeking, let us inquire into its nature.   12
Evidently it is different in different actions and arts: it is not the same thing in medicine as in strategy, and so on. What definition of good will apply to all the arts? Let us say it is that for the sake of which all else is done. In medicine this is health, in the art of war victory, in building it is a house, and in each of the arts something different, although in every case, wherever there is action and choice involved, it is a certain end; because it is always for the sake of a certain end that all else is done. If, then, there is one end and aim of all our actions, this will be the realizable good; if there are several such ends, these jointly will be

---

[6] An ancient Assyrian king to whom is attributed the saying, "Eat, drink, and be merry: nothing else is worth a snap of the fingers." [Translator's note] **Sardanapalus (d. 880 B.C.E.)** Noted for his slothful and decadent life. When it was certain that he was to die — the walls of his city had been breached by an opposing army — he had his wives, animals, and possessions burned with him in his palace.

our realizable goods. Thus in a roundabout way the discussion has been brought back to the same point as before; which we must now try to explain more clearly.

As there is evidently a plurality of ends, and as some of these are chosen only as means to ulterior ends (e.g., wealth, flutes, and instruments in general), it is clear that not all ends are final.[7] But the supreme good must of course be something final. Accordingly, if there is only one final end, this will be the good that we are seeking; and if there is more than one such end, the most complete and final of them will be this good. Now we call what is pursued as an end in itself more final than what is pursued as a means to something else; and what is never chosen as a means we call more final than what is chosen both as an end in itself and as a means; in fact, when a thing is chosen always as an end in itself and never as a means we call it absolutely final. Happiness seems, more than anything else, to answer to this description: for it is something we choose always for its own sake and never for the sake of something else; while honor, pleasure, reason, and all the virtues, though chosen partly for themselves (for we might choose any one of them without heeding the result), are chosen also for the sake of the happiness which we suppose they will bring us. Happiness, on the other hand, is never chosen for the sake of any of these, nor indeed as a means to anything else at all.

We seem to arrive at the same conclusion if we start from the notion of self-sufficiency; for the final good is admittedly self-sufficient. To be self-sufficient we do not mean that an individual must live in isolation. Parents, children, wife, as well as friends and fellow citizens generally, are all permissible; for man is by nature political. To be sure, some limit has to be set to such relationships, for if they are extended to embrace ancestors, descendants, and friends of friends, we should go on *ad infinitum*. But this point will be considered later on; provisionally we may attribute self-sufficiency to that which taken by itself makes life choiceworthy and lacking in nothing. Such a thing we conceive happiness to be. Moreover, we regard happiness as the most choiceworthy of all things; nor does this mean that it is merely one good thing among others, for if that were the case it is plain that the addition of even the least of those other goods would increase its desirability; since the addition would create a larger amount of good, and of two goods the greater is always to be preferred. Evidently, then, happiness is something final and self-sufficient, and is the end and aim of all that we do.

But perhaps it will be objected that to call happiness the supreme good is a mere truism, and that a clearer account of it is still needed. We can give this

13

14

15

---

[7] **not all ends are final**   By *ends* Aristotle means purposes. Some purposes are final — the most important; some are immediate — the less important. When a corporation contributes funds to Public Broadcasting, for example, its immediate purpose may be to fund a worthwhile program. Its final purpose may be to benefit from the publicity gained from advertising.

best, probably, if we ascertain the proper function of man. Just as the excellence and good performance of a flute player, a sculptor, or any kind of artist, and generally speaking of anyone who has a function or business to perform, lies always in that function, so man's good would seem to lie in the function of man, if he has one. But can we suppose that while a carpenter and a cobbler each has a function and mode of activity of his own, man qua man[8] has none, but has been left by nature functionless? Surely it is more likely that as his several members, eye and hand and foot, can be shown to have each its own function, so man too must have a function over and above the special functions of his various members. What will such a function be? Not merely to live, of course: he shares that even with plants, whereas we are seeking something peculiar to himself. We must exclude, therefore, the life of nutrition and growth. Next comes sentient[9] life, but this again is had in common with the horse, the ox, and in fact all animals whatever. There remains only the "practical"[10] life of his rational nature; and this has two aspects, one of which is rational in the sense that it obeys a "rational principle," the other in the sense that it possesses and exercises reason. To avoid ambiguity let us specify that by "rational" we mean the "exercise or activity," not the mere possession, of reason; for it is the former that would seem more properly entitled to the name. Thus we conclude that man's function is an activity of the soul in conformity with, or at any rate involving the use of, "rational principle."

An individual and a superior individual who belong to the same class we   16
regard as sharing the same function: a harpist and a good harpist, for instance, are essentially the same. This holds true of any class of individuals whatever; for superior excellence with respect to a function is nothing but an amplification of that selfsame function: e.g., the function of a harpist is to play the harp, while that of a good harpist is to play it well. This being so, if we take man's proper function to be a certain kind of life, viz. an activity and conduct of the soul that involves reason, and if it is the part of a good man to perform such activities well and nobly, and if a function is well performed when it is performed in accordance with its own proper excellence; we may conclude that the good of man is an activity of the soul in accordance with virtue, or, if there be more than one virtue, in accordance with the best and most perfect of them. And we must add, in a complete life. For one swallow does not make a spring, nor does one fine day; and similarly one day or brief period of happiness does not make a man happy and blessed.

So much, then, for a rough outline of the good: the proper procedure being,   17
we may suppose, to sketch an outline first and afterwards to fill in the details.

---

[8] **man qua man**   Man as such, without reference to what he may be or do.

[9] **sentient**   Knowing, aware, conscious.

[10] **"practical"**   Aristotle refers to the actual practices that will define the ethical nature of the individual.

When a good outline has been made, almost anyone presumably can expand it and fill it out; and time is a good inventor and collaborator in this work. It is in just such a way that progress has been made in the various "human techniques,"[11] for filling in the gaps is something anybody can do.

But in all this we must bear constantly in mind our previous warning: not to expect the same degree of precision in all fields, but only so much as belongs to a given subject matter and is appropriate to a particular "type of inquiry." Both the carpenter and the geometer investigate the right angle, but in different ways: the one wants only such an approximation to it as will serve his work; the other, being concerned with truth, seeks to determine its essence or essential attributes. And so in other subjects we must follow a like procedure, lest we be so much taken up with side issues that we pass over the matter in hand. Similarly we ought not in all cases to demand the "reason why"; sometimes it is enough to point out the bare fact. This is true, for instance, in the case of "first principles"; for a bare fact must always be the ultimate starting point of any inquiry. First principles may be arrived at in a variety of ways: some by induction,[12] some by direct perception, some by a kind of habituation, and others in other ways. In each case we should try to apprehend them in whatever way is proper to them, and we should take care to define them clearly, because they will have a considerable influence upon the subsequent course of our inquiry. A good beginning is more than half of the whole inquiry, and once established clears up many of its difficulties.

18

Confirmation by Popular Beliefs

It is important to consider our ethical "first principle" not merely as a conclusion drawn from certain premises, but also in its relation to popular opinion; for all data harmonize with a true principle, but with a false one they are soon found to be discordant. Now it has been customary to divide good things into three classes: external goods on the one hand, and on the other goods of the soul and goods of the body; and those of the soul we call good in the highest sense, and in the fullest degree. "Conscious actions," i.e., "active expressions of our nature," we take, of course, as belonging to the soul; and thus our account is confirmed by the doctrine referred to, which is of long standing and has been generally accepted by students of philosophy. . . .

19

We are in agreement also with those who identify happiness with virtue or with some particular virtue; for our phrase "activity in accordance with

20

---

[11] **"human techniques"** Arts or skills; in a sense, technology.

[12] **induction** A process of reasoning based on careful observation and collection of details upon which theories are based. "A kind of habituation" may refer to a combination of intellectual approaches characteristic of an individual.

virtue" is the same as what they call virtue. It makes quite a difference, however, whether we conceive the supreme good as the mere possession of virtue or as its employment—i.e., as a state of character or as its active expression in conduct. For a state of character may be present without yielding any good result, as in a man who is asleep or in some other way inactive; but this is not true of its active expression, which must show itself in action, indeed in good action. As at the Olympic games it is not merely the fairest and strongest that receive the victory wreath, but those who compete (since the victors will of course be found among the competitors), so in life too those who carry off the finest prizes are those who manifest their excellence in their deeds.

Moreover, the life of those active in virtue is intrinsically pleasant. For   21
besides the fact that pleasure is something belonging to the soul, each man takes pleasure in what he is said to love—the horse lover in horses, the lover of sights in public spectacles, and similarly the lover of justice in just acts, and more generally, the lover of virtue in virtuous acts. And while most men take pleasure in things which, as they are not truly pleasant by nature, create warring factions in the soul, the lovers of what is noble take pleasure in things that are truly pleasant in themselves. Virtuous actions are things of this kind; hence they are pleasant for such men, as well as pleasant intrinsically. The life of such men, therefore, requires no adventitious[13] pleasures, but finds its own pleasure within itself. This is further shown by the fact that a man who does not enjoy doing noble actions is not a good man at all: surely no one would call a man just who did not enjoy performing just actions, nor generous who did not enjoy performing generous actions, and so on. On this ground too, then, actions in conformity with virtue must be intrinsically pleasant. And certainly they are good as well as noble, and both in the highest degree, if the judgment of the good man is any criterion; for he will judge them as we have said. It follows, therefore, that happiness is at once the best and noblest and pleasantest of things, and that these attributes are not separable as the inscription at Delos[14] pretends:

> Perfect justice is noblest, health is best,
> But to gain one's heart's desire is pleasantest.

For our best activities possess all of these attributes; and it is in our best activities, or in the best one of them, that we say happiness consists.

Nevertheless, happiness plainly requires external goods as well; for it is   22
impossible, or at least not easy, to act nobly without the proper equipment. There are many actions that can only be performed through such instruments

---

[13] **adventitious**   Unnecessary; superfluous.

[14] **inscription at Delos**   Delos is the island that once held the Athenian treasury. It was the birthplace of Apollo, with whom the inscription would be associated.

as friends, wealth, or political influence; and there are some things, again, the lack of which must mar felicity, such as good birth, fine children, and personal comeliness: for the man who is repulsive in appearance, or ill-born, or solitary and childless does not meet the requirements of a happy man, and still less does one who has worthless children and friends, or who has lost good ones by death. As we have said, then, happiness seems to require the addition of external prosperity, and this has led some to identify it with "good fortune," just as others have made the opposite mistake of identifying it with virtue.

Sources of Happiness

For the same reason there are many who wonder whether happiness is attained by learning, or by habituation or some other kind of training, or whether it comes by some divine dispensation,[15] or even by chance. Well, certainly if the gods do give any gifts to men we may reasonably suppose that happiness is god-given; indeed, of all human blessings it is the most likely to be so, inasmuch as it is the best of them all. While this question no doubt belongs more properly to another branch of inquiry, we remark here that even if happiness is not god-sent but comes as a result of virtue or some kind of learning or training, still it is evidently one of the most divine things in the world, because that which is the reward as well as the end and aim of virtuous conduct must evidently be of supreme excellence, something divine and most blessed. If this is the case, happiness must further be something that can be generally shared; for with the exception of those whose capacity for virtue has been stunted or maimed, everyone will have the ability, by study and diligence, to acquire it. And if it is better that happiness should be acquired in this way than by chance, we may reasonably suppose that it happens so; because everything in nature is arranged in the best way possible—just as in the case of man-made products, and of every kind of causation, especially the highest. It would be altogether wrong that what is greatest and noblest in the world should be left to the dispensation of chance. 23

Our present difficulty is cleared up by our previous definition of happiness, as a certain activity of the soul in accordance with virtue; whereas all other sorts of good are either necessary conditions of, or cooperative with and naturally useful instruments of this. Such a conclusion, moreover, agrees with the proposition we laid down at the outset: that the end of statecraft is the best of all ends, and that the principal concern of statecraft is to make the citizens of a certain character—namely, good and disposed to perform noble actions. 24

Naturally, therefore, we do not call an ox or a horse or any other brute happy, since none of them is able to participate in conduct of this kind. For the 25

---

[15] **divine dispensation**   A gift of the gods.

same reason a child is not happy, since at his age he too is incapable of such conduct. Or if we do call a child happy, it is in the sense of predicting for him a happy future. Happiness, as we have said, involves not only a completeness of virtue but also a complete lifetime for its fulfillment. Life brings many vicissitudes and chance happenings, and it may be that one who is now prosperous will suffer great misfortunes in his old age, as is told of Priam[16] in the Trojan legends; and a man who is thus buffeted by fortune and comes to a miserable end can scarcely be called happy.

Happiness and the Vicissitudes of Fortune

Are we, then, to call no one happy while he lives? Must we, as Solon[17] advises, wait to see his end? And if we accept this verdict, are we to interpret it as meaning that a man actually becomes happy only after he is dead? Would not this be downright absurd, especially for us who define happiness as a kind of vital activity? Or if we reject this interpretation, and suppose Solon to mean rather that it is only after death, when beyond the reach of further evil and calamity that a man can safely be said to have been happy during his life, there is still a possible objection that may be offered. For many hold that both good and evil may in a certain sense befall a dead man (just as they may befall a living man even when he is unconscious of them) — e.g., honors and disgraces, and the prosperity or misfortune of his children and the rest of his descendants. And this presents a further problem: suppose a man to have lived to a happy old age, and to have ended as he lived, there are still plenty of reverses that may befall his descendants — some of them will perhaps lead a good life and be dealt with by fortune as they deserve, others not. (It is clear, too, that a man's relationship to his descendants admits of various degrees.) It would be odd, then, if the dead man were to change along with the fortunes of his descendants, becoming happy and miserable by turns; although, to be sure, it would be equally odd if the fortunes of his descendants did not affect him at all, even for a brief time.

    But let us go back to our earlier question,[18] which may perhaps clear up the one we are raising at present. Suppose we agree that we must look to the end of a man's life, and only then call him happy, not because he then *is* happy but because we can only then know him to have been so: Is it not paradoxical to have refused to call him happy during just the period when happiness was present to him? On the other hand, we are naturally loath to apply the term to

26

27

---

[16] **Priam**   King of Troy in Homer's *Iliad*. He suffered a terrible reversal of fortune when Troy was defeated by the Greeks.

[17] **Solon (638–558 B.C.E.)**   Greek lawgiver and one of Greece's earliest poets. He was one of the Seven Sages of Athens.

[18] I.e., whether we are to call no one happy while he still lives. [Translator's note]

living men, considering the vicissitudes to which they are liable. Happiness, we argue, must be something that endures without any essential change, whereas a living individual may experience many turns of fortune's wheel. Obviously if we judge by his changing fortunes we shall have to call the same man now happy now wretched, thereby regarding the happy man as a kind of chameleon and his happiness as built on no secure foundation; yet it surely cannot be right to regard a man's happiness as wholly dependent on his fortunes. True good and evil are not of this character; rather, as we have said, although good fortune is a necessary adjunct to a complete human life, it is virtuous activities that constitute happiness, and the opposite sort of activities that constitute its opposite.

The foregoing difficulty [that happiness can be judged of only in retrospect] confirms, as a matter of fact, our theory. For none of man's functions is so permanent as his virtuous activities — indeed, many believe them to be more abiding even than a knowledge of the sciences; and of his virtuous activities those are the most abiding which are of highest worth, for it is with them that anyone blessed with supreme happiness is most fully and most continuously occupied, and hence never oblivious of. The happy man, then, will possess this attribute of permanence or stability about which we have been inquiring, and will keep it all his life; because at all times and in preference to everything else he will be engaged in virtuous action and contemplation, and he will bear the changes of fortune as nobly and in every respect as decorously as possible, inasmuch as he is truly good and "four-square beyond reproach."[19]   28

But the dispensations of fortune are many, some great, others small. Small ones do not appreciably turn the scales of life, but a multitude of great ones, if they are of the nature of blessings, will make life happier; for they add to life a grace of their own, provided that a man makes noble and good use of them. If, however, they are of an evil kind, they will crush and maim happiness, in that they bring pain and thereby hinder many of our natural activities. Yet true nobility shines out even here, if a multitude of great misfortunes be borne with calmness — not, to be sure, with the calmness of insensibility, but of nobility and greatness of soul.   29

If, as we have declared, it is our activities that give life its character, then no happy man can become miserable, inasmuch as he will never do what is hateful or base. For we hold that the truly good and wise man will bear with dignity whatever fortune sends, and will always make the best of his circumstances, as a good general makes the most effective use of the forces at his command, and a good shoemaker makes the best shoes out of the leather that is available, and so in the case of the other crafts. On this interpretation, the   30

---

[19] A quotation from Simonides. [Translator's note] **Simonides (556?–469 B.C.E.)** Greek lyric poet who lived and wrote for a while in Athens. His works survive in a handful of fragments; this quotation is from fragment 5.

happy man can never become miserable—although of course he will not be blessed with happiness in the full sense of the word if he meets with such a fate as Priam's. At all events, he is not variable and always changing; for no ordinary misfortunes but only a multitude of great ones will dislodge him from his happy state, and should this occur he will not readily recover his happiness in a short time, but only, if at all, after a long period has run its course, during which he has achieved distinctions of a high order.

Is there any objection, then, to our defining a happy man as one whose activities are an expression of complete virtue, and who at the same time enjoys a sufficiency of worldly goods, not just for some limited period, but for his entire lifetime? Or perhaps we had better add the proviso that he shall be destined to go on living in this manner, and die as he has lived; for, whereas the future is obscure to us, we conceive happiness to be an end, something altogether and in every respect final and complete. Granting all this, we may declare those living men to be "blessed with supreme happiness" in whom these conditions have been and are continuing to be fulfilled. Their blessedness, however, is of human order.

So much for our discussion of this question. 32

Derivation of the Two Kinds of Human Excellence

Since happiness is a certain activity of the soul in accordance with perfect virtue, we must next examine the nature of virtue. Not only will such an inquiry perhaps clarify the problem of happiness; it will also be of vital concern to the true student of statecraft, whose aim is to make his fellow citizens good and law-abiding. The Cretan and Spartan lawgivers,[20] as well as such others as may have resembled them, exemplify this aim. And clearly, if such an inquiry has to do with statecraft, it will be in keeping with our original purpose to pursue it.

It goes without saying that the virtue we are to study is human virtue, just as the good that we have been inquiring about is a human good, and the happiness a human happiness. By human virtue we mean virtue not of the body but of the soul, and by happiness too we mean an activity of the soul. This being the case, it is no less evident that the student of statecraft must have some knowledge of the soul, than that a physician who is to heal the eye or the whole body must have some knowledge of these organs; more so, indeed, in proportion as statecraft is superior to and more honorable than medicine. Now all physicians who are educated take much pains to know about the body. Hence as students

31

33

34

---

[20] **Cretan and Spartan lawgivers**   Both Crete and Sparta were noted for their constitutions, based on the laws of Gortyn in Crete. These laws were aristocratic, not democratic as in Athens; they promoted a class system and a rigid code of personal behavior.

of statecraft, too, we must inquire into the nature of the soul; but we must do so with reference to our own distinctive aim and only to the extent that it requires, for to go into minuter detail would be more laborious than is warranted by our subject matter.

We may adopt here certain doctrines about the soul that have been ade- 35 quately stated in our public discourses:[21] as that the soul may be distinguished into two parts, one of which is irrational while the other possesses reason. Whether these two parts are actually distinct like the parts of the body or any other divisible thing, or are distinct only in a logical sense, like convex and concave in the circumference of a circle, is immaterial to our present inquiry.

Of the irrational part, again, one division is apparently of a vegetative 36 nature and common to all living things: I mean that which is the cause of nutrition and growth. It is more reasonable to postulate a vital faculty of this sort, present in all things that take nourishment, even when in an embryo stage, and retained by the full-grown organism, than to assume a special nutritive faculty in the latter. Hence we may say that the excellence belonging to this part of the soul is common to all species, and not specifically human: a point that is further confirmed by the popular view that this part of the soul is most active during sleep. For it is during sleep that the distinction between good men and bad is least apparent; whence the saying that for half their lives the happy are no better off than the wretched. This, indeed, is natural enough, for sleep is an inactivity of the soul in those respects in which the soul is called good or bad. (It is true, however, that to a slight degree certain bodily movements penetrate to the soul; which is the reason why good men's dreams are superior to those of the average person.) But enough of this subject: let us dismiss the nutritive principle, since it has by nature no share in human excellence.

There seems to be a second part of the soul, which though irrational yet 37 in some way partakes of reason. For while we praise the rational principle and the part of the soul that manifests it in the case of the continent and incontinent man alike, on the ground that it exhorts them rightly and urges them to do what is best; yet we find within these men another element different in nature from the rational element, and struggling against and resisting it. Just as ataxic limbs,[22] when we choose to move them to the right, turn on the contrary to the left, so it is with the soul: the impulses of the incontinent man run counter to his ruling part. The only difference is that in the case of the body we see what it is that goes astray, while in the soul we do not. Nevertheless the comparison will doubtless suffice to show that there is in the soul something besides the

---

[21] **our public discourses** Aristotle may be referring to speeches at which the public is welcome, as opposed to his lectures to students.

[22] **ataxic limbs** Aristotle refers to a nervous disorder of the limbs.

rational element, opposing and running counter to it. (In what sense the two elements are distinct is immaterial.) But this other element, as we have said, seems also to have some share in a rational principle: at any rate, in the continent man it submits to reason, while in the man who is at once temperate and courageous it is presumably all the more obedient; for in him it speaks on all matters harmoniously with the voice of reason.

Evidently, then, the irrational part of the soul is twofold. There is the vegetative element, which has no share in reason, and there is the concupiscent,[23] or rather the appetitive element, which does in a sense partake of reason, in that it is amenable and obedient to it: i.e., it is rational in the sense that we speak of "having *logos* of" [paying heed to] father and friends, not in the sense of "having *logos* of" [having a rational understanding of] mathematical truths. That this irrational element is in some way amenable to reason is shown by our practice of giving admonishment, and by rebuke and exhortation generally. If on this account it is deemed more correct to regard this element as also possessing reason, then the rational part of the soul, in turn, will have two subdivisions: the one being rational in the strict sense as actually possessing reason, the other merely in the sense that a child obeys its father.

Virtue, too, is differentiated in accordance with this division of the soul: for we call some of the virtues intellectual and others moral: wisdom, understanding, and sagacity being among the former, liberality and temperance among the latter. In speaking of a man's character we do not say that he is wise or intelligent, but that he is gentle or temperate; yet we praise the wise man too for the disposition he has developed within himself, and praiseworthy dispositions we call virtues.

38

39

---

[23] **concupiscent**   Sexual; Aristotle corrects himself to refer to the general nature of desire.

⠶ QUESTIONS FOR CRITICAL READING

1. Define the following terms: *good, virtue, honor, happiness, truth, soul, body.*

2. In the first paragraphs of the selection, Aristotle talks about aims and ends. What does he mean by these terms?

3. Do you feel that Aristotle's view of the relationship of virtue to happiness is as relevant today as he argued it was in his day?

4. What is Aristotle's attitude toward most people?

5. What characteristics can we assume about the audience for whom Aristotle writes?

6. In what senses is the selection modern? In what senses is it antique or dated?

⬛ SUGGESTIONS FOR CRITICAL WRITING

1. Aristotle discusses the virtuous life in this selection. How would you apply his views to your own life? What ethical issues is Aristotle pointing us toward in this essay? To what extent does his guidance translate to modern life? Explain.

2. In his section on the primacy of statecraft, Aristotle makes a number of assertions regarding the relationship of the happiness of the individual to the welfare (or happiness) of the state. Clarify as much as possible the relationship of the individual's happiness to that of the state. How can a state be happy? Is the term relevant to anything other than an individual? Does Aristotle think that the individual's interests should be subservient to the state's?

3. In paragraph 15, Aristotle talks about the function of man. Relying on that discussion and other aspects of the work, write your own version of "The Function of Man." Be sure to use *man* as a collective term for both men and women. Once you have clarified the function of man, establish the connection between function and happiness. Is it true that the best-functioning person will be the happiest person? Aristotle implies that it is not enough to be, say, honorable or noble, but that one must act honorably or nobly. Is the implication true?

4. Take Aristotle's definition, "Happiness is a certain activity of the soul in accordance with perfect virtue." Define it in terms that are clear not only to you but also to your peers. Take care to include each part of the definition: "certain activity" (or lack of it), "soul" (which in modern terms may be "personality" or "psyche"), "in accordance with," "perfect virtue." You may rely on any parts of the selection that can be of help, but be sure to use the topic of definition to guide you through the selection. You certainly may disagree with Aristotle or amplify aspects of his definitions. In one sense, you will be defining *happiness* for yourself and your times.

5. In his "confirmation by popular beliefs" (para. 19 and following), Aristotle talks about the good. He mentions three classes of good, ranking them in order from lowest to highest: external goods, goods of the body, and goods of the soul. Using concrete examples, define each of these classes of good. Do you agree with Aristotle's order? Do you think that your peers agree with it? Where possible, give examples to help establish the validity of your opinion. Finally, do you think that our society in general puts the same value on these three classes of good that Aristotle does? Again, use examples where possible.

6. Analyze the following quotations from the selection, taking a stand on the question of whether or not Aristotle is generally correct in his assertion about the aim of man:

   It is in our best activities, or in the best one of them, that we say happiness consists. (para. 21)

   A man who does not enjoy doing noble actions is not a good man at all. (para. 21)

> Even supposing the chief good to be eventually the same for the individual as
> for the state, that of the state is evidently of greater and more fundamental
> importance both to attain and to preserve. (para. 4)

> In life . . . those who carry off the finest prizes are those who manifest their
> excellence in their deeds. (para. 20)

> If, as we have declared, it is our activities that give life its character, then no
> happy man can become miserable, inasmuch as he will never do what is hate-
> ful or base. (para. 30)

7. **CONNECTIONS**   Write an essay in which you define happiness by comparing
   Aristotle's views with those in Jean-Jacques Rousseau's "The Origin of Civil
   Society" (p. 99) or in Thomas Jefferson's Declaration of Independence (p. 116).
   Compare their attitudes toward material and spiritual happiness as well as their
   attitudes toward political freedom and the need for possessions. What does
   Aristotle leave out that others feel is important?

HSÜN TZU

Man's Nature Is Evil

© Christoph Rehage

H SÜN TZU (310–c. 220 B.C.E.), also known as Xunzi, was born in interesting and tumultuous times to a moderately aristocratic family in the small state of Chao in the northeast of China. Hsün Tzu means "Master Hsün," and at birth, his family name was Hsün K'uang. His education centered on the writings of the sages of ancient China and a study of Confucian doctrine. The era in China from 453 to 221 B.C.E. is known as the period of the Warring States, during which frequent conflicts arose between competing states. China was not unified until 221 B.C.E., when one of Hsün Tzu's former students, Li Ssu, aided the first emperor of the authoritarian Ch'in Dynasty, ironically enough by using oppressive methods that Hsün Tzu would have opposed.

Hsün Tzu is first mentioned by early biographers at age 50, when he was living in the state of Ch'i where, because of the policies of its governor, many of China's great early philosophers practiced. In terms of the era and the collection of thinkers, the state of Ch'i was comparable to ancient Athens. The doctrines of Confucius (551–479 B.C.E.) had taken root and were interpreted by major figures such as Mencius (372–289 B.C.E.), who became chief interpreter. Like Confucius, Mencius held that human nature was fundamentally good, and he credited a deity with power over the world with a positive moral drive.

Hsün Tzu, however, took a very different stance. He felt that the forces of heaven that Mencius promoted were actually the forces of nature and that there was no divine force operating within nature. He did not credit prayer with any coincidental outcome (such as the sun coming out after one prayed for sunshine). Further, Hsün Tzu became famous for declaring that human nature was evil, somewhat in line with the Christian religion's concept of original sin. The result of his dissension was a bitter disagreement with Mencius, who held the reigning philosophical view of the period. Hsün Tzu came to be considered unorthodox, and his work was widely neglected during his life. He seems to have spent time in the three major states of the period — Ch'i, Ch'in, and Ch'u — but late in life, when

---

From *Hsün Tzu: Basic Writings*. Translated by Burton Watson.

he returned to Ch'i after having lived in its rival state Ch'in, he found himself unwelcome and ultimately retired to Ch'u, where he died.

Despite his philosophy being out of favor, Hsün Tzu's works were exceptionally well preserved. They were edited in 818 C.E. by a court scholar who collected all the individual writings and gathered them into thirty-two sections—an edition that survives today. It is not known whether every one of the sections was written by Hsün Tzu himself, but twenty-five sections are unquestionably authentic. His view that human nature was evil was based on his conviction that following one's natural instincts would almost certainly lead one to an unhappy life. Yet, he also maintained that we are born without any moral leanings or moral knowledge. As a result, Hsün Tzu insisted that we must study the writings of the classics and the sages, that we must follow the Way (the Tao), the path that leads to peace and understanding, and that we must use the rituals of the ancients as aids in self-perfection. As a result, Hsün Tzu is well known for placing great emphasis on education as a lifelong pursuit.

HSÜN TZU'S RHETORIC

Hsün Tzu is a very careful writer who understands language and the principles of rhetoric. He relies on analogy and simile to a much greater extent than the other authors in this book. For example, in paragraph 2, he points to the fact that warped wood needs to be straightened just as blunt metal must be sharpened. These are analogies for his theory that the nature of a person must be shaped and formed by a teacher or a social order. He uses this analogy again and adds, in paragraph 6, the potter and the carpenter, who both shape a material into a desirable form. People, he insists, must also be shaped into a desirable form because, as he tells us often, "man's nature is evil and . . . his goodness is the result of conscious activity" (para. 5).

The important point is that Hsün Tzu links instruction to the achievement of moral perfection. Because he feels that our natural inclinations may lead us astray, we need the rituals of discipline to help us achieve moral perfection. Otherwise, we will lose our way. We will follow our instincts and become materialistic and "petty men" marked by bad behavior and an inclination toward a sensual and selfish life. Like Aristotle, Tzu associates wisdom with virtue and living the good life with pursuing good rather than evil.

Most of the Confucian doctrines and teachers in Hsün Tzu's time were optimistic because they assumed that people are born with a moral character that will lead them to a virtuous life. But Hsün Tzu thought that the sensory life of nature would veer toward immorality and evil behavior resulting from pride, envy, lust, and fear. Following the teachings of the sages, then, is the antidote to his prediction for an undisciplined life. Hsün Tzu recommends that we follow established ritual and, in the process, accrue learning and wisdom. By his own reckoning, the man who does not attend the rituals of behavior is not much different from a beast of the fields because that man, like all animals, gives in to his natural inclinations, which Hsün Tzu sees as leading to degradation and moral destruction. For Hsün Tzu, following the instruction of the sages is the means of becoming truly human, of becoming a moral person bent on achieving wisdom and true happiness.

Because Hsün Tzu disagrees with the major Chinese philosopher, Mencius, his essay constitutes an argument in which he attempts to prove that man's nature is evil. He repeats statements such as, "From this is it obvious, then, that man's nature is evil, and that his goodness is the result of conscious activity" (paras. 5, 9, 10, 12, etc.). Repetition is a powerful rhetorical strategy when handled carefully. The reason he uses it here is that each statement concludes a brief logical analysis. For example, in paragraph 9, Hsün Tzu says that "An understanding of ritual principles is not a part of man's original nature," and therefore, he must be instructed in them. If they are good principles and lead to an ethical life, that proves he began without an ethical understanding — hence, human nature is evil.

▟ PREREADING QUESTIONS: WHAT TO READ FOR

The following prereading questions may help you anticipate key issues in the discussion of Hsün Tzu's "Man's Nature Is Evil." Keeping them in mind during your first reading of the selection should help focus your attention.

1. Why does Hsün Tzu say man's nature is evil?
2. How will proper rituals and the teachings of the sages correct man's evil nature?
3. How does Hsün Tzu describe "conscious activity"?

Man's Nature Is Evil

Man's nature is evil; goodness is the result of conscious activity. The nature of man is such that he is born with a fondness for profit. If he indulges this fondness, it will lead him into wrangling and strife, and all sense of courtesy and humility will disappear. He is born with feelings of envy and hate, and if he indulges these, they will lead him into violence and crime, and all sense of loyalty and good faith will disappear. Man is born with the desires of the eyes and ears, with a fondness for beautiful sights and sounds. If he indulges these, they will lead him into license and wantonness, and all ritual principles and correct forms will be lost. Hence, any man who follows his nature and indulges his emotions will inevitably become involved in wrangling and strife, will violate the forms[1] and rules of society, and will end as a criminal. Therefore, man must first be transformed by the instructions of a teacher and guided by ritual principles, and only then will he be able to observe the dictates of courtesy and humility, obey the forms and rules of society, and achieve order. It is obvious from this, then, that man's nature is evil, and that his goodness is the result of conscious activity.

1

---

[1] Reading *wen* instead of *fen*. [All notes in this selection are from the editor.]

A warped piece of wood must wait until it has been laid against the straight- 2
ening board, steamed, and forced into shape before it can become straight; a
piece of blunt metal must wait until it has been whetted on a grindstone before
it can become sharp. Similarly, since man's nature is evil, it must wait for the
instructions of a teacher before it can become upright, and for the guidance
of ritual principles before it can become orderly. If men have no teachers to
instruct them, they will be inclined towards evil and not upright; and if they
have no ritual principles to guide them, they will be perverse and violent and
lack order. In ancient times the sage kings realized that man's nature is evil, and
that therefore he inclines toward evil and violence and is not upright or orderly.
Accordingly they created ritual principles and laid down certain regulations in
order to reform man's emotional nature and make it upright, in order to train
and transform it and guide it in the proper channels. In this way they caused all
men to become orderly and to conform to the Way. Hence, today any man who
takes to heart the instructions of his teacher, applies himself to his studies, and
abides by ritual principles may become a gentleman, but anyone who gives free
rein to his emotional nature, is content to indulge his passions, and disregards
ritual principles becomes a petty man. It is obvious from this, therefore, that
man's nature is evil, and that his goodness is the result of conscious activity.

Mencius states that man is capable of learning because his nature is good, but 3
I say that this is wrong. It indicates that he has not really understood man's nature
nor distinguished properly between the basic nature and conscious activity. The
nature is that which is given by Heaven; you cannot learn it, you cannot acquire
it by effort. Ritual principles, on the other hand, are created by sages; you can
learn to apply them, you can work to bring them to completion. That part of man
which cannot be learned or acquired by effort is called the nature; that part of him
which can be acquired by learning and brought to completion by effort is called
conscious activity. This is the difference between nature and conscious activity.

It is a part of man's nature that his eyes can see and his ears can hear. But 4
the faculty of clear sight can never exist separately from the eye, nor can the
faculty of keen hearing exist separately from the ear. It is obvious, then, that you
cannot acquire clear sight and keen hearing by study. Mencius states that man's
nature is good, and that all evil arises because he loses his original nature. Such
a view, I believe, is erroneous. It is the way with man's nature that as soon as he
is born he begins to depart from his original naïveté and simplicity, and therefore he must inevitably lose what Mencius regards as his original nature.[2] It is
obvious from this, then, that the nature of man is evil.

---

[2] Mencius, it will be recalled, stated: "The great man is he who does not lose his child's-
heart" (*Mencius* IVB, 12). If I understand Hsün Tzu correctly, he is arguing that this
"child's-heart," i.e., the simplicity and naïveté of the baby, will inevitably be lost by all
men simply in the process of growing up, and therefore it cannot be regarded as the
source of goodness.

Those who maintain that the nature is good praise and approve whatever   5
has not departed from the original simplicity and naïveté of the child. That is,
they consider that beauty belongs to the original simplicity and naïveté and
goodness to the original mind in the same way that clear sight is inseparable
from the eye and keen hearing from the ear. Hence, they maintain that [the
nature possesses goodness] in the same way that the eye possesses clear vision
or the ear keenness of hearing. Now it is the nature of man that when he is
hungry he will desire satisfaction, when he is cold he will desire warmth, and
when he is weary he will desire rest. This is his emotional nature. And yet a
man, although he is hungry, will not dare to be the first to eat if he is in the
presence of his elders, because he knows that he should yield to them, and
although he is weary, he will not dare to demand rest because he knows that
he should relieve others of the burden of labor. For a son to yield to his father
or a younger brother to yield to his elder brother, for a son to relieve his father
of work or a younger brother to relieve his elder brother—acts such as these
are all contrary to man's nature and run counter to his emotions. And yet they
represent the way of filial piety and the proper forms enjoined by ritual principles. Hence, if men follow their emotional nature, there will be no courtesy or
humility; courtesy and humility in fact run counter to man's emotional nature.
From this it is obvious, then, that man's nature is evil, and that his goodness is
the result of conscious activity.

Someone may ask: if man's nature is evil, then where do ritual principles   6
come from? I would reply: all ritual principles are produced by the conscious
activity of the sages; essentially they are not products of man's nature. A potter
molds clay and makes a vessel, but the vessel is the product of the conscious
activity of the potter, not essentially a product of his human nature. A carpenter carves a piece of wood and makes a utensil, but the utensil is the product of the conscious activity of the carpenter, not essentially a product of his
human nature. The sage gathers together his thoughts and ideas, experiments
with various forms of conscious activity, and so produces ritual principles and
sets forth laws and regulations. Hence, these ritual principles and laws are the
products of the conscious activity of the sage, not essentially products of his
human nature.

Phenomena such as the eye's fondness for beautiful forms, the ear's fond-   7
ness for beautiful sounds, the mouth's fondness for delicious flavors, the mind's
fondness for profit, or the body's fondness for pleasure and ease—these are
all products of the emotional nature of man. They are instinctive and spontane-
ous; man does not have to do anything to produce them. But that which does
not come into being instinctively but must wait for some activity to bring it into
being is called the product of conscious activity. These are the products of the
nature and of conscious activity respectively, and the proof that they are not
the same. Therefore, the sage transforms his nature and initiates conscious

activity; from this conscious activity he produces ritual principles, and when they have been produced he sets up rules and regulations. Hence, ritual principles and rules are produced by the sage. In respect to human nature the sage is the same as all other men and does not surpass[3] them; it is only in his conscious activity that he differs from and surpasses other men.

It is man's emotional nature to love profit and desire gain. Suppose now that a man has some wealth to be divided.[4] If he indulges his emotional nature, loving profit and desiring gain, then he will quarrel and wrangle even with his own brothers over the division. But if he has been transformed by the proper forms of ritual principle, then he will be capable of yielding even to a complete stranger. Hence, to indulge the emotional nature leads to the quarreling of brothers, but to be transformed by ritual principles makes a man capable of yielding to strangers. 8

Every man who desires to do good does so precisely because his nature is evil. A man whose accomplishments are meager longs for greatness; an ugly man longs for beauty; a man in cramped quarters longs for spaciousness; a poor man longs for wealth; a humble man longs for eminence. Whatever a man lacks in himself he will seek outside. But if a man is already rich, he will not long for wealth, and if he is already eminent, he will not long for greater power. What a man already possesses in himself he will not bother to look for outside. From this we can see that men desire to do good precisely because their nature is evil. Ritual principles are certainly not a part of man's original nature. Therefore, he forces himself to study and to seek to possess them. An understanding of ritual principles is not a part of man's original nature, and therefore he ponders and plans and thereby seeks to understand them. Hence, man in the state in which he is born neither possesses nor understands ritual principles. If he does not possess ritual principles, his behavior will be chaotic, and if he does not understand them, he will be wild and irresponsible. In fact, therefore, man in the state in which he is born possesses this tendency towards chaos and irresponsibility. From this it is obvious, then, that man's nature is evil, and that his goodness is the result of conscious activity. 9

Mencius states that man's nature is good, but I say that this view is wrong. All men in the world, past and present, agree in defining goodness as that which is upright, reasonable, and orderly, and evil as that which is prejudiced, irresponsible, and chaotic. This is the distinction between good and evil. Now suppose that man's nature was in fact intrinsically upright, reasonable, and orderly—then what need would there be for sage kings and ritual principles? The existence of sage kings and ritual principles could certainly add nothing 10

---

[3] Reading *kuo* instead of *yi*.

[4] Omitting the words *ti-hsiung*, which do not seem to belong here.

to the situation. But because man's nature is in fact evil, this is not so. Therefore, in ancient times the sages, realizing that man's nature is evil, that it is prejudiced and not upright, irresponsible and lacking in order, for this reason established the authority of the ruler to control it, elucidated ritual principles to transform it, set up laws and standards to correct it, and meted out strict punishments to restrain it. As a result, all the world achieved order and conformed to goodness. Such is the orderly government of the sage kings and the transforming power of ritual principles. Now let someone try doing away with the authority of the ruler, ignoring the transforming power of ritual principles, rejecting the order that comes from laws and standards, and dispensing with the restrictive power of punishments, and then watch and see how the people of the world treat each other. He will find that the powerful impose upon the weak and rob them, the many terrorize the few and extort from them, and in no time the whole world will be given up to chaos and mutual destruction. It is obvious from this, then, that man's nature is evil, and that his goodness is the result of conscious activity.

Those who are good at discussing antiquity must demonstrate the validity of what they say in terms of modern times; those who are good at discussing Heaven must show proofs from the human world. In discussions of all kinds, men value what is in accord with the facts and what can be proved to be valid. Hence if a man sits on his mat propounding some theory, he should be able to stand right up and put it into practice, and show that it can be extended over a wide area with equal validity. Now Mencius states that man's nature is good, but this is neither in accord with the facts, nor can it be proved to be valid. One may sit down and propound such a theory, but he cannot stand up and put it into practice, nor can he extend it over a wide area with any success at all. How, then, could it be anything but erroneous? **11**

If the nature of man were good, we could dispense with sage kings and forget about ritual principles. But if it is evil, then we must go along with the sage kings and honor ritual principles. The straightening board is made because of the warped wood; the plumb line is employed because things are crooked; rulers are set up and ritual principles elucidated because the nature of man is evil. From this it is obvious, then, that man's nature is evil, and that his goodness is the result of conscious activity. A straight piece of wood does not have to wait for the straightening board to become straight; it is straight by nature. But a warped piece of wood must wait until it has been laid against the straightening board, steamed, and forced into shape before it can become straight, because by nature it is warped. Similarly, since man's nature is evil, he must wait for the ordering power of the sage kings and the transforming power of ritual principles; only then can he achieve order and conform to goodness. From this it is obvious, then, that man's nature is evil, and that his goodness is the result of conscious activity. **12**

Someone may ask whether ritual principles and concerted conscious activity are not themselves a part of man's nature, so that for that reason the sage is capable of producing them. But I would answer that this is not so. A potter may mold clay and produce an earthen pot, but surely molding pots out of clay is not a part of the potter's human nature. A carpenter may carve wood and produce a utensil, but surely carving utensils out of wood is not a part of the carpenter's human nature. The sage stands in the same relation to ritual principles as the potter to the things he molds and produces. How, then, could ritual principles and concerted conscious activity be a part of man's basic human nature?

As far as human nature goes, the sages Yao and Shun possessed the same nature as the tyrant Chieh or Robber Chih, and the gentleman possesses the same nature as the petty man. Would you still maintain, then, that ritual principles and concerted conscious activity are a part of man's nature? If you do so, then what reason is there to pay any particular honor to Yao, Shun,[5] or the gentleman? The reason people honor Yao, Shun, and the gentleman is that they are able to transform their nature, apply themselves to conscious activity, and produce ritual principles. The sage, then, must stand in the same relation to ritual principles as the potter to the things he molds and produces. Looking at it this way, how could ritual principles and concerted conscious activity be a part of man's nature? The reason people despise Chieh, Robber Chih, or the petty man is that they give free rein to their nature, follow their emotions, and are content to indulge their passions, so that their conduct is marked by greed and contentiousness. Therefore, it is clear that man's nature is evil, and that his goodness is the result of conscious activity.

Heaven did not bestow any particular favor upon Tseng Tzu, Min Tzu-ch'ien, or Hsiao-i that it withheld from other men.[6] And yet these three men among all others proved most capable of carrying out their duties as sons and winning fame for their filial piety. Why? Because of their thorough attention to ritual principles. Heaven has not bestowed any particular favor upon the inhabitants of Ch'i and Lu which it has withheld from the people of Ch'in. And yet when it comes to observing the duties of father and son and the separation of roles between husband and wife, the inhabitants of Ch'in cannot match the filial reverence and respect for proper form which marks the people of Ch'i and Lu.[7] Why? Because the people of Ch'in give free rein to their emotional nature, are content

13

14

15

---

5 Reading *Shun* instead of *Yü* here and in the following sentence to conform to the sentence above.

6 Min Tzu-ch'ien and Tseng Tzu were disciples of Confucius famed for their filial conduct. Hsiao-i is identified by commentators as the heir apparent of Kao-tsung—i.e., King Wu-ting—of the Yin dynasty.

7 Reading *kung* instead of *chü*, *wen* instead of *fu*, and adding the words *Ch'in-jen* at the beginning of the sentence. Ch'i and Lu were of course the main centers of Confucian learning.

to indulge their passions, and are careless of ritual principles. It is certainly not due to any difference in human nature between the two groups.

The man in the street can become a Yü.[8] What does this mean? What made the sage emperor Yü a Yü, I would reply, was the fact that he practiced benevolence and righteousness and abided by the proper rules and standards. If this is so, then benevolence, righteousness, and proper standards must be based upon principles which can be known and practiced. Any man in the street has the essential faculties needed to understand benevolence, righteousness, and proper standards, and the potential ability to put them into practice. Therefore it is clear that he can become a Yü.   16

Would you maintain that benevolence, righteousness, and proper standards are not based upon any principles that can be known and practiced? If so, then even a Yü could not have understood or practiced them. Or would you maintain that the man in the street does not have the essential faculties needed to understand them or the potential ability to put them into practice? If so, then you are saying that the man in the street in his family life cannot understand the duties required of a father or a son and in public life cannot comprehend the correct relationship between ruler and subject. But in fact this is not true. Any man in the street *can* understand the duties required of a father or a son and *can* comprehend the correct relationship between ruler and subject. Therefore, it is obvious that the essential faculties needed to understand such ethical principles and the potential ability to put them into practice must be a part of his make-up. Now if he takes these faculties and abilities and applies them to the principles of benevolence and righteousness, which we have already shown to be knowable and practicable,[9] then it is obvious that he can become a Yü. If the man in the street applies himself to training and study, concentrates his mind and will, and considers and examines things carefully, continuing his efforts over a long period of time and accumulating good acts without stop, then he can achieve a godlike understanding and form a triad with Heaven and earth. The sage is a man who has arrived where he has through the accumulation of good acts.   17

You have said, someone may object, that the sage has arrived where he has through the accumulation of good acts. Why is it, then, that everyone is not able to accumulate good acts in the same way? I would reply: everyone is capable of doing so, but not everyone can be made to do so. The petty man is capable of becoming a gentleman, yet he is not willing to do so; the gentleman is capable of becoming a petty man but he is not willing to do so. The petty man and the gentleman are perfectly capable of changing places; the fact that they do not   18

---

[8] This was apparently an old saying. Cf. *Mencius* VIB, 2: "Chiao of Ts'ao asked, 'It is said that all men may become Yaos or Shuns. Is this so?' Mencius replied, 'It is.'"

[9] Following the rearrangement of the text suggested by T'ao Hung-ch'ing and Kanaya.

actually do so is what I mean when I say that they are capable of doing so but they cannot be made to do so. Hence, it is correct to say that the man in the street is *capable* of becoming a Yü but it is not necessarily correct to say that he will in fact find it possible to do so. But although he does not find it possible to do so does not prove that he is incapable of doing so.

A person with two feet is theoretically capable of walking to every corner of   19
the earth, although in fact no one has ever found it possible to do so. Similarly, the artisan, the carpenter, the farmer, and the merchant are theoretically capable of exchanging professions, although in actual practice they find it impossible to do so. From this we can see that, although someone may be theoretically capable of becoming something, he may not in practice find it possible to do so. But although he does not find it possible to do so, this does not prove that he is not capable of doing so. To find it practically possible or impossible to do something and to be capable or incapable of doing something are two entirely different things. It is perfectly clear, then, that a man is theoretically capable of becoming something else.[10]

Yao asked Shun, "What are man's emotions like?" Shun replied, "Man's   20
emotions are very unlovely things indeed! What need is there to ask any further? Once a man acquires a wife and children, he no longer treats his parents as a filial son should. Once he succeeds in satisfying his cravings and desires, he neglects his duty to his friends. Once he has won a high position and a good stipend, he ceases to serve his sovereign with a loyal heart. Man's emotions, man's emotions—they are very unlovely things indeed! What need is there to ask any further? Only the worthy man is different from this."[11]

There is the understanding of the sage, the understanding of the gentle-   21
man and man of breeding, the understanding of the petty man, and the understanding of the menial. He speaks many words but they are graceful and well ordered; all day he discourses on his reasons, employing a thousand different and varied modes of expression, and yet all that he says is united around a single principle: such is the understanding of the sage. He speaks little but what he says is brief and to the point, logical and clearly presented, as though laid out with a plumb line: such is the understanding of the gentleman and man of breeding. His words are all flattery, his actions irresponsible; whatever he does is shot through with error: such is the understanding of the petty man. His words are rapid and shrill but never to the point; his talents are varied and many but of no practical use; he is full of subtle distinctions and elegant turns of phrase that serve no practical purpose; he ignores right or wrong, disdains

---

[10] Adding *wei-ch'ang* before the negative in accordance with the suggestion of Kubo Ai. But the sentence is far from clear.

[11] A similar passage is found in *Kuan Tzu*, sec. 12, though without the anecdotal setting of a conversation between Yao and Shun.

to discuss crooked or straight, but seeks only to overpower the arguments of his opponent: such is the understanding of the menial.[12]

There is superior valor, there is the middle type of valor, and there is infe- 22 rior valor. When proper standards prevail in the world, to dare to bring your own conduct into accord with them; when the Way of the former kings prevails, to dare to follow its dictates; to refuse to bow before the ruler of a disordered age, to refuse to follow the customs of the people of a disordered age; to accept poverty and hardship if they are in the cause of benevolent action; to reject wealth and eminence if they are not consonant with benevolent action; if the world recognizes you, to share[13] in the world's joys; if the world does not recognize you, to stand alone and without fear: this is superior valor. To be reverent in bearing and modest in intention; to value honor and make light of material goods; to dare to promote and honor the worthy, and reject and cast off the unworthy: such is the middle type of valor. To ignore your own safety in the quest for wealth; to make light of danger and try to talk your way out of every difficulty; to rely on lucky escapes; to ignore right and wrong, just and unjust, and seek only to overpower the arguments of your opponents: such is inferior valor.

Fan-jo and Chü-shu were famous bows of ancient times, but if they had 23 not first been subjected to presses and straighteners, they would never have become true of themselves. Ts'ung of Duke Huan of Ch'i, Ch'üeh of T'ai-kung of Ch'i, Lu of King Wen of the Chou, Hu of Lord Chuang of Ch'u, and Kan-chiang, Mo-yeh, Chü-ch'üeh, and Pi-lü of King Ho-lü of Wu were all famous swords of antiquity, but if they had not been subjected to the grindstone, they would never have become sharp, and if men of strength had not wielded them, they would never have been able to cut anything. Hua-liu, Ch'i-chi, Hsien-li, and Lu-erh were famous horses of antiquity, but if they had not been subjected to the restraint of bit and bridle and the threat of the whip, and driven by a master driver like Tsao-fu, they would never have succeeded in traveling a thousand *li* in one day.

In the same way a man, no matter how fine his nature or how keen his mind, 24 must seek a worthy teacher to study under and good companions to associate with. If he studies under a worthy teacher, he will be able to hear about the ways of Yao, Shun, Yü, and T'ang, and if he associates with good companions, he will be able to observe conduct that is loyal and respectful. Then, although he is not aware of it, he will day by day progress in the practice of benevolence and righteousness, for the environment he is subjected to will cause him to progress. But if a man associates with men who are not good, then he will hear only deceit and lies and will see only conduct that is marked by wantonness,

---

[12] This last is of course aimed at the logicians.

[13] Reading *kung* instead of *k'u.*

evil, and greed. Then, although he is not aware of it, he himself will soon be in danger of severe punishment, for the environment he is subjected to will cause him to be in danger. An old text says, "If you do not know a man, look at his friends; if you do not know a ruler, look at his attendants." Environment is the important thing! Environment is the important thing!

✂ QUESTIONS FOR CRITICAL READING

1. What are the sages?
2. What does a son owe to his father?
3. What role do the emotions play in the life of a gentleman?
4. What is a petty man?
5. What does Mencius believe about human nature?
6. Why does Hsün Tzu introduce the analogy of the potter and the carpenter?
7. What is Hsün Tzu's antidote to human nature?
8. What is the difference between nature and conscious activity?

✂ SUGGESTIONS FOR CRITICAL WRITING

1. Hsün Tzu is creating an argument here to defend his view of human nature. How effective is his argument? In an essay that either defends or attacks his ideas, clarify the strengths and the weaknesses of his argument. What for you are the strongest positions that may convince a reader of his views? Which positions seem the weakest and least convincing? Are you in general agreement with him about how to shape an ethical life?

2. In a brief essay, explain why you feel Hsün Tzu is either a pessimist or an optimist. To what extent is it clear that in our current society his views are held widely? To what extent are his views deemed irrelevant in today's world? Do you find yourself optimistic about the way people live today? Use examples from your own environment when writing about optimism or pessimism.

3. If you followed Hsün Tzu's teaching, how close would you be to living an ethical life? What are the ethical issues that Hsün Tzu establishes in his essay? What does he want you to do, and why? What would be the result of your paying close attention to his teachings and following his advice? In what ways would your "nature" be altered if you were to do as he says and pay attention to the rituals of your elders?

4. In paragraph 7, Hsün Tzu discusses "Phenomena such as the eye's fondness for beautiful forms," and he sees in them a problem for anyone who wishes to overcome instincts and the nature that he claims is evil. However, some modern philosophers see the quest for beauty as a means of discovering a spiritual

understanding of the world. Examine what Hsün Tzu says about this and take a stand. How important is Hsün Tzu's warning? Are you particularly susceptible to the fondness he describes?

5. Hsün Tzu often tells us "the sage transforms his nature and initiates conscious activity; from this conscious activity he produces ritual principles, and when they have been produced he sets up rules and regulations" (para. 7). He does not tell us what the ritual principles or rules and regulations of his time are. What are they for you today? What ritual principles have you been instructed in and practice to make yourself a better person? What rules and regulations help improve your nature?

6. The essay ends with a powerful statement: "Environment is the important thing! Environment is the important thing!" (para. 24). Sociologists today talk a great deal about environment and its shaping of the individual. What is your view about how the environment affects an individual's ethical views? If human nature is evil, why would Hsün Tzu think environment is so important? He talks about associating with "men who are not good" (para. 24) resulting in one's own bad behavior. If this a reasonable assumption, what is the best thing a person can do to try to live an ethical life?

7. **CONNECTIONS**   Hsün Tzu is presenting an argument to convince you to shape your own basic nature by living an ethical life. Aristotle (p. 688) is doing much the same, but these two sages have different starting points and different attitudes. Examine their arguments and identify how they agree with each other and how they are different. Is one pessimistic and one optimistic, or are they both pessimistic or optimistic? Which of them gives you the most useful advice? Which of them seems to be speaking most productively to you?

© FPG/Getty Images

HENRY DAVID
THOREAU
Civil Disobedience

H ENRY DAVID THOREAU (1817–1862) began keeping a journal when he graduated from Harvard in 1837. The journal was preserved and published, and it shows us the seriousness, determination, and elevation of moral values characteristic of all his work. He is best known for *Walden* (1854), a record of his departure from the warm congeniality of Concord, Massachusetts, and the home of his close friend Ralph Waldo Emerson (1803–1882), for the comparative "wilds" of Walden Pond, where he built a cabin, planted a garden, and lived simply. In *Walden*, Thoreau describes the deadening influence of ownership and extols the vitality and spiritual uplift that come from living close to nature. He also argues that civilization's comforts sometimes rob a person of independence, integrity, and even conscience.

Thoreau and Emerson were prominent among the group of writers and thinkers who were referred to as the Transcendentalists. They believed in something that transcended the limits of sensory experience — in other words, something that transcended materialism. Their philosophy was based on the works of Immanuel Kant (1724–1804), the German idealist philosopher; Samuel Taylor Coleridge (1772–1834), the English poet; and Johann Wolfgang von Goethe (1749–1832), the German dramatist and thinker. These writers praised human intuition and the capacity to see beyond the limits of common experience.

The Transcendentalists' philosophical idealism carried over into the social concerns of the day, expressing itself in works such as *Walden* and "Civil Disobedience," which was published with the title "Resistance to Civil Government" in 1849, a year after the publication of Karl Marx's *The Communist Manifesto* (p. 335). Although Thoreau all but denies his idealism in "Civil Disobedience," it is obvious that after spending a night in the Concord jail, he realizes he cannot quietly accept his government's behavior in regard to slavery. He begins to feel that it is not only appropriate but imperative to disobey unjust laws.

In Thoreau's time the most flagrantly unjust laws were those that supported slavery. The Transcendentalists strongly opposed slavery and spoke out against it. Abolitionists in

---

Originally published as "Resistance to Civil Government," 1849.

Massachusetts harbored escaped slaves and helped them move to Canada and freedom. The Fugitive Slave Act, enacted in 1850, the year after "Civil Disobedience" was published, made Thoreau a criminal because he refused to comply with Massachusetts civil authorities when in 1851 they began returning escaped slaves to the South as the law required.

"Civil Disobedience" was much more influential in the twentieth century than it was in the nineteenth. Mohandas Gandhi (1869–1948) claimed that while he was editor of an Indian newspaper in South Africa, it helped to inspire his theories of nonviolent resistance. Gandhi eventually implemented these theories against the British Empire and helped win independence for India. In the 1960s, Martin Luther King Jr. applied the same theories in the fight for racial equality in the United States. Thoreau's essay once again found widespread adherents among the many young men who resisted being drafted into the military to fight in Vietnam because they believed that the war was unjust.

"Civil Disobedience" was written after the Walden experience (which began on July 4, 1845, and ended on September 6, 1847). Thoreau quietly returned to Emerson's home and "civilization." His refusal in 1846 to pay the Massachusetts poll tax — a "per head" tax imposed on all citizens to help support what he considered an unjust war against Mexico — landed him in the Concord jail. He spent just one day and one night there — his aunt paid the tax for him — but the experience was so extraordinary that he began examining it in his journal.

THOREAU'S RHETORIC

Thoreau maintained his journal throughout his life and eventually became convinced that writing was one of the few professions by which he could earn a living. He made more money, however, from lecturing on the lyceum circuit. The lyceum, a New England institution, was a town adult education program, featuring important speakers such as the very successful Emerson and foreign lecturers. Admission fees were very reasonable, and in the absence of other popular entertainment, the lyceum was a major proving ground for speakers interested in promoting their ideas.

"Civil Disobedience" was first outlined in rough-hewn form in the journal, where the main ideas appear and where experiments in phrasing began. (Thoreau was a constant reviser.) Then in February 1848, Thoreau delivered a lecture on "Civil Disobedience" at the Concord Lyceum urging people of conscience to actively resist a government that acted badly. Finally, the piece was prepared for publication in *Aesthetic Papers*, an intellectual journal edited by Elizabeth Peabody (1804–1894), the sister-in-law of another important New England writer, Nathaniel Hawthorne (1804–1864). There it was refined again, and certain important details were added.

"Civil Disobedience" bears many of the hallmarks of the spoken lecture. For one thing, it is written in the first person and addresses an audience that Thoreau expects will share many of his sentiments but certainly not all his conclusions. His message is to some extent anarchistic, virtually denying an unjust government any authority or respect.

Modern political conservatives generally take his opening quote — "That government is best which governs least" — as a rallying cry against governmental interference in everyday affairs. Such conservatives usually propose reducing government interference by reducing the government's capacity to tax wealth for unpopular causes. In fact, what Thoreau opposes is simply any government that is not totally just, totally moral, and totally respectful of the individual.

The easiness of the pace of the essay also derives from its original form as a speech. Even such locutions as "But to speak practically and as a citizen" (para. 3) connect the essay with its origins. Although Thoreau was not an overwhelming orator — he was short and somewhat homely, an unprepossessing figure — he ensured that his writing achieved what some speakers might have accomplished by means of gesture and theatrics.

Thoreau's language is marked by clarity. He speaks directly to every issue, stating his own position and recommending the position he feels his audience, as reasonable and moral people, should accept. One impressive achievement in this selection is Thoreau's capacity to shape memorable, virtually aphoristic statements that remain "quotable" generations later, beginning with his own quotation from the words of John L. O'Sullivan: "That government is best which governs least." Thoreau calls it a motto, as if it belonged on the great seal of a government or on a coin. It contains an interesting and impressive rhetorical flourish — the device of repeating "govern" and the near rhyme of "best" with "least."

His most memorable statements show considerable attention to the rhetorical qualities of balance, repetition, and pattern. "The only obligation which I have a right to assume is to do at any time what I think right" (para. 4) uses the word *right* in two senses: first, as a matter of personal volition; second, as a matter of moral rectitude. One's right, in other words, becomes the opportunity to do right. "For it matters not how small the beginning may seem to be: what is once well done is done forever" (para. 21) also relies on repetition for its effect and balances the concept of a beginning with its capacity to reach out into the future. The use of the rhetorical device of *chiasmus*, a criss-cross relationship between key words, marks "Under a government which imprisons any unjustly, the true place for a just man is also a prison" (para. 22). Here is the pattern:

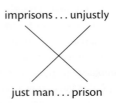

Such attention to phrasing is typical of speakers whose expressions must catch and retain the attention of listeners. Audiences do not have the advantage of referring to a text, so the words they hear must be forceful.

Thoreau relies also on analogy — comparing men with machines, people with plants, even the citizen with states considering secession from the Union. His analogies are effective and thus worth examining in some detail. He draws on the analysis of circumstance throughout the essay, carefully examining government actions to determine their qualities and their results. His questions include comments on politics (para. 1), on the Bible (para. 23), on Confucius (para. 24), and finally on his contemporary Daniel Webster (1782–1852) (para. 42), demonstrating a wide range of influences but avoiding the pedantic tone that can come from using quotations too liberally or from citing obscure sources. This essay is simple, direct, and uncluttered. Its enduring influence is in part due to the clarity and grace that characterize Thoreau's writing at its best. Its power derives from Thoreau's demand that citizens act on the basis of conscience.

✛ PREREADING QUESTIONS: WHAT TO READ FOR

The following prereading questions may help you anticipate key issues in the discussion of Henry David Thoreau's "Civil Disobedience." Keeping them in mind during your first reading of the selection should help focus your attention.

1. What kind of government does Thoreau think would be most ethical and moral?

2. What is the individual's ethical responsibility regarding supporting the government when it is wrong?

3. How does Thoreau deal with unjust laws that seem immoral?

Civil Disobedience

I heartily accept the motto — "That government is best which governs least,"[1] and I should like to see it acted up to more rapidly and systematically. Carried out, it finally amounts to this, which also I believe — "That government is best which governs not at all"; and when men are prepared for it, that will be the kind of government which they will have. Government is at best but an expedient; but most governments are usually, and all governments are sometimes, inexpedient. The objections which have been brought against a standing army, and they are many and weighty, and deserve to prevail, may also at last be brought against a standing government. The standing army is only an arm of the standing

1

---

[1] **". . . governs least"** John L. O'Sullivan (1813–1895) wrote in the *United States Magazine and Democratic Review* (1837) that "all government is evil, and the parents of evil. . . . The best government is that which governs least." Thomas Jefferson wrote, "That government is best which governs the least, because its people discipline themselves." Both comments echo the *Tao-te Ching*.

government. The government itself, which is only the mode which the people have chosen to execute their will, is equally liable to be abused and perverted before the people can act through it. Witness the present Mexican war,[2] the work of comparatively a few individuals using the standing government as their tool; for in the outset the people would not have consented to this measure.

This American government—what is it but a tradition, a recent one, endeavoring to transmit itself unimpaired to posterity but each instant losing some of its integrity? It has not the vitality and force of a single living man; for a single man can bend it to his will. It is a sort of wooden gun to the people themselves. But it is not the less necessary for this; for the people must have some complicated machinery or other, and hear its din, to satisfy that idea of government which they have. Governments show thus how successfully men can be imposed on, even impose on themselves, for their own advantage. It is excellent, we must all allow. Yet this government never of itself furthered any enterprise but by the alacrity with which it got out of its way. *It* does not keep the country free. *It* does not settle the West. *It* does not educate. The character inherent in the American people has done all that has been accomplished; and it would have done somewhat more if the government had not sometimes got in its way. For government is an expedient by which men would fain succeed in letting one another alone; and, as has been said, when it is most expedient the governed are most let alone by it. Trade and commerce, if they were not made of India-rubber, would never manage to bounce over the obstacles which legislators are continually putting in their way; and, if one were to judge these men wholly by the effects of their actions and not partly by their intentions, they would deserve to be classed and punished with those mischievous persons who put obstructions on the railroads.

But to speak practically and as a citizen, unlike those who call themselves no-government men, I ask for, not at once no government, but *at once* a better government. Let every man make known what kind of government would command his respect, and that will be one step toward obtaining it.

After all, the practical reason why, when the power is once in the hands of the people, a majority are permitted, and for a long period continue, to rule is not because they are most likely to be in the right, nor because this seems fairest to the minority but because they are physically the strongest. But a government in which the majority rule in all cases cannot be based on justice, even as far as men understand it. Can there not be a government in which majorities do not virtually decide right and wrong but conscience?—in which majorities decide only those questions to which the rule of expediency is applicable? Must

2

3

4

---

[2] **the present Mexican war (1846–1848)**   The war was extremely unpopular in New England because it was an act of a bullying government anxious to grab land from a weaker nation. The United States had annexed Texas in 1845, precipitating a retaliation from Mexico.

the citizen ever for a moment, or in the least degree, resign his conscience to the legislator? Why has every man a conscience then? I think that we should be men first and subjects afterward. It is not desirable to cultivate a respect for the law, so much as for the right. The only obligation which I have a right to assume is to do at any time what I think right. It is truly enough said that a corporation has no conscience; but a corporation of conscientious men is a corporation *with* a conscience. Law never made men a whit more just; and, by means of their respect for it, even the well-disposed are daily made the agents of injustice. A common and natural result of an undue respect for law is that you may see a file of soldiers, colonel, captain, corporal, privates, powder-monkeys,[3] and all, marching in admirable order over hill and dale to the wars, against their wills, ay, against their common sense and consciences, which makes it very steep marching indeed and produces a palpitation of the heart. They have no doubt that it is a damnable business in which they are concerned; they are all peaceably inclined. Now, what are they? Men at all? or small movable forts and magazines at the service of some unscrupulous man in power? Visit the Navy-Yard,[4] and behold a marine, such a man as an American government can make, or such as it can make a man with its black arts — a mere shadow and reminiscence of humanity, a man laid out alive and standing, and already, as one may say, buried under arms with funeral accompaniments, though it may be —

> Not a drum was heard, not a funeral note,
> As his corse to the rampart we hurried;
> Not a soldier discharged his farewell shot
> O'er the grave where our hero we buried.[5]

The mass of men serve the state thus, not as men mainly, but as machines, with their bodies. They are the standing army, and the militia, jailers, constables, posse comitatus,[6] &c. In most cases there is no free exercise whatever of the judgment or of the moral sense; but they put themselves on a level with wood and earth and stones; and wooden men can perhaps be manufactured that will serve the purpose as well. Such command no more respect than men of straw or a lump of dirt. They have the same sort of worth only as horses and dogs. Yet such as these even are commonly esteemed good citizens. Others — as most legislators, politicians, lawyers, ministers, and office-holders — serve the state chiefly with their heads; and, as they rarely make any moral distinctions, they are as likely to serve the Devil,

[3] **powder-monkeys**   The boys who delivered gunpowder to cannons.

[4] **Navy-Yard**   This is apparently the U.S. naval yard at Boston.

[5] **Not a drum was heard . . .**   These lines are from "Burial of Sir John Moore at Corunna" (1817) by the Irish poet Charles Wolfe (1791–1823).

[6] **posse comitatus**   Literally, the power of the county; the term means a law-enforcement group made up of ordinary citizens.

without *intending* it, as God. A very few, as heroes, patriots, martyrs, reformers in the great sense, and *men*, serve the state with their consciences also and so necessarily resist it for the most part; and they are commonly treated as enemies by it. A wise man will only be useful as a man and will not submit to be "clay" and "stop a hole to keep the wind away," but leave that office to his dust at least:

> I am too high-born to be propertied,
> To be a secondary at control,
> Or useful serving-man and instrument
> To any sovereign state throughout the world.[7]

He who gives himself entirely to his fellow-men appears to them useless and selfish; but he who gives himself partially to them is pronounced a benefactor and philanthropist.   6

How does it become a man to behave toward this American government today? I answer, that he cannot without disgrace be associated with it. I cannot for an instant recognize that political organization as *my* government which is the *slave's* government also.   7

All men recognize the right of revolution; that is, the right to refuse allegiance to, and to resist the government when its tyranny or its inefficiency are great and unendurable. But almost all say that such is not the case now. But such was the case, they think, in the Revolution of '75. If one were to tell me that this was a bad government because it taxed certain foreign commodities brought to its ports, it is most probable that I should not make an ado about it, for I can do without them. All machines have their friction; and possibly this does enough good to counterbalance the evil. At any rate, it is a great evil to make a stir about it. But when the friction comes to have its machine, and oppression and robbery are organized, I say let us not have such a machine any longer. In other words, when a sixth of the population of a nation which has undertaken to be the refuge of liberty are slaves, and a whole country is unjustly overrun and conquered by a foreign army and subjected to military law, I think that it is not too soon for honest men to rebel and revolutionize. What makes this duty the more urgent is the fact that the country so overrun is not our own, but ours is the invading army.   8

Paley,[8] a common authority with many on moral questions, in his chapter on the "Duty of Submission to Civil Government," resolves all civil obligation   9

---

[7] **"clay," "stop a hole . . . wind away," I am too high-born . . .**   These lines are from Shakespeare; the first is from *Hamlet*, V.i.226–27. The verse is from *King John*, V.ii.79–82.

[8] **William Paley (1743–1805)**   English theologian who lectured widely on moral philosophy. Paley is famous for *A View of the Evidences of Christianity* (1794). "Duty of Submission to Civil Government Explained" is Chapter 3 of Book 6 of *The Principles of Moral and Political Philosophy* (1785).

into expediency; and he proceeds to say, "that so long as the interest of the whole society requires it, that is, so long as the established government cannot be resisted or charged without public inconveniency, it is the will of God that the established government be obeyed, and no longer. . . . This principle being admitted, the justice of every particular case of resistance is reduced to a computation of the quantity of the danger and grievance on the one side, and of the probability and expense of redressing it on the other." Of this, he says, every man shall judge for himself. But Paley appears never to have contemplated those cases to which the rule of expediency does not apply, in which a people, as well as an individual, must do justice, cost what it may. If I have unjustly wrested a plank from a drowning man, I must restore it to him though I drown myself. This, according to Paley, would be inconvenient. But he that would save his life, in such a case, shall lose it. This people must cease to hold slaves and to make war on Mexico, though it cost them their existence as a people.

In their practice, nations agree with Paley; but does anyone think that   10
Massachusetts does exactly what is right at the present crisis?

> A drab of state, a cloth-o'-silver slut,
> To have her train borne up, and her soul trail in the dirt.[9]

Practically speaking, the opponents to a reform in Massachusetts are not a hundred thousand politicians at the South but a hundred thousand merchants and farmers here, who are more interested in commerce and agriculture than they are in humanity, and are not prepared to do justice to the slave and to Mexico, cost what it may. I quarrel not with far-off foes but with those who, near at home, co-operate with, and do the bidding of, those far away, and without whom the latter would be harmless. We are accustomed to say that the mass of men are unprepared; but improvement is slow because the few are not materially wiser or better than the many. It is not so important that many should be as good as you as that there be some absolute goodness somewhere; for that will leaven the whole lump. There are thousands who are in opinion opposed to slavery and to the war who yet in effect do nothing to put an end to them; who, esteeming themselves children of Washington and Franklin, sit down with their hands in their pockets and say that they know not what to do, and do nothing; who even postpone the question of freedom to the question of free trade, and quietly read the prices-current along with the latest advices from Mexico after dinner and, it may be, fall asleep over them both. What is the price-current of an honest man and patriot today? They hesitate and they regret and sometimes they petition; but they do nothing in earnest and with effect. They will

---

[9]**A drab . . .**   From Cyril Tourneur (1575?–1626), *Revenger's Tragedy* (1607), IV.iv.70–72. "Drab" is an obsolete term for a prostitute. Thoreau quotes the lines to imply that Massachusetts is a "painted lady" with a defiled soul.

wait, well disposed, for others to remedy the evil, that they may no longer have it to regret. At most, they give only a cheap vote, and a feeble countenance and God-speed, to the right, as it goes by them. There are nine hundred and ninety-nine patrons of virtue to one virtuous man. But it is easier to deal with the real possessor of a thing than with the temporary guardian of it.

All voting is a sort of gaming, like checkers or backgammon, with a slight moral tinge to it, a playing with right and wrong, with moral questions; and betting naturally accompanies it. The character of the voters is not staked. I cast my vote, perchance, as I think right; but I am not vitally concerned that that right should prevail. I am willing to leave it to the majority. Its obligation, therefore, never exceeds that of expediency. Even voting *for the right* is *doing* nothing for it. It is only expressing to men feebly your desire that it should prevail. A wise man will not leave the right to the mercy of chance, nor wish it to prevail through the power of the majority. There is but little virtue in the action of masses of men. When the majority shall at length vote for the abolition of slavery, it will be because they are indifferent to slavery, or because there is but little slavery left to be abolished by their vote. *They* will then be the only slaves. Only *his* vote can hasten the abolition of slavery who asserts his own freedom by his vote.

I hear of a convention to be held at Baltimore,[10] or elsewhere, for the selection of a candidate for the Presidency, made up chiefly of editors, and men who are politicians by profession; but I think, what is it to any independent, intelligent, and respectable man what decision they may come to? Shall we not have the advantage of his wisdom and honesty nevertheless? Can we not count upon some independent votes? Are there not many individuals in the country who do not attend conventions? But no: I find that the responsible man, so called, has immediately drifted from his position, and despairs of his country when his country has more reason to despair of him. He forthwith adopts one of the candidates thus selected as the only *available* one, thus proving that he is himself *available* for any purposes of the demagogue. His vote is of no more worth than that of any unprincipled foreigner or hireling native who may have been bought. O for a man who is a *man* and, as my neighbor says has a bone in his back which you cannot pass your hand through! Our statistics are at fault: the population has been returned too large. How many *men* are there to a square thousand miles in this country? Hardly one. Does not America offer any inducement for men to settle here? The American has dwindled into an Odd Fellow[11]—one who may be known by the development of his organ of gregariousness and a manifest lack of

11

12

---

[10] **Baltimore**   In 1848, the political environment was particularly intense; it was a seedbed for theoreticians of the Confederacy, which was only beginning to be contemplated seriously.

[11] **Odd Fellow**   The Independent Order of Odd Fellows, a fraternal and benevolent secret society, founded in England in the eighteenth century and first established in the United States in 1819 in Baltimore.

intellect and cheerful self-reliance; whose first and chief concern, on coming into the world, is to see that the Almshouses are in good repair; and, before yet he has lawfully donned the virile garb, to collect a fund for the support of the widows and orphans that may be; who, in short, ventures to live only by the aid of the Mutual Insurance Company, which has promised to bury him decently.

It is not a man's duty, as a matter of course, to devote himself to the eradica-   13 tion of any, even the most enormous wrong; he may still properly have other concerns to engage him; but it is his duty, at least, to wash his hands of it and, if he gives it no thought longer, not to give it practically his support. If I devote myself to other pursuits and contemplations, I must first see, at least, that I do not pursue them sitting upon another man's shoulders. I must get off him first, that he may pursue his contemplations too. See what gross inconsistency is tolerated. I have heard some of my townsmen say, "I should like to have them order me out to help put down an insurrection of the slaves, or to march to Mexico — see if I would go"; and yet these very men have each directly by their allegiance and so indirectly, at least, by their money, furnished a substitute. The soldier is applauded who refuses to serve in an unjust war by those who do not refuse to sustain the unjust government which makes the war; is applauded by those whose own act and authority he disregards and sets at naught; as if the State were penitent to that degree that it hired one to scourge it while it sinned, but not to that degree that it left off sinning for a moment. Thus, under the name of Order and Civil Government, we are all made at last to pay homage to and support our own meanness. After the first blush of sin comes its indifference; and from immoral it becomes, as it were, *un*moral, and not quite unnecessary to that life which we have made.

The broadest and most prevalent error requires the most disinterested   14 virtue to sustain it. The slight reproach to which the virtue of patriotism is commonly liable, the noble are most likely to incur. Those who, while they disapprove of the character and measures of a government, yield to it their allegiance and support, are undoubtedly its most conscientious supporters, and so frequently the most serious obstacles to reform. Some are petitioning the State to dissolve the Union, to disregard the requisitions of the President. Why do they not dissolve it themselves — the union between themselves and the State — and refuse to pay their quota into its treasury? Do not they stand in the same relation to the State that the State does to the Union? And have not the same reasons prevented the State from resisting the Union which have prevented them from resisting the State?

How can a man be satisfied to entertain an opinion merely, and enjoy *it*? Is   15 there any enjoyment in it if his opinion is that he is aggrieved? If you are cheated out of a single dollar by your neighbor, you do not rest satisfied with knowing that you are cheated, or with saying that you are cheated, or even with petitioning him to pay you your due; but you take effectual steps at once to obtain the full amount and see that you are never cheated again. Action from principle, the perception and the performance of right, changes things and relations; it is essentially revolutionary and does not consist wholly with anything which was. It not only divides states and churches, it divides families; ay, it divides the *individual*, separating the diabolical in him from the divine.

Unjust laws exist: shall we be content to obey them, or shall we endeavor   16
to amend them and obey them until we have succeeded, or shall we transgress them at once? Men generally, under such a government as this, think that they ought to wait until they have persuaded the majority to alter them. They think that if they should resist the remedy would be worse than the evil. *It* makes it worse. Why is it not more apt to anticipate and provide for reform? Why does it not cherish its wise minority? Why does it cry and resist before it is hurt? Why does it not encourage its citizens to be on the alert to point out its faults and *do* better than it would have them? Why does it always crucify Christ and excommunicate Copernicus and Luther[12] and pronounce Washington and Franklin rebels?

One would think that a deliberate and practical denial of its authority   17
was the only offense never contemplated by government; else why has it not assigned its definite, its suitable and proportionate penalty? If a man who has no property refuses but once to earn nine shillings for the State, he is put in prison for a period unlimited by any law that I know, and determined only by the discretion of those who placed him there; but if he should steal ninety times nine shillings from the State, he is soon permitted to go at large again.

If the injustice is part of the necessary friction of the machine of govern-   18
ment, let it go, let it go: perchance it will wear smooth — certainly the machine will wear out. If the injustice has a spring or a pulley or a rope or a crank exclusively for itself, then perhaps you may consider whether the remedy will not be worse than the evil; but if it is of such a nature that it requires you to be the agent of injustice to another, then I say break the law. Let your life be a counter friction to stop the machine. What I have to do is to see, at any rate, that I do not lend myself to the wrong which I condemn.

As for adopting the ways which the State has provided for remedying the   19
evil, I know not of such ways. They take too much time, and a man's life will be gone. I have other affairs to attend to. I came into this world, not chiefly to make this a good place to live in, but to live in it, be it good or bad. A man has not everything to do, but something; and because he cannot do *everything*, it is not necessary that he should do *something* wrong. It is not my business to be petitioning the Governor or the Legislature any more than it is theirs to petition me; and if they should not hear my petition what should I do then? But in

---

[12] **Nicolaus Copernicus (1473–1543)** and **Martin Luther (1483–1546)**   Copernicus revolutionized astronomy and the way humankind perceives the universe; Luther was a religious revolutionary who began the Reformation and created the first Protestant faith.

this case the State has provided no way: its very Constitution is the evil. This may seem to be harsh and stubborn and unconciliatory; but it is to treat with the utmost kindness and consideration the only spirit that can appreciate or deserves it. So is all change for the better, like birth and death, which convulse the body.

I do not hesitate to say that those who call themselves Abolitionists   20
should at once effectually withdraw their support, both in person and property, from the government of Massachusetts, and not wait till they constitute a majority of one before they suffer the right to prevail through them. I think that it is enough if they have God on their side, without waiting for that other one. Moreover, any man more right than his neighbors constitutes a majority of one already.

I meet this American government or its representative, the State govern-   21
ment, directly and face to face once a year—no more—in the person of its tax-gatherer; this is the only mode in which a man situated as I am necessarily meets it; and it then says distinctly, Recognize me; and the simplest, the most effectual and, in the present posture of affairs, the indispensablest mode of treating with it on this head, of expressing your little satisfaction with and love for it, is to deny it then. My civil neighbor, the tax-gatherer, is the very man I have to deal with—for it is, after all, with men and not with parchment that I quarrel—and he has voluntarily chosen to be an agent of the government. How shall he ever know well what he is and does as an officer of the government, or as a man, until he is obliged to consider whether he shall treat me, his neighbor, for whom he has respect, as a neighbor and well-disposed man, or as a maniac and disturber of the peace, and see if he can get over this obstruction to his neighborliness without a ruder and more impetuous thought or speech corresponding with his action. I know this well, that if one thousand, if one hundred, if ten men whom I could name—if ten *honest* men only—ay, if *one* HONEST man in this State of Massachusetts, *ceasing to hold slaves*, were actually to withdraw from this copartnership and be locked up in the county jail therefor, it would be the abolition of slavery in America. For it matters not how small the beginning may seem to be: what is once well done is done forever. But we love better to talk about it: that we say is our mission. Reform keeps many scores of newspapers in its service but not one man. If my esteemed neighbor,[13] the State's ambassador, who will devote his days to the settlement of the question of human rights in the Council Chamber, instead of being threatened with the prisons of Carolina, were to sit down the prisoner of Massachusetts, that State which is so anxious to foist the sin of slavery upon her sister—though at present she can discover only

---

[13] **esteemed neighbor**   Thoreau refers to Samuel Hoar (1778–1856), a Massachusetts congressman, who went to South Carolina to protest that state's practice of seizing black seamen from Massachusetts ships and enslaving them. South Carolina threatened Hoar and drove him out of the state. He did not secure the justice he demanded.

an act of inhospitality to be the ground of a quarrel with her—the Legislature would not wholly waive the subject the following winter.

Under a government which imprisons any unjustly, the true place for a just   22
man is also a prison. The proper place today, the only place which Massachusetts has provided for her freer and less desponding spirits is in her prisons, to be put out and locked out of the State by her own act, as they have already put themselves out by their principles. It is there that the fugitive slave and the Mexican prisoner on parole and the Indian come to plead the wrongs of his race should find them; on that separate but more free and honorable ground where the State places those who are not *with* her but *against* her—the only house in a slave State in which a free man can abide with honor. If any think that their influence would be lost there, and their voices no longer afflict the ear of the State, that they would not be as an enemy within its walls, they do not know by how much truth is stronger than error, nor how much more eloquently and effectively he can combat injustice who has experienced a little in his own person. Cast your whole vote, not a strip of paper merely, but your whole influence. A minority is powerless while it conforms to the majority; it is not even a minority then; but it is irresistible when it clogs by its whole weight. If the alternative is to keep all just men in prison or give up war and slavery, the State will not hesitate which to choose. If a thousand men were not to pay their tax-bills this year, that would not be a violent bloody measure, as it would be to pay them, and enable the State to commit violence and shed innocent blood. This is, in fact, the definition of a peaceable revolution, if any such is possible. If the tax-gatherer or any other public officer asks me, as one has done, "But what shall I do?" my answer is, "If you really wish to do anything, resign your office." When the subject has refused allegiance and the officer has resigned his office, then the revolution is accomplished. But even suppose blood should flow. Is there not a sort of blood shed when the conscience is wounded? Through this wound a man's real manhood and immortality flow out, and he bleeds to an everlasting death. I see this blood flowing now.

I have contemplated the imprisonment of the offender rather than the   23
seizure of his goods—though both will serve the same purpose—because they who assert the purest right, and consequently are most dangerous to a corrupt State, commonly have not spent much time in accumulating property. To such the State renders comparatively small service, and a slight tax is wont to appear exorbitant, particularly if they are obliged to earn it by special labor with their hands. If there were one who lived wholly without the use of money, the State itself would hesitate to demand it of him. But the rich man—not to make any invidious comparison—is always sold to the institution which makes him rich. Absolutely speaking, the more money, the less virtue; for money comes between a man and his objects and obtains them for him; and it was certainly no great virtue to obtain it. It puts to rest many questions which he would otherwise be taxed to answer; while the only new

question which it puts is the hard but superfluous one, how to spend it. Thus his moral ground is taken from under his feet. The opportunities of living are diminished in proportion as what are called the "means" are increased. The best thing a man can do for his culture when he is rich is to endeavor to carry out those schemes which he entertained when he was poor. Christ answered the Herodians[14] according to their condition. "Show me the tribute-money," said he—and one took a penny out of his pocket—if you use money which has the image of Caesar on it, and which he has made current and valuable, that is, if *you are men of the State* and gladly enjoy the advantages of Caesar's government, then pay him back some of his own when he demands it; "Render therefore to Caesar that which is Caesar's, and to God those things which are God's"—leaving them no wiser than before as to which was which; for they did not wish to know.

When I converse with the freest of my neighbors, I perceive that what-   24
ever they may say about the magnitude and seriousness of the question, and their regard for the public tranquillity, the long and the short of the matter is that they cannot spare the protection of the existing government, and they dread the consequences to their property and families of disobedience to it. For my own part, I should not like to think that I ever rely on the protection of the State. But if I deny the authority of the State when it presents its tax-bill, it will soon take and waste all my property and so harass me and my children without end. This is hard. This makes it impossible for a man to live honestly, and at the same time comfortably, in outward respects. It will not be worth the while to accumulate property; that would be sure to go again. You must hire or squat somewhere and raise but a small crop and eat that soon. You must live within yourself and depend upon yourself always tucked up and ready for a start, and not have many affairs. A man may grow rich in Turkey even, if he will be in all respects a good subject of the Turkish government. Confucius[15] said: "If a state is governed by the principles of reason, poverty and misery are subjects of shame; if a state is not governed by the principles of reason, riches and honors are the subjects of shame." No; until I want the protection of Massachusetts to be extended to me in some distant Southern port, where my liberty is endangered, or until I am bent solely on building up an estate at home by peaceful enterprise, I can afford to refuse allegiance to Massachusetts and her right to my property and life. It costs me less in every sense to incur the penalty of disobedience to the State than it would to obey. I should feel as if I were worth less in that case.

Some years ago the State met me in behalf of the Church and commanded   25
me to pay a certain sum toward the support of a clergyman whose preaching

---

[14] **Herodians**   Followers of King Herod who were opposed to Jesus Christ (see Matt. 22:16).

[15] **Confucius (551–479 B.C.E.)**   The most important Chinese religious leader. His *Analects* (collection) treated not only religious but moral and political matters as well.

my father attended, but never I myself. "Pay," it said, "or be locked up in the jail." I declined to pay. But, unfortunately, another man saw fit to pay it. I did not see why the schoolmaster should be taxed to support the priest, and not the priest the schoolmaster; for I was not the State's schoolmaster, but I supported myself by voluntary subscription. I did not see why the lyceum should not present its tax-bill and have the State to back its demand, as well as the Church. However, at the request of the selectmen, I condescended to make some such statement as this in writing:—"Know all men by these presents, that I, Henry Thoreau, do not wish to be regarded as a member of any incorporated society which I have not joined." This I gave to the town clerk; and he has it. The State, having thus learned that I did not wish to be regarded as a member of that church, has never made a like demand on me since; though it said that it must adhere to its original presumption that time. If I had known how to name them, I should then have signed off in detail from all the societies which I never signed on to; but I did not know where to find a complete list.

I have paid no poll-tax[16] for six years. I was put into a jail once on this account, for one night; and, as I stood considering the walls of solid stone, two or three feet thick, the door of wood and iron, a foot thick, and the iron grating which strained the light, I could not help being struck with the foolishness of that institution which treated me as if I were mere flesh and blood and bones, to be locked up. I wondered that it should have concluded at length that this was the best use it could put me to and had never thought to avail itself of my services in some way. I saw that if there was a wall of stone between me and my townsmen, there was a still more difficult one to climb or break through before they could get to be as free as I was. I did not for a moment feel confined, and the walls seemed a great waste of stone and mortar. I felt as if I alone of all my townsmen had paid my tax. They plainly did not know how to treat me but behaved like persons who are underbred. In every threat and in every compliment there was a blunder; for they thought that my chief desire was to stand on the other side of that stone wall. I could not but smile to see how industriously they locked the door on my meditations, which followed them out again without let or hindrance, and *they* were really all that was dangerous. As they could not reach me, they had resolved to punish my body; just as boys, if they cannot come at some person against whom they have a spite, will abuse his dog. I saw that the State was half-witted, that it was timid as a lone woman with her silver spoons, and that it did not know its friends from its foes, and I lost all my remaining respect for it and pitied it.

Thus the State never intentionally confronts a man's sense, intellectual or moral, but only his body, his senses. It is not armed with superior wit or

26

27

16 **poll-tax**   A tax levied on every citizen living in a given area; *poll* means "head," so it is a tax per head. The tax Thoreau refers to, about $2, was used to support the Mexican War.

honesty but with superior physical strength. I was not born to be forced. I will breathe after my own fashion. Let us see who is the strongest. What force has a multitude? They only can force me who obey a higher law than I. They force me to become like themselves. I do not hear of *men* being *forced* to live this way or that by masses of men. What sort of life were that to live? When I meet a government which says to me, "Your money or your life," why should I be in haste to give it my money? It may be in a great strait and not know what to do: I cannot help that. It must help itself; do as I do. It is not worth the while to snivel about it. I am not responsible for the successful working of the machinery of society. I am not the son of the engineer. I perceive that, when an acorn and a chestnut fall side by side, the one does not remain inert to make way for the other, but both obey their own laws and spring and grow and flourish as best they can till one, perchance, overshadows and destroys the other. If a plant cannot live according to its nature, it dies; and so a man.

The night in prison was novel and interesting enough. The prisoners in   28
their shirt-sleeves were enjoying a chat and the evening air in the doorway when I entered. But the jailer said, "Come, boys, it is time to lock up"; and so they dispersed, and I heard the sound of their steps returning into the hollow apartments. My room-mate was introduced to me by the jailer as "a first-rate fellow and a clever man." When the door was locked, he showed me where to hang my hat and how he managed matters there. The rooms were whitewashed once a month; and this one, at least, was the whitest, most simply furnished, and probably the neatest apartment in the town. He naturally wanted to know where I came from and what brought me there; and when I had told him, I asked him in my turn how he came there, presuming him to be an honest man, of course; and, as the world goes, I believe he was. "Why," said he, "they accuse me of burning a barn; but I never did it." As near as I could discover, he had probably gone to bed in a barn when drunk and smoked his pipe there; and so a barn burnt. He had the reputation of being a clever man, had been there some three months waiting for his trial to come on, and would have to wait as much longer; but he was quite domesticated and contented, since he got his board for nothing and thought that he was well treated.

He occupied one window, and I the other; and I saw that if one stayed there   29
long, his principal business would be to look out the window. I had soon read all the tracts that were left there and examined where former prisoners had broken out and where a grate had been sawed off and heard the history of the various occupants of that room; for I found that even here there was a history and a gossip which never circulated beyond the walls of the jail. Probably this is the only house in the town where verses are composed, which afterward printed in a circular form but not published. I was shown quite a long list of verses which were composed by some young men who had been detected in an attempt to escape, who avenged themselves by signing them.

I pumped my fellow-prisoner as dry as I could, for fear I should never see 30
him again; but at length he showed me which was my bed and left me to blow
out the lamp.

It was like travelling into a far country, such as I had never expected to 31
behold, to lie there for one night. It seemed to me that I never had heard the
town-clock strike before, nor the evening sounds of the village; for we slept
with the windows open, which were inside the grating. It was to see my native
village in the light of the Middle Ages, and our Concord was turned into a Rhine
stream, and visions of knights and castles passed before me. They were the
voices of old burghers that I heard in the streets. I was an involuntary spectator and auditor of whatever was done and said in the kitchen of the adjacent
village-inn — a wholly new and rare experience to me. It was a closer view of
my native town. I was fairly inside of it. I never had seen its institutions before.
This is one of its peculiar institutions; for it is a shire town.[17] I began to comprehend what its inhabitants were about.

In the morning our breakfasts were put through the hole in the door, in small 32
oblong-square tin pans, made to fit, and holding a pint of chocolate, with brown
bread and an iron spoon. When they called for the vessels again, I was green
enough to return what bread I had left; but my comrade seized it and said that I
should lay that up for lunch or dinner. Soon after he was let out to work at hay-
ing in a neighboring field, whither he went every day, and would not be back till
noon; so he bade me good-day, saying that he doubted if he should see me again.

When I came out of prison — for someone interfered and paid that tax — I 33
did not perceive that great changes had taken place on the common, such as he
observed who went in a youth and emerged a tottering and gray-headed man;
and yet a change had to my eyes come over the scene — the town and State
and country — greater than any that mere time could effect. I saw yet more distinctly the State in which I lived. I saw to what extent the people among whom
I lived could be trusted as good neighbors and friends; that their friendship
was for summer weather only; that they did not greatly propose to do right;
that they were a distinct race from me by their prejudices and superstitions, as
the Chinamen and Malays are; that, in their sacrifices to humanity, they ran no
risks, not even to their property; that, after all, they were not so noble but they
treated the thief as he had treated them and hoped, by a certain outward observance and a few prayers, and by walking in a particular straight though useless
path from time to time, to save their souls. This may be to judge my neighbors
harshly; for I believe that many of them are not aware that they have such an
institution as the jail in their village.

It was formerly the custom in our village, when a poor debtor came out of 34
jail, for his acquaintances to salute him, looking through their fingers, which

---

[17] **shire town**   A county seat, which means the town had a court, county offices, and jails.

were crossed to represent the grating of a jail window, "How do ye do?" My neighbors did not thus salute me but first looked at me and then at one another as if I had returned from a long journey. I was put into jail as I was going to the shoemaker's to get a shoe which was mended. When I was let out the next morning I proceeded to finish my errand, and having put on my mended shoe, joined a huckleberry party who were impatient to put themselves under my conduct; and in half an hour—for the horse was soon tackled—was in the midst of a huckleberry field on one of our highest hills two miles off, and then the State was nowhere to be seen.

This is the whole history of "My Prisons." 35

I have never declined paying the highway tax, because I am as desirous 36 of being a good neighbor as I am of being a bad subject; and as for supporting schools I am doing my part to educate my fellow countrymen now. It is for no particular item in the tax-bill that I refuse to pay it. I simply wish to refuse allegiance to the State, to withdraw and stand aloof from it effectually. I do not care to trace the course of my dollar, if I could, till it buys a man or a musket to shoot one with—the dollar is innocent—but I am concerned to trace the effects of my allegiance. In fact, I quietly declare war with the State, after my fashion, though I will still make what use and get what advantage of her I can, as is usual in such cases.

If others pay the tax which is demanded of me from a sympathy with the 37 State, they do but what they have already done in their own case, or rather they abet injustice to a greater extent than the State requires. If they pay the tax from a mistaken interest in the individual taxed, to save his property, or prevent his going to jail, it is because they have not considered wisely how far they let their private feelings interfere with the public good.

This, then, is my position at present. But one cannot be too much on his 38 guard in such a case, lest his action be biased by obstinacy or an undue regard for the opinions of men. Let him see that he does only what belongs to himself and to the hour.

I think sometimes, Why, this people mean well; they are only ignorant; 39 they would do better if they knew how: why give your neighbors this pain to treat you as they are not inclined to? But I think again, this is no reason why I should do as they do or permit others to suffer much greater pain of a different kind. Again, I sometimes say to myself, When many millions of men, without heat, without ill will, without personal feeling of any kind, demand of you a few shillings only, without the possibility, such is their constitution, of retracting or altering their present demand, and without the possibility, on your side, of appeal to any other millions, why expose yourself to this overwhelming brute force? You do not resist cold and hunger, the winds and the waves, thus obstinately; you quietly submit to a thousand similar necessities. You do not put your head into the fire. But just in proportion as I regard this as not wholly a brute force but partly a human force, and consider that I have relations to those millions as to so many millions of men, and not of mere brute or inanimate things, I see that appeal is possible, first and instantaneously, from them to the Maker of them, and secondly, from them to themselves. But if I put my head deliberately into the fire, there is no appeal to fire or to the Maker of fire, and I have only myself to blame. If I could convince myself that I have any right to be satisfied with men as they are, and to treat them accordingly, and not according, in some respects, to my requisitions and expectations of what they and I ought to be, then, like a good Mussulman[18] and fatalist, I should endeavor to be satisfied with things as they are and say it is the will of God. And, above all, there is this difference between resisting this and a purely brute or natural force, that I can resist this with some effect; but I cannot expect, like Orpheus,[19] to change the nature of the rocks and trees and beasts.

I do not wish to quarrel with any man or nation. I do not wish to split hairs, to make fine distinctions, or set myself up as better than my neighbors. I seek rather, I may say, even an excuse for conforming to the laws of the land. I am but too ready to conform to them. Indeed, I have reason to suspect myself on this head; and each year, as the tax-gatherer comes round, I find myself disposed to review the acts and position of the general and State governments, and the spirit of the people, to discover a pretext for conformity.

       40

> We must affect our country as our parents;
> And if at any time we alienate
> Our love or industry from doing it honor,
> We must respect effects and teach the soul
> Matter of conscience and religion,
> And not desire of rule or benefit.[20]

I believe that the State will soon be able to take all my work of this sort out of my hands, and then I shall be no better a patriot than my fellow-countrymen. Seen from a lower point of view, the Constitution, with all its faults, is very good; the law and the courts are very respectable; even this State and this American government are, in many respects, very admirable and rare things, to be thankful for, such as a great many have described them; but seen from a point of view a little higher, they are what I have described them; seen from a

---

[18] **Mussulman**   Muslim; a follower of the religion of Islam.

[19] **Orpheus**   In Greek mythology, Orpheus was a poet whose songs were so plaintive that they affected animals, trees, and even stones.

[20] **We must affect . . .**   From George Peele (1556–1596), *The Battle of Alcazar* (acted 1588–1589, printed 1594), II.ii. Thoreau added these lines in a later printing of the essay. They emphasize the fact that one is disobedient to the state as one is to a parent—with love and affection and from a cause of conscience. Disobedience is not taken lightly.

higher still, and the highest, who shall say what they are, or that they are worth looking at or thinking of at all?

However, the government does not concern me much, and I shall bestow   41
the fewest possible thoughts on it. It is not many moments that I live under a government, even in this world. If a man is thought-free, fancy-free, imagination-free, that which *is not* never for a long time appearing *to be* to him, unwise rulers or reformers cannot fatally interrupt him.

I know that most men think differently from myself; but those whose lives   42
are by profession devoted to the study of these or kindred subjects content me as little as any. Statesmen and legislators, standing so completely within the institution, never distinctly and nakedly behold it. They speak of moving society but have no resting-place without it. They may be men of a certain experience and discrimination and have no doubt invented ingenious and even useful systems, for which we sincerely thank them; but all their wit and usefulness lie within certain not very wide limits. They are wont to forget that the world is not governed by policy and expediency. Webster[21] never goes behind government and so cannot speak with authority about it. His words are wisdom to those legislators who contemplate no essential reform in the existing government; but for thinkers, and those who legislate for all time, he never once glances at the subject. I know of those whose serene and wise speculations on this theme would soon reveal the limits of his mind's range and hospitality. Yet, compared with the cheap professions of most reformers, and the still cheaper wisdom and eloquence of politicians in general, his are almost the only sensible and valuable words, and we thank Heaven for him. Comparatively, he is always strong, original, and, above all, practical. Still his quality is not wisdom but prudence. The lawyer's truth is not Truth but consistency, or a consistent expediency. Truth is always in harmony with herself and is not concerned chiefly to reveal the justice that may consist with wrong-doing. He well deserves to be called, as he has been called, the Defender of the Constitution. There are really no blows to be given by him but defensive ones. He is not a leader but a follower. His leaders are the men of '87.[22] "I have never made an effort," he says, "and never propose to make an effort; I have never countenanced an effort, and never mean to countenance an effort, to disturb the arrangement as originally made, by which the various States came into the Union." Still thinking of the sanction which the Constitution gives to slavery, he says, "Because it was a part of the original compact—let it stand." Notwithstanding his special acuteness and ability, he is unable to take a fact out of its merely political relations

---

[21] **Daniel Webster (1782–1852)**   One of the most brilliant orators of his time. He was secretary of state from 1841 to 1843, which is why Thoreau thinks he cannot be a satisfactory critic of government.

[22] **men of '87**   The men who framed the Constitution in 1787.

and behold it as it lies absolutely to be disposed of by the intellect—what, for instance, it behooves a man to do here in America today with regard to slavery but ventures, or is driven, to make some such desperate answer as the following, while professing to speak absolutely, and as a private man—from which what new and singular code of social duties might be inferred? "The manner," says he, "in which the governments of those States where slavery exists are to regulate it, is for their own consideration, under their responsibility to their constituents, to the general laws of propriety, humanity, and justice, and to God. Associations formed elsewhere, springing from a feeling of humanity, or any other cause, have nothing whatever to do with it. They have never received any encouragement from me, and they never will."[23]

They who know of no purer sources of truth, who have traced up its stream   43
no higher, stand, and wisely stand, by the Bible and the Constitution, and drink at it there with reverence and humility; but they who behold where it comes trickling into this lake or that pool gird up their loins once more and continue their pilgrimage toward its fountain-head.

No man with a genius for legislation has appeared in America. They are   44
rare in the history of the world. There are orators, politicians, and eloquent men by the thousand; but the speaker has not yet opened his mouth to speak who is capable of settling the much-vexed questions of the day. We love eloquence for its own sake and not for any truth which it may utter or any heroism it may inspire. Our legislators have not yet learned the comparative value of free-trade and of freedom, of union, and of rectitude, to a nation. They have no genius or talent for comparatively humble questions of taxation and finance, commerce and manufacturers and agriculture. If we were left solely to the wordy wit of legislators in Congress for our guidance, uncorrected by the seasonable experience and the effectual complaints of the people, America would not long retain her rank among the nations. For eighteen hundred years, though perchance I have no right to say it, the New Testament has been written; yet where is the legislator who has wisdom and practical talent enough to avail himself of the light which it sheds on the science of legislation?

The authority of government, even such as I am willing to submit to—for   45
I will cheerfully obey those who know and can do better than I, and in many things even those who neither know nor can do so well—is still an impure one: to be strictly just, it must have the sanction and consent of the governed. It can have no pure right over my person and property but what I concede to it. The progress from an absolute to a limited monarchy, from a limited monarchy to a democracy, is a progress toward a true respect for the individual. Even the Chinese philosopher[24] was wise enough to regard the individual as the basis of

---

23 These extracts have been inserted since the Lecture was read. [Thoreau's note]

24 **Chinese philosopher**   Thoreau probably means Confucius.

the empire. Is a democracy such as we know it the last improvement possible in government? Is it not possible to take a step further towards recognizing and organizing the rights of man? There will never be a really free and enlightened State until the State comes to recognize the individual as a higher and independent power, from which all its own power and authority are derived, and treats him accordingly. I please myself with imagining a State at last which can afford to be just to all men and to treat the individual with respect as a neighbor; which even would not think it inconsistent with its own repose if a few were to live aloof from it, not meddling with it, nor embraced by it, who fulfilled all the duties of neighbors and fellow-men. A State which bore this kind of fruit and suffered it to drop off as fast as it ripened would prepare the way for a still more perfect and glorious State, which also I have imagined but not yet anywhere seen.

❖ QUESTIONS FOR CRITICAL READING

1. To what extent do you think Thoreau's intended audience agreed with him?

2. What is the relation of justice to the moral view that Thoreau maintains?

3. Thoreau provides us with a detailed account of his imprisonment (paras. 28–35). What is the ethical lesson that Thoreau learned in prison?

4. One example of Thoreau's use of irony is in paragraph 25. What other examples of irony seem effective in his argument?

5. In Thoreau's view, what is the ethical responsibility of a government to a minority population?

6. How clear is Thoreau's position on ethics and morality? What is most convincing to you?

7. It is possible that Thoreau's "Chinese philosopher" is Lao-tzu. How likely is it that Thoreau had read Lao-tzu and agreed with him?

❖ SUGGESTIONS FOR CRITICAL WRITING

1. Thoreau refers to conscience as a monitor of government, yet he says, "Law never made men a whit more just" (para. 4). How does Thoreau's conscience help him establish the ethical principles that he acts by? To what extent do principles of ethics and morality operate in the law of Thoreau's time?

2. Thoreau tells us that the laws of the land were established by the majority population and that if he were to disobey them, he would be in a minority. What are the ethical principles that help Thoreau feel that it is just and right to disobey the laws that the majority population of the country has established?

3. Thoreau's anger is partly directed at proponents of the then-recent Mexican War (1846–1848), which resulted in Mexico's secession from New Mexico and

California and which redrew the national border on the Rio Grande, giving Texas to the United States. He felt it was not an ethical war, for after its end, the nation had to decide whether to permit slavery in the acquired lands. The ensuing debate set the stage for the Civil War. If Thoreau thought the Mexican War was not ethical, what would he have thought about the Civil War?

4. Do some research on the Mexican War and decide whether or not there were any significant ethical concerns that warranted Thoreau's reaction. Who was fighting? Who started the war? What were President Polk's intentions, and were those intentions ethical?

5. Examine quotations from Thoreau that focus on the individual and the question of justice and ethical treatment of the individual by government. What are the values of the government that Thoreau describes, and how might that government see its moral obligations to the governed? How would it treat matters of justice, ethics, and morality? To what extent does the government of Thoreau's time resemble the government of our time?

6. **CONNECTIONS**   Thoreau was especially sympathetic to the plight of African American slaves and would likely have shared the views of Martin Luther King Jr. What advice might Thoreau have given King? Apply the basic ideas of "Civil Disobedience" to the circumstances in which King found himself. What did each of these men learn about themselves while in prison? What did prison mean to them?

7. Slavery in the United States in 1849 was protected by national laws that had to be observed even by states that had abolished slavery. These were federal laws largely created by the slave states for the protection of "property." The Fugitive Slave Laws of 1793 and 1850 were enacted by Congress. Thoreau knew these laws and resisted them. Research these laws and explain how Congress could have imagined them to be ethical and just. Do you think enough attention is paid to ethical issues when Congress enacts such wide-ranging laws?

8. **CONNECTIONS**   One conflict between Aristotle (p. 688) and Thoreau concerns their attitudes toward the state. Thoreau's view suggests that the individual's values are foremost and that the individual must resist the state when he or she thinks the state is in the wrong. Aristotle reveres the state and says that the highest good for humankind is likely to be found in statecraft; therefore, values other than those of the state always come second. Write an essay that attempts to resolve the conflict between these two authors. Which of their arguments can you most effectively support?

FREDERICK DOUGLASS

From *Narrative of the Life of Frederick Douglass, an American Slave*

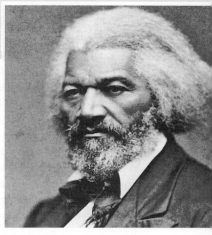

© FPG/Getty Images

F REDERICK DOUGLASS (1817–1895) was born into slavery in Maryland; he died not only a free man but also a man who commanded the respect of his country, his government, and hosts of supporters. Ironically, it was his owner's wife, Mrs. Hugh Auld, a Northerner, who helped Douglass learn to read and write. Until her husband forcefully convinced her that teaching slaves was "unlawful, as well as unsafe," Mrs. Auld taught Douglass enough so that he could begin his own education — and escape to freedom. Mrs. Auld eventually surpassed her husband in her vehement opposition to having Douglass read, leading Douglass to conclude that slavery had a negative effect on slave and slaveholder alike: both suffered the consequences of a political system that was inherently immoral.

The *Narrative* is filled with examples of the injustice of slavery. Douglass had little connection with his family. Separated from his mother, Harriet Bailey, Douglass never knew who his father was. In his *Narrative*, he records the beatings he witnessed as a slave, the conditions under which he lived, and the struggles he felt within himself to be a free man. Douglass himself survived brutal beatings and torture by a professional slave "breaker."

The laws of the time codified the injustices that Douglass and all American slaves suffered. The Fugitive Slave Act of 1793 tightened the hold on all slaves who had gone north in search of freedom. Federal marshals were enjoined to return slaves to their owners. The Underground Railroad helped so many runaway slaves find their way to Canada that a second Fugitive Slave Act was enacted in 1850 with stiff penalties for those who did not obey the law. In retaliation, many northern states enacted personal freedom laws to counter the Fugitive Slave Act. Eventually, these laws became central to the South's

First published 1845; revised 1892.

decision to secede. However, Douglass's fate, when he eventually escaped in 1838 by impersonating an African American seaman (using his papers to board ship), was not secure. Abolitionists in New York helped him find work in shipyards in New Bedford, Massachusetts. He changed his name from Auld to Douglass to protect himself, and he began his career as an orator in 1841 at an antislavery meeting in Nantucket.

To avoid capture after publication of an early version of his autobiography, Douglass spent two years on a speaking tour of Great Britain and Ireland (1845–1847). He then returned to the United States, bought his freedom, and rose to national fame as the founder and editor of the *North Star*, an abolitionist paper published in Rochester, New York. One of his chief concerns was for the welfare of the slaves who had managed to secure their freedom. When the Civil War began, there were no plans to free the slaves, but Douglass managed to convince President Lincoln that it would further the war effort to free them; in 1863, the president delivered the Emancipation Proclamation.

However, the years after the war and Lincoln's death were not good for freed slaves. Terrorist groups in both the North and the South worked to keep them from enjoying freedom, and training programs for former slaves that might have been effective were never fully instituted. During this time, Douglass worked in various capacities for the government — as assistant secretary of the Santo Domingo Commission, as an official in Washington, D.C., and as U.S. minister to Haiti (1889–1891). He was the first African American to become a national figure and to have influence with the government.

DOUGLASS'S RHETORIC

Douglass was basically self-taught, but he knew enough to read the powerful writers of his day. He was a commanding speaker in an age in which eloquence was valued and speakers were rewarded handsomely. This excerpt from the *Narrative* — Chapters 6, 7, and 8 — is notable for its clear and direct style. The use of the first-person narrative is as simple as one could wish, yet the feelings projected are sincere and moving.

Douglass's structure is the chronological narrative, relating events in the order in which they occurred. He begins his story at the point of meeting a new mistress, a woman from whom he expected harsh treatment. Because she was new to the concept of slavery, however, she behaved in ways that were unusual, and Douglass remarks on her initially kind attitude. Douglass does not interrupt himself with flashbacks or leaps forward in time but tells the story as it happened. At critical moments, he slows the narrative to describe people or incidents in unusual detail and lets the reader infer from these details the extent of the injustice he suffered.

By today's standards, Douglass's style may seem formal. His sentences are often longer than those of modern writers, although they are always carefully balanced and punctuated by briefer sentences. Despite his long paragraphs, heavy with example and description, after a century and a half his work remains immediate and moving. No modern reader will have difficulty responding to what Frederick Douglass has to say. His views on education are as accessible and as powerful now as when they were written.

✂ PREREADING QUESTIONS: WHAT TO READ FOR

The following prereading questions may help you anticipate key issues in the discussion of the excerpt that follows from *Narrative of the Life of Frederick Douglass, an American Slave*. Keeping them in mind during your first reading of the selection should help focus your attention.

1. What were the ethical issues involved in Mrs. Auld's helping Douglass learn to read?

2. In what ways was Douglass treated immorally? Was he immoral in his behavior toward others?

3. What was the ethical position of slave owners toward their slaves? Why did they think of themselves as ethical in their behavior?

From *Narrative of the Life of Frederick Douglass, an American Slave*

My new mistress proved to be all she appeared when I first met her at the door,—a woman of the kindest heart and finest feelings. She had never had a slave under her control previously to myself, and prior to her marriage she had been dependent upon her own industry for a living. She was by trade a weaver; and by constant application to her business, she had been in a good degree preserved from the blighting and dehumanizing effects of slavery. I was utterly astonished at her goodness. I scarcely knew how to behave towards her. She was entirely unlike any other white woman I had ever seen. I could not approach her as I was accustomed to approach other white ladies. My early instruction was all out of place. The crouching servility, usually so acceptable a quality in a slave, did not answer when manifested toward her. Her favor was not gained by it; she seemed to be disturbed by it. She did not deem it impudent or unmannerly for a slave to look her in the face. The meanest slave was put fully at ease in her presence, and none left without feeling better for having seen her. Her face was made of heavenly smiles, and her voice of tranquil music.

But, alas! this kind heart had but a short time to remain such. The fatal poison of irresponsible power was already in her hands, and soon commenced its infernal work. That cheerful eye, under the influence of slavery, soon became red with rage; that voice, made all of sweet accord, changed to one of harsh and horrid discord; and that angelic face gave place to that of a demon.

Very soon after I went to live with Mr. and Mrs. Auld, she very kindly com-   3
menced to teach me the A, B, C. After I had learned this, she assisted me in
learning to spell words of three or four letters. Just at this point of my progress, Mr. Auld found out what was going on, and at once forbade Mrs. Auld to
instruct me further, telling her, among other things, that it was unlawful, as well
as unsafe, to teach a slave to read. To use his own words, further, he said, "If
you give a nigger an inch, he will take an ell.[1] A nigger should know nothing but
to obey his master — to do as he is told to do. Learning would *spoil* the best nigger in the world. Now," said he, "if you teach that nigger (speaking of myself)
how to read, there would be no keeping him. It would forever unfit him to be a
slave. He would at once become unmanageable, and of no value to his master.
As to himself, it could do him no good, but a great deal of harm. It would make
him discontented and unhappy." These words sank deep into my heart, stirred
up sentiments within that lay slumbering, and called into existence an entirely
new train of thought. It was a new and special revelation, explaining dark and
mysterious things, with which my youthful understanding had struggled, but
struggled in vain. I now understood what had been to me a most perplexing
difficulty — to wit, the white man's power to enslave the black man. It was a
grand achievement, and I prized it highly. From that moment, I understood the
pathway from slavery to freedom. It was just what I wanted, and I got it at a
time when I the least expected it. Whilst I was saddened by the thought of losing the aid of my kind mistress, I was gladdened by the invaluable instruction
which, by the merest accident, I had gained from my master. Though conscious
of the difficulty of learning without a teacher, I set out with high hope, and
a fixed purpose, at whatever cost of trouble, to learn how to read. The very
decided manner with which he spoke, and strove to impress his wife with the
evil consequences of giving me instruction, served to convince me that he was
deeply sensible of the truths he was uttering. It gave me the best assurance that
I might rely with the utmost confidence on the results which, he said, would
flow from teaching me to read. What he most dreaded, that I most desired.
What he most loved, that I most hated. That which to him was a great evil, to
be carefully shunned, was to me a great good, to be diligently sought; and the
argument which he so warmly urged, against my learning to read, only served
to inspire me with a desire and determination to learn. In learning to read, I
owe almost as much to the bitter opposition of my master, as to the kindly aid
of my mistress. I acknowledge the benefit of both.

    I had resided but a short time in Baltimore before I observed a marked differ-   4
ence, in the treatment of slaves, from that which I had witnessed in the country. A
city slave is almost a freeman, compared with a slave on the plantation. He is much
better fed and clothed, and enjoys privileges altogether unknown to the slave on

---

[1] **ell**   A measure about a yard in length.

the plantation. There is a vestige of decency, a sense of shame, that does much to curb and check those outbreaks of atrocious cruelty so commonly enacted upon the plantation. He is a desperate slaveholder, who will shock the humanity of his nonslaveholding neighbors with the cries of his lacerated slave. Few are willing to incur the odium attaching to the reputation of being a cruel master; and above all things, they would not be known as not giving a slave enough to eat. Every city slaveholder is anxious to have it known of him, that he feeds his slaves well; and it is due to them to say, that most of them do give their slaves enough to eat. There are, however, some painful exceptions to this rule. Directly opposite to us, on Philpot Street, lived Mr. Thomas Hamilton. He owned two slaves. Their names were Henrietta and Mary. Henrietta was about twenty-two years of age, Mary was about fourteen; and of all the mangled and emaciated creatures I ever looked upon, these two were the most so. His heart must be harder than stone, that could look upon these unmoved. The head, neck, and shoulders of Mary were literally cut to pieces. I have frequently felt her head, and found it nearly covered with festering sores, caused by the lash of her cruel mistress. I do not know that her master ever whipped her, but I have been an eyewitness to the cruelty of Mrs. Hamilton. I used to be in Mr. Hamilton's house nearly every day. Mrs. Hamilton used to sit in a large chair in the middle of the room, with a heavy cowskin always by her side, and scarce an hour passed during the day but was marked by the blood of one of these slaves. The girls seldom passed her without her saying, "Move faster, you *black gip!*" at the same time giving them a blow with the cowskin over the head or shoulders, often drawing the blood. She would then say, "Take that, you *black gip!*"—continuing, "If you don't move faster, I'll move you!" Added to the cruel lashings to which these slaves were subjected, they were kept nearly half-starved. They seldom knew what it was to eat a full meal. I have seen Mary contending with the pigs for the offal thrown into the street. So much was Mary kicked and cut to pieces, that she was oftener called "*pecked*" than by her name.

I lived in Master Hugh's family about seven years. During this time, I suc-   5
ceeded in learning to read and write. In accomplishing this, I was compelled to resort to various stratagems. I had no regular teacher. My mistress, who had kindly commenced to instruct me, had, in compliance with the advice and direction of her husband, not only ceased to instruct, but had set her face against my being instructed by any one else. It is due, however, to my mistress to say of her, that she did not adopt this course of treatment immediately. She at first lacked the depravity indispensable to shutting me up in mental darkness. It was at least necessary for her to have some training in the exercise of irresponsible power, to make her equal to the task of treating me as though I were a brute.

My mistress was, as I have said, a kind and tender-hearted woman; and in   6
the simplicity of her soul she commenced, when I first went to live with her, to treat me as she supposed one human being ought to treat another. In entering

upon the duties of a slave-holder, she did not seem to perceive that I sustained to her the relation of a mere chattel, and that for her to treat me as a human being was not only wrong, but dangerously so. Slavery proved as injurious to her as it did to me. When I went there, she was a pious, warm, and tender-hearted woman. There was no sorrow or suffering for which she had not a tear. She had bread for the hungry, clothes for the naked, and comfort for every mourner that came within her reach. Slavery soon proved its ability to divest her of these heavenly qualities. Under its influence, the tender heart became stone, and the lamblike disposition gave way to one of tiger-like fierceness. The first step in her downward course was in her ceasing to instruct me. She now commenced to practice her husband's precepts. She finally became even more violent in her opposition than her husband himself. She was not satisfied with simply doing as well as he had commanded; she seemed anxious to do better. Nothing seemed to make her more angry than to see me with a newspaper. She seemed to think that here lay the danger. I have had her rush at me with a face made all up of fury, and snatch from me a newspaper, in a manner that fully revealed her apprehension. She was an apt woman; and a little experience soon demonstrated, to her satisfaction, that education and slavery were incompatible with each other.

From this time I was most narrowly watched. If I was in a separate room 7 any considerable length of time, I was sure to be suspected of having a book, and was at once called to give an account of myself. All this, however, was too late. The first step had been taken. Mistress, in teaching me the alphabet, had given me the *inch*, and no precaution could prevent me from taking the *ell*.

The plan which I adopted, and the one by which I was most successful, 8 was that of making friends of all the little white boys whom I met in the street. As many of these as I could, I converted into teachers. With their kindly aid, obtained at different times and in different places, I finally succeeded in learning to read. When I was sent to errands, I always took my book with me, and by going one part of my errand quickly, I found time to get a lesson before my return. I used also to carry bread with me, enough of which was always in the house, and to which I was always welcome; for I was much better off in this regard than many of the poor white children in our neighborhood. This bread I used to bestow upon the hungry little urchins, who, in return, would give me that more valuable bread of knowledge. I am strongly tempted to give the names of two or three of those little boys, as a testimonial of the gratitude and affection I bear them; but prudence forbids;—not that it would injure me, but it might embarrass them; for it is almost an unpardonable offense to teach slaves to read in this Christian country. It is enough to say of the dear little fellows, that they lived on Philpot Street, very near Durgin and Bailey's ship-yard. I used to talk this matter of slavery over with them. I would sometimes say to them, I wished I could be as free as they would be when they got to be men. "You will be free as soon as you are twenty-one, *but I am a slave for life!* Have not I as good a right to be free as you have?" These words used to trouble them; they would express for me the liveliest sympathy, and console me with the hope that something would occur by which I might be free.

I was now about twelve years old, and the thought of being *a slave for* 9 *life* began to bear heavily upon my heart. Just about this time, I got hold of a book entitled "The Columbian Orator." Every opportunity I got, I used to read this book. Among much of other interesting matter, I found in it a dialogue between a master and his slave. The slave was represented as having run away from his master three times. The dialogue represented the conversation which took place between them, when the slave was retaken the third time. In this dialogue, the whole argument in behalf of slavery was brought forward by the master, all of which was disposed of by the slave. The slave was made to say some very smart as well as impressive things in reply to his master—things which had the desired though unexpected effect; for the conversation resulted in the voluntary emancipation of the slave on the part of the master.

In the same book, I met with one of Sheridan's[2] mighty speeches on and in 10 behalf of Catholic emancipation. These were choice documents to me. I read them over and over again with unabated interest. They gave tongue to interesting thoughts of my own soul, which had frequently flashed through my mind, and died away for want of utterance. The moral which I gained from the dialogue was the power of truth over the conscience of even a slaveholder. What I got from Sheridan was a bold denunciation of slavery, and a powerful vindication of human rights. The reading of these documents enabled me to utter my thoughts, and to meet the arguments brought forward to sustain slavery; but while they relieved me of one difficulty, they brought on another even more painful than the one of which I was relieved. The more I read, the more I was led to abhor and detest my enslavers. I could regard them in no other light than a band of successful robbers, who had left their homes, and gone to Africa, and stolen us from our homes, and in a strange land reduced us to slavery. I loathed them as being the meanest as well as the most wicked of men. As I read and contemplated the subject, behold! that very discontentment which Master Hugh had predicted would follow my learning to read had already come, to torment and sting my soul to unutterable anguish. As I writhed under it, I would at times feel that learning to read had been a curse rather than a blessing. It had given me a view of my wretched condition, without the remedy. It opened my eyes to the horrible pit, but to no ladder upon which to get out. In moments of agony, I envied my fellow-slaves for their stupidity. I have often wished myself a beast.

---

[2] **Richard Brinsley Sheridan (1751–1816)** Irish dramatist and orator. However, Douglass really refers to a speech by Daniel O'Connell (1775–1847) in favor of Irish Catholic emancipation.

I preferred the condition of the meanest reptile to my own. Any thing, no matter what, to get rid of thinking! It was this everlasting thinking of my condition that tormented me. There was no getting rid of it. It was pressed upon me by every object within sight or hearing, animate or inanimate. The silver trump of freedom had roused my soul to eternal wakefulness. Freedom now appeared, to disappear no more forever. It was heard in every sound, and seen in every thing. It was ever present to torment me with a sense of my wretched condition. I saw nothing without seeing it, I heard nothing without hearing it, and felt nothing without feeling it. It looked from every star, it smiled in every calm, breathed in every wind, and moved in every storm.

I often found myself regretting my own existence, and wishing myself dead; and but for the hope of being free, I have no doubt but that I should have killed myself, or done something for which I should have been killed. While in this state of mind, I was eager to hear any one speak of slavery. I was a ready listener. Every little while, I could hear something about the abolitionists.[3] It was some time before I found what the word meant. It was always used in such connections as to make it an interesting word to me. If a slave ran away and succeeded in getting clear, or if a slave killed his master, set fire to a barn, or did any thing very wrong in the mind of a slaveholder, it was spoken of as the fruit of *abolition*. Hearing the word in this connection very often, I set about learning what it meant. The dictionary afforded me little or no help. I found it was "the act of abolishing"; but then I did not know what was to be abolished. Here I was perplexed. I did not dare to ask any one about its meaning, for I was satisfied that it was something they wanted me to know very little about. After a patient waiting, I got one of our city papers, containing an account of the number of petitions from the north, praying for the abolition of slavery in the District of Columbia, and of the slave trade between the States. From this time I understood the words *abolition* and *abolitionist*, and always drew near when that word was spoken, expecting to hear something of importance to myself and fellow-slaves. The light broke in upon me by degrees. I went one day down on the wharf of Mr. Waters; and seeing two Irishmen unloading a scow of stone, I went, unasked, and helped them. When we had finished, one of them came to me and asked me if I were a slave. I told him I was. He asked, "Are ye a slave for life?" I told him that I was. The good Irishman seemed to be deeply affected by the statement. He said to the other that it was a pity so fine a little fellow as myself should be a slave for life. He said it was a shame to hold me. They both advised me to run away to the north; that I should find friends there, and that I should be free. I pretended not to be interested in what they said, and treated them as if I did not understand them; for I feared they might be treacherous. White men have been known to encourage slaves to escape, and then, to get the reward, catch them and return them to their

11

---

[3] **abolitionists**   Those who actively opposed slavery.

masters. I was afraid that these seemingly good men might use me so; but I nevertheless remembered their advice, and from that time I resolved to run away. I looked forward to a time at which it would be safe for me to escape. I was too young to think of doing so immediately; besides, I wished to learn how to write, as I might have occasion to write my own pass. I consoled myself with the hope that I should one day find a good chance. Meanwhile, I would learn to write.

12   The idea as to how I might learn to write was suggested to me by being in Durgin and Bailey's ship-yard, and frequently seeing the ship carpenters, after hewing, and getting a piece of timber ready for use, write on the timber the name of that part of the ship for which it was intended. When a piece of timber was intended for the larboard side, it would be marked thus—"L." When a piece was for the starboard side, it would be marked thus—"S." A piece for the larboard side forward, would be marked thus—"L.F." When a piece was for starboard side forward, it would be marked thus—"S.F." For larboard aft, it would be marked thus—"L.A." For starboard aft, it would be marked thus—"S.A." I soon learned the names of these letters, and for what they were intended when placed upon a piece of timber in the ship-yard. I immediately commenced copying them, and in a short time was able to make the four letters named. After that, when I met with any boy who I knew could write, I would tell him I could write as well as he. The next word would be, "I don't believe you. Let me see you try it." I would then make the letters which I had been so fortunate as to learn, and ask him to beat that. In this way I got a good many lessons in writing, which it is quite possible I should never have gotten in any other way. During this time, my copy-book was the board fence, brick wall, and pavement; my pen and ink was a lump of chalk. With these, I learned mainly how to write. I then commenced and continued copying the Italics in Webster's Spelling Book, until I could make them all without looking on the book. By this time, my little Master Thomas had gone to school, and learned how to write, and had written over a number of copy-books. These had been brought home, and shown to some of our near neighbors, and then laid aside. My mistress used to go to class meeting at the Wilk Street meeting-house every Monday afternoon, and leave me to take care of the house. When left thus, I used to spend the time in writing in the spaces left in Master Thomas's copy-book, copying what he had written. I continued to do this until I could write a hand very similar to that of Master Thomas. Thus, after a long, tedious effort for years, I finally succeeded in learning how to write.

13   In a very short time after I went to live at Baltimore, my old master's youngest son Richard died; and in about three years and six months after his death, my old master, Captain Anthony, died, leaving only his son, Andrew, and daughter, Lucretia, to share his estate. He died while on a visit to see his daughter at Hillsborough. Cut off thus unexpectedly, he left no will as to the disposal of his property. It was therefore necessary to have a valuation of the property,

that it might be equally divided between Mrs. Lucretia and Master Andrew. I was immediately sent for, to be valued with the other property. Here again my feelings rose up in detestation of slavery. I had now a new conception of my degraded condition. Prior to this, I had become, if not insensible to my lot, at least partly so. I left Baltimore with a young heart overborne with sadness, and a soul full of apprehension. I took passage with Captain Rowe, in the schooner *Wild Cat*, and, after a sail of about twenty-four hours, I found myself near the place of my birth. I had now been absent from it almost, if not quite, five years. I, however, remembered the place very well. I was only about five years old when I left it, to go and live with my old master on Colonel Lloyd's plantation; so that I was now between ten and eleven years old.

We were all ranked together at the valuation. Men and women, old and young, married and single, were ranked with horses, sheep, and swine. There were horses and men, cattle and women, pigs and children, all holding the same rank in the scale of being, and were all subjected to the same narrow examination. Silvery-headed age and sprightly youth, maids and matrons, had to undergo the same indelicate inspection. At this moment, I saw more clearly than ever the brutalizing effects of slavery upon both slave and slaveholder. 14

After the valuation, then came the division. I have no language to express the high excitement and deep anxiety which were felt among us poor slaves during this time. Our fate for life was now to be decided. We had no more voice in that decision than the brutes among whom we were ranked. A single word from the white men was enough—against all our wishes, prayers, and entreaties—to sunder forever the dearest friends, dearest kindred, and strongest ties known to human beings. In addition to the pain of separation, there was the horrid dread of falling into the hands of Master Andrew. He was known to us all as being a most cruel wretch,—a common drunkard, who had, by his reckless mismanagement and profligate dissipation, already wasted a large portion of his father's property. We all felt that we might as well be sold at once to the Georgia traders, as to pass into his hands; for we knew that that would be our inevitable condition,—a condition held by us all in the utmost horror and dread. 15

I suffered more anxiety than most of my fellow-slaves. I had known what it was to be kindly treated; they had known nothing of the kind. They had seen little or nothing of the world. They were in very deed men and women of sorrow, and acquainted with grief. Their backs had been made familiar with the bloody lash, so that they had become callous; mine was yet tender; for while at Baltimore I got few whippings, and few slaves could boast of a kinder master and mistress than myself; and the thought of passing out of their hands into those of Master Andrew—a man who, but a few days before, to give me a sample of his bloody disposition, took my little brother by the throat, threw him on the ground, and with the heel of his boot stamped upon his head till 16 the blood gushed from his nose and ears — was well calculated to make me anxious as to my fate. After he had committed this savage outrage upon my brother, he turned to me, and said that was the way he meant to serve me one of these days, — meaning, I suppose, when I came into his possession.

Thanks to a kind Providence, I fell to the portion of Mrs. Lucretia, and was sent immediately back to Baltimore, to live again in the family of Master Hugh. Their joy at my return equalled their sorrow at my departure. It was a glad day to me. I had escaped a worse fate than lion's jaws. I was absent from Baltimore, for the purpose of valuation and division, just about one month, and it seemed to have been six. 17

Very soon after my return to Baltimore, my mistress, Lucretia, died, leaving her husband and child, Amanda; and in a very short time after her death, Master Andrew died. Now all the property of my old master, slaves included, was in the hands of strangers, — strangers who had had nothing to do with accumulating it. Not a slave was left free. All remained slaves, from the youngest to the oldest. If any one thing in my experience, more than another, served to deepen my conviction of the infernal character of slavery, and to fill me with unutterable loathing of slaveholders, it was their base ingratitude to my poor old grandmother. She had served my old master faithfully from youth to old age. She had been the source of all his wealth; she had peopled his plantation with slaves; she had become a great grandmother in his service. She had rocked him in infancy, attended him in childhood, served him through life, and at his death wiped from his icy brow the cold death-sweat, and closed his eyes forever. She was nevertheless left a slave — a slave for life — a slave in the hands of strangers; and in their hands she saw her children, her grandchildren, and her great-grandchildren, divided, like so many sheep, without being gratified with the small privilege of a single word, as to their or her own destiny. And, to cap the climax of their base ingratitude and fiendish barbarity, my grandmother, who was now very old, having outlived my old master and all his children, having seen the beginning and end of all of them, and her present owners finding she was of but little value, her frame already racked with the pains of old age, and complete helplessness fast stealing over her once active limbs, they took her to the woods, built her a little hut, put up a little mud-chimney, and then made her welcome to the privilege of supporting herself there in perfect loneliness; thus virtually turning her out to die! If my poor old grandmother now lives, she lives to suffer in utter loneliness; she lives to remember and mourn over the loss of children, the loss of grandchildren, and the loss of great-grandchildren. They are, in the language of the slave's poet, Whittier,[4] — 18

> Gone, gone, sold and gone
> To the rice swamp dank and lone,

---

[4] **John Greenleaf Whittier (1807–1892)** New England abolitionist, journalist, and poet. The poem Douglass cites is "The Farewell" (1835).

Where the slave-whip ceaseless swings,
Where the noisome insect stings,
Where the fever-demon strews
Poison with the falling dews,
Where the sickly sunbeams glare
Through the hot and misty air: —
 Gone, gone, sold and gone
 To the rice swamp dank and lone,
 From Virginia hills and waters —
 Woe is me, my stolen daughters!

The hearth is desolate. The children, the unconscious children, who once 19
sang and danced in her presence, are gone. She gropes her way, in the darkness
of age, for a drink of water. Instead of the voices of her children, she hears
by day the moans of the dove, and by night the screams of the hideous owl.
All is gloom. The grave is at the door. And now, when weighed down by the
pains and aches of old age, when the head inclines to the feet, when the beginning and ending of human existence meet, and helpless infancy and painful
old age combine together — at this time, this most needful time, the time for
the exercise of that tenderness and affection which children only can exercise
towards a declining parent — my poor old grandmother, the devoted mother of
twelve children, is left all alone, in yonder little hut, before a few dim embers.
She stands — she sits — she staggers — she falls — she groans — she dies — and
there are none of her children or grandchildren present, to wipe from her
wrinkled brow the cold sweat of death, or to place beneath the sod her fallen
remains. Will not a righteous God visit for these things?

In about two years after the death of Mrs. Lucretia, Master Thomas married 20
his second wife. Her name was Rowena Hamilton. She was the eldest daughter
of Mr. William Hamilton. Master now lived in St. Michael's. Not long after his
marriage, a misunderstanding took place between himself and Master Hugh;
and as a means of punishing his brother, he took me from him to live with
himself at St. Michael's. Here I underwent another most painful separation. It,
however, was not so severe as the one I dreaded at the division of property;
for, during this interval, a great change had taken place in Master Hugh and
his once kind and affectionate wife. The influence of brandy upon him, and of
slavery upon her, had effected a disastrous change in the characters of both; so
that, as far as they were concerned, I thought I had little to lose by the change.
But it was not to them that I was attached. It was to those little Baltimore
boys that I felt the strongest attachment. I had received many good lessons
from them, and was still receiving them, and the thought of leaving them was
painful indeed. I was leaving, too, without the hope of ever being allowed to
return. Master Thomas had said he would never let me return again. The barrier betwixt himself and brother he considered impassable.

I then had to regret that I did not at least make the attempt to carry out my   21
resolution to run away; for the chances of success are tenfold greater from the
city than from the country.

I sailed from Baltimore for St. Michael's in the sloop *Amanda*, Captain   22
Edward Dodson. On my passage, I paid particular attention to the direction
which the steamboats took to go to Philadelphia. I found, instead of going
down, on reaching North Point they went up the bay, in a north-easterly direction. I deemed this knowledge of the utmost importance. My determination to
run away was again revived. I resolved to wait only so long as the offering of a
favorable opportunity. When that came, I was determined to be off.

✖ QUESTIONS FOR CRITICAL READING

1. In paragraph 2, Douglass describes Mrs. Auld as possessing "the fatal poison of irresponsible power." What are the ethical responsibilities of power in her relationship with Douglass?

2. In what sense were the laws of Douglass's time immoral? How can a law be immoral?

3. Did slave owners think it immoral to teach slaves to read and write?

4. Was it ethical for Douglass to learn to read and write even though he knew it was prohibited for him to do so?

5. How does an ethical contract between slave and slaveholder function? What were the responsibilities of each to the other?

✖ SUGGESTIONS FOR CRITICAL WRITING

1. The society in which Douglass lived was governed by laws established by elected officials who had benefited from the authors of the Constitution of the United States, which set itself as the law of the land. How could slaveholders in Maryland have considered it ethical to hold other human beings as slaves? What ethical loopholes were apparent in the Constitution?

2. What is the most important political issue raised in the essay? Douglass never talks about the law, but he implies a great deal about justice and morality. How do justice and morality intersect in Douglass's story of his life as a slave? How aware does he seem to have been that he was being dealt with in an unethical fashion?

3. The vast number of slaveholders during Douglass's time were church-goers and passionate Christians. We often think of religion as a bulwark of morality and ethics, so how could avid religious citizens behave in a way that we now think of as immoral and unethical? Is it possible that there was a disconnect between religion and morality in the slave states? Is it possible that there is no relationship between morality and religion to start with?

4. What, on the whole, is Douglass's attitude toward white people? Examine his statements about them and establish as far as possible his feelings regarding their character. Is he bitter about his slavery experiences? Does he condemn the society that supported slavery as having been immoral?

5. How effective is the detailed description in this selection? Choose the best descriptive passages and analyze them for their effectiveness in context. What does Douglass hope to achieve by giving so much attention to such descriptions? How does his description help you better understand the concept of ethical behavior?

6. **CONNECTIONS**   Which writer would Douglass have expected to understand his views on the ethics of slavery: Henry David Thoreau (p. 720), Thomas Jefferson (p. 116), or Jean-Jacques Rousseau (p. 99)? How do each of their views of ethics intersect with Douglass's? Which of these writers do you think would have most enjoyed being able to discuss slavery with Douglass?

7. **CONNECTIONS**   Aristotle is clear in saying that happiness is the greatest good for man. Yet in Aristotle's Athens, slavery was a simple, accepted fact of everyday life, and Aristotle likely did not have slaves' interests in mind when he wrote "The Aim of Man" (p. 688). How might Frederick Douglass have responded to the way Aristotle connected virtue and happiness? How would Douglass's having been a slave affect his views of Aristotle's respect for the state? Did Douglass consider virtue as a means to happiness? How might Douglass have critiqued Aristotle's views of the ultimate good? For Douglass, what constituted the ultimate good?

8. One of the most constant defenses of the ethics of slavery — even after the Civil War — was that it was for the good of the slaves. Even some of the freed slaves told interviewers in the 1930s that things had been better for them under slavery than they were during the Great Depression. Is the view that slavery was good for the slaves in any way an ethical view? Is it a moral view? What's wrong with it?

9. Douglass escaped from slavery by deceiving the authorities into thinking he was an able-bodied seaman with the right to travel. He broke the law at that time, and he broke it again when he remained free. Why should we not condemn him for immoral behavior and an ethical lapse? The Aulds certainly regarded him as a criminal and as someone who acted immorally. Why should we not agree with them? What would Thoreau have said about his behavior?

IRIS
MURDOCH

Morality and Religion

IRIS MURDOCH (1919–1999) was born in Dublin, Ireland, but her family soon moved to London, where she grew up. Most people know Murdoch as one of the most important novelists in English in the twentieth century. She wrote twenty-six novels that explore interesting aspects of philosophy and psychology. She once said that while she distrusted psychoanalysis, she felt that she was analyzing herself in her novels. Critics have considered her one of the most important literary figures of her time.

Her early schooling prepared her for a degree in Oxford in classics and philosophy. In the 1930s, she became a member of the Communist Party, but she soon rejected its principles and resigned from the party before World War II. During the war, she worked in the British Treasury offices, and afterward she spent time in Belgium and Austria working with the United Nations Relief organization. Murdoch then spent a year trying to sort her life out. She had been given a scholarship to study at Vassar College but could not get a visa because of her Communist past. Eventually, in 1947, she accepted a student-ship at Newnham College, Cambridge, to study philosophy under Ludwig Wittgenstein (1889–1951), one of the age's most influential philosophers. The next year she was elected Fellow of St. Anne's College, Oxford, and remained as a tutor (essentially a professor) until she retired in 1963 to write full time.

She won a number of important prizes for her literary work. Her novel *The Sea, The Sea* won Britain's most prestigious literary award, the Booker Prize, in 1978. The Divinity School at the University of Chicago honored her for "the religious depth of her novels" in 1992. Among the most important and interesting of her novels are *The Flight from the Enchanter* (1956), *The Red and the Green* (1956), *The Black Prince* (1973), *The Sacred and Profane Love Machine* (1974), *The Book and the Brotherhood* (1987), and *The Green Knight* (1993).

From *Metaphysics as a Guide to Morals.*

In addition to novels, Murdoch also wrote a number of influential philosophical studies. Her first book, *Sartre, Romantic Rationalist* (1953), resulted from her meeting Jean-Paul Sartre (1905–1980) in the 1940s and her interest in existentialism. *The Sovereignty of Good and Other Concepts* (1967) is considered a work of first importance in moral studies. *Metaphysics as a Guide to Morals* (1992) developed from the Gifford Lectures she gave at the University of Edinburgh in 1981–82. Her last book, *Existentialists and Mystics: Writings on Philosophy and Literature* (1997), was published near the end of her life when she was suffering from the final stages of Alzheimer's disease.

Murdoch's impressive work *Metaphysics as a Guide to Morals*, from which the following selection is taken, deals with how we interpret and understand the nature of morals. One of the questions she addresses is whether there can be a true moral position outside the confines of religion. Murdoch weighs the arguments on both sides of the issue and lets her readers decide how to resolve them. She herself thrived on contradictions and saw them as energy for understanding.

MURDOCH'S RHETORIC

The first thing one notices about Murdoch's writing is that she relies on very long paragraphs. Each paragraph addresses a position on how religion and morality are related. She does not pose an overarching argument, but how religion affects what we think of as moral behavior is one of the issues she pursues.

Another aspect of her writing is her many references to philosophers such as Kant, Plato, Bentham, and Wittgenstein, and to historical events such as the Cultural Revolution in Mao's China and the murder of kulaks — wealthy farmers — in Stalin's Soviet Union. But these are not essential to our understanding of the issues she discusses.

She begins in paragraph 2 with a consideration of the nature of virtue, which she sees as "[t]he most evident bridge between morality and religion." Yet there are problems with the very idea of virtue, as she points out. For some people in the modern world, the word *virtue* has lost its positive meaning and is related to rigidity and priggishness. Moreover, it is not capable of being applied universally to people because "fear, misery, deprivation" (para. 2) will alter the nature of virtue in people who experience those conditions. Those who suffer from hunger or political oppression may not have much interest in conventional bourgeois theories of virtue. Therefore, Murdoch suggests, virtue may be a relative concept rather than a fixed idea.

In paragraph 3, she continues her discussion of virtue but adds the concept of duty, a sense of obligation that is understood in a social context. According to Murdoch, "Dutifulness could be an account of a morality with no hint of religion" (para. 3). In this extensive paragraph, Murdoch explores the idea of duty, connecting it to eighteenth-century principles of reason, showing that duty and reason fit together rather well. One understands one's duty to others, institutions, and nations, and one performs one's duty without religious intervention. Is that then a virtuous action? Is the performance of duty then irrelevant to the moral views of religion? As she says at the end of the paragraph, after exploring the issue it may be time to refer back to the "clear, rigid rules" of religions to find answers to these questions.

In paragraph 4, Murdoch contrasts secular idealism with religious belief. The question is whether one of these is more likely to produce moral good than the other. Is morality, she continually asks, dependent on religion, or can it be achieved outside religion? She points out a conundrum that continues in modern life: the criminal who constantly breaks the law and yet has a deep religious conviction. She criticizes religion indirectly by examining its nonrational elements, those of pure faith. But near the end of the paragraph she says, "Religion symbolizes high moral ideas which then travel with us and are more intimately and accessibly effective than the unadorned promptings of reason" (para. 4).

In paragraph 5, she begins to discuss the diary of Francis Kilvert (1840–1879), a simple clergyman who found in his rural community moments of intense beauty and moral uprightness. Kilvert is likened to another cleric, Julian of Norwich, who arrives at a deeply philosophical understanding when she holds a "little thing, the size of a hazel nut, which seemed to lie in the palm of my hand; and it was as round as any ball" (para. 5), and in it she saw a metaphor for the wholeness of creation, a sense that was at root a deep religious experience. Murdoch interprets this as a way of exhibiting "God's love for the world" (para. 5).

In paragraph 6, Murdoch proceeds to include religious philosophers such as Søren Kierkegaard (1813–1855), whose views on religion and morality are complex and not easily untangled. Her discussion reaches into the question of whether God exists and the Ontological Proof, a proof of God's existence that dates to the Middle Ages. The proof asserts that we can imagine a perfect being, God, and that because we can imagine it, it must exist because perfection is consistent only with actual existence. Murdoch puts it this way: "Guilt, especially deep apparently incurable guilt, can be one of the worst of human pains. To cure such an ill, because of human sin, God *must* exist" (para. 6).

In her final paragraph, Murdoch explores mysticism, which implies having a direct spiritual experience of God, achieved through prayer, religious discipline, fasting, or a variety of ascetic practices similar to meditation. As she says in her opening sentence, "Religion (even if 'primitive') is generally assumed to be in some sense moral. Mysticism is also assumed to be, by definition, moral" (para. 7). However, despite this assurance, she also points out that in some ages, such as the eighteenth-century Enlightenment period, "institutionalized religion [was] an enemy of morality, an enemy of freedom and free thought, guilty of cruelty and repression" (para. 7). In the remainder of this paragraph she attempts to work out some of the obvious conflicts inherent in these statements.

She ends with an interesting discussion of the relationship of two contradictory forces in the universe: good and evil. As she states in a rather paradoxical fashion: "Discord is essential to goodness" (para. 7). In other words, there can only be a concept of morality in an environment in which there is evil *and* goodness. Murdoch points out that "both morality and religion face the same insuperable difficulty": that if the goal of eradicating evil is achieved "the struggle, the need for devotion, would cease to be real. . . . If there is to be morality, there cannot altogether be an end to evil" (para. 7).

✖ PREREADING QUESTIONS: WHAT TO READ FOR

The following prereading questions may help you anticipate key issues in the discussion of Iris Murdoch's "Morality and Religion." Keeping them in mind during your first reading of the selection should help focus your attention.

1. How is the idea of virtue a bridge between religion and morality?
2. In what senses do religion and morality seem to be different?
3. Is morality impossible without religion?

Morality and Religion

In the background of many of these arguments lies a question about the relation of morality to religion, the difference between them, and the definition of religion. I have already suggested that my whole argument can be read as moral philosophy. In any case moral philosophy must include this dimension whether we call it religion or not. Someone may say that there is only one way to "acquire" religion and that is through being taught it as a small child. You have to breathe it in. It is an ineffable attitude to the world which cannot really be discussed. People who take up religion as adults are merely playing at it, it remains at a level of illusion. So someone could speak, being either a believer or an unbeliever. The unbeliever might add that religion is imbibed in childhood, when it forms part of the infantile child–parent relationship now well-known to psychology; only religion, being a soothing drug, is less easy to give up in later life.

The most evident bridge between morality and religion is the idea of virtue. Virtue is still treated in some quarters as something precious to be positively pursued; yet the concept has also faded, even tending to fall apart between "idealism" and "priggishness." It may be seen as a self-indulgent luxury. It has, perhaps has always had, many enemies. Fear of a perverted ideology or of a too fervent "enthusiasm" may prevent a positive conception of virtue. Cynicism and materialism and *dolce vita*[1] can occlude it, also fear, misery, deprivation, and loss of concepts. Even in a religious context "personal spirituality" may be something that has to be argued for. A utilitarian morality[2] may treat a concern

---

[1] *dolce vita*   The sweet life; the irresponsible life.

[2] **utilitarian morality**   Utilitarianism professed a creed of the greatest good for the greatest number and would insist that any moral principle produce the greatest happiness and the least pain for all involved.

with becoming virtuous as a waste of energy which should be transmitted directly to the alleviation of suffering. Of course numerous people are virtuous without thinking about it, and sages may say that, if thought about, it may *ipso facto*[3] diminish. A saint may perhaps be good by instinct and nature, though saintly figures are also revered as reformed sinners. Perhaps the word itself begins to seem pretentious and old-fashioned.

An idea (concept) of virtue which need not be formally reflective or clari-   3
fied bears some resemblance to religion, so that one might say either that it is a shadow of religion, or religion is a shadow of it. The demand that we should be virtuous or try to become good is something that goes beyond explicit calls of duty. One can of course extend the idea of duty into the area of generalized goodness (virtuous living) by making it a duty always to have pure thoughts and good motives. For reasons I have suggested I would rather keep the concept of duty nearer to its ordinary sense as something fairly strict, recognizable, intermittent, so that we can say that there may be time off from the call of duty, but no time off from the demand of good. These are conceptual problems which are important in the building up of a picture; that is, an overall extension of the idea of duty would blur a valuable distinction, and undermine the particular function of the concept. Duty then I take to be formal obligation, relating to occasions where it can be to some extent clarified. ("Why go?" "I promised." "Why go?" "He's an old friend." "Why go?" "Well, it's somehow that sort of situation.") Duty may be easily performed without strain or reflection, but may also prompt the well-known experience of the frustration of desire together with a sense of necessity to act, wherein there is a proper place for the concept of *will*. Dutifulness could be an account of a morality with no hint of religion. The rational formality of moral maxims made to govern particular situations might make them seem like separated interrupted points of insight rather than like a light which always shines. This could be a picture of human life. Yet Kant[4] also portrays us as *belonging* at every second to the noumenal world of rationality and freedom, the separated pure source. We are orderly because duty is duty, yet also behind the exercise of it we might (surely, after all) glimpse the inspiring light of pure goodness which Kant calls Reason, and sometimes even God. Beyond all this we may picture a struggle in Kant's religious soul over the concept of Reason, so essential, yet so awkward. The rationality (Pure Reason) which enables us to deal with objects and causes *must* be related to that (Practical Reason) which enables us to deal with right and wrong. Well, the concept of truth can relate them. . . . Perhaps Kant felt no awkwardness—it

---

[3] ***ipso facto***   By the very fact itself.

[4] **Immanuel Kant (1724–1804)**   German philosopher who linked pure reason and experiential knowledge. *Noumenal* is a Kantian term that refers to the unknowable world as it is in itself. According to Kant, we can only know the world as it appears to us, as a phenomenon. We can never know it as it is in itself, as a noumenon.

is we who feel awkward, when we connect morality with love and desire. Certainly it does seem possible to set up a contrast between the dutiful man and the virtuous man which is different from the contrast between the dutiful man and the religious man. Here we may think of Christ saying render unto Caesar what is Caesar's. Duty as order, relating morals to politics. Good decent men lead orderly lives. It might also be said in this context that given the abysmal sinfulness of humans, only a strict list of rules can keep them from mutual destruction! The moral (or spiritual) life is both one and not one. There is the idea of a sovereign good, but there are also compartments, obligations, rules, aims, whose identity may have to be respected. These separate aspects or modes of behavior occasion some of the most difficult kinds of moral problems, as if we have to move between *styles*, or to change gear. We have to live a single moral existence, and also to retain the separate force of various kinds of moral vision. Jeanie Deans in Scott's novel[5] loves her sister, but cannot lie to save her life. Isabella in *Measure for Measure* will not save her brother by yielding her chastity to Angelo. Duty is one thing, love is another. These are dramatic examples; one can invent many more homely ones of the conflict of moral requirements of entirely different kinds, wherein one seems to have to choose between being two different kinds of person. This may be a choice between two paths in life, or it may be some everyday matter demanding an instant response. We tend to feel that these dissimilar demands and states of mind must somehow connect, there must be a deep connection, it must all somehow make a unified sense; this is a religious craving, God sees it all. What I earlier called axioms[6] are moral entities whose force must not be overcome by, or dissolved into, other moral streams: a requirement in liberal politics. Axioms may not "win" but must remain in consideration, a Benthamite[7] utilitarian conception of happiness must not, as a frequently relevant feature, be eroded by high-minded considerations about quality of happiness or by theories which make happiness invisible, or of course by political objectives. (The Cultural Revolution, the liquidation of the kulaks.[8]) Equally of course, degraded or evil pleasure cannot count as simple or silly happiness. Such complexities, involving conflicts of moral discernment and moral style, are with us always. So, "keeping everything in mind" is not an easy matter in morals. This may be an

---

[5] **Scott's novel**   *The Heart of Mid-Lothian* (1818) by Sir Walter Scott (1771–1832).

[6] **axioms**   Statements of truth, as in geometry.

[7] **Benthamite: Jeremy Bentham (1748–1832)**   proposed a scheme of "private ethics" in which the aim of one's actions should be to cause the greatest pleasure and least pain. He was influential in developing English utilitarianism.

[8] **The Cultural Revolution . . . kulaks**   The Cultural Revolution (1966–1976), begun by Mao Zedong (1893–1976), chairman of the Chinese Communist Party, was a period of political zealotry characterized by purges of intellectuals and anticommunists. The kulaks were relatively wealthy farmers who opposed Soviet collectivization of their land. Soviet leader Joseph Stalin (1879–1953) sought to execute or deport the kulaks, whom he maligned as "exploiters."

argument for clear rigid rules. Modern clerics who do not feel able to tell newly married couples to be virtuous, tell them to have a sense of humor. This shift is a telling case of a change of style.

Religious belief may be a stronger motive to good conduct than non-religious idealism. Corrupt immoral persons (for instance hardened criminals) who cheerfully break all the "moral rules," may retain the religious images of their childhood which can, at some juncture, affect their conduct. This idea has been (not unsentimentally) dealt with in various novels and films. Indeed, this retention of images, and sensibility to images, might suggest the importance of a religious childhood. (Is it easier to get out of religion, or to get in?) Parents who have had such a childhood themselves, but have "given up religion," may often think along these lines. A kind of sensible well-meaning tolerance is involved here. But, a sterner breed may say, what about *truth*? Religion just *isn't true*. A religious man, even a goodish one, is spoilt and flawed by irrational superstitious convictions; and it is held to be ridiculous for lapsed parents to let their innocent children be tainted with beliefs which the parents know to be false. It is no use talking of a "good atmosphere," what is fundamentally at stake is *truth*. Such arguments come near to familiar problems of today. Is the non-religious good man so like the religious good man that it is merely some point of terminology or superficial style which is at issue? Orthodoxly religious people often tolerantly compliment the unbeliever by saying, "He is *really* a true Christian"; which may well annoy the unbeliever. More positively attempting a distinction to form part of a definition, it might be suggested that religion is a form of heightened consciousness (Matthew Arnold[9] said it was "morality touched by emotion"), it is intense and highly toned, it is about what is deep, what is holy, what is absolute, the emotional imaginative image-making faculties are engaged, the whole man is engaged. Every moment matters, there is no time off. High morality without religion is too abstract, high morality craves for religion. Religion symbolizes high moral ideas which then travel with us and are more intimately and accessibly effective than the unadorned promptings of reason. Religion suits the image-making human animal. Think what the image of Christ has done for us through centuries. Can such images *lie*? Do we not indeed adjust our attitudes to them, as time passes, so as to "make them true"? This continuous adjustment is an aspect of the history of religion.

I intended here, thinking about holiness and reverence, not the exclusive property of believers, to quote from Francis Kilvert's[10] Diary (begun in 1870). Kilvert was a parson in country parishes on the Welsh border, a religious good

4

5

---

[9] **Matthew Arnold (1822–1888)**   Prominent English poet and social commentator.

[10] **Francis Kilvert (1840–1879)**   English clergyman and diarist. Although after his death his widow destroyed many of his notebooks, the remainder were discovered by William Plomer (1903–1973), a South African writer, and published in 1938 and 1940.

man of simple faith. However, it is difficult to quote from the Diary because of the transparent artless lucidity of Kilvert's account of his days. Any particular quotation can sound naive, or sentimental. "I went to see my dear little lover Mary Tavener, the deaf and half dumb child. When I opened the door of the poor crazy old cottage in the yard the girl uttered a passionate inarticulate cry of joy and running to me flung her arms about my neck and covered me with kisses." (12 June 1875.) "Old William Price sat in his filthy den, unkempt, unshaven, shaggy and grey like a wild beast, and if possible filthier than the den. I read to him Faber's hymn of the Good Shepherd. He was much struck with it. 'That's what He has been telling me,' said the old man." (26 January 1872.) "The road was very still. No one seemed to be passing and the birds sang late and joyfully in the calm mild evening as if they thought it must be spring. A white mist gathered in the valley and hung low along the winding course of the river mingled with the rushing of the brooks, the distant voices of children at play came floating at intervals across the river and near at hand a pheasant screeched now and then and clapped its wings or changed his roost from tree to tree like a man turning in bed before he falls asleep." (27 January 1872.) Kilvert spent his days walking all over his territory, visiting everyone, noticing everything (people, animals, birds, flowers) and describing it all in simple humble extremely readable detail. "How delightful on these sweet summer evenings to wander from cottage to cottage and farm to farm." It may be said that Kilvert was lucky, but also that he deserved his luck. There is a serene light and a natural kindly selfless love of people and of nature in what he writes. He felt secure. He had faith. Wittgenstein[11] was struck by a character in a play who seemed to him to feel safe, nothing that happened could harm him. Wittgenstein's "Ontological Proof" or "statement" (*Tractatus* 6.41) places the sense of the world outside the world, outside *all* of the contingent facts. Thinking of Wittgenstein's picture of the world (all the facts) as a self-contained sphere, a sort of steel ball, outside which ineffable value roams, we might look at something similar but different. "He showed me a little thing, the size of a hazel nut, which seemed to lie in the palm of my hand; and it was as round as any ball. I looked upon it with my eye of understanding, and thought 'What may this be?' I was answered in a general way thus: 'It is all that is made.' I wondered how long it could last, for it seemed as though it might suddenly fade away to nothing, it was so small. And I was answered in my understanding: 'It lasts and ever shall last, for God loveth it. And even so hath everything being, by the

---

[11] **Ludwig Wittgenstein (1889–1951)**   Murdoch's philosophy professor. His *Tractatus* approaches problems of language in describing philosophical ideas. His concept of the "world outside the world" implies that we imaginatively observe the world outside itself, much as we observe ourselves. Thus the "little thing" becomes an observable metaphor for a little world.

love of God.'" (Julian of Norwich,[12] *Revelations of Divine Love*, chapter 5.) Julian's showing, besides exhibiting God's love for the world, also indicates our absolute dependence as created things. We are nothing, we owe our being to something not ourselves. We are enlivened from a higher source.

Kierkegaard[13] would object to a moral–religious continuum. We, exist-ing individuals, therefore sinners, feel guilt, feel in need of salvation, to be reborn into a new being. "If any man be in Christ he is a new creature: old things are passed away, behold all things are become new." (2 Corinthians 5:17.) In Kierkegaard's version of Hegelian dialectic[14] it is not endlessly evolv-ing toward totality, but is a picture of levels in the soul, or of different kinds of people, or of the pilgrimage of a particular person. The aesthetic individual is private, the ethical man, including the tragic hero, is public, the religious individual, the man of faith, is once more private. This dramatic triad also suggests the dangerous link between the two private stages, the aesthetic and the religious, so deeply unlike, so easily confused. The idea of repentance and leading a better cleansed and renewed life is a generally understood moral idea; and the, however presented, granting of absolution, God's forgiveness, keeps many people inside religion, or invites them to enter. Guilt, especially deep apparently incurable guilt, can be one of the worst of human pains. To cure such an ill, because of human sin, God *must* exist. (As Norman Malcolm[15] suggested when discussing the Ontological Proof.) The condition of being changed and made anew is a general religious idea, sometimes appearing as magical instant salvation (as in suddenly "taking Christ as Saviour") or as the result of some lengthy ascesis.[16] Here salvation as spiritual change often goes with the conception of a *place* of purification and healing. (We light candles, we bring flowers, we go somewhere and kneel down.) This sense of a safe place is characteristic of religious imagery. Here the outer images the inner, and the inner images the outer. There is a literal place, the place of pilgrimage, the place of worship, the shrine, the sacred grove, there is also a psychological or spiritual place, a part of the soul. "Do not seek for God outside your soul."

6

---

[12] **Julian of Norwich (1332–1416?)**   English mystic and writer. Her book *Revelations of Divine Love* recounts her mystical religious experiences.

[13] **Søren Kierkegaard (1813–1855)**   Danish philosopher whose concept of "Either/Or" explored the choice between an ethical life or one that ignored ethics.

[14] **Hegelian dialectic**   Postulates that the conflict of two opposites ultimately resolves itself through synthesis (a third option). Georg Wilhelm Friedrich Hegel (1770–1831), a German philosopher, has been enormously influential on all modern philosophers. He felt that humans experience a constant and irreconcilable conflict of reason and emotion.

[15] **Norman Malcolm (1911–1990)**   American philosopher whose book *Ludwig Wittgenstein: A Memoir* is referenced in Murdoch's text.

[16] **ascesis**   Ascetic behavior, such as fasting, celibacy, or becoming a hermit.

Religion provides a well-known well-tried procedure of rescue. Particularly in relation to guilt and remorse or the obsessions which can be bred from these, the *mystery* of religion (respected, intuited) is a source of spiritual energy. An orientation toward the good involves a reorientation of desire. Here a meeting with a good person may bring about a change of direction. If Plato had never met Socrates and experienced his death perhaps Western thinking might have been different. The mystical Christ too can be "met" with. (The idea of redemptive suffering is repugnant to some; but such suffering is everywhere around us, where the innocent suffers through love of the guilty.) Of course it may well be argued that there are sound unmysterious secular equivalents to these devices, there are many resources for the afflicted who may use their enlightened common sense, or go to their friends, doctors, therapists, psychoanalysts, social workers, take refuge in art or nature, or say (as the religious too may say) to hell with it all. Many people hate religion, with its terrible history and its irrationality, and would regard resort to religious rituals as a false substitute for real morals and genuine amendment of life. Judaism and Islam, who have avoided the path of image-making, and have revered the name of [God], avoid many of the problems which now beset Christianity. Buddhists live with the mystical Buddha in the soul. (Like Eckhart's[17] God and Christ in the soul.) The Hindu religion also has its philosophical mysticism above its numerous gods. Religion has been fundamentally mystical, and this becomes, in this age, more evident. So will the theologians invent new modes of speech, and will the churches fill with people who realize they do not need to believe in the supernatural?

Religion (even if "primitive") is generally assumed to be in some sense   7
moral. Mysticism is also assumed to be, by definition, moral. Thinkers of the Enlightenment however, and many since, have held, often rightly, that organized, institutionalized religion is an enemy of morality, an enemy of freedom and free thought, guilty of cruelty and repression. This has been so and in many quarters is so. Therefore the whole institution may be rationally considered to be discredited or outmoded. Many other influences from the past support such a line of thought. Kierkegaard saw Hegel as the enemy of religion and of, *ipso facto*, the existing individual. The vast force of Hegel's thinking, followed up by Marx, is inimical to both. The Romantic Movement and the liberal political thinking which went with it have tended to look after the individual, and we associate high morality (idealism, selflessness, goodness) with many people in this century and the last who assumed that religion was *finished*. It must be agreed that, in very many ways, Western society has improved, become more tolerant, more free, more decently happy, in this period. It may also be agreed

---

[17] **Johannes Eckhart (1260?–1327?)**   German theologian who saw a unity in the soul and God: "the core of the soul and the core of God are one."

that with the decline of religious observance and religious "consciousness" (the practice of prayer and the fear of God for instance), some aspects of moral conduct may decline also. (Of course this decline can have other causes.) However that may be, Hegel and Marx, Nietzsche and Freud, have had influence. Virtues and values may give way to a more relaxed sense of determinism. There is a more "reasonable," ordinary, *available* relativism and "naturalism" about. Hegel's *Geist*[18] is the energy which perpetually urges the ever-unsatisfied intellect (and so the whole of being) onward toward Absolute reality. Everything is relative, incomplete, not yet fully real, not yet fully true, dialectic is a continual reformulation. Such is the history of thought, of civilization, or of the "person" who, immersed in the process, is carried on toward some postulated self-consistent totality. Vaguely, such an image as something plausible may linger in the mind. I shall not discuss Hegel here, but look for a moment at a milder form of quasi-Hegelianism in F. H. Bradley's[19] *Appearance and Reality*. According to Bradley both morality and religion demand an unattainable unity. "Every separate aspect of the universe goes on to demand something higher than itself." This is the dialectic, the overcoming of the incomplete, of appearance and illusion, the progress toward what is more true, more real, more harmoniously integrated. "And, like every other appearance, goodness implies that which, when carried out, must absorb it." Religion is higher than morality, being more unified, more expressive of a perfect wholeness. But both morality and religion face the same insuperable difficulty. Morality–religion believes in the reality of perfect good, and in the demand that good be victorious and evil destroyed. The postulated whole (good) is at once actually to be good, and at the same time to make itself good. Neither its perfect goodness nor its struggle may be degraded to an appearance (something incomplete and imperfect). But to unite these two aspects consistently is impossible. If the desired end were reached, the struggle, the need for devotion, would have ceased to be real. If there is to be morality, there cannot altogether be an end to evil. Discord is essential to goodness. Moral evil exists only in moral experience and that experience is essentially inconsistent. Morality desires unconsciously, with the suppression of evil, to become non-moral. It shrinks from this, yet it unknowingly desires the existence and perpetuity of evil. Morality, which makes evil, desires in evil to remove a condition of its own being; it labors to pass into a super-moral and therefore non-moral sphere. Moral–religious faith is make-believe: be sure that opposition to the good is overcome, but act as if it (the opposition) persists. "The religious consciousness rests on the felt unity of unreduced opposites."

---

[18] ***Geist*** The reference is to Hegel's concept of the spirit/mind (geist). Hegel had three categories of spirit/mind: subjective, objective, and absolute. The absolute was reserved for contemplation of religion, fine arts, and philosophy.

[19] **F. H. Bradley (1846–1924)** English philosopher influenced by Hegel who emphasized the force of the mind over the physical world.

✣ QUESTIONS FOR CRITICAL READING

1. Can there be only one concept of virtue?

2. Why is virtue different from duty?

3. How is dutiful behavior different from religious behavior?

4. Does religion foster good behavior more than nonreligious idealism does?

5. How does guilt relate to morality?

6. Is religion essentially moral in nature?

7. Is high morality (idealism, selflessness, goodness) essentially religious?

✣ SUGGESTIONS FOR CRITICAL WRITING

1. One question that underlies Murdoch's views is whether or not a high morality could ever be produced in a completely nonreligious environment. What is your view on this issue? What are the arguments in defense of religion as the essential producer of the high morality Murdoch points to in paragraph 7? Why might it be difficult for such a high morality to be produced by secular means? In a nonreligious context, what would ultimately support high morality?

2. One of Murdoch's assertions is that moral–religious views depend on the existence of evil, otherwise there can be no good behavior. This assertion is commonly made by those who insist on a Hegelian dialectic — a condition in which two opposites collide and a third force emerges. What would the world be like if there were no evil? Would moral behavior then be possible? Would immoral behavior be possible? Would all behavior be morally neutral? Explain.

3. What effects do poverty and the absence of opportunity have on individuals' senses of virtue? Do you agree with Murdoch that virtue "may be seen as a self-indulgent luxury" (para. 2)? Why or why not? Should bourgeois concepts of morality be applied to those without hope of change in their lives? Is morality dependent on social condition? Explain.

4. In paragraph 3 Murdoch states, "Dutifulness could be an account of a morality with no hint of religion." Do you agree? She is obviously tentative in her statement. Examine your own sense of duty and that of someone you know and decide how much duty — as well as the expression of dutiful acts — satisfies our concept of a true morality.

5. Murdoch implies at the end of paragraph 3 that certain political complexities suggest there might be a need to have "clear rigid rules" of behavior in order to establish a morality. She implies that even clerics are viewing contemporary moral standards as flexible, perhaps alterable in some circumstances. How do you feel? Should morality follow the "rules" approach of the Ten Commandments? Or is there a more flexible, "realistic" alternative? Explain.

6. What do you consider virtuous behavior? Try to be as specific as possible. Do you find it difficult to apply your virtues in everyday life? Why or why not? To what extent do you feel an individual's religious beliefs dictate his or her virtuousness? Is religious faith an accurate indicator of virtue? Why or why not? What is Murdoch's view of this issue?

7. **CONNECTIONS**   Aristotle's disregard for religious issues in his position on ethics and morality (p. 688) might disappoint Murdoch. However, as a professional philosopher, Murdoch knew Aristotle's work thoroughly and respected it; she considered the *Nichomachean Ethics* to be a major statement guiding modern ethicists. Therefore, though she found much to agree with him in this essay, she naturally disagreed with him on religion. How can you reconcile these authors' disagreement using the principles that Murdoch defends in her essay? How might she have amended Aristotle's essay to make it more compatible with her views?

8. **CONNECTIONS**   Which of the selections in this section would most satisfy Murdoch's sense of the nature of morality and the relation of morality to religion? Who among these writers is most sympathetic to her views? Is she sympathetic to Martin Luther King Jr.'s ideas in "Letter from Birmingham Jail" (p. 252)? Does she share anything in common with Hsün Tzu in his "Man's Nature Is Evil" (p. 707)? Choose one and compare their views.

CAROL
GILLIGAN

Concepts of Self and Morality

C AROL GILLIGAN (b. 1936) is professor of education at New York University. She concentrates on issues in psychology and has made important contributions to theories concerning the ways in which women develop differently from men from childhood to adulthood. In 1997, she received the Heinz Award in the Human Condition. Her work has involved various aspects of psychological development, but one important focus has been the development of the individual's moral nature. In addressing these issues, she has examined the work of some of the world's most important psychologists, such as Sigmund Freud (1856–1939), Jean Piaget (1896–1980), Erik Erikson (1902–1994), and her own teacher, Lawrence Kohlberg (1927–1987). As she demonstrates in her discussion, the work of these men in establishing parameters of social and moral development depended almost entirely on studying boys, not girls. Gilligan suggests that the differences in early development between boys and girls makes those observations of limited value.

Gilligan's book *In a Different Voice: Psychological Theory and Women's Development* (1982) was the result of many years of research on the ways in which women treat the relational aspects of life differently from men — in part because of the different ways in which girls and boys are raised. Her work establishes the need to account appropriately for women's development by examining how women are socialized in school and at home.

Some of the factors that appear to impede women's success, Gilligan finds, actually confer strength on them. For example, the nature of boys' games differs from that of girls' because boys accept competition — including the need for one party to lose while another wins — as a natural course, provided the rules are followed carefully. Girls tend to treat rules as more elastic if they interfere with the pleasure of the games. This pattern, according to some male psychologists, tends to make it difficult for women to achieve success

---

From *In a Different Voice: Psychological Theory and the Women's Movement.*

in later life. Gilligan, however, explains that this pattern actually helps women succeed on a deeper personal level in ways that men do not normally achieve, especially in midlife when both sexes better understand the need for intimacy and closeness.

Gilligan's efforts to move psychologists away from using only male-based data for establishing norms of behavior and development seem like common sense. Why, then, did people not consider this previously? One reason is that when Gilligan was formulating her ideas in the 1970s, many feminists felt that establishing key differences between men and women would only fuel the controversy about whether women and men should be treated equally. If there was to be complete fairness in gender relations, they reasoned, the false distinctions that Mary Wollstonecraft and her twentieth-century counterparts felt were holding women back would only be accentuated. Fair treatment of the sexes, they thought, demanded that the sexes be considered as more alike than different.

Gilligan fought against this tide at some risk, but her psychological model eventually won out by helping to promote the view that French philosopher Simone de Beauvoir (1908–1986) supported: avoiding the judging of women by men's standards. In Beauvoir's view, men tend to judge women as the Other, or as not-men, rather than as women with their own natures and identities. Gilligan's efforts moved this discourse on gender to a new level by doing what seems natural and reasonable in retrospect: studying the way girls interact and seeing how that interaction is different from that of boys. As one commentator observed, Gilligan "began by posing a deceptively simple question: What are we missing by not listening to half the population?" The answer was a great deal.

GILLIGAN'S RHETORIC

Gilligan relies on testimony in the early part of this selection. She has gathered some comments by female students about their thoughts on what is moral and what constitutes moral behavior. From these samples, and those from earlier studies, she begins an analysis that aims to show how women reflect on the issues of ethics and ethical decisions. One point she makes is that it was common for many of these women to assume major decisions in their life would be made by men, such as fathers, husbands, and clergymen. And since ethical behavior may be defined in terms of choices and decisions, it was natural for these women to defer to their judgment.

However, when acting on their own and making decisions on their own, women displayed a pattern of action that aimed at fairness, equality, empathy, and the avoidance of hurting others. The question she raises is whether or not these qualities are the same as those of men facing similar ethical decisions. If competitiveness is a male quality, then it may be that males can tolerate the fact that someone may have to lose in the competition and thus be hurt. The women and students Gilligan quotes may, in emphasizing fairness and empathy, have a different way of looking at life.

Another kind of testimony characteristic of Gilligan's writing is her reference to literary works. In paragraph 10, she refers to Henrik Ibsen (1828–1906) and his play

A Doll's House, the most famous play of its time proclaiming independence and equality for women. Nora Helmer, the heroine, acted on her own to save her husband and was condemned by him because she had not acted ethically, according to his standards. Maggie Tulliver (paras. 12 and 13), in George Eliot's (1819–1880) novel *The Mill on the Floss*, seems to apply an ethical standard that respects her as a woman rather than applying the masculine standards of her brother.

Gilligan also confronts the issues involved in abortion, an ethical and moral decision that most affects women. Again, she gathers some testimony from women who have had or have considered abortions and examined their reasons for making their decisions. The question of the relation between self and other is central to this issue, and Gilligan makes an effort to understand how women confront it. In paragraph 9, Gilligan says, "The essence of moral decision is the exercise of choice and the willingness to accept responsibility for that choice." This selection focuses on that point primarily from the point of view of women.

⠏ PREREADING QUESTIONS: WHAT TO READ FOR

The following prereading questions may help you anticipate key issues in the discussion of Carol Gilligan's "Concepts of Self and Morality." Keeping them in mind during your first reading of the selection should help focus your attention.

1. How do most of Gilligan's students define morality?

2. How do most of Gilligan's students treat the question of personal responsibility?

3. Why does Gilligan say "the critical moral issue of hurting" is central to abortion (para. 18)?

Concepts of Self and Morality

A college student, responding to the question "If you had to say what morality meant to you, how would you sum it up?" replies: 1

> When I think of the word *morality*, I think of obligations. I usually think of it as conflicts between personal desires and social things, social considerations, or personal desires of yourself versus personal desires of another person or people or whatever. Morality is that whole realm of how you decide these conflicts. A moral person is one who would decide by placing themselves more often than not as equals. A truly moral person would always consider another person as their equal . . .

In a situation of social interaction, something is morally wrong where the individual ends up screwing a lot of people. And it is morally right when everyone comes out better off.

Yet when asked if she can think of someone whom she considers a genuinely moral person, she replies, "Well, immediately I think of Albert Schweitzer, because he has obviously given his life to help others." Obligation and sacrifice override the ideal of equality, setting up a basic contradiction in her thought.

Another undergraduate responds to the question "What does it mean to say   2 something is morally right or wrong?" by also speaking first of responsibilities and obligations:

It has to do with responsibilities and obligations and values, mainly values . . . In my life situation I relate morality with interpersonal relation- ships that have to do with respect for the other person and myself. (*Why respect other people?*) Because they have a consciousness or feelings that can be hurt, an awareness that can be hurt.

The concern about hurting others persists as a major theme in the responses of two other women students to the question "Why be moral?"

Millions of people have to live together peacefully. I personally don't want to hurt other people. That's a real criterion, a main criterion for me. It underlies my sense of justice. It isn't nice to inflict pain. I empathize with anyone in pain. Not hurting others is important in my own private morals. Years ago I would have jumped out of a window not to hurt my boyfriend. That was pathological. Even today, though, I want approval and love, and I don't want enemies. Maybe that's why there is morality—so people can win approval, love, and friendship.

My main principle is not hurting other people as long as you aren't going against your own conscience and as long as you remain true to yourself . . . There are many moral issues, such as abortion, the draft, kill- ing, stealing, monogamy. If something is a controversial issue like these, then I always say it is up to the individual. The individual has to decide and then follow his own conscience. There are no moral absolutes. Laws are pragmatic instruments, but they are not absolutes. A viable society can't make exceptions all the time, but I would personally . . . I'm afraid I'm heading for some big crisis with my boyfriend someday, and someone will get hurt, and he'll get more hurt than I will. I feel an obligation not to hurt him, but also an obligation not to lie. I don't know if it is possible not to lie and not to hurt.

The common thread that runs through these statements is the wish not to   3 hurt others and the hope that in morality lies a way of solving conflicts so that no one will be hurt. This theme is independently introduced by each of the four women as the most specific item in their response to a most general question. The moral person is one who helps others; goodness is service, meeting one's obligations and responsibilities to others, if possible without sacrificing oneself. While the first of the four women ends by denying the conflict she initially introduced, the last woman anticipates a conflict between remaining true to herself and adhering to her principle of not hurting others. The dilemma that would test the limits of this judgment would be one where helping others is seen to be at the price of hurting the self.

The reticence about taking stands on "controversial issues," a willingness   4
to "make exceptions all the time," is echoed repeatedly by other college women:

> I never feel that I can condemn anyone else. I have a very relativistic position. The basic idea that I cling to is the sanctity of human life. I am inhibited about impressing my beliefs on others.
>
> I could never argue that my belief on a moral question is anything that another person should accept. I don't believe in absolutes. If there is an absolute for moral decisions, it is human life.

Or as a thirty-one-year-old graduate student says when explaining why she would find it difficult to steal a drug to save her own life, despite her belief that it would be right to steal for another: "It's just very hard to defend yourself against the rules. I mean, we live by consensus, and if you take an action simply for yourself, by yourself, there's no consensus there, and that is relatively indefensible in this society now."

What emerges in these voices is a sense of vulnerability that impedes these   5
women from taking a stand, what George Eliot[1] regards as the girl's "susceptibility" to adverse judgments by others, which stems from her lack of power and consequent inability "to do something in the world." The unwillingness to make moral judgments that Kohlberg and Kramer (1969) and Kohlberg and Gilligan (1971)[2] associate with the adolescent crisis of identity and belief takes the form in men of calling into question the concept of morality itself. But these women's reluctance to judge stems rather from their uncertainty about their right to make moral statements, or perhaps from the price for them that such judgment seems to entail.

When women feel excluded from direct participation in society, they see   6
themselves as subject to a consensus or judgment made and enforced by the men on whose protection and support they depend and by whose names they

---

[1] **George Eliot (1819–1880)**   Pen name for Mary Ann Evans, a novelist.

[2] **Kohlberg and Gilligan**   A reference to a jointly authored article between Lawrence Kohlberg (1927–1987) and Carol Gilligan called "The Adolescent as a Philosopher: The Discovery of the Self in a Post–conventional World."

are known. A divorced middle-aged woman, mother of adolescent daughters, resident of a sophisticated university community, tells the story:

> As a woman, I feel I never understood that I was a person, that I could make decisions and I had a right to make decisions. I always felt that that belonged to my father or my husband in some way, or church, which was always represented by a male clergyman. They were the three men in my life: father, husband, and clergyman, and they had much more to say about what I should or shouldn't do. They were really authority figures which I accepted. It only lately has occurred to me that I never even rebelled against it, and my girls are much more conscious of this, not in the militant sense, but just in the recognizing sense . . . I still let things happen to me rather than make them happen, than make choices, although I know all about choices. I know the procedures and the steps and all. (*Do you have any clues about why this might be true?*) Well, I think in one sense there is less responsibility involved. Because if you make a dumb decision, you have to take the rap. If it happens to you, well, you can complain about it. I think that if you don't grow up feeling that you ever have any choices, you don't have the sense that you have emotional responsibility. With this sense of choice comes this sense of responsibility.

The essence of moral decision is the exercise of choice and the willingness to accept responsibility for that choice. To the extent that women perceive themselves as having no choice, they correspondingly excuse themselves from the responsibility that decision entails. Childlike in the vulnerability of their dependence and consequent fear of abandonment, they claim to wish only to please, but in return for their goodness they expect to be loved and cared for. This, then, is an "altruism" always at risk, for it presupposes an innocence constantly in danger of being compromised by an awareness of the trade-off that has been made. Asked to describe herself, a college senior responds:

> I have heard of the onion-skin theory. I see myself as an onion, as a block of different layers. The external layers are for people that I don't know that well, the agreeable, the social, and as you go inward, there are more sides for people I know that I show. I am not sure about the innermost, whether there is a core, or whether I have just picked up everything as I was growing up, these different influences. I think I have a neutral attitude toward myself, but I do think in terms of good and bad. Good—I try to be considerate and thoughtful of other people, and I try to be fair in situations and be tolerant. I use the words, but I try and work them out practically. Bad things—I am not sure if they are bad, if they are altruistic or I am doing them basically for approval of other people. (*Which things*

are these?) The values that I try to act out. They deal mostly with inter-personal relations . . . If I were doing things for approval, it would be a very tenuous thing. If I didn't get the right feedback, there might go all my values.

Ibsen's play *A Doll's House*[3] depicts the explosion of just such a world   8
through the eruption of a moral dilemma that calls into question the notion of goodness which lies at its center. Nora, the "squirrel wife," living with her hus-band as she lived with her father, puts into action this conception of goodness as sacrifice and, with the best of intentions, takes the law into her own hands. The crisis that ensues, most painfully for her in the repudiation of that goodness by the very person who was its recipient and beneficiary, causes her to reject the suicide that she initially saw as its ultimate expression and to choose instead to seek new and firmer answers to questions of identity and moral belief.

The availability of choice, and with it the onus of responsibility, has now   9
invaded the most private sector of the woman's domain and threatens a sim-ilar explosion. For centuries, women's sexuality anchored them in passivity, in a receptive rather than an active stance, where the events of conception and childbirth could be controlled only by a withholding in which their own sexual needs were either denied or sacrificed. That such a sacrifice entailed a cost to their intelligence as well was seen by Freud (1908)[4] when he tied the "undoubted intellectual inferiority of so many women" to "the inhibition of thought necessitated by sexual suppression" (p. 199). The strategies of with-holding and denial that women have employed in the politics of sexual rela-tions appear similar to their evasion or withholding of judgment in the moral realm. The hesitance of college students to assert a belief even in the value of human life, like the reluctance to claim one's sexuality, bespeaks a self uncer-tain of its strength, unwilling to deal with choice, and avoiding confrontation.

Thus women have traditionally deferred to the judgment of men, although   10
often while intimating a sensibility of their own which is at variance with that judgment. Maggie Tulliver in *The Mill on the Floss*[5] responds to the accusa-tions that ensue from the discovery of her secretly continued relationship with Phillip Wakeham by acceding to her brother's moral judgment, while at the same time asserting a different set of standards by which she attests to her own superiority:

I don't want to defend myself . . . I know I've been wrong—often contin-ually. But yet, sometimes when I have done wrong, it has been because

---

[3] *A Doll's House*   A play with a feminist theme by Henrik Ibsen (1828–1906).

[4] **Freud**   Sigmund Freud (1856–1939), author of "Civilized Sexual Morality and Modern Nervous Illness."

[5] *The Mill on the Floss*   A novel (1860) by George Eliot.

I have feelings that you would be the better for if you had them. If *you* were in fault ever, if you had done anything very wrong, I should be sorry for the pain it brought you; I should not want punishment to be heaped on you.

Maggie's protest is an eloquent assertion of the age-old split between thinking and feeling, justice and mercy, that underlies many of the clichés and stereotypes concerning the difference between the sexes. But considered from another point of view, her protest signifies a moment of confrontation, replacing a former evasion. This confrontation reveals two modes of judging, two different constructions of the moral domain—one traditionally associated with masculinity and the public world of social power, the other with femininity and the privacy of domestic interchange. The developmental ordering of these two points of view has been to consider the masculine as more adequate than the feminine and thus as replacing the feminine when the individual moves toward maturity. The reconciliation of these two modes, however, is not clear.

Norma Haan's (1975) research on college students and Constance Holstein's (1976)[6] three-year study of adolescents and their parents indicate that the moral judgments of women differ from those of men in the greater extent to which women's judgments are tied to feelings of empathy and compassion and are concerned with the resolution of real as opposed to hypothetical dilemmas. However, as long as the categories by which development is assessed are derived from research on men, divergence from the masculine standard can be seen only as a failure of development. As a result, the thinking of women is often classified with that of children. The absence of alternative criteria that might better encompass the development of women, however, points not only to the limitations of theories framed by men and validated by research samples disproportionately male and adolescent, but also to the diffidence prevalent among women, their reluctance to speak publicly in their own voice, given the constraints imposed on them by their lack of power and the politics of relations between the sexes.

In order to go beyond the question, "How much like men do women think, how capable are they of engaging in the abstract and hypothetical construction of reality?" it is necessary to identify and define developmental criteria that encompass the categories of women's thought. Haan points out the necessity to derive such criteria from the resolution of the "more frequently occurring, real-life moral dilemmas of interpersonal, empathic, fellow-feeling concerns" (p. 34) which have long been the center of women's moral concern. But to derive developmental criteria from the language of women's moral discourse,

---

[6] **Norma Haan . . . Constance Holstein**   Authors of many studies on morality and gender differences in moral development.

it is necessary first to see whether women's construction of the moral domain relies on a language different from that of men and one that deserves equal credence in the definition of development. This in turn requires finding places where women have the power to choose and thus are willing to speak in their own voice.

When birth control and abortion provide women with effective means for   14 controlling their fertility, the dilemma of choice enters a central arena of women's lives. Then the relationships that have traditionally defined women's identities and framed their moral judgments no longer flow inevitably from their reproductive capacity but become matters of decision over which they have control. Released from the passivity and reticence of a sexuality that binds them in dependence, women can question with Freud what it is that they want and can assert their own answers to that question. However, while society may affirm publicly the woman's right to choose for herself, the exercise of such choice brings her privately into conflict with the conventions of femininity, particularly the moral equation of goodness with self-sacrifice. Although independent assertion in judgment and action is considered to be the hallmark of adulthood, it is rather in their care and concern for others that women have both judged themselves and been judged.

The conflict between self and other thus constitutes the central moral   15 problem for women, posing a dilemma whose resolution requires a reconciliation between femininity and adulthood. In the absence of such a reconciliation, the moral problem cannot be resolved. The "good woman" masks assertion in evasion, denying responsibility by claiming only to meet the needs of others, while the "bad woman" forgoes or renounces the commitments that bind her in self-deception and betrayal. It is precisely this dilemma—the conflict between compassion and autonomy, between virtue and power—which the feminine voice struggles to resolve in its effort to reclaim the self and to solve the moral problem in such a way that no one is hurt.

When a woman considers whether to continue or abort a pregnancy, she   16 contemplates a decision that affects both self and others and engages directly the critical moral issue of hurting. Since the choice is ultimately hers and therefore one for which she is responsible, it raises precisely those questions of judgment that have been most problematic for women. Now she is asked whether she wishes to interrupt that stream of life which for centuries has immersed her in the passivity of dependence while at the same time imposing on her the responsibility for care. Thus the abortion decision brings to the core of feminine apprehension, to what Joan Didion[7] (1972) calls "the irreconcilable difference of it—that sense of living one's deepest life underwater, that dark

---

[7] **Joan Didion (b. 1934)**   Acclaimed author of "The Women's Movement," a landmark 1972 essay printed in the *New York Times*.

involvement with blood and birth and death," the adult questions of responsibility and choice.

How women deal with such choices was the subject of the abortion study, designed to clarify the ways in which women construct and resolve abortion decisions. Twenty-nine women, ranging in age from fifteen to thirty-three and diverse in ethnic background and social class, were referred for the study by abortion and pregnancy counseling services. The women participated in the study for a variety of reasons—some to gain further clarification with respect to a decision about which they were in conflict, some in response to a counselor's concern about repeated abortions, and others to contribute to ongoing research. Although the pregnancies occurred under a variety of circumstances in the lives of these women, certain commonalities were discerned. The adolescents often failed to use birth control because they denied or discredited their capacity to bear children. Some women became pregnant due to the omission of contraceptive measures in circumstances where intercourse had not been anticipated. Some pregnancies coincided with efforts on the part of the women to end a relationship and may be seen as a manifestation of ambivalence or as a way of putting the relationship to the ultimate test of commitment. For these women, the pregnancy appeared to be a way of testing truth, making the baby an ally in the search for male support and protection or, that failing, a companion victim of male rejection. Finally, some women became pregnant as a result either of a failure of birth control or of a joint decision that was later reconsidered. Of the twenty-nine women, four decided to have the baby, two miscarried, twenty-one chose abortion, and two who were in doubt about the decision at the time of the interview could not be contacted for the follow-up research.

17

The women were interviewed twice, first at the time they were making the decision, in the first trimester of a confirmed pregnancy, and then at the end of the following year. The referral procedure required that there be an interval between the woman's contacting a counselor or clinic and the time the abortion was performed. Given this factor and the fact that some counselors saw participation in the study as an effective means of crisis-intervention, there is reason to believe that the women interviewed were in greater than usual conflict over the decision. Since the study focused on the relation between judgment and action rather than on the issue of abortion per se, no effort was made to select a sample that would be representative of women considering, seeking, or having abortions. Thus the findings pertain to the different ways in which women think about dilemmas in their lives rather than to the ways in which women in general think about the abortion choice.

18

In the initial part of the interview, the women were asked to discuss the decision they faced, how they were dealing with it, the alternatives they were considering, their reasons both for and against each option, the people

19

involved, the conflicts entailed, and the ways in which making this decision affected their views of themselves and their relationships with others. In the second part of the interview, the women were asked to resolve three hypothetical moral dilemmas, including the Heinz dilemma from Kohlberg's research.

In extending Piaget's[8] description of children's moral judgment to the   20 moral judgment of adolescents and adults, Kohlberg (1976) distinguishes three perspectives on moral conflict and choice. Tying moral development in adolescence to the growth of reflective thought at that time, Kohlberg terms these three views of morality preconventional, conventional, and postconventional, to reflect the expansion in moral understanding from an individual to a societal to a universal point of view. In this scheme, conventional morality, or the equation of the right or good with the maintenance of existing social norms and values, is always the point of departure.

Whereas preconventional moral judgment denotes an inability to construct   21 a shared or societal viewpoint, postconventional judgment transcends that vision. Preconventional judgment is egocentric and derives moral constructs from individual needs; conventional judgment is based on the shared norms and values that sustain relationships, groups, communities, and societies; and postconventional judgment adopts a reflective perspective on societal values and constructs moral principles that are universal in application.

This shift in perspective toward increasingly differentiated, comprehen-   22 sive, and reflective forms of thought appears in women's responses to both actual and hypothetical dilemmas. But just as the conventions that shape women's moral judgment differ from those that apply to men, so also women's definition of the moral domain diverges from that derived from studies of men. Women's construction of the moral problem as a problem of care and responsibility in relationships rather than as one of rights and rules ties the development of their moral thinking to changes in their understanding of responsibility and relationships, just as the conception of morality as justice ties development to the logic of equality and reciprocity. Thus the logic underlying an ethic of care is a psychological logic of relationships, which contrasts with the formal logic of fairness that informs the justice approach.

Women's constructions of the abortion dilemma in particular reveal the   23 existence of a distinct moral language whose evolution traces a sequence of development. This is the language of selfishness and responsibility, which defines the moral problem as one of obligation to exercise care and avoid hurt. The inflicting of hurt is considered selfish and immoral in its reflection of unconcern, while the expression of care is seen as the fulfillment of moral responsibility. The reiterative use by the women of the words *selfish* and *responsible* in

---

[8] **Piaget**   Jean Piaget (1896–1980), an influential psychologist who specialized in childhood development.

talking about moral conflict and choice, given the underlying moral orientation that this language reflects, sets the women apart from the men whom Kohlberg studied and points toward a different understanding of moral development.

The three moral perspectives revealed by the abortion decision study denote a sequence in the development of the ethic of care. These different views of care and the transitions between them emerged from an analysis of the ways in which the women used moral language — words such as *should, ought, better, right, good,* and *had,* by the changes and shifts that appeared in their thinking, and by the way in which they reflected on and judged their thought. In this sequence, an initial focus on caring for the self in order to ensure survival is followed by a transitional phase in which this judgment is criticized as selfish. The criticism signals a new understanding of the connection between self and others which is articulated by the concept of responsibility. The elaboration of this concept of responsibility and its fusion with a maternal morality that seeks to ensure care for the dependent and unequal characterizes the second perspective. At this point, the good is equated with caring for others. However, when only others are legitimized as the recipients of the woman's care, the exclusion of herself gives rise to problems in relationships, creating a disequilibrium that initiates the second transition. The equation of conformity with care, in its conventional definition, and the illogic of the inequality between other and self, lead to a reconsideration of relationships in an effort to sort out the confusion between self-sacrifice and care inherent in the conventions of feminine goodness. The third perspective focuses on the dynamics of relationships and dissipates the tension between selfishness and responsibility through a new understanding of the interconnection between other and self. Care becomes the self-chosen principle of a judgment that remains psychological in its concern with relationships and response but becomes universal in its condemnation of exploitation and hurt. Thus a progressively more adequate understanding of the psychology of human relationships — an increasing differentiation of self and other and a growing comprehension of the dynamics of social interaction — informs the development of an ethic of care. This ethic, which reflects a cumulative knowledge of human relationships, evolves around a central insight, that self and other are interdependent. The different ways of thinking about this connection or the different modes of its apprehension mark the three perspectives and their transitional phases. In this sequence, the fact of interconnection informs the central, recurring recognition that just as the incidence of violence is in the end destructive to all, so the activity of care enhances both others and self.

In its simplest construction, the abortion decision centers on the self. The concern is pragmatic and the issue is survival. The woman focuses on taking care of herself because she feels that she is all alone. From this perspective, *should* is undifferentiated from *would,* and other people influence the decision only through their power to affect its consequences. Susan, an eighteen-year-old, asked what she thought when she found herself pregnant, replies: "I really didn't think anything except that I didn't want it. (*Why was that?*) I didn't want it, I wasn't ready for it, and next year will be my last year and I want to go to school." Asked if there is a right decision or a right way to decide about abortion, she says: "There is no right decision. (*Why?*) I didn't want it." For her, the question of rightness would emerge only if her own needs were in conflict; then she would have to decide which needs should take precedence. This is the dilemma of Joan, another eighteen-year-old, who sees having a baby not only as a way of increasing her freedom by providing "the perfect chance to get married and move away from home," but also as restricting her freedom "to do a lot of things."

⚏ QUESTIONS FOR CRITICAL READING

1. Why does Gilligan emphasize empathy?

2. What do interpersonal relations have to do with morality?

3. Why is hurt an important ethical consideration?

4. When can empathy become pathological?

5. Why might some women refuse to take a stand on controversial subjects?

6. How has possessing birth control changed the decisions women can make?

7. Why is "the thinking of women . . . often classified with that of children" (para. 14)?

8. What is "an ethic of care" (para. 24)?

⚏ SUGGESTIONS FOR CRITICAL WRITING

1. Examine the examples in paragraph 6. Gilligan says they illustrate "The reticence about taking stands on 'controversial issues,' [and] a willingness to 'make exceptions all the time.'" Exactly what does she mean by this? Explain from the examples what Gilligan means, and explore through your own interviews or your own observations about how women make their stand on controversial issues. Do you agree with Gilligan? How different are women's views from those of men?

2. The second example in paragraph 4 talks about "heading for some big crisis with my boyfriend someday, and someone will get hurt." What does this example illustrate about how women make ethical decisions? From personal experience or from observation, how do you deal with the ethical decisions about hurting someone in a romantic relationship? Assuming a breakup, what are the ethical concerns that strike you as most important?

3. Some of the students Gilligan quotes imply that they feel there are no moral absolutes. If you agree with that view, how can you construct an ethical position that will guide you through life with no absolute moral touchstone to test your behavior? If you do not agree with that view, explain what you feel are the moral absolutes that should guide people today. In either event, how do you think our society regards the question of moral absolutes? Do women have a different sense of moral absolutes than men do?

4. After reading and reflecting on the answers that the students gave to Gilligan's question, write a short essay that answers the following question: "If you had to describe what morality meant to you, how would you sum it up?" In the course of your response to this question, try using one of Gilligan's rhetorical strategies by referring to the statements of other students, literary examples, or the research of scholars on the study of ethics and interpersonal relationships.

5. Much of the research on the difference between the moral judgments of women and men depends on studies conducted in the 1970s (see para. 14). More than forty-five years later, much has changed in gender and sexual issues that might not have been imagined then. Do what Gilligan did, and ask a basic moral question of as many people as you can get a response from, and write an essay that takes a stand on whether or not Gilligan's views about the differences between men's moral choices and women's moral choices are pronounced or slight. How well does that older research hold up?

6. Beginning with paragraph 19, Gilligan describes "the abortion study," which involved following twenty-nine women who faced the problem of whether or not to have an abortion. She uses this study as an example of how women make ethical and moral decisions. Write an essay that summarizes what she tells us about this study and what she tells us about how women react to this particular moral choice. Judging from your own personal observations of women who have had to face this choice, how much of what Gilligan tells us seems to be accurate? Based on your observations, what could you add to what Gilligan says? Is abortion all about "the critical moral issue of hurting" (para. 18)?

7. **CONNECTIONS** What insights does your reading of Mary Wollstonecraft (p. 195) and/or Virginia Woolf (p. 220) provide in helping to understand what Gilligan is saying in her selection? How does Wollstonecraft explain the circumstances in which women have been raised and how they have been expected to behave in society? Do her revelations have a meaningful connection with what Gilligan says about the differences in the way women perceive ethical questions? In what ways does the hypothetical situation in which Shakespeare's sister finds herself help explain how Gilligan's students interpret the question of morality?

MICHAEL GAZZANIGA

Toward a Universal Ethics

MICHAEL GAZZANIGA (b. 1939) is professor of psychology at the University of California at Santa Barbara. He is among the most distinguished scientists currently studying the relationship of the mind to the brain. When he was a student at the California Institute of Technology, Gazzaniga's mentor was Roger Sperry, who pioneered important research into the split-brain phenomenon. Sperry relieved severely impaired sufferers of epilepsy by severing the corpus callosum, the informational tissues connecting the left hemisphere to the right hemisphere of the brain. Resultant research at first seemed to indicate that the two hemispheres were so distinct as to almost represent different personalities. Ultimately, research demonstrated that the left hemisphere is usually specialized to deal with language, writing, reading, and math skills, while the right hemisphere is usually specialized to deal with spatial relations and visual, musical, and artistic skills. Gazzaniga's early book *The Bisected Brain* (1970) was among the first general explanations of the implications of this body of brain research.

Since then, various kinds of brain analysis using electromagnetic imaging and other techniques have broadened our understanding of the function of the brain. Research has found with some precision the locations in the brain that govern memory and the acquisition of memories, the areas excited by certain emotions, and the rate of development of important areas of the brain, such as the prefrontal lobe, which governs social and antisocial behavior. The fact that the prefrontal lobe does not develop fully until about twenty-one years of age has been taken as an indication that youthful irrationality is to some extent a matter of immature brain development, not just a matter of character failure.

Gazzaniga is prominent as a cognitive neuroscientist, which is to say as a student of the interaction of the brain and the mind it supports. He has served on the President's

---

From *The Ethical Brain.*

Council for Bioethics, advising the government on a wide variety of ethical issues arising from brain research. One ethical issue, for example, has to do with the concern that there may be people who are "hardwired" to be antisocial and potentially criminal. Some scientists contend that evolutionary forces made some brains naturally prone to violence as a means of survival. Such a characteristic may be helpful in the wild, but in a complex social system that behavior is a deficit. The result is that philosophers and scientists are continually debating the question of how ethically responsible a person who is naturally violent can be.

In his research, Gazzaniga has concluded that even such evolutionary traits do not mean that we are deprived of free will. He feels that people are socialized in ways that may make them prone to violence, but that the very act of socialization implies that people can control themselves if they wish to. One's will is not overridden by one's inclinations. Of course, this is a very hotly contested opinion, particularly in court, where the temporary insanity defense is often used as an excuse for violent behavior. Brain lesions are sometimes blamed for irrational behavior, too, but Gazzaniga has determined that not even lesions can excuse criminal behavior. Yet there are documented instances of patients with brain tumors whose growing masses resulted in changed behavior and personality.

Gazzaniga has written widely on the interconnected subjects of the mind, the brain, and the will. His book *Mind Matters: How Mind and Brain Interact to Create Our Conscious Lives* (1988) addresses many of the problems that have attracted and baffled neuroscientists concerned with consciousness, one of the most intractable puzzles of contemporary science. He reviews the research and the resultant understanding of the nature of the brain as a result of studies of split-brain patients as well as studies of the effects of brain chemistry on behavior. His recent book, *Who's in Charge? Free Will and the Science of the Brain* (2011), examines current research that demonstrates that the brain is a complex of many subsystems that operate at times independently and automatically. As a result, Gazzaniga asks how all of these separately functioning systems can aggregate into a single person who can imagine a freedom of will. Like in much of his earlier work, he is pursuing the issue of how the brain functions to produce a sense of self that we feel is unique and independent.

The following selection is from *The Ethical Brain* (2005), which approaches the issues raised by psychologists who have appropriated neuroscience and tend to connect psychological disorders with anomalies in the physiology of the brain. Some research implies a form of determinism, a concept that has stimulated legal debate over whether humans really have a free will. A number of important studies imply that the brain, rather than a person's will, can determine a person's action, at least to some extent. Gazzaniga reviews the research and cannot give credence to such a view. In his book, he explores the way the brain develops and ages. He takes on the legal issues centered on genetics and on brain enhancement. Finally, he addresses the question of an ethics that takes into consideration what we know about the physiology of the brain.

GAZZANIGA'S RHETORIC

Gazzaniga is exploring a question that may have no absolute answer — yet. He is asking a serious question: Is ethical behavior hardwired in the brain through years of evolution? To begin answering, he has to take into consideration the moral questions raised and answered over the centuries by philosophers and religious leaders who created what he calls "stories" about the way we should behave. These early thinkers were working in what Gazzaniga might consider "the dark" because they knew nothing about the science of brain development and brain systems. Gazzaniga explains that modern observations of the brain indicate that specific responses and resulting behavior can be tracked with some clarity by brain scans. Moreover, specific areas of brain function seem to be responsible for various kinds of actions that all people perform. The seat of personality and the areas involved in moral choice are usually centered in the prefrontal lobe of the brain, while other areas are supportive and functional in decision making. Indeed, Gazzaniga refers to the brain as a "decision-making device" (para. 12).

In the beginning of his essay, Gazzaniga explores the question of evolution and our inheritance of genes from the earliest human population, when there were a mere ten thousand people on the planet. We have inherited their genes, and our genes are virtually the same as theirs. That raises the question, How much of our response when we make moral judgments is built into our brains as a matter of survival? In the process of considering this question, Gazzaniga refers to a great many authorities in the world of neuroscience. This is a key part of his rhetorical strategy, and it is effective because, as a scientist, he feels it is his responsibility to represent the work of other scientists who may or may not agree with him (most are working in similar scientific areas, but some are not). In any event, his rhetorical stance demands that he refer to the testimony of experts and not just tell a "story."

The value of moral empathy, the ability to respond to the distress of others, and the willingness to come to the aid of others are useful to evolutionary survival in the long run. As social animals, we survive when we help others survive. Gazzaniga refers to this as social neuroscience, tying the urge to behave ethically to the evolutionary power of our genes and the physiology of the brain. He devotes quite a bit of time at the end of the passage to the issue of "reading minds." By that, he means our ability to interact with others by imagining what they are possibly thinking, what they are doing, and what they may do. This is a skill that makes social intercourse possible and at the same time helps us secure in our environment. Without that skill, he implies, we would self-destruct and the species itself would not survive. Gazzaniga goes as far as to refer to mirror neurons that are "believed to be responsible for 'action understanding' — that is, understanding the actions of others" (para. 30).

Gazzaniga also explores the question of whether our moral decisions are more rational than they are intuitive. He points to gut instincts that propel people to make moral judgments and ethical decisions that are almost instantaneous. He also refers to some common ethical dilemmas, such as the "trolley problem" (para. 16), which involve making a decision that would influence the fate of either a small number of people or a large number of people. The rational issues in such problems are such that solving them involves thinking more than feeling. But Gazzaniga also establishes that there are emotional issues that combine with rational decisions to behave ethically. His point is that moral decisions have an emotional quotient that is measurable in brain scans.

His central concern is to decide whether on the basis of our evolution and the physiology of our brain there can be a universal ethics that transcends the limitations of our individual cultures. He hopes that scientific discoveries and scientific understandings will either replace or augment our dependence on "tales from the past."

✂ PREREADING QUESTIONS: WHAT TO READ FOR

The following prereading questions may help you anticipate key issues in the discussion of Michael Gazzaniga's "Toward a Universal Ethics." Keeping them in mind during your first reading should help focus your attention.

1. What is the relationship of ethics to the survival of the species?
2. What do studies of the physiology of the brain reveal about moral behavior?
3. Do people have an innate moral sense?

Toward a Universal Ethics

Ever-advancing human knowledge seeps into the assumptions of everyone on earth whether they like it or not. From Harvard Square to a remote village in Sri Lanka, people have concepts of a gene, a brain, the Internet, the good life. Affluent cultures and democracies gain from all this knowledge, even though the lessons of modern knowledge about the nature of the world may produce conflicts with some traditional beliefs. That is what is happening on the surface. Underneath these material gains is another, psychological reality. Modern knowledge is on a collision course with the ubiquitous personal spiritual belief systems of one kind or another that are held by billions of people. Putting it in secular terms, no one has told the kids yet there is no Santa Claus.

We are big animals, and only five thousand generations ago there were just ten thousand of us roaming the world. Our genes stem from those ten thousand people and are 99.9 percent the same. Ever since that time, we have been busy cooking up cultures and stumbling forward. Anyone who does not appreciate this fundamental fact of modern life is either clinging to heartfelt beliefs about the nature of life and the history of the world, or is quite simply out of the loop. This is the single most disturbing reality of modern-day citizenship and our notion of shared values.

Received wisdom — the thoughts of the giants of human history — is stunning, 3 captivating, and intelligent. But for the most part it is based on first guesses, as we know from current scientific and historical information. Aristotle, Socrates, Hume, Locke, Descartes, Aquinas, Darwin, Hobbes[1] — all put forward explanations of human nature that still resonate today. Their thinking about approaches to life are brilliant schemas for how the world must be, based on the information made available to them at the time, and are the products of clear-thinking people. Religious movements throughout human history produced moral codes and interpretations and stories about what it means to be human — indeed, what it means to exist at all. All are part of our rich past. The harsh, cold fact, however, is that these rich, metaphoric, engaging ideas — whether philosophical or religious — are stories, although some are based on more evidence than others. Even if you do not believe or accept this as a given, you should be aware that this is what every modern-day secular university is teaching, either implicitly or explicitly.

What is more fascinating to me is that even though new data provide sci- 4 entific and historical bases for new views about nature and our past, people can still disagree about whether there even *is* a human nature. As Steven Pinker[2] recently remarked before the President's Council on Bioethics, "In much of the 20th Century, there was a widespread denial of the existence of human nature in Western intellectual life, and I will just present three representative quotations. 'Man has no nature,' from the philosopher José Ortega y Gasset. 'Man has no instincts,' from the anthropologist and public intellectual Ashley Montagu. 'The human brain is capable of a full range of behaviors and predisposed to none,' from the evolutionary biologist Stephen Jay Gould."[3]

Yet we know there *is* something we call human nature, with fixed qualities 5 and inevitable expression in any number of situations. We know that some fixed properties of mind come with us from the baby factory, that all humans possess certain skills and abilities other animals don't have, and that all of this makes up the human *condition*. And we now know that we are the products of an evolutionary process that has shaped our species, for better or for worse.

---

[1] **Aristotle . . . Hobbes** Philosophers ranging from early Greeks to nineteenth-century thinkers who posited theories of human behavior and also expressed or implied moral theories.

[2] **Steven Pinker (b. 1954)** Professor of psychology at Harvard University and a student of the evolutionary nature of the language instinct.

[3] **Ortega y Gasset . . . Gould** José Ortega y Gasset (1883–1955) was one of Spain's greatest modern philosophers; Ashley Montagu (1905–1999) was a prominent anthropologist; Stephen Jay Gould (1941–2002) was professor of zoology at Harvard University and author of books studying evidence relating to Darwin's evolutionary theories.

We are big animals. The rest of our stories about our origins are just that, stories that comfort, cajole, and even motivate — but stories nonetheless.

This leaves us in a quandary and with a task. The quandary is daunting: to understand that most of our current beliefs and moral systems derive from theories, perhaps based on the logic of what our species' best minds through the ages, reacting to life's events, could posit about the nature of reality. For those who realize and believe this, the task and the challenge of modern humans is to try to discern whether our highly evolved human nature and culture benefit from an underlying universal ethics, a moral response to life's challenges that has been a feature of our species from the beginning. The question is, Do we have an innate moral sense as a species, and if so, can we recognize and accept it on its own terms? It is not a good idea to kill because it is not a good idea to kill, not because God or Allah or Buddha said it was not a good idea to kill.

Guessing about Our Moral Sense

Until recently, the possibility that our species has a built-in moral sense, a basic human capacity to make judgments about right and wrong, has been argued more by assertion and analysis of human behavior than by demonstrated biological fact. Especially rare, if not missing entirely from the argument, has been the fact that we could not draw upon how the brain works in morally challenging situations. Modern social scientists can get only so far in their efforts to understand human behavior. James Q. Wilson[4] used analysis of social science research in his classic 1993 book, *The Moral Sense*, but admitted, "The truth, if it exists, is in the details . . . I am not trying to discover 'facts' that will prove 'values'; I am endeavoring to uncover the evolutionary, developmental, and cultural origins of our moral habits and our moral sense. But in discovering these origins, I suspect that we will encounter uniformities; and by revealing uniformities, I think that we can better appreciate what is general, nonarbitrary, and emotionally compelling about human nature."[5] Wilson, the distinguished political scientist from Harvard and now UCLA, suggested, "However much the scientific method is thought to be the enemy of morality, scientific findings provide substantial support for its existence and power."[6] Wilson cast an astonishingly wide net to make his case for an innate human moral sense. He reviewed not only the history of philosophy but also evolutionary theory, anthropology, criminology, psychology, and sociology. He concluded that no matter what

6

7

---

[4] **James Q. Wilson (1931–2012)**   Political scientist and professor of government at UCLA.

[5] Wilson, J. Q. (1993). *The Moral Sense* (New York: Free Press), p. 26. [Gazzaniga's note]

[6] Ibid., p. xii. [Gazzaniga's note]

intellectuals argue, there are certain universal, guiding moral instincts. In fact, they are so instinctual that they often get overlooked: "Much of the dispute over the existence of human universals has taken the form of a search for laws and stated practices. But what is most likely to be universal are those impulses that, because they are so common, scarcely need to be stated in the form of a rule . . ."[7] Highest among these are that all societies believe that murder and incest are wrong, that children are to be cared for and not abandoned, that we should not tell lies or break promises, and that we should be loyal to family.

Wilson rejected the idea that morality is purely a social construct—that we are constrained by the need to behave a certain way because of external factors: "For there to be a contract, whether to create a state or manage and exchange, there must first be a willingness to obey contracts; there must be in Durkheim's[8] phrase, some noncontractual elements of contract."   8

Wilson may have been prescient. A series of studies suggesting that there *is* a brain-based account of moral reasoning have burst onto the scientific scene. It has been found that regions of the brain normally active in emotional processing are activated with one kind of moral judgment but not another. Arguments that have raged for centuries about the nature of moral decisions and their sameness or difference are now quickly and distinctly resolved with modern brain imaging. The short form of the new results suggests that when someone is willing to *act* on a moral belief, it is because the emotional part of his or her brain has become active when considering the moral question at hand. Similarly, when a morally equivalent problem is presented that he or she decides not to act on, it is because the emotional part of the brain does not become active. This is a stunning development in human knowledge because it points the way toward figuring out how the brain's automatic response may predict our moral response.   9

Scanning for Moral Reasoning

First, to be able to assess moral reasoning, scientists have analyzed the psychology of different moral theories. In other words, they have asked what kinds of decisions or judgments a person needs to make in order to decide what actions to take. This careful assessment of moral reasoning is obviously tricky, and in a laboratory setting, ascertaining what kinds of decisions trigger what kinds of brain reactions is even trickier; but some clever researchers are doing just that.   10

Evolutionary psychology points out that moral reasoning is good for human survival—the ability to recognize a certain norm for behaving in society and to apply it to others and oneself helps one to survive and thrive. As   11

---

[7] Ibid., p. 18. [Gazzaniga's note]

[8] **Emile Durkheim (1858–1917)**   Considered the father of modern sociology.

William D. Casebeer,[9] a young philosopher at the Air Force Academy, has written, "We are social creatures, and if we are to flourish in our social environments, we must learn how to reason well about what we should do."[10] The question, then, is whether this skill might be built in to the brain, hardwired by evolution.

To me, these kinds of issues may be where the true secrets about the   12
uniqueness of the human brain, the human condition, lie. Research long ago recognized that the essential function of the human brain is to make decisions; it is a decision-making device. On no dimension of human consciousness are more decisions made than on social issues, the second-by-second, minute-by-minute judgments we make all day long about our standing and situation in a social group. The enormous cerebral cortex—the huge expansion of capacity in the human brain—may be there for social processes such as our relentless need for social comparison. Could it be that these decisions are influenced by some kind of universal moral compass we all possess? This issue, along with others, is why the new field of social neuroscience is so exciting and potentially enlightening.

When a scientist wants to design experiments to see what brain centers   13
become active during moral reasoning, he or she needs to examine moral reasoning itself. This is difficult, given how many different moral philosophies exist. Nonetheless, a good place to begin is with the three main Western philosophies: utilitarianism, deontology, and virtue theory—represented by the philosophers John Stuart Mill, Immanuel Kant, and Aristotle, respectively. Utilitarians believe in actions that produce the most happiness for the most people; in other words, they look to the bottom line. Deontologists don't worry about the outcome of an action but focus on the intention that produced it—it's more important not to violate another person's rights than to have an ideal outcome. Virtue theorists look to cultivate virtue and avoid vices.[11]

Casebeer reviewed this trio of philosophies and concluded, "Jokingly,   14
then, it could be said that these approaches emphasize different brain regions: frontal (Kant); prefrontal, limbic, and sensory (Mill); the properly coordinated action of all (Aristotle)."[12] That goes to the heart of the question: Are there

---

[9] **William D. Casebeer**   Former professor of philosophy at the Air Force Academy and current intelligence officer for the U.S. Air Force. His book is *Natural Ethical Facts: Evolution, Connectionism, and Moral Cognition* (2003).

[10] Casebeer, W. D. (2003). "Moral Cognition and Its Neural Constituents," *Nature Reviews Neuroscience* 4: 840–847. [Gazzaniga's note]

[11] Ibid. [Gazzaniga's note]

[12] **frontal . . . all**   The frontal lobe of the brain is the large portion of both hemispheres located behind the forehead; the prefrontal cortex is beneath the forehead and responsible for actions involving moral decisions; the limbic system is responsible for emotional behavior; the sensory is a group of lobes that parse sight, sound, and so on. Casebeer connects each to the philosopher whose "stories" most clearly relate to those portions of the brain.

moral reasoning centers in the brain? It's surely not as simple as that, but it may well be that intricate and distributed neural networks are active when a person is making certain moral decisions. Can they be captured with modern brain-imaging technologies?

Research on moral cognition studies three main topics: moral emotions, [15] theory of mind, and abstract moral reasoning. Moral emotions—those that motivate behavior—are driven mostly by the brain stem and limbic axis, which regulate basic drives such as sex, food, thirst, and so on. *Theory of mind* is the term for our ability to judge what others are thinking so that we can behave appropriately in response to them—an essential in moral reasoning because it guides our social behavior. The "mirror neurons" I discussed [earlier], the orbital frontal cortex, the medial structures of the amygdala, and the superior temporal sulcus are believed to be responsible for theory-of-mind processes. Finally, abstract moral reasoning, brain imaging is showing us, uses many brain systems.

The dilemma in abstract moral reasoning studies most often presented [16] by researchers to volunteers is the trolley problem, one version of which I described [earlier]. In this version, a trolley is hurtling down a track, headed straight for five people. You have to decide whether to let it hit the five people or, up close and personal, throw a person standing next to you onto the tracks to stop the trolley from hitting the other five.

Most people claim they won't throw the nearby person in front of the trol- [17] ley. At the same time, they will pull a switch and divert the train to another track, which will spare the five people even though the switched train will run into and kill a single person. So the question is, Where do these gut reactions come from? Is there a neural basis for these two prevalent responses? Have they been honed through evolution?

Joshua Greene,[13] a neurophilosopher from Princeton, raises two additional [18] commonly used examples. Say you are driving along in your new car and you see a man on the side of the road. He has been in an accident and is bloody. You could take him to the hospital and save his life; however, you would get blood all over your new car. Is it morally okay to leave him there? Or take another scenario. You receive a request in the mail saying that if you send in $100, you will save the lives of ten starving children. Is it okay to not send in the money?

In analyzing these kinds of dilemmas, Greene and his colleagues found [19] that while the choices are the same on the surface—do nothing and preserve your self-interest, or save lives at little cost to yourself—the difference is that the first scenario is personal whereas the second is impersonal. As already mentioned, Greene's studies found that judgments of personal dilemmas such as those seen in the trolley problem involve more brain activity in areas

---

[13] **Joshua Greene**   Professor of psychology at Harvard University and author of *The Moral Brain and How to Use It* (2012).

associated with emotion and moral cognition. Why is this? From an evolutionary perspective the theory is that the neural structures that tie altruistic instincts to emotion may have been selected for over time because helping people immediately is beneficial. Gut instinct, or morality, is a result of processes selected for over the evolutionary process. We have cognitive processes that allow us to make quick moral decisions that will increase our likelihood of survival. If we are wired to save a guy right in front of us, we all survive better. In the case of the money contribution, long-distance altruism just isn't as necessary; out of sight, out of mind. There is no dire need.

This brings us back to the central issue of whether moral truths are really   20
universal truths, or whether they are merely opinions, individual gut instincts. When making moral judgments, are we perceiving external truths or expressing internal attitudes? The new brain imaging results are highly suggestive that our brains are responding to the great underlying moral dilemmas. It is as if all the social data of the moment, the personal survival interests we each possess, the cultural experience we have undergone, and the basic temperament of our species all feed into the subconscious mechanisms we all possess and out comes a response, an urging for either action or inaction. This is the moral spark Wilson was talking about. This is the glue that keeps our species, over the long haul, from destroying itself.

Marc Hauser[14] has addressed this issue, as we saw [earlier]. He reasoned   21
that if moral judgments were derived from rational processes, one would predict that people from different cultures, of different ages and sexes, would respond differently to a common challenge. He also reasoned that they would have readily available and articulate justifications for their decisions. Hauser showed that irrespective of sex, age, and culture, most subjects responded in a similar fashion, making similar moral choices. Further, and most important, none could articulate or justify their responses. In short, there seem to be common subconscious mechanisms that are activated in all members of our species in response to moral challenges. When the participants in Hauser's research were challenged to explain their decision, none of them were particularly rational or logical. Their explanations seemed to be the product of personal interpreters spinning out some theory or other that seemed right to them on the spot.

Most moral judgments are intuitive, as I've noted throughout this book. We   22
have a reaction to a situation, or an opinion, and we form a theory as to why we feel the way we do. In short, we have an automatic reaction to a situation—a brain-derived response. Upon feeling that response, we come to believe we are reacting to absolute truths. What I am suggesting is that these moral ideas are

---

[14] **Marc Hauser (b. 1959)**   Professor of psychology at Harvard University until 2011, where he focused on evolutionary biology and cognitive neuroscience.

generated by our interpreter, by our brains, yet we form a theory about their absolute "rightness." Characterizing the formation of a moral code in this way puts the challenge directly on us. As Greene points out, "It is one thing to care about the plight of the poor, and another to think that one's caring is objectively correct."[15] It looks like it may be correct after all.

Somehow our brains are cued to be alert to the mental states of others   23 as we struggle to play a productive role in developing a moral code in a social group. Somehow it would seem the universally recognized mechanisms of self-survival have been co-opted and are used to work in more social settings. Evolution is saving the group, not just the person, because it would seem that saving the group saves the person. To do this, we have somehow become mind readers, reflexively.

How We Read Minds

There are two major theories about how we "read minds"—that is, how we   24 attribute certain mental or emotional states to others in order to explain or predict their behavior. The first is simulation theory (ST), whereby, very simply, we put ourselves in another person's shoes and figure out what we'd do in his or her situation. This requires us to use our imaginations to feed in "fake" data and to be able to hold the fake data separate from real life so that we don't act on it but only imagine what we would do, given the circumstances.[16]

Rivaling ST is the redundant-sounding theory-theory, or TT. "TT maintains   25 that the mental terms and concepts used in understanding human behavior get their predictive and explanatory credentials by being embedded in a folk theory of mind."[17] This folk psychology, the theory goes, is a set of rules that we use to judge and gauge others' behavior. We need not be conscious of this set of rules, or even of using them; they are just there. But where does the theory come from? Here is where TT comes up against the same problem that Greene raises about where moral truths come from, the nature-nurture dilemma. Are we born with the knowledge, or do the rules exist in the ether, available for us to learn? TT adherents differ on whether the theory is innate or learned, as well as on whether we use a distinct "theory of mind" module in the brain or some more continuous system of representations that produce the same effect. What

---

15 Greene, Joshua (2003). "From Neural 'Is' to Moral 'Ought': What Are the Moral Implications of Neuroscientific Moral Psychology?," *Nature Reviews Neuroscience* 4: 847–850. [Gazzaniga's note]

16 Gallese, V., and A. Goldman (1998). "Mirror Neurons and the Simulation Theory of Mind-Reading," *Trends in Cognitive Sciences* 2: 493–501; Goldman, A. (1989). "Interpretation Psychologized," *Mind and Language* 4: 104–119. [Gazzaniga's note]

17 Ibid. [Gazzaniga's note]

theory-theorists agree on is that we are in fact using knowledge that is encoded in a theory to judge behavior.

ST, on the other hand, denies that we are using a theory or body of knowledge or rules to judge behavior; "rather our own mental processes are treated as a manipulable model of other minds." Even though we may make generalizations that, say, people tend to do X in circumstances like Y, simulation theorists believe this approach is process driven rather than being based strictly on pre-existing knowledge. "The basic idea is that if the resources our own brain uses to guide our own behavior can be put to work as a model of other people, then we have no need to store general information about what makes people tick: We just do the ticking for them."[18]

A long and rich history of psychological research has outlined what is called the empathy altruism hypothesis, which seeks to explain the pro-social behavior we engage in when we watch another human being in distress. We automatically and unconsciously simulate this distress in our minds, which in turn makes us feel bad—not in an abstract way, but literally bad. We become infected by the other person's negative feelings, and in order to alleviate this state in ourselves, we are motivated to action. A number of studies support this idea—that manipulating feelings toward an individual increases helping behavior. Looking at expressions of distress, for example, enhances helping behavior.[19]

Indeed, Adam Smith[20] was onto aspects of this thinking about social contagion. In 1759 he wrote, "When we see a stroke aimed and just ready to fall upon the leg or arm of another person, we naturally shrink and draw back our leg or our own arm; and when it does fall, we feel it in some measure, and are hurt by it as well as the sufferer . . . Persons of delicate fibres and weak constitution of body complain, that in looking at the sores and ulcers which are exposed by beggars on the streets, they are apt to feel an itching or uneasy sensation in the correspondent part of their own bodies."[21]

26

27

28

---

[18] Gordon, R. See www.umsl.edu/~philo/Mind_Seminar/New%20Pages/subject.html. [Gazzaniga's note]

[19] Batson, C. D., and J. S. Coke (1981). "Empathy: A Souce of Altruistic Motivation for Helping," in *Altruism and Helping Behavior: Social Personality and Developmental Perspectives*, J. P. Rushton and R. M. Sorrentino, eds. (Hillsdale, N.J.: Erlbaum), pp. 167–211. Also, Cialdini, R. B., S. L. Brown, B. P. Lewis, C. Luce, and S. L. Neuberg (1997). "Reinterpreting the Empathy-Altruism Relationship: When One into One Equals Oneness," *Journal of Personality and Social Psychology* 73: 481–494; and Hoffman, M. L. (2000). *Empathy and Moral Development: Implications for Caring and Justice* (New York: Cambridge University Press). [Gazzaniga's note]

[20] **Adam Smith (1723–1790)**   Professor of moral philosophy at Glasgow University and author of *Wealth of Nations* (1776).

[21] Hatfield, E., J. T. Caccioppo, and R. L. Rapson (1994). *Emotional Contagion* (New York: Cambridge University Press), p. 17. [Gazzaniga's note]

Countless experiments have been carried out to support this general idea. [29] My former colleague at Dartmouth, John Lanzetta,[22] and his colleagues demonstrated repeatedly that people tend to respond to the sense of touch, taste, pain, fear, joy, and excitement of others with analogous physiological activation patterns of their own. They literally feel the emotional states of others as their own.[23] This tendency to react to the distress of others appears to be innate: it has been demonstrated in newborn infants, who cry in response to the distress of other infants within the first days of life.[24]

In considering all these arguments, I believe the STs have it right. From [30] a neuroscience perspective, the mirror neuron could support the ST view of how this works. Mirror neurons are believed to be responsible for "action understanding"—that is, understanding the actions of others. While we can't ethically do single-cell recording of mirror neurons in humans, some neurophysiological and brain imaging experiments suggest that mirror neurons do exist in humans and that they function to help with action understanding as well as action imitation.[25]

The neurophysiology of what might be called social process started in [31] 1954, when Henri Gastaut[26] and his colleagues in Marseille noted in EEG studies that human subjects have a brain wave response not only when performing actions themselves but when watching others perform actions. Gastaut's research has since been confirmed by many studies using both additional brain measurement techniques, such as the more advanced magnetoencephalographic technique, and stimulation techniques, such as transcranial magnetic stimulation (TMS), a noninvasive technique for electrical stimulation of the nervous system. Another important finding of the more recent studies has been that the spinal cord inhibits the execution of the observed action, "leaving the cortical motor system free to 'react' to that action without the risk of every movement generation."[27] Rizzolatti[28] and his colleagues point out that, in total,

---

[22] **John T. Lanzetta (1926–1989)**   Former professor of psychology at Dartmouth College.

[23] Lanzetta, J. T., and B. G. Englis (1989). "Expectations of Cooperation and Competition and Their Effects on Observers' Vicarious Emotional Responses," *Journal of Personality and Social Psychology* 56: 543–554. [Gazzaniga's note]

[24] Simner, M. L. (1971). "Newborn's Response to the Cry of Another Infant," *Developmental Psychology* 5: 136–150. [Gazzaniga's note]

[25] Rizzolatti, G., and L. Craighero (2004). "The Mirror Neuron System," *Annual Reviews in Neuroscience* 27: 169–192. [Gazzaniga's note]

[26] **Henri Gastaut (1915–1995)**   French neurologist and specialist in epilepsy.

[27] Rizzolatti and Craighero "Mirror Neuron System," citing Baldissera, F., P. Cavallari, L. Craighero, and L. Fadiga (2001). "Modulation of Spinal Excitability During Observation of Hand Actions in Humans," *European Journal of Neuroscience* 13: 190–194. [Gazzaniga's note]

[28] **Giacomo Rizzolatti (b. 1937)**   Italian neurophysiologist at the University of Parma.

the TMS studies indicate that the human mirror system not only exists, but differs from the monkey system in a key way: it seems to recognize meaningless movements, such as vague gestures, as well as goal-directed movements.

Why is that important? Because these are the skills needed to imitate movements. This could suggest that the human mirror neuronal system is the basis for learning by imitation. **32**

Human imaging studies are seeking to identify the complex network that is activated by the human mirror system. This is important to the search for the biology of moral reasoning. If we know what part of the brain is activated when observing an action, we can start to understand what mechanisms the brain uses to understand the world. For instance, if observing a barking dog activates my motor and visual areas, but seeing a picture of a barking dog activates only my visual area, this suggests not only that we process the information from these two situations differently, but that this different processing may evoke a different psychological experience of the observation. Observing a dog barking activates my motor system and therefore creates a deeper resonance with the observed action; seeing a picture of a barking dog just doesn't get "in my bones" in the same way. **33**

Rizzolatti suggests that when we learn new motor patterns, it is possible we break them down into basic movements, via the mirror mechanism, and that once the mirror system activates these basic motor representations, they are recombined into the action. He goes on to argue, as did Robin Allott[29] before him, that the mirror system, with its role in imitation and action understanding, may be the evolutionary precursor to language.[30] In other words, we went from understanding others' gestures, to understanding abstract representations of meaning — speech. This idea is supported by research suggesting hand and mouth gestures are linked in humans. **34**

V. S. Ramachandran's[31] work on anosognosia patients — the stroke patients who deny their paralysis — indicates another crucial role mirror neurons may play in humans. Ramachandran found that some patients deny not only their own paralysis but the obvious paralysis of others — something he suggests may be due to damage to mirror neurons. "It's as if anytime you want to make a judgment about someone else's movements, you have to run a VR [virtual reality] simulation of the corresponding movements in your own brain, and **35**

---

[29] **Robin Allott**   Author of *Motor Theory of Language* (1987) who describes himself as a "higher education professional."

[30] Allott, R. (1991). "The Motor Theory of Language," in *Studies in Language Origins*, vol. 2, W. von Raffler-Enel, J. Wind, and A. Jonker, eds. (Amsterdam: John Benjamins), pp. 123–157. [Gazzaniga's note]

[31] **V. S. Ramachandran (b. 1951)**   Professor of psychology at the University of California at San Diego. Among his books is *The Emerging Mind* (2003).

without mirror neurons you cannot do this."[32] If this is so, it would seem that mirror neurons support the simulation theorists' view that the brain is built to feel not only our own experiences but those of others.

The tension between ST and TT gets us back to the universal ethics dilemma. Are the moral truths we seem to live by a set of rules that exist independently of us, rules that we learn and live by? Or are these rules the result of our brains using built-in systems to empathize and thereby predict behavior and act accordingly? Whatever the answer, one thing is clear: the rules exist.

I believe, therefore, that we should look not for a universal ethics comprising hard-and-fast truths, but for the universal ethics that arises from being human, which is clearly contextual, emotion-influenced, and designed to increase our survival. This is why it is hard to arrive at absolute rules to live by that we can all agree on. But knowing that morals are contextual and social, and based on neural mechanisms, can help us determine certain ways to deal with ethical issues. This is the mandate for neuroethics: to use our understanding that the brain reacts to things on the basis of its hardwiring to contextualize and debate the gut instincts that serve the greatest good—or the most logical solutions—given specific contexts.

I am convinced that we must commit ourselves to the view that a universal ethics is possible, and that we ought to seek to understand it and define it. It is a staggering idea, and one that on casual thought seems preposterous. Yet there is no way out. We now understand how tendentious our beliefs about the world and the nature of human experience truly are, and how dependent we have become on tales from the past. At some level we all know this. At the same time, our species wants to believe in something, some natural order, and it is the job of modern science to help figure out how that order should be characterized.

---

[32] Ramachandran, V. S. "Mirror Neurons and Imitation Learning as the Driving Force Behind 'the Great Leap Forward' in Human Evolution," *Third Edge*. See www.edge.org/3rd_culture/ramachandran/ramachandran_p1.html. [Gazzaniga's note]

❖ QUESTIONS FOR CRITICAL READING

1. What does Gazzaniga mean when he says that modern knowledge is on a collision course with traditional beliefs (para. 1)? Do you agree?

2. How important is it for Gazzaniga's discussion that we think of ourselves as "big animals" (para. 2)?

3. What is the significance of "theory of mind," our ability to judge what other people are thinking and so respond to them (para. 15)?

4. In paragraph 4, the question of human nature is broached. Is there such a thing as human nature?

5. Is morality specifically a social construct? What evidence informs your answer?

6. Do humans have an innate moral sense? What is Gazzaniga's view regarding an innate moral sense?

7. What are the limitations of the philosophical views of human nature described in paragraph 3?

✖ SUGGESTIONS FOR CRITICAL WRITING

1. In paragraph 2, Gazzaniga says, "This is the single most disturbing reality of modern-day citizenship and our notion of shared values." What is he referring to, and how well does the remainder of the essay address the issues that he raises in this and the preceding paragraph? Do you agree that the rise of scientific understanding of brain functions will conflict with the "stories" that constitute much of what we think we know about human nature?

2. Early in the essay, Gazzaniga considers whether human nature exists. He quotes authorities who deny that there are instincts or anything like a human nature and assert that the brain has no predisposition but is adaptable to "a full range of behaviors" (para. 4). Argue the case either for or against the existence of human nature. Consider what role the recent studies of brain physiology might play in this debate. Why is whether or not human nature exists an important question to answer?

3. Review the "trolley problem" (para. 16). If you were in a situation in which you could control the outcome of an event that would kill either one innocent person or five people who may or may not be innocent, what would you do? Construct a different "trolley problem" and explore the possibilities that would face someone making a moral decision in response to that problem. Why are such decisions difficult? Is it possible to have an intuitive response to such problems? Can a gut instinct inform one when dealing with such problems?

4. When considering the question of "an underlying universal ethics," Gazzaniga says, "The question is, Do we have an innate moral sense as a species, and if so, can we recognize and accept it on its own terms?" (para. 6). He then declares, "It is not a good idea to kill because it is not a good idea to kill, not because God or Allah or Buddha said it was not a good idea to kill." What he does he mean? How does this line of reasoning lead us to consider a universal ethics?

5. In paragraph 11, Gazzaniga says that evolutionary psychology supports the view that moral behavior is good for human survival. That leads him to ask "whether this skill might be built in to the brain, hardwired by evolution." What is your view on this possibility? What, in addition to a moral sense, might be hardwired into the brain? Are talents, such as those possessed by musical prodigies, examples of hardwiring in the brain? What about intelligence, athletic skill, or risk taking? If such hardwiring exists, could it be a result of evolution?

6. To what extent do you agree that the emotional parts of the brain control moral behavior? Observe your own emotional reaction to events that demand a moral response and interview others to see if they have similar emotional reactions to morally complex situations. How much are you informed by your emotional responses to immoral behavior or unethical practices? Are your emotions good moral guides? Do you think it is universally true that emotions inform moral decisions?

7. **CONNECTIONS**   For Gazzaniga, Aristotle's "The Aim of Man" (p. 688) is essentially just a "story" because it is not rooted in scientific study and does not take into account what we in the modern world know about brain development and evolution. Yet Aristotle's discussion of ethics still guides the thinking of many modern philosophers and ethicists. Given Gazzaniga's views, how much of Aristotle would he think is still meaningful and relevant to modern society? What would Gazzaniga reject, and what would he accept? On what basis might Gazzaniga disregard entirely the views that Aristotle holds most dear?

8. **CONNECTIONS**   Which of the authors in Part Six would have the most problem with Gazzaniga's views that there might be a universal ethics based on evolutionary developments in the human brain? Consider closely the work of Iris Murdoch in "Morality and Religion" (p. 757) and of Kwame Anthony Appiah in "The Case against Character" (p. 801). Which of these authors would be most opposed to Gazzaniga and which would be most in agreement?

KWAME ANTHONY
APPIAH

The Case against Character

© Greg Martin

KWAME ANTHONY APPIAH was born in London in 1954 and is currently the Laurance S. Rockefeller University Professor of Philosophy at the University Center for Human Values at Princeton University. As a child he was raised in Ghana, the home of his father, Joe Emmanuel Appiah, a lawyer and politician, but he also spent time in England at the family home of his mother, Enid Margaret Appiah. Appiah's grandfather was Sir Stafford Cripps, a noted modern British statesman. Appiah's schooling eventually led him to go to Cambridge University for his Ph.D. in philosophy. His cosmopolitan experience of being raised in Africa and Europe and then having a career in the United States has given him a unique view of international politics and the position of nations both rich and poor in the world today.

Appiah is somewhat skeptical of the ability of well-meaning social groups to help those less fortunate in other nations. He is not opposed to charity, but he sees that the virtuous organizations that try to help the poor have a limited scope and ability to make substantial change. His view is that the responsibility for the well-being of people in Africa, for example, lies in the hands of the governments in Africa. Only local governments can make the changes necessary to improve the lot of their citizens. This view has not met with approval from some Africanists, particularly those who are Afrocentric. For Appiah, Afrocentrism is similar to nineteenth-century Eurocentrism and thus represents a limited view of the world.

Appiah is a philosopher but also a novelist. His work is wide-ranging and remarkable for the variety of interests covered. Among the books that concern themselves with racial issues is *In My Father's House: Africa in the Philosophy of Culture* (1992), which explores the question of African identity, a subject that he has considered deeply. In *Color Conscious: The Political Morality of Race* (1998), he examines the entire question of race: what it is, how it is expressed, and how it has affected different cultures.

From *Experiments in Ethics*.

The moral issues involved in racism are among his chief concerns. In *The Ethics of Identity* (2007), Appiah examines the ways in which people regard their own identity in relation to their religion, their nationality, their race, and the groups to which they choose to belong. He examines the constraints that are imposed on individuals by the choices they make in terms of the organizations and institutions to which they attach themselves.

In *Experiments in Ethics* (2008), from which the following selection is taken, Appiah aims to bring philosophy and the social sciences together in a tradition he sees as tracing back to Aristotle. The book derives from an invitation for him to give the Flexner Lectures at Bryn Mawr College in 2005. The term *experiments* in the title implies much the same as the term *essays*, in that they refer to the writer trying out ideas in ways that help the reader come to a new understanding of the issues at hand.

APPIAH'S RHETORIC

Because Appiah began teaching the philosophy of language and the uses of semantics, or the study of meaning, his care in the use of words is obvious from the start. Yet, his style is direct because his purpose in "The Case against Character" is to reach the general reader, not the specialist in the field of philosophical ethics.

He begins this selection with a story by Lydia Davis, a rhetorical device that acts as an introduction to the question of character and how it is expressed. In that short story, Davis portrays a serious man, a playful man, an angry man, and a patient man — who are all the same man. This fictional description of the complexity of personality is central to Appiah's investigation because he is trying to distinguish between the act of virtue and the agent of virtue in order to understand how virtuous behavior relates to a virtuous person. He is trying to work out the details of the virtue theory and its relation to ethics. In this sense, the story is a good beginning because it shows that people behave in different ways at different times and can be inconsistent despite our feeling that their character is defined by what we think we know about them.

Appiah also relies on a good number of sources by people who write about virtue and ethics. For example, he discusses at length the work of Rosalind Hursthouse, whose book *On Virtue Ethics* (1997) supports the virtue theorists, especially when she says, "To possess a virtue is to be a certain sort of person with a certain complex mindset" (para. 3). Appiah then goes on to discuss Aristotle's concept of *eudaimonia*, which translates as "happiness" or " flourishing," and connects it to the concept of living a virtuous life. For Aristotle, a virtuous life is a better life, a happy life, the life worth living. The point of discussing Hursthouse and Aristotle is to give Appiah the opportunity to analyze their ideas in relation to the issues at hand: the act and agency of virtue.

Definition is also one of Appiah's rhetorical techniques. He defines ethics as "what it means for a life to be well lived" (para. 8), in line with Aristotle's view that virtue is necessary for a happy life. He then defines morality as "the constraints that govern how we should and should not treat other people." His definitions provide the groundwork to deal with the issues that follow and to cope with what he sees as the limits of virtue ethics and the complexities of situationist ethics.

Appiah's reliance on data gathered by social scientists to help shed light on the question of virtue is another important rhetorical technique. For example, take his discussion of situationist ethics, a view that assumes we will act virtuously in some situations, but not in others. He points out studies that show people are helpful to someone who drops a bunch of papers in front of a public telephone if those same people just found a dime in the telephone slot. He also reviews evidence that people will offer change for a dollar if they are enjoying the aromas in front of a bakery. In other words, there are some unconscious situations that affect virtuous behavior.

Appiah also uses an example from popular culture, the protagonist from *Schindler's List*, a film based on the life of a German businessman who saved one thousand Jews in Germany during World War II. Appiah points out that Oskar Schindler's character was marked by both virtuous and vicious behavior and implies that it may be difficult to consider Schindler a virtuous man simply on the basis of his having performed some virtuous acts, despite their magnitude. Underlying this is the question: Does the virtuous act make the agent virtuous, or does the virtuous agent make the act virtuous?

Relating personality traits, such as those manifest in Oskar Schindler, to the likelihood of virtuous behavior was the subject of a psychology experiment performed in the 1920s that gave schoolchildren the opportunity to cheat on tests. The outcome of the experiment demonstrated that there was no way to tell if a child who cheated on one test would cheat on all of them — or any of them. "Knowing that a child cheated on a spelling test didn't even tell you whether he would cheat on a math test" (para. 14). Even seminarians, whom one might expect to put virtuous behavior first, were not consistent in their behavior when offered the opportunity to be "good Samaritans."

In examining the "situationist challenge," Appiah begins to raise interesting questions about motive and intention. If a virtuous act is what a virtuous person does, then how do we interpret that person's intention? Is it important that a virtuous act be considered virtuous only if the person committing that act intended it to be virtuous? Must we do the right thing for the right reason for that act to be virtuous and ethically significant? Is a moral act moral only if we intend it to be so? Is it not possible to commit a moral act accidentally and still have it be considered moral?

▰ PREREADING QUESTIONS: WHAT TO READ FOR

The following prereading questions may help you anticipate key issues in the discussion of Kwame Anthony Appiah's "The Case against Character." Keeping them in mind during your first reading should help focus your attention.

1. What is virtue ethics?
2. What is situationist ethics?
3. What traits of character do we need to live well?

The Case against Character

Les circonstances sont bien peu de chose, le caractère est tout;
c'est en vain qu'on brise avec les objets et les êtres extérieurs;
on ne saurait briser avec soi-même.

(Circumstances don't amount to much, character is everything;
there's no point breaking with exterior objects and things; you
cannot break with yourself.)

—Benjamin Constant, *Adolphe*

The Virtue Revival

Lydia Davis,[1] the fiction writer, once published a short story entitled, signifi-   1
cantly, "Trying to Learn"—and if you know her work, you won't be surprised to
learn that it's a *very* short story indeed. Here's how it goes, in its entirety:

> I am trying to learn that this playful man who teases me is the same
> as that serious man talking money to me so seriously he does not
> even see me anymore and that patient man offering me advice
> in times of trouble and that angry man slamming the door as he
> leaves the house. I have often wanted the playful man to be more
> serious, and the serious man to be less serious, and the patient
> man to be more playful. As for the angry man, he is a stranger to
> me and I do not feel it is wrong to hate him. Now I am learning
> that if I say bitter words to the angry man as he leaves the house,
> I am at the same time wounding the others, the ones I do not want
> to wound, the playful man teasing, the serious man talking money,
> and the patient man offering advice. Yet I look at the patient man,
> for instance, whom I would want above all to protect from such
> bitter words as mine, and though I tell myself he is the same man
> as the others, I can only believe I said those words, not to him, but
> to another, my enemy, who deserved all my anger.

That's the story. It's also the story, more or less, of a growing body of   2
research in the social sciences: we have met that man, many social scientists
say, and he is us. In this chapter, then, I'd like to focus on the seeming clash
between two different pictures of character and conduct: the picture that

---

[1] **Lydia Davis (b. 1947)**   Professor of creative writing at the State University of New York
at Albany. She is noted for her very short stories and is also a renowned translator of
Marcel Proust.

seems to underlie much virtue ethics, on the one hand, and the picture that has emerged from work in experimental psychology, on the other.

What does the first picture look like? The power core of virtue ethics is the idea of the virtuous person. A virtuous act is one that a virtuous person would do, done for the reasons a virtuous person would do it. Character is primary; virtues are more than simple dispositions to do the right thing. Those who draw on Aristotle's ideas are likely to stress, with Rosalind Hursthouse, author of a recent book entitled *On Virtue Ethics*, that the dispositions in question are deep, stable, and enmeshed in yet other traits and dispositions. The character trait of honesty, for instance, is "a disposition which is well entrenched in its possessor, something that, as we say, 'goes all the way down,'" and "far from being a single track disposition to do honest actions, or even honest actions for certain reasons, it is multi-track." For the disposition "is concerned with many other actions as well, with emotions and emotional reactions, choices, values, desires, perceptions, attitudes, interests, expectations, and sensibilities. To possess a virtue is to be a certain sort of person with a certain complex mindset." 3

How complex? Well, Hursthouse explains, an honest person "chooses, where possible, to work with honest people, to have honest friends, to bring up her children to be honest. She disapproves of, dislikes, deplores dishonesty, is not amused by certain tales of chicanery, despises or pities those who succeed by dishonest means rather than thinking they have been clever, is unsurprised or pleased (as appropriate) when honesty triumphs, is shocked or distressed when those near and dear to her do what is dishonest and so on." 4

Virtue ethicists also claim that having a virtue, which is something that comes by degrees, contributes to making one's life a good one—to what Aristotle called *eudaimonia*,[2] or flourishing. A life that exhibits the virtues is for that very reason a better life: not because the acts of the virtuous have good consequences (though they may); not because they lead to satisfaction or give pleasure to the agent (though, for Aristotle at least, learning to take pleasure in what is virtuous is one component of moral development). Virtues are intrinsically worth having. Being virtuous is part, at least, of what makes a life worthwhile. 5

Corresponding to the virtues, as their antitheses, are the vices. They are to be shunned, just as the virtues are to be developed. And their presence in a life makes that life correspondingly less worthwhile. Vices, too, are seen as multi-track, deeper than mere habits. They are certainly multifarious; more so, it seems, than the virtues. Hursthouse, our stalking horse, offers a list of 6

---

[2] **eudaimonia**   Aristotle's idea of highest good, usually translated as "happiness," "welfare," or "flourishing."

dispositions to avoid; we should not be "irresponsible, feckless, lazy, inconsiderate, uncooperative, harsh, intolerant, selfish, mercenary, indiscreet, tactless, arrogant, unsympathetic, cold, incautious, unenterprising, pusillanimous, feeble, presumptuous, rude, hypocritical, self-indulgent, materialistic, grasping, short-sighted, vindictive, calculating, ungrateful, grudging, brutal, profligate, disloyal, and on and on."

Virtue ethics, to be sure, comes in a Baskin-Robbins array of flavors; I take   7
Hursthouse's avowedly neo-Aristotelian account to be representative, because it succeeds in capturing elements that are shared by many of the doctrinal variants in circulation: the basic cream, sugar, and eggs, so to speak. The core of the basic theory, as she formulates it, lies in three claims.

1. The right thing to do is what a virtuous agent would do in the circumstances.
2. A virtuous person is one who has and exercises the virtues.
3. A virtue is a character trait that a person needs in order to have *eudaimonia* — that is, in order to live a good life.

The task of ethics, then, will be to discover what traits of character we need to live well.

This will be as convenient a place as any to announce a terminological   8
convention. Here and elsewhere, I'll generally follow Aristotle in using *ethics* to refer to questions about human flourishing, about what it means for a life to be well lived. I'll use *morality* to designate something narrower, the constraints that govern how we should and should not treat other people. Terminological stipulations of this sort are useful only if they allow us to track distinctions that matter. There are crucial issues that come into view only if we keep in mind the distinction between two general questions, "What is it for a life to go well?" and "What do we owe to other people?" Using the words *ethics* and *morality* in this way will help illuminate the connections between the answers to these two questions. So in making this distinction I wish emphatically to avoid the impression that I think these questions are unconnected.

This may seem obvious enough in virtue ethics, where the rightness of   9
actions is conceptually dependent upon the goodness of lives; and where the goodness of one's life consists, at least in part, in having certain complex traits of character. Its modern practitioners urge us to determine, first, what we must be like to live well (for someone like that is virtuous), and then decide what to do on any particular occasion by deciding what a virtuous person would do. Aristotle wrote that, while everyone agrees that *eudaimonia* is the "highest of all the goods," there is no such agreement as to what it requires; the "popular account of it is not the same as that given by the philosophers." Virtue ethics aims at the wisest answer to the question of what *eudaimonia* requires. Its first answer is: the development of a virtuous character.

Wrongful Attributions

Anscombe,[3] recall, wanted us to become better acquainted with psychology   10
before resuming our moral philosophizing. What sort of psychological findings
might prove relevant to the virtue ethics she helped resurrect? The under-
pinning conception of character shared by most virtue ethicists, including
Aristotle, is what the philosopher John Doris[4] calls "globalist," which is to say, it
involves consistent dispositions to respond across contexts under the guidance of a certain value; and many philosophers have also held some version of
Aristotle's thesis of the unity of the virtues, according to which you fully possess one virtue only if you have them all. But just as modern moral philosophers
were rediscovering the virtues, social psychologists were uncovering evidence
that most actual people (including people ordinarily thought to be, say, honest)
don't exhibit virtues of this sort. The reason wasn't the one that most moralists
would have suspected: that vice far exceeds virtue. The reason was that most
people simply didn't display such multi-track, context-independent dispositions at all, let alone in a unified ensemble.

It's not so surprising to find the unity-of-virtues thesis, in its stronger   11
forms, called into question. Oskar Schindler—as portrayed in the film *Schindler's List*—is mercenary, arrogant, hypocritical, and calculating; but he is also
courageous and compassionate. How many of Jane Austen's young women[5]
are kind but a little bit vain, too? We all know that such traits aren't served up
in a fixed combination like a characterological Happy Meal. (Indeed, a reader
of ecclesiastical hagiography might conclude that the virtues of the saints are
sometimes less spectacular than their vices.) At the same time, there are *some*
reasons for thinking that the virtues would have to be integrated in a virtuous
person: for compassion without courage, say, will too often leave you not doing
the compassionate thing. So there may be, at least in this straightforward way,
something to be said for Aristotle's view. (As there usually is for Aristotle's
views.)

No, the surprising challenge is to the core claim: that character, conceived   12
of in terms of the virtues we ordinarily speak about, is consistent. Yet that is
exactly what many social psychologists today would deny. They find that character traits simply don't exhibit (in the current argot) cross-situational stability.
These psychologists are not globalists but "situationists": they claim—this is

---

[3] **G. Elizabeth Anscombe (1919–1982)**   Professor of philosophy at Cambridge University and one of England's most distinguished philosophers.

[4] **John Doris (b. 1944)**   Professor of philosophy at Washington University, St. Louis, and
author of *Lack of Character* (2002).

[5] **Jane Austen's young women**   The reference is to characters in Jane Austen's (1775–1817)
novels: Elizabeth Bennett in *Pride and Prejudice* (1813); Emma Woodhouse in *Emma*
(1815); and Anna Elliot in *Persuasion* (1818).

a first stab at a definition—that a lot of what people do is best explained not by traits of character but by systematic human tendencies to respond to features of their situations that nobody previously thought to be crucial at all. They think that someone who is, say, reliably honest in one kind of situation will often be reliably dishonest in another. They'd predict that Oskar Schindler was mercenary, arrogant, hypocritical, and calculating sometimes . . . but not always; and that his courage and compassion could be elicited in some contexts but not in others. The playful man, the serious man, the patient man, and the angry man: same fellow, different circumstances.

Now, to ascribe a virtue to someone is, among other things, to say that   13
she tends to do what the virtue requires in contexts where it is appropriate. An honest person, for example, will resist the temptations to dishonesty posed by situations where, say, a lie will bring advantage, or where failing to return a lost wallet will allow one to buy something one needs. Indeed, our natural inclination, faced with someone who does something helpful or kind—or, for that matter, something hostile or thoughtless—is to suppose that these acts flow from their character, where character is understood in the way that "globalism" suggests: as a trait that is consistent across situations and, therefore, insensitive to differences in the agent's environment, especially small ones. But situationists cite experiments suggesting that small—and morally irrelevant—changes in the situation will lead a person who acted honestly in one context to do what is dishonest in another.

This result has been known since the earliest days of modern personality   14
psychology. In the late 1920s, the Yale psychologists Hugh Hartshorne and Mark May[6] studied some ten thousand American schoolchildren, giving them opportunities to lie, cheat, and steal in various academic and athletic situations. What they found is that deceit was, to a surprising extent, a function of situations. It didn't track at all with measurable personality traits or assessments of moral reasoning, and the data gave little support to cross-situational predictions; the child who wouldn't break the rules at home, even when it seemed nobody was looking, was no less likely to cheat on an exam at school. Knowing that a child cheated on a spelling test didn't even tell you whether he would cheat on a math test, let alone in a sporting event.

In the past thirty years or so, broader psychological evidence against globalism has been accumulating. Back in 1972, Alice M. Isen[7] and Paula Levin   15
found that when you dropped your papers outside a phone booth in a shopping mall, you were far more likely to be helped by people if they had just had the good fortune of finding a dime in the phone's coin-return slot. A year later, John

---

[6] **Hartshorne and May**   Hugh Hartshorne (1885–1967) taught at Union Theological Seminary and the Yale Divinity School. Mark A. May was a professor of psychology at Syracuse University. They coauthored *Studies in Deceit* (1928).

[7] **Alice M. Isen**   Professor of psychology at Cornell University.

Darley[8] and Daniel Batson discovered that Princeton seminary students, even those who had just been reflecting on the Gospel account of the Good Samaritan, were much less likely to stop to help someone "slumped in a doorway, apparently in some sort of distress," if they'd been told that they were late for an appointment. In a 1975 study, people were much less likely to help someone who "accidentally" dropped a pile of papers when the ambient noise level was 85 decibels than when it was 65 decibels. More recently, Robert Baron and Jill Thomley[9] showed that you were more likely to get change for a dollar outside a fragrant bakery shop than standing near a "neutral-smelling dry-goods store."

Many of these effects are extremely powerful: huge differences in behavior   16 flow from differences in circumstances that seem of little normative consequence. Putting the dime in the slot in that shopping-mall phone raised the proportion of those who helped pick up the papers from 1 out of 25 to 6 out of 7—that is, from almost no one to almost everyone. Seminarians in a hurry are one-sixth as likely to stop and act like a Good Samaritan. Knowing what I've just told you, you should surely be a little less confident that "she's helpful" is a good explanation next time someone stops to assist you in picking up your papers (especially if you're outside a bakery!).

But, the research also suggests, you will probably go on ascribing good   17 characters to people who do good things and bad ones to those who do bad things, anyway. (Lydia Davis, recall, entitled her story "*Trying* to Learn"—not "I Have Learned.") Experimental research into what psychologists call "attribution theory" shows that people are inclined to suppose that what someone does reflects her underlying character even when you explain to them that she is just putting on a performance. In one classic study, which dates from 1967, subjects were asked to read essays that were either pro- or anti-Castro and decide whether their authors favored or opposed Fidel Castro's regime. People supposed that the writer was pro-Castro if the piece was pro-Castro (and anti-Castro if the essay was anti-Castro, too), even when they had been told both that the authors had been *instructed* to write pro or con, and that whether they were assigned to write for or against Castro was decided by flipping a coin. This tendency to ignore the role of context in determining behavior and to suppose that what people do is best explained by their traits rather than their circumstances is known, in the social-psychology literature, as Correspondence Bias (the supposed correspondence, here, is between conduct and character), or sometimes, more disparagingly, as the Fundamental Attribution Error.

---

[8] **John Darley (b. 1938)**   Professor of psychology at Princeton University and mentor to Daniel Batson (b. 1943), who taught at the University of Kansas.

[9] **Robert A. Baron and Jill E. Thomley**   Baron is a professor of management at Oklahoma State University. Jill E. Thomley is a professor of mathematics at Appalachian State University. Together they authored "A Whiff of Reality: Empirical Evidence Concerning the Effects of Pleasant Fragrances on Work-Related Behavior" (1994).

Nor do we go wrong only when we're explaining the actions of other people; 18
our self-accounting is often untrustworthy. Remember those helpful people who
picked up your papers after getting a free dime, or who made change outside the
fragrant bakery. Who—buoyed by that dime, cheered by that fragrance—would
explain what they themselves had just done by saying, "I helped him because I
was feeling cheerful because I got a dime," or by thinking, "Hey, I did that mostly
because I was in a terrific mood brought on by the wafting smell of croissants"?
And, indeed, when experimenters asked people why they did what they did, they
seldom mentioned these critical variables . . . just as you would have expected.

Now, one rationale for not mentioning these facts is that they don't seem 19
relevant: ask people *why* they do something and they'll expect that you want
not a causal explanation of what they did, but their *reason* for doing it—that
is, what it was about the choice that made it seem a good thing to do. The fact
that there's a splendid aroma of croissants in the air doesn't make offering
change more reasonable; so it wouldn't do as an answer, especially if you're
one of those philosophers who take moral theory to be centrally concerned
with offering justifications for action. But, of course, you fail to mention it not
because it seems like the wrong sort of answer; you fail to mention it because
you have no idea that the aroma is having this effect on you. The researchers,
faced with these data, may hypothesize that when you're cheerful, you're more
inclined to do what you think is helpful; that is, the fact that offering change is
helpful will strike you as a particularly strong reason for doing it when you're
feeling particularly cheerful. But this is not something that the agent herself
will notice in the ordinary course of things. So, even though she's doing what's
helpful, and even though she might give that as her explanation—"He needed
help," she might say—there remains another sense in which she doesn't understand why she's doing what she's doing.

And that, as we've seen, seems consistent with our broader explanatory 20
habits—with the observation that much of what we say when we're explaining what we've done is confabulation: stories we've made up (though quite
sincerely) for ourselves and in response to others. In short—to overstate the
point only slightly—because people don't really know why they do what they
do, they give explanations of their own behavior that are about as reliable as
anyone else's, and in many circumstances actually less so.

The Situationist Challenge

I am not, for the moment, going to worry about whether all these psychological 21
claims are true or whether we can give an account of the results that better
comports with our common sense about why people, ourselves included, do
what they do. The question I want to ask is: Why should ethical theory care
about these claims at all?

Suppose I give you change because (in part) I just got a whiff of my favorite perfume. Of course, if I had a settled policy of never giving change, even that pleasant aroma wouldn't help. So there are other things about me — the sorts of things we would normally assess morally — that are clearly relevant to what I have done. But let's suppose that, other things being equal, if I hadn't had the whiff, I'd have ignored your plaintive plea to stop and change your dollar for the parking meter. I had, in these circumstances, an inclination to do what, according to the virtue theorist, a kind or helpful or thoughtful person — a virtuous person — would do; and I acted on that inclination. A typical virtue theorist will think I have done the right thing because it is the kind thing (and there are no countervailing moral demands on me). But, on the situationist account, I don't act out of the virtue of kindness, and therefore this act doesn't accrue to my ethical credit. Well now, do I deserve praise in this circumstance or not? Have I or haven't I made my life better by doing a good thing?

A situationist might well say that, as a prudential matter, we should, in fact, praise someone who does what is right or good — what a virtuous person would do — whether or not she did it out of a virtuous disposition. After all, psychological theory also suggests that praise, which is a form of reward, is likely to reinforce the behavior. (What behavior? Presumably not helpfulness, but being helpful when you're in a good mood.) For we tend to think that helping people in these circumstances, whatever the reason, is a good thing. But the virtue ethicist cannot be content that one acts *as if* virtue ethics is true. And we can all agree that the more evidence there is that a person's conduct is responsive to a morally irrelevant feature of the situation, the less praiseworthy it is.

If these psychological claims are right, very often when we credit people with compassion, as a character trait, we're wrong. They're just in a good mood. And if hardly anyone is virtuous in the way that virtue ethics conceives of it, isn't the doctrine's appeal eroded? Given that we are so sensitive to circumstances and so unaware of the fact, isn't it going to be wondrously difficult to develop compassion, say, as a character trait? We just can't keep track of all the cues and variables that may prove critical to our compassionate responses: the presence or absence of the smell of baking is surely just one among thousands of contextual factors that will have their way with us. How, if this is so, can I make myself disposed to do or to feel the right thing? I have no voluntary control on how aromas affect me. I cannot be sure that I will have a free dime show up whenever it would be a fine thing to be helpful.

There are some philosophers — among them the aforementioned John Doris (author of *Lack of Character*) and, even more strenuously, my colleague Gilbert Harman[10] — who take the social-science literature about character and conduct to pose a serious and perhaps lethal challenge to the virtue ethicist's worldview. Talk all you like about virtuous dispositions, the challenge goes:

22

23

24

25

---

[10] **Gilbert Harman (b. 1938)**   Professor of philosophy at Princeton University.

we're just not built that way. Owen Flanagan,[11] who has long worked at the cross-roads of psychology and moral theory, once proposed this maxim: "Make sure when constructing a moral theory or projecting a moral ideal that the character, decision processing, and behavior described are possible, or are perceived to be possible, for creatures like us." Plainly, there are costs for those who fail to clear this hurdle.

For one thing, our virtue theorist faces an epistemological difficulty if there are no actually virtuous people. As in all spheres of thought, so in moral deliberation: we sometimes need to think not only about what the right answer is but also about how we discover what the right answers are. Hursthouse, remember, claims that:

1. The right thing to do is what a virtuous agent would do in the circumstances.
2. A virtuous person is one who has and exercises the virtues.
3. A virtue is a character trait that a person needs in order to have *eudaimonia*, in order to live a good life.

No interesting version of virtue ethics holds that doing the right thing is all that matters; we should want to be the kind of person who does the right thing for the right reasons. Still, Hursthouse and others insist that virtue ethics isn't *entirely* "agent-centered," rather than "act-centered"; it can also specify what the right thing to do is—namely, what a virtuous person would do. How are we to follow that advice? If we were fully virtuous, we would find ourselves disposed to think and act and feel the right things. But we are not. If we knew someone who was virtuous, we could see what she would do, I suppose. But, given the depressing situationist reality, maybe no actual human being really is (fully) virtuous. And even if a few people did get to be virtuous against all the odds, we would have to have some way of identifying them, before we could see what they would do. So we would need, first, to know what a good life looks like and then we would need, second, to be able to tell, presumably by reflecting on actual and imaginary cases, whether having a certain disposition is required for a life to be good; and required not in some instrumental way—as nourishment is required for any life at all—but intrinsically.

If experimental psychology shows that people cannot have the sorts of character traits that the virtue theorist has identified as required for *eudaimonia*, there are only two possibilities: she has identified the wrong character traits or we cannot have worthwhile lives. Virtue theory now faces a dilemma.

The problem for the idea that we have gotten the wrong virtues is a problem of method. For virtue theory of the sort inspired by Anscombe, we must discover what the virtues are by reflection on concepts. We can, in principle,

26

27

28

---

[11] **Owen Flanagan**   Professor of neurobiology at Duke University.

reflect on which of the stable dispositions that psychology suggests might be possible—being helpful when we are in a good mood, say—are constitutive of a worthwhile life; or which—being unhelpful when we aren't buoyed up by pleasant aromas—detract from a life's value. But to concede *that* is to accept that we'll need to do the experimental moral psychology before we can ask the right normative questions. On this horn of the dilemma, virtue theory will find itself required to take up with the very empirical psychology it so often disdains.

On the other horn of the dilemma, the prospect that we cannot have worthwhile lives makes normative ethics motivationally irrelevant. What is the point of *doing* what a virtuous person would do if I can't *be* virtuous? Once more, whether I can be virtuous is obviously an empirical question. Once more, then, psychology seems clearly apropos. 29

Still, we should not overstate the threat that situationism poses. The situationist account doesn't, for example, undermine the claim that it would be better if we *were* compassionate people, with a persistent, multi-track disposition to acts of kindness. Philosophical accounts of the character ideal or compassion, the conception of it as a virtue, need make no special assumptions about how easy or widespread this deep disposition is. Acquiring virtue, Aristotle already knew, is hard; it is something that takes many years, and most people don't make it. These experiments might confirm the suspicion that compassionate men and women are rare, in part because becoming compassionate is difficult. But difficult is not the same as impossible; and perhaps we can ascend the gradient of these virtues only through aspiring to the full-fledged ideal. Nor would the ideal be defeated by a situationist who busily set about showing that people whom we take to exemplify compassion—the Buddha, Christ, Mother Teresa—were creatures of environments that were particularly rich in the conditions that (according to situationists) elicit kindly acts. 30

Finally, we could easily imagine a person who, in the virtue ethicists' view, was in some measure compassionate, and who actually welcomed the psychologists' research. Reading about these experiments will only remind her that she will often be tempted to avoid doing what she ought to do. So these results may help her realize the virtue of compassion. Each time she sees someone who needs help when she's hurrying to a meeting, she'll remember those Princeton seminarians and tell herself that, after all, she's not in *that* much of a hurry—that the others can wait. The research, for her, provides a sort of perceptual correction akin to the legend you see burned onto your car's rear-view mirror: *objects may be closer than they appear.* Thanks for the tip, she says. To think that these psychological claims by themselves undermine the normative idea that compassion is a virtue is just a mistake. 31

We might also notice what the situationist research *doesn't* show. It doesn't tell us anything about those seminarians (a healthy 10 percent) who were helpful even when rushing to an appointment; perhaps that subpopulation really 32 did have a stable tendency to be helpful—or, for all we know, to be heedless of the time and careless about appointments. (Nor can we yet say how the seminarians would have compared with, say, members of the local Ayn Rand Society.[12]) There could, consistent with the evidence, be a sprinkling of saints among us. Some will dispute whether the dispositions interrogated by social psychology can be identified with the normative conception of character traits elaborated by the classical virtue theorists. And, of course, the situationist hypothesis is only that, in explaining behavior, we're inclined to overestimate disposition and underestimate situation. It doesn't claim that dispositions don't exist; it hardly could, since one stable disposition it reports is the tendency to commit the Fundamental Attribution Error.

None of these caveats wholly blunts the situationist point that the virtues,   33
as the virtue ethicists conceive them, seem exceedingly hard to develop—a circumstance that must leave most of us bereft of *eudaimonia*. But virtue ethics is hardly alone in assigning a role to elusive ideals. Our models of rationality are also shot through with such norms. In the previous chapter, I mentioned the nineteenth-century hope that, as one formula had it, logic might be reduced to a "physics of thought." What succeeded that project was an approach captured in another formula according to which logic is, in effect, an "ethics of thought." It tells us not how we do reason but how we ought to reason. And it points toward one way of responding to the question we have posed to the virtue ethicist: How might we human beings take seriously an ideal that human beings must fall so far short of attaining?

---

[12] **Ayn Rand Society**   Ayn Rand (1905–1982) was a Russian American novelist and philosopher. Her teachers regarded altruism as a form of weakness.

✂ QUESTIONS FOR CRITICAL READING

1. What is a virtue? What virtues are very important?

2. Are virtues intrinsically worth having?

3. Which virtues do you most respect?

4. Why should one avoid vices? Is it difficult to avoid vices even if you wish to?

5. What are traits and dispositions? (See para. 3.)

6. Appiah mentions globalism in paragraph 13. What is globalism?

7. What are the problems with having compassion as a character trait? (See para. 24.)

◼️ SUGGESTIONS FOR CRITICAL WRITING

1. Look up the word *eudaimonia* and establish what you think Appiah means by the term. What would *flourishing* mean in relation to achieving a happy life? What is the relationship of eudaimonia to the concept of ethics? How would an ethical life be conducive to eudaimonia? Why does Aristotle call it the highest good and declare that it is the most desired thing in one's life? Do you feel that you could achieve eudaimonia? If so, how?

2. Explain why you think a virtuous life is likely to be a happy life. If you think that Aristotle and Appiah are correct that virtue produces happiness, why do you think so many people permit themselves to practice various vices? If people enjoy vices, does that mean that vices make people happy? Are vices universally undesirable and bad? What are the complications involved in relating virtues to vices in the way we live today? Can we measure our life in terms of virtue and vice?

3. Examine Rosalind Hursthouse's three claims (para. 7). According to Hursthouse, what is a virtuous agent? When she says that a virtuous person "exercises the virtues," what does she mean? Do you agree? Do examples from your own experience support that view? Finally, she says that a "virtue is a character trait." Do you agree? How do we define character traits? Is a virtuous character trait essential "to live a good life"?

4. In paragraph 9, Appiah suggests that Hursthouse believes eudaimonia requires "the development of a virtuous character." What is a virtuous character? If the implication is that a virtuous character can be developed, does that suggest that we do not naturally possess one? Does it suggest that there may be a procedure by which we can achieve a virtuous character? Do you have evidence from your observations of people that it is possible to develop a virtuous character? Do you wish to develop a virtuous character?

5. **CONNECTIONS** Appiah is obviously influenced by the position on virtue that Aristotle expressed in the *Nichomachean Ethics* (p. 688). Appiah mentions Aristotle several times and indicates specific agreement with his views, and he also quotes other writers who refer to Aristotle's work. How does Aristotle's position on virtue ethics differ from the positions Appiah and other philosophers hold? Would Aristotle defend the view that virtuous behavior stems from virtuous character? Does Aristotle take character into consideration? Does Aristotle make any allowances for situationist ethics? How does Aristotle help clarify Appiah's thoughts, and how do Appiah's thoughts help clarify those of Aristotle?

6. **CONNECTIONS** Examine Appiah's definition of *ethics* and his definition of *morality* in paragraph 8. Do Appiah's definitions satisfy you with regard to the relationship of ethics to morality? Do you think Iris Murdoch (p. 757) would agree with his definitions and find them acceptable in relation to her views of

religion? Define *ethics* and *morality* in terms that your peers would understand, using examples to bolster your definitions.

7. Write an essay for an audience that has not read this selection and is unaware of the concept of eudaimonia. Explain what situationist ethics is and how it works. Suggest some situations — either genuine ones you have experienced or hypothetical ones that are likely or possible among your peers. What situations might incite a nonvirtuous person to act virtuously? Why would the situation, rather than the character of the actor, control the virtue of the action? What is necessary for a situation ethicist to call an action virtuous?

8. One authority says that the virtues are love, kindness, justice, and service. The Greeks, Aristotle and Plato, say they are temperance, wisdom, justice, and courage. The seven heavenly virtues are chastity, temperance, charity, diligence, patience, kindness, and humility. Research the virtues and explain what they entail, how they are expressed, and why they are important. Decide how many true virtues there are. At the end of your essay, identify which virtues you most value and why.

Reflections on the Nature of Ethics

Now that you have read the selections in "Ethics," consider in what ways these writers have helped further inform your views on the many facets of ethics.

1. What is your view of the idea that happiness is the supreme good? Is this an ethical idea?

2. To what extent is it possible for you to establish "ethical first principles"?

3. Do you agree that happiness is closely related to virtuous behavior?

4. How should people be educated in morality and ethics?

5. To what extent is ethical behavior a result of the company you keep?

6. What is the connection between materialism and ethical behavior?

7. How do ethics and morality operate in the law and government?

8. Where do you stand on the question of whether holding religious views is necessary to ensure moral behavior?

9. What evidence suggests that ethical behavior is gender-linked?

10. What evidence suggests that we accept or not accept the idea of a moral absolute?

Acknowledgments

Kwame Anthony Appiah, "The Case against Character" from *Experiments in Ethics*. Copyright © 2008 by the President and Fellows of Harvard College. Reproduced with permission of Harvard University Press.

Hannah Arendt, "Total Domination" from *The Origins of Totalitarianism*. Copyright © 1973, 1968, 1966, 1958, 1951, 1948 by Hannah Arendt and renewed 2001, 1996, 1994, 1986 by Lotte Kohler. Copyright © renewed 1979 by Mary McCarthy West. Copyright © renewed 1976 by Hannah Arendt. Reproduced with permission of Houghton Mifflin Harcourt Publishing Company. All rights reserved.

Benazir Bhutto, "Islam and Democracy: History and Practice" from *Reconcilation: Islam, Democracy, and the West*. Copyright © 2008 by Benazir Bhutto. Reproduced with permission of HarperCollins Publishers.

Judith Butler, "Doing Justice to Someone: Sex Reassignment and Allegories of Transsexuality" from *Undoing Gender*. Copyright © 2004 by Routledge. Reproduced with permission of Taylor Francis Group, LLC. Permission conveyed through Copyright Clearance Center, Inc. All rights reserved.

Lydia Davis, "Trying to Learn" from *Almost No Memory*. Copyright © 1997 by Lydia Davis. Reproduced with permission of Farrar, Straus and Giroux, LLC.

Alexis de Tocqueville, "Government by Democracy" from *Democracy in America: And Two Essays on America* by Alexis de Tocqueville, translated by Gerald Bevan and edited by Isaac Kramnick. Translation and Translator's Note copyright © 2003 by Gerald Bevan. Introduction and Notes copyright © 2003 by Isaac Kramnick. Reproduced with permission of Penguin Books, Ltd.

Richard Feynman, "The Value of Science" from *The Pleasure of Finding Things Out*. Copyright © 2005 by Richard P. Feynman. Reproduced by permission of Basic Books, a member of the Perseus Books Group.

Sigmund Freud, "The Oedipus Complex" from *The Interpretation of Dreams, the Standard Edition of the Complete Psychology Works of Sigmund Freud* translated and edited by James Strachey. Copyright © 1953 by Sigmund Freud. Copyright © 2010 by James Strachey. Reproduced with permission of Basic Books, a member of the Perseus Books Group.

Milton and Rose Friedman, "Created Equal" from *Free to Choose: A Personal Statement*. Copyright © 1980 by Milton Friedman and Rose D. Friedman. Reproduced with permission of Houghton Mifflin Harcourt Publishing Company. All rights reserved.

Francis Fukuyama, "The Middle Class and Democracy's Future" from *Political Order and Political Decay*. Copyright © 2014 by Francis Fukuyama. Reproduced with permission of Farrar, Straus, and Giroux, LLC.

Howard Gardner, excerpt from *Multiple Intelligences*. Copyright © 2006 by Howard Gardner. Reproduced with permission of Basic Books, a member of the Perseus Group.

Michael S. Gazzaniga, "Toward a Universal Ethics" from *The Ethical Brain*. Copyright © 2005 by Michael S. Gazzaniga. Published by Dana Press, New York. Reproduced with permission.

Carol Gilligan, "Concepts of Self and Morality" from *In a Different Voice: Psychological Theory and Women's Development*. Copyright © 1982, 1993 by Carol Gilligan. Reproduced with permission of Harvard University Press.

F. A. Hayek, "Economic Control and Totalitarianism" from *The Road to Serfdom*. Copyright © 1944, 2007 by F. A. Hayek. Reproduced with permission of University of Chicago Press.

Index of Rhetorical Terms

This tenth edition of *A World of Ideas* presents selections from these important writers and thinkers:

Kwame Anthony Appiah	John Maynard Keynes
Hannah Arendt	Martin Luther King Jr.
Aristotle	Philip Kitcher
Francis Bacon	Lao-Tzu
Benazir Bhutto	Niccolò Machiavelli
Judith Butler	Karl Marx
Andrew Carnegie	Margaret Mead
Charles Darwin	Iris Murdoch
Frederick Douglass	Friedrich Nietzsche
Ralph Waldo Emerson	Robert Nozick
Richard Feynman	Plato
Sigmund Freud	Neil Postman
Milton and Rose Friedman	Lisa Randall
Francis Fukuyama	John Rawls
Howard Gardner	Robert B. Reich
Michael Gazzaniga	Jacob A. Riis
Carol Gilligan	Jean-Jacques Rousseau
F. A. Hayek	Gilbert Ryle
Karen Horney	Adam Smith
Hsün Tzu	Henry David Thoreau
Thomas Jefferson	Alexis de Tocqueville
Carl Jung	Edward O. Wilson
Michio Kaku	Mary Wollstonecraft
Eric Kandel	Virginia Woolf